THE REFORMED FAMILY WORLDWIDE

THE REFORMED FAMILY WORLDWIDE

*A Survey of Reformed Churches,
Theological Schools, and
International Organizations*

Compiled and edited by

JEAN-JACQUES BAUSWEIN
and
LUKAS VISCHER

*A project of the
International Reformed Center John Knox
Geneva, Switzerland*

WILLIAM B. EERDMANS PUBLISHING COMPANY
GRAND RAPIDS, MICHIGAN / CAMBRIDGE, U.K.

© 1999 Wm. B. Eerdmans Publishing Company
255 Jefferson Ave. S.E., Grand Rapids, Michigan 49503 /
P.O. Box 163, Cambridge CB3 9PU U.K.

Printed in the United States of America

04 03 02 01 00 99   7 6 5 4 3 2 1

Library of Congress Cataloging-in-Publication Data

The Reformed family worldwide: a survey of Reformed Churches,
    theological schools, and international organizations / compiled
    and edited by Jean-Jacques Bauswein and Lukas Vischer.
            p.   cm.
        "A project of the International Reformed Center John Knox,
    Geneva, Switzerland."
        ISBN 0-8028-4496-0 (pbk.: alk. paper)
        1. Reformed Church.   I. Bauswein, Jean-Jacques.
    II. Vischer, Lukas.   III. International Reformed Center John Knox.
    BX9422.2.R44   1988
    284′.2 — dc21   98-37771
                                                        CIP

CONTENTS

PREFACE

What we present here is a survey of Reformed churches around the world. The conviction of the usefulness of such a book grew during several consultations about the unity of the Reformed family organized in the early '90s in Geneva by the John Knox Center. Today Reformed churches can be found in almost all countries of the world, but they tend to divide into many groups. In most countries there is more than one Reformed church. Even at the international level, various federations or associations of Reformed churches have been formed, sometimes in opposition to each other. The situation has become so complex that mutual full knowledge about Reformed churches is often impossible even within a single country.

We have tried to establish as complete as possible a list of the churches which currently claim for themselves the heritage of the Reformation, and to provide basic information concerning each. We use the term *Reformed* in a wide sense. All streams of the Reformed tradition (Reformed, Presbyterian, Congregational, Evangelical, and United) have been included in this survey.

The purpose of this handbook is twofold: on the one hand, to allow Reformed churches to become more fully aware of the present situation of their family—its multiplicity, its richness, its potential, but also its weaknesses; and, on the other hand, to serve as an instrument which will facilitate communication within that family.

How did we proceed to gather accurate information on the churches? Having established a preliminary list of Reformed churches on the basis of numerous existing sources, a detailed questionnaire was sent out. Cross-checking of the answers received and information gathered from the churches, from mission and interchurch aid agencies, and from national and regional councils of churches, all helped to establish a list of over 750 different communities. With the help of knowledgeable persons, articles on each country were drafted. The texts were sent to all churches for verification. In the light of their responses, the articles were finalized. It is our hope that the churches will recognize themselves in the present version. We realize that errors may have survived the successive stages of drafting and verification, especially as some churches did not respond to any of our mailings. We apologize in advance for any misrepresentation which may have occurred. We are also aware that, as churches are living entities, facts about them might have changed slightly by the time this book is published.

In addition to an introduction and the survey of the individual churches, the volume also contains a list of various international bodies in which Reformed churches hold membership, as well as an overview of unions and official dialogues in which Reformed churches participate. A special section has been reserved for a list of over 500 Reformed theological schools. We have tried to simplify the use of this volume as much as possible. The section on the churches is organized alphabetically according to the (English) names of countries. To give a clearer idea of the historical developments which have caused the divisions, the churches *within* each country are normally arranged in chronological order.

The authors want to thank the dozens of people in all parts of the world who have contributed to the realization of this volume. We are indebted to all those who provided us with information, especially to those who prepared articles on the churches in the various countries. Their names are listed in chapter 6. We owe a special debt of gratitude to those who made major contributions to the book by serving on the editorial board and by providing detailed information on large countries or continents: John Garret, Hircio de Oliveira Guimarães, Jan A. B. Jongeneel, Seong-Won Park, Paraic Réamonn, Sidney Rooy, Thomas van den End, and Richard Van Houten. We also want to thank churches and foundations which have helped to finance the project. Last, not least, our gratitude goes to Frauke von Essen and Birgit Müller-Marero, who helped in the fact-gathering process, as well as to Rev. Dr. Donald J. Wilson, who helped to harmonize stylistically the texts of this handbook.

ABBREVIATIONS

Abbreviations for Church Statistics

Advent	Seventh-Day Adventist(s)
Angl	Anglican
Assy	Assembly
Bapt	Baptist
Believer	Believer's baptism
BM	Number of baptized members
Catech	Catechist
Ch, ch	Church, churches
ChInst	Church Institutions
ChurchOrg	Organizational structure
CM	Number of communicant members
Congr	Congregation(s)
Congreg	Congregationalist
Counc	Council
Deac	Deacons
Disciples	Churches of Christ (Disciples of Christ)
Distr	District
DoctrB	Doctrinal basis
Eld	Number of elders
EvgHome	Number of evangelists active at home
GenAssy	General Assembly
GenSecr	General Secretary
GenSyn	General Synod
InfantB	Infant baptism
IntlRel	International relationships

ABBREVIATIONS

km^2	Square kilometers
Lang	Language(s)
LangCorr	Language to use when corresponding
Lit, lit	Liturgy, liturgical
Luth	Lutheran
Menn	Mennonite
Meth	Methodist
Mission	Missionaries working abroad
na	not available
nc	not communicated
ne	not existing in a given church
NatRel	National relationships with other churches
OffLang	Official language(s)
OldCath	Old Catholic
OrdM	Ordained Ministers
Orth	Orthodox
Pent	Pentecostal
Pop	Population
Presb	Presbyterian
Presby	Presbytery
Prot	Protestant
PStations	Preaching stations
RCath	Roman Catholic
Ref	Reformed
RegRel	Regional relationships
Syn	Synod
TheolSchool	Theological school(s)
TM	Total Membership
WDeac	Women deacons
WEld	Women elders
Women Ord	Women's ordination

Abbreviations for Confessions of Faith

25 ArtR	25 Articles of Religion
ApC	Apostles' Creed
AthC	Athanasian Creed
Barmen	Barmen Declaration
BelgC	Belgic Confession (1561)
CA	Confessio Augustana
CDort	Canon of Dordt/Dort (1618-19)
HeidC	Heidelberg Catechism (1563)
HelvC	Second Helvetic Confession
Leuenberg	Leuenberg Concordia/Agreement

RochC	La Rochelle Confession of Faith (1559)
NicC	Nicene Creed
SpSt	Special Statement
WestCat	Westminster Catechisms
WestConf	Westminster Confession of Faith

Abbreviations for School Degrees

BA	Bachelor of Arts
BD	Bachelor of Divinity
BMin	Bachelor of Ministry
BPh	Bachelor of Philosophy
BRE	Bachelor in Religious Education
BRS	Bachelor in Religious Studies
BTh	Bachelor of Theology
CertTh	Certificate in Theology
CPE	Clinical Pastoral Education
DD	Doctor of Divinity
Deg	Degree
DiplTh	Diploma of Theology
DPS	Degree in Pastoral Studies
G	Graduate
GTh	Graduate in Theology
Inst	Instruction
LicTh	Licentiate of Theology
MagArt	*Magister Artium* = Master of Arts
MDiv	Master of Divinity
MM	Master of Ministry
MPhil	Master of Philosophy
MRS	Master of Religious Studies
MTh	Master of Theology
MTS	Master in Theological Studies
PhD	Doctor in Philosophy
STM	Master of Sacred Theology
ThD	Doctor in Theology

Abbreviations for Regional and International Organisations

AACC	All Africa Conference of Churches
ABCFM	American Board of Commissioners for Foreign Mission
ACC	Anglican Consultative Council
AEAM	Association of Evangelicals of Africa and Madagascar

AIM	Africa Inland Mission
AIPRAL	Alianza de Iglesias Presbiterianas y Reformadas de América Latina *Alliance of Presbyterian and Reformed Churches of Latin America*
AWF	Alliance World Fellowship
CANAAC	Caribbean and North American Area Council
CANACOM	Caribbean and North American Council of Mission
CCA	Christian Conference of Asia
CCC	Caribbean Conference of Churches
CEEEFE	Commission des Eglises Evangéliques d'Expression Française à l'Extérieur *(Commission of French-speaking Protestant Churches Abroad [outside France])*
CELADEC	Consejo Evangelico Latino Americano de Educación Cristiana *(Latin American Committee on Christian Education)*
CEPPLE	Conférence des Eglises protestantes des pays latins d'Europe *(Conference of Protestant Churches of South-European Countries)*
CEVAA	Communauté Evangélique d'Action Apostolique *(Evangelical Community for Apostolic Action)*
CIEMAL	Consejo Iglesias Evangélicas Metodistas in America Latina *(Latin American Council of Evangelical Methodist Churches)*
CLAI	Consejo Latinoamericano de Iglesias *(Latin American Council of Churches)*
CLIR	Confederación Latinamericana de Iglesias Reformadas *(Federation of Latin American Reformed Churches — Latin-American region of WFRC)*
CMA	Christian and Missionary Alliance
CMS	Church Mission Society
CWM	Council for World Mission
DECC	Disciples Ecumenical Consultative Council
EACA	East Africa Christian Alliance
EECCS	Ecumenical European Commission on Church and Society (Brussels)
EMS	Evangelisches Missionswerk in Südwestdeutschland *(Protestant Mission in Southwest Germany)*
FECCC	Far Eastern Council of Christian Churches
IBPFM	Independent Board for Presbyterian Foreign Missions
ICCC	International Council of Christian Churches
ICF	International Congregational Fellowship
ICRC	International Council of Reformed Churches
IFFEC	International Federation of Free Evangelical Churches
IRF	International Reformed Fellowship
LMS	London Missionary Society

MAF	Missionary Aviation Fellowship
MECC	Middle East Council of Churches
MEFEC	Middle East Fellowship of Evangelical Churches
NAPARC	North American Presbyterian and Reformed Council
NER	Nordiska Ekumeniska Raedet *(Nordic Ecumenical Council)*
OAIC	Organization of African Independent Churches
OMF	Overseas Missionary Fellowship
PCC	Pacific Conference of Churches
QPS	Quaker Peace and Service
REC	Reformed Ecumenical Council
SAARC	Southern African Alliance of Reformed Churches (members of WARC)
UCBWM	United Church Board for World Ministry
VEM	Vereinigte Evangelische Mission *(United Evangelical Mission), Germany*
WAATI	West African Association of Theological Institutions
WACC	World Association for Christian Communication
WARC	World Alliance of Reformed Churches
WCC	World Council of Churches
WCBC	World Council of Biblical Churches
WEC	World Evangelization Crusade
WECF	World Evangelical Congregational Fellowship
WEF	World Evangelical Fellowship
WFRC	World Fellowship of Reformed Churches
WMC	World Methodist Council

1. THE REFORMED TRADITION AND ITS MULTIPLE FACETS

Lukas Vischer

1.0. PREFACE

The nature and message of the Reformed churches cannot be defined by referring exclusively to the Reformation, to relevant texts of John Calvin, and to the confessions of faith formulated in the 16th and 17th centuries. Reformed churches have developed since the Reformation. The original impulse has been enriched by new experiences and new movements. New horizons have appeared and new insights been gained.

Such developments have often led to divisions. The multiplicity of churches points both to the dynamism of the Reformed churches and to their inability to maintain communion in face of new challenges to interpret the Gospel. In many cases, divided churches are monuments to the controversies and struggles of the past.

From the beginning, the Reformed tradition has been characterized by two competing movements — on the one hand an effort to maintain bonds of unity and on the other a trend toward fragmentation. It was not the intention of the Reformers to set up a new church. The Reformation was meant to be a movement to renew the whole church according to God's Word, but separate Reformed churches came into existence because the program of reform was rejected by the Roman church. The need to form separate Reformed churches occurred against the will and hope of the Reformers. For a long time, they hoped that the dividing line would not become permanent. Calvin especially expended many efforts to achieve at least the unity of the Reformed camp; following his example, there have been efforts throughout history to bridge divisions through dialogue, consensus-building and processes of healing. Nevertheless, again and again, almost irresistibly, the centrifugal forces were stronger and new schisms were produced. How shall we interpret these two sides of Reformed tradition? How are the insights gained in history to be valued? What can we learn from historical experience for the life of the church today? What guidance can we derive from earlier attempts to manifest more fully God's gift of communion?

1.1. THE GREAT VARIETY OF NAMES

The complicated history of the Reformed churches finds expression in the variety of names by which Reformed churches designate themselves. The term *Reformed* does not appear in the names of all Reformed churches, although it is the most widely used term to refer to the group of churches presented in this volume. In contrast to other terms, it does not underline a particular characteristic of the church and therefore has a less denominational flavor. It points to the movement initiated by the Reformers and to the commitment to ever renewed reform in conformity with God's revealed Word. The full meaning of the term can be rendered by the phrase "The church reformed according to God's Word."

Reformed is the oldest self-designation of the churches, arising from the Reformation in Switzerland and the south of Germany. They called themselves *ecclesiae reformatae* in distinction from the Lutheran churches. The term was used of the churches identifying with the Swiss Reformation by the churches on the European continent and continues to be used by them today. Generally, the churches which came into existence through European migration, e.g., in the USA or South Africa, or through missionary efforts, e.g., Indonesia, call themselves Reformed.

The designations *Presbyterian* and *Congregationalist* came into use in the Anglo-Saxon world and are closely connected with the history of the Reformation in Britain. For decades of its early history, the Reformed church in Scotland had to defend its identity against the claims of the British crown and the Anglican church. In this struggle, the ministry of elders (presbyters) and the church order arising from it acquired more and more importance. The terms *episcopal* and *episcopalian* stood for the order to be rejected; the church reformed according to God's Word *had* to be *Presbyterian*. Today, the term is widely used throughout the Anglo-Saxon world, especially by churches which came into existence through Scottish and North American migration and missionary work.

The term *Congregationalist* is connected with the congregationalist movement which started in the late 16th century and emphasized, in contrast both to the Church of England and the Presbyterian Church, the role of the locally "gathered church" in worship, witness, and decision-making. Though in agreement with the doctrinal teaching of the Westminster Confession, the movement differed from it in its convictions in the area of church order (Savoy Declaration 1658). Congregationalism spread worldwide primarily through the London Missionary Society. Since many Congregationalist churches united with Presbyterian Churches or became part of even wider unions, fewer and fewer churches call themselves congregationalist, though many of them retain features of their congregationalist heritage. In 1970 the International Congregational Council, originally founded in 1891, united with the World Alliance of Presbyterian Churches to form the World Alliance of Reformed Churches (Presbyterian and Congregational). The specific titles in brackets, which had been regarded as essential in the beginning, were later usually dropped.

Manifold meanings are connected with the term *evangelical,* which appears in many self-designations of Reformed churches. Originally *euangelikos* simply means "related to the Gospel." The adjective does not occur in the Bible, but it came into use in later centuries to point to a life in accordance with the demands of the Gospel. When it is used in church names, it is generally meant to point to the sustaining ground of the Gospel. But there are nuances of meaning in various contexts. While in the first period after the Reformation the term was used to designate the churches that had joined the movement, it served later to point to the bond uniting the various streams of the Reformation: in Europe Lutheran and Reformed churches increasingly called themselves Evangelical-Lutheran or Evangelical-Reformed. In some cases, as, e.g., in the case of Evangelical Presbyterian churches, the term evangelical serves to place the particular characteristic of church order in the wider context of the church's indebtedness and commitment to the Gospel. The revival movement of the 19th century had a preference for the name because it wanted to emphasize both the message of the Gospel and the urgency of bringing it to all people. Today, some churches coming out of the revival bear the name *evangelical* (e.g., Société évangélique de Paris). At the same time, the term evangelical increasingly acquired the connotation of "anti-liberal." People and groups that wanted to distinguish themselves from liberal positions tended to claim the term for themselves. The Evangelical Alliance, founded in 1846, is a typical example of such an identification. In the 20th century, this tendency became even stronger. Those who upheld the doctrine of the inspiration of Scriptures and fought against the erosion of the church's missionary commitment called themselves *evangelicals.* Evangelical and ecumenical increasingly became mutually exclusive terms. There are, however, differences in various languages. While in English and French the term evangelical has come to mean conservative, the older use persists in other languages. In German the two meanings are expressed by two different terms — *"Evangelisch"* and *"Evangelikal."*

The term *Protestant* appears in some church names. It points to the common ground of all movements in the Reformation and is used especially in French (e.g., Eglise *protestante* unie de Belgique).

The issue of the relationship between church and state has been a source of preoccupation throughout the centuries. Especially during the 19th century, it was the reason for splits in several countries, including Scotland, Switzerland, the Netherlands, and Sweden. Movements against the subservience of the established church to the state have led to the formation of *free, liberated, or independent churches,* such as the Free Church of Geneva or the Free Church of Scotland. The term *independent* can also refer to autonomy with regard to mother churches, as in the case of the Independent Presbyterian Church of Brazil.

3

The term *covenant,* which also appears in some church names, is closely related to the congregationalist heritage. Reformed churches in general, and congregationalists in particular, conceived of the church as a covenant community. Faith in Christ leads to a common commitment to praise and serve the God of the covenants — the locally gathered community is a "covenanted community." This concept of covenant played a particularly important role in the revival and free church movements of the 19th century and gave rise to certain churches calling themselves covenant churches (e.g., the Mission Covenant Church in Sweden).

To underline their commitment to the authority of the Bible some churches call themselves *Fundamentalist* or add to their name the word *Bible,* e.g., Bible Presbyterian Church. Other churches, wanting to emphasize their faithfulness to traditional Reformed doctrine, add the term *Orthodox.* These self-descriptions have their roots in 20th-century debates concerning the verbal inspiration of Scriptures and the validity of the classical Reformed confessions.

Quite a number bear the term *united* in their name. In many cases it refers to intraconfessional unions or reunions of Reformed churches. The term is added to the name both to recognize the continuing existence of different Reformed streams and to celebrate their coming together. In other cases, the term designates a wider transconfessional union. In order to underline that all these unions do not yet represent the unity of the Una Sancta and that further steps are to be envisaged, some churches have chosen the name *uniting.*

Some church names are specific and unique. This is particularly the case for the churches pre-dating the Reformation — the Waldensian Church in Italy, named after its founder Peter Waldo (12th century), and the Czech Brethren whose origin goes back to the Hussite movement of the 15th century. Another very particular name appeared at the beginning of the 19th century with the movement of the "Disciples of Christ" (cf. Chapter 2, Appendix and Chapter 5).

Names are more than just labels. Anyone who has been engaged in debates about names, and especially name changes, knows to what extent names are connected with feeling and emotions. Names are also expressions of identity. They point to past experiences and present struggles. While a common name underlines the bonds of communion within one and the same family, particular names distinguish a church from other churches and tend to harden the lines of separation. It is therefore essential not to lose sight, within the great variety of names, of the common heritage all Reformed churches share.

1.2. THE HISTORY OF THE REFORMED CHURCHES: A BRIEF SURVEY

1.2.1. The Reformation

The Reformation of the 16th century was not a sudden or isolated event but the prolongation and culmination of earlier attempts to reform the church. In Western Christianity the idea of reform was alive from at least the 12th century. The appearances of the Waldensian and later the Hussite movements were signals that the structure of the medieval church was not going to last forever. These movements, which later joined the Reformation, are often called the "First Reformation." In the 15th century the Reform movement found expression in the Reform Council of Constance (1414-18) and Basel (1431). The Humanist Movement called for reforms. The urgency of change was widely recognized when Luther, in 1517, began to spread the message of salvation in Christ alone, reinterpreting and at the same time accelerating the movement.

From the very beginning the Reformation occurred in various movements, distinct in their origin and profile but, of course, in constant interaction. Luther's message found wide response in Germany and adjacent countries. For many years the Reformation movement was identified with his name, and those engaged in spreading the message and in renewing and reorganizing the church were generally called Lutherans. Almost simultaneously, other centers sprang up in the south of Germany, in Strasbourg, and in what is today Switzerland. Under the leadership of Ulrich Zwingli (1484-1531) the city of Zurich introduced the Reformation in 1523. Other cities followed — Strasbourg with Martin Bucer (1491-1551), Basel with Johannes Oecolampadius (1482-1531), Berne with Bertold Haller (1492-1536). At a very early date (1525) the Anabaptist movement made its appearance in various places. The whole of Europe was caught in a movement of religious unrest.

The life of Zwingli came to an abrupt end in the war setting Zurich against the Swiss Cantons of central Switzerland, which maintained and defended the traditional faith (1531). Zwingli was replaced by Heinrich Bullinger (1504-1575), who for decades led the church of Zurich and gave to the Zwinglian Reformation its lasting profile. Through his writings and his correspondence he exercised wide influence throughout Europe. He was the author of the Second Helvetic Confession (1561).

The movement of the Reformation was well advanced when, under the leadership of John Calvin (1509-1564), Geneva emerged as a new center of the Reformation. Born in Noyon in France, Calvin studied Latin, logic, and law in Paris, Orléans, and Bourges. A conflict at the university of Paris forced him to leave France in 1533. Three years later Guillaume Farel persuaded him to stay in Geneva, whose citizens had decided to join the Reformation movement. In the following two years Calvin devoted all his strength to consolidating the changes the population had opted for. But soon a controversy about church discipline arose, and Farel and Calvin were forced to leave the city. During the following three years he served the French-speaking community in Strasbourg; he worked there on his *Institutes* and began in his sermons the series of Bible commentaries that were to become characteristic of his spirituality. Called back by the Genevans in 1541, he gradually succeeded in introducing the reform of both the church and the city of Geneva. In 1542 he published his famous Catechism for the religious instruction of children. In the same year he published liturgical material to guide worship in the city. The singing of psalms, already introduced in Strasbourg, also became a practice in Geneva. Soon his activity again met with resistance. For many years his ministry was contested by a group of Geneva citizens. It must also be remembered that the city of Geneva lived under the constant threat of neighboring Savoy, which looked for any opportunity to reconquer the city. Independence could only be maintained through the support of the Swiss cities, especially Berne, which had joined the Reformation. An important step in the history of the Geneva Reformation was the foundation of the Theological Academy in Geneva in 1559, whose first rector Theodore Beza (1519-1605) was to become Calvin's successor.

The impact of Calvin's teaching and leadership was immense. His personality has given rise to different interpretations. To this day, views on him fundamentally diverge. While he is praised for the clarity of his thinking, for his biblical insights, for his commitment to social justice, for his awareness of new problems, and for his extraordinary perseverance in carrying out the reform, his critics denounce the strictness of his thinking both in the doctrinal and ethical fields, and reject his style of leadership as dictatorial. From generation to generation his image has remained controversial. There is unanimity, however, that Calvin regarded himself as the servant of the church of Christ and always warned against attributing excessive significance to his own person. Though he is and remains, no doubt, the primary source of inspiration, the Reformed tradition is not bound to his person, and it would be a mistake to call Reformed Christians "Calvinists." Calvin's passion was to point to Christ and God's Word in the Scriptures and to invite the church to live in accordance with it.

In his letter to Cardinal Sadolet, Calvin explains why the Reformation had become inevitable. He understood his own activity as the effort to "gather the dispersed servants of Christ in the one Church." In his eyes, there was no room for compromise with regard to the inherited teaching, worship, and practice of his time. Unity could only be achieved "in Christ." Calvin was, however, deeply concerned with the unification of the churches of the Reformation. He succeeded in bringing together the churches of Zürich and Geneva through the *Consensus Tigurinus* (1549). His hopes to solve the dispute on the real presence of Christ in the Lord's Supper were not fulfilled. Despite his efforts at mediation (cf. especially his masterful Short Treatise on the Lord's Supper of 1541), the rift between Lutherans and Reformed over the interpretation of the Eucharist could not be healed. The controversies he was drawn into, especially with Westphal in the second half of his ministry in Geneva, led to a hardening of the lines of separation.

At the time of Calvin's death the Reformed churches had spread widely in many parts of Europe. Switzerland remained the heartland of the Reformed churches. The movement had penetrated into France, the Netherlands, England, Scotland, Austria, Czechia, and Bohemia, Hungary, and Poland. In 1537 the Waldensians of Italy also joined the Reformation at the Synod of Chanforan.

Of special importance were the developments in France. King Francis I (1515-1547) was undecided in his attitude toward the Reformation. On the one hand he sympathized with change; on the other hand he took severe measures against the threat of dissidence. Throughout his reign Reformed Christians were arrested and burned. Persecutions continued under his successor, Henry II. Despite these difficulties Reformed leaders were able to convene in 1559 the first National Synod and to decide on both a confession of faith and a church order. While the

Reformation in Switzerland was a magisterial decision, involving cities as a whole, the Reformation in France led to another model — a minority church which could not count on the support of the political authorities and could at any time become the object of persecution. In Geneva, Calvin fought for the relative independence of the church from the state, but, since the Reformation had been introduced by the city, the interdependence of church and state was almost inevitable. In France the pattern of an independent church was forced on the Reformed community. Both models have played a significant role in the history of the Reformed churches. In the second part of the century the tension in France deteriorated into armed conflict which lasted from 1560 to 1598. During the first years a settlement still seemed to be within reach. In 1571 the National Synod met in La Rochelle and issued the Confession of Faith of the French Reformed Church. But a year later the massacre on the "Night of Saint Bartholomew" destroyed all hope for peaceful coexistence. The war resumed until the end of the century. Finally, in 1598, Henry IV (1589-1610) granted the Reformed community freedom of conscience through the Edict of Nantes.

In the middle of the century Reformed influence began to become dominant in the Netherlands. Already in preceding decades, the message of the Reformation had found a favorable response in the country. Increasingly in the 1550s and 60s Reformed theologians and preachers were active in the country. In 1563 the Heidelberg Catechism was translated into Dutch, and in 1566 a Dutch version of the Geneva psalms was published. For the Netherlands, the Reformed tradition took shape in the course of the liberation struggle (1568-1648) against the Spanish occupation. The war led to a clear division within the Netherlands. While the southern provinces under the domination of the House of Hapsburg remained Catholic, the northern provinces gained independence and developed gradually into a powerful Protestant nation. During the war the role of the Reformed tradition was strengthened. At the Synod of Emden (1571), the *Confessio Belgica* (1561) and the *Confessio Gallicana* (1559) were accepted and the Calvinist church order introduced.

The Reformation also took roots in Scotland in the 1550s. The main figure of the Scottish Reformation was John Knox (1505-1572), who in the 1540s had become a fervent defender of anti-Roman convictions. In 1547, he was sentenced to the French galleys but managed to escape. After a period as preacher for the English-speaking refugees in Geneva (1553-1555), he returned to Scotland but met with so much resistance that he had to withdraw again to Geneva. Here he published his famous pamphlet "against the monstrous women's régime" to denounce Queen Mary of Scotland. In 1559 he returned to become the religious leader of the Scottish Reformation. Deeply impressed by Calvin's teaching, he introduced Reformed teaching and practice. Three texts were issued — the *Confessio Scotica* (1560), the Book of Discipline (1560), and the Book of Common Order (1564). With its strong emphasis on the ministry of elders, the church order promoted by John Knox can be called "Presbyterian." In 1567, when Queen Mary left the country, the victory of the Reformation was complete. But there were other struggles ahead. Scottish Presbyterianism had to face the claims of the British crown and the Church of England.

1.2.2. Consolidation of the Reformation Movement

Gradually, the Reformation became a separate tradition. Various stages can be distinguished in the history of the Reformed churches. They can be illustrated by the various statements or confessions of faith that were drawn up. The first stage was the struggle to introduce the new order of the Reformation: to give room to the demands of the Word of God; to replace the celebration of the mass with regular preaching and the common celebration of the Lord's Supper; to simplify the spiritual life and the activities of the church, and so on. In order to reach a decision, the Reformers offered to defend their positions in public. Normally disputations were arranged and in the light of the debate the magistrate decided whether or not to join the Reformation. When a city opted for the Reformation, those who dissented either had to obey or emigrate.

Theses prepared for disputations were the first form of Reformed confessions, e.g., Zwingli's 67 "Schlussreden" of 1523, the Berne Theses of 1528, and the like. Soon the need arose to explain and to defend the Reformation both to the population and to the outside world, in particular to the authorities of the Empire. It had to be shown that the Reformation corresponded to the true Tradition over against the deviations in the medieval church. Also, it had to be made clear that the Reformed cities rejected the extreme position of the Anabaptists and later the Anti-trinitarians. Examples of this new type of confession are the *Fidei ratio* of Ulrich Zwingli addressed to the Diet of Augsburg in 1530, the Synod of Berne formulated by Wolfgang Capito, and the First Helvetic Confession of 1536.

A further stage was reached by the middle of the 16th century. The need arose to give a coherent account of the Christian faith as it was taught by the Reformed churches. The Belgic Confession, the Heidelberg Catechism, and the Second Helvetic Confession are summaries of this kind. They serve both as the source and the criterion of the correct teaching of the church. It is worth noting that no confessional statement ever acquired the adherence of all Reformed churches. While for the Lutheran churches the *Confessio Augustana* (1530) became *the* authoritative confession of faith, throughout the centuries various confessional statements continued to exist side by side among the Reformed churches. Unity among Reformed churches found expression through processes of mutual recognition rather than through the acceptance of a single text. From time to time attempts were made either to suggest a single confession or to underline the unity of doctrine by a harmony or synopsis of all Reformed confessions, but none of these efforts had a lasting impact on the Reformed Churches.

The second part of the 16th century saw the beginning and gradual rise of Reformed Orthodoxy. In contrast to Luther and other Reformers Calvin had developed his teaching in a systematic way. The first edition of his *Institutes*, a full development of Christian doctrine, was published in 1536, even before the beginning of his ministry in Geneva. Throughout his life he worked on the text, refining and completing it. The fullest edition of the *Institutes* appeared a few years before his death. But Calvin never fell prisoner to his own system. His thinking and spirituality were rooted in a constant intercourse with the biblical witness. He was primarily a preacher and biblical scholar. Through biblical studies he was led to teach the doctrines of covenant and predestination, but they do not hold in his thinking the central place often ascribed to them by later generations. Calvin's thinking is characterized by a deep sense for the mysterious nature of God's action. After his death, Reformed doctrine took a more definite form. More and more, Reformed thinking was organized into a coherent system by theologians like Theodore Beza. More and more, Reformed theology appealed to reason to develop the truth revealed in Christ. More and more, the notions of predestination and covenant became the organizing principles of the Reformed doctrinal edifice.

A similar development took place in the field of church order. Increasingly, the ministry of elders which had been introduced by Calvin in Geneva became *the* characteristic of the Reformed churches. In Scotland, in the controversies with the Church of England over episcopacy, the emphasis on eldership acquired the status of a sign of independence. Andrew Melville (1545-1622), a Scottish theologian and teacher who had passed several years of study and teaching in Geneva, promoted the Presbyterian system with fervor. He was the author of the Second Book of Discipline, which was accepted by the General Assembly in 1581. While Calvin was still prepared to accept other forms of church structure, as long as the preaching of God's Word was assured, the Presbyterian order was now regarded as the only biblically valid form of government.

Reformed orthodoxy did not remain unchallenged. In particular, the doctrine of predestination led to controversies and threatened to divide the Reformed family. Jacobus Arminius (1560-1609), professor in Leiden in 1603, called the doctrine of double predestination into question. He found followers but was also sharply attacked by the representatives of Reformed orthodoxy. The real conflict began after Arminius's death. In 1610 Johan van Oldenbarnevelt (1547-1619) published a public declaration, the *Remonstratie,* deviating from the strict doctrine of predestination. He held that God has destined for salvation those who believe, that Christ has died for the whole of humanity; that grace is not within reach of human will but that it is not irresistible. The controversy, which was theological in nature, also had political connotations. The opponents of Arminianism fought for the independence of church from state control. To come to a common mind among the Reformed churches, the authorities called an international synod — the *Synod of Dordrecht* (November 13, 1618, to May 29, 1619). In addition to the Dutch participants, it was attended by 26 delegates from abroad. Arminianism was clearly condemned. The Canons of Dordrecht maintain that election does not depend on faith, that Christ's death brings salvation only to the elect, that human nature is corrupted by sin, that conversion is effected exclusively by God, and that the elect will surely persist in faith. The Remonstrants were removed from the ministry. Oldenbarnevelt was executed by the state, and the famous lawyer Hugo Grotius imprisoned for life. The Canons of Dordrecht acquired the status of a Reformed confession and even today are recognized as such by certain Reformed churches.

In the last decades of the 16th century, England gave birth to two movements which were to have a considerable impact on the Reformed tradition — Puritanism and Congregationalism. The Reformation in England had been a political act. In

1539, Henry VIII had declared independence from Rome. Only under Henry's successor Edward VI (1547-1553) was the reform carried out in depth. In 1549 the Book of Common Prayer and in 1553 the 39 Articles were published. Refugees from all over Europe found protection in England. Under the leadership of Johannes a Lasco the refugee community became a model of Reformed teaching and discipline. But soon the situation changed. Succeeding Edward, Queen Mary (1553-1558) sought to reestablish the Catholic faith. The Protestants had to leave the country, and Archbishop Thomas Cranmer was executed (1556). Following this interlude the long reign of Elizabeth I (1558-1603), who affirmed the reforms introduced under Edward VI, began. Elizabeth I's primary interest was the supremacy of the crown over the church. The maintenance of the episcopal system was therefore beyond any dispute.

For the Puritans, the Reformation in England had not gone far enough. They questioned the validity of the *via media* between Geneva and Rome favored by the queen and called for more thorough changes. For many, the model of the Scottish Reformation served as inspiration. Their theological and spiritual views were radical. Their primary concern was to give honor and glory to God alone. God's Word had to be the guiding principle in all aspects of life. Though they respected political authority, they left no doubt that they were not prepared to accept any compromise when the integrity of God's Word was at stake. Worship had to follow the prescriptions of the Bible. All external forms, such as rites, images, or vestments, were to be rejected. Puritans were, in particular, suspicious of liturgically ordered worship. Though adamant in their demands, they did not impose their views by force but were prepared to bear the consequences of their protest. Among the Puritans the names of the following deserve to be mentioned: William Perkins (1558-1603), William Ames (1576-1633), and John Robinson (1576-1625). Until the middle of the 17th century the movement was a political force. As a type of spirituality it had continuing influence in subsequent centuries. It has left deep marks on the Reformed tradition in North America.

Congregationalists went a step further. They organized independent congregations. The first to advocate the congregationalist order was Robert Browne (ca.1550-ca.1633), who in 1582 defended in two volumes the principle of the gathered church. The concept was new and represented a deviation from both Calvin's and Melville's teaching. When in 1562 the Frenchman Jean Morély defended the thesis that the local church was to be considered the ultimate authority in the life of the church and therefore that church discipline had to be carried out by the community as a whole, Theodore Beza, Calvin's successor in Geneva, rejected the idea. He was as unable to agree with the "Morellian democracy" as with the "Tyranny of Rome." In England, the movement was regarded as a threat to the established order and therefore met with fierce repression. John Greenwood, Henry Barrow, and John Penry, the leaders succeeding Browne, were hanged in 1593. Nevertheless, their number and significance increased. Many independents emigrated to the Netherlands and to America. The Mayflower expedition of the Pilgrim Fathers, which resulted in the establishment of colonies in New England, had a deep impact on the history of the church in America. Congregationalism later developed in various directions — while on the one hand many were deeply engaged in the rising revival movement, others increasingly adopted more liberal positions.

Elizabeth's successors, the Stuarts, James I (1603-1625) and Charles I (1625-1649), had to grapple with all these contesting movements. In Scotland the conflict with the British crown entered into a new stage when, in 1637, the liturgy of the Church of England was to be introduced in Saint Giles in Edinburgh. In response, national leaders declared a National Covenant. Also confronted with resistance in England, in 1640 Charles I finally agreed to call first the "short" and then the "long" parliament. When the king sought to limit its power, the struggle turned into armed conflict. In 1642 the parliament decided to turn its attention to the reform of the church, to abolish the episcopal system, and to call a special synod. Against the declared will of the king the synod convened on July 1, 1643. Its membership consisted of 20 members each of the Upper House and the House of Commons and 121 ministers — Anglicans, Puritans, and Independents. The Synod, called after the place of its meetings the Westminster Synod, quickly set to work and achieved in a relatively short time the revision of the 39 Articles. In the following years the Synod issued guidelines for worship and church order (1645), the Westminster Confession (1647), and two — the shorter and the larger — Catechisms (1648). In 1643 the Scottish leaders had strengthened the authority of both the parliament and the synod by entering the Solemn League and Covenant. In 1647 the Church of Scotland adopted the Westminster Confession, with some amendments, as its confessional basis. It was to become the most widespread of all Reformed confessional writings.

The Westminster Confession follows the teaching of Reformed orthodoxy, stressing the doctrines of predestination and the covenants. Independents had their reservations. In 1648 the Congregationalists in New England formulated their principles of church order in the so-called Cambridge Platform. In England, in 1658, they issued the Savoy Declaration, in which they basically recognized the teaching of the Westminster Confession but developed their own understanding of church order.

In the 17th century Presbyterianism began to develop in Ireland. James I, eager to bring Ireland under English control, consequently implemented a "plantation system" with immigrants from England and southwestern Scotland. Scots settled in the "Plantation of Ulster" in Northern Ireland, taking with them their Presbyterian commitments. Tensions between the Irish and the English grew during the 17th century. In 1641 Irish Catholics revolted and massacred many of the Protestant immigrants. To protect their countrymen the Scots sent troops to strengthen Cromwell's army to suppress the insurrection. Under James II, who was himself Catholic, the Irish Catholics threatened the Protestants in an extended siege of Derry. William of Orange, the new king of England and leader of the Protestant army, lifted the siege and defeated the deposed James II at the battle of the Boyne (1690), a victory which is remembered by the Irish Presbyterians to this day. Problems continued, however. The Anglican Church being recognized as the official church, and Presbyterians were regarded as dissenters. In the 18th century many Irish Presbyterians left the country for North America.

1.2.3. Persecutions and New Horizons

In the course of the 17th century Reformed churches began to take roots in other continents. As result of a French expedition a small Reformed community had come into being in Brazil already in 1557, and in 1562 Huguenots settled in Florida. But the real expansion began in the following century. In the early 17th century several Reformed churches took roots in North America. The emigration of Independents to New England (Plymouth Colony 1620, Massachusetts Bay Colony 1630) has already been mentioned. In 1624 Dutch emigrants founded New York, then called New Amsterdam. Presbyterians followed at the end of the century. Francis Makemie (†1708), an Ulster Scot, settled on the eastern shore of Virginia in 1683, planting churches in Maryland as well as in Virginia. He later played a leading role in organizing the first presbytery in Philadelphia (1706). As the numbers of immigrants increased, this presbytery was transformed into the synod of Philadelphia with three presbyteries — Philadelphia, New Castle, and Long Island (1716). In 1729 the synod adopted the Westminster Confession and the catechisms and required that all members assent to these documents; but the synod also provided for a way of "scrupling," that is, of allowing those who felt the need for it to express disagreement. It declared that the articles of the Westminster Confession dealing with the relation to the civil magistrate were not essential and necessary for faith and life in the American colonies.

Although all major Christian confessions were represented among the immigrants, Christians of Reformed persuasion dominated the early colonization process in the New World. The various streams of immigrants did not, however, come together to form one Reformed church. They all had their particular roots and history, and developed as separate communities with their separate history.

Another important factor in spreading Reformed Christianity internationally was the rise of the Dutch as a leading commercial power. In connection with the activities of the Dutch East India Company (1602), Dutch Reformed congregations were set up in several parts of the world (Caribbean, South Africa [1652], Sri Lanka, Batavia, Formosa). The involvement of the Dutch in northern Brazil (1624-1654) led to the foundation of a Reformed church. Between 1630 and 1648 nineteen presbytery meetings and four synodal assemblies took place in Recife, the political center of the Dutch colony. Fifty pastors served throughout the vast northeastern region; their ministry included Dutch, Portuguese, black, and indigenous people. Generally the Dutch presence had only a limited impact. Their limited understanding of indigenous cultures meant that the efforts of Dutch pastors had no lasting effect. As a rule they ministered to the Europeans, in particular the Dutch, who had settled in the Dutch colonies.

During the period of expansion into other continents, the Reformed churches suffered setbacks in several European countries. The systematic efforts of the Counter-Reformation led to persecutions, especially in the Austro-Hungarian Empire. In the 17th century the Reformed believers in Hungary became victims of severe repression. Roman Catholicism was ruthlessly reimposed in the country. Measures culminated in the "Bloody Tribunal" of Bratislava (1673). Pastors were forced to renounce their faith; many were expelled or sold as galley slaves.

In 1685 an event took place in France that was to have lasting repercussions on the history of the Reformed churches, not only in France but also in other countries. For years, the Reformed churches in France had been the object of harassment and injustice. In the eyes of Louis XIV the presence of dissident communities seemed to undermine the unity of the nation. In 1685 he finally decided to abrogate the *Edict of Nantes* issued by Henry IV in 1598, which granted the Reformed believers freedom of conscience. Protestant Christians were forced to return to the Catholic faith. Though adherents of the Reformed Church were not allowed to emigrate, more than 200,000 left the country and sought new homes in other countries — in Switzerland, the Netherlands, Germany, and the like. Many eventually emigrated to other continents, in particular to South Africa. In almost all Reformed churches, "Huguenot" communities were established. In many respects the "Grand Refuge" was a blessing for the Reformed churches. It challenged their sense of solidarity and brought a new quality to their life. The experience of the French Reformed minority church made manifest what it meant to be a conscious member of the church.

The second part of the 17th century marks the beginning of a new period not only for the Reformed churches but for the whole of Christianity. With the Enlightenment new modes of thinking became dominant. Knowledge was to be based on the criteria of reason and reasonable deduction. While the Reformers of the 16th century had taken for granted God's revelation in Christ, now no truth could be admitted that could not be proved by reason. While the Reformers started from the recognition that human beings, blinded by disobedience and sin, were unable to know God through the capacities of their reason and had therefore to rely on God's redeeming Word, the Enlightenment was guided by a new confidence in the ability of human beings to discover the truth. Generally, philosophers of the Enlightenment did not question the existence of God and the validity of Christ's teaching. But they based their acceptance of the fundamental Christian doctrines on deduction by reason.

Traditional Reformed teaching was called into question primarily in two areas — predestination and the verbal inspiration of the Scriptures. The doctrine of predestination seemed to deny the capacity of human beings to take responsibility for their lives. God's initiative occupies the center; human beings are to glorify God's name. The claim that the Scriptures were divinely inspired and therefore to be accepted in all areas of life as ultimate authority seemed to preclude the free exercise of human reason. Increasingly, in the course of the 18th century, the Enlightenment stressed the historical character of the biblical books. Written by human authors at a particular time and in a particular historical context, they witnessed to the truth. Their truth claims had to be verified.

Though the Synod of Dordrecht had clearly rejected all proposals to attenuate the doctrine of predestination, the criticism increased in subsequent years. For the orthodox mind, the Enlightenment undermined the Christian message. A last attempt to defend the integrity of orthodox Reformed teaching was made in Switzerland in 1675 through the publication of the *Formula Consensus Helvetica,* which reiterated orthodox teaching. It met with only limited approval, and a generation later the teachers in most Swiss theological schools sought ways to reconcile the affirmations based on revelation and the Reformed confessions with the demands of reason ("Enlightened Orthodoxy": Turretini, Ostervald, Werenfels). Gradually, the significance of the Reformed confession diminished. Reformed theology became more and more open to free research.

Orthodox positions were also increasingly shaken by the call for a more personal piety. In all parts of the Protestant world movements arose placing primary emphasis on personal conversion, spiritual renewal and sharing in fellowship — Pietism in Germany, Switzerland, and the Netherlands, Methodism in Britain, and the Great Awakening among the American colonialists. Mere acceptance of the correct doctrine on justification by faith was not sufficient. To be saved Jesus Christ had to touch and to transform the heart. True faith had to transform life and to bear visible fruits. In Germany the movement started with Lutheran Philipp J. Spener (1635-1705) and his famous book *Pia desideria,* published in 1675. The most creative representative of the movement was Count Nikolaus von Zinzendorf (1700-1760), the founder of the Moravian church (Brüderunität) in Herrnhut. Among the Pietists in the Netherlands Jean de Labadie (1610-1674), a former Jesuit, Theodor Undereyck (1635-1693), and Gerhard Tersteegen (1697-1769), a layman and author of outstanding hymns, deserve special mention. The Methodist movement in England was largely inspired by Reformed theology and had a strong impact on the Presbyterian Church both in England and America. George Whitefield (1714-1770) especially had a considerable influence on the Reformed constituency in America during his colonial itineracy. The main representatives of the Great Awakening in America were Gilbert Tennent (1703-1764) and Jonathan Edwards (1703-1758), both powerful preachers of personal conversion. The movement led to a temporary split in the nascent Presbyterian Church of America. For two decades the Presbyterian Synod was divided into the "New Side" and "Old Side" churches. In 1758 re-union was achieved.

Increasingly, in the course of the 18th century, Reformed churches began to advocate tolerance in society. The experience of Reformed minorities and especially the expulsion in France led to a reflection on the rights of minorities. Traditionally, where the Reformation had been magisterial in character, dissidents had no place in society. The Reformed churches' attitude toward religious minorities, in particular the Anabaptists, belongs to the darker chapters of their history. Both in Zurich and in Berne Anabaptists were persecuted or expelled; the repression continued even into the 18th century. To escape hardship, many emigrated to North America. But in the course of the 18th century the mentality began to change; in some areas, in particular in the Netherlands, Germany, and North America, the principles of religious freedom and "human rights" began to be accepted and promoted.

At the end of the 18th century, the Reformed churches found themselves in a deeply contradictory situation. Reformed teaching as it had developed since the Reformation was called into question from many sides. How were the Reformed churches to respond? On the one hand the need for new interpretations and departures was felt. The challenges of the new era needed to be met, and they could not be met within the framework of Reformed orthodoxy. On the other hand, continuity with the past had to be maintained. As basic affirmations of the Christian faith were denied, faithfulness to the heritage of the Reformers and the confessions which had sought to respond to their message was required. Ever since the end of the 18th century the "Reformed tradition" had this double face. On the one hand, there were Reformed Christians who regarded themselves as being on the way, from horizon to horizon, responding to the questions of their time on the basis of the Scriptures and of the witness of the Reformation, affirming but also correcting and reinterpreting the teaching of the past. On the other hand, there were those who regarded the teaching of the Reformed confessions as definitive and unalterable and were therefore determined to "conserve" and protect it against new modes of thinking. Ever since the end of the 18th century, the Reformed tradition has been characterized by the struggle between progressive and conservative approaches. Again and again, Reformed churches have split along this dividing line.

1.2.4. The 19th Century

In the course of the 19th century the profile of the Reformed tradition changed considerably. New interpretations of the Christian heritage became dominant.

Of greatest significance in this respect is Friedrich Daniel Ernst Schleiermacher (1768-1834), Reformed preacher at the Charité in Berlin (1798) and later Professor of Systematic Theology at the universities of Halle (1802) and Berlin (1807). In his theology he sought to develop an alternative to the rationalism of the Enlightenment. He made an attempt to understand Christian teaching as the expression of true religion. Religious experience is part of human existence. Christian teaching has arisen from religious experience and in order to be plausible needs to be retranslated into it. Humanity reaches its fullness in religious experience, in the awareness of being fundamentally dependent on God and the universe. In his theology Schleiermacher sought to show that Christianity is the most adequate expression of this basic experience. Revelation in Christ basically means the recognition of true religion, and redemption the transition from a limited to a more complete understanding of God. Schleiermacher places strong emphasis on the significance of the church. True religion creates community; the church is the place where religious experience is cultivated and developed. Throughout his life Schleiermacher was not only a theological teacher but exercised his ministry as preacher with conviction. His theology remained influential throughout the 19th century, especially in Europe.

Another significant development was the birth of the Revival Movement around the turn of the century. In many respects the revival was the continuation of the 18th century movements already mentioned — Pietism, Methodism, and the Great Awakening. Faced with the rise of anti-Christian forces, the Revival Movement sought to reconquer souls for Christ. Often their message included rationalist elements, e.g., apologetic attempts to "prove" or make plausible revealed truth by rational arguments. From the beginning the movement was characterized by a strong commitment to evangelism and mission. The two brothers Robert (1764-1846) and James Alexander Haldane (1768-1851) belonged to the founders of the movement in Scotland. On the basis of a theology which combined a commonsense philosophy with pietist perspectives they called for the renewal of the Church of Scotland. Robert Haldane traveled widely on the European continent and had a decisive influence on the Revival Movement in Geneva and France. In 1797 James Alexander founded the Society for Propagating the Gospel at Home. The movement swept through the European countries and had its parallel also in America. Its most famous representative in the United States was Charles Grandison Finney (1792-1875).

These developments in theology and spirituality had varying impacts on the Reformed churches. In some places they contributed to unions of Protestant churches, in others they were the cause of new divisions.

In Germany the jubilee of the Reformation in 1817 became the occasion for the Evangelical churches — Lutheran and Reformed — to form united churches. Convinced that "the differences between the two streams of the Reformation did not touch upon the essential content of religion," the King of Prussia, Friedrich Wilhelm II, called on the Protestant churches in his territories to unite. Initially, the response was enthusiastic. In the course of a few years the churches in several German states joined the movement of union, e.g., Hassia in 1817-18, Baden in 1821, and Kurhessen-Waldeck in 1821. Controversy broke out when, in 1822, the Prussian king proposed a common liturgical order (Agendenstreit). In certain areas the move was strongly opposed, and it took some time and much political wisdom to maintain peace in the churches of the Prussian territory.

In America a new situation had arisen with independence from Britain. On the whole the Reformed community, especially the Presbyterian churches, had supported the movement toward independence. John Witherspoon (1732-1794), a Presbyterian pastor, even helped to shape the Declaration of Independence (1776). The new era brought new challenges to the churches. They had to organize themselves within the new nation. Some groups merged, e.g., two Presbyteries related to Scotland, the Associate Presbytery (formed in 1753) and the Reformed Presbytery (formed in 1774), united in 1782 to become the Associate Reformed Synod. Presbyterians gave themselves a national structure in 1788 by forming the General Assembly of the Presbyterian Church in the United States of America (PCUSA). Comparable processes took place in other Reformed churches. At the same time the churches had to come to terms with the general movement to the western part of the continent. New churches had to be set up. The challenge of the "frontier" led to collaborative efforts but also to many tensions. Several splits took place. Deeply affected by the revival experiences in Kentucky, groups of Presbyterians in the Cumberland region wanted to engage in a more effective ministry on the western frontier; their critique of the Westminster Confession eventually led to a split which resulted in the formation of the Cumberland Presbyterian Church (1810).

The foundation of the Christian Churches (Disciples of Christ) is also part of the same context. The church emerged on the frontier, then western Pennsylvania and Kentucky, in the years 1800-1840. Its founders were Alexander Campbell (1788-1866) and Barton Stone (1772-1844), and the two movements initiated by them united in the 1830s. In conflict with a conservative Presbyterian community, Campbell decided to go his own way. He appealed to Protestants of all traditions to form a church exclusively based on the biblical Word of God. The Disciples quickly grew but suffered several splits in subsequent times.

On the European continent, especially in Switzerland, Reformed churches were marked by controversies over the validity of the Reformed confessions. The authority of the *Formula Consensus Helvetica* had already been rejected in the 18th century. In the 19th century the controversies centered on the role to be attributed to the Second Helvetic Confession and, finally, even the Creeds. The question arose especially in state churches, which claimed to represent the whole of the population and therefore had to take into account a wide range of religious and intellectual sensitivities. The abolition of the binding character of confessions and creeds by majority votes sharply raised the question of the independence of the church from the state. The debates on the status of confessions resulted in the formation of a number of Free churches.

The church of Scotland was especially shaken by the debates on the relationship of church and state. It had already been the main issue in the 18th century. The controversies centered on the question of the approval of the election of pastors by the congregation. In 1733, in protest against the claims of the state and against the subservience of the church, the first secession took place (Ebenezer Erskine), and in 1752 a second secession (Thomas Gillespie) followed. In the 19th century a further split occurred. The revival movement had led to a renewal in the Church of Scotland. Under the leadership of Thomas Chalmers the "Evangelicals" sought to give increased significance to local communities. In protest against the rights of patrons to name pastors, they finally decided to leave the Church of Scotland. In 1843, 470 pastors founded the Free Church of Scotland.

The most important development for the future of the family of Reformed churches was the birth of the missionary movement. Mission had not been a central theme of the Reformation. While Roman Catholics, especially the Jesuits, engaged in missionary efforts from the 16th century, the attention of the Reformers concentrated on the proclamation of God's Word and on the renewal of the existing church. It took the Reformed churches almost three centuries to discover the relevance of the missionary mandate. In the 18th and 19th centuries, coinciding with the colonial period, intense missionary activity developed. In a few decades the Gospel was brought to many parts of the world. Gradually the Reformed tradition became a worldwide reality. The breakthrough was due to Pietism and the Revival Movement. Among the pioneers, Nikolaus von Zinzendorf, the founder of the Moravian community, holds a special position. He took the initiative for starting missionary efforts, especially in the Caribbean. At the end of the 18th and in the early 19th centuries centers of missionary outreach were founded in several countries: in England, the London Missionary Society (1795); in Holland, the Nederlandsch Zendelinggenootschap (1797); in South Africa, the South African

Mission Society (1799); in the USA, the American Board of Commissioners for Foreign Mission (1810); in Switzerland and Germany, the Basel Mission (1835); in France, the Mission évangélique de Paris (1822), to mention only a few. Perspectives differed. Most mission societies saw their primary task as bringing the Gospel to the peoples of the world and minimized, at least initially, the importance of links with the churches of their own countries. Others, e.g., the South African Mission Society, sought an explicit mandate from their church. More and more, in the course of the 19th century, mission societies established closer links with the denominations to which they belonged. But the original impulse of the Revival Movement found expression again and again in the foundation of new non-denominational missionary enterprises. Important examples were the China Inland Mission founded by J. Hudson Taylor (1832-1905) and the Sudan Interior Mission (SIM, 1893, since 1989 called Society for International Ministries).

The missionary movement resulted in the founding of churches in all continents. Initially efforts were principally directed to countries in Africa and Asia. In the second part of the 19th century, mainly through efforts from America, Reformed and Presbyterian churches were also established in Latin America. Many of these churches bear the characteristics of the Revival Movement. As a rule, missionary efforts were carried out without much concern for thorough coordination. In many countries, therefore, they led to the foundation of separate churches within the same country. Often splits which had occurred in the home county were reproduced on the mission field.

In the 19th century social witness increasingly became part of the churches' life and activities. A new sense of freedom led many church people to join the struggle against slavery. The issue of whether or not holding of slaves could be reconciled with the biblical witness was hotly debated. Controversies led in 1866 to a split in the Presbyterian Church of the United States into North and South. As the industrial development advanced, the Reformed churches were increasingly challenged by the living conditions of workers. They had to respond to the socialist movement and its vision of a better future. For a long time, the attention of the churches had been confined to alleviating the situation of the poor by relief work. But gradually the awareness grew that their witness had to address the root causes of injustice. Presbyterian witness in the United States was to go in two directions. Presbyterians were numerous among the entrepreneurs responsible for the "Gilded Age" in the USA. In 1900 Andrew Carnegie published the *Gospel of Wealth* in which he defended individualism, private property, competition, accumulation, and plain hard work; he also promoted philanthropy and argued that the rich should not die rich; wealth was to be used as a trust from God. Others, though emphasizing the same values, were more critical of societal developments. Charles Hodge, of Princeton Theological Seminary (1797-1878), wrote on the need to deal with human misery, unrest, and violence caused by industrialization and urbanization. In Europe in the second part of the 19th century more and more theologians and church leaders began to recognize socialism as a sign of the times, pointing the church to the God-given mandate to contribute to the struggle for justice. Among the Reformed representatives of this movement two stand out — Hermann

Kutter (1863-1931) and Leonhard Ragaz (1868-1945). Responsibility for society became an integral part of the witness of many Reformed churches.

The 19th century marked the beginnings of the ecumenical movement. As horizons were widened by the missionary movement and the challenges of the communicating the Gospel in the modern world became more pressing, the divided state of the church appeared increasingly intolerable. The message of reconciliation had no credibility as long as the churches themselves were opposed to one another. A process of reconciliation was required. Among the pioneers of the ecumenical movement, Philip Schaff deserves to be mentioned. Born in Switzerland, he moved in 1841 to the United States and became a leading representative of the Mercersburg School. In the name of the catholicity of Christ and the church he denounced, in a famous and controversial address, the sectarian spirit of the Protestant churches in the New World. He identified rationalism and individualism as the main reasons for the fragmentation of the church. To overcome the trend towards divisions, the place of the church as God's gift had to be more clearly affirmed. Schaff was among the founders of the Evangelical Alliance in 1846 and later, in 1875, of the World Alliance of Reformed Churches throughout the World holding the Presbyterian Order, two attempts to bring together Protestant churches of the various countries. A parallel effort led, in 1892, to the foundation of the International Congregational Council.

1.2.5. Two World Wars and Their Aftermath

With World War I, a new period opened in the history of the Reformed churches. The confidence which had characterized Europe in the 19th century broke down. In many countries World War I meant the end of the "Christian society." Faced with a bewildering variety of philosophical and intellectual approaches, the church had to learn to rely anew on its own resources. The years after the war saw the rise of dialectical theology (Karl Barth, Eduard Thurneysen, Emil Brunner) — a passionate plea to recognize God's majesty and otherness in the face of all attempts to encapsulate God in human schemes and projects. Dialectical theology rejected both pietist and liberal theologies and developed an understanding of Christian faith based on God's revelation in Christ as witnessed to in the Bible. Dialectical theology revived the message of the Reformers. No salvation is possible for sinful human beings except through God's own initiative. At the same time, faced with the spiritual and material destruction of society, religious-socialist thinking gained new strength in the churches.

The United States gradually rose to a dominant position in both world politics and economics, and the churches in the United States began to play a more determinative role on the world scene. Unlike in Europe, there was in the United States considerable optimism about the future. In 1902, characteristically, the Presbyterian Church of the United States adopted an amendment of the Westminster Confession which reads as follows: "God in infinite and perfect love, having provided in the covenant of grace . . . a way of life and salvation, sufficient for and adapted to the whole

19

lost race of man, does freely offer this salvation to all men and women in the Gospel. In the Gospel God declares his love for the world and his desire that all men should be saved." The country had to fulfill a God-given task with the whole of humanity. The experience of World Wars I and II confirmed this conviction. Missionary activity intensified. Developments in the United States increasingly affected the life and witness of the Reformed churches worldwide.

Three distinct but nevertheless connected movements in the last century deserve special mention: Fundamentalism, Evangelicalism, and Pentecostalism.

Fundamentalism developed in North America in the early years of the century. The term refers to fundamental convictions which must be held indisputably by Christian believers. It was first used in a series of pamphlets *The Fundamentals,* which were published from 1910 to 1915. The central convictions concern the inspiration and infallibility of the Bible. In many respects Fundamentalism shares the outlook of the Revival Movement; but, generally, a much stronger emphasis is placed on the second coming of Jesus Christ. An apocalyptic interpretation of history dominates. The church is seen as the group of the elect who are called to meet the Lord and to reign with him in the millennium. Proclaiming God's word means to denounce human sin and to withdraw from fellowship with the unbelieving world. The movement spread into all branches of Protestantism in America and also into other parts of the world. Given the strong emphasis on the verbal inspiration of Holy Scripture, it found a particularly favorable response in Reformed churches. In the 1940s a Presbyterian, Carl McIntire, became one of the prominent leaders of the movement. To counteract the witness of the Federal Council of Churches in the USA, he started the Council of American Churches and, a few years later (1948), took the initiative for the foundation of the International Council of Christian Churches (ICCC). The movement eventually became the cause of many splits in Reformed Churches. Part of the ICCC message was an unconditional rejection of the Roman Catholic Church, of the ecumenical movement, and, in particular, of communism. With the radical political changes occurring in the 1980s and 1990s the movement lost much of its vigor.

Very different perspectives are represented by the Evangelical movement. It can be regarded as the true heir of the Revival movement. Committed to the authority of the biblical Word and to the missionary mandate, it sought to maintain the integrity of the churches' message. It rejected liberal views that had been adopted by theologians and which, in their view, undermined the life and witness of the churches. It viewed with suspicion the churches' political and social activities and warned against the dilution of the central message of the church by secondary concerns. After World War II the movement gained in strength. More and more institutions of evangelical inspiration came into being, and gradually the movement in the United States also became politically influential. In 1960s and 1970s it established itself more and more at the international level as well. In 1974 the International Conference on World Evangelism in Lausanne gave the impetus for new evangelistic and missionary efforts. In many respects, the movement has become an integral part of the Reformed churches. It appealed especially to those in the Reformed pietist tradition.

Pentecostalism emerged as a distinct movement in the early years of the century. Based on older spiritual traditions, the movement emphasized the personal experience of the Holy Spirit in baptism and, generally, in worship. William Joseph Seymour (1870-1922), the son of a black slave, is regarded as its founder. He was at the origin of the Azusa Street Revival in Los Angeles (1906) which brought together people of very different backgrounds — black, white, rich, and poor. In the course of the century these small beginnings grew into a worldwide movement. Pentecostal churches sprang up in many countries. The message was particularly appealing to the lower classes. The experience of the Spirit gave self-respect to marginalized people. The movement also had a considerable impact on existing churches. Pentecostal spirituality constituted a challenge to inherited forms of piety. What place could be attributed to the experience of the Holy Spirit? While in some countries Pentecostalism was successfully integrated into the life and witness of the churches, splits occurred in others. In several countries the Pentecostal revival led to the establishment of new Reformed churches.

A crucial period for the Reformed churches was the confrontation with the regime of National Socialism in Germany in the 1930s. Nazi ideology had made deep inroads into the German churches. The authenticity of the church and its witness was at stake. To clarify the situation, mainly through the inspiration of Karl Barth, an extraordinary synod of the Evangelical Church in Germany was called in 1934 that adopted the *Barmen Declaration*, a text that clearly rejected in six "theses" any compromises with Nazi ideology. The declaration resulted in the formation of a "confessing church" (Bekenntniskirche). In subsequent years many of its members were arrested by the Nazis and some executed. For the Reformed churches the experience of Barmen was important for several reasons. In the first place the declaration was important because it gave tangible expression to the resistance against an anti-Christian regime. But it had wider implications for their witness. For the first time, it had become apparent that the period of confessions was not closed. In confronting the challenges of today, new acts of confessing could take place. The Barmen Declaration was more than a statement concerning the present situation; it was an attempt, in a critical situation, to gather the church around the truth of the Gospel. It was the basis for a confessing church. Without abrogating past confessions, the Barmen Declaration placed them within the perspective of responsible confessing in the present. For many Reformed churches, this experience was to serve as a model in subsequent years.

The persecution and annihilation of the Jewish population by the Nazi regime and the foundation of the Jewish state raised fundamental questions about the relationship between the Jewish people and the church. The debate was conducted with particular vigor in a number of Reformed churches, especially in the Netherlands, Germany, Switzerland, and later also in the United States. How could anti-Semitism reach such atrocious forms? To what extent does Christianity share in the responsibility for it? Are anti-Jewish attitudes perhaps connected with anti-Jewish interpretations of Scripture? Does Christianity not need to recognize its fundamental dependence on the Jewish tradition? Several Reformed churches began to rethink their relation to the Jewish people. To avoid thinking about the

Jews as an item of Christian theology, these churches sought direct contact through dialogues. In several countries Christian-Jewish fellowships were founded.

After World War I the development of the ecumenical movement accelerated. Confronted, on the one hand, with the devastation of the War and, on the other, with increased interaction among the nations, churches began to recognize the need for a new manifestation of the universality of the church. The division of the churches on the mission fields was the subject of a series of conferences culminating in the Missionary Conference in Edinburgh (1910), which led to the foundation of the International Missionary Council. After World War I the ecumenical movement found expression in the two movements of "Faith and Order" and "Life and Work." From the beginning, Reformed Christians were active participants in both movements. In 1939 the unification of these two movements was agreed upon, and after World War II the World Council of Churches was solemnly founded in Amsterdam (1948). The first two General Secretaries of the Council were Willem A. Visser 't Hooft (1948-1966) of the Netherlands Reformed Church and Eugene C. Blake (1966-1972) of the United Presbyterian Church in the USA.

The new ecumenical fellowship found a mixed reception in the Reformed churches. Many Reformed churches welcomed the new departure and joined the organization. Of the founding members about one third were Reformed, Presbyterian, or Congregationalist. The World Alliance of Reformed Churches promoted the ecumenical movement and explicitly encouraged its member churches to participate in it. It even went a step further. Whatever could be done through the World Council of Churches, in the context of the wider ecumenical family, should not duplicated by the Alliance. To strengthen the collaboration, it decided to move its headquarters from London to Geneva.

Other Churches viewed the World Council of Churches with suspicion. A number of Reformed Churches, mainly of Dutch origin and strongly committed to the classical Reformed confessions, set up the Reformed Ecumenical Synod in 1946 as an international platform for an unambiguous Reformed witness. Much more aggressive opposition was launched by fundamentalist circles. One of the main purposes of the International Council of Christian Churches, founded by Carl McIntire in 1948, was to denounce the attempts of the ecumenical movement as betrayal and apostasy. For many Reformed churches participation in the ecumenical movement became a source of controversy and in some cases even division.

1.2.6. Recent Developments

World War II resulted in the defeat of Nazi Germany. But after the victory the conflict between the allied nations of the West and the communist regime of the Soviet Union reemerged. The armistice arrangements divided Europe into two spheres of influence and soon the confrontation of the two superpowers — the USA and its European allies and the USSR and its satellites — became the determining factor in world politics. The conflict also involved the newly independent nations of Asia and Africa, the "Third World," as it was called since the Bandoeng conference of 1955. For Reformed churches the conflict became the source of many tensions, misunderstandings, and suspicions. What witness were the Reformed churches to bear with regard to Communism? Many advocated a radical rejection of Communism. Others, among them Karl Barth, promoted the idea of an independent third way between the radical rejection and the alliance with Communist régimes. While there was no doubt that Marxist ideology was incompatible with the Christian faith, the Christian mind should not be blinded to the injustice inherent in the capitalist system. The World Council of Churches and the World Alliance of Reformed Churches adopted this nuanced approach and were, therefore, the target of violent criticisms from more conservative circles. In some countries the tensions led to disruption and splits. Much of the international activity of the ICCC was based on an unconditional anti-Communist stance.

World War II also meant the end of the colonial period, and the conception of mission as a civilizing arm of colonial expansion also ended. In the decades after the War not only countries but also a large number of churches in Asia and Africa gained independence. In some cases the autonomy of the church preceded, in other cases it followed, the independence of the state. With independence came the need to develop indigenous leadership and become self-supporting. Reformed missions of all stripes carried as an ideal the early development of indigenous leadership in mission churches, but the reality often lagged behind the ideal. In many countries, indigenous leadership had been recruited at an early date and the churches were therefore prepared to take on responsibility for their own ministry. In some countries, such as India, Reformed churches united with other Reformed churches or with churches of other traditions, while in others separate, autonomous churches continued to live side by side. Some churches have become self-supporting. More and more churches in Asia and Africa are engaged in missionary work not only within their own country but also abroad. Others continue to look to a "mother church" or mission agency to provide personnel and finances. The Reformed presence in many former mission fields is deeply divided today.

While there has been a fundamental change in the understanding of the missionary mandate in most "historical" Reformed churches, the more conservative Reformed churches continue in their evangelistic commitment. In the course of the last decades, a large number of small churches have been founded in many countries of Asia, Africa, and Latin America. Reformed churches that maintain strong separation in their home country often feel it necessary to establish separate churches on their mission fields as well.

Recent years have seen a phenomenal growth of churches in many parts of the world. While Reformed churches in Western countries seem to be on the decline, churches in countries recently touched by the Gospel have considerably expanded. The younger churches in Asia, Africa, and Latin America vastly outnumber the historical "white" churches in Europe, North America, South Africa, Australia, and New Zealand. Three countries deserve special mention in this respect: Indonesia, Korea, and Nigeria. In all three countries, Reformed Christianity experienced phenomenal growth in the last few decades, so that they now have the largest Reformed communities in the world. A striking phenomenon is the rapid growth of Reformed Christianity in East Asian countries — Korea, China, and Taiwan. Though Chinese Christians regard themselves as postdenominational, the Reformed tradition is strongly present in their midst. There seems to be a particular affinity between the Reformed tradition and the Confucianist world.

The period since 1960 has been a time of particular ecumenical challenges. From 1962 to 1965 the Second Vatican Council introduced far-reaching reforms in the Roman Catholic Church. Many of the reforms introduced by the 16th century Reformation — the use of the vernacular, the participation of the faithful in the life of the church, the celebration of the Eucharist with bread *and* wine, and in particular the regular preaching of the Word — were now accepted. While the Roman Catholic Church had earlier stood aloof from the ecumenical movement, it now decided to engage in dialogue and discussion. The debate, which had been broken at the time of the Reformation, could now be resumed and carried further. In many parts of the world new relations have developed. Some Reformed churches have explicitly modified their teaching by declaring obsolete certain anti-Roman sentences in the Reformed confessions. Many Reformed churches remain reserved, if not hostile, to sustained contacts with the Roman Catholic Church. The relationship with the Roman Catholic Church continues to be a bone of contention among Reformed churches.

Several important ecumenical developments took place in the '70s. In 1970 the World Alliance of Reformed Churches and the International Congregational Council decided to unite to form the World Alliance of Reformed Churches (Presbyterian and Congregational). From the doctrinal point of view the two traditions had always been close to one another. On issues of church order, a rapprochement had taken place in more recent times. In several countries, Presbyterian and Congregational churches had already united. It therefore seemed appropriate to join forces also at the international level.

Another significant ecumenical advance was the adoption of the Leuenberg Agreement in 1973, which allowed Lutheran, Reformed, and United Churches of Europe to declare full communion. Without denying their particular confessional traditions they were able to formulate a common understanding of the Gospel and the doctrine of justification by faith in Jesus Christ, thus opening the door to full, mutual recognition. A rift that had started in Marburg (1529) and, despite all efforts, could not be overcome in the 16th century, was now seen as a dispute that does not correspond to present positions of the churches on both sides. In 1997 a similar agreement was adopted in the United States.

A particular test for the Reformed churches was the attitude to the apartheid system in South Africa. For a long time the Afrikaans-speaking white Reformed churches in South Africa supported the system. In the eyes of the victims of apartheid, Reformed Christianity was on the side of oppression. The black and Colored churches that had come into existence through Reformed missionary efforts called on the worldwide family to take sides in the conflict. The debates on apartheid led to considerable tensions. In the initial stages of apartheid the response remained ambiguous. Some European and US churches explicitly supported the Dutch Reformed Churches. Others hesitated to take a clear position. Gradually, largely through the insistence of the churches in Africa, the Reformed attitude became more definite. In 1982 the General Council of the World Alliance of Reformed Churches declared the *status confessionis* with regard to apartheid and accordingly suspended the white Dutch Reformed member churches from the exercise of membership rights.

Another issue that increasingly preoccupies Reformed churches since World War II is the place of women in the church. Since the late 19th century both Christian and secular women's organizations have militated for equal rights of men and women in church and society. But in recent decades, more radical questions are being raised. To what degree has Christian teaching contributed to discrimination against women? For centuries, the church has affirmed the leading role of men. The biblical witness seemed to warrant the subordination of women to men. Do we have to admit that the Bible itself reflects in part the thinking of a patriarchal society? How are the biblical passages on the roles of men and women in the church to be interpreted today? The debates on the issue found expression in controversies over inclusive language, the participation of women in decision-making, and the ordination of women to the ministry. In a relatively short time a large number of Reformed churches came to the conclusion that the basic message of the Bible called for the admission of women to the exercise of *all* ministries in the church. A considerable number of churches continue, equally on biblical grounds, to refuse their ordination. For some, the issue has church-dividing significance.

The quest for inclusive communities has brought to the fore still other concerns. In recent years the issue of homosexuality, in particular the question of the place of homosexuals in the church and in the ministries of the church, has been hotly debated in some churches, especially in the industrialized countries; the discussion is likely to expand in the future and may prove to be divisive in many Reformed churches.

In the last decades, faced with challenges from all sides, the churches have increasingly felt the need to rethink their heritage and to express it in modern terms and language. Several churches have issued, on the basis of careful and protracted conversations, new contemporary confessions of faith. The Barmen Declaration had shown that the classical Reformed confessions need not necessarily be understood as the last word. The church could still today respond to God's Word through common statements of faith. In the '50s churches in Great Britain issued new confessions, and in the '60s and '70s several churches in North America followed. A particularly instructive example was "Confession 1967" of the United Presbyterian Church in the United States of America, a confession bearing in its title the date of its proclamation and thus indicating that it was to be considered the expression at a particular moment of history. Even more important were the attempts at formulating new confessions in the younger churches: Cuba, Korea, Indonesia, Taiwan, and South Africa.

The Reformed family today can be described by two terms — dynamism and diversity. In many parts of the world Reformed churches are rapidly growing. There is much creativity in theological thinking, in mission, and in social involvement. At the same time, the diversity among Reformed churches is such that it is difficult to make out elements that are common to all. The diverse forms and expressions represent an immense richness but evidently also lead to controversies, estrangement, and splits. In many places, dynamism becomes paralyzed by unresolved conflicts of the past. To allow for real new departures, a new sense of communion needs to be born — not to kill diversity but to relate churches to one another through a new commitment to mutual understanding and communication.

1.3. THE REFORMED HERITAGE

What is it that characterizes Reformed churches today? The answer is not obvious. The universe of the Reformed churches cannot easily be described, and the descriptions will differ according to the particular background of the authors. The following attempt does not claim to give a complete and definitive exposition but names certain common emphases as well as unresolved issues within the Reformed heritage.

1.3.1. Christus Solus

The Reformed churches emphasize with special passion Jesus Christ as the only and exclusive source of salvation. Calvin writes in his *Institutes*:

"When we see that the whole sum of our salvation, and every single part of it, are comprehended in Christ, we must beware of deriving even the minutest portion of it from any other quarter. If we seek salvation we are taught by the very name of Jesus that he possesses it. If we seek any other gifts of the Spirit, we shall find them in his unction; strength in his government; purity in his conception; indulgence in his nativity, in which he was made like us in all respects, in order that he might learn to sympathize with us; if we seek redemption, we shall find it in his passion; acquittal in his condemnation; remission in the curse of his cross; satisfaction in his sacrifice; purification in his blood; reconciliation in his descent to hell; mortification of the flesh in his sepulchre; newness of life in his resurrection; immortality also in his resurrection; the inheritance of a celestial kingdom in his entrance into heaven; protection, security, and the abundant supply of all blessings in his kingdom; secure anticipation of judgment in the power of judging committed to him." (2,16, 19)

1.3.2. God to Be Glorified in All Things

For the Reformed churches the first commandment is fundamental: "I am the LORD your God . . . you shall have no other gods before me" (Ex. 20:2-3). Human beings have abandoned God and do not have the capacity to restore communion with God. For salvation, they depend entirely on God's initiative. Having sinned and been caught in sin, they cannot expect to be saved. They can only turn to God's grace and give praise for the gift of the new life. The doctrine of predestination has its ultimate root in this emphasis on God's exclusive initiative. Some Reformed confessions go so far as teaching that the effectiveness of Christ's saving work is limited to those whom God has chosen to save. The doctrine of predestination has been the subject of controversies among Reformed churches. Whatever the position taken, two points are not to be forgotten. The doctrine of predestination is not meant to exalt the sense of election but rather to underline the mysterious character of God's dealings with humanity; and it does not reduce the urgency of proclaiming and sharing the good news of salvation to *all* people.

1.3.3. Salvation and Trinitarian Thinking

Reformed teaching affirms Trinitarian teaching — God as Father, Son, and Holy Spirit. God the Creator of all things is the same God who became human in Jesus Christ and fulfills redemption through the power of the Holy Spirit. Reformed theology places particular emphasis on the saving and healing power of the Holy Spirit. In Reformed theology the concept of covenant and covenants has often served to affirm the same truth. Throughout history God's covenant takes ever new forms, but God remains the same God leading humanity and the whole creation to the fulfillment in the coming kingdom.

1.3.4. The Authority of the Bible

All Reformed confessions converge in stressing the authority of the Scriptures of both the Old and the New Testaments. The Scriptures are the source of all decisive knowledge and have to serve as guide in the life of the church. The emphasis on the Bible has had a varied history in the Reformed tradition. In the first period of the Reformation, the Bible was used as the criterion for distinguishing the authentic Christian witness from the distortions of history. Increasingly, beginning with the First Helvetic Confession (1536), the authority of the Bible was affirmed as the unique and all-sufficient source of truth. More and more emphasis was placed on the verbal inspiration of Scriptures. Calvin developed the concept of the testimony of the Holy Spirit in the Bible and today — with readers and listeners of God's Word. Only through the power of the Spirit can the meaning of the Bible be properly understood. Increasingly, the authority of the inspired words of the Bible was stressed in isolation from the community. The recognition of verbal inspiration became the test of orthodoxy. In response to historical-critical biblical research, however, many Reformed churches began to rethink and revise their understanding. They began to see the Bible as a book that witnesses to God's great deeds in creating and redeeming the world; as a response of the community of faith to God's deeds to be read, interpreted, and acted out today by the church. Recent Reformed confessions deal with the authority of Scriptures, as a rule, under the articles on the Holy Spirit and the church.

1.3.5. Confessions of Faith

Reformed churches have formulated confessions of faith to affirm and to give account of the truth of the Gospel. They do not possess the same authority as the Bible but are regarded as "subordinate standards." In principle the church must remain open to new insights gained from the witness of the Bible. There has never been one single Reformed confession. In the early 16th century several confessions existed side by side; they were supplemented in the second part of the century by more comprehensive confessions. Different "generations" of confessions can thus be distinguished. Since the Barmen Declaration (1934), a wide range of new confessions has been formulated, some by progressive, some by more conservative churches. Today the Reformed family is faced with a variety of voices and has the task of bringing the various positions into a constructive dialogue. The passionate struggle for the right response to God's Word belongs to the characteristics of the Reformed family. Diversity without dialogue is bound to harden divisions.

1.3.6. The Church

God calls people to be the church, God's people, Christ's body, and the temple of the Spirit. Throughout history there have been the chosen people who glorify God's name. Now, the church is the place where God's liberating word is announced and can be responded to. There is no way to determine the borderlines of the true church. Ultimately God alone knows the true members of the church. But the church as it exists in history must not be despised. To listen to God's Word and to respond to it we depend on the community; its message can only be proclaimed through the joint efforts of all. Calvin calls the church the mother who nourishes the faithful on the pilgrimage of their life. Justified through God's saving work, we are called to live in the church a life inspired by thankfulness. Justification leads to sanctification.

1.3.7. Prayer and Worship

The first response to God's gift of grace is prayer and praise. Both individually and as a community we are called to glorify God. Worship is primarily a corporate act. It is the occasion to preach the Word and to celebrate the Lord's Supper. Calvin was of the opinion that the Lord's Supper was to be celebrated regularly every Sunday. He stressed the need to receive the signs of bread and wine. As in medieval times the mass had included communion only exceptionally, he suggested that, as a first step, the Lord's Supper should be celebrated four times a year. However his ultimate goal, the weekly celebration of the Lord's Supper, was never realized.

The central elements of corporate worship are prayer, proclamation, and the celebration of the Lord's Supper. Everything detracting attention from these essentials was to be removed from worship. There was, in particular, in the Reformation a clearly negative attitude to images. The Reformed churches took seriously the second commandment. The line was taken even further in the Puritan movement. All external forms were to be rejected. Worship had to be "in spirit and in truth." While Calvin had basically followed the order of the mass, Puritans claimed that no form not explicitly indicated by the Bible should be admitted. Some churches were not prepared to allow hymns other than the psalms. Today there is a wide variety of worship styles in the Reformed churches. A debate on the appropriate forms of worship is urgently required.

1.3.8. Discipleship and Discipline

Justification and sanctification are two sides of the same coin. Communion with Christ is to bear fruits in the practice of love. The law is not only meant to demonstrate our inability to fulfill God's will and demands. It is also a guide for a renewed life *(tertius usus legis)*. Renewed life, in the eyes of the Reformers, especially Calvin, is not only a personal but a communal matter. Through discipleship the community is being built up. Failure in Christian life leads to the destruction of relationships and thus to disintegration. Therefore, not only preaching and the celebration of the sacraments but also the exercise of discipline are characteristics of the true church. Today Reformed churches differ on the form discipline is to take. Only a minority of Reformed churches continue to exercise an institutional form of discipline. For the majority, especially in the secularized countries of the West, discipline is left to the interaction of members of the congregation.

1.3.9. Ministries and Church Order

Generally, in Reformed churches much attention is devoted to the structures of the church. In his *Institutes* Calvin made the attempt to propose an order of ministries that was in harmony with the directions set out in the Bible. According to his view, four ministries were necessary for the life of the church — pastors to preach the Word and administer the sacraments, elders to assist the pastors and to exercise discipline, deacons to look after administrative aspects and to care for the poor, and doctors or teachers who were responsible for the pure teaching of the church. Calvin was prepared to accept other forms of ministry also, as long as the regular preaching of the Word was assured.

Later developments led to stricter views. In particular the Scottish Reformation and its subsequent struggles with the episcopal system of the Church of England gave rise to the conviction that the Presbyterian system was the only biblical way to order the ministries. There is no doubt that the Presbyterian system, with its strong emphasis on the collegial exercise of authority and even more the congregationalist approach, strengthened the sense of participation in the life of the church. An anti-hierarchical element is inherent in both Presbyterianism and Congregationalism. These qualities have become characteristics of Reformed churches. The question is, however, to what extent these qualities can also find a place in other ways of ordering the church, e.g., in an appropriately revised episcopal system. In recent years, a number of unions have taken place which combine presbyterian, congregationalist, and episcopal elements.

1.3.10. The Church — Local and Universal

The Reformers placed strong emphasis on Christ's presence in the local community. God's gifts do not require mediation by a hierarchical order. Christ is present wherever God's Word is proclaimed and the sacraments administered. Congregationalism went even a step further in stressing the primacy of the local community. The Spirit bestows all gifts necessary for the life and witness of the church on the local church. Under God's Word the gathered community has ultimate authority. The positive side of this emphasis is the strong sense of participation and responsibility that often characterizes local Reformed churches.

The mainstream of Reformed churches at the same time stressed the need for common decision-making at regional and national levels. They developed a structure of representation in presbyteries (classes) and synods (assemblies). Decision-making through representative assemblies has become one of the characteristics of the Reformed heritage.

On the whole, the horizon of the Reformed churches remained confined to the national level. Communication between national churches was not a matter of course, and only exceptionally have Reformed churches come together to exchange, debate, and decide on essential issues of faith and witness. None of the international bodies which have been set up by Reformed churches is synodal in nature. They serve as platforms of exchange; some bring together a limited number of like-minded Reformed churches and tend to perpetuate divisions at the local level. The lack of a spontaneous sense of responsibility and commitment to the universal church is the reason for many of the divisions that exist today among Reformed churches.

1.3.11. Called to Be Witnesses of the Gospel

Reformed churches, as a rule, have a strong commitment to the missionary calling of the Church. In the 16th century mission was not a central concern. Calvin was even of the opinion that the missionary mandate had been addressed to apostles and had been fulfilled in the apostolic period. Its relevance was only rediscovered in later centuries. Mainly through the Revival Movement and through the practice of mission since the beginning of the 19th century, it has become a characteristic of the Reformed churches. Most recent confessions speak explicitly of the missionary responsibility of the church; the Church of Scotland amended the Westminster Confession in this sense.

1.3.12. Truth and Unity

Like all churches, Reformed churches face the dilemma of faithfulness to the Gospel and commitment to the oneness of the Body of Christ. Both sides of the dilemma find strong expression in the Reformed tradition. On the one hand, the primary plea of the Reformation was to return to Christ. Unity could be achieved only on the basis of a common commitment to Christ. On the other hand, it was clear from the beginning that commitment to Christ also meant to live in communion with one another. Ways needed to be found to remove obstacles to communion. The dilemma has been dealt with differently by different Reformed churches. While many felt unable to join the ecumenical movement, the majority have become active in endeavors of dialogue, collaboration, and union. The search for unity on the basis of thorough debate on matters of doctrine and church structure has become a characteristic of the Reformed churches.

1.3.13. Church and State

As a rule, Reformed churches advocate the autonomy of the church from state authorities. They recognize the authority of the state in all matters concerning the temporal life of society, but they resist attempts to subordinate the internal life and witness of the church to the magistrate. The church needs to constitute itself, and its structures need to function, without the interference of the state. Since in some countries the Reformation was carried out by the state authorities, churches came into being that to a large extent depended on the state. For centuries, in some cases even today, the struggle for the appropriate relationship to the state has been a major concern for these churches. Basically, the strong emphasis on a coherent, constitutionally established internal order of the church militates in favour of autonomy from the state.

1.3.14. The Witness of the Church in Society

The Reformation was primarily concerned with the life of the church, but from the beginning the witness of the Reformers extended to the whole of society. God's will had to be respected and followed in all realms of life. Society had to be so ordered that justice could prevail. From the beginning, Calvin regularly intervened with the magistrate of Geneva to advocate for justice and the protection of the poor. The Barmen Declaration affirms a genuinely Reformed conviction when it states: "We reject the false doctrine, as though there were areas of our life in which we would not belong to Jesus Christ, but to other lords, areas in which we would not need justification and sanctification through him." However, this witness in society has often been the cause of disputes and even divisions in Reformed churches.

1.3.15. The Church as Wandering People

The Reformed churches are on the Way. In the sense of the Epistle to the Hebrews they regard themselves as the wandering people of God. Facing new situations, they seek to be faithful to God's Word as witnessed to in the Bible and to correct and renew the life of the church accordingly. They are prepared to be led to new horizons. To point to this readiness Reformed Christians like to cite the formula *ecclesia reformata semper reformanda*. The formula should, however, be used with care. It was not created by the Reformers themselves but first appeared in the early 17th century in the Netherlands. The formula can easily be misused to legitimize change for change's sake. Nevertheless, the dictum stands for an important characteristic of Reformed churches — openness to new insights gained through living intercourse with the Bible. *Semper reformanda* must not mean constant adaptation. True reform is always the result of listening to God's Word in the light of a changing situation. There is, today, a wide divergence among Reformed churches about the extent and the validity of such new insights. But there are certain points which, to various degrees, have become part of the common Reformed heritage.

- The missionary commitment of the Reformed churches has already been mentioned.
- The values of tolerance and the commitment to the struggle for human rights have their roots in intellectual and spiritual developments of the 18th century.
- The Reformed churches have developed a special sense of solidarity with the Jewish people. In fact, the strong emphasis on the authority of the Old Testament has always been a cause of special interest in the destiny of the Jewish people. The covenant theology, especially of Johannes Cocceius (1603-1669), reflected on the role of the Jewish people in the fulfillment of God's plans in history. It was through the experience of the persecutions of Jews in World War II that the theme became dominant in Reformed theology. Several churches have adopted statements on the continuing election of the Jewish people. The way of witnessing to the Jews remains an issue of controversy. While a growing number of Reformed churches consider dialogue to be the appropriate form of Christian witness, others continue to think in terms of Paul's mandate "first to the Jews, then to the gentiles."
- The quest for women's rights and the rise of the feminist movement have

deeply affected many Reformed churches. For many, the participation of women in the life of the church, in particular the ordination of women to be pastors and elders, has become a matter of principle. For other churches, the ordination of women continues to be seen as contradicting the words of Scripture. Though a great number of Reformed churches now ordain women to the ministries of the church, the issue is far from resolved.

- The ecological crisis has brought the theme of creation to the fore. Many Reformed churches have become aware of the fact that traditional teaching did not give sufficient place to the need for human beings to live in harmony and communion with the whole of creation. Several churches have adopted statements of faith offering a new and more responsible orientation. In the "Contemporary Testimony," adopted by the Christian Reformed Church in 1983, we read: "We make grateful use of the good products of science and technology, on guard against idolatry and careful to use them in ways that fit within God's demand to love our neighbor and to care for the earth and its creatures."

2. LIST OF REFORMED CHURCHES

The Churches Are Listed Alphabetically
according to the English Form of Countries' Names

ALBANIA

Area in km²	28,748
Population	3,622,400 (Albanian 93.5%, Greek 2.5%, Gypsy 2.5%)
Religions in %	Muslim 40% (Sunnite or Bektashi), Christian ca. 20% (Orth 10.9%, RCath 7%, small Prot communities), large segment of nonbelievers
Official/other languages	Albanian /Tosk is the official dialect, Greek

Present-day Albania is referred to as "Illyricum" in Paul's letter to the Romans (15:19). It became Christian in the 2nd century. In the course of history the church changed jurisdiction several times. From 733 to 1054 it belonged to the Patriarch-ate of Constantinople. After the schism between Rome and Constantinople the northern part of Albania came under the jurisdiction of Rome and was eventually Latinized. With the invasion of the Turks in the 15th century the whole area came under Islamic rule. At the end of World War II a militant Communist regime was established. Churches were systematically persecuted. In 1967 the government proclaimed Albania the first atheist state in the world, and in 1976 all religious practices, even in private, were forbidden. With the fall of Communism in Eastern Europe the situation changed. In 1990/91 religious freedom was guaranteed by law in Albania.

Protestantism has no historical roots in Albania. With the exception of a Baptist community there were, prior to the Communist regime, no Prot churches in the country. In the early '90s about 150 Prot groups started evangelistic work in various parts of Albania, among them several Ref groups. Most of these efforts

35

were independent from one another. Some coordination has been achieved through the Albania Encouragement Project (AEP) with an office in Tirana (K.P. 19, Tirana, +355 30 34 708) which brings together almost 70 agencies currently working in Albania.

1. Greek Evangelical Mission (6005)

In collaboration with the Reformed Congregations in the Netherlands (cf. Netherlands no. 9) the Greek Evangelical Church (cf. Greece) started work in southern Albania. Congregations were founded in Saranda and Delvidon. There are now plans to establish an Evangelical Reformed Church in Albania. A few young Albanians are being trained for the ministry.

Address: Greek Evangelical Mission, c/o Greek Evangelical Church, 24 Markou Botsari Street, Athens, Greece, Tel: +30 1 92 22 684

2. Swiss Evangelical Mission (6006)

Nos Frères de l'Est, an evangelical mission agency in French-speaking Switzerland, has initiated work in northern Albania; congr have been established in Burrel and Baz. Missionaries from German-speaking Switzerland have started a congr in Tirana.

Address: Swiss Evangelical Mission c/o
Christliche Ostmission, Postfach 312, CH-3076 Worb, Tel: +41 31 839 58 11, Fax: +41 839 63 44
Fondacioni Humanitar Albkom, Rt. Budi Pallati 85, 1 Ap. 5, Tirana.

3. Korean Presbyterian Mission (6007)

Korean work has its center in Lezha. In 1992 a missionary of the Presbyterian Church of Korea (PCK; cf. Korea no. 14) started offering computer courses; subsequently a worshiping community was founded. There are plans to build a chapel in Lezha. The mission also intends to initiate campus mission work in Tirana.

Address: Korean Presbyterian Mission, Rev. Hyng Mo Lee, Adenauerstrasse 5, D-36039 Fulda, +49 661 57825

4. Danish Moravian Mission (BDM) (6008)

In 1994 the Danish Moravian Mission (BDM) was invited by the Albanian Ambassador to Scandinavia to start programs in children's religious education. Some 160 Albanian teachers have been in Denmark to study the Danish school system and Christianity. The BDM has sent pastors to work with Bible groups which have been established in eight towns. Services are being held, education for baptism is offered, and Holy Communion celebrated. People make their own choice about the church they want to join. On June 9, 1996, a small congr was founded in Elbasan.

Address: Danish Moravian Mission
           Kristiane Quendra, P.O. Box 2953, Tirana, Albania
           Brodremenighdens Danske Mission, P.O. Box 30, Norregard 14, DK-6070 Christiansfeld,
           Tel: +45 74 56 22 33, Fax: +45 74 56 13 34

ALGERIA

Area in km²	2,381,741
Population	(est. Algeria 1995) 28,600,000
Religions in %	Muslims 99%, Prot 0.1%, RCath 0.9%
Languages	Arabic, French

The Prot presence in the country was established in the middle of the 19th century, soon after Algeria became a French colony. There had been earlier efforts by RCath and Prot churches to minister to both prisoners and British people who lived in Algeria for reasons of health, but they were sporadic and primarily chaplaincies. The Bible Societies began activities in 1830. Around the turn of the century several Prot mission agencies started work in Algeria, some of British, others of French or Swiss origin. In the late '30s a number of Prot churches and missionary agencies formed a consultative association which continued to exist for about a decade after independence. Numerically the most important of the Prot churches active in Algeria was the French Reformed Church (Eglise réformée de France–ERF), whose main purpose was the pastoral care of French settlers. Independence eventually led to an exodus of French people and, accordingly, to a reduction in church membership. Many churches and groups were "invited" to cease their activities. The remaining Christian community is predominantly RCath (priests and members of religious orders constituting a major part of this Catholic presence), but the proportions between RCath and Prot adherents remains about the same as in previous times.

Protestant Church of Algeria (1010)

In 1970 negotiations were initiated among several Protestant groups which led to the establishment, in 1972, of the Protestant Church of Algeria. One of the main reasons for the initiative was the microscopic size of the various groups. Today, this small but dynamic church is established throughout the northern coastal region and counts among its membership Christians representing about 30 different nationalities from all continents and from 25 different Prot traditions. Although half a dozen languages are most commonly used, there are at least twice as many spoken within the community. The Protestant Church of Algeria is committed to ecumenical cooperation, and many of its activities — pastoral, charitable, and administrative — are jointly carried out with RCath. Responsibility for the work of the Bible Society lies with an ecumenical group.

TM: **500** Congr: **8** OrdM: **1** Eld: **1** Deac: **ne** EvgHome: **1** Mission: Women Ord: **yes** As Ministers: **1945/0** as Deac: **nc** as Elders: **nc** ChurchOrg: **synodal** Off/otherLang: **Arabic, French, English, Kabyle, German** DoctrB: **Ref, Meth** Infant or believer's baptism: **both** Periodicals: **none** NatRel: **nc** RegRel: **AACC (1988), MECC (1927)** IntlRel: **WCC (1975), WARC (1950).**

Address: Eglise protestante d'Algérie, 31, rue Reda Houhou, Alger, Algeria, Tel: +213 2 716-238, Fax: +213 2 716-238, E-mail: umc@ist.cerist.dz

---

AMERICAN SAMOA

Area in km²	199
Population	(July 1996 est.) 59,566 Samoan (Polynesian) 89%, Caucasian 2%, Tongan 4%, other 5%
Religions in %	Christian Congreg 50%, RCath 20%, other Prot denominations and indigenous 30%
Official/other languages	Samoan, English

ABCFM (American Board of Commissioners for Foreign Missions)

American Samoa is a group of five volcanic islands with rugged peaks, limited coastal plains, and two coral atolls (Rose Island, Swains Island located in the South Pacific Ocean), all located about halfway between Hawaii and New Zealand. Pago Pago, its capital city, has one of the best natural deepwater harbors in the South Pacific Ocean, sheltered from rough seas by its natural configuration and protected from high winds by peripheral mountains; it has a strategic location in the South Pacific. American Samoa is a territory of the USA, administered by the US Department of Interior. Economic activity is strongly linked to the USA, with which American Samoa conducts between 80% and 90% of its foreign trade. Tuna fishing and tuna processing plants are the backbone of the private sector, with canned tuna the primary export. The tuna canneries and the government are by far the two largest employers. Other economic activities include a slowly developing tourist industry. Subsidies from the US government add substantially to American Samoa's economic well-being.

Congregational Christian Church in American Samoa (CCCAS) (5045)

American Samoa, which had been a naval dependency of the USA since 1900, changed in 1950 to become an American dependent civil territory. The way opened for gradual emergence of the American Samoan church from within the Congregational Christian Church (cf. Western Samoa, no. 1). The latter had always previously spanned both American and soon-to-become-independent Western Samoa.

From 1945 onward the ABCFM (which became the United Church Board of World Ministries after the merger in 1950 of the Congregational Christian and Evangelical and Reformed Churches in the USA) helped and supported the churches in American Samoa.

In 1980 the Congregational Christian Church of American Samoa was formally established. Theology and church government were unchanged. The CCCAS remains in dialogue with the larger Congregational Church in Western Samoa about the possibilitiy of an eventual reunion.

TM: **88,700** Congr: **120** PStations: **380** OrdM: **513** Eld: **nc** Deac: **nc** EvgHome: **nc** Mission: **nc** Women Ord: **yes** As Ministers: **no** as Deac: **yes**, as Elders: **no** ChurchOrg: **nc** Off/otherLang: **Samoan, English** DoctrB: **nc** Periodicals: **Lamp** NatRel: **nc** RegRel: **PCC** IntlRel: **WCC, WARC, WMC.**

Address: Ekalesia Fa'apotopotoga Kerisiano I Amerika Samoa, P.O. Box 1537, Pago Pago 96799, American Samoa, Tel: +684 699-9810, Fax: +684 699-1898

ANGOLA

Area in km²	1,246,700
Population	(July 1996 est.) 10,342,899 Ovimbundu 37%, Kimbundu 25%, Bakongo 13%, Mestico (mixed European and Native African) 2%, European 1%, other 22%
Religions in %	indigenous beliefs 47%, RCath 38%, Prot 15% (est.)
Official/other languages	Portuguese / Bantu and other African languages

CICA (Council of Christian Churches in Angola)

Christianity came to Angola through Portuguese navigators. Though first efforts seemed promising — notably, in 1518 the son of the King of Congo was consecrated as a bishop — Christianity did not really expand. Only after 1866 was the country systematically evangelized. The Spiritan Fathers arrived at that time. To this day they have remained the most important missionary order in Angola. Twelve years later the (British) Baptist Missionary Society, which was working in the Belgian Congo, began missionary activities in Northern Angola. They were followed by other missions of different confessional backgrounds from the USA, Canada, Finland, and even Portugal; there were also individual missionary efforts. Today, Angolan Protestantism represents a heterogeneous reality. In the colonial period the various groups worked together in the Evangelical Alliance without official recognition. The Association of Evangelicals in Angola (AEA) and the Council of Evangelical Churches (CAIE) were founded in 1974 and in 1977 respectively, and later the CAIE was transformed into the Council of Churches in Angola (CICA).

Before independence the RCath church was considered to be *the* church. Through a concordat it was closely linked to the State. The Prot churches were considered a foreign presence by the authorities. Their activities were often restricted.

In the 1950s and '60s various nationalist movements engaged in wars for independence. Portugal finally granted independence in 1975, but the wars continued for many years afterward. Government and liberation movements competed for power. The parties in the conflict were supported by outside partners seeking their own interests. On the one side were the USSR and Cuba and on the other South Africa and the United States. In 1991 a peace agreement was signed in Bicesse, near Lisbon. But conflicts continued. The elections, which had been held in accordance with the Bicesse Agreement, were recognized by the UN and the international community but not by UNITA, one of the liberation movements. The war resumed and brought terrible suffering upon the country. A lasting solution is still not in sight.

1. Evangelical Congregational Church in Angola (1002)

In 1880 the ABCFM (Congr) started work in Sailundo and began to evangelize the central highlands. It was joined by the Congregational Foreign Missionary Society of North America. In the 1950s the congr which had come into existence through their efforts in the Umbundu-speaking region founded the Council of Evangelical Churches in Central Angola (CIEAC). During the period of wars for independence, Prot were mistrusted by the colonial authorities. All foreign missionaries were forced to leave the country. In the conflict following independence the church divided. One group followed the rebels who went underground; the other established itself as the Evangelical Congregationalist Church in the People's Republic of Angola with headquarters in Huambo. The two groups maintained contact and, from the outset of the peace process, the church leaders sought to integrate the two groups within one church. This goal was finally realized in December 1996. The church is a founding member of CICA.

TM: **250,084** BM: **250,084** CM: **15,250** Congr: **160** PStations: **904** OrdM: **150** Eld: **18,500** Deac: **12,000** EvgHome: **nc** Mission: **nc** Women Ord: **yes** As Ministers: **1965/7** as Deac: **1930/1,500** as Elders: **nc** ChurchOrg: **congr, 15 regional synods, national synod** Off/otherLang: **Portuguese** DoctrB: **ApC, NicC, HeidC** Infant or believer's baptism: **both** Frequency of the Lord's Supper: **once per month** Periodicals: **Amossa Jornada (200), Seico (Liturgy/200), Portuguese Agenda da IECA (yearly/2,000), Calendario (300)** NatRel: **CICA (1977)** RegRel: **AACC (1987)** IntlRel: **WCC (1984)** TheolSchool: **Seminario Emanuel Unido**

Address: Igreja Evangélica Congregacional em Angola–IECA, Caixa Postal 551, Huambo, Angola, Tel: +244 3087

2. Evangelical Reformed Church of Angola (1001)

In 1922 Archibald Patterson, an Anglican missionary, founded an indigenous and independent church in the north of the country. At the time of the struggle for liberation from the colonial regime in 1961, it became the victim of severe Portuguese repression. In the following fourteen years many church members went either underground or into exile. A new beginning became possible, however, before political independence. The church was ready in 1977 to constitute itself as the Evangelical Reformed Church of Angola. Headquarters were moved from Uige in the North to the capital Luanda. Though the church seeks to establish itself in other parts of the country (today it has congr and is well implanted in 11 of the 18 provinces of Angola), its primary strength is in the eastern part of the province of Uige.

TM: **100,000** CM: **70,000** Congr: **507** PStations: **85** OrdM: **260** Eld: **yes** Deac: **161** EvgHome: **368** Mission: **2** Women Ord: **yes** As Ministers: **1991/3** as Deac: **4** as Elders: **2** ChurchOrg: **congr, church regions, executive committee, GenAssy** Off/otherLang: **Portuguese / Kikongo, Fioti, Kimbundu, Chokwe, Umbundu** DoctrB: **ApC, HeidC, HelvC** Infant or believer's baptism: **both** Frequency of the Lord's Supper: **1st Sunday of the month** Periodicals: **Novidades da IERA (Gen./4per year/1,000)** NatRel: **CICA (1977)** RegRel: **SAARC, AACC** IntlRel: **WCC (1995), WARC (1980)** TheolSchool: **Instituto Biblico de Kinkuni, Seminario Basico de Teologia (Luanda), Seminario Emmanuel Unido (Huambo) Seminario Evangelico Teologico (Lisbon)**

Address: Igreja Evangélica Reformada de Angola–IERA, Caixa Postal 2594 C, Karl Marx 45R/ C47-B, Luanda, Angola, Tel: +244 2 394-632 or 394-638, Fax: +244 2 394-586

3. United Evangelical Church of Angola (1006)

When the Evangelical Reformed Church of Angola (cf. no. 2) was about to be constituted, differences of opinion arose about the way the heritage of Archibald Patterson should be preserved in the future. There were also tensions concerning the leadership of the new church. Rev. Domingos Alexandre decided, together with others, to found a separate church in the north of Angola. He later founded the United Evangelical Church of Angola–Anglican Communion, in relationship with the Anglican Church of Mozambique. The two churches are both members of CICA, but there are no plans at this stage to reunite.

TM: **2,205** BM: **1,500** CM: **705** Congr: **11** PStations: **24** OrdM: **5** Eld: **0** Deac: **35** EvgHome: **12** Mission: **0** Women Ord: **yes** As Ministers: **nc** as Deac: **15/1959** as Elders: **nc** ChurchOrg: **local, regional, GenAssy** Off/otherLang: **Portuguese / Kikongo, Lingala, Frances, Kimbundu, Umbundu** DoctrB: **ApC** Infant or believer's baptism: **believer** Frequency of the Lord's Supper: **monthly** Periodicals: **none** NatRel: **UCAH (1993), FONGA (1993)** RegRel: **none** IntlRel: **none**

Address: Igreja Evangelica Unida de Angola, 18139 Vila Alice, Golf ex. Correios, Luanda, Angola

4. Presbyterian Church of Angola–PCA (1007)

This church also arose from an unresolved conflict in the IERA (cf. no. 2) about ways of exercising leadership in the church. In 1984 Pastor Neves Mussaqui was repudiated as pastor by the IERA for having advocated polygamy and the free use of alcohol. Close relations with the Presbyterian Church of Brazil (cf. Brazil no. 1) fostered the secession. The center of activities is in Luanda and in Uige, the home region of the founder.

TM: **7,528** BM: **7,528** Congr: **28** PStations: **50** OrdM: **11** Eld: **68** Deac: **200** EvgHome: **nc** Mission: **ne** Women Ord: **no** ChurchOrg: **congr, presby, synod, GenAssy** Off/otherLang: **Portuguese / Kikongo, Umbumbu, Chiluba** DoctrB: **ApC, WestConf** Infant or believer's baptism: **both** Frequency of the Lord's Supper: **monthly** Periodicals: **A Trombeta (general/twice a year)** NatRel: **Aliança Ev. de Angola (1985)** TheolSchool: **International Institute Timothy, Biblical Institute (under consideration)**

Address: Igreja Presbiteriana de Angola–IPA, C.P. 14470 SP, Luanda, Funchal n 1, Luanda, Angola

5. Independent Presbyterian Church in Angola (1008)

The church was founded in 1991 by Angolan refugees who returned from Zaire and had become identified with the "Communauté presbyterienne de Kinshasa" during their exile (cf. Congo-Kinshasa). When they returned, they experienced difficulties in relating to another church and decided to be maintain their independence based on their spiritual experience in Zaire.

TM: **1,052** BM: **350** CM: **95** Congr: **4** PStations: **10** OrdM: **8** Eld: **11** Deac: **nc** EvgHome: **4** Mission: **nc** Women Ord: **yes** As Ministers: **0** as Deac: **1994/2** as Elders: **1997/9** ChurchOrg: **consistories, presby, Synod, GenAssy** Off/otherLang: **Portuguese, national languages (Kikongo, Kimbundu, Umbundu)** DoctrB: **ApC** Infant or believer's baptism: **both** Frequency of the Lord's Supper: **12 times per year and "emergency"**

Address: Igreja Presbiteriana Independente em Angola, José Kumenda, C.P. 5207, Marien Nganaky 102, 1a, andar E, Ex-Antonio Barraso, Luanda, Angola, Tel: +244 2 390-414

AOTEAROA NEW ZEALAND

Area in km²	268,680
Population	(July 1996 est.) 3,547,983 European 88%, Maori 8.9%, Pacific Islander 2.9%, other 0.2%
Religions in %	Angl 24%, Presb 18%, RCath 15%, Meth 5%, Bapt 2%, other Prot 3%, unspecified or none 33% (1986)
Official/other languages	English / Maori

CCANZ (Conference of Churches in Aotearoa New Zealand)

Christianity came to New Zealand when in 1814 Rev. Samuel Marsden, Church of England chaplain to the British settlement in Sydney, preached on Christmas Day in that country. In the following two decades the Church of England, the Methodists and the RCath began mission work among the Maoris. In 1840 the British Crown signed a treaty with many Maori chiefs. In the following years migrants from Europe, mainly from the British Isles, began to arrive in the country in growing numbers. Also arriving were settlers who were Ref, Presb, and Congreg; they formed settler churches and did not carry out missions to the Maori. There has never been an established church in New Zealand; the state was always secular. In the 19th century denominational rivalry could at times be intense over issues like temperance and the place of the Bible and religion in schools. Toward the end of the century other denominations such as Bapt, Brethren, Quakers, and the Salvation Army founded congr. The Seventh-Day Adventists made their entry in 1924, and the Assemblies of God started in 1927.

In the early 20th century church union negotiations began among Congreg, Meth, and Presb. At a later stage they also included Angl. But these did not ultimately lead to union — though there are in New Zealand almost 150 union congr. Many Christian activities are carried out ecumenically. The National Council of Churches, founded in 1941, was the first such Council in the world.

After World War II new immigrants, especially of Dutch origin, entered the country. An important development was the changing status of the Maori population in the churches' life. In 1945 the Presbyterian Church set up Te Hinota Synod (Maori Synod) to regulate its own affairs. In 1973 the Methodist Church set up a separate Maori division. The first Angl Maori bishop was consecrated in 1928, though it took 50 years for him to achieve full diocesan status; the RCath appointed their first Maori bishop in 1988.

The role of women has changed considerably. The Congregationalist Church was the first to ordain women (1951). Now all Prot churches practice women's ordination. The first Angl woman diocesan bishop was consecrated in New Zealand.

1. Presbyterian Church of Aotearoa New Zealand (5031)

The first Presb congr was founded in 1840 in Wellington by the Church of Scotland for settlers arriving from Glasgow. After the disruption in 1848 the Free Church sent ministers to care for the many immigrants throughout the country. Most notable was the Free Church settlement in Dunedin in the South Island where Presb formed the majority. The 19th century was a time of expansion among settlers; the church did not carry out missionary work among the Maori; however, it sent missionaries to the New Hebrides, China, and India, and worked among the Chinese in New Zealand. A number of heresy trials gave rise in 1892 to a Declaratory Act allowing "liberty of conscience in such matters as do not enter into the substance of faith." Initially there were two churches, the Northern and the Southern; they united in 1901.

In 1876 Knox Theological Hall was established for the training of ministers and in the early 20th century secondary schools were opened in all the main cities. In 1902 the Young Men's Bible Class Union, and two years later the Young Women's Bible Class Union, were formed. For 50 years they were powers in the church. The New Life Movement in the '50s and early '60s brought rapid growth of new congr, and membership and Sunday school attendance. In 1945 a special Synod was set up for the relatively few Maori Presb. In 1970 when many Pacific Island Congreg joined the church, several Pacific Island congr were formed; the establishment of a special synod is currently under consideration.

TM: **540,675** CM: **58,325** Congr: **442** PStations: **950** OrdM: **780** Eld: **ne** Deac: **ne** EvgHome: **ne** Mission: **15** Women Ord: **yes** As Ministers: **1965/91** as Deac: **ne** as Elders: **1955** ChurchOrg: **Presbyterian (presby, annual GenAssy)** Off/otherLang: **English, Maori, Samoan, CookIsland, Niuean, Tokelaun, Korean, Taiwanese, Mandarin, Indonesian** DoctrB: **ApC, WestConf, WestCat, Faith we affirm together (NZ Statement of Faith)** Infant or believer's baptism: **both** Frequency of the Lord's Supper: **varies — monthly or quarterly, the former becoming more the norm** Periodicals: **Crosslink (gen/monthly/60,000), Harvest Field (gen./monthly/7,300)** Close relations with: **Meth Church of NZ, Associated Churches of Christ, Congregational Union of NZ, Anglican Church of NZ and 11 Churches in Pacific and Asia** NatRel: **CCANZ (1940), Churches Education Commission (1973), Council of Christian Social Services, Churches Broadcasting Commission (1963), Forum of Cooperative Ventures** RegRel: **PCC (1957), CCA** IntlRel: **WARC, WCC (1948), CWM (1977), WACC** TheolSchool: **Knox Theological Hall (Dunedin), Centre for Advanced Ministry Studies.**

Address: Presbyterian Church of Aotearoa New Zealand, P.O. Box 9049, 100 Tory Street, Wellington, Aotearoa New Zealand, Tel: +64 4 801-6000, Fax: +64 4 801-6001, E-mail: aes@pcanz.org.nz

2. Congregational Union of New Zealand (5033)

The Congregational Fellowship was founded in the far north by Pastor Barzillai Quaife in 1840. Forty years later there were still only 12 ministers in the whole country. The first Congregational Union was held in 1887. In 1893 women were admitted to the Assembly as full members, and a few years later a woman became president of the Assembly. In 1920 the Congregational Union approached the Presbyterian Church with a view to church union, but it later withdrew "until the Meth could join in." In 1947 the Assembly accepted responsibility for Samoan, Cook Island, and Niuean Christians in New Zealand (former London Missionary Society Churches). But in 1963 The Pacific Island Congregational Church (PICC) split over matters of language and culture to form a Samoan Church. The majority of the remaining PICC joined the Presbyterian Church (cf. no. 1).

TM: **850** Congr: **15** PStations: **15** OrdM: **14** Eld: **nc** Deac: **nc** EvgHome: **1** Mission: **6** Women Ord: **yes** As Ministers: **1946/nc** as Deac: **10** as Elders: **0** ChurchOrg: **districts and annual National Assembly** Off/otherLang: **English, Samoan, Cook Island, Maori, Niuean** DoctrB: **ApC, Savoy Declaration** Infant or believer's baptism: **both** Frequency of the Lord's Supper: **monthly** Periodicals: **Congreg (quarterly/300)** NatRel: **NCUN, CCANZ Ecumenical Board** Broadcasting IntlRel: **CWM, ICF, WECF** TheolSchool: **Congregational College of New Zealand, Auckland.**

Address: Congregational Union of New Zealand, P.O. Box 112, 14 St. Catherine Crescent, West Habour, Auckland 4066, Aotearoa New Zealand, Tel: +64 9 416 7463, Fax: +64 9 378 9563

3. Reformed Churches of New Zealand (5034)

After World War II many Dutch people immigrated to New Zealand. Most joined existing churches. But some felt that the Presbyterian Church of New Zealand had strayed from sound doctrine and in 1953 founded a new denomination: the Reformed Churches of New Zealand. Ministers came from Holland or were sent by the Christian Reformed Church of North America or the Orthodox Presbyterian Church (cf. United States). Initially, the church belonged to several international bodies. Due to tensions, membership in the ICCC was discontinued in 1969. Formal ties with the Gereformeerde Kerken in the Netherlands (cf. Netherlands no. 5) and with the Christian Reformed Church of North America (cf. United States) ended respectively in 1986 and 1995. The church adheres strictly to the Ref confession and seeks to be faithful to God's Word according to the Ref confessions.

TM: **3,117** BM: **1,375** Congr: **17** PStations: **1** OrdM: **18** Eld: **91** Deac: **46** EvgHome: **0** Mission: **1** Women Ord: **no** ChurchOrg: **presby in 3 regions, synod at national level** Off/otherLang: **English** DoctrB: **ApC, NicC, AthC, HeidC, WestConf, CDort, BelgC, 66 books of the Bible as interpreted by confessions** Infant or believer's baptism: **both** Frequency of the Lord's Supper: **every two months** Periodicals: **Faith in Focus (gen/monthly/900)** Close relations with: **Ref. Churches of Australia, Orth Presb Ch (USA), Christian Ref Ch (USA), Christian Ref Ch (NL), Ref Ch of South Africa** IntlRel: **ICRC** TheolSchool: **Reformed Theological College (Geelong, Australia).**

Address: Reformed Churches of New Zealand, P.O. Box 1301, Hastings, Aotearoa New Zealand, Tel: +64 6 826-4351, Fax: +64 6 826-4351, E-mail: bhoyt@voyager.co.nz

4. Evangelical Presbyterian Church (5032)

This church is the result of a split in 1974. Members of the Presbyterian Church of Aotearoa New Zealand felt that true Ref teaching had been abandoned and there was need for a more authentic witness. They placed strong emphasis on evangelism. The Church is part of the Westminster Churches in Australia (cf. Australia).

TM: **73** BM: **26** CM: **47** Congr: **1** PStations: **1** OrdM: **na** Eld: **5** Deac: **1** EvgHome: **na** Mission: **nc** Women Ord: **no** ChurchOrg: **presby, synod** Off/otherLang: **English** DoctrB: **WestConf, WestCat** Infant or believer's baptism: **both** Frequency of the Lord's Supper: **every 2 months** Periodicals: **none** Close relations with: **Westminster Presbyterian Church of Australia (1991)** NatRel: **none** RegRel: **none** IntlRel: **none** TheolSchool: **Grace Theological College.**

Address: Evangelical Presbyterian Church, P.O. Box 31-210, 166 Waimairi Rd., Ilam, Christchurch, Aotearoa New Zealand, Tel: +64 3 338-2508, Fax: +64 3 348-0551, E-mail: rvanrij @clear.net.nz

5. Free Presbyterian Church of Scotland–Australia and New Zealand Presbytery (5035)

These three congr belong to the "Australia and New Zealand Presbytery" of the Free Presbyterian Church of Scotland. They are served by one minister. With the split among Presb in Scotland (cf. United Kingdom no. 6), there has been a similar split in NZ and Australia in 1893 leading to the formation of a new denomination.

TM: **211** BM: **128** CM: **74** Congr: **3** PStations: **2** OrdM: **2** Eld: **17** Deac: **2** EvgHome: **ne** Mission: **ne** Women Ord: **no** ChurchOrg: **presb (annual synod)** Off/otherLang: **English** DoctrB: **WestConf, WestCat** Infant or believer's baptism: **both** Periodicals: **Free Presbyterian (magazine, monthly)**

Address: Free Presbyterian Church of Scotland–Australia and New Zealand Presbytery, 14 Thomson St., Gisborne, Aotearoa New Zealand, Fax: +64 6 868 5809, E-mail: johannes.vandorp @clear.net.nz

ARGENTINA

Area in km²	2,766,890
Population	(July 1996 est.) 34,672,997 white 85%, mestizo, Indian, or other nonwhite groups 15%
Religions in %	RCath 80% (less than 20% practicing), Prot 12%, Jewish 2%, other 6%
Official/other languages	Spanish / English, Italian, German, French

ISEDET (Instituto superior evangélico de estudios teológicos)

The Argentine Republic forms, together with Chile and Uruguay, the southern cone of Latin America. One third of its population lives in the capital — Buenos Aires and Greater Buenos Aires. Due to the length of the country, the climate varies from semi-tropical to polar, and due to its width the topography varies from coastal to mountainous zones in the Andes. Historically, the country was colonized by the Spaniards and gained independence in 1816. The majority religion has been Roman Catholicism. The first Protestant groups to arrive were Presb from Scotland and Angl (1825-1829); they were authorized to work in English only. The Meth church made its appearance in 1836, followed in 1881 by the Bapt. The first immigrants, who later established the Argentine Reformed Church, arrived from Holland in 1886. By now, most of the historical churches have celebrated the 100th anniversary of their presence in the country. The historical churches also include the Waldensian Church in Argentina and Uruguay (cf. Uruguay), the Evangelical Church of the River Plate in Argentina, Uruguay, and Paraguay, the Disciples of Christ, and the United Lutheran Church. In the last few years the country has seen the emergence of a great number of Pentecostal churches, some open for ecumenical contacts, others based on a strong personal and individual ministry. All religious communities have to register with the Foreign Ministry.

For many years now, most of these churches have united in cooperative efforts. More than 25 denominations, including the Salvation Army and some Pentecostal churches, are members of the Argentine Federation of Protestant Churches; nine churches share the Faculty of Theology (ISEDET) for the training of their ministers. A few years ago the Waldensian, United Lutheran, Reformed, and Evangelical Church of the River Plate agreed on the mutual recognition of membership and ministry on the basis of the Leuenberg Concord. The Reformed and Waldensian Church have gradually begun to share their work. They jointly issue the magazine *Dialogo* and together run a student hostel in Buenos Aires. In 1994 the Synods celebrated a joint Assembly.

1. St. Andrew's Presbyterian Church (2002)

This church has its historical roots in the Church of Scotland. It was established in 1829 primarily to give spiritual assistance to the Scots people who had come to Argentina. Evangelistic work in Spanish started only 13 years ago. As the Church of Scotland withdrew its support, the church sought contacts with the Reformed Church of Argentina and receives, at present, support from the Evangelical Presbyterian Church in the USA of which it is the Argentine presby (cf. United States). The church is engaged in evangelistic-social work in Villa Paranacito in the periphery of Buenos Aires.

TM: **2,000** CM: **500** Congr: **7** PStations: **18** OrdM: **10** Eld: **40** Deac: **yes** EvgHome: **3** Mission: **ne** Women Ord: **yes** As Ministers: **none** as Deac: **none** as Elders: **1969/1** ChurchOrg: **Presby, sessions of organized churches** Off/otherLang: **Spanish, English** DoctB: **ApC, WestConf** Infant or believer's baptism: **both** Frequency of the Lord's Supper: **once per month** Periodicals: **Revista de la Iglesia Presbiteriana san Andres (gen/bi-monthly)** NatRel: **FAIE, FRA** IntlRel: **Asociación de Iglesias Reformadas, Fradernidad Reformada de Fe** TheolSchool: **ISEDET, Instituto Bíblico Buenos Aires (IBBA)**

Address: Iglesia Presbiteriana San Andrés en Olivos, P.O. Box 1636, Acasusso 1131, Olivos, Buenos

Aires, Argentina, Tel. +54 1 790-0974, Fax +54 1 792-2983, E-mail bq858538 @bed
.bvnayre.com.ar

2. Evangelical Church of the River Plate (2012)

The first congregation of this church was founded in 1843 by European immigrants. At the end of the last century another congregation was founded in Entre
Rios with Russian-German immigrants and a third with Swiss immigrants. In
1899 the Evangelical German Synod of the River Plate was founded. In 1965 the
church established itself as the Evangelical Church of the River Plate with full
self-government. Since the end of the 1970s the church has sought to go beyond
being an ethnic church serving exclusively the descendants of German and Swiss
immigrants and to become more and more a national church. The church has expanded into the neighboring countries of Uruguay and Paraguay.

TM: **45,000** BM: **45,000** Congr: **60** PStations: **200** OrdM: **70** Eld: **0** Deac: **15** EvgHome: **0** Mission: **5**
Women Ord: **yes** As Ministers: **1985/11** as Deac: **1985/6** ChurchOrg: **synod** Off/otherLang: **Spanish /
German** DoctrB: **ApC, NicC, AthC, HeidC, CA, Luther's Catechism** Infant or believer's baptism:
both Frequency of the Lord's Supper: **monthly** Periodicals: **Revista Parroquial (gen/monthly/
4,000), Lecturas Diarias (meditation/yearly/9,000)** NatRel: **Federación Argentina de Iglesias
Evangélicas (1955/56) Federación de Iglesias Evangélicas del Uruguay (1955/65)** RegRel: **CLAI
(1978), Leuenberg (1980)** IntlRel: **WARC (1991), WCC (1957), LWF (1991)** TheolSchool: **partner
in ISEDET**

Address: Iglesia Evangelica del Río de la Plata, Mariscal Antonio Sucre, 2855-3 piso, 1428 Buenos
Aires, Argentina, Tel: +54 1 787-0436, Fax: +54 1 787-0335, E-mail: iglesia@ierp.cci
.org.ar

3. Evangelical Waldensian Church of Argentina (2004)

The first Waldensian immigrants reached Argentina in 1860 and settled in the
province of Santa Fé. This led to the foundation of other colonies, including
Colonia Belgrano, where the first church was erected. Beginning in the 1970s the
migration extended to the north of Argentina; both in the Pampa and the region of
Chaco new colonies and churches were founded. These congr were rural. The
foundation of churches in cities of Argentina and Uruguay occurred much later.
Without losing its spiritual and cultural roots the church adopted Spanish as its
current language. In Argentina the Church has 10 congr and 2,760 members of
whom 927 are communicant members. Three presby of the church are in Argentina. The centre of the Church is in Uruguay.

See under Uruguay for statistics.

Address: Iglesia Evangélica Valdense en Argentina, Mariscal Antonio Sucre, 2855-2, Buenos Aires,
Argentina

4. Reformed Churches in Argentina (2011)

This Church was founded in the last decade of the last century with the arrival of the second wave of Dutch immigrants to Argentina. The congr were established mainly in the center of the province of Buenos Aires and in Patagonia. The ecclesiastical structure is Presb, with men and women participating in all ministries. The church participates in ISEDET. At present, the church is going through a period of redefinition of its priorities, renewal of leadership, and revitalization of its missionary action. The church seeks closer links with the Waldensian Church of the River Plata. The synods of the two churches have held joint sessions, and there has even been a joint General Assembly. Some 20 families living in Patagonia which had dissolved their church, the Iglesia Galesa (Welsh Church), have joined the Reformed Churches in Argentina.

TM: **669** BM: **669** CM: **500** Congr: **13** PStations: **6** OrdM: **6** Eld: **nc** Deac: **nc** EvgHome: **2** Mission: **ne** Women Ord: **yes** As Ministers: **1** as Deac: **yes** as Elders: **yes** ChurchOrg: **national synod every 18 months with each congregation represented by 1 elder, 1 deacon, and 1 pastor** Off/otherLang: **Spanish** DoctrB: **ApC, NicC, AthC, HeidC, CDort, Calvinist teaching** Infant or believer's baptism: **both** Frequency of the Lord's Supper: **at least every 2 or 3 months, maximum once per month and on special occasions** Periodicals: **Dialogo (bi-monthly/2,000), Encuentro y Fe Liga** NatRel: **Bible Society, Argentine Federation of Evangelical Churches, Ecumenical Movement for Human Rights, United Mission Council, Ecumenical Council for Christian Education** RegRel: **CLAI** IntlRel: **WARC** TheolSchool: **partnership in ISEDET.**

Address:　Iglesias Reformadas en la Argentina (I.R.A.), C.P. 1296, Barracas, Benito Quinquela Martin 1763/7, Buenos Aires, Argentina, Tel: +54 1 301-1441, Fax: +54 1 301-3982, E-mail gerk@iragob.cci.org.ar

5. Evangelical Congregational Church (IECA) (2010)

This Church was founded in Concordia in 1922 when, after the Russian revolution, German congr from the Volga region immigrated to Argentina. Since they could not adjust themselves to the model of the Lutheran Church in the region, they asked the Congregationalist Churches in the USA (cf. United States no. 12) to provide assistance. They received some help from the itinerant pastor Jorge Geir. The first member of the church to be ordained was Carlos Holzer. In 1940 a seminary was founded in Concordia by pastor Otto Tiede.

TM: **20,000** BM: **20,000** CM: **5,500** Congr: **130** PStations: **30** OrdM: **32** Eld: **ne** Deac: **yes** EvgHome: **nc** Mission: **yes** Women Ord: **no** ChurchOrg: **Congreg** Off/otherLang: **Spanish, German** DoctrB: **ApC, NicC, HeidC, Luther's Small Catechism** Infant or believer's baptism: **both** Periodicals: **Crecimiento (magazine/monthly/1,400)** NatRel: **Argentine Federation of Evangelical Churches** RegRel: **CLAI** IntlRel: **WARC (1988), WCC** TheolSchool: **Instituto de Teologia de la IECA.**

Address:　Iglesia Evangélica Congregacional Argentina (IECA), Asunción 29, Concordia, Prov. Entre Ríos 2826, Argentina, Tel: +54 45 211-721

6. Hungarian Christian Evangelical Reformed Church (2014)

This Hungarian Reformed Church started in 1938 with the missionary work of Daniel Háry. In 1954 the church was constituted by Rev. Balász Dezsö Nagy, who had arrived in the country in 1953. He was succeeded by the pastors Imre Szábo and István Kotsis and, at present, Gyula Süto. In 1956 the church and the pastor's house were dedicated. In 1960 part of the congregation joined the Luth congregation in Buenos Aires. The congregation uses the same liturgy as the Reformed Church in Hungary. The congregation is also involved in social work. The pastor seeks to give pastoral assistance to a group of Hungarian Ref members in the interior of Argentina and in Uruguay and Chile.

TM: **360** BM: **360** CM: **60** Congr: **1** PStations: **3** OrdM: **2** Eld: **yes** Deac: **yes** EvgHome: **nc** Mission: **nc** Women Ord: **yes** As Ministers: **yes** as Deac: **yes** as Elders: **yes** ChurchOrg: **local session** Off/otherLang: **Hungarian, Spanish** DoctrB: **ApC, HelvC, HeidC** Infant or believer's baptism: **both** Frequency of the Lord's Supper: **once a month.**

Address: Iglesia Cristiana Evangélica Reformada Húngara, Calle Ramon Freire, C.P. 1428, Buenos Aires, Argentina, Tel: +54 1 551-4093

7. Che Il Korean Presbyterian Church (2001)

This Church was founded in 1969. The pioneers were Hong Jong Jin, a deacon, and Key Hwa Sam, a pastor of the Presbyterian Church of Korea–HapDong (cf. Korea no. 15). The main objective of their missionary activities is evangelism among Argentineans. They send candidates for the ministry to theological schools of other denominations

TM: **1,500** BM: **1,500** CM: **1,350** Congr: **1** PStations: **7** OrdM: **4** Eld: **yes** Deac: **nc** EvgHome: **nc** Mission: **7** Women Ord: **no** As Ministers: **no** as Deac: **yes** as Elders: **0** ChurchOrg: **Presb** Off/otherLang: **Korean, Spanish** DoctrB: **ApC, WestConf** Infant or believer's baptism: **both** NatRel: **Korean Churches in Argentina.**

Address: Iglesia Presbiteriana Coreana Che Il, Carabobo 1295, 1046 Flores, Buenos Aires, Argentina, Tel: +54 1 631-1788

8. Taiwanese Presbyterian Church (Sin-Heng) (2003)

This church came into existence in 1982. The first missionary was Rev. Lin. At present, the church does not have a pastor living in Argentina. Under lay leadership the community seeks to prepare the members for evangelistic outreach. They maintain an educational institution (Colégio Chino) in Buenos Aires.

TM: **125** BM: **100** CM: **70** Congr: **1** PStations: **1** OrdM: **0** Eld: **5** Deac: **10** EvgHome: **nc** Mission: — Women Ord: **yes** As Ministers: **nc** as Deac: **3** as Elders: **1** ChurchOrg: **local session** Off/otherLang: **Taiwanese, Spanish** DoctrB: **ApC** Infant or believer's baptism: **both.**

Address: Iglesia Presbiteriana Taiwan (Sin-Heng), Mendoza 1660, Belgrano, Buenos Aires, Argentina, Tel: +54 1 781-8809, Fax: +54 1 501-5552

9. Central Presbyterian Church of Buenos Aires (2009)

This Church was founded in 1985 by missionaries sent by the Korean Presbyterian Church of America (cf. United States). It is part of the South American Presbytery of this church. With considerable missionary commitment it seeks to evangelize both Korean immigrants and Argentineans; for this purpose it has hired the services of a local pastor. The church offers Bible courses not only for its own pastors and missionaries but also for the staff of other denominations; it provides financial help for missionaries and evangelists of other churches.

TM: **2,800** BM: **2,800** CM: **2,000** Congr: **1** PStations: **0** OrdM: **4** Eld: **yes** Deac: **yes** EvgHome: **nc** Mission: **1** Women Ord: **no** ChurchOrg: **Presbyterian** Off/otherLang: **Korean, Spanish** DoctrB: **ApC, WestConf** Infant or believer's baptism: **both** Periodicals: **newsletter** NatRel: **Evangelical Churches in Argentina.**

Address: Iglesia Presbiteriana Central de Buenos Aires, Calle Castañares 1435, 1406–Parque Chacabuco, Buenos Aires, Argentina, Tel: +54 1921-0509, Fax: +54 921-8860, E-mail nc.

10. Argentine Presbyterian Church (2013)

This Church was founded in 1988 in Rosario (central region) by Rev Antonio Andrés Gomez on behalf of the Evangelical Presbyterian Church in the USA (cf. United States no. 16). After it had been constituted it lost its links with the American church and became self-supporting. It entertains contacts with the Presbyterian Church San Andrés (cf. no. 1) with the intention of forming one presby in the region. It supports social projects in the region and participates in the ecumenical movement. It hopes to initiate evangelistic work in the center of the city and to expand to other areas, to start a theological school, and to build a center for homeless people.

TM: **360** BM: **360** CM: **300** Congr: **1** PStations: **3** OrdM: **1** Eld: **4** Deac: **4** EvgHome: **nc** Mission: **2** Women Ord: **yes (but not beyond presby level)** As Ministers: **nc** as Deac: **1988/6** as Elders: **1988/1** ChurchOrg: **local session** Off/otherLang: **Spanish** DoctrB: **ApC, NicC, WestConf, CDort,** Infant or believer's baptism: **both** Frequency of the Lord's Supper: **once a month** Periodicals: **newsletter (quarterly/100)** NatRel: **Ecumenical Movement of Rosario, Christian Alliance of Evangelical Churches in the Republic of Argentine.**

Address: Iglesia presbiteriana Argentina, Cochabamba 1555, Rosario, Argentina, Tel: +54 41 827-877, Fax: +54 41 827-877

11. Iglesia Presbiteriana Mui (Taiwanesa) (2017)

In March 1991 the Taiwanese pastor Chuang Chiou Wei arrived in Buenos Aires with the intention of establishing a church among immigrants of Taiwanese nationality. The Presbyterian Church Mui was formally inaugurated in 1995. Because work began only recently, the church has not yet ordained leaders. Attention is concentrated on the capital, but there is also a preaching station to look after Taiwanese in the interior of the country. The church participates financially in missionary work among Argentineans under the leadership of a Taiwanese pastor.

TM: **80** BM: **60** CM: **50** Congr: **1** PStations: **0** OrdM: **1** Eld: **no** Deac: **no** EvgHome: **nc** Mission: **1** Women Ord: **no** ChurchOrg: **nc** Off/otherLang: **Taiwanese, Chinese** DoctrB: **ApC, WestConf** Infant or believer's baptism: **both** IntlRel:.

Address: Mui Presbyterian Church, Marcos Sastre, 2875, Buenos Aires, Argentina, Tel: +54 1 503-8662, Fax: +54 1 503-8662

12. Swiss Evangelical Church (2015)

The Church was founded in 1944 in the Province of Misiones to look after immigrants in the area. In 1995 the church sought affiliation with the Evangelical Church of the River Plate (cf. no. 2). It entertains a project among aborigines and runs a technical and an agro-technical school.

TM: **600** BM: **600** CM: **140** Congr: **1** PStations: **6** OrdM: **1** Eld: **nc** Deac: **nc** EvgHome: **nc** Mission: **nc** Women Ord: **yes** As Ministers: **yes** as Deac: **yes** as Elders: **yes** ChurchOrg: **Presb** Off/otherLang: **Spanish, German** DoctrB: **ApC, NicC, HeidC, WestConf, HelvC.**

Address: Iglesia Evangelica Suiza en la Argentina, 3334 Ruiz de Montoya–Provincia Misiones, Ruiz de Montoya, Argentina, Tel: +54 7 439-5032, Fax: +54 7 439-5076

13. Korean Evangelical Presbyterian Church (2006)

Founded in 1966.

TM: **450** CM: **450** Off/otherLang: **Korean, Spanish** DoctrB: **ApC, WestConf** Infant or believer's baptism: **both**.

Address: Iglesia Evangelica Presbiteriana Coreana, Rev Sung Woo Lee, Senillosa 1769, Parque Chacabuco, Buenos Aires, Argentina

AUSTRALIA

Area in km²	7,686,850
Population	(July 1996 est.) 18,260,863 Caucasian 95%, Asian 4%, aboriginal and other 1%
Religions in %	Angl 26.1%, RCath 26%, Uniting 12.7%, other Christian 24.3%
Official/other languages	English, native languages

NCCA (National Council of Churches in Australia)

Though Australia was visited several times in the 16th and 17th centuries by Portuguese and Dutch navigators, Western colonization began only in 1788 when Britain established a convict colony in what is now Sydney. At that time the aboriginal population — which had existed since at least 60,000 years — is thought to have numbered about 300,000; it drastically decreased in subsequent years. Christian mission contributed to assuring their survival but at the same time alienated them from their traditional heritage. Today the churches seek to strengthen the awareness of their cultural identity; their number has again increased considerably in both traditional communities and urban areas.

Christianity in Australia is multiform and reflects various streams of immigration. The first Ref Christians to arrive were Presb from Scotland and Congreg from England. Congregations were established in various parts of Australia. In the course of the 19th century they gradually organized themselves at the national level. In 1977, after protracted negotiations, Methodists, Presb, and Congreg formed the *Uniting Church of Australia* (cf. no. 1).

The first Scottish Presb settled in 1802 in Hawkesbury River near Portland Head, west from Sydney. A church was built in 1809 in Ebenezer. The first minister on the mainland was John Dunmore Lang, who arrived in 1823 and started the Scots Church in Sydney. Other ministers followed. After a period of disputes, two groups in New South Wales formed in 1840 *The Synod of Australia in connection with the Established Church of Scotland*. But soon afterward a disruption occurred — reproducing on Australian soil the split in the Church of Scotland and the formation of the Free Church of Scotland (1843). In Scotland the issue was the power the state came to exercise in church affairs, especially the imposition on parishes of ministers approved by the patron (cf. United Kingdom) but not approved by the church members. The majority of the Australian Synod refused to break their moral and legal tie to the Established Church of Scotland. Division came in 1846 with the formation of the Presbyterian Church of Eastern Australia (New South Wales and Queensland) and the Free Presbyterian Church of Victoria, both of which were independent but maintained fellowship with the Free Church of Scotland. In addition, the United Presbyterian Church of Scotland was represented in

Australia from 1847 (cf. United Kingdom, Introduction on Scotland). Several other Presbyterian groups established themselves in Australia, representing dissenting groups in their home countries — e.g., the Welsh Calvinistic Methodist Church (1857, no. 6) and the Reformed Presbyterian Church of Australia (1857, no. 4). As time went on, the need for a common witness in Australia became more manifest. Unions of most Presb were achieved in all the then separate colonies. Each union resulted in the name Presbyterian Church with the name of the colony. Toward the end of the 19th century the general feeling was that the colonies should federate into one country comprising six states. The churches followed this movement. The Presb started to meet together in a Federal Assembly. In 1901, they formed the Presbyterian Church in Australia. In 1977 70% of the Presb joined the Uniting Church (cf. no. 1), but a minority of almost one third decided to continue as the Presbyterian Church of Australia (cf. no. 2).

The Congreg presence is due mainly to work of the LMS. The first congregation was founded in 1809 in Sydney by W. P. Crook. Others followed in several other parts of Australia. They expanded considerably in Melbourne and Sydney and had a remarkable impact on politics and the press. Before 1900 South Australian Congreg represented 3.5% of the population but provided 40% of the members of the Legislative Council and 12.5% of the House of Assembly. Their influence diminished in the 20th century. In the second part of the 19th century Congreg unions were formed in several states. Congr participated in church union negotiations and decided by an overwhelming majority to join the Uniting Church of Australia (1977). Only 40 of the 300 congr opted for a continuing separate existence. There are still several Congreg churches outside the membership of the Uniting Church — some of them have formed the Congregational Federation of Australia (no. 14), others belong to the Fellowship of Congregational Churches in NSW (no. 15), and still others are entirely independent.

In addition to the groups so far mentioned there are quite a number of Presb and Ref Churches which came into existence through immigration, doctrinal disputes, or particular missionary initiatives after World War II — Dutch Reformed (no. 11-12), Irish Presb (no. 13), and, in recent years, more and more Korean Presb groups (no. 18-21).

While the Uniting Church of Australia participates in the ecumenical movement and is an active member of the National Council of Churches in Australia, most Presb and Ref bodies view the ecumenical movement with scepticism, some even with hostility. These hold to conservative interpretations of the Ref tradition.

1. Uniting Church in Australia (5012)

The Uniting Church was inaugurated on June 22, 1977, after more than sixty years of negotiations. At the time of union, the Methodists represented about 60%, the Presb about 35%, and the Congreg about 5% of the membership. The Church has not only transcended denominational boundaries but has become a multicultural church. It includes a large number (80) of ethnic congr following their own traditions. In 1985 the National Assembly opposed re-baptism as espoused by the charismatic movement, a decision which led to a loss of membership, mainly to the Assemblies of God. The Uniting Church is known for its witness in the social and political field and its involvement in the cause of the Aborigines. It has relatively strong roots in rural areas.

The Basis of Union includes reference to the ApC and NicC as authoritative statements of faith framed in the language of their day, which are to be studied, taught, and interpreted in the light of a later age; while affirming the abiding teaching value of the documents embodying the doctrinal heritage of the three churches before union, the Uniting Church seeks to learn how to confess its faith in fresh words and deeds in the light of changing circumstances; among Ref Confessions the HeidC and WestConf are listed.

TM: **1,386,000** BM: **900,000** CM: **183,000** Congr: **2,921** PStations: **ne** OrdM: **2,230** Eld: **4,500** Deac: **30** EvgHome: **ne** Mission: **25** Women Ord: **yes** As Ministers: **1977/250** as Deac: **1977/50** as Elders: **1977/5500** ChurchOrg: **congr, 54 presby, 7 state synods, national Assembly** Off/otherLang: **English** DoctrB: **ApC, NicC, Scots Confession, HeidC, WestConf, Savoy Decl, Wesley's 44 sermons, Basis of Union** Infant or believer's baptism: **both** Frequency of the Lord's Supper: **weekly to monthly** NatRel: **NCCA (1977)** RegRel: **CCA (1977), PCC (observer)** IntlRel: **WARC (1977), WCC (1977), WMC (1977)** TheolSchool: **six theological colleges: Perth, Melbourne, Adelaide, Sydney, Brisbane, Darwin (for indigenous people)** Service infrastructure: **11 hospitals, hundreds of nursing homes and social services, 30 kindergartens** Periodicals: **each synod publishes a monthly magazine**

Address: Uniting Church in Australia, P.O. Box A 2266, 5th floor / 222 Pitt St., Sydney South 1235, Australia, Tel: +61 2 9287-0900, Fax: +61 2 9287-0999, E-mail: assysec@nat.uca.org.au.

2. Presbyterian Church of Australia (5009)

While before union (1977) the Presbyterian Church was predominantly liberal in outlook, the position of the "continuing" Presbyterian Church has become increasingly conservative. A resurgence of traditional Ref theology has taken place. In 1991 the General Assembly repealed the approval of the ordination of women which had been introduced by the church before union (1974). Women elders continue to be admitted in a number of states. In 1982 the church became a member of the REC and withdrew from the WARC. In 1987 a new hymnbook was introduced which is used by about 50% of the congr. The church is committed to missionary work — about 130 missionaries are serving in more than 20 countries, especially in the Pacific, Korea, and India.

TM: **70,000** CM: **36,176** Congr: **412** PStations: **356** OrdM: **502** Eld: **3,186** Deac: **ne** EvgHome: **ne** Mission: **ne** Women Ord: **yes** As Ministers: **1991/6** as Deac: **nc** as Elders: **nc** ChurchOrg: **nc** Off/otherLang: **English** DoctrB: **WestConf** Infant or believer's baptism: **both** IntlRel: **REC, having relations with ICRC** TheolSchool: **Presb Theol Center (Sydney), Presb Theol College (Melbourne), Presb Theol Hall (Brisbane)** Service infrastructure: **Presb (local congr, presby, annual state assy, national assy every three years)** Periodicals: **Australian Presbyterian Living Today**

Address: Presbyterian Church of Australia, P.O. Box 100, 420 Elizabeth St., Surry Hills, Sydney, NSW 2001, Australia, Tel: +61 2 9310-3724, Fax: +61 2 9310-2148

3. Presbyterian Church of Eastern Australia (5007)

This church was founded in 1846 by three ministers and an elder who withdrew from the *Synod of Australia in connection with the Established Church of Scotland*. While part of the membership returned in 1865 to the mainstream Presb church, a minority continued as a separate church. The church is a free church strictly adhering to Presb standards of faith.

TM: **870** BM: **327** CM: **543** Congr: **15** PStations: **18** OrdM: **9** Eld: **45** Deac: **28** EvgHome: **ne** Mission: **0** Women Ord: **no** ChurchOrg: **Presb (3 regional presby, 1 national synod)** Off/otherLang: **English** DoctrB: **ApC, NicC, AthC, WestConf** Infant or believer's baptism: **both** Frequency of the Lord's Supper: **2 to 6 times per year** Close relations with: **Free Church of Scotland** NatRel: **none** RegRel: **none** IntlRel: **ICRC (1985)** TheolSchool: **Free Ch. of Scotland College (Edinb.), Presb. Theol. College (Melbourne)** Periodicals: **Presbyterian Banner (gen/monthly/450)**

Address: Presbyterian Church of Eastern Australia, 23 Gleneagles Crescent, Albany Creek, Queensland 4035, Australia, Tel: +61 7 3264-3270, Fax: +61 7 3264-3270, E-mail: w.hanna @qut.edu.au.

4. Reformed Presbyterian Church of Australia (Covenanters) (5017)

This church has its roots in the history of Scottish Presbyterianism. In 1690 a Presb group denounced the acquiescence of the Church of Scotland in its alliance with the state. The protest resulted in the formation of the Reformed Presbyterian Church in 1743. In 1876 part of this church joined the Free Church of Scotland, but a remnant continued in Scotland; in the meantime, Reformed Presbyterian Churches had been established in Ireland and North America. In 1857 a pastor of the Reformed Presbyterian Church in Ireland (cf. Ireland no. 4) came to Australia and founded a congregation in Geelong in 1857. From 1954 to 1979 a presby operated as part of the Reformed Presbyterian Church in Ireland, but it is now independent with its own constitution. Discussion, with a view to union with the Presbyterian Church of Eastern Australia (1983-86), did not succeed.

TM: **100** CM: **100** Congr: **3** OrdM: **3** Eld: **8** Deac: **nc** EvgHome: **none** Mission: **none** Women Ord: **no** ChurchOrg: **presb (one presby)** Off/otherLang: **English** DoctrB: **WestConf** Infant or believer's baptism: **both** Close relations with: **Ref Presb Church in Ireland** NatRel: **none** RegRel: **none** IntlRel: **none** TheolSchool: **Ref Theol College (Geelong)** Periodicals: **none**

Address: Reformed Presbyterian Church of Australia, 2 Fenwick St., Geelong 3220, Australia, Tel: +61 39 744-3921, E-mail: rpgelong@ne.com.au.

5. Free Presbyterian Church of Scotland (5004)

This church is the result of a schism in the Presbyterian Church of Eastern Australia (no. 3), which occurred in 1880s. A dissenting group was eventually received (1911) into communion by the Free Presbyterian Church of Scotland (cf. United Kingdom no. 6), which had come into existence in 1893. Today the three congr are under the Presbytery of Australia and New Zealand. There are three congr in New Zealand.

TM: **60** BM: **60** CM: **50** Congr: **2** PStations: **1** OrdM: **1** Eld: **5** Deac: **5** EvgHome: **0** Mission: **0** Women Ord: **no** ChurchOrg: **Presbyterian (one presby for Australia and New Zealand)** Off/otherLang: **English** DoctrB: **WestConf** Infant or believer's baptism: **both** Close relations with: **Free Presbyterian Church of Scotland** TheolSchool: **training in Scotland** Periodicals: **Free Presbyterian (magazine)**

Address: Free Presbyterian Church of Scotland, 90 Victoria Street, Grafton, NSW 2460, Australia

6. Welsh Calvinistic Methodist (Presbyterian Church) (5018)

In Wales the Meth revival of the 18th century followed Presb patterns, and the converts were organized as a genuinely Presb body. The first services in Welsh were held in Melbourne in 1852, and a Welsh minister arrived in 1857. In the period of the gold rush work flourished, but today only two congr are left — in Melbourne and in Sebastopol (near Ballarat). Initially all services were in Welsh, but prior to the turn of the century English services were introduced to meet the needs of the first generation Welsh Australians.

TM: **90** BM: **90** CM: **90** Congr: **2** OrdM: **2** Eld: **8** Deac: **ne** EvgHome: **ne** Mission: **ne** Women Ord: **yes** As Ministers: **nc** as Deac: **nc** as Elders: **1991/1** ChurchOrg: **Presbyterian** Off/otherLang: **English, Welsh** DoctrB: **ApC** Infant or believer's baptism: **both** Frequency of the Lord's Supper: **monthly** Close relations with: **Carmel Welsh Church (Sebastopol, Victoria)** NatRel: **none** RegRel: **none** IntlRel: **none** Service infrastructure: **none** Periodicals: **The Dawn (gen/monthly/240)**

Address: Welsh Calvinistic Methodist (Presbyterian Church), Latrobe St. 320, Melbourne, Vic 3000, Australia, Tel: +61 3 9329-6961

7. Presbyterian Reformed Church of Australia (5010)

In recent years more small Presb churches have been founded. The Presbyterian Reformed Church resulted from a split in the Presbyterian Church (no. 2) in 1967 in protest against modernist teachings.

TM: **720** BM: **410** CM: **410** Congr: **13** PStations: **6** OrdM: **14** Eld: **39** Deac: **29** EvgHome: **0** Mission: **4** Women Ord: **no** ChurchOrg: **Presb (1 presby for Australia and New Zealand)** Off/otherLang: **English** DoctrB: **WestConf** Infant or believer's baptism: **both** Frequency of the Lord's Supper: **monthly** Close relations with: **Presbyterian Ch of Eastern Australia, Sovereign Grace Baptist Church** TheolSchool: **John Knox Theological College, Sydney** Service infrastructure: **none** Periodicals: **The Prot Review (gen/monthly/450), Proclaim (mission/monthly/115)**

Address: Presbyterian Reformed Church of Australia, 1, Cassandra Place, Stanwell Park, NSW 2508, Australia, Tel: +61 2 42 942-579, Fax: +61 2 42 942-579

8. Evangelical Presbyterian Church of Australia (5002)

Originally called the Reformed Evangelical Church, this body was constituted in 1961 in Launceston, Tasmania, by three men who had been ordained for this purpose by a special presby of ministers of the Presbyterian Church of Eastern Australia (cf. no. 3). Its position is close to this church, with a special emphasis on the limited effect of the work of atonement. The church maintains relations with the Protestant Reformed Church of America (cf. United States).

TM: **320** BM: **128** CM: **192** Congr: **6** PStations: **3** OrdM: **6** Eld: **18** Deac: **6** EvgHome: **1** Mission: **ne** Women Ord: **no** ChurchOrg: **Presbyterian** Off/otherLang: **English** DoctrB: **WestConf, WestCats, historic confessions of the Ref Ch of Scotland** Infant or believer's baptism: **both** Frequency of the Lord's Supper: **average 4 times a year** Close relations with: **Presb Ref Ch of Ireland; Free Presb Ch of Scotland, Presb Ch of Eastern Australia; Prot Ref Ch of America; Ev. Ref Ch of Singapore Presb Australia; Prot Ref Ch of N Zealand; Presb Heritage/USA** NatRel: **none** RegRel: **none** IntlRel: **none** TheolSchool: **in the church and other Ref Churches** Periodicals: **The Evangelical Presbyterian (gen/quarterly/300)**

Address: Evangelical Presbyterian Church of Australia, 116, Hyde Street, North Rockhampton, Queensland 4701, Australia, Tel: +61 7 928-1316

9. Bible Presbyterian Churches (5003)

These churches grew out of the movement initiated by Carl McIntire (cf. United States no. 7; Singapore). The first congregation was established in 1969 in Adelaide. Close links exist with the Bible Presb in Singapore. Through missionary efforts three large, principally Chinese-speaking, congr were founded in Perth, Adelaide, and Melbourne.

TM: **500** Congr: **nc** OrdM: **nc** Eld: **nc** Deac: **nc** EvgHome: **ne** Mission: **ne** Women Ord: **yes** As Ministers: **1991/111** as Deac: **nc** as Elders: **nc** ChurchOrg: **nc** Off/otherLang: **English** DoctrB: **nc** TheolSchool: **Fundamental Bible College of Australia**

Address: Bible Presbyterian Church, Brahan, Springton, SA 5235, Australia

10. Westminster Presbyterian Church (5016)

The church grew out of work initiated by a woman missionary — Mary Jones — in the mid-1960s among the aborigines in the Brookton area about 130 km southeast of Perth. In 1967 the World Presbyterian Missions, related to the Reformed Presbyterian Church, Evangelical Synod, in the US (cf. United States), took responsibility for the mission. Several centers were formed (in Perth, Brisbane, Penrith, Canberra).

TM: **900** BM: **900** Congr: **16** PStations: **5** OrdM: **26** Eld: **50** Deac: **34** EvgHome: **nc** Mission: **nc** Women Ord: **no** ChurchOrg: **Presbyterian (congr, presby, synod)** Off/otherLang: **English, Indonesian** DoctrB: **ApC, NicC, WestConf** Infant or believer's baptism: **both** Close relations with: **none**

NatRel: **none** RegRel: **none** IntlRel: **none** TheolSchool: **Westminster Theological College** Periodicals: **Westminster Messenger (magazine/6x a year/400)**

Address: Westminster Presbyterian Church, 54 Fingleton Cres., Gordon, ACT 2906, Australia, Tel: +61 2 6294 2242, E-mail: rwilson@cos.com.au.

11. Reformed Churches of Australia (5006)

After World War II many immigrants arrived from the Netherlands. Most of them joined the Presbyterian Church (no. 2) and eventually the Uniting Church (no. 1). The Gereformeerde Kerken in the Netherlands (cf. Netherlands no. 5) initially advised its members to join the Presbyterian Church of Eastern Australia. When this failed, steps were taken to found separate churches. The first was established in 1951 in Tasmania. The church is active in evangelism and education.

TM: **9,210** BM: **3,629** CM: **5,881** Congr: **46** PStations: **4** OrdM: **48** Eld: **268** Deac: **85** EvgHome: **1** Mission: **1** Women Ord: **no** ChurchOrg: **local: session, classes, synod** Off/otherLang: **English** DoctrB: **ApC, NicC, AthC, HeidC, CDort, WestConf** Infant or believer's baptism: **both** Frequency of the Lord's Supper: **6 to 12 per year** IntlRel: **REC** TheolSchool: **Reformed Theological College (Geelong)** Periodicals: **Trowel & Sword (gen/monthly)**

Address: Reformed Churches of Australia, 9 High Street, Saratoga, NSW 2251, Australia, Tel: +61 2 4369 6494, Fax: +61 2 4369 6494, E-mail: rca@magnet.com.au.

12. Free Reformed Churches of Australia (5005)

The first Free Reformed Church was instituted in the early '50s in Armadale, Western Australia. Like its parallel body in Canada, the church came into existence because its members came to the conclusion that they were unable to join any of the existing churches. The church opposes liberalism and higher criticism of the Bible.

TM: **3,300** BM: **1,638** CM: **1,662** Congr: **9** PStations: **2** OrdM: **10** Eld: **60** Deac: **32** EvgHome: **ne** Mission: **ne** Women Ord: **no** As Ministers: **none** as Deac: **none**, as Elders: **none** ChurchOrg: **Reformed (consistories, classes, synods)** Off/otherLang: **English** DoctrB: **ApC, NicC, AthC, HeidC, CDort, BelgC** Infant or believer's baptism: **both** Frequency of the Lord's Supper: **6 times per year** Close relations with: **Canadian Reformed Churches, Reformed Churches in the Netherlands (Liberated), Free Reformed Churches of South Africa, Presb Church in Korea-Koshin (cf. Korea no. 1)** NatRel: **none** RegRel: **CRC** IntlRel: **none** TheolSchool: **Theol University of Ref Ch (NL), Theol Coll of Can Ref Ch (Canada)** Service infrastructure: **3 primary and 2 secondary schools, one high school** Periodicals: **Una Sancta (gen/fortnightly/700), Together We Serve (Women's magazine/monthly/300), Thy Way (Youth magazine/monthly/500)**

Address: Free Reformed Churches of Australia, P.O. Box 191, Armadale, W.A. 6112, Australia, Fax: +61 89 497 3280

13. Presbyterian Reformed Church of Ireland (5014)

For the background of this church cf. Ireland (no. 4). Two congr exist in Port Lincoln and in Perth.

No data have been made available.

14. Congregational Federation of Australia (5015)

In September 1992 representatives of the Congregational Churches in New South Wales and Queensland which had continued to uphold the Congreg way after the formation of the Uniting Church in Australia (in 1977) resolved to establish the Congregational Federation of Australia as successor to the former Congregational Union of Australia. It links in fellowship churches in New South Wales, Queensland, and New Zealand, the Church of Jesus Christ in India, the Congregational Church in India, and the Congregational Church of Myanmar.

TM: **3,102** BM: **2,363** CM: **3,102** Congr: **33** PStations: **ne** OrdM: **27** Eld: **ne** Deac: **198** EvgHome: **ne** Mission: **ne** Women Ord: **yes** As Ministers: **1995/0** as Deac: **nc** as Elders: **ne** ChurchOrg: **Congreg (Congregational Federations [state level], Congr Federation of Australia)** Off/otherLang: **English, Samoan** DoctrB: **ApC, NicC, Savoy Declaration, Trinitarian** Infant or believer's baptism: **both** Frequency of the Lord's Supper: **monthly** Close relations with: **Congr Churches in India, Myanmar, Pacific, New Zealand; Uniting Church in Australia** NatRel: **NCCA, Queensland Churches Together (1993), North South Wales Ecumenical Council (1997)** RegRel: **PCC (1997)** IntlRel: **ICF (1992), CWM (1996), WARC (1996)** Periodicals: **The Congregationalist (gen/quarterly/100), Year Book (special/annually/40)**

Address: Congregational Federation of Australia, Inc., 127 Rusden Road, Blaxland, NSW 2774, Australia, Tel: +61 2 47 39-1760, Fax: +61 2 47 39-1760

15. Fellowship of Congregational Churches in NSW (FCC) (5000)

This fellowship consists of 25 congr in New South Wales which did not join the Uniting Church in 1977 (cf. no.1); in subsequent years membership was enlarged by the addition of other congr. There are today congr in Tasmania, South Australia, and Queensland.

TM: **2,500** CM: **1,800** Congr: **33** OrdM: **27** Eld: **nc** Deac: **nc** EvgHome: **nc** Mission: **16** Women Ord: **yes** As Ministers: **no** as Deac: **yes**, as Elders: **no** ChurchOrg: **Congreg** Off/otherLang: **English, Mandarin, Cantonese** DoctrB: **Savoy Declaration, FCC's own statements of faith** Infant or believer's baptism: **both** NatRel: **North South Wales Council of Churches** IntlRel: **WECF** TheolSchool: **Presbyterian Theological Center, Sidney Missionary and Bible College, Moore Theological College** Periodicals: **Congregational Communications (monthly), The Australian Congregationalist (quarterly)**

Address: Fellowship of Congregational Churches in NSW, P.O. Box 475, Bexley South, NSW 2207, Australia, Tel: +61 2 9588-5128, Fax: +61 2 9587-0640

16. Huon Community Churches (HCC) (5019)

This is another small group of four congr in Tasmania which stayed out of the Uniting Church in 1977. They sought fellowship with the Churches of Christ and are associated with the Fellowship of Congregational Churches. The churches define themselves as "Ref in outlook, but upholding the independence of the local congregation" and underline that they "are not an ordaining body."

TM: **80** BM: **60** CM: **40** Congr: **4** OrdM: **?** Eld: **0** Deac: **0** EvgHome: **ne** Mission: **ne** Women Ord: **no** ChurchOrg: **Congreg** Off/otherLang: **English** DoctrB: **Reformed** Infant or believer's baptism**: both** NatRel: **Fellowship of Congregational Churches (FCC) as associate member**

Address: Huon Community Churches (HCC), The Manse, 12 Brownell St., Geeveston, Tas 7116, Australia, Tel: +61 3 6297-7116, Fax: +61 3 6297-7116, E-mail: jzandt@tassie.net.au.

17. Hungarian Reformed Church of Australia (5020)

A Hungarian pastor arrived in Melbourne in 1949, and in 1973 a separate Hungarian-speaking congregation was founded. There are also Hungarian-speaking Ref communities in other cities. In Melbourne a second congregation was started in 1982 by a young pastor; it is known under the name Free Hungarian Reformed Church of Australia (2 Mill Avenue, Forest Hill, Australia 3131).

No data have been made available.

Address: Hungarian Reformed Church of Australia, P.O. Box 66, Fitzroy, Victoria 3065, Australia, Tel: +61 42 850-8639

18. Korean Central Presbyterian Church (5021)

This church is of Korean origin and has congr in Belfield, Sydney, and Wollongong. Its background in Korea is the Presbyterian Church of Korea–Kosin (cf. Korea no. 1).

ChurchOrg: **together with two congr in Auckland and one in Fiji they form the Oceania Synod** Off/otherLang: **English, Korean**

No other data have been made available.

Address: Korean Central Presbyterian Church, 72 Burwood Rd., Belfield 2191, Australia

19. Korean Presbyterian Church (Gae-Hyuk) (5022)

In 1995 three congr, which had been part of the Presbyterian Church of Australia, withdrew and formed a separate presby within Gae-Hyuk, a Korean denomination having its origin in the HapDong Church (cf. Korea no. 15).

TM: **300** Off/otherLang: **English, Korean**

No other data have been made available.

20. Sun Presbyterian Church (5023)

The background of these three congr in Adelaide, Riverland SA, and the Gold Coast is a Presbyterian Church in Korea which was founded in 1938 in protest against the imposition of Shinto shrine worship (cf. Korea).

Congr: **3** Off/otherLang: **English, Korean**

No other data have been made available.

Address: Sun Presbyterian Church, 12 Scott St., Beulah Park 5067, Australia

21. Saesoon (New Branch) Presbyterian Church (5024)

An independent group of about 200 members in Sydney.

TM: **200** Congr: **3**

No other data have been made available.

Address: Saesoon (New Branch) Presbyterian Church, P.O. Box 710 4/28 High Street, Epping Sydney NSW 2121, Australia, Tel: +61 2 98697150, Fax: +61 2 98697150, E-mail: ghl@comuni.com.au.

22. Presbyterian Church (Evangelical) (5001)

TM: **700** CM: **300** Congr: **9** Off/otherLang: **English** DoctrB: **WestConf**

No other data have been made available.

Address: Presbyterian Church (Evangelical), 53 Alberfeldy Street, Kenmore, Qld 4069, Australia

AUSTRIA

Area in km²	83,856
Population	7,938,000
Religions in % 1992	RCath 84.3%, Luth 5.6%, OldCath 0.2%, Muslim 2%, Jews 0.1%, others 7.6%
Official/other languages	German / Hungarian, Slovenian, Croatian, Czech

Reformed Church in Austria (6010)

Luth and Ref Christians have existed in this country since the early 1520s. Around 1600 over 90% of the population were Prot. There was no organizational delimitation between Luth and Ref congr during the 16th and 17th centuries. During the Counter-Reformation the whole country became RCath, with the exception of the Ref congregation of Oberwart, which belonged then to the Hungarian Kingdom. During the following period of "underground Protestantism" Ref worship services were held only in Vienna in the chapel of the Dutch diplomatic mission. The first legal congregation was opened in Vienna after the Edict of Tolerance in 1781; two years later a church building was erected but "without belfry nor main entrance from the street." In 1821 what is now called the "Evangelical Theological Faculty" was established, became incorporated into the University of Vienna, and was state-sponsored after 1921. The *"Protestantenpatent"* of Emperor Franz Joseph of 1861 guaranteed equal treatment to RCath and Prot. In the wake of the "getaway from Rome" movement, groups of RCath joined Ref congr around 1900.

After World War I the Church faced a crisis through the loss of parishes located in Bohemia and Moravia which had become constitutive parts of newly created Czechoslovakia. After World War II successive "streams of refugees" (Hungary/ 1956; Czechoslovakia/1968; Romania/1969) brought numerous Ref believers into Austria. A new and ninth congregation was established in Linz (1954).

In 1949 the Ref and the Luth churches decided to cooperate within the "Evangelical Church of the Ausgburg and Helvetic Confessions." This body acts in the name of the two churches on public and ecumenical matters as well as in their relations with the Austrian state, but the two churches remain independent denominations.

The Preamble of the joint constitution speaks of "two churches brought together by God in the course of their history." The Ref and Luth in Austria have been forerunners of the Leuenberg Agreement (1973) by practicing full pulpit and altar fellowship, running their welfare and educational institutions in common, and deciding on matters of mutual concern during a joint general synod.

During the period of the Cold War both churches used the neutrality of Austria for bridge-building activities with sister churches in Eastern Europe. Pastors from East and West met regularly at the "Oberwart conferences." Numerous East-West consultations were held during this period of political tension. Since Vatican II meaningful ecumenical initiatives have also been undertaken. More recently Korean communities started using the facilities of the Reformed Church in Austria. Since 1989 the Ref congr celebrate annually a "Day of the Ref Congregations."

TM: **14,394** BM: **14,394** CM: **8,205** Congr: **9** PStations: **16** OrdM: **20** Eld: **98** Deac: **0** EvgHome: **ne** Mission: **ne** Women Ord: **yes** As Ministers: **1965/4** as Deac: **1997/4** as Elders: **nc** ChurchOrg: **Reformed (parishes, synod)** Off/otherLang: **German, Hungarian, English, Korean** DoctrB: **ApC, NicC, HeidC, HelvC, Leuenberg, "Declaration of Principles" (1996)** Infant or believer's baptism: **infant** Frequency of the Lord's Supper: **monthly with each parish having its own tradition** Periodicals: **Reformiertes Kirchenblatt (info/monthly/ 5,500), Wiener Predigten (homiletics/twice a year/**

500), Aktuelle Reihe (church&theol info/2xyear/ 500) NatRel: **Ecumenical Council of Austria (1957), Austrian Mission Council (1972), Austrian Bible Society (1958)** RegRel: **CEC (1964)** IntlRel: **WARC (1884), WCC (1948)** TheolSchool: **Evangelical Theological Faculty (Vienna) jointly with the Luth.**

Address: Evangelische Kirche HB (Reformiert) in Oesterreich, Dorotheegasse 16, A-1010 WIEN, Austria, Tel: +43 1 513-6564, Fax: +43 1 512-4490

BAHAMAS

Area in km²	13,939
Population	(1993) 268,000 80% Black
Religions in %	Bapt 29%, Angl 23%, RCath 22%
Official/other Languages	English

St. Andrew's Presbyterian Church (3005)

In the 18th century there was already a "dissenter" presence in the Bahamas. The Ref community considerably increased by the end of the century when the British colonists who had remained loyal to the British crown in the revolutionary war in the United States were forced to leave and a substantial number of Scottish Presb settled in the Bahamas in 1783. In 1798 they formed the St. Andrew's Society, and in 1810 the foundation stone of St. Andrew's church was laid in Nassau. Close links with the state were severed through a parliamentary act in 1869. In 1966 an additional community was started in Freeport. Another important missionary effort was undertaken in 1995 in Marsh Harbour, Abaco. St. Andrew's Church is an overseas congregation of the Church of Scotland.

TM: **210** BM: **210** CM: **210** Congr: **200** PStations: **17** OrdM: **1** Eld: **25** Deac: **0** EvgHome: **0** Mission: **0** Women Ord: **Yes** As Ministers: **1945/0** as Deac: **ne** as Elders: **1963/10** ChurchOrg: **Presb** Off/otherLang: **English** DoctrB: **ApC, NicC, HeidC, HelvC, WestConf** Infant or believer's baptism: **both** Frequency of the Lord's Supper: **monthly** Close relations with: **Presbytery of Tropical Florida, PCUSA, Church of Scotland** RegRel: **Affiliated Presbytery Tropical Florida (1988)** IntlRel: **Church of Scotland (1810)**

Address: St. Andrew's Presbyterian Kerk, P.O. Box 1099, Princes' Street at Peck's Slope, Nassau, Bahamas, Tel: +1 242 393-2534, Fax: +1 242 393-2534

BAHRAIN

See also GULF REGION

Area in km²	620
Population	(July 1996 est.) 590,042 Bahraini 63%, Asian 13%, other Arab 10%, Iranian 8%, other 6%
Religions in %	Shi'a Muslim 75%, Sunni Muslim 24.9%, expatriate Christians, Hindus and other 0.1%
Official/other languages	Arabic / English, Farsi, Urdu

Bahrain is an archipelago consisting of 33 islands, only 5 of them inhabited. Most of the population of Bahrain is concentrated in the two principal cities, Manama and Al Muharraq. The indigenous people, representing 63% of the population, are from the Arabian Peninsula and Persia. The most numerous minorities are South and East Asians and Europeans.

Archeological artifacts reveal the pre-Islamic existence of Nestorian Christianity in the archipelago as well as along the coast of southeastern Arabia. In fact, prior to Islam, Bahrain was the residence of a Nestorian Bishop, and one of its villages still bears a name which means "monastery" in Arabic.

Islam is the dominant religion. Though Shiite Muslims make up more than two-thirds of the indigenous population, Sunni Islam is the prevailing belief held by those in the government, military, and corporate sectors. RCath and Prot churches, as well as a tiny indigenous Jewish community, also exist in Bahrain.

National Evangelical Church of Bahrain (4398)

The Ref family is, as in most other countries of the Arabian Gulf, one among several confessional denominations included under an umbrella church structure named the National Evangelical Church of Bahrain. The actual number of Ref members is very small, because the NEC is an interdenominational church composed of congr. with seven different languages. Only the pastors of the English and Arabic congr come from Ref backgrounds. The total number of Ref members is estimated at some 200. A division occurred in the Arabic congregation in 1990, and the church remains in a very weakened condition.

The main English service is on Sunday evenings and is mostly attended by Asians. Arabic services are on Saturday evening. In addition to supplying a pastor for the English-language congregation of the NEC, the Refomed Church in America (RCA) also has mission personnel working in the American Mission Hospital and Al Raja School. The NEC sponsors a youth worker supplied by Youth for

Christ and a Bible resource center manager supplied by the Bible Societies in the Levant.

The American Mission Hospital is the oldest hospital in the Arabian Gulf and the whole of southeastern Arabia. Its origin dates from 1902 when it was established as a result of Samuel Zwemer's entry onto the island ten years earlier. The hospital chaplaincy is filled by a member of the Ref community.

In addition to the American Mission Hospital, the RCA founded a girls school and an orphanage. The orphanage work was taken over by the government; the school, Al Raja (meaning "hope"), became coed in the late 1960s and today has an entirely new facility with a student body numbering 1,000 boys and girls. The headmaster of Al Raja School is supplied by the RCA. The school is no longer under the mission, but has ties to the NEC.

Bahrain is overrun with "tent-makers" from a variety of independent mission groups based in Europe, America, and Korea. In addition to the 7 different-language congr of the NEC, 33 other congr exist in Bahrain. These represent charismatic, evangelical, Jacobite, Coptic, Roman Catholic, Syrian Orthodox, and Anglican/Episcopal church groups.

TM: **700** CM: **320** Congr: **5**

Address: National Evangelical Church of Bahrain, P.O. Box 1, American Mission, Manamah, Bahrain, Tel: +973 254-508, Fax: +973 275-190

BANGLADESH

Area in km²	144,000
Population	(July 1996 est.) 123,062,800 Bengali 98%, Biharis 250,000, tribal (Garo, Santal, Chittagong Hill Tracts tribes) less than 1 million
Religions in %	Muslim 83%, Hindu 16%, Buddhist, Christian (less than 0.3%), other
Official/other languages	Bangla (official), English

NCCB (National Council of Churches, Bangladesh)

In 1947, when India won independence from Britain, East Bengal became part of Pakistan. The large majority of the country is Muslim. The sizeable minority of Hindus considerably diminished after 1947, especially during the civil war (1971-1972), when many fled to West Bengal in India. In 1971 Bangladesh was proclaimed an independent secular state with a socialist orientation. Through a military coup it was turned into an Islamic state.

The Christian churches represent only a small minority. RCath arrived in the area in the 16th century, but the first diocese was not established until 1886. Today there are four dioceses. Bapt are the largest Prot community. Baptist missionary work started as early as 1793. Angl and Presb missions started early in the 19th century; Angl and Presb united in 1970 to form the Church of Pakistan.

1. Church of Bangladesh (4001)

The Church of Bangladesh is a united church with a similar background to other united churches on the Indian subcontinent, i.e., Church of Pakistan and the Churches of North and South India. The Anglican roots go back to the 17th century when Church of England chaplains came to the area to minister to traders with the East India Company. Mission work in the area started in the first decades of the 19th century. Presb came to East Bengal in 1817 when Church of Scotland missionaries, based in Calcutta, began to work in Rajshahi. In the 1920s a Christian Mission Hospital was established there; it is still operating today. In 1924 Presb churches in East Bengal, along with the Congreg churches, joined the United Church of North India. In 1930 the Anglican Church in India became independent; after partition in 1947 it was known as the Church of India, Pakistan, Burma, and Ceylon. In 1970 the two churches united to form the Church of Pakistan. Following the war with Pakistan and the independence of Bangladesh, the former diocese of Dhaka became independent and was named the Church of Bangladesh.

TM: **12,500** BM: **12,500** CM: **7,500** Congr: **nc** PStations: **50** OrdM: **20** Eld: **nc** Deac: **2** EvgHome: **nc** Mission: **nc** Women Ord: **yes** As Ministers: **nc** as Deac: **nc** as Elders: **nc** ChurchOrg: **2 dioceses, 1 combined synod** Off/otherLang: **Bengali, 2 English-speaking congregations** DoctrB: **ApC, NicC,** Frequency of the Lord's Supper: **weekly to monthly depending on availability of clergy in predominantly Presb areas** Close relations with: **RCath, Bapt, Luth, Presb Fellowship** NatRel: **National Council of Churches in Bangladesh (NCCB)** RegRel: **CCA** IntlRel: **WCC, ACC, CWM** TheolSchool: **St Andrews Theological School** Service infrastructure: **2 hospitals, 1 social service org, 2 kindergartens, 2 nursing institutes, schools, hostels** Periodicals: **Kopot (gen/bi-monthly/ 200)**

Address: Church of Bangladesh, St. Thomas Church, 54 Johnson Rd., Dhaka 1, Bangladesh, Tel: +880 2 234-650 or 238-218, Fax: +880 2 832-915

2. Hill Tracts Presbyterian Church (HPC) (4000)

The Chittagong Hill Tracts are an area inhabited by tribal people. The region is divided into three administrative units under the authority of tribal chiefs whose task it is to maintain their cultural heritage. Until the recent past the tribes enjoyed real self-government. Since Independence from Britain in 1947, the situation has changed. Due to the general increase of population, many additional people have moved to the Hill Tracts.

The Hill Tracts Presbyterian Church has roots particularly in the Bawm Tribe. In an extraordinary vision a famous Bawm priestess, Sialdarnu, was shown

67

a threatening future: "We are afraid of the time when a peculiar white man, just as white as cotton, will come to our country from beyond the ocean, bearing great light; then we shall no longer exist; when this white man appears we shall disappear." The Bawm believe that the light turned out to be the Light of Life.

In 1918 the Welsh missionary, Edwin Rowland, accompanied by native Gospel volunteers, came to the area; he had served for 20 years in the Mizo Hills. The Mission responsible for the work in the following years was the North East India General Mission with headquarters in Philadelphia, USA. The first conversions took place in 1926, and three years later the first church was built. In 1968 missionaries withdrew and the Evangelical Christian Church became self-supporting. Eventually several splits took place which resulted in the formation of five groups. The Hill Tracts Presbyterian Church was constituted in 1980. In recent years attempts have been made to restore Christian unity in the Hill Tracts. They resulted in the foundation of the "Hill Tracts Tribal Churches Fellowship" in 1996 (Evangelical Christian Church, Christian Fellowship of Bangladesh, Bangladesh Baptist Sangha, Tribal Baptist Church, and the Hill Tracts Presbyterian Church). The Hill Tracts Presb have no affiliation with any church abroad.

TM: **2,236** BM: **1,581** CM: **1,558** Congr: **26** PStations: **2** OrdM: **5** Eld: **42** Deac: **30** EvgHome: **7** Mission: **ne** Women Ord: **no** ChurchOrg: **Presbyterian** Off/otherLang: **Bawm, Mizo, Pangkhua, Tripera, Meru** DoctrB: **ApC** Infant or believer's baptism: **believer** Frequency of the Lord's Supper: **at least 4 times per year** Close relations with: **Mizoram Presbyterian Church–Synod, India** NatRel: **National Council of Churches in Bangladesh (NCCB) (1980)** IntlRel: **WCC** Service infrastructure: **expected and proposed: small local social service organizations** Periodicals: **Gospel Cheu-nak (Light of the Gospel) (mission/monthly/150), Topic on Sunday School (bi-monthly/150)**

Address: Hill Tracts Presbyterian Kawhmi (HPC), P.O. Box 5, Ujani Para Bandarban Hill Tracts, Bandarban 4600, Bangladesh

3. Sylhet Presbyterian Synod (SPS) (4002)

This church has its roots in the Greater Sylhet District in the northeast of Bangladesh. Its members belong mostly to the ethnic minority population — Khasi, Garo, and Santal. One presby is completely composed of Khasi communities, another of Santal communities. The church was founded by Welsh missionaries; the missionary effort is the fruit of the Welsh revival in 1905. With the partition of India the church was cut off from its larger constituency in North East India. SPS is running a primary school program, an adult literacy program, and some boarding schools. It maintains Sunday schools, youth work, and a women's program.

TM: **5,549** BM: **3,048** CM: **2,501** Congr: **87** PStations: **38** OrdM: **8** Eld: **nc** Deac: **36** EvgHome: **7** Mission: **nc** Women Ord: **no** ChurchOrg: **Presb (congr, subdistricts, 4 presby, Synod, GenAssy)** Off/otherLang: **Bengali, Khasi, Garo, Santal, Uria** DoctrB: **ApC** Infant or believer's baptism: **both** Frequency of the Lord's Supper: **twice per year** Close relations with: **Santal Mission Norwegian Board–Dhaka (Lutheran Church)** NatRel: **National Christian Fellowship of Bangladesh Dhaka (NCFB)** RegRel: IntlRel: **Norwegian Santal Mission (Oslo, Norway)** TheolSchool: **CCTB (Dhaka)** Service infrastructure: **Mafiz Filty Memorial Clinic Social Service (like literacy, primary educa-**

tion, school scholarships), financial support for 13 other projects by Santal Mission Norwegian Board, youth hostels, sewing projects Periodicals: **none**

Address: Sylhet Presbyterian Synod (SPS), P.O. Moulvibazar 3200, 3100 Dt Moulvibazar, Bangladesh, Tel: +880 861-52486, Fax: +880 861-52261, E-mail: smnb@citechco.net.

BELARUS

Area in km²	207,595
Population	(July 1996 est.) 10,415,973 Byelorussian 77.9%, Russian 13.2%, Polish 4.1%, Ukrainian 2.9%, other 1.9%
Religions in %	Eastern Orthodox 60%, other (including RCath and Muslim) 40% (early 1990s)
Official/other languages	Byelorussian (since 1990), Russian, other

Belarusian Evangelical Reformed Church (6562)

This small community was established and officially registered in 1992. Ref communities had been present in the territory of Belarus since the 16th century. The first Ref church was founded in 1553 in Brest-Litowsk; at the same time a publishing house was started. At the end of the 16th century more than 200 congr existed in Belarus. In 1617 a Ref high school was established in Slutsk; in the 18th and 19th centuries a theological school functioned in Koidanava (Dziarzynsk), Minsk region. During the Communist regime all activities were suppressed; the school was closed and several church buildings blown up. The community which came into existence in 1992 seeks to revive the Ref presence in Belarus.

TM: **40** BM: **30** CM: **20** Congr: **1** PStations: **2** OrdM: **0** Eld: **1** Deac: **3** EvgHome: **3** Mission: **0** Women Ord: **yes** As Ministers: **1992/1** as Deac: **1994/3** as Elders: **1992/1** ChurchOrg: **synods, congregational assembly: 2 times a year** Off/otherLang: **Byelorussian** DoctrB: **ApC, HeidC, CDort, BelgicC** Infant or believer's baptism: **both** Frequency of the Lord's Supper: **every Sunday.**

Address: Bielaruski evangelicny refarmacki zbor, Tsnianskaya str. 17–17, 220100 Minsk, Belarus, Tel: +375 17 232-1672, Fax: +375 17 232-1672, E-mail: unilit@radivil.belpak.minsk.by

BELGIUM

Area in km²	30,528
Population	(1995) 10,600,000
Religions in %	RCath 80%, Prot 1%, Muslims 3%, non-religious 15%, others 1%
Official/other languages	Flemish 58%, French 32%, / Bilingual 9%, German 1%

In the 16th century the Reformation found a favorable reception in the area now called Belgium. Large parts of the country joined the Reformation. Two monks of the monastery of Augustins in Antwerp, Heinrich Voes and Johann Esch, were the first martyrs of the Reformation (1523). The *Confessio Belgica* by Guido de Brès became a representative text for churches both in the Netherlands and in France (1561). The occupation by Spain (1585) meant the end of this movement. Freedom of religion was granted toward the end of the 18th century and when, in 1830, Belgium gained independence, Protestantism was able to reconstitute itself. Several Prot bodies came into existence. Major moves toward unity were undertaken in the late sixties.

United Protestant Church of Belgium (6020)

In 1969 the Union of Evangelical Protestant Churches joined with the Belgian Conference of the United Methodist Church to become the Protestant Church of Belgium. Negotiations with the Belgian Christian Missionary Church and the Belgian District of the Gereformeerde Kerken in the Netherlands (GKN) led finally to the official constitution, on September 30, 1978, of the *United Protestant Church of Belgium (UPCB)*.

Belgian Protestantism, though in the minority, has significantly contributed to the missionary movement (former Zaire, Rwanda). Today, the UPCB is particularly active in promoting the integration of immigrants and refugees.

TM: **40,000** Congr: **109** PStations: **10** OrdM: **86** Eld: **nc** Deac: **nc** EvgHome: **ne** Mission: **ne** Women Ord: **Yes** As Ministers: **1979/10** as Deac: **nc** as Elders: **nc** ChurchOrg: **local church–district–synod assembly** Off/otherLang: **French, Dutch, German** DoctrB: **ApC, NicC, AthC, HeidC, BelgC, CA, 25 ArtR, Leuenberg** Infant or believer's baptism: **both** Frequency of the Lord's Supper: **different from parish to parish: weekly to communion at feasts only** Periodicals: Info (**gen/monthly/1,500**) NatRel: **Concertation d'Eglises Chrétiennes en Belgique (1988) — Organe de Concertation entre Chrétiens et Juifs en Belgique (1992)** RegRel: **CEC, CEPPLE** IntlRel: **WARC (1948), WCC (1948), WMC** TheolSchool: **Faculté Universitaire de Théologie Protestante**

Address: Eglise Protestante Unie de Belgique/ Verenigde Prote Kerk in België, 5, rue du Champ-de-Mars, B-1050 Bruxelles, Belgium, Tel: +32 2 511-4471, Fax: +32 2 511-2890

BELIZE

Area in km²	22,965
Population	(1993) 210,000 Mestizo 44%, Creole 30%, Maya 11%, Garifuna 7%, White 4%, Hindus 2%
Religions in %	Christian 90% consisting of RCath 62%, Protestant 30% (Anglican 12%, Meth 6%, Mennonite 4%, Advent 3%, Pentecostal 2%, Ref), indigenous Indian religion, Jews
Official/other languages	English / Créole, Spanish, Maya ketchi

Belize (or British Honduras, as it was called until 1973) is part of the Yucatan peninsula and is believed to have been the center of the Maya civilization with over two million people at its height in 1000 A.D. Maya ruins are so common that they have provided the building materials for whole towns and roads in the recent past.

The small, essentially private enterprise economy is based primarily on agriculture, agro-based industry, and merchandizing, with tourism and construction assuming increasing importance. Agriculture accounts for about 30% of the GNP and provides 75% of export earnings, while sugar, the chief crop, accounts for almost 40% of hard currency earnings. The US, Belize's main trading partner, is assisting in efforts to reduce dependency on sugar with an agricultural diversification program.

Presbyterian Church of Belize (2000)

The origin of Presbyterianism in Belize is associated with the arrival of Scottish settlers in the middle of the 19th century. They were granted public financial support for building a Presb Church in the country (July 24, 1850). The new church affiliated with the (Presbyterian) Free Church of Scotland. The first pastor, David Arthur from Scotland, served for almost twenty-five years. In 1905 affiliation was changed to the (State Presb) Church of Scotland. For several decades, the church had an intermittent life. Sometimes it was closed (1903-1905). For long periods it was pastored by Meth (1914-1919, 1939-1953, 1955-1968) or Bapt ministers (1922-1923). In 1933/34 an attempt was made to unite the Presb with the Angl church, and in 1945 another attempt was proposed to unite with the Meth; both times the church preferred to maintain its independence.

Until well after World War II the church remained confined to the white population in the capital city. In 1958, with the help of the National Presb Church in Mexico, mission work started among the Mayan population in the northern part of Belize. Mainly due to the evangelistic activity of Don Manuel Beltram a few

71

new communities came into existence. In 1985 St. Andrew's Church in Belize joined with these Spanish-speaking communities to form a provisional presby and on June 7, 1987, a National Presbyterian Church was established. In a message addressed to all churches in the country the church declared: "As we, a new member of the family of churches of the Lord Jesus Christ, come into being we necessarily profess the Biblical doctrine of unity of all who are in Christ; we know that what happens in one part of His Church affects all the body of Christ." In 1988 a ministry among the Chinese population was founded.

TM: **400** BM: **450** CM: **400** Congr: **8** PStations: **7** OrdM: **5** Eld: **20** Deac: **20** EvgHome: **2** Mission: Women Ord: **Yes** As Ministers: **no** as Deac: **8/1960** as Elders: **no** ChurchOrg: **1 presby** Off/otherLang: **English (1 church), Chinese (1 church), Spanish (remainder)** DoctrB: **ApC, NicC, AthC, HeidC, HelvC, CDort (recognized) WestConf** Infant or believer's baptism: **both** Frequency of the Lord's Supper: **quarterly** Close relations with: **PCUSA** NatRel: **Belize Council of Churches (1956).**

Address: Presbyterian Church of Belize, P.O. Box 348, Regent Street, Belize City, Belize, Tel: +501 2 73-841, Fax: +501 2 35-462

BERMUDA

Area in km²	53
Population	(1993) 60,800
Religions in %	Angl 37,8%, Meth 16,4%, RCath 13%, other 32,8%
Official/other languages	English

This group of 360 islands, of which only 20 are inhabited, was discovered by the Spaniard Juan Bermudez in 1503. Uninhabited until then, they were colonized by the British in 1609. Since 1968 Bermuda has been a self-governing dependent territory of the United Kingdom. Tourism (1/3 of the GNP) and offshore finance (of equal importance) place Bermuda in the top four worldwide *per capita* income economies.

Today Bermuda has 100 churches of 25 denominations including Advent, Angl, Brethren, Bapt, Meth, RCath, and Salvation Army. The first minister in Bermuda, the Rev. George Keith, was sent in 1609 as chaplain for the Bermuda Company. This was ostensibly a Church of England ministry, but the Church of England was not uniform at that time and he was Scottish, Calvinist, and perhaps of Presbyterian ordination. In the 17th century there were largely ineffective objections to Anglican liturgy and practice before the lasting establishment of Presbyterian worship in the 18th century.

1. Christ Church of Warwick (Church of Scotland) (3350)

The first Presb congr was Christ Church of Warwick, established in 1719. It remained an independent congr, served by ministers mainly from Scotland but also from Canada and the USA, until 1845, when it affiliated with the Free Church of Scotland. In 1843 services were started in Hamilton by Mr. Morrison, minister of Christ Church, and a new church was opened there for worship in 1846 (cf. no. 2). Christ Church, Warwick became a congr first of the United Free Church of Scotland (1900) and then of the Church of Scotland (1929). Ministers serving the congr remained members of the presby in Scotland to which they previously belonged and came already trained and ordained, generally with experience in a number of parishes.

TM: **600** CM: **500** Congr: **1** PStations: **0** OrdM: **1** Eld: **40** Deac: **ne** EvgHome: **ne** Mission: **ne** Women Ord: **yes** As Ministers: **1971/0** as Deac: **ne** as Elders: **1971/9** ChurchOrg: **one congregation** Off/otherLang: **English** DoctrB: **ApC, NicC, WestConf** Frequency of the Lord's Supper: **quarterly** Periodicals: **Life and Work (gen info/monthly)** IntlRel: **(same as Church of Scotland).**

Address: Christ Church, Warwick, PG 88, Paget, Bermuda, Tel: +1 441 236-0400, Fax: +1 441 232-0552

2. St. Andrew's Presbyterian Church (3351)

In 1843 Presb living in the town of Hamilton approached the minister and Church Session in Christ Church, Warwick, to have Rev. James Morrison come to Hamilton to preach each fortnight if a suitable facility could be found. The church sanctuary was built in 1846 with the donation of land from the Governor. James Morrison ministered to both congr until his death in 1849. In 1873 the congregation of St. Andrew's Church petitioned the Presbytery of Halifax (Canada) to sever the pastoral connection with Warwick and to ordain and induct Kenneth Junor as their minister. In 1875 the Presbyterian Church in Canada was formed and St. Andrew's became part of that body. Today the congregation is under the pastoral care of the Presbytery of Toronto West.

TM: **90** BM: **90** CM: **75** Congr: **1** PStations: **1** OrdM: **1** Eld: **13** Deac: **ne** EvgHome: **ne** Mission: **ne** Women Ord: **yes** As Ministers: **1960s** as Deac: **ne** as Elders: **1960s** ChurchOrg: **part of presby of West Toronto of Presbyterian Church in Canada** Off/otherLang: **English** DoctrB: **ApC, NicC, WestConf, Living Faith (Statememt of Faith of the Presb Ch of Canada)** Infant or believer's baptism: **both** Frequency of the Lord's Supper: **6 times a year and on Christmas Eve** Periodicals: **none** Close relations with: **none** NatRel: **none** RegRel: **none.**

Address: St. Andrew's Presbyterian Church, P.O. Box HM 193, Hamilton, Bermuda, Tel: +1 441 292-7601, Fax: +1 441 236-4826, E-mail: stard.prs@ibl.bm

BOLIVIA

Area in km²	1,098,581
Population	(est. July 1996) 7,165,257 Quechua 30%, Aymara 25%, mestizo (mixed European and Indian ancestry) 25%-30%, European 5%-15%
Religions in %	RCath, Prot, Bahaï
Official/other languages	Spanish, Quechua, Aymara (all official)

The first Prot came to the country in connection with the liberation by Simon Bolivar at the beginning of the 19th century. Diego Thompson, representative of the British Bible Society, who was associated with various leaders of the liberation movement, visited Bolivia in 1824. He started the translation of the New Testament in Quechua, and in 1829 he produced, with the help of Vincente Pazos Kanki, the translation of the Gospel of Luke in Aymara. Other representatives of Bible Societies followed. José Mongiardino, representing the American Bible Societies, was assassinated in 1877. In 1898 the Free Brethren from Canada started work in Oruro. Many other denominations followed. Presb groups did not enter the country until the late seventies. Today there are seven Presbyterian groups, mainly of Korean origin. Efforts are being undertaken to bring these various groups closer to one another. Churches in La Paz, Cochabamba, Tarija, and St. Cruz have their own presbyteries.

1. Evangelical Presbyterian Church in Bolivia (2200)

Evangelistic activities were initiated in 1983 by a Korean missionary, Chong-Moo Park, in La Paz and in El Alto. After three months he withdrew, but he returned, together with other Korean missionaries, in the same year and opened a first church in Bairro de Rio Secco (El Alto). Evangelistic efforts led to the establishment of other churches. The Korean mission opened a college which was later transformed into a university. In 1990 Chong-Moo Park was replaced by Ki Joon Choi; in 1996 he in turn was succeeded by Joi-Wook Kwak. The church's counterpart in Korea is the Presbyterian Church of Korea (TongHap, cf. Korea no.14).

TM: **1,500** BM: **1,250** CM: **600** Congr: **12** PStations: **0** OrdM: **12** Eld: **ne** Deac: **10** EvgHome: **5** Mission: **ne** Women Ord: **under discussion** As Ministers: **not yet** as Deac: **not yet** as Elders: **not yet** ChurchOrg: **La Paz = one presby with 12 churches; churches in St. Cruz/ Cochabamba/Tarija have their own presbys** Off/otherLang: **Spanish, Aymara, Korean, bilingual and monolingual priests** DoctrB: **ApC, WestConf** Infant or believer's baptism: **both** Frequency of the Lord's Supper: **twice per year (Easter, Christmas)** Close relations with: **none** NatRel: **Presbyterian Church of Korea (TongHap), Fraternidad de Educadores de Instituciones Teologicas** RegRel: **AIPRAL (1984),**

WARC IntlRel: **WARC** TheolSchool: **Universidad Union Evangélica Boliviana (founded and administered by Korean missionaries)** Periodicals: **None**

Address: Iglesia Evangélica Presbiteriana en Bolivia, Casilla 15110, Av. Rgto Castillo #49, San
Antonia Baja, La Paz, Bolivia, Tel: +591 2 710-249 or 710-251

2. Presbyterian Church in Bolivia (2202)

In 1990 a new Presb church came into existence. Various issues, among them the
question of women's ordination, led to conflicts within the IEBP (cf. no. 1). Under
the leadership of José J. Barrau one of the congr dissociated itself from the IEPB
and constituted itself as an independent church. It sought to relate more construc-
tively to the Bolivian context.

TM: **130** BM: **110** CM: **70** Congr: **1** PStations: **6** OrdM: **1** Eld: **1** Deac: **2** EvgHome: **ne** Mission: **ne**
Women Ord: **yes** As Ministers: **nc** as Deac: **1982/4** as Elders: **1989/2** ChurchOrg: **none** Off/otherLang:
Spanish DoctrB: **ApC, NicC, HeidC, WestConf, BelgC** Infant or believer's baptism: **both** Frequency
of the Lord's Supper: **biweekly** Close relations with: **Iglesias Unidas de La Paz** NatRel: **Centro de
Entrenamiento Cristiano (1993), Iglesias Unidas de La Paz (1982)** TheolSchool: **Seminario
Evangélico Teologico La Paz (interconfessional)** Periodicals: **newsletter (gen/weekly/40)**

Address: Iglesia Presbiteriana en Bolivia, Casilla 22577, La Paz, Bolivia, Tel: +591 2 782-101

3. Evangelical Presbyterian Church in Bolivia–Cochabamba (2204)

In 1987 Kwang Ho Choo, assisted by the Korean mission in La Paz, established
himself in Cochabamba and started vigorous evangelistic work. Sometime later he
separated himself from the mission in La Paz and proceeded to start churches in
Cochabamba. In recent years more missionaries arrived from Korea, and the work
was extended to neighboring cities. They started a seminary and a health center to
serve people in need and especially the members of the church.

TM: **1,000** BM: **1,000** Congr: **23** PStations: **30** OrdM: **4** Eld: **yes** Deac: **nc** EvgHome: **nc** Mission: **20**
Women Ord: **no** ChurchOrg: **Presb** Off/otherLang: **Spanish, Korean** DoctrB: **ApC, WestConf** Infant
or believer's baptism: **both** Close relations with: **Presbyterian Church of Korea (TongHap; cf. Korea no. 14)**

Address: Iglesia Evangelica Presbiteriana en Bolivia–Cochabamba, Casilla Correo 1430,
Cochabamba, Bolivia, Tel: +591 42 88080, Fax: +591 42 87721

4. Presbyterian Church of Bolivia (2207)

In 1988 a Brazilian missionary, João Carlos de Paula Mota, sent by the Presbyterian Church of Brazil (cf. Brazil), started to evangelize in Cochabamba. Later,
more Brazilian pastors arrived to strengthen the work. Though Cochabamba remained the center of activities, the work extended to other cities as well. The
church seeks recognition as a juridical entity by the authorities. Among its goals

are the acquisition of land for church buildings and the training of national leaders to consolidate church life. The church runs a dental clinic and offers relief work.

TM: **120** BM: **120** CM: **100** Congr: **2** PStations: **3** OrdM: **4** Eld: **6** Deac: **no** EvgHome: **nc** Mission: **2** Women Ord: **no** ChurchOrg: **Presb** Off/otherLang: **Spanish** DoctrB: **ApC, WestConf** Infant or believer's baptism: **both** Close relations with: **Igreja Presbiteriana do Brasil** NatRel: **Asosiación de Iglesias Evangelicas de Cochabamba**

Address: Iglesia Presbiteriana de Bolivia, Casilla Correo 5801, Cochabamba, Bolivia, Tel: +591 42 83145, E-mail: pipcipbo@bo.net.

5. Korean Presbyterian Mission in Santa Cruz de la Sierra I (2203)

In 1982 a Korean missionary, Eun-Sil Chung, started work in Santa Cruz della Sierra. He also opened a college there, which was later transformed into a university. Rev. Eun-Sil Chung is connected to the Presbyterian Church in Korea (TongHap, cf. Korea no. 14)

TM: **1,500** CM: **400** Congr: **nc** OrdM: **7** Eld: **nc** Deac: **nc** EvgHome: **nc** Mission: **nc** Women Ord: **no** As Ministers: **nc** as Deac: **nc** as Elders: **nc** ChurchOrg: **nc** Off/otherLang: **nc** DoctrB: **nc**

Address: Korean Presbyterian Mission in Santa Cruz I, Casilla 4320, Santa Cruz de la Sierra, Bolivia

6. Korean Presbyterian Mission in Santa Cruz de la Sierra II (2205)

In 1986 another Korean group began working in Santa Cruz, independently from the work already started by Eun-Sil Chung (cf. no. 5). The primary responsibility for this missionary initiative was with Ik-Bae (Pedro) Moon, who is also connected to the Presbyterian Church in Korea (TongHap, cf. Korea no. 14). The church runs two schools and 13 kindergartens.

TM: **5,000** CM: **2,000** Congr: **nc** OrdM: **3** Eld: **nc** Deac: **nc** EvgHome: **nc** Mission: **nc** Women Ord: **no** As Ministers: **nc** as Deac: **nc** as Elders: **nc** ChurchOrg: **Presb** Off/otherLang: **Spanish** DoctrB: **ApC, WestConf**

Address: Korean Presbyterian Mission in Santa Cruz II, Casilla 5130, Santa Cruz de la Sierra, Bolivia

7. Korean Presbyterian Mission in La Paz (KPCA) (2206)

Another Korean initiative led to the foundation of still another church. In 1993 a Korean student, Do-Gun Yoon, who had started theological studies in Seoul, arrived in Bolivia. Having completed studies at the Korean theological seminary (cf. no. 1), he was ordained and worked with the IEPB. Later he decided to separate and, with the support of Grace Church, New York, of the Korean Presbyterian Church in the US, organized a new church. Two pastors, Sung-Duck Suh and Eshik Kim, work with the church; it is located in La Paz, Cochabamba, and Sta Cruz. The group has not yet obtained official governmental recognition.

TM: **230** BM: **45** Congr: **3** PStations: **3** OrdM: **3** Eld: **nc** Deac: **nc** EvgHome: **nc** Mission: **nc** Women Ord: **no** As Ministers: **nc** as Deac: **nc** as Elders: **nc** ChurchOrg: **Presb** Off/otherLang: **Spanish, Aymara** DoctrB: **ApC, WestConf** NatRel: **KPCA**

Address: Korean Presbyterian Mission in La Paz, P.O. Box 3159, La Paz, Bolivia, Tel: +591 2 71 2444

BOTSWANA

Area in km²	583,000
Population	(est. July 1996) 1,477,630 Tswana 95%, Kalanga, Basarwa, and Kgalagadi 4%, white 1%
Religions in %	indigenous beliefs 50%, Christian 50%
Official/other languages	English / Setswana

BCC (Botswana Christian Council), **SAARC** (Southern Africa Alliance of Reformed Churches)

Botswana covers 2/3 of the Kalahari Desert. Until 1966 it was under British rule. Constitutionally it is now a multiparty democracy; thus far political life has been dominated by the Botswana Democratic Party. Mining, the main industry of the country, is primarily in the hands of transnational corporations. Economically, Botswana is dependent on South Africa.

Prot missionaries came to Botswana in the 19th century. The London Missionary Society (LMS) was among the first societies to start mission work. By 1857 the whole Bible was translated into Setswana, the first such translation into an African language south of Ethiopia; this achievement owes to the efforts of the LMS missionary, Moffat, in South Africa. In 1863 the Cape Synod of the Dutch Reformed Church (cf. South Africa no.1) started work among the Bagkatla, laying the ground for the Dutch Reformed Church in Botswana. Other missionaries followed. Luth missions especially played a significant role in Botswana. RCath efforts started in 1928. Today 18 churches, among them the RCath Church, cooperate through the Botswana Christian Council.

1. United Congregational Church of Southern Africa (1021)

The United Congregational Church in Botswana grew out of the work the LMS had initiated in the country. The church is part of the United Congregational Church of Southern Africa (cf. South Africa no. 12).

TM: **20,364** BM: **20,364** CM: **15,726** Congr: **51** OrdM: **44** Eld: **nc** Deac: **300** EvgHome: **3** Mission: **nc**

Women Ord: **since beginning** As Ministers: **5** as Deac: **300** as Elders: **nc** ChurchOrg: **local church, region, synod, Assy** Off/otherLang: **Setswana, English** DoctrB: **nc** Infant or believer's baptism: **both** Periodicals: **Congregational Chronicle (gen/quarterly/nc)** NatRel: **Botswana Council of Churches** RegRel: **SAARC** IntlRel: **CWM, WCC, WFRC** TheolSchool: **seminaries and universities in Southern Africa.**

Address: United Congregational Church of Southern Africa, P.O. Box 96014, 150 Caroline Street, Bridon, Johannesburg 2019, South Africa, Tel: +27 11 837 9997, Fax: +27 11 837 2570

2. Dutch Reformed Church in Botswana (1020)

Sent by the Cape Synod of the Dutch Reformed Church, the Swiss missionary Henri Gonin began to work in 1863 among the tribe Bakgatla ba ga Kgafela in the area of Saulspoort, near Rustenburg in South Africa. In 1870, under the leadership of Chief Kgamanyane, part of the tribe moved north and finally settled in Mochudi, Botswana. Missionaries from South Africa followed them (Pieter Brink and later E. B. Beyer). In 1892 the great chief of the Bakgatla, Linchwe I, was baptized; his example was followed by many members of the tribe. The missionaries placed strong emphasis on social, educational, and medical work. Following negotiations starting in 1976, the church gained autonomous status in 1979. Today, the church is no longer confined to Bakgatla in Kgatleng district, but has expanded to include the Basarwa, Bakalanga, coloured, whites, and others.

TM: **5,380** BM: **1,180** CM: **4,200** Congr: **10** PStations: **47** OrdM: **9** Eld: **81** Deac: **107** EvgHome: **1** Mission: **none** Women Ord: **yes** As Ministers: **1994/0** as Deac: **1979/75** as Elders: **1994/5** ChurchOrg: **2 presby, 1 Synod every 3 years** Off/otherLang: **English, Setswana, Afrikaans** DoctrB: **ApC, NicC, AthC, BelgC, HeidC, CDort** Infant or believer's baptism: **both** Frequency of the Lord's Supper: **at least 4 times a year and often at Easter** Periodicals: **Morning Star (official/month/500)** Close relations with: **Dutch Reformed Church in SA (Northern Cape)** NatRel: **Botswana Christian Council (1979)** RegRel: **SAARC (1985), Federal Council of Dutch Reformed Churches (1979)** IntlRel: **REC (1979), WARC (1979).**

Address: Dutch Reformed Church in Botswana, P.O. Box 846, Gaborone, Botswana, Tel: +267 352-272, Fax: +267 313-966

BRAZIL

Area in km²	8,456,510
Population	(July 1996 est.) 162,661,214 white (includes Portuguese, German, Italian, Spanish, Polish) 53%, mixed white and African 22%, African 12%, other (includes Japanese, Arab, Korean, Amerindian) 13%
Religions in %	The majority of the population is Catholic, although part of this majority practices a syncretistic religion and, in addition to the Catholic Church, frequents terreiros (holy places) of Umbanda, Macumba, and Candomblé (Afro-Brazilian religions). Prot represents today about 14%; Pentecostalism is growing especially quickly
Official/other languages	Portuguese / Spanish, English, French

CONIC (National Council of Christian Churches)
CIEF (Confederação das Igrejas Evangelicos Fundamentalistas do Brasil)
CESE (Ecumenical Coordination)
MPB (Presbyterian Mission of Brazil)

Portuguese navigators discovered Brazil in 1500. The colonization which followed focused upon establishing a metropolitan center to the detriment of the indigenous population, which exceeded four million at the time of discovery. As a result, the indigenous population was dramatically reduced until today it numbers 250,000. At the same time the traffic in slaves from Africa, which stretched over more than 300 years, brought in the black cultural element, which is of utmost importance for anyone who wishes to understand the Brazilian soul in depth.

The churches of the Ref tradition in Brazil form a contingent of approximately 1.5 million persons in over 3,000 congr; they represent more than 20 distinct denominations. All claim for themselves the Calvinist tradition but constitute separate bodies, not only for historical reasons but also for reasons of ethnic origin, theology and doctrine, and ecclesiastical polity. Some of these factors have caused deep divisions, turning the churches into distant sisters.

Nevertheless, it must also be recognized that the churches of the Ref tradition have played an important role in Brazilian Protestantism. The first attempts at planting Reformation churches on Brazilian soil were of Calvinist inspiration. The initial effort was part of the French project to establish an economic and political "bridgehead" in the New World, "Antarctic France," in 1551, with the added motive of enabling the French government to resolve a social problem by finding a haven for the Huguenots, who were being persecuted for religious reasons. On the orders of John Calvin himself, pastors were incorporated into the project of the

French commander, Villegaignon. On March 10, 1557, the first Protestant worship service was held in Brazil, a Ref worship service with a Genevan liturgy. Misunderstandings between Villegaignon (a Catholic Templar) and the pastors, however, caused the former to turn against the Calvinists in his group. They were persecuted; some of them were even tortured and killed. The French were expelled by the Portuguese in 1566.

A second Calvinist incursion took place between the years 1624 and 1654, through the initiative of an association of Dutch citizens of Ref confession who sought to settle in Brazil for economic purposes. Churches were established, and attempts were made to evangelize indigenous people and black slaves. As in the previous case, the Dutch were driven out by the Portuguese with the support of the natives in the land. Thus nothing remained of the Ref church's activities, except for the impression that invaders were always Prot and that Protestantism was therefore an enemy of Brazil.

It was not until the 19th century that the Ref tradition interacted anew with Brazilian society. The new contact took place in the context of the transformations which the Brazilian monarchy began to introduce in 1822, especially with regard to religious liberty and tolerance, fruits of the liberal spirit of the times. In 1855 Robert Kalley, a Scotsman and medical doctor of the Presbyterian tradition, arrived in Rio de Janeiro. In 1858 the first Protestant Church of missionary inspiration, the Igreja Evangélica Fluminense, was founded. This church became the beachhead of the Congreg movement in Brazil, which culminated in the organization of a denomination in 1913. Another Congreg group was later organized in the south of the country in 1920. The latter group was originally united with the Iglesias Evangélicas Congregacionales de Argentina and was made up of German immigrants and their descendants.

In 1859 Ashbel Green Simonton, the first missionary sent by the Presb church in the United States, arrived in Rio de Janeiro. Young and dynamic, Simonton founded the first Brazilian Presbyterian Church in the city of Rio de Janeiro in 1863. He organized a seminary and founded a Prot newspaper. In the beginning, Simonton received aid and assistance from the Rev. R. Kalley. Later, the Presbyterian presence in Brazil was strengthened by a number of missionaries from both the Northern and the Southern Presb churches and, by the end of the 19th century, the Presbyterian Church was the strongest Prot denomination in the country, although Meth, Angl, Bapt, and Free churches were already present. The growth of Presbyterianism was attributed to preaching in the countryside, which contrasted biblical texts with the practices of the Catholic Church to foster strong opposition to Catholicism. Further, the growth of Presbyterianism and Brazilian Protestantism generally paralleled the advance of liberal political ideas.

The final years of the 19th century were years of tension between Brazilian Presbyterian leaders and the missionary establishment. There was a desire for autonomy from the North American mother churches. The unity of the Brazilian independence movement, however, was undermined by the "Masonic question," with some Brazilians insisting on the incompatibility of the profession of Christian faith and membership in a Masonic Lodge. In 1903 a group of Brazilian pastors and elders, led by the Rev. Eduardo Carlos Pereira, organized the Independent Presbyterian Church of Brazil under the banners of nationalism, autonomy, and anti-Masonry. It was the first significant division within Brazilian Presbyterianism, which had yet to complete its first 50 years.

A second division, which took place within the Independent Presbyterian Church of Brazil and which came to be known as the "doctrinal question," gave rise to a third Presbyterian denomination in Brazil: The Conservative Presbyterian Church. Led by the Rev. Bento Ferraz, several pastors and elders maintained a rigid theological stance from 1938 to 1940.

Dissident movements of a Pentecostal nature were a source of tensions in both the Presbyterian Church and the Independent Presbyterian Church. These Pentecostal segments united in 1975 to form the Renewed Presbyterian Church.

There were three more Presbyterian denominations to come out of dissident movements: (1) The United Presbyterian Church of Brazil, which was born in 1978 under the name of the National Federation of Presbyterian Churches. The United Presbyterian Church was organized by a group of churches and pastoral leaders who were discontent with the internal policies of the Presbyterian Church of Brazil. They called for more freedom of thought and of expression for their theological ideas. (2) The Fundamentalist Presbyterian Church, which was established under the leadership of a very conservative Presbyterian group in the northern region of Brazil in 1956. (3) The Traditional Presbyterian Church of Brazil, which began its activities in 1993 in the central region of Brazil.

In addition to the churches so far mentioned, there are a large number of ethnic churches, consisting of immigrants and their descendants. In this category the following churches should be mentioned: The Central Armenian Evangelical Church of São Paulo (1927), The Christian Reformed Church of Brazil (Hungarian, 1932), The Reformed Evangelical Churches in Brazil (Dutch, 1933), The Arabic Evangelical Church of São Paulo (1954), The Swiss Evangelical Church (1958), The Cumberland Presbyterian Church of Bahia (Japanese, 1960), The Central Presbyterian Church of Formosa in Brazil (Taiwanese, 1962), The Korean United Presbyterian Church of São Paulo (1964), The Evangelical Church of São Paulo (Japanese, 1967), The Korean Presbyterian Church of Brazil (1969), The Antioch Presbyterian Church (Korean, 1984), The Reformed Church of Brasolandia (Dutch 1991), The Reformed Church of Brazil (1994), and The Reformed Church of Colombo (1905).

There are encouraging signs on the Ref horizon in Brazil, in terms of efforts to strengthen the bonds within the Calvinist family. Since 1989 the Independent Presbyterian Church, the United Presbyterian Church, and the Presbyterian Church of Brazil, along with the ethnic Ref churches, have been in dialogue, holding meetings, tightening bonds of friendship, and preparing to take bolder steps such as the setting up of joint projects. Recently in Campinas, in the State of São Paulo (August, 1995), almost all branches of the Ref tradition in Brazil, except for those of a fundamentalist or Pentecostal type, participated in a consultation sponsored by the Latin American Association of Presbyterian and Reformed Churches (AIPRAL), which has contributed significantly to this growing spirit of coopera-

81

tion and unity. The prospect for Brazilians of the Ref tradition in the next century is for the acceleration of the process of unity and of cooperation.

1. Presbyterian Church of Brazil (2305)

The church was organized in 1859. Its founder was Rev. Ashbel Green Simonton, of the United States. Another pioneer was the Rev. John Rockwell Smith. Simonton arrived in the city of Rio de Janeiro on August 12, 1859, with the objective of evangelizing Brazilians. The work bore fruit and has obviously been consolidated over a period of more than 130 years of activity, evangelism, and mission. In the course of its history the church has undergone several schisms. The most recent split resulted in the organization of the United Presbyterian Church of Brazil.

TM: **480,000** BM: **450,000** CM: **350,000** Congr: **820** PStations: **5,215** OrdM: **2,600** Eld: **8,040** Deac: **8,700** EvgHome: **nc** Mission: **245** Women Ord: **no** ChurchOrg: **Presb** Off/otherLang: **Portuguese** DoctrB: **ApC, WestConf** Infant or believer's baptism: **both** Close relations with: **PCUSA, Presb Ch of America, Free Ref Church of the Netherlands, Presb Ch of Australia, National Presb Ch of Chile, Presb Ch of Korea** NatRel: **Brazilian Evangelical Association, Biblical Society of Brazil, Trinity Bible Society** IntlRel: **WARC** TheolSchool: **6** Periodicals: **Brasil Presbyterian Newspaper and three theological magazines**

Address: Igreja Presbiteriana do Brasil, Caixa Postal 17, Rua Silva Jardin 23 Centro, 20050-060, Rio de Janeiro RJ, Brazil, Tel: +55 21 240 8466, Fax: +55 21 240-8374

2. Independent Presbyterian Church of Brazil (2302)

Organized on July 31, 1903, this church was the fruit of a schism within the Presbyterian Church of Brazil. It identifies itself as an indigenous church and is present in most of the states of Brazil. In recent years the church has provided leadership in a number of dialogues with the different churches of the Ref family in Brazil seeking to strengthen the ties of fraternal relationship and of affirmation of the Ref faith. Without neglecting its work of missionary expansion, the church has given strong emphasis to social work through more than a hundred social projects, most of them oriented toward meeting the needs of needy children and adolescents. At the same time it promotes Christian Education and produces its own educational material. This material is being translated into Spanish for use in Presb and Ref churches in Latin America.

TM: **100,000** BM: **80,000** CM: **45,000** Congr: **420** PStations: **442** OrdM: **550** Eld: **850** Deac: **950** EvgHome: **190** Mission: **60** Women Ord: **yes** As Ministers: **no** as Deac: **1,350** as Elders: **no** ChurchOrg: **Presbyterian** Off/otherLang: **Portuguese** DoctrB: **ApC, WestConf** Infant or believer's baptism: **both** NatRel: **Bible Society of Brazil CESE (Ecumenical coordination), GTME (Mission group), ASTE (Association of Evangelical Theological Seminaries) Presb Mission of Brazil, Caiuá Evangelical Mission** RegRel: **AIPRAL, CLAI, CELADEC** IntlRel: **WARC** TheolSchool: **3** Periodicals: **O Estandarte** (newspaper/monthly), **Alvorada** (magazine)

Address: Igreja Presbiteriana Independente do Brasil (IPI), Rua Amaral Gurgel 452, São Paulo SP
01221-000, Brazil, Tel: +55 11 258-1422, Fax: +55 11 259-0009

Joint mission effort of no. 1 and no. 2

Caiuá Evangelical Mission (2307)

This mission among the Caiuá, Guarani, and Tereno in the central-west part of the country was founded in 1928 by the American missionaries Albert Sidney and Mabel Maxwell. The success of the project was in large part due to the indefatigable efforts of these two missionaries and of the Brazilians who followed them — Rev. Orlando Andrade and his wife Loide Bonfim, who devoted more than 30 years of their life to it. The mission is supported by the Independent Presbyterian Church of Brazil, the Presbyterian Church of Brazil, and the Presbyterian Church (US). The objective of the mission is to care for the spiritual and material needs of the Amerindian people. Emphasis is placed on education, health services, and evangelism. In collaboration with various cities in the area, the mission succeeded in setting up 10 schools with 1,340 pupils (90% indigenous). In the area of health the mission established a hospital and a maternity clinic for indigenous people in Dourados — the "Door of Hope" — with 100 beds, 50 being reserved for the treatment of tuberculosis and other diseases often occurring among the indigenous. Free services are offered in a dental clinic. Medical doctors and nurses are sent regularly to the villages together with pupils of the Bible Institute. The Mission has stationed workers in 10 different indigenous villages. There are now 6 organized churches, 18 congr, and 2 preaching stations. Among the pastors, elders, and missionaries, 20 are indigenous persons and have been trained in the Bible Institute, Felipe Landes, which was founded for developing indigenous leadership.

TM: **1,200** BM: **1,000** CM: **600** Congr: **6** PStations: **20** OrdM: **5** Eld: **15** Deac: **no** EvgHome: **no** Mission: **91** Women Ord: **no** ChurchOrg: **Presbyterian** Off/otherLang: **Portuguese, Caiuá, Guarani** DoctrB: **WestConf** Infant or believer's baptism: **both** Close relations with: **PCUSA** TheolSchool: **Bible Institute Felipe Landes**

Address: Missão Evangélica Caiuá, Caixa Postal 4, 79804-970 Dourado MS, Brazil, Tel: +55 67
421-4197

3. Conservative Presbyterian Church of Brasil (2325)

This church resulted from a doctrinal schism within the Independent Presbyterian Church of Brazil. It was officially organized on June 27, 1940, when the first presby of the denomination, consisting of 11 churches and 5 pastors, was established. The difficulties which resulted from the small number of pastors to minister to the communities, some of them over a great distance, began to be overcome with the organization of a seminary in 1954. Although numerically small, the church began to experience a period of expansion following the creation of a Missionary Department and the organization of pioneer camps in several states of Brazil, some among indigenous people.

TM: **4,532** BM: **4,532** CM: **2,935** Congr: 42 PStations: 18 OrdM: 44 Eld: **175** Deac: **159** EvgHome: **7** Mission: Women Ord: **no** ChurchOrg: **5 presby, 1 synod** Off/otherLang: **Portuguese** DoctrB: **ApC, WestConf** Infant or believer's baptism: **both** NatRel: **Trinitarian Bible Society of Brazil** RegRel: **none** IntlRel: **none** TheolSchool: **Conservative Presbyterian Seminary** Service infrastructure: **Presb Church of America** Periodicals: **O Presbiteriano Conservador (newspaper/bimonthly)**

Address: Igreja Presbiteriana Conservadora do Brasil (IPC), Rua Santa Maria 23, Riacho Grande, 09830-320 São Bernado do Campo SP, Brazil, Tel: +55 11 451 9952, Fax: +55 11 451 9952

4. Fundamentalist Presbyterian Church of Brazil (2326)

This church came into existence in 1956 in the northeastern region of Brazil under the leadership of Rev. Dr. Israel Gueiros; it resulted from a schism in the Presbyterian Church of Brazil over doctrinal questions, especially the inspiration of the Bible. Today the church has six presby and is about to organize itself as a synod. Until recently the church has collaborated with others in missionary endeavors, but it is now planning to set up its own evangelistic project. The journal of the church, *O Presbiteriano Bíblico,* is being reactivated. The church maintains relations with churches and organizations having a fundamentalist following, in particular the ICCC of Dr. Carl McIntire.

TM: **2,000** BM: **2,000** CM: **1,500** Congr: nc PStations: 50 OrdM: 30 Eld: **yes** Deac: **yes** EvgHome: **nc** Mission: **yes** Women Ord: **no** ChurchOrg: **Presbyterian** Off/otherLang: **Portuguese** DoctrB: **ApC, WestConf, CIEF** Infant or believer's baptism: **both** IntlRel: **ICCC**

Address: Igreja Presbiteriana Fundamentalista do Brasil, Rua José Gustavo Macedo Soares Busch, 265, 13481-311 Limeira SP, Brazil, Tel: +55 49 452-7807, Fax: +55 19 451-8539

5. Renewed Presbyterian Church (IPRB) (2331)

The church has two roots. In 1968, groups of Presb, members of the IPB (cf. no. 1), who were influenced by the Pentecostal movement, left their church and founded the Christian Presbyterian Church (Igreja Cristã Presbiteriana). A similar process took place in the Independent Presbyterian Church (IPIB). In response to the Pentecostal movement, groups of Presb left their church and founded in 1972 the Independent Renewed Presbyterian Church (Igreja Presbiteriana Independente Renovada). On January 8, 1975, the two groups became one and the Renewed Presbyterian Church of Brazil was officially constituted. Its work has spread all over Brazil, but its greatest strength is in the states of Paraná (16,334 members) and São Paulo (15,427 members). Some of the local churches have given special attention to social work. The church has a missionary institution (Missão Priscila e Aquila) that gives support to 27 missionaries in Brazil and 8 abroad. It is also active in the Amazon region. It has a ship which sails in the south of the state of

Paraná in the north of Brazil and gives assistance to communities that live along the riverbanks. Two theological schools are available for the formation of pastors. The church also runs a publishing house.

TM: **57,033** BM: **57,033** CM: **57,033** Congr: **267** PStations: **615** OrdM: **342** Eld: **1,289** Deac: **1,471** EvgHome: **nc** Mission: **8** Women Ord: **no** ChurchOrg: **Presbyterian** Off/otherLang: **Portuguese** DoctrB: **ApC, Pentecostal Doctrines** Infant or believer's baptism: **believer** TheolSchool: **2 Bible Institutes** Periodicals: **Jornal Aleluia (newspaper/monthly/6,000), Revista de estudios Biblicos Aleluia (Bible studies/quarterly/20,000)**

Address: Igreja Presbiteriana Renovada do Brasil (IPRB), Caixa Postal 655, Rua Gaviao de Caude Curta, 115, 86700-970 Arapongas PR, Brazil, Tel: +55 43 252-3858, Fax: +55 43 252-3858

6. United Presbyterian Church of Brazil (2303)

This church was organized September 10, 1978, as the result of a protest movement in the 1970s within the Presbyterian Church of Brazil (IPB, cf. no.1) against both the doctrinal and the political positions of the church. Some years earlier, several pastors and communities, upon leaving the IPB, constituted themselves as the National Federation of Presbyterian Churches. The church is present in several states of Brazil and is distinguished by its ecumenical character, positive valuation of the ministry of women, and public positions against the social injustices that have been inflicted on the people.

TM: **5,200** BM: **5,200** CM: **3,600** Congr: **80** PStations: **78** OrdM: **110** Eld: **420** Deac: **yes** EvgHome: **nc** Mission: **yes** Women Ord: **yes** As Ministers: **4** as Deac: **100** as Elders: **100** ChurchOrg: **Presbyterian** Off/otherLang: **Portuguese** DoctrB: **ApC, NicC, Scottish Conf, HelvC, HelvC, Barmen, Confession of 1967, Atibaia Doc of 1978** Infant or believer's baptism: **both** NatRel: **CONIC, CESE, MPB** RegRel: **AIPRAL, CLAI** IntlRel: **WARC, WCC** TheolSchool: **1 interconfessional** Periodicals: **Imprensa Evangelica (journal)**

Address: Igreja Presbiteriana Unida do Brasil (IPU), Caixa Postal 01-212, 29001-970 Vitoria ES 29001-970, Brazil, Tel: +55 27 222-8024, Fax: +55 27 222-8024

7. Traditional Presbyterian Church of Brazil (2335)

This church came into existence in 1993. The reason for establishing a separate church was the doctrinal infiltration of charismatic teaching and liturgical practices which it felt were contrary to the worship tradition of the Presbyterian Church of Brazil (IPB). Under the leadership of Major Daldyr Aguiar da Silva, members of the Presb communities in the region of Brazilia-DF expressed their disapproval. They established themselves as a separate community and invited Rev. Benon Wanderley Pais, a retired pastor, to provide pastoral assistance. In September 1993 the church was organized, affirming the Ref tradition. In worship services traditional hymns, accompanied by the organ or the piano, are sung. Participation in these services has increased considerably; people have responded to the call to return to authentic Calvinism and are attracted by the evangelistic commitment of the church.

TM: **100** BM: **60** CM: **60** Congr: **1** PStations: **1** OrdM: **1** Eld: **5** Deac: **4** EvgHome: **ne** Mission: **ne** Women Ord: **yes** As Ministers: **no** as Deac: **2** as Elders: **no** ChurchOrg: **Presbyterian** Off/otherLang: **Portuguese** DoctrB: **WestConf** Infant or believer's baptism: **both** NatRel: **none** RegRel: **none** IntlRel: **none** TheolSchool: **none** Periodicals: **Boletim Dominical (gen/weekly)**

Address: Igreja Presbiteriana Tradicional do Brasil, Rua Q N D 8, casa 20, 72120-080 Taguatinga DF, Brazil, Tel: +55 61 562-1214.

8. Union of Congregational Churches of Brazil (2306)

This church was founded in the middle of the 19th century. It started on August 19, 1855, when Dr. Robert Reid Kalley and his wife Sarah opened the first Portuguese-language Sunday School in Brazil. After arriving in Brazil, Dr. Kalley invited evangelicals from the island of Madeira, who had fled to the United States, to participate in the work of evangelizing the people of this country (cf. Portugal). Three Madeirans responded to this invitation and arrived in Brazil in 1856. An Englishman, William Pitt, joined the movement, beginning a work of evangelization and colportage in Rio de Janeiro. In 1858 the Igreja Evangelica Fluminense was opened. Dr. Kalley became a friend of the Emperor of Brazil, Dom Pedro II. This facilitated the recognition of the rights of non-RCath, such as the right to a birth certificate and to burial in public cemeteries, although in separate areas. The Kalleys made a distinctive contribution in the area of hymnology through the translation and composition of hymns; they published *Salmos e Hinos,* which has become the traditional hymnbook and which, in its present form, is still in use in the majority of the historic Brazilian churches.

TM: **50,000** BM: **42,000** CM: **42,000** Congr: **582** PStations: **578** OrdM: **260** Eld: **no** Deac: **no** EvgHome: **no** Mission: **18** Women Ord: **no** ChurchOrg: **Congregational** Off/otherLang: **Portuguese** DoctrB: **Savoy Declaration of Faith and Order** Infant or believer's baptism: **believer** Close relations with: **Congreg Ev Church of Portugal** TheolSchool: **Theological Seminaries in: Rio, Recife; Bible Schools in: Alcantara, Niteroi, São Paulo, Belo Horizonte** Periodicals: **O Cristão (newspaper)**

Address: União das Igrejas Evangelicas Congregacionais do Brasil, Rua Visconde de Inhauma, 134– sala 1309, 20091-000 Rio de Janeiro RJ, Brazil, Tel: +55 21 216-4178

9. Evangelical Congregational Churches of Brazil (2309)

In 1920 Congregationalist missionaries from Argentina began to work in Brazil, entering through the state Rio Grande of the South. The church which resulted from this effort acquired autonomy in 1942. The church developed and began to spread also to other states. In the seventies a missionary outreach took place to Paraguay; in the border region new communities were planted (cf. Paraguay no. 3). In this church women play an important role. Though they cannot be ordained for the ministry they share in church government and participate with voice and vote both in regional synods and the General Assembly.

TM: **42,000** BM: **38,000** CM: **38,000** Congr: **52** PStations: **375** OrdM: **48** Eld: **no** Deac: **no** EvgHome: **nc** Mission: **5** Women Ord: **no** ChurchOrg: **Congregational** Off/otherLang: **Portuguese, German, Spanish (in Paraguay)** DoctrB: **ApC, Reformed doctrines** Infant or believer's baptism: **both** NatRel: **CONIC** RegRel: **AIPRAL, CLAI** TheolSchool: **3**

Address: Igrejas Evangélicas Congregacionais do Brasil (de alemaes), C.P. 374, Linha 4 Leste, 98700-000 Ijui RS, Brazil, Tel: +55 55 522-2093

10. Christian Reformed Church of Brazil (2300)

This church was founded on October 31, 1932, by the Rev. Janos Apostol under the supervision of the Reformed Church of Hungary. The first parish was organized in the city of São Paulo by Hungarian immigrants, the majority of them being from the region of Transylvania. Other congr were implanted in the states of São Paulo and Paraná. The church reached its high point between 1945 and 1980 when it had a total membership of 700 with three pastors. With the death of the Rev. Janos Apostol in 1991 the church entered into a period of difficulties and used the services of Luth Hungarian pastors. At the present time a Brazilian pastor of Hungarian descent is serving the church, holding worship services in both Hungarian and Portuguese.

TM: **500** BM: **500** CM: **400** Congr: **1** PStations: **1** OrdM: **1** Eld: **13** Deac: **no** EvgHome: **nc** Mission: **no** Women Ord: **yes** As Ministers: **yes** as Deac: **no** as Elders: **5** ChurchOrg: **Presbyterian** Off/otherLang: **Hungarian, Portuguese** DoctrB: **ApC, HelvC, Fluminense Confession of 1557** Infant or believer's baptism: **both** NatRel: **CONIC, DIACONIA** RegRel: **AIPRAL, CLAI** IntlRel: **WCC, WARC**

Address: Igreja Cristã Reformada do Brasil, Caixa Postal 2808, Lapa Rua Domingos Rodrigues, 306, 05075-000 São Paulo SP, Brazil, Tel: +55 11 260-2395

11. Evangelical Reformed Churches of Brazil (IERS) (2301)

This church started in 1911 when the first Dutch immigrants arrived in Brazil. Under the leadership of two laymen, Leonard Erschoor and Jacob C. Voorsluys, a church was established in the city of Carambeí, Paraná state. In the beginning they sought the assistance of Luth pastors for the administration of the sacrament of baptism. Some years later, after contacts with the Reformed Church of America in the USA, with the Ref Churches in the Netherlands, and with the Buenos Aires presby of the Reformed Churches of Argentina, they decided to organize officially the first Reformed Evangelical Church in Brazil, and did so on September 14, 1933. On February 18, 1962, the Brazilian communities decided to separate from the Buenos Aires presby and organize themselves as the Association of Evangelical Reformed Churches in Brazil; the name was later changed to Evangelical Reformed Churches in Brazil (IER).

87

TM: **2,700** BM: **2,700** Congr: **7** PStations: **8** OrdM: **11** Eld: **yes** Deac: **yes** EvgHome: **4** Mission: **nc** Women Ord: **yes** As Ministers: **no** as Deac: **yes** as Elders: **yes** ChurchOrg: **Presbyterian (presby, synod)** Off/otherLang: **Portuguese, Dutch** DoctrB: **WestConf, HeidC, BelgC, Three Ecumenical Creeds** Infant or believer's baptism: **both** Close relations with: **Gereformeerde Kerken** IntlRel: **WARC** TheolSchool: **no** Periodicals: **Informe (monthly/750)**

Address: Igrejas Evangelicas Reformadas no Brasil (IERs), Rua Saladino de Castro, 605, 86510-000 Arapoti PR, Brazil, Tel: +55 43 857 1396, Fax: +55 43 857 1396

12. Arab Evangelical Church of São Paulo (2304)

The first attempt at implanting an Arab church in Brazil was made in 1920 by a Lebanese immigrant pastor, The Rev. Khalil Simão Ragi. He organized the Syrian Evangelical Church of São Paulo. Though it experienced progress and numerical growth, this church was dissolved in 1935. Evangelistic work in Arabic was resumed in 1954 by another Lebanese immigrant, Rev. Ragi Azar Khouri. He opened the doors of his own house in Campinas, São Paulo state, for a small community to gather. He set up preaching points in the states of São Paulo and Goiás. Until the dedication of its own church building in São Paulo in 1979, the community met on the premises of various Evangelical denominations. The church maintains a library, the Salão Internacional de Leitura e Orientação (International Reading and Counselling Room) in the city of Campinas, São Paulo state.

TM: **90** BM: **85** Congr: **1** PStations: **3** OrdM: **2** Eld: **6** Deac: **no** EvgHome: **2** Mission: **no** Women Ord: **yes** As Ministers: **nc** as Deac: **no** as Elders: **15** ChurchOrg: **Presbyterian** Off/otherLang: **Arabic, Portuguese** DoctrB: **ApC, WestConf** Frequency of the Lord's Supper: **monthly** Close relations with: **Evangelical Synod of Syria and Lebanon; Independent Presb Church of Brazil** NatRel: **nc** RegRel: **AIPRAL, CLAI** IntlRel: **WCC, WARC (1980)** Periodicals: **Boletim de Igreja (gen/weekly/70)**

Address: Igreja Evangélica Arabe de São Paulo, C.P. 590, Rua Vergueiro, 1845, Campinas SP 13001-970, Brazil, Tel: +55 1 9242-0537, Fax: +55 1 9234-6118

13. Swiss Evangelical Church of São Paulo (2330)

This church was organized in 1958 to serve the Swiss community in São Paulo. Rev. Middendorp was sent by the Swiss Protestant Federation. For several reasons, such as the acculturation of the second generation and the return of immigrant families to their country of origin, the church has experienced a marked loss in membership. At the present time the church is served by a pastor of the Presbyterian Church of Brazil, replacing a Swiss pastor who left at the end of 1994 and returned to Switzerland.

TM: **720** BM: **680** CM: **120** Congr: **2** PStations: **1** OrdM: **10** Eld: **yes** Deac: **yes** EvgHome: **nc** Mission: **no** Women Ord: **yes** As Ministers: **yes** as Deac: **yes** as Elders: **yes** ChurchOrg: **Presbyterian** Off/otherLang: **Portuguese, German** DoctrB: **HelvC** Infant or believer's baptism: **both** Close relations with: **Swiss Protestant Church Federation** TheolSchool: **no**

Address: Igreja Evangelica Suiça de São Paulo, Caixa Postal 21369, Rua Gabriele d'Annuncio 952, 04619-000 São Paulo SP, Brazil, Tel: +55 11 240-5802, Fax: +55 11 240-6530

14. Cumberland Presbyterian Church of Bahia (2332)

This community started in March 1960 when a Japanese Presbyterian, Mitsuo Sasaki, settled in the interior of Bahia state with his family. They held Bible studies. When the community began to grow, the Cumberland Presbyterian of Koza in Japan (cf. Japan no. 5) decided in 1982 to send a pastor with the special mandate to ordain Mitsuo Sasaki as presbyter. The church in Brazil belongs to the twelfth region of the Cumberland Presbyterian Church in Koza. In the period from 1986 to 1994, pastors were sent to assist the community in Brazil. Elder Mitsuo Sasaki continues to be the spiritual leader of the church. The members of the community are mainly farmers. Thirty percent of the community live in the city of Salvador, 75 km away, but participate regularly in the services held in Japanese.

TM: **80** BM: **80** CM: **60** Congr: **1** PStations: **1** OrdM: **0** Eld: **1** Deac: EvgHome: **nc** Mission: **nc** Women Ord: **no** ChurchOrg: **Presbyterian** Off/otherLang: **Japanese, Portuguese** DoctrB: **WestConf** Infant or believer's baptism: **both** Close relations with: **Cumberland Presb Ch of Koza (Japan)** TheolSchool: **no**

Address: Igreja Presbiteriana Cumberland da Bahia, Apto 402-A, Rua Ubarana 330, 91910-070 Salvador BA, Brazil

15. Presbyterian Church of Formosa in Brazil (2329)

The Taiwanese Presbyterian Church began in 1962 with the arrival of a Chinese physician who had also studied theology and had immigrated to Brazil. Activities started with meetings in homes in São Paulo. The first Taiwanese immigrant church was organized in the same year. With the arrival of new groups of immigrants, the church began to develop, with new churches being organized in several cities in Brazil. The church structured itself as a denomination in 1970, with ties to the General Assembly of the Presbyterian Church of Taiwan. There is at present a movement in the presby toward dialogue, with the thought of eventual incorporation into one of the Synods of the Independent Presbyterian Church of Brazil.

TM: **2,000** BM: **1,000** CM: **800** Congr: **11** PStations: **1** OrdM: **12** Eld: **yes** Deac: **yes** EvgHome: **nc** Mission: **5** Women Ord: **yes** As Ministers: **2** as Deac: **yes** as Elders: **yes** ChurchOrg: **Presbyterian** Off/otherLang: **Taiwanese, Mandarin, Portuguese** DoctrB: **ApC, WestConf** Infant or believer's baptism: **both** Close relations with: **Taiwanese Presb Church** TheolSchool: **1 (interconfessional)**

Address: Igreja Presbiteriana de Formosa no Brasil (de chineses), Rua Topazio 368, 04105 060 São Paulo SP, Brazil, Tel: +55 11 575-8795

16. Korean United Presbyterian Church of São Paulo (2308)

The first Korean Presbyterian immigrants arrived in Brazil in 1956. Among them was Kang Hi Dong, who, after studying theology at the Presbyterian Theological Seminary of Campinas, became a pastor and remains active to this day. Presbyterian work among Koreans began in April 1964 in the interior of São Paulo state, with the arrival of an evangelist, Myoung Jae Lee, along with four other families. Today, Koreans and persons of Korean descent number more than 50,000; about 10% of them are naturalized. Over 7,000 belong to Evangelical denominations, most of them Presbyterian, with approximately seventeen communities linked to different Presbyterian denominations in South Korea. The Korean immigrants have demonstrated concern for the second generation with the founding of the "Korean Campus Mission Mocidade do Brazil" (Korean Campus Mission Youth of Brazil), whose objective is the evangelization of adolescents and youth of Korean origin. The Korean United Presbyterian Church of São Paulo is structurally linked to the Presbyterian Church of Korea (PCK-TongHap; cf. Korea no. 14).

TM: **950** BM: **950** CM: **650** Congr: **1** PStations: **3** OrdM: **3** Eld: **9** Deac: **11** EvgHome: **nc** Mission: **4** Women Ord: **no** ChurchOrg: **Presbyterian** Off/otherLang: **Korean, Portuguese** DoctrB: **ApC, WestConf** Infant or believer's baptism: **both** Close relations with: **Presb Church of Korea (TongHap)** TheolSchool: **no**

Address: Igreja Presbiteriana Unida Coreana de São Paulo, Rua Mituto Mizumoto, 220, 01513-010
São Paulo SP, Brazil, Tel: +55 11 278-2555, Fax: +55 11 277-8936

17. Evangelical Church of São Paulo (2327)

Japanese Evangelicals have been present in Brazil for a period of 60 years. During the '50s they began to structure themselves as an organized church. In 1958 the Kyodan (cf. Japan no. 1) sent a pastor, Motoi Munakata, to minister to the group's spiritual needs. He first served the church, which is today the Evangelical Alliance Church and which unites persons of Reformed and Arminian persuasions. In 1967 he left the leadership of this church and founded the Evangelical Church of São Paulo, where he remained until 1979 when he returned to Japan. The problems which led to the division of the church in Brazil had more to do with ideology than with theology. Although the community consisted of a small number of members, one has to take into consideration that, given the presence of Japanese immigrants in Brazil over a period of more than 80 years, the second and third generations, being acculturated, have joined a variety of Brazilian Evangelical Churches.

TM: **40** BM: **40** CM: **40** Congr: **1** PStations: **1** OrdM: **1** Eld: **no** Deac: **no** EvgHome: **nc** Mission: **no** Women Ord: **yes** As Ministers: **nc** as Deac: **nc** as Elders: **nc** ChurchOrg: **Congregational** Off/otherLang: **Japanese, Portuguese** DoctrB: **Calvinism, Arminianism** Infant or believer's baptism: **both** Close relations with: **Kyodan (cf. Japan no. 1)** TheolSchool: **no**

Address: Igreja Evangelica de São Paulo (de Japoneses), Rua Dr. Tomas Carvalhal, 471, 04006-001
São Paulo SP, Brazil, Tel: +55 11 885-7665

18. Korean Presbyterian Church of Brazil (2333)

The Korean Presbyterian Church was founded on August 21, 1969, by Korean immigrants belonging to the Presbyterian Church Hapdong (cf. Korea no. 15). The first missionary was Pastor Sung Man Kim, who stayed in Brazil until 1983. He was succeeded by Pastor Sung Chuel Kang, who came to Brazil in September 1983, and has served ever since as the pastor of the first church of the denomination, the Han-In church in Sao Paulo. Today the church has 7 organized congr and 8 preaching stations; it has started missionary work among Brazilians. Among its evangelistic and social activities, the church holds the so-called "Beggar's Service" with an attendance of over 700 persons, who receive a modest meal and hear the Gospel preached, all under the leadership of evangelists and the assistance of the church youth. In the perspective of evangelism the church maintains, under the responsibility of missionaries with special training in the field of health, a center of medical and dental care; it is also developing a program for the rehabilitation of alcoholics and drug addicts.

TM: **1,800** BM: **1,800** CM: **1,500** Congr: **7** PStations: **8** OrdM: **18** Eld: **50** Deac: **20** EvgHome: **nc** Mission: **20** Women Ord: **yes** As Ministers: **no** as Deac: **yes** as Elders: **yes** ChurchOrg: **Presbyterian** Off/otherLang: **Korean, Portuguese** DoctrB: **ApC, WestConf** Infant or believer's baptism: **both** Close relations with: **Presb Church in Korea (HapDong, cf. Korea no. 15))** TheolSchool: **no**

Address: Igreja Presbiteriana Coreana do Brasil, Rua Livreiro Alves 16, 01505-010 São Paulo SP, Brazil

19. Antioch Presbyterian Church (2334)

The existence of this church is also due to a Korean initiative. It was started on April 15, 1984, by Korean Presbyterian immigrants under the leadership of Kae Man (Presbyterian Church of Kora, TongHap). At present there are three congr, self-supporting and independent. One of the pastors was ordained by the Independent Presbyterian Church of Brazil. The church employs a Brazilian woman theologian to coordinate youth work, Sunday school, and camps.

TM: **1,400** BM: **1,400** CM: **1,200** Congr: **3** PStations: **3** OrdM: **6** Eld: **16** Deac: **no** EvgHome: **nc** Mission: **5** Women Ord: **no** ChurchOrg: **Presbyterian** Off/otherLang: **Korean, Portuguese** DoctrB: **ApC, WestConf** Infant or believer's baptism: **both** Close relations with: **Presb Church of Korea (TongHap, cf. Korea no. 14)** TheolSchool: **no**

Address: Igreja Presbiteriana Antioquia, Rua Rio Bonito 1804, 03023-000 São Paulo SP, Brazil

20. Reformed Church of Brasolandia (2321)

Dutch immigrants, who belonged to the Reformed Churches–Liberated (cf. Netherlands no. 8), decided in 1965 to establish an agricultural settlement in Brazil. They started to work in the state of Paraná. After some unsuccessful years, the group was dissolved. In 1970 a member of this group, Jan Glas, organized another group with four families in Unaí in the state Minas Gerais in central Brazil. They succeeded in founding the agricultural settlement, Brasolandia, and organized a community. In 1991 the congregation was formally established.

TM: **130** BM: **112** CM: **54** Congr: **1** PStations: **1** OrdM: **ne** Eld: **2** Deac: **1** EvgHome: **ne** Mission: **ne** Women Ord: **no** ChurchOrg: **no regional or national structure** Off/otherLang: **Dutch, Portuguese** DoctrB: **ApC, NicC, AthC, HeidC, CDort, BelgC** Infant or believer's baptism: **both** Frequency of the Lord's Supper: **4 times per year** Close relations with: **De Gereformeerde Kerken (Vrijgemaakt) in the Netherlands** NatRel: **none** IntlRel: **none** Service infrastructure: **elementary school**

Address: Igreja Reformada de Brasolandia, Caixa Postal 154, 38610-000 Unai MG, Brazil, Tel: +55 61 505-2345

21. Reformed Church of Brazil (2322)

In the 1970s Canadian Reformed Churches sent missionaries to the northeastern region to start evangelistic work among Brazilians. Their efforts led to the foundation of the first two congr in the states of Alagoas and Pernambuco in 1994. Soon, two more congr and preaching stations came into existence. The Canadian missionaries are supported in their work by two Brazilian Presbyterian students. The church has organized an elementary school. There is the hope that before long a presby can be organized.

TM: **195** BM: **195** CM: **89** Congr: **2** PStations: **5** OrdM: **3** Eld: **2** Deac: **2** EvgHome: **2** Mission: **ne** Women Ord: **no** ChurchOrg: **no national or regional structure** Off/otherLang: **Portuguese** DoctrB: **ApC, NicC, AthC, HeidC, CDort, BelgC** Infant or believer's baptism: **both** Frequency of the Lord's Supper: **six times per year** Close relations with: **Canadian Reformed Churches** NatRel: **none** RegRel: **none** IntlRel: **none** TheolSchool: **use of Seminario Presbiteriano do Norte (Presbyterian Church of Brazil)** Service infrastructure: **1 elementary school, 1 nursery**

Address: Igreja Reformada do Brasil, Padre José Vennekes, 257, 57955-000 Maragogi AL, Brazil, Tel: +55 82 296 1186, Fax: +55 82 296 1186

22. Reformed Church of Colombo (2323)

The Reformed Churches (Liberated) in the Netherlands decided in 1963 to start mission work in Curitiba, Paraná, among Dutch immigrants who had moved to the area since 1950. Though the Dutch colony Monte Alegre was dissolved in 1971, the evangelistic work continued in Curitiba among Brazilians. A difficult time arose in the '80s when many members left the church. The center of activities moved at that time from Curitiba to Colombo, an independent municipality in the metropolitan area of Curitiba. A church was registered there in 1995. Mission work is also expanding in other places. The Reformed Church in Colombo has close contacts with the Reformed Church of Brasolandia at Unaí, Minas Gerais, where some of the old immigrants of Monte Alegre have established themselves (no. 21), with the Reformed Churches of Brazil (no. 22), and with the Presbyterian Church of Brazil (no. 1).

TM: **80** BM: **80** CM: **46** Congr: **1** PStations: **2** OrdM: **2** Eld: **1** Deac: **ne** EvgHome: **2** Mission: **ne** Women Ord: **no** ChurchOrg: **no national or regional structure** Off/otherLang: **Portuguese, Dutch** DoctrB: **ApC, NicC, AthC, HeidC, CDort, BelgC, Reformed** Infant or believer's baptism: **both** Frequency of the Lord's Supper: **6 times per year** Close relations with: **De Gereformeerde Kerken (Vrijgemaakt) in the Netherlands, Canadian Reformed Churches; Presb Church of Brazil, Ref Church of Brasolandia, Ref Churches of Brazil** NatRel: **none** IntlRel: **ICRC** TheolSchool: **Theological University of Reformed Churches (Liberated) in Kampen NL** Service infrastructure: **na** Periodicals: **newsletter (gen/monthly)**

Address: Igreja Reformada de Colombo, Caixa Postal 4171, 82501-970 Curitiba PR, Brazil, Tel: +55 41 253-2494, Fax: +55 41 256-0686, E-mail: roelof@penguin.super.com.br.

BULGARIA

Area in km²	110,842
Population	(July 1996 est.) 8,612,757 Bulgarian 85.3%, Turk 8.5%, Gypsy 2.6%, Macedonian 2.5%, Armenian 0.3%, Russian 0.2%, other 0.6%
Religions in %	Bulgarian Orthodox 85%, Muslim 13%, Jewish 0.8%, RCath 0.5%, Uniate Catholic 0.2%, Protestant, Gregorian-Armenian and other 0.5%
Official/other languages	Bulgarian / Turkish (1992)

Evangelical Congregational Churches in Bulgaria (6025)

Protestantism came to the region of Bulgaria at a time when it still belonged to the Turkish empire. Its presence was due to the ABCFM (Boston). The first congregational mission station was established in 1831 in Asia Minor, and in 1840 a school was opened in Babek (Istanbul) which had a considerable impact on the younger generation. In 1840 Elias Riggs began work among the Bulgarians, and in 1844 the first journal in Bulgarian — *Luboslovie* — with Constantine Fotinov as editor, began to appear. In 1868 the first church was built in Bansko, and several others followed in subsequent years. With the help of Dr. Long, Christobul Kostovich, and Petko Slaveikov, Riggs translated the Bible into Bulgarian (1871). In 1875 the Evangelical Association was founded, consisting initially of the Congregational Union and the Methodist Church, one working in the south and the other in the north. Later the Association was joined by the Baptists (1925) and the Adventists. In 1876, *Zornitza*, the first Bulgarian weekly church journal, started to appear. Several kindergartens, the first in Bulgaria, were opened.

After their liberation from Turkish occupation several members of the Prot community played a particular role in the formation of the Bulgarian state. Andrew Tsanov, Velko Shopov, and Andrew Sharenkov were parliamentarians, and

Georgi Yordanov served in the government. Some outstanding Communists were raised in Prot families (Georgi Dimitrov and the poets, Nicola Vaptzarov and Geo Milev). After World War II the church suffered persecution and restrictions. Schools were closed and the journal *Zornitza* discontinued. Prot pastors were accused of collaboration with the West. In a trial in 1949, and continuing in subsequent years, some were sentenced to prison and camps: Vasil Ziapkov, Lambri Mishkov, Stefan Gradinarov, Georgi Sivriev, Simeon Iliev, Gerasim Popov, Cyril Yotov, and Constantine Bozovaiski. In 1985, in a new surge of oppression, Dimitar and Hristo Kulichev were sent to prison.

After the fall of the Communist regime, the church was reconstituted. In search of its identity, it went through a difficult period of internal tension which has not yet fully been overcome. The church continues to suffer from restrictions imposed by the state authorities. At the same time a new evangelistic outreach is taking place. Missionaries from various countries are working with the church (Mission to the World of the Presbyterian Church of America, Presbyterian Evangelistic Fellowship, Korean and Dutch missionaries).

TM: **5,000** BM: **5,000** CM: **5,000** Congr: **34** PStations: **8** OrdM: **10** Eld: **ne** Deac: **22** EvgHome: **6** Mission: **0** Women Ord: **no** ChurchOrg: **Congregational (local communities, synod)** Off/otherLang: **Bulgarian, Armenian, Turkish** DoctrB: **ApC, NicC, local creed based on Savoy Declaration** Infant or believer's baptism: **both** Frequency of the Lord's Supper: **quarterly** Periodicals: **Zornitza-gen (monthly/3,000)** Close relations with: **Meth, Bapt** NatRel: **Bulgarian Evangelical Alliance (1993)** IntlRel: **WARC (1990), IFFEC (1994).**

Address: Evangelska Kongreschanska Zerkwa, Solunska St. 49, BG-1225 Sofia 1000, Bulgaria, Tel: +359 2 880-593 or 394-117, Fax: +359 2 394-117, E-mail: 103640.1047@compuserve.com

---

BURKINA FASO

Area in km²	274,200
Population	(July 1996 est.) 10,623,323 Mossi about 50%, Gurunsi, Senufo, Lobi, Bobo, Mande, Fulani
Religions in %	indigenous beliefs 25%, Muslim 52%, Christian 22% (RCath 17%, Prot 5%), other 1%
Official/other languages	French / tribal languages belonging to Sudanic family, spoken by 90% of the population

FEME (Federation of Churches and Missions in Burkina Faso)

Burkina Faso (until 1984 called Upper Volta) is part of the Sahel region. Its climate is dry, and the country is vulnerable to the process of desertification. Only about 25% of the country can be cultivated. In the 13th century the Mossi invaded the country from the east and established five kingdoms. They resisted French colonization in the 1880s until their defeat at the beginning of this century. The country became part of French West Africa. Since 1947 the region has been separately administered. It gained independence in 1960. In 1965, 1980, and 1987, the army established military regimes.

Until recently it was thought that the country would turn Muslim. But Christianity has experienced rapid growth. The largest among the Protestant communities are the Assemblies of God, which are also rapidly increasing. Due to the fact that they live in different parts of the country and speak different languages, the Protestant communities so far have little contact with one another. In addition to the three communities mentioned below, special note needs to be taken of the Protestant Evangelical Church, which was founded by the World Evangelical Crusade (WEC) and has roots in the western part of Burkina Faso (headquarters in Gaoua). A large number of Protestant communities in Burkina Faso, including the Assemblies of God, are part of the Federation of Churches and Missions in Burkina Faso (FEME).

1. Church of the Christian Alliance (1027)

The initiative for establishing this church came from the Christian and Missionary Alliance, a missionary movement founded in the United States by Albert Benjamin Simpson (1843-1919). The first missionaries of the Alliance came to Burkina Faso in 1923. They established themselves in Bobo-Dioulasso, in the western part of the country. In 1962 the church became autonomous and was officially recognized by the state. The church runs several schools. The church is organized into 10 districts: Banfora, Bobo-Dioulasso, Dedougou, Djibasso, Pouna, Ouagadougou, Ouroué, Santodougou, Solenzo, and Tougan; each district is governed by a district committee, and the entire church by a national committee.

TM: **47,900** CM: **13,400** Congr: **550** OrdM: **nc** Eld: **nc** Deac: **nc** EvgHome: **nc** Mission: **nc** Women Ord: **nc** As Ministers: **nc** as Deac: **nc** as Elders: **nc** ChurchOrg: **Congregational (ten districts, GenAssy)** Off/otherLang: **French** DoctrB: **nc** NatRel: **FEME**

Address: Eglise de l'Alliance chrétienne (EAC), B.P. 909, Bobo-Dioulasso, Burkina Faso, Tel: +226 97 24 03, Fax: +226 97 22 55, E-mail: cmaburkina@maf.org.

2. Association of Evangelical Churches in Burkina Faso (A.E.E.B.F.) (1028)

The church came into being in 1931 through the efforts of the Sudan Interior Mission (SIM) among the Gourma and the Mossi. Its congr are mainly located in the east, but they have spread through migration also to other parts of the country. The church places strong emphasis on health services and Christian education.

TM: **80,000** CM: **10,200** Congr and PStations: **334** OrdM: **250** Eld: **nc** Deac: **nc** EvgHome: **nc** Mission: **nc** Women Ord: **no** ChurchOrg: **Congregational (congr, districts, synod)** Off/otherLang: **French, Mossi, Gourma** DoctrB: **ApC, Evangelical** Infant or believer's baptism: **believer** NatRel: **FEME** TheolSchool: **Bible School (Fada N'Gourma), Centre Biblique (Nyamey), Theological School (Bangui)**

Address: Association des églises évangéliques au Burkina Faso (A.E.E.B.F.), B.P. 1552, Ouaga-
           dougou, Burkina Faso

3. Reformed Evangelical Church of Burkina Faso (1025)

This is the youngest of the Ref churches in the country. It was started in 1977 in
Zimtenga by an association of 30 members led by Kinda Lazare, a pastor from
Burkina Faso. Its work is concentrated in the north. Apart from evangelizing, the
church is engaged in rural development work.

TM: **3,220** BM: **2,700** CM: **2,100** Congr: **30** PStations: **15** OrdM: **9** Eld: **ne** Deac: **54** EvgHome: **6** Mission: **0** Women Ord: **yes** As Ministers: **0** as Deac: **1989** as Elders: **ne** ChurchOrg: **parishes — regional
synods — one general synod** Off/otherLang: **French** DoctrB: **ApC, NicC, HeidC** Infant or believer's
baptism: **believer** Frequency of the Lord's Supper: **monthly** NatRel: **FEME** RegRel: **AACC** IntlRel:
WARC (1989) Service infrastructure: **social service organization**

Address: Eglise évangélique réformée du Burkina Faso, B.P. 3946, Ouagadougou 01, Burkina Faso,
           Tel: +226 34 03 78, Fax: +226 310-648; other address: B.P. 269 Kongoussi (Burkina Faso).

CAMBODIA

Area in km²	181,000
Population	10 million (Khmer 80%, Vietnamese 8%, Chinese 7%, Malay 2,5%)
Religions in %	Buddhist 87%, Muslim 2%, Animist 3%, Christian 0.1% (Prot around 10,000, RCath 4,000)
Official/other languages	Khmer, Vietnamese, Chinese, and minority languages in the hill areas

Cambodia is basically a Buddhist country. For centuries Buddhism was closely
linked to the worship of the king ruler (devarajaia cult). In the 13th century
Theravada Buddhism was brought to the country by Thai monks and was officially
recognized by King Jayavarman Parameswara (1327-1336). The royal constitution
(1956) recognizes Buddhism as the state religion. In 1970 General Lon Nol overthrew the royal house, and King Norodom Sihanouk went into exile. Under the extreme Communist regime of the Khmer Rouge led by Pol Pot, hundreds of thousands were massacred (1975-1979). The churches suffered persecution. Many
died or fled to other countries. In the '80s Vietnam occupied Cambodia and established a pro-Vietnamese regime. After many years of internal strife, elections were
held and Sihanouk was able to return to the country.

RCath missionary efforts began in the 16th century, but the Christian presence developed slowly. In 1842 there were four churches and a little over 200 RCath Christians. By 1962 their number had increased to 62,000, but most of them were Vietnamese, Chinese, or European. Under Lon Nol's anti-Vietnamese regime many of them were killed, and under Pol Pot RCath missionaries were expelled. As a result the number of RCath drastically diminished.

A Prot mission was started in 1923 by the Christian and Missionary Alliance (CMA) among the Khmer population. Their center was in Phnom Penh. By 1964 the mission had founded 13 congr in 9 of the 17 provinces. In 1970 Evangelicals numbered about 10,000 to 12,000 members, many of them among the Khmer population. Work was also initiated among the Muong, Biet, and Kuoy in the northeastern part of the country. In 1965 the missionaries were forced to leave. Many of them returned under Lon Nol. Thousands of Christians were massacred during the Pol Pot regime (1975-1978); many fled abroad. Only about 2,000 remained in the country. A sizeable number of Cambodian congr were established among the refugees in neighboring Thailand.

During the pro-Vietnamese regime Prot were again able to gather, and in 1990 religious freedom was granted. At present more than 30 denominations and congr with about 10,000 members are to be found, mainly in the areas of Phnom Penh and Battembang, as well as among the Muong. In 1996 an Evangelical Fellowship of Cambodia was founded. A new translation of the Bible into Khmer is in preparation. Reliable figures are difficult to report.

Addresses: Evangelical Fellowship of Cambodia, P.O. Box 543, Phnom Penh, Cambodia

General Assembly of Presbyterian Church of Cambodia, P.O. Box 161, Phnom Penh, Cambodia

CAMEROON

Area in km²	475,440
Population	(July 1996 est.) 14,261,557 Cameroon Highlanders 31%, Equatorial Bantu 19%, Kirdi 11%, Fulani 10%, Northwestern Bantu 8%, Eastern Nigritic 7%, other African 13%, non-African less than 1%
Religions in %	indigenous beliefs 51%, Christian 35% (RCath 21%, Prot 14%), Muslim 16%
Official/other languages	English, French / 24 major African language groups with 220 dialects

FEMEC (Fédération des Eglises et Missions du Cameroun / *Federation of Prot Churches and Missions in Cameroon*)
CUEC (Comité d'union des Eglises du Cameroun / *Church Union Committee*)

In 1472 the mouth of the river Wouri (Duala) was discovered by Portuguese navigators. The first Prot missionaries were freed slaves from Jamaica who were sent in 1841 by the London Baptist Missionary Society to visit the West African coast. In 1842 a British missionary, Alfred Saker, started work in Fernando Po (Bioko), but, due to the intolerance of the Spanish rulers, he left three years later with a Jamaican, Joseph Merick, for the area of Duala. The converts of Fernando Po joined him in 1858. Saker concentrated his energy on the translation of the Bible, while his colleagues carried the Gospel further inland. Saker's New Testament was published in Duala in 1862, and the Old Testament in 1872.

In 1877 leading Duala chiefs wrote to Queen Victoria offering their territory to be protected by the British government. Before then British and German traders had been operating in Duala without any formal protection by a European government. Since Britain was hesitating, German traders persuaded the German government to accept the offer. In 1884 the German flag was hoisted over Duala. From then on British traders and missionaries were considered to be a threat to German interests. After World War I the Cameroon was divided — while West Cameroon came under British rule, the main part of the country, four-fifths of the territory, became French. Independence was achieved in 1960. Due to the double colonial past the country uses both English and French as official languages.

Four of the five churches with Ref background are very close to one another both in teaching and in practice. Separation is primarily due to mission history and geographical distance, though all churches have begun to have congr in the "territory" of the others. Efforts toward union were made in the '60s and early '70s but so far have not led to tangible results. A Church Union Committee continues to exist but is practically inoperative.

1. Presbyterian Church in Cameroon (PCC) (1031)

The policy of the German government was to admit only German missionaries to their colonial territories. After some negotiation, the English Bapt withdrew from the Cameroon and concentrated their efforts on the Congo, where they also had a mission field. The Basel Mission was requested to take their place in 1885 and soon sent a first team of four missionaries to the country. In 1890 German Pallotin Fathers were also permitted to start work in Cameroon. The Basel Mission introduced church discipline and infant baptism to the church. Since Christians in Duala and Victoria were mainly Bapt, they revolted against these innovations and, since the Basel Mission was unwilling to change its policy, a split occurred which resulted in the formation of the Native Baptist Church in 1889, a church which remained in subsequent years independent from white influence. By World War I the Basel Mission had opened 22 mission stations. Much emphasis was placed on educational work and on health care and agriculture.

In 1914 all German missionaries were forced to leave the country. Africans continued the work. When the Basel Mission returned after the War (1925), it was confined to the British-controlled part of Cameroon. The disturbances of World War II led to the recognition that leadership had to be handed over. In 1957 the Presbyterian Church in Cameroon was constituted. Fraternal relations between the Basel mission and the church continued in relation to schools, hospitals, health centers, and agricultural institutions. In 1968 the schools were handed over. The Church sees its priority in evangelizing the area. There are several movements such as the Christian Women's Fellowship, the Christian Men's Fellowship, and the Christian Youth Fellowship. Lay training has been intensified. Among the Africans who gave leadership to the Church the following stand out: Esoka Diso, Abraham Ngole, Aaron Su, and Jeremiah Chi Kangsen.

TM: **300,000** CM: **200,000** Congr: **291** PStations: **1,215** OrdM: **192** Eld: **500** Deac: **28** EvgHome: **42** Mission: **1** Women Ord: **yes** As Ministers: **1978/2** as Deac: **no ordination** as Elders: **nc** ChurchOrg: **Presbyterian (congr, presby, synod)** Off/otherLang: **Douala, Mungara (local languages), English, French** DoctrB: **ApC, NicC** Infant or believer's baptism: **both** Frequency of the Lord's Supper: **monthly (not enough pastors to celebrate every week)** Periodicals: **Presb newsletter (gen/quarterly/1,500)** NatRel: **FEMEC (1963), CUEC (1964)** RegRel: **AACC** IntlRel: **WCC, WARC** TheolSchool: **Theological Seminary (Kumba)**

Address: Eglise presbytérienne camérounaise, P.O. Box 19, Buea, Cameroon, Tel: +237 322-336, Fax: +237 322-113

2. Evangelical Church of Cameroun (ECC) (1034)

This Church was born out of the work of three successive European missions — the English Bapt, the Basel Mission, and the Paris Mission. In 1917, during World War I, the Basel Mission handed over 15 of its 22 stations to the Paris Mission. Since the Paris Mission was lacking in money and personnel, the Africans had a large share in the activities of the church. Preparations for the constitution of an independent church began in 1947, and in 1957 the EEC gained autonomy from the Paris Mission. Among the African leaders of the Church the following deserve to be mentioned: Modi Din, Eugène Mallo, and Jean Kotto.

The EEC has close links with the Union des Eglises Baptistes du Cameroun (UEBC), which had also been under the supervision of the Paris Mission and became independent in the same year as the EEC. They jointly run certain church institutions. The two churches are federated in the Council of Baptist and Evangelical Churches (CEBEC).

TM: **1,175,000** CM: **543,000** Congr: **700** OrdM: **287** Eld: **23,000** Deac: **nc** EvgHome: **500** Mission: **1** Women Ord: **Yes** As Ministers: **1989/9** as Deac: **nc** as Elders: **nc** ChurchOrg: **consistories, 13 regional synods, 1 executive commission for the synod, 1 general synod** Off/otherLang: **French, Douala, Bamoun, Bangangté, Ghom, Nufi** DoctrB: **ApC** Infant or believer's baptism: **both** Frequency of the Lord's Supper: **monthly** Periodicals: **L'Appel (popular+religious/monthly/3,000), En Marche (special+information/3 times per year/3,000)** Close relations with: **Evangelical-Reformed Church in the NL, Evangelical Church of Westphalia (Germany)** NatRel: **FEMEC** RegRel: **AACC** IntlRel: **WCC, CEVAA, VEM** TheolSchool: **Theological College (Ndoungué).**

Address: Eglise évangélique du Cameroun, B.P. 89, Douala, Cameroon, Tel: +237 423-611, Fax: +237 424-011

3. Presbyterian Church of Cameroon (1030)

In 1875 American Presb who had been active in Gabun since 1871 established themselves in Batanga, Southern Cameroon. In 1884 the area came under German influence. Four years later the Presbyterian Board of Mission asked the German government for permission to extend their work into Cameroon. The request was granted on certain conditions; the German government specifically insisted on the use of German in mission schools. In 1892 work started among the Bulu people; the first converts were baptized in 1900. In 1897 a mission station was opened in Lolodorf. Between 1898 and 1901 an uprising took place among the Bulu people who sought to defend their trade monopoly against competing caravans from Yaoundé to the port of Kribi. In the course of events the Germans confiscated the American mission station in Lolodorf because of its strategic location. In response to protests by the US government the mission was compensated for the damages. But the relations between the colonial authorities and the American mission deteriorated. Their schools did not receive any subsidies, and their students were not admitted to German examinations. The American Mission sought to improve its situation by recruiting German-speaking missionaries. Stations were opened in Elat (1895), Lolodorf (1897), Metet (1901), Foulassi (1916), Yaoundé (1922), Bafia (1924), Abong Mbang (1926), Momjepom (1935), and Batouri (1940). By 1894 the Bible and some hymns had been translated into Bulu. In 1920 the Paris Mission handed over to the American Mission the former Basel Mission area around Edea and the upper Sanaga extending to Sakbayene with 94 congr. Since the Bassa people in this region refused to adopt the Bulu language, efforts were made to translate the Bible into their own language (1960).

In 1957 the EPC was granted autonomy. At the time of independence the Church numbered about 69,000 members with 79 African pastors. Outstanding leadership was given by Moubitang, Jega, and Albert Nyemb. In May 1997 one synod has been split into two, making a total of 5 synods (Municam, Bassa, East, Center, and Metet).

TM: **600,000** BM: **391,883** CM: **208,117** Congr: **500** PStations: **2,637** OrdM: **387** Eld: **4,226** Deac: **5,008** EvgHome: **nc** Mission: **1** Women Ord: **yes** As Ministers: **not yet** as Deac: **6,000** as Elders: **3,132** ChurchOrg: **19 classes, 5 synods** Off/otherLang: **French, Bulu, Bassa, Bafia, Makai** DoctrB: **ApC, NicC, HeidC, WestConf** Infant or believer's baptism: **both** Frequency of the Lord's Supper: **quarterly (and on Christmas and Easter)** Periodicals: **Mefoé (Lumière)** Close relations with: **PCUSA, EZE (German development aid)** NatRel: **FEMEC (1969), CUEC** RegRel: **AACC (1962)** IntlRel: **WARC (1961), WCC (1961)** TheolSchool: **Dager Theological School (Bibia), Faculty of Prot Theology (Yaoundé)**

Address: Eglise presbytérienne camerounaise, B.P. 519, Yaoundé, Cameroon, Tel: +237 206-472, Fax: +237 206-472

4. African Protestant Church (1032)

This Church is the result of a secession from the Eglise Presbytérienne du Cameroun (cf. no. 3). In 1921 the Mission had opened a Bible School in Bibia, near Lolodorf, for the training of African leaders. It was soon raised to the level of a theological college; some of its brighter students continued their studies in Europe or North America. In 1934 a group of Christians in Ngoumba, led by Martin Bamba Minkio, broke away from the Mission over the issue of language; he was joined by two other pastors, Abraham Nzie Beaud and Rudolph Ngouah Beaud. The number quickly rose to 2,000. Lolodorf was the administrative center of the church. The choice of the name proved difficult. The first name, Eglise Protestante autochtone, was changed to Eglise Protestante Ngoumba, but, since this name seemed too restrictive, the church was renamed Eglise Protestante Africaine. The church has extended its work to areas like Mbalmayo, Abong-Mbang, Yaoundé, and Douala.

TM: **8,000** Congr: **29** PStations: **45** OrdM: **16 pastors** Eld: **200 to 250** Deac: **3 to 400** EvgHome: **1** Women Ord: **yes** As Ministers: **1985/1** as Deac: **since beginning / 80%** as Elders: **since beginning / 70%** ChurchOrg: **2 consistories, 1 evangelization zone (East province), 1 synod** Off/otherLang: **Kwassio, French (local languages in the Eastern part)** DoctrB: ApC Infant or believer's baptism: **both** Frequency of the Lord's Supper: **on church feast days** Periodicals: **Echos de l'esprit — Mapwo ma kyos (popular/4 times per year/200)** Close relations with: **Département Missionnaire de la Suisse Romande, Brot für die Welt (Germany)** NatRel: **FEMEC (1963)** RegRel: **AACC (1968)** IntlRel: **WCC (1968)**

Address: Eglise protestante africaine (E.P.A.), B.P. 6754, Yaoundé, Cameroon, Tel: +237 28 43 56, Fax: +237 28 43 75

5. Orthodox Presbyterian Church of Cameroon (EPCO) (1033)

This Church resulted from a breakaway from the EPC (cf. no. 3). In January 1967, a group of pastors left the 10th General Assembly of the EPC in protest against a series of decisions with ecumenical implications — joining the WCC, starting union negotiations, and founding a jointly run theological college in Douala. Under the leadership of Pastor Jean Andjongo they started the Eglise Presbytérienne Initiale. In February 1967 the EPC appealed to court denouncing the illegal appropriation of churches, manses, and schools by the new church. In December 1967, a court message began to circulate indicating that the court had decided in favor of the Eglise Presbytérienne Initiale. It turned out that the message originated, in fact, from a catechist by the name of Billé Ze Etienne in Douala. The authorities took severe action and arrested more than 100 pastors and laypeople. After a few months they were released, with the exception of Andjongo and Billé Ze Etienne, who were sentenced, respectively, to two and four years of imprisonment.

The EPC was prepared to readmit the secessionist group, but they remained separate. It was encouraged and supported by anti-ecumenical groups in the US and Europe, in particular the ICCC. Initially the government sought to prevent outside support. In 1970 the Church was officially registered. The name Eglise Presbytérienne Initiale was changed into the present name, and in the following decades the church experienced considerable growth.

TM: **100,000** BM: **97,800** CM: **78,600** Congr: **200** PStations: **365** OrdM: **70** Eld: **653** Deac: **1,362** EvgHome: **265** Mission: **nc** Women Ord: **yes** As Ministers: **no** as Deac: **1970/1362** as Elders: **1970-1985/23** ChurchOrg: **11 consistories, 3 synods, GenAssy** Off/otherLang: **French** DoctrB: **ApC, WestConf** Infant or believer's baptism: **both** Frequency of the Lord's Supper: **each trimester and during church meetings** IntlRel: **ICCC (1970)**

Address: Eglise Presbytérienne Camerounaise Orthodoxe (E.P.C.O.), B.P. 1418, Yaoundé, Cameroon, Tel: +237 206-770

CANADA

Area in km^2	9,976,140
Population	(July 1996 est.) 28,820,671 British Isles origin 40%, French origin 27%, other European 20%, indigenous Indian and Eskimo 1.5%, other, mostly Asian 11.5%
Religions in %	RCath 45%, United Church 12%, Angl 8%, Presb 1.5%, Greek Orth 0.8%, other 32% (1991)
Official/other languages	English (60.5%), French (23.8%), others (13%)

CCC (Canadian Council of Churches)

The world's second-largest country in land area, Canada had in 1995 a relatively small population of about 27 million. Most of its territory is sub-arctic and supports only a small population. Canada was first settled by French explorers and traders, but eventually came under English rule. The demands of the minority French constituency are a major feature of Canadian cultural life, and in recent years Quebec separatists have strained attempts to forge a new national unity. If Quebec were to separate, further fragmentation of the country is possible. Its well-organized aboriginal peoples are also a prominent feature in the large wilderness spaces of Canada. And on its western coast and interior urban areas, Asian immigration has increased rapidly in recent years.

Reformed presence came first with the French Huguenots, but they did not survive as an effective presence after the Catholic counter-reformation of 1685. Catholic pressure kept them from settling along the St. Lawrence River, where the population was concentrated.

In the 18th century immigrants from Scotland and Ireland, as well as Presb loyal to the English, came from the USA, firmly establishing a Reformed presence. The first presby was established in 1795 among Scottish immigrants. These early immigrants were from two groups of secession churches who left the Church of Scotland over the issue of who chose the minister — a patron or the people of the congregation. In 1817, they formed the Synod of Nova Scotia.

Church of Scotland immigrants formed two other synods in 1833. The Free Church, however, broke from the Church of Scotland in 1843, again over the patronage law, and this division was carried over into Canada. So by the 1850s there were three main strands of Presbyterianism: the secessionists who held a voluntary separation from the state, the Free Church followers who accepted state support but refused interference, and the Old Church branch who accepted some control and support from the state. In addition, there were several smaller groups, so that seven distinct bodies could be identified.

When state support of churches declined drastically in 1854, the differences in the main strands diminished. In 1860 the secession and free church streams in Nova Scotia joined to form one synod, and several similar unions followed in other areas. When Canada became a single nation in 1867, the Presb were also uniting across the nation. And in 1875, four churches, two from the secession/free church line and two in covenant with the Church of Scotland, joined to form the Presbyterian Church of Canada. In the late 19th century, the need for mission in the west stimulated cooperation and solidified the union the Presb had accomplished.

The same need to minister to the vast western provinces that kept the Presb together also drove them to cooperate with other groups in seeing that churches and mission stations appeared all over the western frontier. This led to another major union in 1925, when 70% of the Presbyterian Church joined three other bodies to form the United Church of Canada, Canada's largest church (cf. no. 17).

The Reformed Church in America made efforts in the 19th century to establish congr in Canada, but there was not a large immigrant base for this Dutch and German style of the Ref faith, and they remain among the smaller Ref churches.

In the 20th century, the relatively open border with the United States created or strengthened a number of cross-border churches. Several of the smaller denominations are part of international churches with members in Canada and the United States. Dutch immigration after World War II added significantly to one of these, the Christian Reformed Church, now the third largest of the churches surveyed here.

Denominations are listed below in alphabetical order.

1. Alliance of Reformed Churches (3244a)

Although half of the Alliance members are found in Canada, the administration is based in the United States (cf. United States).

TM: **nc** Congr: **nc** OrdM: **37**

Address: Alliance of Reformed Churches, 10532 Paw Paw Dr., Holland, MI 60438, USA, Tel: +1 616
772-2918

2. Associated Presbyterian Churches in Canada (3032)

These two congr, in Toronto and Vancouver, left the Free Presbyterian Church of Scotland in 1989.

Congr: **2** Off/otherLang: **English**

No other data have been made available

Address: Associated Presbyterian Churches in Canada, 646 Percival Court, Oshawa, ON L1K 1M4, Canada, Tel: +1 416 434-5334

3. Associate Reformed Presbyterian Church (Presbytery) (3019)

There are three congr, in Nova Scotia, New Brunswick, and Ontario, that are members of the Northeast Presbytery of the Associate Reformed Presbyterian Church (cf. United States).

Address: Associate Reformed Presbyterian Church, 1324 Marion Street, Columbia, S.C. 29201, USA

4. Canadian Reformed Churches (3029)

During a 1944 struggle in the Reformed Churches in The Netherlands, a group of churches that refused to obey the synod was expelled. They called themselves the Reformed Churches (Liberated). Immigrants from that church formed the Canadian Reformed Churches in 1950. They are found mainly in Ontario and the Western provinces, with three congr in the United States. Their closely knit communities usually support their own Christian day schools, and they run a teachers' college. They report their main challenges as secularism, materialism, and feminism.

TM: **14,200** BM: **6,800** CM: **7,400** Congr: **45** PStations: **2** OrdM: **49** Eld: **300** Deac: **140** EvgHome: **nc** Mission: **3** Women Ord: **no** ChurchOrg: **classes, regional synods, general synod** Off/otherLang: **English** DoctrB: **ApC, NicC, AthC, BelgC, CDort, HeidC,** Frequency of the Lord's Supper: **4 or 6 times per year** IntlRel: **ICRC (1993)** TheolSchool: **Theological College (Hamilton, Ontario)** Periodicals: **Clarion (gen/bi-weekly), Reformed Perspective (monthly), Diakonia (church personnel/ monthly/1,000), Mission News (mission/bi-monthly), In Holy Array (youth/monthly), Evangel (evangelism/4 times per year/1,500)**

Address: Canadian Reformed Churches, 5734 191 A Street, Surrey, B.C. V3S 7M8, Canada, Tel: +1 604 576-2124, Fax: +1 604 576-2101

5. Christian Reformed Church in North America (Canadian Branch) (3228a)

Congregations of the Christian Reformed Church in North America have been present in Canada since 1908. However, real growth of this branch of the CRCNA began after World War II, when many Dutch immigrants came to Canada and found a home in this church. Today the Canadian branch of the church is about one fourth of the whole CRCNA. It operates separate agencies for the distinct interests of the Canadian churches. It also participates ecumenically with other Canadian churches through its Canadian offices. A prime example of this has been its cooperation in the Canadian Food Grains Bank, through which churches can distribute excess Canadian production when they have proportional grants from their own sources. For further history, see the article on this church in the United States section.

TM: **81,805** BM: **33,255** CM: **48,550** Congr: **244** PStations: **21** OrdM: **218** Eld: **3,300** Deac: **nc** EvgHome: **36** Mission: **50** Women Ord: **Yes** As Ministers: **1995/1** as Deac: **nc** as Elders: **16** ChurchOrg: **12 classes in Canada, Council of Christian Reformed Churches in Canada, with synod as the broadest assembly, covering North America** Off/otherLang: **English** DoctrB: **BelgC, CDort, HeidC, Contemporary Testimony** Infant or believer's baptism: **both** Frequency of the Lord's Supper: **at least 4 times per year** Close relations with: **RefChurch in Canada** NatRel: **CCC (1996), Evangelical Fellowship of Canada (1988)** TheolSchool: **Calvin Theological Seminary** Periodicals: **Banner (mag/bi-weekly/nc)**

Address: Christian Reformed Church in North America (Canadian Branch), P.O. Box 5070, 3475 Mainway, Burlington, Ontario L7R 3Y8, Canada, Tel: +1 905 336-2920, Fax: +1 905 336-8344, E-mail: CassidyJ@CRCnet.mhs.compuserve.com.

6. Congregational Christian Churches in Canada (3017)

Organized in 1821, the Congregational Christian Churches left their original denominations, adding to their name the term *Christian*. The official national organization was formed only in 1989. It is a member of the World Evangelical Congregational Fellowship.

TM: **7,000** Congr: **70** OrdM: **123** Eld: **nc** Deac: **nc** EvgHome: **nc** Mission: **nc** Women Ord: **nc** As Ministers: **nc** as Deac: **nc** as Elders: **nc** ChurchOrg: **nc** Off/otherLang: **English** DoctrB: **nc** IntlRel: **WECF**

Address: Congregational Christian Churches in Canada, 222 Fairview Dr., Ste. 202, Brantford, ON, N3T 2W9, Canada, Tel: +1 519 758-1315, Fax: +1519 751-0852

6a. The Evangelical Covenant Church (3215a)

The Evangelical Covenant Church finds its roots in the Luth traditions of Sweden. As a fruit of the 19th-century revival movement and in protest against the Lutheran state church the Swedish Mission Covenant Church was founded in 1878 with a Reformed emphasis. The Evangelical Covenant Church is made up of immigrants from the Mission Covenant Church, and is its sister church in North America. Its main challenges have been the process of emerging from its immigrant roots into a North American body. The church emphasizes the personal freedom of its members and thus acknowledges both the practice of infant baptism and the practice of believer's baptism.

This church has 23 congr in Canada, but no organizational center. For further information cf. United States no. 15a.

7. Free Church of Scotland (3033)

This church has six congr, three of them on Prince Edward Island. They are represented at the Free Church Assembly in Edinburgh.

Congr: **6** Off/otherLang: **English** IntlRel: **ICRC**

No other data have been made available.

Address: Free Church of Scotland, P.O. Box 977, Montague PEI, COA 1R0, Canada, Tel: +1 902 838-4271

8. Free Presbyterian Church of North America (Irish) (3234a)

Affiliated with the Free Presbyterian Church of Ulster, this church has congr in Alberta, British Columbia, New Brunswick, and Ontario.

TM: **nc** Congr: **4** OrdM: **nc** Eld: **nc** Deac: **nc** EvgHome: **nc** Mission: **nc** Women Ord: **nc** As Ministers: **nc** as Deac: **nc** as Elders: **nc** ChurchOrg: **nc** Off/otherLang: **English** DoctrB: **nc**

Address: Free Presbyterian Church of North America, 209 N. Newtown Street Road, Newtown Square, PA 19073, Tel: +1 215 353-2309

9. Free Reformed Churches of North America (3220a)

Some immigrants from the Christian Reformed Churches in The Netherlands formed their own churches when they moved to Canada. There are 12 congr in Canada, most in Ontario and British Columbia (cf. United States).

10. Netherlands Reformed Congregations of North America (3227a)

(Cf. United States)

11. Federation of Orthodox Christian Reformed Churches (3016)

This group counts 14 congr in Canada and the USA. Most families in these congr broke away from the Christian Reformed Church in North America beginning in 1979. There are eight congr in Canada and six in the USA.

TM: **1,400** BM: **800** CM: **610** Congr: **14** OrdM: **14** Eld: **nc** Deac: **nc** EvgHome: **nc** Mission: **none** Women Ord: **no** ChurchOrg: **classes, synod** Off/otherLang: **English** DoctrB: **ApC, NicC, AthC,**

HeidC, CDort, BelgC, Calvinistic Reformed Infant or believer's baptism: **both** Frequency of the Lord's Supper: **at least 4 times per year** TheolSchool: **in various Reformed institutions** Periodicals: **The Trumpet (general/monthly/450)**

Address: Federation of Orthodox Christian Reformed Churches in North America, P.O. Box 26202, 242 Elmhurst Dr., Cambridge ON N1R 8E9, Canada, Tel: +1 519 623-9830, E-mail: trumpetocr@aol.com.

12. Presbyterian Church in America (Canadian Section) (3213a)

Canadian congr of the Presbyterian Church in America entered that body when the Reformed Presbyterian Church, Evangelical Synod joined the Presbyterian Church USA in 1982. Others have been added through evangelism since the merger. The Canadian churches report that secularism and unbelief provide an opportunity for their churches to witness, and they express concern about the ongoing issue of Quebec sovereignty (cf. United States no. 31).

TM: **1,100** BM: **500** CM: **600** Congr: **15** PStations: **none** OrdM: **16** Eld: **25** Deac: **20** EvgHome: **2** Mission: **2** Women Ord: **no** ChurchOrg: **presby, GenAssy** Off/otherLang: **English / Japanese, Arabic, French** DoctrB: **ApC, WestConf, WestCat** Infant or believer's baptism: **both** Frequency of the Lord's Supper: **from weekly to 4 times per year** Close relations with: **as per the PCA** NatRel: **via PCA** TheolSchool: **use schools of the PCA** Periodicals: **Periodicals of the PCA**

Address: Presbyterian Church in America (Canadian Section), 2581 E. 45th Ave., Vancouver, BC V5R 3B9, Canada, Tel: +1 604 438-8755

13. Presbyterian Church in Canada (3010)

The first Presbyterian church was set up by Irish settlers in Nova Scotia in 1761. The subsequent history of the Presbyterian Church may properly be said to begin with the cession of much of what became Canada to Britain in 1763. Among the settlers and fur traders to come to this newly available land were many Scots Presb. Scots and Scots-Irish would make up the bulk of most Presbyterian congr until very recent years. The English-speaking settlement of Canada was also hastened by the results of the American Revolution; defeated loyalists crossed into what remained British territory. Missionaries from northern American states followed these settlers and established some of the older congr.

Early Presbyterianism in Canada was shaped to a considerable degree by the quarrels and divisions of the Scottish Church. Most particularly, the disruption of 1843 out of which the Free Kirk of Scotland was formed affected church life in Canada. Canadian Presb churches aligned themselves with mother churches in the homeland. The folly of division over Scottish issues was early apparent, however, and strenuous efforts were made to overcome these divisions. In 1875 all the various strands of Presbyterianism came together to form the Presbyterian Church in Canada. This church body was by 1925 the largest Protestant body in Canada.

In 1902 the idea of a union with the Methodist Church, almost identical in size to the Presbyterian Church, was advanced by certain key Presbyterian leaders. Such a union would facilitate mission work, particularly in the West, and enable the churches more strongly to combat many social evils. Negotiations for union began in earnest in 1904. An early promise was made (and later regretted) that union must "carry the consent of the entire membership." Opposition, led by lay people and women in particular, grew through the subsequent years, however. When the new United Church of Canada was formed in 1925, all Methodists and all Congregationalists, but only two-thirds of Presbyterians, joined the new church.

The continuing Presb faced an enormous challenge in rebuilding a national structure. Approximately 90% of ministers had joined the United Church, so there was a desperate shortage of educated clergy. Subsequent years would be marked by an ultimately successful struggle to survive and rebuild as a national church. The theological course of the continuing church was also uncertain. In the end a dynamic professor of Knox College (later principal), Walter Bryden, influenced the church in a Barthian and neoorthodox direction.

Through the 1950s the Presbyterian Church profited, as did other churches, from the growth of the nation. Since that time social trends have caused great difficulties for this and all the so-called mainline churches of North America. The rise of secularism, a more permissive culture, the challenge of different views of sexuality, and a host of other difficulties face all North American churches. Like many mainline churches, the PCC has experienced a worrying decline in membership, especially among the young.

To some degree this trend has been counteracted by immigration. The church is no longer Scots and Scots-Irish alone. Infusions of vigor have come from Dutch, Guyanese, Chinese, and Korean immigration, to name but a few. The Presbyterian Church in Canada faces the new millennium as an increasingly multi-ethnic and multicultural body, searching for a renewed sense of mission in a world and country with an unpredictable future.

TM: **236,822** CM: **153,928** Congr: **1,100** PStations: **1,180** OrdM: **1,211** Eld: **nc** Deac: **nc** EvgHome: **nc** Mission: **nc** Women Ord: **yes** As Ministers: **1966/na** as Deac: **ne** as Elders: **1966/na** ChurchOrg: **Presbyterian** Off/otherLang: **English, French, Chinese, Korean, Hungarian** DoctrB: **ApC, NicC, HeidC, HelvC, WestConf** Infant or believer's baptism: **both** Frequency of the Lord's Supper: **4 times per year** Close relations with: **Angl Church, United Church of Canada, Christian Reformed Church** NatRel: **CCC** RegRel: **CANAAC** IntlRel: **WCC, WARC (1988)** TheolSchool: **Knox College (Toronto), Presbyterian College (Montreal), Vancouver School of Theology** Periodicals: **Presbyterian Record (gen/11 times a year/70,000), The Message Glad Tidings (mission/quarterly/na)**

Address: Presbyterian Church in Canada, 50 Wynford Drive, North York, Ontario M3C 1J7, Canada, Tel: +1 416 441-1111, Fax: +1 416 441-2825, E-mail: Thomas.Gemmell@presbyterian.ca.

14. Reformed Church in America (Regional Synod of Canada) (3206a)

The Regional Synod of Canada of the Reformed Church in America has 41 congr organized in three classes or districts. It is also known informally as the Reformed

Church in Canada. It has national membership in the Evangelical Fellowship of Canada and the Canadian Council of Churches (cf. United States).

TM: **4,096** BM: **6,700** CM: **4,096** Congr: **41** PStations: **51** OrdM: **40** Eld: **200** Deac: **150** EvgHome: **nc** Mission: **0** Women Ord: **yes** As Ministers: **1979/0** as Deac: **1979/10** as Elders: **1979/2** ChurchOrg: **consistory, classes, regional synod, general synod** Off/otherLang: **English** DoctrB: **ApC, NicC, HeidC, CDort** Infant or believer's baptism: **both** Frequency of the Lord's Supper: **monthly** Close relations with: **Council of Christian Churches in Canada** NatRel: **Evangelical Fellowship of Canada (1990), CCC (1990)** IntlRel: **WARC (via RCA in the USA)** Periodicals: **The Pioneer (home mission/ bi-monthly/2,500)**

Address: Reformed Church in America (Regional Synod of Canada), Reformed Church Center, R.R. 3, Cambridge, Ontario N1R 5S5, Canada, Tel: +1 519 622-1777, Fax: +1 519 622-1993, E-mail: RSCMoerman@aol.com.

15. Reformed Church of Quebec (3026)

The Reformed Church of Quebec (RCQ) was formally established in 1988; however, there was a Reformed presence in Quebec much earlier. Huguenot settlers were numerous among the settlers of New France, and some governors of the French territory were Huguenot. Following the Edict of Nantes (1685), which outlawed the Protestant church, Huguenot refugees were among many of the francophone settlers. After the Napoleonic reforms, churches were founded. When the mission society turned these congr over to the Presbyterian church in Canada, some 25 parishes with churches and schools were established. As the mission interests of the Presb turned west, however, the churches in Quebec declined, reaching a low point of three congr in 1975.

At that point the Christian Reformed Church began mission work, with the goal of establishing one francophone Ref church. They were assisted by the Presbyterian Church in America. In 1984 a council of Ref churches was formed, and it proposed to form a single church. In 1988 nine congr joined to establish the RCQ. The RCQ has officially adopted the Heidelberg Catechism and the Westminster Confession as its creedal basis.

TM: **297** BM: **111** CM: **145** Congr: **6** PStations: **6** OrdM: **8** Eld: **7** Deac: **1** EvgHome: **1** Mission: **ne** Women Ord: **yes** As Ministers: **no** as Deac: **yes/0** as Elders: **no** ChurchOrg: **congregations, synod** Off/ otherLang: **French** DoctrB: **ApC, NicC, AthC, RochC, CDort, HeidC, WestConf** Infant or believer's baptism: **both** Frequency of the Lord's Supper: **weekly to monthly** Close relations with: **Canadian Reformed Churches, Presbyterian Church of America** NatRel: **none** IntlRel: **none** Periodicals: **"En lui" (parish news bulletin /quarterly/300)**

Address: L'Eglise Réformée du Québec, 5377 Maréchal Joffre, Charny, Québec G2E 5E7, Canada, Tel: +1 418 832-9143, Fax: +1 418 871-8452, E-mail: Farel@Qbc.clic.net.

16. Reformed Presbyterian Church of North America (3211a)

(Cf. the United States section)

17. United Church of Canada (3011)

In 1925, four church bodies joined to form the United Church of Canada. The founding members were the Methodist Church, Canada, the Congregational Union of Canada, the General Council of Union Churches, and 70% of the Presbyterian Church in Canada. The Wesleyan Methodists of Bermuda joined in 1930, and the Evangelical United Brethren in 1968. The union was the first in the world to cross historic denominational lines. Impetus for union came from the need to serve Canada's vast northwest and the desire for more effective overseas mission.

The United Church is Canada's largest Protestant church and includes various strata of the population. It is known for its consistent stand on social and environmental issues. It also has to face challenges of a large and diverse body, with debates about sexual ethics and other controversial questions. It maintains its ecumenical ties with the families from which it arose, being a member not only of the WCC but also of the WARC and the WMC.

The United Church has eleven theological training institutions, with some attached to major universities. The *United Church Observer* is the principal publication; there are three other periodicals covering liturgy and music, education, and mission.

TM: **3,093,120** CM: **728,134** Congr: **2,413** OrdM: **3,965** Eld: **na** Deac: **260** EvgHome: **na** Mission: **45** Women Ord: **yes** As Ministers: **1936/831** as Deac: **1980/244** as Elders: **1925/nc** ChurchOrg: **13 regional conferences, 94 districts presby** Off/otherLang: **English, French / other ethnic/aboriginal languages** DoctrB: **ApC, Basis of Union, and short, contemporary Creed** Infant or believer's baptism: **both** Frequency of the Lord's Supper: **monthy to quarterly** NatRel: **CCC (1944)** IntlRel: **WARC (1875), WMC (1881), WCC (1948)** Service infrastructure: **5 hospitals, 45 rest homes, 10 educational and 6 conference centers** Periodicals: **The United Church Observer (gen/monthly/ 119,000), Mandate (mission/quarterly/20,000), Exchange (adult education/twice yearly/4,500), Gathering (liturgy/music/ 3 times a year/3,500)** TheolSchools: **6 postsecondary universities, 6 colleges, 11 theological centers and colleges**

Address: United Church of Canada, 3250 Bloor St. W, Suite 300, Etobicoke, Ontario M8X 2Y4, Canada, Tel: +1 416 231-5931, Fax: +1 416 231-3103, E-mail: webmaster@uccan.org.

18. United Reformed Churches in North America (3250a)

This bi-national church has 27 congr in Canada (cf. the United States section).

TM: **nc** Congr: **27**

No other data have been made available.

Address: United Reformed Churches in North America, 3646 193rd Place, Lansing, IL, Tel: +1 718 418-5321, Fax: +1 718 418-5591

CENTRAL AFRICAN REPUBLIC

Area in km²	622,980
Population	(July 1996 est.) 3,274,426 Baya 34%, Banda 27%, Sara 10%, Mandjia 21%, Mboum 4%, M'Baka 4%, Europeans 6,500 (including 3,600 French)
Religions in %	indigenous beliefs 24%, Prot 25%, RCath 25%, Muslim 15%, other 11%
Official/other languages	French, Sangho (lingua franca and national language), Banda, Baya, Mandja, Arabic, Hausa, Swahili

AEEC (Association des Eglises évangéliques du Centrafrique)

The Central African Republic was first known as the "Ubangi-Shari" (from the name of the two major rivers in the area). It was part of the former French Equatorial Africa until its independence in 1960. The country is predominantly agricultural, with more than 70% of the population living in outlying areas. Its main export earnings come from the export of lumber (13%) and of diamonds (80%). Between 1966 and 1979 the country was ruled by Jean Bedel Bokassa, who had served in the French army as captain and proclaimed himself field marshall and then Emperor. His demise was followed by several coups d'etat. In 1994 Ange Félix Patassé became the first democratically elected head of state.

RCath work in the area started first in the late 1880s, entering by way of Gabon and Congo-Brazzaville and spreading to the north and the east during the following decades. Prot were to follow with the Baptist Mid Mission, which arrived in 1912 in the eastern part of the area. Their emphasis was on evangelism, church planting, leadership training, and Bible translation. The Church of the Brethren came in 1919 and worked among the Karre tribe in the western part of the Ubangi-Shari. By 1940 they had 13 centers including Bangui, the capital. Their emphasis was on religious education, Christian literature, and medical care. The Swedish Baptist Mission started work in the southwestern part of the country. The Africa Inland Mission began its work in 1924 among the Zande tribe. The Swiss Pentecostal Mission started in 1927. Since the 1960s several other mission societies have arrived into the country. In 1977 the Bangui Evangelical School of Theology was opened as an initiative of the Association of Evangelicals of Africa and Madagascar (AEAM). Today it has some 60 students.

Although half of the population are Christians, animistic beliefs and practices continue to influence the people strongly.

1. Protestant Church of Christ The King (1300)

This church was established to serve the Prot French-speaking expatriates of different countries and backgrounds (including Presb, Ref, Meth, and Bapt). It has been strongly supported by the Société des Missions Evangéliques de Paris (Paris Mission Society), which provided the needed pastors. After independence, this church grew by inclusion of indigenous Prot. Today it relies almost exclusively on Central African personnel. Its Prot Youth Center has become, since its inception in 1968, a vital feature of the local public scene as a meeting place for various associations, for the school and university chaplaincy, for Bible camps, and for major socio-cultural events.

TM: **678** BM: **566** CM: **450** Congr: **2** OrdM: **4** Eld: **ne** Deac: **20** EvgHome: **ne** Mission: **ne** Women Ord: **yes** As Ministers: **1980/1** as Deac: **0** as Elders: **20** ChurchOrg: **Congregational (congr, GenAssy)** Off/otherLang: **French, Sangho (national language)** DoctrB: **nc** Infant or believer's baptism: **both** Frequency of the Lord's Supper: **monthly** NatRel: **AEEC (1984)** RegRel: **AACC** IntlRel: **WARC (1989), WCC, CEVAA** TheolSchool: **training at the Theological Faculty of Yaoundé (Cameroon)** Periodicals: **Partage (news bulletin/quarterly/400), Focus Maseka (women's magazine/bi-monthly)**

Address: Eglise protestante du Christ-Roi, B.P. 608, Rue des Missions, Bangui, Central African Republic, Tel: +236 618-070, Fax: +236 613561

2. Evangelical Church of Central Africa (1301)

This denomination is the fruit of the work done by the Africa Inland Mission.

No data have been made available.

Address: Eglise évangélique centrafricaine, Mission Protestante, Obo via Bangasson, Central African Republic

CHAD

Area in km²	1,259,200
Population	(July 1996 est.) 6,976,845 North and Center: Muslims (Arabs, Toubou, Hadjerai, Fulbe, Kotoko, Kanembou, Baguirmi, Boulala, Zaghawa, and Maba). South: non-Muslims (Sara, Ngambaye, Mbaye, Goulaye, Moundang, Moussei, Massa). Nonindigenous 150,000, of whom 1,000 are French
Religions in %	Muslim 55%, Christian 20%, indigenous beliefs (mostly animism) 25%
Official/other languages	French and Arabic / Sara and Sango (in South), more than 100 different languages and dialects

SUM (Sudan United Mission)

Chad, formerly part of French Equatorial Africa, became independent in 1960. The country is economically weak. More than 80% of the work force is involved in subsistence farming and fishing. Cotton accounts for at least half of the exports. The country is highly dependent on foreign aid, especially food credits, given chronic shortages in several regions. In the late 1980s the country was ravaged by civil war. Half of the population is Muslim and consists mainly of nomads living in the northern semi-desert area of the country. The south has rich vegetation and is inhabited by animists and Christians.

RCath missions started in the late 1920s. Today about half of the Christian population in the country is Catholic, organized in five dioceses: the first Chadian bishop was consecrated in 1987. Prot missions entered the country in the early 1920s. Several mission agencies were at work establishing different communities. In 1923 the Baptist Mid Mission started work in southern Chad among the Sara. In 1924 the Brethren Mission penetrated into Chad, coming from Cameroon, where it had established roots. SUM played a significant role in providing some coordination among various efforts. Substantial church growth took place in the 1940s. Churches planted by SUM agencies generally are self-supporting. In 1925 the Canadian branch of SUM started work in the southwestern province of Logone. In 1927 Dr. Olley, with the support of the Christian Mission to Many Lands, set up missionary work in southern Chad. In 1946 a dissident missionary of the Baptist Mid Mission established a new mission field in Central Chad which later became the Evangelical Mission of Guera (Mission évangélique du Guéra). In 1958 the Mission franco-romande du Tchad was set up as a SUM branch. It started work in the Ouaddaï region, the eastern part of Chad which is predominantly Muslim. Since then it became the Mission protestante franco-suisse du Tchad. In 1962 it received substantial personnel support from a British mission agency, the Worldwide Evangelization Crusade (WEC). The SUM branches of North America, Switzerland, and France, as well as the Mennonite Mission (EMEK) and WEC, decided to create the SUM Mission, which the Chadian government recognized in January 1963. In 1968 some missionaries left the SUM North American Branch to join TEAM (USA); in 1969 they became the United Evangelical Mission (MEU).

Occasional joint ventures are conducted by the Entente des Eglises et Missions évangéliques (EEMET), a loose association of evangelical missions and churches, which was established in 1964 and officially recognized by the civil authorities in 1988.

Address: EEMET, Secr. gen. Pasteur A Agouna Deliat, B.P. 2006, N'Djamena, Chad, Tel. +235 51 53
93, Fax +235 51 53 93

Evangelical Church of Chad (EET)

The fragmentation of Prot communities and tensions between mission bodies and local communities increasingly called for clarification. In 1962 extensive discussions took place among the various partners and led to the creation of the Evangelical Church of Chad. Basically, this denomination is the fruit of the joint efforts of the Sudan United Mission, the French Mennonites, and the Worldwide Evangelization Crusade (WEC). In the strict sense of the term, it does not belong to the Ref tradition. It claims some 200,000 members, worshiping in over 1,000 different places. It runs several tribal Bible schools as well as ESTES (Ecole supérieure de théologie évangélique). COCOAM (Comité de Coordination des Activités Missionnaires), set up in January, 1991, seeks to ensure closer collaboration.

Address: Eglise évangélique du Tchad, B.P. 821, N'Djamena, Chad

CHILE

Area in km²	756,950
Population	(July 1996 est.) 14,333,258 European and European-Indian 95%, Indian 3%, other 2%
Religions in %	RCath 76.7%, Prot 18.9%, Jewish 0.2%, others 4.2%
Official /other languages	Spanish

Originally inhabited by Indians (Araucans), Chile was conquered by the Spaniards in the middle of the 16th century. Santiago de Chile was founded in 1541, but Chile remained under the administration of Lima until 1778. The country became independent in 1818. The constitutions of 1833 and 1925 assured a democratic system. Increasingly the country became economically dependent on foreign powers. Attempts of the Democracia Cristiana (Edoardo Frei 1964-1970) and, later, of the socialist Unidad Popolar (Salvador Allende 1970-73) to introduce economic reforms failed. With the support of the United States, General Pinochet took power in 1973 and exercised repressive rule until 1990. Democratic elections were again held in 1994.

The RCath Church began to take root in the 16th century. The diocese of Santiago was founded in 1559. Until the middle of the 19th century the RCath was recognized as the state church. In 1865 religious freedom was granted to other religious communities; in 1875 the first non-Catholic community was registered as a juridical entity (Anglican Church). Today a wide variety of religious groups can be found in Chile. About 42 communities belong to the Concilio Evangélico de Chile.

Chilean Presbyterianism began with the arrival in Chile of Dr. David Trumbull in 1845. Trumbull, who was sent to Chile by the American and Foreign Missions Society of the Congregational Churches in the United States, began his work in Valparaiso, Chile's principal port. He was the first Protestant in Chile to engage in evangelism of the Spanish-speaking population. In the early years of his ministry his efforts focused on gaining legal and civil rights for non-Catholics in Chile. Supported since 1870 by the Presbyterian Church in the United States, the church gradually established congr in the principal cities, particularly in Santiago, the central valley of Chile, and the northern nitrate-mining areas, where English influence was strong.

Following Trumbull's death in 1889, other Presbyterian missionaries assumed direction of the **Iglesia Presbiteriana de Chile** (no. 1), which was at that time the Chile Presbytery under the Synod of New York of the Presbyterian Church in the United States of America. During the 20th century tensions became increasingly apparent between the American missionaries and the Chilean national pastors and elders. In the mid-1930s, younger Chilean pastors formed an evangelistic group which eventually allied itself with fundamentalist forces in the US. A first division occurred in 1944, when the **Iglesia Presbiteriana Nacional** (no. 2) separated from the Iglesia Presbiteriana de Chile. The Iglesia Presbiteriana Nacional established its congregations in Santiago, Valparaiso, and the central valley. Many of these were new congr, formed with a nucleus of persons who had left the Iglesia Presbiteriana de Chile.

By the 1950s there was increasing questioning of fundamentalist theology in the Iglesia Presbiteriana Nacional. As a consequence, in 1960 the fundamentalists left the church and formed the **Iglesia Presbiteriana Nacional Fundamentalista** (no. 3). They maintained relations with Carl McIntire's ICCC, while the Iglesia Presbiteriana Nacional established relations with the Presbyterian Church in America and with the Mission League of the Reformed Churches in the Netherlands.

Meanwhile, tensions continued in the **Iglesia Presbiteriana de Chile** between Chilean nationals and the American missionaries. By the late 1950s the US church began to reduce the number of missionaries assigned to Chile. In 1964 the Iglesia Presbiteriana de Chile became an independent and completely self-supporting denomination.

However, the end of the relationship with American missionaries did not put an end to division in the Iglesia Presbiteriana de Chile, and in 1972 the church divided yet again, with the congregations in the north of Chile and many in Valparaiso forming the **Iglesia Evangelica Presbiteriana** (no. 4). The Iglesia Evangelica Presbiteriana renewed relationships with the United Presbyterian Church in the United States of America, and became active in the WARC as well as in the Latin American Council of Churches (CLAI) and other ecumenical groups.

In the late 1980s the Presbyterian Church in America (PCA), a new denomination which split off from the PCUS (cf. United States no. 31) decided that missionaries in Chile ought to dedicate themselves to the establishment of new congregations instead of working in existing ones, and this resulted in the departure of the PCA missionaries from the Presby of the Iglesia Presbiteriana Nacional and the formation of the **Presbyterian Church in America (in Chile)** (cf. no. 5). The PCA missionaries have been successful in establishing several new congregations, particularly in Santiago.

The 1980s also saw the arrival of several missionaries of the Presbyterian Church of Korea in Chile. The **Korean Presbyterian Church** (no. 6) was founded in 1982 by Rev. Lim Soon-Sam, a missionary sent by the Presbyterian Church in Korea — TongHap (cf. Korea no. 14). While this church mainly consisted of Koreans living in Chile, the **Christian Presbyterian Church of Chile** (no. 7) owes its existence to an effort of evangelization among Spanish-speaking people. The **Korean United Church in Chile** (no. 8) was founded by missionaries of the Presbyterian Church in Korea — HapDong (cf. Korea no. 15); later it established relations with the Korean American Presbyterian Church (cf. United States no. 23). Recently, it has been joined by missionaries of Pentecostal churches; its character has thus been transformed.

In the 1990s efforts toward the reunion of the churches gained momentum. In 1994 the Iglesia Presbiteriana Nacional, the Iglesia Presbiteriana Cristiana, and the Iglesia Evangélica Presbiteriana formed the Association of Presbyterian and Reformed Churches in Chile (AIPRECH), with the Presbyterian Church of America (PCA) and the Iglesia Presbiteriana de Chile (cf. no. 1) as observers. In 1996 the Iglesia Presbiteriana Nacional, the Iglesia Presbiteriana Cristiana, and the Iglesia Evangélica Presbiteriana decided to form the General Assembly of a new united church as the next step toward the organic unity of the Presbyterian churches in Chile. However, in January 1998, the Iglesia Presbiteriana Nacional decided to withdraw from the Assembly, raising questions about the theological stance of the Iglesia Evangélica Presbiteriana. The spirit of unity has thus been diminished.

1. Presbyterian Church of Chile (2031)

TM: **1,850** BM: **600** CM: **1,250** Congr: **25** PStations: **23** OrdM: **16** Eld: **97** Deac: **58** EvgHome: **ne** Mission: **ne** Women Ord: **yes** As Ministers**: no** as Deac: **108** as Elders: **40** ChurchOrg: **consistories, 3 presby, 1 synod** Off/otherLang: **Castillano** DoctrB: **ApC, NicC, AthC, WestConf, HeidC** Infant or believer's baptism: **both** Frequency of the Lord's Supper**: 4 times a year and special occasions** Close relations with: **nc** NatRel: **Coordinación Evangélica (1993)** RegRel: **AIPRAL (1993)** IntlRel: **WARC (1984)** TheolSchool: **nc** Periodicals: **Acontario Presbiterano (info/gen)**

Address: Iglesia Presbiteriana de Chile, Casilla 22-58, Nuñoa Exeguel Fernandez 1144, Nuñoa-Santiago, Santiago D.F., Chile, Tel: +56 2 238-1188, Fax: +56 2 238-1188

2. National Presbyterian Church (IPNA) (2032)

TM: **1,390** BM: **1,390** CM: **700** Congr: **25** PStations: **5** OrdM: **16** Eld: **nc** Deac: **nc** EvgHome: **nc** Mission: **nc** Women Ord: **no** ChurchOrg: **nc** Off/otherLang: **Spanish** DoctrB: **ApC, NicC, HeidC, BelgC, WestConf, CDort** Infant or believer's baptism: **both** NatRel: **COE (Coordinación evangélica)** RegRel: **AIPRAL** IntlRel: **WARC (1994)** TheolSchool: **Evangelical Institute of Chile (IECH) (formerly John Calvin Seminary), IREP (Reformed Institute for Pastoral Studies)**

Address: Iglesia Presbiteriana Nacional de Chile, Casilla 14060, Avenida Brasil 153, Santiago de Chile D.F., Chile, Tel: +56 2 698-4838, Fax: +56 2 643-2251, E-mail: nc.

3. National Fundamentalist Presbyterian Church (2036)

TM: **500** CM: **200** Congr: **nc** OrdM: **nc** Women Ord: **na** ChurchOrg: **nc** Off/otherLang: **Spanish**
DoctrB: **nc** TheolSchool: **seminary in Quinta**

Address: Iglesia Presbiteriana Nacional Fundamentalista, Chile

4. Evangelical Presbyterian Church in Chile (2030)

TM: **600** CM: **480** Congr: **16** OrdM: **7** Women Ord: **yes** ChurchOrg: **nc** Off/otherLang: **Spanish**
DoctrB: **nc** NatRel: **Christian Brotherhood of Churches** RegRel: **CLAI** IntlRel: **WARC (1988)**
TheolSchool: **Evangelical Theological Community**

Address: Iglesia Evangélica Presbiteriana en Chile, Casilla 91, Nuble 658, Vallenar D.F., Chile, Tel:
+56 51 613811, Fax: +56 51 531464

5. Presbyterian Church in America (2037)

Congr: **5**

No other data have been made available.

Address: Iglesia Presbiteriana in America, Chile

6. Korean Presbyterian Church of Chile (2035)

The church was founded in 1982 by Rev. Lim Soon-Sam. It consists of one congregation, and its members are almost exclusively Koreans living in Chile. The
church is part of the Korean Presbyterian Church in America (cf. United States no.
24). Currently the congregation is served by Rev. Choi Chong-Nam.

TM: **400** BM: **150** CM: **250** Congr: **1** OrdM: **1** Eld: **2** Deac: **2** Women Ord.: **no** Off/otherLang: **Korean, Spanish** NatRel: **Iglesia Cristiana Presbiteriana de Chile (no. 7)**

Address: Iglesia Presbiteriana Coreana de Chile, Casilla 13970, Correo 21, Eusebio Lillo 333,
Recoleta, Santiago, Tel. +56 2 737 3672 or 737 2559, Fax: +56 2 732 0442

7. Christian Presbyterian Church of Chile (2038)

Rev. Lim Soon-Sam did not limit his efforts at evangelization to Koreans living in
Chile but started, in cooperation with the National Presbyterian Church (no. 2), to
plant congregations among Chilean people. Five congregations came into existence in Santiago and its suburbs; Rev. Lim trained Chilean pastors for evangelistic work. In 1987 three more missionaries from the Presbyterian Church in Korea
— TongHap (cf. Korea no. 14) joined him, and they succeeded in expanding the
church to Vinya and Temuco; in 1990 they also started work in Concepción. In the

first years the four missionaries formed a "Council of Korean Presbyterian Missionaries" in cooperation with the National Presbyterian Church. In 1994 they organized the Christian Presbyterian Church of Chile (ICP). While the first two moderators were Koreans, Chileans began to take leadership responsibility. Three Korean missionaries are still members of the Presbytery.

TM: **692** BM: **336** CM: **356** Congr: **12** PStations: **1** OrdM: **11** EvgHome: **5** Eld: **2** Deac: **21** WomenOrd: **no** Off/otherLang: **Spanish** DoctrB: **ApC, NicC, HeidC, WestConf** NatRel: **Iglesia Presbiteriana de Chile** IntlRel: **PCK (TongHap), PCUSA** TheolSchool: **Instituto Reformado de Estudios Pastorales, IREP**

Address: Iglesia Cristiana Presbiteriana de Chile, Casilla 560, Philippi 416, Temuco, Chile, Tel. +56 45 271062 or 272559, Fax +56 45 271062, E-mail: misangte@lazos.cl

8. Korean United Church in Chile (2034)

Founded by missionaries from the Presbyterian Church in Korea — HapDong (cf. Korea no. 15), the church today has adopted a Pent style. It has close relations with the Korean American Presbyterian Church (cf. United States no. 24).

TM: **342** BM: **159** CM: **159** Congr: **1** PStations: **0** OrdM: **1** Eld: **2** Deac: **72** EvgHome: **nc** WomenOrd: **no** As Ministers: **no** as Deac: **no** as Elders: **no** ChurchOrg: **family church** Off/otherLang: **Korean, Spanish** DoctrB: **ApC, HeidC, WestConf** Infant or believer's baptism: **both** Frequency of the Lord's Supper: **nc** Close relations with: **Iglesia Presbiteriana de Chile, Union Biblica Chilena, Korean American Presbyterian Church — GenAssy (1982)** NatRel: **Union Biblica Chilena (1993)** RegRel: **nc** TheolSchool: **nc** Service infrastructure: **nc** Periodicals: **El Jubileo (gen/1,500)**

Address: Iglesia Presbiteriana de Union Coreana en Chile, Casilla 325, Correo 3 Juan Vicuña, 1505, Santiago, Chile, Tel: +56 2 556-1732 or 341-0389, Fax: +56 2 556-7628, E-mail: kimJK@enteichile.net.

CHINA, PEOPLE'S REPUBLIC OF

Area in km^2	9,564,500
Population	1,185,000,000 55 national minorities
Religions in %	no statistics available
Official language / other languages	Mandarin / Han (92%), Cantonese, 55 major regional languages

There are currently no Reformed denominations in China, but Ref and Presb churches were an integral part of the history of Christianity in China. Missions from various countries have made a long and significant contribution to the Christian presence in China.

The first Prot missionaries, Robert and Mary Morrison, were **Scots Presbyterians** sent to China by the London Missionary Society (LMS) in 1807. Morrison's work on the translation of the Bible is well known.

- The first Americans to work in China were Elijah Bridgman, whose primary work was in the publication of Christian literature, and Peter Barker, the first medical missionary. Both were supported by the **ABCFM**. This early missionary society was nondenominational. The ABCFM was founded by members of the Congregational Church in New England but became the missionary society of Presb as well. Later, various Presbyterian and Reformed mission boards were in the vanguard of the growing number of societies at work in China.
- In 1842 missionaries of the **Reformed Church in America** (RCA) established a mission station in Xiamen (Amoy), and their work later spread to the other areas of Fujian (Fukien) Province. In 1848 they built the first Prot church in China.
- In 1844 the **Presbyterian Church in the United States of America** opened work in Ningbo (Ningpo). Over the next 50 years they founded eight other China missions in North China — Shandong, Jiangsu, Zhejiang (Chekiang), Anhui, Guangzhou (Kwangtung), Hunan, Hainan, and Yunnan.
- In 1847 the **English Presbyterians** began work in Shantou (Swatow) and quickly established a close working relationship with the RCA missionaries in the same province.
- In 1867 the **Presbyterian Church in the United States (South)** joined their Northern colleagues and founded two missions in Jiangsu and Zhejiang provinces.
- Irish Presbyterians began work in Manchuria in 1869, working in close cooperation with missionaries of the United Free Church of Scotland who arrived in 1872.
- The **Church of Scotland** established its one mission station at the Yangtse river port of Yichang (Ichang) in the interior province of Hubei in 1878.
- The **Presbyterian Church of Canada** began work in the province of Henan (Honan) in 1887.
- In 1897 the **Cumberland Presbyterian Church** in the United States began work at Changde (Changteh) in the fiercely anti-foreign province of Hunan. Later, when the Cumberlands united with the Presbyterian Church in the USA, their work was merged with that of the Northern Presb.
- The **Presbyterian Church of New Zealand** began work in Guangdong province in 1901.
- At the invitation of the American Presb (North), the **Korean Presbyterian Church** began a highly successful mission in Shandong in 1913.

By the first decade of the 20th century, eleven different Presb/Ref mission bodies were at work in China. They formed a substantial portion of the total Prot missionary presence. At an early date discussions began about establishing one

119

united Chinese Presbyterian Church. Essential theological differences appeared between the various bodies. Distances and dialects presented an even more serious problem. Moreover, each related differently to their home boards, which presented an obstacle for unity in China.

The first successful **plan of church union** was effected by the Reformed Church in America and English Presb in Fujian Province. Here a united presby ("Tai-hoe") was formed in 1864 which was independent of its mother churches both in America and Great Britain. Known as the **"Amoy Plan,"** it placed strong emphasis on self-government, self-support, and self-propagation.

The first attempt at establishing a united church on a national scale came in 1874 when the Northern Presb sponsored a conference to explore ways of establishing one Presbyterian Church for all of China. All Reformed and Presbyterian bodies plus the English Bapt and the ABCFM sent representatives to the conference. As a first step toward general union, a confederation of Presb churches was established which encouraged a greater degree of cooperation in local areas.

American Presb, North and South, established the "Synod of the Five Provinces" in 1906 which united the various missions at work in Central China. The newly formed synod was independent of control from mother churches in the USA. In the following year **a Council of Presbyterian churches** was formed which included the following eight Presb/Ref missions:

- The Presbyterian Church in the USA (North)
- The Presbyterian Church in the USA (South)
- The Reformed Church in America
- The Church of Scotland
- The United Free Church of Scotland
- The Presbyterian Church of Canada
- The Presbyterian Church in Ireland
- The Presbyterian Church of England

A "Declaration and Resolution of Union of the Presbyterian Church of Christ in China" was adopted, which noted the substantial doctrinal agreements of the eight denominations but agreed that "The Presbyterian Church of China, being autonomous, will have the prerogatives of formulating its own standards. But these will, we believe, in the Providence of God, and under the teaching of His Holy Spirit, be in essential harmony with the creeds of the parent churches. Until such standards are adopted, the different sections of the church may adhere to their own standards."

The third meeting of the Council convened in Jinan (Tsinan) in 1914, with delegates from churches with approximately 60,000 communicant members in Manchuria, Hebei, Shandong, Henan, Anhui, Jiangsu, Zhejiang, Fujian, and Guangdong. The Chinese delegates without exception were in favor of moving as soon as possible toward consummating the union by forming a General Assembly. The issue was referred to the presby for a vote.

The next year the Council met in Shanghai, with the overwhelming number of

120

presby reporting in favor of establishing a General Assembly; shortly afterward a committee was appointed to work on a proposed constitution. The General Assembly of the new Presbyterian Church met in Shanghai on April 1922, representing 6 synods, 25 presby, and 77,000 communicant members. The Rev. P. Frank Price of the Southern Presbyterian Mission was elected the first moderator. An extensive debate on the name of the new church was held. The Chinese delegates were strongly opposed to including any denominational name and also opposed to including the word "united" on the grounds that the new church was to be in its own right a Chinese church and not just a "union of Western denominations." The name chosen was "The Church of Christ in China" (Chung Hua Chi Tu Chiao Hui). An invitation was extended to other church bodies to join in a wider church union.

As the momentum for church union continued to build, two of the oldest and most prestigious mission boards — the London Missionary Society (LMS) and the ABCFM — decided to enter the negotiations even though they were congregational in polity. Later the following bodies joined the union movement: English Bapt, the Disciples, the Swedish Missionary Society, some indigenous Chinese churches, and some affiliated with the China Inland Mission.

But undertaking a wider union so soon after the Presb had united was risky business. The broader the union became, the more difficult it would be to include missions and churches with different views on theology and polity. The Rev. Asher R. Kepler, Presb, USA, was asked to serve as the organizing secretary of the proposed union. For the next five years negotiations continued toward translating the high ideals of the union movement into practical reality.

The **Church of Christ in China** (CCC) was consummated when the first Assembly met in Shanghai in October 1927. Present were 88 commissioners (66 of whom were Chinese) representing 11 synods and 46 district associations with 120,000 communicant members. The new church included approximately one-third of the Prot Christians of China. Dr. C. Y. Cheng, whose background was with the LMS in Peking, was elected moderator.

In general, church polity followed the historic Presb form, with local sessions governed by either elders or deacons. District associations corresponded to presby. Synods, based on geographic areas covering one or more provinces, formed the basic structure of the CCC. Each synod had the freedom to organize itself according to its own principles — in many cases following the predominant denominational polity of the church or mission in that area. Matters such as baptism by sprinkling or immersion, infant or believer's baptism, and ministerial ordinations were left to each synod. The Assembly representing the national church met every three or four years.

The constitution included a "Bond of Union" and a brief statement of faith which affirmed (1) "Our faith in Jesus Christ as Redeemer and Lord . . . (2) The Holy Scriptures of the Old and New Testaments as the divinely inspired word of God, and the supreme authority in matters of faith and duty, and (3) the Apostles' Creed as expressing the fundamental doctrines of our common evangelical faith." A committee was appointed to draw up a more complete confession of faith, but it was never completed because of the turbulent nature of the times.

121

The history of the Church of Christ in China spanned twenty years of war and revolution. During the critical years of the conflict with Japan (1937-48), the CCC operated two headquarters — one in Shanghai and one in Chengdu in West (Free) China. During these years the CCC engaged in numerous relief activities, including service to wounded soldiers, and expanded its pioneer missionary witness to China's western frontier. In 1948 it reported an adult communicant membership of 166,000 with a Christian constituency of half a million. The fifth and last meeting of its General Assembly was held in Suzhou in 1948.

While it never achieved the hope of bringing together the bulk of Prot Christianity in China, the Church of Christ in China represented a substantial proportion of the whole. It sought to establish an identity as an indigenous Chinese church and, with the exception of distinctively indigenous Chinese movements, came nearer to that goal than any other church in China. Many Chinese involved in the history of the CCC bore a significant witness in the ecumenical movement (Cheng Chingyi at the Edinburgh Conference in 1910, Timothy Tingfang Lew at the Lausanne Conference in 1927).

Reference should be made to the continental European mission societies working in China during the 19th and 20th centuries. Though their mission work was not specifically Reformed, the Ref heritage played a role in their interdenominational efforts. In 1847 the first four missionaries of the "Evangelische Missionsgesellschaft in Basel" (Basel Mission) and of the Rhenish Mission Society in Wuppertal-Barmen arrived in Hong Kong. Both societies had finally responded positively to the requests repeatedly issued by Karl A. F. Gützlaff. After a brief period of common efforts the two societies began to work independently: the Basel Mission among the Hakka, mainly in the east of Guangdong province, and the Rhenish Mission among the Cantonese in the south of Guangdong province. The two missions did not seek to set up denominational churches. Missionaries were of both Luth and Ref background. The Rhenish Mission, with its roots in the Prussian Union (cf. Germany), recruited its missionaries among both Luth and Reformed. The churches which resulted from their work merged with other existing churches in 1957 when all denominations in China became defunct. In 1980 they became part of the China Christian Council (cf. below). In Hong Kong, the Tsun Tsin Mission and the Rhenish Mission joined the Lutheran World Federation in the '70s.

The Berlin Mission Society began work in Guangdong and Jiangxi provinces in 1882, and was active in Jiaozhou, Shandong province, from 1898 to 1924. Though missionaries were both Luth and Reformed, the congr which resulted from their work were integrated into the Lutheran Church and later became part of the China Christian Council (cf. below).

An important Christian community has developed in the northeastern part of China among the population of Korean origin. Koreans immigrated into the area from the second half of the 19th century to the end of World War II. They number today about two million. At an early date Korean and Canadian missionaries were active among them. The congr which were founded belonged to various presby in Korea. In 1921 the independent Gando Presbytery was established; its name was later changed into Dong Man Presbytery. In 1938 there were altogether about

22,000 Presb in the area. In 1940 all Christian communities, regardless of their denominational identity, were forced by the Japanese occupation authorities to organize themselves as the Korean Christian Federation of Manchuria, later called the Korean Church of Christ in Manchuria. After World War II the number of Koreans drastically decreased and only a few Korean Christian communities survived. With the end of the Cultural Revolution their situation was eased and their numbers began to grow again rapidly. When in 1992 China and Korea established diplomatic relations, more and more Korean missionaries became active in northeastern China. Most of them operate without coordination with the China Christian Council. Many regard northeastern China as the base for future missionary work in North Korea.

After the establishment of the People's Republic of China in 1949 all missionaries had to leave the country and all church councils, assemblies, and synods with ties to the historic Western churches were dissolved. Their place was taken by the distinctive Chinese church organization called the Protestant "Three Self Movement." Many leaders, at both national and provincial levels, took part in this movement and saw it consistent with what their Ref heritage taught them (H. H. Tsui, Peter W. H. Tsai, and Peter Wong). In eclipse during the ten years of the Cultural Revolution (1966-1976), it reemerged in 1979 when religious activities were again officially admitted.

During the years of repression Christianity, especially Prot Christianity, has grown considerably and has increasingly taken root in China. Today, several million confess the Christian faith. In 1980 the **China Christian Council** was founded; it includes practically all former Prot churches. There are, however, Protestant communities which exist apart from the China Christian Council and the Three-Self Movement. Prot Christianity in China considers itself "post-denominational"; the China Christian Council seeks to serve all Protestant communities in the country. The China Christian Council seeks to become one united Christian — Protestant — Church. This process has not yet been completed. But a common order, designed in 1992, has been officially adopted by the Sixth National Chinese Christian Conference in January 1997. The order incorporates Ref elements in its recognition of the role of elders and the laity.

The China Christian Council was accepted as a member of the World Council of Churches in 1991; it maintains close relations with many Ref and Presb Churches around the world.

Through the 19th and 20th centuries, Ref churches contributed to the educational, medical, and social welfare developments of the Chinese nation. Although there are no Presb or Ref churches in the People's Republic of China today, the Presb/Ref church heritage has made a distinctive contribution to the vital and growing Christian movement in that land in terms of worship, liturgy, theological education, and polity.

Since the Presb or Ref churches do not exist in China as separate bodies, no detailed statistical data are given here. The estimates of Prot Christianity in China vary considerably. A recent publication of the Amity Foundation in China gives 9.85 million as the lowest and 13.7 million as the highest estimate.

Address: China Christian Council, 169 Yuan Ming Yuen Road, Shanghai 200002; Nanjing Office: 17 Da Jian Yin Xiang, Nanjing 210029, E-mail: cccnjo@public1.ptt.js.cn

HONG KONG
(SPECIAL ADMINISTRATIVE REGION OF PEOPLE'S REPUBLIC OF CHINA)

Area in km²	1,040
Population	(July 1996 est.) 6,305,413 Chinese 95%, other 5%
Religions in %	mixture of local religions 90%, Christian 10%
Official/other languages	Chinese (Cantonese), English

HKCC (Hong Kong Christian Council)

In 1842/43 Hong Kong became a British Crown colony. Several times the territory was expanded. In 1860 Kowloon was added, and in 1898 a treaty was concluded for a period of 100 years. After the victory of the revolution in mainland China the population of the city increased massively. In July1997 the colonial territory returned to Chinese sovereignty.

The Christian community numbers about 500,000 — about equally divided between RCath and Prot. The Ref churches are a minority among the very diverse groups of the Prot community.

1. Church of Christ in China, The Hong Kong Council (4040)

This Church represents the Hong Kong part of the Church of Christ in China, which was formed in 1927 (see above). The Hong Kong Council was organized in 1950. It is an interdenominational church within which the Presb and Ref traditions play a significant role. Strong emphasis is placed on educational work; the church operates 25 secondary and 34 primary schools.

TM: **24,271** CM: **20,000** Congr: **44** PStations: **31** OrdM: **52** Eld: **nc** Deac: **nc** EvgHome: **nc** Women Ord: **nc** ChurchOrg: **nc** Off/otherLang: **Cantonese, English, Mandarin** DoctrB: **nc** NatRel: **HKCC** RegRel: **CCA** IntlRel: **WCC, WARC, CWM, WMC** TheolSchool: **Theological Division of Chung Chi College (Chinese University of Hong Kong)** Service infrastructure: **34 primary and 25 secondary schools**

Address: The Hong Kong Council of the Church of Christ in China, Morrison Memorial Centre, 191 Prince Edward Road, Kowloon, Hong Kong (Special Administrative Region of China), Tel: +852 2397-1022 or 1050, Fax: +852 2397-7405

2. Cumberland Presbyterian Church (4041)

This church owes its existence to missionary efforts of the Cumberland Presbyterian Church (cf. United States). After an initial presence at the end of the 19th century, missionary work was launched in 1908 in the province of Canton by a Chinese, Rev. Gam Sing-Quah, who had been converted to Christianity in the United States. By 1949 there were 13 congr with about 1,500 members. In 1952, after the takeover of the Communist regime, the Cumberland Presbyterian Church concentrated its efforts on Hong Kong. In 1980 the seven congr — six in Hong Kong and one in Macao — were organized as a presby. In 1989 the church made a statement in support of the democratic movement in China.

TM: **780** CM: **450** Congr: **8** PStations: **13** OrdM: **4** Eld: **6** Deac: **na** EvgHome: **2** Mission: **none** Women Ord: **yes** As Ministers: **1** as Deac: **0** as Elders: **2** ChurchOrg: **Presbyterian** Off/otherLang: **Chinese, English** DoctrB: **same as Cumberland Church (USA)** NatRel: **Hong Kong Council of Churches** RegRel: **none** IntlRel: **none** Periodicals: **none**

Address: Cumberland Presbyterian Church, 1F Cheng Hong Building, 47-57 Temple Street, You Ma Tei Kowloon, Hong Kong (Special Administrative Region of China), Tel: +852 2783-8923, Fax: +852 2771-2726

3. Hong Kong Swatow Christian Church (4042)

Prot Christianity came to Swatow through the Basel Mission. The Basel missionary Lechler worked there from 1848 to 1852. After his expulsion English Presb missionaries arrived there in 1856. The LMS continued the work of this Presb Church. The first Swatow church was founded in Hong Kong in 1909 by Swatow traders who had settled there.

TM: **6,492** CM: **3,410** Congr: **10** PStations: **27** OrdM: **7** Eld: **13** Deac: **nc** EvgHome: **nc** Mission: **nc** Women Ord: **yes** As Ministers: **1** as Deac: **nc** as Elders: **3** ChurchOrg: **Presbyterian** Off/otherLang: **Chinese (Qiao Zhu, Putonghua)** DoctrB: **ApC**

Address: Hong Kong Swatow Christian Church, 20 Shelly Street, Hong Kong (Special Administrative Region of China), Tel: +852 2524-7915 or 7914, Fax: +852 2721-0256

4. The Man Lam Christian Church (4046)

This Church was founded in Hong Kong in 1938. In 1953 the congr acquired its first church building and soon associated itself with the Hong Kong Council of the Church of Christ in China. The church has close relations with the Reformed Church in America (cf. United States).

TM: **1,408** CM: **800** Congr: **3** OrdM: **4** Eld: **18** Deac: **nc** EvgHome: **nc** Mission: **nc** Women Ord: **yes** As Ministers: **nc** as Deac: **nc** as Elders: **yes** ChurchOrg: **nc** Off/otherLang: **Chinese (Fujian, Cantonese)** DoctrB: **nc**

Address: The Man Lam Christian Church, 9 Village Road, Happy Valley, Hong Kong (Special Administrative Region of China), Tel: +852 2838-0577, Fax: +852 2832-7141

5. The Chinese Christian Church of Amoy (4043)

After 1949 more and more Christians came to Hong Kong from Fujian. They first worshiped in homes in Kowloon city. In 1958 a church was founded by Rev. Kan Su Kok at 14 Tin Kwong Road, Kowloon.

TM: **682** CM: **682** Congr: **1** PStations: **1** OrdM: **1** Eld: **ne** Deac: **14** EvgHome: **nc** Mission: **nc** Women Ord: **nc** As Ministers: **nc** as Deac: **nc** as Elders: **nc** ChurchOrg: **Presbyterian** Off/otherLang: **Chinese (Fujian, Cantonese)** DoctrB: **nc**

Address: The Chinese Christian Church of Amoy, 14 Tin Kwong Road, Kowloon, Hong Kong (Special Administrative Region of China), Tel: +852 2711-1964 or 2463, Fax: +852 2714-0635

6. Hong Kong Chinese Presbyterian Church (4044)

This Church was founded in 1948 by Christians coming to Hong Kong mainly from the area of Si Yi, Guangdong Province.

TM: **160** CM: **120** Congr: **1** PStations: **3** OrdM: **1** Eld: **0** Deac: **nc** EvgHome: **nc** Mission: **nc** Women Ord: **nc** As Ministers: **nc** as Deac: **nc** as Elders: **nc** ChurchOrg: **Presbyterian** Off/otherLang: **Cantonese** DoctrB: **nc**

Address: Hong Kong Chinese Presbyterian Church, 80 Tai Po Road, 2/F B2, Kowloon, Hong Kong (Special Administrative Region of China), Tel: +852 2777-8485, Fax: +852 2490-2195

COLOMBIA

Area in km²	1,038,700
Population	(July 1996 est.) 36,813,161 mestizo 58%, white 20%, mulatto 14%, black 4%, mixed black-Indian 3%, Indian 1%
Religions in %	RCath 95%
Official/other languages	Spanish

CEDECOL (Confederación Evangélica de Colombia / Evangelical Federation of Colombia)

The first Prot arrived in Colombia through the British Legion, which supported Simon Bolivar and his struggle to free Venezuela, Colombia, Ecuador, Peru, and Bolivia from the Spanish empire. The first missionary, Henry Barrington Pratt, was sent by the Presb Church in the US; he arrived in Santa Maria in 1856 and soon after celebrated the first Prot service in Santa Fe de Bogotá. The first church was established in 1861. As in other Latin American countries, primary emphasis was placed on education. In 1868 Kate McFarren came to Bogotá or educational work. Under the direction of the Presb Church, the Colegio Americano for girls and in 1885 another school for boys were founded. Later, four other primary and high schools in Barranquilla, Bucaramanga, Ibagué, and Girardot were opened. Until the Second Vatican Council the situation of Prot in Colombia was precarious. Under varying pretexts they suffered discrimination and persecution. In recent decades their number has increased. In 1982 a theological seminary was founded to serve the churches in Colombia, Venezuela, and Ecuador.

Besides the Presb Church in Colombia there are other churches of Ref background. The Cumberland Presbyterian Church (cf. United States) has roots in the area of Cali, where it also runs a big high school. The Evangelical Reformed Church of Colombia owes its existence to Korean efforts. In 1987 Rev. Kim Wui-Dong arrived in the country and founded in Bogotá the Colombia Presbyterian Theological Seminary. Several congr were founded by Korean missionaries in Bogotá.

1. Presbyterian Church of Colombia

In recent years this church has gone through a period of conflicts. They were primarily due to struggles for leadership. In 1993 a mutual understanding was reached to separate into two synods. The properties of the church were divided between the two synods. But they continue to recognize each other as part of the same church. Many regard the situation as unsatisfactory, and there have been attempts in recent times to heal the rift.

a) Presbyterian Synod (2040)

This synod comprises three presbys (Central, Uraba, Costa/North) and about one third of the total membership.

TM: **4,500** BM: **4,500** CM: **4,500** Congr: **35** PStations: **25** OrdM: **30** Eld: **50** Deac: **175** EvgHome: **15** Mission: **0** Women Ord: **yes** As Ministers: **Oct. 1975** as Deac: **250** as Elders: **250** ChurchOrg: **Presbyterian (3 presby, 1 synod)** Off/otherLang: **Spanish** DoctrB: **ApC, NicC, WestConf** Infant or believer's baptism: **both** Frequency of the Lord's Supper: **monthly** NatRel: **CEDECOL (founding member)** RegRel: **CLAI** IntlRel: **WARC, WCC** TheolSchool: **Presbyterian Theological Seminary (Barranquilla)** Service infrastructure: **kindergartens, colleges, social services**

Address: Iglesia Presbiteriana de Colombia (Sinodo presbiteriano), AA 562 Carrera 46, No. 48-50, Barranquilla Atlco, Colombia, Tel: +57 5 351-2576, Fax: +57 5 351 2576, E-mail: precosta@b-quilla.cetcol.net.co.

b) Presbyterian Church of Colombia (Reformed Synod) (2042)

The Reformed Synod comprises four presbys.

TM: **5,673** BM: **5,673** CM: **5,600** Congr: **15** PStations: **65** OrdM: **42** Eld: **425** Deac: **340** EvgHome: **18** Mission: **2** Women Ord: **yes** As Ministers: **1980/8** as Deac: **1960/160** as Elders: **1950/280** ChurchOrg: **Presbyterian (4 presbys, one synod)** Off/otherLang: **Spanish** DoctrB: **ApC, NicC, HeidC, WestConf** Infant or believer's baptism: **both** Frequency of the Lord's Supper: **monthly** Close relations with: **Confederación Evangélica de Colombia** NatRel: **Alianza Reformada (1960), CEDECOL (1958)** RegRel: **AIPRAL (1978)** IntlRel: **WCC** TheolSchool: **Biblical Institute (Monteria), Presbyterian Theological Faculty of the South (Ibagué), Corporate Presbyterian Faculty (Bogotá)** Service infrastructure: **5 rest homes, 33 social service stations, 8 kindergartens, 16 colleges, and primary schools** Periodicals: **Evangelista Colombiano (mission/3 times a year), Liturgia Presbiteriana (liturgy/annual)**

Address: Iglesia Presbiteriana de Colombia (Sinodo Reformado), Carrera 4a # 4-11, Ibagué, Tolima, Colombia

2. Cumberland Presbyterian Church (2041)

This church grew out of missionary work of the Cumberland Presbyterian Church (cf. United States no. 14) in Cali, which started in 1929.

TM: **4,320** BM: **3,670** CM: **3,528** Congr: **32** PStations: **12** OrdM: **18** Eld: **75** Deac: **68** EvgHome: **0** Mission: **0** Women Ord: **yes** As Ministers: **1994/1** as Deac: **1928/nc** as Elders: **1928/nc** ChurchOrg: **Presbyterian (presby of the Andes, presby of Cauca Valley)** Off/otherLang: **Spanish** DoctrB: **ApC, NicC, HeidC, HelvC, WestConf, CDort, Confession of Faith of the Cumberland Presb Church** Infant or believer's baptism: **both** Frequency of the Lord's Supper: **monthly** NatRel: **CEDECOL (1950)** Service infrastructure: **American College, primary and secondary schools** Periodicals: **El Pregon Evangelico (gen/monthly/4,000)**

Address: Iglesia Presbiteriana Cumberland de Colombia, AA 7611 Avenida de las Américas 19 No. 18, Cali, Valle, Colombia, Tel: +57 2 668-7109, Fax: +57 2 339-1579

3. Evangelical Reformed Church of Colombia (2043)

This church was founded by Korean missionaries. Initially they worked within the Reformed Presbyterian Synod but then established, together with a number of members of the Synod, a separate church. They have congr in Bogotá.

No data have been made available.

Address: Iglesia Evangélica Reformada de Colombia, AA 103633 Transversal 40, # 150-46, local 274, Bogotá, D.C, Colombia, Tel: +57 1 615-0505, Fax: +571 258-0936

CONGO

Area in km²	341,821
Population	(July 1996 est.) 2,527,841 Kongo 48% (South); Sangha 20%, M'Bochi 12% (North); Teke 17%, Europeans 8,500 (mostly French) (Center)
Religions in %	RCath 53%, Prot 24.4%, Animists 19%, other 4%
Official/other languages	French / African languages (Lingala and Kikongo are the most widely used)

COEECC (Conseil oecuménique des églises chrétiennes du Congo — Ecumenical Council of Christian Churches of Congo)
ACEEDAC (Association pour la coopération des églises, l'environnement et le développement de l'Afrique — Association for the Cooperation of the Churches, the Environment and the Development of Africa)

The kingdom of Congo had been established in the 14th century. The Congo River was discovered in 1484 by the Portuguese Diogo Cão. In 1880 Pierre Savorgnan de Brazza established a French protectorate by a treaty with King Makoko. In 1910 Brazzaville became the capital of French Equatorial Africa. The country gained autonomy in 1957 and independence in 1960. In 1969 it became the first popular republic in Africa. For the last 25 years political troubles, including frequent bloodshed, have marked the development of Congo.

The Evangelical Church of the Congo (1045)

In 1909 missionaries from the Mission Covenant Church of Sweden came to Madzia in the then French Equatorial Africa (Moyen Congo) across the border from Belgian Congo (later called Zaïre, then Democratic Republic Congo) to start mission work. The Swedes were later joined by missionaries from the Covenant Churches of Norway and Finland. In 1961 an independent church was formed, The Evangelical Church of the Congo. It regards the Holy Scripture as the sole source of faith, and it has no creeds. Only adult baptism is practiced. Communion is celebrated by the pastor, and members distribute the elements. Pastors have been trained at the church's seminary at Ngouedi and Mansimou. The church has a fairly large social and community work program, especially in the health and medical sector, three schools for girls, and an "Institute for Training and Information," a joint undertaking with the Covenant Church of Sweden at Pointe Noire.

In 1947 a revival occurred at the Ngouedi pastors seminary and spread throughout the whole of Congo in the following years. It is considered to be one of the great African revivals. The number of members rose to 120,000 in the '70s from a population of 1.5 million people. The Synod is the highest decision-making body, and all the property — church buildings, schools, etc. — is owned by this central church body. The executive board is elected by the Synod. The church is divided into districts with superintendents. The church has cooperated with the RCath Church, the Kimbangist Church, and the Salvation Army in the "Conseil Oecuménique des Eglises chrétiennes du Congo" since 1970. A monthly paper, *Le Chemin*, is published by one of the local congr in Brazzaville.

The EEC is working in a country which has had great upheavals and economic problems during the last five years. The church is itself facing an economic and leadership crisis aggravated by ethnic tensions within the church. The EEC is actively trying to influence the democratic process in the Congo Republic through the Institute at Pointe Noire and through its seminaries and local congr. During the civil war in 1997 church property was heavily damaged by violence and looting.

The EEC cooperates in mission and development with evangelical churches in Sweden, Denmark, Ecuador, Finland, India, Japan, Nicaragua, Norway, and Congo-Kinshasa. In the mid-80s a pastor was sent to serve for some years as a missionary to Ecuador.

TM: **135,264** BM: **116,154** CM: **107,114** Congr: **111** PStations: **1,670** OrdM: **153 (38 retired)** Eld: **nc** Deac: **3,200** EvgHome: **210 (11 retired)** Mission: **1** Women Ord: **yes** As Ministers: **1985/6** as Deac: **1911/5120** as Elders: **nc** ChurchOrg: **synod, synod council consistories, parishes** Off/otherLang: **French, Lingala, Kituba** DoctrB: **ApC** Infant or believer's baptism: **believer** Frequency of the Lord's Supper: **monthly and on special feast days** Close relations with: **Covenant Church (Sweden), Evangelical Church (Norway), Evangelical Church (Finland)** NatRel: **COEECC (1970), ARCK (1994)** RegRel: **AACC (/1963), ACEEDAC (1988),** IntlRel: **WCC (1960), WARC (1994)**

Address: Eglise évangélique du Congo (EEC) — Dibundu ya nsangu ya mbote na Congo, Bacongo 3205, 1 rte de Djoué-Moukounizgouaka, Brazzaville, Congo, Tel: +242 834-037 or 830-263, Fax: +242 837-733

CONGO-KINSHASA

Area in km²	2,345,410
Population	(July 1996 est.) 46,498,539 over 200 African ethnic groups, the majority are Bantu; four largest tribes — Mongo, Luba, Kongo (all Bantu), and the Mangbetu-Azande (Hamitic) make up about 45% of the population
Religions in %	RCath 55%, Prot 25%, Kimbanguist 9%, Muslim 1%, syncretistic sects and traditional beliefs 10%
Official/other languages	French, Lingala (a lingua franca trade language), Kingwana (a dialect of Kiswahili or Swahili), Kikongo, Tshiluba, and many tribal languages

ECC (Eglise du Christ au Congo — Church of Christ in Congo)
ARCK (Alliance Réformée du Congo-Kinshasa — Reformed Alliance of
Congo-Kinshasa, formerly GOREZA)

The recent history of the country begins with the discovery of the Congo area by H.
M. Stanley (1841-1904) and the colonial domination which followed. Until June 30,
1960, the Congo was under Belgian domination. Decolonization threw the country
into a deep crisis. The major events were the attempted secession of the Katanga, the
assassination of Patrice Lumumba, nationalist prime minister of Meth origin, the rebellion of the Neo-Lumumbists, and the victory of Mobutu Sese Seko (1965).
Mobutu ruled the country for more than thirty years. In 1967 he founded the
Mouvement Populaire de la Révolution (MPR). In 1971, as part of a program of
Africanization *(authenticité)*, he renamed the country Zaire. As resistance to his dictatorial regime mounted, he agreed to certain concessions but at the same time succeeded for a long time in maintaining power. When he was forced to abdicate in
1997, the country was politically and economically ruined. Through a military action Laurent Désiré Kabila took power and proclaimed himself president.

Evangelization began in 1878 through two British missions. They were
followed by RCath missions. Soon, they also began courageously to denounce
the atrocities perpetrated by the colonial regime against the Congolese population, especially the system of forced labor. The Belgian administration encouraged and systematically supported the implantation and the development of
RCatholicism, especially through educational and social institutions. Until 1948
the official line followed by the administration was clearly anti-Prot. When ten
years later the colonial regime ended, Catholicism was one of the dominant factors in the country.

Of particular religious significance is the Kimbanguist movement, which
started after World War I. After a very short ministry in public the prophet Simon
Kimbangu was arrested by the Belgian authorities and kept in prison until his
death in 1954. The movement which he had initiated was forbidden but continued
to grow in secret. When, toward the end of the colonial period, it was officially
recognized, its adherents appeared in public and constituted themselves in a very
short time as a church. Today, the Church of Jesus Christ by the Prophet Simon
Kimbangu counts several million members.

At an early date the Prot missions affirmed their common ground and developed forms of ecumenical collaboration. The idea of a Church of Christ in
the Congo (ECC) was launched. Established in 1924, the Prot Council of Congo
(CPC) included 47 denominations. It was, together with the South African
Council of Churches, the first attempt within the framework of the International
Missionary Council (IMC) to coordinate structurally the work of missions. Prot
missions were active in the medical and educational fields. There were two tendencies among Prot. While the smaller denominations were rather conservative,
the larger churches tended to be more open to contemporary issues. The tension
between these two groups led in 1958 to the withdrawal of the CPC from the
IMC. Together with the Bapt and the Methodists the Presb churches were influ-

ential in the liberal camp and defended the idea of unity and collaboration within the CPC.

In 1970, under pressure from Mobutu and with the support of the World Council of Churches, those churches and mission agencies which were more open to the ecumenical movement and to new methods of mission work agreed to establish the Eglise du Christ au Congo, later called the Eglise du Christ au Zaire. Ref church leaders played an important role in realizing this union. The risks of the church being controlled by the Mobutist system were not immediately and sufficiently recognized. When the ambiguity of the situation became clearer, the same leaders began to criticize the authoritarian style of the ECZ leadership and, cautiously, also the political system.

In this context, in 1988, the Reformed Conference of Zaire (COREZA, now ARCK) was founded; it includes the following churches: the Community of the Disciples of Christ (CDC), the Evangelical Community in Congo (CEC), the Presbyterian Community in Occidental Kasai (CPKOC), the Presbyterian Community in Oriental Kasai (CPKOR), the Presbyterian Community of Kinshasa (CPK), the Presbyterian Community in Congo (CPCA), the Reformed Community of Presb (CRP), the Prot Community of Shaba/Katanga (CPSHA). The ARCK did not wish to separate itself from the ECC but rather to strengthen its unity though maintaining a separate framework of communion and Ref witness within the Protestantism of the country. The ARCK militates for democracy and reconstruction of the country and seeks to promote inter-ethnic relations. In 1997 its name was changed to Alliance Réformée du Congo-Kinshasa (ARCK)

1. Presbyterian Community in the Congo (CPC) (1240)

The Presbyterian Community in the Congo, formerly CPZa, is numerically the most important Ref community in the Congo. It counts more than a million members. It grew out of the work of the American Presbyterian Congo Mission (APCM), which started in 1891. This was one of the three biggest mission agencies working in the Belgian Congo. It carried out an impressive work in the Kasai, through a large number of institutions (schools, hospitals, etc.). From the beginning the mission cooperated with other denominations. It has close links with the CPK (cf. no. 5) and the CPSHA (cf. no. 11). The APCM reacted at an early date against the repressive policy of the colonial administration. The heritage of protest against the violation of human rights marks the church to this day.

The CPC suffered from controversies and schisms in the decade from 1960 to 1970. The conflicts, magnified by inter-ethnic tensions, led to the foundation of three separate denominations: the Presbyterian Community of Eastern Kasai (cf. no. 2), the Presbyterian Community of Western Kasai (cf. no. 4), and the Reformed Community of Presb (cf. no. 3). Soon the separate groups began to feel the need for collaboration. Thus the split led to the foundation of the COREZA, now ARCK.

TM: **1,250,000** BM: **1,010,000** CM: **1,001,000** Congr: **525** PStations: **215** OrdM: **964** Eld: **810** Deac: **496** EvgHome: **38** Mission: **2** Women Ord: **yes** As Ministers: **1989/6** as Deac: **1962/204** as Elders: **1961/440** ChurchOrg: **congr, consistories, presby, GenAssy** Off/otherLang: **French, Tchiluba** DoctrB: **ApC, WestConf** Infant or believer's baptism: **both** Frequency of the Lord's Supper: **monthly** Close relations with: **Presbyterian Church USA** NatRel: **Eglise du Christ au Congo, no. 31 ARCK (1989)** RegRel: **AACC (1969)** IntlRel: **WARC (1968), WCC (1956)** TheolSchool: **Faculté de Théologie Réformée Kananga (Kasaï)** Service infrastructure: **5 hospitals, 2 orphanages, various schools**

Address: Communauté presbytérienne au Zaïre (CPZ), B.P. 117, Kananga Kasaï Occidental, Congo-Kinshasa

2. Presbyterian Community of Eastern Kasaï (CPKOR) (1244)

The church separated in 1967 from the Presbyterian Community in Congo (cf. no. 1). The split was primarily due to ethnic tensions. It has its roots in one of the most dynamic regions of the country. Unfortunately the church suffers from internal strife. The church belongs to ARCK and WARC but has no other international relations. A segment of the church functions separately, having obtained a provisional recognition from the government, but it has not been recognized by either ARCK or WARC.

TM: **27,210** BM: **19,316** CM: **16,203** Congr: **104** PStations: **46** OrdM: **148** Eld: **556** Deac: **605** EvgHome: **60** Mission: **ne** Women Ord: **yes** As Ministers: **0** as Deac: **1891/417** as Elders: **1891/215** ChurchOrg: **consistories, presby, synod** Off/otherLang: **Tchiluba, French** DoctrB: **ApC** Infant or believer's baptism: **both** Frequency of the Lord's Supper: **monthly** NatRel: **ECC no. 58 (1981)** ARCK **(1988)** IntlRel: **WARC (1989)** Service infrastructure: **4 medical centers, schools, pastoral institute (Kasonji)** Periodicals: **none**

Address: Communauté presbytérienne au Kasaï Oriental (CPKOR), B.P. 1692, Av. Mukelenge Ntumba, Mbuji-Mayi Kasaï Oriental, Congo-Kinshasa

3. Reformed Community of Presbyterians (C.R.P.) (1246)

The church split from the Presbyterian Community in Eastern Kasai (cf. no. 2) as a result of both theological and ethical tensions. Its present leader, Moise Kalonji Kaja, originally a minister of the Presbyterian Community in the Congo (cf. no. 1), identifies with the charismatic movement. He first became a member of CPKOR (cf. no. 2) but then decided to set up his own group within the Reformed Community of Presb. The church combines fundamentalist and Pentecostal features. A literalist reading of the Bible undergirds doctrinal orthodoxy. At the same time, elements of African religion are being reinterpreted in the light of the Bible, especially the Old Testament. New revelations, obtained through dreams and visions, are admitted by the church. In addition to the Apostles' Creed the Church has formulated its own confession of faith, called la "cerpéinne." Though the church remains attached to its Presbyterian origin, it has, in fact, become an Afro-Christian church. Theological education presents a challenge. The church belongs to both ARCK and WARC.

TM: **11,194** BM: **8,289** CM: **8,289** Congr: **21** OrdM: **28** Eld: **91** Deac: **66** EvgHome: **29** Mission: **ne** Women Ord: **no** ChurchOrg: **nc** Off/otherLang: **nc** DoctrB: **nc** Infant or believer's baptism: **nc** NatRel: **ECZ no. 60, ARCK** IntlRel: **WARC**

Address: Communauté Réformée des Presbytériens (C.R.P.), B.P. 875, 13 Salongo no. 3, Zone de la Kanshi, Mbuji Mayi Kasaï Oriental, Congo-Kinshasa

4. Presbyterian Community of Western Kasaï (CPKOC) (1243)

The church came into existence in 1982, following a controversy within the Presbyterian Community in the Congo. The leaders of the Eglise du Christ au Zaire made an attempt to impose an episcopal system on the Presbyterian community in Zaire. The church resisted, but Pastor Jean Bakatushipa, one of the important leaders of the church, was in favor of the proposal. He was consecrated as bishop. The General Assembly of the CPC (cf. no. 1) decided to excommunicate him. He and his followers became part of the Presbyterian Community in Eastern Kasai but then decided to set up their own group. In contrast to other divisions, this split did not cause too many ill feelings because Pastor Bakatushipa avoided any court action against his church of origin. He continues to seek reconciliation and to restore unity among Presb in the country.

TM: **28,000** BM: **28,000** CM: **15,000** Congr: **496** PStations: **92** OrdM: **124** Eld: **283** Deac: **222** EvgHome: **51** Mission: **0** Women Ord: **yes** As Ministers: **1982/8** as Deac: **1981/92** as Elders: **1981/68** ChurchOrg: **Presbyterian (congr, executive committee, GenAssy)** Off/otherLang: **French, Tchiluba** DoctrB: **ApC** Infant or believer's baptism: **both** Frequency of the Lord's Supper: **bi-monthly** NatRel: **ECC (1982), ARCK (1984)** IntlRel: **WARC (1989)** TheolSchool: **none** Service infrastructure: **4 health care centers, schools** Periodicals: **none**

Address: Communauté presbytérienne au Kasaï occidental (CPKOC), B.P. 153, Kananga, Congo-Kinshasa, E-mail: presb.-Kin@maf.org.

5. Presbyterian Community of Kinshasa (CPK) (1241)

The CPK was founded in 1955 by the Presbyterian Mission in Leopoldville, which was a branch of the American Presbyterian Congo Mission (APCM). It considered the evangelization of the urban population to be its principal vocation. Since many Presb, especially educated people, migrated to the capital, pastoral care needed to be provided. The church developed in close touch with the Presb community in the Kasai and other communities in the neighborhood of Kinshasa. The CPK was deeply involved in the unification of the Prot churches within the framework of the ECC. The lay members of the church were particularly dynamic and played a significant role in society; they gave the church a degree of visibility beyond its numerical strength.

After independence the church was shaken by tensions and divisions. More than 1,500 members separated in 1964 to form a Pentecostal community. Step by step the community regained its stability, largely due to the leadership of the Rev.

Josué Tshimungu. Though the CPK was a catalyst in the formation of the ECC, it now criticizes its clericalism and authoritarian style of leadership. It also speaks out on issues such as the democratization of the country and human rights. Working together with an important Baptist community in the same region, the CPK represents in the eyes of the public a progressive force. It has been a member of WARC since 1982 and provides the secretariat for the ARCK.

TM: **67,436** BM: **40,000** CM: **20,994** Congr: **74** PStations: **152** OrdM: **87** Eld: **705** Deac: **694** EvgHome: **21** Mission: **nc** Women Ord: **Yes** As Ministers: **1987/1** as Deac: **1968/250** as Elders: **1968/ 245** ChurchOrg: **Presbyterian (74 consistories, 11 presbyteries, 3 synods, GenAssy)** Off/otherLang: **Lingala, French** DoctrB: **ApC** Infant or believer's baptism: **both** Frequency of the Lord's Supper: **monthly** Close relations with: **PCUSA, PC Korea** NatRel: **ECC no. 32, ARCK (1987)** RegRel: **AACC (1963), ACEEDAC (Association pour la cooperation des églises l'environement et le dévelopement de l'Afrique) (1987)** IntlRel: **WARC (1982)** Service infrastructure: **6 health centers, 1 maternity ward (staff: 93), 45 primary schools (17,445 students), 33 secondary schools (10,461), 1 professional school**

Address: Communauté presbytérienne de Kinshasa (CPK), B.P. 91, Boulevard Lumumba no. 2860, Limete, Kinshasa, Congo-Kinshasa, Tel: +243 12 70661

6. Community of Disciples of Christ (CDCC) (1248)

The church owes its existence to the Disciples of Christ Congo Mission (DCCM) and has its roots in the Equator region. Missionary efforts began in 1897. American Bapt having done the groundwork, the DCCM found open doors. Certain DCCM missionaries courageously denounced the inhuman practices of the colonial régime. The DCCM promoted the cooperation of Prot missions, and had a leading role in education and health services. It worked together with Presb missionaries in the Kasai in the field of theological education. The mission agency in the USA encouraged the autonomy of the church and continued to support the new African leaders. The Disciples of Christ in the Congo became one of the important denominations, and its leaders were prominent in the creation and the life of the ECC. Rivalries between Disciples leaders and the negative role played by Mgr. Bokoleale as president of the ECC have damaged the reputation of the church among Prot of the Congo. The church does not belong to WARC. Though a founding member of COREZA, it suspended its participation in 1992.

TM: **720,000** CM: **470,000** Congr: **206** PStations: **1306** OrdM: **208** Eld: **48** Deac: **613** EvgHome: **54** Mission: **nc** Women Ord: **yes** As Ministers: **1994/7** as Deac: **1940/306** as Elders: **1952/8** ChurchOrg: **Presbyterian (congr, consistory, GenAssy)** Off/otherLang: **Lomongo, Lingala, some French** DoctrB: **Matt 16:16: You are the Christ, the Son of the living God** Infant or believer's baptism: **believer** Frequency of the Lord's Supper: **every Sunday** Close relations with: **Christian Church (Disciples of Christ) (USA), VEM (Germany)** NatRel: **ECZ no. 10** IntlRel: **WCC (1948)** Service infrastructure: **6 hospitals, 1 kindergarten, primary schools (171 staff), secondary schools (52 staff)** Periodicals: **Bulletin d'information des Disciples (monthly)**

Address: Communauté de Disciples du Christ (CDCZ), B.P. 178, Avenue du Zaire no. 5, Mbandaka, Congo-Kinshasa, Tel: +243 31 062 2314

7. Evangelical Community in Congo (CEC) (1242)

The church came into being through the missionary action of the Svenska Missionsförbundet (SMF, cf. Sweden), which started in 1881. Choosing as their center the Lower-Congo, where British and American Baptists were already at work, the SMF contributed to the Prot presence in this region especially through the interdenominational center of Kimpese. SMF shared with the Bapt the practice of believer's baptism. One of the SMF missionaries became General Secretary of the CPC. The indigenous community resulting from the Swedish mission was strongly marked by a revival movement of Pentecostal inspiration. After independence, the church, now called the Evangelical Church of Manyanga-Matadi, pursued the task of evangelization. Together with two Baptist groups, it founded the Theological School in Kinshasa. It was active in creating the ECC. Through the participation of several of its leaders in the work of the WCC the church became more conscious of its Ref heritage. The CEC is a founding member of the COREZA (ARCK). It has recently developed programs of political education in rural areas. The Swedish government supports some church projects.

TM: **64,453** BM: **3,023** CM: **64,453** Congr: **71** PStations: **519** OrdM: **91** Eld: **ne** Deac: **4,471** EvgHome: **2,073** Mission: **1** Women Ord: **yes** As Ministers: **1975/6** as Deac: **2,700** ChurchOrg: **parish, consistory, synodal council, synod** Off/otherLang: **Kikongo, Lingala, French** DoctrB: **ApC** Infant or believer's baptism: **believer** Frequency of the Lord's Supper: **monthly** NatRel: **ECC no. 23, ARCK** RegRel: **AACC** IntlRel: **WCC, WARC** Service infrastructure: **5 hospitals (10 doctors, 174 nurses), 74 primary and 39 secondary schools (21,973; 6,371 students, 706; 676 teachers)**

Address: Communauté évangélique du Congo (CEC), B.P. 36, Luozi Bas-Congo, Congo-Kinshasa

8. Evangelical Community in Ubangi-Mongala (CEUM) (1237)

The church came into existence through missionary efforts of the (Swedish) Mission Covenant Church in the United States (cf. United States no. 15a). The Mission Covenant Church in the USA has close links with the Svenska Missionsförbündet (cf. Sweden). In 1927 a delegation of the Church in Sweden visited the Swedish Evangelical Mission Covenant Church in the United States. In 1937 the church changed its name to Evangelical Covenant Church of America. In the same year the church developed plans for missionary work in central Africa. As investigations in the French Congo failed, the missionaries of the Covenant Church, with the support of the Conseil Protestant du Congo and the Svenska Missionsförbündet, started work in the far northwest of the Belgian Congo. Before independence this church closely collaborated with the Disciples of Christ (cf. no. 6), especially in the field of education. It also sent students to the medical school of Kimpese (cf. CEC, no. 7). Having its roots in the region of origin of late president Mobutu, the church enjoyed certain advantages but was also faced with considerable difficulties. The church belongs to the Eglise du Christ au Congo (ECC), but it is not a member of WARC or ARCK.

136

No statistical data have been made available.

Address: Communauté évangélique en Ubangi-Mongala (CEUM), B.P. 140, Gemena, Congo-Kinshasa

9. Evangelical Community of Christ in Ubangui (CECU) (1247)

The church grew out of missionary efforts of the Evangelical Free Church of America, a small denomination of Swedish origin, closely related but distinct from the Evangelical Covenant Church of America (cf. Evangelical Community of Christ in Ubangi-Mongala, above). After exploratory journeys by T. M. Johnson, the mission settled in 1923 in the northwest of the then Belgian Congo. It was first called the Swedish American Mission and later renamed the Evangelical Mission in Ubangi. Like its sister church, the Evangelical Community of Christ in Ubangi-Mongala (cf. no. 8), the CECU is implanted in the region whose population had the same ethnic background as late President Mobutu; it is therefore somewhat suspect in the eyes of those from other parts of the country. The church belongs to the Eglise du Christ au Congo (ECC), but it is not a member of WARC or ARCK.

No statistical data have been made available.

Address: Communauté évangélique du Christ en Ubangui (CECU), B.P. 145, Gemena Equateur, Congo-Kinshasa

10. Evangelical Community of Kwango (CKE) (1236)

Mission work in the Kwango area was initiated in 1924 by a mission agency called Unevangelized Tribe Mission (UTM). This resulted in the foundation of mission stations in Wamba-Luadi (1939), Matamba-Solo (1941), and Kasongo-Lunda (1945); the headquarters of the church are in Kasongo-Lunda, where the king of the Bajaka is also residing. At the end of the 1940s another mission agency, the Baptist Mid Mission, started activities in the Kwango area. As tensions arose, the UTM decided to leave the country. Since 1952 missionaries from Switzerland and Germany have been active in the area. In 1958 the church was officially recognized by the state authorities, and in 1960 the Deaconess House *Ländli* in Switzerland accepted responsibility for the mission station in Wamba-Luadi. Both educational work and health services expanded. During the turbulence subsequent to independence the church went through difficult times. Missionaries resumed work in 1968. In 1970 the church gained independence. The church belongs to the Eglise du Christ au Congo.

No data have been made available.

Address: Communauté évangélique du Kwango (CKE), B.P. 4830, Kinshasa-Gombe, Congo-Kinshasa

11. Protestant Community of Shaba (CPSHA) (1245)

The CPSHA started in 1953 through an effort of Belgian Prot. The church was then called Protestant Church of Katanga (EPROKAT). Though it includes Prot of other denominations, it remains attached to the Ref tradition. Like the CPK (cf. no. 5) it sought to respond to the emerging urban population. The members of the CPSHA are mainly Presb who have moved from Kasai to the mining centers in Shaba. Attempts at collaboration with CPC (cf. no. 1) failed. Out of fear of being absorbed by the CPSHA, the CPC creates its own congr in the region. In the course of the last decades it has been decisively weakened.

TM: **18,000** BM: **8,200** CM: **8,200** Congr: **28** PStations: **34** OrdM: **28** Eld: **300** Deac: **480** EvgHome: **54** Mission: **ne** Women Ord: **yes** As Ministers: **1992/22** as Deac: **1960/168** as Elders: **1960/84** ChurchOrg: **consistories, presby, synod or regional council, GenAssy** Off/otherLang: **nc** DoctrB: **ApC, HeidC** Infant or believer's baptism: **both** Frequency of the Lord's Supper: **3 to 6 times a year** Close relations with: **Belgic founders** NatRel: **ECC no. 46 (1972)** IntlRel: **WARC (1989), ICCC (1995)** Service infrastructure: **6 centers for young women and mothers, 10 kindergartens, 30 primary schools, 12 secondary schools, 4 professional schools**

Address: Communauté Protestante au Shaba (CPSHA), B.P. 400, Avenue Kaniama No. 1, Zone de Katuba II, Lubumbashi, Congo-Kinshasa

12. Confessing Reformed Church in Congo (ERCC) (1239)

The church grew out of a broadcasting program "Reformed Perspectives," which was started in 1978 by Rev. A. R. Kayayan. He was financially and spiritually supported by the Dutch Reformed Church (NGK) from South Africa and by the Christian Reformed Church in North America. The church was officially registered by the state authorities in 1991.

TM: **24,000** BM: **16,283** CM: **13,500** Congr: **200** PStations: **200** OrdM: **3** Eld: **600** Deac: **400** EvgHome: **542** Mission: **ne** Women Ord: **no** ChurchOrg: **Presbyterian (congr, consistories, regional synods, general synod)** Off/otherLang: **French** DoctrB: **ApC, NicC, AthC, HeidC, CDort, RochC, Calvinistic** Infant or believer's baptism: **both** Frequency of the Lord's Supper: **Christmas, Easter, Pentecost, Ascension Day** Close relations with: **Reformed Churches (Liberated) (NL), NGK, Reformed Church US, Christian Reformed Church NA** NatRel: **none** RegRel: **none** IntlRel: **very loose relations with ICRC** TheolSchool: **school for preachers and evangelists** Service infrastructure: **4 primary schools, 2 secondary schools** Periodicals: **none**

Address: Eglise Réformée Confessante au Congo (ERCC), 7, avenue Boulangerie, Mungomba, rte Munama zone Kampemba, Lubumbashi, Congo-Kinshasa

COOK ISLANDS

Area in km²	240
Population	(July 1996 est.) 19,561 Polynesian (full blood) 81.3%, Polynesian and European 7.7%, Polynesian and non-European 7.7%, European 2.4%, other 0.9%
Religions in %	Christian (majority of population are members of Cook Islands Christian Church)
Official/other languages	English, Maori

This country is constituted by a group of islands in the South Pacific Ocean, about halfway between Hawaii and Aotearoa New Zealand. Since August 4, 1965, it has been independent in free association with New Zealand and has had a self-governing parliamentary government. Cook Islands is fully responsible for internal affairs; New Zealand retains responsibility for external affairs, in consultation with the Cook Islands. It has the right at any time to move to full independence by unilateral action. Agriculture provides the economic base. The major export earners are fruit, copra, and clothing. Manufacturing activities are limited to a fruit-processing plant and several clothing factories. Economic development is hindered by the isolation of the islands from foreign markets and a lack of natural resources and good transportation links. A large trade deficit is annually made up for by remittances from emigrants and by foreign aid, largely from New Zealand.

Cook Islands Christian Church (5100)

The Cook Islands Christian Church traces its beginnings to the Tahitian missionary Papeiha, who was brought to the southern island of Aitutaki in 1821 by John Williams of the London Missionary Society. The Gospel was successfully introduced. In the following years Charles Pitman, John Williams, Aaron Buzacott, and others undertook Bible translation and trained many Cook Islander missionaries at the Tacamoa Theological College. They went for the LMS to Samoa, Niué, Vanuatu, Loyalty Islands,Torres Straits, and Papua New Guinea while at the same time all the Cook Islands came under the overall care of the LMS.

In the 20th century, the Cook Islands churches kept ethnic and linguistic identification with their mother church in Tahiti, but they became dependent on New Zealand, particularly between the two world wars. After churches within the Congregational Union of New Zealand united with the NZ Presbyterian Church in 1970, the church accepted a presb form of government.

TM: **10,898** BM: **10,000** CM: **8,000** Congr: **34** PStations: **42** OrdM: **40** Eld: **46** Deac: **288** EvgHome: **10** Mission: **0** Women Ord: **no** ChurchOrg: **Presbyterian** Off/otherLang: **English, Cook Islands Maori** DoctrB: **ApC, NicC** Infant or believer's baptism: **both** Frequency of the Lord's Supper: **monthly** Periodicals: **Karere (mission/monthly/1,000), Lamepa (gen/monthly/1,000), Nuti Evangelia (gen/monthly/2,000)** Close relations with: **Presbyterian Church of New Zealand** NatRel: **nc** RegRel: **PCC (1968)** IntlRel: **WCC (1968)** TheolSchool: **Tacamoa Theological College.**

Address: Ekalesia Keresitiano ote Kuki Airani, P.O. Box 93, Avarua. Rarotonga, Cook Islands, Tel: +682 26540, Fax: +682 26174 (Post Office)

COSTA RICA

Area in km²	51,100
Population	(July 1996 est.) 3,463,083 white (including mestizo) 96%, black 2%, Indian 1%, Chinese 1%
Religions in %	RCath 95%
Official/other languages	Spanish / English spoken around Puerto Limon

In 1502 Columbus entered Costa Rica through the Belen River seeking riches and taking with him two captive Indians to serve as guides and translators. During the following centuries until 1821 the area was part of the Spanish empire. With independence, agricultural exploitation came mainly through expatriate businessmen, first British and German, then North American, who developed the coffee and banana trade. They were also instrumental in starting English worship services in private homes. The first services were held in 1848 by Captain William Le Lacheur from Guernsey Islands, with the cooperation of Dr. R. L. Brealey of Heredia. Both were active in Bible distribution. The first Protestant chapel, the Church of the Good Shepherd, was built in 1865. The free exercise of non-Catholic worship was assured by the constitution of 1882; the "Apostolic RCath Church" was declared the official religion of the land. This status has continued to the present.

The Church of the Good Shepherd was served by Congreg and Meth pastors until 1896 when it established ties with the Anglican diocese in Belize and became officially related to the Episcopal Church in the USA. Through the years it ministered to the needs of the English-speaking expatriate community. Meanwhile, due to the construction of the railway and other projects which required a labor force, black immigrants from Jamaica and the Antilles, mostly Protestant, arrived during the last decades of the 19th and the beginning of the 20th century. Several churches sent missionaries and pastors: the Jamaican Missionary Society (Baptist) in 1887, the Methodist Missionary Society from Great Britain in 1894, and the Anglican Society for the Propagation of the Gospel in 1896.

The Central American Mission, founded by the dispensationalist C. I. Scofield (1843-1921), was the first North American missionary society to begin work in Costa Rica, in 1891; it was followed by the American Methodists in 1917. The interdenominational Latin American Mission began work in Costa Rica in 1921; in 1924 it founded the Seminario Biblico Latinoamericano, which developed into an important theological center of Central American Protestantism. Several missionaries of the Latin American Mission came from Presb and Ref churches, but Reformed and Presb communities have come into existence only in recent years. Recently missionaries from Asia, especially from Korea, have come into the country and have organized several churches. In addition to those mentioned under nos. 3-5, the following two deserve to be mentioned: the Asociación Presbiteriana Coreana (in Tibas, tel. 506 240-8620) and Iglesia Evangélical Formsana (in San José, tel. 506 231-4803).

1. Christian Reformed Church (2051)

In 1982 the Christian Reformed Church in North America began mission work in the capital city of San José. Through the efforts of Rev. Michael Van Hofwegen and several other missionaries, three congr were established; later, work expanded to the Pacific province of Punta Arenas, where congr were founded in the towns of Esparza and El Roble. Pastoral training is carried out by Instituto Farel, basically using the extension method. A national consistory defines the general objectives and policy for the five congr, while local committees and consistories carry out the church's ministry.

TM: **219** BM: **75** CM: **144** Congr: **5** PStations: **1** OrdM: **3** Eld: **4** Deac: **3** EvgHome: **ne** Mission: **ne** Women Ord: **yes** As Ministers: **no** as Deac: **yes/3** as Elders: **ne** ChurchOrg: **local congr and national consistory** Off/otherLang: **Spanish** DoctrB: **ne** Infant or believer's baptism: **both** Close relations with: **Christian Reformed Church in NA** NatRel: **none** RegRel: **none** IntlRel: **none** TheolSchool: **Instituto Farel (Costa Rica), IMDELA (Missiological Institute of Latin America)** Periodicals: **none**

Address: Iglesia Cristiana Reformada en Costa Rica, APDO 10250-1000, c/o World Mission 455, San José, Costa Rica, Fax: +506 255 4779

2. Fraternity of Costarrican Evangelical Churches (FIEC) (2050)

The FIEC was organized officially in 1985 with five congr from the metropolitan area of San José as constituent members. All five had separated from the Asociación de Iglesias Biblicas Costarricenses (AIBC) because of the conviction that the church bears a serious responsibility for its social context and that there should be room for different theological approaches with respect to its faith and action in this area. These convictions were not shared by the leadership of the AIBC. However, the leaders of the FIEC believe that these views reflect the spirit and activity of the founders of the AIBC, Harry and Susanna Strachan and their son Kenneth, who were Presb missionaries working through the Latin American Mission. Harry, a Scotsman, and Susanna, from Ireland, arrived from Argentina in San José in 1921 and founded several ministries that have continued to the present: the Biblical Clinic (now hospital), Caravans of Good Will, the Latin American Biblical Seminary, and others. Several pastors and members of the FIEC teach or carry administrative functions in the Seminary (now a university).

TM: **1,000** BM: **600** CM: **450** Congr: **12** PStations: **3** OrdM: **7** Eld: **25** Deac: **40** EvgHome: **5** Mission: **0** Women Ord: **yes** As Ministers: **1990/1** as Deac: **1985/15** as Elders: **1985/5** ChurchOrg: **local parishes and missions, presby (the denomination is one "civil society")** Off/otherLang: **English, Spanish** DoctrB: **ApC** Infant or believer's baptism: **believer** Frequency of the Lord's Supper: **monthly** Close relations with: **PCUSA, PCCanada, Disciples of Christ USA, United Church of Christ USA** NatRel: **CELADEC** RegRel: **AIPRAL, CLAI** IntlRel: **WARC** TheolSchool: **Latinamerican Biblical University (Costa Rica), in Scotland, France, and USA.** Service infrastructure: **none** Periodicals: **Revista Shalom (twice a year)**

Address: Fraternidad de Iglesias Evangélicas Costarricenses (FIEC), Apartado 1473-1002, Paseo los Estudiantes, San José, Costa Rica, Tel: +506 225-0442, Fax: +506 225-4058

3. Korean Presbyterian Church (2053)

This community grew out of work initiated by Chang Hak Kwen. For several years worship services were held in the house of the Korean Ambassador. In 1982 the community adopted the name Korean Church. In the same year Rev. Yong Guel Choi arrived from California to organize the church. Three years later the name of the church was changed to Korean Presbyterian Church. In 1992 a church building was inaugurated. In 1995 an unfortunate split occurred in the church.

TM: **127** BM: **80** CM: **127** Congr: **1** PStations: **5** OrdM: **1** Eld: **1** Deac: **36** EvgHome: **none** Mission: **none** Women Ord: **yes** As Ministers: **no** as Deac: **22** as Elders: **no** ChurchOrg: **under the Synod of Los Angeles** Off/otherLang: **Korean, Spanish** DoctrB: **ApC, NicC, WestConf** Infant or believer's baptism: **both** Frequency of the Lord's Supper: **two to three times per year** Close relations with: **Asamblea de Dios, but "interested in more relations with Reformed Churches"** NatRel: **Alianza Evangelica de Costa Rica** RegRel: **none** IntlRel: **none** Service infrastructure: **community center for Korean members and vicinity**

Address: Iglesia Presbiteriana Coreana, Apartado 1652-2050 San Pedro Monte de Ocas, San José, Costa Rica, Tel: +506 240-8620, 240-9310, Fax: +506 236-9491.

4. Korean Sion Church of Costa Rica (2052)

No historical data have been made available.

TM: **55** BM: **35** Congr: **1** OrdM: **1** Eld: **2** Deac: **2** EvgHome: **nc** Mission: **nc** Women Ord: **nc** As Ministers: **nc** as Deac: **nc** as Elders: **nc** ChurchOrg: **nc** Off/otherLang: **nc** DoctrB: **nc** Infant or believer's baptism: **infant**

Address: Iglesia Coreana Sion de Costa Rica, Apartado 690, Bario Socoro, San Miguel de Santo Domingo, Heredia, San José, Costa Rica, Tel: +506 236-9959, 236-9963, Fax: +506 236-1100

5. Presbyterian Mission of Korea (2054)

No data have been made available.

Address: La Misión Presbiteriana de Corea, Apartado 870/2050, San José, Costa Rica, E-mail: mprbcr@sol.racsa.co.cr.

CROATIA

Area in km²	56,538
Population	(July 1996 est.) 5,004,112 Croat 78%, Serb 12%, Muslim 0.9%, Hungarian 0.5%, Slovenian 0.5%, others 8.1% (1991)
Religions in %	RCath 76.4%, Orth 11.1%, Prot 0.4%, Muslim 1.2%, others and unknown 10.7%
Official language	Serbo-Croatian 96%, other 4% (including Italian, Hungarian, Czech, and German)

Reformed Christian Church in Croatia (6234)

The Reformed Christian Church in Croatia (Reformirana Krscanska Crkva U Hrvatskoj) came into existence following the disintegration of Yugoslavia in 1993 (cf. also Yugoslavia). The Reformed congr organized themselves as the Reformed Christian Church of Yugoslavia in 1933, after World War I, when the southern areas of the Austro-Hungarian empire became part of the Kingdom of Yugoslavia. With the recognition of Croatia as an independent state the congr in Croatia became a separate entity. Historically, the church has served the Hungarian-speaking population, but there are also congr worshiping in Croatian and Czech. The church has special relations with the Reformed Church of Hungary. Due to the pressures of war many members of the church have emigrated to Hungary and to other countries.

TM: **4,750** BM: **4,750** CM: **1,000** Congr: **20** PStations: **10** OrdM: **7** Eld: **110** Deac: **nc** EvgHome: **nc** Mission: **nc** Women Ord: **yes** As Ministers: **1970/nc** as Deac: **ne** as Elders: **1960/nc** ChurchOrg: **synod, 2 delegates from every organized church** Off/otherLang: **Hungarian, Croatian, Czech** DoctrB: **ApC, NicC, AthC, HeidC, HelvC** Frequency of the Lord's Supper: **weekly to 6 times a year** Close relations with: **The Ref Ch in Hungary** NatRel: **Protestant Evangelical Council** IntlRel: **WARC (1993)**

Address: Reformirana Krscanska Crkva U Hrvatskoj, Vladimir Nazora 31, HR 34 300 Vinkovci, Croatia, Tel: +385 32 333-056, Fax: +385 32 333-055

CUBA

Area in km²	110,860
Population	(July 1996 est.) 10,951,334 mulatto 51%, white 37%, black 11%, Chinese 1%
Religions in %	RCath 85% prior to Castro assuming power; Prot (Angl, Meth, Bapt, Presb, Pent), Jehovah's Witnesses, Jews, and Santeria
Official/other languages	Spanish

Reached by Christopher Columbus in 1492, the island was occupied by Spain in 1510-1511. In 1514 the Dominican priest Montesinos preached his famous sermon denouncing the abuse of the Indians in Cuba. It had a decisive impact on Bartolomé de Las Casas, who became the Spanish conscience for Latin America and was later officially titled "the Defender of the Indians." The first RCath diocese was created in 1518.

For more than three centuries Cuba remained under Spanish domination. The indigenous population of Cuba (Taino) had already been extinguished after a few decades. In 1762 the British conquered Havana and controlled the island from Matanzas to Mariel. Religious liberty for Prot and RCath was declared. However, in 1763 the English agreed to return Cuba to Spain in exchange for Florida. Slave rebellions (1812) and two liberation wars (1868-78, 1895-98) led to independence (1898). Cuba was constituted as a republic. In place of Spain the dominating power now became the United States, which obtained the use of the base of Guantánamo in 1934. In 1959 Fidel Castro overthrew the dictatorship of Fulgencio Batista (1952-59) and established a revolutionary regime based on Marxist principles. Despite persistent American intervention and massive emigration of Cubans to the USA, the regime has continued to survive.

The RCath missionary work began in the early 16th century. Until independence in 1898 Roman Catholicism was the official religion. The Constitution of 1902 declared the separation of church and state and the freedom of worship. This was reaffirmed by Article 35 of the Constitution of 1940 and by the basic laws of the Cuban revolution of 1959.

The earliest Protestant presence in Cuba consisted of pirates and corsairs. "In 1641 many Portuguese and French, some Jews and others, Luth and Calvinists, were expelled from Cuba" (Fernando Ortiz). Following the British invasions in the 18th century, Anglican services were held in 1741. At the beginning of the 19th century, Protestant influence increased. Though open evangelistic work was impossible in this period, Protestant political and commercial representatives played a significant role, both in the struggle for the emancipation of the blacks and in the distribution of Bibles. In 1855 a civil law against Bible distribution was passed.

During the 19th century, the number of foreign residents increased, and more and more Cubans sent their children abroad for university and professional training. The process of "Americanization" was facilitated by commercial interests, the importation of literature, overseas visits, and cultural influences.

Until 1880 the Protestant presence was basically limited to foreign residents. However, in 1883 the Episcopal Church was established through the emigration of black people from the USA, followed by the Bapt in 1886, the Presb in 1890, and the Advent in 1920. Today about 40% of the population consider themselves members of the RCath Church. A substantial part of the population has no connection with any church. A sizeable group adheres to Afro-American cults.

1. Presbyterian Reformed Church in Cuba (3300)

This church was founded in 1890 by Evaristo Collazo, a layman who came from Tampa, Florida, in the United States. He founded communities in Havana and Santa Clara, Placetas. He was ordained by a Presb missionary who had come from the USA for the same purpose. Collazo's intention was to support the struggle of the revolutionary party of José Marti for the independence of Cuba. He participated in the war for independence and obtained the grade of lieutenant in the revolutionary army. In 1902 the church was reopened. American missionaries engaged in evangelistic activities. The communities constituted themselves as a presby of the Presbyterian Church in the USA, Synod of New Jersey. In 1945 the Theological Seminary of Matanzas was founded as an ecumenical venture of Presb, Methodists, and Episcopalians. In 1967, eight years after the revolution, the church became autonomous. A year later it adopted its own confession of faith. The church runs a center with a capacity for 120 persons and publishes three journals — *Heraldo Cristiano, Juprecu* (for youth) and *Su Voz.* Since 1990 the church has experienced rapid growth.

TM: **15,000** BM: **15,000** CM: **5,600** Congr: **59** PStations: **17** OrdM: **26** Eld: **450** Deac: **102** EvgHome: **15** Mission: **nc** Women Ord: **yes** As Ministers: **1967/7** as Deac: **1960/60** as Elders: **1950/220** ChurchOrg: **Presb (3 presbys, national synod)** Off/otherLang: **Spanish** DoctrB: **ApC, NicC, HeidC, HelvC, WestConf, Barmen, Cuban Confession (1968)** Infant or believer's baptism: **both** Frequency of the Lord's Supper: **4 times per year** Close relations with: **Christian Reformed Church** NatRel: **CEC** RegRel: **CLAI, CCC** IntlRel: **WCC (1967), WARC (1967)** TheolSchool: **Evangelical Theological Seminary (Matanzas)** Service infrastructure: **conference center** Periodicals: **Heraldo Cristiano (mission/monthly/2,500), Juprecu (youth), Su Voz (devotional/3 times a year/2,500)**

Address: Iglesia Presbiteriana-Reformada en Cuba, Salud 222 E/ Lealtad y Campanario, La Habana 10200, Cuba, Tel: +53 7 984-818, Fax: +53 7 331-788, E-mail: ceham@tinored.cu.

2. Christian Reformed Church in Cuba (3302)

In 1940 a young woman from the Christian Reformed Church, Bessie Vander Valk of Paterson, New Jersey, decided to follow the Lord's call to work in Cuba. At first she worked with the Cuban Evangelical Association, which had mission stations in the province of Matanzas. Most of her 22 years in Cuba were spent in Jaguey Grande. There she married a young Cuban pastor, Vicente Izquierdo. In 1944 the Cuban Evangelical Association was dissolved for lack of funds. The newly married couple continued their work as faith missionaries, receiving help from the United States, especially from Christian Reformed members and congr. They established the Interior Gospel Mission, which was officially adopted by the Christian Reformed Church in North America (cf. United States) in 1958. A missionary with his family was sent in 1958; however, because of the political situation after the Cuban revolution in 1959, they left Cuba in 1960. The national Iglesia Cristiana Reformada continued to grow, and by 1974 there were eight pastors and twelve churches. The work is basically centered in the provinces of La Habana and Matanzas. In addition to the 12 congr there are at least 26 active Bible groups.

TM: **1,143** BM: **496** Congr: **12** PStations: **24** OrdM: **4** Eld: **20** Deac: **20** EvgHome: **nc** Mission: **nc** Women Ord: **no** ChurchOrg: **local consistory, central consistory** Off/otherLang: **Spanish** DoctrB: **nc** Infant or believer's baptism**: believer** Close relations with**: Christian Reformed Church in North America (CRCNA)** NatRel: **Ecumenical Committee of Cuba** RegRel: **none** IntlRel: **none** TheolSchool: **Evangelical Theological Seminary (Matanzas)**

Address: Iglesia Cristiana Reformada en Cuba, APDO 19, Jagüey Grande, Matanzas, Cuba, Fax: +53 7 331-788

CZECH REPUBLIC

Area in km²	78,864
Population	10,000,000 Czech 94.4%, Slovak 3%, Polish 0.6%, German 0.5%, Gypsy 0.3%, Hungarian 0.2%, other 1%
Religions in %	atheist 39.8%, RCath 39.2%, Prot 4.6%, smaller minorities of Eastern Orthodox (3%) and Jews, other 13.4%
Official/other languages	Czech, Slovak

The Christian era began in the Czech lands in 863 through the missionary activity of Constantine (Cyril) and Methodius, who had been sent by the Byzantine emperor. While Czech Christianity was influenced by Eastern tradition, it nevertheless became an integral part of the Western Church.

Czech Protestantism has its roots in the 14th and 15th centuries. Under the reign of Charles IV (1346-1378), Prague became the political and spiritual center of the Holy Roman Empire. At that time radical voices regarding the interpretation of Scriptures, church organization, and the papacy began to be voiced. The preaching activity of men such as Milic of Kromeríz, Konrad Waldhauser, and Matej of

146

Janov, the ideas of John Wycliffe, and the activity of Waldensians prepared the soil for the struggle of Jan Hus (1370-1415). His death at the stake in Constance led to the creation of the Hussite Church, which for two hundred years — until 1620 — represented an island in the heart of late medieval Europe which was no longer controlled by Rome. The Hussite Church emphasized the free proclamation of the Word of God, the administration of the Eucharist in both kinds to lay people, and the renewal of the church according to the model of the early church.

Under the influence of the lay theologian Petr Chelcicky (1380-1415) a separatist movement grew within the Hussite Church which organized itself in 1457 into the Unity of Brethren. The Unity preached nonviolence, separation from the world, refusal to take oaths, and the upbuilding of spiritual community life in a secluded place. In the 16th century the Unity abandoned these restrictions and entered fully in the cultural life of Czech lands. It became famous especially in the fields of education, diaconal activity, church organization, and discipline. One of its great contributions to Czech national culture was the translation of the whole Bible, including the apocryphal books, accompanied by a commentary, and called the Bible of Kralice (1579-1593). The last bishop of the Unity, Jan Amos Comenius (1592-1676), was the founder of modern pedagogy. As a result of the Counter-Reformation he had to live in exile.

Before 1620 it is believed that 90% of the Czech population were Prot. During the Counter-Reformation the Protestant faith became illegal and for more than 150 years was maintained only in families of farmers and agricultural workers. When, in 1781, the Edict of Toleration was issued by Emperor Joseph II, only remnants of the former Protestant communities, approximately 100,000, registered as Reformed or Luth. They were not allowed to organize themselves in continuity with their own indigenous tradition but depended on the consistory in Vienna. Congr, mainly those established in the countryside, were served by Slovak and Hungarian pastors. The first Czech students of theology studied in Sárospatak, Debrecen, and later in Vienna.

Not until the second half of the 19th century was the church given more freedom. In this period contacts were made with sister churches in Germany, Scotland, etc. German and Anglo-Saxon hymns were translated into Czech. Theological thinking was enriched by emphases coming from abroad (Scottish spirituality, H. F. Kohlbrügge, E. Böhl). The Czech Reformed Church became a member of the World Alliance of Reformed Churches in 1877.

1. Evangelical Church of Czech Brethren (6030)

In 1918, when the state of Czechoslovakia came into existence, the two churches, the larger Reformed and the smaller Luth church, which had been artificially separated from one another, decided to unite and to form the Evangelical Church of the Czech Brethren. In 1919, a Theological Faculty was established outside Charles University (first called Hus Faculty and, later, Comenius Faculty). Theological thinking was influenced by J. L. Hromádka (1889-1969). At the time of World

War II part of the church was involved in resistance against the German occupation. After 1948, under the influence of Hromádka and others, the church adopted an attitude of critical loyalty to the regime. This approach was put to the test after the Soviet occupation of Czechoslovakia in 1968. A number of pastors lost their license as ministers because of their critical attitude to the "process of normalization." Since the demise of Communism the church is faced with new challenges. Many diaconal projects have been started and the Comenius Faculty has been incorporated into Charles University.

TM: **150,371** BM: **150,371** CM: **14,532** Congr: **264** PStations: **279** OrdM: **215** Eld: **2,600** Deac: **590** EvgHome: **nc** Mission: **0** Women Ord: **Yes** As Ministers: **1953/36** as Deac: **1953/0** as Elders: **1953/9** ChurchOrg: **Presbyterian (264 congr, 13 seniorates, synod)** Off/otherLang: **Czech (German-speaking parish in Prague)** DoctrB: **ApC, NicC, HeidC, CA, HelvC, 4 Articles of Prague (1420), Confession of Brethren (1535), Czech Confession (1575)** Infant or believer's baptism: **both** Frequency of the Lord's Supper: **monthly in general** Close relations with: **Ev. Churches in Germany, Ev. Churches in Austria, Slovakia, Alsace-Lorraine, Netherlands, Hungary, Ch of Scotland, United Ref Ch (UK), PCUSA, PC Korea** NatRel: **Czech National Council of Churches (1955), Konstanzer Unität (1905), Czech Bible Society, Alliance of Prot Churches (1990)** RegRel: **CEC (1957)** IntlRel: **WARC (1877), WCC (1948)** TheolSchool: **Theological Faculty in Prague or Bratislava** Periodicals: **Cesky bratr (gen/every 3 weeks/4,600), Bratrstvo (gen for youth/10 per year/2,300), Sermons (homiletics/semesterly/750), Na kazdý den (for daily meditation/8,000)**

Address: Ceskobratrská Církev Evangelická, Postfach 466, Jungmannova 9, CZ-1112 Praha 1, Czech Republic, Tel: +42 2 2422-2219, Fax: +42 2 2422-2218

2. The Church of the Brethren (6031)

A spiritual revival in 1868 led to the formation of a community of evangelical spirit and congregational structure in Bystré, Eastern Bohemia. Later a similar movement began in Prague which, with the help of the Free Church of Scotland and missionaries of the ABCFM (Congregational) in Boston, resulted in the foundation of the Free Reformed Church. Soon friendly contacts developed between the two spiritual streams, and in 1891 the two congr merged under a single leadership. As the movement gained momentum it became the target of discriminatory measures on the part of the Austrian authorities. After World War I the church adopted a new name, calling itself the Unity of Czech Brethren. In doing so it sought to express its allegiance to the spiritual legacy of the old Bohemian Unitas Fratrum. The church eventually also expanded into Slovakia (cf. Slovakia no. 2) and the Transcarpatian Ukraine. After World War II it gained new members especially of Polish and Slovak origin. Because of this new situation the church decided in 1967 to change its name again to the Church of the Brethren. The church is congregationalist in character but has an increasingly Reformed profile.

TM: **8,140** BM: **5,174** CM: **5,174** Congr: **44** PStations: **250** OrdM: **50** Eld: **250** Deac: **1** EvgHome: **200** Mission: **ne** Women Ord: **no** ChurchOrg: **congr (local congr, GenAssy)** Off/otherLang: **Czech, Polish** DoctrB: **ApC, NicC, HeidC, HelvC, WestConf** Infant or believer's baptism: **both** Frequency of the Lord's Supper: **monthly** Close relations with: **Federation of Free Ev. Churches** NatRel: **Czech National Council of Churches (1990), Ecumenical Council of Churches, Federation of Evangelical**

Churches (1990) RegRel: **none** IntlRel: **IFFEC, WCC, WARC (1970)** TheolSchool: **Theological Faculty in Prague or Bratislava** Periodicals: **Bratrská rodina (general/monthly/5,000)**

Address: Církev bratrská, P.O. Box, Soukenická 15, CZ-11000 Praha 1, Czech Republic, Tel: +42 2 231-8131, Fax: +42 2 231-8131

DENMARK

Area in km²	43,070
Population	(July 1996 est.) 5,249,632 Scandinavian, Eskimo, Faroese, German
Religions in %	Luth 91%, other Prot and RCath 2%, other 7% (1988)
Official/other languages	Danish/Faroese, Greenlandic (an Eskimo dialect), German (small minority)

Over 90% of the population of Denmark is Luth. At the end of the Peasants' Revolt in 1536/1537 Lutheranism prevailed. At least since 1683 it has been the state religion of this Nordic country. For many decades RCath were granted religious freedom only if they were foreign diplomatic representatives. Because they could help to foster the economic growth of the country, Jews and Reformed were granted special privileges at the end of the 17th century. The Basic Law of 1849 introduced full religious freedom but not equal religious rights to all. Only after the introduction of a parliamentary democracy in 1901 did a clearer differentiation between state and church appear in public affairs.

Today most Reformed belong to one of the four ethnic communities regrouped as the

Reformed Synod of Denmark (6040)

TM: **1,000** BM: **1,000** Congr: **4** PStations: **2** OrdM: **4** Eld: **18** Deac: **nc** EvgHome: **nc** Mission: **nc** Women Ord: **yes** As Ministers: **1** as Deac: **nc** as Elders: **nc** ChurchOrg: **Reformed (synod)** Off/otherLang: **Danish, German, French** DoctrB: **ApC, NicC, HeidC** Infant or believer's baptism: **both** Frequency of the Lord's Supper: **monthly** NatRel: **Ecumenical Council of Denmark, Danish Council of Free Churches** IntlRel: **WARC**

Address: Den reformerte Synode i Danmark, Norrebrogade 32 A 1ter, DK-1123, Fredericia, Denmark, Tel: +45 75 920551

No other data have been made available.

1. The Reformed Church of Copenhagen

Before marrying Christian V of Denmark, Charlotte-Amelia of Hessen-Cassel had requested, and had been granted for herself and her court, the right to profess freely the Ref faith. However, the hostility of the Luth clergy was so strong that she never was crowned Queen of Denmark. The Reformed Church of Copenhagen was founded in 1685, and three years later Charlotte-Amelia personally financed the erection of the first Ref church building in Denmark. In April 1685 the King also granted special privileges to the French Huguenots, whose skill and courage were greatly appreciated. This explains why even today both French and German are spoken in this church.

a) French Reformed Church (6040c)

This church consists of a single congregation of about 50 members. The French pastor of Stockholm comes once a month to preside over the service of Eucharist. This parish has 4 elders who lead worship on the other Sundays; it is a member of the CEEFE (Commission of French Evangelical Churches Abroad).

Address: Eglise réformée française, Gothersgade 107-111, DK-Kopenhagen, Denmark, Tel: +45 33 14 97 05

b) German-Reformed Church of Kopenhagen (6040b)

This German-speaking congregation is composed of Reformed Germans, Dutch, Hungarians, Swiss, Americans, and also some Danes, living in and around Copenhagen. It numbers some 300 members, has a pastor from Germany, and is a member of the Reformed Alliance in Germany.

Address: Deutsch-Reformierte Kirche zu Kopenhagen, Gothersgade 109,3, DK-Kopenhagen, Denmark, Tel: +45 33 138753, Fax: +45 33 138753

2. Reformed Congregation in Fredericia (6040a)

At the invitation of King Frederick IV, the first Huguenots arrived in Fredericia in 1719. Their reputation as skilled farmers, in particular as tobacco planters and assiduous workers, had preceded them. They were granted royal privileges (freedom of religion, exemption from taxes and from draft, free land, royal and financial support for their pastors and their church buildings). The Huguenots settled down in the garrison town of Fredericia. Their way of farming soon became a model for the whole of Denmark. The congregation spoke the language of the resident garrison — first French, later German, and, since 1938, Danish. Pastors have come from France, Switzerland, and now Germany.

Today the congregation has one pastor and 300 members; about one fifth of them live scattered throughout Denmark.

Address: Den reformerte Meighed i Fredericia, Norrebrogade 32 A 1ter, DK-1123, Fredericia, Denmark, Tel: +45 75 920551

3. Korean-Reformed Church in Denmark (6040d)

In 1989 a small Korean congregation was formed in Copenhagen. It consists of a Korean pastor and some 50 members. Since 1997 this congregation has also been a member of the Reformed Synod of Denmark.

Address: Korean-Reformed Church in Denmark, Gothersgade 109,3, DK-Kopenhagen

DJIBOUTI

Area in km²	23,700
Population	(est. July) 421,320 Somalis Issas (37%), other Somalis (11%), Afar (35%), Europeans, including 10,000 French (8%), Arab (6%), many refugees
Religions in %	Muslim 96%, RCath 2%, Orth. 1%, Prot. 1%
Official/other languages	French, Arabic/Somali, Afar

In 1862 France bought the bay of Obock for 10,000 thalers from the Sultan of Raheito. Later it occupied the regions of Tadjourah and of Djibouti. First known as French Coast of the Somalis (1892), this strategic position at the exit of the Red Sea (opposite to Yemen) was named by the French the "Territory of the Afars and the Issas." It was given its own local government in 1967 before becoming independent under the name of the Republic of Djibouti in 1977.

The country is almost totally Muslim. Christian churches — both Catholic and Protestant — which existed already before independence are allowed to minister, but further expansion and church planting is impossible.

Protestant Church of Djibouti (1290)

This denomination was founded in 1960 by the army chaplain of the French troops stationed there. After independence and the official departure of the French troops, the buildings became the property of a commission related to the Federation of Protestant Churches. The DEFAP (mission department of the French Prot churches) took responsibility for this single parish, which developed a growing threefold activity: a) regular worship life and Bible school; b) running of language and vocational schools; and c) refugee work, serving as local agent of the UNHCR.

The church building is also used as a place of worship by Ethiopian and Malagasy Christian groups. The Protestant Church of Djibouti houses in its worship life Christians from various countries (Ethiopia, France, Zaire, Burundi, United States, etc.) as well as from various confessions (Reformed, Luth, Bapt, Advent, Mennonites, etc.). Church members normally stay in Djibouti for not more than two or three years.

TM: **100** BM: **100** CM: **100** Congr: **1** PStations: **0** OrdM: **1** Eld: **ne** Deac: **5** EvgHome: **ne** Mission: **ne** Women Ord: **no** As Ministers: **no** as Deac: **ne** as Elders: **no** ChurchOrg: **the only Protestant church in a Muslim environment and society** Off/otherLang: **French** DoctrB: **ApC, NicC, RochC** Infant or believer's baptism: **both** Frequency of the Lord's Supper: **monthly** Periodicals: **none** Close relations with: **Fédération protestante de France (C.E.E.E.F.E.)** NatRel: **ne** RegRel: **AACC** IntlRel: **none** TheolSchool: **none.**

Address: Eglise Protestante Evangélique de Djibouti (EPED), P.O. Box 416, Bd. de la République, Djibouti 1981, Tel: +253 351-820, Fax: +253 350-706

DOMINICAN REPUBLIC

Area in km²	48,734
Population	7,515,899
Religions in %	RCath 69%, Prot 11%, no religion 20%
Official/other languages	Spanish

The island Hispaniola was the first territory to be conquered by the Spaniards in 1493. Santo Domingo became the capital. After twenty years of Spanish rule the Taino, the original population, had almost entirely disappeared. Initially the whole island was Spanish, in 1659 the French occupied the part which today forms Haiti. In 1804 Haiti became independent, and from 1822 to 1844 the Haitians invaded the eastern part, then still under Spanish domination.

The first Prot came to the country during this period. In 1824, upon the invitation of the Haitian government, several thousand Afro-Americans, among them some freed slaves, settled in several areas of the island; they were accompanied by pastors of the African Episcopal Methodist Church. Prot centers were established in several places, especially in Port-au-Prince, Haiti, and Samana, Puerto Plata, Dominican Republic. Methodists started formal missionary work in 1841. They were followed in the 20th century by several denominations, among them the Free Methodists (1908), the Adventists (1908), Assemblies of God (1931), Plymouth Brethren (1921), Church of God (1940), Southern Bapt (1962), and, more recently, by a wide range of evangelical groups.

1. Dominican Evangelical Church (3325)

In 1919 three North American missions meeting in New York — Methodist, Presb, and United Brethren — organized the Alliance for Christian Service in Santo Domingo. Their aim was to work toward an indigenous church in Santo Domingo. In January 1922 the Dominican Evangelical Church was founded with, at that time, 29 baptized adult members. The church quickly grew and spread over the whole country. In 1932 the church united with the Wesleyan Methodists, and in 1960 with the Moravians. By the time of World War II it had a little more than one thousand members. Today it is the second largest Prot church in the Republic. The church is independent and self-supporting.

TM: **6,280** BM: **6,280** CM: **6,280** Congr: **72** PStations: **55** OrdM: **29** Eld: **17** Deac: **12** EvgHome: **nc** Mission: **nc** Women Ord: **yes** As Ministers: **1985/4** as Deac: **1985/2** as Elders: **none** ChurchOrg: **Reformed (local churches, GenAssy)** Off/otherLang: **Spanish** DoctrB: **ApC, NicC, AthC** Infant or believer's baptism: **both** Frequency of the Lord's Supper: **monthly** Periodicals: **Nuestro Amigo (gen/quarterly/1,500), Anuario (gen/quarterly/1,500)** NatRel: **SSID, Dominican Bible Society, ECLOF** RegRel: **CCC, CIEMAL, AIPRAL, CLAI** IntlRel: **WARC (1997)** TheolSchool: **Seminario teologico (Iglesia Evangelica Dominicana)**

Address: Iglesia Evangelica Dominicana, Apartado 727, Rosa Duarte 41-A, Esq. Ave. México 31, Santo Domingo, Dominican Republic, Tel: +1 809 682-4945, Fax: +1 809 689 4088

2. Christian Reformed Church in the Dominican Republic (3326)

In the 1970s Christian Reformed missionaries from Puerto Rico visited the country, following up on radio program contacts. The first American missionaries, Ray and Gladys Brinks and Neal and Sandy Hegeman, began work among the Haitian immigrants working in the cane fields and marginal areas of urban centers in 1981. People of Haitian origin, speaking French Creole, continue to make up 90% of the church membership. During the 1980s several Spanish-speaking groups were formed among national Dominicans. These were organized in 1990 into a separate branch of the church.

TM: **10,000** BM: **2,971 (adult) and 2,833 (children)** Congr: **88** PStations:**133** OrdM: **82** Eld: **nc** Deac: **nc** EvgHome: **nc** Mission: **nc** Women Ord: **nc** ChurchOrg: **Reformed (synod)** Off/otherLang: **Spanish, French Creole** DoctrB: **HeidC, CDort, BelgC, Reformed** IntlRel: **REC**

Address: Iglesia Cristiana Reformada en la Republica Dominicana, Apartado 747-2, Santo Domingo, Dominican Republic

ECUADOR

Area in km²	276,840
Population	(July 1996 est.) 11,466,291 mestizo (mixed Indian and Spanish) 55%, Indian 25%, Spanish 10%, black 10%
Religions in %	RCath 95%, Prot and other 5%
Official/other languages	Spanish/Indian languages (especially Quechua)

Prot mission work started toward the end of the 19th century—the Gospel Missionary Union (1895), the Christian and Missionary Alliance (1896), the Methodist Episcopal Mission (1897), and Advent (1904). For several decades progress was slow. From 1931 the Radio Missionary Fellowship began evangelistic work through La Voz de los Andes, which proved to be effective. In 1945 the first national church was formed — the Iglesia Evangelica Ecuatoriana Alianza Cristiana e Misionera. A wide range of Prot missions began work after World War II. Prot also expanded through the growth of the Pent movement and of indigenous churches. In 1964 the Presb, the Church of the Brethren, the Disciples of Christ, and the Methodists decided to form the United Evangelical Church of Ecuador. More recently, Korean missionaries entered the country and founded separate communities.

1. Ecuadorian Evangelical Church of the Christian and Missionary Alliance (2068)

The Christian and Missionary Alliance (CMA) began its work in Ecuador in 1897. The first church was founded in the town of Junin. The Alliance founded the first evangelical church in Quito in 1922. In 1945 the National Church was formed. Today the CMA has about 25 churches in the area of Guayaquil and some 20 churches in the area of Quito. Encouraging growth among the Quechua-speaking population in Otavalo has also been reported. The Alliance Bible Seminary has been training national pastors and leaders for almost sixty years.

TM: **31,480** BM: **15,740** Congr: **109** PStations: **60** OrdM: **43** Eld: **nc** Deac: **nc** EvgHome: **nc** Mission: **ne** Women Ord: **no** ChurchOrg: **nc** Off/otherLang: **Spanish, Quechua** DoctrB: **nc** Infant or believer's baptism: **believer** Frequency of the Lord's Supper: **monthly** Close relations with: **CMA USA, CMA Canada** NatRel: **Confraternidad Evangelica** RegRel: **none** IntlRel: **CMA World Fellowship** TheolSchool: **CMA Bible Seminary (Guayaquil)**

Address: Iglesia Evangelica Ecuatoriana Alianza Cristiana y Misionera, Casilla 09-011-3995, Guayaquil, Ecuador, Tel: +593 4 530-540, Fax: +593 4 329-571, E-mail: misione @pi.pro.ec.

2. United Evangelical Church of Ecuador (2066)

This church is the result of a merger in 1964 of the Church of the Brethren and the United Andean Indian Mission (UAIM) in which the missions of the following four US churches had federated: United Methodist Church, United Church of Christ, Presbyterian Church in the USA, and United Presbyterian Church in the USA. The church started with 10 congr, five from the Church of the Brethren, four from the UAIM, and one independent congr. The first president of the Church was Pastor Gonzalo Carvagal, who was trained in Brazil and returned to Ecuador. The church is socially active, e.g., through a project for street children; it also participates in the plan for a Christian University in Ecuador.

TM: **1,500** BM: **600** CM: **500** Congr: **15** PStations: **20** OrdM: **10** Eld: **20** Deac: **20** EvgHome: **10** Mission: **3** Women Ord: **yes** As Ministers: **1995/2** as Deac: **10** as Elders: **10** ChurchOrg: **Congregational (congr, classes: Region Costal and Region Sierra, national synod)** Off/otherLang: **Spanish, Quechua, English** DoctrB: **ApC** Infant or believer's baptism: **believer** Frequency of the Lord's Supper: **monthly** Close relations with: **Meth and Presb in the USA** NatRel: **Confraternidad Ev Ecuatoriana (1980)** RegRel: **CLAI (1974), AIPRAL (1997)** IntlRel: **WARC (1997)** TheolSchool: **none** Service infrastructure: **day nursery, kindergarten** Periodicals: **none**

Address: Iglesia Evangelica Unida del Ecuador, P.O. Box 17-03-236 A, Rumipamba 915, Y Yugoeslavia, Quito, Ecuador, Tel: +593 2 456-714, Fax: +593 2 553-996

3. Evangelical Covenant Church of Ecuador (2067)

TM: **1,500** CM: **657** Congr: **17** OrdM: **nc** Eld: **nc** Deac: **nc** EvgHome: **nc** Mission: **nc** Women Ord: **nc** As Ministers: **nc** as Deac: **nc** as Elders: **nc** ChurchOrg: **nc** Off/otherLang: **nc** DoctrB: **nc**

Address: Iglesia del Pacto Evangelico en el Ecuador, Casilla 17-17-778, Quito, Ecuador

4. Reformed Presbyterian Church of Ecuador (IRPE) (2065)

This church was organized in 1991 through the work of Mission to the World (Presbyterian Church of America). It states that it is conservative and evangelical and claims to be "the only Ref or Presb denomination in Ecuador." The presby in Quito presently has five churches. There is also a presby in formation in Guayaquil with two mission churches.

TM: **nc** Congr: **5** PStations: **20** OrdM: **nc** Eld: **nc** Deac: **nc** EvgHome: **nc** Mission: **nc** Women Ord: **no** ChurchOrg: **Presbyterian (one presby with 5 churches in Quito, another presby in formation)** Off/otherLang: **Spanish** DoctrB: **WestConf, WestCat**

Address: Iglesia Reformada Presbiteriana del Ecuador (IRPE), Casilla 17-08-8403, Quito, Ecuador, Tel: +593 2 504-087, Fax: +593 2 468 993

EGYPT

Area in km²	1,001,450
Population	(est. July 1996) 63,575,107 Eastern Hamitic stock (Egyptians, Bedouins, and Berbers) 99%, Nubian, Greek, Armenian, European (primarily Italian and French) 1%
Religions in %	Muslim (mostly Sunnites) 94% (official estimate), Coptic Christian and other 6% (official estimate)
Official/other languages	Arabic

Christianity came to Egypt during the first century A.D.; the founder of the church of Alexandria was St. Mark. In the following centuries, Egypt was the cradle of many important Christian movements, including the catechetical schools of Clemens and Origen (2nd and 3rd centuries), monasticism under St Anthony (4th century), the Arian-Athanasian controversy (4th century), Cyril's opposition to Nestorianism (5th century), and the controversy over the nature of Christ, which came to a head at the Councils of Ephesus and Calcedon in 451. Monophysitism gained so much strength that by the middle of the 7th century Monophysites became the majority. At about that time Islam had conquered Egypt, and during the following five centuries massive conversions occurred, in part as a result of opposition to Byzantine administration.

The majority of Christians in Egypt belong to the Coptic Orthodox Church under the Patriarchate of St. Mark—the See of Alexandria. There is, in addition, a (Greek) Patriarchate of Alexandria in communion with the Patriarchate of Constantinople. During the 17th century, concurrent with the French campaigns, the Capuchins and Jesuits began to work in Egypt, which eventually led to the formation of several Uniate Catholic churches.

The first Prot missionaries, Presb from the USA, began work in Egypt in 1854; the Moravians had attempted an earlier initiative, but they withdrew within a short time. Drawing its membership only from nominal Orthodox Christians through evangelism, Bible study in Arabic, and educational and medical work, the church grew rapidly. By 1899 there were four presby, and by 1972 there were seven, extending from the Delta in the north to the Upper Regions of the south — at one point including Sudan, whose churches are now independent from the Evangelical Church of Egypt (cf. Sudan).

In addition to the Anglican Church, which formed a presence in Egypt in 1882, a large independent body split from the Evangelical Church in 1869, identifying itself as the Christian Brethren (sometimes called the Plymouth Brethren). Since their separation, the Brethren have been entirely under Egyptian leadership. Several Holiness missions entered Egypt toward the end of the 19th century; they are responsible for the establishment of two churches: the Faith Church, and the larger Holiness Movement, i.e., the Free Methodist Church. Advent and Pent communities also owe their origin to that period.

1. The Evangelical Church—Synod of the Nile (1040)

Originally part of the United Presbyterian Church of North America, the Evangelical Church of Egypt (sometimes called the Coptic Evangelical Church of Egypt) has been autonomous since 1957; it became officially independent in 1958. The highest judicatory of the church is the Synod of the Nile, encompassing the various presby.

TM: **300,000** Congr: **300** OrdM: **220** Eld: **nc** Deac: **nc** EvgHome: **nc** Mission: **nc** Women Ord: **no** ChurchOrg: **nc** Off/otherLang: **nc** DoctrB: **nc** Close relations with: **PCUSA** IntlRel: **WARC (1980), WCC** TheolSchool: **Evangelical Theological Seminary (Abbasiah, Cairo)**

Address: El-Kanisah El-Injiliyah, P.O. Box 1248, Cairo, Egypt, Tel: +20 2 591-5448, Fax: +20 2 591-8296

2. Armenian Evangelical Church (1041)

A small Armenian Prot community exists in Egypt; since they had diminished in numbers considerably in the early 1990s, their building was turned over to the Evangelical Church. The church belongs to Union of the Armenian Evangelical Churches in the Near East.

TM: **500** CM: **200** Congr: **1** OrdM: **nc** Eld: **nc** Deac: **nc** EvgHome: **nc** Mission: **nc** Women Ord: **nc** Off/otherLang: **nc** DoctrB: **nc**

Address: Armenian Evangelical Church, Ahmed Fouad Nour Street (Ex. Canope Street), Ibrahimieh, Alexandria, Egypt, Tel: +20 3 845-187

EL SALVADOR

Area in km²	21,040
Population	(July 1996 est.) 5,828,987 mestizo 94%, Indian 5%, white 1%
Religions in %	RCath 75% Prot (est.) 22%
Official/other languages	Spanish/Nahua (among some Indians)

The country was conquered by the Spaniards in the early 16th century. A relatively long period (1524-1547) was required to impose Spanish rule on the 168 Indian communities. Scant attention was paid to the country because it lacked precious metals. During the colonial reign it belonged to Guatemala. Through a fierce struggle the country gained independence from Spain in the early 19th century (1811-1821). Eventually, it also succeeded in establishing a separate Salvadorian diocese (1822, fully recognized in 1842). Toward the end of the century El Salvador was governed by Liberals who sought to promote, in their own interests, the economic development of the country: coffee became the main item of export. In particular, the doors were opened to Protestant groups from North America. Salvadorans live in poverty, and in recent decades the country has been ruled by repressive regimes. The conflicts deteriorated in 1980 into a civil war which lasted for several years with thousands of victims.

Missionary efforts started in 1540 when the military conquest was about to be completed. In the following centuries the church was close to the colonial power. During the struggle for independence several Creole priests were among the revolutionaries. Under the Liberal regime the RCath Church lost many of its privileges, but the church and the oligarchic government remained mutually supportive. The constitution of 1871 declared freedom of press, education, and religion, but Roman Catholicism continued to be recognized as the official religion of the country. The Second Vatican Council brought far-reaching changes. The church committed itself more and more to the cause of the poor and thus became the target of repressive violence. Many priests, catechists, and simple believers were killed, notably the Archbishop of San Salvador, Oscar A. Romero, who was shot while celebrating mass (March 24, 1980).

Protestantism came to the country in the wake of Liberalism. The Misión Centroamericana, founded by the dispensationalist C. I. Scofield in Texas, began work in 1896 and quickly gained ground in the country. Today the Central American Mission has 176 congr in the central and western parts of the country, mainly led by indigenous pastors. Several other churches followed. In 1904 Pentecostalism was introduced to the country by the missionary Frederick Mebius, in 1911 Baptists started work, and from 1930 the Assemblies of God began to expand.

The Panama Congress of 1916, organized by Prot mission agencies in the USA, assigned El Salvador to the Bapt (Northern Branch), with the result that Reformed and Presb missions concentrated their effort on other countries. Their presence in the country is therefore of recent date.

1. Christian Reformed Church in El Salvador (2061)

Missionaries from the Christian Reformed Church in North America had been working several years within the country before this church was founded in 1978. During El Salvador's unrest this church suffered a split. Both the Reformed Church of El Salvador (no. 2) and a newly formed Christian and Reformed Church (no. 3) broke away from it. It has diminished to a small size but remains quite active.

TM: **60** BM: **25** CM: **35** Congr: **2** PStations: **0** OrdM: **0** Eld: **0** Deac: **0** EvgHome: **2** Women Ord: **no** ChurchOrg: **local directorate, national directorate** Off/otherLang: **Spanish** DoctrB: **nc** Infant or believer's baptism: **both** Close relations with: **Reformed Church of El Salvador** NatRel: **Committee for Calvinist Education and Literature** IntlRel: **none**

Address: Iglesia Cristiana Reformada en El Salvador, Calle 5, poniente 2-4, Nueva San Salvador, El Salvador, Tel: +503 228-5283

2. Reformed Church of El Salvador (2060)

The church was officially inaugurated August 1979 in San Salvador. It maintains a Reformed Biblical Center for lay training. It has an agreement with the Lutheran University of San Salvador for advanced theological education. In the social area it runs a training center and several kindergartens.

TM: **3,212** BM: **2,248** CM: **2,030** Congr: **6** PStations: **10** OrdM: **5** Eld: **10** Deac: **20** EvgHome: **5** Mission: **5** Women Ord: **yes** As Ministers: **1988/-** as Deac: **1988/10** as Elders: **1988/4** ChurchOrg: **local consistories, presbys, national synods** Off/otherLang: **Spanish** DoctrB: **ApC, NicC, AthC, HeidC, HelvC, WestConf, CDort** Infant or believer's baptism: **both** Frequency of the Lord's Supper: **monthly** Close relations with: **CLAI, Bible Society, Luth Church, Episc, Bapt, LWF** NatRel: **Consejo Nacional de Iglesias (1990), Alfalit de El Salvador (1988), Asociación Cristiana de Jóvenes (1990), Communidad Cristiana de Jóvenes (FUMEC — El Salvador) (1989)** RegRel: **AIPRAL (1995)** IntlRel: **WARC (1993), CWM** TheolSchool: **Biblical Center** Service infrastructure: **social service center, center for lay people, home for retired people** Periodicals: **Boletin (gen/quarterly/2,000), Cartas Pastorales (2 per year/3,000)**

Address: Iglesia Reformada de El Salvador, Ap 2241centro de gobierno Av., San José, No. 367, San Salvador, El Salvador, Tel: +503 235-8603, Fax: +503 226-4144

3. Christian and Reformed Church (2062)

Very little reliable information could be found on this church. Its leadership is said to claim a total of 8 preaching stations.

Address: Iglesia Cristiana y Reformada, El Salvador

EQUATORIAL GUINEA

Area in km²	28,052
Population	(est. 1995) 420,260 Bioko (primarily Bubi, some Fernandinos), Rio Muni (primarily Fang), Europeans fewer than 1,000, mostly Spanish
Religions in %	Large RCath majority (90%), Prot minorities
Official language	Spanish (official), pidgin English, Fang, Bubi, Ibo

The country is divided into two parts: on the one hand there are the islands, especially Bioko, with the capital Malabo; on the other hand is the much larger continental area, Rio Muni (20,000 km^2). The two parts also have different histories. Bioko (formerly Fernando Po) was first Portuguese but became Spanish in 1777. Malabo (formerly Santa Isabel) was an important port. Rio Muni was French territory until 1901, when it came under Spanish rule. Catholic missionaries had a strong impact on the country. In 1968 Equatorial Guinea became independent. Ever since, it has experienced brutal dictatorships — first under Macias Nguema (†1979), and later under his nephew Obiang Nguema.

Presbyterian Church of Equatorial Guinea

In 1840 Presbyterian missionaries from the United States started missionary work on the island of Corisco. They soon began to expand into the interior. After 1901, under Spanish rule, the church had to face many difficulties. In 1952 churches were closed and pastors prohibited from working. Nevertheless, the Presbyterian Church continued to grow. Under Macias Nguema's regime the church again experienced fierce repression, and its freedom is limited even today. In 1969 the Presbyterian Church united with the church which had resulted from the missionary work of the World Evangelical Crusade in the area of Akurenam, and in 1973 the two churches formed, together with the Methodist Church, the Reformed Church of Equatorial Guinea (Iglesia Reformada de Guinea Ecuatorial, IRGE). The Methodist Church had come into existence in Bioko through the efforts of the British Methodists. The union was ambiguous because there was no real agreement on the authority of the new church over the three preexisting churches. Tensions were therefore bound to arise. Conversations toward a deeper common understanding are underway. Since January 1996 IRGE functions as a federation of churches; its name has been changed to Council of Evangelical Churches in Equatorial Guinea (CIEGE)

TM: **8,000** CM: **4,629** Congr: **25** PStations: **60** OrdM: **20** Eld: **172** Deac: **nc** EvgHome: **3** Mission: **ne** Women Ord: **yes** As Ministers: **none yet** as Deac: **none yet** as Elders: **none yet** ChurchOrg: **Presbyterian (congr, Synod)** Off/otherLang: **Spanish, local dialects** DoctrB: **ApC, WestConf** Infant or believer's baptism: **both** NatRel: **CIEGE (Concilio de Iglesias evangélicas en Guinea Ecuatorial)** RegRel: **AACC** IntlRel: **WCC, WARC (1988)** TheolSchool: **training in Cameroun**

Address: Iglesia Presbiteriana de Guinea Ecuatorial, Apartado 195, Bata Litoral, Equatorial Guinea, Tel.: +240 8 2052, Fax: +240 8 2131, E-mail: nc

ETHIOPIA

Area in km²	1,127,127
Population	(July 1996 est.) 57,171,662 Oromo 40%, Amhara and Tigrean 32%, Sidamo 9%, Shankella 6%, Somali 6%, Afar 4%, Gurage 2%, other 1%
Religions in %	Muslim 45%-50%, Ethiopian Orthodox 35%-40%, animist 12%, other 5% (Prot 4%, RCath 1%)
Official/other languages	Amharic, Tigrinya, Orominga, Guaraginga, Somali, Arabic, English (major foreign language taught in schools)

The Ethiopian population can roughly be divided into three groups: the Semitic tribes in the north (one third of the population) of which the Tigreans and Amharas are numerically the most important; the Cushitic tribes in eastern, southern, and western Ethiopia (about half the population), the most significant within this group being the Oromos (16 to 18 million); and the Nilotic group living on the border with Sudan. About half of the population belongs to the Orthodox Church, and a very large segment is Muslim. Ethiopia is one of the oldest Christian countries of the world. Christianity was introduced in the north in the fourth century by two Syrian brothers, Frumentius and Aedesius. For several centuries the Christian Axumite Kingdom (Abyssinia) flourished. But Islam spread rapidly, surrounding the kingdom and isolating the church from the rest of Christendom. Despite adverse circumstances the Abyssinian empire succeeded in surviving. In the 16th century a prolonged war between Christians and Muslims decisively weakened both parties and made it possible for the Oromos to move to territories formerly held by Christians or Muslims. Modern Ethiopia begins with Emperor Menelik II (1889-1913), who defeated the Italians in 1896 and extended the empire into the area of the Oromos. His successor, Haile Selassie I, sought to maintain the conquests. When, in 1935, Italy invaded and occupied the country, he went into exile; after his return in 1941 he continued to rule the country as an independent nation. In 1974 he was overthrown and the country was governed for 17 years by a military regime of Communist inspiration. After its fall in 1991 Ethiopia became a republic.

Protestant missions entered the country in the 19th century. Their intention originally was to contribute to the renewal of the Orthodox church and with its help to spread the Gospel within the non-Christian population. In fact, their witness resulted in the formation of Protestant churches. The first missionaries came from the Swedish Lutheran church; they were later joined by missionaries from Denmark, Norway, Germany, and the United States. In 1899 the Bible was translated into Oromo by Nesib (or Onesimus, his Christian name), an Oromo who had converted to Christianity.

The Reformed presence in Ethiopia dates to the beginning of the 20th century. A decision in 1869 by the United Presbyterian Church of North America (UPCNA) to send missionaries did not materialize until 1919. The effort began when a deadly epidemic, the Spanish flu, swept across the country. Thomas Alexander Lambie (1885-1954), a medical missionary of the UPCNA, stationed in Sudan, received from the governor of Qellem an urgent invitation to provide medical services. The efforts began within the framework of the Sudan Mission, but the UPCNA decided in 1922 to establish a separate mission. In 1924 the Ethiopia Missionary Association was formed. Work concentrated on the provinces of Wolega and Illubabour in the western part of Ethiopia. The policy of the Missionary Association was explicitly to revive the Orthodox Church and not to set up a separate church. But the missionaries decided to establish a church anyway. While the issue was still being debated, Italy invaded Ethiopia and the missionaries were forced to leave. The unexpected development led to the birth of the Evangelical Church Bethel in 1940. In 1947 it was constituted as an independent church under national leadership, holding Presbyterian doctrine and polity. The church became a member of WARC in 1970.

Ethiopian Evangelical Church Mekane Yesus (EECMY) (1043)

Soon after liberation from Italian occupation, initiatives were taken to bring together the various evangelical groups in the country. Beginning in 1944 Conferences of Ethiopian Evangelical Churches were held. Through the initiatives of Swedish missionaries and even more through the efforts of Ethiopian leaders, consensus was reached and, on January 21, 1959, the Ethiopian Evangelical Church Mekane Yesus was inaugurated. Emmanuel Gebre Selassie was elected as the first president.

At its foundation the church consisted of four synods, all of Lutheran background. Fifteen years later (1974), one year after the adoption of the Leuenberg Agreement, the churches resulting from Presbyterian missions decided to join this church. The Reformed congregations maintain their identity within the EECMY and continue to carry the name Bethel. The EECMY is basically a united church with a Lutheran majority, but since it was constituted as a Lutheran church, membership of the Bethel Church in the WARC became ineffective. Today the EECMY is made up of ten synods, two areas, and two presbyteries. The following belong to the Bethel tradition: the Western Wolega Bethel Synod, the Illubabour Bethel Synod, the Southwest Bethel Synod (formerly the Kaffa Bethel Presbytery), the Eastern Gambella Bethel Presbytery, and the Western Gambella Bethel Presbytery. A special office within EECMY provides the coordination which is needed (Bethel Synod Co-ordination BSCO). In recent times a remarkable development has taken place. The number of congregations both of the Bethel synods and of the EECMY as a whole has rapidly increased. At the time of joining, the Bethel Church had 55 congregations, 16,000 members, and 14 ordained ministers. Today the Bethel synods and presbyteries have a total membership of about 415,000 (Wollega 145,000, Illubabour 123,000, South-West 64,200, and Gambella 86,000). The Bethel synods are economically poor but are committed to spreading the Gospel; they understand mission as a service to the whole person, both spiritual and physical.

TM: **2,091,851** CM: **969,198** Congr: **3,748** PStations: **1,514** OrdM: **497** Eld: **nc** Deac: **85,561** EvgHome: **876** Mission: **nc** Women Ord: **yes** As Ministers: **1997/0** as Deac: **yes/nc** as Elders: **yes/nc** ChurchOrg: **United; the Bethel Synods, in particular, maintain Presbyterian polity (congr, parish, presby-district, synod, GenAssy)** Off/otherLang: **Oromo, Amharic, Tigrean, Sidama, Kombato** DoctrB: **ApC, NicC, AthC** Infant or believer's baptism: **both** Frequency of the Lord's Supper: **monthly** Close relations with: **PC (USA), ELCA (USA)** NatRel: **Evangelical Churches Fellowship of Ethiopia (1976)** (there are plans for an Ethiopian Evangelical Churches Union) RegRel: **AACC (1972)** IntlRel: **WCC (1972), LWF (1963), WARC (1970, discontinued in 1974)** TheolSchool: **Mekane Yesus Seminary (Addis Ababa), Terfa Jarso Bible School (P.O. Box 11 Metlu, Illubabour), Gidada Bible School (c/o P.O. Box 16, Western Wolega Bethel Synod, Dembi Dollo), Southwest Bethel Synod Bible School (P.O. Box 48, Mizan Teferi)**

Addresses: Ye Etiopia Wangelawit Betakristian Makane Yesus, P.O. Box 2087, Addis Ababa Wollega, Ethiopia, Tel: +251 1 55 32 80, Fax: +251 1 55 29 66

> Bethel Synod Coordination (BSCO), P.O. Box 1111, Addis Ababa, Tel. +251 1 75088/89, Fax +251 1 75 43 21
> Western Wollega Bethel Synod (WWBS), P.O. Box 16, Dembi Dollo, Ethiopia
> Illubabour Bethel Synod (IBS), P.O. Box 11, Mettu, Illubabour, Ethiopia
> Southwest Bethel Synod, P.O. Box 48, Mizan Teferi, Ethiopia
> Eastern Gambella Bethel Presbytery, P.O. Box 6, Gambella, Ethiopia
> Western Gambella Bethel Presbytery, P.O. Box 135, Gambella, Ethiopia

FEDERATED STATES OF MICRONESIA (FSM)

Area in km²	702
Population	(July 1996 est.) 125,377 nine ethnic Micronesian and Polynesian groups
Religions in %	RCath 50%, Protestant 47%, other and none 3%
Official/other languages	English/Trukese, Pohnpeian, Yapese, Kosrean

The United Church of Christ in Micronesia

In the 19th century the ABCFM evangelized the Marshall Islands (cf. Marshall Islands), together with Pohnpei, Kosrae, Chuuk (Truk), and Yap, the four island states which form the Federated States of Micronesia. They became a sovereign state in 1986, freely associated with the USA, the former administering power under UN mandate. The name The United Church of Christ in Micronesia has been chosen in analogy to the United Church of Christ in the United States of America (UCCUSA), which brought together the previous Congregational and Evangelical and Reformed Churches (cf. United States). The church's collective memory and international contacts reflect previous successive political occupations by Spain, Germany, Japan, and the USA.

The Marshall Islands church, being outside the federation, shares the UCCUSA form of church order within the wider United Church of Christ in Micronesia and participates in assemblies of the whole church. Headquarters of the church in the FSM are located in Pohnpei, the Federation's capital. The church includes a majority (over 90%) of the population of Kosrae, but is only lightly represented in the other two states of the federation. The ABCFM, which became the United Church Board of World Ministries from 1957 onward, introduced Congreg church government, though some of its missionaries were originally Presb. Links continue with the Mission Board of the United Church of Christ in Hawaii. They date back to 1857, when Hawaiian Islander missionaries accompanied the ABCFM pioneers. On Kosrae, a mission training school educated future pastors and lay leaders for the area, including the Marshall Islands, and earlier for Kiribati (the Gilbert Islands). Communication was maintained by a succession of mission vessels called *Morning Star*. Bible use in English and local languages was promoted through the mission school until its closure in 1963. Modern communications and membership in the Pacific Conference of Churches, together with theological education programs provided through the Pacific Theological College in Fiji, have ensured Micronesian participation in the ecumenical movement in the Pacific as a whole.

1. United Church of Christ in Kosrae (5142)

No data have been made available.

Address: United Church of Christ in Kosrae, P.O. Box 25, Tafunsak, Kosrae State, FSM 96 944, Micronesia (Federated States).

2. United Church of Christ in Pohnpei (5140)

No data have been made available.

Address: United Church of Christ in Pohnpei, P.O. Box 864, 96 941 Kolonia—Pohnpei, Micronesia (Federated States), Tel: +691 320 2271, Fax: +691 320 4044

3. Namoneas Congregational Church in Chuuk (5141)

No data have been made available.

Address: Namoneas Congregational Church, P.O. Box 542, Weno Chuuk, Truk State, FM 96942 Micronesia (Federated States), Fax: +691 330 3192

FIJI

Area in km²	18,270
Population	(July 1996 est.) 782,381 Fijian 49%, Indian 46%, European, other Pacific Islanders, overseas Chinese, and other 5%
Religions in %	Christian 52% (Meth 37%, RCath 9%), Hindu 38%, Muslim 8%, other 2% (Fijians are mainly Christian, Indians are Hindu, and there is a Muslim minority)
Official/other languages	English, Fijian, Hindustani

Fiji, with its 332 islands, of which approximately 110 are inhabited, is richly endowed with forest (65% of its aerial surface), mineral, and fish resources; it has one of the most developed economies among the Pacific Islands. Sugar exports and tourism are the major sources of foreign exchange. It has been independent from the United Kingdom since October 10,1970.

The first missionaries — British and French — arrived in the 19th century. Whites came mainly from Australia and New Zealand. Between 1879 and 1916 some 60,000 Indians were solicited to immigrate for work on the sugar cane plantations.

St. Andrew's Presbyterian Church (5130)

This church is part of the Auckland Presbytery of the Presbyterian Church of Aotearoa New Zealand. It was established when Fiji was a British Crown colony, partly in response to the needs of Scots and New Zealanders employed in the Colonial Service, teaching, trade, or the mercantile marine, and who had made Fiji their home for shorter or longer periods. Relationships with the New Zealand church were also facilitated by the fact that people in the islands of New Zealand were part of Polynesia and included a Maori population. Since World War II personnel and English-speaking teachers and students from other Reformed areas in the Pacific (Vanuatu, Tahiti, New Caledonia, Niué, Kiribati, Tuvalu, and the Solomon Islands, for example) joined in the life and worship of the church during their time in Fiji. They are now the substantial core of the church, giving it a predominantly Pacific Island flavor under the care of Islander ministers. The Kirk session is cross-cultural and avails itself of the services of elders and some ordained ministers from other parts of Oceania, working closely with the Fiji Council of Churches and the Pacific Conference of Churches based in Fiji. The Pacific Theological College (PTC) also has its home in Fiji.

165

TM: **300** BM: **250** CM: **200** Congr: **3** PStations: **3** OrdM: **1** Eld: **15** Deac: **ne** EvgHome: **ne** Mission: **ne** Women Ord: **yes** As Ministers: **0** as Deac: **0** as Elders: **4** ChurchOrg: **belongs to Auckland Presbytery of Presbyterian Church of Aotearoa-New Zealand** Off/otherLang: **English** DoctrB: **ApC, NicC, WestConf** Infant or believer's baptism: **both** Frequency of the Lord's Supper: **monthly** Close relations with: **Uniting Church Papua New Guinea, Methodist Church, Cook Islands Christian Church, Church of Christ Marshall Islands, Kiribati Protestant Church** NatRel: **Fiji Council of Churches** IntlRel: **none** TheolSchool: **in Pacific or regional theological colleges** Service infrastructure: **na** Periodicals: **na**

Address: St. Andrew's Presbyterian Church, P.O. Box 25, 74 Gordon Street, Suva—Fiji, Fiji Islands, Tel: +679 301-204, Fax: +679 303-205

FINLAND

Area in km²	337,030
Population	(July 1996 est.) 5,105,230 Finn, Swede, Lapp, Gypsy, Tatar
Religions in %	Luth 89%, Greek Orth 1%, none 9%, other 1%
Official/other languages	Finnish 93.5%, Swedish 6.3%, small Lapp- and Russian-speaking minorities

IFFEC (International Federation of Free Evangelical Churches)

Since the 9th century Finland has been at the intersection of Western and Eastern Christendom. From the time of the Crusades in the 12th century RCath gained in influence while Byzantine Christianity was predominant among the population of Karelia, a region which over the centuries came to the zone of influence of either Russia or Sweden. Since the Reformation, Finland has remained, like the other Scandinavian countries, an almost exclusively Luth country. After 1860 small Bapt, Meth, and Free Church congr developed. They were followed around the 1900s by Pentecostals, Salvation Armyists, and Jehovah's Witnesses; Mormons arrived after World War II. The Law on Religious Freedom (1923) defined the rights and obligations of these communities. By 1982 some 24 denominations other than Luth were registered, with a total of 46,000 members. Strongest among them today are the Advent (some 40,000) and the Free Churches. The Orth Church (3 bishops and 25 congr) is an autonomous church in communion with the Ecumenical Patriarchate of Constantinople. RCath number less than 3,000.

1. Evangelical Free Church of Finland (6531)

The first congr sprang up in various parts of Finland during the revivals of the 1870s. The first chapel was built in 1877. In 1889 the Free Mission of Finland was organized. After 1923 the Free Church of Finland was constituted. Over the past decade this church has experienced a revival, created a Bible course by correspondence, and increased publishing work. It supports mission work in 7 Asian and 3 African countries.

TM: **13,807** CM: **8,477** Congr: **91** OrdM: **75** Eld: **487** Deac: **nc** EvgHome: **10** Mission: **52** Women Ord: **no** ChurchOrg: **congr, general meeting twice yearly (each local church is independent; common concerns are discussed in a general meeting in summer and fall)** Off/otherLang: **Finnish** DoctrB: **ApC** Infant or believer's baptism: **believer** Periodicals: **Suomen Viikkolehti (weekly)** NatRel: **Ecumenical Council (observer), Council of Finnish Free Christians, Finnish Missionary Council** IntlRel: **IFFEC** TheolSchool: **Theological Institute and Bible school**

Address: Suomen Vapaakirkko, Pl 198, FIN—13, 100 Hameenlinna, Finland, Tel: +358 3 644-5150, Fax: +358 3 612-2153, E-mail: svk@svk.fi

2. Free Mission Covenant Church in Finland (6530)

The first local congr was founded in 1880. The Fria Missionen (the Free Mission) was constituted in 1889 as a result of revivals in the 1880s and 1890s. In 1921 the Free Mission was divided into a Finnish and a Swedish group. As a rule pastors of this church baptize only believers, while children are baptized by a pastor of the Finnish Lutheran Church. The church emphasizes renewal, teaching, prayer, and personal evangelism. It does not have congr abroad, but it cooperates in mission with other denominations in some eight countries around the world.

TM: **900** BM: **700** Congr: **20** PStations: **5** OrdM: **15** Eld: **75** Deac: **na** EvgHome: **nc** Mission: **12** Women Ord: **yes** As Ministers: **1980/0** as Deac: **yes** as Elders: **25** ChurchOrg: **congr, special general meetings** Off/otherLang: **Swedish** DoctrB: **Bible only** Infant or believer's baptism: **believer** Frequency of the Lord's Supper: **monthly** NatRel: **Council of Free Churches of Finland, Ecumenical Council of Finland** RegRel: **nc** IntlRel: **IFFEC** TheolSchool: **Theol. Seminary of the Mission Covenant Church of Sweden (Lidingö), Disciple School (Borga, SF), Free Christian People's College (FIN)** .

Address: Fria Missionsförbundet, Högbergsgatan 22, FIN SF-00, 130 Helsingfors 13, Finland, Tel: +358 9-60 20 33, Fax: +358 9 60 20 90

FRANCE

Area in km²	551,602
Population	58,087,000
Religions in % (1994)	RCath 67%, Muslims 2%, Prot 1%, Jews 1%, other 3%
Official language	French

CPLR (Permanent Luth-Ref Council—*Conseil permanent luthero-réformé*)
DEFAP (French Prot Churches Mission arm—*Département évangélique français d'Action Apostolique*)
ERF (Reformed Church of France—*Eglise réformée de France*)
FPF (French Protestant Church Federation—*Fédération protestante de France*)

The Reformation movement started in France in the early 16th century. Mainly under the influence of Calvin, Ref churches were organized during the 1540s and 1550s. Very quickly their membership added up to 1,500,000 people, approximately 10% of the population. They held their first National Synod in 1559 in Paris, at which they approved the "Confessio Gallicana" and rules for church government. They were granted legal status in 1598 (the Edict of Nantes), though the King of France and his kingdom were Roman Catholic. In 1685 the Edict of Nantes was repealed, and France reverted to the rule generally applied in Europe: *cujus regio, ejus religio*. Many reformed people had already left France. Many more fled. Those that remained, 600-700,000, were thought to have joined the RCath Church. Yet, all through the 18th century, though outlawed, the Reformed Churches of France carried on; ministers in hiding visited the scattered flocks, services were held in the "wilderness," and so on.

Just before the Revolution began in 1789, the king granted that the Prot could have their births, marriages, and deaths registered without undergoing RCath baptism, marriage and burial. During the revolutionary years the Reformed people were briefly, for the first time in their history, fully free to enjoy their church life. In 1802 Napoleon settled the framework in which the RCath Church, the Luth and Reformed churches were to live all through the 19th century. The Reformed churches were granted a state-paid clergy but denied full freedom of government and the authority to convene national synods. The evangelical revivals renewed the spiritual life of the churches and led lay people to take the initiative in many fields, such as evangelization, schools, hospitals, and charities of all sorts. The French Reformed also took part in the missionary adventure through the Paris Missionary Society, started at the beginning of the 1820s.

Under the strain brought about by the spread of new ideas, with no real church government and synodical life to hold the different parties together, the unity of the Reformed people broke down. Some chose to be free of all links with the state (cf. no. 3). Free churches like the Methodist Church, the Plymouth Brethren, and, in the 20th century, the Pentecostalists made their entry in France.

In 1906 all French churches were disestablished. Three national Reformed Churches, which soon became two, were set up. One was more strict in doctrine, the other more liberal. But both took part in the ecumenical movement and had members attending the meetings of Life and Work and Faith and Order. In 1938 those two churches decided to unite and, with some Free and Methodist Churches, became the present Reformed Church of France.

The history of the churches in Alsace and the department of Moselle was somewhat different from that in the rest of France. The churches there were under German rule from 1870 to 1918 and remained within the framework of the Napoleonic arrangement. When France recovered Alsace and Lorraine, the RCath, the Ref, and the Luth churches kept their same state-linked status. The Reformed Church of Alsace and Lorraine is in close communion with the Reformed Church of France and represented at its national synod; yet it remains distinct.

1. Reformed Church of France (6051)

The Reformed Church of France (ERF) believes it is called to express and bear out the unity of all those of different spiritual and theological trends that claim to belong to the Ref tradition. All congr and ministers must subscribe to the Declaration of Faith of 1938. The ERF covers practically the whole of France, except Alsace and Moselle and an area in the east (Pays de Montbéliard), traditionally Luth. It shares many responsibilities, including the theological faculties, with the Lutheran Church and with the other churches who belong to the French Protestant Federation and has an old practice of partnership with the RCath Church in certain fields. Its life is organized on a regional basis (8 regions). The national headquarters are in Paris.

TM: **182,000** Congr: **350** PStations: **1,715** OrdM: **630** Eld: **nc** Deac: **nc** EvgHome: **nc** Mission: **nc** Women Ord: **yes** As Ministers: **94** as Deac: **nc** as Elders: **nc** ChurchOrg: **nc** Off/otherLang: **French** DoctrB: **ApC, RochC** Infant or believer's baptism: **both** Frequency of the Lord's Supper: **once per month, some parishes every Sunday** Periodicals: **Réforme (gen/weekly), Le Christianisme au XXe siècle (gen/weekly), Mission (monthly), Information-Evangélisation (6 times per year/8,000), Regional papers (gen/monthly)** Close relations with: **member churches of CPLR** NatRel: **CECEF (Council of Christian Churches in France), CPLR, DEFAP (Mission Service), ACAT (Association against Torture)** RegRel: **CEC** IntlRel: **CEVAA, WCC, WARC, EECCS** TheolSchool: **three faculties of Protestant theology (Paris, Montpellier, Strasbourg)**

Address: Eglise Réformée de France (ERF), 47, rue de Clichy, F-75 009 Paris Cedex 09, France, Tel: +33 1 48 74 90 92, Fax: +33 1 42 81 92 40

2. Reformed Church of Alsace and Lorraine (ERAL) (6050)

In the 16th and 17th centuries some small areas in Alsace belonged to Reformed princes; they have remained Reformed since then. The Republic of Mulhouse was also Reformed when it became French at the time of the Revolution. Between 1870 and 1918 the Germans set up congr belonging to the Church of the Union in Lorraine. The Reformed Church of Alsace and Lorraine (ERAL) has inherited those different churches. ERAL is in close fellowship with ERF. Its delegates are full members of the ERF National Synod. It is also a close partner of the Augsburg Confession Church in Alsace and Lorraine: the two have the same headquarters (in Strasburg), same departments and offices for the different areas of the life of the church. With the Augsburg Confession Church, the RCath Church, and the Jewish community, it enjoys official status. Most ministers are paid by the government.

TM: **33,000** BM: **33,000** Congr: **52** PStations: **91** OrdM: **50** Eld: **406** Deac: **0** EvgHome: **1** Mission: **nc** Women Ord: **yes** As Ministers: **1930/5** ChurchOrg: **5 consistories, synod (each congr represented by pastor and two lay people), synodal council (consisting of the lay people and four pastors)** Off/otherLang: **French** DoctrB: **ApC, NicC, HeidC, HelvC, RochC, Declaration of ERF/1938** Infant or believer's baptism: **both** Frequency of the Lord's Supper: **monthly and special feast days** Periodicals: **Le Ralliement protestant (pop and gen/monthly/6,200), Le Renouveau (pop and gen/monthly/ 5,000), Ensemble (pop and gen/7times per year), Le Messager Evangélique (gen/weekly/12,000)** Close relations with: **Evangelical Lutheran Church of Alsace-Lorraine (1960)** NatRel: **DEFAP (1971), ERF (1950), CPLR (1972), FPF Conseil Eglises chrétiennes France** RegRel: **CEC** IntlRel: **CEVAA (1971), WCC, WARC, Leuenberg (1973)** TheolSchool: **Faculties of Protestant Theology (Strasbourg, Paris, Montpellier)**

Address: Eglise Réformée d'Alsace et de Lorraine (ERAL), 1, Quai St. Thomas, F-67 081 Strasbourg Cedex, France, Tel: +33 3 88 25 90 10, Fax: +33 3 88 25 90 80

3. Union of Free Evangelical Churches in France (6055)

The Union of Free Evangelical Churches in France was founded on September 1, 1849. Most of the churches joining the new organization were previously independent churches which grew out of the revival that spread over France between 1820 and 1830. A few were Ref churches which had left the Protestant State Church several months before because of spiritual and doctrinal "confusion." In 1939 a split occurred, and a number of congr joined the Reformed Church of France (cf. no. 1).

TM: **4,000** BM: **2,400** CM: **2,200** Congr: **54** OrdM: **47** Eld: **nc** Deac: **nc** EvgHome: **nc** Mission: **nc** Women Ord: **yes** As Ministers: **no** as Deac: **yes** as Elders: **yes** ChurchOrg: **semi-synodal system for matters of general interest** Off/otherLang: **French** DoctrB: **ApC, NicC, Church's own Confession of Faith** Infant or believer's baptism: **both** Frequency of the Lord's Supper: **weekly on Sundays** Periodicals: **Pour la Vérité (For the Truth) (gen/monthly/1,500)** Close relations with: **ERF, EREI, Federation of Evangelical Baptist Churches** NatRel: **FPF, Confederation of United Evangelical Churches** RegRel: **Association of Professing Churches in Francophone Countries** IntlRel: **IFFEC (1949)** TheolSchool: **Free Faculty of Evangelical Theology (Vaux-sur-Seine)**

Address: Union des Eglises évangéliques libres de France, 12, rue Claude Perrault, F-92 120 Toulouse, France, Tel: +33 5 6126-0618, Fax: +33 5 6199-9282

4. National Union of Independent Reformed Evangelical Churches of France (6052)

When the present Reformed Church of France was formed in 1938, some congr, though also deeply desiring to share in this demonstration of the unity of the Body of Christ, did not deem it right to belong to this new institution. Instead they joined together to form the denomination now known as the Independent Evangelical Reformed Church (EREI). The preaching and teaching provided in the EREI are required to agree with the Declaration of Faith (1872) and the Confession of Faith (1559) "because there is one Truth, not a plurality of truths." The EREI stresses that personal faith also be in agreement with what the Church confesses. The headquarters of the church is in Nimes. The congregations are mainly in the southeast, though there are some in the southwest and a few in the Paris area

TM: **10,600** BM: **1,860** Congr: **51** PStations: **65** OrdM: **37** Eld: **360** Deac: **1** EvgHome: **6** Mission: **2** Women Ord: **yes** As Ministers: **1994/1** as Deac: **1938/1** as Elders: **1938/140** ChurchOrg: **Presbyterian-synodal (3 annual regional synods, 1 annual national synod, general national synod every third year)** Off/otherLang: **French** DoctrB: **ApC, NicC, CDort, AthC, HeidC, RochC, Ref Decl of Faith (1872)** Infant or believer's baptism: **both** Frequency of the Lord's Supper: **varies from congr to congr, twice per month** Periodicals: **Bulletin d'Information et de Liaison special (3-4 per year), Cahier Lumières des hommes (pop/occasional), Nuance (pop/monthlyl/1,500) Entente Evangélique (pop/quarterly/1,600)** Close relations with: **Mission to the World/USA, Gereformeerde Zendingsbond in de Nederlandse Hervormde Kerk; Stichting Steun Gereformeerde Kerken in Fankrijk — both NL** NatRel: **FPF, DEFAP, CEVAA, Alliance Evangélique Française** IntlRel: **REC (1952)** .

Address: Union Nationale des Eglises Réformées Evangéliques Indépendantes de France EREI, 74, rue Henri Revoil, F-34 000 Nîmes, France, Tel: +33 4 66 23 95 05, Fax: +33 4 66 23 95 98

5. Malagazy Protestant Church (FPMA) (6058)

The FPMA, as this church is known, was set up in 1959 by Malagasy students in France with the agreement of the Federation of Protestant Churches in Madagascar. Its membership is composed of Malagasies belonging to the Church of Jesus Christ in Madagascar and the Lutheran Church of Madagascar living in France. It considers itself the firstfruit of the United Protestant Church of Madagascar.

TM: **3,000** BM: **2,500** CM: **2,500** Congr: **24** PStations: **none** OrdM: **0** Eld: **ne** Deac: **80** EvgHome: **ne** Mission: **ne** Women Ord: **yes** As Ministers: **0** as Deac: **1996/70** as Elders: **ne** ChurchOrg: **23 parishes, 5 regional synods** Off/otherLang: **Malagazy** DoctrB: **ApC, NicC, AthC, HeidC** Infant or believer's baptism: **both** Frequency of the Lord's Supper: **monthly** Periodicals: **Jour 'Vatsy' (Info/twice a month/300)** NatRel: **FPF (1979), FFKM (1992, see under Madagascar)** RegRel: **CEC (1992)** TheolSchool: **none**

Address: Eglise Protestante Malgache/Fiangonana Protestanta Malagasy 47, rue de Clichy, F-75 311 Paris Cedex 09, France, Tel: +33 1 45 96 03 05, Fax: +33 1 42 81 40 01

FRENCH GUIANA

Area in km²	83,534
Population	150,000 including ca. 5,000 Amerindians, 30,000 "Metropolitains," 5,000 Chinese, 2,000 Syro-Lebanese. 65% of the country's population lives in Cayenne, 27% on the coast, 8% in the forest.
Religions in %	RCath 66%, Prot 1.6%
Official language	French

French Guiana is an overseas district ("département d'Outre-mer") located in South America, 7,000 km distance from Paris, France. Its capital city, Cayenne, was founded in 1544 by Spaniards looking for the mythical gold country of El Dorado. French settlers arrived in the early 1600s. Protestant families began to arrive after 1624 and remained, despite having, unlike the RCath Church, no governmental support. No indigenous Protestant church was started until the 20th century. The "département" served between 1795 and 1953 as a prison for banned French political prisoners and for common law criminals with long sentences. Since 1979 French Guiana has housed thousands of families working for Ariane Espace, the French satellite launching company.

Evangelical Church of French Guiana (3323)

This denomination was officially created in summer of 1997. It serves an ethnic group of French military and civilians coming mostly from France (also called "metropolitains"). One of the congr meets in the military fort in Cayenne. It maintains a chaplaincy within the French army stationed in this country. The denomination is a member of the CEEEFE (Commission of French-speaking Evangelical Churches Abroad) and thus has close relationships with the Fédération protestante de France, which incorporates some 14 Protestant denominations and missions within France.

TM: **1,000** CM: **500** Congr: **1** PStations: **4** OrdM: **1** Eld: **nc** Deac: **nc** EvgHome: **ne** Mission: **ne** Women Ord: **ne** ChurchOrg: **nc** Off/otherLang: **French** DoctrB: **ApC, NicC** Infant or believer's baptism: **both** Close relations with: **Fédération protestante de France (CEEEFE)** TheolSchool: **none.**

Address: Eglise Evangélique de la Guyane française, B.P. 6019, Cayenne, Département de la Guyane française

FRENCH POLYNESIA

Area in km²	4,000,000
Population	(est. 1992) 200,000 Polynesians (68.5%), Europeans (11.6%), Polyn./Europeans (9.5%), var. Chinese groups (9.3%), others (1.1%)
Religions in %	RCath (34.3%) Prot (45.2%), Latter Days Saints (6%) Advent (4.8%), Sanitos (3.8%), others (5.9%)
Official/other languages	French, Tahitian/local dialects

French Polynesia consists of 118 islands grouped in 5 archipelagos scattered across four million km² of the Pacific Ocean, an area the size of Europe (without the former USSR). Tahiti, with 1,042 km², is the largest among these islands, which total a land surface of only 4,000 km².

First settlements took place between 300 and 600 A.D. The Spanish navigator Magellan was in 1521 the first "Westerner" to arrive in this region. He was followed by Mendana (1595); various Dutch, English, and Spanish ships sailed through the Tuamotu islands between 1606 and 1765. In 1767 Samuel Wallis "discovered" Tahiti and took possession of it in the name of King George III. A year later the French explorer L. A. de Bougainville "discovered" it in the name of the French King. In 1769, 1773, and 1771 the English captain James Cook conducted three expeditions through the region. The famous "mutiny on the Bounty" and the survival journey back to England of Captain Bligh greatly captured the imagination of Europeans.

The London Missionary Society (LMS) became in 1797 the first mission body present in the Pacific by sending missionaries to Polynesia. In 1815 King Pomare II was converted and with him most of the population ("cujus regio, ejus religio" was not only true in Europe!). The first RCath missionaries arrived in the archipelago of the Gambiers in 1834 and progressed to Tahiti in 1836. They were not welcome since Protestantism was by law the only established religion. French commander La Place threatened to fire on Tahiti's main city, Papeete, unless the RCath were allowed freely to exercise their religion. Queen Pomare IV gave in. After more threats and bluffs a protectorate treaty was signed with France in 1842.

Between 1856 and1866 a first wave of over 1,000 Chinese from mainland China and Hong Kong arrived on the cotton and coffee plantations, mainly in the archipelago of the Marquises. A second wave arrived between 1907 and 1930.

In 1880 France annexed the archipelago of Tahiti, then the Leeward Islands and the Austral Islands (1897-1900). During World War II Bora Bora was used as a US military air base; until then Polynesia could be reached by boat only. In 1945 all Polynesians became French citizens. An independence movement started in

1947 under the leadership of Pouvanaa a Oopa. In 1949 he was elected into the Parliement of France, and reelected in 1951 and 1956. In 1958 General de Gaulle asked all French colonies by way of a referendum to decide their political future. In French Polynesia only 36% voted for independence. Within 12 months Pouvanaa was arrested, imprisoned for 8 years, and sent "into exile" in France for 15 years. He later became a senator and a lay preacher of the Evangelical Church. Progressively (1977 and 1984) autonomy was handed over to the local elected authorities. Today Polynesia is a French "overseas territory with internal autonomy." Although a growing number of voices are in favor of cutting all links with France, the Legislative Assembly of the Territory voted in 1996, by a two-thirds majority, in favor of a sustained relationship with France.

Between 1963 and 1996 France tested, under mounting international protest, almost 200 nuclear bombs (first 41 in the atmosphere, later 152 underground). Launching sites in Moruroa and Fangataufa have since been dismantled.

The **Evangelical Church of French Polynesia** (EEPF) (cf. no. 1) includes some 45% of the total population and over 98% of all Prot Reformed believers in French Polynesia, while several dozen other small to tiny denominations also claim the Protestant heritage. There are some Reformed among them, mostly individual splinter congr of which three constitute today a loose **Confederation of Reformed Churches of French Polynesia**. This body has become the "omnium gatherum" for all those who are in favor of independence and who disagree with the policies, structure, administration, or theological direction of the EEPF. It once counted up to 13 congr, but barely more than 3, with a total of less than 500 members, are really active today. Most of these autonomous Reformed single-congregation churches have been founded and/or led by former pastors of the EEPF who had previously studied at the Pacific Theological College (PTC) in Suva (Fiji).

1. Evangelical Church of French Polynesia (EEPF) (5060)

This church dates back to the arrival of the first missionaries of LMS on March 5, 1797. After 1815, the majority of the population identified themselves with Christianity; they formed this national Prot church, which spread from Tahiti over to the other four archipelagos. Following political developments in 1863, LMS handed its control over the church to the Paris Evangelical Missionary Society. In 1963 the church became autonomous under the name of Eglise évangélique de Polynésie française. Except for the Marquises and the Tuamotu-Gambier archipelagos where RCath come first in numbers, the Evangelical church is predominant in the rest of French Polynesia. Almost all the income of the church is collected each year during special offering services held during the month of May. This church also has a parish of over 5,000 migrant workers in New Caledonia.

Burning issues for the Church today are the declining numbers in membership and of pastors; growing unemployment on Tahiti, which is crowded by the influx of islanders; the conflicts arising between conservative traditionalists and modernists; and the efforts toward independence which had been linked for a long time with antinuclear demonstrations and, since the closure of the testing sites, with the economic future of the area. On the religious scene various attitudes, ranging from maintaining the heritage of the early missionaries to rebirth by cultivating the ancient traditions, have drastically changed the religious scene in French Polynesia and given birth to dozens of different denominations and religious groupings.

TM: **95,000** BM: **45,000** CM: **30,000** Congr: **81** PStations: **81** OrdM: **65** Eld: **yes** Deac: **900** EvgHome: **800** Mission: **none** Women Ord: **yes** As Ministers: **1995/0** as Deac: **1950/55** as Elders: **nc** ChurchOrg: **Reformed (congr, districts, general synod)** Off/otherLang: **Reo Maohi, French** DoctrB: **ApC** Infant or believer's baptism: **both** Frequency of the Lord's Supper: **monthly** Close relations with: **Christian Church of Cook Islands, Evangelical Church of New Caledonia** NatRel: **nc** RegRel: **PCC (1963)** IntlRel: **CEVAA (1972), WCC (1963), WARC (1992)** TheolSchool: **Hermon Theological College (Tahiti), Pacific Theological College (Suva, Fiji)** Service infrastructure: **center for young girls, education center, 3 nursing houses, 1 high school, 1 college, 1 technical school, 3 schools** Periodicals: Veà Porotetani (gen/monthly/6,000)

Address: Etaretia Evaneria no Porinetia Farani (Eglise évangélique de Polynésie française), B.P. 11, 3 Bvd. Pomare 403, Papeete, Tahiti, French Polynesia, Tel: +689 460 600, Fax: +689 419 357

2. Independent Church of French Polynesia (5061)

This church is the result of a split in the late 1940s when the parish of Afaahiti went on its own after having refused a decision of the "Mission protestante" to move its pastor to another parish. Today this church is led by a layman, Mr. Jean-Pierre Aumeran.

TM: **100** Congr: **1** OrdM: **0** Eld: **yes** Deac: **yes** EvgHome: **nc** Mission: **none** Women Ord: **nc** ChurchOrg: **Congregational** Off/otherLang: **Reo Maohi, French** DoctrB: **nc** NatRel: **Confederation of Reformed Churches of French Polynesia** RegRel: **none** IntlRel: **none**

Address: Eglise autonome de Polynésie française. B.P. 7336, Route de Ceinture, Taravao, Tahiti, French Polynesia

3. Christian Church (5067)

The Christian Church is the result of a split which occurred in 1958, when the parish of Taunao left the EEPF. It protested against the decision of the EEPF to appoint its pastor to another parish. The move was also motivated by its political stance at the time of the referendum of 1958 (see above). This church was in favor of independence from France, while the EEPF was against. In those days the EEPF (called the "Mission protestante") was still under the leadership of French missionaries. There is not much difference between the order of service and basic teachings of the Christian Church and the Evangelical Church, except that each parish of the former is autonomous and all its pastors are "tent-makers."

TM: **1,000** Congr: **8** OrdM: **8** Eld: **yes** Deac: **yes** EvgHome: **nc** Mission: **none** Women Ord: **nc**

ChurchOrg: **Congregational** Off/otherLang: **Reo Maohi, French** DoctrB: **nc** NatRel: **nc** RegRel: **none** IntlRel: **none**

Address: Te faaroo Cheretesiano, Avenue Prince Hinoi, Papeete Tahiti, French Polynesia

4. Church of the Living Bread (5062)

This church consists of one congregation. It was founded by the late Rev. Tupai Tahua, a former pastor of the parish of Papara (EEPF). He had previously served as pastor in New-Caledonia. After his death his sister-in-law, Ms. Aurore Reid, took over the leadership from him.

TM: **200** Congr: **1** OrdM: **1** Eld: **yes** Deac: **yes** EvgHome: **nc** Mission: **none** Women Ord: **yes** As Ministers: **0** as Deac: **0** as Elders: **0** ChurchOrg: **Congregational** Off/otherLang: **Reo Maohi, French** DoctrB: **nc** NatRel: **Confederation of Reformed Churches of French Polynesia** RegRel: **none** IntlRel: **none**

Address: Pane Ora (Le Pain de Vie), pk 34,5, Papara, Tahiti, French Polynesia, Tel: +689 574-081

5. Free Church of French Polynesia (5061)

The Free Church represents the most liberal or radical faction in the whole spectrum of Christian religion in French Polynesia. It was founded in the 1970s by Hubert Bremond, a student in theology trained at the Pacific College of Theology in Fiji, but who was expelled from the Evangelical Church (EEPF) while he was still a pastor-assistant. Since its beginning this church has had no ordained clergy, and Holy Communion could be celebrated whenever and wherever members met, even in a restaurant. Today it consists of a tiny parish in Parea, on the island of Huahine.

TM: **30** Congr: **1** OrdM: **0** Eld: **yes** Deac: **yes** EvgHome: **nc** Mission: **none** Women Ord: **nc** ChurchOrg: **nc** Off/otherLang: **Reo Maohi** DoctrB: **nc** NatRel: **nc** RegRel: **none** IntlRel: **none**

Address: Eglise libre de Polynésie Française, Parea Huahine, French Polynesia, Tel: +689 688-520

6. New Evangelical Reformed Church (5063)

This church was founded in 1982 by another former minister of the EEPF, Rev. Ferdinand Teura. He had studied at the Pacific College of Theology in Fiji. In the beginning of his ministry in Pueu he had been impressed by a "Youth with a Mission" campaign. After a few years of service he left the EEPF because he disagreed with the church's leadership and the handling of funds at the local level. He founded, in the early 1990s, the Confederation of Reformed Churches (see above), which he qualified as "a badly needed renewal movement." He was expelled from this church and created a new one (cf. no. 7). The present pastor of the church,

Rev. Arona Temu (another former student of the PTC and pastor of the EEPF), is also the president of the Confederation.

TM: **nc** Congr: **1** OrdM: **1** Eld: **yes** Deac: **yes** EvgHome: **nc** Mission: **none** Women Ord: **nc** ChurchOrg: **Congregational** Off/otherLang: **Reo Maohi, French** DoctrB: **nc** NatRel: **Confederation of Reformed Churches of French Polynesia** RegRel: **none** IntlRel: **none**

Address: Paroita Galilea, pk 4,5, Pueu Tahiti, French Polynesia, Tel: +689 571-722

7. Protestant Reformed Church of French Polynesia (5066)

This tiny church was created by Rev. Ferdinand Teura after he was expelled from the New Evangelical Reformed Church (cf. no. 6).

TM: **20** Congr: **1** PStations: **none** OrdM: **1** Eld: **yes** Deac: **yes** EvgHome: **nc** Mission: **none** Women Ord: **nc** ChurchOrg: **Congreg** Off/otherLang: **Reo Maohi, French** DoctrB: **nc** NatRel: **nc** RegRel: **none** IntlRel: **none**

Address: Eglise réformée protestante de Polynésie française, B.P. 806, Uturoa, Raiatea, French Polynesia, Tel: +689 662-537

GABON

Area in km^2	267,670
Population	(July 1996 est.) 1,172,798 Bantu tribes including four major tribal groupings (Fang, Eshira, Bapounou, Bateke), other Africans and Europeans 100,000, including 27,000 French
Religions in %	Christian 55%-75%, Muslim less than 1%, animist
Official/other languages	French (official), Fang, Myene, Bateke, Bapounou/Eschira, Bandjabi

Formerly part of French Equatorial Guinea, Gabon is a rich and densely forested territory south of Cameroon. Notwithstanding its serious ongoing economic problems, Gabon enjoys a per capita income more than three times that of most nations of sub-Saharan Africa. Gabon depended on timber and manganese until offshore oil was discovered in the early 1970s. The oil sector now accounts for 50% of its GDP.

The first Prot to arrive in this country were an American missionary and a handful of pastors from Palm Cape (present-day Liberia) who landed in June 1842 at a former Portuguese slave pier. They represented the American Board of Commissioners for Foreign Mission (ABCFM) who later, in 1870, handed over its mission fields to the Presbyterian Church of the USA. In 1892 the "Société des Missions Evangéliques de Paris" (SMEP) took responsibility for this area. Today several other Protestant denominations, including the Christian and Missionary Alliance, are active in Gabon, where the famous Lambaréné Hospital, built by Dr. Albert Schweitzer in 1913, is also located.

Evangelical Church of Gabon (EEG) (1095)

In 1949 the SMEP had in Gabon "eight stations under the Equator" with some 20 missionaries (pastors, teachers, doctors, and nurses) from France, Switzerland, and Italy. In the same year five former Gabonese schoolteachers returned from the Theological School of Ndoungué (Cameroon). They became the first indigenous pastors of Gabon. As early as 1951 efforts toward autonomy and independence were felt within the MPF. Gabon became a republic in 1960. Under the expert leadership of the then President of the SMEP, Rev. Marc Boegner, the mission church was declared independent in June 1961 in Port-Gentil, under the name "Eglise évangélique du Gabon" (EEG).

The church was soon to become the scene of a power-play among its leaders. In 1967 the first signs of dissent emerged and gradually hampered church life. At the Synod in 1971, Rev. Sima Ndong challenged the outgoing head of EEG, Nang Essono, but lost the election. A clear division occurred within the EEG which, according to observers, "had been provoked neither by theological nor by ecclesiological issues, but because of an incompatibility between persons." For a few years the two church communities existed side by side, using the same building in a given town for worship, listening to pastors who had studied together at the same theological schools but now obeying two different "church leaderships." In 1972 the dissident pastors were taken off the pastoral enrollment list by the "official" EEG.

Numerous attempts to settle the dispute were undertaken by different outside partners. For the next twenty years the Communauté Evangélique d'Action Apostolique (CEVAA) was to play a leading role in sending numerous delegations to Gabon and initiating many meetings in an effort to mediate between a growing number of parties in conflict. The CEVAA is a joint venture of churches and missions in Europe, Africa, Madagascar, and the Pacific. In 1976 it invited to Yaoundé (Cameroon) all the parties involved for a reconciliation meeting. But the commitments made there by all present were not implemented in the following years.The CEVAA finally suspended EEG from membership from 1984 till 1990; a single Synodal Council was elected in 1989, and, for the first time in twenty years, the EEG met again as a whole.

Unfortunately, tensions soon rose again. Endless disputes between leaders about synodal election procedures, quarrels within local congr, ending in some instances with shootings, deteriorated the situation again. This time the EEG was split into several groups called "Baraka," "Foyer," "Gros Bouquet." Once more the CEVAA intervened and in 1996 sent one of its vice-presidents, Rev. Harry Henry, as a resident mediator between the groups. A sign of hope came as the groups

178

jointly agreed to cover his living costs. After 1989 the Synod met several times, but until 1997 on no occasion were its decisions considered valid by all factions. Finally, in the summer of 1997, "Baraka" and "Gros Bouquet" met as a synod and elected a joint leadership to form the National Council of the EEG headed by its new president, Rev. Jean Noël Ogouliguendé. The third group did not participate.

The latest reliable figures about this church are those of June 1990. The church is present in five out of the nine provinces of Gabon.

TM: **96,652** Congr: **59** OrdM: **58** Eld: **nc** Deac: **nc** EvgHome: **8** Mission: **nc** Women Ord: **nc** ChurchOrg: **nc** Off/otherLang: **French, Fang** DoctrB: **nc** Infant or believer's baptism: **both** NatRel: **nc** RegRel: **AACC** IntlRel: **WCC, CEVAA** TheolSchool: **Theological Faculty (Yaoundé, Cameroon)**

Address: Eglise évangélique du Gabon, B.P. 10080, Libreville, Gabon, Tel: +241 72 41 92, Fax: nc

GAMBIA

Area in km²	11,300
Population	(est. 1993) 930,249 (Mandingo/Malinke 45%, Dsholov, Fulla)
Religions in %	wazzu Muslim (90%), Christian (Angl, Meth, RCath) 5%, Indigenous 1%
Official/other languages	English/Mandinka, Wolof, Fula

The Gambia, a British crown colony since 1843, became independent in 1965. It is ruled by a presidential regime elected on the basis of a multiparty system. In 1981 Gambia and Senegal established the Senegambian Confederation. While maintaining their sovereignty the two countries have a common government and parliament.

Canaan Christian Community Church (1310)

In 1982 Jae Hwan Lee, a Korean missionary sent by the Presbyterian Church in Korea—Hapdong (cf. Korea no. 15), started work in Gambia. He organized a small congr in Brikama. In 1992 two more missionaries arrived from Korea. A new congr came into being in Somita. A small Bible college has been established with five students currently being trained as church workers. Two students have been sent for advanced studies to the Philippines. In addition, a school for administrators and carpenters has been opened, with 90 students at present.

TM: **175** BM: **50** CM: **50** Congr: **3** OrdM: **1** Eld: **nc** Deac: **nc** EvgHome: **8** Mission: **10** Women Ord: **no** ChurchOrg: **nc** Off/otherLang: **English, Mandika** DoctrB: **nc** NatRel: **Evangelical Fellowship of the Gambia** TheolSchool: **Bible Institute and Canaan Christian Community Centre.**

Address: Canaan Christian Community Church, P.O. Box 2864, West Africa Mission, Serrekundna,
Gambia, Tel: +220 48 41 86, Fax: +220 48 41 86

GERMANY

Area in km²	356,910
Population	(July 1996 est.) 83,536,115 German 95.1%, Turkish 2.3%, Italians 0.7%, Greeks 0.4%, Poles 0.4%, other 1.1% (made up largely of people escaping from the war in former Yugoslavia
Religions in %	Prot 45%, RCath 37%, unaffiliated or other 18%
Official/other languages	German

ACK (Arbeitsgemeinschaft Christlicher Kirchen — *Fellowship of Christian Churches*)
DW (Diakonisches Werk)
EKD (Evangelische Kirche in Deutschland — *Evangelical Church in Germany*)
EKU (Evangelische Kirche der Union — *Evangelical Church of the Union*)
VEM (Vereinte Evangelische Mission — *United Evangelical Mission*)

The evangelical churches in Germany have their origin in the Reformation of the 16th century. The main impulse came from Wittenberg. Most evangelical churches in Germany followed Martin Luther's teaching. But other centers of the Reformation — Zurich with Huldrych Zwingli, Geneva with John Calvin, and southern Germany, especially Strasbourg, with Martin Bucer — also had a lasting influence and led to the foundation of Reformed congr and denominations. In the course of later confessional conflicts the Ref churches became more and more minority churches. Only through the peace treaty of Westphalia (1648) were they legally recognized as a confessional group. Later, French-speaking refugees (Huguenots, Walloons) and Dutch immigrants founded new Reformed congr in several parts of Germany, especially in the north.

According to the generally accepted rule of that period, the territorial authority, the prince or the city magistrate, had the right to decide which faith the population had to follow. Though the political order has fundamentally changed in subsequent centuries, the system of territorial churches (Landeskirchen) continues to exist to this day. In the early 19th century, largely at the initiative of secular powers, Luth and Ref churches were brought together into united churches. After World War II the 24 evangelical Landeskirchen, while maintaining their internal autonomy, decided to establish the Evangelical Church of Germany (EKD), which allows them to act together and to represent common convictions in society and in the ecumenical movement.

The Ref churches constitute a minority within German Protestantism. Like all Reformed and Presb churches they have adopted a presbyterian-synodal church order. On the whole, the order of the Luth churches has developed in the same direction, but while for the Ref church order is the expression of their confession of faith and their particular understanding of the church, for the Luth churches the synodal order is understood more in the sense of parliamentarian representation within the church. The common confession of the Reformed in Germany is the Heidelberg Catechism. Today most Reformed Christians in Germany are part of one of the Landeskirchen. In some areas they maintain their separate confessional identity as Reformed congr, in other areas they are fully integrated into united churches. There are two autonomous Ref churches — the Church of Lippe and the Evangelical–Reformed Church of Bavaria and northwest Germany. In addition, there is a Reformed Free Church, as well as a number of free Reformed congr which form a federation of Ref churches.

1. Church of Lippe (6203)

This church is one of the two churches in Germany with a Reformed majority. The Ref faith was introduced by the Duke of Lippe in 1605. At that time the city of Lemgo, where Martin Luther's message had already been preached in 1522, refused to accept the change. Through a peace agreement with the Duke, they were given the right to remain Luth. This arrangement has survived to this day. The Church of Lippe is a Reformed Landeskirche with a Luth minority. During the Nazi period the Church of Lippe accepted into its ministry many pastors and assistants who were persecuted in other Landeskirchen.

TM: **219,000** BM: **219,000** Congr: **72** OrdM: **142** Eld: **989** Deac: **30** EvgHome: **20** Mission: **0** Women Ord: **yes** As Ministers: **1983/29** as Deac: **16** as Elders: **413** ChurchOrg: **congr, classis, synod** Off/otherLang: **German** DoctrB: **ApC, NicC, HeidC** Infant or believer's baptism: **both** Frequency of the Lord's Supper: **monthly** Close relations with: **Ref Ch in Hungary, Ref Ch in Poland, EPC Ghana, EEPT (Togo), URCSA (South Africa)** NatRel: **Reformed Alliance, United Ev Mission (VEM), ACK** RegRel: **CEC** IntlRel: **WARC, LWF, WCC** TheolSchool: **Theological School of Wuppertal (jointly with the churches of Rhineland and Westfalen)** Service infrastructure: **14 resting homes, 22 care stations, 60 kindergartens, various other institutions** Periodicals: **Synodendokumentationen (Synod papers) (semiannual)**

Address: Lippische Landeskirche, Postfach 2153, Leopoldstrasse 27, D-32756 Detmold, Germany, Tel: +49 5231 976-60, Fax: +49 5231 976-850, E-mail: kirche_lippe@t-online.de

2. Evangelical Reformed Church (6205)

While in many parts of Germany in the 19th century Luth and Ref churches decided to form united churches, the two confessions continued to exist side by side in the former kingdom of Hanover, when Hanover became part of Prussia. In 1882 the Reformed congr were permitted by the king of Prussia to found an autonomous

Evangelical-Reformed church in the Province of Hanover. Reformed congr from other provinces became part of this church: Reformed congr of East Frisia, of the Dukedoms of Bentheim and Lingen, of Plesse (in the neighborhood of Göttingen), and of Bremen; in addition, several Huguenot congr joined the church.

Much later, in 1988, the Evangelical-Reformed Church in Bavaria also united with this church. Some of the congr in Bavaria were founded by Huguenots, others go back to the time of the Reformation (under the influence of the Reformation in Zurich, several congr were founded in the Allgäu), still others came into existence through refugee settlement from the Palatinate, e.g., the Reformed congregation in Munich. In 1920 they adopted their own constitution and existed in close collaboration with the Evangelical-Lutheran Church of Bavaria.

Today this church consists of 142 congr with over 200,000 members spread all over Germany. It is one of the smaller churches in Germany, and, in contrast to the Church of Lippe, it is not a territorial church but a federation of congr fully responsible for themselves in all matters.

TM: **204,348** BM: **204,348** CM: **45,000** Congr: **142** PStations: **165** OrdM: **165** Eld: **790** Deac: **20** EvgHome: **28** Mission: **nc** Women Ord: **yes** As Ministers: **1967/30** as Deac: **ne** as Elders: **ne** ChurchOrg: **11 synods of Reformed congregations** Off/otherLang: **German** DoctrB: **ApC, NicC, HeidC, Barmen** Infant or believer's baptism: **both** Frequency of the Lord's Supper: **minimum 4 times a year** Close relations with: **Confederation of Ev Churches in Niedersachsen, EPC Ghana (cf. Ghana no. 2), EEPT Togo, Karo-Batak Ch in Indonesia (cf. Indonesia no. 3)** NatRel: **Reformed Alliance (since beginning), EKD, VEM** RegRel: **Leuenberg (1973)** IntlRel: **WARC, WCC (1948)** TheolSchool: **at several German universities** Service infrastructure: **3 hospitals, 4 rest homes, 22 social services, 25 kindergartens, 1 family center, 5 youth centers** Periodicals: **Sonntagsblatt für ev.-ref. Gemeinden (gen/weekly/4,000), "Reformiert" (gen/6 per year/45,000)**

Address: Ev.-Ref. Kirche, Postfach 1380, Saarstrasse 6, D-26789 Leer, Germany, Tel: +49 491 91980, Fax: +49 491 9198 251

3. Evangelical-Oldreformed Church of Niedersachsen/Germany (6202)

This church came into existence in the 1830s as part of the movement which protested against the spirit of the Enlightenment and advocated the return to the confessions of the Reformation. Since 1923 it has associated as a particular synod with the Gereformeerde Kerken in the Netherlands (cf. Netherlands) but also maintains contacts with the churches in Germany and is a member of the Reformed Alliance.

TM: **7,500** Congr: **14** PStations: **14** OrdM: **15** Eld: **100** Deac: **nc** EvgHome: **0** Mission: **nc** Women Ord: **yes** As Ministers: **1970/0** as Deac: **1970** as Elders: **1970** ChurchOrg: **parishes belong to one Synod, divided into 2 "Synodalverbände" (classes); synod is part of the Generalsynod of the GKN (Gereformeerde Kerken in the Nederlands, cf. Netherlands no. 5))** Off/otherLang: **German** DoctrB: **ApC, NicC, AthC, CDort, HeidC** Infant or believer's baptism: **both** Frequency of the Lord's Supper: **4 times a year** NatRel: **Reformed Alliance (1967), DW, AGK (1973)** IntlRel: **WCC (via Gereformeerden Kerken NL)** Periodicals: **Der Grenzbote (gen/bi-weekly/2,000), Der Jugendbote (youth/monthly/700)**

Address: Evangelisch-Altreformierte Kirche in Niedersachsen, Hauptstr. 33, D-48527 Laar, Germany, Tel: +49 5947 242

4. Alliance of Evangelical Reformed Churches of Germany (6218)

The Federation is an association of the Reformed congr located in various Lutheran Landeskirchen. The congr were founded in past centuries by refugees from the Netherlands and France (Huguenots).

TM: **14,000** BM: **14,000** Congr: **6** PStations: **11** OrdM: **10** Eld: **52** Deac: **4** EvgHome: **27** Mission: **none** Women Ord: **yes** As Ministers: **1976/2** as Deac: **1949/nc** as Elders: **1949/nc** ChurchOrg: **synod** Off/otherLang: **German** DoctrB: **ApC, HeidC, Barmen** Infant or believer's baptism: **both** Frequency of the Lord's Supper: **monthly** NatRel: **Reformed Alliance (1945)** RegRel: **none** IntlRel: **none** TheolSchool: **none** Service infrastructure: **2 nursing homes, 2 social centers, 1 kindergarten, 3 recreational centers** Periodicals: **none**

Address: Bund Evangelisch-reformierter Kirchen Deutschlands, Ferdinand Str. 21, D-20095 Hamburg, Germany, Tel: +49 40 337 260, Fax: +49 331 659

5. Reformed Alliance (6204)

The Reformed Alliance was founded in 1884 in order to resist the loss of Ref identity and the growing "Lutheranization" of the German churches. It is a free association of churches, congr, and individuals who adhere to the Ref confessions. It seeks to fulfill the following tasks: a) to give a common direction to congregations of Ref origin; b) to establish contacts with Ref churches in other countries and to contribute to the activities of the World Alliance of Ref Churches and generally of the ecumenical movement; c) to deepen communion with the evangelical churches within Germany and to participate in its common efforts and in its institutions. Legally the Alliance is an association, but it is recognized by the Evangelical Church in Germany as representing the Ref churches. The Reformed Alliance has close contacts with Ref churches in eastern Europe (Romania, Hungary, Poland, etc.) and supports the Ref churches in South Africa in their effort to overcome racism in church and society. The members of the Alliance are: Church of Lippe (cf. no. 1), the Evangelical-Reformed Church (cf. no. 2), the Evangelical–Old Reformed Church in Niedersachsen (cf. no. 3) and the Alliance of Evangelical-Ref churches of Germany (cf. no. 4); in addition, it includes about 400 congr from within united churches and 600 individuals.

Org: **General Assembly every second year which elects an executive committee (Moderamen) and a Moderator (elected for eight years)** Off/otherLang: **German** DoctrB: **ApC, NicC, HeidC** NatRel: **EKD** RegRel: **same as EKD** IntlRel: **WARC, WCC** TheolSchool: **none** Service infrastructure: **none** Periodicals: **Reformierte Kirchenzeitung (gen/monthly/1,700)**

Address: Reformierter Bund, Vogelsangstr. 20, D-42109 Wuppertal, Germany, Tel: +49 202 755-111, Fax: +49 202 754-202

6. Evangelical Church of Anhalt (6201)

The Church of Anhalt covers the territory of the former princedom, which in 1918 became the state of Anhalt. Prince Wolfgang of Anhalt supported the Reformation in the late 1520s and in 1534 introduced new forms of worship. In 1541 the pastors officially accepted the Reformation. In 1606 the whole princedom changed from the Luth to the Ref confession. Anhalt-Zerbst returned to the Luth tradition in 1644, but ever since the two confessions have coexisted in the area of the princedom. In the 19th century the church joined the movement toward united churches. In 1865 the consistories were unified, and in 1875 a new church order introduced. The constitution of 1920 does not mention any confession, either Luth or Ref, in order to avoid reviving old controversies. The church is a member of the Evangelical Church of the Union (EKU) and the Evangelical Church in Germany.

TM: **76,000** Congr: **196** OrdM: **85** Eld: **nc** Deac: **nc** EvgHome: **nc** Mission: **nc** Women Ord: **yes** ChurchOrg: **United (5 regional synods: Dessau, Köthen, Zerbst, Bernburg, Ballenstedt), general synod of 33 members)** Off/otherLang: **German** DoctrB: **see above in introduction** Service infrastructure: **40 staff members for catechism and music teaching**

Address: Evangelische Landeskirche Anhalts, Postfach 1424, Friedrich Str. 22/24, D-06844 Dessau, Germany, Fax: +49 340 25 26 1 30

7. Evangelical Church in Baden (6206)

The beginnings of this church go back to the Reformation of both Luther and Zwingli. In the course of the conflict between Wittenberg and Zurich, the neighboring Strasbourg sought to mediate, though with little success. Since dynasties often changed in the following decades and centuries, the population was often forced to change confession. For a period the area even returned to Roman Catholicism. At the initiative of the Grand Duke of Baden the Luth and Ref congr formed a United Church in 1821. At that time about 80% were Luth and 20% Ref. After 1918 the function of the supreme bishop, which had thus far been vested in the Grand Duke, was transferred to an independent church government. The General Synod of Baden is elected directly by the members of the congr, not by the congr and districts.

TM: **1,300,000** BM: **1,300,000** CM: **10,690** Congr: **700** PStations: **670** OrdM: **1,579** Eld: **5,582** Deac: **150** Mission: **9** Women Ord: **yes** As Ministers: **1955/245** as Deac: **nc** as Elders: **nc** ChurchOrg: **presbys, Synod** Off/otherLang: **German** DoctrB: **ApC, NicC, AthC, HeidC, Luther's Small Catechism** Infant or believer's baptism: **both** Close relations with: **Presbyterian Churches in Cameroon, Ghana, Republic of Korea, Indonesia (Bali, Sulawesi), Japan, Luth. Bolivia, Peru, Chile, and the Moravian Ch in Republic of South Africa, Ch of South India** NatRel: **CEC (since foundation), EECCS (1994)** RegRel: **Conference of Churches along the Rhine (1987)** IntlRel: **WCC (1950)** Service infrastructure: **652 kindergartens/nursing homes, 84 rest homes, 17 work projects/help for unemployed people, 5 mission stations, 8 support groups for cancer patients** Periodicals: **Mitteilungen (general/6 times per year/14,000), Standpunkte (general/monthly/30,000)**

Address: Evangelische Landeskirche in Baden, Postfach 2269, Blumenstr. 1, D-76133 Karlsruhe, Germany, Tel: +49 721 9175-0, Fax: +49 721 9175-553

8. Evangelical-Reformed Council Berlin-Brandenburg (6207)

In the 16th century the Electorate (Kurfürstentum) of Brandenburg adopted the Luth Reformation. In 1613 Prince Johann Sigismund decided to follow the Ref tradition, but, despite the rules then in force, he did not succeed in changing the confessional status of the territory, even though the Hohenzollern dynasty continued to adhere to the Ref confession and actively supported the Ref minority. The number of Ref considerably increased with the arrival of Huguenots following the abolition of the Edict of Nantes (1685). Brandenburg was particularly generous in receiving refugees. Within the United Church of Berlin-Brandenburg the Ref congr are organized into two consistories — one French-Ref and the other German-Ref. Together they form the United Synod of the Evangelical-Reformed congr in Berlin-Brandenburg. They are also represented in the general synod of the United Church.

TM: **2,160** Congr: **17** PStations: **20** OrdM: **12** Eld: **200** Deac: **nc** EvgHome: **12** Mission: **nc** Women Ord: **yes** As Ministers: **1945/5** as Deac: **ne** as Elders: **ne** ChurchOrg: **nc** Off/otherLang: **German** DoctrB: **ApC, NicC, HeidC, Confessio Gallicana** Infant or believer's baptism: **both** Frequency of the Lord's Supper: **monthly** Close relations with: **ERAL (cf. France no. 2), Reformed churches in Hungary, Netherlands, Switzerland, Poland** Service infrastructure: **home for senior citizens** Periodicals: **Reformierte Kirchenzeitung (gen/monthly)**

Address: Evangelisch-Reformiertes Moderamen Berlin-Brandenburg, Freiheit 14, D-12555 Berlin, Germany, Tel: +49 30 655 7032, Fax: +49 30 655 7032

Evangelische Kirche in Berlin Brandenburg, Bachstr. 1-2, D-10555 Berlin, Tel: +49 30 3 90 91 0

9. Evangelical Church of Bremen (6208)

In the 16th century Luth preaching and teaching predominated in the Church of Bremen. After the Synod of Dort (1618) relations were gradually established with the Netherlands. Ref patterns of church order were adopted, not in the city itself, but in the region around the city. In subsequent centuries confessional differences increasingly lost importance. The Evangelical Church of Bremen considers itself as a "free" Landeskirche; each of the 69 congr decides independently which confession and which church order it adopts. Besides Luth and united congr there are also Ref congr. The latter are a minority and are mainly located in the area of the Unterweser.

TM: **316,000** Congr: **69** OrdM: **nc** Women Ord: **nc** Off/otherLang: **German** DoctrB: **nc**

Address: Bremische Evangelische Landeskirche, Postfach 106929, D-28069 Bremen, Germany, Tel: +49 421 5 59 70, Fax: +49 421 5 59 72 65

10. Evangelical Church in Hessen and Nassau (EKHN) (6209)

This church is one of the youngest Landeskirchen in Germany. It was formed in 1947 through the union of three formerly independent churches — Hessen-Darmstadt, Nassau, and Frankfurt. The church does not adhere to one confession of faith but leaves the decision about confessions to the individual congr. The first president of the church was Martin Niemöller, known for his leading role in the Confessing Church during the Nazi period. In the course of its existence the church went through several controversies, notably the debate about the WCC Program to Combat Racism, about the possibility of pastors belonging to the Communist party, and about the enlarging of the Airport Frankfurt am Main. The confessions referred to in the constitution include the Barmen Declaration.

TM: **2,041,000** BM: **1,940,000** CM: **768,185** Congr: **1,196** PStations: **1,689** OrdM: **2,041** Eld: **12,300** Deac: **250** EvgHome: **1,250** Mission: **20** Women Ord: **yes** As Ministers: **571** as Deac: **180** as Elders: **6,200** ChurchOrg: **congr, district, synod** Off/otherLang: **German** DoctrB: **ApC, NicC** Infant or believer's baptism: **both** Frequency of the Lord's Supper: **monthly** NatRel: **Ev Mission SW Germany, VEM (Wuppertal), ACK, Leuenberg** TheolSchool: **at several German universities** Service infrastructure: **20 hospitals, 81 rest homes, 84 social centers, 560 kindergartens, etc. (full-time staff: 12,500; half-time staff: 7,000)** Periodicals: **EKHN Mitteilungen (internal/monthly/nc)**, **Echt (gen/quarterly/nc)**

Address: Evangelische Kirche in Hessen und Nassau, Postfach 10 01 52, Paulus Platz 1, D-64285 Darmstadt, Germany, Tel: +49 6151 405-0, Fax: +49 6151 405 220

11. Evangelical Church of Kurhessen-Waldeck (6210)

At the time of the Reformation the Landgrave of Kurhessen also took responsibility for church affairs. In 1529 Prince Philip sought to unify the opposing streams of the Reformation by arranging for conversations on the understanding of the Lord's Supper in Marburg. In the 17th and 18th centuries many Huguenots found refuge in Kurhessen, and in the 19th century the ground was laid for the coexistence of the Luth and Ref confessions in a united church. The close relations with the state ended after World War I; the church was given the freedom to constitute itself independently from the state. In 1924 the constitution for the Evangelical Landeskirche Hessen-Cassel was adopted. Ten years later the area of Waldeck was joined to the territory of the Landeskirche. From a confessional point of view the Evangelical Church of Kurhessen-Waldeck is a united church.

TM: **1,022,088** BM: **1,022,088** CM: **374,490** Congr: **971** OrdM: **708** Eld: **3,870** Deac: **150** EvgHome: **1** Mission: **4** Women Ord: **yes** As Ministers: **257** as Deac: **228** as Elders: **4,121** ChurchOrg: **United (congr, 28 districts, 4 regional classes, synod)** Off/otherLang: **German** DoctrB: **ApC, NicC, CA** Infant or believer's baptism: **both** Frequency of the Lord's Supper: **monthly and feast days or 4/5 times a year** Close relations with: **Ev Luth. Church of Estonia, Namibia, Southern Africa, Church in South India, in Russia, Ukraine, Kasachstan, and Middle Asia, Hervormde Kerk in the Netherlands, North German Convent of Churches** NatRel: **Conference of Arnoldshain (1967), EKD (1945), Council of Christian Churches in Nordhessen, ACK Rhein-Main, ACK Thüringen, VEM** RegRel: **Leuenberg (1973)** IntlRel: **WCC (1948)** Service infrastructure: **54 social services, 190 kin-**

dergartens, 1 school (47 teachers), 1 academy (5 staff), 1 pastoral seminary (7 staff), 1 pastoral training institute (11 staff) Periodicals: **Blick in die Kirche (staff news/monthly/20,000), Kasseler Sonntagsblatt (general/weekly/18,000)**

Address: Evangelische Kirche von Kurhessen-Waldeck, Wilhelmshöher Allee 330, D-34131 Kassel, Germany, Tel: +49 561 93780, Fax: +49 561 93784-400

12. Evangelical Church of Silesian Oberlausitz (6219)

In 1815 the Eastern Oberlausitz became part of Silesia. The Evangelical Church of this area was the Evangelical Church in the Province of Silesia. Before World War II the Church of Silesia had more than two million members in 700 congr served by 900 pastors. In 1951 the western districts of the church, i.e., west of the Neisse border, were reconstituted as the Evangelical Church of Silesia. In 1968 the name of the church was changed to Evangelical Church of the Area of Görlitz. The present name was adopted in 1992. The church's background is primarily Lutheran, but the church is a member of the Evangelical Church of the Union. There is one Ref congregation in Görlitz.

TM: **72,230** BM: **72,230** CM: **5,950** Congr: **73** OrdM: **68** EvgHome: **nc** Mission: **nc** Women Ord: **yes** As Ministers: **yes** as Deac: **na** as Elders: **na** ChurchOrg: **Congregational, four districts, synod** Off/ otherLang: **German** DoctrB: **ApC, NicC, AthC, Barmen and, for Reformed congr, HeidC** Infant or believer's baptism: **both** Close relations with: **Luth Church in Poland, Church of the Brethren** NatRel: **EKD, EKU** RegRel: **CEC** IntlRel: **WCC**

Address: Evangelische Kirche der schlesischen Oberlausitz, Schlaurother Str. 11, Postfach 300334, D-02827 Görlitz, Germany, Tel: +49 3581 744-0, Fax: +49 3581 744 299

13. Church of the Palatinate (6211)

The Church of the Palatinate owes its existence to both Luth (Wittenberg) and Ref (Zurich, Geneva, and Strasbourg) influence. In the wake of the Counter-Reformation the RCath Church had regained strength. In order to consolidate the Reformation in his area and to end the controversies between strict and moderate Luth, as well as the Ref, the prince elector, Frederick III, introduced the Palatinate church order whose main feature is the well-known Heidelberg Catechism. The efforts to achieve a rapprochement among Prot was pursued after the Thirty Years War. The changing confessional allegiance of the princes in the 16th and 18th centuries led to bitter controversies as well as disenchantment with religion. Only the French Revolution, which had gained considerable influence in the Palatinate, opened the door to a new era. In 1818 the Prot churches united to form the Evangelical Church of the Palatinate. The project of union was put to a vote. While 40,167 family heads voted for the union, only 539 voted against it. In order to avoid confessional disputes, the Church did not adopt any particular confessions but declared Holy Scripture to be the only basis for the teaching of the church.

TM: **657,035** Congr: **430** PStations: **500** OrdM: **626** Eld: **3,525** Deac: **390** EvgHome: **ne** Mission: **30** Women Ord: **yes** As Ministers: **1958/154** as Deac: **ne** as Elders: **ne** ChurchOrg: **Presbyterian (congr, 20 districts [Dekanate], Synod)** Off/otherLang: **German** DoctrB: **ApC, NicC, church's own catechism based on HeidC** Infant or believer's baptism: **both** Frequency of the Lord's Supper: **4 times to 25 times a year according to congr.** Close relations with: **UCR (GB), Presbyterian Church of Ghana** NatRel: **ACK (1975) Leuenberg (1973)** IntlRel: **WCC (through EKD)** TheolSchool: **none** Service infrastructure: **5 hospitals, 27 homes for seniors, 36 care centers, 241 kindergartens** Periodicals: **Der Kirchenbote (gen/weekly), Liturgische Blätter (liturgical material (3 times a year/650), Religionspädagogische Blätter (teaching/quarterly/1,000), Informationen (gen for elders/ monthly/5,000)**

Address: Evangelische Kirche der Pfalz, Domplatz 5, D-67346 Speyer, Germany, Tel: +49 6232 667-0, Fax: +49 6232 667-246

14. Pomeranian Evangelical Church (6212)

The Reformation was introduced in Pomerania at an early date. Under the leadership of Johannes Bugenhagen, called Doctor Pomeranus, the area adopted the Reformation in 1534. Thirty years later Jakob Runge published a collection of Confessions for use in the church. The territory of Pomerania often changed its rulers. After the peace of Westphalia (1648) the eastern part of Pomerania was consigned to Brandenburg. The whole area became part of Prussia in 1815. The plans of union introduced in 1817 by the Prussian kings initially met with much resistance but finally were generally accepted. The end of World War II brought far-reaching changes. The eastern part of Pomerania became part of Poland. The center of the church moved from Stettin to Greifswald. The numerical strength of the church diminished. While it had 1,761,000 members in 1932, today it has only 143,000. To a large extent this is due to secularization.

TM: **143,000** BM: **143,000** Congr: **173** PStations: **400** OrdM: **173** Eld: **2,000** Deac: **25** EvgHome: **80** Mission: **nc** Women Ord: **yes** As Ministers: **1947** as Deac: **nc** as Elders: **nc** ChurchOrg: **regional synods** Off/otherLang: **German** DoctrB: **ApC, NicC, CA** Frequency of the Lord's Supper: **monthly** NatRel: **EKU (1947), EKD (1948), ACK (1948)** RegRel: **CEC (1959 via EKD membership)** IntlRel: **LWF (1955), WCC (1948 via EKD membership)** Service infrastructure: **3 hospitals, 24 homes for senior citizens, 23 social care centers, 21 kindergartens, 19 homes for differently abled persons: managed by Diakonisches Werk with staff of ca. 3,200)** Periodicals: **Die Kirche (The Church) (gen/weekly/3,500)**

Address: Pommersche Evangelische Kirche, Postfach 3152/PLZ 17461 Bahnhofsstr. 35/38, D-17489 Greifswald, Germany, Tel: + 49 3834 5546, Fax: + 49 3834 554 799

15. Evangelical Church in the Rhineland (6213)

This church came into existence in 1817 when the Prussian King William III called for the union of the congr of Luth and Ref background. Despite forming one church, the individual congr retain their own confession of faith. In its structure the church follows the Ref tradition. In the struggle with the Nazi regime the Ref congregations of the Rhineland gave the signal for resistance by calling the Barmen synod in 1934. The Barmen Declaration continues to play a significant role in most united churches of Germany. The first free synod after the Nazi regime was held in 1948. The Ref congr are mainly situated in the following regions: Niederrhein, Bergisches Land (area of Wuppertal), Mittelrhein, Hunsrück, and the Hessian part of the church.

TM: **3,172,498** BM: **3,172,498** CM: **1,111,900** Congr: **833** PStations: **2,337** OrdM: **2,904** Eld: **11,698** Deac: **nc** EvgHome: **ne** Mission: **0** Women Ord: **yes** As Ministers: **23/5%** as Deac: **nc** as Elders: **nc** ChurchOrg: **parish, region, Church (Landeskirche)** Off/otherLang: **German** DoctrB: **ApC, NicC, AthC, HeidC, Luther's Catechisms** Infant or believer's baptism: **both** Frequency of the Lord's Supper: **minimum once a month** Close relations with: **United Prot Ch in Belgium, Eglise réformée de France, Churches in Alsace (France), Waldensian Ch (Italy), Ch in Hungary, Ev Ch in Poland, Ev Ch A.B. in Romania, Ev Ch in NL, ELCRN-Namibia, Batak churches in Indonesia, United Ch Christ/USA** NatRel: **EKD (1952), EKU (1952), United Evangelical Mission (EUM) (1996)** RegRel: **Leuenberg, CEC** IntlRel: **WCC (1948)** TheolSchool: **universities, Kirchliche Hochschule Wuppertal-Barmen** Service infrastructure: **church regions run all institutions, church is responsible for 5 high schools, 2 secondary schools, 1 academy** Periodicals: **Evangelisch (for members/2 times a year/700,000), Kirchliches Amtsblatt (gen/monthly/3,000), Faltblatt (gen/annual/50,000), Der Weg (magazine/weekly/50,000)**

Address: Evangelische Kirche im Rheinland, Postfach 32 03 40 Hans-Böckler-Str. 7, D-40476 Düsseldorf, Germany, Tel: +49 211 45 62-0, Fax: +49 211 45 62-4 44

16. Evangelical Church of the Church-Province of Sachsen (6215)

The province of Sachsen is the part of Sachsen which was attributed to Prussia by the Congress of Vienna (1815). It covers the area of Sachsen-Anhalt, Altmark, the eastern part of the Harz, the industrial centers of Halle, Leuna, and Bitterfeld, and the city of Wittenberg. The churches in this area were integrated into the Prussian union between Luth and Ref. Despite the union which was introduced in 1817, the Ref congr maintained their identity and form a special unit within the United church. It includes the following congr: Aschersieben, Burg, Calbe, Halberstadt, Halle/Saale, Magdeburg, Stendal, and Wettin. At the initiative of the Prussian kings, a special chair for Ref theology was established at the University of Halle.

TM: **593,674** BM: **593,674** Congr: **2,185** PStations: **0** OrdM: **656** Deac: **na** EvgHome: **ne** Mission: **na** Women Ord: **yes** As Ministers: **1929** as Deac: **ne** as Elders: **ne** ChurchOrg: **national: synod and church headquarters, regional: Propsteien, Kirchenkreise** Off/otherLang: **German** DoctrB: **ApC, NicC, HeidC, CA, Barmen, Leuenberg** Infant or believer's baptism: **both** Frequency of the Lord's Supper: **monthly** Close relations with: **Luth Ch in Tanzania, Angl Diocese of Worcester (UK), Central Atlantic Conference of the United Ch of Christ/USA, Ref Ch in NL, NL Ref Ch** NatRel: **EKD, EKU, Arnoldshainer Konferenz, AGK in Sachsen-Anhalt, Thüringen** IntlRel: **WCC (1948)** Service infrastructure: **19 hospitals (3,591 staff), 50 rest homes (1,694 staff), 35 social service stations (498 staff), 110 kindergartens (876 staff), various schools** Periodicals: **Die Kirche, Aufbrüche**

Address: Evangelische Kirche der Kirchenprovinz Sachsen, Am Dom 2, D-39104 Magdeburg, Germany, Tel: +49 391 56 81 80, Fax: +49 391 56 81 81 11

17. Evangelical Church of Westphalia (6217)

In 1835 the Prussian state issued a church order for both the Rhineland (cf. no. 15) and Westphalia through which Luth and Ref congr were united into one church. The Church of Westphalia is a united church within which both Luth and Ref confessions continue to exist side by side. The majority of congr in the industrial area of the Ruhrgebiet recognize both confessional traditions and consider themselves as united *(uniert)*. The church maintains the Ref tradition in its structure.

TM: **2,868,654** BM: **2,868,654** CM: **1,075,442** Congr: **658** PStations: **1,953** OrdM: **1,629** Eld: **7,118** Deac: **ne** EvgHome: **ne** Mission: **11** Women Ord: **yes** As Ministers: **1975/512** as Deac: **nc** as Elders: **nc** ChurchOrg: **Presb, Synod** Off/otherLang: **German** DoctrB: **ApC, NicC, AthC, HeidC, Luther's Small Catechism** Infant or believer's baptism: **both** Frequency of the Lord's Supper: **usually monthly** Close relations with: **Hungary, Poland, Russ Orthodox, Evangelical Lutheran Church in Russia (ELKRAS), Waldensian, Tanzania, Rwanda, Cameroon, Botswana, Namibia, Congo (Kinshasa), Sri Lanka, China (Hong Kong), China, United Church of Christ-USA, Indonesia, Philippines** NatRel: **EKD, EKU, Arnoldshainer Konferenz, Leuenberg, VIM** IntlRel: **WCC** Service infrastructure: **11 hospitals, 21 homes for older people, 766 kindergartens, 40 centers for conference/education/leisure, 37 meeting centers for older people, 141 homes for adolescents, 7 schools** Periodicals: **Unsere Kirche**

Address: Evangelische Kirche von Westfalen, Postfach 10 10 51 Altstädter Kirchplatz 5, D-33602 Bielefeld, Germany, Tel: +49 521 5 94-0, Fax: +49 521 5 94-129, E-mail: lka@ekvw.de.

GHANA

Area in km²	238,540
Population	(July 1996 est.) 17,698,271 black African 99.8% (major tribes: Akan 44%, Moshi-Dagomba 16%, Ewe 13%, Ga 8%), European and others 0.2%
Religions in %	Christians 62% (Prot 22%, RCath 12%, Pent 16%, African Indig. Churches 12%), Muslims 14.5%, Afr Rel 23.5%
Official/other languages	English, Akan (Twi, Fante) 45%, Ewe 13%, Ga-Adanme 6%, Guan, Nzema, Dagbani, Mampruli, Gur, and others

CCG (Christian Council of Ghana)

Christian missionary activity began with the arrival of Europeans in 1481, whereas Islamic influence had made itself felt from the 9th century, mainly in the trading centers and kingdoms of the north. Portuguese and, later, Dutch, British, and Dutch seafarers and traders built fortified trading posts along the coast. Their missionary efforts failed primarily because of their association with the slave trade and the low moral standards at the forts.

The first deliberate missionary effort in the interior by Moravians in the 18th century ended in disaster because of the high death toll among missionaries. Missionaries from the Basel Mission who arrived in 1828 would have suffered the same fate but for the fact that Black Moravian missionaries from the West Indies — freed slaves — had been called to assist. Other missions followed: Angl (who had been present already in the 18th century but fully developed their work in the 19th century), Methodists (1835), Bremen Mission among the Ewe (1847), French RCath Mission (1880). Until the end of the century the growth of the church was restricted to the south; only after the defeat of the Ashanti Kingdom in 1896 by the British was mission work extended to the Ashanti heartland. The north of Ghana, falsely declared Islamic territory by the colonial power, remained officially off limits for Christian mission work until 1945.

During the first decades of the 20th century many African Independent churches emerged, often founded by catechists of the mainline churches. Likewise, Apostolic and Pent churches gained momentum due to the rise of the new charismatic movement. By 1929 five Prot churches founded the Christian Council of Ghana, then called the Gold Coast, and which today comprises 14 member churches (CCG); it closely cooperates with the RCath Bishops' Conference (CBC). Pent, Apostolic, and African Indigenous churches formed separate umbrella organizations; however, they cooperate with CCG and CBC. An attempt by Presb, Meth, and, initially, the Angl and Menn churches failed in 1980. Theological training is done cooperatively by the Presb, Meth, and Angl churches at Trinity College Legon.

The history of Christian missions is closely connected with the history of colonial power. The churches had, especially through their schools, a decisive impact on the development of modern African nationalism and the formation of an educated elite. Christians played a significant role in economic development, public life, and the process of decolonization. In 1957 the Gold Coast became independent as the first African independent colony. The relationship between the churches and the state has generally been one of close collaboration in the fields of education, health, and other social services. Politically, however, relations have repeatedly experienced strains during the first republic under Dr. Kwame Nkrumah and under the various military governments which followed. Both the CCG and the CBC played a prophetic role in the defense of human rights, freedom of worship, democracy, and moral standards.

The Ref tradition is represented in Ghana primarily by two churches: the Presbyterian Church of Ghana founded by the Basel Mission and the Ewe-speaking Evangelical Presbyterian Church, founded by German missionaries. During World War I German and Swiss missionaries had to leave the country. Scottish missionaries stepped in and, through their witness, contributed a distinctly Ref self-understanding and promoted the indigenization of the churches.

191

1. Presbyterian Church of Ghana (1061)

From 1828 missionaries of the Basel Mission, mainly from South West Germany, Switzerland, and the West Indies, established stations in the Ga- and Twi-speaking eastern part of the Gold Coast, later spreading to other parts of the country. The first indigenous pastor, David Asante, was trained in Basel and ordained in 1864. First called the Basel Mission of the Gold Coast, the church was renamed the Scottish Mission Church after World War I and became, in 1926, with a Presbyterian Constitution, the Presbyterian Church of the Gold Coast. In 1957 Gold Coast became known as Ghana. Today the church is one of the largest Prot churches, comprising 13 presby all over the country and the "northern mission field," covering the three northern regions and other rural mission fields within various presby. The church is running primary, secondary, and vocational schools, teacher training colleges, lay training centers, hospitals, clinics, primary health care programs, and agricultural and other social services. The main challenges are charismatic renewal, firmly established within the church through Bible study and prayer groups, and the issue of social institutions, which constitute a great financial burden but also as a means of evangelism.

TM: **444,382** BM: **444,382** CM: **158,981** Congr: **1,865** PStations: **400** OrdM: **455** Eld: **nc** Deac: **nc** EvgHome: **152** Mission: **10** Women Ord: **yes** As Ministers: **1977/20** as Deac: **1977/14** as Elders: **1920/ nc** ChurchOrg: **Presbyterian (13 presbys, synod)** Off/otherLang: **English/Ga, Twi, Ewe, Danme, Dagbani, Kusal, Chumuru** DoctrB: **nc** Infant or believer's baptism: **both** Periodicals: **Christian Messenger (gen/monthly/nc), Presbyterian (gen/quarterly/nc)** NatRel: **CCG, Christian Health Association of Ghana** RegRel: **AACC** IntlRel: **WCC, WARC** TheolSchool: **Trinity College, Legon; Ramseyer Training Center Abetifi, Akrofi-Christaller Centre Akropong**

Address: Presbyterian Church of Ghana, P.O. Box 1800, Thorpe Road, Accra, Ghana, Tel: +233 21 662-511, Fax: +233 21 665-594

2. Evangelical Presbyterian Church, Ghana (1060)

In 1847 German missionaries of the Bremen (or North German) Mission Society, closely cooperating with the Basel Mission, started work among the Ewe people in the east of present-day Ghana. After a period of rapid growth, at the outbreak of World War I, the church had two stations in the British Gold Coast colony and seven stations in the German territory of Togoland. Later the mission work also spread to the Twi, Guan, Konkomba, Kabre, and Akposso-speaking areas. After World War I the former German colony of Togo was divided into two mandated territories of the League of Nations, the western part under the British and the eastern part under French rule (cf. Togo). Yet, in May 1922, the first synod of the mission stations declared itself the supreme governing body of the one "Ewe Church." The congregational order of the North German Mission became the church order. In 1923 Scottish missionaries began to work in British Togo, and in 1929 the Paris Mission took over in French Togo. For practical reasons divisional synods had to be set up in the two territories, which led to separate developments.

192

To this day, however, the two churches share the same constitution and hold common synod meetings every four years.

In 1954 tensions arose in the church over the issues of language and of polygamy. Twenty congr in Buem- and Krachi-speaking areas separated and formed their own church. Most of them reintegrated the mother church in 1964. In response to this tension the church changed its name from Ewe Presbyterian Church to Evangelical Presbyterian Church.

The Evangelical Presbyterian Church is strongest in the Volta region but has congr all over the country.

In the course of its history it suffered several splits when individual members gathered followers to establish new churches (the Apostolic Revelation Society, the White Cross Society, the Evangelical Presbyterian Reformed Church, and the Lord's Pentecostal Church). The reason for a fifth schism in 1991 was differences with the charismatic movement within the church. These led to the formation of the Evangelical Presbyterian Church *of* Ghana under new leadership but based on the church's constitution and representing a substantial minority of the constituency. However, it was not officially recognized by the CCG. So far, attempts to reconcile and reunite have not been successful. The following statistical data do not include the congr that broke away.

TM: **143,107** BM: **143,107** CM: **41,968** Congr: **748** PStations: **748** OrdM: **195** Eld: **7,000** Deac: **ne** EvgHome: **33** Mission: **1** Women Ord: **yes** As Ministers: **1979/11** as Deac: **1900/na** as Elders: **1900/na** ChurchOrg: **Presbyterian (congr, districts, presbys, 1 synod)** Off/otherLang: **English, Ewe, Twi, Kokomba** DoctrB: **ApC** Infant or believer's baptism: **both** Frequency of the Lord's Supper: **monthly** Periodicals: **The Youth Catechist (quarterly) The Message (monthly)** Close relations with: **Eglise Evangélique Presbyterienne du Togo, United Church Board for World Ministries (USA), Bremen Mission Board (Bremen, Germany), Evangelische Zentrale für Entwicklung (Bonn, Germany), Bread for the World (Stuttgart, Germany)** NatRel: **CCG Christian Council of Ghana (1929)** RegRel: **AACC** IntlRel: **WCC, WARC** TheolSchool: **Trinity College, Legon (shared with Presb, Meth, and Angl churches), EP Seminary, Peki**

Address: Presbiteria Nyanyui Hame le Ghana, P.O. Box 18, Ho-Kpodzi, HO Volta Region, Ghana, Tel: +233 91 755, Fax: +233 91 8275

GREECE

Area in km²	130,918
Population	10,300,000
Religions in %	Orth (97%)
Official language	Greek (demotiki)

Greek Evangelical Church (6330)

The origins of the Greek Evangelical Church go back to the work of Jonas King, a missionary of the ABCFM who settled in Greece after the Greek War of Independence (1821-1828). He was engaged in educational and welfare work as well as in preaching. In 1848 he was brought to court and expelled from the country. Later he was able to return to Athens, where he died in 1869. A young student who had been present at his trial, Kalopothakis, converted to the Ref faith and became one of the leading figures in the history of the Evangelical Church. The movement met with much hostility in Orthodox circles.

In 1866 the first Evangelical community was organized, and in 1871 the first church building was erected. In 1885 a synod, consisting of three small congr, was established. Evangelistic work had also been started in Asia Minor. When, after the Greek-Turkish War in 1922, Greek people were forced out of Asia Minor, a significant number of Greek Evangelical refugees either joined existing communities or established new ones. The situation of Evangelicals became particularly precarious during the dictatorial regime of the Colonels in the early '70s. The democratic climate which followed that period gave them greater freedom, though they continue to be regarded as an element foreign to Greek religion and culture.

The church is engaged in both evangelistic and social work. There are two centers for marginalized people in Thessaloniki and Athens. New missionary work has been undertaken in Albania (cf. Albania).

TM: **5,000** BM: **4,900** CM: **1,600** Congr: **34** PStations: **4** OrdM: **17** Eld: **85** Deac: **65** EvgHome: **1** Mission: **3** Women Ord: **yes** As Ministers: **no ordination** as Deac: **10/from beginning** as Elders: **no ordination** ChurchOrg: **local church sessions (presby), regional synods, GenAssy** Off/otherLang: **Greek** DoctrB: **NicC, Conf of the Greek Evangelical Ch (modified WestConf)** Frequency of the Lord's Supper: **6-10 times/yearn** Periodicals: **Astir tis anatolis (gen/monthly/1,000)** NatRel: **nc** RegRel: **CEC** IntlRel: **REC (1984), WARC (1886), WCC (1946)** TheolSchool: **nc**

Address: Helleniki Evangeliki Ekklesia, 24 Markou Botsari Str., GR-11 741, Athens, Greece, Tel: +30 1 922-2684, Fax: +30 1 653-1498

GRENADA

Area in km²	340
Population	(July 1996 est.) 94,961 black African 82%, Coloured 13%, other 5%
Religions in %	RCath 64%, Angl 22%, various Prot
Official/other languages	English/French patois

Grenada was discovered in 1498 by Christopher Columbus. In 1650 it was colonized by the French, and it was given to the English in 1783. In 1974 it became a parliamentary monarchy headed by the Queen of England with a residing governor.

The recent history of this island has been shaped by a coup of the New Jewel (Joint Endeavour for Welfare, Education and Liberation) in 1979 which made the pro-Cuban, M. Bishop, Prime Minister. He was overthrown in 1983, liberated by a crowd of followers, but died in the following bloody rebellion. This prompted the Caribbean Organization of States to call for help from the USA. In October 1983, "Operation Urgent Fury," led by US marines and Grenadian troops, "cleaned" the island and restored peace in five days. All foreign pro-Communist advisors had to leave the country.

Over 35% of Grenada's GNP is generated by tourism. Of the 300,000 annual visitors over 70% come on luxury cruise ships.

Presbyterian Church in Grenada (PCG) (3370)

The first Presb church (St. Andrew's Kirk) was built in 1833 by Scottish plantation owners. The church was associated with the Church of Scotland. Its first minister was William Haig, who was ordained in British Guyana. Government grants which the church received in its early years were withdrawn in 1860. After the abolition of slavery and with the advent of East Indians as indentured workers in 1880, mission work was established in various parts of the island, especially in Belair (St. Andrew's) and Samaritans (St. Patrick's). The missionaries who served at these stations were drawn from the Canadian mission in Trinidad. Schools were opened in Belair and Samaritan. In 1945 the Church of Scotland withdrew its support for the mission work both in Grenada and in St. Vincent. The suggestion was made that the church unite with the Methodists. Resisting the proposal, the church associated itself with the Presb Church of Trinidad. Through the resources and assets of a large East Indian population, this church had grown considerably (cf. Trinidad). It had the support of the United Church of Canada. The congr in Grenada became part of the Northern Presbytery of the Church of Trinidad. In the 1980s the will for autonomy became stronger in Grenada, and on April 20, 1986, the Presbyterian Church in Grenada was founded.

TM: **876** BM: **1,320** CM: **620** Congr: **4** OrdM: **1** Eld: **16** Deac: **nc** EvgHome: **nc** Mission: **nc** Women Ord: **yes** As Ministers: **nc** as Deac: **nc** as Elders: **1950s/6** ChurchOrg: **sessions (elders), presby, GenAssy** Off/otherLang: **English** DoctrB: **ApC, NicC, WestConf, Living Faith (A Statement of Faith adopted by the Presbyterian Church of Canada)** Infant or believer's baptism: **both** Frequency of the Lord's Supper: **quarterly and on special occasions (Easter, Pentecost, Confirmation)** Close relations with: **Meth Ch in Grenada, Presb Ch in Trinidad, United Church of Canada** NatRel: **Conference of Churches in Grenada (1950), St. Andrew's People's Assoc. (1985), Agency for Rural Transformation (1983)** RegRel: **CCC (1973), CANACOM (1986), Caribbean Alliance of Ref Churches (1983), CANAAC (1983)** IntlRel: **WARC (1983)** TheolSchool: **nc**

Address: Presbyterian Church in Grenada (PCG), Knox House, Grand Etang Rd., West Indies St. George's, Grenada, Tel: +1 809 440-2436, Fax: +1 809 440-2436, E-mail: pcgknox @caribsurf.com

GUADELOUPE

Area in km²	1,438
Population	Total 408,000 métropolitains 8,000
Religions in %	vast majority is officially RCath, Prot. 1.9%
Official/other languages	French/créole

This archipelago of 9 islands was discovered by Christopher Columbus on his second trip to the Americas and settled by the French, including Huguenot families, in 1635. It was annexed to France in 1674. French Huguenots were few in number by the end of the 18th century and had to go to neighboring islands, like St. Kitts or St. Thomas, to conduct Ref church life openly. The Prot community remained small in number, having, unlike the RCath Church, no governmental support. Guadeloupe was declared a "département" (district) of France in 1946; thus French law prevails. France provides over 80% of the GNP through various forms of subsidies. In 1995 unemployment was over 30% of the active population.

The first Prot to come to this Caribbean group of islands were the Moravians. Today they are the smallest of the eight Prot groups, totalling altogether 34 congr. Protestant sects have made deep inroads into the Guadeloupean population.

Reformed Church of the Antilles (3324)

This church is the only Ref denomination in Guadeloupe. It serves mainly French military and an immigrant ("métropolitains") population from France. It has ties to the government through its chaplaincy services; the chaplain resides in Martinique and comes regularly to Guadeloupe. The Reformed Church of the Antilles is a member of CEEEFE and thus has close relationships with the "Fédération protestante de France," which includes some 14 Protestant French denominations and missions.

Precise data have not been made available.

Address: Eglise réformée des Antilles, B.P. 606, F 97 261 Fort de France, Guadeloupe, Tel: +596 39 55 57, Fax: +596 39 55 57

GUATEMALA

Area in km²	108,000
Population	(est. 1997) 11,200,000
Religions in %	RCath 70%, Prot 25%, others 5%
Official/other languages	Spanish (official), plus 20 Mayan languages, Xinca, and Garifuna

The "Reino de Guatemala" included all of Central America and Chiapas during the colonial period. In 1524 the process of evangelization began, especially by Franciscan and Dominican priests. In 1534 Pope Paul III founded the bishopric of Guatemala, which was raised to the status of an archbishopric in 1742. Since the center of the Spanish government for Central America was based in Guatemala, few Prot were found there during the colonial period. However, some cases of persons accused of being "Luth" were processed by the office of the Inquisition in Guatemala.

During the first part of the 19th century, a strong conservative pro-Catholic dictatorship prevented a Protestant presence. However, from 1843 to 1846 the Bible colporteur Frederick Crowe, a lay Baptist from England, established a school and distributed Bibles until he was forcibly evicted by a military convoy. With the establishment of the liberal government in 1873, the door opened to the mission societies. The first, by invitation of the country's president, Justo Rufino Barrios, in 1882, was Rev. John Clark Hill from the Presbyterian Church in the USA. He was followed by the Central American Mission of C. I. Scofield in 1896. Other groups which arrived at an early date were: the Friends in 1902, the Nazarenes in 1904, the Advent in 1908, and the Primitive Methodists in 1914.

The overwhelming majority of Guatemalan Prot are Pent. Pentecostal pioneers Charles Furman and Thomas Pullin had both experienced the baptism of the Holy Spirit at the Christian and Missionary Alliance Bible School in Nyack, N.Y., in 1907. Furman worked with the Primitive Methodists from 1922 to 1929 but encountered strong resistance to his Pent emphasis. The Full Gospel Church of God, related to the Church of God (Cleveland, Tennessee), marks its founding date as 1932, the year when Furman's Guatemalan co-workers experienced the baptism of the Holy Spirit. Another major Pent denomination, the Assemblies of God, currently the largest denomination in the country, arrived in 1935 from their base in El Salvador.

Today, Guatemala's Prot community includes more than two million people, is divided into some 300 different denominations, and is made up of about 14,000 local churches.

The Guatemalan Ref family today consists basically of the following denominations:

197

1. National Evangelical Presbyterian Church of Guatemala (IENPG) (2070)

This church is the fruit of missionary work started by the Presbyterian Church in the USA in 1882. In its first period the church took roots in the milieu of the urban liberal middle class. Various educational and welfare projects were launched.

A synod was established in 1950; and the church became independent in 1962.

In the course of the century the church grew in membership among the lower classes, especially among indigenous peoples. In 1959 the first indigenous (Maya) presby was founded. Since then church growth has primarily taken place within the indigenous population. Today the majority in the synod is held by indigenous believers. Another factor in its growth was a ten-year major promotion campaign launched in 1972 with a view to the centennial of the church.

However, in the last 20 years the serious social, ethnic, and military conflicts of the country have had their repercussions on the life of the church. At the same time the impact of the Pent movement has grown. One result of these develop-ments is the lower growth rate of the church; another is the secession of, at least, one major group (cf. no. 2).

TM: **25,000** CM: **11,500** Congr: **155** PStations: **130** OrdM: **188** Eld: **ne** Deac: **nc** EvgHome: **0** Mission: **0** Women Ord: **1998/yes** As Ministers: **yes** as Deac: **yes** as Elders: **yes** ChurchOrg: **congr, consistories, 15 presby, synod** Off/otherLang: **Spanish, Quiche, Kakchiquel, Mam, Quekchi, Kanjobal** DoctrB: **ApC, WestConf** Infant or believer's baptism: **both** Frequency of the Lord's Supper: **monthly** Close relations with: **PC (USA), Reformed Missionary League of Holland, Presb Church of Canada, Church of Scotland** NatRel: **Evangelical Alliance of Guatemala** RegRel: **AIPRAL** IntlRel: **WARC** TheolSchool: **Evangelical Presbyterian Seminary, Maya Quiche Bible Institute, Mam Bible Institute, Edward Haymaker Institute** Service infrastructure: **2 schools in Quetzaltenango and Guatemala City; Monte Sion retreat center (Amatitlan)**

Address: Iglesia Evangélica Nacional Presbiteriana de Guatemala, Apartado 655, Ave. Simeon Canas 7-13, zona 2, 01002 Guatemala C.A., Guatemala, Tel: +502 2 288-4444, Fax: +502 2 254-1242.

2. Presbyterian Synod of the Southwest of Guatemala (2071)

This church split in 1993 from the NEPCG (cf. no. 1) and sought legal registration from the government of Guatemala. Both churches are in court with a dispute over ownership of land which is presently occupied by the Synod of the Southwest. When the Sinodo applied for membership in AIPRAL in 1994, it was denied such a status on the basis of its "unclear situation." The Sinodo then became a founding member of CLIR (Confederaçao Latinamerica de Igrejas Reformadas), a more conservative counterpart to AIPRAL.

TM: **6,540** BM: **6,540** CM: **6,540** Congr: **nc** OrdM: **180** Eld: **350** Deac: **nc** EvgHome: **nc** Mission: **nc** Women Ord: **yes** As Ministers: **no** as Deac: **yes** as Elders: **yes** ChurchOrg: **consistory (session), presby, synod** Off/otherLang: **Spanish** DoctrB: **ApC, WestConf** Infant or believer's baptism: **believer** Frequency of the Lord's Supper: **monthly** IntlRel: **CLIR** TheolSchool: **4 theological study cen-**

ters (no seminary) Periodicals: **Ecos Femeniles del Suroeste (quarterly/nc), El Esforzador del Suroeste (quarterly/nc)**

Address: Sinodo Evangélico Presbiteriano Sur Oeste de Guatemela, 13 Ave. A 52, zona 1, Quetzaltenango 09001, Guatemala, Tel: +502 872-0740 or 872-1611

3. Bethlehem Bible Presbyterian Church (Synod of Guatemala) (2075)

TM: **1,000** BM: **900** CM: **900** Congr: **45** OrdM: **10** Eld: **nc** Deac: **nc** EvgHome: **4** Mission: **nc** Women Ord: **no** ChurchOrg: **congr, 5 presby (with 6-12 congr), synod** Off/otherLang: **Spanish, Quiche, Kakchikel** DoctrB: **WestConf** Infant or believer's baptism: **believer** Frequency of the Lord's Supper: **monthly** Close relations with: **National Evangelical Presbyterian Church of Guatemala (cf. no. 1)** NatRel: **none** RegRel: **none** IntlRel: **none** Service infrastructure: **medical clinic, vacation Bible school**

Address: Iglesia Presbiteriana Biblica Belen, Apartado postal 443, 11 calle 15-11, zona l, Guatemala City, Guatemala, Tel: +502 232-9369

4. Independent Fundamental Presbyterian Church (2072)

This church was founded on Palm Sunday 1967. Composed of people from various church backgrounds, it affirms as its goal to become more Presb and Ref. It rejects ecumenism but is committed to "Biblical cooperation." Its members are to support three foreign missionary families from the Independent Board for Presbyterian Foreign Missions.

TM: **90** BM: **85** CM: **74** Congr: **1** PStations: **1** OrdM: **2** Eld: **2** Deac: **4** EvgHome: **1** Mission: **nc** Women Ord: **no** ChurchOrg: **congr** Off/otherLang: **Spanish** DoctrB: **WestConf, WestCats** Infant or believer's baptism: **both** Frequency of the Lord's Supper: **every second month** Close relations with: **Bible Presbyterians** NatRel: **Confederación de Iglesias Fundamentalistas in Guatemala** RegRel: **Alianza Latinoamericana de Iglesias Cristianas** IntlRel: **ICCC** TheolSchool: **training in Chile and USA** Periodicals: **occasional**

Address: Iglesia Presbiteriana Independiente Fundamentalista, 2 Avenida 3-22, zona 4 de Mixco, Colonia Monte Verde, Guatemala City, Guatemala, Tel: +502 597-1235, Fax: +502 594-7633

5. St. John Apostle Evangelical Church (2076)

This church is the product of a split within the NEPCG (cf. no. 1). It serves as a kind of refuge for ex-fundamentalists. The pioneer pastor, who led this dissenting group, is Rev. Guillermo Debrot, who continues to be considered "pastor emeritus" although he does not take part in the community's life anymore. From the nine ordained ministers this church claims, only three (one full-time, one half-time, and a volunteer) are still active.

TM: **250** BM: **150** CM: **130** Congr: **1** OrdM: **9** Eld: **8** Deac: **1** EvgHome: **2** Mission: **nc** Women Ord:

199

yes As Ministers: **0** as Deac: **7** as Elders: **2** ChurchOrg: **consistory, presby** Off/otherLang: **Spanish** DoctrB: **WestConf** Frequency of the Lord's Supper: **weekly** Close relations with: **IENPG, Missouri Synod Lutheran Church in Guatemala, Disciples, United Church of Christ USA** NatRel: **United Bible Society** TheolSchool: **Central American Theological Seminary (Guatemala City), Evangelical Presbyterian Seminary (Guatemala City), Christian Theological Seminary (Indianapolis, USA)** Service infrastructure: **clinic, vocational school, agricultural loans**

Address: Iglesia Evangélica San Juan Apostol, 1 Calle 1-73, zona 4, Mixco, Guatemala, Tel: +502 592-5159

GUIANA — *See* FRENCH GUIANA

GULF REGION

The Gulf region traditionally includes the countries bordering the Arabian Gulf: Bahrain, Iraq, Kuwait, Oman, Qatar, Saudi Arabia, and United Arab Emirates.

The Christian presence in the region goes back to the first centuries. Early Christianity expanding eastward reached the area of today's Iraq. Even today most Christians in the area belong to the Assyrian (Chaldean) and Syrian churches which survived through the centuries from ancient times. There are in Iraq, mainly in Baghdad, also a small Armenian community of pre-genocide origin, and in Baghdad a very small Greek Orthodox community. When after World War I Turkey was established and an aggressive "turkification" became state policy, many Assyrian and Syrian Orthodox Christians emigrated from southeast Turkey to Iraq.

Western Christian missions in the Gulf region began in 1623 with Carmelite Catholic missionaries founding a chapter house in Basrah (now in Iraq). Carmelites, along with other RCath orders and priests, continue to be active in the region.

A Prot presence did not exist until the Arabian Mission (then a nondenominational mission) "occupied" Basrah in 1891 and progressed throughout the area: Bahrain (1893), Oman (1893), Amarah (1895, but real work started only in 1925), Kuwait (1910). A few other "stations" were established, but did not survive. The Arabian Mission officially came under the Ref Church in 1894 and was fully amalgated with the denomination's other mission endeavors only in 1925. Pioneering work for the Reformed Church in America (RCA) had been done by Samuel Zwemer and James Cantine, the first missionaries to go there. The work in northern Iraq was under a joint mission named The United Mission of Mesopotamia (to become after 1930 The United Mission in Iraq). It was officially founded by a coalition in the USA of three American Reformed Churches: the Presbyterian Church (cf. United States of America no. 30), the Reformed Church in the US (also known as German Reformed and which later became part of the United

Church of Christ, cf. United States no. 43), and the Reformed Church in America (also known as the Dutch Reformed Church; cf. United States no. 36)

Since the RCA was the only church with work in the area, the other churches, such as the Angl and the RCath (Carmelite monks did not establish church institutions or worshiping communities of their own), used the RCA facilities when they began their work. This means actually that all church activities in the area are related to the work of the RCA.

The work began with personal witness and Bible distribution. The colporteurs from Lebanon, Syria, and Iraq made valuable contributions to this part of the world. The need for schools and hospitals became evident. The first physician was appointed in 1892, but he was dismissed within a year for "theological incompatibility." A second arrived in 1893, but had to leave for health reasons. With the arrival in 1895 of Dr. Lankford Worrall (a Meth) and, in 1898, of Dr. Sharon and Marion Thoms (also Meth) the mission policy shifted from that practiced by Samuel Zwemer to an evangelism through educational and medical involvement. Starting in the early 1900s schools and hospitals were built along with churches. Everyone was welcomed regardless of religious background. Between 1895 and 1925 a substantial number of Prot Christians who had been proselytized by Congreg mission work in Anatolia fled into Iraq and neighboring countries. A good number of these were later recruited by mission organizations in Baghdad, Basrah, Kuwait, and Bahrain to serve as colporteurs, evangelists, and medical assistants.

A big change came about through the discovery of oil. Workers came from all parts of the world, but mostly from Asia, to share in the wealth from the "black gold." All church activities rapidly expanded, particularly the English language services. While the missionaries were there primarily for the Arabs, the missionaries felt that they could not neglect the witness to non-Arabic-speaking people. The English-language groups were a mixture of Arabs, Indians, Pakistanis, Europeans, Americans, and, later, Koreans and Filipinos, organized into loose congr to work together in planning the use of the buildings, worshiping together, etc. As more and more people of a particular language and denomination arrived, the various groups would organize themselves, have their own time of worship, and, as soon as financially possible, call their own pastor or priest.

While some countries have given land to the church, or allowed land to be purchased for building a church, local governments have made it clear that they prefer that Christians all worship in one or two places, rather than the various congr each having their own building. Each congregation has its own church council to plan its services and deal with such things as baptisms and funerals. There is also an overall council that deals primarily with the use and upkeep of the building, official relations with the government, and the like.

This church structure, found only in the Gulf region, is unique : it is a sort of coalition of groups identified by language and culture, while accommodating a variety of denominationally specific and clearly separate groups.

Bahrain
See Bahrain, National Evangelical Church of Bahrain (4398)

Iraq
See Iraq, Evangelical Churches of Iraq (4303)

Kuwait
See Kuwait, National Evangelical Church in Kuwait—NECK (4393)

Oman, Sultanate of
See Oman, the Protestant Church in Oman (4357)

Saudi Arabia
Ref Church missionaries arrived there at the invitation and permission of the Saudi government and were active between 1917 and 1955, often providing medical treatment to the royal family. Christians used to gather in "fellowships" led by "special teachers." But there are no longer any RCA missionaries in Saudi Arabia.

United Arab Emirates
In the early 1950s Dr. Sarah Hosman, formerly of the RCA, opened a maternity ward in the town of Sharjah. The work was later associated with the Independent Board of Foreign Missions of the Bible Presbyterian Church (cf. United States no. 6). In the late 1950s, when the Reformed Presbyterian Church–Evangelical Synod (cf. United States no. 31) was formed by churches that withdrew from the Bible Presbyterian Church, Glen and Helen Fearnow (male nurse and midwife) left Sharjah and opened a small clinic in the town of Ras Al Khaimah (RAK). However, due to governmental restrictions placed upon the work in RAK in the late 1970s, the work was closed down. About this same time the maternity work of the Bible Presb in Sharjah was taken over by MECO (Middle East Christian Outreach); it operated under their care until 1996, when it was closed for lack of a doctor.

In 1959 RCA missionaries received a request from the ruler of the Shaikhdom (now Emirate) of Abu Dhabi requesting a doctor to establish medical work. The request was passed on to Drs. Burwell (Pat) and Marian Kennedy, members of TEAM (The Evangelical Alliance Mission), who had worked with RCA missionaries in Iraq prior to the forced closure in 1958 of the RCA work there due to the revolution. TEAM sent the Kennedys along with other workers, and in 1961 Oasis Hospital was established in the village (now major city) of Al Ain in the hinterland of the Shaikhdom of Abu Dhabi, where it continues to function as a respected medical facility.

In the mid-1960s a maternity ward was established by workers from WEC (Worldwide Evangelism Crusade) in the village of Fujairah on the coast of the Gulf of Oman.

Arabic congr, made up primarily of expatriate Arab Christians, exist in the cities of Al Ain, Abu Dhabi, and Dubai. Each has its own Arabic-speaking pastor.

Depending upon the population, from time to time Arabic congr exist in Sharjah and RAK, but usually in the form of loosely organized small groups that meet occasionally for Bible study and mutual encouragement.

In this part of the Gulf region, the Evangelical Alliance Mission (EAM) has been particularly active. Its original founders are Dr. Pat and Marian Kennedy, who started the "Oasis Hospital" at Al Ain. The EAM runs another hospital in Sharja. In each place there is a hospital chaplain who also serves a small local congregation. There are other churches in Abu Dhabi and Dubai. The Church of Pakistan has a very active Urdu congregation made of migrant workers.

A number of charismatic and evangelical groups are active in the Emirates, where they work as "tent-makers."

GUYANA

Area in km²	214,970
Population	(July 1996 est.) 712,091 East Indian 51%, black and mixed 43%, Amerindian 4%, European and Chinese 2%
Religions	Christian 57%, Hindu 33%, Muslim 9%, other 1%
Official/other languages	English/Hindi, Urdu, Créole, and 9 dialects

The first Europeans settled in present-day Guyana after the arrival of the Dutch West India Company in 1616. It became a Dutch colony in 1621, but was taken by the English in 1796. The area soon became an object of disputes between several countries. In 1815 the Congress of Vienna confirmed the division of Guyana between England (later British Guyana), Holland (Surinam), and France (Cayenne). The partition was ratified by the Paris Agreement of 1899; but there is still a claim from Venezuela over 140,000 km² of territory taken by Great Britain in 1841. Until the 1830s sugar cane and 110,000 black slaves made up the wealth of Guyana. The abolition of slavery in 1834, the dropping of sugar cane prices, and the subsequent need to compensate with the cultivation of rice and coffee prompted planters to bring hired laborers into the country. Between 1846 and 1917 over 240,000 workers where hired from India alone. The first serious autonomy movement came in 1949 with the PPP (People's Progress Party). In 1961 Great Britain granted internal autonomy to the country; riots and bloodshed followed in 1963/64. Guyana became independent in 1966 but remained a member of the British Commonwealth. Since 1980 Guyana is a "cooperative Republic in transition from capitalism to socialism." About 90% of the population of Guyana live solely on the 20-30-km-wide coastal area. Guyana is also the last country in the Caribbean region where one can still find a few small communities of true descendants of the indigenous people whom Christopher Columbus met in the 15th century.

Christian mission work was started in 1657 by the Capuchins. It took a century and a half before a RCath diocese could be established. In the 17th century Dutch Ref churches and missions, especially the Netherlandse Hervormde Kerk (NHK), spread to Brazil, Curaçao, and what would become Surinam. They arrived in Guyana in the 1620s, soon to be followed by the Brethren (the latter were almost exterminated in 1763 by rebelling black slaves). The first Dutch Ref church building in Guyana was erected in 1720. The Dutch Reformed Church, together with the Angl Church, became a state church supported financially through colonial taxes. When Great Britain took over the country from the Dutch, it withdrew its financial support from the Dutch Reformed Church and confined subsidies to Presb and Angl. The Dutch Reformed Church was therefore bound to disappear; the NHK had furthermore not permitted blacks and Indians to become members, so its membership was slowly absorbed by Presb and Angl churches. By 1860 there were no Ref congr left in Guyana.

A Presb presence dates back to the arrival in 1766 of planters from Scotland. It became vocal through the Scottish Presb Lachal Cuming, also called the "Patriarch of Scotland in Guyana." A Presb Missionary Society was formed in 1860 to evangelize the East Indians. Canadian Presb cooperated in this venture. They concentrated their work among East Indians, teaching them in English.

1. Presbyterian Church of Guyana (3322)

On September 23, 1815, Scotsmen in the new British Guyana resolved that it was desirable to establish a Presb Church in the colony. An unfinished building, which was intended to become a church, was bought at cost from the Dutch. The first minister — Mr. Archibald Brown — arrived on September 18, 1816, in the colony. Many of the Scottish church members were slave owners; given the liberal stance of the Scots toward slaves, Africans were admitted into the congr as soon as 1821. Church planting proved successful, and the Presbyterian Church of Guyana was established on February 9, 1837, during a session in St. Andrew's Kirk. By 1860 it had absorbed the remnant members of the NHK. The presby would be largely supported by government grants. Partial disestablishment began in 1899. In 1945 a capital sum was paid to the presby and the state ceased its financial aid. On May 25, 1967, the Church of Scotland dissolved the presby, which then became an autonomous church.

TM: **5,600** CM: **3,250** Congr: **25** OrdM: **41** IntlRel: **WARC**

Address: Presbyterian Church of Guyana, P.O. Box 10151, 81 Coral Str., Georgetown, Guyana

2. Guyana Congregational Union (GCU) (3320)

Its beginnings date back to 1808 when John Wray, from the London Missionary Society (LMS), arrived in Guyana, which was then ruled by the Dutch. He and his successors experienced strong opposition in church planting. The congr, however, spread quickly after the abolition of slavery in 1834. The British Congregational Union of Guyana was formed in 1883. When the LMS withdrew its support, it almost ceased to exist. In 1908 the Colonial Missionary Society gave its support instead. In 1942 the Union started mission work among the Arawak Indians living in the interior. After 1942 the Union undertook a joint ministry with other denominations among bauxite miners. Ministerial and financial support was still required and given by the Congregational Council for World Mission.

TM: **2,452** CM: **2,300** Congr: **40** PStations: **6** OrdM: **9** Eld: **nc** Deac: **ne** EvgHome: **nc** Mission: **1** Women Ord: **yes** As Ministers: **1990/1** as Deac: **ne** as Elders: **nc** ChurchOrg: **committee meeting, quarterly executive, Annual Assy** Off/otherLang: **English** DoctrB: **ApC** Infant or believer's baptism: **both** Frequency of the Lord's Supper: **monthly** Close relations with: **Presb Ch of Guyana, Guyana Presb Ch** NatRel: **Guyana Council of Churches** RegRel: **CANAAC, CCC, CANACOM** IntlRel: **WARC, CWM** TheolSchool: **United Theological College of the West Indies (Jamaica)** Periodicals: **Beacon (general/semesterly)**

Address: Guyana Congregational Union (GCU), Quamina House, Third and Light Streets, AlbertTown, Georgetown, Guyana, Tel: +592 2 70758, Fax: +592 2 70758

3. Guyana Presbyterian Church (3321)

In 1880 John Morton, a Canadian Presb missionary from Trinidad, visited British Guyana and recommended setting up a mission there. The Presbyterian Church in Canada sent John Gibson, who started work five years later in Demerara County. After his death it took several years before a new minister, J. B. Cropper, arrived at Better Hope in 1895. He spoke fluent Hindi with the Indians working on the plantations. By 1905 his endeavor had spread to all three colonies. Until 1945 the Guyana Presbyterian Church worked almost exclusively among East Indians employed on the sugar plantations. Schools and churches were established, but the church suffered from the heavy turnover of missionaries. A presby was formed in 1945, and the church became autonomous as the "Canadian Presbyterian Church in British Guyana." In 1961 the name was changed to "Guyana Presbyterian Church."

TM: **2,500** BM: **1,890** CM: **2,000** Congr: **44** PStations: **44** OrdM: **3** Eld: **32** Deac: **ne** EvgHome: **ne** Mission: **ne** Women Ord: **yes** As Ministers: **1992/1 (resigned)** as Deac: **nc** as Elders: **1936/75** ChurchOrg: **sessions, presby** Off/otherLang: **English, Hindi** DoctrB: **ApC, NicC, WestConf, Presb** Infant or believer's baptism: **both** Frequency of the Lord's Supper: **monthly** Close relations with: **Guyana Congregational Union; Presb Ch of Guyana** NatRel: **Guyana Council of Churches (1957)** RegRel: **Caribbean Association of Ref Churches, CCC, CANAAC, CNACM** IntlRel: **WARC (1977)** TheolSchool: **Bethel Theological College (opening Fall 1998)** Service infrastructure: **none** Periodicals: **The Torch (gen/quarterly/200)**

Address: Guyana Presbyterian Church, 22 Princess Elizabeth Rd., New Amsterdam Berbice, Guyana, Tel: +592 3 2831

GUYANE FRANCAISE — *see* FRENCH GUIANA

HAITI

Area in km²	27,750
Population	(July 1996 est.) 6,731,539 black 95%, mulatto and European 5%
Religions in %	RCath 80% (of which an overwhelming majority also practice Voodoo), Protestant 16% (Bapt 10%, Pent 4%, Advent 1%, other 1%), none 1%, other 3% (1982)
Official/other languages	French 10%, Creole 90%

The island was discovered by Christopher Columbus in 1492. In 1657 the territory of Haiti passed from the Spanish to the French. In 1791 the black population rose against the white ruling class; it was the first country in Latin America to become independent (under Toussaint Louverture in 1804). From 1822 to 1844 Haiti also ruled over the Dominican Republic. Prompted by an anarchic situation, the US marines occupied the country in 1915; it remained dependent on the USA after their departure (1934). The mulattos played the dominant role. In 1957 François Duvalier won the elections on the basis of the promise to defend the rights of the blacks. In fact, he and, after 1971, his son Jean-Claude ruled as brutal dictators. In 1990 Aristide, a priest, was elected to the presidency, but he was soon removed by a military putch. Through US intervention the democratic order was reestablished in 1994. Haiti is the poorest country of the Western hemisphere.

Prot first came to the country in the early part of the 19th century when slaves, fleeing from the USA, found refuge in Haiti. The oldest Prot churches are the Meth and Angl, the largest body are the Bapt, followed by the Pent and Advent. In the '60s evangelical Prot denominations founded a Council of Evangelical Churches, and in 1986 the Protestant Federation of Haiti, which brings together the majority of Protestant Churches, came into existence. The two bodies cooperate in some fields.

Christian Reformed Church of Haiti (3311)

The history of this church is closely connected with the history of the Christian Reformed Church in the Dominican Republic (cf. no. 2). In the 1980s a missionary of the Christian Reformed Church in North America (CRCNA) brought two pastors of the Christian Reformed Church in the Dominican Republic, Obelto

Cheribin and Emilio Martinez, to Haiti to start theological education on an extension basis in the evangelical community. They were joined by several Haitian nationals in forming the John Calvin Institute in Port-au-Prince. They also founded a Christian Ref congr. In 1991 a major repatriation of Haitians (70,000) from the Dominican Republic took place, among them one-fifth of the Haitian membership of the Christian Reformed Church; they settled in the mountains of Thiotte and Jacmel, on the central plateau, and in the slums of Port-au-Prince. The decision to establish the Christian Reformed Church in Haiti was taken in 1993 at a joint meeting of Haitian and Dominican church leaders, with participation of CRC missionaries from the United States.

TM: **1,220** BM: **520** CM: **520** Congr: **26** PStations: **3** OrdM: **12** Eld: **na** Deac: **na** EvgHome: **14** Mission: **ne** Women Ord: **yes** As Ministers: **nc** as Deac: **1992/nc** as Elders: **nc** ChurchOrg: **zonal committees, loose association of Christian Reformed Churches at national level** Off/otherLang: **Haitian, Creole, French** DoctrB: **ApC, HeidC, WestConf** Infant or believer's baptism: **believer** Frequency of the Lord's Supper: **monthly** Periodicals: **none** Close relations with: **Christian Reformed Church in North America (Christian Reformed World Mission)** NatRel: **none** RegRel: **none** IntlRel: **none** TheolSchool: **Juan Calvino Training Centre (Port-au-Prince)**

Address: Eglise Chrétienne Réformée d'Haiti, P.O. Box 1693, N 3, rue Pelican (Delmas 56), Port-au-Prince, Haiti, Tel: +509 46 13 41, Fax: +509 46 13 41

HONDURAS

Area in km²	112,090
Population	(July 1996 est.) 6,605,193 mestizo (mixed Indian and European) 90%, Indian 7%, black 2%, white 1%
Religions in %	RCath 80%, Prot 20%
Official/other languages	Spanish/Indian dialects

The area was originally inhabited by the Maya. Copán was one of the most significant Maya sanctuaries. In 1538 the area became part of the Spanish dominion of Guatemala. In 1823 it obtained independence: first as part of the Federation of Central America and then, in 1838, as an independent state. In this century Honduras became economically more and more dependent on the United States, especially on the United Fruit Company. In the '50s tensions between the campesinos and the government began to mount. In 1972 masses of campesinos marched on the capital to protest against their exploitation. But the economic situation has hardly changed. Some 63% of the land is in the hand of 4% of the population, and 75% of the population have very low incomes. In 1990 four-fifths of the children were undernourished.

The RCath Church came to Honduras in the early period of Spanish domination. In 1531 the first bishopric was established. In the 1550s the Franciscans began to undertake systematic missionary efforts. For centuries the RCath faith was the state religion until, in 1880, state and church were definitively separated. Today the RCath Church is organized as an archdiocese with four dioceses. About one-fifth of the 300 priests are indigenous. The presence of Prot began in the 18th century with Angl and Moravian missions; they were followed in the 19th century by the Advent (1887), the Central American Mission (1896), the Sala Evangélica (1898), the Holiness Church (1903); in 1930 the Moravians established a presence among the natives; and since 1931 the Assemblies of God have grown rapidly.

1. Evangelical Reformed Church of Honduras (3308)

This church was founded in 1922 by Haroldo Auer, a missionary of the United Church of Christ in the USA (cf. United States). In its teaching it follows the lines of Calvinist theology and seeks at the same time to affirm its own theological identity. Its main emphases are the spiritual and prophetic vocation of the church, a program of evangelism, and medical and educational projects among the destitute. An Association of Evangelical Institutions in Honduras (AIEH) has been established under the authority of the Synod to coordinate the social activities of the church: clinics, feeding centers for children, kindergarten, primary, and secondary schools, and a center of professional training.

TM: **15,000** BM: **15,000** CM: **15,000** Congr: **45** PStations: **105** OrdM: **50** Eld: **nc** Deac: **120** EvgHome: **nc** Mission: **1** Women Ord: **no** ChurchOrg: **congr, synod** Off/otherLang: **Spanish** DoctrB: **ApC, HeidC** Infant or believer's baptism: **believer** Frequency of the Lord's Supper: **monthly** Close relations with: **UCC (USA)** NatRel: **Sociedad Biblica de Honduras** TheolSchool: **Seminario Teologico de la Iglesia Evangelica Reformada de Honduras**

Address: Iglesia Evangelica y Reformada de Honduras, Ap. 17, 5 Ave 5a Calle, Apdo 17, San Pedro Sula, Honduras, Tel: +504 52 67 67, Fax: +504 52 97 15

2. Christian Reformed Church (3305)

The Christian Reformed Church has its roots in a group of 26 members from the Evangelical and Reformed Church who moved in 1962 from San Pedro Sula to the capital city of Tegucigalpa. After various attempts to start another Evangelical and Reformed Church they requested the help of the Christian Reformed Church in the United States (cf. United States). The first two CRCNA missionaries were sent in 1972. Work has developed in four areas — first in the central area with eight congr today, then in the south with nine and in Olancho with 22 churches, and most recently in the north with two churches. In 1990 a national synod was formed. A theological seminary, four theological centers, and a polytechnical school were opened.

TM: **1,500** BM: **1,200** CM: **1,000** Congr: **18** PStations: **39** OrdM: **11** Eld: **54** Deac: **72** EvgHome: **2** Mission: **0** Women Ord: **yes** As Ministers: **nc** as Deac: **1972/60** as Elders: **nc** ChurchOrg: **sessions of**

organized churches Off/otherLang: **Spanish** DoctrB: **ApC, NicC, AthC, HeidC, CDort** Infant or believer's baptism: **both** Frequency of the Lord's Supper: **monthly** Close relations with: **Evangelical Reformed Church** NatRel: **none** TheolSchool: **SETERA** Periodicals: **none**

Address: Iglesia Cristiana Reformada (de Honduras), Apto 1109, Colonia 3 de Mayo, Sector 1, Bloque 3, N 2036, Comayagüela, Tegucigalpa, Honduras, Tel: +504 32 34 94, Fax: +504 32 34 94, E-mail: jwin@gbm.hn.

3. Presbyterian Church of Honduras (3306)

The existence of this church is due to the arrival, in 1960, of Presb immigrants from Guatemala — Antonio Farfan and Benjamin Jacob — in the region of Piedra Bonita. These pioneers made contact with the Presbyterian Church of Guatemala and asked for missionaries. Since then the church developed its activities, and several congr and preaching stations were established. The work was strengthened through proposals by the leadership of the church; they suggested various social activities such as health care, education, youth work, fighting drug addiction, and forming of young people in the Christian faith.

TM: **650** BM: **400** CM: **400** Congr: **7** PStations: **18** OrdM: **5** Eld: **40** Deac: **60** EvgHome: **nc** Mission: **0** Women Ord: **no** ChurchOrg: **consistories, presby** Off/otherLang: **Spanish** DoctrB: **ApC, NicC, HeidC, WestConf** Infant or believer's baptism: **believer** Frequency of the Lord's Supper: **monthly** NatRel: **Comision Cristiana de Desarollo, Sociedad Biblica de Honduras** TheolSchool: **Instituto Presbiteriano de Honduras.**

Address: Iglesia Presbiteriana de Honduras, Ap 906, Comayagüela, Honduras, Tel: +504 27 22 64, Fax: +504 27 22 64

HONG KONG — *See* CHINA, PEOPLE'S REPUBLIC OF

HUNGARY

Area in km²	93,030
Population	10,318,000 Hungarian 89.9%, Gypsy 4%, German 2.6%, Serb 2%, Slovak 8%, Romanian 7%
Religions in %	RCath 67.5%, Reformed 20%, Luth 5%, atheist and other 7.5%
Official language	Magyar (Hungarian)

Reformed Church of Hungary (6335)

The Reformation movement reached Hungary in the 16th century. By the middle of the century large parts of Hungary had joined the Reformation, especially the eastern part where the population enjoyed the protection of the princes of Transylvania. Though Lutheran in its initial inspiration, the movement came under Calvinist influence; the churches adopted Presb polity. In the 17th century the movement was severely repressed through the combined efforts of the Hapsburg dynasty and the RCath hierarchy. The work of the Counter-Reformation culminated in Archbishop Szelepcsényi's "Bloody Tribunal" in Bratislava (1673). Catholicism was ruthlessly reimposed all over the country. Pastors were forced to renounce their faith, many were expelled, and some sold as galley-slaves.

Repression did not end until the end of the 18th century. The Diet of 1790-1791 granted Prot basic civil rights. The Reformed Church suffered further reprisals, however, after the War of Independence (1848-1849). Finally, the Agreement of 1867 set the pattern for church-state relations until the end of World War II (1945).

In the 17th and 18th centuries the Presb system was developed; elders held a dominant position in the life of the congr. The synod of 1881 laid the basis for the Constitution, which, with additions, is still in force today. One of the church's particularities is the retention of the office of bishop, though the position carries administrative rather than hierarchical authority.

After both World Wars Hungarian-speaking territories were distributed to neighboring states. Hungarian-speaking churches can be found in the following countries: Croatia, Czech Republic, Romania, Slovakia, Ukraine, and Yugoslavia. There is also a large Diaspora around the world. In 1995 a (consultative) Synod of Hungarian-speaking churches was formed.

After World War II Hungary came under Communist rule. In 1948 Marxist-Leninist ideology, with its strong anti-religious bias, became the official position of the regime. Though freedom of conscience was officially guaranteed, the churches came under tight government control. Church institutions (schools, hospitals, etc.) were confiscated and religious life confined within church walls. While there was courageous resistance by individuals, the church generally sought to survive by working together with the authorities. A new era began in 1989. After the first democratic elections in 1990, the parliament passed a constitutional law guaranteeing the enactment of freedom of conscience and religion. Many properties were returned to the churches.

The Reformed Church of Hungary now has the immense task of grasping those new opportunities offered to her today in a society which is deeply affected by secularization. In many fields new initiatives have been launched — in the field of evangelism (e.g., evangelistic work among the gypsies), education (e.g., church schools), and social work. The text of a new church constitution is under consideration. The church works closely with other Prot churches, in particular through the Ecumenical Council of Hungarian churches (founded in 1943). As a result of the new religious freedom, the country is also exposed to an influx of foreign missionaries sent by various religious groups and sects.

TM: **1,600,000** BM: **1,530,197** Congr: **1,100** PStations: **1,519** OrdM: **1,152** Eld: **20,223** Deac: **nc** EvgHome: **nc** Mission: **nc** Women Ord: **yes** As Ministers: **1981/249** as Deac: **nc** as Elders: **nc** ChurchOrg: **congregations, seniorates (27), church districts (4), General synod** Off/otherLang: **Hungarian** DoctrB: **ApC, HeidC, HelvC** Infant or believer's baptism: **both** Frequency of the Lord's Supper: **monthly to 6 times per year** Periodicals: **Reformátusok Lapja (general/weekly/20,000), Confessio (theol/6 times a year/2,500), Református Egyház (monthly/2,000)** Close relations with: **Hungarian-speaking Ref Churches, Ch of Scotland, Dutch Churches, German Churches, Swiss Prot Fed, PCUSA, PROK (Korea) United Reformed Ch (UK)** NatRel: **Ecumenical Council of Hungarian Churches (ECHC)** RegRel: **CEC** IntlRel: **WARC (1909), WCC (1948)** TheolSchool: **Theological schools in Debrecen, Budapest, Sárospatak**

Address: Magyarországi Református Egyház, P.O. Box 5, Abonyi-u 21, H-Budapest 1146, Hungary, Tel: +36 1 227-870, Fax: +36 1 218-0903

INDIA

Area in km²	3,287,590
Population	(July 1996 est.) 952,107,694 Indo-Aryan 72%, Dravidian 25%, Mongoloid and other 3%
Religions in %	Hindu 82%, Muslim 12.5%, Christian 2.4%, Sikh 2%, Buddhist 0.7%, Jains 0.5%
Official/other languages	English, Hindi, Bengali, Telugu, Marathi, Tamil, Urdu, Gujarati, Malayalam, Kannada, Oriya, Punjabi, Assamese, Kashmiri, Sindhi, Sanskrit, Hindustani/ note: 24 languages each spoken by a million or more persons; numerous other languages and dialects, for the most part mutually unintelligible

NCCI (National Council of Churches in India), **NEICC** (Northeast India Church Council affiliated to NCCI))

According to a widely held tradition Christianity came to India through the apostle Thomas. In any case, the Christian faith reached India at a very early time, facilitated by the maritime trade which existed between India and the Mediterranean region. RCath missionaries began to work in India in the context of the Portuguese colonial enterprise. They were followed by the Angl in the context of British domination of India.

The Prot witness began in 1706 at Tranquebar with the arrival of two German Luth missionaries Batholomäus Ziegenbalg and Heinrich Plutschen. They came as a result of the pietist revival movement in Northern Europe. The

Tranquebar mission engaged in the translation and printing of the Bible and, after 1719, started to attack the caste system. The English Society for the Propagation of Christian Knowledge (SPCK) worked closely with the Luth mission.

In the early 19th century several newly formed mission societies established themselves in the country. In 1800, the Baptist Missionary Society initiated work in Serampore. The Bapt were active in many fields — translation of the Bible in several Indian languages, printing Bibles, books, and newspapers, protesting against infant sacrifices and the burning alive of Hindu widows. They were the first to introduce theological education; the theology department of Serampore College was opened in 1820. Other British mission societies followed — the London Missionary Society, Church Missionary Society, and Wesleyan Methodist Society. After the removal of restrictions on non-British societies in 1833 they were joined by continental European societies. The first among them were the Basel Mission, which started work in South Kanara on the West Coast in 1834, and the Luth Leipzig Mission, which became active in Tranquebar and Tamilnadu in 1841. In 1813 the ABCFM began work in Bombay, in 1831 it extended its activities to Ahmednagar, and in 1841 it started its Madura Mission in South India. Several other American mission societies set foot on Indian soil — American Presb in Punjab (1834) and Uttar Pradesh (1838), American Bapt in Andhra Pradesh and Assam (1836), American Luth in Northern Circars and Andhra Pradesh (1842). All these missions contributed to the spread of education for women and had considerable influence through schools and colleges.

After 1870, almost all Christian missions experienced a rapid growth in membership. The converts came from outcast groups which opted in large numbers for Christianity in order to move out of the caste system which denied them human dignity. They came from tribal or indigenous groups such as the Orans, Munda, and Kolha in Chota Nagpur, from aboriginal people such as the Santals in Bengal and Bihar, the Gonds and Bhils in Central India, and the Konds and Panis in Orissa, the Garo, Naga, Khasi-Jaintia, Lushai, and others in Assam, the Nadars in Tirunavelly and Kanyakumari, the Adi-Dravidas and Chakkaliyana in Tamilnadui, the Adi-Andhras (such as the Malas and Nadigas) in Andhra Pradesh, the Adi-Karnataks (such as the Holeyas, Pulayas, Kuravas, and Ezhavas) in Kerala, the Mongs and Mahars in Maharastra, the Mazabi Sihks, Chamars, and Chuhras in Uttar Pradesh and Punjab. The result of these conversion movements was that, today, Assam and northeast India rank with Kerala, Tamilnadu, and Andhra Pradesh as the regions where the Christian population of the country is chiefly concentrated. Mass conversion became possible because Christianity was seen as fighting against social evils and for the rights of the downtrodden.

As missionaries witnessed to the Gospel in a multireligious context they increasingly felt the need for cooperation. Interdenominational missionary conferences started as early as 1855. The series of decennial conferences which began in 1872 contributed to the convening of the World Missionary Conference in Edinburgh in 1910. YMCA, YWCA, the Student Volunteer Movement (SVM), and the Student Christian Movement (SCM) played a significant role in promoting collaboration among Christians. Church Union became a central theme of Indian Christianity in the latter 19th century.

Ref Churches were particularly active in this respect. The Presbyterian Churches in South India united in 1901, thus bringing together the American Arcot Mission and the two Scottish Presb Missions (Church of Scotland and Free Church of Scotland). In 1904 this church united with several Presb churches in North India to form the Presbyterian Church of India. The Madras Arcot group indicated that it would prefer an interdenominational union in the South if this should become possible. In 1905, the Congreg of the LMS and the American Madura Mission in Tamilnadu established a loose federation. In 1908, the first interdenominational union took place, bringing together Presb and Congreg in the South and in the Jaffna District (which is today part of Sri Lanka). In 1919, the Basel Mission joined the union. Finally, on September 27, 1947, after years of negotiations, the Church of South India (CSI) was inaugurated, bringing together all major traditions of the Reformation. A parallel movement took place in North India, leading in 1924 to the formation of the United Church of North India, again a union of Presb and Congreg. Union negotiations of a wider scope started in 1929 and lasted till 1965; in 1970 the Church of North India (CNI) was inaugurated in Nagpur. The CSI and CNI have declared communion with the Mar Thoma Church and have established the CSI-CNI–Mar Thoma Joint Council.

The Lutheran Churches are united under the umbrella of the United Evangelical Lutheran Church in India (UELCI). Pentecostalism began to spread in the first decade of the century, and the charismatic movement entered the scene after World War II.

As a small minority the churches in India have to struggle with the issue of identity. How can they maintain their Christian identity and profile? How can they serve the wider society without being overwhelmed and conquered by the religious majority of the country? What significance does conversion have in a pluralistic society? The churches represent parts of the population which, at least in the past, were exploited and oppressed. How can they today continue to be a church of the poor and bear a witness of solidarity with them? What role are they prepared to give to women? How can the churches overcome barriers of language, region, caste, and tribal community and develop a sense of the universality of the church?

1. Church of South India (CSI) (4052)

The union resulting in the formation of the CSI took place in autumn 1947 in Madras, only a few months after India attained independence from Britain. For the first time in the history of Prot churches Episcopal and non-Episcopal traditions united in one church. Ways were found for full mutual recognition of ministries. The constitution distinguishes three levels: local parishes, dioceses, and synod. Each diocese (a total of 21, including the diocese of Jaffna and Sri Lanka) is led by a bishop. He exercises his functions collegially in council. The Synod is the highest policy-making body. All properties and institutions are under what is known as the CSI Trust Association.

The church is spread over the whole south, i.e., in all four southern states. In addition, for the diaspora, CSI congr have been formed in the USA and elsewhere.

TM: **2,100,000** Congr: **9,405** OrdM: **1,050** Eld: **nc** Deac: **nc** EvgHome: **nc** Mission: **nc** Women Ord: **yes** ChurchOrg: **5 councils: parish council, presbyteral, synodal, organizing council, council of administration; 21 dioceses, General Synod** Off/otherLang: **English, all southern languages** DoctrB: **ApC, Confession of faith** Infant or believer's baptism: **both** Frequency of the Lord's Supper: **before Easter, special events** NatRel: **NCCI** RegRel: **CCA** IntlRel: **WARC (1990), WCC, CWM** TheolSchool: **United Theological College (Bangalore), Tamil Nadu Theological Seminary (Madras)** Service infrastructure: **2,000 colleges, 130 schools, 104 hospitals, 50 development projects, 50 youth training centers, 500 residential hostels for 35,000 children**

Address: Church of South India, P.O. Box 688, 5 Whites Road, Royapettah, Madras Chemni 600 014, India, Tel: +91 44 852 1566, Fax: +91 44 852 3528

2. Church of North India (CNI) (4050)

Partners in union negotiations which lasted for 41 years were the United Church of Northern India (Presb and Congreg), the (Anglican) Church of India, Pakistan, Burma, and Ceylon, the Methodist Churches (of British, Australasian, and North American background), and the Council of Baptist Churches. In 1957 the Church of the Brethren and the Disciples of Christ also joined in the conversations. Just before the Church of North India was inaugurated in 1970, the Methodist Church of Southern Asia, i.e., the Methodists of American origin, withdrew from the negotiations.

In the course of the negotiations agreement on the understanding and the practice of baptism and the Lord's Supper, the threefold ministry of bishops, presbyters, and deacons and the organizational patterns of the church (pastorates, dioceses, and synod) was achieved. Episcopacy was integrated in the church order and found its place in the constitution. Provision was made for diverse liturgical practices and understanding of divine revelation, provided that these do not violate the basic Faith and Order of the church or disrupt the unity and fellowship within the church.

The church covers a vast area, in fact, all states of the Indian Union with the exception of the four states in the south. This amounts to 80% of the surface and 75% of the population of India. Apart from English and Hindi, five regional languages are in use — Marathi, Punjabi, Bengali, Oriya, and Assamese — along with six major tribal languages. Almost all the cultural differences of India's people are to be found within the CNI with its congr spread throughout the cities, towns, and villages. The pastoral and organizational problems of the church are considerable.

TM: **1,250,000** CM: **900,000** Congr: **3,000** PStations: **none** OrdM: **1,000** Eld: **none** Deac: **none** EvgHome: **none** Mission: **1** Women Ord: **yes** As Ministers: **1980/7** as Deac: **5** as Elders: **nc** ChurchOrg: **parishes, pastorates, dioceses, synod** Off/otherLang: **English, Hindi, Marthi, Punjabi, Bengali, Oriya, Assamese** DoctrB: **ApC, NicC, Basis of Union** Infant or believer's baptism: **both** Frequency of the Lord's Supper: **weekly to monthly according to local tradition** Close relations with: **CSI (cf. no. 1), Mar Thoma Church** NatRel: **NCCI** RegRel: **CCA** IntlRel: **WCC, CWM, WARC, WACC** TheolSchool: **in various theological colleges and seminaries** Service infrastructure: **61 hospitals, 210 social service stations, 500 kindergartens, 12 degree colleges, 30 inter colleges, 3 technical institutes, 2 agricultural institutes** Periodicals: **North India Ch Review (monthly/2,500)**

Address: Church of North India, P.O. Box 311, CNI Bhavan, 16 Pandit Pant Marg, New Delhi 110 001, India, Tel: +91 11 371-6513 or 373-1081, Fax: +91 11 371-6901, E-mail: gscni@giasdloivsnl.

3. Presbyterian Church of India (PCI) (4051)

The PCI resulted from efforts of Welsh missionaries. Rev. Thomas Jones and his wife arrived in Cherrapunji on June 22, 1841. Even before, around 1813, the (Bapt) Serampore mission had started evangelistic work at the foot of the Khasi Hills; very soon two persons, U Duwan and U Anna, accepted the Christian faith. But this mission was closed down in 1838. The Welsh mission revived the work. In 1850 Rev. William Pryse arrived to strengthen the work. The first presby was formed in 1867 in the Khasi Hills; five presbys were established in 1895, resulting in 1896 in what was then called the Assembly. Work was also started in the plains of Sylhet and Cachar, where eventually another Assembly was formed. But since in 1947, when India and Pakistan were divided, the greater part of the area came under Pakistan, the Assembly was discontinued. Toward the end of the century the mission extended to Mizoram. In January 1894 the first Welsh missionary reached Aizawl in Mizoram; soon strengthened by the arrival of another missionary, the work began to develop in 1897. Through revival movements the church grew rapidly and includes today virtually the whole of the population. Various tribes in the North Cachar Hills who had been evangelized by missionaries and local workers were also organized as an Assembly in 1930. Finally, in 1978 the Manipur Presb Synod was formed. Initially, the local community of Manipur consisted of Christians of various tribal backgrounds. They were received into the Presb family in 1959 and since then recognized as a special field.

The Assembly for the whole Presbyterian Church in Northeast India was established in 1926. Today it comprises four Synods. The PCI is the largest denominational body in northeast India. The organization of the Church as a whole is rather loose. The synods enjoy considerable autonomy and in fact have more authority than the Assembly. Some of the synods are highly centralized, while others exercise little control over the congr.

TM: **797,732** BM: **380,054** CM: **389,385** Congr: **2,896** PStations: **647** OrdM: **615** Eld: **6,357** Deac: EvgHome: **984** Mission: **26** Women Ord: **yes** As Ministers: **0** as Deac: **nc** as Elders: **nc** ChurchOrg: **presbys, four Synod, Assembly,** Off/otherLang: **English, 23 languages used in the church** DoctrB: **ApC, WestConf** Infant or believer's baptism: **both** Frequency of the Lord's Supper: **at least once a month** Close relations with: **CNI, PCUSA, PC Korea, PC Taiwan** NatRel: **NCCI (1975)** RegRel: **CCA** IntlRel: **WARC (1970) CWM (1978)** Service infrastructure: **3 hospitals (300 staff)** Periodicals: **Presbyter (gen/quarterly/500) Didakhe (theol/quarterly/1,600) Kristian Tlangall (gen/monthly/40,000) Agape (women/monthly/18,000), Kristion Thalai (youth/monthly/20,000), Ramthar (mission/monthly/30,000)**

Address: Presbyterian Church of India, Presbyterian Assembly House, Central Ward, OPP, State Library, Shillong Meghalaya 793 001, India, Tel: +91 364 226-828, Fax: +91 364 228-166

4. Evangelical Church of Maraland (ECM) (4049)

For the origin of this church see under Myanmar (no. 1). The church became autonomous in 1961. In 1976 its name was changed from Mara Independent Evangelical Church into Independent Church of Maraland to avoid the impression that church membership was limited to Mara people. In 1989 the term "Independent" was dropped. The administrative center was moved in the same year from Serkawr to Saiha. A controversy arose which eventually led to a split. A minority opposing the changes decided on June 9, 1989, to form the Congregational Church of India (Maraland); cf. no. 5. The majority stayed with the Evangelical Church of Maraland.

TM: **25,228** BM: **15,208** CM: **15,208** Congr: 65 PStations: 2 OrdM: **24** Eld: **410** Deac: **420** EvgHome: **4** Mission: **120** Women Ord: **yes** As Ministers: **no** as Deac: **1965/4** as Elders: **nc** ChurchOrg: **Presbyterian (local circle, presby, assembly/synod)** Off/otherLang: **Mara, Mizo, English** DoctrB: **ApC, NicC, AthC** Infant or believer's baptism: **believer** Frequency of the Lord's Supper: **monthly** Close relations with: **Presbyterian Ch of Mizoram (1963)** NatRel: **NEICC (1961)** IntlRel: **WARC (1995)** TheolSchool: **Peniel Bible Institute** Service infrastructure: **orphanage, 1 primary to higher school, kindergartens, school in the mission field, Bible school, mission houses at Lalung mission field** Periodicals: **ECM News letter (gen+mission/weekly/1,200)**

Address: Evangelical Church of Maraland, P.O. Box 796901, P.O. Saiha, Chhimtuipui District, Mizoram, India, Tel: +91 3835 2206 and 2207

5. The Congregational Church of India (Maraland) (4064)

This church seeks to continue the missionary heritage of the Independent Church of Maraland (cf. no. 4). It resulted from the dispute over the innovations decided upon in 1989 by the Evangelical Church of Maraland. Under the leadership of Rev. Mark Lapi, the son-in-law of the last missionaries, a sizeable group decided to continue in the missionary tradition. The headquarters remained at Serkawr. The dispute has led to much ill feeling on both sides. The church is growing in both India and Myanmar.

TM: **5,500** BM: **5,000** CM: **4,500** Congr and PStations: **23** OrdM: **5** Eld: **109** Deac: **120** EvgHome: **4** Mission: **12** Women Ord: **yes** As Ministers: **1994/1** as Deac: **1994/1** as Elders: **none** ChurchOrg: **Congregational (congr, circles, Assy)** Off/otherLang: **Mara, Mizo, English** DoctrB: **ApC, NicC** Infant or believer's baptism: **both** Frequency of the Lord's Supper: **monthly** Close relations with: **Presbyterian Church (cf. no. 3), Isua Krista Kohhran (cf. no. 11), Congregational Federation of North South Wales (Australia) (1992)** IntlRel: **ICF (1993)** TheolSchool: **training in Bangalore and in Cherrapunjee (India), in Sydney (NSW, Australia)** Periodicals: **none**

Address: Congregational Church of India (Maraland), P.O. Box 796901 Serkawr, Chhimtuipui District, Mizoram, India

6. Free Church of Central India (4057)

Toward the end of the 19th century the Free Church of Scotland initiated missionary work in Seoni at Lakhnadon and Chhapara villages. Two congr were established. In 1976 the church spread to Jabalpur; two more congr came into existence. When the Central India State government prohibited the entry of foreign missionaries, the Foreign Missions Board of the Free Church of Scotland helped national leaders to set up the Free Church of Central India Presbytery (FCCI). The last missionaries left in 1988.

TM: **450** BM: **360** CM: **160** Congr: **4** PStations: **5** OrdM: **4** Eld: **8** Deac: **16** EvgHome: **1** Mission: **1** Women Ord: **no** ChurchOrg: **Regional Presbytery** Off/otherLang: **English, Hindi** DoctrB: **WestConf** Infant or believer's baptism: **both** Frequency of the Lord's Supper: **twice to four times per year** Close relations with: **Free Church of Scotland, Ev. Presb Ch of Northern Ireland (cf. Ireland no. 5), Presb Church of Eastern Australia (cf. Australia no. 3)** NatRel: **seeking relationship with Faith Bible Ref Church in Delhi, Dehradun, Kalempong North-East India** IntlRel: **ICRC (1993)** TheolSchool: **Presb Theological Seminary, Faith Academy Prasadnagar New Delhi, Union Biblical Seminary** Service infrastructure: **2 hospitals with community health project, 3 guests rooms, 2 libraries with reading rooms, 2 kindergartens, 2 schools** Periodicals: **Darpan (gen/monthly/2 issues)**

Address: Free Church of Central India, Free Church Premnagar, Jabalpur PIN 482001, India, Tel: +91 761 422-713

7. Reformed Presbyterian Church of India (4055)

The church is the result of a union between Bible Presb and Ref Presbyterian Churches. It is located in Dehra Dun in Uttar Pradesh.

TM: **3,000** BM: **2,500** Congr: **5** OrdM: **14** Eld: **15** Deac: **nc** EvgHome: **nc** Mission: **nc** Women Ord: **no** ChurchOrg: **Presbyterian (congr, presby, synod)** Off/otherLang: **Hindi, English, Nepali** DoctrB: **ApC, NicC, HeidC, WestConf** Infant or believer's baptism: **both** IntlRel: **ICRC**

Address: Reformed Presbyterian Church of India, 51-c Rajpur Road, Dehra Dun U.P. 248001, India, Tel. +91 135 658-417, Fax +91 135 655-078

8. Hindustani Covenant Church (4058)

Having been expelled in 1938 from East Turkestan (Sinkiang), missionaries of the Mission Covenant Church of Sweden came in 1940 to Bombay and Poona in Maharastra. They worked primarily among the Muslim population. In 1948 they started medical and health care work in Sholapur. In 1963 the Hindustani Covenant Church was formed. It regards mission to Muslims as its primary task.

TM: **600** BM: **400** CM: **400** Congr: **20** PStations: **4** OrdM: **16** Eld: **6** Deac: **0** EvgHome: **4** Mission: **2** Women Ord: **yes** As Ministers: **1990/2** as Deac: **nc** as Elders: **nc** ChurchOrg: **congreg (congr, annual council)** Off/otherLang: **Urdu, Hindi** DoctrB: **ApC** Infant or believer's baptism: **both** Frequency of the Lord's Supper: **monthly** Close relations with: **Mission Covenant Church of Sweden** NatRel: **NCCI** RegRel: **CCA** IntlRel: **IFFEC** TheolSchool: **Union Biblical Seminary, United Theol Semi-**

nary (Pune) Service infrastructure: **2 hospitals, social work in Maharashtra and Karnataka states, 2 kindergartens, no theol school**

Address: Hindustani Covenant Church, HCC Church Centre, 15 Sholapur Road, Pune 411 001, India,
Tel: +91 212 66 69 44, Fax: +91 212 66 02 04

9. Kolhapur Church Council (KCC) of the United Church Northern India (4060)

The congr belonging today to the Kolhapur Church Council (KCC) is the fruit of missionary work by American Presb which started in 1852. In 1924 the Kolhapur Presb became part of the United Church of Northern India, which brought together Presb and Congreg; they formed the Kolhapur Church Council within the United Church of Northern India. Though the United Church joined the Church of North India (CNI) in 1970, the KCC claims that it continued to exist as a juridical entity. A dispute between the Presbyterian Church USA and KCC over properties was finally settled in 1997 by mutual agreement. The KCC does evangelistic work in Western Maharashtra and is represented in the political districts of Kolhapur, Sangli, Ratnagiri, Sindhurga, and Belguam (Karnatak).

TM: **10,000** BM: **10,000** CM: **10,000** Congr: **45** PStations: **400** OrdM: **35** Eld: **400** Deac: **20** EvgHome: **nc** Mission: **nc** Women Ord: **no** ChurchOrg: **congr, synod, GenAssy** Off/otherLang: **Marathi, English** DoctrB: **ApC** Infant or believer's baptism: **infant** Frequency of the Lord's Supper: **monthly** TheolSchool: **Maharashtra Synod Theological College** Service infrastructure: **six high schools, 4 primary schools, 3 hostels, kindergartens, two hospitals** Periodicals: **Prarthana Jeevan Prkash Digant Suwasta**

Address: Kolhapur Church Council (of the former United Church of Northern India), New Palace
P.O., Church Council House, E. Patton School Compound, Kolhapur 3, Maharashtra 416
003, India, Tel: +91 231 654-738, Fax: +91 231 654-738

10. North India Synod—Presbyterian Church (4062)

This church is a former constituent of the Church of North India (CNI). Claiming that CNI is too centralized and that its bishops have not demonstrated much care about rural churches, they decided in 1994 to secede from the CNI and to revive the United Church of Northern India (UCNI) to which it belonged in the past and through which it became part of the CNI in 1970. At a synod in Etah in 1994 the decision was taken "to withdraw union from the Agra and Lucknow diocese of the CNI." Currently the North India Synod is a registered society of the United Church of Northern India, having four church councils, namely Allahabad, Farrukhabad, Mainpuri, and Bundelkhanad (in process of formation). As a consequence of the withdrawal legal cases are before court. The main emphasis of the church is on the life of rural communities.

TM: **432** CM: **215** Congr: **25** PStations: **432** OrdM: **11** Eld: **nc** Deac: **30** EvgHome: **14** Mission: **ne** Women Ord: **yes** As Ministers: **1996/0** as Deac: **nc** as Elders: **nc** ChurchOrg: **rural congr, urban** churches, church councils, synod, GenAssy Off/otherLang: **Hindi, English, Urdu** DoctrB: **to be found in Blue Book of the UCNI** Infant or believer's baptism: **both** Frequency of the Lord's Supper: **monthly** Service infrastructure: **none** Periodicals: **none**

Address: United Church of Northern India—Presbyterian Synod, P.O. Allahabad Agricultural Institute, Allahabad Uttar Pradesh 211007, India, Tel: +91 532 697-442

11. The Church of Christ (4053)

The Church of Christ (Isua Krista) has its roots among the tribes of the Lais in the Chhimtuipui District, Mizoram. The origins of the church are closely related to the history of the churches of Mizoram (cf. no. 3) and Maraland (cf. no. 4). The Lais were evangelized by two missionary agencies — the Baptist Mission and the Lakher Pioneer Mission. In 1958 a Lai elder, Mr. F. Hniarkunga, started a movement for an independent Church of the Lais in India. In 1964, a meeting of delegates representing both missions agreed to the project. After protracted negotiations the church was inaugurated on May 23, 1970. Headquarters were established in Balpui (NG). For some time the new church was not recognized by the neighboring churches, and it was prevented from joining the North East Indian Council of Churches. Eventually the obstacles were overcome; the church is now a member of the Council. Faithful to its Bapt origins, the church practices believer's baptism. The worship services are conducted by the church elders, who are elected by the local church community once every month. Challenges to the church include mission to Myanmar and Bangladesh.

TM: **12,800** BM: **6,399** CM: **6,399** Congr: 57 PStations: 0 OrdM: 10 Eld: **248** Deac: 0 EvgHome: 18 Mission: 62 Women Ord: **yes** As Ministers: **yes** as Deac: **yes** as Elders: **1970/2** ChurchOrg: **congr, area church, GenAssy** Off/otherLang: **Lai, English, Mizo, Mara** DoctrB: **ApC** Infant or believer's baptism: **believer** Frequency of the Lord's Supper: **monthly** Close relations with: **Congregational Church of India, Presbyterian Church of India (Mizoram), Congregational Federation of Australia** NatRel: **NEICC (1996)** IntlRel: **WARC (1996)** TheolSchool: **Serampore Colleges** Service infrastructure: **11 primary and middle schools, home for unwed mothers, orphanages**

Address: Isua Krista Kohhran, P.O. Box, Balpui (NG) Chhimtuipui District, Mizoram 796901, India

12. Reformed Presbyterian Church, North East India (4054)

The history of this church begins in 1835 when an American Presb missionary, the Rev. James R. Campbell, started work at Saharanpur, U.P. The Presbyterian Mission in Mizoram later exercised a great influence on many churches of Manipur South. Rev. Watkins R. Robert came to Lushai Hills (now Mizoram) in 1908, from where he entered Senvawn, Manipur, in 1910.

The Reformed Presbyterian Church in North East India has existed officially since 1979.

TM: **4,200** BM: **4,200** CM: **2,515** Congr: 29 OrdM: 14 Eld: **33** Deac: yes EvgHome: 3 Mission: **6** Women Ord: **no** ChurchOrg: **Presbyterian** Off/otherLang: **Hmar, English, Manipuri, Karbi,**

Assamese DoctrB: **ApC, WestConf, WestCat** Infant or believer's baptism: **both** Frequency of the Lord's Supper: **monthly** NatRel: **Evangelical Fellowship of India** IntlRel: **WARC (1996), having relations with ICRC** TheolSchool: **Presbyterian Theological Seminary (Dehra Dan, U.P.)** Service infrastructure: **460 orphanages, schools, and high schools** Periodicals: **Kohran (The Church) (sermons/monthly/400), Makedonia (news/bi-monthly/na)**

Address: Reformed Presbyterian Church, North East India, P.O. Box 4, Peace Lane, Luocia Rd., Churachandpur, Manipur 795128, India, Tel: +91 3874 22545

13. Evangelical Convention Church (4059)

This church was originally called Manipur Christian Convention and was a constituent body of the then North East India General Mission, Inc. (NEIGM), founded in 1910. This mission had been founded as a result of the Welsh Revival of 1904 prompted by members of the Dutch Reformed Presbyterian Church settled in the area of Philadelphia (Pennsylvania, USA). The Evangelical Convention Church is an indigenous church and since 1975 independent from the NEIGM.

TM: **49,600** CM: **18,778** Congr: **354** OrdM: **188** EvgHome: **nc** Mission: **64** Women Ord: **na** ChurchOrg: **nc** Off/otherLang: **nc** DoctrB: **nc**

Address: Evangelical Convention Church, P.O. Box 6, Dorcas Hall, Lamka, Manipur 795128, India

INDONESIA

Area in km²	1,919,317
Population	(February 1997) 200 million, 120 million on the island of Java alone; of 13,677 islands some 3,000 are inhabited.
Religions in %	There are five religions recognized by the state: Islam (87%), Prot (7%), RCath (3%), Hinduism (2%), Buddhism (less than 1%); especially in Java, mystical groups *(kebathinan)* rooted in traditional Javanese culture are influential. Every inhabitant of Indonesia is expected to belong to one of the five recognized religions
Language	Indonesian and many local languages

Key to Abbreviations

AMIN   Gereja Angowuloa Indonesia Nias, *cf. no. 2*
BNKP   Banua Niha Keriso Protestan, Nias, *cf. no. 1*
CMA   Christian and Missionary Alliance
DGI   Dewan Gereja-Gereja di Indonesia (Council of Churches in Indonesia, became PGI in 1984)

EIC	East India Company
GBKP	Gereja Batak Karo Protestan, Sumatra, *cf. no. 3*
GGMM	Gereja-Gereja Masehi Musyafir, *cf. no. 4*
GJPI	Gereja Jemaat Protestan di Irian Jaya, *cf. no. 5*
GK	Gereja Kristus, *cf. no. 44*
GPIIJ	Gereja Protestan Indonesia di Irian Jaya, *cf. no. 45*
GKE	Gereja Kalimantan Evangelis, Kalimantan, *cf. no. 6*
GKI	Gereja Kristen Indonesia, Java, *cf. no. 7*
GKII	Gereja Kemah Injil Indonesia, *cf. no. 48*
GKISS	Gereja Kristen Indonesia Sulawesi Selatan, *cf. no. 46*
GKI Sumut	Gereja-Gereja Kristen Indonesia Sumatera Utara, Sumatra, *cf. no. 8*
GKI Irja	Gereja Kristen Injili di Irian Jaya, *cf. no. 9*
GKJ	Gereja Kristen Jawa, Java, *cf. no. 10*
GKJTU	Gereja Kristen Jawa Tengah Utara, Northern Java, *cf. no. 11*
GKJW	Gereja Kristen Jawi Wetan, East Java, *cf. no. 12*
GKKB	Gereja Kristen Kalimantan Barat, West Kalimantan, *cf. no. 13*
GKKK	Gereja Kristen Kalam Kudus, *cf. no. 47*
GKLB	Gereja Kristen di Luwuk Banggai, Sulawesi, *cf. no. 14*
GKN	Gereformeerde Kerken in Nederland
GKP	Gereja Kristen Pasundan, Java, *cf. no. 15*
GKPI	Gereja Kristen Pemancar Injil, Kalimantan, *cf. no. 16*
GKPB	Gereja Kristen Protestan di Bali, *cf. no. 17*
GKS	Gereja Kristen Sumba, *cf. no. 21*
GKSBS	Gereja Kristen Sumatera bagian Selatan, Sumatra, *cf. no. 20*
GKSS	Gereja Kristen Sulawesi Selatan, *cf. no. 18*
GKST	Gereja Kristen Sulawesi Tengah, *cf. no. 19*
GKT	Gereja Kristus Tuhan, *cf. no. 22*
GKT-Mamasa	Gereja Kristen Toraja Mamasa
GKTT	Gereja Kristen di Timor Timur, East Timor, *cf. no. 23*
GMIBM	Gereja Masehi Injili Bolaang Mongondow, Sulawesi, *cf. no. 24*
GMIH	Gereja Masehi Injili Halmahera, *cf. no. 25*
GMIM	Gereja Masehi Injili di Minahasa, Sulawesi, *cf. no. 26*
GMIST	Gereja Masehi Injili Sangir Talaud, *cf. no. 27*
GMIT	Gereja Masehi Injili di Timor, *cf. no. 28*
GPI	Gereja Protestan di Indonesia, Java, *cf. no. 29*
GPIB	Gereja Protestan di Indonesia bagian Barat, Java, *cf. no. 30*
GPIBT	Gereja Protestan Indonesia di Buol Toli-Toli, Sulawesi, *cf. no. 31*
GPID	Gereja Protestan Indonesia di Donggala, Sulawesi, *cf. no. 32*
GPIG	Gereja Protestan Indonesia di Gorontalo, Sulawesi, *cf. no. 33*
GPIL	Gereja Protestan Indonesia Luwu, Sulawesi, *cf. no. 34*
GPKB	Gereja Gereja Protestan Kalimantan Barat, West Kalimantan, *cf. no. 35*
GPM	Gereja Protestan Maluku, Moluccas, *cf. no. 36*

GEPSULTRA	Gereja Protestan di Sulawesi Tenggara, *cf. no. 37*
GGRI	Gereja-Gereja Reformasi Indonesia, Irian Jaya, Nusatenggara Timur and West Kalimantan, *cf. no. 38*
GRII	Gereja Reformed Injili Indonesia *cf. no. 39*
GT	Gereja Toraja, Sulawesi, *cf. no. 40*
GTM	Gereja Toraja Mamasa, Sulawesi, *cf. no. 41*
HKBP	Huria Kristen Batak Protestan
KGPM	Kerapatan Gereja Protestan Minahasa, Sulawesi, *cf. no. 42*
NHK	Nederlandse Hervormde Kerk (Netherlands Reformed Church)
NTT	Nusatenggara Timur, Eastern Lesser Sunda Islands *cf. no. 38B*
NVZ	Nederlandsche Zendingsvereeniging
NZG	Nederlandsch Zendelinggenootschap
OMF	Overseas Missionary Fellowship
ONKP	Orahua Niso Keriso Protestan, Nias, *cf. no. 43*
PARKINDO	Partai Kristen Indonesia
PERMESTA	Perjuangan Semesta (Total struggle)
PGI	Persekutuan Gereja-Gereja di Indonesia (Communion of Churches in Indonesia, cf. also DGI)
PGIW	Persekutuan Gereja-gereja Indonesia Wilayah
PII	Persekutuan Injili Indonesia (Indonesian Evangelical Fellowship)
RMG	Rheinische Missionsgesellschaft
SAAT	Seminari Alkitab Asia Tenggara (South-east Asia Bible Seminary)
SAG	Sinode Am Gereja-gereja (Sulawesi Utara dan Tengah)
VEM/UEM	Vereinte Evangelische Mission/United Evangelical Mission (Germany)
VOC	(Dutch) East India Company

Introduction

Indonesia consists of approximately 13,000 islands on both sides of the equator between the southeast Asia mainland and Australia. The most important islands are: Java, Sumatra, Kalimantan, and Sulawesi. Important island groups are the Moluccas, with Ambon and Ceram in the center and Ternate and Halmahera in the north, and Nusatenggara Timur (NTT) with the islands of Flores, Sumba, and Timor.

The population of approximately 200 million (1997) is unevenly distributed between western Indonesia, including Sumatra, Java and Bali (85%), and the rest of the country. There are about 300 ethnic groups, with ± 250 different languages. The Malay language, originally spoken by the coastal people of East Sumatra and Malaya, who embraced Islam at an early stage (1400), has become the *lingua franca* in the whole archipelago, and has been adopted and developed as the official language of Indonesia.

In the first centuries A.D. contact with India was established, and Hinduism and Buddhism flourished in a number of kingdoms on Java and Sumatra. Contacts with China were much more transitory. Islam entered Indonesia about 1300 A.D. It established itself first in Aceh, then in the coastal regions of East Sumatra, Java, and in the North Moluccas (the sultanate of Ternate). In 1525 and 1527, the Hindu kingdoms in the interior of Java collapsed. In the next two centuries the coastal regions of West Sumatra, Kalimantan, and Sulawesi were islamicized. Only the interior of Sumatra, Kalimantan, and Sulawesi, as well as Bali and southeast Indonesia, including Irian, remained outside the sphere of Islam.

In the meantime Europeans found their way to Indonesia; first the Portuguese, who in 1511 conquered Malacca and from 1522 to 1574 had a trade center protected by a fort on Ternate; then the Dutch, who in 1605 established a stronghold on Ambon and in 1619 founded their capital city of Batavia on the ruins of Jakarta (from 1945 onward named Jakarta again). In the next three centuries the whole of Indonesia gradually came under Dutch rule, but not without fierce resistance in many regions. In the 20th century, a movement for independence came into being. In 1942 the country was occupied by the Japanese, but after the capitulation of Japan, on August 17, 1945, the Republic of Indonesia was established, with Soekarno as President. Only after a colonial war which lasted until 1949 did the Dutch recognize the Republic of Indonesia.

The Republic of Indonesia is founded upon the *Pancasila*, the Five Principles, which include belief in God, humanity, national unity, consultative democracy, and social justice. In one of the first drafts, belief in God was linked to the obligation of Muslims to keep to the law of Islam; but under pressure of the nationalists this clause was dropped. So the republic is neither a Muslim nor a secular state. The Constitution of 1945 gave great powers to the President. Western individualism as well as Marxism was rejected, and a collectivistic "guided" democracy was introduced, modeled upon the structures of village society, and concentrating all political activities in one political party. However, between 1946 and 1959 this "Pancasila democracy" was attacked from three sides. In 1946 it was made more pluralistic and a number of political parties were founded, including a Protestant party (PARKINDO) and a Catholic party (Partai Katolik). The Communists tried to establish a Communist state, first through an armed insurgency (1948) and then through the elections of 1955 and political agitation in the following years. Extreme Muslims established a Muslim state in West Java and South Sulawesi, and the Muslim parties tried to strengthen the influence of Islam in a legal way. In the 1955 elections these parties got 45% of the vote, the Communists 15%. In 1957 parts of Sumatra and Sulawesi started a rebellion known as PERMESTA (Perjuangan Semesta = Total Struggle) against the central government. This rebellion was not religious in character, Muslims and Christians both being involved in it, but it caused much suffering, especially to the churches in North and Central Sulawesi.

In 1959 Soekarno, with the support of the armed forces, disbanded the Constituent Assembly formed after 1955 and returned to the Constitution of 1945. In the next few years, Soekarno incorporated Communism into the national identity, and Communist influence and agitation increased. Tensions came to a head in October 1965. After the top army commanders were murdered, Communism was eliminated both physically and politically. General Suharto became president and a New Order was launched, which stressed economic development using a Western capitalistic model. Politically, however, the country was remodeled on the base of the 1945 Constitution. The Golkar ("functional groups") became the national party. The political parties were forced to merge into PDI (PNI, Socialist, and Christian parties) and PPP (Muslims). Both played a marginal role in the state. Golkar and PDI include Christians as well as Muslims. The Pancasila remains the nation's foundation, so that around 1984 all organizations, including the churches, had to recognize Pancasila as the only foundation of national life. In the '70s and '80s, Christians occupied important posts in the successive cabinets, in the bureaucracy, and in the armed forces. The Muslims, however, were making up for their disadvantage in the field of education, economics, and politics, the effects making themselves felt in the '90s. Essential to the New Order was the influence on government of the Armed Forces, which is based upon the doctrine of the *Dwifungsi ABRI*, the dual function of the Armed Forces.

History of Christianity

Possibly from the 7th century onward Christian merchants from Persia and India came to Indonesia (North Sumatra and possibly Java), but they left only very faint traces. In the 16th century, the Portuguese brought Roman Catholicism to Halmahera, Ambon, and Nusatenggara Timur, and in the 17th century the extreme north of the archipelago was missionized by the Spanish from Manila. This mission was hampered by its subordination to trade interests. From 1546 Francis Xavier brought a fresh spirit. After 1570, the mission suffered heavily from attacks by the sultanate of Ternate (North Moluccas). What remained of it was taken over and protestantized by the Dutch after 1605. Only in East Timor and Flores could the Portuguese maintain themselves and their religion.

Missionary activities were restricted by the Dutch East India Company (VOC, 1602-1799), which also forbade Roman Catholicism in its territories, to areas where they served its interests, i.e., mainly to eastern Indonesia. Even there, they were deployed in earnest mostly in areas which were vital to the VOC, like Ambon and the surrounding islands. Christians were also found on a number of more remote islands as a result of the Portuguese-Spanish mission or of Protestant activities. But these groups were more or less neglected; they had no pastors or church councils and were rarely visited by ministers from the centers. The church could do little to improve this situation since organizationally and logistically it depended completely on the Company. The complete Bible was available in Malay in 1733 (the New Testament in 1668). Formally, the Christianity brought by the Dutch was of the Ref type, the central (town) congr being led by church councils, which in some areas also had Indonesian members. However, due to geographical and political circumstances, there were no national or regional synods, the church council of Batavia acting as a kind of central governing body. Government influence in the church was very noticeable, but no more so than in Europe in the same

224

period. Indonesians could only serve as unordained teacher-preachers without authority to administer the sacraments, or, in some centers, as members of the church council. As a result, in this period there were no Indonesian pioneers, and no first ordained leaders can be named. At the end of the 18th century, there were 55,000 Protestant Ref Christians and a smaller number of RCath in the archipelago.

In the 19th century, the situation changed. In 1799, the Dutch state took over all assets of the bankrupt VOC. Freedom of religion was proclaimed (an influence of the French Revolution). As a consequence, Catholic priests could enter the country again (1808). The existing Prot congr were organized into the *Protestant Church in the Netherlands Indies*, which had no mission work of its own because it was financed by the state, which professed to be neutral in religious matters. However, the way was also open to missionaries from the newly formed Prot missionary bodies. Between 1811 and 1850, a number of English and Americans (Bapt, Meth, and Congreg) worked in Java and Sumatra (where two of them were murdered) and West Borneo/Kalimantan. The first Dutch missionaries of the *Nederlandsch Zendelinggenootschap* (NZG, 1797) were put in charge of the neglected Christian parishes in Java and Eastern Indonesia. After 1830 the Dutch Prot missions gradually spread out to the neglected Christians in the outer regions, such as North Sulawesi and the Sangir archipelago, which had never been served by resident ministers or missionaries. At the same time, through the efforts of a number of lay people, Europeans and Eurasians, the Christian faith first put roots among the Javanese (± 1850).

In the meantime, as a result of theological conflicts, a number of new missionary bodies, most of which were informally linked with the Netherlands Reformed Church, came into being. Most of these had a pietist outlook. They started work in New Guinea (Irian, 1855), North Sumatra (1857), the North Moluccas (Halmahera, 1866), Central Sulawesi (1892) and South Sulawesi (1852/1913/ 1930). Southern Central Java and Sumba became the mission field of the *Gereformeerde Kerken*. In 1836 the German *Rheinische Mission* (RMG), a united Lutheran-Ref body, started mission work among the Dayak in South Kalimantan, and in 1861 the first RMG missionaries arrived in North Sumatra. After World War I the *Basel Mission* took over work in Kalimantan from the RMG. These missions stressed the use of tribal languages instead of Malay, aimed at individual conversion, and kept the congr under close supervision, church independence being postponed until a long nurturing process resulted in sufficient Christian maturity. The Salvation Army came to Indonesia in 1894, the Advent in 1900, the American CMA in 1930. After several Baptist missionaries had been working without any lasting result in the 19th century, Bapt reentered Indonesia in 1951. The Pentecostal movement was brought from Europe and America around 1920. In the 20th century the government allowed the Protestant Church to do missionary work in Sulawesi, the South Moluccas, and Timor.

The RCath concentrated their work in Flores (1860) and in Central Java (1894), but they also had important fields in North Sumatra (1878), West Kalimantan (1885), North Sulawesi (1868), Timor (1883), the Southeast Moluccas (1888), and Southern New Guinea (1905). They had a later start than the Prot, and in most of those territories a certain rivalry developed between RCath and Prot missions, which only diminished after 1960. From 1859 until 1902 all mission fields in Indonesia were served by the Jesuits; after 1902 most areas were gradually handed over to other orders and congr, the Jesuits retaining only the capital city of Batavia (Jakarta) and the culturally important region of Central Java.

In colonial times missionary work was accompanied by the conviction that Western civilization and Western models of Christianity, and even Western people, were superior. As a consequence, throughout the 19th century no Indonesians were ordained as ministers or priests except by the RMG in North Sumatra (RMG, first 1885). In the Prot missions, and even more so in the Protestant church, there was a functional hierarchy in which Europeans invariably held the top positions. Almost without exception Indonesian mission personnel worked as local teacher-preachers, with only a basic education. They served as the essential link between the "white" church government and the indigenous church members. In contrast with the VOC period, however, local church councils were established in purely Indonesian village congr.

This is not to say that Indonesians received the Gospel in a passive way. Those who became Christians did so of their own will, consciously, and for their own reasons, which mostly were not those expected and often assumed by the missionaries. And in many areas Indonesians played a decisive role in bringing their fellow countrymen to the faith, often without any formal tie to the mission.

In the 20th century things gradually changed. Between 1878 and 1886, theological seminaries had been founded in North Sumatra, Java, North Sulawesi, and Ambon. In 1934 a Theological Academy was established in Jakarta. The RCath opened their first seminary in Java in 1911 and in Flores in 1925. A number of Indonesians were ordained, and some of these worked on an equal footing with Europeans. The first RCath priest of Indonesian descent was ordained in 1926, and the first Indonesian bishop was consecrated in 1940. Between 1927 and 1940 a number of Prot churches in North Sumatra, Java, North Sulawesi, and the Moluccas became independent. In consequence of the division of the mission field among the missionary societies, these churches were all of the regional and/or ethnic type. On the Prot side, Hendrik Kraemer (1922-1936 in Indonesia) was instrumental in bringing about this development. However, European influence remained very strong even in the independent churches. Until 1940, all synods were chaired by white missionaries, the general idea being that the character, moral soundness, and organizational abilities of the Indonesian Christians still had to be brought up to European level. In the meantime the number of Christians steadily grew; in 1941 there were about 1.7 million Prot and 600,000 RCath in a population of 60 million.

In 1942 Indonesia was occupied by Japan. In the confusion of the transition period there were bouts of persecution by fanatical Muslims in some areas. Christianity was tolerated by the Japanese, and, up to a certain point, protected, even if among the Dutch-oriented Ambonese scores of congregation leaders were killed. The Japanese tried consistently to make the churches into channels for their war propaganda and confiscated almost all mission schools and hospitals. The churches were forced to join regional councils of churches (*Kiristokyo Rengokai*) which included mainline Prot, RCath, and other Prot groups. Japanese clergy were sent to Indonesia and, within the narrow margins allowed them, succeeded in providing protection and practical assistance to the churches.

Since nearly all foreign missionaries were interned, the war proved that Indonesian Christianity was able to govern itself. The declaration of national independence in 1945, too, caused quick progress in church independence. Most Prot churches which had not been independent before the war became so between 1946 and 1949, following the war of independence (1945-1949), and their infrastructure expanded. A Christian publishing house was established. Theological education grew quantitatively and qualitatively, most larger churches founding a theological school or faculty of their own. Christian universities sprang up in Pematangsiantar, Jakarta, Salatiga, and elsewhere. Leading Indonesian theologians were J. L. Ch. Abineno, P. D. Latuihamallo, and S. A. E. Nababan. The laymen T. S. G. Mulia and T. B. Simatupang were instrumental in founding and leading the Indonesian Council of Churches. In politics J. Leimena and A. M. Tambunan can be mentioned. The status of the missionaries changed from that of guardians to fraternal workers. In the RCath Church Indonesianization proceeded at a slower pace. The hierarchy was established in 1961, but of the bishops, Indonesians were not in the majority until 1979, and of the priests not until 1982. RCath set up an excellent infrastructure in education; their daily *Kompas* became the biggest newspaper in southeast Asia.

After World War II the growth of the church accelerated, especially in tribal societies, and in the aftermath of the 1965 coup d'état in Muslim Java as well. In 1994 the number of RCath was reported to be 5.8 million (including East Timor); the number of Prot is more difficult to estimate but might be put at 13 to 16 million. The government tends to give higher numbers, owing to the phenomenon that many people (especially in Java) have themselves registered as Christians even if they have no ties with a church. Among the Prot, 45% belong to the Ref denomination, 25% are of a mixed Lutheran-Calvinist type, and 30% are members of Evangelical and Pentecostal church bodies. It is to be noted that in 1950 the last group comprised about 1% of Indonesian Protestantism. Most of its growth came from outside existing Christian churches.

The percentage of Christians (including RCath) is highest in the provinces of Eastern Indonesia, which are relatively thinly populated: East Timor (90%), Irian (85%), and NTT (75%); North Sulawesi follows with 55%. Between 25% and 50% is Christian in the Moluccas, North Sumatra, and West Kalimantan; 10 to 25% in Central Sulawesi, Central and East Kalimantan, and the capital city of Jakarta; 5 to 10% in the Autonomous Region of Yogyakarta (Central Java) and South Sulawesi; 3 to 5% in Central and East Java and Southeast Sulawesi; 1 to 3% in Sumatra outside North Sumatra and South Kalimantan; under 1% in West Java, Bali, and West Nusatenggara. Of the total number of Christians, more than 25% are living in Java (mostly ethnic Javanese), more than 20% in North Sumatra (mostly Batak), less than 10% in Kalimantan (mostly Dayak), more than 10% in Sulawesi (mostly Minahasans and Torajans), and 30% in the rest of Eastern Indonesia. Of the RCath, 35% are living on the islands of Flores and Timor, the other areas of concentration being Java, West Kalimantan, and North Sumatra.

Some characteristics of the development of the churches during the last decades are: the tendency to experiment with decentralizing and recentralizing the church order; expanding the confession formulas in church orders or even formulating new confessions of faith (of which eight were received between 1951 and 1984); the prospering of initiatives by Indonesian authors and composers to create new church hymns and church music; the broadening of ecumenical relations in general and aid relations in particular from the former mission body to churches and other organizations in other European countries, Australia, the United States, and, of course, Asia; the decreasing of the number of foreign church workers due to both government policy and the rising level of training of Indonesian theologians.

Present Situation

The present situation of the churches is partly determined by their mutual relations, and partly by their relation to government and Islam. Originally, Christianity was planted by the Dutch Ref. The RMG, with its mixed Ref-Luth background, brought a Lutheran strain to North Sumatra; the Dutch Mennonites founded churches in Central Java and the Methodists in Sumatra. In 1950 churches of these denominations founded the Council of Churches in Indonesia (*Dewan*; after 1984, *[Persekutuan] Gereja-Gereja di Indonesia*, DGI/PGI); in 1997 the membership of the 70 affiliated churches totalled more than 10.5 million, of whom 2.5 million were in the HKBP alone. In 1984 the PGI accepted a Common Understanding of the Christian Faith (*Pemahaman Bersama Iman Kristen*, PBIK) consisting of five articles. The member churches of the PGI have formed regional councils of churches (*Persekutuan Gereja-Gereja di Indonesia Wilayah*, PGI-W), which in one case (Northern and Central Sulawesi) has developed into a synod (*Sinode Am Gereja-Gereja Sulawesi Utara/Tengah*, SAG).

The Indonesian Bapt (± 100,000 baptized members) are in part affiliated with the Indonesian Baptist Alliance (*Gabungan Gereja Baptis Indonesia*, GGBI). Most churches issuing from CMA mission work have united in the *Gereja Kemah Injil Indonesia*, whose six member churches total about 500,000 members, more than half of whom are in Irian Jaya. Between 1930 and 1970 Pentecostalism experienced a number of schisms. In 1979 the Indonesian Pentecostal Council (*Dewan Pentakosta Indonesia*, DPI) was founded. Very tentatively, the combined membership can be put at 1.5 to 2 million, of whom many are of Chinese descent. Advent (numbering about 200,000) and a number of independent bodies do not belong to any national church council. It should be noted that the lines between the denominations are not rigid. Within the PGI members now there are also churches of Bapt, CMA, and Pent stock. Moreover, since the 1970s an Evangelical movement has developed, mainly stimulated from America, which has led to the founding of a number of new church bodies and of an Indonesian Evangelical Fellowship (*Persekutuan Injili Indonesia*, PII), which also counts many CMA and Pent churches among its members.

In the '50s and '60s, the main ecumenical challenge faced by Indonesian Prot-estantism was the effort to bring together the DGI member churches into one church body. That effort resulted in the renaming of the "Council" (*Dewan*) as "Fellowship" (*Persekutuan*) in 1984, but it did not really change the relationship between the member churches. In the meantime, no attempts were made to realize church union between single churches. On the contrary, a number of regional churches (North Su-matra, South Sulawesi, North Sulawesi) split, usually on ethnic or regional lines. Af-ter 1970 a theological reorientation in DGI/PGI circles and the increasing influence of American evangelicalism caused a growing antithesis between evangelicals and ecumenicals, which makes itself felt in evangelization, literature work, and theologi-cal education, even though the Indonesian cultural and religious context does not seem to warrant such an American-style antithesis. Moreover, the charismatic move-ment influences a number of traditional churches and eventually generates tensions that threaten to cause them to break up. Relations between Prot and RCath, which were strained until the '60s, have improved. There is a common Bible translation and regular consultation between PGI and the Conference of Bishops, but no organized cooperation. Twenty-six Indonesian churches are members of the WCC, 30 have joined the CCA, 28 the WARC, and 8 the LWF.

Relations with the government are partly determined by the Christians' mi-nority position. Because of this the churches tend to conform to the government policy of the moment, even to the point of making "revolution" a theological issue in the early 1960s and doing the same with "development" in the 1970s. In the 1980s there was a clash with the CCA over the East Timor issue. In 1984-1985 all churches and church organizations had to insert a formula into their church order or statutes recognizing the *Pancasila* as the sole foundation for the life of the na-tion. On daily matters the churches communicate with the government through the Ministry of Religion (*Departemen Agama*), which has departments for each of the five recognized religions; the Minister is always a Muslim.

Relations with Islam are uneasy. In 1996 and 1997 existing tensions came to the surface in riots on Java and West Kalimantan. Islam has long considered Chris-tianity the "religion of the Dutch," and Muslim fears that the process of Westernization will bring Christianization in its trail were fueled by the large num-bers of Muslim youth in Christian schools converting to Christianity in the 1970s and 1980s. Christians tend to suspect the Muslims of striving for an Islamic state and do not appreciate that they may have to take a step back, now that Muslims are overcoming their disadvantage in education, economics, and politics. In a minority situation Christians have problems in obtaining permission to use church build-ings; where Christians are a majority, Muslim presence may be felt to be ostenta-tious. In recent years a significant number of Christian churches and other build-ings have been destroyed by Muslim mobs, especially on Java; these incidents were more or less explicitly approved by part of the Muslim leadership. In Catho-lic East Timor, with its long history of armed resistance against the annexation to Indonesia in 1976, a mosque was destroyed, as well as several Prot churches, in an anti-immigrant riot. Very few Christians have a thorough theological knowledge of Islam, and dialogue on an academic and national level has hardly been practiced

(Th. Sumartana). However, since 1945 Christians have earned their legitimate place as members of the nation, and the majority of people on both sides want to live together in peace.

Types of Reformed Christianity

The differences between the various types of Ref Christianity in Europe, especially in the Netherlands, make themselves felt in the Indonesian churches. Even now, four types can be distinguished.

a) There are churches originating from the former established church (the Protestant Church in the Netherlands Indies). After 1934 a number of regional churches were carved out of the former Protestant Church. These churches accepted Ref church orders. However, they still have a tradition of their own which distinguishes them from the other Ref Churches in Indonesia. A tendency to think in top-down terms still remains; in their church orders no confessions of faith are named except those of the early church (Apostles' Creed, Nicene Creed, Athanasian Creed); none of these churches has formulated a confession of faith of its own; nowhere, except in the Batak Church (HKBP), are church and Christianity so much interwoven with regional (ethnic) identity as in these churches. The churches belonging to this group are: GKLB (cf. no. 14), GMIM (cf. no. 26), GPM (cf. no. 36), GMIT (cf. no. 28), GPIB (cf. no. 30), GPID (cf. no. 32), GPIG (cf. no. 33), GPIBT (cf. no. 31), GPKB (cf. no. 35), GPI-Irja and, historically speaking, the KGPM (cf. no. 42). With the exception of the GPI-Irja all of them are PGI members. Until the mid-50s, the then existing churches of this type still functioned as a loose confederation, convening in General Synods of the Protestant Church (Gereja Protestan Indonesia, GPI), but today, after having lost its function, the GPI continues as an empty shell, with an office and board but no congr or pastors. Taken together, the membership of these churches amounts to ± 2.5 million, or about 20% of Prot Christianity in Indonesia.

b) There are churches originating from 19th- and 20th-century mainline Dutch and German mission bodies. In general these bodies consciously avoided transferring the confessional, organizational, and liturgical identity of their own denomination to the congr on the mission field. The missions were hierarchically organized, with the European missionary at the top. The missionaries introduced their congr to the liturgy they had known in their home churches; in many cases they also introduced the Heidelberg Catechism. After 1925 their character and policy changed, and most of the churches were founded with a simply worded church order of the Ref type. Initially the confessions of faith included in these church orders were very succinct; in the following decades in many churches these formulas were enlarged and the Creeds of the Early Church, in some cases also the Heidelberg Catechism, were named explicitly as belonging to the fundamentals of the church. To this group of churches belong the GBKP (cf. no. 3), GEPSULTRA (cf. no. 37), GKI (cf. no. 7), GKI Irja (cf. no. 9), GKJW (cf. no. 12), GKP (cf. no. 15), GKSS (cf. no. 18), GKST (cf. no. 19), GMIBM (cf. no. 24), GMIH (cf. no. 25), GMIST (cf. no. 27). Among the churches springing from the RMG mission, AMIN (cf. no. 2), BNKP (cf. no. 1), GKE (cf. no. 6), and ONKP (cf. no. 43) could be added, the other churches of this stock having opted for the membership of the LWF. Their combined membership amounts to 2.5 million, about 20% of Prot Christianity in Indonesia. All churches belonging to this category are members of the PGI.

c) Another group of Ref churches in Indonesia derives from conservative Ref mission bodies in the Netherlands. In contrast to the mainline missions, these bodies include both missionary societies and church missions. They stressed their denominational identity and up to a certain point tried to transfer this identity to the congr on the mission field. When these congr became independent churches, the HeidC and, in most cases, the BelgC and the CDort were included in their church order. In one case (GT, cf. no. 40) these three confessions were replaced by a new confession formulated by the church itself. The transfer of identity also included the exclusion of women from office in the church and the introduction of the exclusive use of the Psalm Book (with Genevan melodies) in church services. To this group belong GGRI (cf. no. 38), GJPI (cf. no. 5), GKI-Sumut (cf. no. 8), GKJ (cf. no. 10), GKS (Cf. no. 21), GT (cf. no. 40), and GT-Mamasa. Together they have ± 750,000 members, which amounts to 6% of Indonesian Prot Christianity. The older churches of this group are all PGI members and admit women to church office; the younger churches still follow the pattern of their Dutch mother-churches.

d) Among the churches affiliated with the Indonesian Evangelical Fellowship (PII) there are some which consciously present themselves as Ref or Presb. In the list below one of these churches, on which data could be obtained, has been included (GRII, cf. no. 39). This type of Ref Christianity is characterized by a conservative Calvinist theology and an energetic rejection of modern theology. These churches are not affiliated with the PGI.

It should be noted that for all types of Ref Churches, the Presb church structure is sometimes under overt pressure from cultural factors (e.g., traditional feudalism, government and army hierarchy). Also, all Ref churches in Indonesia practice infant baptism exclusively (with the exception, of course, of adult converts). During the last decades many churches have been afflicted by schisms, mostly caused by regionalism.

1. Protestant Christian Church of Nias (BNKP) (4253)

Christianity was first brought to the island of Nias by the Catholic *Missions Etrangères de Paris*, who had a short-lived mission there from 1832 to 1835. Prot missions in the island of Nias were started in 1865 by the RMG, after it had been temporarily expelled from Kalimantan. At the time, the population of the island (now over 500,000, of whom 73% are Prot, 18% RCath, and 7% Muslim) adhered to the ancestral religion. Until 1900, when the Dutch colonial power came in, growth was slow (first baptism in 1874; 706 baptized by 1890; 20,000 by 1915). From 1915 to 1920 the Christian community on Nias experienced a great revival which resulted in accelerated growth (1921: 62,000 baptized). In 1936 the first synod of the BNKP was convened, chaired, until 1940, by a German missionary. Subsequent revivals (1938-1942, 1945-1949) brought not only growth but also schisms (Fa'awösa khö Geheha and Fa'awösa khö Jesu). Other schisms, starting in 1946 and 1952, were regional in character and were rooted in the traditional social structure (cf. Gereja Angowuloa Masehi Indonesia Nias, AMIN no. 2, and Orahua Niha Keriso Protestan, ONKP no. 43). In 1994 a new schism occurred in southern Nias. Moreover, Advent and, especially, the RCath Church acted as competitors with the BNKP. Nevertheless, the BNKP remains the church of the majority, including 60% of the population. As such, the church was an important factor in welding the population of the various parts of island into an ethnic and linguistic unity, the language of northern Nias being made the language of the Bible (complete Bible printed 1913) and the church. In the future, for the BNKP as for other churches on the rim of Sumatra, the confrontation with Islam will become a greater challenge than that with other Christian groups. The BNKP is active in the field of education, medical care, and social work. It publishes a magazine, *Turia Röfa* (Message of the Cross). The church considers May 15, 1938 (the first church order), as its birthday.

TM: **325,750** Congr: **78** OrdM: **87** Eld: **nc** Deac: **nc** EvgHome: **nc** Mission: **nc** Women Ord: **yes** As Ministers: **8** as Deac: **nc** as Elders: **nc** ChurchOrg: **Presbyterian** Off/otherLang: **Indonesian/Niasan** DoctrB: **ApC, NicC, "as explained by the Churches of the Reformation, especially Luther's Short Catechism and HeidC"** NatRel: **PGI** RegRel: **CCA** IntlRel: **WCC, VEM, UEM** TheolSchool: **Theol Academy Gunung Sitoli, Univer. HKBP Nommensen (Pemantang Siantar), STT Jakarta** Service infrastructure: **education, medical care, social work** Periodicals: **Turia Röfa (Message of the Cross)**

Address: Banua Niha Keriso Protestan (BNKP), Jalan Soekarno 22, Gunungsitoli 22813 Nias Sumatera Utara, Indonesia, Tel: +62 639 21448

2. Christian Communion of Indonesia Church in Nias (AMIN) (4239)

Prot missions in the island of Nias started in 1865 (RMG). At the time, the population of the island (now over 500,000, of whom 73% are Prot, 18% RCath, and 7% Muslim) adhered to the ancestral religion. Until 1900, when the Dutch colonial power came in, growth was slow (706 in 1890). From 1916 to 1929 the Christian community on Nias experienced a great revival which resulted in accelerated growth. In 1936 the first Synod of the BNKP (cf. no. 1) convened. The AMIN split off from the BNKP in 1946. Among the issues was the supposedly legalistic style of the BNKP leadership and the authority of traditional leaders in the church. Accordingly, the church was restricted to the territory of one traditional chief. The congr are independent in financial mattters. In the '60s relations between AMIN and BNKP were normalized, but an attempt at church reunion failed. The church considers May 1, 1946, as its birthday.

TM: **21,142** BM: **19,075** CM: **12,500** Congr: **70** OrdM: **19** Eld: **332** Deac: **ne** EvgHome: **4** Mission: **ne** Women Ord: **yes** As Ministers: **1991/3** as Deac: **none**, as Elders: **1975/100** ChurchOrg: **Presb synodal** Off/otherLang: **Indonesian/Niasan** DoctrB: **ApC, NicC, AthC, LuthC** Infant or believer's baptism: **both** Frequency of the Lord's Supper: **quarterly** Close relations with: **VEM** NatRel: **PGI (1980)** Service infrastructure: **1 kindergarten** Periodicals: **none**

Address: Gereja Angowuloa Masehi Indonesia Nias (AMIN), P.O. Box 9, Tetehösi Idanoi, Gunungsitoli Nias 22871 Sumatera Utara, Indonesia

3. Karo Batak Protestant Church, GBKP (4214)

The Karonese were the only Batak tribe not to be served by the RMG. Christianity came to Karoland (North Sumatra) in 1890 with the first missionaries of the Nederlandsch Zendelinggenootschap. As the Karonese considered the mission part of a white conspiracy to rob them of their lands, growth was very slow initially. In 1941, when the church became independent and the first Karonese pastors were ordained, there were 5,000 Karo Christians. During the turbulent 1940s the church maintained itself, but after 1950 mass movements toward Christianity occurred. From 1980 onward evangelization among the Karonese had to be carried out in competition with Islam. In 1979 the church demonstrated its internal growth with the drawing up of a confession of faith (*Pengakuan Dasar*), which was expanded in 1984. Also, the church abandoned the negative attitude toward traditional culture it had inherited from the mission, and reformulated its church order (1959, 1971, 1976). The GBKP has a number of schools and clinics, and supports a Christian orphanage, home for the elderly, and credit bank. It had woman elders from the beginning, woman deacons from 1961, and ordained woman ministers from 1987. The church considers April 18, 1890, as its birth date.

TM: **225,552** Congr: **293** PStations: **353** OrdM: **135** Eld: **3,301** Deac: **1,938** EvgHome: **54** Mission: **ne** Women Ord: **Yes** As Ministers: **1987/5** as Deac: **1961/784** as Elders: **1985/269** ChurchOrg: **Presbyterian (congr, synod)** Off/otherLang: **Indonesian, Karonese** DoctrB: **ApC, NicC, AthC, HeidC, Pemahaman Bersama Iman Kristen (PGI), Confession of Faith of the GBKP** Infant or believer's baptism: **both** Frequency of the Lord's Supper: **4 times per year** Close relations with: **CMS (Australia), VEM (Germany), NHK (NL), ELCA (Chicago, USA)** NatRel: **PGI (1950)** RegRel: **CCA** IntlRel: **WARC (1988) WCC** Service infrastructure: **schools, nursing homes, orphanages, credit bank, clinics** Periodicals: **Maranatha GBKP (magazine/gen/monthly/3,000)**

Address: Gereja Batak Karo Protestan (GBKP), Jalan Kapten Pala Bangun no. 66, Kabanjahe 22115—Sumatra Utara, Indonesia, Tel: 162 628 20466, Fax: +62 628 20932

4. The Pilgrim's Churches (GGMM) (4241)

In 1947 the Gereja Masehi Injili di Timor (GMIT cf. no. 28) became independent. However, Dutch ministers still occupied some of the leading positions in the church. Some members of GMIT disliked the continuing Dutch presence, and in 1950 they separated and formed the Gereja Masehi Musyafir, which was recognized by the Indonesian government in 1951. Contacts with an orthodox Calvinist mission working on the island of Sumba (cf. GGRI no. 38) led the GMM to find its identity in Calvinism (synod of 1985) and change its name into Gereja-Gereja Masehi Musyafir (1992). The GGMM has no schools or medical facilities and no church magazine. The church considers December 17, 1950, as its date of birth.

TM: **5,315** Congr: **20** PStations: **0** OrdM: **15** Eld: **46** Deac: **30** EvgHome: **7** Mission: **nc** Women Ord: **yes** As Ministers: **no** as Deac: **15** as Elders: **nc** ChurchOrg: **Presbyterian** Off/otherLang: **Indonesian** DoctrB: **ApC, NicC, AthC, HeidC, BelgC, CDort** Close relations with: **Free Reformed Churches (NL)** NatRel: **PII** IntlRel: **ICRC** TheolSchool: **Theological School of GGRI-NTT (Waimarangu)** Service infrastructure: **none** Periodicals: **none**

Address: Gereja-Gereja Masehi Musyafir (GGMM), P.O. Box 102, Deputat Penghubung GGMM-NTT, Jalan Phalawan, Kupang NTT Nunbaun Delha 85223, Indonesia, Tel: +62 380 31736, 21905

5. Protestant Congregations Church in Irian Jaya (GJPI) (4231)

In 1963 the Gereformeerde Gemeenten (GG, Netherlands Reformed Congregations), a conservative Calvinist church, began pioneer mission work in the Pass Valley district of the Yali territory east of the Baliem Valley in the central part of a mountain range. The first baptism took place on December 28, 1969. In 1974 a central Bible School was established at Landikma; in 1978 the first congr were established; and in 1979 the first classis was installed. In 1981 the first CBS class graduated and six young men were admitted by the classis to the administration of Word and sacraments. In 1984 the GJPI was instituted and the leadership of the missionary work was transferred to the native church. In the meantime mission work had expanded to other valleys in the area with the active participation of the local Christians. In each of these valleys a different language is spoken. In the Nipsan Valley the mission post was destroyed and six Yali missionaries killed in 1974; however, in 1978 Nipsan was reopened. A second classis in the Una-speaking eastern part of the mountain range was formed in 1984. Parts of Holy Scripture were translated into the Yali (NT 1976, parts of the OT 1982) and Una languages. The mission is a pioneer mission which for logistical support depends on the Missionary Aviation Fellowship.

The GG mission intends to transfer the characteristics of Ref Christianity as perceived by the mother church without forcing its own identity upon the incipient church. The three confessions of Dutch Calvinism are used by the GJPI as an explanation of scriptural doctrine, but in the 1984 church order of the GJPI only the Apostles' Creed, the Nicene Creed, and the Athanasian Creed are named explicitly as confessions agreed to by the church; following these, 23 brief articles of faith have been accepted. The structure of the church is presbyterial; the Synod convenes once every two years. Women are not admitted to church office. The liturgy follows the pattern used by the mother church, but part of the hymn singing is done with indigenous melodies. Theological education is given in preparatory Bible Schools, Bible School, and Theological School; some graduates are sent to the KINGMI (CAMA) Theological School on the coast for further studies. Mission and church are also active in education, health care, and agricultural development. The GJPI has joined the Persekutuan Injili Indonesia (PII) as a guest member. The church considers June 25, 1984, as its birth date.

TM: **10,000** CM: **4,000** Congr: **65** OrdM: **24** Eld: **nc** Deac: **nc** EvgHome: **nc** Mission: **nc** Women Ord: **no** ChurchOrg: **Presb** Off/otherLang: **Indonesian/Yali, Una, Mek, and other local ones** DoctrB: **ApC, NicC, AthC, 23 Articles of Faith (1987)** NatRel: **PII as a guest member** TheolSchool: **Bible and Theological schools (Pass Valley); CMA Theological School**

Address: Gereja Jemaat Protestan di Irian Jaya (GJPI), P.O. Box 1042, Jalan Gueriliawan, Jayapura Irian Jaya, Indonesia, Tel: +62 967 81675

6. Evangelical Church in Kalimantan (GKE) (4220)

From the 16th century the coastal areas of Kalimantan (Borneo) were Islamicized, but the Dayak tribes in the interior kept to their ancestral faith. The first RMG missionary in Southern Kalimantan arrived in 1835; in 1838 the mission started work in the interior, among the Dayak Ngaju and Maanyan tribes. The resistance of the tribal religion was fierce, and in 1859 the mission was nearly destroyed by an uprising against Dutch colonial rule. Contrary to the experience of the RMG in North Sumatra, from 1866 to 1904 progress was slow (1901: 2,000 Christians), in spite of great efforts by the mission. The causes were the self-determination mentality of the Dayak, which made them skeptical of new things, the paternalism of the mission, and its negative attitude toward local culture. In 1920, due to the situation in Germany after World War I, the RMG had to hand over its Kalimantan mission to the Basel Mission. In 1935 the church was declared autonomous with the name of Gereja Dajak Evangelis, and the first five ministers were ordained. Among these was F. Dingang, son of a traditional chief who had made an active contribution to the spread of Christianity. Until 1942 the Synod Board was chaired by a European missionary; only after the arrival of the Japanese, when Europeans could not fill such posts, was a Dayak appointed President. In 1950 the church decided to abandon its tribal base, changing its name into Gereja Kalimantan Evangelis (GKE). This indicated clearly that the church welcomed Christians from other parts of Indonesia to join and fully participate as members of the church, and, if elected, on the church boards at any level. This development helped to encourage real fellowship and witness by Indonesian Christians, an idea which in the same year materialized in the constitution of the newly founded Indonesian Council of Churches (DGI, now PGI). It also led to support for building a united Indonesian nation, which by its very nature is a diverse and multi-cultural society.

235

To improve the economic and social life of inland people, GKE established the Centre of Agricultural Training in Tumbang Lahang in 1955. As a contribution to the national development plan, in 1967 the GKE founded the Technical High School for woodworking in Mandomai, which became known nationwide. The church has clinics, student homes, and a number of schools on all levels, from kindergarten to university. A Christian University was established in 1987 in Palangka Raya, the capital of Central Kalimantan. This church publishes a tri-monthly magazine, *Berita GKE*. The GKE considers April 4, 1935, as the date of its birth.

TM: **219,145** Congr: **785** PStations: **118** OrdM: **215** Eld: **nc** Deac: **nc** EvgHome: **14** Mission: **nc** Women Ord: **Yes** As Ministers: **1935/16** as Deac: **1935**, as Elders: **1935** ChurchOrg: **congr, presby, synod, general synod** Off/otherLang: **Indonesian, Dryale, Ngaju** DoctrB: **ApC, NicC** Infant or believer's baptism: **both** Frequency of the Lord's Supper: **monthly** NatRel: **PGI (1950)** RegRel: **CCA** IntlRel: **WCC, WARC (1988)** TheolSchool: **Sekolah Tinggi Theol. GKE** Service infrastructure: **Agricultural Training Center (1955), Technical High School for wood-cutting, polyclinics, student homes, all levels of schools, Christian University (1987)** Periodicals: **Berita GKE (gen/quarterly/nc)**

Address: Gereja Kalimantan Evangelis (GKE), P.O. Box 86, Jalan Jenderal Sudirman, No. 4, Rt. 1, Benjarmasin-Jolly 70114 Kalimantan, Indonesia, Tel: +62 511 54 856, Fax: +62 511 65 297

7. Indonesian Christian Church (GKI) (4200)

The GKI has its origins in mission work among the Chinese and people of Chinese descent on Java in the 19th century by a number of Dutch missionary societies and the American Methodists (1905-1928). Chinese evangelists and lay people played a large part in the spreading of Christianity, and the congr were relatively independent from the missions and their missionaries. Their common history starts with the Cipaku Conference in 1926, which aimed at the unity of the Christians of Chinese descent on Java. The founding of the Church of Christ in China (1927) was a stimulus toward independence. After 1930 a number of these congr coalesced into four regional churches (East Java 1934, Central Java 1935 and 1936, West Java 1938), each of which more or less bore the stamp of its founding mission. At the time the combined membership was ± 3,500. With a view toward future unity, these churches initially had the status of classis. However, in the fifties they constituted themselves into four Synods. Three of these took the name of Gereja Kristen Indonesia Jawa Barat/Tengah/Timur. In 1962 for the first time the three churches convened in a General Synod, but not until August 1988 was the projected church union finally realized. This union was strengthened when the united GKI declared itself as a member of the PGI instead of the three constituent churches (1994). Currently the church is in the process of drawing up a church order which will replace the constitutions of the separate churches. Gradually the GKI is taking on a multi-ethnic character. It encompasses only a minority of the Indonesians of Chinese descent, as many belong to the RCath Church and to Prot churches of Pentecostal, Mennonite, and other denominations. The church has general health clinics, several older people's homes, and a social welfare organization. It publishes a tri-monthly theological magazine, *Penuntun*, and a general monthly, *Kairos*. The GKI considers February 22, 1934, as its date of birth.

TM: **161,677** BM: **161,371** CM: **118,306** Congr: **168** PStations: **109** OrdM: **254** Eld: **3,314** Deac: **612** EvgHome: **43** Mission: **3** Women Ord: **Yes** As Ministers: **1965/25** as Deac: **nc** as Elders: **nc** ChurchOrg: **congr, classis, regional synod, national synod** Off/otherLang: **Indonesian** DoctrB: **ApC, NicC AthC, HeidC, "Common Understanding of the Faith"** Infant or believer's baptism: **both** Frequency of the Lord's Supper: **4 times per year** Close relations with: **PGI, GKP, Gereja Kristus, GKJ, GPIB, AMIN, ONKP, BNKP** NatRel: **PGI (1950)** RegRel: **CCA (1962)** IntlRel: **WARC (1965), WCC (1963)** TheolSchool: **Jakarta Theological Seminary (STTJ), Christian University Duta Wacana, Theological Faculty, Christian University Satya Wacana** Service infrastructure: **clinics, rest homes, kindergartens** Periodicals: **Penuntun (theology/quarterly/2,000), Kairos (monthly/4,000)**

Address: Gereja Kristen Indonesia—Jawa Barat (GKI), P.O. Box 1200, Jakarta 13012 Puri Grand Center B/38 Jalan Seulawah—Kalimalang, Jakarta 13620, Indonesia, Tel: +62 21 862-6523, Fax: +62 21 862-6522

8. Indonesian Christian Church of North Sumatera (GKI-Sumut) (4238)

This church has its roots in the Dutch Reformed (Gereformeerde) Church, which existed in the city of Medan between 1915 and 1957. Through the missionary work of this church, a number of Javanese and Toba and Karo Batak joined the church. When the Dutch had to leave (1957), the Indonesian members remained. In 1969 the congr constituted themselves into an independent Synod, which in the same year enacted a church order of a strictly Presb character (no permanent Synod). In 1970 the membership was 5,000, with 4 ordained ministers, 16 evangelists, and 120 elders, in 12 congr and 56 places of worship. The church sent some of its young people to Yogyakarta to receive theological education at the Theological Academy of the Gereja Kristen Jawa. In the 1960s most church members were ethnic Javanese, but in the meantime Bataks, originating from the Toba Batak and the Karo Batak churches, constitute the majority. In time the church changed its name from Gereja-Gereja Gereformeerd Synode Sumatera Utara to its present name. The GKI Sumut is very active in the social sphere. In 1976 the church became a member of the PGI. It considers September 1, 1969, as its date of birth.

TM: **12,400** Congr: **34** OrdM: **19** Eld: **nc** Deac: **nc** EvgHome: **nc** Mission: **nc** Women Ord: **nc** ChurchOrg: **Presbyterian** Off/otherLang: **Indonesian, regional languages** DoctrB: **nc** NatRel: **PGI (1976)**

Address: Gereja-gereja Kristen Indonesia Sumatera Utara (GKI-Sumut), Bakordep Sinode GKI Sumut, Jalan Gunung Simanuk-manuk 5, Pematang Siantar 21115 Sumatera Utara, Indonesia, Tel: +62 622 23143

9. Evangelical Christian Church in Irian Jaya (GKI Irja) (4217)

In 1855 two German carpenter missionaries landed on the coast of northwestern Irian. They had been selected by J. E. Gossner and sent by an independent faith mission in Holland. In 1862 the Utrechtsche Zendingsvereeniging took over the Irian mission, which in the first decade was more or less confined to the east coast of the Bird's Head. The Dutch missionaries were assisted by teacher-preachers from other islands, mainly Moluccans. Progress was very slow, so that after 25 years the number of missionary graves was greater than that of converted Irianese. The extremely negative attitude of most missionaries toward local religion and culture may be considered one of the causes, but also the fact that the Irianese were caught in a vicious circle of revenge (head-hunting) from which a single village or tribe could not escape. In 1907, however, a great revival started which brought thousands into the church. The mission spread to the whole north coast of Irian and the islands, the south coast being allotted by the Dutch colonial government to the RCathMission. The period 1907-1942 was one of gradual development, in which the teacher training school at Miei played a great role. Its leader, I. S. Kijne (1923-1958 in Irian), used his wide range of talents in educating Irianese evangelists and teachers and creating hymnbooks which were used all over Indonesia. However, at the time of the Japanese invasion in 1942, there was no church assembly other than at the local level, and the first Irianese were not ordained as ministers until as late as 1950. By then development was hastened by the political circumstances. In 1956 the first Synod convened. In 1963, when Irian Jaya was surrendered to Indonesia, most Dutch missionaries left Irian.

Even though the visible manifestations of tribal religions have disappeared, except for some remote areas in the interior, they still remain a challenge to the church. One of the key elements in those religions was what is commonly called the "cargo cult" (*Koreri*-movements). These movements occurred periodically throughout the missionary period and into the era of independence. The church also faces serious problems in the social-economic field. After 1963 the island, with its great economic potential, was open to immigration from other parts of Indonesia. The ethnic Irianese were not always ready to face economic competition. Locally this led to symptoms of social disintegration. With immigration, Islam, which until then had been marginal, entered Irian. The extreme ethnic and linguistic fragmentation of the island and the rivalry between the dominant ethnic units also created difficulties. However, it has to be noted that these difficulties did not cause the church to split. In the 1970s the church had to cope with the tensions generated by an insurrection against the Indonesian government. The Evangelical missionary organizations which worked in the interior since 1938 refused cooperation with the GKI, as this church was supposed not to meet their doctrinal and moral standards. The Catholic Church invaded the North and attracted many young GKI members with its excellent schools. Nevertheless the GKI-Irja, with its approximately 650,000 members (1997), still includes the mass of the population in northern and western Irian and is the greatest single church in Irian (about 30% of the total population). The church has some hospitals, a diaconal foundation, and a large number of schools from primary (467) to academic level. It publishes a bi-monthly magazine, *Serikat* ("Bond").

TM: **650,000** Congr: **1,869** OrdM: **246** Eld: **nc** Deac: **nc** EvgHome: **344** Mission: **2** Women Ord: **Yes** As Ministers: **1971/81** as Deac: **nc** as Elders: **nc** ChurchOrg: **congr, classis, synod** Off/otherLang: **Indonesian/regional languages** DoctrB: **ApC, NicC, AthC** Infant or believer's baptism: **both** Frequency of the Lord's Supper: **4 times per year** Close relations with: **VEM (Germany), NHK (NL), Basel Mission** NatRel: **PGI** RegRel: **CCA** IntlRel: **WCC, WARC (1985)** TheolSchool: **Sekolah Tinggi Theologia I. S. Kijne (Abepura)** Service infrastructure: **hospitals, diaconal foundation, schools from primary (467) to university level** Periodicals: **Serikat ("Bond") (monthly/1,000)**

Address: Gereja Kristen Injili di Irian Jaya (GKI Irja), P.O. Box 1160, Jalan Argapura No. 21, Jayapura 99222 Irian Jaya, Indonesia, Tel: +62 967 31472, Fax: +62 967 33192

10. Christian Churches of Java (GKJ) (4218)

The GKJ is one of a number of churches on Java which originate from a movement toward Christianity which was initiated by Javanese and European lay people. Afterward the mission bodies came in and organized the Christians into congr under their care. One of these missions was the Nederlandsche Gereformeerde Zendingsvereeniging, which in 1894 was absorbed by the Zending der Gereformeerde Kerken in Nederland. This mission rejected Javanese Christianity as it had developed since the 1870s under the leadership of Sadrach, a Javanese religious leader who had converted to Christianity and spread the Gospel in a truly Javanese way through debates with heads of other religious groups. Most missionaries and the mission agencies in the Netherlands had a negative view of him, mainly because of the honor bestowed on him by his followers, including practices which could be explained as magical. After the rupture with the Sadrach, about 1890, the mission had to make a fresh start. About 1900 it set out to build a new church with a more traditional Western outlook. The negative attitude of the mission toward expressions of traditional Javanese culture, such as the *wayang* (puppet play), has to be seen as the reverse side of the introduction of Western (Dutch-language) education and modern health care on a scale not equalled in any mission field in Indonesia. The mission also stressed its activity in (Christian) organizations in the social and political field, although it frowned on Indonesian nationalism. In accordance with its Calvinist principles it systematically built up the church organization, starting from the local congregation (1900) to the Synod level. In 1931, when there were 7,500 Christians in 31 congr, the first Synod was held, under Javanese leadership; in 1932 the church accepted a church order. However, as in other mission fields, the missionaries held an important position as advisors until 1942.

After World War II the missionaries were received back, with the condition that they should not interfere in the internal affairs of the church. The GKJ was more ready than its mother church to join ecumenical organizations (1948 WCC, which was joined by GKN only in 1969; 1950 PGI). Many or its members joined the struggle for Indonesian independence, and many played an important role in the Christian political party PARKINDO and other mass organizations. The church experienced sustained growth, with a peak occurring after the suppression of leftist parties in 1965-1967. The union of the four Javanese-speaking churches in Central and East Java, which at one time had been set as a distant goal by the missions, was never realized. In 1949 the GKJ united with the congregationalist-type congr in the northern half of Central Java; in 1953 a number of those congr split off again and formed what was to become the GKJTU. In 1997 the GKJ accepted a new confession of faith, *Poko-poko ajaran Gereja Kristen Jawa*, written in the form of a catechism. Through several foundations, in which GKJ and GKI-Jawa Tengah work together, the church is active in the field of education (Lembaga Perencanaan dan Pembinaan Pendidikan Kristen) and health care (YAKKUM, which runs the great Bethesda hospital in Yogyakarta). The Lembaga Pembinaan dan Pengaderan runs a lay training center. The church publishes a magazine. The GKJ considers February 17, 1931, as its birth date.

TM: **211,279** CM: **91,205** Congr: **218** PStations: **460** OrdM: **291** Eld: **nc** Deac: **nc** EvgHome: **nc** Mission: **nc** Women Ord: **yes** As Ministers: **3** as Deac: **nc** as Elders: **nc** ChurchOrg: **nc** Off/otherLang: **Indonesian** DoctrB: **nc** NatRel: **PGI (1950)** RegRel: **CCA** IntlRel: **WCC (1948), WARC (1959), REC** Periodicals: **Warta Gereja**

Address: Gereja-Gereja Kristen Jawa (GKJ), Jalan Dr. Sumardi No. 10, Salatiga 50711 Java Tengah, Indonesia, Tel: +62 298 26351, Fax: +62 298 23985

11. Javanese Christian Church of Northern Central Java (GKJTU) (4232)

Like its sister church in the southern part of Central Java, the GKJTU originates from the spontaneous movement which arose in the middle of the 19th century. But unlike it, it subsequently was cared for by the Neukirchener Mission from Germany together with the Ermelo Mission in Holland, two faith missions which were congregationalist and pietist in their outlook. Christianity grew slowly in this strongly Muslim country. In 1937, when a Synod convened (Parapatan Agung), there were 6,000 baptized Christians. Little had been done to organize them or to make them self-supporting. After the troubled years of Japanese occupation and war against the Dutch (1942-1949), the church, which had lost its buildings and half of its members, united with the GKJ. However, after 1953 several congr left the united church. They felt they were the legitimate continuation of the Parapatan Agung but took the name GKJTU. The lack of theological training and leadership, which were a legacy of the mission, still plagued the church, and its financial position was weak. After 1980 a certain consolidation took place. Through the Sion Foundation, the church is active in the field of education and social work. The GKJTU considers April 4, 1937, as its birth date.

TM: **18,644** Congr: **53** OrdM: **14** Eld: **nc** Deac: **nc** EvgHome: **nc** Mission: **nc** Women Ord: **nc** As Ministers: **na** as Deac: **nc** as Elders: **nc** ChurchOrg: **Presbyterian** Off/otherLang: **Indonesian/Javanese** DoctrB: **ApC** NatRel: **PGI Badan, Musyawarah Gereja-Gereja Jawa** TheolSchool: **UKSW Salatiga, UK Duta Wacana (Yogyakarta), Institut Theol. Abdiel (Ungaran)** Service infrastructure: **education and social work**

Address: Gereja Kristen Jawa Tengah Utara (GKJTU), P.O. Box 105, Jalan Letjen Sukowati 74, Salatiga 50715 Jawa Tengah, Indonesia, Tel: +62 298 21149, Fax: +62 298 21149

12. The East Java Christian Church (GKJW) (4219)

The GKJW has been a missionary church from the beginning. Like its sister churches in Central Java, it grew from a spontaneous movement among the Javanese in the middle of the 19th century. In the 1830s groups of Muslims near Surabaya were brought into contact with the Gospel by the activities of European lay people, an Indo-Russian farmer and a German watchmaker; the first baptism occurred December 12, 1843. In the 1850s the Dutch mission (NZG) took over and started what it considered to be a necessary long process of bringing the congr to maturity. Under the influence of H. Kraemer, this process was concluded by the convening of the first Synod in 1931, when the church had 23,000 baptized members, but, as elsewhere in Indonesia, the mission remained as a "guide toward adulthood" until 1942. So great was its influence that the GKJW considers itself a daughter church of the NHK. The coming of the Japanese brought the end of missionary domination. During and after World War II the church went through hard times. After 1950 a slow but steady growth began, which peaked after the elimination of Communism in 1965-1967. From the beginning, the GKJW has been a rural church; many congr were founded by clearing forests and establishing Christian villages on the reclaimed land. The other churches in East Java are based in the cities. Together they constitute 2.0 million (including RCath) of the 34 million population of East Java, the overwhelming majority (97.5%) being Muslim. In 1995 and 1996 riots occurred several times, resulting in severe damage to Christian lives and property. The GKJW has a number of clinics, an orphanage, and a small number of schools for all levels. In 1987 the church commenced its first Six-year Comprehensive Church Development Plan, which consists of programs for the development of theological activities, community life, Christian service, Christian witness, and stewardship. The GKJW publishes a monthly magazine, *Duta*. The church considers December 11, 1931, as its birth date.

TM: **153,000** BM: **153,000** CM: **97,442** Congr: **118** PStations: **5** OrdM: **133** Eld: **1,985** Deac: **1,525** EvgHome: **nc** Mission: **1** Women Ord: **yes** As Ministers: **1985/11** as Deac: **nc** as Elders: **nc** ChurchOrg: **Synodal-Presbyteral** Off/otherLang: **Indonesian, Javanese, Madurese** DoctrB: **ApC** Infant or believer's baptism: **both** Frequency of the Lord's Supper: **5 times per year** Close relations with: **NHK, VEM, PCUSA** NatRel: **PGI (1950)** RegRel: **CCA** IntlRel: **WARC, WCC** TheolSchool: **Institut Pendidikan Theologia Bale Wiyata (Malang), Fak. Theol. Univer. Kristen Duta Wacana (Yogyakarta)** Service infrastructure: **5 hospitals, clinics, 12 kindergartens, orphanages** Periodicals: **Duta (general/monthly/nc)**

Address: Gereja Kristen Jawi Wetan (GKJW), Jalan Shodanchoo Supriadi 18, Malang 65147 Jawa Timur, Indonesia, Tel: +62 341 25946 or 25873 or 62604, Fax: +62 341 62604

13. West Kalimantan Christian Church (GKKB) (4249)

In 1906 an American Meth mission brought the Gospel to West Kalimantan (Singkawang), where a great number of ethnic Chinese were living. In 1927/28 the mission handed its work over to the Chinese Christian Church, which, in the meantime, had been established there. In 1928 the church was assisted by the Basel Mission and the Protestant Church in the Netherlands Indies; it also received support from China. In 1935 the Chinese Christian Church in Pontianak, the capital of the province West Kalimantan, was established. During the Japanese occupation the Chinese of West Kalimantan went through much suffering; one of their pastors was murdered. After 1950 the church was assisted by the OMF, the former China Inland Mission. After 1965 the "Indonesianization" of the ethnic Chinese in Kalimantan accelerated, and, as a consequence, in 1967 the church changed its name from Tiong Hoa Kie Tok Kauw Hwe (Chinese Christian Church) to GKKB, with a more Presb structure. The change was completed when the church joined the PGI (1972). According to the church order, the doctrinal basis of the GKKB is belief in Holy Trinity, and in Jesus Christ as the only Savior, Head of the Church and source of Truth and Life; the church accepts the inspired Scriptures of the Old and the New Testament as the living guideline for the faithful. Today the church has a number of schools from kindergarten to secondary school. It publishes a tri-monthly periodical, *Zion*. The GKKB considers 1935 as the year of its birth.

TM: **7,853** Congr: **28** OrdM: **7** Eld: **nc** Deac: **166** EvgHome: **nc** Mission: **nc** Women Ord: **yes** As Ministers: **nc** as Deac: **67** as Elders: **nc** ChurchOrg: **Presbyterian** Off/otherLang: **Indonesian/Mandarin, other Chinese languages** DoctrB: **nc** Close relations with: **Charismatic Consultation on World Evangelization** NatRel: **PGI (1972)** Service infrastructure: **schools from kindergartens to secondary level.** Periodicals: **Zion (gen/quarterly)**

Address: Gereja Kristen Kalimantan Barat (GKKB), Jalan Gajah Mada 250, Pontianak 78122 Kalimantan Barat, Indonesia, Tel: +62 561 34487

14. Christian Church in Luwuk Banggai (GKLB) (4209)

The Gospel was brought to Luwuk Banggai in 1912 (first baptism: January 31, 1912) by Dutch and Indonesian functionaries of the established Protestant Church (GPI) in a way typical of that church at the time: group conversion, brief preparation for baptism, use of a foreign language (Malay), and a negative attitude toward local culture. In 1934, when the Prot congregations in nearby Minahasa became independent (GMIM), Luwuk Banggai was transferred to that church as a mission field. So the church here belongs to the "established" variety of Indonesian Presbyterianism. After the war, however, the congr there were combined with those on the NZG mission field, in adjoining Poso, to become the Gereja Kristen Sulawesi Tengah (1947). The amalgam did not last. Regionalism and differences in tradition caused the congr in Luwuk Banggai to break away and found an independent church (1966). Half of the church classes are situated on the mainland of Sulawesi and half on the islands of the Banggai Archipelago. In 1992 some leaders of island classes seceded and formed a new church, the Gereja Protestan Indonesia Luwuk Banggai (GPILB). The GKLB requested the government to intervene, and to declare the new church illegal. The GKLB has a number of schools. It considers January 27, 1966, as its birth date.

TM: **73,000** Congr: **226** PStations: **none** OrdM: **70** Eld: **na** Deac: **450** EvgHome: **ne** Mission: **ne** Women Ord: **yes** As Ministers: **19** as Deac: **nc** as Elders: **nc** ChurchOrg: **congr, classis, synod (every five years)** Off/otherLang: **Indonesian/regional languages** DoctrB: **ApC, NicC, AthC** Infant or believer's baptism: **both** Frequency of the Lord's Supper: **4 times per year** Close relations with: **Nederlandse Hervormde Kerk (NHK), Gereformeerde Kerken in Nederland (GKN)** NatRel: **PGI, GPI, SAG** IntlRel: **WARC (1982)** TheolSchool: **none** Service infrastructure: **schools** Periodicals: **none**

Address: Gereja Kristen di Luwuk Banggai (GKLB), P.O. Box 13, Jalan Sam Ratulangi 261, Luwuk Kabupaten Banggai 94714, Indonesia, Tel: +62 461 22218

15. Pasundan Christian Church (GKP) (4221)

West Java was Islamized in the 16th century. Christian missionary work was started in 1863 by a Dutch mission body, the NZV. The missionaries took a very antithetic attitude toward Islam and Sundanese culture. Progress among the Sundanese was extremely slow. In the meantime a Dutch layman, member of the Supreme Court of the Dutch Indies, gathered a number of converts using less orthodox methods together with the forms of Javanese magical learning. In 1885 the two streams converged, and in 1934, when there were 4,000 Sundanese Christians, the first Synod of the Gereja Kristen Pasundan convened. Until World War II the Synod was chaired by a missionary. In 1942 a troubled period began which, for the GKP, lasted into the fifties due to an Islamistic revolt which broke out in West Java after the War of Independence ended in 1949. However, the church survived, and after the revolt petered out, it entered upon a period of quiet consolidation. The church has a number of schools and a large hospital in Bandung. The church publishes a monthly magazine. It considers November 14, 1934, as its birth date.

TM: **30,000** CM: **8,000** Congr: **45** OrdM: **46** Eld: **na** Deac: **na** EvgHome: **nc** Women Ord: **yes** As Ministers: **4** as Deac: **nc** as Elders: **nc** ChurchOrg: **nc** Off/otherLang: **Indonesian/Sundanese** DoctrB: **nc** Close relations with: **NHK, OMF** NatRel: **PGI** RegRel: **CCA** IntlRel: **WCC, WARC (1988)** TheolSchool: **Sekolah Theologia Tinggi (Jakarta)** Service infrastructure: **schools, big hospital in Bandung** Periodicals: **Berita Gereja Kristen Pasundan**

Address: Gereja Kristen Pasundan (GKP), P.O. Box 1051, Jalan Pasirkaliki 121-123, Bandung 40010 Jawa Barat, Indonesia, Tel: +62 22 614 803, Fax: +62 22 614 803

16. Gospel Propagating Christian Church (GKPI Tarakan) (4254)

The GKPI has its origin in the 1950s. It arose from a secession from the Gereja Kemah Injil Indonesia, one of the CAMA churches in Indonesia. The founders of the church, who belonged to the Dayak people, felt the Gospel should have a greater impact on the living conditions of the Dayak, especially their health situation and agricultural methods. As Indonesians from outside Kalimantan joined the church, it lost its exclusive character as a rural church for the Dayak. The GKPI Tarakan has one secondary school and a clinic where traditional medicines are promoted. It publishes a tri-monthly magazine, *Wagi*. The church considers May 30, 1959, as its birth date.

TM: **13,255** Congr: **75** OrdM: **60** Eld: **na** Deac: **na** EvgHome: **nc** Mission: **nc** Women Ord: **yes** As Ministers: **2** as Deac: **nc** as Elders: **nc** ChurchOrg: **Presb** Off/otherLang: **Indonesian/regional ones** DoctrB: **ApC, NicC, AthC** NatRel: **PGI** Service infrastructure: **1 secondary school, 1 clinic with traditional medicine** Periodicals: **Wagi (general/quarterly)**

Address: Gereja Kristen Pemancar Injil (GKPI), P.O. Box 112, Jalan Gunung Belah n. 6, Tarakan 77101 Kalimantan Timur, Indonesia, Tel: +62 551 21154

17. Protestant Christian Church in Bali (GKPB) (4213)

Bali resisted political and religious conquest by Islam. Only here in the Indonesian archipelago does Hinduism still dominate society and daily life. The island had been in contact with the Dutch since 1597, but not until 1864 was a mission post established there. Until 1881 only one Balinese was baptized, but then the missionary was murdered. As a result, the colonial government banned missionary work on Bali. In 1929 Tsang To Hang, a Chinese CAMA missionary, entered Bali, and on November 11, 1931, a group of Balinese were baptized. In 1933 Tsang To Hang was banished. The Dutch mission in neighboring East Java was not permitted to care for the Balinese Christians, but then the Christian Church in East Java (GKJW) took over. Pressure from the closed village societies was heavy; nevertheless, in 1947 there were 1,700 Balinese Christians. In 1949 the church became independent. Growth remained slow, but, of the Balinese who emigrated from the densely populated island to other parts of Indonesia, thousands entered churches there. Since the 1970s the Balinese church has made serious attempts to adapt its forms to Balinese culture. For example, the pastors do not don a black gown when leading the church service, black symbolizing evil, but a white gown instead. In several places elements of Balinese architectural style have been applied. Other Christian bodies on Bali are the RCath Church (8,000) and a number of Pentecostal and CAMA congr. The church has a small number of primary and secondary schools, a training school for the tourist industry, a hospital, and several health care centers. It publishes a magazine every four months under the name *Galang Kangin*. The GKPB considers August 11, 1949, its birth date.

TM: **6,871** Congr: **50** OrdM: **38** Eld: **327** Deac: **nc** EvgHome: **nc** Mission: **nc** Women Ord: **yes** As Ministers: **1** as Deac: **53** as Elders: **nc** ChurchOrg: **Presbyterian** Off/otherLang: **Indonesian/Balinese, English (in tourist areas)** DoctrB: **ApC, NicC, AthC,** NatRel: **PGI** RegRel: **CCA** IntlRel: **WCC (assoc. member), WARC (1988)** TheolSchool: **STT Jakarta, Duta Wacana (Jogyakarta), Satya Wacana (Salatiga), INTIM (Ujung Pandang), Bandung** Service infrastructure: **primary and secondary schools; training school for tourist industry, one hospital, health care centers** Periodicals: **Galang Kangin (gen/3 times per year)**

Address: Gereja Kristen Protestan di Bali (GKPB), P.O. Box 72, Jalan Dr. Sutomo 101A, Denpasar
80118 Bali, Indonesia, Tel: +62 361 424-862, Fax: +62 361 51463

18. Christian Church South in Sulawesi (GKSS) (4223)

The southern half of South Sulawesi is inhabited by two peoples, the Makassarese in the southwest and the Buginese in the southeast and center. Christianity first came to the region in the 16th century through the Portuguese mission. Some local rulers were baptized. But the mission was not followed up, and in the 17th century Islam spread northward from Makassar. From 1667 the Dutch had a factory and a fort in Makassar, but they did not attempt to preach the Gospel to the local population. In 1848 the Dutch Bible Society sent a Bible translator who translated the complete Bible into the two local languages. An attempt by the mission to start missionary work was thwarted by the government (1858). A second attempt (1895-1905) was abandoned because it did not yield any result. But in the 1930s, in the island of Salayar, a heterodox Muslim movement offered points of contact with the mission which, from 1933 onward, had been established by the Protestant Church. At the same time, European congr of the GKN on Java started a mission on the mainland of South Sulawesi. Before World War II several hundred people were baptized. World War II and the Muslim rebellion, which started in 1950 and lasted until the sixties, caused much suffering for the congr. When peace returned, the congr of the two missions were gathered into the GKSS (1966). The church has been able to maintain itself but has made no headway among the Muslim population. The GKSS has a number of primary schools and provides elementary health care in some isolated areas. Social work is being done by several foundations. The church considers June, 12, 1966, as its birth date.

TM: **6,555** BM: **6,540** CM: **4,786** Congr: **41** OrdM: **34** Eld: **328** Deac: **287** EvgHome: **8** Mission: **ne** Women Ord: **yes** As Ministers: **1966/5** as Deac: **1966/432** as Elders: **1966/480** ChurchOrg: **congr, presby, synod** Off/otherLang: **Indonesian/Buginese Makassarese** DoctrB: **ApC, "the principles of the testimony of the Reformation"** Infant or believer's baptism: **both** Close relations with: **GKN and NHK (NL) EMS (Stuttgart, Germany)** NatRel: **PGI (1950), PGIW Sulselra (1962)** IntlRel: **WARC (1974), WCC (1981)** Service infrastructure: **primary schools, elementary health care centers** Periodicals: **Warta GKSS (internal/monthly/nc)**

Address: Gereja Kristen i Sulawesi Selatan (GKSS), P.O. Box 1186, Jalan Ketilang No. 4, Ujung
Pandang 90011 Sulawesi Selatan, Indonesia, Tel: +62 411 854-436, Fax: +62 411 854-436

19. Christian Church in Central Sulawesi (GKST) (4228)

As an isolated mountain area, Central Sulawesi remained outside the Dutch sphere of influence until the end of the 19th century. A mission was established here in 1892, after the Minahasa to the north had been Christianized. A. C. Kruyt, who worked here from 1892 until 1932, was one of the first Dutch missionaries in Indonesia to use a new approach: being positive toward local culture, thus preventing

Christians from being excluded by society. The first individuals who converted were not baptized until a large group was ready to become Christians (first baptism December 25, 1909). From then on, the number of Christians and the territory of the mission gradually increased until World War II (1939: 42,000 Christians). As in other parts of Sulawesi during World War II, the congr received protection and help from a Japanese minister turned civil servant, S. Mijahira. After the war the first Synod convened (1947). In the '50s and early '60s, while under the leadership of F. Lumentut, the GKST was hard-pressed in the south by the Muslim guerillas in South Sulawesi, while in Central Sulawesi the secession movement PERMESTA created much unrest. Not until the 1970s could the church embark on a period of stabilization. In 1974 it adopted a new church order. Attempts were made to improve the economy of the economically backward region and to give training to the church members. To this end, an agricultural college was founded. The church has a large number of elementary and secondary schools and a hospital. Until recently the GKST published a magazine, *Berita GKST*. It considers October, 18, 1947, as its birth date.

TM: **160,000** CM: **50,000** Congr: **342** OrdM: **257** Eld: **na** Deac: **na** EvgHome: **nc** Mission: **nc** Women Ord: **yes** As Ministers: **91** as Deac: **nc** as Elders: **nc** ChurchOrg: **Presbyterian** Off/otherLang: **Indonesian/regional languages** DoctrB: **ApC, Pemahaman Iman Bersama PGI** Close relations with: **World Vision, Mission Aviation Fellowship, Mennonite Central Committee, EMS** NatRel: **PGI, SAG** RegRel: **CCA** IntlRel: **WARC, WCC (1989)** TheolSchool: **Akademi Theologia GKST (Tentena)** Service infrastructure: **agricultural college, elementary and secondary schools, one hospital** Periodicals: **Berita GKST**

Address: Gereja Kristen Sulawesi Tengah (GKST), Jalan Setia Budi 93, Tentena Sulawesi Tengah 94663, Indonesia, Tel: +62 458 21050, Fax: +62 458 21318

20. Christian Church of Southern Sumatra (GKSBS) (4229)

The GKSBS did not originate from foreign mission work but from the migration of millions of Javanese from their densely populated island to Southern Sumatra. In the 1930s Christians began to be among these migrants. The Christian Church of Central Java (GKJ) concerned itself with these diaspora Christians, and in 1938 this church officially made Lampung, the southernmost district of Sumatra, its mission field. Four years later the first missionary arrived from Central Java. He guided the small groups of Javanese Christians through World War II and the war of liberation (1945-1949). In 1952 the five congr formed a classis, which then joined the GKJ. From 1938 the mission in Lampung had also been supported by the GKN congregation in nearby Palembang (mainly consisting of Europeans), which sent and paid some evangelists. After the Dutch had been forced to leave Indonesia, the GKN in the Netherlands took over (1959) and provided considerable financial support. Nevertheless, Dutch influence was always limited; only two Dutch missionaries ever worked in the church. On the contrary, the GKJ provided all missionary workers and most of the ministers serving in congr. However, the members came from five churches on Java and Bali. In 1987 the church on Sumatra became independent from the mother church in Central Java, taking the name of GKSBS. Initially, the church was a member of the Consultative Body of Javanese Churches (BMGJ), but, as it did not wish to be an ethnic church, in 1996 it left this body. At the same time the GKJ church order, which had been provisionally accepted, was replaced by a new church order and the name of the church was changed from *Gereja-Gereja* (plural) into *Gereja* (singular). The church has opened church offices to women.

For sixty years the mission and the church in South Sumatra have gathered the Christians among the migrants and also brought the Gospel to the Muslims and Hindus among them. However, they did not work among the indigenous population of the region, which is strongly Muslim and considers the migrants as strangers. The GKSBS has a number of schools which have played an important part in the education of the church members. This despite the fact that the first generation consisted of landless and jobless farm laborers. It publishes a general magazine, *Berita GKSBS*, and one for the church cadre, *Buletin PWG Sinode GKSBS*. The GKSBS considers October 15, 1987, as its birth date.

TM: **39,900** BM: **39,900** CM: **31,598** Congr: **62** PStations: **36** OrdM: **44** Eld: **na** Deac: **na** EvgHome: **23** Mission: **1** Women Ord: **yes** As Ministers: **1987/5** as Deac: **(about 20%)** as Elders: **(about 20%)** ChurchOrg: **Presbyterian (congr, presb, regional synod, synod)** Off/otherLang: **Indonesian/ Javenese** DoctrB: **ApC, NicC, HeidC, AthC** Infant or believer's baptism: **both** Frequency of the Lord's Supper: **quarterly** Close relations with: **GKN, GKJ, GKI** NatRel: **PGI (1988)** RegRel: **none** IntlRel: **WARC (1992), REC (1992)** TheolSchool: **Fak. Theol. Univ. Kristen Duta Wacana (Yogyakarta)** Service infrastructure: **hospital, foundation for Christian education** Periodicals: **Berita GKSBS (gen), Buletin PWG Sinode GKSBS (for church workers/quarterly/300)**

Address: Gereja Kristen Sumatera Bagian Selatan (GKSBS), P.O. Box 146, Jalan Yos Sudarso 15 Polos, Metro Lampung 34101, Indonesia, Tel: +62 725 42598, Fax: +62 725 42598

21. Christian Church of Sumba (GKS) (4225)

In the 19th century the Dutch government, which did not effectively dominate Sumba until 1906, moved inhabitants of the island of Sawu to Sumba in order to establish a foothold there. When Christianity came to Sawu, two congr came into existence among these immigrants (± 1875). In 1881 a conservative Calvinist mission body in the Netherlands sent a missionary to Sumba; in 1892 the GKN took over. It was hoped that the Sawunese Christians would be a stepping-stone for the mission among the Sumbanese proper. But as relations between Sumbanese and Sawunese were bad, during the next quarter of a century hardly a Sumbanese accepted the Gospel. In 1907 the mission made a fresh start by establishing a mission post among the Sumbanese. Teacher-preachers from Ambon, Rote, and Sawu, together with the Dutch missionaries, slowly (first baptism of Sumbanese proper in December 1915) founded a number of congr. Gradually a number of these were given autonomy, but, unlike the GKN mission on Java, the evangelists pastoring them were not ordained as ministers. Not until 1942, when there were more than

5,000 baptized Christians, was the first Sumbanese minister ordained. Two years later he was executed by the Japanese.

During World War II Sumba was occupied by a large Japanese army, and the population suffered accordingly. After the war the mission sped up the process of building an independent church. On January the first Synod of the Gereja Kristen Sumba convened. Numbers of missionaries remained on Sumba, but in the next ten years their role gradually changed into that of advisors. They were active in theological education, lay training programs, but also in agriculture ("comprehensive approach"). In 1972 the relationship with the GKN was reformulated in a new agreement of cooperation. During the last decade the church has been going through a process of contextualization, which is leading to a more positive attitude toward traditional custom. The GKS has a number of schools and two hospitals and publishes a magazine, *Berita GKS*. It considers January 15, 1947, as its birth date.

TM: **173,000** Congr: **72** OrdM: **82** Eld: **na** Deac: **na** EvgHome: **nc** Mission: **na** Women Ord: **yes** As Ministers: **5** ChurchOrg: **Presbyterian** Off/otherLang: **Indonesian/regional languages** DoctrB: **HeidC**, NatRel: **PGI** IntlRel: **REC, WARC (1988)** TheolSchool: **Fak. Theol Univ. Kristen Artha Wacana Kupang, STT Jakarta, STT INTIM Ujung Pandang** Service infrastructure: **schools, two hospitals** Periodicals: **Berita GKS**

Address: Gereja Kristen Sumba (GKS), Jalan R. Suprapto 23, Waingapu Sumba NTT 87113, Indonesia, Tel: +62 386 21342, Fax: +62 386 21333

22. The Church of Christ the Lord (GKT) (4247)

Unlike the Dutch Mission in West Java (cf. Gereja Kristen Pasundan, no. 15) the 19th-century mission in East Java did not work among people of Chinese descent. Christianity among the Chinese in East Java has its origins in mission work by the Chinese themselves (cf. Gereja Kristen Indonesia, no. 7) and, in the first decades of the 20th century, by the mission of American Methodists (1905-1928). In 1928 this mission was taken over by a small Calvinist church in the Netherlands. At the time there was only one Chinese congregation, in Surabaya, which was divided into three sections according to the Chinese dialects spoken. The mission started working among the Malay-speaking Chinese, and on August 9, 1934, eight congr were united into one General Assembly. In 1940 the combined membership was 900, of whom half were Malay-speaking, the total Chinese population of East Java being a little more than 150,000. However, this small church split over the language issue. Part of the Chinese-speaking Christians founded a separate Church, Gereja Kristus Tuhan, which now considers itself as Calvinist Evangelical. The church has a theological school, Institut Theologia Aletheia, a publishing house, Gandum Mas, and a small number of schools. The GKT considers December 7, 1939, as its date of birth.

TM: **11,000** Congr: **37** OrdM: **21** Eld: **nc** Deac: **nc** EvgHome: **nc** Mission: **nc** Women Ord: **no** ChurchOrg: **Presbyterian** Off/otherLang: **Chinese** DoctrB: **ApC**, NatRel: **PGI** TheolSchool: **Institut Theologia Aletheia (Jalan Argopuro 28-34, Lawang, Jawa Timur)** Service infrastructure: **Gandum Mas Publishing House, some schools**

Address: Gereja Kristus Tuhan (GKT), Kotak Pos 13, Jalan Argopuro 6, Malang 65112 Jawa Timur, Indonesia, Tel: +62 341 25826

23. Christian Church in East Timor (GKTT) (4227)

The Gospel came to East Timor at about the same time as to other parts of the Nusatenggara Timur islands, in the second half of the 16th century (cf. Gereja Masehi Injili Timor, no. 28). As this eastern half of Timor belonged to the Portuguese sphere of influence, even after the Dutch established themselves in Indonesia, the Catholic Church remained the only Christian body in the area until far into the 20th century. Protestantism won a few adherents, but it was suppressed by the colonial government and could expand only after 1975, when East Timor was abandoned by Portugal and annexed by Indonesia. Among the government officials and military moving in were a number of Prot who established congr. Numbers of Timorese, who had not or had only nominally become RCath during the centuries before, also joined the Prot community. In 1979 a Coordinating Agency of Prot Christian Congregations in East Timor was established, under the auspices of the PGI (NCC). This agency made preparations for the formation of a regional church, according to the pattern prevailing in Indonesia since the days of the mission, and on July 9, 1988, the first Synod convened. The membership grew from 6,668 in 1979 to 34,625 in 1996. The close relationship with the NCC made it easier for the GKTT to insert itself into the international oecumene; in 1989 it joined the WARC and in 1993 the WCC. The GKTT has a foundation which is active in education (four maternity schools), health care (one clinic), and social work. Since November 1996, the church has published a monthly magazine under the name *Tatoli* ("Message" in one of the Timorese languages). It considers July 9, 1988, as its date of birth.

TM: **34,625** Congr: **67** OrdM: **20** Eld: **250** Deac: **150** EvgHome: **nc** Mission: **nc** Women Ord: **yes** As Ministers: **3** as Deac: **nc** as Elders: **nc** ChurchOrg: **Presbyterian** Off/otherLang: **Indonesian/regional ones** DoctrB: **ApC, NicC, AthC** NatRel: **PGI** IntlRel: **WARC (1989), WCC (1993)** TheolSchool: **STT: Artha Wacana (Kupang); Duta Wacana (Yogyakarta; Tomohon (Sulawesi)** Service infrastructure: **four maternity schools, one clinic, social work** Periodicals: **Tatoli (Message) (gen/nc/nc)**

Address: Gereja Kristen di Timor Timur (GKTT), P.O. Box 1186, Jalan Martires de Patria, Dili 88110 Timor Timur, Indonesia, Tel: +62 390 22318, Fax: +62 390 22318

24. Christian Evangelical Church in Bolaang Mongondow (GMIBM) (4215)

Christianity entered the kingdom of Bolaang Mongondow, situated west of the Minahasa, in the 17th century, at about the same time as Islam. However, during the 18th and 19th century no attention was given to this region, and by 1900 the majority of the population had entered Islam. In 1904 the Muslim king requested the mission to establish schools in his territory. At the same time Christians from the densely populated Sangir islands and the Minahasa immigrated to Bolaang Mongondow. In 1970 about 80% of GMIBM members consisted of immigrants and their descendants. The church became independent in 1950. Between 1958 and 1961 the GMIBM, like its sister churches in North and Central Sulawesi, suffered from a revolt against the central government (PERMESTA). The church is active in the field of education and health care and publishes a monthly magazine, *Bulletin GMIBM*. It considers June 28, 1950, as its date of birth.

TM: **86,200** BM: **79,000** CM: **50,000** Congr: **176** OrdM: **51** Eld: **1,029** Deac: **504** EvgHome: **nc** Mission: **nc** Women Ord: **Yes** As Ministers: **1967/21** as Deac: **1995/243** as Elders: **1995/340** ChurchOrg: **congr, classis, synod** Off/otherLang: **Indonesian/Mongondow, Sangir, Minahasa** DoctrB: **nc** Infant or believer's baptism: **both** Frequency of the Lord's Supper: **3 to 6 times per year** Close relations with: **Dutch Missionary Council** NatRel: **PGI** RegRel: **CCA** IntlRel: **WARC (1974), WCC** TheolSchool: **Fakultas Theologia Universitas Kristen (Tomohon)** Service infrastructure: **Christian primary and secondary schools, clinics** Periodicals: **Buletin GMIBM (spec/monthly/250)**

Address: Gereja Masehi Injili di Bolaang Mongondow (GMIBM), P.O. Box 104, Jalan Ahmad Yani No. 720, Kotamobagu 95711Sulawesi Utara, Indonesia, Tel: +62 434 21 280, Fax: +62 434 22 446

25. The Christian Evangelical Church in Halmahera (GMIH) (4244)

From the 15th century Halmahera belonged to the sphere of influence of four regional sultanates, among which Ternate was the most important. Christianity arrived after 1520 with the Portuguese and Spanish. In 1534 thousands of inhabitants of Halmahera were baptized. However, the wars between the Portuguese and Ternate destroyed these congr. Around 1600 the Prot Dutch arrived. They established a church in the Central Moluccas but left Halmahera to Ternate. Not until 1866 did a Dutch missionary society send missionaries to the island. Until 1900 the mission was characterized by a very negative attitude toward *adat* (customary law) and a careful selection and preparation of individuals to be baptized. This policy and the opposition of Islam from its center in Ternate caused progress to be extremely slow. After 30 years of missionary work there were 150 Christians on Halmahera. But in 1896 a group movement toward Christianity started. The young missionary, Hueting, let himself be guided by it to a new approach. In 1938 there were 17,000 Christians. As on many Dutch mission fields in Eastern Indonesia, Halmaheran Christianity was ill prepared for the events of World War II. The population of Halmahera, including the Christians, had a particularly hard time as Halmahera was an important Japanese base; they had to labor for the Japanese; meanwhile their villages were bombed by the Allies. An independent church was established with the name of Gereja Protestan Halmahera. After the Allies reconquered, Halmahera church independence was renegotiated with the missionaries. In 1949 the GMIH was constituted as an independent church with a membership of 30,000, and, not much later, all Dutch missionaries had to leave, since during the conflict between the Indonesian Republic and the Netherlands, Halmahera was on the front line. After 1965 government pressure on the adherents of the ancestral religion to choose one of the state-recognized religions resulted in increased church growth. The church has a hospital, several homes for the elderly, and a considerable number of schools from kindergarten to university level. It publishes a tri-monthly magazine, *Buletin GMIH*. It considers September 6, 1949, as its birth date.

TM: **150,000** BM: **150,000** CM: **57,342** Congr: **328** PStations: **0** OrdM: **141** Eld: **4,256** Deac: **4,537** EvgHome: **260** Mission: **ne** Women Ord: **yes** As Ministers: **1975/27** as Deac: **1949/2,536** as Elders: **1955/1,928** ChurchOrg: **congr, presby, synod** Off/otherLang: **Indonesia/Daerah Suku** DoctrB: **ApC, NicC** Infant or believer's baptism: **both** Frequency of the Lord's Supper: **4 times per year** Close relations with: **NHK (NL), Presbyterian Church of Ireland, EMS, Uniting Church of Australia** NatRel: **PGI (1950)** RegRel: **CCA (1979)** IntlRel: **WARC (1979), WCC (1979)** TheolSchool: **Sekolah Tinggi Theologia GMIH (Ternate); Sekolah Tinggi Theologia INTIM (Ujung Pandang)** Service infrastructure: **schools at all levels (101 primary, 9 secondary, 4 high schools, 1 university), hospital, nursing homes** Periodicals: **Buletin GMIH (magazine/three monthly)**

Address: Gereja Masehi Injili Halmahera (GMIH), Jalan Kemakmuran, Tobelo, Halmahera Halmahera Maluku Utara 97762, Indonesia, Tel: +62 924 21302, Fax: +62 924 21302

26. Christian Evangelical Church in Minahasa (GMIM) (4211)

Christianity came to the Minahasa in 1563 when the Portuguese sent a missionary who, after two weeks of preparations, baptized 1,500 people. The war with Ternate, which broke out in 1570, prevented the expansion of the mission to other regions of North Sulawesi where a request for missionaries had been made; as a result, in the next century these regions became Islamicized. Even in the Minahasa, the mission was continued only in a desultory way by the Portuguese and the Spaniards, their successors in the North Moluccas. When the Dutch arrived, what remained of the local Christians, about 2,500 souls, were protestantized (1666, cf. Gereja Protestan Maluku, no. 36, and Gereja Masehi Injili Sangir Talaud, no. 27). But the Dutch never placed a resident church minister in the Minahasa, as they did in Ambon. Thus until the 19th century the number of Christians did not increase, and Christian influence was so shallow that no fusion of the Christian faith and Minahasan religion took place and no Minahasan parallel of the "Ambonese religion" and the Moluccan Corpus Christianum developed.

In 1817 Joseph Kam (*see* GPM, no. 36) came to the Minahasa for the first time. He arranged for missionaries to be sent. In the next half century the Minahasa became the showpiece of the Dutch mission. In 1880 more than 80% of the population had been baptized and numbers of well-educated teacher-preachers were in charge of the congr. But no independent church was created, and around 1875 the congr were handed over to the established Protestant Church (*see* GPI). At the same time, the Rcath Mission penctrated into the Minahasa and became a competitor of Protestantism. Under the GPI regime the church continued to grow in numbers, and hundreds of Minahasan teacher-preachers brought the Gospel to mission fields in Central and Western Indonesia. But the church was not prepared for self-government and self-support. It was not until after 1927 that the combined pressure of nationalism and new insights within the mission (H. Kraemer) and the GPI rapidly led to independence. In 1934 the GMIM was instituted. One of the features of the Minahasa in those days was the openness of its people toward modernity and even secularism.

During the first years the Synod of the GMIM was still chaired by a Dutch minister. In 1942, however, the Minahasan minister, A. Z. R. Wenas, took his place. From 1942 until his death in 1967 he was the most visible and influential leader of the GMIM. During World War II he found a way to maintain reasonable relations with the Japanese authorities without renouncing the faith; in 1957-1961 he had to cope with the consequences of the PERMESTA rebellion against the central government. Both wars brought much destruction to the Minahasa, while the civil war of 1958-1961 created bitterness between individuals and villages. Another factor which threatened to tear apart Minahasan society was politics, especially the rise of the Communist party. As early as 1956 this church issued a manifesto against Marxist ideology; the church leadership consistently tried to maintain church unity in the midst of political strife. After 1971 political discord receded into the background, and the church had to face more practical problems caused by corruption, the introduction of large-scale lotteries, and the boom of the clove market which brought sudden wealth to the Minahasa. In the meantime, the church tried to adapt its order, rewriting it to give more autonomy to the local congr in 1951, and centralizing again 20 years later. The church has several hospitals and a large number of clinics; it is very active in school education. Besides the Universitas Kristen Tomohon, which was founded starting from the Theological Academy already there, the large lay training center in Kaaten should be mentioned. It publishes a magazine, *Warta GMIM*. The GMIM considers September 30, 1934, as its birth date.

TM: **632,705** CM: **200,000** Congr: **677** OrdM: **586** Eld: **nc** Deac: **nc** EvgHome: **nc** Mission: **nc** Women Ord: **yes** As Ministers: **307** as Deac: **nc** as Elders: **nc** ChurchOrg: **Presbyterian** Off/otherLang: **Indonesian** DoctrB: **ApC, NicC, AthC,** NatRel: **PGI, SAG** RegRel: **CCA** IntlRel: **WCC, WARC (1985)** TheolSchool: **Fakultas Theologia Universitas Kristen Tomohon** Service infrastructure: **several hospitals, a large number of clinics, lay training center (in Kaaten)** Periodicals: **Warta GMIM (magazine)**

Address: Gereja Masehi Injili di Minahasa (GMIM), P.O. Box 5, Tomohon Minahasa 95362, Indonesia, Tel: +62 431 35162, Fax: +62 4313 51036, E-mail: azer@manado.wasantara.net.id.

27. Sangir-Talaud Evangelical Church (GMIST) (4222)

The Gospel came to the Sangir archipelago at the same time and in the same way as to the Minahasa (cf. GMIM no. 26). Throughout the 18th century the number of Christians was larger, around 10,000, but the mission was later in returning to Sangir. In 1857 four carpenter missionaries came to Sangir; in 1859 four more started work in the Talaud Islands, more to the north. By that time Christianity had disappeared in Talaud. In Sangir the congr were still there, but they still followed the old EIC pattern, which was not to the liking of the pietist missionaries. The leading missionary was E. T. Steller, who with his own hands cleared the forest and laid out a plantation which became the center where leaders of the church and society were formed. A theocratic society was built, and the number of Christians increased from 20,000 in 1855 to 121,000 in 1936. Today 90% of the inhabitants of the Sangir-Talaud Islands belong to the GMIST. In 1921 the missionaries abandoned the paternalism that had been dominant until then. They ordained 16 indigenous ministers. In the beginning these ministers still functioned as a link in a hierarchical chain, but then the missionaries started discussing the building of a presbyterial structure. The process took much time; in 1947 the first Synod of the GMIST convened. Problems which the new church had to face were the relationships between the two island groups and with the Sangirese emigrants in Western Indonesia and in the Philippines. Like its sister church the GMIM, the GMIST made an experiment in granting more autonomy to the local congr (1961). By 1970 this experiment had matured even more radically than in the GMIM, but in 1978 the classis had to be restored. The church suffered much from the political tensions accompanying the rise and fall of the Indonesian Communist Party. Around 1984 a younger generation took over and the rising self-assurance of the Indonesian nation made itself felt in the church. Currently, the church has to cope with a secession movement on the northern islands, the Talaud archipelago. The Synod held in December 1996 agreed to the founding of an independent church in that region. The church has a large number of elementary and vocational schools and some clinics. It publishes a magazine, *Marimba*. The GKST considers May 15, 1947, as its birth date.

TM: **220,000** CM: **70,000** Congr: **355** OrdM: **122** Eld: **nc** Deac: **nc** EvgHome: **nc** Mission: **nc** Women Ord: **nc** ChurchOrg: **Presbyterian** Off/otherLang: **Indonesian, regional languages** DoctrB: **confessional passage in Church Order (1947)** NatRel: **PGI, SAG** RegRel: **CCA** IntlRel: **WCC, WARC (1985)** TheolSchool: **Theol. School (Tahuna, Sangir); Fakultas Theol. Univ. Kristen (Tomohon)** Service infrastructure: **elementary and vocational schools, clinics** Periodicals: **Marimba (magazine)**

Address: Gereja Masehi Injili in Sangir-Talaud (GMIST), P.O. Box 121, Tahuna, Sangir-Talaud Sulawesi Utara, Indonesia, Tel: +62 432 21370

28. Christian Evangelical Church in Timor (GMIT) (4212)

Christianity was brought to the Timor archipelago about 1550 by missionaries of the Dominican Order (OP). When the Dutch came (1613) they did not drive out the Catholic clergy, as they had done in the Moluccas. As a consequence, Catholicism and also the Portuguese could maintain themselves. Nowadays RCath in the region are three times as numerous as Prot. Kupang became the center of Protestantism, but as the region was not economically important to the Dutch, until the end of the 19th century development was slow, with the exception of a group movement on the island of Rote in the 1740s. About 1800 there were 10,000 Prot Christians. In the 19th century an attempt by a Dutch missionary society to effect a breakthrough failed. Only after 1900, when the colonial government had established an effective administration on Timor, did the Protestant Church start an active evangelistic program which adopted elements from the methods developed by the missionary societies. Between 1912 and 1938 the number of Prot Christians increased tenfold. During the 1930s preparations for church independence began, which were completed in 1947. In the 1950s a certain weariness dominated, but in the '60s the church experienced a great revival (1966-1969). Some of the causes were the general feeling of insecurity after the 1965 coup, and the influence of the charismatic movement which had its center in Batu, East Java. In a few years the GMIT membership doubled. After 1970 a period of consolidation began. The GMIT has a number of hospitals, homes for the elderly, orphanages, and social centers, and a large number of kindergartens. It publishes a tri-monthly, *Berita GMIT*. The church considers October 31, 1947, as its birth date.

TM: **850,000** BM: **830,000** CM: **700,000** Congr: **1,500** PStations: **1,390** OrdM: **439** Eld: **18,000** Deac: **14,500** EvgHome: **900** Mission: **2** Women Ord: **Yes** As Ministers: **1954/150** as Deac: **1947/7,500** as Elders: **1954/8,000** ChurchOrg: **nc** Off/otherLang: **Indonesian, Atoni, Savunese, Rotenese** DoctrB: **ApC, NicC, AthC** Infant or believer's baptism: **both** Frequency of the Lord's Supper: **4 times per year** Close relations with: **NHK (Netherlands), Presb Ch of Ireland, Uniting Ch (Australia), UCC (USA)** NatRel: **PGI (1950)** RegRel: **CCA** IntlRel: **WCC (1948), WARC (1950)** TheolSchool: **Fak. Theol. Univ. Kristen Artha Wacan (Kupang)** Service infrastructure: **4 hospitals, 2 social centers, 500 kindergartens, 7 nursing homes, orphanages, one bookshop** Periodicals: **Berita GMIT (gen/quarterly/nc)**

Address: Gereja Masehi Injili Timor (GMIT), P.O. Box 85228, Jalan Perintis Kemerdekaan, Walikota Baru, Kupang 85228 NTT, Indonesia, Tel: +62 391 32943, Fax: 0062 391 32943

29. Protestant Church in Indonesia (GPI) (4204)

In the 19th century the colonial state took over responsibility for the ± 50,000 Indonesian Prot Christians it had inherited from the Dutch East India Company (VOC). These Christians lived mainly in the Minahasa, the Moluccas, the Timor archipelago, and in the towns of Western Indonesia. They were organized into the Protestant Church in the Netherlands Indies. This church had a hierarchical structure, the ministers being appointed and transferred by the central Church Board (Kerkbestuur) in Batavia (Jakarta), and all costs, except poor relief, were borne by the government. The church had no confession of faith and was not supposed to proclaim the Gospel to non-Christians, as it was an organ of a neutral state. However, the Church Board wanted congr resulting from the activities of the missionary societies to be incorporated into the church, as indeed was done in the Minahasa (± 1875). In the early decades of the 20th century the church started missionary work in its traditional territories (Timor, Moluccas). The government tolerated these activities because it considered them as a preventive measure against Islam. As a result, in 1938 about 40% of Prot Christians in Indonesia belonged to the GPI. At the same time, the spiritual situation of the church improved thanks to an intensification of pastoral care and an influx of new members from the Netherlands. After protracted negotiations, in 1935 the administrative separation of church and state was implemented; in 1950 this process was completed when the Indonesian state relinquished its financial obligations toward the GPI. In 1936 the church adopted a new, more Presb church order, including a brief confessional formula which included the Apostles' Creed. In these years the congr in the Minahasa (1934), the Moluccas (1935) and Timor (1947) were allowed to form autonomous churches under the aegis of the Church Board; the congr in the towns of Western Indonesia were organized into a fourth church (GPIB, 1948). The GPI remained in existence as an umbrella organization. The Church Board even wanted the mission churches to join the GPI, so that the church would become the ecumenical organization of Indonesian Protestantism. However, history went a different way. The Indonesian churches founded a Council of Churches (DGI, from 1984 onward PGI), and even the bond with the autonomous churches within the GPI decreased to the point of becoming meaningless. The sixth and last General Synod of the GPI was held in 1956. Attempts in the 1980s to revive the unity of the GPI churches under the Church Board met with little or no response. However, the family of "Protestant" Churches, now numbering nine, still constitutes a separate strain within Indonesian Protestantism.

Address: Gereja Protestan di Indonesia (GPI), Jalan Medan Merdeka Timur 10, Jakarta-Pusat 10110, Indonesia, Tel: +62 21 351-9003, Fax: +62 21 385-9250

30. Protestant Church in West Indonesia (GPIB) (4208)

The GPIB is one of nine churches belonging to the "Protestant" church family in Indonesia (cf. General Introduction and GPI). It was founded in 1948 as the church of GPI members, mostly immigrants from Eastern Indonesia, in the towns of Western Indonesia. At the time the church still included a considerable number of European members and ministers. After the exodus of the Dutch in 1956-1957, the church became purely Indonesian. During the first decade of the GPIB, it still understood itself, colonial-style, as an organization for the pastoral care of the Christians who had immigrated from the traditional GPI areas into Western Indonesia. Gradually, however, the GPIB's sense of mission broadened to include missionary work among non-Christians (Central Kalimantan, 1973) and involvement in the life of the society and church in Indonesia as a whole. This meant that the lay people were given a clear place and task in the church. This was more important as the church had a proportionally great number of members in the government bureaucracy and in the army. This new self-understanding was incorporated into the church order of 1962, which was revised in 1972. The GPIB is active in the field of medical care and education, and it has homes for the elderly and orphanages. It publishes two weekly magazines, which contain homiletical materials and Bible studies respectively. The church considers October 31, 1948, as its birth date.

TM: **242,938** BM: **nc** CM: **132,168** Congr: **223** OrdM: **307** Eld: **2,868** Deac: **2,813** EvgHome: **30** Mission: **ne** Women Ord: **Yes** As Ministers: **1952/95** as Deac: **nc/1,298** as Elders: **nc/1,035** ChurchOrg: **Presbyterian (regional synods, general synod)** Off/otherLang: **Indonesian** DoctrB: **ApC, NicC, Pemahaman Iman GPIB** Infant or believer's baptism: **both** Frequency of the Lord's Supper: **4 times**

255

per year NatRel: **PGI, Indonesian Bible Society, Dutch Missionary Council** RegRel: **CCA** IntlRel: **WARC (1984)**, **WCC (1992)** TheolSchool: **Sekolah Tinggi Theologia (Jakarta)** Service infrastructure: **nursing homes, orphanages, foundation for health care** Periodicals: **Sabda Guna Dharma (homiletics/weekly/3,000)**, **Sabda Bina Umat (homiletics, liturgy/nc/5,000)**, **Sabda Guna Krida (Bible studies/nc/3,000)**

Address: Gereja Protestan di Indonesia Bagian Barat (GPIB), P.O. Box 10110, Medan Merdeka Timur 10, Jakarta-Pusat, Indonesia, Tel: +62 21 384-2895 or 384-9917, Fax: +62 21 385-9250

31. Indonesian Protestant Church in Buol Toli-Toli (GPIBT) (4205)

Buol Toli-Toli, in the northern arm of Sulawesi, was Islamicized in the 16th to 18th centuries. In the 19th century European and Indonesian (mostly Minahasan) Christians immigrated into the area. They were visited by Minahasan ministers of the established Protestant Church (GPI). In 1937 the region was transferred to the Minahasan Church (GMIM). Attempts by the GPI and the GMIM to bring the Gospel to the indigenous population failed, so that the church still consists of people who came from other parts of Indonesia. Because of the geographical distance, it was considered advisable that the church would not remain a part of the GMIM, so in 1965 the congr in the region were constituted into an independent church. The GPIBT has one kindergarten and one secondary school. There is no church magazine. The GPIBT considers April 4, 1965, as its birth date.

TM: **14,434** Congr: **43** OrdM: **28** Eld: **245** Deac: **125** EvgHome: **nc** Mission: **nc** Women Ord: **yes** As Ministers: **no** as Deac: **52** as Elders: **50** ChurchOrg: **Presbyterian** Off/otherLang: **Indonesian** DoctrB: **ApC, NicC, AthC** NatRel: **PGI, SAG** IntlRel: **WARC (1988)** Service infrastructure: **1 kindergarten, 1 secondary school**

Address: Gereja Protestan Indonesia di Buol Toli-Toli (GPIBT), P.O. Box 105, Jalan Kapten Piere Tendean 50, Kotakpos 105, Toli-Toli Sulawesi Tengah 94501, Indonesia, Tel: +62 453 21780

32. Indonesian Protestant Church in Donggala (GPID) (4206)

The history of the church in the Donggala region is similar to that in Buol Toli-Toli (cf. no. 31) and Gorontalo (cf. no. 33). However, the outreach to the indigenous inhabitants of the region was more successful here than in the neighboring regions. On April 7, 1965, the church became independent. It has three orphanages and a small number of schools (nursery and secondary). It has no magazine of its own. It considers financial and economic weakness as one of the main problems it faces. The GPID considers April 7, 1965, as its birth date.

TM: **23,959** BM: **22,823** Congr: **130** OrdM: **49** Eld: **440** Deac: **418** EvgHome: **nc** Mission: **ne** Women Ord: **Yes** As Ministers: **since beginning/13** as Deac: **since beginning/139** as Elders: **since beginning/ 149** ChurchOrg: **Presbyterian** Off/otherLang: **Indonesian** DoctrB: **ApC, NicC, AthC** Infant or believer's baptism: **both** Frequency of the Lord's Supper: **4 times per year** Close relations with: **NHK**

(Netherlands), GKN (Netherlands), EMS NatRel: PGI, SAG IntlRel: WARC (1965), WCC Service infrastructure: **3 orphanages, 8 kindergartens, 4 high schools** Periodicals: **none**

Address: Gereja Protestan Indonesia Donggala (GPID), Jalan Pattimura No. 5, Palu Sulawesi Tengah 94112, Indonesia, Tel: +62 451 22358

33. Indonesian Protestant Church in Gorontalo (GPIG) (4207)

The history of the church in the Gorontalo region is similar to that in Buol Toli-Toli and Donggala. On July 18, 1965, the congr in Gorontalo were constituted into an independent church.

TM: **14,185** Congr: **56** OrdM: **38** Eld: **na** Deac: **na** EvgHome: **nc** Mission: **nc** Women Ord: **yes** As Ministers: **18** as Deac: **nc** as Elders: **nc** ChurchOrg: **Presbyterian** Off/otherLang: **Indonesian** DoctrB: **ApC, NicC, AthC** NatRel: **PGI, GPI, SAG** IntlRel: **WARC (1982)**

Address: Gereja Protestan Indonesia di Gorontalo (GPIG), Kotak Pos 43, Jalan P. Kalengkongan 220, Gorontalo Sulawesi Utara 96101, Indonesia, Tel: +62 435 23815

34. Luwu Indonesian Protestant Church (GPIL) (4235)

Up to 1965 the history of Christianity in Luwu coincides with that of the Gereja Toraja, Luwu being part of the same mission field. However, not until 1930 was a missionary placed in Luwu proper. As the coastal areas had been Islamicized from the 17th century, the mission could only make headway in the mountain villages (first baptism April 21, 1918). After political independence was reached (1949), an Islam-inspired rebellion against the central government broke out. As a consequence the congr suffered, and some of the Christians had to settle in the coastal area. After order had been restored, the number of Christians in Luwu increased through immigration from the densely populated Toraja highlands. Regional feelings caused a number of Luwurese Christians to split off from the Gereja Toraja and constitute the GPIL. The church considers February 6, 1966, as its date of birth.

TM: **10,000** Congr: **98** OrdM: **17** Eld: **na** Deac: **na** EvgHome: **nc** Mission: **nc** Women Ord: **no** ChurchOrg: **Presbyterian** Off/otherLang: **Indonesian/Torajan** DoctrB: **nc** NatRel: **PGI** TheolSchool: **Theol. Institute (Palopo), STT INTIM (Ujung Pandang)**

Address: Gereja Protestan Indonesia Luwu (GPIL), Kotak Pos 113, Jl Veteran no. 83, Palopo 91923, Sulawesi Selatan, Indonesia, Tel: +62 471 23 616

35. Protestant Church of West Kalimantan (GPKB) (4252)

This church was founded by immigrants, mainly public officers originating from other regions in Indonesia, apparently because they did not feel at home in the existing Christian churches (Meth, Pent). Initially development was slow. In the

1990s the church reached out to the numerous Dayak people (15% of the population) and grew rapidly. In West Kalimatan 9% of the population are Prot, 20% RCath, and 52% Muslim. This church has no relations with any church or mission abroad.It considers February 10, 1963, as its birth date.

TM: **6,635** Congr: **19** OrdM: **6** Eld: **56** Deac: **ne** EvgHome: **nc** Mission: **nc** Women Ord: **yes** As Ministers: **1** as Deac: **6** as Elders: **na** ChurchOrg: **Presbyterian** Off/otherLang: **Indonesian** DoctrB: **no specific creeds in the Church Order** Close relations with: **none** NatRel: **PGI** RegRel: **none** IntlRel: **none** TheolSchool: **none** Periodicals: **none**

Address: Gereja Protestan Kalimantan Barat (GPKB), Jalan Rajawali 57, Pontianak 78112 Kalimantan Barat, Indonesia, Tel: +62 561 37523

36. Protestant Church in the Moluccas (GPM) (4210)

The territory of the GPM is the Central and South Moluccas. Christianity in its RCath form was brought here by the Portuguese (first baptism 1538). In 1605 the Dutch drove out the Portuguese and the Catholic clergy and Protestantized the indigenous Christians (on February 27, 1605, the first Prot church service was held ashore in the Moluccas and even in Asia). Ambon city and Banda became centers of a church which stretched from Ceram to the South Moluccas; here the Dutch ministers resided, six of them in Ambon alone at the end of the 17th century; here, too, a church council was formed. The villages, even on the central islands, were served by teacher-preachers with a modest education. Gradually they were provided with the materials needed for Christian education: a catechism (before 1625; the complete HeidC was translated into Malay as early as 1625); the New Testament (1668), the complete Bible (1733), and a Psalm Book (1735); and collections of sermons which the teacher-preachers were supposed to read before their congr. In this way Christianity became rooted in the Moluccan soil as a mixture of pre-Enlightenment European Christendom and traditional Moluccan religiosity ("agama Ambon," "religion of the Ambonese").

In the 19th century this Moluccan Christian community became the springboard for the mission work in the whole of eastern Indonesia. In 1815 the first NZG missionaries arrived in Indonesia. They were immediately enlisted by the established church. Joseph Kam was sent to Ambon. For 18 years (1815-1833) he had a powerful ministry in a large part of eastern Indonesia, bringing pietistic fervor to the old congr. Between 1840 and 1940 the Central Moluccas were a fertile recruiting ground for the missionary societies, who needed teacher-preachers for their mission fields in eastern Indonesia. These teacher-preachers were the backbone of the mission in the region, especially in the Southern Moluccas and in Irian. From about 1865 the mission terminated its activities in the Moluccas proper; however, in the next decade the established church improved its organization, intensified the care for the existing congr, and started missionary work in the Southern Moluccas. In this way the church was prepared for autonomy, which it gained in 1935. At first the GPM was within the Prot Church, and important decisions were subject to approval by the Church Board in Jakarta. However, after 1948 this bond became increasingly meaningless. Since 1950 the PGI became the channel for the ecumenical relations of the GPM with other churches within Indonesia.

During World War II the GPM suffered more than any other Indonesian church. As many as 54 church workers were killed by the Japanese, not including scores of Ambonese teacher-preachers in other parts of Indonesia. In 1944 buildings and archives of the church, the oldest Protestant Church in Asia, were lost when Ambon city suffered a heavy bombardment by the Allies. In 1950 heavy damage was suffered again when an insurrection against the central government was quelled. After that a period of consolidation began. The church order was revised in a presbyterian manner, the relation of the Christian faith with *adat* was reflected upon (1960 *Pesan Tobat*, "Message of Conversion"), theological education was raised to a higher standard, and the new congr on the southern islands were more and more integrated into the church. Problems facing the church are: the economic situation and its relation with the local Islamic population, which is rapidly making up for the lag in education and political influence, while the old Christian majority in the Central Moluccas is turning into a minority due to immigration from other islands. The GPM has a number of schools, mostly on the Southern Moluccas, and it is active in health care, with a hospital in Ambon City. The church considers September 6, 1935, as its birth date.

During the colonial era, including the years of armed struggle for national independence (1945-1949), many Moluccans served as soldiers in the colonial army. In 1950 the Dutch government brought 4,000 of these soldiers, with their families and their Ambonese army chaplains, to the Netherlands. There they continued the ecclesiastical tradition of their homeland.

TM: **453,978** CM: **nc** Congr: **796** OrdM: **625** Eld: **na** Deac: **na** EvgHome: **nc** Mission: **nc** Women Ord: **yes** As Ministers: **244** as Deac: **nc** as Elders: **nc** ChurchOrg: **Presbyterian** Off/otherLang: **Indonesian** DoctrB: **ApC, NicC, AthC, "Testimony of Reformation"** NatRel: **PGI** RegRel: **CCA** IntlRel: **WCC, WARC (1985)** TheolSchool: **Fakultas Theol. Univ. Kristen Indonesia Maluku (Ambon)** Service infrastructure: **schools, health care, one hospital**

Address: Gereja Protestan Maluku (GPM), Jalan Mayjend, D.I. Panjaitan 2, Ambon 97124 Maluku, Indonesia, Tel: +62 911 42442 or 52248, Fax: +62 911 43360

37. Protestant Church in Southeast Sulawesi (GEPSULTRA) (4224)

Christianity entered southeast Sulawesi for the first time in 1885-1887, when the RCath Mission had a post in Kendari. Around 1910 the Protestant Church had a congregation there, consisting of government officials and military. The Prot mission effort began in earnest in 1916, when Islam had already gained a foothold; so it had to fight an uphill battle. Only a small percentage of the population became Christian (first baptism September 1, 1918). During World War II the church suffered from the Japanese, the more so because the mission had not made preparations by ordaining ministers and registering property in the name of the congr. In 1950 a missionary and several church workers, who were traveling around to make preparations for church independence, were killed by Muslim guerillas. In 1957 the political situation had stabilized sufficiently for the GEPSULTRA to become constituted as an independent church. After 1968, when the Muslim rebellion had been stamped out, the central government started a development program which included the transmigration of large numbers of settlers from other provinces to sparsely populated southeast Sulawesi. As a result, the church now consists of elements belonging to 27 ethnic entities, among them Torajans, Javanese, and Balinese; its ministers belong to 12 ethnic entities. The number of Christians in the area attached to different churches has increased from 6,000 (1966) to 40,000 (1995), out of a total population of 1,400,000 now. A related problem was the great difference in agricultural methods between the indigenous population, including the Christians, still using slash-and-burn technology, and the new arrivals, who were familiar with sawah culture. The church responded with a village development program founded upon a "village theology," which brought together people of both categories and combined agricultural training with spiritual upbuilding. The GEPSULTRA has two orphanages, 1 elementary school, and 4 secondary schools. It publishes a magazine, *Bulletin Gepsultra*. The church considers February 10, 1957, as its birth date.

TM: **25,135** BM: **24,335** CM: **22,335** Congr: **88** PStations: **12** OrdM: **43** Eld: **435** Deac: **379** EvgHome: **29** Mission: **1** Women Ord: **yes** As Ministers: **1957/7** as Deac: **117** as Elders: **56** ChurchOrg: **Presbyterial-Synodal** Off/otherLang: **Indonesian/regional languages** DoctrB: **ApC, NicC** Infant or believer's baptism: **both** Frequency of the Lord's Supper: **6 times per year** NatRel: **PGI** RegRel: **CCA** IntlRel: **WARC (1982), WCC** TheolSchool: **Sekolah Tinggi Theol. INTIM (Ujung Pandang)** Service infrastructure: **2 orphanages, 1 elementary and 4 secondary schools** Periodicals: **Bulletin Gepsultra**

Address: Gereja Protestan di Sulawesi Tenggara (GEPSULTRA), P.O. Box 3, Jalan Dr. Ratulangi 121, Kendari 93121 Sulawesi Tenggara, Indonesia, Tel: +62 401 21506, Fax: +62 401 22626

38. Reformed Churches in Indonesia (GGRI)

Actually the GGRI consists of three regional churches, in Irian Jaya, Nusatenggara Timur, and West Kalimantan, which every four years meet together in conferences, and are pursuing greater unity through a General Synod to be convened for the first time in 1999. Two of these three churches have originated from mission work by the Gereformeerde Kerken in Nederland (Vrijgemaakt/Liberated, GKN(V)), which seceded from the Gereformeerde Kerken in Nederland (GKN) in 1944; the third came into existence through a split in the GKN Sumba mission which occurred in 1938.

A. Reformed Churches in Indonesia—Irian Jaya (GGRI-Irja) (4230)

In 1956 some local GKN(V) churches in the Netherlands and Canada decided to start a mission in an isolated and thinly populated region in southeast Irian (Upper

Digul). The Gospel was first proclaimed in that region on August 10, 1958. The first baptisms took place in 1967. Due to social structures prevailing in the region, conversions were individual, not in groups, while the first converts were young people. After 1969 new posts were opened, and through local migration congr sprang up also in the coastal cities of Irian. In villages where a number of Christians were found a provisional church council was installed, and when material and spiritual progress was considered sufficient a congregation was established. In 1976 for the first time classes were formed (at the moment there are 3 classes), and after delegates of the congr had met several times in preparatory conferences, the first general synod was held in 1988. The GGRI–Irian Jaya has a theological seminary in Boma. Schools and clinics have been surrendered to the Indonesian government.

TM: **4,000** Congr: **58** OrdM: **10** Eld: **115** Deac: **na** EvgHome: **30** Mission: **nc** Women Ord: **nc** ChurchOrg: **Presb** Off/otherLang: **Indonesian/local languages** DoctrB: **ApC, NicC, AthC, BelgC, CDort, HeidC** IntlRel: **ICRC** TheolSchool: **Sekolah Tinggi Theol. Ref. Injili Indonesia (Jakarta), Theol. Seminary (Boma)** Service infrastructure: **none**

Address: Gereja-Gereja Reformasi di Indonesia (GGRI), Kotak Pos 178, Abepura Irian Jaya, Indonesia, Tel: +62 967 71586, Fax: +62 967 71416, E-mail: kantorggri@MAF.org.

B. Reformed Churches in Indonesia—Nusatenggara Timur (GGRI-NTT) (4240)

Mission work on the island of Sumba started in 1881 (cf. Gereja Kristen Sumba no. 21). In 1938 one of the GKN missionaries was suspended, but most Christians in East Sumba remained loyal to this person and seceded from the GKN mission. After World War II a relationship was established between these congr and the GKN(V). Conflicts in the Netherlands (within the GKN(V)) and on Sumba led to a new schism. In 1976 the relation between GKN(V) and part of the Sumbanese congr was consolidated, the latter taking the name GGRI. The church has an agricultural center and a theological seminary at Wai Marangu (Melolo). There are also congr on the island of Sawu and in the provincial capital, Kupang.

TM: **4,200** Congr: **14** PStations: **38** OrdM: **10** Eld: **104** Deac: **20** EvgHome: **25** Mission: **na** Women Ord: **no** ChurchOrg: **Reformed (congr, classis, regional synod)** Off/otherLang: **Indonesian** DoctrB: **ApC, NicC, AthC, CDort, HeidC, HelvC, WestConf** Infant or believer's baptism: **both** Frequency of the Lord's Supper: **4 times per year** Close relations with: **GGRI in Iryan Jaya and West Kalimantan, Free Ref Chs in the Netherlands, Free Ref Ch of Australia** NatRel: **National Conference of Reformed Churches in Indonesia (1974) (meets every 4 years)** RegRel: **none** IntlRel: **none** TheolSchool: **Theological School (1980—Wai Marangu, East Sumba)** Service infrastructure: **social service organizations, hospital** Periodicals: **Church Bulletin (gen/monthly/600)**

Address: Gereja-Gereja Reformasi di Indonesia (GGRI), P. Hawu, Melolo-Waingapu 87181Sumba Timur NTT, Indonesia

C. Reformed Churches in Indonesia—Kalimantan Barat (GGRI-Kalbar) (4251)

The GGRI Kalimantan Barat originates from mission work by two GKN(V) churches in the Netherlands, which was started in 1949. Between 1960 and 1993 eight local churches were established. As in the other GGRI churches, the autonomy of the local church was a central issue. Since 1983 contacts exist with the sister churches in Irian and Sumba. The church has a theological seminary at Sentagi (Bengkayang).

TM: **3,000** Congr: **19** OrdM: **6** Eld: **na** Deac: **na** EvgHome: **na** Mission: **nc** Women Ord: **yes** As Ministers: **none** as Deac: **nc** as Elders: **nc** ChurchOrg: **Presbyterian** Off/otherLang: **Indonesian** DoctrB: **ApC, NicC, AthC, CDort, HeidC,** NatRel: **Konperensi nasional GGRI** TheolSchool: **Theological Seminary (Sentagi, Bengkayang)**

Address: Gereja-Gereja Reformasi di Indonesia Kalimantan Barat, Sentagi/Bengkayang 79182 Kalimantan Barat, Indonesia, Tel: +62 362 41 416

39. Reformed Evangelical Church (GRII) (4234)

The GRII is one of the churches which sprang from SAAT, a theological institute in Malang, East Java, founded in 1952. Stephen Tong (1940, Amoy), a lecturer at SAAT and minister of the Gereja Kristus Tuhan and Gereja Kristen Abdiel, became convinced of the value of Ref doctrine for the Christian church in our times. In 1986 he founded the Lembaga Reformed Injili Indonesia (LRII, Indonesian Evangelical Reformed Foundation), and in 1989 the GRII, followed by the Sekolah Tinggi Theologi Reformed Injili Indonesia (Reformed Theological Seminary) in 1991 and the Reformed Institute for Christianity and the Cultural Mandate in Jakarta and Washington, D.C. (1966).

For direct evangelization there exists a Stephen Tong Evangelistic Ministry International (STEMI, begun in 1987, formally founded in 1986) that conducts evangelistic meetings and annual lay theological seminars in Taipeh, Hong Kong, Singapore, Jakarta, etc. The more specific goal of all these institutions is to spread orthodox Ref doctrine, especially among the well-educated, in order to give a solid doctrinal basis to evangelical and charismatic Christianity. This endeavor is supported by publishing activities through the LRII and the publishing house, Momentum.

The GRII has congr in 5 Indonesian cities and among Indonesian citizens in Melbourne and Taipei. The number of attendants at Sunday services is over 3,000, of whom 1,400 are baptized members. The congr are led by church councils; as yet there are no ordained elders and deacons. Part of the money collected in the church services is used to support the evangelistic enterprise among students and intellectuals (Campus Crusade, IVF, etc.). The church and its affiliated institutions have woman evangelists, lecturers, and church council members, but as yet no ordained woman ministers.

TM: **2,000** Congr: **8** OrdM: **12** Eld: **na** Deac: **na** EvgHome: **na** Mission: **na** Women Ord: **no** ChurchOrg: **Presbyterian** Off/otherLang: **Indonesian, Mandarin** DoctrB: **Pemahaman Iman GRII (Indonesian Statement of Faith)** TheolSchool: **Sekolah Tinggi Theologi Reformed Injili (Jakarta); in the USA: Reformed Theological Seminary (Jacksonville, MI), Calvin Seminary, and Westminster Seminary**

Address: Gereja Reformed Injili Indonesia (GRII), Jl Tanah Abang III/1, Jakarta 10160, Indonesia, Tel: +62 21 381 0912, Fax: +62 21 381 1021

40. Toraja Church (GT) (4242)

The Toraja country in the southern part of the central highlands of Sulawesi warded off Islamicization during the 17th through 19th centuries, but with the establishment of Dutch authority in 1906 the region was opened to foreign influences. In 1912-1913 the established Protestant Church started a mission, which resulted in a first group baptism on March 16, 1913. In the same year a Dutch mission body, the conservative Calvinist Gereformeerde Zendingsbond, took over. Until 1942 the GZB made a sustained and well-organized effort to bring Christianity to Tana Toraja and to make preparations for the founding of an independent church starting with the congr. Church councils on the local and classis level were constituted, and in 1941, when there were about 15,000 baptized Christians, the first congregation was declared independent and called its own minister. World War II interrupted the process of building a church starting from these congr. In March 1947 a synod was convened and the Toraja Church was constituted, which included all congr. In the 1950s the church suffered heavily because of an Islam-inspired rebellion against the central government. At the same time tens of thousands entered the church because they were faced with the choice: Islam or Christianity. In the '60s peace returned, and the church entered on a phase of consolidation. It established itself as the church of the (Sa'dan) Toraja people, including about 70% of those who consider themselves Torajans, 10% belonging to the RCath Church, and 10% still adhering to the ancestral religion. It has also founded congr among emigrants to the cities outside Toraja land, in Sulawesi, Kalimantan, and Java.

The church has retained the moderate stance toward local culture taken by the mission, and it devotes much energy to thinking and living the relation between that culture and the Christian faith. In the church order of 1947, the Heidelberg Catechism, Belgic Confession, and Canons of Dordt were introduced as the confessions of the church, but in 1981 the Synod accepted a new confession of faith drafted by Toraja theologians. In 1984 women were admitted to church office (deacons, elders, ministers). The Gereja Toraja still maintains a cordial relationship with the founding mission, but it has also entered into relation with other churches and missions abroad. The Gereja Toraja has two hospitals, an orphanage, a number of schools, and a training center for women motivators in the villages. It publishes a magazine, *Berita Gereja Toraja*. The church considers March 25, 1947, as its birth date.

TM: **300,000** Congr: **709** PStations: **250** OrdM: **239** Eld: **na** Deac: **na** EvgHome: **nc** Mission: **nc** Women Ord: **yes** As Ministers: **1984/25** as Deac: **1984/nc** as Elders: **1984/nc** ChurchOrg: **Presbyterian** Off/otherLang: **Indonesian/Torajan** DoctrB: **ApC, NicC, AthC, HeidC, "Confession of the Toraja Church" (1981)** NatRel: **PGI** RegRel: **CCA** IntlRel: **WCC, WARC** TheolSchool: **Sekolah Tinggi Theologia Gereja Toraja (Rantepao), Sekolah Tinggi Theologia INTIM (Ujung Pandang)** Service infrastructure: **2 hospitals, 1 orphanage, schools, training center for women motivators** Periodicals: **Berita Gereja Toraja (magazine)**

Address: Gereja Toraja (GT), Jalan Jenderal Ahmad Yani 45, Rantepao—Tana Toraja 91831 Sulawesi Selatan, Indonesia, Tel: +62 423 21460 and 21539, Fax: +62 423 21742

41. Toraja Mamasa Church (GTM) (4236)

While the coastal areas of Sulawesi were Islamicized between the 17th and 19th century, the inhabitants of the central highlands adhered to their ancestral religion. When the established Protestant Church started missionary work in the highlands after 1910, it also sent preachers to Mamasa and the neighboring districts in the southwestern part of Central Sulawesi (first baptism 1913). One Dutch minister and a number of Ambonese and Minahasan teacher-preachers worked here until 1928, following the usual Protestant method of Christianization by mass baptism as a preventive measure against Islamicization. In 1928, when this area was taken over by the mission of the Christelijke Gereformeerde Kerken (CGK), a conservative Calvinist church body in the Netherlands, the mission made a fresh start, recognizing baptisms administered by its predecessor but counting as Christians only those who went through an intensive process of religious education. The church organization was built up in the same systematic way as in the neighboring GZB mission field (cf. Gereja Toraja no. 40). The elders especially were carefully selected and prepared for their task before they were ordained. GZB and CGK intended the congr on their respective mission fields to coalesce into one church, and in fact around 1950 the church in Mamasa was considered as a regional synod of the Christian Toraja Church. However, several factors, among them the long isolation caused by the Muslim guerilla action between 1950 and 1965, which brought much suffering, caused the Gereja Toraja Mamasa to consider itself as an independent church. After 1965 the church entered upon a phase of reconstruction and consolidation. Around 1982, however, most congr in the northern region of Galumpang seceded and formed a regional church, which took the name Gereja Protestan Sulawesi Selatan. The GTM is active in education, health care (hospital in Mamasa), and agricultural development, and has lay training programs. The church considers June 7, 1947, as its birth date.

TM: **80,000** CM: **36,000** Congr: **353** PStations: **38** OrdM: **73** Eld: **nc** Deac: **na** EvgHome: **2** Mission: **ne** Women Ord: **yes** As Ministers: **1992/8** as Deac: **nc** as Elders: **nc** ChurchOrg: **congr, presby, synod** Off/otherLang: **Indonesian, Torajan** DoctrB: **ApC, HeidC** Infant or believer's baptism: **both** Frequency of the Lord's Supper: **4 times per year** Close relations with: **ZCGK, EMS** NatRel: **PGI** IntlRel: **REC, WARC (1996)** Service infrastructure: **education, health care, one hospital** Periodicals: **Buletin Prog GTM (monthly/400)**

Address: Gereja Toraja Mamasa (GTM), Kab. Polmas, Kecamatan Mamasa, Sulawesi Selatan 91362, Indonesia

42. Minahasa Protestant Church Assemblies (KGPM) (4237)

The origins of the KGPM are closely related to the attempts of Minahasan Christians to reorganize the Protestant Church in Minahasa to become an independent church (cf. GMIM no. 26). When it turned out that the GMIM was to became an autonomous church under the supervision of the Dutch-dominated GPI Church Board, a number of anti-colonial Minahasans seceded and founded an independent church, not tied to the GPI and the government. As both considered the KGPM illegal, relations with the GMIM were strained. The tensions continued after national independence; as a result, not until 1979 could the KGPM join the Indonesian Council of Churches (PGI). Nevertheless, in the case of doctrine and worship there never was any difference between the KGPM and the GMIM. During the regional PERMESTA rebellion (cf. GMIM), the nationalist past of the KGPM made itself visible in the anti-regionalist stance taken by the church. As for the form of church administration, KGPM in the beginning submitted to congregationalism. Currently, however, the church does not follow the rules of this system but rather seeks a church administration which is colored by a central leadership. Typical of the structure of the church is that there are two boards of leadership, one for organizing business and one for the ministry of the Word of God on all levels (center, district, and congregation). The church has a number of schools from kindergarten to secondary school level and a number of agricultural training centers. The church considers October 29, 1933, as its birth date.

TM: **47,767** Congr: **165** OrdM: **87** Eld: **na** Deac: **na** EvgHome: **nc** Mission: **nc** Women Ord: **nc** ChurchOrg: **Congregational** Off/otherLang: **Indonesian** DoctrB: **ApC, NicC** NatRel: **PGI (1979)** TheolSchool: **Fakultas Theologia Univ. Kristen Tomohon** Service infrastructure: **schools of all levels, agricultural training centers**

Address: Kerapatan Gereja Protestan Minahasa (KGPM), Kotak Pos 1239, Jalan Sea Malalayang Satu, Manado 95012 Sulawesi Utara, Indonesia, Tel: +62 431 65941

43. Communion of Protestant Christian Church of Nias (ONKP) (4255)

Protestant missions in the island of Nias started in 1865 (RMG). At the time, the population of the island (now over 500,000, of whom 73% are Prot, 18% RCath, and 7% Muslim) adhered to the ancestral religion. Until 1900, when the Dutch colonial power came in, growth was slow (706 in 1890). From 1916 to 1929 the Christian community on Nias experienced a great revival which resulted in accelerated growth. In 1936 the first Synod of the Banua Niha Keriso Protestan (BNKP, Christian Church of Nias, 1996 340,000 members) convened. After several secessions had occurred (cf. AMIN, BNKP), a number of congr split off from the BNKP in 1952, under the leadership of four ministers, because they felt neglected, especially in the field of pastoral care. However, traditional social structures played a role, for the ONKP membership belongs in great part to two clans. The congr are independent in financial matters. The relationship with the BNKP was long strained. The church considers April 16, 1952, as its birthday.

TM: **57,000** Congr: **179** OrdM: **40** Eld: **na** Deac: **na** EvgHome: **nc** Mission: **nc** Women Ord: **yes** As Ministers: **1** as Deac: **na** as Elders: **na** ChurchOrg: **nc** Off/otherLang: **Indonesian** DoctrB: **nc** NatRel: **PGI**

Address: Orahua Niso Keriso Protestan (ONKP), Pusat Tagala Lahomi, Kecamatan Sirombu, Kab Nias 22863 Sumatera Utara, Indonesia

44. Church of Christ (GK) (4264)

Spreading the Gospel among the Chinese immigrants in Indonesia, who have lived there from at least the beginning of the colonial era, was only begun in earnest in the second half of the 19th century. In a number of cities in the island of Java, small congr sprang up, which cooperated with Dutch missionaries. In 1905, the Episcopal Methodists' Board of Missions started work in West Java. When the Methodists left Java again (1927), the congregation which had formed in the Manggabesar area of Jakarta became independent, with the name Tiong Hoa Kie Tok Kauw Hwee (THKTKH, January 1928, in 1939 the name changed into CHCTCH). What moved them to opt for a separate existence was not only their Meth background, but also a difference in cultural (Malay or Mandarin) and political (Netherlands Indies or China) orientation. However, there was a gradual adaptation to the Indonesian environment.

In 1950, the CHCTCH was among the founding members of the Council of Churches in Indonesia (DGI/PGI; the church did not join any international denominational or ecumenical organization). In 1958 the church took an Indonesian name, Gereja Kristus, and in 1963 it adopted a presbyterial-synodal church order instead of the congregationalist structure it had had up to that year.

Of its 17 congr in West Java and Southern Sumatra, 9 are in Metropolitan Jakarta. Only in one of these is Mandarin still in use besides Indonesian. The Lord's Supper is celebrated four times a year, as in most churches. The church has a theological school in Cipanas (West Java), a number of elementary and secondary schools, and several medical and social facilities. It considers June 12, 1939, as its birthday.

TM: **18,000** Congr: **17** OrdM: **51** Eld: **nc** Deac: **nc** EvgHome: **nc** Mission: **nc** Women Ord: **yes** As Ministers: **5** as Deac: **na** as Elders: **na** ChurchOrg: **Presbyterian-Synodal** Off/otherLang: **Indonesian, Mandarin** DoctrB: **ApC** Close relations with: **Gereja Kristen Indonesia** NatRel: **PGI** IntlRel: **none** TheolSchool: **STT Cipanas; STT Jakarta; Duta Wacana (Yogyakarta); SAAT (Malang); III (Batu Malang)**

Address: Gereja Kristus (GK), Jalan Patra Raya I-I, Duri Kepa, Jakarta 11440, Indonesia, Tel: +62 21 911-0536, Fax: +62 21 563-4118

45. Indonesian Protestant Church in Irian Jaya (GPIIJ) (4261)

In 1912 the colonial government decided that northern New Guinea was to remain an exclusively Prot mission field, while the southern half of the island was reserved for the Catholic missions. In 1928, however, the latter started work in Prot territory, whereupon the Protestant Church invaded the regions of Fak-Fak and Merauke in the south. In 1935, when the Protestant Church in the Moluccas (GPM no. 36) was given autonomy, these regions were incorporated into the GPM. However, as the center of the church in Ambon was far away and an increasingly large part of the membership belonged to the indigenous population of Irian, the GPM classes in Irian became an independent church (May 25, 1985).

TM: **30,000** Congr: **169** OrdM: **86** Eld: **nc** Deac: **0** EvgHome: **nc** Mission: **nc** Women Ord: **no** As Ministers: **no** as Deac: **nc** as Elders: **nc** ChurchOrg: **Presbyterian** Off/otherLang: **Indonesian, local languages** DoctrB: **ApC, NicC, AthC, "Pemahaman Iman Gereja Protestan di Indonesia"** Close relations with: **Gereja Protestan di Indonesia** IntlRel: none TheolSchool: **Fak. Theol. Univ. Kristen Indonesia Maluku (Ambon); STT INTIM (Ujung Pandang)**

Address: Gereja Protestan Indonesia di Irjan Jaya (GPIIJ), Jalan Jenderal A. Yani, Kotak Pos 39, Fak-Fak, Irian Jaya, Indonesia, Tel: +62 956 22426

46. Indonesian Christian Church of South Sulawesi (GKISS) (4265)

The GKISS has an ethnic Chinese background, like its sister church in Java (GKI). Groups of Chinese Christians sprang up for the first time in South Sulawesi about 1930. In 1932 the "Min Nan Kie Tok Kauw Hwee" (classis of South Sulawesi) was formed. In 1963 the classis took the name of GKISS. However, until 1972 there was only one congregation — in Ujung Pandang, the capital city of South Sulawesi. A synod was not convened until 1980; GKISS considers this year as its birth date. In 1997 this church had 4 congr and seven preaching stations in Southern and Central Sulawesi. In 1994 this church joined the council of Churches of Indonesia (PGI). It also maintains special ties with other churches in the region, mainly of Chinese background. The church owns a radio station, CRISTY RIA, as a means of evangelization as well as a magazine, *Sola Gratia*.

TM: **2,200** Congr: **4** PStations: **7** OrdM: **4** Eld: **15** Deac: **15** EvgHome: **11** Mission: **nc** Women Ord: **yes** As Ministers: **0** as Deac: **5** as Elders: **no** ChurchOrg: **Presbyterian** Off/otherLang: **Indonesian/ Mandarin** DoctrB: **ApC** NatRel: **PGI** RegRel: none IntlRel: none TheolSchool: **institutions in Sulawesi and Java** Service infrastructure: **kindergartens to high schools, radio station CRISTY RIA** Periodicals: **Sola Gratia**

Address: Gereja Kristen Indonesia Sulawesi Selatan (GKISS), Jalan Samiun 17, Ujung Pandang 90111 Sulsel, Indonesia, Tel: +62 411 319-622, 322-984, Fax: +62 411 326-871

47. Holy Word Christian Church (GKKK) (4268)

Like the GRII (cf. no. 39), the Gereja Kristen Kalam Kudus is one the churches which sprang from the Gereja Kristus Tuhan (cf. no. 22) and its theological Institute SATT in Malang, East Java, which was founded in 1952. Also like the GRII, the GKKK belongs to the Reformed Evangelical denomination. The church originated around 1965 in Javanese villages in the Malang area, East Java, but now most congregations are in the cities and most members are ethnic Chinese. The church has no classes (presby); the deputies of the 16 congregations convene directly in a national synod. Educational activities are considered very important as a means of evangelization; in fact several congregations have sprung from schools founded by GKKK members. The church publishes a magazine, *Solid*. It considers February 25, 1987, as its date of birth.

TM: **13,477** BM: **nc** CM: **nc** Congr: **16** OrdM: **20** Eld: **na** Deac: **na** EvgHome: **na** Mission: **na** Women Ord: **nc** ChurchOrg: **Presbyterian/synodal** Off/otherLang: **Indonesian** DoctrB: **Reformed Evangelical** Infant or believer's baptism: **nc** NatRel: **PGI** RegRel: **nc** IntlRel: **nc** TheolSchool: **Sekolah Alkitab Asia Tenggara, Malang** Periodicals: **Solid** (mag)

Address: Gereja Kristen Kalam Kudus, Jl Tangkilio Timur No. 48-49, Jakarta 1170, Indonesia, Tel: +62 21 649 5147, Fax: +62 21 601 0840

48. Indonesian Gospel Tabernacle Church (GKII) (4266)

The GKII belongs to the "Alliance" family. The founder of the Alliance movement was A.B. Simpson, a minister of the Presbyterian Church in New York, who first laid down his ministry because he wanted to devote himself to the poor and sinners, and subsequently left the Presbyterian Church because he had been persuaded that baptism could only be administrated to adults. In 1897 the Christian and Missionary Alliance (CMA) was founded. Its doctrine can be summarized in four short sentences: Jesus Christ saves; Jesus Christ sanctifies; Jesus Christ heals; Jesus Christ will come again as Lord. The fourth sentence includes the adoption of chiliastic doctrine.

The conviction that Christ will come again soon gives the CMA a strong missionary impetus. The mother organization in America had to be as simple as possible, and on the mission field all energy had to be directed to direct preaching of the Gospel. Consequently no costly institutions, such as schools and hospitals, were to be founded.

In 1926 the CMA Board in New York decided to start missionary work in what was then the Netherlands Indies. When it seemed this decision would not be implemented because of lack of funds, Robert A. Jaffray (1873-1945), who from 1897 until 1927 worked in South China and had received reports about the thousands of Chinese immigrants in southeast Asia, together with Chinese Christians founded the Chinese Foreign Mission Union (CFMU, president Leland Wang, vice president/treasurer R. A. Jaffray). Beginning in 1928 the CFMU sent several Chinese missionaries to Indonesia, who worked mainly among Chinese immigrants in urban areas but baptized more than 2,000 tribal people in the Mahakam area of East Kalimantan. In 1930 Jaffray himself settled in Makassar (now Ujungpandang). It became the center of CMA work in Indonesia, which was mainly among ethnic Indonesians.

Within a few years, missionary work was begun in a number of regions which were not or hardly touched by the Dutch and German missionary societies working in the colony, such as East Kalimantan (1929, George Fisk and David Clench), Lombok (1929, J. Wesley Brill), Bali (1931, Tsang To Hang), Southern Sumatra (1933, David Griffin), West Kalimantan (1935, D. A. Patty and Luther Adipatty), Sumbawa (1937, S.W. Chu), Malaya (1937, Tsang To Hang and Gustave Woerner), North Kalimantan (1937, Einar Mickelson), West Irian (Paniai region 1939, W. Post and R. Deibler; Baliem Valley 1954, E. Mickelson, Elisa and Ruth Gobai). Eventually, East Kalimantan and Irian became the most important fields from a statistical point of view.

In this mission work, students and graduates from the Bible School which in 1932 was opened in Makassar took an important part. In some cases it was these students who opened up new mission fields. Another important general tool was colportage, the materials for which were provided by the publishing house Kantor (1930). The CAMA magazine was *Kalam Hidup*, with P. H. Pouw as editor. Pouw also published a hymnbook, *Nafiri Perak* (The Silver Trumpet). In East Kalimantan, the work was particularly blessed, so that a second Bible School was founded there (1938). It used the same simple facilities as had been applied by Jaffray at the Makassar Bible School, so that the students might not become alienated from the environment they came from and were destined for. In 1939 Fisk was the first missionary in Indonesia to use a plane in the service of the mission, to overcome the difficulties of traveling in the jungle.

The mission fields mentioned above were mainly inhabited by adherents to tribal religions, sometimes by Muslims (Lombok, Sumbawa) or Hindus (Bali). In Sumatra and Malaysia missionary work was directed to isolated ethnic groups which had not embraced Islam. Because of lack of funds and personnel, the Dutch and German mission bodies, weighed down by educational and medical work, had not started work in these fields. However, as a number of Bible School students originating from christianized regions returned there to bring the Gospel as they had come to understand it, CMA churches came into existence in those regions, too (Toraja, Minahasa, Alor). Even preceding this development, the Dutch mission held the CMA in low esteem because of the supposedly low level of its theological education and its "American" methods. The colonial government was mainly interested in preventing unrest. For that reason, in 1934 the CMA workers were expelled from Bali. In 1941 CMA worked in 139 places. There were 11,694 baptized members, served by 20 foreign and 140 Indonesian workers; the Bible School in Makassar had 209 students, and there were 13 lower-level Bible Schools with 479 students.

During World War II, the work survived without funds from abroad and sometimes under heavy Japanese pressure. Four Americans and ten Indonesian workers were killed, and two more Americans, including Jaffray, died in Japanese internment. The CMA churches had to join the regional councils of Christian

Churches (*Kiristokyo Rengokai*) set up by the Japanese. After the war, the work continued to expand, including to other Christianized regions (Eastern Sunda Islands, Sangir-Talaud) and to Java, where in 1981 an ambitious program was launched to found 500 new congr within 10 years. In 1947 for the first time inhabitants of the Paniai region, Irian Jaya, were baptized; in 1964 the Ekagi New Testament was published. In 1954 the first CMA missionaries entered the Baliem Valley (Irian), by plane. More Bible Schools were founded; in 1987 there were 19 of them. The central Bible School in Ujungpandang was upgraded and became Jaffray Bible College (1958) and Sekolah Tinggi Theologia [Theological Academy] Jaffray (1966). The mass media, including radio, continued to be used extensively. Church workers from 1967 onward had their own journal for pastors, the *Sahabat Gembala*. In 1951 the CMA congr were assembled into three regional churches, in East Indonesia, East and West Kalimantan. Five years later, the Indonesian daughter churches were considered to have reached maturity. The foreign workers were put under the supervision of these churches; at the same time the CMA stopped the allowances which until then were given to a great number of Indonesian church workers. However, the Indonesian Church and the CMA, though separated organizationally, continued to cooperate closely.

In 1965 the regional churches entered into a fellowship named the Kemah Injil Gereja Masehi Indonesia (KINGMI), which in 1983 was transformed into a united church named Gereja Kemah Injil Indonesia (GKII), with its central office in Jakarta. The regional churches which made up the united church were:

1. GKII Bahagian Timur (KINGMIT, 21,000 members),
2. GKII Kalimantan Timur (98,000), GKII Kalimantan Barat (62,000),
3. GKII Toraja (Kerapatan Injil Bangsa Indonesia, ca. 40,000),
4. GKII Bahtera Injil Menado (6,500),
5. GKII Irian Jaya (138,000),
6. GKII Jawa-Sumatera (3,000).

(Membership figures are given for 1990 and include those not yet baptized.) The Board was all-Indonesian; first chairman was Matias Abai, from East Kalimantan. The congr which had originated from the CFMU mission kept apart and formed several independent churches. The GKII has not joined the Indonesian Council of Churches, but it is a full member of the Indonesian Evangelical Fellowship (PII) and of the Alliance World Fellowship which was formed in 1975. Once every four years conferences of the Alliance Churches in Asia are held.

TM: **323,288** Congr: **1,661** PStations: **334** OrdM: **783** Eld: **nc** Deac: **nc** EvgHome: **1,698** Mission: **nc** Women Ord: **yes** As Ministers: **1961** as Deac: **nc** as Elders: **nc** ChurchOrg: **social service centers, kindergartens** Off/otherLang: **Indonesian** DoctrB: **ApC** Infant or believer's baptism: **believer** Frequency of the Lord's Supper: **monthly** NatRel: **PII** RegRel: **Evangelical Fellowship of Asia** IntlRel: **Alliance World Fellowship** Periodicals: **Bulletin Kemah Injil (gen/quarterly/1,000), Kalam Hidup (bi-monthly/7,000), Sahabat (bi-monthly/7,000)**

Address: Gereja Kemah Injil Indonesia (GKII), Jl Jambrut 24, Kelurahan Kenari, Jakarta 10430, Indonesia, Tel: +62 21 314-2148

IRAN

Area in km²	1,648,000
Population	(est. July 1996) 66,940,244 Persian 51%, Asserbaidjani 24%, Kurdish 7%, others 18%
Religions in %	Muslim 99% (Shi'a 89%, Sunni 10%), Zoroastrian, Jews, Baha'i, Christian 1%
Official/other languages	Persian 58%, Turkish 26%, Kurdish 7%, other 9%

There are three churches of the Ref tradition presently in this country. They find their origin in the work of American missionaries sent by the Presbyterian Church. Until the Second World War they were linked with the mission work in Pakistan.

They differentiate by language and culture and are today regrouped together under the overall umbrella of the Evangelical Church of Iran. Since the "Islamic Revolution" of 1979 their situation has become more tense. They are members of the Middle East Council of Churches (MECC) and of the Fellowship of Middle East Evangelical Churches (FMEEC).

Evangelical Church of Iran (4300)

TM: **3,100** Congr: **41** PStations: **4** RegRel: **FMEEC, MECC** IntlRel: **WARC**

Address: Klesoy Injili Iran, P.O. Box 11365-4464, Teheran, Iran, Tel: +98 21 674097, Fax: +98 21 674095

IRAQ

See also GULF REGION

Area in km²	437,072
Population	(est. July 1996) 21,422,292 Arab 75%-80%, Kurdish 15%-20%, Turkoman, Assyrian, or other 5%
Religions in %	Muslim 97% (Shi'a 60%-65%, Sunni 32%-37%), Christian or other 3%
Official/other languages	Arabic, Kurdish, Assyrian, Armenian

The Christian message reached the region of Iraq in the first century. According to tradition, the founder of the Christian community was the apostle Thomas. Church structures developed under the patriarch of Antioch in the 4th century, but a century later the church in Mesopotamia declared itself independent from Antioch and subsequently became almost entirely Nestorian. Until the 10th century the Nestorians were involved in energetic missionary activity toward the east; but Islam, which entered the country in the 7th century, became increasingly more important.

From the 13th century onward, Latin missionaries made strenuous efforts toward obtaining Nestorian reunion with Rome. They were partly successful; in 1553 the Uniate Chaldean Catholic Church was established in Baghdad. A Latin diocese was formed in 1632, but no resident Latin bishop was permitted until 1820. RCath (Chaldean, Syrian, and Armenian) are today the largest Christian community in Iraq (70%).

The Ancient Church of the East, or the Assyrian Church, is the oldest Christian church in Iraq. Together with the Syrian Orthodox Church, the Armenian Apostolic Church, and the Greek Orthodox Church, they form a strong presence in the country. Protestantism made its appearance in the 19th century.

The Evangelical Churches of Iraq (4303)

The earliest Prot mission in Iraq was launched by the London Jews Society in 1820. In 1850 the ABCFM, representing Presb and Congreg, opened a mission station in Mosul. The Church Missionary Society (Anglican) entered in 1882 and was active until World War I. The Arabian Mission of the Ref Church in America (cf. United States no. 36) entered Basra in 1889, initiating work which, during the 1920s, received support from two other American denominations — the Evangelical and Reformed Church, and the United Presbyterian Church in the USA (the church in the northern United States before the reunion in 1983). The United Mission, as it was later called, was joined in 1957 by yet a fourth body, the Presbyterian Church in the USA (the church in the southern USA before the reunion of 1983).

Strongly involved in educational work, the United Mission had little success in the evangelistic sphere. The result was basically four separate Evangelical (Presb-Ref) congr in Baghdad, Kirkuk, Basra, and Mosul, all served by Egyptian pastors. There are two Evangelical churches in Baghdad and Mosul, which are independent of each other. The Armenian Evangelical Church is related to the Union of Armenian Evangelical Churches and consists of one small congregation in Baghdad.

There have been a variety of other Prot churches in Iraq, with some relative degree of success in the years immediately preceding the Iran-Iraq War and the Gulf War. Those included the Assembly of God, the Basra Assembly, the Evangelical Alliance of Mission, and the Adventists. In 1969 all American missionaries were expelled from the country and their schools nationalized or closed. However, the churches continued to function under national leadership.

Iraq has been largely isolated from the international community since the Gulf War of 1991 and the subsequent sanctions imposed by the United Nations at the instigation of the United States. As a result, contact with the churches has been impossible. Statistics and information about the status of these churches and how well they are functioning are therefore not known.

No statistical data have been made available.

Address: Evangelical Churches of Iraq, Rev. Karam Farag, P.O. Box 3446, Aloubah, Baghdad, Iraq, Tel: +964 1 71 95 80, Fax: +964 1 71 95 80

IRELAND

Ireland	70,280 km²
Population	(July 1991 est.) 3,566,833 Celtic, English
Religions in %	RCath 91.6%, Anglican 2.53%, Presb 0.37%, Meth 0.14%, other rel. 5.36%
Official/other languages	Irish (Gaelic), spoken mainly in areas located along the western seaboard; English is the language generally used
Northern Ireland	13,359 km²
Population	(July 1991 est.) 1,577,836 Celtic, English
Religions in %	RCath 41%, Presb 23%, Anglican 18%, Meth 4%, other rel. 14%
Official/other languages	English is the language generally used; Irish (Gaelic) is spoken mainly in areas located along the western seaboard

ICC (Irish Council of Churches)

The great missionary apostle of Ireland was the fifth-century St. Patrick. The church which he established had its ecclesiastical capital at Armagh, and churches and monasteries of the distinctive Celtic tradition soon spread all over the island. It was largely through the Irish monastic schools, famous for their learning and missionary zeal, that the Christian faith was reestablished in a Europe which had been overrun by Germanic tribes. With the 12th-century Norman invasion of Ireland, the fortunes of England and Ireland became intertwined. The church also developed a diocesan structure and hierarchy. With the establishing of the Church of England in the 16th century, the government of Ireland passed into the hands of

Angl in a manner similar to England. The church was reinforced by the "planting" of English people faithful to the government in England. For the first century of its life, this church was dominated by prelates and professors who belonged to the Calvinist tradition. Indeed, the Irish Articles of Religion, developed by Bishop Ussher, became the foundation for the Westminster Confession of Faith.

Presb began to settle in Ireland, particularly in Northern Ireland, through a succession of "plantations" by the government and through the military campaigns of Oliver Cromwell. Unfortunately the continued close links with Scotland, where university education was a possibility for members of the Ref tradition, also meant that the numerous divisions in Scottish Presbyterianism were transposed to Irish soil. Under pressure of penal laws, many Scots-Irish Presb emigrated to the United States, where they had a profound influence on the institutions of church, state, and university.

At the beginning of the 18th century, Presb became known as Dissenters (from the Angl government in Ireland) and began to champion RCath emancipation and movements for Home Rule. The Penal Laws also created an atmosphere in which numbers of important Presb responded enthusiastically at the end of the 18th century to the writings of Thomas Paine and Wolfe Tone on human rights and on civil liberties. These impulses, however, were largely reversed by the middle of the 19th century.

Although in 1922 the island was divided into Northern Ireland, which is part of the United Kingdom, and the South, which became the Republic of Ireland, the churches have remained organized on an all-island basis. The majority of the Ref family live in Northern Ireland, where they are seen to be Ulster-Scots in cultural and social terms. The Ref churches have maintained a strong missionary tradition.

Throughout this century, the Ref churches have on the whole supported the Union with Great Britain, rather than the aspirations of Irish nationalists for "united" or "agreed" Ireland. Statements from these churches have been critical of nationalists and of the British and Irish governments for initiatives which seem to bring the two countries into a relationship which allows for discussion and cooperation in Northern Ireland. There has been a Ref anxiety about the influence of the RCath Church on the government and educational institutions in Ireland. The Ref churches have increasingly felt isolated within Ireland and Great Britain. While they have welcomed the recent ceasefire in the hostilities of the para-military groups and have done much to foster cross-community projects and reconciliation, the next atrocity could lead to a return to an ethos of suspicion and noncooperation between the communities.

1. The Presbyterian Church in Ireland (6300)

The presence of chaplains in the Scottish army with the forces of Oliver Cromwell brought about the formal organization of Presb into the Presbytery of Ulster in 1642. The Presb Church in Ireland emerged from this presby and through union with other synods of different Scottish presby, culminating in the union of the synods of Ulster and the Secession Church in 1840. Throughout the 19th and 20th centuries the Presb Church has had a strong missionary presence in different parts of the world, and it was a founding member of the World Presb Alliance in 1870.

TM: **307,863** BM: **307,863** CM: **125,053** Congr: **562** PStations: **0** OrdM: **614** Eld: **7,210** Deac: **ne** EvgHome: **9** Mission: **56** Women Ord: **yes** As Ministers: **1973-76/20** as Deac: **none** as Elders: **1926/ 714** ChurchOrg: **Presbyterian (Kirk session—22 presby—5 synods—GenAssy)** Off/otherLang: **English** DoctrB: **ApC, NicC, WestConf** Frequency of the Lord's Supper: **4 times a year** Close relations with: **other members of the ICC** NatRel: **ICC (1922)** RegRel: **CEC (1977)** IntlRel: **WARC (1873)** TheolSchool: **Union Theological School (Belfast)** Service infrastructure: **7 rest homes (223 staff), 2 social service organizations (20 staff)** Periodicals: **Presbyterian Herald (gen/monthly/ 17,000), Wider World (mission/quarterly/28,000), Christian Irishman (mission/monthly/10,500)**

Address: The Presbyterian Church in Ireland, Church House, Fisherwick Place, UK—Belfast BT1 6DW, Northern Ireland, Tel: +44 1232 32 22 84, Fax: +44 1232 23 66 09

2. Congregational Union of Ireland (6540)

This community emerged in Ireland at the time of the activity of the Puritan army of Oliver Cromwell. The contemporary church has strong links with the World Congregational Evangelical Fellowship.

TM: **3,100** CM: **2,030** Congr: **26** PStations: **nil** OrdM: **30** Eld: **na** Deac: **na** EvgHome: **22** Mission: **17** Women Ord: **no** ChurchOrg: **executive committee comprising representations of each church, annual assembly** Off/otherLang: **English** DoctrB: **Savoy Declaration (1658)** Infant or believer's baptism: **both** Frequency of the Lord's Supper: **monthly** Close relations with: **Evangelical Fellowship of Congregational Churches (England and Wales)** NatRel: **British Evangelical Council (1986)** IntlRel: **WECF (1983)** Service infrastructure: **Irish Evangelical Society and Congregational Home Missions** Periodicals: **The Congregationalist (quarterly/1,300)**

Address: Congregational Union of Ireland, 38 Edgecumbe Gardens, UK—Belfast BT4 2EH, Northern Ireland

3. Non-Subscribing Presbyterian Church of Ireland (6542)

In 1725 the Presbytery of Antrim, originally attached to the General Synod of Ulster (cf. no. 1), was rearranged so as to consist solely of the Presb ministers and congr in Ulster who objected to subscription to the Westminster Confession. They were joined by the Remonstrant Synod of Ulster, formed in 1830, and the Synod of Munster, to form the Association of Non-Subscribing Presb.

TM: **3,716** BM: **3,716** Congr: **34** OrdM: **18** Eld: **200** Deac: **ne** EvgHome: **nc** Mission: **ne** Women Ord: **yes** As Ministers: **1982/1** as Deac: **ne** as Elders: **1950/880** ChurchOrg: **Presbyterian (Antrim, Bangor), Synod of Munster, General Synod** Off/otherLang: **English** DoctrB: **Faith based on Scripture without addition of man-made creeds or confessions of faith** Frequency of the Lord's Supper: **twice a year** Close relations with: **Christian Aid** NatRel: **ICC, Irish Inter-Church meeting** IntlRel: **none** Service infrastructure: **none** Periodicals: **The Non-Subscribing Presbyterian (gen/monthly/1,100)**

Address: Non-Subscribing Presbyterian Church of Ireland, 102 Carrickfergus Road, UK—Larne, Co., Antrim BT40 3JX, Northern Ireland, Tel: +44 1574 272-600

4. Reformed Presbyterian Church of Ireland (6545)

When the National Covenant (1638) and Solemn League of Covenant (1643) were no longer championed by the Church of Scotland at the Revolution Settlement in 1690, a group of Cameronian Covenanters continued their adherence. In 1743 a presby was established in Scotland which sent ministers to work among Covenanters in Ireland, a presby being established in Ireland from 1761 onward, while a synod was constituted in 1811. The Irish Reformed Presbyterian Church has supported mission work in Australia, Canada, Syria, Lebanon, Ethiopia, and Cyprus and is currently working in France, Cyprus, and the Republic of Ireland.

TM: **3,100** CM: **2,417** Congr: **35** PStations: **3** OrdM: **39** Eld: **167** Deac: **9** EvgHome: **5** Mission: **5** Women Ord: **no** ChurchOrg: **Presbyterian (4 presby: North, South, West, East) Synod** Off/ otherLang: **English** DoctrB: **WestConf** Infant or believer's baptism: **both** Frequency of the Lord's Supper: **twice to six times a year** Close relations with: **Sister Reformed Presbyterian Churches in Scotland, North America, and Australia** IntlRel: **ICRC (1986)** TheolSchool: **Ref Theol College (Belfast)** Service infrastructure: **"Covenanter Flats," Bally money, one full-time warden; "Renwick House"/Belfast—accommodation for young people (social service)** Periodicals: **The Covenanter Witness (gen/monthly/1,200), Reformed Vision (mission/quarterly/1,000), The Messenger (youth/ bi-monthly/nc), The Reformed Theological Journal (theol/yearly)**

Address: Reformed Presbyterian Church of Ireland, 98 Lisburn Road, UK—Belfast BT9 6AG, Northern Ireland, Tel: +44 1232 660-689, Fax: +44 1265 823-794, E-mail: clerk@rpc.org.

5. Evangelical Presbyterian Church in Ireland (6541)

Rooted in the historical setting of Presb immigrants from Scotland in the 17th century, the Evangelical Presbyterian Church in Ireland (EPCI) emerged from the Presbyterian Church in Ireland (cf. no. 1) in 1927. At that time liberal theology dominated the teaching in the Theological College responsible for training most of the ministers in PCI. A heresy trial involving one of the professors resulted, but he was acquitted on five clearly substantiated charges. When the General Assembly instituted measures to discipline those who continued to call the church back to the Word of God, there was a spontaneous uncoordinated separation from PCI by many members of evangelical persuasion throughout Northern Ireland. The result was the formation of The Irish Evangelical Church, later to be renamed The Evangelical Presbyterian Church. The church began without any church buildings or manses and with only two ordained ministers, and has grown steadily throughout its 70-year history. It has 11 congr in Northern Ireland, one in the Republic of Ireland, and one in England.

TM: **655** BM: **175** CM: **480** Congr: **13** PStations: **1** OrdM: **10** Eld: **27** Deac: **35** EvgHome: **0** Mission: **4** Women Ord: **no** ChurchOrg: **1 presby covering Ireland and 1 congregation in England** Off/ otherLang: **English** DoctrB: **WestConf, WestCat** Infant or believer's baptism: **both** Frequency of the Lord's Supper: **monthly** Close relations with: **Ref Presb Church in Ireland, Ev Presb Church in England and Wales, Free Church of Scotland, Ref Church in Netherlands (Liberated), Orth Presb Church (USA), Free Church in Southern Africa** NatRel: **British Evangelical Council**

IntlRel: **ICRC (1981)** TheolSchool: **Free Church College (Edinburgh)** Service infrastructure: **none** Periodicals: **Evangelical Presbyterian (gen/bi-monthly/800)**

Address: Evangelical Presbyterian Church in Ireland, 15 College Square East, UK—Belfast BT1 6DD, Northern Ireland, Tel: +44 1232-320529, Fax: +44 1232 438-330

6. Free Presbyterian Church of Ulster (6543)

This church came into existence through a secession of congr which felt that the Irish Presbyterian Church had abandoned true Ref teaching. From its beginnings in 1951, the driving force was Dr. Ian R. K. Paisley, a leading figure of the loyalist movement in Northern Ireland. The first congr was Crossgar, County Down, soon joined by a congr in Ravenhill which had seceded from the Irish Presbyterian Church. The church spread in subsequent years to all counties of Northern Ireland. It places strong emphasis on doctrinal standards and evangelism, and it is fiercely opposed to all ecumenical efforts. The church has worldwide connections with Free Presbyterian Churches and is responsible for mission work in Kenya.

TM: **14,000** Congr: **75** PStations: **22** OrdM: **83** Eld: **300** Deac: **na** EvgHome: **3** Mission: **7** Women Ord: **no** ChurchOrg: **Presbyterian (congr, presby)** Off/otherLang: **English** DoctrB: **WestConf, WestCat** Infant or believer's baptism: **both** Frequency of the Lord's Supper: **monthly** Close relations with: **represented in meetings like World Congress of Fundamentalist Churches but no relationships** NatRel: **none** RegRel: **none** IntlRel: **none** TheolSchool: **Theological College in Northen Ireland, Theological College (Greenville, SC, USA)** Service infrastructure: **7 independent Christian day schools, 1 Bible college and theological hall** Periodicals: **The Revivalist (gen/monthly/6,000), Truth for Youth (gen/bi-monthly/3,500)**

Address: Free Presbyterian Church of Ulster, 356-376 Ravenhill Road, GB-Belfast BT6 8GL, Northern Ireland, Tel: +44 1232 457-106, Fax: +44 1232 651-574

ISRAEL

Area in km²	21,646
Population	(1995) 5,460,000 (Israeli 80%, Arab Palestinians 18%)
Religions in %	Jewish (1993: 4,242,000), Samaritans (500,000), Muslims (725,400), 140,000 Christians (RCath 57%, Orth 40%, Prot 3%)
Official/other languages	Hebrew and Arabic

The majority of the Christian minority in Israel are Eastern Orthodox or Catholic. They have lived in the country for many centuries. Today the situation of Arab Christians is delicate as they have to live, against their will, with the reality of the

Jewish state. Prot churches arrived in the region in the 19th century. In 1842 Luth
and Angl established a common bishopric in Palestine and appointed a bishop of
Jewish descent in the hope of winning Jewish converts. In 1885 the Free Church of
Scotland started missionary work in Palestine. In the 20th century they more and
more adopted an attitude of dialogue and service toward the Jewish population.
The political events of this century, especially the establishment of the State of Israel, motivated many Christians to come to the country. There are active missionary organizations, mainly from Scandinavia and from the United States, some of
which are dispensationalists drawn to Israel in expectation of the events preceding
the end times. Others have come for the purpose of dialogue with Jews. Three Ref
Churches in the Netherlands, for instance (Nederlandse Hervormde Kerk, Gereformeerde Kerken in Nederland, Christelijk Gereformeerde Kerken in Nederland),
are represented by theologians functioning as a link with the Jewish community.
These churches are also doing pastoral work with Christians visiting Israel. There
are also Christians of Jewish parentage who relate either to Hebrew-speaking
Christian — either RCath or Prot — communities or meet in small local assemblies and prefer to be called Messianic Jews.

1. St. Andrew's Scots Memorial Church (6594)

This church has grown out of the missionary work of the Church of Scotland and
is still part of the Church of Scotland. There are two congr, one in Jerusalem and
the other in Tiberias. The church runs a school and two pilgrim guest houses. In
the past the guest house in Tiberias served for many years as a hospital and a maternity clinic. In St. Andrew's Church in Jerusalem, close to the walls of the ancient city, Dutch, French, and Korean groups are regularly worshiping.

TM: **40** BM: **40** CM: **35** Congr: **2** PStations: **2** OrdM: **1** Eld: **5** Deac: **3** EvgHome: **0** Mission: **1** Women
Ord: **yes** As Ministers: **1971** as Deac:, as Elders: **1965** ChurchOrg: **belongs to the Church of Scotland, is governed by presby and GenAssy, there is a presby of Jerusalem** Off/otherLang: **English,
also Dutch, French, Korean groups worshiping in St. Andrew's** DoctrB: **ApC, NicC, WestConf** Infant or believer's baptism: **both** Frequency of the Lord's Supper: **monthly** Close relations with: **Diocese of Episcopal Church in Jerusalem** NatRel: **United Christian Council in Israel (1963), various
organizations in Israel/Palestine, Action of Churches Together in Scotland (ACTS)** IntlRel:
WARC (via Ch of Scotland), WCC, ICCC (associated member 1980) TheolSchool: **nc.**

Address: St. Andrew's Scots Memorial Church, P.O. Box 8619, David Remer St., Jerusalem 91086,
Israel, Tel: +972 2 732-401, Fax: +972 2 731-711

2. Baraka Bible Presbyterian Church (6595)

In 1946 Dr. Thomas Lambi of Pennsylvania, USA, serving with his wife under the
Board of the Presbyterian Foreign Mission, started a sanatorium with about 90
beds in Aroub, about 13 km south of Bethlehem. At the same time they built a
church in the town of Bethlehem. In 1954 the first service in the new building was

conducted by Tabra Khalil, one of the local Arab elders. Recently, land was purchased for building a church center in Shepherd Field Town.

TM: **50** BM: **42** CM: **30** Congr: **7** PStations: **2** OrdM: **1** Eld: **2** Deac: **3** EvgHome: **0** Mission: **1** Women Ord: **no** ChurchOrg: **Presbyterian (congregation, church session-pastor, elder, deacons)** Off/otherLang: **Arabic, English** DoctrB: **ApC, WestConf** Infant or believer's baptism: **both** Frequency of the Lord's Supper: **monthly** Close relations with: **Baptist** IntlRel: **associated member of the ICCC (1950)** TheolSchool: **nc.**

Address: Baraka Bible Presbyterian Church, P.O. Box 26, Hebron Road, Bethlehem, Israel, Tel: +972 2 742-480, Fax: +972 2 929288, E-mail: 106024.523@compuserve-com

3. Grace and Truth Christian Congregation (6596)

This community of Jewish origin was founded by Rev. Baruch Maoz in Rishon LeTsion. After initial steps in 1974 it was officially established in May 1978. It seeks to witness to Jews and celebrates worship on Saturdays. Ref in theology and congregational in ecclesiology, it practices believer's baptism. The community has grown steadily in recent years and also includes immigrants from Russia.

TM: **223** BM: **187** CM: **187** Congr: **1** PStations: **3** OrdM: **1** Eld: **4** Deac: **3** EvgHome: **2** Mission: **ne** Women Ord: **no** ChurchOrg: **none** Off/otherLang: **Hebrew, Russian, English** DoctrB: **adapted WestConf, Calvinistic Conf, Congreg ecclesiology, bapt view of baptism** Infant or believer's baptism: **believer** Frequency of the Lord's Supper: **monthly** Periodicals: **none** TheolSchool: **nc.**

Address: Grace and Truth Christian Congregation, P.O. Box 75, Smitkin 8, Rishon Le'Zion 75100, Israel, Tel: +972 3 966 1898

4. Nes Ammin Christian Settlement

Nes Ammin is a solidarity project founded in 1960 by Dr. Johan Pilon and supported by three Ref Churches in the Netherlands, by several Prot Churches in Germany, and by Friends Organizations in countries such as Switzerland and the USA. About 150 people, mainly Dutch and German, are living in Nes Ammin. From the beginning, the community rejected any missionary attitude toward the Jewish people. The village has a guest house and receives about 25,000 visitors annually. Nes Ammin is accepted by Israelis as an integral part of the multicolored landscape of Israel. The community also entertains friendly relations with Arab Christians. Various study projects of the community concentrate on themes showing the Jewish roots of Christianity.

Address: Nes Ammin, Doar Na, Western Galilee 25225, Israel, Tel:+972 4 982-5522, Fax: +972 4 995 0000

ITALY

Area in km²	301,270
Population	(1995) 57,910,000
Religions in %	RCath majority, Prot minorities with a total member-ship of about 325,000
Official/other languages	Italian/French, English

The Ref presence in Italy has its roots in the medieval lay movement of the Waldensians. Around 1170 Peter Waldo of Lyon, France (the name Peter was given to him later as a title) started the movement of the "poor of Lyon." It spread quickly, especially in Italy. In 1184 the movement was officially condemned by the Council of Verona, and the Waldensians were scattered around Europe. Many withdrew into the valleys of the Piemontese Alps. Waldensian history throughout the Middle Ages was a history of persecution and suffering. In the 15th century re-lations were established with the Hussite movement in Bohemia. At the Synod of Chanforan in 1532, in the presence of Farel and Saulnier, the Waldensians agreed to join the Reformation. But they continued to be exposed to severe persecution by both the Dukes of Piedmont and Savoy and the French kings. These culminated in 1655 in a cruel massacre, the so-called "Piemontese Easter." After the revocation of the Edict of Nantes (1685) the Dukes of Piedmont and Savoy gave them the choice to renounce their faith or to emigrate. In 1689 a group of refugees, under the leadership of Henri Arnaud, took the risk of returning to the valleys — the "glorious return" — and were eventually granted permission to stay. 1848 marks a new stage in Waldensian history: through the Emancipation Edict of King Carlo Alberto they were given equal rights and could establish themselves in other parts of Italy. A theological faculty was founded in Torre Pellice (1855), moved to Flor-ence (1860), and later (1920) to Rome. At the end of the 19th and the beginning of the 20th centuries, mainly for economic reasons, many Waldensians emigrated to Uruguay and Argentina and founded Waldensian churches there (cf. Uruguay). Gradually the church obtained more freedom. In connection with the Concordate between Italy and the Holy See (1929) the Waldensians were "tolerated"; the Con-stitution of 1948 guaranteed religious liberty, and finally in 1984 the Italian state signed an agreement granting the Waldensian church full recognition.

Waldensian Evangelical Church (Union of Waldensian and Methodist Churches) (6340)

In 1975 Waldensians and Meth in Italy decided to integrate their synods. The Meth movement had started in Italy in the early 19th century through a combined effort of British and American Methodists. Following its independence from the British Methodists in 1962, the Methodist Church in Italy sought closer relations with the Waldensians. Today they are practically one church — the Waldensian Evangelical Church *(Chiesa Evangelica Valdese)*. An agreement has also been reached with the Baptist churches about the mutual recognition of baptism.

TM: **27,846** BM: **27,846** Congr: **137** PStations: **0** OrdM: **103** Eld: **ne** Deac: **24** EvgHome: **0** Mission: **0** Women Ord: **Yes** As Ministers: **1967/17** as Deac: **since beginning/12** as Elders: **ne** ChurchOrg: **Presbyterian (circuits) districts synod** Off/otherLang: **Italian** DoctrB: **ApC, NicC, Confession of Faith of 1655** Infant or believer's baptism: **both** Frequency of the Lord's Supper: **monthly** Periodicals: **Riforma Eco delle Valle (gen/weekly/6,000), Gioventù Evangelica (gen/3-4per year/1,200), Confronti (interconfessional/monthly/3,100), NEV (press agency/weekly/500) L'Amico dei Fanciulli (children/monthly/600), Protestantesimo (theol/quarterly/980)** Close relations with: **Baptist Union (UCEBI), Luth Church in Italy (CELI), Federation of Evangelical Churches in Italy (FCEI)** NatRel: **FCEI (Federation of Evangelical Churches in Italy) (1967), FDEI (Women's Federation) (1976), FGEI (Youth Federation) (1969)** RegRel: **CEC, CEPPLE, Leuenberg** IntlRel: **WCC (1948), CEVAA (1971), WARC (1988)** TheolSchool: **Faculty of Theology (Rome).**

Address: Chiesa Evangelica Valdese, Via Firenze n. 38, I—00184 Roma, Italy, Tel: +39 06 474-5537, Fax: +39 06 474-3324

IVORY COAST

Area in km²	332,462
Population	(est. 1993) 13,340,000
Religions in %	Animists (63%,) Muslim (23%)
Official/other languages	French/Baoulé, Dioula

Evangelical Protestant Church of the Christian and Missionary Alliance (1340)

The Ref presence in this country is due to efforts undertaken by the Christian and Missionary Alliance. The first mission station was in Kankan in Guinea; from there American missionaries moved to the Ivory Coast and settled in Bouaké in 1930. The first baptisms took place in 1932. Work expanded in the following years to Bocanda, M'Bahiakro, Toumodi, and Dimbokro. In the early 40s a Bible school was established with Baoulé as the teaching language. Further outreach took place in subsequent years. In 1955 the first African pastor, Diéké Koffi Joseph, was ordained. Four years later the church was granted autonomy by the central direction of the Christian and Missionary Alliance in the USA. In 1995 it adopted its present name.

TM: **250,000** Congr: **50** PStations: **247** OrdM: **149** Eld: **nc** Deac: **nc** EvgHome: **nc** Mission: **nc** Women

281

Ord: **no** ChurchOrg: **Congregational (communities, parishes, districts, and 7 regions, GenAssy)** Off/otherLang: **French, Baoulé** DoctrB: **ApC, Statement of Faith (in Constitution)** Infant or believer's baptism: **believer** Frequency of the Lord's Supper: **monthly** NatRel: **Federation of Evangelical Churches of Ivory Coast (FECI) (1960)** RegRel: **Association of Evangelical Churches in Africa (AEA)** IntlRel: **World Union of the CMA** TheolSchool: **Biblical Institute (Yamoussoukro), Faculty of Evangelical Theology (BP 309 Abidjan 06).**

Address: Eglise protestante évangélique de l'Alliance chrétienne et missionnaire (CMA), B.P. 4329, Abidjan, Ivory Coast, Tel: +225 45 28 55

JAMAICA

Area in km²	10,991
Population	(July 1996 est.) 2,595,275 African 76.3%, Afro-European 15.1%, East Indian and Afro-East Indian 3%, white 3.2%, Chinese and Afro-Chinese 1.2%, other 1.2%
Religions in %	Protestant 55.9% (Church of God 18.4%, Baptist 10%, Angl 7.1%, Advent 6.9%, Pent 5.2%, Meth 3.1%, United Church 2.7%, other 2.5%), RCath 5%, other, including some spiritual cults, 39.1% (1982)
Official/other languages	English/Creole

SMS (Scottish Missionary Society), **LMS** (London Missionary Society), **CCC** (Caribbean Council of Churches)

Arrawak Indians were living on Jamaica when Christopher Columbus arrived there on April 5, 1494. First a Spanish colony (1509-1655), later a British colony (1655-1962), Jamaica is today a parliamentary democracy and a member of the British Commonwealth. Some 60% of the state income and 75% of the jobs are provided by tourism alone.

The earliest recorded Ref presence on the island was in 1688 when Presb and members of other denominations worshiped together in Hampden Trelawn. Organized missionary work began after 1800 with the arrival of the Scottish Missionary Society (SMS). Until 1824 schooling of Afro-American children was the only church activity tolerated by the colonial government. From 1832 to 1838 Presb greatly contributed to the gradual abolition of slavery. The emancipation in 1838 of more than 300,000 slaves led to a boom in conversions and church planting. In 1836 the Jamaican Missionary Presbytery (JMS) and the Presbyterian Academy were established. The first ministers graduated in the early 1840s.

1. United Church in Jamaica and the Cayman Islands (3330)

This church was formed in 1965 by the Union of the Presbyterian Church of Jamaica and Grand Cayman and the Congregational Union of Jamaica. The Presbyterian Church was the result of the work of the SMS (cf. above). As early as 1846, Jamaican missionaries were sent by this church to Calabar and thus became the first non-European Presb from the Caribbean islands to minister in Africa. They planted the church which became the Presbyterian Church of Nigeria (cf. Nigeria no. 1). They also sent missionaries to Rajputana (NW India) while evangelizing East Indians in Jamaica itself.

Congreg churches originated in 1834 from the activities of the LMS. The Congregational Union of Jamaica was formed in 1877 to give coherence to the individual churches. But a financial crisis and the lack of manpower explain why the Congregational Union of England and Wales, as well as the International Congregational Council, had to be called for help. The Congreg churches later moved toward independence before ultimately merging with the Presbyterian church.

TM: **20,000** CM: **18,000** Congr: **200** OrdM: **nc** Eld: **nc** Deac: **nc** EvgHome: **nc** Mission: **nc** Women Ord: **yes** As Ministers: **nc** as Deac: **nc** as Elders: **nc** ChurchOrg: **nc** Off/otherLang: **English (official), dialect** DoctrB: **nc** NatRel: **Jamaica Council of Churches, Jamaica Ecumenical Mutual Mission** RegRel: **CANAAC, CCC** IntlRel: **WCC, WARC (1985)**

Address: United Church in Jamaica and the Cayman Islands, P.O. Box 359, 12 Carlton Crescent, Kingston 10, Jamaica, Tel: +1 876 926-8734, Fax: +1 876 926-6509

2. The Protestant Reformed Churches of Jamaica (PRCJ) (3331)

In 1962 a church in England asked the Protestant Reformed Churches of the USA (cf. USA no. 33) to come to Jamaica and assist a group of 23 parishes and 3 pastors whose roots went back to the "holiness movement." The presence of PRC missionaries did not, however, bring the expected success. By 1987 only seven parishes with 4 pastors constituted the Protestant Reformed Church in Jamaica (PRCJ). The others had returned to the holiness movement. The differing assessments of the situation prevailing between leaders of the PRC and the PRCJ hampered significant church growth. The PRC has finally discontinued its work in Jamaica.

TM: **121** BM: **73** CM: **48** Congr: **4** PStations: **3** OrdM: **nc** Eld: **4** Deac: **nc** EvgHome: **nc** Mission: **nc** Women Ord: **no** ChurchOrg: **office bearers (twice monthly), four classes annually** Off/otherLang: **English** DoctrB: **ApC, NicC, AthC, HeidC, HelvC, CDort, WestConf, Five points of Calvinism** Infant or believer's baptism: **both** Frequency of the Lord's Supper: **4 times per year**

Address: Protestant Reformed Church in Jamaica (PRCJ), Belmont Dist., Bluckfields P.O., Westmoreland, Jamaica, Tel: +1 809 955-8085, Fax: +1 809 955-8085

JAPAN

Area in km²	376,520
Population	125,500,000 Japanese (99.4%), Koreans and Ainu (0.6%)
Religions in %	Shintoism and Buddhism 84%, others 15%, including Christians 1.577% (Prot 600,350, RCath 463,300, others 879,000)
Official language	Japanese

NCCJ (National Council of Churches in Japan)

Christianity first came to Japan in 1543. The first missionary efforts were suppressed by violent persecution and only survived in small communities. In the 19th century, with the beginning of the era of modernization, Prot missions from America and Europe entered the country (1859), among them several agencies belonging to the Ref tradition.

The first Prot congr was established in 1872. Congr of various Prot backgrounds followed. In 1923 the Christian Alliance of Japan was founded, which brought together Prot of different persuasions. Protestantism began to face the challenge of unity.

In 1941, shortly before the outbreak of the war with the United States, the United Church of Christ in Japan (Kyodan) was formed under the pressure of the government. It included 34 different denominations and had over 240,000 members. After the War, in 1945, several of these churches left the Kyodan and reconstituted themselves. The majority, however, stayed within the Kyodan. In the decades since the War, several new Ref denominations have come into existence.

1. United Church of Christ in Japan (Kyodan) (4317)

After World War II the churches which decided to stay within the Kyodan faced the difficult task of clarifying the identity of the United Church—both with regard to the many traditions which were represented within its fold and with regard to the new political authorities. In 1954 a statement of faith was adopted, and in 1967 the church issued a confession concerning Japan's involvement in the Second World War. In 1968 the Kyodan united with the United Church of Okinawa, located on the islands of Okinawa, which had remained under American occupation. The Kyodan has gone through turbulent times in the '60s and '70s, but it has succeeded in overcoming tendencies toward separation. Today the Kyodan is organized in the following 16 districts: Hokkai, Ou, Tohoku, Kanto, Tokyo, Kanagawa, Tokai, Chubu, Kyoto, Osaka, Hyogo, Higashichugoku, Nishichugoku, Shikoku, Kyushu, and Okinawa.

TM: **205,244** BM: **102,758** CM: **127,816** Congr: **1,721** OrdM: **2,181** Eld: **nc** Deac: **nc** EvgHome: **nc** Mission: **23** Women Ord: **yes** As Ministers: **1933/nc** as Deac: **nc** as Elders: **nc** ChurchOrg: **congr, districts, GenAssy** Off/otherLang: **Japanese** DoctrB: **ApC, Confession of Faith of Nihon Kirisuto Kyodan** Infant or believer's baptism: **both** NatRel: **NCCJ (1955)** RegRel: **CCA (1957)** IntlRel: **WCC (1948)** TheolSchool: **Tokyo Union Theological Seminary (Tokyo Shingaku Daigaku), Kwansei Gakuin Univ. (Tokyo), Tokyo Bible School, Theol Seminary (Nihon Seisho Shing Shing Shingakko)** Periodicals: **Fukuin Shibun (Evangelical News)(gen/monthly), RAIK Tsushin (Korean Issues)(bi-monthly/1,000), Dodai (Lighthouse) (youth/annual), Ko-gae (Ridge) (women mag/bi-annually), An-nyung (Hello) (gen English/quarterly)**

Address: Nihon Kirisuto Kyodan, #31 Japan Christian Centre 3-18 Nishi-Waseda, 2-chome, Shinjuku-ku, Tokyo 169, Japan, Tel: +81 3 3202-0541, Fax: +81 3 3207-3918

2. Church of Christ in Japan (4311)

Before World War II, the Church of Christ was one of the larger churches. Its origins go back to the first Prot missionaries who came to Japan. The first congrs were founded in 1872 by the American Presbyterian J. C. Hepburn, by S. R. Brown, and by J. H. Ballagh of the Ref tradition. The beginnings were in Yokohama. In 1877, after the union with the Presbyterian Association in Japan, the church had 623 members. By 1890 membership had increased to 10,495 in 72 congr. In the following fifty years it was the largest among the churches and exercised a leading role. It did missionary work in Korea, Taiwan, China, Hong Kong, and Singapore. In 1941 it became part of the Kyodan. After the War the majority of the congr stayed with the Kyodan, but thirty-nine congr reconstituted themselves in 1951 as the Church of Christ in Japan.

TM: **13,450** BM: **13,842** CM: **7,673** Congr: **174** PStations: **5,384** OrdM: **157** Eld: **502** Deac: **474** EvgHome: **nc** Mission: **nc** Women Ord: **yes** As Ministers: **1930/22** as Deac: **1951/305** as Elders: **1951/129** ChurchOrg: **Presbyterian (congr, four presbys, GenAssy)** Off/otherLang: **Japanese** DoctrB: **ApC, Confession of Faith of Nippon Kirisuto Kyokai** Infant or believer's baptism: **believer** Frequency of the Lord's Supper: **monthly** NatRel: **none** RegRel: **none** IntlRel: **WARC (1967)** TheolSchool: **Nippon Kirisuto Kyokai Theological Seminary** Periodicals: **FuKuin Giho (gen/monthly)**

Address: Nippon Kirisuto Kyokai, 2-2 Yoshida, Kawagoe 350, Japan, Tel: +81 492 335-542, Fax: +81 492 337-039

3. Reformed Church in Japan (4313)

Prior to World War II, several teachers already practiced Ref teaching as it was done in the West. Due to political pressure they had also joined the Kyodan in 1941. After the War, when religious freedom was proclaimed, they decided to form a separate church. The church was constituted in Tokyo in 1946. At that time the group had nine teachers and three elders. In 1950 the Synod of the Christian Reformed Church in North America (cf. United States no. 11) accepted the request of the Reformed Church in Japan to send missionaries. The denomination has grown steadily throughout the years.

TM: **8,986** BM: **6,921** CM: **5,014** Congr: **217** OrdM: **130** Eld: **341** Deac: **476** EvgHome: **nc** Mission: **1** Women Ord: **no** ChurchOrg: **Reformed (congr, 4 districts, synod)** Off/otherLang: **Japanese** DoctrB: **WestConf, WestCat** Infant or believer's baptism: **both** Close relations with: **CRCNA (Christian Reformed Church in North America)** IntlRel: **REC (close rel. with ICRC)** TheolSchool: **Theological Seminary of Kobe**

Address: Nippon Kirisuto Kaikakuha Kyokai, 7-16 6-Bancho Koshien, Nishinomiya Hyogo-ken 663, Japan, Tel: +81 3 3461-4616

4. Presbyterian Church in Japan (4314)

This church represents a union of two Presb churches which were founded after World War II — the Christian Presbyterian Church (1956) and the Evangelical Presbyterian Church (1979). The two churches began collaborating in 1980 and united in 1993.

TM: **2,781** BM: **2,295** CM: **1,601** Congr: **46** OrdM: **52** Eld: **87** Deac: **83** EvgHome: **3** Mission: **3** Women Ord: **no** ChurchOrg: **3 presby** Off/otherLang: **Japanese, Korean** DoctrB: **WestConf, WestCat** Infant or believer's baptism: **both** NatRel: **Japanese Evangelical Alliance** RegRel: **none** IntlRel: **none** TheolSchool: **Tokyo Christian Theological Seminary, Covenant Seminary, Senkyokai Seminary** Periodicals: **General Assembly Magazine (gen/3 times a year/2,000)**

Address: Nihon Choro Kyokai, 1-8-15 Hikawadai Higashikurume-City, Tokyo 23 nc, Japan, Tel: +81 424 763-305, Fax: +81 424 763-306

5. Cumberland Presbyterian Church (4312)

Cumberland Presb missionaries (cf. United States) began to work in Japan in 1873. J. B. Hall, the first among them, was active in Osaka and Wakayama. The congrs which were established at that time formed the Union Church of Christ in Japan (Nihon Kirisuto Itchi Kyokai) in 1889. After World War II Pastor Yoshizaki Tadao, a pastor of the Kyodan (cf. no. 1), joined the Cumberland Church with his congr; in the course of subsequent years other congrs followed.

TM: **1,789** BM: **1,789** CM: **1,789** Congr: **11** OrdM: **15** Eld: **42** Deac: **55** EvgHome: **nc** Mission: **nc** Women Ord: **yes** As Ministers: **no** as Deac: **1950/40** as Elders: **1984/5%** ChurchOrg: **Presbyterian** Off/otherLang: **Japanese** DoctrB: **ApC, NicC, AthC, Confession of Cumberland Presb Church** Infant or believer's baptism: **both**

Address: Kambarando Choro Kirisuto Kyokai Nihon Chukai, 2-chome, Minami Rikan, 14-21, Yamato-shi, Kanagawa 242, Japan, Tel: +81 4 6274-1371, Fax: +81 4 6274-6350

6. Christian Association in Japan (4320)

This church has emerged from the Union Church of Christ (cf. no. 5). It was founded by Oshima Shinji, pastor of the former Union Church of Christ. There is one congr in Tokyo and three in the district of Shimane.

TM: **161** BM: **125** CM: **117** Congr: **4** PStations: **0** OrdM: **8** Eld: **10** Deac: **10** EvgHome: **0** Mission: **0** Women Ord: **yes** As Ministers: **1941/2** as Deac: **1941/2** as Elders: **1941/2** ChurchOrg: **Reformed** Off/ otherLang: **Japanese** DoctrB: **Statement of Faith of Nippon Kirisuto Kai** Infant or believer's baptism: **both** NatRel: **Nihon Kirisutokyo Rengokai**

Address: Nihon Kirisuto Kai, 1-25-6 Matsudo Shibuya-ku, Tokyo 150, Japan, Tel: +81 3 3466-3414

7. Korean Christian Church in Japan (KCCJ) (4310)

In 1909 the Presb Church of Korea sent Pastor Han Sok-Po to Japan. He evangelized primarily among Korean students in Tokyo. Since 1915 the Presb Church in Korea has regularly sent pastors to Japan, and as the church in Korea grew stronger, its mission in Japan also increased. As a result congr were founded in all parts of Japan. In 1934 the Korean Christian Church was established. It was forced in 1939 to become part of the Church of Christ in Japan (cf. no. 2) and eventually had to join the Kyodan. After World War II it left the Kyodan and constituted itself as the General Assembly of the Korean Christian Churches in Japan.

TM: **6,453** BM: **4,603** CM: **4,205** Congr: **60** PStations: **15** OrdM: **73** Eld: **83** Deac: **56** EvgHome: **16** Mission: **0** Women Ord: **yes** As Ministers: **1980/2** as Deac: **51** as Elders: **4** ChurchOrg: **KCCJ is divided into 5 regions: Kanto (eastern), Chubu (central), Kansai (central western), Seibu (western), Seinan (south western)** Off/otherLang: **Korean, Japanese** DoctrB: **ApC, WestConf** Infant or believer's baptism: **both** Frequency of the Lord's Supper: **3 times per year** NatRel: **NCCJ** RegRel: **CCA** IntlRel: **WCC, WARC (1988)** TheolSchool: **Christian Bible School (Tokyo), Bible Institute Kansai**

Address: Zainichi Daikan Kirisuto Kyokai Sokai, Japan Christian Center, Room 55, 2-3-18 Nishi-Waseda, Shinjuku-ku, Tokyo 191, Japan, Tel: +81 3 3202-5398, Fax: +81 3 3202-4977

8. The Reformed Presbyterian Christian Church of Japan (4321)

The existence of this church owes to the efforts of missionaries of the Presbyterian Church in the USA who had been active in China and moved to Japan in 1950. They started work in Kobe. They continued to be part of the General Assembly of the Presbyterian Church in the USA but have since gained autonomy.

TM: **213** CM: **134** Congr: **7** PStations: **na** OrdM: **7** Eld: **na** Deac: **na** EvgHome: **nc** Mission: **na** Women Ord: **no** As Ministers: **nc** as Deac: **nc** as Elders: **nc** ChurchOrg: **nc** Off/otherLang: **Japanese** DoctrB: **WestConf, WestCat**

Address: Nihon Kirisuto Kaikaku Choro Kyokai, 4-2-26, Oote-Machi, Suma-ku, Kobe-City 654, Japan

9. Biblical Church (4322)

This church was founded by Pastor Oyama Reiji. He graduated in 1953 from the Tokyo Theological Seminary and started to evangelize in Takadanobaba, near

Waseda University. Over the years a group grew up around him, and "The Biblical Church" was organized as a Presb-Ref denomination in 1978.

TM: **908** BM: **775** CM: **546** Congr: **19** PStations: **na** OrdM: **15** Eld: **15** Deac: **41** EvgHome: **5** Mission: **3** Women Ord: **no** ChurchOrg: **Synod** Off/otherLang: **Japanese** DoctrB: **ApC, NicC, AthC, HeidC, WestConf, HelvC, Conf of Faith of Seisho Kirisuto Kyokai** Infant or believer's baptism: **both** Frequency of the Lord's Supper: **4 times a year** TheolSchool: **Tokyo Graduate School of Theology** Periodicals: **Kyokai Shimpo (gen/monthly/1,000)**

Address: Seisho Kirisuto Kyokai, 1-12-3, Toyotama-Kita, Nerima-ku, Tokyo 176, Japan, Tel: +81 3 5984-3571, Fax: +81 3 5984-3572

10. Japan Evangelical Reformed Church (4319)

In 1956 J. P. Visser, a missionary from South Africa, founded a congr in the district of Oita. He was joined by Japanese pastors. Together they founded an association for rural mission. In 1992 two more mission congrs were established.

TM: **31** BM: **27** CM: **17** Congr: **1** PStations: **2** OrdM: **3** Eld: **nc** Deac: **nc** EvgHome: **nc** Mission: **nc** Women Ord: **yes** As Ministers: **not yet** as Deac: **1982/1** as Elders: **not yet** ChurchOrg: **aims for a synodal structure** Off/otherLang: **Japanese, English** DoctrB: **ApC, WestConf, Reformed** Infant or believer's baptism: **both** Frequency of the Lord's Supper: **once every 2 months** Close relations with: **Synod of the Orange Free State (Bloemfontein, S.A. 1986), Dutch Reformed Church of S. Africa (1986)** Periodicals: **Japan Rural Mission Newsletter (gen/bi-monthly/5,000)**

Address: Nihon Fukuin Kaikakuha Kyokai, P.O. Box 142, 46 Mitsuyoshi Gyoen 800-42 Soda, 870-11 Oita City, Japan, Tel: +81 975 691-195, Fax: +81 975 691-196

KENYA

Area in km^2	582,650
Population	(est. 1996) 28,176,686 Kikuyu 22%, Luhya 14%, Luo 13%, Kalenjin 12%, Kamba 11%, Kisii 6%, Meru 6%, Asian, European, and Arab 1%, other 15%
Religions in %	RCath 28%, Prot (including Angl) 38%, indigenous beliefs 26%, other 8%
Official/other languages	English, Swahili/numerous indigenous languages

AIC (Africa Inland Church)
EACA (East Africa Christian Alliance, the regional body of the ICCC)
IBPFM (Independent Board for Presbyterian Foreign Missions)
NCCK (National Council of Churches of Kenya)

Eastern Africa was the cradle of humankind, and paleontological evidence traces human presence there back over 3 million years. In more recent times, from the 10th century onward, Bantu groups settled the area later to become Kenya and started trading with the Arabs. In the 15th century Nilohamite tribes arrived. The slave trade which was active between 1735 and the end of the 19th century destroyed many tribal structures and traditions inside Kenya. Kenya came under British colonial rule after the Berlin Congo Conference (1884/85). In 1895 the British government officially took over the country from the Imperial British East Africa Company (IBEA). Kenya and Uganda were at that time one and the same British protectorate. Indians were brought in to build the Lake Victoria–Mombassa railroad and work on plantations, while the Europeans developed agriculture, trade, and administration. Kenya became a British colony in 1920. Soon a growing movement in favor of independence generated the creation in 1922 of the Kikuyu Central Association (KCA). The Mau-Mau revolt (1952-55) in favor of land and freedom was followed by elections which granted limited political participation to Kenyans. The Kenya African National Union (KANU) won the elections in 1961. On December 12, 1963, Kenya became independent, and Jomo Kenyatta (1891-1978) was appointed as Prime Minister. A constitutional amendment of 1982 made Kenya a "de jure" one-party state. In 1992 a multiparty system was introduced. The legal system is based on English common, tribal, and Islamic law. President Daniel Toroitich arap MOI has been in office since 1978.

Mission work has taken place in two phases. The first started after the arrival of Portuguese sailors in 1498 and ended in the middle of the 17th century. The second began with the arrival in 1844 of the Angl Church Missionary Society (CMS) under the leadership of J. L. Krapf; other European missions were soon to follow: British Meth (1862), RCath orders (1889), Scottish Presb (1891), Salvation Army (1921), and many others. The interdenominational Africa Inland Mission (AIM), founded by Peter Cameron Scott in 1895 with the vision to establish a string of mission stations stretching from the East Coast of Africa to Lake Chad, has developed into the largest Prot body in Kenya today with about 2,500 congr. The first African Independent Church started in 1914 among the Luo people. In the meantime over 230 Independent African Churches have developed in Kenya. Almost all denominations are active in educational, social, and medical programs.

Throughout history efforts for unity were a major concern of the churches. A representative missionary conference was already called in 1909, and in 1913 a Federation of Churches was set up which brought four missions into a consultative body — the Church of Scotland, the AIM, the Church of England, and the Meth mission. Plans for a United Church were pursued in the '50s and '60s. In 1954 St. Paul's United Theological College was officially inaugurated in Limuru. But the unification process of the churches was abandoned in 1972.

A number of national and regional church organizations are headquartered in Kenya: the All Africa Conference of Churches (AACC), the Association of Evangelicals of Africa and Madagascar (AEAM), East African Christian Alliance (EACA), and United Orthodox Independent Churches Organization. The major national church organization is the National Council of Churches of Kenya (NCCK).

1. Presbyterian Church of East Africa (1070)

This church grew out of a private venture. In 1891 a group of missionaries established a station at Kibwezi. At the end of the century, a new site was chosen in Kikuyu. In 1901 the Church of Scotland took responsibility for the work, continuing to combine evangelistic, educational, medical, and agricultural work. The development of the church was slow. The first baptism took place in 1907, and by 1913 membership had grown to only 87. In 1920 the first Kikuyu Kirk Session was set up which, together with the (white) Nairobi Kirk Session, formed the Presbytery of Kenya Colony. In 1926 the first eight Kenyans were ordained to the ministry (three came from Thoyoto, five from Tumutumu). In 1929 the issue of female circumcision led to a controversy both in the church and the public arena. The decision of the church to declare circumcision incompatible with the Christian faith was regarded by Kikuyu leaders as an interference with their traditional customs and was rejected. Gradually church leadership passed into African hands. In 1945 the presby of Chania, which had resulted from the work of the (American) Gospel Missionary Society, became part of the Presbyterian Church of East Africa. In the '40s and '50s membership quickly rose, and in 1956 the church became fully independent, with a new constitution. The independent church also included the (white) Overseas Presbytery of Kenya (with a congregation in Dar es Salaam and one in Kampala), which had constituted itself separately in 1936. In 1964 the first Kenyan General Secretary, John Gatu, was appointed (1964-1979).

TM: **3,000,000** BM: **3,000,000** Congr: **1,020** OrdM: **300** Eld: **nc** Deac: **nc** EvgHome: **150** Mission: **1** Women Ord: **yes (since 1976)** As Ministers: **1982/13** as Deac: **1926** as Elders: **1965** ChurchOrg: **parishes, presby, GenAssy** Off/otherLang: **Gikuyu (over 75%), Kimeru, Kiswahili, Kikamba, Masai, occasionally English** DoctrB: **ApC, NicC, WestConf** Infant or believer's baptism: **both** Frequency of the Lord's Supper: **monthly** Close relations with: **PCUSA, Ch of Scotland, Ch of Ireland, PC Canada, PROK in Korea** NatRel: **NCCK** RegRel: **AACC** IntlRel: **WARC (1956), WCC (1956)** TheolSchool: **United Theological College (Limuru), PCEA Pastoral Institute (Thogoto), overseas** Service infrastructure: **hospitals, social service organizations, kindergartens, dispensaries, community health centers, teacher's training college, pastoral institute** Periodicals: **The Jitegemea (magazine/quarterly/5,000)**

Address: Presbyterian Church of East Africa, P.O. Box 48268, Nairobi, Kenya, Tel: +254 2 504-417 or 8, Fax: +254 2 504-442

2. Reformed Church of East Africa (RCEA) (1071)

The origin of the Reformed Church of East Africa goes back to 1944, when the Dutch Reformed Church of Eldoret, a church of South African origin, started mission work and called a missionary from South Africa. In 1961 the work was taken over by the Reformed Mission League of the Netherlands Reformed Church. Since that time all aid and all missionaries have come from the Netherlands.

The RCEA became autonomous in July 1963. Until 1970 a Missionary Conference served as Executive Committee of the Synod. From 1970 to 1979 a Joint Committee, composed of seven missionaries (from the Reformed Mission League) and five Africans representing the Synod of the RCEA, functioned as the Executive Committee of the Synod of the RCEA. Since November 20, 1979, new structures made the RCEA fully independent.

TM: **110,000** BM: **85,000** CM: **85,000** Congr: **205** PStations: **75** OrdM: **300** Eld: **8,000** Deac: **1,000** EvgHome: **10,000** Mission: **nc** Women Ord: **yes** As Ministers: **no** as Deac: **1920/40** as Elders: **no** ChurchOrg: **preaching station, local church, parish, presby, synod** Off/otherLang: **English, Kiswahili** DoctrB: **ApC, NicC, HeidC, WestConf, CDort** Infant or believer's baptism: **both** Frequency of the Lord's Supper: **4 times a year depending on availability of the minister** Close relations with: **Presb Ch of East Africa (cf. no. 1)** NatRel: **NCCK (1965)** IntlRel: **WARC, REC** Service infrastructure: **4 health centers and 12 dispensories, two rest homes; every parish has its own kindergarten** Periodicals: **Tuzungurize "Let's Talk" (quarterly/1,050)**

Address: Reformed Church of East Africa (RCEA), P.O. Box 99, Kisumu Rd., Eldoret, Kenya, Tel: +254 321 32984, Fax: +254 321 62870

3. Independent Presbyterian Church of Kenya (1072)

The church was started in 1948 by missionaries of the IBPFM and was until 1963 called the Independent Presbyterian Mission. The split in 1956 within the Bible Presbyterian Church in the US also caused a split within the Church of Kenya in 1960. A minority group left and set up the African Evangelical Presbyterian Church (cf. below, no. 4). Since 1964 the Independent Presbyterian Church has been self-governing and carried its present name.

Following a dispute in 1984 with the mission on "questions of ecclesiastical compromise" a number of parishes left and organized themselves under the same name of Independent Presbyterian Church of Kenya but without any relations with the parent body. In 1984 the Independent Presbyterian Church joined with other churches of the EACA in founding the Faith College of the Bible.

TM: **2,500** CM: **1,500** Congr: **70** OrdM: **22** Eld: **140** Deac: **15** EvgHome: **14** Mission: **none** Women Ord: **no** ChurchOrg: **session, classis, presby, synod; only up to national level** Off/otherLang: **English, Kiswahili, Kikamba** DoctrB: **ApC, WestConf, Reformed** Infant or believer's baptism: **both** Frequency of the Lord's Supper: **monthly** Close relations with: **East Africa Christian Alliance** NatRel: **none** RegRel: **EACA (1964)** IntlRel: **ICCC (1964-84)** TheolSchool: **Faith College of the Bible, Mwingi IPC Bible School** Service infrastructure: **Bible schools** Periodicals: **none**

Address: Independent Presbyterian Church of Kenya, P.O. Box 37, Mwingi, Kenya, Tel: +254 1 42 22 035

4. Africa Evangelical Presbyterian Church (AEPC) (1076)

The AEPC was registered in 1962. Its roots go back to the work started in 1946 by missionaries of the IBPFM at the invitation of the Africa Inland Mission. Mr. and Mrs. Saunders Campbell were active since the early days when the mission began in Mwingi (North Kitui). In 1956 the crisis within the IBPFM in the US affected also church life in Kenya. The Campbells created, with some pastors who went with them, a new mission station in Muruu. This was the beginning of what be-

291

came the AEPC. In 1973 the church embarked on a "church planting vision." Rev. Campbell was sent to Nairobi, where he founded a congregation, the Community Presbyterian Church. New efforts in 1986 to go "Beyond Mwingi" saw the creation of congr in Nairobi, Limuru, Nakuru, and Meru. In 1990 three Kenyan missionaries were sent to Meru, Mombasa, and Embu.

TM: **10,000** BM: **1,000** CM: **9,000** Congr: **46** PStations: **4** OrdM: **17** Eld: **52** Deac: **30** EvgHome: **5** Mission: **0** Women Ord: **no** As Ministers: **none** as Deac: **none** as Elders: **none** ChurchOrg: **Presbyterian (sessions, presby, GenAssy)** Off/otherLang: **English, Swahili, local dialects** DoctrB: **ApC, WestConf** Infant or believer's baptism: **both** Frequency of the Lord's Supper: **monthly** Close relations with: **Presb Ch in America, Orth Presb Ch (USA), Gen Assembly of the Presbyterians of Korea** NatRel: **looking for a biblical organization** RegRel: **none** IntlRel: **CWM** TheolSchool: **Grace Bible College, Trinity Bible Institute (Muruu)** Service infrastructure: **1 health center (47 staff), 4 kindergartens, and 1 primary school (20 staff for both)** Periodicals: **none**

Address: Africa Evangelical Presbyterian Church, P.O. Box 7554, Nairobi, Kenya, Tel: +254 2 503-807, E-mail: compres@umsg.sasa.unon.org.

5. Africa Gospel Unity Church (AGUC) (1069)

The AGUC was formed in 1964 by an untrained pastor who left the National Holiness Mission after a dispute over administrative matters. Due to negligence and insufficiently qualified personnel, disorder in the membership and in the church grew (for example, polygamists were admitted to church office). Fellowship in 1970 with the EACE and the ICCC (membership was later dropped) brought the church in touch with missionaries of the IBPFM and with Ref theology. A group of younger pastors, trained at the Bible College of East Africa, were instrumental in reforming the church in 1982 by removing polygamous leaders and rewriting its constitution. The AGUC maintains the Baptist Confession of Faith (1689).

Most of the congr are in rural areas. The need for worship places within walking distance has been met by establishing numerous preaching stations and training additional lay preachers. Two thirds of Sunday worshipers are not communicant members yet. Every month each regional council holds an "evangelistic outreach" in which visits from house to house are made.

TM: **2,000** BM: **2,000** CM: **2,000** Congr: **65** PStations: **65** OrdM: **7** Eld: **7** Deac: **60** EvgHome: **0** Mission: **0** Women Ord: **no** ChurchOrg: **local church, district, region, and central church councils** Off/otherLang: **English, Swahili, other local languages** DoctrB: **ApC, Baptist Conf of Faith (1689) (similar to WestConf), Reformed** Infant or believer's baptism: **believer** Frequency of the Lord's Supper: **4 times a year** Close relations with: **Evangelical churches committed to biblical separation** NatRel: **East Africa Christian Alliance (1969)** TheolSchool: **Bomet Bible Institute** Service infrastructure: **1 kindergarten, 1 primary school** Periodicals: **none**

Address: Africa Gospel Unity Church (AGUC), P.O. Box 33, Bomet, Kenya, Tel: +254-360-22049

6. Bible Christian Faith Church (1075)

The church was founded in 1980 by 15 dissident congr of the Africa Inland Church. Reasons invoked for the move were disagreement on issues like "Biblical Separation and involvement in worldly politics affecting the spiritual life and power of the church." The church has been registered by the government since 1996. Ten congr left, in the meantime, to join other denominations already registered, although not sharing the same theological stance.

The Bible Christian Faith Church has from its beginning closely worked with the Free Presbyterian Church of Ulster (cf. Ireland no. 6), which has provided it with two female missionaries (one in 1984, a second one in 1996). The church has been touched by tribal clashes which are said to have caused the murder of two relatives of the general secretary of the church.

TM: **600** BM: **120** CM: **120** Congr: **6** PStations: **7** OrdM: **3** Eld: **18** Deac: **15** EvgHome: **3** Mission: **none** Women Ord: **no** ChurchOrg: **local church council, classical session, synod, assembly** Off/otherLang: **English, Kiswahili** DoctrB: **ApC, WestConf, strictly Reformed** Infant or believer's baptism: **believer** Frequency of the Lord's Supper: **monthly** Close relations with: **Independent Presbyterian Church, East Africa Christian Alliance** NatRel: **none** RegRel: **EACA** IntlRel: **World Christian Fundamentalist Congress** Service infrastructure: **kindergartens, sponsoring 2 state-owned primary schools, plans for church-owned primary and secondary school (1997/98)** Periodicals: **none**

Address: Bible Christian Faith Church, P.O. Box 179, Kapenguria, Nairobi, Kenya, Tel: +254 2 324 2473, Fax: +254 2 324 2233

KIRIBATI

Area in km²	717
Population	(July 1996 est.) 80,919 Micronesian
Religions in %	RCath 52.6%, Prot (Congreg) 40.9%, other (1985) 5.5% (Advent, Baha'i, Church of God, Mormon)
Official/other languages	English/Gilbertese

ABCFM (American Board of Commissioners for Foreign Mission)

Kiribati, the former Gilbert Islands, is a remote country of 33 scattered coral atolls, straddling the equator and the International Date Line, about halfway between Hawaii and Australia. Kiribati has few national resources. Commercially viable phosphate deposits were exhausted at the time of independence in 1979. Some 20 of the 33 islands are inhabited; Banaba (Ocean Island) in Kiribati is one of the three great phosphate rock islands in the Pacific Ocean: the others are Makatea in French Polynesia and Nauru.

Kiribati Protestant Church (5180)

Prot in Kiribati trace the beginnings of their church to "the coming of the light," when Hiram Bingham II, from Hawaii, settled on the island of Abaiang in 1852, as the first resident missionary. He had been sent by the Hawaiian Board of Mission, working closely with the ABCFM. His co-workers on the other islands were all Hawaiian Islander missionaries. The ABCFM evangelized the northern region of the Gilbert Islands until handing over the field to the LMS in 1917. The LMS was active in the southern part since 1872, working there with trained Samoan Islander missionaries. After 1920 the LMS and its successor bodies (first Congreg Council for World Missions and later Council for World Mission) oversaw the gradual growth of the church which became independent in 1969, ten years before Kiribati became an independent Republic.

TM: **28,359** BM: **28,359** CM: **10,000** Congr: **131** OrdM: **90** Eld: **ne** Deac: **300** EvgHome: **20** Mission: **2** Women Ord: **Yes** As Ministers: **1983/7** as Deac: **1969** as Elders: **no elders** ChurchOrg: **village church meeting, island church council, Synod (region), GenAssy** Off/otherLang: **Kiribati, English** DoctrB: **ApC, NicC** Infant or believer's baptism: **infant** Frequency of the Lord's Supper: **monthly** Periodicals: **News Share (mission and gen/monthly/25)** Close relations with: **Uniting Church of Australia** NatRel: **Kiribati National Council of Churches (1987), Kiribati Bible Society (1970s)** RegRel: **PCC (1970s)** IntlRel: **CWM (1968), WCC (1981), WARC (1985)** TheolSchool: **Tangintebu Theological College.**

Address: Ekaretia ni Boretetanti i Kiribati, P.O. Box 80, Antebuka Tarawa, Kiribati, Tel: +686 21195, Fax: +686 21453

KOREA, REPUBLIC OF

Area in km²	99,394
Population	46,433,920
Religions in %	Buddhist 36%, Confucian 16%, Christian 28% (Prot 23%, RCath 5%), Donghak 1.7%, Shamanism, folk religions etc. 18.3%
Official/other languages	Korean

CBS Christian Broadcasting System (founded August 31, 1954), **CCA** Christian Conference of Asia, **CCAK** Conservative Christian Association of Korea (founded December 19, 1983), **CCLK** Council of Christian Leaders in Korea, **CCK** Christian Council of Korea (founded April 28, 1989), **CMPC** Council for Mission of Presbyterian

Churches (1893), **CJPC** Council of Jesus Presbyterian Churches in Korea (founded in 1991), **CPCA** Central Office of Police and Church Agency (founded in 1966), **CPCJCC** The Chosun Presbyterian Church of Japan Christ Church (founded May 5, 1943), **CPC** Council of Protestant Churches in Korea, **CPCK** Council of Presbyterian Churches in Korea (founded September 22, 1981) **CRCK** Council of Ref Churches in Korea, **GAPCC** General Assembly of the Presbyterian Church in Chosun (1912), **GCPCK** General Council of Presbyterian Churches in Korea (founded in 1997), **ICCC** International Council of Christian Churches, **IPCC** Independent Presbytery of Jesus Christ in Chosun (1907), **KBS** Korean Bible Society, **KCCC** Korean Council of Christian Churches (founded May 11, 1965), **KHC** Korean Hymnal Committee (1956), **KHS** Korean Hymnal Society (founded April 9,1981), **KSCF** Korean Student Christian Federation (founded April 25, 1948), **NCCK** National Council of Churches in Korea (1949), **NEA** National Association of Evangelicals

The history of Korea goes back to the third millennium before Christ. In 2333 B.C. the kingdom of Chosun was founded by the legendary king Tangun. Since the first century before Christ there were three kingdoms on the peninsula — Koguryo, Paekche, and Silla. In the 7th century the Silla kingdom acquired a dominating position. In 935 the Koryo kingdom was established; it lasted until 1392. It was followed for several centuries by the Chosun kingdom under the Yi dynasty. In 1910 Korea was annexed by Japan and came, for 35 years, under Japanese colonial rule. The years of Japanese occupation are remembered by Koreans as a time of humiliation and suffering. As national consciousness grew, the Japanese occupation became increasingly oppressive. Koreans were forced to bow before the Shinto shrine, the symbol of the divine power of the Japanese emperor. Japanese colonial rule ended in 1945. The country was liberated but at the same time divided. Subsequent decades brought new suffering. Korea became the battlefield of superpowers (1950-53). Ever since the division of the country into the Democratic People's Republic of Korea (North) and the Republic of Korea (South) the situation has been tense, and all attempts at reunification of Korea have so far proved to be unsuccessful. The North regime, officially Marxist, became more and more of a dictatorship under the autocratic leadership of Kim Il Sung. Under a succession of authoritarian regimes the South experienced an astonishing economic development; today it is one of the rich nations in Asia.

The first Christian influence reached Korea in the 18th century. Korean neo-Confucian scholars contacted Jesuits in China and brought the Christian faith into the country. For a long time Christians were persecuted. In the years 1839, 1846, and 1866-1871 several thousand Christians became martyrs. Today the RCath has about two million adherents. Protestantism reached Korea in the 19th century. Even before missionaries arrived in Korea (or Chosun, as it was then called), lay people like Suh Sang-Yoon and Baek Hong-Joon spread the Gospel in the country. Suh was converted in 1876 in Manchuria by Scottish missionaries and helped with the translation of the New Testament into Korean. He brought copies of Gospel portions back to Korea and in 1883 formed a small Christian community in his home village. In the following year the first American missionaries landed in Korea. Horace N. Allen of the northern Presbyterian Church started medical work (1884). A year later he was joined by Horace G. Underwood, the first ordained missionary. Several more missions were established in the following years: the Presbyterian Church of Victoria in Australia (1889), the Presbyterian Church in the USA (1892), and the Presbyterian Church of Canada (1898). In 1893 they formed the Council for Mission of Presbyterian Churches (CMPC) and opened the theological seminary of Pyongyang (1901).

In response to the Great Revival Movement (1907), missionaries of various backgrounds established the Independent Presbytery of Jesus Church in Chosun (IPCC) and ordained seven Koreans as pastors (1907). Some years later (1912) missionaries and Korean ministers together formed the General Assembly of the Presbyterian Church in Chosun (GAPCC) and sent three Korean missionaries to China. In 1921 GAPCC set up two important lay organizations — the National Youth Association of the Presbyterian Church and the National Association of Women's Meetings for Evangelism.

Under the Japanese occupation (1910-1945) many Christian lay people participated in the struggle for independence. Toward the end of Japanese occupation the worship of the Shinto shrine was more and more forced on the churches. Under police threat the GAPCC illegally approved the worship of the shrine (1938). Many pastors and lay people resisted and started a movement against "bowing to the emperor's shrine." Many were arrested and sentenced to prison or death. Almost all missionaries were expelled (1941). GAPCC was dissolved and integrated into the newly founded Chosun Presbyterian Church of Christ in Japan (1943). After World War II different responses to the Japanese oppression became the reason for the first divisions among the Presb churches.

With the victory of the Allied forces Japanese colonialism came to an end. But with the division of the countries new problems arose. In the North the churches were dissolved (cf. People's Republic of Korea). In the South the Presbyterian Church was reconstituted (1946). The 33rd Assembly held in DaeGu in 1947 claimed to represent the whole of Korea. Two years later the church adopted the name Presbyterian Church of Korea.

In the following years the Presb churches in Korea grew rapidly. Many reasons can be given for this astonishing development. In the first place it must be emphasized that Christian missions in Korea, in contrast to so many other countries, was not identified with a colonial power. The Christian message was brought to Korea at a time when the religious and cultural heritage of Korea had lost much of its inner strength. Equally important was the policy, the so-called Nevius method, which missionaries adopted. They urged each convert to become an evangelist and to convert others. Much of the growth is due to Korean initiative. Koreans developed a strong commitment to the Christian faith. Spiritual discipline and prayer are characteristic of Korean Christians. A special feature of Korean church life is, for instance, the dawn prayer meeting. Another important factor in church growth was the revival movement. Finally, the Korean Christians generally did not allow evangelism and social action to fall apart.

Korean churches are also found in many other countries. Through migration Korean communities have come into existence in many parts of the world. Since

296

the late seventies the Korean churches have also begun to send out increasing numbers of missionaries. Today several thousand Korean missionaries are active outside Korea. In some countries Korean Presb churches have been founded.

Church growth was accompanied by a succession of schisms. Today Korea presents a bewildering picture. Christianity represents close to 28% of the population. But Presb Christianity alone consists of around 100 separate denominations in Korea.

Immediately after World War II a dispute arose over the readmission of those who had bowed to the shrine (KoShin [no. 1], JaeGun [no. 6]). A few years later Presb Christianity was shaken by the conflict between conservative and progressive theological interpretations of the biblical tradition (KiJang [no. 13]), followed by the conflict over the participation in the ecumenical movement (TongHap [no. 14], HapDong [no. 15]). The influence of ICCC, struggle for leadership and power, and the impact of seminaries on the life of the churches were divisive. Division was exacerbated by the fact that the Korean church had been cut off from the universal church in its early mission history as well as during Japanese colonial rule. The social disruption resulting from the Korean War also strengthened the trend toward division.

Despite their divisions the Presb churches hold common convictions. They all adhere to the Apostles' Creed and the Westminster Confession. They all maintain the same patterns of organization and, generally, use the same hymnal (which is also used by other denominations such as the Meth and Bapt). Again and again attempts have been made to bring the churches closer to one another. In recent years the movement has gained momentum. In 1981, in response to the need for common witness, the five largest Presb churches (TongHap [no. 14], HapDong [no. 15], KoShin [no. 1], KiJang [no. 13], DaeShin [no. 16]) decided to organize the Council of Presbyterian Churches in Korea (CPCK). In 1995 three more churches joined the council (GaeHyuk [no. 23], HapDongJeongTong [no. 37], and HoHun [no. 18]). At the initiative of HapDong (no. 15) an even larger association, mainly of conservative churches, came into existence in 1991. For several years these two councils existed side by side, but in 1997 they decided to merge. The new Council (GCPCK) represents most Presb churches in Korea. At its second Assembly in November 1997 the Council emphasized the need for closer collaboration with the wider Ref family.

A. List of Presbyterian Churches in Korea

I. Churches Arising from Protest against the Shrine Worship

1. Presbyterian Church in Korea (KoShin = Korean Theology)
2. Korea Jesus Presbyterian (KyeShin = Ref Theology)
3. Korean Reformed Presbyterian Church (KoRyuPa = Korean Theology Group)
4. Presbyterian Church in Korea (KoRyu = Anti-accusation)
5. Presbyterian Church (HapDongJangShin = United Presb Theology)
6. Korea Presbyterian Reconstruction Church (JaeGun = Reconstruction)
7. Pure Presbyterian Church of Korea (SunJang = Pure Presb)

8. Presbyterian Church of Korea (DokNoHoe I = Independent presby)
9. Presbyterian Church of Korea (DokNoHoe II = Independent presby)
10. Presbyterian Church in Korea (DongShin = Eastern Theology)
11. Presbyterian Church in Korea (BoSu I = Conservative)
12. Presbyterian Church in Korea (BoSu II = Conservative)

II. Churches Arising from Two Major Breaks in the Fifties

13. Presbyterian Church in the Republic of Korea (KiJang = Christ Presb, PROK)
14. Presbyterian Church of Korea (TongHap = Ecumenical, PCK)
15. Presbyterian Church of Korea (HapDong = United)

III. The Divisive Impact of the International Council of Christian Churches (ICCC)

16. Presbyterian Church of Korea (DaeShin I = Korean Theology)
17. Presbyterian Church of Korea (DaeShin II = Korean Theology)
18. Korean Presbyterian Church (HoHun = Protecting Constitution)
19. Presbyterian Church of Korea (HwanWon = Returned)
20. Presbyterian Church in Korea (HapDongHwanWon = United Returned)
21. Presbyterian Church of Korea (BubTong = Legitimate Succession)
22. Presbyterian Church in Korea (JangShin = Presb Theology)

IV. The Aftermath of the Division of HapDong into Mainline and Non-Mainline (1979)

23. Korean Presbyterian Church (GaeHyuk I = Ref)
24. Presbyterian Church in Korea (BoSuHapDong I = Conservative United)
25. Presbyterian Church in Korea (GaeHyuk II = Ref)
26. Presbyterian Church in Korea (BoSuHapDong II = Conservative United)
27. Presbyterian Church in Korea (BoSuHapDong III = Conservative United)
28. Presbyterian Church in Korea (HapDongSeong Hoe = United Holy Assembly)
29. Presbyterian Church in Korea (HapDongBoSu I = United Conservative)
30. Presbyterian Church in Korea (HapDongBoSu II = United Conservative)
31. Presbyterian Church in Korea (HapDongBoSu III = United Conservative)
32. Presbyterian Church in Korea (HapDongBoSu IV = United Conservative)
33. Presbyterian Church of Korea (HapDongGaeHyuk = United Ref)
34. Presbyterian Church in Korea (HapDongJinRi = United for Truth)
35. Presbyterian Church in Korea (HapDongChongShin I = United General Assembly)
36. Presbyterian Church in Korea (HapDongChongShin II = United General Assembly)
37. Presbyterian Church in Korea (HapDongJeong Tong = United Orthodox)
38. Presbyterian Church in Korea (YeJeong = Jesus Presb)
39. Presbyterian Church in Korea (BokUm I = Gospel)

40. Presbyterian Church of Korea (YeJangHapBo = United Conservatives of Jesus Presb)

V. Churches Based on JungAng

41. Presbyterian Church in Korea (HapDongJungAng = United Central)
42. Presbyterian Church in Korea (JungAng = Central)
43. Presbyterian Church in Korea (BoSuTongHap = Conservative United)
44. Women Pastors' Presbyterian Church (YuMok = Women Ministry)
45. Korean Presbyterian Union of Women Pastors (YunHapYerMok = United Women Ministry)
46. Union Presbyterian Church of Korea (YunHap = United)

VI. Fundamentalist Churches

47. Korean Christian Fundamentalist Assembly (GunBon — Fundamentalist I)
48. Fundamentalist Presbyterian General Assembly (GunBon — Fundamentalist II)

VII. Churches Connected with BoSu Seminary

49. Conservative Presbyterian Church in Korea (BoSuChuk = Conservative Group)
50. Korea Presbyterian Church (YeJang = Jesus Presb)
51. Presbyterian Church of Korea (SungHapChuk = Holy United Group)

VIII. Other Churches

52. Conservative-Reformed Presbyterian Church in Korea (BoSuGeHyuk = Conservative Ref)
53. Union Presbyterian Church of Korea (YunHapChuk = United Group)
54. Presbyterian Church of Korea (Logos)
55. Presbyterian Church in Korea (JeongRip = Stand Rightly)
56. Presbyterian Church in Korea (HapDongBoSu = United Conservative)
57. Korea Presbyterian United Church General Assembly (JongHap = United)
58. General Co-operation of the Presbyterian Church in Korea (HyupDong = Cooperation)
59. Presbyterian Church in Korea (HapDongChongYun = United)
60. Presbyterian Church in Korea (JungRip = Neutral Position)
61. Presbyterian Church in Korea (JeongTongChongHap = Orthodox United)
62. Union General Assembly (HapDongChongHoe = Union Assembly)
63. Presbyterian General Assembly in Korea (ChanYang = Praise)
64. Presbyterian Church of Korea (PyungHap = General Union)
65. Presbyterian Church of Korea (HapDongBokUm = United Evangelical)
66. Presbyterian Church in Korea (HapDongYeChong I = United Jesus Assembly)
67. Presbyterian Church in Korea (HapDongYeChong II = United Jesus Assembly)
68. Presbyterian Church in Korea (HyukShin = Renovation)

69. Presbyterian Church in Korea (GaeHyukHapDong I =Ref United)
70. Presbyterian Church in Korea (GaeHyukHapDong II = Ref United)
71. Presbyterian Church in Korea (GaeHyukHapDong III = Ref United)
72. Presbyterian Church in Korea (NamBuk = South and North)
73. Presbyterian Church in Korea (DaeHanShinChuk = Korean Theology Group)
74. Presbyterian Church in Korea (BoSuJeongTong = Conservative Orthodox)
75. Presbyterian Church in Korea (BoSuChuk = Conservative Group)
76. Presbyterian Church in Korea (SunGyo = Mission)
77. Presbyterian Church in Korea (YunShin = Yonsei Theology)
78. Presbyterian Church in Korea (YeJeong = Predestined)
79. Presbyterian Church in Korea (JeongTongGyeSeung = Succession of Orthodox)
80. Presbyterian Church in Korea (ChongHoe I = General Assembly)
81. Presbyterian Church in Korea (ChongHoe II = General Assembly)
82. Presbyterian Church in Korea (TongHapBoSu = United Conservative)
83. Presbyterian Church in Korea (PyungAhn I = Peace)
84. Presbyterian Church in Korea (PyungAhn II = Peace)
85. Presbyterian Church in Korea (HanGukBoSu = Korean Conservative)
86. Presbyterian Church in Korea (HapDongSunGyo I = United Mission)
87. Presbyterian Church in Korea (HapDongSunGyo II = United Mission)
88. Presbyterian Church in Korea (HapDongSunMok = United Sacred Ministry)
89. Presbyterian Church in Korea (HapDongYunHap = United Union)
90. Presbyterian Church in Korea (HapDongYeSun = United Jesus Mission)
91. Presbyterian Church in Korea (HapDongEunChong = United Grace)
92. Presbyterian Church in Korea (HapDongJeongShin = United Orthodox Theology)
93. Presbyterian Church in Korea (HapDongJungRip = United Neutral Position)
94. Presbyterian Church in Korea (HapDongTongHap = United Union)
95. Presbyterian Church in Korea (HoHun II = Protecting Constitution)
96. Presbyterian Church in Korea (HoHun III = Protecting Constitution)

B. Origin and History of the Presbyterian Churches

I. Presbyterian Churches Arising from the Protest against the Shrine Worship

Until the end of World War II Presb in Korea formed one church. After the attempts of the Japanese to neutralize the witness of the church, the need arose after Liberation to "reconstruct" the church. Attempts in this direction led to violent debates on the issue of the readmission of those who had bowed before the Shinto shrine. Divisions began to occur in this process.

Presbyterian Churches Arising from the Protest against Shrine Worship (nos. 1-12)

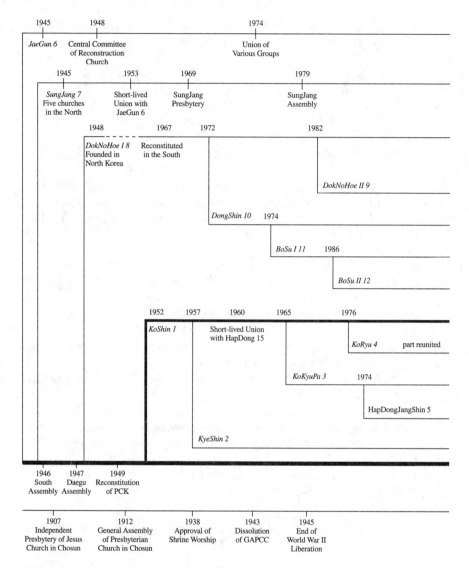

1. Presbyterian Church in Korea (KoShin) (4604)

This denomination was founded by pastors and lay people who had resisted the shrine worship and had been imprisoned by the Japanese. After liberation in 1945 on September 18, 1945, they organized the KyungNam Reconstruction Presbytery in Pyongyang and called for full investigation and repentance of the pastors who

had worshiped the shrine. Their request was rejected. Three pastors who had suffered imprisonment in Pyongyang (Joo Nam-Sun, Han Sang-Dong, and Park
Yun-Sun) moved to the South and in 1946 founded KoRyu Seminary (now
KoShin University) in Pusan. The General Assembly of the Presbyterian Church,
however, refused to recognize the seminary. Originally the three pastors belonged
to the KyungNam Reconstruction Presbytery. But due to internal tensions, this
presby divided into five parts (1950). The founders of KoRyu Seminary formed
the KyungNam (BubDong = legitimate succession) presby (1952). They continued to call for a full investigation and repentance of shrine worshipers. They refused fellowship with them. Their presby later became the KoShin denomination.

Several splits occurred in KoShin. In 1957 secession took place which resulted in the foundation of KyeShin (no. 2). A conflict between two leaders, Park
Yun-Sun and Song Sang-Suk, which started in the 1950s, eventually led to the
foundation of the Presbyterian Church in Korea (KoRyuPa [no. 3]). When in 1960
TongHap (no. 14) and HapDong (no. 15) divided (for details cf. below, no. 15), the
suggestion was made that HapDong and KoShin should unite. The union did not
last long. KoShin withdrew from the united church; only about 150 local churches
stayed with HapDong.

A further split occurred in 1976. Song Sang-Suk, then rector of KoShin University in Pusan, sought to maintain himself in his position beyond his term. The
KoShin Assembly decided to bring him to court. Some members of the Assembly,
led by Suk Won-Tae, objected to this decision on biblical grounds (1 Cor. 6:1-11).
Together with Song Sang-Suk they withdrew from KoShin and founded the Presbyterian Church in Korea (KoRyu — Anti-Accusation [no. 4]). Some members of
this new denomination later returned to KoShin.

In the following years KoShin developed steadily. In 1993 an Assembly
building was erected.

TM: **362,620** CM: **146,339** Congr: **1,361** OrdM: **1,365** Eld: **3,046** Deac: nc EvgHome: **1,485** Mission:
nc Women Ord: **no** DoctrB: **ApC, WestConf** ChurchOrg: **Presbyterian (30 presby, GenAssy)** Off/
otherLang: **Korean** DoctrB: nc NatRel: **CCK, CPCK, KHS** IntlRel: **ICRC** TheolSchool: **KoShin
University (Pusan)**

Address: 58 10 Banpo-Dong, Sucho-Gu, 137-040 Seoul, Korea, Tel: +82 2 592-0433, Fax: +82 2
592-1468

2. Korea Jesus Presbyterian Church (KyeShin) (4605)

This church resulted from a split within KoShin in 1957 (cf. no. 1). Kim
Suk-Chan, pastor of MunChang Church in Masan, wanted to join HapDong (no.
15) together with his congr. Song Sang-Suk, who had succeeded him as pastor, respected his personal decision but questioned his right to involve the congr as a
whole. He decided to bring him to court. KoShin people were divided on the issue.
Some felt that the church should not go to court if fellowship with a congr was at
stake. The GenAssy leaders were hesitant. Dissatisfied with their lack of clarity,
one of the presby (KyungKi) suspended relations with the GenAssy. The opposi-

tion to the GenAssy was divided into three groups (Kim Chang-In, Jang Yur-Jae, and Lee Byung-Gyu). Nevertheless they agreed to organize a council (1960), to open a high school (1967), to found the Covenant Seminary (1969), and to start a new denomination (1975). In 1980 the name KeyShin was adopted. Eventually Kim Chang-In joined HapDong (no. 15) and Jang Yur-Jae joined GaeHyuk (no. 23). Lee Byung-Gyu became the leading figure of this denomination.

TM: **21,712** BM: **nc** CM: **14,474** Congr: **135** OrdM: **122** Eld: **52** Deac: **nc** EvgHome: **65** Mission: **nc** Women Ord: **no** DoctrB: **ApC, WestConf** ChurchOrg: **Presbyterian (11 presby, GenAssy)** Off/otherLang: **Korean** DoctrB: **nc** NatRel: **CCK, CPCK, KHS** IntlRel: **ICRC** TheolSchool: **Covenant Seminary**

Address: 20-5 ChangCheong-Dong, SuDaeMoon-Gu, Seoul, Korea, Tel: +82 2 392-2936, Fax: +82 2 393-9249

3. Korean Reformed Presbyterian Church (KoRyuPa) (4607)

This church resulted from a split within KoShin (no. 1). Due to tensions at KoRyu Seminary (cf. above) Professor Park Yun-Sun moved to Seoul and there founded the Reformed Theological Seminary. Many students of KoRyu Seminary followed him. To avoid division Park returned to KoShin, but Pastor Chung Hun-Taek took over as director of the Reformed Theological Seminary at DongSan Church in Seoul. In 1965 about 50 pastors related to this seminary founded KoRyuPa. KoRyuPa has entertained relations with conservative Ref churches in Japan, the Netherlands, and the USA. The church has often been accused of being heretical because of the similarity of its name with the heretical group DongBang (= Eastern Direction). Since 1977 the leading figure of the church has been Yoo Don-Sik, who also directs the Reformed Theological Seminary.

TM: **76,900** BM: **nc** CM: **58,700** Congr: **497** OrdM: **501** Eld: **105** Deac: **35,000** EvgHome: **250** Mission: **nc** Women Ord: **no** DoctrB: **ApC, WestConf** ChurchOrg: **Presbyterian (16 presby, GenAssy)** Off/otherLang: **Korean** TheolSchool: **Reformed Theological Seminary**

Address: 43-46 ManSuk-Dong, Dong-Gu, Inchon, Korea, Tel: +82 32 762-1209, Fax: +82 32 764-1839

4. Presbyterian Church in Korea (KoRyu — Anti-Accusation) (4608)

This church also split from KoShin (cf. no. 1) on the ground that Christians should not go to secular courts. The KoShin GenAssy divided into the "Accusation" and the "Anti-Accusation" groups. When the GenAssy decided to bring Song Sang-Suk to court, the "Anti-Accusation" group withdrew and formed KoRyu (Anti-Accusation) in 1976. Later KoRyu divided again, and part of its members returned to KoShin (no. 1).

TM: **66,345** BM: **nc** CM: **nc** Congr: **194** OrdM: **391** Eld: **3,046** Deac: **nc** EvgHome: **131** Mission: **nc** Women Ord: **no** DoctrB: **ApC, WestConf** ChurchOrg: **Presbyterian** Off/otherLang: **Korean** NatRel: **CCK, CCLK**

Address: 53 Young-Deong Po-Dong, YoungDeung Po-Gu, Seoul, Korea, Tel: +82 2 780-0614, Fax: +82 2 780-0615

5. Presbyterian Church (HapDongJangShin) (4609)

This denomination separated in 1974 from KoRyuPa 4. The new church was founded in 1980 by Kil Young-Bok.

TM: **32,163** Congr: **112** OrdM: **143** Eld: **nc** Deac: **nc** EvgHome: **76** Mission: **nc** Women Ord: **nc** As Ministers: **nc** as Deac: **nc** as Elders: **nc** ChurchOrg: **nc** Off/otherLang: **Korean** DoctrB: **ApC, WestConf** NatRel: **CCAK, CPCA, KHC**

Address: 255-116 JamSil-Dong, SongPa-Gu, Seoul, Korea, Tel: +82 2 422-4258

6. Korea Presbyterian Reconstruction Church (JaeGun) (4610)

This church represents the most radical approach to the issue of shrine worship. After liberation in 1945 the Reconstruction movement took three different forms: **a)** Reconstruction within the established church (Pastor Ko Hung-Bong); **b)** Reconstruction through an act of repentance of all pastors who had worshiped the shrine (Pastors Lee Ki-Sun, Han Sang-Dong; cf. no. 1); **c)** Forming a new "reconstructed" church outside the established church (Choi Duk-Ji, Kim Rin-Hee). The movement adopting the third line was started simultaneously in the North and the South. In the North the Central Committee of the Reconstructed Church was founded with Pastor Kang Sang-Eun as moderator and Mrs. Choi Duk-Ji as vice-moderator (1948). Pastor Han Sang-Dong (see KoShin [no. 1]) in the South proposed that the movement should unite, but Mrs. Choi rejected the proposal.

During the Korean war (1950-1953) the movement in the North suffered oppression from the Communists and was also torn apart by the extremist positions held within its fold. They moved to the South and united with another reconstruction group (cf. under SunJang [no. 7]). But the union did not last. In 1954 their GenAssy decided to ordain women to both the ministry of the Word and to eldership. The decision led to dissension. The 1955 GenAssy confirmed the decision and dismissed the opposition through a disciplinary act. In 1959 the church adopted the name JaeGun. In the seventies JaeGun united with some other reconstruction groups (1973-1974).

TM: **23,569** Congr: **113** OrdM: **135** Eld: **nc** Deac: **nc** EvgHome: **20** Mission: **nc** Women Ord: **nc** As Ministers: **nc** as Deac: **nc** as Elders: **yes** ChurchOrg: **Presb (13 presby, GenAssy)** DoctrB: **ApC, WestConf**

Address: 640-243 ChangSing2-Dong, Chongro-Gu, Seoul, Korea, Tel: +82 2 763-3679

7. The Pure Presbyterian Church of Korea (SungJang) (4611)

The origins of this group are in the North. During the Japanese rule and struggle against shrine worship, five churches in HamKyungNamDo province separated from the HamNam presby and kept their faith in the spirit of martyrdom (Dukchun, East Dukchun, Kigock, Sangsuri, and JangHung). Their leader was Pastor Lee Gye-Sil. After liberation they went their own way. During the Korean War Pastor Lee, with hundreds of church members, fled to the South; they were rescued from HungNam by the US Army. They built a church and a seminary on GuJae Island (1953). In the same year they united with JaeGun (no. 6), which held similar views and had also moved to the South. Both introduced the system of a general meeting for the formation of a presby. The union was soon dissolved, but six congr of JaeGun (no. 6) stayed with SunJang. They founded the Dukchun Church and an independent seminary (1956) in YoungDeungPo in Seoul. Pastor Lee Gye-Sil became the first president of the independent presby. The church grew and developed international relations; it participated in the 10th ICCC Assembly with observer status. In 1979 the church adopted the name SungJang. The church is active in missions abroad.

TM: **12,775** CM: **3,509** Congr: 25 ChurchOrg: **Presbyterian (9 presby, 3 of which are outside Korea)** DoctrB: **ApC, WestConf**

Address: 632-31 SinDaeBang-Dong, DongJak-Gu, Seoul, Korea, Tel: +82 2 845-771, Fax: +82 2 849-9545

8. Presbyterian Church of Korea (DokNoHoe I) (4612)

The conflict over shrine worship led to the formation of still other churches. DokNoHoe has its roots in the North. After liberation those who were released from prison together celebrated a worship service in Sanjunghyun Church in Pyongyang (17 August 1945). While Han Sang-Dong moved to the South and founded KoShin (no. 1) and Kim Chang-In (cf. KyeShin [no. 4]) and Mrs. Choi Duk-Ji (cf. JaeGun [no. 6]) formed Reconstruction Churches, the pastors Lee-Ki-Sun, Bang Gye-Sun and Oh Yun-Sun organized an Independent presby (DokNoHoe) in the North in 1948, which was joined by about 30 churches. In their five principles program they insisted on the reconstruction of the church at a national scale and asked for the full repentance of the pastors who had worshiped the shrine; they should withdraw from their ministry for two months. During the Korean War Pastor Lee Ki-Sun suffered martyrdom (1950). Many members of DokNoHoe fled to the South. Chang Ki-Ryur and Lee Il-Hwa came to Pusan City and started a tent church (1951). They also established themselves in Seoul and there founded the Sangjunghyung church (1954). In 1967 they reorganized the Independent presby (DokNoHoe). Further splits occurred (cf. nos. 9 to 12). In 1974 DokNoHoe organized itself as an Assembly. Pastor Ahn Do-Myung was the first moderator.

TM: **14,900** CM: **1,000** Congr: **87** OrdM: **91** Eld: **nc** Deac: **nc** EvgHome: **91** DoctrB: **ApC, WestConf** ChurchOrg: **Presbyterian**

Address: 406-5 HuAm-Dong, YoungSan-Gu, Seoul, Korea, Tel: +82 2 754-0904, Fax: +82 2 755-8349

9. Presbyterian Church of Korea (DokNoHoe II) (4613)

A leadership issue led to a further split in 1982. When moderator Ahn Do-Myung (cf. no. 8) went to the USA in 1981, Pastor Chung Nam-Young acted as proxy. But the Assembly elected Pastor Yoo Yong-Hyun as moderator. In response Pastors Chung Nam-Young and Bang Byung-Duk withdrew from the church and formed DokNoHoe II.

TM: **3,952** CM: **2,811** Congr: **25** OrdM: **23** Eld: **32** Deac: **821** EvgHome: **2** Mission: **nc** Women Ord: **no** ChurchOrg: **nc** Off/otherLang: **Korean** DoctrB: **nc** NatRel: **CCK (1989)**

Address: 279-422 Sangdo-Dong, Dongjak-Gu, Seoul, Korea, Tel: +82 2 821-0387, Fax: +82 2 824-7517

10. Presbyterian Church in Korea (DongShin) (4614)

This church is the result of a tension within DokNoHoe I (cf. no. 8). Two groups under the leadership of Chung Dae-Shin and Kim Chang-Gil opposed one another within DokNoHoe I. Kim Chang-Gil, leader of DongA Seminary, in 1972 formed the Presbyterian Church in Korea (BoSu or DongShin). For four years he acted as moderator of this church. The church grew. But it suffered further divisions. While Kim Chang-Gil, Lee Hong-Pyun, and Bang Boo-Shin continued with DongShin, Cho Chang-Hyun and Choi Han Yong formed BoSu I (cf. no. 11). The issue at stake was leadership prerogatives. Later Bang Boo-Shin also seceded from DongShin and founded GaeHyukJeongTong, a small denomination which continues to exist in Seoul.

TM: **5,264** CM: **3,509** Congr: **56** OrdM: **56** Eld: **nc** Deac: **nc** EvgHome: **37** DoctrB: **ApC, WestConf** ChurchOrg: **Presbyterian**

Address: 111-270 Gong-Duk-Dong, MaPo-Gu, Seoul, Korea, Tel: +82 2 712-2874

11. Presbyterian Church in Korea (BoSu I) (4615)

The division of DongShin and BoSu took place in 1974 (cf. no. 10). BoSu I started a seminary in Sinsuldong under the direction of Choi Sung-Gon. In 1978 the GenAssy of BoSu I adopted a revised constitution. But soon the church passed through turbulent times. For some years, in order to strengthen its numbers, BoSu I had uncritically received pastors from other churches into its fellowship. Some of them had been under the influence of Elder Na Un-Mong, the founder of

YongMun movement. Pastor Park Young-Kwan of BoSu regarded the teaching of Elder Na Un-Mong as heresy and opposed him in public debates. When the Assembly of BoSu I named Park Young-Kwan as professor at the seminary, many of the pastors who had recently been received into the church objected. About 60 churches withdrew from BoSu I and entered other denominations individually.

TM: **10,700** Congr: **92** OrdM: **89** Eld: **nc** Deac: **nc** EvgHome: **3** DoctrB **ApC, WestConf** ChurchOrg: **Presbyterian**

Address: 73-11 Jak-Dong, OhJeong-Gu, Buchon, Korea, Tel: +82 32 677-5715, Fax: +82 32 681-6667

12. Presbyterian Church in Korea (BoSu II) (4616)

In 1986 Pastor Cho Chang-Hyun, the founder of BoSu I (no. 11), separated from the church and founded, together with Pastor Cha Eung-Hyun, the Presbyterian Church in Korea (BoSu II).

TM: **5,264** CM: **3,509** Congr: **56** OrdM: **64** Eld: **nc** Deac: **nc** EvgHome: **29** DoctrB: **ApC, WestConf**

Address: 2239 BangBaebon-Dong, Sucho-Gu, Seoul 137-069, Korea, Tel: +82 2 536-9953, Fax: +82 2 534-7194

II. Two Major Breaks in the Fifties

13. Presbyterian Church in the Republic of Korea (KiJang, PROK) (4601)

This church is the result of a conflict over theological positions within the Presbyterian Church of Korea. The conflict arose in Chosun Seminary. Because of refusal to worship at the emperor's shrine, the Theological Seminary in Pyongyang was closed down by force in 1938. Some of the leaders went into exile. One year later Chosun Seminary was reopened in the South; the new seminary was to become the nucleus of KiJang. In contrast to the Pyongyang seminary Chosun Seminary adopted a progressive theological line. After liberation the South Assembly of the Presbyterian Church in Korea recognized Chosun Seminary as the seminary under the authority of the Assembly (1946). But an essay published by Dr. Kim Jae-Joon, president of the seminary, caused a violent debate between conservative and progressive theological positions. Dr. Park Hyung-Ryong decided to leave the seminary and to found a new Presb seminary; he was followed by 51 students (1947). The Assembly also recognized the new seminary. Now there were two competing seminaries under the authority of the Assembly. In order to unite them the Assembly withdrew both recognitions and urged them to give up separate management. In the process of the negotiations it became clear that the line adopted by Chosun Seminary was not shared by the Assembly. Dr. Kim Jae-Joon was expelled from the church by the 37th Assembly in 1952. A year later the Chosun Group formed the Presbyterian Church in the Republic of Korea (PROK).

Major Breaks in the Fifties (nos. 13-15)

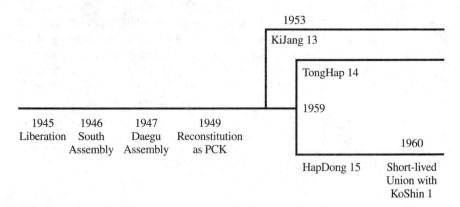

In 1954 the church adopted the name Han Kun Ki Dok Kyo Jang No Hoe (abbreviated KiJang).

The church is the most progressive among the Presb churches in Korea. In 1956 it voted in favor of the ordination of women for the ministry and for eldership. In 1974 the first women were ordained, and in 1987 *Confession 1987* was adopted. The church places strong emphasis on social and political action and has promoted the "Peace-Reunification Movement" since 1987. In 1993 the denomination celebrated its fortieth anniversary and began to develop the "Peace-Unity Movement" and the "Restoration of Life Movement."

TM: **326,076** CM: **173,619** Congr: **801** PStations: **631** OrdM: **1,734** Eld: **2,624** Deac: **19,919** EvgHome: **572** Mission: **35** Women Ord: **yes** As Ministers: **1974/70** as Deac: **47,769** as Elders: **1956/ 76** ChurchOrg: **Presbyterian (10 presby, GenAssy)** Off/otherLang: **Korean** DoctrB: **ApC, WestConf, Confession 1987** Close relations with: **EMS** NatRel: **NCCK, KSCF, CBS, CLS, KBS, KHC** RegRel: **CCA** IntlRel: **WARC, WCC** TheolSchool: **Theological Seminary Seoul, HanShin University Suwon**

Address: #1501 Korean Ecumenical Building, 136-56 YunJi-Dong, ChongRo-Gu, Seoul 110-470, Korea, Tel: +82 2 708-4021, Fax: +82 2 708-4027

14. Presbyterian Church of Korea (TongHap, PCK) (4600)

After World War II this church was reconstituted. After two Assemblies in 1946 and 1947 the church adopted the name Presbyterian Church of Korea at its 35th Assembly. Despite heavy losses through divisions arising from the controversies over shrine worship, the majority of members continued to adhere to that church. Today it represents the major stream in Korean Presbyterianism.

In the '50s the issue of participation in the ecumenical movement caused increasing tensions in the church. While one party promoted the idea of membership in the World Council of Churches (WCC), others opted for the National Association of Evangelicals (NAE). At the 44th Assembly in 1959 the church broke into two churches of about equal size — TongHap (no. 14) and HapDong (no. 15). A few years later (1962) TongHap celebrated the 50th Assembly of the Presbyterian Church of Korea. In 1984 a commemorative event for the 100th anniversary of the Presbyterian Church in Korea was organized by the church; at that time an Assembly building was inaugurated. In 1986 PCK adopted its present confession of faith. TongHap is open to the ecumenical movement and allows for a wide range of theological positions. In 1995 it introduced the ordination of women.

TM: **2,094,338** CM: **929,424** Congr: **5,890** OrdM: **7500** Eld: **14,804** Deac: **472,312** EvgHome: **4,516** Mission: **nc** Women Ord: **yes** As Ministers: **1995/nc** as Deac: **yes/nc** as Elders: **yes/nc** ChurchOrg: **Presbyterian (56 presby, GenAssy)** Off/otherLang: **Korean** DoctrB: **ApC, WestConf** NatRel: **NCCK, KSCF, KBS, CBS, CPCK** RegRel: **CCA** IntlRel: **WARC, WCC, CWM**

Address: P.O. Box 1125 135 YunChi-Dong, ChongRo-ku, Seoul 100-611, Korea, Tel: +82 2 741-4350, Fax: +82 2 766-2427

15. Presbyterian Church of Korea (HapDong) (4618)

At the 44th Assembly (1959) the Presbyterian Church of Korea divided into two churches of about equal size (cf. no. 14). While TongHap maintained membership in the WCC and allowed for a relatively wide range of theological positions, HapDong represents the more conservative line. After the break, HapDong, with the help of ICCC, built a seminary. On the basis of its strict doctrinal positions it seemed logical that the church would unite with KoShin (no. 1). The union decided upon in 1960 did not last. It turned out that their seminaries were too different in their theological approaches. Some 150 KoShin congrs stayed with HapDong. Like TongHap, HapDong celebrated (in 1962) the 50th Assembly of the Presbyterian Church of Korea. In 1965 it started the newspaper *KiDokSinBo* and founded ChongShin Seminary in SaDangDong.

At the 64th Assembly (1979) HapDong suffered a further division. The church divided into mainline and non-mainline groups. The debate centered around two issues. The first was the authorship of the Pentateuch, and the second the relationship of the church to ChongShin Seminary. Rev. Kim Hee-Bo, the president of ChongShin Theological Seminary, advocated biblical criticism by denying Moses' authorship of the Pentateuch. As he was censured, 15 directors of ChongShin Seminary withdrew from the authority of the Assembly, changed the school into a university, and ran it privately. The non-mainline group soon fragmented further and gave birth to several more denominations (cf. below, nos. 3-40). HapDong, however, continued to grow and developed in the following years into the largest denomination in Korea. In 1986 an Assembly building was inaugurated, and in 1992 HapDong celebrated the 80th anniversary of the first General Assembly in 1912.

TM: **2,158,908** Congr: **5,123** OrdM: **6,251** Eld: **nc** Deac: **nc** EvgHome: **7,002** Mission: **nc** Women Ord: **no** ChurchOrg: **nc** Off/otherLang: **Korean** DoctrB: **ApC, WestConf** ChurchOrg: **Presbyterian**

NatRel: **KBS, KHS, CCK, CBS, CPCK** TheolSchool: **ChongShin Seminary (SaDangDong)** Periodicals: **KiDokSinBo**

Address: 1007-3 DaeChi-Dong, KangNam-GU, Seoul, Korea, Tel: +82 2 564-5004, Fax: +82 2 568-7456

III. The Divisive Impact of the International Council of Christian Churches (ICCC)

16. Presbyterian Church of Korea (DaeShin I) (4602)

The origin of this church goes back to 1948 when Dr. Kim Chi-Sun, Pastor Kim Sun-Do, and Pastor Yun Phil-Sung started evening courses for the formation of candidates for the ministry. The school later became DaeHan Seminary. The history of the denomination is closely connected with the history of DaeHan Seminary.

In 1960, after the split of TongHap and HapDong, ICCC began to be active in Korea. Under the influence of Dr. Carl McIntire and with the financial support of the ICCC, Dr. Kim Chi-Sun, who belonged to HapDong, founded in 1961 the Bible Presbyterian Church. He became the director of the DaeHan Seminary. Soon tension developed between the Mission Department of the Bible Presbyterian Church and DaeHan Seminary, represented respectively by Dr. Bak Joon-Gul and Dr. Kim Chi-Sun. In 1968 Kim Chi-Sun withdrew from the ICCC. But new problems developed. Kim Chi-Sun was running DaeHan Seminary by himself, and he even tried to get his son Kim Sae-Chang appointed as director of the seminary. The idea was opposed by a professor of the seminary, Choi Soon-Jik, who together with some seminary students founded a new denomination called HapDongJinRi. The movement was joined by several groups. A leading figure of HapDongJinRi was Huh Kwang-Jae (cf. no. 34). In 1972 Dr. Kim Chi-Sun and his son withdrew from DaeShin I (cf. no. 17).

Gradually, DaeShin I sought to clarify the position of the church. The constitution was revised (1970) and the name of the church changed to DaeShin (1972). The church adopted the "Declaration of the Church" (1974), amended the new constitution (1976), and joined the Council of Presbyterian Churches in Korea (1980) and WARC (1992). DaeShin has experienced a rapid development and has actively participated in efforts of cooperation among the churches. DaeShin runs a seminary and a school and publishes a weekly church newspaper.

TM: **139,916** Congr: **1,170** OrdM: **1,256** Eld: **406** Deac: **27,036** EvgHome: **949** Mission: **nc** Women Ord: **no** ChurchOrg: **Presbyterian (30 presby in Korea, 3 abroad, GenAssy)** Off/otherLang: **Korean** DoctrB: **ApC, WestConf** NatRel: **CPCK, CCK** IntlRel: **WARC (1992)** TheolSchool: **DaeShin Seminary** Service infrastructure: **one school, own theological seminary**

Address: 381-1 SukSu 1 Dong, ManAn-Gu, Anyang, Korea, Tel: +82 34 373-6881, Fax: +82 34 371-6884

**The Divisive Impact of the International Council of Christian Churches
(nos. 16-22)**

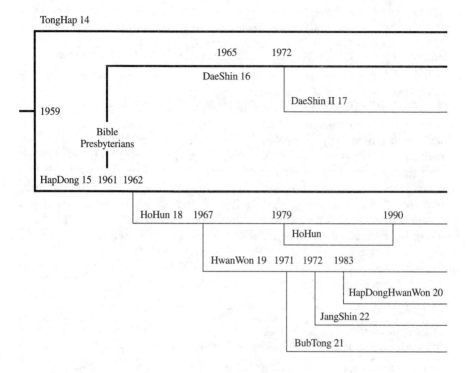

17. Presbyterian Church in Korea (DaeShin II) (4620)

This church resulted from a split in 1972. Dr. Kim Chi-Sun separated from
DaeShin I (no. 16) in connection with a dispute over the seminary and founded
DaeShin II. They founded another DaeShin Seminary, which later (1980) was rec-
ognized as a college. The denomination developed around the college.

TM: **15,200** CM: **12,300** Congr: **125** OrdM: **155** Eld: **12** Deac: **2,900** (the church names committed
Christians as deacons) EvgHome: **85** Mission: **nc** Women Ord: **nc** As Ministers: **nc** as Deac: **nc** as El-
ders: **nc** ChurchOrg: **Presbyterian (9 presby, GenAssy)** Off/otherLang: **Korean** DoctrB: **ApC,
WestConf** NatRel: **CRCK, NEA** TheolSchool: **DaeShin College**

Address: 158 GaRak-Dong, SongPa-Gu, Seoul, Korea, Tel: +82 2 431-1005, Fax: +82 2 3474-2347

18. Korean Presbyterian Church (HoHun) (4621)

HoHun also split from HapDong (no. 15). In 1961 some 25 delegates to the Assembly, among them Pastor Park Byung-Hun and Kim Yun-Chan, formed a special association for the safeguard of the conservative faith. They declared their in-

311

tention to join ICCC. In the following year they formed the General Assembly HoHun. Park Byung-Hun was elected as moderator.The church joined ICCC and was financially supported by it.

An unfortunate conflict over leadership arose in the early '60s. A group led by Pastor Lee Do-Bong sought to prolong Park Byung-Hun in his leadership functions. A clash developed with the new moderator Song Jae-Muk, who left the denomination and founded the Presbyterian Church of Korea (HwanWon [no. 19]) in 1967. HwanWon enjoyed the support of the ICCC.

For a time, HoHun found itself in a precarious situation. Under the leadership of Pastor Sin Eun-Kyun, the church succeeded in overcoming its financial difficulties. It united with ChongYun (1977). Pastor Sin Eun-Kyun was elected as moderator (1978). A year later Park Byung-Hun and a group of his followers separated from HoHun (1979); after Park's death most of them returned to HoHun eleven years later (1990). HoHun adopted a policy of integrating small denominations into church fellowship, e.g., BoKum (Pastor Park Myung-Bin) and SuBu (Pastor Hwang Jong-Ik). In 1982 the church established a Committee for Combining Denominations. As a result several small groups joined HoHun. In 1987 HoHun sought to unite with BoSu (Pastor Lee Hyun-Jae). But two years later controversies over this union and over the presidency of HoHun Seminary (founded in 1985) led to a division within the General Assembly of HoHun.

TM: **120,000** CM: **90,000** Congr: **910** OrdM: **930** Eld: **120** Deac: **42,000** (the church names committed Christians as deacons) EvgHome: **230** Mission: **nc** Women Ord: **no** ChurchOrg: **Presbyterian (39 presby, GenAssy)** Off/otherLang: **Korean** DoctrB: **ApC, WestConf** NatRel: **CPCK, CCK, CPC, CPCA, KHS** IntlRel: **ICCC (1962)** TheolSchool: **HoHun Seminary**

Address: 419-42 HapJeong-Dong, MaPo-Gu, Seoul, Korea, Tel: +82 2 322-6711, Fax: +82 2 322-6713

19. Presbyterian Church of Korea (HwanWon) (4622)

The existence of this church owes to a controversy over leadership (cf. no. 18). In 1967, with the financial support of the ICCC, Pastor Song Jae-Muk, former moderator of HoHun, separated from HoHun and founded HwanWon. Soon complications developed. In 1969 the GenAssy of HwanWon accepted the services of a missionary of the Westminster Biblical Mission, Robert S. Rapp, sent by the ICCC. Rapp took responsibility for a theological seminary which was to train conservative candidates for the ministry. A disagreement between Pastor Ma Du-Won, the ICCC representative for Korea, and Rapp on the appropriate management of the theological seminary ended with the dismissal of Rapp by the ICCC. But Rapp stayed with HwanWon, while the group supporting and supported by Pastor Ma Du-Won started BubTong (no. 21). In 1977 HwanWon suffered a further split: JangShin (no. 22) came into existence. Since HwanWon had lost much of its strength, the new moderator, Kim Dong-Hyuk, decided to unite with the independent JungAng presby and with JeongTong (cf. no. 20). The united church was given the name HapDongHwanWon (no. 20). The group refusing these new developments continued membership in HwanWon.

No statistical data and addresses have been made available.

20. Presbyterian Church in Korea (HapDongHwanWon) (4623)

The church is the result of a union of three groups. Under the leadership of its moderator, Kim Dong-Hyuk, HwanWon (no. 19) decided to unite with two small denominations, the independent JungAng presby (Pastor Kim Sun) and JeongTong (Pastor Yun Sung-Duk). The church was given the name HapDongHwanWon (1983).

TM: **9,776** CM: **6,517** Congr: **46** OrdM: **46** Eld: **nc** Deac: **nc** EvgHome: **35** ChurchOrg: **Presbyterian** DoctrB: **ApC, WestConf**

Address: 23-87 Dae-Bang-Dong, DongJak-Gu, Seoul, Korea, Tel: +82 2 814-5323

21. Presbyterian Church of Korea (BubTong) (4624)

The denomination came into existence in 1971 (see HwanWon [no. 19]). Founded by Pastor Jun Seong-Soo in close cooperation with Pastor Ma Du-Won, the representative of the ICCC in Korea, the church has been the Korean stronghold of the ICCC. The church was therefore in the center of the controversies around the ICCC. In 1974 Carl McIntire, the founder of the ICCC, visited Korea. He took a strong anti-Communist stand and supported the dictatorship of President Park Jung-Hee. The National Council of Churches in Korea (NCCK), which stood for the democratization of the country, denounced McIntire "as an isolated figure, known as tactician of church division." The KCCC, the Korean counterpart of the ICCC, counterattacked: "The WCC is pro-communist. . . . NCCK is part of the WCC. . . . To be against the government is non-biblical." BubTong is conservative in theology and strongly anti-Communist in political orientation.

TM: **33,920** Congr: **229** OrdM: **334** Eld: **nc** Deac: **nc** EvgHome: **125** Mission: **nc** Women Ord: **nc** As Ministers: **nc** as Deac: **nc** as Elders: **nc** ChurchOrg: **Presbyterian** Off/otherLang: **Korean** DoctrB: **ApC, WestConf**

Address: 1130 KeumHo-Dong, SungDong-Gu, Seoul, Korea, Tel: +82 2 234-1408, Fax: +82 2 235-5028

22. Presbyterian Church in Korea (JangShin) (4625)

In 1977 a group of young ministers who had graduated from HwanWon Seminary under the leadership of Robert S. Rapp (cf. no. 19) held an emergency assembly and started the JangShin denomination (Rev. Bae Soo-Ho, Rev. Im Joo-Ern, Rev.

Im Yun-Taek, Rev. Jun Yo-Han, and Rev. Sim Sang-Do). The reason was the continuing divergence of opinion between Ma Du-Won, the ICCC representative in Korea, and Rapp, the director of the seminary. JangShin maintained close relations with the seminary but became independent as a church body. Eventually JangShin integrated other church bodies and increased in numbers.

TM: **18,987** Congr: **209** OrdM: **290** Eld: **nc** Deac: **nc** EvgHome: **29** Mission: **nc** Women Ord: **nc** As Ministers: **nc** as Deac: **nc** as Elders: **nc** ChurchOrg: **Presb (9 presby, GenAssy)** Off/otherLang: **Korean** DoctrB: **ApC, WestConf** NatRel: **CCLK (1978), CCAK** IntlRel: **Westminster Biblical Society (USA)**

Address: 948-29 BongChon-Dong, KwankAk-Gu, Seoul, Korea, Tel: +82 2 889-2145, Fax: +82 2 873-4350

IV. The Aftermath of the Division of HapDong into Mainline and Non-Mainline (1979)

At the 64th General Assembly held in DaeGu in 1979, a major division occurred in HapDong (no. 15). The church fell apart into the "mainline" and "non-mainline" groups. Eventually the division led to many ramifications. The controversy centered around two issues. The first was theological and concerned the authorship of the Pentateuch; the second had to do with the management of the HapDong Seminary ChongShin. Fifteen directors of the seminary, representing the mainline, succeeded in changing the status of the school; it was changed into a privately run university.

The division into two parties created a complex situation. Before the split was consummated, a neutral group had sought, for two years, to mediate and to maintain the unity of the church; but it failed. Pastors close to the neutral group then decided to found a new denomination — GaeHyuk I (no. 23). The non-mainline group soon divided further. Two groups opposed one another — JongAm and BangBae. JongAm again divided into two parts but, a year later, reunited under the new name ChungAm. There were now three groups — GaeHyuk, ChungAm, and BangBae. At the end of 1980 they decided to form a united assembly. But the union did not last. According to the government's policy at that time a denomination could run one seminary only. Since each of the three groups had its own seminary, the union could not be maintained. In 1981 and 1982 the three groups were reestablished under the names GaeHyuk, HapDongBoSu (BangBae), and HapDongBoSu (ChungDam). All three groups divided further in subsequent years.

23. Korean Presbyterian Church (GaeHyuk I) (4626)

Before HapDong divided in 1979, a neutral group representing about 400 congr formed a committee of 17 members with the mandate to work for the maintenance of unity. For two years they promoted reconciliation under the slogan "Be one." The effort remained unsuccessful. The neutral group then sided with the directors

Division of HapDong into Mainstream and Non-Mainstream Churches (nos. 23-40)

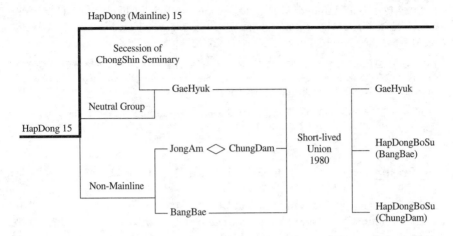

of HapDong Seminary, who had seceded from the mainline group (Park Yun-Sun, Park Hyung-Ryong, Yoon Yung-Tak and Kim Myung-Hyuk), and planned for the foundation of a new denomination, GaeHyuk.

Meanwhile the non-mainline group had divided into two denominations — JongAm and BangBae. An attempt was made to unite the three groups. In 1980 a united assembly was held (moderator: Kim In-Sung). But soon the three groups separated again since none of them was prepared to give up its seminary. In 1981 the neutral group, strengthened by representatives of ChongShin Seminary, constituted GaeHyuk I. JongAm and BangBae also founded separate denominations. Three new denominations had thus come into being: GaeHyuk, HapDongBoSu (BangBae), and HapDongBoSu (ChungDam).

TM: **633,600** CM: **400,000** Congr: **2,030** OrdM: **2,010** Eld: **2,800** Deac: **280,000** (the church names committed Christians as deacons) EvgHome: **700** Mission: **nc** Women Ord: **no** ChurchOrg: **Presbyterian (31 presby, 1 presby abroad, GenAssy)** Off/otherLang: **Korean** DoctrB: **ApC, WestConf** NatRel: **CCLK, CPC, CPCK**

Address: 201 BanPo-Dong, SuCho-Gu, Seoul, Korea, Tel: +82 2 2596-1702, Fax: +82 2 569-1704

24. Presbyterian Church in Korea (BoSuHapDong I) (4629)

This church came into existence in 1983 through separation from GaeHyuk I (no. 23).

No data have been made available.

Address: 397-14 HongEun 3-Dong, SuDaeMoon-Gu, Seoul, Korea, Tel: +82 2 302-3346, Fax: +82 2 302-3902

25. Presbyterian Church in Korea (GaeHyuk II) (4627)

In 1984 GaeHyuk I united with part of HapDongBoSu (ChungDam). One of the GaeHyuk leaders, who did not approve of this merger, Kim Myung-Hyuk, separated from the church and started GaeHyuk II.

TM: **83,567** CM: **55,711** Congr: **433** OrdM: **696** Eld: **nc** Deac: **nc** EvgHome: **139** Mission: **nc** Women Ord: **nc** As Ministers: **nc** as Deac: **nc** as Elders: **nc** ChurchOrg: **Presbyterian (16 presby, GenAssy)** Off/otherLang: **Korean** DoctrB: **ApC, WestConf** NatRel: CCK

Address: 136-56 YunChi-Dong, ChongRo-Gu, Christian Bldg. Room 1601, Seoul, Korea, Tel: +82 2 708-4458, Fax: +82 2 708-4464

26. Presbyterian Church in Korea (BoSuHapDong II) (4628)

In 1983 the General Assembly of HapDongBoSu (BangBae), the second of the three denominations, had to face the issue of non-province presby which were composed of refugees from the North after the Korean War. Since no agreement could be reached, the Assembly adjourned for an unlimited period. The Assembly leaders proceeded with the reform, beginning with SuDo presby. The opponents interpreted the action as an illegitimate attempt to gain hegemony in the church and submitted "four demands." A period of three years should be allowed for adjusting presby boundaries and for achieving a fully democratic administration of the Assembly. But the leaders of HapDongBoSu (BangBae) ignored these demands. A group within the church under the leadership of Pastor Kang Young-Suh separated from HapDongBoSu (BangBae) and founded BoSuHapDong II in 1984.

TM: **101,400** CM: **67,600** Congr: **408** OrdM: **456** Eld: **nc** Deac: **nc** EvgHome: **223** Mission: **nc** Women Ord: **nc** As Ministers: **nc** as Deac: **nc** as Elders: **nc** ChurchOrg: **Presbyterian (17 presby, GenAssy)** DoctrB: **ApC, WestConf**

Address: 595-43 ChangSin-Dong, Jonglo-Gu, Seoul 11-542, Korea, Tel: +82 2 742-3610

27. Presbyterian Church in Korea (BoSuHapDong III) (4630)

In 1989 BoSuHapDong I (no. 24) split to give life to two more groups. BoSuHapDong is one of these two. Rev. Kim Dae Hyung was elected as moderator. No data has been made available on the other group.

TM: **19,100** CM: **14,569** Congr: **120** OrdM: **120** Eld: **nc** Deac: **nc** EvgHome: **55**

Address: 258-8 DoRim 2-Dong, YoungDeungPo-Gu, Seoul, Korea, Tel: +82 2 835-0567 and 69

Second Stage of Splits (after 1980)

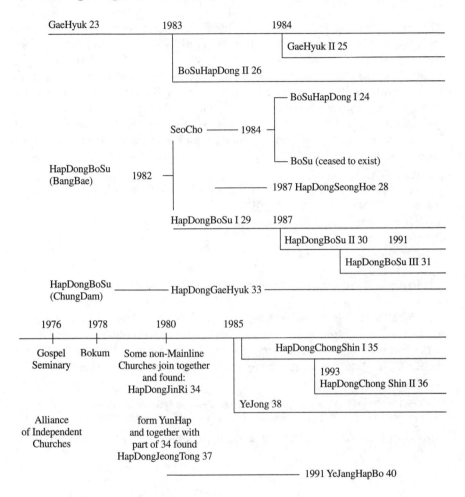

28. Presbyterian Church in Korea (HapDongSeongHoe) (4631)

This church came into existence out of a desire to prevent divisions in BoSuHapDong from becoming permanent. To counteract the trend toward splits, a number of concerned pastors formed HapDongSeongHoe in 1987. Their intention was to "gather the members in a holy meeting." The movement ended up as an additional denomination.

TM: **10,013** CM: **7,486** Congr: **78** OrdM: **64** Eld: **17** Deac: **4,008** EvgHome: **38** Mission: **nc** Women Ord: **yes** As Ministers: **no** as Deac: **2,815**, as Elders: **no** ChurchOrg: **Presb (5 presby, GenAssy)** DoctrB: **ApC, WestConf**

Address: 314-8 SamJeong-Dong, Jung-Gu, Buchon-City, Korea, Tel: +82 32 638-0578

29. Presbyterian Church in Korea (HapDongBoSu I) (4632)

The second of the three major non-mainline churches was HapDongBoSu (BangBae). When, after the short-lived union of 1980, the three denominations had reestablished themselves, a further split occurred in HapDongBoSu (BangBae). The church divided into HapDongBoSu and SeoCho, which later divided further into BoSuHapDong I (no. 25) and another BoSu group. HapDong-BoSu, under the leadership of Park Byung-Jin and Baek Dong-Sup, sought union with HapDongGaeHyuk (no. 33). Together they formed HapDongBoSu I (no. 29) in 1982. In 1987-1988 an attempt at reunion with HapDong (no. 15) was made but failed. The church joined the ICCC in 1989.

TM: **199,701** CM: **133,134** Congr: **945** OrdM: **1,466** Eld: **nc** Deac: **nc** EvgHome: **134** Mission: **nc** Women Ord: **nc** As Ministers: **nc** as Deac: **nc** as Elders: **nc** ChurchOrg: **Presbyterian** Off/otherLang: **Korean** DoctrB: **ApC, WestConf** IntlRel: **ICCC (1989)**

Address: 171-1 NaengChun-Dong, DuDaeMoon-Gu, Seoul, Korea, Tel: +82 2 363-5005, Fax: +82 2 362-2513

30. Presbyterian Church in Korea (HapDongBoSu II) (4633)

The church separated from HapDongBoSu I (no. 29). It had participated in the union movement to restore unity with HapDong, but after its failure it became an independent denomination. It is very conservative, opposed to both the WCC and the ICCC. It is one of the larger conservative bodies and runs nine seminaries and ten Bible schools.

TM: **669,346** CM: **446,232** Congr: **1,293** OrdM: **1,003** Eld: **nc** Deac: **nc** EvgHome: **200** ChurchOrg: **Presbyterian** DoctrB: **ApC. WestConf** TheolSchool: **9 seminaries and 10 Bible schools**

Address: 460 HongEun3-Dong, SuDaeMoon-Gu, Seoul, Korea, Tel: +82 2 394-3220, Fax: +82 2 379-4751

31. Presbyterian Church in Korea (HapDongBoSu III) (4634)

This church resulted from a further split in HapDongBoSu, due to the heresy trial of Park Yun-Sik of DaeSung Church.

TM: **197,511** CM: **31,674** Congr: **807** OrdM: **1,243** Eld: **nc** Deac: **nc** EvgHome: **144** ChurchOrg: **Presbyterian** DoctrB: **ApC, WestConf**

Address: 930-42 Bong-Chon-Dong, KwanAk-Gu, Seoul, Korea, Tel: +82 2 888-2151, Fax: +82 2 888-2253

32. Presbyterian Church in Korea (HapDongBoSu IV) (4635)

No historical data have been made available.

TM: **30,122** Congr: **127** OrdM: **nc** Eld: **nc** Deac: **nc** EvgHome: **600** ChurchOrg: **Presbyterian** DoctrB: **ApC, WestConf**

Address: 877-186 GilEum-Dong, SungBuk-Gu, Seoul, Korea, Tel: +82 2 941-0262

33. Presbyterian Church of Korea (HapDongGaeHyuk) (4636)

The third of the three major non-mainline denominations was HapDongBoSu (ChungDam), or, as it called itself later (1984), HapDongGaeHyuk.

TM: **84,000** CM: **68,000** Congr: **1,200** OrdM: **1,250** Eld: **150** Deac: **27,000** EvgHome: **700** Mission: **nc** Women Ord: **yes** As Ministers: **nc** as Deac: **19,500**, as Elders: **nc** ChurchOrg: **Presbyterian (26 presby, GenAssy)** Off/otherLang: **Korean** DoctrB: **ApC, WestConf** NatRel: **CCK, CPC, CPCA, CRCK**

Address: 59-7 OnSu-Dong, GuRo-Gu, Seoul, Korea, Tel: +82 2 611-2891, Fax: +82 2 688-2799

34. Presbyterian Church in Korea (HapDongJinRi) (4637)

The origins of this church go back to Pastor Hur Kwang-Jae, who founded the Gospel Seminary in 1976. This institution became the nucleus of the BoKum denomination (1978). When the break occurred in HapDong (1979), they sought contacts with the non-mainline churches. But they soon separated because of the power struggle which was going on and because of their wish to maintain their own characteristics. In 1980 they organized themselves as a denomination under the name HapDongJinRi. One of the pastors of this church, Jang Jong-Hyun, separated from this denomination, merged with YunHap (Pastor Lee Young), and founded HapDongJeongTong (no. 37).

TM: **44,747** CM: **29,831** Congr: **397** OrdM: **375** NatRel: **CCK, CPC** ChurchOrg: **Presbyterian** DoctrB: **ApC, WestConf**

Address: 604 ChoJi-Dong, AnSan City, Kyunggi-Do, Korea, Tel: +82 34 584-8344, Fax: +82 34 584-8343

35. Presbyterian Church in Korea (HapDongChongShin I) (4638)

The church is an offspring of HapDongJinRi 34. Its founder originally belonged to that church. The church was constituted in 1985. The first Assembly elected Pastor Lee Geun-Su as Moderator.

TM: **11,765** Congr: **99** OrdM: **128** Eld: **nc** Deac: **nc** EvgHome: **15** ChurchOrg: **Presbyterian** DoctrB: **ApC, WestConf**

Address: 72-1GaJoa3-Dong, Sur-Gu, Inchon, Korea, Tel: +82 32 572-1023, Fax: +82 32 572-9685

36. Presbyterian Church in Korea (HapDongChongShin II) (4639)

A further division, which occurred in 1993, was due to the initiative of the vice-moderator of HapDongChongShin I, Pastor Kim Jung-Gon.

No data have been made available.

Address: 799-1BuPyung1-Dong, Buk-Gu, Inchon, Korea, Tel: +82 32 523-5893

37. Presbyterian Church in Korea (HapDongJeongTong) (4603)

Over the past years HapDongJeongTong has developed into a strong denomination. Its origins go back to the beginnings of the mainline and non-mainline division in 1979. In 1980 representatives of the non-mainline churches, together with Gospel Seminary, founded HapDongJinRi (no. 34). A year later some members of HapDong JinRi joined forces with YunHap. YunHap had started in 1976 as an alliance of independent churches and had integrated in 1981 with the Grace denomination. HapDongJinRi and YunHap united and in 1982 formed a new denomination under the name HapDongJeongTong. In subsequent years the denomination grew rapidly, both through evangelism and through integration with smaller denominations. It runs a theological college and a press.

TM: **610,818** CM: **183,482** Congr: **1,695** OrdM: **2,905** Eld: **514** Deac: **39,538** EvgHome: **1,000** Mission: **nc** Women Ord: **no** ChurchOrg: **Presbyterian (39 presby, GenAssy)** Off/otherLang: **Korean** DoctrB: **ApC, WestConf** NatRel: **CPCK, CCK** IntlRel: **WARC**

Address: 981-56 Bang-Bae 3 Dong, Seo-Cho Ku, Seoul, Korea, Tel: +82 2 584-9845, Fax: +82 2 521-2729

38. Presbyterian Church in Korea (YeJong) (4640)

HapDongJinRi (no. 34) sought union with YunHap (cf. no. 37) and eventually formed HapDongJeongTong (no. 37). In the course of these developments a split occurred in HapDongJinRi (no. 34) due to theological differences and leadership struggles. In 1983 the dissenting group moved its headquarters and seminary to DokSanDong, chose Pastor Park Young-Hwa as moderator, and in 1985 adopted the name YeJong. It concentrates on work in rural areas.

TM: **4,900** CM: **2,750** Congr: **40** OrdM: **35** Eld: **14** Deac: **520** EvgHome: **nc** Mission: **nc** Women Ord: **nc** As Ministers: **nc** as Deac: **nc** as Elders: **nc** ChurchOrg: **Presbyterian (5 presby, GenAssy)** Off/otherLang: **Korean** DoctrB: **ApC, WestConf** NatRel: **CCAK, KHC**

Address: 236-488 sinDang 1-Dong, Jung-Gu, Seoul, Korea, Tel: +82 2 234-9201, Fax: +82 2 236-2845

39. Presbyterian Church in Korea (BokUm I) (4641)

In the course of the struggles following the split in HapDong, an independent presby was established which was later (1988) developed into a denomination.

TM: **26,880** Congr: **112** OrdM: **162** Eld: **nc** Deac: **nc** EvgHome: **94** ChurchOrg: **Presbyterian** DoctrB: **ApC, WestConf**

Address: 1-87 HyunJur-Dong, SuDaeMoon-Gu, Seoul, Korea, Tel: +82 2 392-8826, Fax: +82 2 392-8828

40. Presbyterian Church of Korea (YeJangHapBo) (4642)

This denomination is the result of an attempt to bring together members of various HapDong groups, both from the mainline and the non-mainline side. In 1980 No Jin-Young of the mainline group, You Je-Suh and Son Chi-Ho of the neutral group, and Bak Dong-Sup of the non-mainline group formed a new denomination which they called HapDongBoSu. They included people from other denominations. In 1991 the church was renamed YeJangHapBo.

TM: **187,500** CM: **109,700** Congr: **293** OrdM: **249** Eld: **86** Deac: **86,700** EvgHome: **358** Mission: **nc** Women Ord: **nc** As Ministers: **nc** as Deac: **nc** as Elders: **nc** ChurchOrg: **Presbyterian (16 presby, GenAssy)** DoctrB: **ApC, WestConf**

Address: 193-180 EuengBong-Dong, SungDong-Gu, Seoul, Korea, Tel: +82 2 281-9191, Fax: +82 2 281-1191

V. Churches Connected with JungAng

The group of churches presented in the following chapter are concerned with an incident in the Methodist Church of Korea. Wesley Seminary of the Methodist Church operated without proper government authorization. As a result, the Meth bishop, Mun Dae-Gol, was arrested and put in prison. A controversy arose between the bishop and Lee Won-Hwang, the president of the seminary. Lee left the Methodist Church and founded a Presbyterian seminary and later, together with elder Kang Yong-Sik of TongHap 14, founded the General Assembly JangShin (1970); in 1976 the name JangShin was changed to JungAng.

41. Presbyterian Church in Korea (HapDongJungAng) (4643)

The aim of the seminary founded in 1970 by Lee Won-Hwang was to give a chance to candidates for the ministry who felt they had a calling but could not succeed in their studies. The undertaking turned into a scandal: the seminary produced too many unqualified candidates. A controversy arose. Pastor Baek Kee-Wan and Pastor Chung Yun-Song called an assembly. In order to redress the situation and to restore the good name of the denomination, the name was changed from JangShin to JungAng (1976). In 1979 the church revised its constitution and introduced women's ordination. Since 1980 JungAng has grown rapidly. The first woman was ordained in 1983. In order to avoid friction with opponents of women's ordination, women pastors and women evangelists formed a separate presby. Soon this presby separated from JungAng and formed a distinct denomination (cf. no. 44). Baek Kee-Wan seceded from JungAng (see under no. 42) and formed a separate denomination. The remaining body changed its name to HapDongJungAng.

TM: **132,000** CM: **43,000** Congr: **550** OrdM: **528** Eld: **198** Deac: **417** EvgHome: **601** Mission: **nc** Women Ord: **yes** As Ministers: **1983/210** as Deac: **nc** as Elders: **nc** ChurchOrg: **Presbyterian (25 presby, GenAssy)** Off/otherLang: **Korean** DoctrB: **ApC, WestConf** NatRel: **CCK (1990)**

Address: 448-3 HongEun-Dong, SeoDaeMoon-Gu, Seoul, Korea, Tel: +82 2 353-3777, Fax: +82 2 353-0639

42. Presbyterian Church in Korea (JungAng) (4644)

In 1986 Pastor Baek Kee-Hwan left HapDongJungAng and started a separate church. He maintained the practice of ordaining women.

TM: **60,479** Congr: **355** OrdM: **294** Eld: **198** Deac: **417** EvgHome: **nc** Mission: **nc** Women Ord: **yes** As Ministers: **221** as Deac: **nc** as Elders: **nc** ChurchOrg: **Presbyterian** DoctrB: **ApC, WestConf**

Address: 383-30 WolKyel-Dong, NoWon-Gu, Seoul, Korea, Tel: +82 2 943-3124, Fax: +82 2 943-2946

43. Presbyterian Church of Korea (BoSoTongHap) (4645)

This church was founded by Chung Yun-Song, who, together with Baek Kee, had participated in the reconstitution of JungAng (1976). He criticized the Assembly of JungAng for its contradictory attitudes and founded BoSuJaeGun in 1984. He opened a new seminary in 1985. Later BoSuJaeGun merged with another denomination and changed its name to BoSoTongHap.

TM: **5,914** Congr: **102** OrdM: **128** Eld: **nc** Deac: **nc** EvgHome: **18** Mission: **nc** Women Ord: **yes** As Ministers: **1** as Deac: **nc** as Elders: **nc** ChurchOrg: **Presb** DoctrB: **ApC, WestConf**

Address: 433-3 JangAn-Dong, DongDemun-Gu, Seoul, Korea, Tel: +82 2 246-4524, Fax: +82 2 267-831

44. Women Pastors Presbyterian Church (YuMok) (4646)

YuMok was founded by women who, in a patriarchal world dominated by men, were unable to exercise their leadership qualities. In 1979 JungAng introduced women's ordination (cf. no. 41). The first women pastors were ordained in 1983. But they had a difficult time in their church and therefore decided to form a women pastors' presby within JungAng. Soon they left JungAng and started their own GenAssy, YuMok (moderator: Park Jeong-Ho). A year later they opened a seminary. Park Jeong-Ho unduly dominated both the seminary and the assembly and was dismissed by the assembly in 1987.

TM: **15,407** Congr: **103** OrdM: **65** Eld: **nc** Deac: **nc** EvgHome: **nc** Mission: **nc** Women Ord: **yes** As Ministers: **1983/136** as Deac: **nc** as Elders: **nc** ChurchOrg: **Presbyterian** DoctrB: **ApC, WestConf**

Address: DaeRim1-Dong, YungDungPo-Gu, Seoul, Korea, Tel: +82 2 848-5875

45. Korean Women Pastors Presbyterian Union (YunHapYerMok) (4647)

After her dismissal by the Assembly of YuMok, Pastor Park Jeong-Ho founded a new denomination, YunHapYerMok (1987). She continues as moderator even today.

TM: **5,418** Congr: **125** OrdM: **9** Eld: **nc** Deac: **nc** EvgHome: **nc** Mission: **nc** Women Ord: **yes** As Ministers: **147** as Deac: **nc** as Elders: **nc** ChurchOrg: **Presbyterian** DoctrB: **ApC, WestConf**

Address: 977-22 SinJeong4-Dong, YangChun-Gu, Seoul, Korea, Tel: +82 2 698-0583, Fax: +82 2 607-2173

46. Union Presbyterian Church of Korea (YunHap) (4655)

In 1990 another YuMok presby was organized. It eventually changed its name to YunHap Assembly. In 1992 the Assembly adopted a constitution for the church. The moderator of YunHap Assembly I is a woman, Rev. Lee Young-Ja.

TM: **10,448** Congr: **18** OrdM: **18** Eld: **nc** Deac: **nc** EvgHome: **18** ChurchOrg: **Presbyterian** DoctrB: **ApC, WestConf**

Address: 830-53 SanBon-Dong, GunPo, KyungKiDo, Korea, Tel: +82 34 329-2201

VI. Fundamentalist Churches

47. Korean Christian Fundamentalist Assembly (GunBon — Fundamentalist I) (4648)

This church was founded in response to influence from Western countries. In 1968 Rev. Gerald Johns, a fundamentalist missionary from Bob Jones College in the United States, came to Korea and established the Maranata Seminary in 1972. In February 1976, Bob Jones and Ian Paisley organized the World Fundamentalist Conference in Edinburgh, followed in November of the same year by a conference of Korean fundamentalists. The fundamentalist movement found a favorable echo in Korea. In 1987 the Korean Christian Fundamentalist Assembly was founded.

TM: **18,262** Congr: **116** OrdM: **104** Eld: **nc** Deac: **nc** EvgHome: **23** ChurchOrg: **Presbyterian** DoctrB: **ApC, WestConf**

Address: 414-8 JangAhn-Dong, DongDaeMun-Gu, Seoul, Korea, Tel: +82 2 217-0718, Fax: +82 2 215-3004

48. Fundamentalist Presbyterian General Assembly (GunBon — Fundamentalist II) (4649)

The denomination was founded in 1983 by Pastors Yum Haeng-Soo and Hwang Oh-Gyu. The reason for this initiative was the conviction that the Korean churches were bowing to mammonism, secularism, and syncretism and had to return to the fundamental spirit of the Bible. Yum Haeng-Soo was originally a fundamentalist who had graduated from Bob Jones Seminary. Emerging doubts about dispensationalism caused him to turn to Ref theology and to begin to promote a form of fundamentalist Ref theology.

TM: **69,638** Congr: **216** OrdM: **243** Eld: **nc** Deac: **nc** EvgHome: **53** ChurchOrg: **Presbyterian** DoctrB: **ApC, WestConf**

Address: 244-1HangGangLo-1, YongSan-Gu, Seoul, Korea, Tel: +82 2 795-2915, Fax: +82 2 795-2916

VII. Churches Connected with BoSu Seminary

BoSu means conservative. The name applies to a group of churches which split from HoHon churches, e.g., nos. 18, 94, and 95. They felt that the neoorthodox teaching of Barthian theology was the main cause for the division of the Presbyterian Church into TongHap and HapDong. They wanted to remain faithful to conservative teaching. They were, however, not satisfied with the positions of the HoHon either. The BoSu group is committed to a stricter conservative line.

49. Conservative Presbyterian Church in Korea (BoSuChuk) (4650)

In 1963 Pastor Choi Sung-Gon of HoHun (no. 18) and Kim Oh-Sung gathered 102 churches and formed a new denomination at Sungdongjaeil Church. Choi Sung-Gon served as moderator. The initiative was largely financed by Choi Sung-Gon's private money. SungHwa seminary was opened and was directed by Kim Oh-Sung. Their conviction was that neoorthodox theology was the main reason for the division of TongHap and HapDong, and therefore they promoted a conservative approach. But soon BoSu could no longer maintain its activities, and, when Pastor Choi left for the USA in 1965, many churches left the denomination. For five or six years the church was inactive. Graduates from SungHwa seminary — Cho Won-Kuk, Kim Duk-Sun, and Chung In-Young — met in 1972 and succeeded in restoring the denomination. When HapDong divided in 1979, many

324

ministers and about 200 congr joined non-mainline churches of HapDong. Only 22 stayed in BoSu.

TM: **12,779** Congr: **109** OrdM: **nc** Eld: **nc** Deac: **nc** EvgHome: **nc** Mission: **nc** Women Ord: **nc** As Ministers: **nc** as Deac: **nc** as Elders: **nc** ChurchOrg: **Presbyterian (8 presby, GenAssy)** Off/ otherLang: **Korean** DoctrB: **ApC, WestConf** TheolSchool: **SungHwa Seminary**

Address: 467-24 BangBae3 Dong, SuCho-Gu, Seoul, Korea, Tel: +82 2 587-1616, Fax: +82 2 586-2044

50. Korean Presbyterian Church (YeJang) (4651)

After the division of HapDong into mainline and non-mainline, under the leadership of Pastor Chung Bong-Kuk and Chung Na-Yul three small denominations united and formed a new assembly under the name of SungHap (1981). SungHap was responsible for BoSu Seminary, which later was renamed Paul Seminary (1984). SungHap collaborated closely with government policies. Chung BongKuk left SungHap in 1984 and founded SungHapChuk (no. 51). SungHap changed its name to YeJang.

TM: **345,325** CM: **185,000** Congr: **425** OrdM: **720** Eld: **1,120** Deac: **140,000** EvgHome: **850** Mission: **nc** Women Ord: **no** ChurchOrg: **nc** Off/otherLang: **Korean** DoctrB: **ApC, WestConf** NatRel: **CPC** IntlRel: **ICCC (1985)** TheolSchool: **Paul Seminary**

Address: 717 DaeRim-Dong, YoungDeungPo-Gu, Seoul, Korea, Tel: +82 2847-5091, Fax: +82 2 847-5092

51. Presbyterian Church of Korea (SungHapChuk) (4652)

This church separated from YeJang (no. 50) in 1984. Chung Bong-Kuk was the leading figure in the process of separation.

TM: **39,040** CM: **25,020** Congr: **155** OrdM: **104** Eld: **nc** Deac: **nc** EvgHome: **212** Mission: **nc** Women Ord: **nc** As Ministers: **nc** as Deac: **nc** as Elders: **nc** ChurchOrg: **Presbyterian (9 presby, GenAssy)** DoctrB: **ApC, WestConf**

Address: 90 HanGangRo 2Ga, YongSan-Gu, Seoul, Korea, Tel: +82 2 795-8165

VIII. Other Churches

52. Conservative-Reformed Presbyterian Church in Korea (BoSuGaeHyuk) (4653)

This denomination was founded in 1980 by Pastor Oh Gyun-Yul.

TM: **7,687** CM: **4,777** Congr: **126** OrdM: **129** Eld: **27** Deac: **1,321** EvgHome: **58** Mission: **nc** Women Ord: **nc** As Ministers: **nc** as Deac: **nc** as Elders: **nc** ChurchOrg: **Presbyterian** Off/otherLang: **Korean** DoctrB: **ApC, WestConf** NatRel: **CCK**

Address: 1-1 YunChi-Dong, ChongRo-Gu, The Korean Women's Associations' Building, Room 1007, Seoul, Korea, Tel: 82 2 764-3580, Fax: +82 2 764-3561

53. United Presbyterian Church of Korea (YunHapChuk) (4654)

The denomination was founded by Kim Se-Yul, Kang-Heung-Mo, and Kim Yong-An in 1972 at YoungSeng Church in ChunJu City. They were joined in the same year by Kim Gil-Chang. They adopted the name Christian United Church and prepared for an Assembly in 1973. At the 13th Assembly in 1984, the name was changed to United Presbyterian Church. Since 1987 the church has been called YunHapChuk.

TM: **7,925** BM: **nc**: Congr: **96** OrdM: **102** Eld: **nc** Deac: **nc** EvgHome: **46** ChurchOrg: **Presbyterian** DoctrB: **ApC, WestConf**

Address: 31-1 TaePyung-Dong, Wansan-Gun, ChunJoo ChunKaBukDo, Korea, Tel: +82 652 251-1185

54. The Presbyterian Church of Korea (Logos) (4656)

In 1970 Kim Hyun-Bong and the pastors of seven churches met to assure the cooperation of independent churches. Later they decided to set up an organization for the promotion of the cooperation of independent churches called Logos Council (1971, Moderator An Gil-Hong). Since 1971 Logos has run a seminary. In 1990 the denomination became the Logos Assembly.

TM: **800** CM: **500** Congr: **20** OrdM: **14** Eld: **4** Deac: **190** EvgHome: **6** ChurchOrg: **Presbyterian** DoctrB: **ApC, WestConf** TheolSchool: **own theological seminary**

Address: 13-7 SangDo2-Dong, DongJak-Gu, Seoul, Korea, Tel: +82 2 814-1813

55. The Presbyterian Church in Korea (JeongRip) (4657)

The history of this denomination goes back to the '60s. In 1964 Pastors Lee Eun-Kyu, Kim Guk-In, and Choi Soo-Haeng set up the denomination SaeKye-BokUm (= World Mission) at DongWon Church in Seoul. All three came from the Presbyterian Church (SuBu), a church which later was united with HapDong-JangShin (no. 5). Without permission from the government, they opened DongWon Seminary. In the beginning the church had considerable financial difficulties, but it received help from Pastor Hosino Aizi in Japan. The government closed DongWon Seminary. As a result many congr left the denomination. To make a new start Pastors Chung Kyu-Wan, Kim Guk-In, and others started JeongRip.

TM: **16,786** Congr: **309** OrdM: **358** Eld: **nc** Deac: **nc** EvgHome: **332** ChurchOrg: **Presbyterian** DoctrB: **ApC, WestConf**

Address: 265-5 EeungBong-Dong, SungDong-Gu, Seoul, Korea, Tel: +82 2 292-3450, Fax: +82 2
           294-2100

56. The Presbyterian Church in Korea (HapDongBoSu) (4658)

A non-mainline group established relations with part of JeongRip (no. 55) and established a separate denomination (1984). Pastors Han Chun-Keun, Kim Kuk-In, and Lee Sun-Sik, together with 50 pastors, formed HapDongJeongRip. Its name was changed to HapDongBoSu in 1989.

TM: **3,795** CM: **2,528** Congr: **74** OrdM: **68** Eld: **nc** Deac: **492** EvgHome: **38** Mission: **nc** Women Ord: **yes** As Ministers: **13** as Deac: **1,548** as Elders: **nc** ChurchOrg: **Presbyterian (4 presby, GenAssy)** DoctrB: **ApC, WestConf**

Address: 1-59 DoRim1-Dong, YoungDeungPo-Gu, Seoul, Korea, Tel: +82 2 841-6061, Fax: +82 2
           845-0934

57. Korea Presbyterian Church (JongHap) (4659)

This church started in the Gospel Mission Seminary founded by Pastor Park Young-Bin in Seoul. The first moderator of the new church was Pastor Kil Jin-Kyung. After 1970, under the leadership of Pastor Cho Jyun-Jong, the church revised its constitution. In subsequent years it divided several times.

TM: **1,050** CM: **550** Congr: **21** OrdM: **22** Eld: **9** Deac: **45** EvgHome: **25** Mission: **nc** Women Ord: **yes** As Ministers: **yes/3** as Deac: **yes/185** as Elders: **yes** ChurchOrg: **Presbyterian (4 presby, GenAssy)** DoctrB: **ApC, WestConf**

Address: 466-3 MangWoo2-Dong, JungRyang-Gu, Seoul, Korea, Tel: +82 2 432-7656, Fax: +82 2
           432-7657

58. General Cooperation of the Presbyterian Church in Korea (HyupDong) (4660)

This church separated from JongHap (no. 57) in 1973. Its founders were: Oh Kyung-Shin, Park Sang-Gul, Choi Hong, and Chan Chul-Ung.

No statistical data and addresses have been made available.

59. Presbyterian Church in Korea (HapDongChongYun) (4661)

In 1976 ChongYun (Pastor Chung Young-Jin) separated from JongHap. In 1984 they united with HapDongHyunHap (Pastor Ser Tae-Jin) and HyukShin (Pastor Park In-Bon) from Koryu to form one denomination, HapDongChongYun.

TM: **58,317** Congr: **386** OrdM: **348** Eld: **nc** Deac: **nc** EvgHome: **268** ChurchOrg: **Presbyterian** DoctrB: **ApC, WestConf** TheolSchool: **ChongHoe Seminary**

Address: 1038-27 SaDang 1-Dong, DongJak-Gu, Seoul, Korea

60. Presbyterian Church in Korea (JungRip) (4662)

The existence of this church owes to an attempt to unite divided Presb. When HapDong divided in 1979 into mainline and non-mainline groups, pastors in both TongHap (no. 14) and HapDong (no. 15) gathered under the slogan "Return to the early church and aim at one Gospel Church!" They held a prayer meeting and decided in 1981 to form JungRip assembly and denomination. They started with the 66th Assembly. Some members of the group had already opened PyungYang Seminary in 1975. The name was later changed to Seoul Westminster Seminary (1978) and ChongHoe Seminary (1981). The church teaches the verbal inspiration of the Bible.

TM: **75,007** Congr: **451** OrdM: **454** Eld: **nc** Deac: **nc** EvgHome: **23** Mission: **nc** Women Ord: **nc** As Ministers: **nc** as Deac: **nc** as Elders: **nc** ChurchOrg: **Presbyterian (13 presby, GenAssy)** DoctrB: **ApC, WestConf** TheolSchool: **ChongHoe Seminary**

Address: 186-16 GaePo3-Dong, DongIn Church, GangNam-Gu, Seoul, Korea, Tel: +82 2 575-5904

61. Presbyterian Church in Korea (JeongTongChongHap) (4663)

The founder of this denomination, Pastor Park In-Soo, was ordained by Pastor Bang Shin-Wung of JeongTong (1976). When Pastor Bang left for America, Park joined DokNoHoe (no. 8). Later (1981) he became a member of JongHap (no. 57) and was elected vice-moderator. Two years later he left JongHap with a group of supporters and founded JeongTongChongHap (1983).

TM: **60,000** Congr: **120** OrdM: **110** ChurchOrg: **Presbyterian** DoctrB: **ApC, WestConf**

Address: 528 AnYang-Dong, ManAn-Gu, Anyang, HoJeong Tower Off 907, Korea, Tel: +82 34 343-1848

62. The Union General Assembly (HapDongChongHoe) (4664)

This church was founded in 1982. Its seminary was originally called HoHun. At the 60th Assembly (1984) the name was changed to HapDongChongHoe.

TM: **6,235** Congr: **128** OrdM: **117** Eld: **nc** Deac: **nc** EvgHome: **11** ChurchOrg: **Presbyterian** DoctrB: **ApC, WestConf** TheolSchool: **HapDongChongHoe Seminary**

Address: 97-7 DaeBang-Dong, DongJak-Gu, Seoul, Korea, Tel: +82 2 831-6100

63. Presbyterian General Assembly (ChanYang) (4665)

Plans for an Assembly were worked out in 1987 (Pastor Park Jong-Hwa). A committee established five presby and founded the denomination at El Bethel Church ChanYang in 1988.

TM: **13,748** Congr: **57** OrdM: **54** Eld: **46** Deac: **501** EvgHome: **19** Mission: **nc** Women Ord: **no** ChurchOrg: **Presbyterian (8 presby, GenAssy)** DoctrB: **ApC, WestConf**

Address: 13-2 UuMyun-Dong, SuCho-Gu, Seoul, Korea, Tel: +82 2 573-2192, Fax: +82 2 579-6215

64. Presbyterian Church of Korea (PyungHap) (4666)

This denomination was started in 1989 by pastors who had graduated from Pierson Seminary in Seoul. The first moderator was Ji Byung-Sur.

No statistical data and addresses have been made available.

65. Presbyterian Church of Korea (HapDongBokUm) (4667)

In 1960 Pastor Jang Sung-Ho established Seoul Seminary, and three years later he founded a denomination. In 1964 he started Immanuel Central Committee and developed it into BokJi (= welfare) Seminary and BokJi Bible School (1971). The denomination united with seven smaller denominations and became HapDong-BokUm in 1984. In 1986 the church started the HanRim Educational Institute. Under the leadership of Jang Sung-Ho and Byun Dong-Ho the denomination has grown through the witness of its schools and through integration with small churches.

TM: **34,420** CM: **16,812** Congr: **272** OrdM: **265** Eld: **nc** Deac: **nc** EvgHome: **2,481** Mission: **nc** Women Ord: **yes** As Ministers: **3** as Deac: **nc** as Elders: **nc** ChurchOrg: **Presbyterian** DoctrB: **ApC, WestConf**

Address: 3-135 ChangChun-Dong, MaPo-Gu, Seoul, Korea, Tel: +82 2 324-0580, Fax: +82 2 332-6798

66. Presbyterian Church in Korea (HapDongYeChong I)

The existence of this church owes to a split in a church called HapDongBoSu. Under the leadership of Pastor Dogo Bong-Mun four presby left this church and formed HapDongYeChong.

TM: **2,260** Congr: **45** OrdM: **66** Eld: **nc** Deac: **nc** EvgHome: **29** Mission: **nc** Women Ord: **nc** As Ministers: **nc** as Deac: **nc** as Elders: **nc** ChurchOrg: **Presbyterian (4 presby, GenAssy)** DoctrB: **ApC, WestConf**

Address: 90-8 ChoRyang3-Dong, Dong-Gu, Pusan, Korea, Tel: +82 51 465-6122

67. Presbyterian Church in Korea (HapDongYeChong II) (4669)

The church places special emphasis on the arts. Under the leadership of Pastor Chun Byung-Hun, Choi Young-Su, and Lee Sang-Yun the denomination was founded at Seoul YeSin Church in 1988. The church is responsible for the Seoul Artistic Seminary, teaching students drama, literary arts, fine arts, music, and dance. It publishes the *Christian Artistic Paper.*

TM: **32,178** CM: **20,057** Congr: **65** OrdM: **70** Eld: **nc** Deac: **nc** EvgHome: **15** Mission: **nc** Women Ord: **nc** As Ministers: **nc** as Deac: **nc** as Elders: **nc** ChurchOrg: **Presbyterian (7 presby, GenAssy)** Off/otherLang: **Korean** DoctrB: **ApC, WestConf** Service infrastructure: **Seoul Artistic Seminary** Periodicals: **Christian Artistic Paper**

Address: 24-12 ChunHo-Dong, GangDong-Gu, Seoul, Korea, Tel: +82 2 474-9664, Fax: +82 2 485-5846

68. Presbyterian Church in Korea (HyukShin) (4670)

The founders of this church originally founded a church called BoSu (1973). In 1987 the church was renamed GaeHyukBoSu, and two years later the name was changed again to HyukShin.

TM: **62,814** Congr: **72** OrdM: **175** Eld: **nc** Deac: **nc** EvgHome: **7** Mission: **nc** Women Ord: **nc** As Ministers: **nc** as Deac: **nc** as Elders: **nc** ChurchOrg: **Presbyterian (7 presby, GenAssy)** DoctrB: **ApC, WestConf**

Address: 96-4 BanPo2-Dong, SuCho-Gu, Seoul, Korea, Tel: +82 2 831-6100

69. Presbyterian Church in Korea (GaeHyukHapDong I) (4671)

No historical data have been made available.

TM: **24,000** CM: **11,000** Congr: **179** OrdM: **193** Eld: **169** Deac: **4,000** EvgHome: **227** Mission: **nc** Women Ord: **yes** As Ministers: **no** as Deac: **7,000** as Elders: **no** ChurchOrg: **Presbyterian (7 presby, GenAssy)** Off/otherLang: **Korean** DoctrB: **ApC, WestConf** NatRel: **CCK**

Address: 553-2 SeRuy3-Dong, KwunSun-Gu, Suwon, Korea, Tel: +82 331 5222-5630

70. Presbyterian Church in Korea (GaeHyukHapDong II) (4672)

TM: **13,272** Congr: **125** OrdM: **171** Eld: **nc** Deac: **nc** EvgHome: **7** ChurchOrg: **Presbyterian** DoctrB: **ApC, WestConf**

Address: 1637-10 SuChol-Dong, SuCho-Gu, Seoul, Korea, Tel: +82 2 586-7434

71. The Presbyterian Church in Korea (GaeHyukHapDong III) (4673)

TM: **4,065** Congr: **23** OrdM: **29** Eld: **nc** Deac: **nc** EvgHome: **7** ChurchOrg: **Presbyterian** DoctrB: **ApC, WestConf**

Address: 134-2 Chang5-Dong, DoBong-Gu, Seoul, Korea, Tel: +82 2 995-1906

72. Presbyterian Church in Korea (NamBuk) (4674)

TM: **310,400** Congr: **213** OrdM: **250** Eld: **nc** Deac: **nc** EvgHome: **nc** Off/otherLang: **Korean** Church Org: **Presbyterian** DoctrB: **ApC, WestConf**

Address: 174-13 YumRi-Dong, MaPo-Gu, Seoul, Korea, Tel: +82 2 715-6735

73. Presbyterian Church in Korea (DaeHanShinChuk) (4675)

TM: **3,552** Congr: **58** OrdM: **33** Eld: **nc** Deac: **nc** EvgHome: **35** ChurchOrg: **Presbyterian** DoctrB: **ApC, WestConf**

Address: 885-27 BongCun10-Dong, KwanAk-Gu, Seoul, Korea, Tel: +82 2 488-9944

74. Presbyterian Church in Korea (BoSuJeongTong) (4676)

TM: **3,729** Congr: **45** OrdM: **58** Eld: **nc** Deac: **nc** EvgHome: **6** ChurchOrg: **Presbyterian** DoctrB: **ApC, WestConf**

Address: 109 DonSoMunDong 6 Ga, SungBuk-Gu, Seoul, Korea, Tel: +82 2 926-1416

75. Presbyterian Church in Korea (BoSuChuk II) (4677)

TM: **700** Congr: **45** OrdM: **37** Eld: **nc** Deac: **nc** EvgHome: **19** ChurchOrg: **Presbyterian** DoctrB: **ApC, WestConf**

Address: 31-7 SinJeong1-Dong, YangChun-Gu, Seoul, Korea, Tel: +82 2 652-9358

76. Presbyterian Church in Korea (SunGyo) (4678)

TM: **1,000** Congr: **10** OrdM: **56** Eld: **nc** Deac: **nc** EvgHome: **15** ChurchOrg: **Presbyterian** DoctrB: **ApC, WestConf**

Address: 13-35 DonAm1-Dong, SungBuk-Gu, Seoul, Korea, Tel: +82 2 929-1474

77. Presbyterian Church in Korea (YunShin) (4679)

TM: **6,469** Congr: **88** OrdM: **84** Eld: **nc** Deac: **nc** EvgHome: **45** ChurchOrg: **Presbyterian** DoctrB: **ApC. WestConf**

Address: Il Won-Dong, KangNam-Gu, Seoul, Korea, Tel: +822 2 573-6743

78. The Presbyterian Church in Korea (YeJeong) (4680)

TM: **3,731** Congr: **37** OrdM: **42** Eld: **nc** Deac: **nc** EvgHome: **13** ChurchOrg: **Presbyterian** DoctrB: **ApC, WestConf**

Address: 236-488 SinDang1-Dong, Jung-Gu, Seoul, Korea, Tel: +82 2 234-9201

79. Presbyterian Church in Korea (JeongTongGyeSeung) (4681)

TM: **1,200** Congr: **56** OrdM: **35** Eld: **nc** Deac: **nc** EvgHome: **20** ChurchOrg: **Presbyterian** DoctrB: **ApC, WestConf**

Address: 522-8 SungNael-Dong, GangDong-Gu, Seoul, Korea, Tel: +82 2 486-5897

80. Presbyterian Church in Korea (ChongHoe I) (4682)

TM: **3,511** Congr: **64** OrdM: **64** Eld: **nc** Deac: **nc** EvgHome: **36** ChurchOrg: **Presbyterian** DoctrB: **ApC, WestConf**

Address: 613-21 Suyu 1-Dong, DoBong-Gu, Seoul, Korea, Tel: +82 2 906-9837

81. Presbyterian Church in Korea (ChongHoe II) (4683)

TM: **30,186** Congr: **123** OrdM: **132** Eld: **nc** Deac: **nc** EvgHome: **108** ChurchOrg: **Presbyterian** DoctrB: **ApC, WestConf**

Address: 1675-7 BongChun 6-Dong, KwanAk-Gu, Seoul, Korea, Tel: +82 2 887-2133

82. Presbyterian Church in Korea (TongHapBoSu) (4684)

TM: **18,309** Congr: **159** OrdM: **199** Eld: **nc** Deac: **nc** EvgHome: **17** ChurchOrg: **Presbyterian** DoctrB. **ApC, WestConf**

Address: 135-5 BangLee-dong, SongPa-Gu, Seoul, Korea, Tel: +82 2 417-7601

83. Presbyterian Church in Korea (PyungAhn I) (4685)

TM: **1,997** Congr: **43** OrdM: **45** Eld: **nc** Deac: **nc** EvgHome: **23** Mission: **nc** Women Ord: **nc** As Ministers: **nc** as Deac: **nc** as Elders: **nc** ChurchOrg: **Presbyterian** Off/otherLang: **Korean** DoctrB: **ApC, WestConf**

Address: 568 DoHwa-Dong, MaPo-Gu, Seoul, Korea, Tel: +82 2 706-8588

84. Presbyterian Church in Korea (PyungAhn II) (4686)

TM: **3,172** Congr: **40** OrdM: **59** ChurchOrg: **Presbyterian** DoctrB: **ApC, WestConf**

Address: 150 HongIk-Dong, SungDong-Gu, Seoul, Korea, Tel: +82 2 296-19740

85. Presbyterian Church in Korea (HanGukBoSu) (4687)

TM: **6,906** Congr: **132** OrdM: **145** Eld: **nc** Deac: **nc** EvgHome: **12** ChurchOrg: **Presbyterian** DoctrB: **ApC, WestConf**

Address: 207-9 JungHwa-Dong, JungRang-Gu, Seoul, Korea, Tel: +82 2 492-4968

86. Presbyterian Church in Korea (HapDongSunGyo I) (4689)

TM: **11,510** Congr: **77** OrdM: **77** Eld: **nc** Deac: **nc** EvgHome: **43** ChurchOrg: **Presbyterian** DoctrB: **ApC, WestConf**

Address: 373-5 IeeMoon 1-Dong, DongDAeMoon-Gu, Seoul, Korea, Tel: +82 2 652-9358

87. Presbyterian Church in Korea (HapDongSunGyo II) (4690)

TM: **16,375** Congr: **161** OrdM: **135** Eld: **nc** Deac: **nc** EvgHome: **6** ChurchOrg: **Presbyterian** DoctrB: **ApC, WestConf**

Address: 621-6 Mok 3-Dong, Yang-Chun-Gu, Seoul, Korea, Tel: +82 2 642-1101

88. Presbyterian Church in Korea (HapDongSunMok) (4691)

TM: **44,120** Congr: **82** OrdM: **47** Eld: **nc** Deac: **nc** EvgHome: **40** ChurchOrg: **Presbyterian** DoctrB: **ApC, WestConf**

Address: 63-3 HwiGyung 2-Dong, DongDaeMoon-Gu, Seoul, Korea, Tel: +82 2 245-9204

89. Presbyterian Church in Korea (HapDongYunHap) (4692)

TM: **85,841** Congr: **391** OrdM: **317** Eld: **nc** Deac: **nc** EvgHome: **65** ChurchOrg: **Presbyterian** DoctrB: **ApC, WestConf**

Address: 192-2 JanChung 2-Dong, Jung-Gu, Seoul, Korea, Tel: +82 2 277-0079

90. Presbyterian Church in Korea (HapDongYeSun) (4693)

TM: **2,814** Congr: **31** OrdM: **71** ChurchOrg: **Presbyterian** DoctrB: **ApC, WestConf**

Address: 298-13 SinGil-Dong, YoungDeoungPo-Gu, Seoul, Korea, Tel: +82 2 831-1277

91. Presbyterian Church in Korea (HapDongEunChong) (4694)

TM: **2,392** Congr: **67** OrdM: **51** Eld: **nc** Deac: **nc** EvgHome: **16** ChurchOrg: **Presbyterian** DoctrB: **ApC, WestConf**

Address: 32-63 DangSan 4 Ga, YoungDeungPo-Gu, Seoul, Korea, Tel: +82 2 631-6967

92. Presbyterian Church in Korea (HapDongJeongShin) (4695)

TM: **112,275** Congr: **186** OrdM: **194** Eld: **nc** Deac: **nc** EvgHome: **102** ChurchOrg: **Presbyterian** DoctrB: **ApC, WestConf**

Address: 27-4 YongDu 1-Dong, DongDaeMoon-Gu, Seoul, Korea, Tel: +82 2 969-3976

93. Presbyterian Church in Korea (HapDongJungRip) (4696)

TM: **4,537** Congr: **102** OrdM: **88** Eld: **nc** Deac: **nc** EvgHome: **39** ChurchOrg: **Presbyterian** DoctrB: **ApC, WestConf**

Address: 856-1 BangDae 4-Dong, SuCho-Gu, Seoul, Korea, Tel: +82 2 537-3777

94. Presbyterian Church in Korea (HapDongTongHap) (4697)

TM: **22,932** Congr: **133** OrdM: **202** Eld: **nc** Deac: **nc** EvgHome: **64** ChurchOrg: **Presbyterian** DoctrB: **ApC, WestConf**

Address: 82-27 YukChob 2-Dong, EunPyung-Gu, Seoul, Korea, Tel: +82 2 386-9960

95. Presbyterian Church in Korea (HoHun II) (4698)

TM: **51,481** Congr: **310** OrdM: **309** Eld: **nc** Deac: **nc** EvgHome: **34** ChurchOrg: **Presbyterian** DoctrB: **ApC, WestConf**

Address: 209-2 JamSilBon-Dong, SongPa-Gu, Seoul, Korea, Tel: +82 2 417-2409

96. Presbyterian Church in Korea (HoHun III) (4699)

TM: **8,850** Congr: **73** OrdM: **79** Eld: **nc** Deac: **nc** EvgHome: **13** Mission: **nc** ChurchOrg: **Presbyterian** DoctrB: **ApC, WestConf**

Address: 661-11 GongLeung 1-Dong, NoWon-Gu, Seoul, Korea, Tel: +82 2 948-9111

KOREA, DEMOCRATIC PEOPLE'S REPUBLIC (DPRK)

Area in km²	120,540
Population	(July 1996 est.) 23,904,124
Religions in %	no statistics available
Official language	Korean

From the beginning of Christian mission in Korea in the 19th century to the division of Korea into two states, the church had particular strength in the North. The famous Korean Pentecost movement in 1907 was initiated in Pyongyang, and the Presbyterian Theological Seminary in Peyong Yang was the spiritual center of the church in the whole country. Pyongyang was called the Korean Jerusalem. However, the Christian churches had to face an entirely new situation when the Socialist state was established after World War II. As soon as Korea was liberated from Japanese colonial rule, Christians in the North took initiatives for reconstructing the nation. They organized societies such as the "Self-government Society (Ja Chi Hoi)" or the "National Establishment Preparatory Society (Ku Kuk Chun Bi Woi Won Hoi)." Some leaders even organized political parties such as the Christian Social Democratic Party or the Christian Liberal Party. These Christian initiatives caused concern to the Communists and inevitably led to sharp conflict.

The first clash with the Communist regime arose around the issue of the anniversary celebrations of the March First Independence Movement in 1946. The church planned a special memorial service for this occasion but was forbidden to celebrate it and instead ordered to join the Communist celebration. The churches persisted in their plan. After the service Christians even went into the streets to demonstrate for religious freedom. A number of leaders were arrested. Another significant confrontation occurred in connection with the elections which were scheduled to take place on Sunday, November 3, 1946. Prior to this the government had already chosen Sundays for important political demonstrations and misappropriated church buildings as lecture rooms for political propaganda. Faced with the demand to vote on Sunday, the Joint Presbytery issued a statement on Christian freedom and refused participation.

In order to facilitate the control of the churches, the Communist government organized the "Christian League (Ki Dok Kyo Kyo Do Yen Mange)" at the national as well at provincial and local levels. Protestant leaders were urged to join. More severe measures followed. The Presb and Meth theological seminaries were forced to unite. Many church buildings were taken over by the state. Before the Korean war (1950-1953) there were around 120,000 Christians and 1,400 congr in the North. During the war buildings were destroyed, and many people were killed or scattered. Many fled to the South.

From the time of the war until the 1980s the Christian churches in the North

335

had no contact with the outside world. Little is known about their life and witness. The organization representing Christians in North Korea is the Korean Christian Federation (KCF). Under its auspices the Bible and a new hymnbook were published in 1983. From the beginning of the 1980s the World Council of Churches sought to establish contacts with the Korean Christian Federation. A delegation visited Korea for the first time in November 1985, and in 1986 a meeting of Protestant representatives from the North and the South took place in Glion, Switzerland. Since then contacts have become more frequent. They also included the World Alliance of Reformed Churches. In 1997 a delegation of four church observers from North Korea participated in the 23rd General Council of the Alliance in Debrecen, Hungary.

The Prot church in North Korea is in a post-denominational situation. But the teaching and the structure of the church are in line with the Presb heritage. The highest authority of the Korean Christian Federation is the Central Committee. Every province has its own committee; similar structures apply to cities and the countryside. According to the Federation there are 10,000 Prot Christians in North Korea today. In P'yongyang there are two Prot church buildings; a RCath church was built in 1988. Federation leaders indicate that there are 500 house churches throughout the country. Since there are at present only 25 pastors, most of the pastoral activities, including the administration of the sacraments, are performed by elders and deacons.

No statistical data have been made available.

Address: Korean Christian Federation (KCF), Rev Kang Yong-Sub, Chairperson of Central Committee of KCF, and Rev. Hwang Si-Chon, Executive Secretary of International Affairs Department of KCF, Konguk-Dong, Man Gyung Dae District, Pyongyang, Democratic People's Republic of Korea, Tel: + 850 2 422 2405, Fax: +850 2 381 2100

KUWAIT

See also GULF REGION

Area in km²	1,818
Total population	(July 1996 est.) 1,950,047 Kuwaiti 45%, other Arab 35%, South Asian 9%, Iranian 4%, other 7%
Religions in %	Islam Muslim 85% (Shi'a 30%, Sunni 45%, other 10%), Christian, Hindu, Parsi, and other 15%
Official/other languages	Arabic/English widely spoken

National Evangelical Church in Kuwait — NECK (4393)

Christian work started in Kuwait in 1910 when the *Arabian Medical Mission* of the Reformed Church in America (RCA; see United States no. 36)) opened a clinic in Kuwait. It was followed by a Men's Hospital and later also by one for Women. The income from oil soon made this ministry unnecessary, and the hospitals were closed in 1967. By that time the church consisted of three distinct language-based congregations. They constitute the National Evangelical Church in Kuwait (NECK), formerly also called the Church of Christ in Kuwait. There exist, in addition, ten Christian organizations in Kuwait.

At present there are within NECK 45 different congregations with over 4,800 people — Arabs (mostly expatriate, but also a few Kuwaiti families), Europeans, Americans, Indians (several different denominational and language congregations), Pakistanis, Koreans, and Filipinos. Services are held every day of the week, especially Fridays, Saturdays, and Sundays. There is a much more positive attitude from the Kuwaiti people and government since the help the USA gave during the Iraqi invasion.

Under the present organization each congregation has its own council; there is one common council, made up of representatives from the larger congregations, charged with overseeing times of worship, use of the building, etc. The main church building is in the city of Kuwait. At present it belongs to the government and is rented by the church for 150 dollars a year.

Among the congregations within NECK the more historical ones are:

- the **English** congregation, which was formally established in 1962 and maintains warm links with the RCA. It is an independent congregation within NECK.
- the **Arabic** congregation, which has in the past been pastored by ministers from the Coptic Evangelical Church of Egypt and is now nondenominational.
- the **Malayalam** congregation, which is served by a pastor from the Church of South India.

TM: **4,850** BM: **1,200** CM: **1,200** Congr: **45** PStations: **1** OrdM: **3** Eld: **8** Deac: **8** EvgHome: **1,200** Mission: **1** Women Ord: **yes** As Ministers: **1980/0** as Deac: **1980/10** as Elders: **1980/10** ChurchOrg: **none** Off/otherLang: **17, including English, Arabic** DoctrB: **ApC, spirit-filled evangelical** Infant or believer's baptism: **both** Frequency of the Lord's Supper: **weekly** Close relations with: **Reformed Church in America (RCA)** NatRel: **none** RegRel: **MECC (1975)** IntlRel: **none** TheolSchool: **none** Periodicals: **none**

Address: The National Evangelical Church in Kuwait, P.O. Box 80, Safat Kuwait 13001, Kuwait, Tel: +965 240 7195, Fax: +965 243 1087

LAOS

Area in km²	230,800
Population	(July 1996 est.) 4,975,772 Lao Loum (lowland) 68%, Lao Theung (upland) 22%, Lao Soung (highland) including the Hmong ("Meo") and Yao (Mien) 9%, ethnic Vietnamese/Chinese 1%
Religions in %	Buddhist 57.8%, traditional beliefs 33.6%, Muslim 1%, RCath 0.9%, Prot 0.9%, others 6.6%
Official/other languages	Lao/French, English, and various ethnic languages

Christianity was first brought to Laos at the end of the 19th century. RCath missionaries began work both in the north (1881) and in the south (1886) of the country. The first Prot witness was that of a Presb missionary, Daniel McGilvray, from the USA, who started evangelistic work in the north. He was based in Chiang Mai, Thailand, and from there made several journeys to Laos between 1872 and 1898. A few communities came into existence. The first Prot church was founded by two Swiss missionaries in the south. Gabriel Contesse and Maurice Willy established a mission station in Sing-Khône in 1902. Work proved to be very difficult. Epidemics took a high toll. Contesse and his wife died prematurely in 1908. Other missionaries followed, and by 1936 twelve communities had been founded. In 1928 they were joined by missionaries of the Christian and Missionary Alliance.

Three Gospels were translated into Lao in 1908; a translation of the full Bible was published in 1932.

The small Christian minority met with many difficulties, especially in the decades after World War II. In 1975, religious activities were curtailed by the Communist regime. Some leaders were imprisoned, some were killed. Many left the country. The main witness came from Christians in Laos who continued to communicate the Gospel.

Lao Evangelical Church (4510)

The Christian communities in the south and the north, who were at first two independent entities, progressively reorganized themselves to form the Lao Evangelical Church, which was officially recognized in December 1982; it regards itself as nondenominational. A small measure of outside help continues in the form of medical and agricultural work.

TM: **40,000** CM: **19,000** Congr: **150** OrdM: **nc** Eld: **nc** Deac: **nc** EvgHome: **nc** Mission: **nc** Women Ord: **nc** ChurchOrg: **Congregational/Presbyterian** Off/otherLang: **Lao** DoctrB: **ApC** NatRel: **nc** RegRel: **CCA** IntlRel: **nc** TheolSchool: **nc.**

Address: Lao Evangelical Church, P.O. Box 4200, Vientiane, Lao P.D.R., Tel: +856 21 169-136 or
           169-313

NB: In the United States, under the umbrella of the Presbyterian Church USA, a number of Lao communities have formed the Lao Presbyterian Council, P.O. Box 165, Cornelia, GA 30531, USA

LATVIA

Area in km²	61,400
Population	(July 1996 est.) 2,468,982 Latvian 51.8%, Russian 33.8%, Byelorussian 4.5%, Ukrainian 3.4%, Polish 2.3%, other 4.2%
Religions in %	Luth 24.3%, RCath 21.1%, Russian Orth 4.1%, Ref. 0.03%, other 50.47%
Official/other languages	Lettish/Lithuanian, Russian

The Baltic country of Latvia consists of four geographic regions: Latgale, Kurzeme, Vidzeme, and Zemgale. The Christian faith was introduced at the beginning of the 13th century mainly by missionaries from Germany. In the course of history the major part of the country was also called Livonia or Courlandia. In 1581 the first Bibles in Lettish were introduced in Riga by the Swedish pastor, Gothfriedd Glick. Jesuits began to teach in Latvian. For centuries the country was under the control of Germany, Sweden, Poland, and Russia. In 1918 Latvia obtained the status of an independent Democratic Republic. On June 17, 1940, on the basis of the Hitler/Stalin pact, the country was annexed by the Soviet Union. It remained under Soviet domination from the end of World War II until 1992. On May 4, 1992, the Republic of Latvia again became independent. As a result of the policy generally pursued by the Soviet Union nearly half of the population in Latvia today is of non-Latvian origin.

Luth, RCath, and Russian Orthodox are the most important religious bodies in Latvia.

Reformed Church in Latvia (6460)

Since the 16th century a number of Calvinist congregations had been established along the routes used by English, Dutch, French, and Swiss carrying on business between Copenhagen and Latvia. Today the denomination consists of a single Ref church, which was built by German traders in 1733. Up to World War II the church was predominantly of German origin. In 1938 there were still about 1,000 members, including those living in Mitau and a group of Lithuanians. When in 1939 the

German repatriation took place, the majority of the congregation left Latvia. The church buildings were handed over to the Evangelical Lutheran Church. After World War II, on December 10, 1949, the Ref congregation was joined by the Evangelical Church of the Brethren and the Evangelical Bethlehem Community. A new community, the Evangelical Reformed–Brethren community, was formed. Funding for church repairs was unavailable. In 1964 the state took over the building and transformed it into a sound studio. The building was returned to the church in December 1993 and rededicated on May 15, 1994. Since 1996 an ordained minister from Toronto has been serving this church.

TM: **40** BM: **40** CM: **40** Congr: **1** PStations: **1** OrdM: **1** Eld: **1** Deac: **2** EvgHome: **nc** Mission: **nc** Women Ord: **no** ChurchOrg: **Reformed** Off/otherLang: **Latvian** DoctrB: **nc** Infant or believer's baptism: **both** Frequency of the Lord's Supper: **during each service** Periodicals: **none** Close relations with: **Ev. Resurrection Church (Lübeck/Germany since 1994)** NatRel: **none** RegRel: **none** IntlRel: **WARC** TheolSchool: **training in Great Britain**

Address: Evangeliska Reformatu-Braju Draudze, P. 12.337 Marstalu 10, LV-1050 Riga, Latvia, Tel: +371 2 273-409, Fax: +371 722 4283

LEBANON

See also SYRIA

Area in km^2	10,400
Population	(July 1996 est.) 3,776,317 Arab 95%, Armenian 4%, other 1%
Religions in %	Islam 70% (5 legally recognized Islamic groups — Alawite or Nusayri, Druze, Isma'ilite, Shi'a, Sunni), Christian 30% (11 legally recognized Christian groups — 4 Orthodox Christian, 6 Catholic, 1 Prot), small Jewish communities
Official/other languages	Arabic, French/Armenian, English

MECC (Middle East Council of Churches)

Lebanon as a state has existed only since 1920. But its history dates back to the Phoenician empire. Beirut was founded around 4,000 B.C. For more than 50 centuries various civilizations have molded its people, and the region has been ruled by Assyrian, Egyptian, Persian, Greek, Roman, and, later, Arab and Turkish occupants. British troops intervened in 1840 to master a major revolt. After the massacre in 1860 of 22,000 Christians by the Druzes, France intervened and from then on played a leading role in the region. At the end of World War I, when the Ottoman empire was dissolved, Lebanon was placed by the League of Nations under French mandate; this came to an end in 1943 when the independent Republic of

Lebanon was proclaimed. In recent times a devastating civil war (1975-1991) brought Lebanon almost to collapse. It has since made much progress toward rebuilding its political institutions and regained its national sovereignty, although neighboring Syria continues to maintain (in 1997) about 30,000 troops on its territory. Under the Ta'if Accord — the blueprint for national reconciliation — the Lebanese have established a more equitable political system, particularly by giving Muslims a greater say in the political process.

For nearly 1,300 years, with the exception of the two centuries of Christian Crusades, the region has lived under Muslim rule. Christianity, however, survived, and since 1861 a special administrative district with Christian administrators exists in the area of Mount Lebanon traditionally inhabited by Maronite Christians. Lebanon offers a particular model of society inherited from the Ottoman system. Religious communities have equal rights and handle most matters of daily life as internal affairs. They have their own jurisdictions in matters of personal status and register legal acts concerning birth, marriage, divorce, and matters of inheritance. At the political level official functions have been clearly distributed among the confessional bodies; according to the unwritten "National Pact," the president of Lebanon has to be a Maronite, the Prime Minister a Sunnite, the president of Parliament a Shiite.

The Maronite Church is the largest Christian church in the Lebanon. It has a close relationship with the Holy See in Rome. Christianity in Lebanon includes further Greek-Orthodox, Catholic-Orthodox (Melkites), Apostolic Armenians (they arrived in 1918 as survivors from the massacres in Turkey), Armenian Catholics, Syrian Orthodox (Jacobites), Syrian Catholics, Assyrian Orthodox, Chaldean Catholics, and Arab Catholics.

The Evangelical presence in this part of the former Ottoman Empire owes to the work of Ref missionaries, who arrived in the early 19th century from the United States and the British Isles. They worked primarily in Mount Lebanon and in major portions of the Syrian interior. The Ottoman authorities recognized the Prot faith already in 1848.

Today most Prot are gathered under the umbrella of the Supreme Council of the Evangelical Community in Syria and Lebanon (1936). The Ref churches are part of the Middle East Council of Churches. For several decades the Near East School of Theology, which operates under the responsibility of various Prot churches, has provided theological training for candidates to the ministry.

1. Union of the Armenian Evangelical Churches in the Near East (4391)

This church is an autonomous body of 24 congregations throughout Lebanon, Syria, Turkey, Greece, Egypt, and Iran. It began as an indigenous reform movement in the 1820s from within the Armenian Orthodox Church. It became an independent community in 1846 in Istanbul. It once counted over 60,000 members in the Ottoman Empire. After the massacres of Armenians and, following World War I, the deportation of the remnant Armenian population from what is now Turkey, the Union was reorganized in Syria and Lebanon. Today it is the second strongest Prot community in Lebanon. Its headquarters are in Beirut. It also provides a ministry for a number of Syriac Prot congr whose ancestry came from regions predominantly Armenian. The Union stresses the importance of education; it operates 15 schools and owns Haigazian University College — the only such college in the Armenian diaspora — with over 360 students.

TM: **10,000** BM: **10,000** CM: **1,000** Congr: **23** OrdM: **22** Eld: **nc** Deac: **nc** EvgHome: **nc** Mission: **2** Women Ord: **yes** As Ministers: **not yet** as Deac: **yes** as Elders: **yes** ChurchOrg: **12-member central committee, elected by the union of autonomous churches (acts as supervisor and coordinates activities of member churches and church-related institutions)** Off/otherLang: **Armenian (Arabic in 2 congr, Turkish in one)** DoctrB: **ApC, NicC** Infant or believer's baptism: **both** Frequency of the Lord's Supper: **4-5 times a year and special occasions** Close relations with: **National Presbyterian Synod, Armenian Ev. Union of North America, Union of the Ev. Churches of France** NatRel: **nc** RegRel: **MECC (1974)** FMEEC (since beginning) IntlRel: **WCC (1948), WARC, Armenian Evangelical World Council** TheolSchool: **Near East School of Theology (NEST)(Beirut)** Service infrastructure: **1 hospital in partnership with Arm Apostolic Ch; 2 rest/nursing homes with Apostolic and Cath. ch, 2 social sevice org., 15 kindergartens,** Periodicals: **Chanasser (gen/monthly/1,200) Badanegan Artzakank (youth/monthly/2,500), Louys (devotional/quarterly/2,500)**

Address: Union of the Armenian Evangelical Churches in the Near East, P.O. Box 11-377, Ibrahim Pasha Mar Mikhael, Beirut, Lebanon, Tel: +961 1 443-547, Fax: +961 1 582-191

2. National Evangelical Union of Lebanon (4392)

The first congr was established in Beirut in 1848 as the Evangelical Church of Beirut. A dozen others were created in the following decades in various parts of the country. After the fall of the Ottoman Empire and the creation of "Greater Lebanon" in 1920 Beirut became the capital. Soon several parishes around Beirut sought communion with the Beirut church for spiritual sustenance, thus depending heavily on the Beirut church for pastoral and administrative care. In the early 1960s it was decided to set up the National Evangelical Union of Lebanon, a loose federative structure. The congregations remain largely independent. Before the civil war the Union counted over 8,000 communicant members. The Union runs a number of schools, including a Schneller School as well as an orphanage.

TM: **2,800** BM: **1,800** CM: **1,800** Congr: **9** PStations: **4** OrdM: **2** Eld: **30** Deac: **ne** EvgHome: **2** Mission: **ne** Women Ord: **yes in principle** As Ministers: **0** as Deac: **0** as Elders: **0** ChurchOrg: **as a congregational union of 9 independant churches united only spiritually and socially** Off/otherLang: **Arabic** DoctrB: **ApC, NicC, HeidC, Ref Creeds** Infant or believer's baptism: **both** Frequency of the Lord's Supper: **monthly** Close relations with: **EMS** NatRel: **Supreme Council of Evangelical Churches in Syria and Lebanon (1936)** RegRel: **MECC (1974), MEFEC (1974),** IntlRel: **WARC** TheolSchool: **Near East School of Theology (NEST)(Beirut)** Service infrastructure: **National Prot College (kindergarten to senior high school), Schneller School (kindergarten, junior high, orphanage, technical school)** Periodicals: **Risalat al Kanissah (gen/quarterly/1,000) NEC Beirut Newsletter (first church e-mail newsletter)**

Address: National Evangelical Union in Lebanon, P.O. Box 11 5224, Al Kanissa Al Injiliah, Beirut, Lebanon, Tel: +961 3 690 116, Fax: +961 1 652-780 or 781, E-mail: nec.beirut@tnet.com.lb

3. National Evangelical Synod of Syria and Lebanon (4390)

The Synod is the administrative body for some sixty Arabic-speaking churches and centers in Syria and Lebanon who share the Evangelical faith and have adopted Ref teaching and Presb order. The Synod was organized in 1920 as a union of several presbyteries. In 1959 it assumed responsibility for the direction of almost all work of former mission bodies from the USA, France, Denmark, Holland, and Switzerland.

The congr are found in the Fertile Crescent, between the Mediterranean and the Tigris and Euphrates rivers. After steady growth over the years the Synod more recently experienced continuous emigration of large numbers of Evangelicals to the USA and to Australia. During the civil war in Lebanon many church buildings were destroyed or heavily damaged. The Synod carries a large educational ministry with some 20 schools and kindergartens as well as a hospital.

TM: **8,000** BM: **7,000** CM: **4,000** Congr: **36** PStations: **37** OrdM: **22** Eld: **150** Deac: **0** EvgHome: **3** Mission: **0** Women Ord: **yes** As Ministers: **0** as Deac: **0** as Elders: **1940s/15** ChurchOrg: **one presbytery, representation in the Synod of 8 regions (4 in Syria, 4 in the Lebanon)** Off/otherLang: **Arabic** DoctrB: **ApC, NicC, Ref Calvinist** Frequency of the Lord's Supper: **every two weeks to once or twice a year** Close relations with: **Armenian Evangelical Union of the Near East, National Evangelical Ch of Beirut** NatRel: **Supreme Council of the Evangelical Community in Syria and Lebanon (1937)** RegRel: **MECC (1974), MEFEC (1974)** IntlRel: **WCC (1948), WARC** TheolSchool: **nc** Service infrastructure: **Hamlin Hospital, Hammana Nursing Home, 9 kindergartens, 5 elementary schools, 6 secondary schools** Periodicals: **Al-Nashrah (gen and spiritual/monthly/1,000)**

Address: National Evangelical Synod of Syria and Lebanon, P.O. Box 70890, Rabieh St. 34, Antelias, Lebanon, Tel: +961 1 411-179, Fax: +961 1 411-184

LESOTHO

Area in km²	30,350
Population	(July 1995) 1,992,960 Sotho 99.7%, Europeans 1,600, Asians 800
Religions in %	Christian 92% (RCath 43.5%, Evangelical 29.8%, Angl 11.5%), Afr Rel 8%
Official/other languages	English/Sesotho, Zulu, Xhosa

Lesotho Evangelical Church (1080)

Sent by the freshly founded *Mission de Paris,* three French missionaries — Thomas Arbousset, Eugène Casalis, and Constant Gosselin — arrived in Lesotho in 1833. They received the support of King Moshoeshoe I (1786-1870), who sought to gather the Basotho population under his reign. Under his protection the mission work began to develop. A first mission station was built in Morija; others followed but, as a result of wars, much of the work had to be discontinued. In response to expansionist threats by South Africa, King Moshoeshoe I established an alliance with Britain. In 1868 Basotholand, as it was then called, became a colony of the British crown. Mission stations could be reopened and, gradually, the church was organized. In 1887 a theological school for the formation of African pastors was opened, and in 1898 the Seboka (Synod) was established, an assembly in which both missionaries and Basotho pastors were represented. With the arrival of other missions (1862 RCath, 1875 Angl) a sense of competition developed and the evangelical mission lost some of its impact, especially in the period between the two World Wars. In the 1950s the church began to gain autonomy, and in April 1964 the independent Evangelical Church of Lesotho was inaugurated. In 1966 the British colony became a sovereign state within the Commonwealth, now called Lesotho.

The following years were a period of trial and hardship. In 1970 Prime Minister Leabuda Jonathan suspended the constitution and ruled as dictator. Once the church joined the resistance, it suffered persecution and repression. Edgar Motuba, editor of the church paper, who had published detailed analyses of the situation, was murdered, and the vice-president of the church, Ben Masilo, had to leave the country. The church consistently called for true national reconciliation which could only be achieved through free elections. In 1986, with the help of South Africa, Jonathan was overthrown and replaced by Lekhanya. The regime remained dictatorial, however, and in 1990 King Moshoeshoe II was sent into exile. He was able to return two years later. Democratic elections were held in 1993, which brought an overwhelming victory by the opposition Congress Party. In 1994 Moshoeshoe II was replaced by his son Letsie, who now has the difficult task of guaranteeing the unity of the country.

In recent years the church has experienced considerable internal tensions due to different visions of the future of the church among pastors and lay people.

TM: **211,000** Congr: **56** PStations: **106** OrdM: **65** Eld: **nc** Deac: **none** EvgHome: **120** Mission: **none** Women Ord: **yes** As Ministers: **1985/3** as Deac: **none** as Elders: **over 2,000** ChurchOrg: **church council, consistory, presby, gen synod** Off/otherLang: **Sesotho, English** DoctrB: **ApC HeidC** Infant or believer's baptism: **both** Frequency of the Lord's Supper: **quarterly** Periodicals: **Leselinyana La Lesotho (gen/bi-weekly/10,000)** NatRel: **CCL (1970)** RegRel: **SAARC** IntlRel: **WCC, WARC (1985)** TheolSchool: **nc**

Address: Kereke ea Evangeli Lesotho, P.O. Box 260, Old Busstop, Casalis House, Maseru 100, Lesotho, Tel: +266 313-942, Fax: +266 310-555, E-mail: none

LIBERIA

Area in km²	111,370
Population	(est. July 1996) 2,109,789 Ethnic divisions: indigenous African tribes 95% (including Kpelle, Bassa, Gio, Kru, Grebo, Mano, Krahn, Gola, Gbandi, Loma, Kissi, Vai, and Bella), Americo-Liberians 5% (descendants of former slaves)
Religions in %	traditional 70%, Muslim 20%, Christian 10%
Official/other languages	English 20%/Niger-Congo language group: about 20 local languages come from this group

Liberia was declared a colony in 1822 in order to settle freshly liberated American slaves. More slaves were to be unloaded in the following years from American and British warships. The international community recognized Liberia as a Republic after a Constitution was adopted in 1847. For over a century (from 1870 to 1980) the country was ruled by the "True Whig" Party, often chaired by church people like its latest leaders, W. V. S. Tubman and W. R. Tolbert. Samuel Kanyon Doe came to power in 1980 through a coup d'etat but was assassinated 10 years later. The ensuing civil war killed more than 150,000, displaced nearly 800,000 people within Liberia, and forced 750,000 refugees to live in neighboring countries. Less than a year after the August 1995 Abuja Peace Accord, war resumed when forces loyal to faction leader Charles Taylor and Alhaji Kromah attacked rival factions in Monrovia, further damaging the capital's already dilapidated infrastructure and causing panic among the remaining foreign residents. Thousands sought refuge in American facilities. Prospects for peace became extremely uncertain again. Years of civil strife have destroyed much of Liberia's economic infrastructure, made civil administration nearly impossible, and brought economic activity virtually to a halt.

The population of Liberia belongs in its majority to traditional African religions. Less than 10% are Christians (5.4% belonging to Prot. denominations). Since the '50s a growing number of Muslim missionaries have come from Egypt and Pakistan. The Constitution had not changed from 1847 to 1985, when it was revised.

The largest Prot denominations are the Meth Church (Meth were already among the freed slaves in 1822), the Presbyterian Church in the USA (PCUSA) (1833), the Luth Church (dates back to 1860), and the Pent Church (1908). Among other Christian churches are the Angl Church, originating from the Prot Episcopal Church of the USA, and the RCath Church, which started mission work in 1841 only. The 12 mainline churches, including the Presbytery of Liberia in West Africa, constitute the Liberian Council of Churches (LCC). The LCC tries to keep political and church interests clearly separated, but often without success. The Li-

345

berian independent churches are organized in groups like the Pent Fellowship Union, the Association of Evangelicals of Liberia, and the National Union of Christian Alliance of Liberia.

Presbytery of Liberia in West Africa (1090)

In 1833 the Board of Foreign Missions, set up by the PCUSA, started work in Liberia. The policy of sending only black missionaries from the USA was abandoned when it became clear that they were not less subject to malaria than the white missionaries. One of them signed the Monrovian Declaration of Independence (1847). The last missionaries arrived in 1887. The Presbytery of Liberia in West Africa became independent in 1928. In 1944 it started its own mission work in the Todee District and opened a school and a clinic. Women have traditionally played an important role in church life and have been ordained at an early stage to the various ministries. In 1980 the Presbytery of Liberia became a provisional Presbytery of the Cumberland Presbyterian Church of the USA.

TM: **3,000** Congr: **12** OrdM: **12** Eld: **yes** Deac: **yes** EvgHome: **8** Mission: **ne** Women Ord: **yes** As Ministers: **1950s/3** as Deac: **1940s/yes** as Elders: **1940s/yes** ChurchOrg: **Presbyterian** Off/otherLang: **English** DoctrB: **ApC, NicC** Infant or believer's baptism: **both** Frequency of the Lord's Supper: **monthly** Periodicals: **none** NatRel: **LCC** RegRel: **AACC** IntlRel: **WCC, WARC (1985)** TheolSchool: **none.**

Address: Presbytery of Liberia in West Africa, P.O. Box 3350, Broad and Johnson Street, Monrovia, Liberia, Tel: +231 226 630, Fax: +231 226 132, E-mail: none

---

LIECHTENSTEIN

Area in km²	160
Population	(1993) 30,310
Religions in %	RCath 80.6%, small Prot (Ref and Luth) minority 7.3%, other
Official language	German

Evangelical Church in Liechtenstein (6015)

With the beginning of industrialization, Prot from neighboring countries began to settle in Liechtenstein. In 1880 the Duke of Liechtenstein granted permission to hold Prot worship services and to organize religious instruction for the children of Prot families. For several decades pastors from parishes across the border in Switzerland and Austria served the small community. In 1952 a pastor was named for Liechtenstein, and in 1963 a church was built in Vaduz, the capital of Liechtenstein. The Evangelical Church comprises Prot of Ref and Luth background; through a special agreement it is linked to the Evangelical-Reformed Church of St. Gallen in Switzerland (cf. Switzerland no. 13). In addition to the Evangelical Church, there is also an Evangelical-Luth congr in Liechtenstein.

TM: **1,600** Congr: **1** PStations: **2** OrdM: **1** Eld: **12** Deac: **nc** Women Ord: **yes** As Ministers: **nc** as Deac: **nc** as Elders: **nc** ChurchOrg: **single congregation, regrouping Luth, Ref, and other Prot**; **United/ Congreg (from the point of view of public law the church is constituted as an association)** Off/ otherLang: **German** DoctrB: **ApC, NicC, AthC, United** Infant or believer's baptism: **both** Frequency of the Lord's Supper: **church festivals, occasional** Close relations with: **Ch of St. Gallen (Switzerland)**

Address: Evangelische Kirche im Fürstentum Liechtenstein, Fürst Franz Josef Str. 11, FL-9490 Vaduz, Liechtenstein, Tel: +41 75 232 2142

LITHUANIA

Area in km^2	65,200
Population	(July 1996 est.) 3,646,041 Lithuanian 80.1%, Russian 8.6%, Polish 7.7%, Byelorussian 1.5%, other 2.1%
Religions in %	RCath 80%, Russian Orth 0.7% Prot (Ref, Luth, Free Ch) 2%, Jews 0.3% (8% in 1939), other 17%
Official/other languages	Lithuanian until 1864, 1918-1940, and since 1989/ Russian

Christianity officially took root in Lithuania in 1387 when King Gediminas renounced paganism and married the RCath queen Hedwig of Poland. The dual kingdom of Lithuania-Poland was thus born, and the fortunes of the two peoples became intertwined. From the 13th till the 16th century the Grand Duchy of Lithuania, which is sometimes called the state of Belarusan-Lithuanian by historians, was one of the largest, most powerful, and most flourishing states in medieval Eastern Europe. It comprised the lands of contemporary Belarus, Lithuania, Ukraine, and a part of Russia.

Protestantism came to Lithuania in the early Reformation years. Lutheranism arrived in the beginning of the 1520s. Young people of prominent families went to schools in Scotland, Bohemia, France, and Switzerland and helped to promote the Calvinist religion upon returning to their home country. The first Ref church was founded in 1555. John Calvin himself corresponded with Duke Radvila (in Polish "Radziwill"), the leading magnate of the country. Vilnius, with its numerous nationalities, also became a religious center. Under the "Magna Charta Libertatum," issued in 1563, Luth and Calvinists enjoyed equal rights with all other faiths.

During the Counter-Reformation Prot, like other minorities, lost their civil rights. Though subjected to discrimination, the Lithuanian Reformed church survived and met regularly in synods. In 1795 tsarist Russian troops invaded the country. Religious discrimination affected all non-Russian Orthodox believers. During the time of national independence, i.e., 1918-1940, the country gained new strength.

During World War II Lithuania was invaded by the Soviet Union, then by Germans. Fierce fights destroyed part of the country. Over 300,000 died. Hundreds of thousands fled when Russian troops came back in 1944. Many Lithuanians escaped to Western countries. Today over 850,000 Lithuanians still live in the USA alone. For five decades the Soviet Union imposed its rule and its atheist system on the country. Church property was confiscated, preaching restricted, teaching forbidden. Over 250,000 Lithuanians died in camps in Siberia. An equal number of Russian immigrants settled in Lithuania.

On March 11, 1990, in the wake of the changes in the Soviet Union, the Lithuanian parliament proclaimed independence. Lithuania is today an independent republic within the Baltic free zone of exchange and is a member of the Council of Europe.

Reformed Church in Lithuania (6461)

The church was founded in 1553 in Vilnius. At its first synod meeting in 1557 the church was officially named the "Unitas Lithuanie" (Lithuanian Unity); from its beginning it has been open to various national groups and accepted the use of several languages. The Huguenot cross and *Soli Deo Gloria* are used as popular symbols. During the Russian occupation theological training was forbidden. Pastors were not replaced.

In 1982 the last minister of the church died. A Luth pastor helped out. The church split into two groups: "conservatives" (in favor of a limited collaboration with the authorities) and "reformers" (wanting to take more risks). In the late 1980s Ref communities emerged in unexpected places. Since 1992 the Lithuanian Bible Society has been working on an ecumenical translation of the Bible. There is a sister congregation in Chicago (Ill., USA) formed by emigrants (cf. United States no. 25).

TM: **10,762** BM: **6,000** CM: **2,000** Congr: **11** OrdM: **1** Eld: **0** Deac: **0** EvgHome: **2** Mission: **ne** Women Ord: **ne** ChurchOrg: **Congregational (congr, synod council, annual synod)** Off/otherLang: **Lithuanian** DoctrB: **ApC, HeidC, HelvC** Infant or believer's baptism: **both** Periodicals: **none** NatRel: **none** RegRel: **none** IntlRel: **WARC** TheolSchool: **training in Poland, USA, Germany**

Address: Lietuvos Evangeliku Reformatu Baznycia, P.O. Box 661, LT-2049 Vilnius, Lithuania, Tel.:
           +370 2 450-656, Fax: +370 2 450-656

LUXEMBOURG

Area in km²	2,586
Population	(1994) 400,900
Religions in %	RCath (97%) Prot (1%) Jews (.2%)
Official language	Luxemburgish

Historically, Luxembourg is a RCath country. Protestantism, officially tolerated since 1768, came to Luxembourg through migration. The first Prot community was a garrison church. After the Vienna Congress of 1815 the country was awarded to King Wilhelm I of the Netherlands, who was a Calvinist. In 1817 the Trinity Church in the city of Luxembourg was built for Prussian soldiers serving the Duke and later made available to the Prot community. With the industrialization of the country Prot became more numerous, especially in the region of Esch-sur-Alzette.

In 1894 the Prot community in the city of Luxembourg was officially recognized; it included all Prot of the Helvetic and the Augsburg Confessions ("communauté protestante, confession unie").

In 1961 French-speaking immigrants established the "Eglise protestante européenne d'expression française." In 1982 the Prot in the region of Esch-sur-Alzette formed the Protestant-Reformed Church of Luxembourg (Helvetic Confession); they were granted the status of an officially recognized church by the state.

In addition to these churches there are in the city of Luxembourg several language communities which are under the jurisdiction of the churches in their country of origin (Germans, Danes, Dutch, English, Swedish). Since 1976 there is a "Council of Parishes and Communities in Luxembourg" in which the majority of the Prot communities are federated.

1. Protestant Church of Luxembourg (6351)

This church consists of five congr located in the city of Luxembourg, in Ettelbruck, Wiltz, and Obercorn. From the beginning of its history (in 1894) it was a united church. It is in conversation with the French-speaking community, and it is expected that they will unite in the near future.

TM: **900** BM: **900** CM: **650** Congr: **5** PStations: **4** OrdM: **1** Eld: **7** Deac: **nc** EvgHome: **ne** Mission: **ne** Women Ord: **yes** As Ministers: **nc** as Deac: **nc** as Elders: **8** ChurchOrg: **consistories, presbyterian-council** Off/otherLang: **Luxemburgish, French, German** DoctrB: **ApC, NicC, HelvC, CA** Infant or believer's baptism: **both** Frequency of the Lord's Supper: **monthly** Periodicals: **Glaubensbote (info/monthly/500)** Close relations with: **Evang. Ref Ch of Alsace-Lorraine (ERAL), other Prot**

churches in Luxembourg NatRel: **Alliance of the Prot Churches in Luxembourg (1993) Euregion (1995)** RegRel: **CEC** IntlRel: **WCC (1995)** TheolSchool: **none.**

Address: Eglise Protestante de Luxembourg et Eglise Protestante d'Expression Française, 5, rue de la Congregation, L-1352 Ville de Luxembourg, Luxembourg, Tel: +352 229-670, Fax: +352 467-198

2. Evangelical Protestant Church of Luxemburg H.B. (6350)

When this church was established in l982, it clearly opted for the Ref heritage. It asked for membership in the World Alliance of Reformed Churches.

TM: **3,500** BM: **3,500** CM: **250** Congr: **4** PStations: **3** OrdM: **2** Eld: **6** Deac: **1** EvgHome: **nc** Mission: **nc** Women Ord: **Yes** As Ministers: **1982/0** as Deac: **1982/0** as Elders: **1982/2** ChurchOrg: **"consistoires" of parishes and church** Off/otherLang: **German** DoctrB: **ApC, NicC, AthC, HeidC, HelvC** Infant or believer's baptism: **both** Frequency of the Lord's Supper: **at least 8 times per year** Close relations with: **Protestant Church of Rhineland (Düsseldorf)** NatRel: **Alliance of Protestant Churches in Luxembourg (1997) Council of Christian Churches in Luxembourg (1997)** RegRel: **CEC Reformed Alliance (Germany) (1994) Arbeitsgemeinschaft Christlicher Kirchen (Germany) (1995)** IntlRel: **WARC (1982), Leuenberger Concord (1995)** TheolSchool: **none**

Address: Protestantisch-Reformierte Kirche von Luxembourg H.B., P.O. Box 295, 11, rue de la libération, L-4003 Esch-sur-Alzette, Luxembourg, Tel: +352 540-345, Fax: +352 540-346, E-mail: none

MADAGASCAR

Area in km²	587,040
Population	(July 1996 est.) 13,670,507 Malayo-Indonesian (Merina and related Betsileo), Cotiers (mixed African, Malayo-Indonesian, and Arab ancestry, Betsimisaraka, Tsimihety, Antaisaka, Sakalava), French, Indian, Comoran
Religions in %	indigenous beliefs 52%, Christian 41% (RCath 26%, Prot 22%: Ref, Luth, Ev., Pent, Angl), Muslim 7%
Official/other languages	French, Malagasy/dialects

FFKM (Christian Council of Madagascar — *Conseil des Eglises Chrétiennes à Madagascar*)
FFPM (Fédération of the Protestant Churches of Madagascar — *Fédération des Eglises Protestantes de Madagascar*)

The first missionary efforts in Madagascar were made by RCath in the 16th century. Further efforts by Portuguese Jesuits and French Lazarists in the 17th and

18th centuries were made without lasting fruits. The first Ref missionaries were sent by the London Missionary Society (LMS). On August 18, 1818, Pastor David Jones and Thomas Bevan arrived in Toamasina, the harbor at the Eastern coast of Madagascar. They enjoyed the protection of King Radama I (1810-1828). They opened a school and succeeded in attracting many young people from noble Malagasy families. In subsequent years many more schools were opened. Though all missionaries, with the exception of Jones, died soon after their arrival, the work went on. Until the death of King Radama other LMS missionaries were allowed to come to the island. One of their important achievements was reducing the Malagasy language into Latin script; the first translation of the Bible was published in Antananarivo in 1835.

Under Radama's widow and successor Ranavalona I (1828-1861) a period of brutal persecution began. In 1835, the same year as the Bible was published, the missionaries were forced to leave the country and many Malagasy converts suffered martyrdom. The first to be executed was a woman called Rasalama. This time of persecution also gave birth to indigenous leadership (Rafaravavy Mary and Andriambelo +1904). The memory of this dark period plays a significant role in the life of the churches in Madagascar.

Under the short reign of Ranavalona's son the situation changed again. He sought to modernize the country and favored mission work. Queen Ranavalona II converted to the Ref faith in 1869, and large numbers of the upper class followed her example. Other Prot missions began work in various parts of the island (Angl 1864, Norwegian Luth 1866, Quaker 1867). The growing influence of France led to tensions between RCath and Prot. To strengthen their work, the Prot mission asked for the support of the Paris Evangelical Missionary Society in 1895. In 1896 Madagascar became a French colony. The rivalry between RCath and Prot continued throughout the following decades.

1. Church of Jesus Christ in Madagascar (FJKM) (1100)

After the Second World War the churches began to become independent. In 1958 the churches founded by the LMS and by French mission efforts constituted themselves respectively as the Church of Christ in Madagascar and the Evangelical Church in Madagascar; the Quaker mission was transformed into the Malagasy Friends' Church. Since the three groups were very close in doctrine and outlook, they decided to form a single church. In August 1968, during the commemoration celebration of the 150th anniversary of the arrival of Prot missions, the Church of Jesus Christ in Madagascar was inaugurated.

The church was not immediately recognized by the state. The conflict centered on an article of the church constitution stipulating that the state had no right to make its authority manifest within church buildings; the government wanted agreement that, on the occasion of ceremonies at which state representatives were present, the national flag would be exhibited. The church was recognized only after the fall of the first republic. In 1972 the synod agreed to hand over church primary schools to the state as a contribution to general education. In the same year a central fund was created to assure the same salaries for all pastors. In the following years the church sought to become self-supporting. The church did not employ any more expatriate personnel; financially, however, the church remained heavily dependent on foreign church aid (25% of its total expenditures, nearly 100% of all development projects). In 1980 the National Council of Christian Churches in Madagascar was founded (together with the RCath, Angl, and Luth churches). Efforts were made to unify Christian language, in particular to agree on a common version of the name of Christ — the name of Jesus Christ was changed from Jesosy Kristy into Jesoa Kristy. In 1991 the Church, together with other churches, took an active part in the fall of the second republic and in the development of the new constitution of the third republic.

The church is active in many fields. Since 1990 activities have been focused in four areas: a) church, ministry, and evangelization; b) Christian education and schooling; c) administration; d) development and finances. Among new spiritual developments, the creation of the community of sisters of Mamre deserves special mention.

TM: **2,500,000** BM: **2,200,000** CM: **1,200,000** Congr: **4,510** OrdM: **900** Eld: **20,000** Deac: **200,000** EvgHome: **500** Mission: **6** Women Ord: **Yes** As Ministers: **1960/100** as Deac: **since beginning/50,000** as Elders: **since beginning/5,000** ChurchOrg: **parish, 35 regional synods, gen synod (every 4 years)** Off/otherLang: **Malagasy** DoctrB: **ApC, NicC, AthC, Statement of Faith (1958), catechism in the Malagasy language** Infant or believer's baptism: **both** Frequency of the Lord's Supper: **monthly** Close relations with: **Département Missionnaire (Switzerland)** NatRel: **FFKM (1980), FFPM (1913)** RegRel: **AACC** IntlRel: **WCC (1968), WARC (1968), CWM, CEVAA, QPS** TheolSchool: **Three theol. colleges in Mandritsara, Fianarantsoa, and Ivato, Theological Faculty in Antananarivo** Service infrastructure: **30 ambulant hospitals, 70 community pharmacies, about 50 kindergartens, 340 schools** Periodicals: **Rojo (laity/quarterly/300), Vaovao FJKM (news of church/monthly/500), Mpanolotsaina (spec/3 per year/500), Ny Teny soa (homiletics/2per year/ 1,500)**

Address: Fiangonan'i Jesoa Kristy Eto Madagasikara (FJKM), P.O. Box 623, Lot II B 18, Tohato-habato Ranavalona I, Trano, Analakely, 101 Antananarivo, Madagascar, Tel: + 261 20 22 268 45, Fax: + 261 20 22 263 72, E-mail: fjkm@dts.mg.

2. Tranozozoro Atranobiriky (FMTA) (1102)

This church resulted from a conflict between the LMS missionaries and a group led by a Malgache pastor. The church started on October 8, 1893, when Pastor Rajaonary was refused entry into the church by the LMS missionary and decided to hold the worship service in open air. Tranozozoro means "house of reed," and recalls the first building the group used for worship. In 1900 the building was replaced by a stone construction, and the church accordingly changed its name to Tranobiriky "house of stones." The "mother community" is located in Ambatonakanga. Today the church has its roots mainly in the central part of the country. It is Congreg in character and maintains close relations with the OAIC.

TM: **100,000** Congr: **120** OrdM: **60** Eld: **nc** Deac: **nc** EvgHome: **nc** Mission: **nc** Women Ord: **yes** As

Ministers: **nc** as Deac: **nc** as Elders: **nc** ChurchOrg: **Congregational** Off/otherLang: **Malagazy** DoctrB: **nc** Infant or believer's baptism: **both** Frequency of the Lord's Supper: **no limit** NatRel: **none** RegRel: **Organization of African Independent Churches (OAIC)** IntlRel: **nc** TheolSchool: **FMTA headquarters**

Address: Tranozozoro Atranobiriky (FMTA), B.P. 5162 Lot VB 48 Ambatonakanga, Antananarivo 101, Madagascar, Tel: +261 2 34934

3. Evangelical Indigenous Mission in Madagascar (METM) (1101)

This church was founded by Pastor Rakotobe Andriamaro who was, until 1955, a pastor of the church related to the Paris Evangelical Missionary Society. Its teaching and its structure is Ref, though, in recent years, it tends to place increased emphasis on Congreg positions. It is associated with the ICCC and with the Africa Inland Mission, which provides missionaries and teachers. Its present head is the son of the founder.

TM: **105,000** BM: **87,500** CM: **100,000** Congr: **350** OrdM: **210** Eld: **7,500** Deac: **nc** EvgHome: **ne** Mission: **10** Women Ord: **yes** As Ministers: **23** as Deac: **5,700** as Elders: **277** ChurchOrg: **Reformed Evangelical (congr, 28 regional synods, gen synod)** Off/otherLang: **Malagasy** DoctrB: **nc** Infant or believer's baptism: **both** NatRel: **nc** RegRel: **AIM** IntlRel: **ICCC** TheolSchool: **Theological Faculty and College** Periodicals: **(newspaper for preachers/250)**

Address: Misiona Evanjelika Teratany eto Madagasikara (METM), Lot VX 50 Antsahatsiroa, Antananarivo, Madagascar, Tel: +261 2 30-880

MALAWI

Area in km²	118,480
Population	(July 1996 est.) 9,452,844 Chewa, Tumbuka, Yao, Lomwe, Sena, Tonga, Ngoni, Ngonde, Asian, European, American
Religions in %	Prot 52%, RCath 11%, Muslim 17%, traditional indigenous beliefs 20%
Official/other languages	English/Yao, Lomwe, Sena, Chichewa, Tumbuka

CCM (Christian Council of Malawi)

In the middle of the 19th century southeast Africa was visited by David Livingstone. Appalled by the slave trade and its devastating effects on the people of East and Central Africa, he appealed on his return to the British public to fight the scourge of slavery by the introduction of commerce and Christianity. The Angl Church, which responded first (1861), is today represented by three dioceses. In

353

1875 two Scottish churches joined the missionary effort. The Free Church of Scotland established itself in Northern Malawi with headquarters in Khondowe (Livingstonia). In 1876 the Church of Scotland settled in southern Malawi with headquarters in Blantyre. In 1889 the Cape Synod of the Dutch Reformed Church in South Africa (NGK) began work in Central Malawi. Initially its base was Mvera; it was later moved to Nkhoma.

As British commercial interests in Malawi grew, the country was declared a British protectorate (1891). In the early years missions participated in the effort to combat slavery through "commerce and Christianity" and collaborated with commercial entrepreneurs when actions seemed to serve the interests of both parties. Increasingly, however, the attitude of missionaries toward planters and British officials became critical. Missionaries acquired for themselves the label of an "unofficial" opposition to the colonial administration. During the colonial period basic education and medical services spread throughout the country, but no priority was given to higher education. The plan of both education and evangelism aimed at the destruction of the local cultural heritage. In spite of all this, Western education and increasing contacts with other people in Africa (partly due to the participation of Malawians in the two World Wars) began to sow the seeds of political awakening and resistance. There was, for example, in 1915 an uprising against British rule by Rev. John Chilembwe of the Providence Industrial Mission. From 1953 to 1962 there was increasing opposition against the Federation of Rhodesia and Nyasaland. At that time many members of the church in Central Africa (mainly from the Blantyre and Livingstonia Synods) were detained in Nyasaland and Southern Rhodesia. In 1964 the country became self-governing; two years later it constituted itself as an independent republic.

In 1924 the Livingstonia and Blantyre Synods decided to form the Church of Central Africa Presbyterian (CCAP). The Nkhoma Synod joined in 1996. Thirty years later the three synods established the General Synod of the Church of Central Africa Presbyterian. Since 1956 two more Synods have joined the General Synod — in 1960 the Synod of Harare (cf. Zimbabwe) and in 1980 the Lundazi Synod, now called the CCAP Synod in Zambia (cf. Zambia).

In 1933 a sizeable split in the Northern Synod (Livingstonia) resulted in the formation of the Blackman's Church of Central Africa Presbyterian.

1. Church of Central Africa Presbyterian (General Synod) (1111)

After independence the churches, the CCAP included, tended to work closely with the Malawi Congress Party and the Malawi government. There were, however, a few outspoken leaders who suffered for their witness. In April 1992, the Southern Africa Alliance of Reformed Churches issued a statement expressing solidarity with a Lenten Letter the RCath Bishops had published a month before, criticizing human rights violations in Malawi. In June 1992, a joint delegation of the WARC and the CCAP presented a memorandum to the president of Malawi calling for the establishment of a "broadly based commission" which would make specific proposals for the structural reform of the political system in Malawi, review the judicial system, and look into the distribution of income and wealth. These proposals led to a referendum being held in 1993. As a result of the 1994 elections, the Malawi Congress Party regime came to an end and was replaced by a democratically elected government.

The General Synod is a loosely knit federal structure which comprises three churches or church traditions. There are, for instance, three catechisms, three Sunday school curriculums, and three liturgies. The synods enjoy considerable autonomy. One of the few areas of competence of the General Synod is theological training, which is currently done at Zomba Theological College and University. Today the CCAP is faced with the question of how the three synods can advance to greater unity. The viability of the present union with the synods in Zimbabwe and Zambia needs to reexamined.

TM: **769,051** CM: **595,000** Congr: **503** PStations: **2,251** OrdM: **296** Eld: **19,920** Deac: **12,013** EvgHome: **41** Mission: **5** Women Ord: **no (Nk)/yes (Bl; Liv)** As Ministers: **no (Nk)/yes (Bl; Liv)** as Deac: **B68/200 L46/-** as Elders: **Bl68/500 L46/-** ChurchOrg: **Presbyterian (congr, presby, synods, General Synod)** Off/otherLang: **Chichewa, Tumbuka, English** DoctrB: **ApC, NicC, WestConf (Bl; L), CDort, HeidC, WestC** Infant or believer's baptism: **both** Frequency of the Lord's Supper: **monthly to quarterly** Close relations with: **Church of Scotland** NatRel: **each synod by itself is member of CCM** RegRel: **AACC, SAARC (1989)** IntlRel: **REC (only Nkhoma Synod), WCC (observer), WARC** TheolSchool: **Zomba Theological College (Zomba)** Service infrastructure: **property is owned by synods individually** Periodicals: **Kuunika of Nkhoma Synod**

Address: Church of Central Africa Presbyterian (General Synod), P.O. Box: 30398 Capital City, Lilongwe 3, Malawi, Tel: +265 734-187, Fax: +265 734-187, E-mail: none.

Addresses of Synods:

1. CCAP Synod of Livingstonia, General Secretary, P.O. Box 112, Mzuzu, Malawi, tel. +265 332 403, fax +265 332 344, e-mail: synod-of-livingstonia@eo.wn.apc.org
2. CCAP Synod of Blantyre, P.O. Box 413, Blantyre, Malawi, tel. +265 636 744 or 633 942, fax +265 636 957
3. CCAP Synod of Nkhoma, P.O. Box 45, Nkhoma, Lilongwe, Malawi, tel. +265 723 688

2. Blackman's Church of Africa Presbyterian (1114)

This church was founded in 1933 under the leadership of a former minister of the Northern Synod (Livingstonia), Rev. Yesaya Zerenje Mwase. Some of the reasons for the split were: delays by the missionaries to integrate Africans fully into the life and work of the mission church; and strict discipline in the mission church, which led to delays in the admittance of new members.

No statistical data have been made available.

Address: Blackman's Church of Africa Presbyterian, P.O. Box 2411, Blantyre, Malawi

MALAYSIA

Area in km²	329,750
Population	(July 1996 est.) 19,962,893 Malay and other indigenous 59%, Chinese 32%, Indian 9%
Religions in %	Peninsular Malaysia: Muslim (Malays), Buddhist (Chinese), Hindu (Indians), Christian 2% Sabah: Muslim 38%, Christian 27%, other 45% Sarawak: tribal religion 35%, Buddhist and Confucianist 24%, Muslim 20%, Christian 29%, other 5%
Official/other languages	Peninsular Malaysia: Malay (official), English, Chinese dialects, Tamil Sabah: English, Malay, numerous tribal dialects, Chinese (Mandarin and Hakka dialects predominate) Sarawak: English, Malay, Mandarin, numerous tribal languages

CCM (Council of Churches of Malaysia)

The Malaysian Confederation comprises two geographical areas — the Malaysian peninsula (Melaka) and the northern part of Borneo (Sarawak and Sabah). The Malaysian peninsula became independent from Great Britain in 1957. In 1963 Britain also incorporated the crown colony of Singapore and the colonial territories of Sarawak and Sabah into the Confederation. Two years later Singapore withdrew and became a separate state (cf. Singapore). The two areas, lying at a distance of about 600 km apart, are very different in cultural background and social conditions and have had different histories. The population of the peninsula is basically composed of three ethnic groups — Malayan, Chinese, and Hindu. In North Borneo indigenous peoples — Iban, Dayak, Kadazan, etc. — make up a significant part of the population. The Malayan population is generally Muslim; Christianity is primarily represented among the Chinese and the indigenous peoples. While Christians on the peninsula represent not more than 2%, they are stronger in North Borneo — 29% in Sarawak and 27% in Sabah.

The earliest contact of Malaysia with the Ref tradition was through the Dutch who conquered Catholic Melaka in 1641 and built the now famous Christ Church Melaka in 1753. In 1815 the LMS began mission work in Melaka (Penang and Singapore); they decided, however, to leave for China in the 1840s. At that time the Scottish community took steps to call its own ministers. Missionaries arrived in Penang in 1851 and in Singapore in 1856. They took evangelistic initiatives beyond the boundaries of the Scottish communities. The Malay chapel at

Prinsep Street in Singapore became the center of a major outreach among Malay-speaking Chinese whose ancestors had been in Malaya for several hundred years.

A new chapter began in 1861. The Orchard Road congregation in Singapore obtained the services of a full-time missionary, A. B. Cook, who was to work among the Chinese, who were arriving in considerable numbers from Swatow and South Fukien. This new departure was eventually chosen as marking the founding of the present Presbyterian Churches in Malaysia and Singapore. Missionaries from the Presbyterian Church in England who had been working in these areas in China and had seen many of their converts migrating to Malaysia supported this arrangement. Therefore, from this time, the church in Malaysia has been related to the Presbyterian Church of England rather than to the Church of Scotland. The number of Chinese congregations steadily increased, and in 1901 the Singapore Presbyterian Synod was established. An important witness was given by the first Chinese missionary, Pastor Tay Sek Tin, who started work in Malaysia in 1897. From 1901 to 1938 the mission grew from 8 to 16 congregations and 3 preaching stations, about equally divided between Singapore and Johor.

Meanwhile the expatriate English-speaking communities continued separately. Two new churches for expatriates were opened in Kuala Lumpur and Ipoh.

After World War II a further expansion of the Presbyterian Synod occurred. In 1962 the Chinese Presbyterian Synod gave itself a new structure; three presbyteries were formed — Singapore, South Malaysia and North Malaysia; some churches outside presbytery boundaries were placed under the direct authority of the synod. At the end of 1967 the Chinese congregations numbered 13 in Singapore and 15 in Malaya with a communicant membership of 2,650. In 1971 the expatriate congregations, which in 1958 had become more independent from the Presbyterian Church in England by forming their own presbytery, decided to join the Chinese Synod and to form the Presbyterian Church of Singapore and Malaysia. It was the union of two Presbyterian groups from different cultural backgrounds (British and Chinese) which had established them in a country of different culture, language, and religion (Malaysia).

The formation and history of the churches in North Borneo are closely connected with that of China. When the Taiping Revolution, a social and religious revolt against the Mandschu dynasty, failed in 1864, hundreds of thousands of Chinese farmers and landless laborers were in great difficulty. Many emigrated to various southeast Asian countries. The British Chartered Company entered North Borneo in 1878 and offered new homes to Chinese settlers. With these settlers the RCath and Angl churches came to North Borneo, and the Basel Mission also began work there. The victory of the Communist revolution under Mao Tse-Tung in 1949 brought a new influx of Christian refugees to North Borneo.

1. Presbyterian Church in Malaysia (4340)

With the withdrawal of Singapore from the Malaysian Confederation in 1965, a new situation also arose for the churches. In 1975 the Synod of the Presbyterian Church in Singapore and Malaysia decided to establish two synods — one for Singapore and another for Malaysia. The structure and organization of these synods remained basically unchanged. The synod in Malaysia considered moving headquarters to Kuala Lumpur but decided, given the preponderance of membership in Johor, to maintain its offices in Batu Pahat. Despite adversities, new communities were established.

TM: **7,000** CM: **105** Congr: **33** PStations: **1** OrdM: **1** Eld: **3** Deac: **8** EvgHome: **nc** Mission: **nc** Women Ord: **Yes** As Ministers: **1991/1** as Deac: **1986** as Elders: **1989/1** ChurchOrg: **Presbyterian (congr, presby, synod)** Off/otherLang: **Malay, English, Mandarin, Tamil, Javanese** DoctrB: ApC, **Presbyterian Constitution** Infant or believer's baptism: **both** Frequency of the Lord's Supper: **monthly** Close relations with: **Meth, Luth, Angl; House of Hope; Agape counseling center** NatRel: **CCM (1974), CCCOWE (1986), Chinese Christian Churches in Malaysia (1991)** RegRel: **CCA (1984)** IntlRel: **CWM (1978), WARC, REC** TheolSchool: **Trinity Theological College (Spore), Disciple Training Center (Malaysia)** Periodicals: **Weekly News**

Address: Gereja Presbyterian Malaysia, 7 Jalan SG Buya Batu 3 1/2 Jl Klang Lama, 58100 Kuala Lumpur, Malaysia, Tel: +60 3 784-7361, Fax: +60 3 780-9037

2. The Basel Christian Church of Malaysia (BCCM) (4343)

The origin of this church is to be found in China (Kwantung Province), an area of the Hakka. In 1847 missionaries of the Basel Mission had started evangelistic work among the Hakkas in Hong Kong and, more generally, in South China. For political and economic reasons many Hakkas emigrated to North Borneo, which had come under indirect British rule in 1878. The first Christian group reached Kudat in 1882; others were to follow and to settle at different places in North Borneo. They set up a loose association of "Basel congregations." In 1907, at the request of the colonial regime, the Basel Mission established direct relations with them, intending to establish an independent church in North Borneo. The realization of the project was prevented by World War I. In 1925 the church became independent. After the formation of Malaysia (1963), the church adopted its present name.

In 1974 the church began evangelistic work among the indigenous people of the area (Bumiputra). The number of indigenous believers quickly increased, and today Malay-speaking Christians outnumber Chinese-speaking members. The new congregations plan to form their own synod by the year 2000.

The BCCM is the leading member of an association of different Sabah churches, which run the Theological Seminary of Sabah (Seminari Theologi Sabah) in Kota Kinabatu.

Though the structure of the BCCM is genuinely Ref (autonomy of congregations, elected lay president, strong lay participation in decision-making bodies, periodical election of head-pastor, who is called bishop), the church is a full member of the LWF. This is because the Basel Mission combined Luth and Ref traditions from the very beginning; it also chose to have close relations with the Tsung Tsin Mission in Hong Kong (TTM).

TM: **45,000** CM: **20,000** Congr: **112** OrdM: **58** Eld: **100** Deac: **500** EvgHome: **nc** Mission: **nc** Women Ord: **yes** As Ministers: **yes** as Deac: **yes** as Elders: **yes** ChurchOrg: **Reformed** Off/otherLang: **Bahasa Malaysia, Chinese, English** DoctrB: **ApC** Infant or believer's baptism: **both** NatRel: **CCM, Christian Federation of Malaysia (CFM)** RegRel: **CCA** IntlRel: **LWF** TheolSchool: **Sabah Theological Seminary (Kora Kinabalu)** Periodicals: **BCCM Information (quarterly)**

Address: Gereja Basel Malaysia, P.O. Box 11516, Kota Kinabalu Sabah, East Malaysia 88816, Malaysia, Tel: +60 88 428-595, Fax: +60 88 427-900, 901, 902, E-mail: bccm@tm.net.my

3. Protestant Church in Sabah (Rungus Church) (4342)

In 1948 the Advent began to evangelize the Kudat peninsula in North Borneo. At that time the indigenous people in this area began to realize that their religious taboos represented a hindrance to economic progress. Some became Advent; others were hesitant to replace old taboos with new ones (no pork, no alcohol, etc.). Soon representatives of the Rungus people, a tribe of poor rice farmers in the north of Sabah, approached the Basel mission in Kudat and asked for missionaries. Two years later Heinrich Honegger of the Basel Mission began work among them. He found open doors. Evangelistic work went hand in hand with educational efforts. Since the economic situation of the Rungus was precarious, an agricultural school on Tinangol was opened. In 1965 a Bible School was established. By 1965 the church became independent.

   In the years from 1969 to 1976 the church came under heavy pressure due to an Islamicization campaign of the Sabah government. All European personnel had to leave the country. In recent years the church has grown rapidly and has also reached other tribes. There is also a congr in West Malaysia for the many migrant workers from Sabah. As far as structure is concerned, the church is similar to the BCCM (cf. no. 2). It entertains close relations with the BCCM, especially in the field of theological education. Despite its Presbyterian structure the church also became a member of the LWF in 1995.

TM: **29,200** Congr: **298** PStations: **7** OrdM: **117** Eld: **349** Deac: **nc** EvgHome: **nc** Mission: **nc** Women Ord: **yes** As Ministers: **1** as Deac: **nc** as Elders: **nc** ChurchOrg: **Reformed (18 districts, Synod)** Off/otherLang: **Rungus, Malay** NatRel: **CCM (1975), Sabah Council of Churches (1975)** RegRel: **CCA** IntlRel: **WCC (1975), LWF (1995)** TheolSchool: **nc**

Address: Gereja Protestan di Sabah, P.O. Box 69, Kudat, Sabah, East Malaysia 89057, Malaysia, Tel: +60 88 612-440, Fax: +60 88 614-697

4. Evangelical Assembly of Borneo (4344)

This church originated from efforts of the Australian Borneo Evangelical Mission (BEM), which was founded by committed individuals of different church affiliation. BEM worked in rural Sarawak and Sabah. The congregations enjoy great autonomy. To different degrees they have been influenced by the Pent and the charismatic movements. Their common language is Malay. The church is also present among migrant workers in West Malaysia.

No statistical data have been made available.

Address: Sidang Injil Borneo, P.O. Box 12 306, 88825 Kota Kinabu Sabah, Malaysia, Tel: +60 88
420-788, Fax: +60 88 420-784

MARSHALL ISLANDS

Area in km²	181,300
Population	(July 1996 est.) 58,363 Micronesian
Religions in %	Christian (mostly Prot)
Official/other languages	English/two major Marshallese dialects, Japanese

ABCFM (American Board of Commissioners for Foreign Missions)

The Marshall Islands are located in the North Pacific Ocean, about halfway between Hawaii and Papua New Guinea. They are constituted by two archipelagic island chains of 30 atolls and 1,152 islands; Bikini and Enewitok are former US nuclear test sites; Kwajalein, the famous World War II battleground, is now used as an American missile test range. Agriculture and tourism are the mainstays of the economy.

Missionaries of the Boston-based ABCFM first came to the Marshall Islands in 1857-1858. The atolls of the Marshalls were part of a wider field of the ABCFM — the Micronesian Mission (cf. Federated States of Micronesia). Some early missionaries were Hawaiians. The work of the American Board was delegated to the Hawaiian Church's Board of Missions from 1865 onward. American and Hawaiian ABCFM missionaries worked in close partnership with Hawaiian Islanders, whose style of mission was to plant churches on all the northern atolls with the help of local converts along Congreg lines; the office of deacon became a means of localized administration and spiritual oversight at an early stage. Close relationships emerged with the Congreg church, later to become the Congreg Christian Churches in the USA. When the latter merged with the Evangelical and Ref Church to form the United Church of Christ (cf. United States no. 43), the ABCFM was transformed into the United Church Board of World Ministries. The new board continued relations, from Boston and New York and through the Hawaiian Board, with the church in the Marshall Islands.

After World War II developments all over Micronesia led to independence of the present self-governing church, with headquarters in Uliga, Majuro, adjacent to the national capital of the Marshall Islands. The church is a member body of the United Church of Christ in Micronesia, which also has member churches in the states of Kosrae and Pohnpei within the Federated States of Micronesia.

1. Marshalls United Church of Christ-Congregations (5191)

TM: **38,599** BM: **31,272** CM: **7,000** Congr: **88** PStations: **92** OrdM: **35** Eld: **92** Deac: **2,000** EvgHome: **400** Mission: **4** Women Ord: **no** As Ministers: **no** ChurchOrg: **Board of Directors (meets twice a year), Church Conference (every second year)** Off/otherLang: **Marshallese, English** DoctrB: **ApC** Infant or believer's baptism: **both** Frequency of the Lord's Supper: **quarterly** Close relations with: **UCBWM, PCC, WCC, WCE, MCUCC, SPATS** NatRel: **Micronesian Council of United Churches of Christ (1958)** RegRel: **South Pacific Association of Theological Schools, PCC (1965)** IntlRel: **World Christian Endeavor (1895), WCC (1994), WARC (1997)** TheolSchool: **Marshalls Theological College (Majuro).**

Address: Jarin Parik Dron, P.O. Box 75, 96 960 Uiliga-Majuro, Marshall Islands, Tel: +692 625-3342, Fax: +692 625-5246

2. Reformed Congregational Churches (RCC) (5190)

This church is the result of a split in 1985 within the United Church of Christ-Congregations in the Marshalls. The RCC leadership claims that the break-away was not caused by doctrinal differences but by personal problems when a minister refused to take an assignment with the Marshall Islands Museum. Other sources within the church add that there was also a desire to return to the patterns of the original Congreg Church as they were before the merger in 1966 with the Evangelical and Reformed Church in the USA.

TM: **4,000** CM: **1,000** Congr: **9** PStations: **18** OrdM: **9** Eld: **80** Deac: **68** EvgHome: **nc** Mission: **nc** Women Ord: **yes** As Ministers: **9** as Deac: **68** as Elders: **80** ChurchOrg: **Congregational** Off/otherLang: **Marshallese, English** DoctrB: **nc** Periodicals: **Christian Endeavor** NatRel: **nc** RegRel: **nc** IntlRel: **WARC (1988)**

Address: Reformed Congregational Churches (RCC), P.O. Box 1651, Majuro 96960, Marshall Islands, Tel: +692 247-8811, Fax: none, E-mail: none

MARTINIQUE

Area in km²	1,106
Population	(July 1996 est.) 399,151 African and African-white-Indian mixture 90%, white 5%, East Indian, Lebanese, Chinese less than 5%
Religions in %	RCath 95%, Hindu and traditional African 5.5%, Prot 0.5%
Official/other languages	French/Creole patois

The island of Martinique was first inhabited by Arawaks. It was discovered by Christopher Columbus on Saint Martin's day in 1493. French, including Huguenot families, began to settle on the island in 1635; in 1674 Martinique was annexed by France. No Prot church came into existence until the 20th century. The Prot community remained small in number, having, unlike the RCath Church, no governmental support. Martinique was declared a French "department" (district) in 1946, and so French law prevails. This island has had several natural catastrophes, such as the eruption of Mount Pelée in 1902, which wiped out all but two of the 30,000 inhabitants of the city of St. Pierre and also meant the end of the Arawaks.

Reformed Church of the Antilles (3319)

This church is the smallest of the seven Prot denominations present in Martinique. The denomination ministers to French civilians and military who comprise less than 1% of the population of the island. Closely linked to the military chaplaincy, this denomination shows no significant signs of cross-cultural evangelism among the local population. This denomination is not an independent church, but a member of the CEEEFE (Commission of French-speaking Evangelical Churches Abroad) of the "Fédération protestante de France," which incorporates some 14 Prot denominations and missions within France. The military chaplain is also in charge of the same church in Guadeloupe (cf. Guadeloupe).

TM: **300** Congr: **1** OrdM: **1** Eld: **5** Deac: **0** EvgHome: **0** Mission: **0** Women Ord: **yes** As Ministers: **none** as Deac: **none** as Elders: **none** ChurchOrg: **Presbyterian** Off/otherLang: **French** DoctrB: **ApC** Infant or believer's baptism: **both** Close relations with: **CEEEFE** NatRel: **nc** RegRel: **none** IntlRel: **none** TheolSchool: **pastors are trained in France.**

Address: Eglise Réformée des Antilles, B.P. 606, F-97 261 Fort de France Cedex, Martinique, Tel: +33 5 96 39 55 57, Fax: +33 5 96 39 55 57

MAURITIUS

Area in km²	1,860
Population	(July 1996 est.) 1,140,256 Indo-Mauritian 68%, Creole 27%, Sino-Mauritian 3%, Franco-Mauritian 2%
Religions in %	Hindu 52%, Christian 28.3% (RCath 26%, Prot 2.3% [Presb 0.26%]), Muslim 16.6%, other 3.1%
Official/other languages	English/Creole, French, Hindi, Urdu, Hakka, Bojpoori

When Europeans reached Mauritius, there was no indigenous population. Portuguese were the first to arrive (1507); they were followed, toward the end of the 16th century, by the Dutch, who established a small harbor in Mahébourg but eventually abandoned the island. In 1721 Mauritius was occupied by the French, who began to cultivate and develop it. African and Malegassi slaves were imported to do the hard labor; in particular, to clear the fields of the basalt rock covering nearly the entire volcanic island. In 1814 the island was taken over by the British.

RCath mission work began in 1722. The first Prot were Huguenots who had been deported out of France. In 1814 the London Missionary Society sent missionaries to Mauritius; they discovered the small communities of Huguenots, who had continued, together with their servants and slaves, to practice their faith. Among the missionaries, Jean Le Brun (+1865) deserves special mention. He founded free primary schools for the children of slaves, first for boys and then for girls. In 1825 Mr. Ménard, a Huguenot, built the first chapel on his property in St. Pierre. Other churches were built in the north (Port Louis/St. Jean 1842, Grand'Gaube/St. Joseph 1867) and later in the south (Mahébourg/St. Paul 1876, St. André 1878).

In 1851 the Church of Scotland began evangelistic activities on the island. In 1876 its congr united with the existing LMS congr. From then on responsibility for the missionary work was with the Church of Scotland. A great opportunity was missed when the Presb church did not open itself for converts among the Indian population which, after the abolition of slavery, had been brought to the island to replace the former slaves; several thousands eventually joined the Angl church. However, their church, St. Columba, eventually joined the French-speaking Presbyterian communities which today form the Presbyterian Church of Mauritius.

Independence came in 1968. The change also had implications for the church, which had to reorganize itself. A synod was constituted, and more local people were trained for church ministries. Despite heavy losses through the migration of Creoles to Europe, the USA, and Australia, the church was able to maintain its level of membership and to develop a strong social work program.

Presbyterian Church of Mauritius (1125)

This church plays an important role in society by participating as much as possible in decision-making groups concerned with social issues and the welfare of the country. The youth of St. John's parish in the capital have shown interest in a ministry to battered women and generally in family counseling. The church seeks to fulfill an ecumenical ministry among the denominations.

TM: **843** BM: **823** CM: **662** Congr: **6** PStations: **6** OrdM: **4** Eld: **46** Deac: **2** EvgHome: **nc** Mission: **nc** Women Ord: **yes** As Ministers: **nc** as Deac: **1992/1** as Elders: **18** ChurchOrg: **parish council, synodal council, synod** Off/otherLang: **French, Créole, English, Chinese (Hakka)** DoctrB: **ApC, NicC** Infant or believer's baptism: **both** Frequency of the Lord's Supper: **monthly** Periodicals: **La Sève et la Vigne (gen/monthly/250)** Close relations with: **Angl, RCath** NatRel: **Ecumenical Working Committee, Bible Society** RegRel: **SAARC (1992)** IntlRel: **WARC (1979), CEVAA (1980)** TheolSchool: **nc.**

Address: Eglise Presbytérienne de Maurice, Farquhar/Coignet, Rose Hill, Mauritius, Tel: +230 464 5265, Fax: +230 696 6608

MEXICO

Area in km²	1,972,550
Population	(July 1996 est.) 95,772,462 mestizo (Indian-Spanish) 60%, Amerindian or predominantly Amerindian 30%, Caucasian or predominantly Caucasian 9%, other 1%
Religions in %	RCath 90 %, Prot 10%
Official/other languages	Spanish/various Mayan dialects

From the *Conquista* (by the Spaniards) until the 19th century, the RCath church was the only accepted religion. A new era began with the independence from Spain (1810-1821) and the rise of the militant anticlerical liberalism of Benito Juárez (1806-1872), who granted religious freedom in 1857. From that time Prot influence from the USA made itself increasingly felt in Mexico. Around 1872 four Ref churches started mission work in Mexico: the Presbyterian Church USA (Northern Presbyterian Church), the Presbyterian Church US (Southern Presbyterian Church), the Associate Presbyterian Church (ARPC), and the Congregationalist Church in the United States. These churches built on work that had been accomplished by missionaries during the previous years. For instance, an important role for the nascent Presbyterian Church was played by Arcadio Morales Escalona (1850-1922). He was a Mexican who came to a living faith in 1869 and was ordained pastor in 1878 with ten other national leaders.

The Northern Presbyterian Church USA began work in Mexico City, Villa de Cos, Zacatecas, and San Luis Potosi. From Mexico City it extended its efforts to other parts of the Federal District and from there to the states of Mexico, Morelos, Hidalgo, Puebla, Guerrero, Michoacan, Oaxaca, Veracruz, Tabasco, Campeche, and Yucatan. The Southern Presbyterian Church was active in Matamoros Tamaulipas and spread to the whole state of Brownsville, Texas, a region that then still belonged to Mexico.

The work of these churches developed rapidly. The first presbyteries were established in Zacatecas (1883), Tamaulipas (1884), Mexico City (1885), and Comalcalco, Tabasco (1896). In 1882 a theological seminary was opened in Mexico City, where Mexican pastors began to be trained. In 1894 the two Presbyterian missions decided to unite their work, and in 1901 the first synod of the **National Presbyterian Church in Mexico (1)** was held. At that time the church had 5,500 members, 73 churches, and 190 smaller congregations, which were served by 46 ministers. Strong emphasis was placed on educational and medical work; several schools and Presbyterian hospitals were established.

The Associate Presbyterian work resulted in the formation of the **Associate Reformed Presbyterian Church of Mexico (2),** mainly in the area of the states of San Luis Potosi, Tamaulipas, and Hidalgo. The Congreg work started in 1872 in the states of Jalisco, mainly Guadalajara, Sinaloa, Mazatlan, and some small towns of these states. The **Christian Congregational Churches in Mexico (3)** are the fruit of these efforts.

The Mexican revolution, which culminated in the adoption of a new constitution in 1917 hastened the indigenization of the church. More and more responsibility had to be taken over by Mexicans. In the 1920s a new field of expansion opened in Chiapas. With the help of missionaries John and Mabel Kempers of the Reformed Church in America (RCA), the National Presbyterian Church in Mexico developed important evangelistic work in Chiapas, first among the Spanish-speaking population and then in the 1950s among the Mayan-speaking people, such as Chol, Tzotil, and Tzeltzal indigenous groups. Today Chiapas is one of the strongholds of the National Presbyterian Church.

In the years after World War II two splits occurred in the National Presbyterian Church. First, in 1947, due to doctrinal, administrative, and personality conflicts, the Independent Presbyterian Church was formed, and in the early '50s, largely through the activities of Carl McIntire, the **National Conservative Presbyterian Church (4)** came into existence.

In 1962 the Independent Presbyterian Church entered into relations with the Christian Reformed Church in North America, which sent missionaries to strengthen its evangelistic work. After a period of stagnation it began to expand its work to the south. In 1984 it suffered further division; while the larger group changed its name in 1992 to **Presbyterian Ref Church (5)**, the other maintained the name **Independent Presbyterian Church (6)**.

In recent times initiatives have been taken to bring the various Presbyterian churches in Mexico closer to one another. On July 4, 1995, three Presbyterian Churches — the National Presbyterian Church, the Presbyterian Reformed Church, and the Associate Presbyterian Reformed Church — decided to form the

Alliance of Presbyterian and Reformed Churches in the Republic of Mexico (La Alianza de Iglesias Presbiterianas y Reformadas de la Republica Mexicana — AIPREM).

1. National Presbyterian Church in Mexico (IPNM) (2095)

This church is by far the largest of the Presbyterian churches in the country, in fact the second-largest among the non-RCath communities, after the Assemblies of God Church. It is present in the whole country and among the whole population; it is particularly strong in the states of Tabasco, Chiapas, Campeche, Yucatan (South-east), Nuevo Leon, and the Federal District (Mexico City).

TM: **1,200,000** BM: **1,200,000** CM: **1,200,000** Congr: **4,800** OrdM: **700** Eld: **4,200** Deac: **3,500** EvgHome: **0** Mission: **0** Women Ord: **no** ChurchOrg: **Presbyterian (50 presby, 8 synods, GenAssy)** Off/otherLang: **Spanish, Maya, Cho'l, Tzetal, Tojolabal, Mixe, Mixteco, and 200 more Indian languages and dialects** DoctrB: **ApC, WestConf, CDort, BelgC, HeidC** Infant or believer's baptism: **both** NatRel: **AIPREM** RegRel: **AIPRAL** IntlRel: **WARC (1988)** TheolSchool: **Presb. Theol. Seminary of Mexico, 5 others in various provinces, school for women missionaries in Mexico** Periodicals: **El Faro (since 1888) (pastoral/bi-monthly/3,000)**

Address: Iglesia Nacional Presbiteriana de Mexico, Arenal 36, Col. Agric. Chimalistac, 01050 Mexico D.F., Mexico, Tel: +52 5 661-4774, Fax: +52 5 661-3643, E-mail: none

2. Associate Reformed Presbyterian Church of Mexico (2094)

In 1875 the Associate Reformed Presbyterian Church in the USA (cf. United States) began to send missionaries to Mexico for the distribution of Bibles. On June 29, 1878, a small presbytery was formed in Tampico. For many years Rev. Neill E. Prestly and his wife Rachel worked at Tampico. Due to illness Prestly had to abandon the work in 1917. Under the leadership of the Mexican pastor Pedro Trujillo, the presbytery of Tampico became independent. In 1891 a group of women missionaries opened the Instituto Juárez — named after President Benito Juárez. The church has worked in the northeastern part of the country, mainly in the states of Tamaulipas, Northern Veracruz, and San Luis. Recently congregations have been established in the capital and in Guadalajara (state of Jalisco)

TM: **2,365** BM: **1,857** CM: **975** Congr: **63** PStations: **103** OrdM: **27** Eld: **92** Deac: **115** EvgHome: **0** Mission: **0** Women Ord: **no** ChurchOrg: **congr, 5 presby, GenAssy** Off/otherLang: **Spanish, Totonaco, Huasteco, Nahuatl** DoctrB: **ApC, HeidC, WestConf, CDort** Infant or believer's baptism: **both** Frequency of the Lord's Supper: **4 times a year** NatRel: **AIPREM (Alliance of Reformed and Presbyterian Churches of Mexico)** RegRel: **AIPRAL** IntlRel: **WARC** TheolSchool: **Seminario Teologico Eben-Ezer (Tampico)** Periodicals: **Lecciones para Escuela Dominical (gen/monthly/ 300) Avante Reformado/gen/bimestral/500)**

Address: Iglesia Presbiteriana Asociada Reformada de Mexico, C.P. 89800, J J de la Garza 206 PTE, Mante Tamaulipas, Mexico, Tel: +52 123 2 02 22, Fax: +52 123 2 06 15

3. Christian Congregational Churches in Mexico (2093)

The history of this group goes back to the 19th century. In the '50s and the '60s a Congreg missionary, Melinda Rankin, founded several communities which she later directed to join the Presbyterian mission. Some of these communities maintained their independence, however. Other congregations were founded by missionary efforts of the Congreg Board of Mission in Boston, USA. David Watkins and his wife started a community in Guadalajara in 1872. A year later Juan L. Stephens, who had founded a community in Ahualulco, was assassinated by fanatic people. Similar violence took place in Santa Maria del Oo, Tecolotlán, Atengo. The work expanded to Chihuahua (1896) and to other places.

TM: **800** BM: **450** CM: **723** Congr: **12** PStations: **1** OrdM: **6** Eld: **nc** Deac: **nc** EvgHome: **nc** Mission: **2** Women Ord: **yes** As Ministers: **1975/1** as Deac: **nc** as Elders: **nc** ChurchOrg: **Congregational (council of churches)** Off/otherLang: **Spanish** DoctrB: **ApC, NicC, AthC** Infant or believer's baptism: **both** Close relations with: **Christian Church (Disciples of Christ, USA), United Church of Christ (USA)** NatRel: **nc** RegRel: **nc** IntlRel: **nc** TheolSchool: **Edinburgh, Texas, Instituto Evangelisto de Mexico** Service infrastructure: **1 kindergarten, 3 schools, "Alberto Remba Center"** Periodicals: **Enlaces (gen/semester/3,000)**

Address: Iglesias Cristianas Congregacionales in Mexico, Casilla 82000 5 de Mayo y Melchor Ocampo, #1714, Mazatlán Sinaloa, Mexico, Tel: +52 69 85 16 87, Fax: +52 69 13 58 25

4. National Conservative Presbyterian Church of Mexico (2098)

This church resulted in the early '50s from a conflict within the National Presbyterian Church (cf. no. 1). It was established by Eleazar Z. Perez, pastor of the El Divino Salvador parish in Mexico City, and, under the influence of Carl McIntire, adopted conservative and fundamentalist views. The church consists of three presbyteries.

TM: **1,600** OrdM: **20** Eld: **nc** Deac: **nc** EvgHome: **nc** Mission: **nc** Women Ord: **nc** ChurchOrg: **3 presby** Off/otherLang: **Spanish** DoctrB: **nc** Infant or believer's baptism: **infant** NatRel: **nc** RegRel: **nc** IntlRel: **nc** TheolSchool: **Seminario "Juan Calvino" II**

Address: Iglesia Nacional Presbiteriana Conservadora de Mexico, Calle del Parque no. 85, Col. Del Parque, Mexico D.F., Mexico, Tel: +52 5 523-6138

5. Presbyterian Reformed Church of Mexico (2096)

In 1947 a group of pastors came into conflict with the National Presbyterian Church (no. 1). As a result the Independent Presbyterian Church came into existence. In 1984 a split occurred in the church. The issue at stake was the relationship with the missionaries of the Christian Reformed Church in North America. In 1983 the Synod had decided to discontinue the presence of missionaries. The decision provoked a schism. Two presbyteries maintained relations with the CRCNA; in 1992 the church adopted the name Presbyterian Reformed Church of Mexico.

The center of its activities is Mexico City, but, with the help of US missionaries, work has expanded to several other states. Linked to this church are the Theological Seminary, Juan Calvino, in Mexico City and three Bible institutes in Mexico City, Yucatan, and Tabasco.

TM: **26,000** CM: **12,000** Congr: **102** OrdM: **43** Eld: **nc** Deac: **nc** EvgHome: **60** Mission: **nc** Women Ord: **no** ChurchOrg: **Presbyterian (6 presby, GenAssy)** Off/otherLang: **Spanish, Indian languages** DoctrB: **nc** NatRel: **nc** RegRel: **nc** IntlRel: **WARC (1994)** TheolSchool: **Juan Calvino Theol Seminary (Mexico), 3 Bible institutes**

Address: Iglesia Presbiteriana Reformada de Mexico, Cuahutemoc 117, ESQ. Allende, Col. de Carmen, 04000 Coyoacan D.F., Mexico, Tel: +52 5 554 3467, Fax: +52 5 562-9755

6. Independent Presbyterian Church (IPIM) (2099)

This church is the result of the split in 1984 (cf. no. 5). The reason was tension between the Mexican leaders and the missionaries of the Christian Reformed Church (CRCNA). While the majority decided to maintain cooperation with the CRCNA, three of the five presbyteries of the Independent Presbyterian opted for independence. They were registered with the Mexican government as the Independent Presbyterian Church and also obtained control of the property, including the site of Juan Calvino Theological Seminary II (Mexico).

TM: **2,500** Congr: **35** PStations: **30** OrdM: **28** Eld: **145** Deac: **nc** EvgHome: **nc** Mission: **nc** Women Ord: **no** ChurchOrg: **parish, presby, gen synod** Off/otherLang: **Espanol, Maya, Cho'l** DoctrB: **ApC, NicC, AthC, HeidC, CDort, WestConf, WestCat** NatRel: **nc** RegRel: **nc** IntlRel: **nc** TheolSchool: **nc**

Address: Iglesia Presbiteriana Independiente, P.O. Box 21-818 Viena 99, Col. Carmen Coyoacan, Mexico D.F. 04100, Mexico, Tel: +52 5 554-4901, Fax: +52 5 554-4662

MOROCCO

Area in km²	443,300
Population	(1995) 28,300,000
Religions in %	Muslims 98.7%, Christians 1.1% Jews 0.2%
Languages	Arabic, French

Various Prot mission societies, including the Southern Morocco Mission of Scottish origin, the North Africa Mission, the Gospel Missionary Mission, and the Emmanuel Mission worked in this country since 1875. The Eglise Réformée de France (ERF) started work in Morocco in 1922, mainly to serve people of French origin living in this country. With the arrival of independence from France in 1956 a new situation arose. In recognition of independence and also as an accommodation to the increasing numbers of Germans, Swiss, Scandinavians, and French, the ERF decided in 1958 to establish an autonomous church — the Evangelical Church in Morocco (Eglise évangélique du Maroc, EEM). In accordance with the legal requirements (since 1963 most mission work is prohibited) the EEM foregoes all proselytism. Its purpose is to strengthen the faith of the local and expatriate Prot living in various parts of the country. The Prot Christian community does not exceed 3,000 members worshiping in some 20 places.

Several other Christian traditions are represented in the country; the RCath church with Archbishoprics in Tanger and Rabat, the Angl with two parishes in Tanger and Casablanca, and various Orth communities.

Evangelical Church in Morocco (EEAM) (1130)

TM: **1,600** BM: **1,000** CM: **170** Congr: **6** PStations: **6** OrdM: **1** Eld: **32** Deac: **nc** EvgHome: **none** Mission: **none** Women Ord: **no** As Ministers: **no** ChurchOrg: **synod** Off/otherLang: **French** DoctrB: **ApC, NicC, RochC same as Ref. Ch of France** Infant or believer's baptism: **both** Frequency of the Lord's Supper: **once or twice monthly** Periodicals: **Vie Nouvelle (church-life/occasional/400)** Close relations with: **FPF and ERF** NatRel: **Christian Council of Churches (1989)** RegRel: **nc** IntlRel: **WARC (CEEEFE), WCC** TheolSchool: **nc.**

Address: Eglise évangélique au Maroc (EEAM), 33, rue d'Azilal, 20000 Casablanca, Tel: +212 2 30 21 51, Fax: +212 2 44 47 68

MOZAMBIQUE

Area in km²	801,590
Population	(July 1996 est.) 17,877,927 indigenous tribal groups 99.66% (Shangaan, Chokwe, Manyika, Sena, Makua, and others), Europeans 0.06%, Euro-Africans 0.2%, Indians 0.08%
Religions in %	indigenous beliefs 50%, Christians 30% (RCath 3 million, Prot 2.2 million), Muslim 20%
Official/Other languages	Portuguese/indigenous dialects

CCM (Christian Council of Mozambique)

Until 1975 the country was under Portuguese colonial rule. As an independent country, Mozambique became a People's Republic with Marxist-Leninist orientation. In the 1980s the country was devastated by a civil war which was instigated and supported by the Republic of South Africa and Western countries to counteract the influence of Communism in Africa; it took a toll of more than a million lives. With the

369

end of the apartheid system in South Africa a new era also began for Mozambique. Civil war was ended by the Rome peace agreement of October 4, 1992.

RCath missionary work began with the arrival of the Portuguese (1497/98). There were missionaries on Vasco da Gama's vessels. The first church was built in 1505 in Sofala. The missionaries were primarily Jesuits and Dominicans. In 1616 Mozambique, which had been part of the Archdiocese of Goa, was recognized as a separate ecclesiastical area. Generally, the Christianization of the country was slow. By the middle of the 19th century there were no priests in the interior, and only four or five Goan priests were serving parishes along the coast. New efforts were made in the second part of the 19th and in the 20th century. In recent times the RCath Church has rapidly grown. Today there are eight dioceses.

Protestantism came to Mozambique in the 19th century. The first missionaries were not Europeans but Mozambicans who had come into contact with Prot missionaries and catechists in the neighboring countries and returned home. Prot missions had great difficulty in being accepted by the colonial authorities, who feared that foreign ideas might penetrate the culture. "Everybody recognizes that it is not good colonial policy to allow foreign missionaries . . . instilling in the natives religious convictions and, who knows, giving them the inspiration for political ideas that suit their purpose or that of those who pay them (Statement on the District of Lourenço Marques, December 22, 1888)." Due to the pressure of other colonial powers Prot missionaries were increasingly admitted after the Berlin Conference of 1885. Ref missionaries came from Switzerland (Mission suisse en Afrique du Sud), Scotland, South Africa, and the United States. Apart from Ref and Congreg churches Meth, Bapt, Angl, Nazarenes, Advent, and several Pent and Independent churches are today implanted in the country. In 1948 the Prot churches decided to form a Christian Council of Mozambique; today it has 18 member churches. In 1978 an Alliance of Independent Churches was established.

1. Presbyterian Church of Mozambique (1140)

This church was founded by Swiss missionaries, especially Paul Berthoud (1847-1930). Before his arrival in 1887, Josefa Mhalamhala preached the Gospel he had enountered through missionaries in South Africa. In the early period the church was working in the two southern provinces of Maputo and Gaza, but today it is also spreading to the rest of the country. Beginning in 1948 the church became autonomous in several stages. The founder of the Liberation Front of Moçambique (FRELIMO), Eduardo Chivambo Mondlane, was raised in the Presbyterian Church. In 1972 the first Synod president, Zedekias Manganhela, together with other members of the church, was arrested by the Portuguese authorities; he died in prison as a consequence of torture.

TM: **100,000** BM: **80,000** CM: **100,000** Congr: **350** PStations: **400** OrdM: **35** Eld: **5** Deac: **1,200** EvgHome: **6** Mission: **1** Women Ord: **yes** As Ministers: **1985/2** as Deac: **1912/24** as Elders: **nc** ChurchOrg: **Presbyterian (congr, presby, synods, GenAssy)** Off/otherLang: **Tsonga, Ronga, Portuguese, Chewa-Nyanya, Macua, Lomwe, Chopi** DoctrB: **ApC, NicC, HeidC, Ref** Infant or believer's baptism: **both** Frequency of the Lord's Supper: **monthly** Close relations with: **Département Missionnaire (Switzerland)** NatRel: **CCM (1948)** RegRel: **AACC (1976), SAARC (1988)** IntlRel: **WARC (1960), WCC (1962), CEVAA (1976)** TheolSchool: **Theological Institute of Ricatla, Theological School of Khovo** Periodicals: **Khwezi (quarterly)**

Address: Igreja Presbiteriana de Moçambique, Caixa Postal, 21 Av. Ahmed Sekou Touré 1822, Maputo, Mozambique, Tel: +258 1 422-950 and 424-763, Fax: +258 1 428-623

2. United Congregational Church of Southern Africa (1146)

The church goes back to work done by Edwin Richards, who was sent to Mozambique in 1880 by the American Board of Commissioners for Foreign Missions (Congreg). Since this mission decided to close the work, most members followed Richards in joining the Meth Church. A small group maintained the Congreg tradition. Today the church is active in the Inhambane, Gaza, and Maputo provinces. (cf. South Africa: United Congregational Church of Southern Africa).

TM: **13,400** BM: **13,400** CM: **8,496** Congr: **27** OrdM: **19** Eld: **nc** Deac: **200** EvgHome: **nc** Mission: **nc** Women Ord: **since beginning** As Ministers: **1** as Deac: **100** as Elders: **nc** ChurchOrg: **local church, region, synod, Assy** Off/otherLang: **Xitxe, Portuguese, Tsonga, Tyopi** DoctrB: **nc** Infant or believer's baptism: **both** NatRel: **CCM** RegRel: **SAARC** IntlRel: **CWM, WARC, WCC (through UCCSA)** TheolSchool: **training in South African seminaries and universities** Periodicals: **Congregational Chronicle (quarterly)**

Address: Igreja Congregacional Unida do Africa do Sul, C.P. 930, Maputo, Mozambique, Tel: +258 1 470-572, Fax: +258 1 470-572

3. United Church of Christ in Mozambique (1141)

Since the 1870s the ABCFM had shown interest in working in Mozambique. The effort leading to the foundation of the church was prompted by Mozambicans who had been converted to the Christian faith in South Africa or in Lourenço Marques. In 1905 an American missionary, Fred Bunker, with the help of Zulu volunteers from South Africa and new Vandau converts, started missionary work in the region of Manica and Sofala. The mission suffered much hardship from the Portuguese authorities. The authorization to open a mission station in Beira was granted in 1915 but was withdrawn a few years later. In 1931 work was continued by Gulhierme Tapera Nkomo, the first ordained Mozambican pastor. He was supported and helped by Swiss missionaries, in particular Pierre Loze. Today the church works in the Manica, Sofala, Tete, Inhambane, Zambêzia, and Maputo provinces. The headquarters are in Beira.

TM: **9,000** BM: **6,500** Congr: **19** PStations: **60** OrdM: **15** Eld: **19** Deac: **nc** EvgHome: **30** Mission: **ne** Women Ord: **yes** As Ministers: **1993/1** as Deac: **ne** as Elders: **0** ChurchOrg: **nc** Off/otherLang: **Portuguese, Cindau, Cisena** DoctrB: **ApC** Infant or believer's baptism: **both** Frequency of the Lord's Supper: **monthly and feasts** Close relations with: **CCM, IPM (cf. no 1), IMUM (Meth United Church), ICUM (United Congregational Church)** NatRel: **CCM (1948), SUR (1958)** RegRel: **SAARC (1993) AACC (1994)** IntlRel: **WARC (1993)** TheolSchool: **United Seminary of Ricatla (SUR)** Service infrastructure: **1 rest house (Munhava), plans for 4 schools and 2 health centers** Periodicals: **Manasse (gen/3 times per year/200)**

Address: Igreja de Cristo Unida em Moçambique (Ex-Missão American Board), Caixa Postal 396, Av. Samora Machel N 2537, Beira, Mozambique, Tel: +258 3 325 430

4. Evangelical Church of Christ in Mozambique (1142)

This church goes back to 1876 when Presbyterian missionaries from Scotland came from Malawi to explore the region of Lake Nyama in Mozambique. Missionary efforts were initiated by Christians who had been converted in Malawi (1885). In 1910 a Scottish missionary, James Reid, accompanied by an African elder, Luis Mataka Bandawe, started working for spiritual revival in the Zambesi region. In 1912 a mission station was opened in Alto Molocue, 200 km southeast from Nampula. In 1913 they officially founded the Scottish Presbyterian Church, later called the Evangelical Mission of Nauela, and today known as the Evangelical Church of Christ in Mozambique. In the 1930s Pastor John C. Procter translated the Psalms and the NT into Lomwe. The Scottish missionaries discontinued their work in 1933, and one year later the work was transferred to the Church of the Brethren, who, only five years later, handed it over to the South African General Mission. The Portuguese government closed the mission in 1959, charging that it was responsible for an incident of religious folly. A troubled period followed. For several years the church had to rely on its own resources. In 1969, through an inter-denominational initiative, Pastor Felix Cossa was made available to the congregation of Nampula. Today some of the congr are part of the Bapt church, others have remained faithful to their origins. Now the church is witnessing in the Zambêzia and Nampula provinces as well as in Maputo. Headquarters are in Nampula.

TM: **40,000** BM: **25,000** Congr: **500** PStations: **10** OrdM: **8** Eld: **nc** Deac: **1** EvgHome: **3** Mission: **0** Women Ord: **yes** As Ministers: **nc** as Deac: **1994/3** as Elders: **nc** ChurchOrg: **Congregational (local congr, annual conference)** Off/otherLang: **Portuguese, Makhua, Lomwe, Nyanja** DoctrB: ApC Infant or believer's baptism: **believer** Frequency of the Lord's Supper: **3-4 times per year** NatRel: **CCM** RegRel: **SAARC** IntlRel: **WARC (1995)** TheolSchool: **nc** Periodicals: **Despertar (mission/quarterly)**

Address: Igreja Evangélica de Cristo em Moçambique, P.O. Box 284, Nampula, Mozambique, Tel: +258 621-5302, Fax: +258 621-5302

5. Reformed Church in Mozambique (1147)

This church is rooted primarily in Angónia and Tete in the north and Gaza and Maputo in the south. In 1908 Rev. A. C. Murray of the Dutch Reformed Church in Malawi founded stations at Mphatso, and later at Mwenzi Chiputu and Benga in Angonia. Murray's co-workers included Rev. Jaubert, A. L. Liebenberg, D. P. V. Z. Laurie, among others. The church devoted primary attention to educational and health services. In 1922 work was discontinued by the Portuguese colonial government. In the years which followed, the CCAP in Malawi gave valuable assistance to the church. In 1973 the Mphatso Synod was formed. In 1981 the first two elders were ordained. Since 1991 work developed rapidly. The first 5 pastors trained at Hefsiba Christian Training Center were ordained in 1997.

In Gaza and Maputo work was started by Rev. P. D. Tembe; he founded the community of Trigo de Morais (Chokwe today) in 1971, and in Maputo in 1978. The two churches of Angónia and Gaza united in 1977 to form one Synod.

a) *Reformed Church of Mozambique (Mphatso Synod) (1144)*

TM: **29,000** BM: **4,000** CM: **25,000** Congr: **17** PStations: **420** OrdM: **5** Eld: **780** Deac: **780** EvgHome: **4** Mission: **6** Women Ord: **no** As Ministers: **no** ChurchOrg: **Presbyterian (2 presby in Tete, 1 in Zambesi)** Off/otherLang: **Portuguese, Chichewa** DoctrB: **ApC, HeidC, BelgC, CDort** Infant or believer's baptism: **believer** Frequency of the Lord's Supper: **4 times per year** Close relations with: **Dutch-Reformed Church in South Africa, CCAP–Nkhoma Synod (Malawi)** NatRel: **CCM, Evangelical Fellowship of Mozambique** RegRel: **none** IntlRel: **applied to REC** TheolSchool: **Hefsiba Christian Training Center** Service infrastructure: **Hefsiba Christian Training Center, small schools in rural areas, adult literacy training** Periodicals: **none**

Address: Igreja Reformada em Moçambique (Mphatso Sinodo), P.O. Box 312, Dezda Malawi, Mozambique, Tel: none, Fax: none, E-mail: hchamber@iafrica.com.

b) *Reformed Church in Mozambique (1147)*

TM: **28,000** BM: **14,000** Congr: **18** PStations: **112** OrdM: **18** Eld: **120** Deac: **120** EvgHome: **3** Mission: **0** Women Ord: **yes** As Ministers: **no** as Deac: **9** as Elders: **no** ChurchOrg: **2 mission zones, 18 consistories, 4 presby, 2 synods (synod meets every second year)** Off/otherLang: **Portuguese, Tsonga, Afrikaans, Nkau, Sena, Cinyanja, Makua, Ciyao, Lomwe** DoctrB: **ApC, HeidC, CDort, BelgC** Infant or believer's baptism: **both** Frequency of the Lord's Supper: **4 times per year** NatRel: **CCM (1982), Associaçao Evangélica de Moçambique (1992)** RegRel: **nc** IntlRel: **REC (1997)** TheolSchool: **Hefsiba Theological School (CP 3, Vila Ulongue, Tete Province)** Service infrastructure: **Trichardt school, 3 clinics, 2 medical centers** Periodicals: **none**

Address: Igreja Reformada em Moçambique, 2373 Rua dos Pioneiros No 71, Machava, Maputo, Mozambique, Tel: +258 1 492-961 and 752-586, Fax: +258 1 492-961

6. The Evangelical Church of the Good Shepherd (1148)

This church was founded in 1965 by Rev. Fernando M. Magaia, who previously was a pastor of the Reformed Church in South Africa.

TM: **10,130** Congr: **17** OrdM: **18** Eld: **43** Deac: **nc** EvgHome: **nc** Mission: **nc** Women Ord: **yes** As Ministers: **6** as Deac: **nc** as Elders: **19** ChurchOrg: **Evangelical (local congr, synod, with a bishop leading the executive board)** Off/otherLang: **Portuguese, Ronga, Changana, Zulu, English** DoctrB: **nc** NatRel: **CCM, Bible Union, Bible Society** RegRel: **nc** IntlRel: **nc** TheolSchool: **nc**

Address: Igreja Evangélica do Bom Pastor, C.P. 1948, rua Lacerda de Almeida, Maputo, Mozambique, Tel: +258 1 475-499, Fax: +258 1 475-499

MYANMAR

Area in km²	678,578
Population	(July 1996 est.) 45,975,625 Burman 68%, Shan 9%, Karen 7%, Rakhine/Arakanese 4%, Chinese 3%, Mon 2%, Indian 2%, other 5%
Religions in %	Buddhist 89%, Christian 4% (Bapt 50%, RCath 21%, others 29%), Muslim 4%, animist beliefs 1%, other 2%
Official/other languages	Burmese/tribal languages (Karen, Mon, Shan, Kachin, Chin. Rakhine)

MCC (Myanmar Council of Churches)
MECF (Myanmar Evangelical Christian Fellowship)

Christianity came first to Burma in the 16th century (1554) through RCath missionaries. At the beginning of the 19th century (1813) Adoniram Judson of the American Bapt Mission began working in Burma. He translated the Bible (1834) and published an English-Burmese dictionary (1852). Evangelistic efforts made slow progress. While the Burmese Buddhist population hardly responded, the Gospel was received by the Hill people (Karen 1828, Shan 1861, Kachin 1876, and Chin 1886). Other missions followed: Angl (1852), Meth (1879), Advent (1915), and Assemblies of God (1924). The Ref churches represent a minority within the Christian minority. The various groups owe their existence to both missionary efforts and spontaneous movements. They serve different parts of the Hill population, especially in Chin State.

1. Mara Evangelical Church (4012)

The Mara people live in the northeastern part of the country. The first missionaries were a British couple, Rev. and Mrs. Reginald Arthur Lorrain (1907). Two years before they had founded the Lakher Pioneer Mission in London. A church was founded in Serkawr (India), and the number of converts increased rapidly. With the independence of India (1947) and Burma (1948), the church was divided into two bodies (cf. India no. 4) in the respective territories. In 1970 the church in Burma suffered a split over the location of the headquarters (Mara Independent Evangelical Church and Mara Independent Church). Efforts at reconciliation succeeded in 1987. The church is self-supporting and active in evangelism among the neighboring tribes.

TM: **17,170** BM: **10,638** CM: **10,938** Congr: **96** PStations: **2** OrdM: **43** Eld: **495** Deac: **310** EvgHome: **32** Women Ord: **yes** As Ministers: **none** as Deac: **1986/0** as Elders: **1985/0** ChurchOrg: **local church committee, circle committee, presbytery, GenAssy** Off/otherLang: **Mara dialect** DoctrB: **ApC,**

NicC Infant or believer's baptism: **believer** Frequency of the Lord's Supper: **4 times a year** Close relations with: **no official working relations with any church or organization** NatRel: **MCC (1984)** RegRel: **CCA (1991)** IntlRel: **WARC (1992)** TheolSchool: nc Service infrastructure: **kindergarten in preparation, 9 primary schools, 1 middle school** Periodicals: **Christian Herald (gen/quarterly/ 300), newsletter (gen/monthly/300) Mission Voice (mission/quarterly/300)**

Address: Mara Evangelical Awnanopa, Evangelical Mission Myanmar, 7-68 Chinpyan Road, Sittwe
Rakhine State, Myanmar, Tel: +95 43 21873

2. Independant Church of Myanmar (4010)

This church was formed in 1938 in Doikhel, a village in Chin State, in response to the preaching of Thawng Khaw Zam, an independent evangelist from Tonzang. His charismatic style was rejected by the American Bapt Church. The movement constituted itself as the Independent Church of Myanmar. The church suffered splits in 1963 and 1969 but reconstituted itself in 1979. In recent years it has grown rapidly. Its congr are in the Chin State, Sagaing Division (Upper Chindwin), and elsewhere in Myanmar. Its missionary work centers in southern Chin and Rakhine State. About ten different dialects are spoken in the church; the main languages are Falam and Mizo.

TM: **4,932** Congr: **182** OrdM: **24** Eld: **150** Deac: nc EvgHome: **20** Mission: **1** Women Ord: **no** ChurchOrg: **Presbyterian** Off/otherLang: **Chin** DoctrB: **ApC, NicC, WestConf** Infant or believer's baptism: **both** NatRel: nc RegRel: **CCA** IntlRel: **WARC (1987)** TheolSchool: **Bethany Theological Seminary (Yangoon)** Service infrastructure: **CMC** Periodicals: **The Light of the Church (gen/ bi-monthly/250)**

Address: Independant Church of Myanmar, P.O. Box 446, Sagaing Division, Yangoon Tahan
Kalemyo 02092, Myanmar, Tel: +95 21206

3. St. Gabriel's Church Union (Congregational) (4014)

This is one congregation in Yangoon of Congreg origin.

No statistical data have been made available.

Address: St. Gabriel's Church Union (Congregational), P.O. Box 722, Yangoon, Union of Myanmar

4. The Presbyterian Church of Myanmar (4017)

In the period from 1914 to 1950 Mizo immigrants, some of them Presb, moved into the Kalay and Kabaw valleys in the Upper Chindwin. They were served first by a Bapt missionary and later by Meth ministers. But the Mizo Presb decided to maintain their tradition. Presbyterianism also spread in the Chin Hills. The first congregation was founded in 1956 in Losau village. As time went on, the Mizo Presb Church (cf. India no. 3) recognized that the church in the Kalay and Kabaw valleys and in the Chin Hills needed pastoral care and decided to send Pastor

Lalthanga (1959-1969) to serve them. In 1962 the church was constituted at the national level; at that time it had 5,000 members. The church has extended its activities to the Southern Chin Hills, Upper Sagain Division, and Rakhine States.

TM: **29,496** CM: **11,785** Congr: **256** PStations: **160** OrdM: **41** Eld: **339** Deac: **ne** EvgHome: **78** Mission: **ne** Women Ord: **no** ChurchOrg: **Local congregation, pastorate (37), presbs (17), synod (3), Assy** Off/otherLang: **Burmese/Mizo, hilltribe dialects such as Falam, Haka, Matupi, Tedim** DoctrB: **ApC, NicC** Infant or believer's baptism: **both** Frequency of the Lord's Supper: **at least three times a year** Close relations with: **Ind. Ch. of Myanmar, Bapt and Meth Church, Presb. Ch. of Wales, United Ref Church (UK)** NatRel: **Myanmar Council of Churches (1965)** RegRel: **CCA (1990)** IntlRel: **CWM (1977), WARC** TheolSchool: **Tahan Theological College** Service infrastructure: **1 clinic, 1 baby home** Periodicals: **Church's Herald (gen/monthly/753) Mission Newsletter (specialized/bi-monthly/1,200), Women's Newsletter (specialized/3 times per year/1,200),** Youth Newsletter (gen andspec/monthly/1,075)

Address: Kawlram Presb Kohhran, General Assembly Office, Tahan-Kalaymyo, Upper Myanmar, Union of Myanmar, Tel: +95 21216

5. Evangelical Presbyterian Church in Myanmar (4016)

This church came into existence in 1983. All members once belonged to diverse denominations, but seceded as these churches, in their eyes, succumbed to liberalism, modernism, and ecumenical and charismatic movements. The church was founded by Rev. Robert Thawm Luai. It has its roots in Chin State.

TM: **1,000** BM: **900** Congr: **49** PStations: **ne** OrdM: **37** Eld: **118** EvgHome: **12** Mission: **nil** Women Ord: **no** ChurchOrg: **49 sessions, 3 presbys, GenAssy** Off/otherLang: **Chin, Burmese, English** DoctrB: **WestConf** Infant or believer's baptism: **both** Frequency of the Lord's Supper: **monthly** NatRel: **nc** RegRel: **nc** IntlRel: **nc** TheolSchool: **Far Eastern Fundamental School of Theology** Periodicals: **Special announcement (gen/occasional/500)**

Address: Evangelical Presbyterian Church in Myanmar, P.O. Box 532, 6-D Nanthani Street, Insein, Sawbwagyigone Yangoon, Union of Myanmar, Tel: +95 1 41123

6. Christian Reformed Church of Myanmar (4013)

The CRCM was founded by Pastor Chan Thleng, who was a former ordained minister of the Presbyterian Church of Myanmar (cf. no. 4). He belongs to a Matu tribe in Southern Chin State. Born in 1954, he became a Christian in 1974 and after some years of study began, with the help of the Christian Reformed Church in North America, to evangelize the mountain people. In 1985 he founded the United Christian Church. When he returned in 1992, after a few years of studies at Calvin Theological Seminary in Grand Rapids, USA, he changed the name of the church to Christian Reformed Church of Myanmar. In 1991 he completed the translation of the NT into the Matu dialect.

TM: **5,000** BM: **4,047** Congr: **50** PStations: **21** OrdM: **10** Eld: **45** Deac: **60** EvgHome: **21** Mission: **ne** Women Ord: **no** ChurchOrg: **local consistory, regional classes, GenAssy** Off/otherLang: **Matu, Makang, Burmese** DoctrB: **ApC, NicC, AthC, HeidC, CDort, BelgC** Infant or believer's baptism:

both Frequency of the Lord's Supper: **4 times a year** Close relations with: **Evangelical Presb Church of Myanmar** (cf. no. 5) NatRel: **MECF** RegRel: **nc** IntlRel: **REC (1996)** TheolSchool: **nc** Service infrastructure: **goat farms and orange plantation** Periodicals: **Christian News (gen and mission/ bi-monthly/200)**

Address: Tlaihpan Kri Thlangboel, 53/c, Taungtugone Road, Insein, Yangoon, Myanmar

7. Reformed Presbyterian Church of Myanmar (4015)

This church was founded in 1995 by Dr. Tial Hlei Thanga, a former school teacher. He belongs to a Hualngo (Mizo) tribe from northern Chin State. He studied from 1987 to 1994 at the Reformed Theological Seminary in Jackson, Mississippi. He was ordained in 1996 by Mission to the World (Presbyterian Church of America gave him initial support). The Reformed Presbyterian Church of Myanmar is self-supporting, active in discipleship ministry and church planting. Members come primarily from the Church Missionary Alliance and the Upper Myanmar Meth Church.

TM: **1,356** BM: **1,348** Congr: **11** PStations: **8** OrdM: **2** Eld: **33** Deac: **ne** EvgHome: **4** Mission: **2** Women Ord: **no** ChurchOrg: **11 local sessions, 2 presby, GenAssy** Off/otherLang: **Burmese, Mizo, often also English** DoctrB: **ApC, WestConf, WestCat, 5 points of Calvinism (TULIP)** Infant or believer's baptism: **both** Frequency of the Lord's Supper: **monthly** NatRel: **MECF** RegRel: **nc** IntlRel: **ICCC** TheolSchool: **Reformed Theological Seminary** Periodicals: **Ram Ni Eng (quarterly)**

Address: Burmese Mizo, G.P.O. Box 1256, 292 AB-7 Bangya Dala Rd., Kyauk Myaung, Tamwe, Yangoon, Union of Myanmar, Tel: +95 1 541-316, Fax: +95 1 549-750

8. United Reformed Church in Myanmar (4019)

TM: **nc** Congr: **21** OrdM: **7** Eld: **nc** Deac: **nc** EvgHome: **nc** Mission: **nc** Women Ord: **nc** ChurchOrg: **nc** Off/otherLang: **nc** DoctrB: **ApC, Three Forms of Unity, WestConf** NatRel: **nc** RegRel: **nc** IntlRel: **nc** TheolSchool: **nc**

Address: United Reformed Church in Myanmar, 35/1277-1278 Kanthayar Str. Dagon, North 11421, Yangoon, Union of Myanmar

NAMIBIA

Area in km²	825,418
Population	(July 1996 est.) 1,677,243 black 86%, white 6.6%, mixed 7.4% note: about 50% of the population belong to the Ovambo tribe and 9% to the Kavango tribe; other ethnic groups are: Herero 7%, Damara 7%, Nama 5%, Caprivian 4%, Bushmen 3%, Baster 2%, Tswana 0.5%
Religions in %	Christian 80% to 90% (Luth 50% at least, other Christian denominations 30%), native religions 10% to 20%)
Official/other languages	English 7%, Afrikaans common language of most of the population and about 60% of the white population, German 32%, indigenous languages: Oshivambo, Herero, Nama

In 1884 South-West Africa, as it was then called, became a German protectorate. In 1904 the Herero tribe rebelled against German domination; thousands were killed. After World War I the territory was placed, by decision of the League of Nations, under the control of South Africa, which in 1948 began to apply the apartheid system. As a consequence, the UN withdrew the mandate in 1966, and two years later renamed the country Namibia. When, finally, in 1990 free elections took place the South-West African People's Organization (SWAPO) obtained the majority; its leader, S. Nujoma, became the first president.

The strong Christian presence is the result of various missionary efforts in the 19th and 20th centuries. The first mission to reach the country was the LMS (1805). The Lutheran Rhenish and Finnish missions followed in 1842 and 1870. The relatively small Reformed churches have their origin in South Africa and reflect the situation of the churches there. In 1978 a large number of churches, including the RCath Church, founded the Council of Churches in Namibia.

1. Dutch Reformed Church in Namibia (DRCN) (1117)

Mission work by the Dutch Reformed Church in South Africa started in Great Namaqualand in the 1880s. The first congregation was established in 1898. In subsequent decades the church grew. It is autonomous but essentially one with the Dutch Reformed Church in South Africa (see South Africa no. 1). There is the hope that the church will achieve unity with the Uniting Reformed Church in South Africa.

TM: **25,342** CM: **17,300** Congr: **46** OrdM: **61** Eld: **681** Deac: **nc** EvgHome: **nc** Mission: **nc** Women Ord: **yes** As Ministers: **1991/0** as Deac: **1987/na** as Elders: **1987/na** ChurchOrg: **the church is a regional synod of the Dutch Reformed Church in SA, 7 presby** Off/otherLang: **Afrikaans, English, Bushman** DoctrB: **ApC, NicC, AthC, HeidC, CDort, BelgC** NatRel: **Council of Churches in Namibia (1995, observer status)** RegRel: nc IntlRel: nc TheolSchool: nc

Address: Nederduitse Gereformeerde Kerk in Namibië, Postbus 389, Windhoek 9000, Namibia, Tel: +61 225-073, Fax: +61 227-287

2. Uniting Reformed Church of Southern Africa (1116)

The church was established through missionary work of the Dutch Reformed Church in South Africa (cf. no. 1). The first synod was constituted in 1975 with only three congregations. The church grew in subsequent years. In 1987 it was divided into three independent regional synods which were held together by an umbrella body called the General Meeting of the Evangelical Reformed Church in Africa (ERCA). Four years later the three churches decided to merge again as a General Synod with the three churches functioning as regional synods (ERCA Kavango, Central, and Ovambo Regional Synods). In 1995 the Reformed Church in Caprivi, which had also originated from DRC missionary efforts, joined the ERCA and became the fourth Regional Synod of the Church. In 1995 the General Synod decided in principle to join the Uniting Reformed Church in Southern Africa (cf. South Africa no. 4). Union was officially announced in April 1997 at the synod of the Uniting Church in East London, South Africa.

TM: **6,850** CM: **2,950** Congr: **31** OrdM: **24** Eld: **102** Deac: **57** EvgHome: **15** Mission: nc Women Ord: **no (Caprivi: yes)** As Ministers: **(yes/8)** as Deac: **(yes/12)** as Elders: nc ChurchOrg: nc Off/otherLang: **Afrikaans, English, Herrero, Kwangali, Lozi, Ndonga, Damara, Portuguese** DoctrB: **ApC, NicC, AthC, HeidC, CDort, Belhar Confession** NatRel: **Council of Churches in Namibia** RegRel: nc IntlRel: **REC (1980)** TheolSchool: **Namibia Evangelical Theological Seminary**

Address: Verenigende Gereformeerde Kerk in Suider-Africa, P.O. Box 20764, Windhoek, Namibia

3. Reformed Churches in Namibia (1120)

The Reformed people who formed this church came to Namibia in 1929 from Angola. The "Dorslandtrekkers" from the Transvaal (South Africa) — most of them Reformed — lived as farmers in Angola for half a century before they moved to Namibia. In 1930 three congr were established in their new country. Later, more came from South Africa as government employees. Missionary work was started in 1969 under the Bushman of the Gobabis region in Botswana (see Botswana). A Bible translation in the Gobabis-Kung language by Pastor P. J. W. S. van der Westhuizen is close to completion.

TM: **2,757** CM: **924** Congr: **14** PStations: OrdM: **12** Eld: **123** Deac: nc EvgHome: nc Mission: nc Women Ord: **no** As Ministers: **no** ChurchOrg: **two classes gathering annually as a regional synod of the Reformed Churches in SA** Off/otherLang: **Afrikaans, Gobabis-Kung (Bushman dialect)**

DoctrB: **ApC, NicC, AthC, HeidC, CDordt, BelgC** NatRel: **Council of Churches in Namibia (1996, observer status)** RegRel: **nc** IntlRel: **nc** TheolSchool: **nc.**

Address: Gereformeerde Kerk in Namibië, P.O. Box 20004, Potchefstroom, 2522 South Africa, Namibia

4. United Congregational Church of Southern Africa (Namibia Regional Council) (1118)

Since 1933, members of the Congregational Church in South Africa have moved to Namibia to find work and places to settle. They came mainly from Keimoes and Upington in the northwestern Cape. Seven congregations were eventually established: Duineveld, Rehoboth, Karlfeld, Windhoek (1959), Luderitz (1966), Walvis Bay (1966), Swakopmund (1976), and Grootfontein (1975). In 1982, the seven congregations became an independent regional council.

TM: **2,879** CM: **2,163** Congr: **7** OrdM: **6** Eld: **50** Deac: **nc** EvgHome: **nc** Mission: **nc** Women Ord: **yes** As Ministers: **0** as Deac: **30** as Elders: **0** ChurchOrg: **local church, region, synod, Assembly** Off/otherLang: **Afrikaans, English** DoctrB: **nc** NatRel: **Council of Churches in Namibia** RegRel: **SAARC** IntlRel: **WARC, WCC, CWM (all through the Church in South Africa)** TheolSchool: **nc**

Address: United Congregational Church of Southern Africa, P.O. Box 8332, Bachbrecht, Windhoek, Namibia, Tel: +61 206-3038, Fax: +61 206-3806

5. Dutch Reformed Church (NHK) (1121)

The members of this church constitute a presbytery of the Nederduitsche Hervormde Kerk in South Africa (see South Africa no. 2)

Address: Nederduitsche Hervormde Kerk (NHK), P.O. Box 2368, Jacob Maré Str., Pretoria, 0001 South Africa, Tel:+ 27 12 322-8885, Fax: +27 12 322-7909, E-mail: hervormd@pixie.co.za

6. Afrikaans Protestant Church (APK) (1122)

This church resulted from a split in the Dutch Reformed Church (see no. 1). When, in 1986, the Dutch Reformed Church began to denounce apartheid, a group within the church founded in protest the APK. (For statistics see under APK in South Africa no. 7.)

Address: Afrikaanse Protestantse Kerk, P.O. Box 11488, Hatfield, Pretoria 028 South Africa, Namibia, Tel: +27 12 362-1390, Fax: +27 12 362-2023

NAURU

Area in km²	21
Population	(July 1996 est.) 10,273 Nauruan 58%, other Pacific Islander 26%, Chinese 8%, European 8%
Religions in %	Prot 66%, RCath 34%
Official/other languages	Nauruan (a distinct Pacific Island language) , Kiribati, Chinese, Tuvaluan, English widely understood, spoken, and used by most

Nauru Congregational Church (NCC) (5150)

The British sailor John Fearn was the first European to visit the island, which he named Pleasant Island. In 1888 the island was annexed by Germany. After World War I Nauru came under Australian trusteeship, and during World War II under Japanese control. After the war Australia recovered the island.

The origins of the Nauru Church date back to 1887, when Timoteo Tabwia, its pioneer missionary and a Gilbert Islander, landed on the island under the auspices of the ABCFM. He preceded white resident ABCFM missionaries Philip A. and Salome Delaporte, who studied the unique language of Nauru and began Bible translation and a hymnbook with the help of the Nauruan high chief, Timothy Detudamo.

After discovery of the island's rich reserves of calcium phosphate in 1900, the deposits were mined by British, German, and Australian-based companies, which gave patronage to the church and supported the ABCFM. After 1917 the London Missionary Society (LMS) took over from the ABCFM. Congreg church government, promoting lay deacons as preachers and teachers, closely aligned the island's local church congregations with the work of the Congregational Union of Australia, especially after many Nauruans suffered a period of severe trial and exile in Chuuk (Truk) and Pohnpei (cf. Federated States of Micronesia) under Japanese occupation during World War II. LMS white resident missionaries from Australia and New Zealand gave leadership until Nauru's first internationally trained and locally born minister, Itubwa Amram, was ordained and returned to the island in 1956.

The church gained full autonomy from the LMS, though it preserved links with Australia and the International Congregational Council. Many Gilbertese Prot came to work in the phosphate industry and received pastoral care and opportunities for worship in their own language. Movements toward full church autonomy and political status, independent of the postwar Australian UN mandate, were led by Prot Nauruan chiefs and church deacons. Nauru's national independence and full repossession of the phosphate industry followed in 1968. Today the phos-

381

phate industry is declining and reserves will run out soon. The exploitation has left 80% of the island uninhabitable and non-arable.

The church has assumed its place in the Pacific Conference of Churches and the Council for World Mission (CWM). Most Nauruans have links with the Congregational Church; there are also Independent and RCath congr on the island.

TM: **7,000** Congr: **nc** OrdM: **nc** Eld: **nc** Deac: **nc** EvgHome: **nc** Mission: **nc** Women Ord: **no** Off/otherLang: **Nauruan, English** ChurchOrg: **Congregational (congr, 7 church districts)** DoctrB: **nc** Infant or believer's baptism: **infant** Frequency of the Lord's Supper: **nc** RegRel: **Prot Churches in Tuvalu and Kiribati, PCC** IntlRel: **CWM** TheolSchool: **nc**.

Address: Nauru Congregational Church, P.O. Box 232, Nauru, Central Pacific, Nauru, Tel: nc, Fax: +674 444 3752

NEPAL

Area in km²	147,181
Population	(July 1996 est.) 22,094,033 Newars, Indians, Tibetans, Gurungs, Magars, Tamangs, Bhotias, Rais, Limbus, Sherpas
Nepali living abroad	(est.) 6,000,000
Religions in %	Hindu 90%, Buddhist 5%, Muslim 3%, Christians 0.58% (Prot 0.56%, RCath 0.02%), other 1.42%
Official/other languages	Nepali/20 other languages divided into numerous dialects

The Himalayan Kingdom of Nepal dates back to the 8th century B.C. when the Gopal and Ahir dynasties arrived from India and, later, the Kirats from Tibet. The country's history has been shaped by numerous struggles among dozens of local principalities, and by regular strife with its neighbors Tibet and India as well as with the British and the East India Company. In the second half of the 18th century the country was unified under the first king of the present dynasty.

Calling itself "the world's only Hindu Kingdom" (Hinduism was the state religion until 1990), Nepal remained officially closed to Christian missions until the 1950s when a change of government brought an end to isolation and an openness to foreign aid.

In 1953 the first Prot were called into the country to build a hospital. They received other Prot groups and missions into this project, thus creating in 1954 the **United Mission to Nepal** (UMN), an interconfessional organization. At that time Prot missions, as well as Nepalis converted to the Christian faith in India, entered the country. Their activities were restricted to aid and development. Churches had no legal entity and could not own property. The pastors would often support themselves, and they usually had no formal training. There were no denominational structures; most churches practiced adult baptism only.

Today UMN includes over 40 agencies and churches with more than 400 staff. They are active all over Nepal in the fields of health, education, and development. They all continue to have their headquarters outside Nepal. Other active organizations include the Nepal Evangelistic Band, the International Nepal Fellowship (deals with lepers), and the Evangelical Alliance Mission (medical care).

Since the revolution in 1990, freedom of religion is granted. Foreign Christians (including many Indian groups) have been active, and Western-style denominations have grown rapidly. Today the vast majority of local churches are, however, independent or loose members of one of the church fellowships (Nepal Church Fellowship, Agape Christian Fellowship, Evangelical Christian Fellowship of Nepal). Though every religion now has a right to maintain its religious places and institutions, it has proved difficult to register with the government. Christians continue to face difficulties since hostility to this "foreign religion" and discrimination in education and employment are still common and persecutions in villages or extended families are regularly reported. Accurate statistical information is not available. A widely quoted figure in 1996 is 240,000 Christians. The vast majority belong to groups such as the Assemblies of God, Foursquare Gospel Church, Bapt Church, and Evangelical Friends Church.

Presbyterian Church of the Kingdom of Nepal (4530)

The Presbyterian Church of the Kingdom of Nepal claims some 18 congregations and entertains privileged links with Korean and Mizoram Presb. It held its first General Assembly in 1996. With the support of the Presbyterian Church in the USA it runs the Ebenezer Bible College as well as a pastor and leadership training center.

THE NETHERLANDS

Area in km²	37,330
Population	(July 1996 est.) 15,568,034 Dutch 96%, Moluccans, Turks, and other 4% (1988)
Religions in %	RCath 34%, Prot 25%, Muslim 3%, other 2%, unaffiliated 36% (1991)
Official/other languages	Dutch/Frisian, ethnic minority languages (Surinam Creole, Turkish, Moroccan Arab, Moluccan, etc.)

CCN (Council of Churches in the Netherlands)

In 1648, after the Eighty Years' War with Spain, the Netherlands became free and independent and the Republic of the United Netherlands, comprising the seven Northern provinces, was established. In 1814 this republic was transformed into the Kingdom of the Netherlands. In the 19th and the first half of the 20th century this kingdom also included the Netherlands Indies in Southeast Asia, Surinam, and the Netherlands Antilles in the Caribbean. After the Second World War both the Netherlands Indies/Indonesia and Surinam became independent. The Netherlands Antilles became a self-governing part of the kingdom.

The reformation of the church in the Netherlands was closely associated with the struggle for political and religious freedom under William of Orange (1533-1584) and his successors. In 1651 the Reformed Church became the privileged religion. However, the Batavia Revolution (1795), influenced by the French Revolution (1789), led to the separation of church and state, and the Reformed Church lost its privileged position. Since then other Prot churches, the RCath Church, and the Jewish religion have been granted greater religious liberty. The constitution of 1848 affirmed religious freedom for all. Until World War II the Netherlands Reformed Church remained influential, but thereafter secularism and nonaffiliation gradually became dominant.

Through the centuries the Netherlands Reformed Church has experienced several schisms, separations, or secessions, starting with the Remonstrants, who were expelled from the Reformed Church in 1618/1619 (cf. no. 2). The churches rooted in the Afscheiding (Separation 1834) and in the Doleantie (Abraham Kuyper 1886) were afflicted by a number of further schisms. All churches, however, which have separated from the Netherlands Reformed Church, with the exception of the Covenant of Free Evangelical Congregations in the Netherlands (cf. no. 4), are one in maintaining the three classical confessions of the Dutch Reformation: the Belgic Confession (1561), the Heidelberg Catechism (1563), and the Canons of Dordrecht (1618/19). Some of these churches follow these confessions strictly and others more moderately. It should also be noted that the Reformed Churches in the Netherlands (cf. no. 5), the most important church of the secession, modified the Belgic Confession in 1905, deleting from Article 36 the passages which entrusted the government with the task of suppressing all false religions and "destroying the reign of Antichrist."

In 1830, when the first census took place, 59.1% of the Dutch population was Prot (mainly Reformed), 39% RCath, and 1.0% Jewish and 0.1% adhered to other religions or professed no faith. Since then the situation has changed remarkably. In 1971 the RCath outnumbered the Prot, while the number of people with no church allegiance increased from 0.3% in 1879 to 23.3% in 1971. After 1971 church membership continued to decline, with the Church of the Nazarenes and the Pent being the main exceptions. According to some sociological studies the percentage of people who are not affiliated to any church increased to 48.7% in 1985. If this is true, the Netherlands is now one of the most secularized countries in the West. Recently the Dutch government decided to stop registering the religious affiliation of its citizens.

In addition, since the end of World War II the religious situation has become

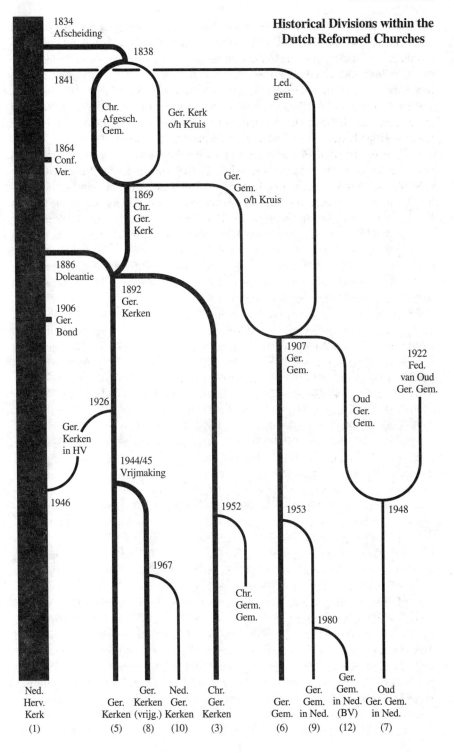

**Historical Divisions within the
Dutch Reformed Churches**

1834
Afscheiding

1838

1841

Led.
gem.

Chr.
Afgesch.
Gem.

Ger. Kerk
o/h Kruis

1864
Conf.
Ver.

Ger.
Gem.
o/h Kruis

1869
Chr.
Ger.
Kerk

1886
Doleantie

1892
Ger.
Kerken

1906
Ger.
Bond

1907
Ger.
Gem.

1922
Fed.
van Oud
Ger. Gem.

Oud
Ger.
Gem.

1926

Ger.
Kerken
in HV

1944/45
Vrijmaking

1946

1952

1953

1948

1967

Chr.
Germ.
Gem.

1980

Ned. Herv. Kerk		Ger. Kerken	Ger. Kerken (vrijg.)	Ned. Ger. Kerken	Chr. Ger. Kerken		Ger. Gem.	Ger. Gem. in Ned.	Ger. Gem. in Ned. (BV)	Oud Ger. Gem. in Ned.
(1)		(5)	(8)	(10)	(3)		(6)	(9)	(12)	(7)

385

more diverse and complex through immigration, especially from Surinam, North Africa,,and Turkey. Among the immigrants there are many Christians, but the greater part belongs to Islam. Hinduism and other non-Western religions can also be found in many of the larger cities. Muslims have established mosques in practically all towns and even in a good number of villages. Today, therefore, the Reformed churches in the Netherlands are called to cope not only with secularism but also with non-Christian religions, especially Islam and new religious movements.

The following survey of the Reformed churches in the Netherlands cannot claim to be complete. In addition to the 17 churches (with a nationwide ministry) at least ten small and independent Reformed congregations, mainly at the local level, could have been mentioned. The survey presented here lists first the "historical" churches in the Netherlands (nos. 1-11) and then mentions the communities which resulted from recent immigration (nos. 12-17). Since World War II the number of immigrants has rapidly grown. Many immigrants have joined one of the existing Dutch churches, while others have set up their own Bible groups, congregations, or churches. A first group of churches came into existence in connection with decolonization (nos. 12-15), and the others are due to other immigrations (nos. 16-17). In addition to the churches listed in this survey, the Indonesian community in the Netherlands (Indonesische Christelijke Gemeenschap in Nederland/ Persekutuan Kristen Indonesia di Nederland PERKI), an association of Prot, mainly Reformed, Christians from Indonesia, could have been mentioned.

In Dutch there are two words for the term Reformed — *hervormd* and *gereformeerd*. They have the same meaning but differ in emotional value. Since 1814 the term *hervormd* is primarily linked with the Netherlands Reformed Church, the former state church, while *gereformeerd* is used for the separated churches and congregations since the Afscheiding of 1834. The orthodox wing within the Netherlands Reformed Church, however, bears the name *gereformeerd* (Gereformeerde Bond/Reformed Alliance).

1. Netherlands Reformed Church (NHK) (6361)

The NHK was established during the struggle for freedom from Spain (1568-1648). The seven northern provinces became largely Reformed. Since the revolt of William of Orange the House of Orange belongs to this church.

The national Synod of Dordrecht (1618/1619) consolidated the position of the Reformed Church in the Netherlands, ordered its ecclesiastical life, and dealt with the control of the church by the state. It accepted the five canons of Dordrecht which set forth unconditional election and faith as a gift of God; the death of Christ as fully sufficient to expiate the sins of the whole world, and so on. These canons condemned the views of the Remonstrants who attacked the Calvinistic doctrine of predestination, especially the doctrine of reprobation. Their adherents were expelled by the synod (cf. no. 2)

The Synod of Dordrecht also discussed Christian missions. These had already been established by the Netherlands Reformed Church in the East Indies

(1612), and in the following years work was started in Taiwan (1624), New York (1626), India (1633), Brazil (1640), and South Africa (1652). Netherlands Reformed ministers were the first Prot missionaries to preach the Gospel among the Indians in North America (with New York, then known as New Amsterdam, serving as their base), in northeast Brazil, as well as among the indigenous people of Formosa. In the 19th and 20th centuries Dutch immigrants to North and South America, South Africa, and other countries established their own ethnic Reformed churches. During the first decades after their arrival they maintained Dutch as their language, both in their church services and in their Bible reading at home, but later they accommodated themselves more and more to the new context, adopted the national language, and started their own missionary work.

Since the time of the establishment of state universities Netherlands Reformed ministers were trained at the theological faculties of Leiden (1575), Groningen (1614), Utrecht (1636), and, more recently, Amsterdam. Through the centuries both professors and staff of these faculties were members of the NHK. Since the 1960s the teaching staff has become interdenominational and even interreligious and secular; they include Jews, Muslims, and nonaffiliated persons. The student body is also diverse. Nevertheless the NHK continues to be affiliated with these faculties and has the right to appoint the professors of systematics and pastoral theology. The Remonstrants (cf. no. 2) and the Covenant of Free Evangelical Congregations (cf. no. 4) exercise the same privilege in Leiden and Utrecht respectively.

In 1685, because of the Revocation of the Edict of Nantes, many Huguenots fled from France to the Netherlands, where they joined the already existing French-speaking Reformed congregations, the "Eglises wallones." In 1816 these congregations were integrated into the NHK. At the same time they maintained their identity as a French-speaking classis within the NHK.

In 1816 King William I (1772-1843) reorganized the NHK as a whole. He gave it its present name and introduced a new church order, which was redrafted in 1852. Though liberalism gained momentum in the Netherlands after 1848, the NHK remained under government control. Only the order of 1951 brought the end of all forms of tutelage by the state.

Throughout its history the NHK had a typically Reformed organizational structure — local congregations, classes at the regional level, and particular and general synods at the provincial and national levels. Since the beginning of the 20th century it is characterized by a vast variety of theological convictions: confessionalism in the Confessionele Vereniging (Confessional Association 1864), orthodoxy in the Gereformeerde Bond (Reformed Alliance 1906), theological liberalism (organized in 1904/1913), and Neo-Orthodoxy (Barthianism) have influenced theology, practice, and the life of the church and its congregations. Liberalism and Neo-Orthodoxy are strong in the faculties, but confessionalism and orthodoxy maintain a strong influence in many large congregations. Recently, the Evangelicals have decided to set up their own organization within the NHK.

Though membership has been declining since the 19th century (54.7% in 1869, 48.4% in 1899, 34.4% in 1930, 28.3% in 1960, and 23.6% in 1971), the

NHK continues to be the largest Prot church in the Netherlands. The loss of members is not exclusively due to the process of secularization but also to a series of separations. Since the 1970s the NHK is involved in a process of unification with the Gereformeerde Kerken (cf. no. 5) and the Evangelical-Lutheran Church in the Kingdom of the Netherlands, which was established in the first decades of the 16th century. A union scheme has been adopted by the synods in 1997. The name of the new church will be United Protestant Church in the Netherlands (Verenigde Protestantse Kerk in Nederland, VPKN). Union is likely to be consummated in the first years of the new millennium.

The NHK has strong ecumenical ties with the World Council of Churches, which was founded in 1948 in Amsterdam and whose first general secretary, W. A. Visser 't Hooft, was of Dutch origin; with the World Alliance of Reformed Churches; with daughter churches in South Africa, the Caribbean, and North America; with many Indonesian churches which originated from its missionary involvement; and with some Moluccan churches in the Netherlands (cf. nos. 12-14).

TM: **2,314,510** BM: **988,773** CM: **744,849** Congr: **1,354** PStations: **1,770** OrdM: **1,753** Eld: **19,380** Deac: **8,680** EvgHome: **ne** Mission: **19** Women Ord: **yes** As Ministers: **1958/275** as Deac: **1958/3212** as Elders: **1958/5212** ChurchOrg: **regional: classes (presby), provincial synods, gen synod** Off/ otherLang: **Dutch, French (16 communities), English (2 Scots Churches)** DoctrB: **ApC, NicC, AthC, HeidC, CDort, BelgC** Infant or believer's baptism: **both** Frequency of the Lord's Supper: **monthly to quarterly** Close relations with: **Evang.-Luth Ch in the Kingdom of the NL, Ref Ch in the NL, Remonstrant Brotherhood** NatRel: **CCN (1968)** RegRel: **CEC (1957), Leuenberg Concord (1973)** IntlRel: **WCC (1948), WARC (1876)** TheolSchool: **affiliated with the Theological Faculties of the State Universities of Leiden, Utrecht, and Groningen and of the Municipal University of Amsterdam** Service infrastructure: **none** Periodicals: **Kerkinformatie (gen/monthly/23,000), Woord en Dienst (gen/twice a month)**

Address: Nederlandse Hervormde Kerk (NHK), Postbus 405 Overgoo 11, NL-2260 AK Leidschendam, Netherlands, Tel: +31 70 313 1131, Fax: +31 70 313 1202

2. Remonstrant Brotherhood (RB) (6362)

After having been expelled from the NHK in 1619, the Remonstrants, or Arminians, as they were also called, founded their own church in that same year. In 1621 they adopted their own confession of faith. It has always been a small but influential church. Until 1795 the Remonstrants were not officially tolerated. Many, among them Hugo Grotius (1583-1645), the "father" of international law, had to leave the country. In the 18th century the church had significant influence on Methodism and in the 19th century on theological liberalism. In 1634 the Remonstrants set up their own seminary in Amsterdam, and in 1873 it was integrated into the theological faculty of Leiden. After World War II the church adopted progressive policies; it is one of the few churches in the Netherlands which allows homosexuals to marry in the church. There is a congregation in Friedrichsstadt, Germany, which is affiliated with the church.

TM: **8,175** BM: **8,010** CM: **8,175** Congr: **48** PStations: **40** OrdM: **20** Eld: **200** Deac: **100** EvgHome: **ne** Mission: **1** Women Ord: **yes** As Ministers: **since 1921/18** as Deac: **150** as Elders: **150** ChurchOrg:

Presbyterian-Congregational Off/otherLang: **Dutch, English** DoctrB: **Remonstrant Confession (1940), Declaration of Principle (1928)** Infant or believer's baptism: **both** Frequency of the Lord's Supper: **6 times a year** Close relations with: **Mennonites** NatRel: **CCN (1968)** RegRel: **CEC (from the beginning)** IntlRel: **WCC (1948), WARC (1981)** TheolSchool: **Remonstrant Seminary (affiliated with the Theological Faculty of the University of Leiden)** Periodicals: **Ad Rem (monthly/ 3,000)**

Address: Remonstrantse Broederschap, Nieuwe Gracht 27a, NL-3512 LC Utrecht, Netherlands, Tel: +31 30 231 69 70, Fax: +31 30 231 1055, E-mail: info@zemonstrante.org.

3. Christian Reformed Churches in the Netherlands (CGKN) (6363)

In 1834 Rev. Hendrik de Cock (1801-1842) was suspended from the ministry by the NHK, mainly because of his vociferous criticisms of the new church order of 1816 (cf. no. 1). This measure led to the separation of his congregation in Ulrum from the NHK. Other ministers also protested against theological liberalism and state influence in the church and decided to leave as well. Within two years more than one hundred independent congregations were established throughout the country. They were known as the Christelijke Afgescheiden Gemeenten or the Gereformeerde Kerk onder het Kruis (Reformed Church under the Cross).

In 1869 the main stream of these congregations established the Christelijke Gereformeerde Kerk. In 1892 most of them joined the GKN (cf. no. 5). A few congr, however, objected to this union, mainly on the ground that the independence of local congregations was not sufficiently recognized. This remnant of the Reformed Church under the Cross reorganized itself and established its own classes and particular and general synods. In 1947 the church changed its name into Christelijke Reformed Churches in the Netherlands. In 1952 it suffered a division: Rev. J. G. van Minnen and a few others decided to leave the church. Since 1894 the church has had its own theological seminary. In 1917 it moved to Apeldoorn, and it has recently been transformed into a theological faculty. From 1950 to 1977 the church belonged to the ICCC. In 1989 it withdrew from the REC, and in 1995 it joined the ICRC. It has close ties with several churches in North America, Australia, New Zealand, and Southern Africa. Its missionary work in Sulawesi, Indonesia, resulted in the foundation of the Gereja Toraja Mamasa/ GTM (cf. Indonesia).

TM: **75,243** BM: **30,679** CM: **44,564** Congr: **107** OrdM: **179** Eld: **2,000** Deac: **1,600** EvgHome: **6** Mission: **8** Women Ord: **no** ChurchOrg: **13 classes (twice per year), 4 synods (annual), 1 gen synod (tri-annual)** Off/otherLang: **Dutch** DoctrB: **ApC, NicC, AthC, BelgC, CDort, HeidC** Frequency of the Lord's Supper: **4 times a year** Close relations with: **Free Reformed Church of N. America, Reformed Presb Churches of New Zealand, Gereformeerde Kerke in Suid Afrika, Gereja Toraja Mamasa (Indonesia)**, NatRel: **nc** RegRel: **nc** IntlRel: **ICRC (1995)** TheolSchool: **Theological University (Apeldoorn)** Periodicals: **De Wekker (gen/weekly), Doorgeven (mission/quarterly), Vrede over Israel (mission/quarterly), Echo (home mission/weekly), Mit de Levensbron (homiletics/ weekly), Adma Info (diaconate/quarterly)**

Address: Christelijke Gereformeerde Kerken in Nederland (CGKN), P.O. Box 334 Vijftien Morgen 1, NL-3900 AL Veenendaal, Netherlands, Tel: +31 8 52 91 76, Fax: +31 8 51 89 32

4. Covenant of Free Evangelical Congregations in the Netherlands (VEG) (6370)

The church was established in 1881 by a group of independent congregations which originated from the Afscheiding and were influenced by Methodism and the Revival Movement. Like the Christian Reformed Church (cf. no. 3) it objected to liberal theology and to state influence on the life of the church, but it did not seek to collaborate with this church because it rejected Reformed confessionalism. In 1993 ten congregations left the VEG. They became independent. The VEG maintains fraternal relations with evangelical congregations in several European countries and belongs to the IFFEC. Its seminary is affiliated with Faculty of Utrecht, and the church has officially agreed to collaborate with the NHK (cf. no. 1) and GKN (cf. no. 5).

TM: **7,000** BM: **2,500** CM: **7,000** Congr: **40** PStations: **3** OrdM: **45** Eld: **yes** Deac: **yes** EvgHome: **ne** Mission: **7** Women Ord: **yes** As Ministers: **1972/5** as Deac: **1935/na** as Elders: **1935/na** ChurchOrg: **congr, annual Assy** Off/otherLang: **Dutch** DoctrB: **no doctrinal creeds** Infant or believer's baptism: **both** Frequency of the Lord's Supper: **every second month** NatRel: **Ecumenical Council of the Netherlands** RegRel: **nc** IntlRel: **IFFEC (1948)** TheolSchool: **Seminary of the Covenant Free Evangelical Churches (Utrecht)** Periodicals: **Ons Orgaan (gen/monthly/4,700)**

Address: Bond van Vrije Evangelische Gemeenten in Nederland (VEG), President Kennedylaan 311, NL-6883 AK Velp, Netherlands, Tel: +31 26 364 8249, Fax: +31 26 364 5031

5. Reformed Churches in the Netherlands (GKN) (6360)

After the Afscheiding of 1834 some smaller schisms from the NHK followed during the 1840s. In 1841, for instance, Rev. L. G. C. Ledeboer (1808-1863) was suspended from the ministry in the church and established several independent congregations (cf. no. 6).

There was another major separation from the NHK in 1886 in Amsterdam. Abraham Kuyper (1837-1920) initiated the Doleantie (from the Latin verb *dolere* = "to suffer"). Six years later the Doleantie congregations, together with the majority of the congregations of the Christian Reformed Church (cf. no. 3), formed the Gereformeerde Kerken in the Netherlands (GKN) in Amsterdam.

In 1896 the General Synod of the GKN at Middelburg adopted a mission statement. It regarded mission not as a responsibility of mission societies but as a task of the church itself. Another General Synod in Utrecht in 1905 rejected Abraham Kuyper's doctrine of presumptive regeneration (veronderstelde wedergeboorte).

In 1926 and 1944 the GKN suffered divisions. In 1926 the General Synod of Assen expelled Dr. J. G. Geelkerken (1879-1960), who no longer accepted the literal interpretation of Genesis 2 and 3. The small group of ministers and congregations which left the church with him united in 1946 with the NHK. In 1944 a larger separation took place under the leadership of Professor K. Schilder which led to the foundation of the Reformed Churches — Liberated (cf. no. 8). After World

War II both ecumenism and theological liberalism became influential in the GKN. Orthodox members of the church protested against these trends. They objected, in particular, to the decision of the 1967 General Synod to regard the classical Reformed confessions of faith in the Netherlands as primarily historical documents. They established their own organizations within the GKN — Schrift en Getuigenis (Scripture and Witness) and Confessioneel Gereformeerd Beraad (Confessional Reformed Consultation).

In 1973 the first joint synod with the NHK was held. Later the project of union was transformed into a tripartite effort *Samen op weg* (Together on the Way). The Evangelical-Lutheran Church in the Kingdom of the Netherlands also joined the union project .

The ministers of the GKN are trained in the Theological University of Kampen (1854) and the theological faculty of the Free University at Amsterdam, founded in 1880 by Abraham Kuyper.

The GKN includes two classes outside the Netherlands — the German presbyteries of East Friesland and Bentheim of the Evangelical Old Reformed church in Niedersachsen. It also has close ties with daughter churches in Java, Sumba, and some other Indonesian islands as well as with immigrant churches, especially some Moluccan churches (cf. nos.12-14). The GKN is a member of REC, WARC (1966), and the WCC (1971).

TM: **727,483** BM: **299,251** CM: **428,232** Congr: **850** PStations: **ne** OrdM: **1249** Eld: **8,000** Deac: **3,000** EvgHome: **none** Mission: **30/35** Women Ord: **yes** As Ministers: **1968/70/52 out of 1,188** as Deac: **1968/many** as Elders: **1968/many** ChurchOrg: **synod, particular synods (= regional synods), classes, and church councils(local)** Off/otherLang: **Dutch and Frisian (only in Friesland)** DoctrB: **ApC, NicC, AthC, BelgC, CDort, HeidC** Infant or believer's baptism: **both** Frequency of the Lord's Supper: **weekly to 6 times a year** Close relations with: **Netherlands Reformed Church, Ev.-Luth Church in the Kingdom of the Netherlands** NatRel: **CCN (1968), Contactorgaan voor de Gereformeerde Gezindte (1963)** RegRel: **CEC (1959)** IntlRel: **WARC (1966), WCC (1971), REC (1946), CWM (1978), Leuenberg Concord (1973)** TheolSchool: **Theological Faculty of the Free University of Amsterdam, Theological University of Kampen** Service infrastructure: **none** Periodicals: **Kerkinformatie (gen/monthly/24,000), Vandaar (mission/monthly/125,000), Uniting (gen/quarterly), Ouderlingenblad (gen/monthly/19,000), Central Weekblad (gen/weekly/15,000), Cred. (gen-confessional/monthly/4,000)**

Address: Gereformeerde Kerken in Nederland (GKN), Postbus 202 Burg de Beaufortweg 18, NL-3830 AE Leusden, Netherlands, Tel: +31 33 496-0360, Fax: +31 33 494-8707, E-mail: oecumene@gkn.nl

6. Reformed Congregations (GG) (6375)

Several congr which in 1834 or thereafter (Pastor L. G. C. Ledeboer, 1841) separated from the NHK joined neither the CGKN (cf. no. 3) nor the GKN (cf. no. 5) but remained independent and were called the "Ledeboeriaanse gemeenten (Ledeboer Congregations)" or "Reformed Congregations under the Cross." In 1907 Rev. G. H. Kersten (1892-1948) succeeded in uniting 35 of these independent congregations into the GG. From the beginning this church had a close connection with the Netherlands Reformed Congregations in the USA (cf. United States no. 27). It also has links with a congregation in St. Catharines, Ontario, Canada.

The GG emphasizes the need for experiencing conversion and heartfelt piety (cf. nos. 7, 9, 11). Its spirituality is less rational and activist than that of the GKN (cf. no. 5) and parts of the CGKN (cf. no. 3). The GG has its own theological seminary in Rotterdam. In 1953 a teacher of this seminary caused a split in the church (cf. no. 9). The GG did missionary work in Indonesia, Nigeria, and South Africa. It was involved in the establishment of the Gereja Jemaat Protestan di Irian Jaya (GJPI; cf. Indonesia no. 5) and of the Nigeria Reformed Church among the Izi (cf. Nigeria no. 7).

TM: **95,973** BM: **44,723** Congr: **157** OrdM: **53** Eld: **nc** Deac: **nc** EvgHome: **nc** Mission: **5** Women Ord: **no** ChurchOrg: **congr, 4 particular synods, 12 classes** Off/otherLang: **Dutch** DoctrB: **ApC, NicC, AthC, HeidC, CDort, BelgC** Infant or believer's baptism: **both** Frequency of the Lord's Supper: **4 times a year** Close relations with: **Netherlands Reformed Congregations in North America** NatRel: **nc** RegRel: **nc** IntlRel: **nc** TheolSchool: **Theologische School der Gereformeerde Gemeenten (Rotterdam, NL)** Service infrastructure: **nursing home** Periodicals: **De Sahmbinder (weekly/14,500)**

Address: Gereformeerde Gemeenten (GG), Houttuinlaan 7, NL-3447 GM Woerden, Netherlands, Tel: +31 348 420-776, Fax: +31 348 424-192

7. Old Reformed Congregations in the Netherlands (OGG) (6367)

In 1907 a few independent congregations accepted the invitation of Pastor G. H. Kersten to consider a union of (old) Reformed congregations, but finally they decided to stay apart. They established their own even more conservative church — the OGG. Pastor L. Boone (1860-1935) was its leader. He disagreed with Pastor Kersten because the latter was willing to adopt the name "Reformed" instead of "Old Reformed," to replace the psalmbook of Petrus Dathenus (1531-1588) with that of 1773, and to change the dress code of ministers.

After World War II some congregations separated from the OGG but others joined it. In 1948 the church united with the Federation of Old Reformed Congregations (Federatie van Oud Gereformeerde Gemeenten), a small group of congregations founded in 1912. In 1952 some congregations of the CGKN (cf. no. 3) also joined the church.

The church has no theological seminary. It has one congregation in Salford, Canada. In missions it collaborates with the Free Presbyterian Church of Scotland.

TM: **nc** Congr: **65** OrdM: **5** Eld: **ne** Deac: **nc** EvgHome: **ne** Mission: **ne** Women Ord: **no** ChurchOrg: **synod, divided into classis Oost and classis West** Off/otherLang: **Dutch, in Salford (Canada), English** DoctrB: **HeidC, CDort, Dutch Confession, Staten Bijbel (1618-1619)** Frequency of the Lord's Supper: **annually** NatRel: **nc** RegRel: **nc** IntlRel: **nc** TheolSchool: **none** Service infrastructure: **rest homes** Periodicals: **Kerkblad der Oud Ger. Gemeenten (gen/monthly)**

Address: Oud Gereformeerde Gemeenten in Nederland, Postbus 137, 3771 DE 't Achterdorp 17, 3772 BZ, NL-3770 AC Barneveld, Netherlands, Tel: +31 34 242-0012, Fax: +31 34 241-6440

8. Reformed Churches (Liberated) (GK[v]) (6371)

In the midst of World War II a major schism took place in the GKN (cf. no. 5). The split is known as the Vrijmaking (Liberation). It was the outcome of ongoing theological conflicts on common grace, the covenant of grace, presumptive regeneration (Abraham Kuyper), etc., which the Synod of the GKN sought to overcome by the adoption of doctrinal statements.

Professor K. Schilder (1890-1952) protested against binding decisions on these issues. The Synod excluded him from the ministry. This decision led to an exodus of many congregations which wanted to be "liberated from synodal power structures." In 1944 they established the GK(v) at the Hague, emphasizing their loyalty to Art. 31 of the church order which was drawn up by the Synod of Dordrecht (1618/1619).

In 1965 the GK(v) experienced its own schism (cf. no. 10). The church runs a university in Kampen. With the establishment of this university, Kampen has two universities (cf. no. 5) which do not cooperate. It also has its own political party, schools, and the like. The church is a member of the ICRC (1982) and cooperates with other members of this organization. It is engaged in missionary work in Indonesia (especially in Sumba, Kalimantan, and Irian Jaya), South Africa, Brazil, DR Congo, and Ukraine.

TM: **122,749** BM: **122,749** CM: **73,865** Congr: **280** OrdM: **nc** Eld: **na** Deac: **na** EvgHome: **4** Mission: **18** Women Ord: **no** ChurchOrg: **communities, classes, provincial synods, gen synod (every 3 years)** Off/otherLang: **Dutch** DoctrB: **HeidC, CDort, Nederlandse Geloofsbelijdenis** Infant or believer's baptism: **both** Frequency of the Lord's Supper: **4 times a year** Close relations with: **Christian Reformed Churches in the Netherlands** NatRel: **nc** RegRel: **nc** IntlRel: **ICRC** TheolSchool: **Theologische Universiteit Broederweg (Kampen)** Periodicals: **Nederlands Dagblad (daily/24,000), De Reformatie (weekly/5,000), Tut Aan de Einden der Aande (mission/monthly/24,000), Lux Mundi (quarterly/550)**

Address: Gereformeerde Kerken (Vrijgemaakt), Postbus 138, NL-8000 AC Zwolle, Netherlands, Tel: +31 38 427-0470, Fax: +31 38 427-0471, E-mail: bbk@epsilon.nl.

9. Reformed Congregations in the Netherlands (GGN) (6368)

In 1953 Dr. C. Steenblok was dismissed as a teacher at the theological seminary of the GG (cf. no. 6) in Rotterdam because he taught that God does not offer grace to all sinners but only to those persons who are elected and acknowledge their sins. When he left the church he was joined by three ministers. They established a small new church — the GGN. In 1980 a few congregations left the church (cf. no. 11). The GGN cooperates with the Reformed Congregations in North America and with a congregation in Pretoria. In missions it relates to the Free Presbyterian Church of Scotland.

TM: **19,828** BM: **10,505** CM: **9,323** Congr: **53** PStations: **3** OrdM: **2** Eld: **100** Deac: **130** EvgHome: **ne** Mission: **ne** Women Ord: **no** As Ministers: **no** ChurchOrg: **3 classes, 1 synod** Off/otherLang: **Dutch** DoctrB: **ApC, NicC, AthC, BelgC, CDort, HeidC** Infant or believer's baptism: **both** Frequency of the

Lord's Supper: **1-4 times per year** Close relations with: **Ref Congr in N. America, Free Presbyterian Church of Scotland (cf. United Kingdom no. 6)** NatRel: **nc** RegRel: **nc** IntlRel: **nc** TheolSchool: **nc** Service infrastructure: **1 rest home, 1 social service organization, 20 primary schools, 1 home for mentally handicapped children** Periodicals: **De Wacher Sions (gen/weekly/ 6,000)**

Address: Gereformeerden Gemeenten in Nederland (GGN), 's-Gravenweg 240, NL-2903 LW Capelle aaw den Yssel, Netherlands, Tel: +31 10 450-0721

10. Netherlands Reformed Churches (NGK) (6365)

In the 1960s serious discord within the Reformed Churches (Liberated) (cf. no. 8) led to the foundation of the Reformed Church (Liberated, Unconnected). In 1969 this church adopted its present name (Netherlands Reformed Churches). Various factors played a role. The believers who formed the new church were critical of the tendency within the GK(v) to consider itself the only true church in the Netherlands. They also disagreed with the GK(v) on its strong emphasis on the classical confessions of faith and on the need for distinct political parties and schools. The NGK does not provide its own theological training, though there is a theological seminary in Amersfoort, run by some ministers on a private basis, which is held in high esteem by the congregations. The official policy of the church is to send its students for training to the Theological University of the CGKN (cf. no. 3) in Apeldoorn. The NGK entertains close relations with the following denominations: Liberated Churches in East Sumba (Indonesia), Christian Reformed Church in North America, Eglises réformées évangéliques indépendantes (France), Reformed Churches in Australia, Reformed Church in Japan, Gereformeerde Kerk in Suid-Afrika, and Geformeerde Kerk in Suid-Africa (Sinode Middelande).

TM: **29,570** BM: **10,627** CM: **18,943** Congr: **94** OrdM: **72** Eld: **nc** Deac: **nc** EvgHome: **nc** Mission: **11** Women Ord: **Yes** As Ministers: **nc** as Deac: **1995** as Elders: **nc** ChurchOrg: **regional assemblies (all churches in region), national Assy (every three years)** Off/otherLang: **Dutch** DoctrB: **ApC, NicC, AthC, HeidC, BelgC, CDort, 3 Forms of Unity** Infant or believer's baptism: **infant** Frequency of the Lord's Supper: **every second month** Close relations with: **Christian Reformed Church in North America (CRCNA), EREI (France), Ref Churches of Australia, Reformed Church in Japan, Gereformeerde Kerkg in Suid-Afrika** (cf. South Africa no. 3) NatRel: **nc** RegRel: **nc** IntlRel: **nc** TheolSchool: **Theological University of the CGKN (Apeldoorn); in addition, a theological seminary run in Hellevoetsluis by the initiative of a few ministers** Periodicals: **Opbouw (opinion/every 2 weeks)**

Address: Nederlands Gereformeerde Kerken (NGK), Franklinstraat 46, NL-171 BM Badhoevedorp, Netherlands, Tel: +31 20 659-5464

11. Reformed Congregations in the Netherlands (Unconnected) (6356)

In 1980 the GGN (cf. no. 9) suffered a split. A small group of congregations separated from the GGN and established a church "buiten het verband" (= unconnected, i.e., outside the structure of the GGN). The secession was not primarily for doctrinal reasons but rather due to conflicts between a number of ministers. The controversy began with a complaint of an elder in the congregation of Gouda against Pastor A. van den Berg. Seven congregations now belong to this church.

TM: **3,000** BM: **950** CM: **2,050** Congr: **7** OrdM: **0** Eld: **12** Deac: **22** EvgHome: **0** Mission: **0** Women Ord: **no** ChurchOrg: **one classis** Off/otherLang: **Dutch** DoctrB: **ApC, NicC, AthC, HeidC, CDort, BelgC** Infant or believer's baptism: **infant** Frequency of the Lord's Supper: **4 times a year** NatRel: **none** RegRel: **none** IntlRel: **none** TheolSchool: **nc** Service infrastructure: **2 primary schools (500 pupils each)** Periodicals: **Kerkblad (gen/bi-weekly/nc)**

Address: Gereformeerden Gemeenten in Nederland (buiten verband), Johan den Haenstraat 26, NL-806 DK Gouda, Netherlands, Tel: +31 182 517-850

12. Moluccan Evangelical Church (GIM) (6374)

The Moluccans are the largest group of Reformed immigrants after World War II. Moluccans arrived in the Netherlands as a consequence of decolonization. They had supported the Dutch colonial regime in the hope of establishing an independent Moluccan Republic. In 1951 a first group of 12,500 Moluccans disembarked in Rotterdam. Today their number has reached some 40,000. Most of them continue to defend the idea of an independent Moluccan state, a proposal which is totally incompatible with the policies of both Indonesia and the Netherlands. Religiously, the Reformed Moluccans originate from the Moluccan Protestant Church, GPM (cf. Indonesia no. 36). While the church in Indonesia never suffered any secessions, the Moluccan community in the Netherlands experienced one split after another. Today there are no less than 18 Moluccan Reformed churches in the Netherlands. Fifteen consist only of one, two, or three congregations. In this survey only the three largest are presented.

The Malay-speaking Moluccan Prot community wanted to organize itself as a classis of the GPM in Indonesia. The church in Indonesia did not accept this request of the Moluccan community in the Netherlands. The Moluccan Prot community then decided to set up its own independent church.

The GIM is the largest Moluccan Church in the Netherlands. It has its own congregations, classes, and synods. It cooperates with both the NHK (cf. no. 1) and the GKN (cf. no. 5) and has also established a link with the VEG (cf. no. 4). The GIM applied for membership in the WCC. When the request was rejected, it became a member of the ICCC. In 1994 it reapplied to the WCC. At the same time it started conversations with the Community of Churches in Indonesia (PGI) and the GPM. The classis west of GIM opposed this policy of rapprochement; it regards it as a betrayal of the political ideal of an independent Moluccan state.

TM: **11,215** BM: **3,560** CM: **7,655** Congr: **65** PStations: **ne** OrdM: **35** Eld: **nc** Deac: **nc** EvgHome: **ne** Mission: **ne** Women Ord: **yes** As Ministers: **1978/7** as Deac: **1952/95** as Elders: **1978/30** ChurchOrg: **congr, presby, classes, synod** Off/otherLang: **Malayan. Dutch** DoctrB: **ApC** Infant or believer's baptism: **both** Frequency of the Lord's Supper: **twice a year** Close relations with: **Netherlands Reformed Church, Reformed Churches in the Netherlands** NatRel: **Commissie Contact Molukse en**

Nederlandse Kerken (1979), Raad van deputaten "Samenop Weg" (1995), SKIN (1997), Communion of Churches in Indonesia (1995) RegRel: **none** IntlRel: **ICCC (1954-1996)** TheolSchool: **nc** Service infrastructure: **"Muhabbat" Foundation (staff of 3)** Periodicals: **Madjalah (gen/quarterly/ 7,500)**

Address: Geredja Indjili Maluku, Standerdmolen 8-029, NL-995 AA Houten, Netherlands, Tel: +31 30 635-0416, Fax: +31 30 634-0441

13. Moluccan Protestant Church in Exile in the Netherlands (NGPMB) (6373)

In contrast to GIM (cf. no. 12) this church did not wish to establish a new Moluccan church in the Netherlands. It continues to regard itself as part of the GPM in Indonesia (cf. Indonesia no. 36). Its members consider themselves to be living in exile. Today the NGPMB is the second largest Moluccan group in the Netherlands. Like the GIM it cooperates officially with the NHK (cf. no. 1) and GKN (cf. no. 5).

TM: **2,383** BM: **689** CM: **1,694** Congr: **23** OrdM: **16** Eld: **35** Deac: **29** EvgHome: **ne** Mission: **ne** Women Ord: **yes** As Ministers: **1985/6** as Deac: **1955/15** as Elders: **1952/12** ChurchOrg: **congr, presby, classes, synod** Off/otherLang: **Malayan, Dutch** DoctrB: **ApC** Infant or believer's baptism: **both** Frequency of the Lord's Supper: **twice to four times a year** Close relations with: **Netherlands Reformed Church, Reformed Churches in the Netherlands** NatRel: **Commissie Contact Molukse en Nederlandse Kerken (1979), Raad van deputaten "Samenop Weg" (1995), Communion of Churches in Indonesia (1995)** RegRel: **none** IntlRel: **none** TheolSchool: **nc**

Address: Noodgemeente Geredja Protestan Maluku di Belanda, NL-841 BN Moordrecht, Netherlands, Tel: +31 182 374-391

14. Moluccan Protestant Church in Exile in the Netherlands (March 1953) (NGPMB '53) (6372)

The NGPMB '53 was established in 1975. The driving force was a group of people who did not originate from the Moluccans but from Irian Jaya, the former Dutch New Guinea. They did not feel at home in the Moluccan "other church" which was established in 1953 (cf. no.13). The NGPMB '53 is the third largest Moluccan Prot Church in the Netherlands. It has fewer relations with other churches, both in the Netherlands and in Indonesia, than the preceding two Moluccan churches (cf. nos. 12-13).

TM: **nc** Congr: **28** PStations: **ne** OrdM: **na** Eld: **nc** Deac: **na** EvgHome: **ne** Mission: **ne** Women Ord: **yes** As Ministers: **1975/2** as Deac: **na** as Elders: **na** ChurchOrg: **congr, presby, synod** Off/otherLang: **Malayan, Dutch** DoctrB: **ApC** Infant or believer's baptism: **both** Frequency of the Lord's Supper: **twice a year** Close relations with: **none** NatRel: **none** RegRel: **none** IntlRel: **none** TheolSchool: **nc**

Address: Noodgemeente Protestan Maluku di Belanda (NGPMB '53), van Herwynemplantsoen 250, NL-3431 VR Niemwegein, Netherlands, Tel: +31 30 604-5598, Fax: +31 30 604-5598, E-mail: none.

15. Indonesian Christian Church in the Netherlands (GKIN) (6376)

The GKIN is another ethnic minority church which has its roots in Indonesia. The church was established in 1985. It originated in Chinese-Indonesian circles. Today the church also includes members from other ethnic backgrounds in Indonesia and the Netherlands.

TM: **782** BM: **332** CM: **450** Congr: **8** PStations: **15** OrdM: **5** Eld: **26** Deac: **0** EvgHome: **0** Mission: **0** Women Ord: **yes** As Ministers: **nc/0** as Deac: **nc/0** as Elders: **1985/11** ChurchOrg: **national organiza-tion with 5 regions** Off/otherLang: **Dutch, Indonesian** DoctrB: **ApC** Frequency of the Lord's Supper: **4 times a year** Close relations with: **none except with other Indonesian organizations** NatRel: **Amstelveen-Buitenveldert Council of Churches (1989)** RegRel: **none** IntlRel: **none** TheolSchool: **none** Service infrastructure: **none** Periodicals: **Overdenkingen (daily Bible readings/nc) 6 times per year/1,000)**

Address: Gereja Kristen Indonesia Nederland, Borsenburg 28, NL-1181 NV Amstelveen, Nether-lands, Tel: +31 20 641-6571, Fax: +31 20 647-9888, E-mail: none

16. Korean Reformed Church in the Netherlands (KRC) (6357)

There are other ethnic minority churches in the Netherlands which have no con-nection with the colonial past of the country. Some of these churches (e.g., the Chinese and Vietnamese churches) are nondenominational, while others are clearly Reformed. An example is the KRC, which was founded in 1983 and brings together members of different Presb churches in Korea. It cooperates with the con-gregation of the NGK in Amstelveen (cf. no. 10), which offers its building for the worship services of the Koreans.

TM: **159** BM: **81** Congr: **1** PStations: **na** OrdM: **1** Eld: **2** Deac: **6** EvgHome: **na** Mission: **na** Women Ord: **nc** ChurchOrg: **Ref** Off/otherLang: **Korean, English** DoctrB: **ApC, NicC, BelgC, HeidC** Infant or believer's baptism: **both** Frequency of the Lord's Supper: **twice a year** Close relations with: **na** NatRel: **none** RegRel: **none** IntlRel: **none** TheolSchool: **training in Korea** Service infrastructure: **none** Periodicals: **Faith, Hope, Love (gen/quarterly), First 10 years of Korean Reformed Church: 1980-1990**

Address: Korean Reformed Church in the Netherlands, De Ruyschlaan 147, NL-1181 PE Amstel-veen, Netherlands, Tel: +31 20 409-0638, Fax: +31 20 409-0639

17. Church of the Urdu Congregation, Holland (CUCH) (6377)

The CUCH was established in 1985 in Rotterdam. Most of its members come from Pakistan. It cooperates with the GKN (cf. no. 5) and is now considering becoming part of the GKN.

TM: **nc** Congr:**1** OrdM: **1** Eld: **nc** Deac: **nc** EvgHome: **nc** Mission: **nc** Women Ord: **nc** Off/otherLang: **Dutch, Urdu** DoctrB: **nc** NatRel: **nc** RegRel: **nc** IntlRel: **nc** TheolSchool: **nc**

Address: The Church of Urdu Congregation, De Raephorstraat 41b, NL-VB Rotterdam, Netherlands, Tel: +31 10 466-2831

NETHERLANDS ANTILLES
(Curaçao, Aruba, Bonaire, St. Maarten, Saba, St. Eustatius)

Area in km^2	960
Population	(July 1996 est.) 208,968 mixed African 85%, Caribbean Indian, European
Religions in %	RCath 82%, Prot 2%, Jewish, Advent
Official/other languages	Dutch (official), Papiamento (a Spanish-Portuguese-Dutch-English dialect) predominates, English widely spoken, Spanish

CCC (Council of Churches of Curaçao)
WIC (West Indies Company)

The Netherlands Antilles consist of a total of six islands divided into two groups "sitting" on each side of the Caribbean Sea, over 1000 km apart from one another. Curaçao (444 km^2, 160,000 inhabitants), Bonaire (288 km^2, 11,300 inhabitants), and Aruba (190 km^2, 58,000 inhabitants) are situated just outside Venezuela. St. Maarten (288 km^2, with half of it belonging to France, 65,839 inhabitants); Saba (13 km^2, 1,180 inhabitants), and St. Eustatius (21 km^2, 1,844 inhabitants) are "hidden" in the north of the Lesser Antilles, east of the Virgin Islands.

Discovered in 1599 by Alfonso de Ojeda, Curaçao became Dutch in 1527, British in 1634, and Dutch again in 1816. In the 17th century other islands became Dutch: St. Maarten in 1631, Bonaire, Aruba, and St. Eustatius in 1636, and Saba in ca. 1640. The West Indian Company (WIC), established in 1635, closed down in 1791. In 1816, after the Napoleonic period, Dutch rule was restored on the islands. In 1948 the name Netherlands Antilles was introduced. Since 1954 the Netherlands Antilles are autonomous but remain in the framework of the kingdom of the Netherlands.

Christianity, as in most Central and South American countries, arrived with the conquistadors. RCath were the first to reach the region. The Nederlandse Hervormde Kerk (NHK) followed in 1635. Efforts to convert the Indians from Catholicism to the Reformed faith failed. The Synod of Dordrecht (1618-1619) had accepted only adult baptism of "heathen," and few Indian children were prepared to follow catechetical lessons. The labor force was enlarged by the importation of more and more African slaves. The WIC's economic interests needed to be satisfied. The NHK, being more a WIC chaplaincy than a regular denomination, had little freedom of initiative and demonstrated nearly no opposition to slavery. The Dutch were among the last in the Caribbean region to abolish slavery in 1863.

At the beginning of the 19th century, the NHK in Curaçao, Aruba, and Bonaire was transformed into the Protestant Church of Curaçao, Aruba, and Bonaire respectively. In 1968, responding to the new situation, these three churches adopted a new church order by which they became the Protestant Church of the

398

Netherlands Antilles. The development in St. Maarten, Saba, and St. Eustatius was different. The NHK disappeared on these islands because most people did not speak Dutch any longer but only English. Presb tried, without success, to take over the heritage of the NHK. Today Protestantism is represented by the Meth, especially in St. Maarten and St. Eustatius, and the Angl, especially in Saba. Reformed people attend their services.

1. United Protestant Church of Netherlands Antilles (3360)

The church consists of the three Prot churches of Curaçao, Aruba, and Bonaire.

a. United Protestant Church of Curaçao (VPG)

The denomination was created by Dutch King William I in 1825 as a union between Reformed and Luth. It is basically a Dutch-speaking church, but now it also uses English and Papiamento — a mixture of Portuguese, Dutch, Spanish, and English. It has received leaders and members from both traditions, but it is predominantly Reformed. It has always been the major Prot church.

In 1931 several members, originating from the Reformed Churches in the Netherlands (GKN), created their own denomination — the Reformed Church in Curaçao (GKC). Some 10 ministers, sent by the mother church, served consecutively on Curaçao. In addition, five chaplains ministered among the merchant sailors. With its periodical *Gids* the GKC established a valuable link over the years with dispersed GKN members throughout the world. In 1984 the VPG and the GKC merged. Through this association the church has become more ecumenical and open to society. Ministers from both churches now serve the community. The more frequent use of Papamiento in worship and Bible readings is the expression of a process of growing contextualization.

In 1937 the Ebenezer Church affiliated with the VPC, and it was later integrated into it. This church originates from the ministry of Obed Anthony, a Meth lay preacher from Dominica, and served through the years particularly with English-speaking migrants from other Caribbean countries.

TM: **3,200** BM: **3,000** CM: **1,800** Congr: **3** PStations: **1** OrdM: **2** Eld: **12** Deac: **1** EvgHome: **ne** Mission: **ne** Women Ord: **yes** As Ministers: **1995/1** as Deac: **7** as Elders: **12** no ChurchOrg: **Reformed (3 local boards, central board)** Off/otherLang: **Dutch, English, Papiamento** DoctrB: **same as in use in the Reformed Church in the Netherlands and in the Netherlands Reformed Church** Infant or believer's baptism: **both** Frequency of the Lord's Supper: **monthly** Close relations with: **Moravian Church, Meth Church, Reformed Church in the Netherlands, Netherlands Reformed Church** NatRel: **CCC (1962)** RegRel: **CCC (1973), CANACOM (1997)** IntlRel: **WCC** TheolSchool: **training in the Netherlands** Service infrastructure: **2 youth centers (in Tamaryn and "Oleander"), Prot schools** Periodicals: **Gids tot Eenheid (newspaper/monthly/1,500)**

Address: Verenigde Protestantse Gemeente van Curaçao, Fortkerk, Willemstad Curaçao, Netherlands Antilles, Tel: +599 9 461-1139, Fax: +599 9 465-7481

b. Protestant Church in Aruba

Though the Dutch conquered Aruba in 1636, they settled there much later. In the 18th century no regular church life developed. In 1816 the total population of Aruba was 1732 persons, 564 Indians included. Among them were 279 Reformed. In 1822 the Protestant Church of Aruba was established. In 1825 Luth and Reformed united in this church. Usually Reformed ministers from Curaçao visited Aruba a few times every year. In 1858 the first full-time minister started his service on the island. At that time the United Church of Curaçao regarded the church in Aruba as independent. Sermons were also preached in Papiamento. As the church grew, a second minister was appointed in 1947, and in 1969 a third followed. In the years from 1949 to 1953 members of the GKN tried to establish a Reformed church but finally abandoned the project. In 1968 the three congr in Aruba had 1,268 members.

Address: Protestant Church in Aruba, Bilderdijkstraat 7, Oranjestad Aruba, Netherlands Antilles,
Tel: +297 8 21961 and 21435

c. Protestant Church in Bonaire

The historical data about early religious activities are scarce. In 1816, 64 Dutch Reformed and 27 Luth were reported to live on the island. The first worship service took place in 1843, the first church was built in 1847, and the first minister was ordained in 1860. Church records report that on Bonaire the discriminatory practice of the NHK, not to baptize slave children, was ignored. In the absence of resident pastors lay people read sermons approved by the NHK. In 1934 a second church was built. In 1968 there were 215 members in two congr. Church services are held not only in Dutch but also in English and Papiamento.

Address: Protestant Church in Bonaire, Kaya Hulanda 21, Kralendijk Bonaire, Netherlands Antilles,
Tel: +599 7 8086

2. Reformed Church in the Netherlands (Liberated) in Curaçao (GKNVC) (3361)

The existence of this church is closely linked to developments in the Netherlands. In 1944 a split occurred in the Reformed Churches in the Netherlands, resulting in the foundation of the Reformed Church in the Netherlands (no. 5). Immigrants to Curaçao, originating from this new denomination, created their own congregation called GKNVC in 1947. The congregation consisted entirely of Dutch people. The church was committed, however, to preaching the Gospel to the inhabitants of the island and to gathering as a church. Efforts were made in the 1960s to reach those outside. But after 20 years the mission work was still closely related to the main immigrant community. Immigrants wanted classical Dutch worship services, while most of the 16 missionaries, who worked for the GKNVC, were seeking to contextualize the services to Curaçaon needs. Records show that progress was made in the 1980s, with over one-third of the members being Antilleans. But the GKNVC has no autochthonous minister or preacher yet. Its challenge resides in trying to find a balance between two mission motives: the preservation/extension of the classical Reformed church, on one side, and the evangelization/indigenization of the Gospel among the Antilleans, on the other side.

TM: **135** BM: **67** CM: **68** Congr: **1** PStations: **2** OrdM: **2** Eld: **3** Deac: **1** EvgHome: **ne** Mission: **ne** Women Ord: **no** ChurchOrg: **nc** Off/otherLang: **Dutch, Papiamento** DoctrB: **same as Reformed Church (Liberated) in the Netherlands** Infant or believer's baptism: **both** Frequency of the Lord's Supper: **6 times a year** Close relations with: **none** NatRel: **none** RegRel: **Reformed Faith Christian Church in Venezuela (no. 3)** IntlRel: **Reformed Churches in the Netherlands (Liberated)** TheolSchool: **Theological University of Kampen (NL)** Service infrastructure: **Fundashon Nos Prohimo (development organization)** Periodicals: **Kuentanan for di Beibel**

Address: Iglesia Reforma, Arowakenweg 28, Willemstad Curaçao, Netherlands Antilles, Tel: +599 9 737-3152, Fax: +599 9 737-8508

NEW CALEDONIA

Area in km²	19,103
Population	(July 1996 est.) 187,784 Melanesian (Kanak) 42.5%, European 37.1%, Wallisian 8.4%, Polynesian 3.8%, Indonesian 3.6%, Vietnamese 1.6%, other 3%
Religions in %	RCath 67%, Prot 25% (Ref, Advent, Pent), Other 8%
Official/other languages	French/37 Melanesian-Polynesian dialects

SMP (Société des Missions de Paris — Paris Mission Society)
LMS (London Missionary Society)

Discovered in 1774 by James Colnett, a midshipman of Captain Cook, New Caledonia — also nicknamed "le caillou" (the stone) — is located some 2,000 km east of Australia. It comprises the main island and the Loyalty Islands (Ouvéa, Lifou, and Maré). It was first settled by the British, then in 1853 by the French, who also used the islands for the banning of their convicts. Nickel and cobalt mines soon attracted settlers and called for a labor force from abroad. In 1996 nickel comprised 90% of the country's exports; New Caledonia is presently the second largest cobalt producer in the world. The development of agriculture in the early 1890s by settlers coming from France created serious land disputes. Land is an essential part of Melanesian culture and self-understanding. As early as 1878 the indigenous Kanak people revolted against the French occupiers. First steps toward autonomy were made after World War II. Since 1956 New Caledonia has been a French Overseas Department (District). In the 1980s political life was marked by serious and frequent bloodshed.

New parties like the FLNKS (Front de libération national kanak et socialiste) fought for independence. The "Accords of Matignon," signed in 1988, foresaw a number of steps, including a referendum on "self-determination" to settle the political future of the "caillou."

The first Christian missionaries arrived in New Caledonia in 1840. They were Polynesian Prot catechists. Twelve years later the first European missionaries arrived; they were sent by the LMS. RCath presence dates back to 1851 — two years before France took possession of the islands — when a mission was created on the Pines Island. The SMP took over in 1897 by sending the missionary Delord to the island of Maré. He was soon to be followed by the pastor and ethnologist Maurice Leenhard, who settled on the eastern coast of the main island.

1. Evangelical Church in New Caledonia and Loyalty Islands (EENCIL) (5070)

The EENCIL is a direct fruit of the LMS and the SMP; it became independent in 1962. Since 1979 the church has supported the Kanak people, their rights and their wish for independence. All of its pastors are Kanak except for two European pastors sent by CEVAA: one of them teaches at the church's own Pastoral School of Béthanie (on the island of Lifou), while the other serves the congregation of the "Vieux Temple," the only multi-ethnic parish of the EENCIL.

TM: **30,000** Congr: **72** PStations: **105** OrdM: **65** Eld: **nc** Deac: **100** EvgHome: **nc** Mission: **nc** Women Ord: **yes** As Ministers: **1992/2** as Deac: **1994/4** as Elders: **nc** ChurchOrg: **consistory — regional synod — gen synod** Off/otherLang: **French and 32 dialects** DoctrB: **ApC, NicC, HeidC, HelvC** Infant or believer's baptism: **both** Frequency of the Lord's Supper: **monthly** Close relations with: **KEM (1971), Free Evangelical Church** NatRel: **Fédération Protestante de France (1862), DEFAP (formerly 'Société des Missions év. de Paris') (1862), Ecumenical Committee with the RCath Church (1962), Reconciliation Committee with the Free Evangelical Church (1992)** RegRel: **PCC (1966)** IntlRel: **WCC (1962), CEVAA (1971), WARC (1992)** TheolSchool: **Ecole pastoral Béthanie**

Address: Eglise évangélique en Nouvelle Calédonie et aux Iles Loyauté (EENCIL), Boîte Postale 277
8, rue Fernande Leriche, Noumea 98845, New Caledonia, Tel: +687 283-166, Fax: +687
273-898

2. Free Evangelical Church (5071)

The Evangelical Free Church split from the EENCIL in 1957. It was created by a former missionary of the SMP, Raymond Charlemagne, who had been deeply involved in the teaching and the moral instruction of the Kanak people. The SMP requested him to return to France. But numerous teachers supported him and asked him to stay. This incident created a split within the Prot population and provoked the foundation of the Evangelical Free Church. Since 1992 the church has launched a reconciliation process with the EENCIL.

TM: **2,000** BM: **200** CM: **1,200** Congr: **74** PStations: OrdM: **25** Eld: **70** Deac: **60** EvgHome: **6** Mission: **0** Women Ord: **no** ChurchOrg: **"mini synods," synod** Off/otherLang: **French** DoctrB: **ApC, NicC** Infant or believer's baptism: **believer** Frequency of the Lord's Supper: **twice monthly** Close relations with: **EENCIL, Evangelical Free Church of Vanuatu (1958)** NatRel: **Union of Free Churches in France (1993), Reconciliation Committee with the EENCIL (1992), Ecumenical Committee of New Caledonia (1996)** RegRel: **nc** IntlRel: TheolSchool: **Institut de l'Eglise libre (IEL)**

Address: Eglise évangélique libre, B.P. 568, Carcopino 3, Nouméa 98845, New Caledonia, Tel: +687 35 40 83

NEW ZEALAND — *See* AOTEAROA/NEW ZEALAND

NICARAGUA

Area in km²	129,494
Population	(July 1996 est.) 4,272,352 mestizo (mixed Amerindian and white) 69%, white 17%, black 9%, Indian 5%
Religions in %	RCath 95%, Prot 5%
Official/other languages	Spanish

The evangelization of Nicaragua by the Catholic Church accompanied the conquest in 1523, at first by force, later by indoctrination, especially by the Franciscans. The diocese of Nicaragua included the province of Costa Rica during the colonial period.

Pirates and corsairs from Prot lands, especially England, such as Drake, Hawkins, and Morgan, made contacts with the inhabitants of some Caribbean islands and the coastal areas of Central America, which were used as bases for provisions and refuge. By 1630 Puritans conquered two islands and established Cape Gracias a Dios on the Nicaraguan coast. After the conquest of Jamaica by Cromwell's forces in 1655, such incursions of Prot were made easier.

The English presence was motivated primarily by economic reasons. However, chaplains accompanied the traders who established centers on the Misquito Coast and became allies with the Misquito Indians in their struggle against the Spanish. In 1678 England assumed the protectorate of the Misquito Indians, which was maintained until 1850. Permanent English populations were established by 1730 in Rio Negro, Bluefields, and Cape Gracias a Dios.

In 1705 Angl priests started catechizing some of the indigenous inhabitants. Nathan Price was sent by the Society for the Propagation of the Gospel to evangelize the Misquito people, and died among them in 1748. In 1815 an Angl cathedral

403

was built in Belize, in whose archives is registered the coronation of Federico, king of the Misquito Coast in Nicaragua. The diocese of Belize included the whole Caribbean coast, and eventually all of Central America.

From 1824 to 1838 Nicaragua became part of the Central American Federation, whose constitution guaranteed the RCath Church as the only religion "with the exclusion of the public exercise of any other." According to the "Concordato" signed by the government of Nicaragua and Rome in 1862, the Roman church maintained its official status until 1892, education conformed to its doctrine, and the Catholic religion supported by the state. However, with the advent of the Liberal government in 1893, the new constitution established the separation of church and state, the secularization of cemeteries and matrimony, and the spoliation of much of the church's income. With the fall of the liberal government, the separation of church and state continued, though the Conservative governments from 1912 to 1928 favored the Catholic Church, and the expelled monastic orders were permitted to return.

During the Somoza family regime, from 1936, salaries were paid to the Catholic priests, and other financial assistance was given. With parental consent, the RCath Church was allowed to teach religion at public schools. Only after 1969 did its difficulties with the state begin.

The tendency toward liberalization made room for the arrival of the Moravians from Germany beginning in 1849 and has continued to the present. Responsibility for the mission changed to the North American Moravian branch during World War I. Besides the Moravians representatives of the Bible Societies campaigned in the country, e.g., Francisco Penzotti (1892, 1894). Other groups followed: the Central American Mission of C. Scofield in 1900, and several Pent missionaries from the Assemblies of God.

Christian Reformed Church of Nicaragua (3335)

The destructive earthquake of 1972 that devastated Managua, the capital city, and killed 10,000 persons, leaving 300,000 homeless, prompted immediate assistance from the Christian Reformed world diaconate agency from North America. This included nurses, community development, medical assistance, builders, literature, and literacy aid. Soon spiritual guidance was provided by two Mexican evangelists from the Christian Reformed Church of Mexico City. The first regular missionary was sent in 1975. Few missionaries have served there, and most for only brief periods, because of the unstable political situation. At present one missionary cooperates with the national church. Some of the areas where church groups are present include: Managua, Tipitapa, Muy Muy, Chinandega, El Tamarindo, and Nagarote.

TM: **200** BM: **50** CM: **150** Congr: **8** OrdM: **3** Eld: **6** Deac: **11** EvgHome: **nc** Mission: **nc** Women Ord: **yes** As Ministers: **no** as Deac: **yes/11** as Elders: **no** ChurchOrg: **nc** Off/otherLang: **Spanish** DoctrB: **ApC, HeidC, BelgC, CDort, WestConf** Infant or believer's baptism: **both** Frequency of the Lord's Supper: **monthly to quarterly** Close relations with: **CRCNA (USA)** NatRel: **nc** RegRel: **nc** IntlRel: **nc** TheolSchool: **none**

Address: Iglesia Cristiana Reformada de Nicaragua, Apartado 3410 Km. 13 1/2 Carretera Sur, Apto 3410, Managua, Nicaragua

NIGER

Area in km²	1,266,700
Population	(July 1996 est.) 9,113,000 Hausa 56%, Djerma 22%, Fula 8.5%, Tuareg 8%, Beri Beri (Kanouri) 4.3%, Arab, Toubou, and Gourmantché 1.2%, about 4,000 French expatriates
Religions in %	Muslim 80%, remainder indigenous beliefs and Christians
Official/other languages	French/Hausa, Djerma

The presence of Christianity in the country owes to the RCath Church, the Bapt churches, and the SIM (Sudan Interior Mission, now Société Internationale Missionnaire). SIM work started in 1924 in the east of the country and moved later to its central region. The missionaries established various institutions — a home for lepers in Danja, a hospital in Galmi, and a school in Maradi. While RCath and Bapt worked primarily in the west, SIM efforts concentrated on the east and the center. In recent years the three churches have tended to spread over the whole country. For almost four decades the evangelical communities which had been established were part of the Evangelical Church in West Africa in Nigeria (cf. Nigeria no. 9).

1. Evangelical Church of the Republic of Niger (EERN) (1320)

In 1961 the Evangelical Church of the Republic of Niger (EERN) was constituted and officially recognized by the national authorities. Due to the considerable autonomy of the local churches unity was difficult to establish. Some congregations founded by the SIM, e.g., the International Evangelical Church and the Gourmantché Church, both in Niamey, remain independent. In 1991 a split occurred in the church. A dispute arose over the admission of church members moving from one place to another and asking for recognition as members of another community. It led eventually to the formation of two new churches (cf. no. 2 and no. 3).

TM: **3,000** BM: **1,800** Congr: **31** PStations: **59** OrdM: **17** Eld: **155** Deac: **nc** EvgHome: **83** Mission: **ne** Women Ord: **yes** As Ministers: **no** as Deac: **yes** as Elders: **yes** ChurchOrg: **in regional districts with a central office** Off/otherLang: **French** DoctrB: **ApC** Infant or believer's baptism: **believer** Frequency of the Lord's Supper: **first Sunday of the month** Periodicals: **Matashi (youth/quarterly/300)** Close relations with: **Société Internationale Missionnaire (SIM), Service des Relations islamo-chrétiennes en Afrique (SRICA)** NatRel: **nc** RegRel: **nc** IntlRel: **WARC (1994)** TheolSchool: **Faculté de Theologie (Bangui)**

Address: Ekklisiyar Bishara Ta Kasar Nige, B.P. 250, Maradi, Niger, Tel.: +227 410 454, Fax: +227 510 216

2. Union of Evangelical Protestant Churches of Niger (1321)

The existence of this church owes to a split from the EERN in 1991 (cf. no. 1).

Address: Union des églises évangéliques protestantes (UEEPN), B.P. 2360, Niamey, Niger

3. Evangelical Church Salama of Niger (1322)

The church also split from the EERN; it comprises several congr in and also beyond the capital, Niamey.

Address: Eglise évangélique Salama du Niger (EENS), B.P. 12644, Niamey, Niger

NIGERIA

Area in km²	923,768
Population	(July 1996 est.) 103,912,489 Hausa and Fulani, Yoruba, and Ibos together make up 65% of population, many small tribes
Religions in %	Muslim 50%, Christian 40% (Prot 26.3%, RCath 12.1%, other 1.6%), indigenous beliefs 10%
Official/other languages	English/Hausa, Yoruba, Ibo, Fulani, many other dialects

CAN (Christian Association of Nigeria)
CCN (Christian Council of Nigeria)
CRUDAN (Christian Rural Development Association of Nigeria)
RECON (Reformed Ecumenical Council of Nigeria)
TEKAN (Fellowship of Christian Churches in Nigeria)

Nigeria is the country with the largest population on the African continent. The official administrative language is English, but more than 500 Nigerian languages are spoken by the various tribes. The main ethnic groups are the Hausa, Yoruba, Igbo, Efik, Annang, Tiv, Kanuri, Ijaw, Beni, and Fulani.

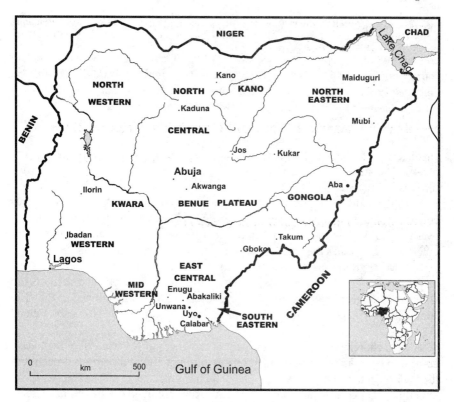

Nigeria

After initial contacts with Great Britain in 1849, Lagos became a colony of the British Crown in 1861. In 1924 the northern and southern protectorates established by the British in 1900 were united to form Nigeria. Nigeria became a confederation in 1954, and it acquired independence in 1960. It was constituted as a republic in 1963. In 1966 a military government took over. With the exception of the period from 1979 to 1983 Nigeria was ruled by a succession of military governments. From 1967 to 1970 the country was shaken by a civil war between the eastern region which, under the name of Biafra, had declared independence and the army of the central government. In 1992 the capital was moved from Lagos to Abuja in the center of the country.

A large percentage of the population, especially in the North, is Muslim. Historically Christianity is mainly represented in the South, though it is also spreading among the adherents of African religions in the North. Islam penetrated into Nigeria before Christianity. From the 9th century onward the North was gradually Islamicized, and in the 14th century Islam became the official religion in the North. Though Portuguese missionaries had reached the country already in the 15th century, the expansion of Christianity began only with the colonial period in

407

the 19th century. The first RCath order to reach Nigeria was the French "Société des missions africaines" (1861). Today the RCath Church is the largest Christian community in Nigeria (38 dioceses). The Anglican Church Mission Society started work in 1845 and gradually extended its activities toward the North. The Anglican Province of Nigeria was established in 1979. Meth had arrived in Nigeria even earlier (1842), followed by Presb (1846) and Bapt (1850).

In principle Nigeria is a secular state. The constitutions of 1963, 1979, and 1989 guarantee religious freedom. But the recent history of the country has been characterized by tensions between the two religions, often leading to violent outbreaks. The stability of Nigeria depends on constructive relations between Muslims and Christians.

Reformed Christianity came to Nigeria at different times and from various countries. There are today eleven Reformed Churches with a total membership of over five million. These churches have never deliberately separated from one another; they are rather the fruit of separate missionary enterprises.

Several groups can be distinguished. The earliest missionary work was done in the South. The Scottish Mission led to the foundation of the **Presbyterian Church of Nigeria (1)** (1846). The second church to be mentioned is the **Qua Iboe Church (2)**; it resulted from missionary efforts from Northern Ireland (1887).

Five churches are active in the central provinces of Nigeria. All of them have come into being in the 20th century, mostly through efforts of various branches of the Sudan United Mission (SUM). The churches involved are all — directly or indirectly — Dutch in background. The **Christian Reformed Church of Nigeria (3)** (1904), the **Church of Christ in the Sudan among the Tiv (4)** (1911), the **Evangelical Reformed Church of Christ (5)** (1916), the **Church of Christ in Nigeria (6)** (1920), and the most recent among the Reformed churches: the **Nigeria Reformed Church (7)** (1970).

In the predominantly Muslim northern part of the country there are four more churches which can be considered Reformed: the **Church of the Brethren in Nigeria (8)** (1922), the **Evangelical Church of West Africa (9),** the **Church of Christ in Nigeria (COCIN) (10),** and the **United Church of Christ in Nigeria (UCCN) (11).**

Recognizing the need for better coordination of their witness, several of these churches decided in 1991 to form an association of Reformed Churches in Nigeria **(Reformed Ecumenical Council of Nigeria — RECON).** Most of them also belong to interdenominational associations such as TEKAN (Fellowship of Christian Churches in Nigeria), CCN (Christian Council of Nigeria), and CAN (Christian Association of Nigeria).

1. Presbyterian Church of Nigeria (PCN) (1150)

"The PCN began with the enthusiasm of freed slaves in Jamaica." Following the abolition of the slave trade Jamaican missionaries were sent to Nigeria by the

Church of Scotland. Missionary work began in 1846 in Calabar (Duke Town and Creek Town). In the following year another group of missionaries arrived and opened a second station in Calabar (Old Town). From Calabar the church spread to Upper Cross River. In 1888 work was started in Unwana, in 1904 in Arochukwu, and so on. In the more recent past the church also began to be present in other parts of Nigeria. The church gained autonomy in 1954.

TM: **123,919** BM: **7,173** CM: **90,000** Congr: **645** PStations: **700** OrdM: **250** Eld: **2,756** Deac: **21** EvgHome: **80** Mission: **nc** Women Ord: **Yes** As Ministers: **1982/7** as Deac: **14** as Elders: **1954/nc** ChurchOrg: **Presbyterian**Off/otherLang: **Efik, Igbo, Tiv, English** DoctrB: **ApC, NicC, WestConf** Infant or believer's baptism: **both** Frequency of the Lord's Supper: **4 times per year** Close relations with: **Angl and Meth Church** NatRel: **CCN, CAN, RECON (1992), Bible Society of Nigeria** RegRel: **AACC** IntlRel: **WCC, WARC (1984), REC** TheolSchool: **Presb. Theol. College (Goldie)** Service infrastructure: **Marx Slessor Hospital, Ejah Memorial Hospital, Presb joint Hosp. Uburu, Leprosy Hospital Mbembe, 10 kindergartens, Lay Training Center Abia State**

Address: Presbyterian Church of Nigeria (PCN), P.O. Box 2635, 26-29 Ehere Road, Ogbor Hill, ABA, Abia State, Nigeria, Tel: +234 82 222-551, Fax: +234 82 226-554

2. Qua Iboe Church (PIC) (1158)

The church was founded in 1887 by the Irish missionary Samuel Alexander Bill. He came from Belfast in Northern Ireland. Bill named the mission after the Qua Iboe River in the southeastern area of Nigeria. In 1932 mission work was extended to northern Nigeria (among Igala and Bassa people). In 1944 the mission stations were constituted into a church. Today the church has spread throughout the country, but it continues to have its strongest roots in Akwa Ibo State, Imo State, and Benue State. In 1960 the church started establishing churches in the larger towns of Nigeria.

TM: **80,000** Congr: **1,000** PStations: **800** OrdM: **36** Eld: **nc** Deac: **nc** EvgHome: **nc** Mission: **nc** Women Ord: **no** ChurchOrg: **Presbyterian (congregational session, local session, 5 superintendencies, church conference)** Off/otherLang: **(mainly) Ibibo, Ibo, Igala, Igbirri Bassa, Mgem Wepo-Wane** DoctrB: **detailed doctrinal statement and constitution adopted in 1972** Close relations with: **Qua Iboe Fellowship (Belfast)** NatRel: **CCN** RegRel: **nc** IntlRel: **nc** TheolSchool: **Bible School College Abak, Church Training Centre (Ankba), Samuel Bill Theological College (SBTC, Abah, Akwa Ibon State)**

Address: Qua Iboe Church (PIC), P.O. Box IT 91, 168 Aka Road, Uyo Akwa, Ibon State, Nigeria

3. Christian Reformed Church of Nigeria (CRCN) (1155)

The Church came into existence in 1904 through missionary efforts of the Sudan United Mission (SUM) — British Branch. From 1920 to 1993 Johanna Veenstra, a Christian Reformed woman, worked for the church. Her witness had a deep impact on the life of the church. She was joined by other missionaries of the Christian Reformed Church, and in 1940 the Christian Reformed Church made an official commitment to this activity by joining the SUM as the CRC branch. Nigerian converts, such as Timon Mamma Irmiya, Filibus Ashu Angyu, Simon Atajiri, and others, made an important contribution to the evangelistic work. In 1951 the church was officially established. It is today rooted in Gongola State, and in parts of Benue State and Borno State, but it has also spread to the Federal Capital Territory.

TM: **160,000** CM: **65,000** Congr: **62** PStations: **245** OrdM: **65** Eld: **nc** Deac: **nc** EvgHome: **35** Mission: **nc** Women Ord: **no** As Ministers: **no** ChurchOrg: **Reformed (local councils or consistories, district church councils or classes, gen church council or synod)** Off/otherLang: **Hausa** DoctrB: **ApC, NicC, AthC, HeidC, HelvC, WestConf, BelgC, CDort,** Close Rel with: **CRCNA** (cf. United States no. 11) NatRel: **TEKAN, CAN, National Evangelical Missionary Association** RegRel: **nc** IntlRel: **REC** TheolSchool: **Johanna Veenstra Seminary (Wukari, Taraba State)**

Address: Christian Reformed Church of Nigeria (CRCN), P.O. Box 31, CRCN Secretariat, Takum Taraba State, Nigeria, Tel: +234 73 54689, Fax: +234 73 57719

4. Church of Christ in the Sudan among the Tiv (NKST) (1154)

The church is the fruit of missionary work undertaken by the Dutch Reformed Church in South Africa. Work began in 1911 among the Tiv people in Gongola and Benue States. The beginnings were slow — only 25 baptized Christians in 25 years. In 1960, due to the apartheid system, the South African missionaries were no longer tolerated in Nigeria and had to leave. In their place the SUM–Christian Reformed branch related to NKST and gave it strong support until about 1985. In 1957 the church was formally organized as an autonomous, self-supporting, and self-propagating church with four Nigerian pastors. A full translation of the Bible into Tiv was completed in 1964.

TM: **900,000** BM: **150,000** CM: **150,000** Congr: **215** PStations: **3,000** OrdM: **280** Eld: **33** Deac: **na** EvgHome: **750** Mission: **1** Women Ord: **no** ChurchOrg: **Reformed (local consistory, 23 classes, and gen synod)** Off/otherLang: **English, Tiv, Hausa, Fulani, Yukun** DoctrB: **ApC, NicC, HeidC, WestC, CDort** Infant or believer's baptism: **both** Frequency of the Lord's Supper: **4 times per year** Close relations with: **CRCNA, Gereformeerde Kerken (vrijgemaakt) (NL)** NatRel: **TEKAN (1955), CAN (1985), RECON** RegRel: **CCN** IntlRel: **REC (1960), WARC (1995), relations with ICRC** TheolSchool: **Reformed Theological College, Bible Institute** Service infrastructure: **9 hospitals, 150 health clinics and posts, 15 comprehensive health centers, orphanage, 450 primary schools, 1 liberal arts college, 1 Bible institute, 1 agricultural cooperative company** Periodicals: **NKST Newsletter (gen/bi-monthly/10,000), NKST Mkaanem (gen/bi-monthly/15,000)**

Address: Nongo u Kristu u ken Sudan hen Tiv (NKST), NKST Secretariat Office, PA Mkar, P.O., Gboko, Benue State, Nigeria, Tel: +234 44 70473, Fax: +234 44 70631

5. Evangelical Reformed Church of Christ (ERCC) (1152)

The origins of this church go back to 1916. It came into existence through missionary efforts of the Sudan United Mission (SUM) — South Africa Branch. The first missionary establishment was at Keana, Plateau State, but the church has expanded into Southern Zaria, Southern Plateau State, the eastern part of Kwara State, Niger State, and Akwa Ibom State. In the course of its history the name of the church has been modified; it was first called Church of Christ in Nigeria, later Church of Christ in Central Nigeria; the present name was recently adopted. In 1972/73 the South African missionaries were expelled. The church has grown considerably in the last two decades.

TM: **1,500,000** Congr: **267** OrdM: **152** Eld: **nc** Deac: **nc** EvgHome: **nc** Mission: **nc** Women Ord: **yes** As Ministers: **nc** as Deac: **nc** as Elders: **yes** ChurchOrg: **Reformed (congr, local council, district council, 11 regional councils, gen council)** Off/otherLang: **Hausa** DoctrB: **ApC, NicC, AthC, HeidC, HelvC, WestConf, CDort,** Close relations with: **Netherlands Reformed Church (NHK)** NatRel: **RECON, TEKAN, CAN, CCN, Nigerian Evangelical Fellowship** RegRel: **nc** IntlRel: **REC, WARC (1991), WCC** TheolSchool: **Obi Pastoral College, Ayu Theological Seminary**

Address: Evangelical Reformed Church of Christ (ERCC), P.O. Box 104, Akwanga, Plateau State, Nigeria

6. Reformed Church of Christ in Nigeria (RCCN) (1151)

The church has its roots in the Christian Reformed Church in Nigeria (cf. no. 3). In 1973 a split occurred and the Reformed Church of Christ was established. It consists mainly of people of the Kuteb tribe. The church is self-governing, self-supporting, and self-propagating. In 1993 the church decided to change the name from Church of Christ in Nigeria (COCIN) to Reformed Church of Christ in Nigeria (RCCN). Since 1973 the church has grown rapidly.

TM: **500,000** CM: **277,202** Congr: **50** PStations: **300** OrdM: **41** Eld: **500** Deac: **300** EvgHome: **208** Mission: **ne** Women Ord: **no** ChurchOrg: **Reformed (50 consistories, 10 classes, 1 synod)** Off/otherLang: **Kuteb, English, Hausa, Jukun, Tvu, Ichean** DoctrB: **ApC, NicC, AthC, CDort, HeidC, WestConf** Infant or believer's baptism: **both** Frequency of the Lord's Supper: **4 times per year** Close relations with: **Ch of Christ in the Sudan among the Tiv, Christian Reformed Church (USA), UCC (Nigeria), Ev. Ref. Church of Christ** NatRel: **RECON (1992), Christian Rural Development Association of Nigeria (CRUDAN) (1994), CAN (1991)** RegRel: **AACC (Probational 1994)** IntlRel: **REC (1996), WARC (1991)** TheolSchool: **Veenstra Bible College and Seminary (Wakari, Tabata State)** Service infrastructure: **4 clinics, Apura social service, RCCN rural development, school of health, RCCN vocational school and training** Periodicals: **Apura**

Address: Reformed Church of Christ in Nigeria (RCCN), P.O. Box 42, Lupwe Road n 2 ussa, Takum, Taraba State, Nigeria, Tel: +234 73 466-475

7. The Nigerian Reformed Church (NRC) (1157)

The Izi tribes, comprising a population of about half a million, live in the area north of Abakaliki in Anambra State. Though there are distinct subtribes they share a common language. The RCath Church and the Assemblies of God were the first Christian communities in the area. The Reformed presence is due to missionary efforts of the Netherlands Reformed Congregations (cf. Netherlands no. 6) operating under the Sudan United Mission (SUM). Work started in 1970. The first baptisms were celebrated in 1977. In April 1988 the missionary congregations were constituted as an independent church.

411

TM: **2,500** BM: **2,500** CM: **1,300** Congr: **5** PStations: **66** OrdM: **6** Eld: **25** Deac: **15** EvgHome: **25** Mission: **ne** Women Ord: **no** ChurchOrg: **one classis** Off/otherLang: **Izi, Igede, Ikwo, Ezaa, Igbo, English** DoctrB: **ApC, NicC, AthC, HeidC, BelgC, CDort,** Infant or believer's baptism: **both** Frequency of the Lord's Supper: **four times per year** Close relations with: **Netherlands Reformed Congregations (in Holland and North America)** NatRel: **CAN (1989), TEKAN (1991)** RegRel: **nc** IntlRel: **NKST, Qua Iboe Church** TheolSchool: **Bible School (Abakaliki), Nigeria Reformed Theological College (NRTC) (Izzilga, Ebonyi State)** Service infrastructure: **one health center, one orphanage, secondary school** Periodicals: **none**

Address: Nigerian Reformed Church in Iziland (NRC), P.O. Box 538, Abakaliki, Ebonyi State, Nigeria

8. Brethren Church of Nigeria (EYN) (1156)

Missionary work was started by missionaries from the Church of the Brethren in the USA who engaged in medical, educational, and evangelical activities among the Bura in and around Garkida in the north of Nigeria. The pioneer missionaries were Stover Kulp and Albert Hesler, who arrived in 1923. The first worship service was held on March 17, 1923, at Garkida. From 1930 evangelistic work was extended to the Marghi, one of the largest non-Muslim communities in northeastern Nigeria. Further mission stations opened in Bille (1927), Chibuk (1941), Gulak (1948), Uba (1955), and Mbororo (1957). In 1963 the Church of the Brethren Mission was joined by the Basel Mission from Switzerland. The two mission bodies worked cooperatively up to 1973, when the church became independent.

TM: **150,000** BM: **140,000** CM: **140,000** Congr: **339** PStations: **500** OrdM: **320** Eld: **ne** Deac: **nc** EvgHome: **400** Mission: **nc** Women Ord: **yes** As Ministers: **not yet** as Deac: **0** as Elders: **0** ChurchOrg: **Congregational (local committees, 13 districts, annual council)** Off/otherLang: **Hausa, English, tribal dialects** DoctrB: **ApC** Infant or believer's baptism: **believer** Frequency of the Lord's Supper: **quarterly with footwashing** Close relations with: **Basel Mission, Church of the Brethren** NatRel: **CCN, CAN** RegRel: **nc** IntlRel: **WCC** TheolSchool: **Kulp Bible College** Service infrastructure: **women's center, many kindergartens, five district Bible schools, one technical school, a secondary school**

Address: Ekklesiyar Yan'uwa a Nigeria (EYN), PMB 1, Mubi, Adamawa State, Nigeria

9. Evangelical Church of West Africa (ECWA) (1160)

The beginnings of this church owe to missionary work of the Sudan Interior Mission (SIM), which established a station in Kukar Gadu in the Borno province near the border with the Bauchi province in 1935. The SIM strategy was to start mission centers in each of the four non-Muslim ethnic communities of the area: the Kare-Kare, Bade, Ngamo, and Ngizim. Stations were opened in Gashua among the Bade (1938), in Gadaka among the Ngamo (1951), and in Garin Maje among the Ngamo and Ngizim (1952). In 1954 the SIM congregations were organized into the Association of Evangelical Churches of West Africa. The church grew

412

quickly in the following years. A church was opened in Maiduguri, the capital of North-East State. The church also spread to other parts of Borno state: Biu, Buni Yadi, Kukawa, and Hildi.

TM: **2,200,000** BM: **1,200,000** CM: **1,200,000** Congr: **3,500** PStations: **200** OrdM: **2,800** Eld: **nc** Deac: **0** EvgHome: **1,500** Mission: **35** Women Ord: **no** ChurchOrg: **Congregational (local councils, 18 districts with bi-annual meetings, gen council)** Off/otherLang: **English, Hausa, Yoruba, Igbo, Nupe, Igala** DoctrB: **ApC** Infant or believer's baptism: **believer** Frequency of the Lord's Supper: **monthly** Close relations with: **All Evangelical Churches** RegRel: **nc** IntlRel: **WEF** TheolSchool: **nc** Service infrastructure: **3 hospitals, 160 clinics, 1 pharmacy, 4 guest houses, rural development projects, 2 seminaries, 3 theological colleges, 15 Bible training schools, 65 nursery/primary schools, 7 secondary schools, 3 medical training institutions** Periodicals: **Today's Challenge (gen/ bi-monthly/nc)**

Address: Evangelical Church of West Africa (ECWA), P.O. Box 63, Jos, Plateau State, Nigeria, Tel: +234 73 54484 or 54482 or 54481

10. Church of Christ in Nigeria (COCIN or EKAN in Hausa) (1159)

The history of this church goes back to the vision of Charles Kumm (1874), a German, who initiated the Sudan United Mission, an effort to bring the Gospel to the black people of the interior of Africa (the term Sudan does not refer to today's Republic of Sudan but has the meaning "black people"). Missionary work was started by the British branch of the SUM in Borno province among the Kanuri, a Muslim tribe. In 1936 a leper station was established in Molai. Of special importance for later developments was the opening of a bookshop in Maiduguri. Special emphasis was laid on post-primary schools. Christian communities could be formed in the urban centers. In 1966 the Church of Christ in Nigeria was formed. While growth was rather slow in the first decades, the church has rapidly expanded since then.

TM: **1,000,000** CM: **400,000** Congr: **1,300** OrdM: **nc** Eld: **nc** Deac: **nc** EvgHome: **nc** Mission: **nc** Women Ord: **nc** ChurchOrg: **nc** Off/otherLang: **Hausa** DoctrB: **nc** NatRel: **TEKAN** RegRel: **nc** IntlRel: **nc** TheolSchool: **nc**

Address: Church of Christ in Nigeria (COCIN), PMB 2127, Jos, Plateau State, Nigeria

11. United Church of Christ in Nigeria (UCCN or HEKAN in Hausa) (1153)

In 1956 representatives of the Sudan Interior Mission (SIM), the Sudan United Mission (SUM; cf. no. 9), and the Church of the Brethren (cf. no. 8) agreed to build a church for the armed forces in Kaduna. The membership of this new community increased quickly. But a controversy arose between SIM and SUM over doctrinal issues, especially infant baptism, with the result that the SUM members of the Kaduna congr in 1962 decided to form a separate church. Under the leadership of Pastor Habila Aleiyedeno the church grew quickly in the area of Kaduna and more generally in the Hausa-speaking North.

TM: **65,855** BM: **35,650** CM: **31,650** Congr: **81** PStations: **12** OrdM: **18** Eld: **567** Deac: **567** EvgHome: **36** Women Ord: **no** ChurchOrg: **congr, regional council, district council, gen council** Off/ otherLang: **Hausa, English** DoctrB: **ApC** Infant or believer's baptism: **both** Frequency of the Lord's Supper: **monthly** Close relations with: **The Fellowship of the Church of Christ in Nigeria, RECON** NatRel: **CAN, TEKAN** RegRel: **nc** IntlRel: **WARC** TheolSchool: **nc** Service infrastructure: **nursery and primary schools**

Address: Habaddiyar Ekklisiyar Kristi a Nigeria, P.O. Box 302, Kapsima Road, Kaduna, Kaduna State, Nigeria, Tel: +234 62 210-950

NIUE

Area in km^2	260
Population	2,300 Polynesian (with some 200 Europeans, Samoans, and Tongans)
Religions in %	Ekalesia Niue (Niuean Church) 85%, other 15% (RCath, Jehovah's Witnesses, Advent)
Official/other languages	Polynesian closely related to Tongan and Samoan, English

Church of Niue (5055)

The people of Niue, the world's largest coral island, were first evangelized by Samoan missionaries stationed there by the London Missionary Society during the 1840s and 1850s. The church they molded was organized along Congreg lines under William George Lawes (1861-1868) and his brother Frank E. Lawes (1868-1910), both of the LMS. W. G. Lawes trained, and afterward supervised, Pacific Islander missionaries from Niue, who were stationed under him when he went to serve the LMS in Papua. A further succession of LMS missionaries between 1910 and 1973 moved the church toward independence, in close association with the Congregational Union in New Zealand. As the administering political power, New Zealand established strong political and economic ties with Niue. Approximately 15,000 Niueans live in Aotearoa New Zealand. The island's political independence goes together with a special relationship with New Zealand, where Niueans have citizenship rights.

The Ekalesia (Church) of Niue is independent (since 1966) but related to Presb and Congreg churches in New Zealand (and in Fiji), serving among laity and ministers living in those countries. There are several Niuean congr in New Zealand. The Ekalesia Niue is a member of the Pacific Conference of Churches, WARC, and the Council for World Mission (CWM).

TM: **1,675** Congr: **16** OrdM: **10** Eld: **nc** Deac: **nc** EvgHome: **nc** Mission: **nc** Women Ord: **no** ChurchOrg: **nc** Off/otherLang: **Niuean, English** DoctrB: **nc** NatRel: **nc** RegRel: **PCC** IntlRel: **WARC, CWM** TheolSchool: **Theological College (Niue), Pacific Theological College (Fiji), Knox Theological Hall (Dunedin, NZ)** Periodicals: **none**

Address: Ekalesia Niue, P.O. Box 25, Alofi, Niue (via New Zealand), Tel: +683 4012, Fax: +683 4010

OMAN, SULTANATE OF

See also GULF REGION

Area in km²	212,460
Population	(July 1996 est.) 2,186,548 Arab, Baluchi, South Asian (Indian, Pakistani, Sri Lankan, Bangladeshi), African
Religions in %	Ibadhi Muslim 75%, Sunni Muslim, Shi'a Muslim, Hindu
Official/other languages	Arabic/English, Baluchi, Urdu, Indian dialects

Oman is large, about 1,000 miles long and 300 miles wide. The population has grown rapidly since the discovery of oil there. The country has developed even more rapidly since the beginning of the present Sultan's rule in 1970, bringing many expatriates in to do the work. A good number of them are Christians. While among the Westerners some are medical workers sent to staff the growing medical expansion, many are connected with the oil business. Migrants from India, Pakistan, Korea, and the Philippines are mostly laborers, street cleaners, construction workers, tailors, and maids.

The Protestant Church in Oman (4357)

This Church is the fruit of the active presence of the Reformed Church in America (RCA), which has ministered in this area since the 1890s. The first missionaries arrived in 1893. Services were held for many years on the mission compound. Four large tracts of land, two in the capital area, one in Salalah and one in Sohar, were granted by the government for Christian worship. In the capital area, the Prot church, the RCath church, a Prot church office building, and six houses have been built.

Although the mission was originally for the Arabs, the large influx of other people could not be neglected. There are today in Muscat over 30 different denominational and language congregations worshiping in these buildings and forming one common council; they are composed of Westerners, Indians, Pakistanis, and other Asians. The main services are on Friday, with a few on Sundays.

415

The main church building is in Ruwi, five miles or so outside the capital city of Muscat. A second building is at Ghala, about 30 miles from Muscat. While the work was begun by missionaries of the RCA, the Protestant Church of Oman invited the Angl church to share in the work there by sending one of its priests. He is considered a member of the Arabian Mission of the RCA, and the Reformed pastor is, in return, a member of the Diocese of Cyprus and the Arabian Gulf. The two men participate actively in the work of all the churches in Oman. There are four services in English and over two dozen other worship services each week. They are led by over a dozen professional clergy and several lay leaders. At Ruwi there is a small Angl service on Sunday morning, with a large interdenominational service in the evening. Once a month this service is led by the Angl priest.

Address: The Protestant Church in Oman, P.O. Box 1982, Ruwi — 112, Sultanate of Oman, Tel: +968
799-475; 702-372, Fax: +968 789-943 or 799-475, E-mail: pcomct@gto.net.om.

PAKISTAN

Area in km^2	803,940
Population	(July 1996 est.) 133,500,000 Punjabi, Sindhi, Pashtun (Pathan), Baloch, Muhajir (immigrants from India and their descendants)
Religions in 1992	Muslim 95% (Sunni 76%, Shi'a 19%), Hindu 1.8% and others 1.2%, Christian 2% (RCath 40%, Prot 60%),
Off/other languages	Urdu/English (official and lingua franca of Pakistani elite and most government ministries) 8%, Punjabi 48%, Sindhi 12%, Siraiki (a Punjabi variant) 10%, Pashtu 8%, Balochi 3%, Hindko 2%, Brahui 1%, Burushaski, and other 8%

NCP (National Council in Pakistan)

Pakistan became a sovereign state on August 14, 1947. For centuries the area had been under Muslim rule. Islam entered the Indian subcontinent first in 711 and spread in various stages in subsequent centuries. The high point of Muslim power was the period of the Great Moghuls (1526-1857). The influence of Britain began to make itself felt through the presence of the East India Company from 1600 onward. The battle of Plassey (Bengal) in 1757 opened for Britain access to the eastern part of the subcontinent. By the end of the 18th century British rule over the Moghuls was practically complete. In 1835 English was introduced as the official language. In 1857, after a last attempt of rebellion, the administration was taken over entirely by the British crown. The idea of an independent Muslim state in northwestern India was first put forward in 1930 by Muhammed Iqbal (1877-

1938) and later, during the independence struggle, pursued by M. A. Jinnah (†1948). It was realized through the partition of India and Pakistan, which caused mass movement between the two countries and led to conflicts which cost many lives. Bangladesh, which was initially part of Pakistan, became an independent state in 1971.

Christianity is a small minority (2%) within a vast Muslim majority. The first missionaries in the area of today's Pakistan were RCath. Several Prot missions followed. Large numbers became Christian during the so-called Indian mass movement between 1880 and 1930, when in the whole of India about two million untouchables accepted the Christian faith. In 1970 the Presb, Luth, Angl, and Meth churches decided to unite and to form the Church of Pakistan (cf. no 2), initially consisting of four dioceses, now of eight.

1. Presbyterian Church of Pakistan (4350)

United Presb missionaries from the USA started work in 1834 in Ludhiana (East Punjab). A year later J. C. Lowrie, the pioneer Presb missionary, moved from Ludhiana to Lahore. In 1849, after the second Sikh war, the Presb began missionary work in Lahore under John Newton and Charles Forman; soon they extended their work to Rawalpindi. Their efforts resulted in the foundation of the Lahore Church Council.

In 1855 the United Presbyterian Mission of the USA opened work in Lahore under Andrew Gordon; two years later he established a mission station in Sialkot, where he was soon joined by other missionaries. They opened schools and an orphanage. In 1859 the Sialkot Presbytery was formed. The church grew, and other presbyteries were established. In 1893 the Synod of the Punjab was formed as one of the synods of the United Presbyterian Church in the USA. The Synod of Punjab became autonomous in 1961 and constituted itself as the United Presbyterian Church of Pakistan. The church went through several crises. In 1968, as a result of the McIntire movement, a serious split occurred which, in subsequent years, has been largely healed. The United Presbyterian Church has made an impact on Christianity in Pakistan. The "Sialkot Conventions" held since 1904 have been instrumental in deepening the faith of many believers. The *Sialkot Convention Hymnbook* with psalms and hymns in Punjabi and Urdu with Indian tunes is widely used in all churches, including the RCath Church. The United Presbyterian Church founded the seminary of Gujiranwala, which became a united seminary in 1954.

In 1904, long before other Presb communities, the Lahore Church Council joined the United Church of Northern India. In contrast to the United Presbyterian Church, it became administratively independent from the USA. On November 18, 1993, the United Presbyterian Church and the Lahore Church Council of the United Church united to form the Presbyterian Church of Pakistan.

TM: **400,000** BM: **300,000** Congr: **200** PStations: **10** OrdM: **220** Eld: **1300** Deac: **nc** EvgHome: **10** Mission: **0** Women Ord: **nc** As Ministers: **no** as Deac: **no** as Elders: **3/4** ChurchOrg: **Presbyterian (sessions, 19 presby, GenAssy)** Off/otherLang: **Urdu, Punjabi, English** DoctrB: **ApC, NicC, AthC,**

HeidC, WestConf Infant or believer's baptism: both Frequency of the Lord's Supper: once a month Close relations with: Church of Pakistan, ARPChurch, Salvation Army, charismatic groups NatRel: NCCP RegRel: CCA IntlRel: WARC, WCC TheolSchool: Gujranwala Theological Seminary Periodicals: Presbyterian Newsletter (gen/monthly/4,000), Pasban (theological/monthly/ 1,000).

Address: Presbyterian Church of Pakistan, P.O. Box 13, 2 Empress Road, Lahore 54000, Pakistan, Tel: +92 42 630-5867, Fax: +92 42 636-9745

2. Sialkot Diocese of the Church of Pakistan (4351)

The Church of Scotland began work in the Sialkot area in 1856. One of the pioneer missionaries was Rev. Hunter. Activities developed through a hospital, clinics, an orphanage, pastoral care, and a seminary. In 1953 the Sialkot Church Council took responsibility for all affairs of the church. At this time the Sialkot Church Council was a presbytery of the General Assembly of the United (Presb) Church in North India and Pakistan. In 1970 Presb, Luth, Angl, and Meth united to form the Church of Pakistan. The church is now part of the united church; it forms the Sialkot District of the Church of Pakistan. Many Christian leaders have received their Christian education in Murray College in Sialkot.

TM: 40,436 BM: 37,896 Congr: 45 PStations: 28 OrdM: 30 Eld: 174 Deac: 4 EvgHome: 11 Mission: 0 Women Ord: yes As Ministers: no as Deac: 0 as Elders: 1920/12 ChurchOrg: 8 dioceses, 1 synod Off/ otherLang: Penjabi, Urdu, English DoctrB: ApC, NicC, HeidC, WestCat Infant or believer's baptism: both Frequency of the Lord's Supper: monthly Close relations with: Church of Scotland NatRel: National Council of Churches in Pakistan RegRel: CCA IntlRel: WCC (1953), WARC (1994) TheolSchool: Murray College in Sialkot

Address: Sialkot Diocese of the Church of Pakistan, Synod Secretariat, Barah Patthar, Christian Town Sialkot 2, Pakistan, Tel: +92 432 264895, Fax: +92 42 26 48 28

3. Pakistan Synod of the Associate Reformed Presbyterian Church (4352)

In 1906 the Associate Reformed Presbyterian Church of the USA (cf. United States no. 3) sent out Minnie Alexander to work with the United Presb (cf. no. 1); she was joined in 1911 by Rev. and Mrs. Ranson. After their language studies they were offered a site for a mission station in Sahiwal District. In the years following 1911 considerable numbers of Chuhras, a group of untouchables, moved into the area. A hospital and several schools were founded by the mission, and churches were planted. Church planting continues today outside the Sahiwal district among untouchables in the Bahawalpur area and among migrants from the villages to the big cities of Multan and Karachi.

TM: 150,000 Congr: 50 OrdM: nc Eld: nc Deac: nc EvgHome: nc Mission: 0 Women Ord: nc ChurchOrg: Presbyterian (4 presby, synod) Off/otherLang: nc DoctrB: ApC, NicC, AthC, WestC, WestCat Infant or believer's baptism: both NatRel: nc RegRel: nc IntlRel: nc TheolSchool: Gujranwala Theological Seminary

Address: Pakistan Synod of the Associate Reformed Presbyterian Church, Knox Home, Sahiwal,
57004, Pakistan

PAPUA NEW GUINEA

Area in km²	451,710
Population	(July 1996 est.) 4,394,537 Melanesian, Papuan, Negrito, Micronesian, Polynesian
Religions in %	RCath 22%, Luth 16%, Presb/Meth/London Missionary Society 8%, Angl 5%, Ev. Alliance 4%, Advent 1%, various Prot sects 10%, indigenous beliefs 34%
Official/other languages	English spoken by 1%-2%, pidgin English widespread, Motu spoken in Papua region, 715 indigenous languages

MCC (Melanesian Council of Churches)
EASPI (the Evangelical Alliance of the South Pacific Islands)

Christianity came to Middle Melanesia in three waves. First came the historic confessions in the 19th century. The churches resulting from their efforts are today federated in the Melanesian Council of Churches (MCC). Second were the conservative evangelical and fundamentalist missions which are today collaborating in the Evangelical Alliance of the South Pacific Islands. After World War II Pentecostalism began to appear as the third force.

RCath work began on the Solomon Islands in 1845 through Marianists; after failures at first they made a new and more successful beginning in 1898. Angl activities started on the Solomon Islands in 1855 and in northeast Papua in 1891. German Luth missionaries appeared on the scene in the '80s. Today the churches which are united in the United Church owe their existence to the Congreg London Missionary Society (LMS), which initiated activities along the coast of New Guinea in 1871, and to the Australian Meth, whose work began in 1875 and concentrated on the Bismarck archipelago and the islands east and south of the main island, among them Dobu, a center of traditional beliefs. J. Chalmers, a LMS missionary, together with 11 indigenous believers, paid with their lives for their witness among the Gaoribari (1901).

At a relatively early stage both the LMS and the Australian Meth Mission began to prepare for the independence of the churches. In 1963 the Congreg Church was constituted, and five years later Congreg, Meth, and the United Church of Port Moresby (two congr serving primarily expatriates and being part of the United Church of North Australia) formed the United Church of Papua New Guinea and the Solomon Islands. Leadership of both churches was to a large ex-

419

tent indigenous, and soon local congr became financially independent. The life of the church took roots in the Melanesian culture. The work of the United Church began to extend into the interior of Papua.

In 1996 the United Church in Papua New Guinea and the Solomon Islands decided by mutual agreement to separate into the United Church in Papua New Guineas and the United Church of the Solomon Islands (for details, see Solomon Islands)

United Church in Papua New Guinea (4540)

TM: **1,000,000** BM: **600,000** CM: **600,000** Congr: **nc** PStations: **2,600** OrdM: **600** Eld: **2,000** Deac: **2,000** EvgHome: **20** Mission: **10** Women Ord: **yes** As Ministers: **8** as Deac: **200** as Elders: **200** ChurchOrg: **congregation, circuit, region, Assembly** Off/otherLang: **English, Pidgin, Motu, Toaripi, Hula, Kuanua, Dobu, Roviana** DoctrB: **ApC, NicC, AthC** Infant or believer's baptism: **both** Frequency of the Lord's Supper: **monthly** Periodicals: **United Church Mission Link (Life and Mission/monthly), Rarong Theological Col. News (Theology and Mission/monthly)** Close relations with: **RCath, Luth, Angl, Salvation Army, Advent** NatRel: **Papua New Guinea Council of Churches (1970), National Council of Women (1992), Christian Women's Association (1970)** RegRel: **Asian Association of Theological Schools (1970s), PCC (1970s), Pacific Assoc. of Theological Schools (1970s), Australia National Council of Churches (1970s)** IntlRel: **WCC (1970), CWM (1970), CEC of NZ (1970s)** TheolSchool: **Theological Seminary of Rabaul**

Address: United Church in Papua New Guinea, P.O. Box 1401, United Church Assembly Office, Port Moresby, Papua New Guinea, Tel: +675 321-1744, Fax: +675 321-4930

For more details cf. Solomon Islands.

PARAGUAY

Area in km^2	406,400
Population	(July 1996 est.) 5,504,146 mestizo (mixed Spanish and Indian) 95%, whites plus Amerindians 5%
Religions in %	RCath 96%, Mennonite and other Prot denominations
Official/other languages	Spanish/Tupi-Guarani

The first Prot were teachers who had been invited by the government to improve the educational system of the country. In 1886 missionary work was started by the Meth and the Disciples of Christ. The Meth withdrew in 1918; their mission was continued by the Disciples. In 1889 the Angl initiated evangelistic and social work among the indigenous people of Chaco. A German Luth Church was established in 1893. Other Prot groups followed: Evangelical New Testament Mission (1902), Free Brethren (1911), Bapt (1919), Menn (1926), and several Pent groups.

The Presb and Reformed presence is of relatively recent date and is mainly due to evangelistic efforts by Brazilians and Koreans. In addition to the denominations listed below, there are a number of individual Korean mission congregations.

1. Presbyterian Church in Paraguay (2152)

In 1968 the Board of Foreign Mission of the Presbyterian Church of Brazil (cf. Brazil no. 1) decided to start evangelistic work in Paraguay. The first missionary was Evandro Luiz da Silva, who arrived in Paraguay in 1970. The responsibility for the work was with Brazilians until 1984, when two Paraguayan ministers who had been trained in Campinas, Brazil, were able to take over.

TM: **200** BM: **85** CM: **65** Congr: **5** PStations: **5** OrdM: **5** Eld: **none** Deac: **none** EvgHome: **1** Mission: **none** Women Ord: **no** ChurchOrg: **no regional or national structures** Off/otherLang: **Spanish, Guarani** DoctrB: **ApC, WestConf, Ref** Infant or believer's baptism: **both** Frequency of the Lord's Supper: **monthly** Periodicals: **newsletter (gen/monthly/100)** Close relations with: **Presb Church of Brazil** NatRel: **nc** RegRel: **nc** IntlRel: **nc** TheolSchool: **nc**

Address: Iglesia Presbiteriana en el Paraguay (Missão da Igreja Presbiteriana do Brasil), Casilla D 4055, Lambaré, Paraguay, Tel: +595 21 332-943, Fax: +595 21 332-943

2. Evangelical Congregationalist Churches in Paraguay (2153)

In 1970 the Congreg Churches in Brazil started evangelistic work primarily among Brazilian farmers in the border area between Brazil and Paraguay. The church has acquired juridical recognition in Paraguay but ecclesiastically continues to be part of the Brazilian church (cf. Brazil).

TM: **2,000** BM: **2,000** CM: **1,500** Congr: **10** PStations: **40** OrdM: **6** Eld: **none** Deac: **none** EvgHome: **none** Mission: **none** Women Ord: **no** ChurchOrg: **no national structures in Paraguay** (the church has acquired juridical recognition in Paraguay but ecclesiastically continues to be part of the Brazilian Church) Off/otherLang: **Portuguese, Spanish, German** DoctrB: **ApC** Infant or believer's baptism: **both** Frequency of the Lord's Supper: **na** Close relations with: **Evangelical Congregrational Chs of Brazil** NatRel: **nc** RegRel: **nc** IntlRel: **nc** TheolSchool: **nc**

Address: Iglesias Evangelicas Congregacionalistas en el Paraguay, C.P. 374, Ijuí-Rs Brazil, Paraguay

3. Reformed Presbyterian Church — Korean Mission in Paraguay (2151)

The church came into existence in 1975, when Pastor Seung Yong Kim arrived in Asunción to serve the growing Korean community in Paraguay. The Church was first called Iglesia Presbiteriana Asunción de los Coreanos. In 1986, with the arrival of more Korean missionaries, a Presb Reformed Mission was formed which integrated four different Korean missionary groups. In the same year a pastor of the National Presbyterian Church of Chile, Rev. Pedro Vega, was entrusted with establishing a theological seminary; the teaching language was to be Spanish. In 1993 the present name was adopted. The church is affiliated with the Korean Presbyterian Church of America (cf. United States no. 23) and depends on the South American Presbytery of this church.

TM: **2,500** CM: **1,200** Congr: **2** PStations: **21** OrdM: **6** Eld: **yes** Deac: **yes** EvgHome: **nc** Mission: **yes** Women Ord: **no** ChurchOrg: **South America Presbytery — KPCA** Off/otherLang: **Spanish, Korean** DoctrB: **ApC, WestConf, Ref** Infant or believer's baptism: **both** Frequency of the Lord's Supper: **once a month** Periodicals: **newsletter (liturgy/weekly)** Close relations with: **Korean Presb Ch of America** NatRel: **nc** RegRel: **nc** IntlRel: **nc** TheolSchool: **Seminario Presbiteriano Reformado, Von Polesky y Americo Picco, Vitla Elisa — Paraguay**

Address: Iglesia Presbiteriana y Reformada en el Paraguay — Missão Coreana en el Paraguay, Casilla 2544 Lomas Valentinas 1460, Asunción, Paraguay

4. Korean United Church (2150)

The church was founded in 1965 by a group of Korean immigrants. The theological basis is Reformed, and the polity is Congregational with some Presb ingredients. It is an autonomous church which claims to be independent from outside financial aid. It runs a clinic and a secondary school and has started a small theological school.

TM: **730** BM: **730** CM: **427** Congr: **1** PStations: **1** OrdM: **1** Eld: **12** Deac: **14** EvgHome: **2** Mission: **nc** Women Ord: **no** ChurchOrg: **session of organized church** Off/otherLang: **Korean, Spanish** DoctrB: **ApC, WestConf** Infant or believer's baptism: **both** Frequency of the Lord's Supper: **6 times per year** NatRel: **nc** RegRel: **nc** IntlRel: **nc** TheolSchool: **nc**

Address: Iglesia Unida Coreana, Casilla 3072, Coronel Irazabal con Herrera 787, Asunción, Paraguay, Tel: +595 21 206-244, Fax: +595 21 213-809

5. Taiwanese Presbyterian Church in Asunción (2154)

This church was started on May 28, 1978, in Asunción by Rev. Chou Shen Chong, a Taiwanese pastor in Brazil who succeeded in bringing together a number of Taiwanese Presb living in the capital of Paraguay. As the group grew, a church was formally established in 1980. For some time, the congr had the services of a pastor. At present it is led by presbyters and deacons. Though small in numbers, the church has been engaged in relief work among destitute people. The work of this church also extends to Ciudad del Este, at the Brazilian border.

TM: **92** BM: **92** CM: **73** Congr: **nc** PStations: **2** OrdM: **nc** Eld: **6** Deac: **7** EvgHome: **nc** Mission: **nc** Women Ord: **yes** As Ministers: **nc** as Deac: **1980/1** as Elders: **1980/2** ChurchOrg: **Presbyterian** Off/otherLang: **Taiwanese/Spanish** DoctrB: **ApC, NicC, HeidC, WestConf** Infant or believer's baptism: **both** Frequency of the Lord's Supper: **quarterly** Close relations with: **Presb Church of Formosa in Brazil, Presb Church of Taiwan** NatRel: **nc** RegRel: **nc** IntlRel: **nc** TheolSchool: **none**

Address: Iglesia Presbiteriana Taiwanesa en Asunción, 33 Orientales, Asunción, Paraguay, Tel: +595 21 227-103, Fax: +595 21 227-103

PERU

Area in km²	1,285,220
Population	(July 1996 est.) 24,523,408 Indian 45%, mestizo (mixed Indian and European ancestry) 37%, white 15%, black, Japanese, Chinese, and other 3%
Religions in %	RCath majority (89.6% in 1981), rapidly growing Prot minorities (5% in 1984)
Official/other languages	Spanish, Quechua/Aymara

CONEP (Consejo Nacional Evangélico del Peru — National Evangelical Council of Peru)

Prot witness in Peru began in the early 19th century with the struggle for liberation from Spain. In 1822 James Thomson, a representative of the British and Foreign Bible Society, started a number of schools with the help of the political authorities. Angl worked among the English-speaking residents and among seamen (1849). Meth evangelism led to the foundation of a Meth church in 1890. Other groups followed (Advent 1906, Salvation Army 1910, Pent 1922, Bapt 1927). The earliest Reformed effort came from independent evangelists who aligned themselves in 1897 with the British missionary society Regions Beyond Missionary Union (RBMU). Its most dynamic representative was John Ritchie, a Scottish Presb who came to Peru in 1906 (†1952). Around the same time efforts by other Reformed groups were undertaken. In 1911 the Evangelical Union of South America (EUSA), based in London, and a few years later the Christian and Missionary Alliance (CMA), based in New York, began to send missionaries to the country.

Out of the RBMU work grew the Iglesia Evangélica Peruana (IEP), established largely through the efforts of John Ritchie. For a long time EUSA and CMA worked closely with the IEP, but in the '50s increasing tensions between national leaders and missionaries led to conflicts. This resulted in the withdrawal of the CMA from the IEP and the formation of a separate church — the Iglesia Alianza Cristiana y Misionera (ACM).

Through Scottish and American initiative two Presb churches came into existence — the Iglesia Evangélica Presbiteriana del Peru and the Iglesia Nacional Presbiteriana.

Since 1940, 75% of all Prot are federated through the National Evangelical Council of Peru (CONEP). The largest and fastest growing group is the Pent.

1. Evangelical Church of Peru (2083)

The first congr of this church was formed in 1894 in Negreiros, Lima. In 1919 the regional synod of Central Peru decided to name the church, nine communities at that time, the Evangelical Church of Peru. The church has always placed strong emphasis on national leadership. The church was formally constituted in 1946. Since the crisis in the early '50s (see above) it has grown rapidly and is now represented in the whole country. About 80% of the congr are to be found in the Andine highlands. In the 1980s the church actively engaged in the human rights struggle.

TM: **20,000** BM: **18,000** CM: **18,000** Congr: **1,960** OrdM: **800** Eld: **nc** Deac: **4,000** EvgHome: **nc** Mission: **nc** Women Ord: **yes** As Ministers: **no** as Deac: **4,000** as Elders: **no** ChurchOrg: **Presbyterian (congr, presby, synods, GenAssy)** Off/otherLang: **Spanish, Quechua** DoctrB: **ApC, WestConf** Infant or believer's baptism: **believer** Frequency of the Lord's Supper: **monthly** Periodicals: **Renacimiento (gen/semesterly/3,000)** Close relations with: **Christian and Missionary Alliance, Presb and Ref Chs of Peru** NatRel: **CONEP** RegRel: **nc** IntlRel: **nc** TheolSchool: **nc**

Address: Iglesia Evangélica Peruana, Apartado 2866, Luis Gonzaga 709 esquina Cajamarquila, Lima 100, Peru, Tel: +51 1 459-6170, Fax: +51 1 477-2161

2. Evangelical Presbyterian and Reformed Church in Peru (2082)

This church is a result of a recent union. In January 1995 the Iglesia Evangélica Presbiteriana del Peru and the Iglesia Presbiteriana Nacional del Peru united to form the Iglesia Presbiteriana y Reformada en el Peru (IEPRP). The two churches were very close in their teaching (WestConf).

a) Iglesia Evangélica Presbiteriana del Peru

The church is the fruit of missionary efforts of the Scottish Free Church. In 1915 John A. Mackay came to Peru to found the Anglo-Peruvian College, today San Andrés College, the most renowned Prot school in Peru. He was followed by Calvin Mackay, who arrived in Lima in 1921 and later settled in Cajamarca. The first church was built there in 1936. The first GenAssy was held in 1963. At the time of union the church had five presbyteries — Amazonas, Cajamarca, Celendin (Cajamarca), Lima, and San Martin — and about 3,000 members. The church used Spanish only.

b) Iglesia Nacional Presbiteriana

Another Presb church was planted in Peru in 1936. The principal missionary was the American Alonso D. Hitchcock, who began to work in the area of Ayocucho. A team under the leadership of Homer Emerson, together with Florencio Segura, Simon Izarra, Rafael Yupanqui, Fernando Quicana, and Romulo Saune, engaged in the task of translating the Bible into the Quechua of the area. In 1970 the first GenAssy was held. In 1983 the church had 8,000 members and was

424

organized into two synods (Ayacucho and Selva del Valle Apurimac) and 11 presbyteries. In addition to Spanish, Quechua was in use.

TM: **15,000** Congr: **136** PStations: **11** OrdM: **20** Eld: **730** Deac: **100** EvgHome: **nc** Mission: **nc** Women Ord: **no** ChurchOrg: **consistories, presb, reg. synod, GenAssy** Off/otherLang: **Spanish, Quechua** DoctrB: **ApC, HeidC, HelvC, WestConf, CDort** Infant or believer's baptism: **both** Frequency of the Lord's Supper: **monthly to quarterly** Periodicals: **Pasos sobre Fundamento Solide (history/1,000), Vida Y Mision de la IEPP (mission/500)** Close relations with: **Free Ch of Scotland, Liga Misionera Reformada (Netherlands)** NatRel: **Concilio Nacional Evangélico del Peru (1964)** RegRel: **nc** IntlRel: **nc** TheolSchool: **Seminario evangélico (Lima)**

Address: Iglesia Evangélica Presbiteriana y Reformada en el Peru, Parque San Carlos n 191, Lima 21, Peru, Tel: +51 1 462-3754, Fax: +51 1 337-6911, E-mail: none

3. Christian and Missionary Alliance (2084)

This church was formed in 1957. For many years the Christian and Missionary Alliance had worked with the IEP (cf. no. 1). Conflicts over leadership led to the withdrawal of CMA and the formation of a separate church. About 35% of the congrs which had worked with CMA in IEP joined the new group.

No statistical data have been made available.

Address: Iglesia Alianza Cristiana y Misonera, Ap. 11-0216, Lima 11, Peru

PHILIPPINES

Area in km²	298,170
Population	(July 1996 est.) 74,480,848 Christian Malay 91.5%, Muslim Malay 4%, Chinese 1.5%, other 3%
Religions in %	RCath 83%, Prot 9%, Muslim 5%, Buddhist and other 3%
Official/other languages	Filipino (based on Tagalog), English/many vernacular languages

NCCP (National Council of Churches in the Philippines)
PCEC (Philippine Council of Evangelical Churches)

The Philippines are a group of over 7,100 islands, of which 800 are inhabited. The two main islands are Luzon in the North (105,000 km²) and the capital, Manila, and Mindanao in the South (95,000 km²). The original indigenous population, the Negritos and the old Malay groups (Igorot, Kalinga, Bontok), are now a minority of 10% to 20%. The majority Malay population consists of over 80 groups with an equal number of different languages. Tagalog/Filipino is being promoted as the national language; about 65% of the population have some knowledge of English. The islands were reached by Magellan in 1521 and conquered by the Spaniards in 1565 and 1571. In the course of the centuries there have been many revolts against the colonial regime. The Spanish domination ended with the war between Spain and the USA in 1898, but the Philippines were eventually annexed by the USA. The country gained independence after World War II (1946). American economic influence and military presence, however, continued. Several governments succeeded one another — the dictatorship of Ferdinand Marcos (1966-1986), Corazon Aquino (1986-1992), and today Fidel Ramos. Filipino democracy remains fragile. The population is rapidly increasing.

Christianity came to the Philippines in the 16th century. In contrast to other countries in Asia the Philippines have a vast RCath majority. The liberation from Spain was accompanied by a strong anti-RCath movement which led at the end of the 19th century to the foundation of the Filipino Independent Church. The Prot presence began with the Spanish-American War in 1898. Many American missions arrived in the Philippines — Presb and Meth (1899), Bapt and CMA (1900), Episcopal, United Brethren, and Disciples (1901), Congreg (1902), and Advent (1906). Prot missions found a response especially among intellectuals and in the middle class. Since the 1970s Korean Presb have started missionary activities in the Philippines. They have led to the foundation of the Presbyterian Church of the Philippines (no. 5); Koreans have also set up a number of smaller communities.

1. United Church of Christ in the Philippines (4360)

The UCCP is the result of an organic union of three Philippine Prot churches, i.e., the United Evangelical Church in the Philippines, the Evangelical Church in the Philippines, and the Philippine Meth Church, plus a few independent congr in 1948. In 1929 the United Evangelical Church in the Philippines brought together Presb, Congreg, and United Brethren. The Disciples from South Luzon joined the United Church in 1962. The UCCP is self-governing, self-propagating, and well on its way to being self-reliant. The church is a strong advocate for justice and peace in the Philippines. It has been in the forefront in fighting for the protection of human rights under successive regimes, including the present regime of Fidel Ramos, himself a member of the UCCP. The church runs 18 high schools and colleges and four hospitals. The most prominent educational institution is Silliman University in Dumaguete City in Central Visayas, founded by Presb missionaries in 1901.

TM: **950,000** Congr: **1,699** PStations: **787** OrdM: **743** Eld: **na** Deac: **118** EvgHome: **na** Mission: **14** Women Ord: **Yes** As Ministers: **nc** as Deac: **nc** as Elders: **nc** ChurchOrg: **United (Jurisdictions: North Luzon; South Luzon; Visayas and Mindanao)** Off/otherLang: **English and dialects (Filipino)** DoctrB: **ApC, NicC, WestConf (occasional), the UCCP Statement of Faith, Trinitarian doctrine** Infant or believer's baptism: **both** Frequency of the Lord's Supper: **monthly** NatRel: **NCCP**

426

(1963). UCCP was a member of the former Phil. Federation of Evangelical Churches (created in 1938) and of the Phil. Federation of Christian Churches (created in 1949) RegRel: **CCA (1959)** IntlRel: **WCC (1948), WMC, WARC, REC** TheolSchool: **Divinity School, Silliman University; Union Theological Seminary, Philippine Christian University; College of Theology, Southern Christian College** Service infrastructure: **3 hospitals and clinics, Metro Manila Health Program, Palawan Mission (social service), kindergartens in almost every urban local church, 18 schools** Periodicals: **United Church Letter (gen/quarterly/3,000), Batingaw (national issues/bi-monthly/ 3,000)**

Address: United Church of Christ in the Philippines, P.O. Box 718, C.P.O. 877, EDSA, Quezon City, Ermita Manila, Quezon City 1099, Philippines, Tel: +63 2 924-0215, Fax: +63 2 924-0207, E-mail: Cable: UNICHURCH.

2. United Evangelical Church of Christ (4361)

Inspired by the sense of independence of the Filipino clergymen and lay leaders, who founded the Iglesia Evangélica de los Cristianos Filipinos in 1906, representatives of 13 evangelical churches met in Manila at the invitation of Don Toribio Teodoro and started the groundwork for a church union in November 1931. However, of the 13 churches, only six evangelical and independent churches of different denominational backgrounds and traditions such as Presb, Reformed, and the Iglesia Evangélica de los Cristianos eventually united to form what is now known as the United Evangelical Church of Christ (January 3, 1932). All these churches had earlier affirmed their independence and selfhood from foreign mission boards and missionaries. The church has since grown considerably. More and more it focuses on the economic and social needs of the community.

TM: **30,000** Congr: **72** PStations: **24** OrdM: **89** Eld: **nc** Deac: **100** EvgHome: **nc** Mission: **nc** Women Ord: **yes** As Ministers: **nc** as Deac: **35** as Elders: **nc** ChurchOrg: **Reformed (15 member board of directors, GenAssy with delegates from all congrs)** NatRel: **NCCP** RegRel: **CCA** IntlRel: **WARC** TheolSchool: **Union Theological School**

Address: Iglesia Evangélica Unida de Cristo, Unida Development Center, Biga, Silang Cavite 4118, Philippines, Tel: +63 219-511 and 219-296

3. Christian Reformed Church in the Philippines (CRCP) (4362)

The existence of this church owes to the missionary efforts of the Christian Reformed Church in the USA, which began in 1962 on Negros Island. By 1976 three congrs had been established and the Philippine denomination was officially organized. By 1990 there were 25 fully organized congrs and more than 20 emerging churches in Luzon, Negros, and Panay Islands. As the number of churches grew, the need to form a synod followed. A synodal church order was adopted in 1983.

TM: **4,575** Congr: **37** PStations: **34** OrdM: **50** Eld: **185** Deac: **nc** EvgHome: **nc** Mission: **nc** Women Ord: **yes** As Ministers: **no** as Deac: **1975/185** as Elders: **no** ChurchOrg: **Reformed (consistories, 5 classis, synod)** Off/otherLang: **English, Filipino** DoctrB: **ApC, NicC, AthC, HeidC, CDort** Infant or believer's baptism: **both** Frequency of the Lord's Supper: **monthly** NatRel: **nc** RegRel: **nc** IntlRel:

REC (1997) TheolSchool: **Asian Theological Seminary (Manila), Manila Christian Reformed Seminary and Bible College (Bacolod City), Presb Theological Seminary (Cavite)** Service infrastructure: **kindergartens run by congr, Manila Christian Reformed Seminary and Bible College (Bacolod City)**

Address: Christian Reformed Church in the Philippines (CRCP), # 301, 3rd floor, Lola Taya Bldg., 1165 Quezon Avenue, Quezon City, Philippines, Tel: +63 2 924-0534, Fax: +63 2 924-1002

4. Presbyterian Church of the Philippines (Korean) (4365)

Korean missions in the Philippines started with Pastor Choi Chan-Young from the Presbyterian Church in Korea (TongHap; cf. Korea no. 14), who worked in the Philippines for the Bible Society from 1974 to 1977. At about the same time Rev. Han Sang-Hyu, a Meth missionary, began work for the Meth church. In 1977 Rev. Kim Hwal-Young, who had to leave Vietnam after the victory of the socialist revolution, arrived in the Philippines and began work in Manila in 1978. Since he was unable to establish constructive relations with the United Church of Christ in the Philippines (cf. no. 1), he sought to revive the Presbyterian Church, which had become part of the United Church in 1948. Very soon the Evangelical Presbyterian Mission (EPM) was registered with the government. The Mission became the instrument through which missionaries from both Korea and Japan were invited to start work in the Philippines. In 1981 Korean missionaries agreed to establish one Presb denomination.

As the number of missionaries grew, conflicts arose among them. But more serious were the tensions between the Korean missionaries and the local Filipino church. The need for harmonious collaboration among missionaries became even more evident. In 1983 the Presbyterian School of Theology was founded, later renamed Presbyterian Theological Seminary. Soon students who had graduated from the seminary were ordained. In 1987 the General Assembly of the Presbyterian Church of the Philippines was established. In 1989 the first split occurred in the church. Rev. Kim You-Shik from the Presbyterian Church in Korea (HapDong; cf. Korea no. 15) started the Reformed Church in the Philippines. But new efforts toward unity were undertaken. In 1989 twenty Korean missionaries from various Presb churches in Korea (PCK, cf. Korea no. 14; KoShin, cf. Korea no. 1; HapDongBoSu, cf. Korea no. 29) expressed their commitment to unity in the Manila Manifest. They appealed to leaders at home to approve of their action. They were joined by some American missionaries from the Orthodox Presbyterian Church in America (cf. United States). In 1996 four presbyteries were organized in the country, and the General Assembly of the Presbyterian Church of the Philippines was ecclesiastically organized.

Many Korean missionaries are working outside the PCP and setting up their own congregations. While in 1977 there were 266 Korean missionaries in the Philippines, today they number around 800 (from various Prot denominations). Most missionaries of PCK (cf. Korea no. 14), KoShin (cf. Korea no. 1), HapDong (cf. Korea no. 15), and HapDongBoSu (cf. Korea no. 29) work with PCP; others are acting independently: HapDongChongShin (cf. Korea nos. 35 and 36), HapDong-JungAng (cf. Korea no. 41), GaeHyuk (cf. Korea no. 23). The allegiance of missionaries in certain churches is under discussion (DaeShin, cf. Korea no. 16; HapDongJeong Tong, cf. Korea no. 37).

TM: **5,000** Congr: **145** OrdM: **64** Eld: **16** Deac: **nc** EvgHome: **none** Mission: **none** Women Ord: **no** ChurchOrg: **Presbyterian** Off/otherLang: **English, Filipino, local dialects** DoctrB: **WestConf** Infant or believer's baptism: **both** Frequency of the Lord's Supper: **monthly** Close relations with: **Christian Reformed Church** (no. 3) NatRel: **PCEC (1993)** RegRel: **Evangelical Fellowship in Asia** IntlRel: **WEC** TheolSchool: **Presb Theological Seminary** Periodicals: **Presbyterian Herald (newsletter/ bi-annually/nc)**

Address: Presbyterian Church of the Philippines (PCP), 22 Dona Isidora Street, Kapalaran Suburb, Quezon City M.M., Philippines, Tel: +63 2 931-0145 or 932-6150, Fax: +63 2 931-0145 or 932-6150

5. Christian and Missionary Alliance Churches of the Philippines (4364)

CMA missionary work in the Philippines started in 1901 in the Western Mindanao and the Sulu regions. The first church was inaugurated in Tetuan Zamboanga region on December 25, 1904. Growth was slow, and by 1924 the missionaries were so discouraged that they were on the point of abandoning the Philippines. But an effort to recruit indigenous leadership was successful, and the church began to grow. During World War II missionaries either went into hiding or were detained in Japanese camps. Leadership had to be exercised by national workers. In 1947 the denomination was officially established. Thirteen of the 42 congregations were self-supporting at that time. Two years later a constitution was adopted. In 1982 the church officially decided to be present, not only in Mindanao, but in the whole of the Philippines. In recent years the church has grown rapidly. The number of congregations increased from 1,537 in 1990 to 2,167 in 1997. The church is active in educational work. Very early on the church also began to take responsibility for mission work abroad.

TM: **249,500** BM: **113,430** Congr: **1,897** PStations: **270** OrdM: **603** Eld: **3,794** Deac: **2,372** EvgHome: **25** Mission: **32** Women Ord: **no** ChurchOrg: **local church, circuits, districts, regional, national** Off/ otherLang: **English, Filipino** DoctrB: **ApC, NicC** Infant or believer's baptism: **believer** Frequency of the Lord's Supper: **monthly** Close relations with: **Christian Reformed Church** NatRel: **PCEC (1965)** RegRel: **Evangelical Fellowship of Asia** IntlRel: **WEF (1990), AWF (1975)** TheolSchool: **Alliance Bible Seminary, Philippines Alliance College of Theology, 7 others** Service infrastructure: **241 preschools, 13 grade schools, 1 high school** Periodicals: **publications temporarily stopped**

Address: Christian and Missionary Alliance Churches of the Philippines, 13 West Capitol Drive, 1603 Pasig City, Metro Manila, Philippines, Tel: +63 2 361-1363, Fax: +63 2 631-7947, E-mail: camacop@phil.gn.apc.org

POLAND

Area in km²	311,730
Population	(1994) 38,400,000
Religions in %	RCath majority (95%), Orth, Luth, Ref, and other even smaller minorities (5%)
Official language	Polish

Evangelical Church in Poland (6395)

The beginnings of the Reformed Church in Poland go back to the 1540s, when the teaching of the Swiss Reformers Zwingli and Calvin began to penetrate the country. The return of Jan Laski (1499-1560) to Poland, famous for his reforming activities in Western Europe, strengthened the young church. In 1570 three churches — the Ref, Luth, and the Czech Brethren — adopted the Consensus of Sandomir, which allowed them to unite their forces. For some decades the Reformation movement constituted an important factor in the national life of Poland. The Counter-Reformation not only put an end to the Reformation's expansion but led to its marginalization. In the 18th century, when the rights of dissenters were recognized (1768), the church was reconstituted and was able to continue its witness despite the loss of national independence (1795-1918). During this period the Reformed community in Lithuania became an independent church. Today the church in Poland is a small minority. Three elements constitute its membership — native Polish people, immigrants from Western Europe, and Czech Brethren who are the descendants of groups seeking refuge in Poland in the 18th century because of religious persecution in their country. They each preserve their own language and customs.

TM: **4,000** BM: **3,800** CM: **2,500** Congr: **9** PStations: **10** OrdM: **8** Eld: **27** Deac: **nc** EvgHome: **nc** Mission: **nc** Women Ord: **yes** As Ministers: **nc** as Deac: **nc** as Elders: **1930/28** ChurchOrg: **Presbyterian synodal organization: synod has a governing function at the national level, consistory as an executive organ, parish councils and council of elders at the local level** Off/otherLang: **Polish (Czech)** DoctrB: **ApC, NicC, HelvC, Sandomerian Conf. (1570) based on HelvC** Infant or believer's baptism: **both** Frequency of the Lord's Supper: **5 to 20 times a year** Periodicals: **Jednota (gen/monthly/ 1,200)** Close relations with: **Luth Ch in Poland, Evangelical-Meth Ch in Poland, Bapt Ch in Poland** NatRel: **Polish Ecumenical Council (1946)** RegRel: **CEC (1957)** IntlRel: **WARC (after 1945)** TheolSchool: **nc**

Address: Kosciol Ewangelicko-Reformowany w Rzeczypospolitej Polskiej, AI. Solidarnosci 76 A, PL-00 145 Warszawa, Poland, Tel: +48 22 831 45 22, Fax: +48 22 8310827

PORTUGAL

Area in km²	92,072
Population	(1992) 9,850,000 (+ 4,535,000 living abroad)
Religions in %	RCath (90%) with various Prot minorities totalling 1% of the population (Meth, Lusitanian Church, Ev. Ref, Bapt, and others)
Official language	Portuguese

COPIC (Portuguese Council of Christian Churches)

Portugal was hardly touched by the Reformation; thus in subsequent centuries only a few individuals affirmed Reformed convictions. João Ferreira de Almeida (1628-1698), who became acquainted with the Reformed message in Java and was ordained pastor of the Dutch Reformed Church, translated the Bible into Portuguese (1688). The first Reformed community was founded on May 8, 1845, in Funchal (Madeira) by a Scottish medical doctor, Robert Reid Kalley. Soon persecution began; most members of the community emigrated and found refuge in Brazil, Trinidad, and the United States. Some of them, among them Antonio de Matos, returned to Portugal later, and in 1871 the first Evangelical Presbyterian Church in Lisbon was founded. Slowly the Presb work expanded. Missionaries from both Brazil and the United States played a significant role in strengthening the movement.

Congreg work began in the 1880s. The founding figure was Manuel dos Santos Carvalho (+1916). In the early years of his ministry he had served Meth and Presb communities, but he was an independent spirit, mainly concerned with planting evangelical communities. The Congreg movement found the support of the Evangelical Church of Rio de Janeiro. Together they established the Evangelical Union and Mission of Brazil and Portugal. The movement spread under the impulse of strong leaders, among them Eduardo Henriques Moreira (1886-1981), a poet and preacher. Internal dissensions during and after World War II weakened the movement.

1. Evangelical Presbyterian Church of Portugal (6380)

In the 1940s the first efforts toward forming a national church were made among the Presb communities. One of the promoters was Pastor Natanael Emmerich, who had come from Brazil to serve the congr in Lisbon. On May 12, 1947, the statutes for an Evangelical Presbyterian Church of Portugal were adopted, and on October

31, 1952, the first synod was held. The church also included the majority of the Congreg churches.

The new church enjoyed the strong support of the United Presbyterian Church in the USA. Dr. Michael P. Testa (1912-1981), a missionary sent from the USA, was of great help in solving initial problems. A theological seminary was opened in 1946; it serves all Prot churches. A new situation arose with the Second Vatican Council. In 1966 the church started the Centro Ecumenico Reconciliaçao in Figueira da Foz, a place for encounters and consultations also containing an important social community project.

TM: **1,350** CM: **870** Congr: **22** PStations: **32** OrdM: **15** Eld: **60** Deac: **22** EvgHome: **ne** Mission: **ne** Women Ord: **Yes** As Ministers: **1** as Deac: **10** as Elders: **12** ChurchOrg: **22 community councils, 4 regional councils (presby), 1 synod** Off/otherLang: **Portuguese** DoctrB: **ApC, NicC, AthC, HeidC, Luth and Calvinistic teaching** Infant or believer's baptism: **both** Frequency of the Lord's Supper: **weekly to monthly** Close relations with: **Meth, Lusitanian Church (Angl)** NatRel: **COPIC, CER** RegRel: **CEC, Leuenberg Concord, CEPPLE** IntlRel: **WARC, WCC** TheolSchool: **ne** Service infrastructure: **1 nursery home, 1 social service station, 2 kindergartens** Periodicals: **info and liaison bulletin (spec/3-4 times per year/650), Portugal Evangélico (spec/monthly/1,500)**

Address: Igreja Evangélica Presbiteriana de Portugal, Rua Tomás da Anunciação n 56, 1-D, P-1300 Lisboa, Portugal, Tel: +351 1 397-4959, Fax: +351 1 395-6326

2. Union of Evangelical Congregationalist Churches (6382)

In 1947 the decision to join the Evangelical Presb Church had to be taken individually by the congreg communities. While the majority opted for the union, some decided to maintain their independence. They hold to the 28 Articles of the Christian Faith. The Congregationalist Union has its headquarters in Lisbon. There are presently some 20 churches and missions, including several preaching stations in the areas of Portalegre and Santarém.

TM: **325** Congr: **12** PStations: **8** OrdM: **ne** Eld: **ne** Deac: **ne** EvgHome: **ne** Mission: **ne** Women Ord: **yes** As Ministers: **4** as Deac: **ne** as Elders: **ne** ChurchOrg: **Congregational (congr, annual Assy)** Off/otherLang: **Portuguese** DoctrB: **28 Articles of the Christian Faith** Infant or believer's baptism: **both** NatRel: **Portuguese Evangelical Christian Alliance** RegRel: **ne** IntlRel: **ne** TheolSchool: **ne**

Address: União das Igrejas Evangélicas Congregacionais Portuguesas, Estrada de Chelas, 145, P-1900 Lisboa, Portugal, Tel: +351 1 859-2602

3. Reformed Church in Portugal (6381)

This church was founded by a missionary of the Dutch Reformed Church of South Africa. It presently has two congregations, one in the metropolitan area of Lisbon, the other in Porto.

TM: **45** Congr: **2** OrdM: **1** Eld: **ne** Deac: **ne** EvgHome: **ne** Mission: **ne** Women Ord: **yes** As Ministers: **ne** as Deac: **ne** as Elders: **ne** ChurchOrg: **ne** Off/otherLang: **ne** DoctrB: **ne** NatRel: **ne** RegRel: **ne** IntlRel: **ne** TheolSchool: **ne**

Address: Igreja Reformada em Portugal, R. Norton de Matos 11A Massama, P-2745 Queluz, Portugal,
Tel: +351 1 439-4219, Fax: +351 1 437-16 12, E-mail: nop46549@mail.telepac.pt

4. Christian Presbyterian Church of Portugal (6383)

TM: **nc** Congr: **3** ChurchOrg: **one presbytery (1991)** Off/otherLang: **Portuguese** DoctrB: **nc** Close relations with: **Presb Church of Brazil** NatRel: **nc** RegRel: **nc** IntlRel: **nc** TheolSchool: **nc**

Address: Igreja Cristiana Presbiteriana de Portugal, Rua Prof. Fernando Fonseca, 28, C/V Dt, 1600, Lisboa, Portugal, Tel: +351 1 355-5752, Fax: +351 1 983-5636, E-mail: www.geocities. com/Athens/Acropolis/7154.

Other contact: Rev. Thomas D. Hudson, Rua dos Cedros, 3A P-2670 Loures, E-mail: 74152.326 @compuserve.com

PUERTO RICO

Area in km²	9,104
Population	(July 1996 est.) 3,819,023
Religions in %	RCath 85%, Prot and other 15%
Official/other languages	Spanish, English

With the arrival of Columbus in 1493 the RCath religion was established in Puerto Rico; the first diocese was approved in 1511. The indigenous population rapidly disappeared because of the conquest, slavery, and disease, and was replaced by black slaves; though the present population is 75% white, 15% is black and 10%, mulatto. In 1952, the Commonwealth of Puerto Rico became a self-governing political unit associated voluntarily with the Unites States. Religious vocations among Puerto Ricans have traditionally been few, with the result that a significant majority of the RCath clergy is foreign, especially from the USA and Spain.

Although there had been occasional worship services during brief occupations by the British as early as 1598, and by the Dutch in 1625, no significant Prot mission work occurred until religious tolerance was allowed after the Spanish Revolution in 1868. The first continuous Prot presence was that of the Episcopal Church, established in 1872. The Church of Jesus, founded by Manuel Ferrando in 1902, which had grown to over 2,000 members, united with the Episcopal Church in 1922.

The North American Prot churches established a comity agreement for work in the former Spanish territories in 1898, and in the following year five denominations began to send missionaries: the Bapt, Disciples of Christ, Luth, Presb, and Evangelical United Brethren. But the two largest groups on the island are the Meth, who arrived in 1900, and the Advent in 1909. Both have carried out significant educational projects, while the Advent have also emphasized medical work. The Evangelical United Brethren, the Christian Church, and the Congreg Church formed the United Evangelical Church of Puerto Rico in 1931 (cf. no. 1). As in most of Latin America, however, with the establishment of the Pent Church of God in 1916 the Pent groups have become more numerous than the older churches.

In 1954 nine denominations organized the Evangelical Council of Puerto Rico in which the Presbyterian Church and the IEUPR participate. The Evangelical Seminary (Seminario Evangélico de Puerto Rico), which serves twelve of the Caribbean countries, is constituted by ten of the island's denominations. Since the Spanish American War of 1898, the separation of church and state follows the pattern of the USA closely.

1. United Evangelical Church of Puerto Rico (IEUPR) (3317)

This church was founded on January 28, 1931, in Fajardo, Puerto Rico. It is the product of the union of the Congregational Church, the Evangelical United Brethren, and the Christian Church. It is also the result of an effort started in the earlier part of this century to bring together all evangelical churches in Puerto Rico.

In Humaco, on February 9, 1990, its General Assembly ratified that the IEUPR is a Conference of the United Church of Christ in the USA, keeping its legal and theological order, its traditions and institutions.

TM: **4,951** CM: **4,931** Congr: **61** PStations: **42** OrdM: **0** Eld: **ne** Deac: **ne** EvgHome: **ne** Mission: **none** Women Ord: **yes** As Ministers: **1975/5** as Deac: **ne** as Elders: **ne** ChurchOrg: **national general assembly** Off/otherLang: **Spanish** DoctrB: **ApC, NicC** Infant or believer's baptism: **believer** Frequency of the Lord's Supper: **monthly** Close relations with: **Presb, Meth, Disciples** NatRel: **Concilio evangélico de Puerto Rico** RegRel: **none** IntlRel: **none** TheolSchool: **Evangelical Seminary of Puerto Rico** Service infrastructure: **colleges and schools, kindergartens**

Address: Iglesia Evangélica Unida de Puerto Rico, Apartado 00919-5427, San Juan, Puerto Rico, Tel: +787 759-9707, Fax: +787 756-5459

2. Synod Boriquén in Puerto Rico (PC USA) (3315)

Presb missionaries (J. M. Greene, Milton E. Cadwell) arrived in Puerto Rico in 1899. On the basis of a comity agreement their work concentrated on the area of Aguadilla and Mayagüez. The first church was opened in 1900, and a presby established in 1902. It depended first on Iowa and later on New York. On January 7, 1973, the Synod Boriquén was officially founded.

TM: **8,385** Congr: **71** OrdM: **97** Eld: **169** Deac: **119** Mission: **7** Women Ord: **yes** As Ministers: **13** as Deac: **319** as Elders: **227** ChurchOrg: **Presb (three presby — Surocate, Noroeste, San Juan — synod)** Off/otherLang: **Spanish, English** DoctrB: **nc** Infant or believer's baptism: **both** Frequency of the Lord's Supper: **nc** TheolSchool: **Centro de Estudios Theologicos del Caribe**

Address: Sinodo Boriquén in Puerto Rico, Condominio Medical Center Plaza, Oficina 216, Mayaquez, Puerto Rico 00680, Tel: +1 809 832-8375

3. Christian Reformed Church in Puerto Rico (3316)

This church has 6 congregations totalling about 250-300 in attendance on Sundays. It is served by 3 ordained ministers and by one foreign missionary; a further minister is being trained. It runs its own theological seminary with about 30 students. There is also a book distribution center called "Sola Scriptura" with one full-time person. There is a real need for more ordained ministers.

TM: **300** Congr: **6** OrdM: **4** Eld: **nc** Deac: **nc** EvgHome: **nc** Mission: **nc** Women Ord: **no** ChurchOrg: nc Off/otherLang: **Spanish** DoctrB: **nc** NatRel: **nc** RegRel: **nc** IntlRel: **nc** TheolSchool: **own theological seminary** Service infrastructure: **book distribution center "Sola Scriptura"** Periodicals: **nc**

Address: Iglesia Cristiana Reformada en Puerto Rico, Calle 8, M-1 La Milagrosa, Bayamon, Puerto Rico, 00959, Puerto Rico, Tel: +1 787 755-0350

REUNION ISLAND

Area in km²	2,510
Population	(July 1996 est.) 679,198 French, African, Malagasy, Chinese, Pakistani, Indian
Religions in %	RCath 94%, Hindu, Islam 2%, others 8.4%
Official/other languages	French/Creole widely used

Protestant Church of Reunion Island (1330)

The first Prot community came into existence in the 1950s. From time to time the French military chaplain stationed in Tananarive held services on the island. In 1976 the community was transformed into a church (Eglise Protestante de la Réunion), and in 1992 a church sanctuary was built. The pastors serving the congr in St. Denis are sent by the Fédération Protestante de France. The congr brings together people of different cultural backgrounds: Créoles, French, and especially immigrants from Madagascar.

TM: **600** BM: **600** CM: **580** Congr: **2** PStations: **2** OrdM: **1** Eld: **14** Deac: **4** EvgHome: **nc** Mission: **1** Women Ord: **yes** As Ministers: **none** as Deac: **1979/1** as Elders: **1979/7** ChurchOrg: **member of the Prot Federation of France, synodal system = GenAssy** Off/otherLang: **French, Malgache, Créole** DoctrB: **ApC, NicC, HeidC** Infant or believer's baptism: **both** Frequency of the Lord's Supper: **monthly** Periodicals: **Réforme (gen/monthly), Mission (gen/monthly)** Close relations with: **Bapt, Pent, Evangelicals** NatRel: **nc** RegRel: **nc** IntlRel: **WARC (1986), WCC (1979)** TheolSchool: **nc**

Address: Eglise Protestante de la Réunion, B.P. 818 123, Allée des Saphirs, F — St. Denis Cedex, Reunion Island, Tel: +262 215-535 or 416-391, Fax: +262 414-292

ROMANIA

Area in km²	237,500
Population	(July 1996 est.) 21,657,162 Romanian 89.1%, Hungarian 8.9%, German 0.4%, Ukrainian, Serb, Croat, Russian, Turk, and Gypsy 1.6%
Religions in %	Romanian Orthodox 70%, RCath 6% (of which 3% are Uniate), Prot 6%, unaffiliated 18% (Romanian-speaking population largely Orthodox with RCath and Prot minorities, Hungarian-speaking population in Transylvania evenly divided between Ref and RCath, Luth and Bapt minorities)
Official/other languages	Romanian, Hungarian, German

The history of the Ref churches in Transylvania is closely connected with the history of the Ref churches in Hungary (cf. Hungary). At an early date (1541-1550) the Reformation took roots in the Hungarian-speaking population. Though various influences were at work, Ref theology soon began to dominate. In 1559 the Synod of Márosvasarhely adopted the Ref teaching on the Lord's Supper, and in 1564 the Ref and Luth churches separated. In 1577 the Second Helvetic Confession and the Heidelberg Catechism became official teaching. The princes of Transylvania favored the Reformation and sought to guarantee through laws the peaceful coexistence of the Ref, Luth, and RCath churches. In 1604 Istvan Bosckai (1557-1606), Ref prince of Transylvania, went to war to defend the religious rights of the Prot and obtained from the emperor the recognition of his reign in Transylvania. Throughout the 17th century the Ref Church could freely live and develop. In 1622 the first theological academy was established.

In the 18th century Transylvania was incorporated into the Hapsburg empire. Many difficulties arose, but the Ref church was able to maintain its integrity and to defend the spiritual identity of the people. One of the significant figures of this period was Peter Bod, pastor, historian, and encyclopedist. In the middle of the 19th century the Ref church identified with the liberation struggle from the Hapsburg empire, hoping for a new Christian and democratic order. In 1867 Transylvania once more became part of Hungary. In 1895 the theological school of Kolozsvár was opened. The church enjoyed a period of growth: churches were built and schools opened.

A new period began with the end of World War I, when Transylvania became part of Romania. The Hungarian-speaking population in Transylvania became a minority within the Romanian-speaking Orthodox majority. Between World Wars I and II the church experienced spiritual renewal. The leading figure during this time was Bishop Sandor Makkai (1926-1936). After a brief period of re-integration into Hungary (1940-1944), Transylvania returned to Romania. Four decades of Communist rule followed. All public institutions of the church were confiscated and church life limited to worship in church buildings. Especially in the late '50s and early '60s many pastors were imprisoned; several died or were executed. Admission of candidates for pastoral training was severely curtailed. While in the '70s and '80s the bishops collaborated with the state authorities, many pastors and church members suffered violation of their rights.

The fall of the Communist regime brought to the church in Romania, on the one hand, more freedom, on the other, new challenges and opportunities. More than 120 new buildings have been constructed or are in construction, among them about 30 new churches, a diaconal center, conference and youth centers, orphanages, old people's homes, and parish buildings. High expectations are placed on the church. At the same time, however, the church continues to face the difficulties of being a linguistic, cultural, and political minority. The major problems are that the buildings, e.g., schools, as well as other goods expropriated during the Communist regime, have not yet been returned and that religious education has not been restored as requested by the churches.

The Reformed Church of Romania is organized in two districts — the Transylvanian District and the District of Oradea. They have a common synod for legislative purposes but two independent administrations.

1. Reformed Church in Romania — Transylvanian District (6390.A)

TM: **404,066** BM: **404,066** CM: **323,248** Congr: **506** PStations: **760** OrdM: **465** Eld: **8,500** Deac: **nc** EvgHome: **none** Mission: nc Women Ord: **yes** As Ministers: **25** as Deac: **nc** as Elders: **10%** ChurchOrg: **parishes, deaneries, districts, synod (legislative)** Off/otherLang: **Hungarian** DoctrB: **ApC, HeidC, HelvC** Infant or believer's baptism: **both** Frequency of the Lord's Supper: **7-8 times per year** Periodicals: **Üzenet (gen/bi-weekly/10,500), Igehirdetö (homiletics/monthly/1,250), Református Szemle (theol/bi-monthly/800), Ertesítö (official news/monthly/800), Református Család (family/quarterly/10,000)** Close relations with: **Ref Alliance (Germany), Church of Lippe (Germany), Ev. Ref Church (Germany), SEK/FEPS (CH), PCUSA, PC Ireland, Ref Churches in Hungary, Slovakia, Yugoslavia, Ukraine, Hungarian-speaking in USA** NatRel: **AIDROM (Ecumenical relief) (1990), Consultative Synod of Hungarian Ref Churches (1995)** RegRel: **CEC** IntlRel: **WARC (1923), WCC (1961), Hungarian Ref World Alliance (1991)** TheolSchool: **Theological Seminary in Kolozsvár (Cluj)**

Address: Rönániái Református Egyház — Erdélyi Egyházkerület, Strada I.C. Bratianu Nr. 51, R-3400 Cluj-Napoca, Romania, Tel: +40 64 197-472, Fax: +40 64 195-104

2. Reformed Church in Romania — Oradea (6390.B)

TM: **320,000** BM: **311,500** Congr: **271** PStations: **342** OrdM: **225** Eld: **6,450** Deac: nc EvgHome: **0** Mission: nc Women Ord: **yes** As Ministers: **1950/15** as Deac: nc as Elders: **1950/690** ChurchOrg: **congr (elders), deaneries (each has one dean), 8 deaneries form the church district led by the GenAssy** Off/otherLang: **Hungarian** DoctrB: **ApC, HeidC, HelvC** Infant or believer's baptism: **both** Frequency of the Lord's Supper: **6-10 times per year** Periodicals: **Közlöny (church news — ecum/2,000), Harangszó (gen/17,000), Elö Reménység (hospital newsletter/1,000)** Close relations with: **RCath, Luth, Unitarian Bapt** NatRel: **AIDROM (ecumenical relief) (1990)** RegRel: nc IntlRel: **WARC, WCC, CEC** TheolSchool: **Theological Seminary in Kolozsvár (Cluj)**

Address: Királyhágómelléki Református Egyházkerület (Oradea District), J. Calvin nr. 1, R-3700
Oradea Bihor 3700, Romania, Tel: +40 59 43 1710, Fax: +40 59 432-837

RUSSIA

Area in km²	17,075,200
Population	(July 1996 est.) 148,178,487 Russian 81.5%, Tatar 3.8%, Ukrainian 3%, Chuvash 1.2%, Bashkir 0.9%, Byelorussian 0.8%, Moldavian 0.7%, other 8.1%
Religions in %	Russian Orthodox ca. 50%, Muslim, Jew, Bapt, Ref, other
Official/other languages	Russian, other

There are only a few Ref communities in the vast territory of Russia. Their existence owes to particular historical circumstances. Russia belongs to the sphere of Eastern Orthodoxy. For a long time the message of the Reformation did not find an entrance into the country. Protestantism was brought to Russia through migration and later through intentional missionary efforts. The earliest trace of a Ref community goes back to the 17th century (cf. no. 1). In the 18th century the Russian Tsars, especially Catherine the Great, invited German farmers to establish themselves in the Volga area; among them there were many Prot, Luth, and Ref. In the first half of the 19th century the Basel Mission was active among them. During World War II the German-speaking population was deported to Siberia by Stalin. The scattered communities today belong to the Evangelical Lutheran Church. The fall of the Marxist regime of the Soviet Union and the introduction of religious freedom gave rise to new developments. In certain circles Ref teaching met with spontaneous interest; Ref communities were founded by Russian Christians (cf. no. 2). The new opportunities were also seized by many evangelistic and missionary movements in all parts of the world. Hundreds of groups became active in Russia — some with considerable, others with limited success. These efforts caused resentment and hostility within the Russian Orthodox Church and vast parts of the population. Government and parliament have responded by introducing a more restrictive law on religious freedom (1997).

1. Reformed Fundamental Church (6561)

The first Ref Church with Russian members was established in Tula in 1632. The church was founded by Dutch and French immigrants who came to work with a Dutch iron producer and merchant, Andrew Vinius. To confess Calvinism at that time in Russia was considered a crime. In 1714 Thomas Ivanov, a surgeon in the Moscow Infantry Regiment, was executed for publicly preaching Ref convictions. Foreigners were allowed to practice their faith, but the Russian Ref church had to operate underground. In Tula many educated merchants were members of the Ref Church. Under the Communist regime many Ref suffered martyrdom. The Ref Church was reconstituted in 1992 and officially registered in 1994 as the Reformed Fundamental Church. Apart from this community there continue to be underground Ref communities which do not trust the democratic changes in Russia. The community in Tula confesses a strict form of Calvinism. Only members of the church participate in communion.

TM: **2,261** BM: **1,376** CM: **891** Congr: **7** PStations: **8** OrdM: **1** Eld: **5** Deac: **1** EvgHome: **2** Mission: **5** Women Ord: **yes** As Ministers: **no** as Deac: **yes/1** as Elders: **yes/2** ChurchOrg: **congr, consistories, synod** Off/otherLang: **Russian** DoctrB: **NicC, HeidC, CDort** Infant or believer's baptism: **both** Frequency of the Lord's Supper: **twice to four times a year** Close relations with: **Siberian "underground" Bapt Church** NatRel: **none** RegRel: **nc** IntlRel: **nc** TheolSchool: **Bible School in Tula** Service infrastructure: **Program on creationism (has published over 35 articles with circulation of 1,500,000), pastoral help program against Chechenya war syndrome** Periodicals: **The Reformed Russia (gen/bi-weekly/900)**

Address: Reformirovannaya Fundamentalistskaya Tserkow, 71 "A," Sovetskaya, 300000 Tula, Russia, Tel: +7 872 36 24 25 or 26 50 30, Fax: +7 872 36 24 25, E-mail: www.cterra.com.

2. Union of the Evangelical Reformed Churches of Russia (6560)

This group came into existence after the fall of the Soviet regime and the changes which followed. The initiative came from Evgenyi D. Kashirski and Vladimir M. Lotsmanov in Tver and Moscow. In 1991 congregations were established in these two cities, and one year later the Union of Evangelical Reformed Churches was formed. The aim of the movement was and is to introduce Calvinist thinking into Russia. It places strong emphasis on communicating pure Reformation thinking. The church has begun to publish in Russian a series of pamphlets on Calvinist teaching.

TM: **40** BM: **40** CM: **40** Congr: **2** PStations: **2** OrdM: **2** Eld: **2** Deac: **2** EvgHome: **2** Mission: **none** Women Ord: **no** ChurchOrg: **congr, consistory, regional synod** Off/otherLang: **Russian** DoctrB: **ApC, HeidC, WestConf, CDort** Infant or believer's baptism: **both** Frequency of the Lord's Supper: **monthly** Close relations with: **Ref Churches in the Netherlands (Liberated)** NatRel: **none** RegRel: **none** IntlRel: **none** TheolSchool: **none** Service infrastructure: **none** Periodicals: **none**

Address: Soyus Evangelichesko-Reformatskich Tserkvey Rossii,

1. 1-Zavokzalnaya Str., Apt. 64, 1700042, Tver, Russia
2. P.O. Box 27, Chudova 14-41, 123424, Moscow, Russia, Tel: +7 095 490 2289, E-mail: 76135.2425@compuserve.com.

3. Korean Missions and Communities in Russia

Korean evangelistic efforts directed toward the Soviet Union started with the establishment in 1956 of the Keuk Dong (Far East) Broadcasting System. Actual mission work began in the late 1980s. Elder Kim Young-Kuk from KoShin (cf. Korea no. 1) founded a mission agency called "Mission for Russia" in 1986. In 1990 Korean missionaries began activities within Russia. In the same year one Meth and two Presb congregations were founded — the Ban Suk Meth Church in Moscow, the Presbyterian Church in Moscow (by Pastor Hwang Sang-Ho), and the Presbyterian Church in Sakhalin (by Elder Kim Young-Kuk). In the following year a course for missionaries to Russia was organized and nine missionaries sent to various cities such as Tashkent, Alma Ata, Viskek, Khabarovsk, Sakhalin, and Vladivostok. More missionaries followed. In 1993 an association of Korean missionaries to Russia was formed; it was later transformed into the Council of Korean Missionaries in Moscow. In 1994 a Council of Presbyterian Missionaries in Russia was organized to meet requirements of official registration with state authorities.

Currently a little over one hundred congregations have come into existence. Sixty-three congregations are led by Koreans, forty congregations by Russians. Membership varies from 40 to 100. The pattern of congregational life is similar to the patterns in Korea.

A sizeable group of Koreans lives in Russia. According to the 1989 census Korean-Russians number 457,000. About half of the Korean-Russians continue to regard Korean as their mother tongue and would like to be in touch with the mother country, though they regard Russia as their permanent home. Originally Koreans lived mainly in the Maritime Provinces of Siberia. During the period of Japanese rule many Koreans left their home country. Vladivostok became a center of Korean exile. Today large numbers can be found in Uzbekistan because in 1937 about 200,000 Koreans were deported by Stalin and forced to resettle in Central Russia. Many continue to live in Vladivostok. Since the city is close to North Korea, many North Koreans have found refuge there. In 1991 South Korean missionaries began to arrive in Vladivostok, and their numbers increased in subsequent years. Today, besides Presb, several other South Korean denominations are represented. Currently there are 23 congregations in the Maritime Province of Russia, eleven in Vladivostok alone.

Koreans have started a number of theological schools in Russia. In 1991 Korean missionaries from the USA founded Grace Presbyterian Theological Seminary in Moscow. In the following year missionaries from KoShin (cf. Korea no. 1) and HapDong (cf. Korea no. 15) opened the Presbyterian Theological Seminary for Russia in Moscow; it has recently been placed under the authority of the Council of Presbyterian Missionaries in Russia. In 1994 the Presbyterian Church in Korea (TongHap, cf. Korea no. 14) set up the Moscow Presbyterian Theological Academy (Elder Lee Hong Rae, 105173 Moscow Savhoz, 1 Maya Dom 11). There are two theological schools in Vladivostok. Other Korean denominations have also established seminaries in Russia.

Address: a) Council of Presbyterian Missionaries in Russia, Rev. Chung-Soo Kang, Chairman, Moscow, Tel: +7 095 307 1768

b) For Vladivostok: Rev. Yun Mi-Kyung, KB 49 Russkaya, 59/4 Vladivostok 105, Russia, Fax: +7 4232 32 98 17

RWANDA

Area in km²	26,340
Population	(July 1996 est.) 6,853,359 Hutu 80%, Tutsi 19%, Twa (Pygmoid) 1%
Religions in %	RCath 65%, Prot 9%, Muslim 1%, indigenous beliefs and other 25%
Official/other languages	Kinyarwanda, French/Kiswahili (Swahili) used in commercial centers

Because of its mountainous landscape and its being enclaved in the interior of the African continent, Rwanda was one of the last African countries conquered by colonial powers. Before the Berlin Conference (1885) which placed the country under German rule, cutting off half of its territory, political and military authority was exercised by a monarchy which succeeded in unifying the three social classes known as Hutu, Tutsi, and Twa. After World War I the Germans were forced to leave and Rwanda was placed under Belgian protection until independence was gained on July, 1, 1962. As a result of insufficient preparation for the transition, Hutu and Tutsi were stirred up against each other, with the consequence that many Tutsi were exterminated and others driven into exile. In 1990 descendants of these refugees, who had not been authorized to return to the country, invaded Rwanda from Uganda with foreign help. In 1994 an unprecedented massacre took place which resulted in over a million victims among the Tutsi and a number of Hutu political leaders.

The first missionaries were RCath White Fathers (1900). The first Prot mission was the German Bethel Mission (1907), a new body established for missionary work in the African territories of Germany, whose spiritual direction was decisively influenced by Friedrich von Bodelschwing (1831-1910). Besides the RCath and the Presbyterian Church the following churches have taken root in Rwanda: Angl, Free Meth, Bapt, Pent, and Advent. The country has been famous for its participation in the East Africa Revival movement in the '30s. Today all churches suffer from the consequences of the genocide which has carried away many of its members, including many clergy.

441

Presbyterian Church in Rwanda (1350)

The church resulted from the work of the Bethel Mission. After the departure of the German missionaries (1916) the work was taken over, after some years, by the small Belgian Protestant Missionary Society. In 1959 the church gained independence and adopted the name Presbyterian Church in Rwanda. At that time it strengthened its relationship with the Dutch and Swiss churches, and later with the Presbyterian Church USA and the Evangelical Church in Germany. The church experienced strong growth up to 1994. It maintained many primary and several secondary and professional schools as well as three hospitals and several local clinics. Three presidents have served the church since independence: Naasson Hitimana (until 1977), Michel Twagirayesu (until 1994), and André Karamaga (from 1995). Today, the church faces the difficult task of rebuilding its life, of consoling and reconciling its members, and of creating new confidence for Rwandan people both inside and outside the country. The tribal composition of the church corresponds to the proportions of the populations in the country.

TM: **120,000** Congr: **74** PStations: **47** OrdM: **38** Eld: **712** Deac: **712** EvgHome: **nc** Mission: **nc** Women Ord: **yes** As Ministers: **2** as Deac: **407** as Elders: **304** ChurchOrg: **Presbyterian (congr, regional synods, GenAssy)** Off/otherLang: **Kinyarwanda, French** DoctrB: **ApC** Infant or believer's baptism: **both** NatRel: **Christian Council of Rwanda** RegRel: **AACC** IntlRel: **WCC, WARC, VEM** TheolSchool: **Theological Faculty (Butare) jointly with other Prot denominations, CORVT (Centre oecuménique de Recherche et de Vulgarisation Théologique)**

Address: Eglise presbytérienne au Rwanda, B.P. 56, Kigali, Rwanda, Tel.: +250 7 6929, Fax: +250 7 6929, E-mail: epr@maf.org

---

SENEGAL

Area in km²	196,190
Population	(July 1996 est.) 9,092,749 Wolof 36%, Fulani 17%, Serer 17%, Toucouleur 9%, Diola 9%, Mandingo 9%, European and Lebanese 1%, other 2%
Religions in %	Muslim 92%, indigenous beliefs 6%, Christian 2% (mostly RCath)
Official/other languages	French/Wolof, Pulaar, Diola, Mandingo

The RCath Mission started in Senegal in 1659. In the 19th century several attempts were made by the Société des Missions évangéliques de Paris (SMEP) to establish mission work. A first group of missionaries arrived in 1862 in Sedhiou (Casamance), but it had to abandon the Casamance region as a result of the death of two members of the team as well as other incidents. Later attempts started from the then capital, St. Louis. Until the end of the century 25 missionaries followed one another, without much response from the people. François Villegier translated the Gospel into Wolof, and Walter Taylor from Sierra Leone, a descendant of freed slaves and ordained in Paris in 1878, did evangelistic work among freed slaves. In 1882 he founded a small community in Khor (near St. Louis). In 1894 the first chapel was built in Khor. After Dakar became the capital of Senegal in 1904, SMEP stationed a missionary there in 1906, and eventually a church was built in 1913. In 1952 the community was constituted as the Protestant Church of Dakar and the diaspora in French West Africa with two pastors — one to serve the community in Dakar and the other the Prot scattered in other parts of the country. Several institutions were created (dispensary, primary school, meeting center). In 1972 when the church became independent, it became the Protestant Church of Senegal (Eglise protestante du Sénégal). Since then leadership is entirely in African hands. Membership of the two communities consists largely of foreigners living in Senegal.

Apart from the Eglise protestante de Sénégal a great number of small evangelical communities have come into existence in recent times.

Protestant Church of Senegal (1180)

TM: **250** CM: **200** Congr: **2** PStations: **3** OrdM: **2** Eld: **10** Deac: **20** EvgHome: **1** Mission: **nc** Women Ord: **no** ChurchOrg: **parish council, GenAssy — executive committee elected for 2 years** Off/otherLang: **French** DoctrB: **ApC, NicC** Infant or believer's baptism: **both** Frequency of the Lord's Supper: **monthly** NatRel: **nc** RegRel: **AACC** IntlRel: **WARC, WCC, CEVAA** TheolSchool: **nc**

Address: Eglise protestante du Sénégal (EPS), P.O. Box 22.390, Ponty 65, rue Wagane Diouf, Dakar, Senegal, Tel: +221 21 55 64, Fax: +221 21 71 32

SINGAPORE

Area in km²	6,326
Population	(July 1996 est.) 3,396,924 Chinese 76.4%, Malay 14.9%, Indian 6.4%, other 2.3%
Religions in %	Buddhist (Chinese) 65%, Muslim (Malays) 15%, Christian 9%, Hindu 5%, other (Sikh, Taoist, Confucianist) 6%
Official languages	Chinese, Malay, Tamil, English

Until 1965 the city of Singapore was part of the Federation of Singapore and Malaysia. In the last three decades the city has experienced rapid economic growth. For details on the history of the Ref presence in Singapore see under Malaysia.

443

1. Presbyterian Church in Singapore (4370)

In 1975, ten years after the withdrawal of Singapore from the Malaysian Federation, the Presbyterian churches in Singapore and Malaysia decided to establish their own synods. The Presbyterian Church in Singapore held its first synod meeting in January 1975 and elected an executive committee holding term for two years. Since then there has been significant growth in terms of congregations and preaching stations; welfare work and education programs have been established. In 1992 two language presbyteries (Chinese and English) were formed, a decision which helped to make synod proceedings more focused. The church runs four schools (primary and secondary). Welfare services are provided for the elderly and other needy people. Several congregations have recently expanded their facilities. A theological response commission has been established to grapple with contemporary issues.

TM: **9,000** CM: **6,232** Congr: **28** PStations: **5** OrdM: **30** Eld: **8** Deac: **152** EvgHome: **nc** Mission: **yes** Women Ord: **yes** As Ministers: **3** as Deac: **nc** as Elders: **nc** ChurchOrg: **Presbyterian (congr, 2 presby [Chinese and English], Synod)** Off/otherLang: **Mandarin, English** DoctrB: **ApC, WestConf** Periodicals: **Presbyterian Express (in English), Presbyterian Messenger (in Mandarin)** NatRel: **nc** RegRel: **nc** IntlRel: **CWM, WARC** TheolSchool: **Trinity Theological College, Singapore Bible College**

Address: Presbyterian Church in Singapore, Church House, 132 Sophia Rd., Singapore 228186, Singapore, Tel: +65 338-5837, Fax: +65 339-4076, E-mail: twpc1@swiftech.com.sg

2. Life Bible Presbyterian Church (4371)

This church separated in the 1950s from the Presbyterian Church of Singapore and Malaysia (cf. Malaysia no. 1). The inspiration for the new movement came from Pastor Timothy Tow Siang Hui, a follower and supporter of Carl McIntire, the leader of the International Council of Christian Churches (ICCC). He defended fundamentalist convictions and opposed all forms of modernism, especially the ecumenical movement led by the WCC. After a few years of struggle within the Presbyterian Church, in 1955 Pastor Tow founded the Life Bible Presbyterian Church. The movement grew. In 1956 three pastors were ordained, and in 1960 the Singapore Presbytery of the Bible Presbyterian Church in Singapore and Malaysia was inaugurated. In 1962 the Far Eastern Bible College was opened. By 1971 eight congregations had been founded and the church began to extend its witness abroad, e.g., in Australia, Indonesia, Saipan, Malaysia, Thailand, Burma, Africa, and Canada. Dissensions arose within the church. The militant anti-modernist and anti-ecumenical stance of its leaders was not accepted by a sizeable minority. In the 1980s, in addition, a controversy occurred over the place of speaking in tongues in the life of the church. In November 1988 the tensions had become so strong that the decision was taken to dissolve the synod. Individual Bible Presbyterian Churches, separately registered with the government, continue to exist under their respective names.

TM: **1,300** BM: **1,300** Congr: **6** PStations: **5** OrdM: **3** Eld: **8** Deac: **20** EvgHome: **1** Mission: **8** Women Ord: **no** As Ministers: **ne** as Deac: **ne** as Elders: **ne** ChurchOrg: **Synod dissolved in 1988** Off/otherLang: **English, Chinese, Indonesian, Thai, Filipino, Burmese** DoctrB: **ApC, WestConf** Infant or believer's baptism: **both** Frequency of the Lord's Supper: **monthly** Periodicals: **Life Bible Presbyterian Church (weekly/1,000), Burning Bush by FEBC (2 per year/2,000)** Close relations with: **half a dozen Bible Presb churches since dissolution of Bible Presb Synod in 1988** NatRel: **none anymore** RegRel: **Far Eastern Council of Christian Churches (1951)** IntlRel: **ICCC (1955)** TheolSchool: **Far Eastern Bible College (Singapore)**

Address: Life Bible Presbyterian Church, 9A Gilstead Road, Singapore 1130, Singapore, Tel: +65 256-9256, Fax: +65 250-6955, E-mail: febc@pacific.net.sg

3. Evangelical Reformed Churches in Singapore (4373)

This church was founded by Pastor Lau Chin Kwec, who had been active in various Prot groups in Singapore, but who adopted in 1976, under the influence of visiting guests of the Reformed Church in America, a decidedly Ref confessional position. In 1982 the Evangelical Reformed Church in Singapore was founded. It was eventually joined by another congregation, the Covenant Evangelical Reformed Church.

TM: **328** BM: **208** CM: **208** Congr: **2** PStations: **2** OrdM: **1** Eld: **7** Deac: **7** EvgHome: **0** Mission: **0** Women Ord: **no** As Ministers: **ne** as Deac: **ne** as Elders: **ne** ChurchOrg: **classis** Off/otherLang: **English, occasionally Chinese and dialects** DoctrB: **ApC, HeidC, CDort, Three Forms of Unity** Infant or believer's baptism: **both** Frequency of the Lord's Supper: **every 2 months** Close relations with: **Prot Ref Ch of America** (cf. USA no. 33) NatRel: **nc** RegRel: **nc** IntlRel: **nc** TheolSchool: **nc**

Address: Evangelical Reformed Churches in Singapore, 652 Yio Chu Kang Road S 787076, Singapore 787076, Tel: +65 452-4388, Fax: +65 452-4638, E-mail: lckferc@mbox2.singnet.com.sg

---

SLOVAKIA

Area in km^2	48,845
Population	(July 1996 est.) 5,374,362 Slovak 85.7%, Hungarian 10.7%, Gypsy 1.5%, Czech 1%, Ruthenian 0.3%, Ukrainian 0.3%, German 0.1%, Polish 0.1%, other 0.3%
Religions in %	RCath 60.3%, atheist 9.7%, Prot 8.4%, Orth 4.1%, other 17.5%
Official/other languages	Slovak/Hungarian

Up to World War I the present territory of Slovakia belonged to the Austrian-Hungarian Empire. In 1918, through the Trianon Treaty, it became part of newly formed Czechoslovakia. In 1993 Czechoslovakia was divided into two independent states — the Czech and the Slovak Republics.

1. Reformed Church of Slovakia (6132)

Until the end of World War I the Ref church in Slovakia, as well as in the Carpatho-Ukraine (cf. Ukraine), was part of the Reformed Church in Hungary. The Reformation movement reached the region in the early 1520s. The soil had been prepared by the Hussite movement a century before. In the beginning, Luther's influence was dominant; later, Calvinist thinking prevailed. In 1564 four presbyteries were formed in eastern Slovakia in which Slovaks and Hungarians lived side by side. After the Synod in Debrecen, where the Reformed Church of Hungary adopted the Second Helvetic Confession, the Ref faith also spread to central and western Slovakia. During the period of the Counter-Reformation in the 17th century the Ref churches were protected by the princes of Transylvania, who extended their supremacy to parts of Slovakia. Literature (catechism, hymnbook, liturgy) in Slovak was printed in Debrecen.

The church was revitalized after the Edict of Toleration (1781). The Synod of Buda (1791) opened the way for the presbyterian-synodal constitution. The Synod of Debrecen (1881) gave a unified structure to the Reformed Church of Hungary. Within this framework the Reformed Church of Slovakia was exposed to nationalist Hungarian tendencies. By 1918 the indigenous Slovak culture was almost extinct.

The Reformed Church of Slovakia was established in its present form after World War I. At that time it had a membership of 216,000 in Slovakia and 20,000 in Carpatho-Ukraine. In 1923 a General Synod was convened in Levice to adopt the constitution. The relationship between Slovaks and the Hungarian minority proved to be difficult. Some Hungarians did not recognize the results of the Trianon Treaty and refused to accept the new constitution. In 1925 a Hungarian-speaking theological seminary was founded in Lucenec. During the time of the puppet Slovak state established by the Nazis (1939-1945), the majority of the congr again became part of the Reformed Church of Hungary.

World War II brought new changes. The Carpatho-Ukrainian region became part of the Ukraine (USSR). In 1951 the Reformed Church of Slovakia adopted a new constitution. The supreme organ was the Synod, with a Synodal Council as its executive arm. Seven presbyteries were created. After the separation in 1993 a Theological Institute was opened in Komarno (1995); catechetical schools began to function in Komarno and Kosice.

TM: **120,000** BM: **120,000** CM: **40,000** Congr: **327** PStations: **76** OrdM: **135** Eld: **2,957** Deac: **30** EvgHome: **40** Mission: **6** Women Ord: **yes** As Ministers: **1972/32** as Deac: **1925/12** as Elders: **1970/ 380** ChurchOrg: **congr, classis, presby, synod** Off/otherLang: **Hungarian, Slovak** DoctrB: **ApC, HeidC, HelvC** Infant or believer's baptism: **both** Frequency of the Lord's Supper: **6 times per year** Close relations with: **Ev. Luth Ch AC, Slovak Bible Society** NatRel: **Hungarian Ref World Federation (1995), Ecumenical Council of Churches in Slovakia** RegRel: **nc** IntlRel: **WARC (1948), REC**

(1948), WCC (1948), ICRC (1948) TheolSchool: **Theological Seminary in Komarno, Catechetical School in Komarno and Kosice** Periodicals: **Kálvinista Szemle-Kalvínske hlasy (gen/monthly/ 7,300), Református Újság (gen/monthly/2,000), Duchovná obnova (gen/6per year/1,300)**

Address: Reformovaná krest. církev na Slovensku, Jókaiho 34, 94 501 Komárno 945 01, Slovakia, Tel: +42 1 819 701 826, Fax: +42 1 819 701 827

2. Church of the Brethren in the Slovak Republic (6133)

As a consequence of the separation of the Czech and Slovak republics, the church was also divided. For the history of the church cf. Czech Republic.

TM: **2,200** BM: **1,250** CM: **1,200** Congr: **9** PStations: **35** OrdM: **12** Eld: **60** Deac: **10** EvgHome: **4** Mission: **0** Women Ord: **yes** As Ministers: **0** as Deac: **8** as Elders: **4** ChurchOrg: **regional level: no structure, national level: church council and GenAssy** Off/otherLang: **Slovak** DoctrB: **ApC, NicC, AthC, HeidC, HelvC, WestConf, Conf of Faith of the Brethren Ch** Infant or believer's baptism: **both** Frequency of the Lord's Supper: **monthly** Close relations with: **Bapt, Meth, Pent** NatRel: **Ecumenical Council (1990), Evangelical Alliance (1991), Association of Evangelical Churches (1997)** RegRel: **nc** IntlRel: **WARC (1990), IFFEC (1989)** TheolSchool: **Matej Bel University (Banská Bystrica), Theological Faculty (Bratislava)** Periodicals: **Bratská rodina (magazine/monthly/350)**

Address: Cirkev Bratská na Slovensku, 93401 ul. 29, augusta 27, Levice 934 01, Slovakia, Tel: +42 1 813-23848, Fax: +42 1 813-23848, E-mail: cblv@uvt.uniag.sk.

SLOVENIA

Area in km²	20,256
Population	(July 1996 est.) 1,951,443 Slovene 91%, Croat 3%, Serb 2%, Muslim 1%, other 3%
Religions in %	RCath 96% (including 2% Uniate), Muslim 1%, other 3%
Official/other languages	Slovenian 91%/Serbo-Croatian 7%, other 2%

Reformed Church in Slovenia (6400)

Until World War I Slovenia was part of Austro-Hungarian Empire. At that time there were about 800 Ref Hungarians living in Slovenia. They belonged to three parishes of the Reformed Church of Hungary which were close to the Slovenian border— Bajánsenye, Kercaszomor, and Szentgyörgyvölgy. After World War I, through the Trianon Treaty, Slovenia became part of Yugoslavia, and the Reformed Church in Yugoslavia became independent in 1921. The scattered communities in Slovenia were served by a minister until 1950. Thereafter Slovenia was considered a missionary field of the Reformed Christian Church in Yugoslavia located beyond the river Mura.

Early in the Yugoslavian War of the 1990s Slovenia became an independent state. Eventually a separate church was also set up for Slovenia. In 1993, at a meeting attended by elders, the Hungarian Reformed Christian Church in Slovenia was established. A constitution was adopted and submitted to the Slovenian government to obtain the registration of the church. The Reformed Church of Hungary has accepted responsibility for pastoral care. At present there are five places of worship. The church hopes to extend its work to the cities where several hundred Ref followers have migrated. The church maintains fraternal relations with the Luth living in the same area. By mutual support, they seek to implement the Leuenberg Agreement.

TM: **400** Congr: **3** PStations: **2** OrdM: **nc** Eld: **nc** Deac: **nc** EvgHome: **nc** Mission: **nc** Women Ord: **yes** As Ministers: **1975/nc** as Deac: **nc** as Elders: **nc** ChurchOrg: **nc** Off/otherLang: **Hungarian** DoctrB: **ApC, NicC, AthC, HeidC, HelvC** Close relations: **Reformed Church in Hungary** NatRel: **nc** RegRel: **nc** IntlRel: **WARC** TheolSchool: **training in Hungary**

Address: Reformed Church in Slovenia, Motvarjevci, SLO — Prosenjakovci 699207, Slovenia, Tel: +386 69 44027, Fax: +386 69 44027

SOLOMON ISLANDS

Area in km²	27,540
Population	(July 1996 est.) 412,902 Melanesian 93%, Polynesian 4%, Micronesian 1.5%, European 0.8%, Chinese 0.3%, other 0.4%
Religions in %	Angl 34%, RCath 19%, Bapt 17%, United (Meth/Presb) 11%, Advent 10%, other Prot 5%, traditional beliefs 4%
Official/other languages	Melanesian pidgin is lingua franca in much of the country, English spoken by 1%-2% of population, 120 indigenous languages

United Church of the Solomon Islands (4541)

The Solomon Islands, formerly a British protectorate, became independent in 1978. In 1902 John F. Goldie, an Australian missionary, was sent by the Australian Meth Overseas Mission Board to the archipelago's Western Solomons Province. The Meth mission expanded within the major western islands from its base at Munda Point, New Georgia, helped by Islander missionaries from Fiji and Samoa.

From 1913 onward the church extended northwestward into the large island of Bougainville, which had been administered by Germany, then by Australia, and under League of Nations and United Nations trusteeship, finally becoming part of independent Papua New Guinea. New Zealand Meth were major partners in the mission from 1913. Meanwhile, after World War II, the church of the London Missionary Society in Papua became the independent Papua Ekalesia in 1962, which in 1968 united with Meth churches in Papua New Guinea and the Solomon Islands to form the United Church of Papua New Guinea and Solomon Islands.

The Bougainville area of the Solomon Islands straddled the political divide. In the Western Solomons, from 1955 onward, British relocation of a substantial group of Gilbert Islander Prot of LMS background on the Western Solomons island of Wagina led to their integration, by agreement between Meth and the LMS, into the Solomon Islands Meth Church. The United Church, which in this way acquired people of Ref backgrounds, included 15% of the population on Bougainville. The Solomon Islands attained political independence in 1978. A movement on Bougainville seeking secession from Papua New Guinea led, in the 1980s, to fighting against the Papua New Guinea government and disrupted communication within the church, which it unsuccessfully sought to mediate. The Solomons half of the church and the Papua New Guinea half separated (by mutual agreement) in 1996. Wider connections for the Solomon Islands church continue through the membership of both churches in the Pacific Conference of Churches (PCC), the ecumenical Solomon Islands Christian Association (SICA), and the World Council of Churches. Leslie Boseto of the Solomon Islands, a former bishop and presiding moderator in the previously undivided church, was elected as a president of the WCC in 1992.

TM: **50,000** Congr: **300** OrdM: **50** Eld: **nc** Deac: **nc** EvgHome: **nc** Mission: **nc** Women Ord: **yes** As Ministers: **1978** as Deac: **nc** as Elders: **nc** ChurchOrg: **nc** Off/otherLang: **Melanesian pidgin, English** DoctrB: **nc** Infant or believer's baptism: **both** Periodicals: **none** Close relations with: **Uniting Church in Australia, PC USA, United Church of Canada** NatRel: **Solomon Islands Christian Association (SICA)** RegRel: **PCC** IntlRel: **WARC (1997), WCC (1997), CWM** TheolSchool: **Raratonga Theological College**

Address: United Church of the Solomon Islands, P.O. Box 82, Kokeqolo, Munda Western Province, Solomon Islands, Tel: +677 61125, Fax: +677 61265

SOUTH AFRICA

Area in km²	1,219,912
Population	(July 1996 est.) 41,743,459 black 75.2%, white 13.6%, colored 8.6%, Indian 2.6
Religions in %	Christians 75% (African Independent Churches 26%, Ref 15%, RCath 12%, other Prot and Pent 12%), Muslim (2%), Hindu (60% of Indians), Jewish communities, African traditional religions
Official/other languages	11 official languages, including Afrikaans, English, Ndebele, Pedi, Sotho, Swazi, Tsonga, Tswana, Venda Xhosa, Zulu

SACC (South African Council of Churches)
CUC (Church Unity Commission)
SAARC (Southern African Alliance of Ref Churches)

The Ref tradition came to South Africa with Dutch colonists who settled in the Cape in 1652. Originally the Dutch Reformed Church consisted only of white settlers. But mission work was started, first among slaves and later among the indigenous population. Ultimately, as the hinterland was opened up by explorers, traders, and mission societies, Ref missionaries also moved further and further into the interior, first into what is today the Northern Province of South Africa, and later into neighboring countries such as Swaziland, Zimbabwe, Botswana, Zambia, Malawi, and Mozambique. In this way the Ref churches of South Africa extended the Ref tradition over much of Southern Africa, creating links which still exist today. The first split in the Dutch Reformed Church, possibly better known by its Afrikaans acronym NGK, occurred about two centuries after its arrival in the Cape. Afrikaners, who had settled in the then Transvaal in the northern interior of South Africa, suspicious of what they considered to be liberal tendencies in the Cape-dominated NGK, and insisting on a rigid policy of "no equality between white and black in church or state," formed the Nederduitsche Hervormde Kerk (NHK — in English the name also translated to Dutch Reformed Church, cf. no. 2) in 1857. Two years later another split occurred in the Transvaal, when the Gereformeerde Kerk (Reformed Church — the Afrikaans acronym is GKSA, cf. no. 3) was formed. Differing interpretations about the three traditional Ref confessions of faith inherited from the Dutch Reformation (HeidC, BelgC, CDort), as well as the issue of whether only psalms or also other spiritual songs should be sung in church, played an important role in this split. In this way three major white Afrikaans-language Ref churches came into being.

The white Ref churches in South Africa are well known for their policy of instituting racially separated churches for converts from their missionary efforts.

The Dutch Reformed Mission Church for "colored" South Africans (DRM, cf. no. 4) was instituted in 1881, to be followed in the 20th century by separate churches for Africans (Dutch Reformed Church in Africa, DRCA, cf. no. 4) and Indians (Reformed Church in Africa, RCA, cf. no. 5).

In the meantime English-speaking Presb Christians and missionaries had settled in the Eastern Cape. From this work grew four separate Presb Churches in Southern Africa (cf. below nos. 8-11). In the course of the last decades several attempts have been made to bring these, or at least some of these churches, closer to one another. In recent years, the Reformed Presbyterian Church in South Africa (cf. no. 10) has made another attempt by proposing negotiations for unity with the Presbyterian Church of Southern Africa (cf. no. 8)

Another branch of Ref Christianity can be found in the United Congregational Church of Southern Africa (cf. no. 12), mainly the fruit of the work of the LMS. The Church of England in South Africa (CESA) came into being in 1865 after the split between Bishop Colenso and the Anglican Church of England. Today this church considers itself to belong to the Ref tradition.

South African churches have been active in mission work. Efforts by the Dutch Reformed Church gained momentum in the 18th century, especially as a result of the work of two ministers, H. R. van Lier and M. C. Vos. The first LMS missionary to arrive in Cape Town, John Philip, was, together with M.C. Vos, responsible for the founding of the South African Mission Society (1799). This society was widely supported by DRC members in its mission work throughout the Cape colony. In 1824 the first Cape Synod of the DRC decided to commence church-related mission work; it was one of the first, if not the first, Ref synods to make such a decision. Another branch of the Ref family to take up mission work in South Africa was the (Congreg) American Board of Commissioners for Foreign Mission (ABCFM), which started work in Natal in 1835. Scottish Presb were active in the Eastern Cape. The South African General Mission, an "undenominational" mission, strongly supported by DRC members such as Andrew Murray, was formed in 1889 and started mission work in Swaziland, which was later extended to Natal and also to Malawi and Zambia.

Much of the 20th-century history of the Ref tradition in South(ern) Africa centers around the official policy of racial separation existing in most of these churches. The problem became especially acute after the Sharpeville massacre in 1960. The WCC called the Cottesloe Consultation of all its member churches in South Africa. The NHK, as well as the Cape and Transvaal synods of the NGK, withdrew from membership in the WCC. The Cottesloe Consultation led to a lasting break in relationships between the white Ref churches and most other South African denominations. The NGK and the NHK remained members of the WARC. In 1982, however, the WARC General Council in Ottawa declared apartheid a sin and its theological justification a heresy and suspended both churches from the exercise of their membership rights. This motion of censure by the worldwide Ref family had a strong influence in both the ecclesiastical and the socio-political history of Southern Africa. One of these was the adoption by the DRMC in 1986 of the Belhar Confession of Faith as the fourth standard of faith for the church. After the synod meeting the DRCM and DRCA set in motion a process of negotiation to unite the racially separated Dutch Ref churches. The process culminated in 1994 in the formation of the Uniting Reformed Church. The NGK and the RCA so far have not joined the movement of union negotiations.

The broken ecumenical relationships are slowly on the mend. The black Ref churches, the UCCSA (cf. no. 12), and the various Presb churches have been members of the South African Council of Churches for a long time. Subsequent to the political liberalization announced by President de Klerk in 1990, the NGK joined the Council, first as an observer and later as a member. The WARC General Council in Debrecen (1997) decided to restore the NGK to full membership on the condition that its General Synod will unanimously rejected apartheid as sin and heresy. It seems clear that problems will continue to exist until the painful history of racial separation between white and black Ref Christians has been confronted and rectified by a process of restitution and reconciliation.

1. Dutch Reformed Church (NGK) (1201)

Started by Dutch settlers in 1652, this church severed ties with the Reformed Church in the Netherlands at the beginning of the 19th century when the British annexed the Cape of Good Hope. It held its first synod as an independent church in 1824. In 1862 the Supreme Court ruled that representatives of congregations outside the Cape colony could not sit in the Cape Synod. This led to the formation of independent churches in Orange Free State, Natal, Transvaal, and, later, South West Africa. These churches always maintained a close relationship with one another, and in 1907 they established a Federal Council of Churches. In 1962 the five churches came together to form a single united Nederduitse Gereformeerde Kerk.

Apart from extensive missionary activity within South Africa, the DRC (NGK) initiated work and was instrumental in establishing churches beyond its borders, e.g., in Malawi, Zimbabwe, Zambia, Mozambique, Nigeria, Kenya, and Namibia.

TM: **1,292,850** BM: **365,513** CM: **927,337** Congr: **1,260** OrdM: **2,021** Eld: **32,245** Deac: **32,745** EvgHome: **nc** Mission: **139** Women Ord: **yes** As Ministers: **1990/3** as Deac: **1982/9,345** as Elders: **1990/2,076** ChurchOrg: **presby, classes, synod, General Synod** Off/otherLang: **Afrikaans, English, Portuguese** DoctrB: **ApC, AthC, CDort, HeidC** Infant or believer's baptism: **both** Frequency of the Lord's Supper: **at least 5 times per year (once every quarter and Good Friday)** NatRel: **SACC (1995)** RegRel: **nc** IntlRel: **REC** TheolSchool: **nc** Service infrastructure: **6 hospitals, 10 social service organizations, 110 homes for aged, children's homes, 10 homes/schools for the disabled** Periodicals: **Die Kerkbode (gen/weekly/22,000), Die Voorligter (family mag/monthly/90,000)**

Address: Nederduitse Gereformeerde Kerk (NGK), P.O. Box 4445, Pretoria 00001 234, Visagie-straat, Pretoria 0001, South Africa, Tel: +27 12 322-7658, Fax: +27 12 322-3803, E-mail: ngkdrc@cis.co.za.

2. Dutch Reformed Church (NHK) (1210)

Die Nederduitsch Hervormde Kerk van Afrika has existed since the settlement of Jan van Riebeeck on the Cape in 1652. Van Riebeeck founded the church which he named the Nederlands Hervormde Kerk (Dutch Reformed Church). The principles of Dutch Church canonical law, liturgy, etc., were applied in the Cape Church and parishes.

Simultaneously with British attempts to anglicize the Cape and the church, the Great Trek occurred. As the ministers in the Cape were in the service and under the authority of the British Government, they did not participate in the "Groot Trek." Two missionaries, Erasmus Smit and Daniel Lindley, tended to the spiritual needs of the Voortrekkers. The first congregation was founded in Potchefstroom, Transvaal, in 1842, followed by further and rapid expansion, especially in the Transvaal. In 1885 an amalgamation of the Nederduitsch Hervormde Kerk and the Nederduitse Gereformeerde Kerk was effected. This was initiated by the enormous feeling of solidarity among the Afrikaners after the First War of Independence of 1880-1881.

A single congregation, however, did not merge, and it was around this parish, Witfontein, that the Hervormers rallied after they had forfeited their property and a vast number of their members.

In its missionary endeavors the church has notched up major achievements. A theological training center is operating at Klipdrift, where the ministers of the different language black church, the Hervormde Kerk van Suidelike Afrika (HKSA), are trained. It has been the consistent conviction and view of the church that the gospel can best be served to people in their own language. The most recent church law has just been completed and is indigenous to the church.

TM: **129,759** BM: **176,338** CM: **176,338** Congr: **330** PStations: **none** OrdM: **444** Eld: **9,900** Deac: **9,900** EvgHome: **0** Mission: **5** Women Ord: **yes** As Ministers: **1981/35** as Deac: **1981/3,300** as Elders: **1981/1,650** ChurchOrg: **congr, 38 dioceses or regional synods (meeting annually), GenAssy (every third year)** Off/otherLang: **Afrikaans, Dutch, English** DoctrB: **ApC, NicC, AthC, HeidC, CDort** Infant or believer's baptism: **both** Frequency of the Lord's Supper: **4 to 5 times per year** Close relations with: **Nederduitse Gereformeerde Kerk, Afrikaanse Protestanse Kerk, Presb Church** NatRel: **none** RegRel: **none** IntlRel: **none** TheolSchool: **University of Pretoria** Service infrastructure: **none** Periodicals: **Die Hervormer Konteks, Die Hervormde Teologiese Studies (HTS)**

Address: Nederduitsch Hervormde Kerk van Afrika (NHK), P.O. Box 2368, Jacob Mare Street 224, Pretoria RSA 0001, South Africa, Tel: +27 12 322 8885, Fax: +27 12 322 7909, E-mail: hervormd@pixie.co.za.

3. Reformed Churches in South Africa (GKSA) (1211)

This church came into existence in 1859 as the result of a split from the NGK (cf. no. 1). It organized its churches into racially exclusive synods within its General Synod. The Synod Soutpansberg and the Midlands Reformed Churches are two such synods with exclusively black membership.

TM: **114,350** BM: **29,637** CM: **77,449** Congr: **297** PStations: **200** OrdM: **300** Eld: **yes** Deac: **nc** EvgHome: **20** Mission: **none** Women Ord: **no** ChurchOrg: **Presbyterian** Off/otherLang: **Afrikaans, English** DoctrB: **BelgC, CDort, HeidC** Infant or believer's baptism: **both** NatRel: **none** RegRel: **none** IntlRel: **related to ICRC** TheolSchool: **Potchefstroom University for Christian Higher Education** Periodicals: **Die Kerkblad Die Vroveblad Die Almanak**

Address: Gereformeerde Kerke in Suid-Afrika (GKSA), P.O. Box 525, Potchefstroom, South Africa, Tel: +27 148 297 3989, Fax: +27 148 293 1042, E-mail: rtsmk@packnet.eok.ac.za.

4. Uniting Reformed Church in Southern Africa (URCSA) (1202)

After a long process of negotiations the two "daughter churches" of the Dutch Reformed Church united in 1994 to form the Uniting Reformed Church of Southern Africa. The union is doctrinally based on the classic Ref confessions, and, in addition, the Belhar Confession which was formulated by the Dutch Reformed Mission Church in 1982 and adopted in 1990. The Uniting Church aims at the union of all Ref churches in Southern Africa.

a) Dutch Reformed Church in Africa
(Nederduitse Gereformeerde Kerk in Afrika)

This church was the result of a merger in 1963 of three churches — the Nederduitse Gereformeerde Bantoekerk in Suid-Afrika, the Nederduitse Gereformeerde Sendingkerk van Transvaal, and the Nederduitse Gereformeerde Sendingkerk in the Orange Free State. The church's first work was started in the northeastern Cape in 1859 in the towns of Burgersdorp and Middleburg. The year 1864 was a landmark because Henri Gonin started mission work then at Saulspoort among the Kgatla tribe and McKidd in Zoutpansberg at Kranspoort in the Transvaal. Shortly after 1872 a new initiative was taken at Kimberley and in the Free State. Work in Natal started much later except for a few towns on the border to Transvaal. The first synod was constituted in the Orange Free State in 1910. Transvaal followed in 1932, the Cape in 1951, and Natal in 1952. The first General Synod was held on May 7, 1963. The church consists mainly of Sozho and Nguni groups, with small minorities from other northern tribes. It has four theological seminaries.

b) Dutch Reformed Mission Church in South Africa
(Nederduitse Gereformeerde Sendingkerk in Suid Afrika)

This church was founded as a separate church alongside the Dutch Reformed Church because of various factors, e.g., a growing racial prejudice among the whites, the establishment of mission congregations by foreign missionary societies in South Africa, and the strong influence of German missiological thinking. In 1880 the Synod of the Dutch Reformed Church decided to establish a separate daughter church for colored people. The church was constituted in October 1881, in Wellington, and consisted then of four ministers and two elders. The church received a seminary for the training of its own ministers from the Dutch Reformed Church. Ministers have the same title and status as ministers in the Dutch Reformed Church, although they are not licensed to become ministers in the Dutch Reformed Church. At the synods of 1974 and 1978 unprecedented decisions were taken denouncing apartheid and separate development, as well as South African laws undergirding the system, such as the ban on mixed marriages, separate townships, and job reservations. The principle of free worship and free church membership regardless of race or color was also accepted. In 1982 a further step was taken. Following the decision of the WARC General Council in Ottawa, the *status confessionis* was declared regarding apartheid, and a new confession, the Belhar Confession, took a strong stand against all forms of apartheid in church and state. It was officially adopted by the synods in 1986 and 1990.

TM: **1,227,345** BM: **1,227,345** CM: **516,274** Congr: **694** OrdM: **636** Eld: **7,282** Deac: **12,135** EvgHome: **nc** Mission: **nc** Women Ord: **yes** As Ministers: **1990/2** as Deac: **1986/na** as Elders: **nc** ChurchOrg: **presbys, regional synods, gen synod** Off/otherLang: **all 11 official languages** DoctrB: **ApC, NicC, AthC, HeidC, HelvC, CDort, Conf of Belhar** Infant or believer's baptism: **both** Frequency of the Lord's Supper: **5 times per year** Close relations with: **Federation of Swiss Protestant Churches, Lippische Landeskirche Church (Germany), Reformierter Bund, Gereformeerde Kerken in Nederland, Nederlands Hervormde Kerk, Presb Church in USA, Ref Church in America** NatRel: **SACC (1994)** RegRel: **SAARC (1994)** IntlRel: **WCC (1995), WARC (1994)** Theol School: **nc** Service infrastructure: **rehabilitation centers for drugs and alcohol abusers, old age homes service, center for handicapped, preschools, children's homes, schools for hearing impaired/epileptics/handicapped, development projects in social services, life skills training** Periodicals: **Die Ligdraer/Ligstraal (gen/monthly/22,000)**

Address: Verenigende Gereformeerde Kerk in Suider Afrika, Private Bag 1, Belhar 7507, South Africa, Tel: +27 21 9522151, E-mail: vgk@cis.co.2a

5. Reformed Church in Africa (Indian) (1206)

The RCA was founded in Pietermaritzburg in 1968. Although it works primarily among the Indian community in South Africa, who number around 800,000, it is a nonracial church with an open membership. Most of its members are converts from Hinduism. The church is strongly evangelical in doctrine and spirituality and seeks to reach Hindus and Muslims especially.

TM: **2,000** Congr: **12** PStations: **14** OrdM: **9** Eld: **36** Deac: **31** EvgHome: **5** Mission: **1** Women Ord: **yes** As Ministers: **no** as Deac: **1990/6** as Elders: **no** ChurchOrg: **church council, presby, synod** Off/otherLang: **English** DoctrB: **ApC, NicC, AthC, BelgC, CDort, HeidC** Infant or believer's baptism: **both** Frequency of the Lord's Supper: **monthly** Close relations with: **United Congreg Church of South Africa, Ref Presb Ch in South Africa, Meth Ch of South Africa, Angl Ch, Evangelical Pres Ch, PCUSA, Ch of Scotland, United Ref Ch UK, Pres Ch of Aotearoa New Zealand** NatRel: **SACC (1980)** RegRel: **nc** IntlRel: **WARC (1976), REC (1990)** TheolSchool: **RCA Bible School** Periodicals: **Perspective (gen/monthly/8,000)**

Address: Reformed Church in Africa, P.O. Box 33320, Montclair, 144 Amos Street, Colbyn, 0083, Durban 4061, South Africa, Tel: +27 12 434977

6. Reformed Church in Southern Africa (1217)

Lufafa was a congregation of the Free Church of Scotland, under the superintendency of Rev. J. Dewar. Rev. Mlaba, then 55 years old, protested against the use of unordained persons for work requiring ordained persons. When his complaint was not heeded, he broke away in April 29, 1923. In January 1923, he had approached Rev. A. R. Smith of a newly established church in Pietermaritzburg, the Nederduitsch Hervormde Kerk van Natal (NHKN), for recognition and membership. (NHKN had broken away from the Nederduitse Gereformeerde Kerk.) Rev. Smith and Rev. Mlaba and their church councils agreed to cooperate, one as the mssion church, under the official name Zulu Hervormde Zending Kerk (ZHZK), and the other as the sending church. But in 1925 the NHK van Natal applied successfully to be incorporated into the Nederduitsch Hervormde Kerk van Afrika (NHK, cf. no. 2). However, the NHK would not accept the ZHZK as its mission church. In 1928 a pro-mission lobby in the NHK formed its own mission society, the Nederduitsch Hervormde Sendinggenootskap, and established formal relations with the ZHZK until 1951, when the NHK accepted responsibility to do mission as a church.

In 1948 a new name, the Bantoe Hervormde Kerk, was adopted. The church grew in Natal. In 1951 it was established in Pretoria. It also spread to the Orange Free State, and in the early '60s it reached the Transkei. Around 1953 the training of ministers started under ad hoc conditions. In 1966 the training of ministers and evangelists continued under the Stofberg Teologiese Gedenkskool of the Nederduits Gereformeerde Kerk. In 1977 a new constitution was adopted, and the name of the church changed to Hervormde Kerk in Suidelike Afrika. The church also declared itself open to *all* peoples. This church can be considered the "black daughter church" of the Dutch Reformed Church (NHK, cf. no. 2).

TM: **23,950** BM: **23,950** CM: **13,643** Congr: **68** OrdM: **66** Eld: **445** Deac: **425** EvgHome: **5** Mission: **nc** Women Ord: **yes** As Ministers: **1991/6 in training** as Deac: **1977** as Elders: **1985** ChurchOrg: **church council, circuit, GenAssy** Off/otherLang: **Afrikaans, English, various African languages** DoctrB: **ApC, NicC, AthC, BelgC, CDort, HeidC** Infant or believer's baptism: **both** Frequency of the Lord's Supper: **quarterly** Close relations with: **Uniting Reformed Church of Southern Africa, Gereformeerde Kerk van Suid Afrika** NatRel: SACC **(1992)** RegRel: SAARC **(request)** IntlRel: **WARC (requested)** TheolSchool: **Hervormde Teologiese Opleiding, Klipdrif near Hammanskraal** Periodicals: **Montshafatsi (The Reformer) (quarterly, depending on funds)**

Address: Hervormde Kerk in Suidelike Africa, P.O. Box 12162, Tremshed Jacob Maré Str. 224, Pretoria 0002, South Africa, Tel: +27 12 322-8885, Fax: +27 12 322-7909, E-mail: hervormd @pixie.co.za.

7. Afrikaans Protestant Church (1220)

This church came into existence in 1987. It was founded mostly by members of the NGK (cf. no. 1), who could no longer identify with the course the general synod took in 1986 by adopting a report entitled "Church and Society." They were convinced that the policy of the NGK would contribute to "open South Africa to anti-Christian

Communism" and that it failed "to appreciate the diversity in God's creation and the necessity for the church to be indigenous." A minority of members and ministers from the Ref churches in South Africa (cf. no. 3) and the NHK (cf. no. 2) also joined the church. In 1988 a theological seminary was opened. The APK is a church for Afrikaners. It is growing and could grow further if the NHK should initiate union negotiations with the black churches. It also exists in Namibia (cf. Namibia).

TM: nc BM: **14,445** CM: **37,684** Congr: **245** PStations: **none** OrdM: **154** Eld: nc Deac: nc EvgHome: nc Mission: nc Women Ord: **no** ChurchOrg: **local church, presby (meet annually), Synod (meets bi-annually)** Off/otherLang: nc DoctrB: **ApC, NicC, AthC, HeidC, BelgC, CDort** Infant or believer's baptism: **both** Frequency of the Lord's Supper: **4 to 5 times per year** Close relations with: **conversational relations with various Ref churches** NatRel: nc RegRel: nc IntlRel: nc TheolSchool: **Theological Seminary of the APK** Periodicals: **Die Bookskapper (10 times per year), Die Jeugbookskappen (10 times per year)**

Address: Afrikaanse Protestantse Kerk (APK), P.O. Box 11488, Hatfield, Pretoria 0028, South Africa, Tel: +27 12 43 44 61, Fax: +27 12 362-2023

8. Presbyterian Church of Southern Africa (PCSA) (1205)

This church originated from the missionary work of the United Presbyterian Church (Scotland) among white settlers, especially the soldiers of the Scottish regiments stationed in Cape Town in the early 19th century. The first church was opened in 1829. As the British settlement grew, congregations were founded in other parts of South Africa as well. In 1897 the mission stations of the United Presbyterian Church were consolidated into a denomination. Today the church has congregations throughout South Africa, Zambia, and Zimbabwe. About two-thirds of the membership are white; the remainder are mainly black, though there is a small, but growing work among the Indian community and among the colored people. The church is strong in urban areas.

TM: nc CM: **90,000** Congr: **253** PStations: **26** OrdM: **259** Eld: nc Deac: nc EvgHome: nc Mission: **2** Women Ord: **yes** As Ministers: **1973** as Deac: nc as Elders: **1968** ChurchOrg: **presby and synod (in Zambia only)** Off/otherLang: *S. Africa:* **English, Lulu, Xhosa, S. Sotho, N. Sotho, Setsana, Venda, Tsonga, Afrikaans;** *Zambia:* **Tumbuka, Chibemba;** *Zimbabwe:* **Sindebele, Shona** DoctrB: **ApC** Frequency of the Lord's Supper: **monthly** NatRel: **SACC, CUC(SA)** RegRel: **AACC** IntlRel: **WCC** TheolSchool: nc Service infrastructure: **2 old-age homes, kindergartens, 8 schools in Zimbabwe, 1 school in Zambia**

Address: Presbyterian Church of Southern Africa (PCSA), P.O. Box 96188, 150 Caroline Street, 1st Floor, Joseph Wing Centre, Brixton 2019, South Africa, Tel: +27 11 837-1258, Fax: +27 11 837-1653

9. Presbyterian Church of Africa (PCA) (1204)

This church was founded in 1898. Under the leadership of Pastor Pambani Mzimba six black ministers and a strong group of followers constituted the first synod in Alice, Cape Colony. Mzimba had a dispute with the Free Church of Scotland over the use of money. To this day the PCA is a black church concentrated in the eastern Cape and Natal as well as in Malawi. The church is a founding member of the African Independent Churches Association.

TM: **927,000** BM: **426,000** CM: **927,000** Congr: **9,000** PStations: 600 OrdM: 58 Eld: **800** Deac: **2,600** EvgHome: 50 Mission: 4 Women Ord: **yes** As Ministers: **1986/2** as Deac: **300** as Elders: **29** ChurchOrg: nc Off/otherLang: **English** DoctrB: **ApC, WestConf** Infant or believer's baptism: **both** Frequency of the Lord's Supper: **monthly** Close relations with: **Presb Ch USA, Taiwan Presb Ch** NatRel: **SACC (1964), Diakonia Council of Churches (1976), Kwazula-Natal Church Leaders' Group (1990), Ministers' Fraternal (1992), Ecumenical Center Trust (1984)** RegRel: **AACC (1975)** IntlRel: **WCC (1973), WARC (1973)** TheolSchool: nc Service infrastructure: **clinics, day care centers**

Address: Presbyterian Church of Africa (PCA), P.O. Box 54840, Central Office, 21 St. Andrews Street, Durban 4001, South Africa, Tel: +27 31 305-5489, Fax: +27 31 306-2742, E-mail: celula 0837756913.

10. Reformed Presbyterian Church in Southern Africa (RPCSA) (1207)

This church was formerly called the Bantu Presbyterian Church. It originated from mission work of various Scottish churches and became independent in 1923. The church consists mainly of Africans (and a few Coloured) and is spread over the whole country, although with a stronger presence in the Cape and Natal. The church is largely located in rural areas.

TM: **52,000** CM: **43,877** Congr: **91** PStations: 4 OrdM: 78 Eld: nc Deac: nc EvgHome: nc Mission: nc Women Ord: **yes** As Ministers: 2 as Deac: **790** as Elders: **2,000** ChurchOrg: nc Off/otherLang: nc DoctrB: nc Infant or believer's baptism: **both** NatRel: **SACC** RegRel: **AACC** IntlRel: **WCC, WARC** TheolSchool: nc Periodicals: **none**

Address: Reformed Presbyterian Church in Southern Africa (RPCSA), P.O. Box 144, Umtata, Transkei 5100, South Africa

11. Evangelical Presbyterian Church in South Africa (1200)

This church grew out of the work of Swiss missionaries who began their activities in 1875 among the Tsonga people. It was formerly called the Tsonga Presbyterian Church. A network of mission stations was established in the northern and eastern parts of Transvaal. The rapid growth of mining industry drew many people into the towns. Congregations were also established in Pretoria, Reef, and later Welkom areas (Orange Free State), and also in Zululand. The church has a strong ethnic character. Tsonga is the official language, both in worship and the courts of the church. Since 1962 the church has been independent but not yet self-sufficient. Gradually, a new sense of autonomy is pervading the church. It finds expression in the revival of liturgy and African music, as well as in the acceptance of greater social and political involvement in the life of the country.

TM: **30,000** Congr: **32** PStations: **7** OrdM: **26** Eld: **1920** Deac: **nc** EvgHome: **nc** Mission: **nc** Women Ord: **yes** As Ministers: **nc** as Deac: **nc** as Elders: **nc** ChurchOrg: **nc** Off/otherLang: **Tsonga** DoctrB: **nc** Infant or believer's baptism: NatRel: **SACC** RegRel: **AACC** IntlRel: **WCC** TheolSchool: **nc**

Address: Evangelical Presbyterian Church in South Africa, P.O. Box 31961, Braamfontein 2017, Johannesburg, South Africa, Tel: +27 11 339-1044, Fax: +27 11 339 7274

12. United Congregational Church of Southern Africa (UCCSA) (1208)

Congregationalism took root in Southern Africa when Johannes van der Kemp, a missionary of the LMS, arrived in Cape Town in 1799. He was the first missionary to take the Gospel to the Bantu-speaking people in Southern Africa. The first Congreg churches were founded at Graaff-Reinet in 1801 and at Bethelsdorp (Port Elizabeth) in 1802. Within a few years the LMS was moving north from its famous mission station at Kuruman. Robert Moffat, David Livingstone, and other pioneers brought the Gospel to almost every part of Southern Africa. In order to pursue its evangelistic thrust into the interior, the LMS withdrew from the Cape in 1854. Five years later the congregations it had founded, together with a number of English-speaking congregations in larger centers, formed the Evangelical Voluntary Union, which became the Congregational Union of South Africa in 1877.

At the invitation of the LMS, the American Board of Commissioners for Foreign Mission sent their first group of missionaries to South Africa in 1835. They worked among the Zulu people in Natal and the Batswa people in Mozambique, and the congregations they established eventually constituted themselves into the Bantu Congregational Church.

For more than a century the three churches of congregational origin, while having close fraternal relations, operated as separated denominations. In 1967, the three strands of Congregationalism came together to form the United Congregational Church of Southern Africa. In 1972 the South African Association of the Disciples also merged with the United Congregational Church. Union talks are proceeding with the Angl, Meth, and Presb Churches. The UCCSA operates in South Africa, Botswana, Mozambique, Namibia, and Zimbabwe.

TM: **277,527** BM: **345,801** CM: **277,527** Congr: **353** OrdM: **271** Eld: **na** Deac: **na** EvgHome: **na** Mission: **na** Women Ord: **yes** As Ministers: **19th cent/15** as Deac: **nc** as Elders: **nc** ChurchOrg: **assy, executive committee, synods/regional councils** Off/otherLang: **English, Afrikaans, Xhosa, Zulu, Tswana, Indebele, Xixswa, Sotho, Venda** DoctrB: **ApC, NicC** Infant or believer's baptism: **both** Frequency of the Lord's Supper: **monthly** Close relations with: **Presb Church of Southern Africa, UCC (cf. United States no. 43), URC** (cf. UK no. 14) NatRel: **SACC, CUC** RegRel: **AACC, SAARC** IntlRel: **WCC, CWM, WARC** TheolSchool: **nc** Service infrastructure: **none** Periodicals: **Congregational Chronicle (news sharing/quarterly)**

Address: United Congregational Church of Southern Africa (UCCSA), P.O. Box 96014, 150 Caroline
Street, Brixton, Johannesburg 2019, South Africa, Tel: +27 11 837-9997, Fax: +27 11
837-2570

13. The Church of England in South Africa (1222)

The Church of England in South Africa has its historical roots in the Angl tradition but is Ref in its theology and teaching. The church originated in services held in Cape Town in 1795. In the early 19th century tensions arose in the Angl Church between Evangelical ministers in the church and the newly appointed Tractarian bishop Robert Gray. As a result a number of congregations remained aloof from Gray's leadership, and when in 1870 Gray formed the Church of the Province of South Africa, the dissenting congregations remained as the Church of England in South Africa, holding to the Ref faith of the church as set out in the 39 Articles of 1563, and rejecting the innovations, doctrine, vestments, and ritual. Later in the 19th century it "inherited" the mission work among the Zulus initiated by Bishop John William Colenso (1814-1883). In 1938 the churches which remained faithful to the principles of the Church of England in South Africa adopted a constitution defining themselves as a "Ref and Protestant Church . . . adhering to the faith and doctrine of the Church of England . . . embodied in the 39 Articles of Religion, and the Book of Common Prayer of 1662." In 1955 Fred Morris, formerly bishop of North Africa, became the bishop of the church. Today the church has a large number of congregations in the western Cape, in most of the provinces of South Africa, as well as in Namibia.

TM: **10,945** CM: **10,000** Congr: **160** OrdM: **125** Eld: **nc** Deac: **nc** EvgHome: **31** Mission: **8** Women Ord: **no** ChurchOrg: **autonomous local congr, provincial area councils, synod, nat. exec. committee with presiding bishop** Off/otherLang: **English** DoctrB: **ApC, NicC, 39 Articles of Religion** Infant or believer's baptism: **infant** Frequency of the Lord's Supper: **weekly** NatRel: **nc** RegRel: **nc** IntlRel: **nc** TheolSchool: **George Whitefield College, Trinity Academy** Periodicals: **New Paper (bi-monthly/ nc)**

Address: Church of England in South Africa, P.O. Box 23622, Claremont 7735, South Africa, Tel: +27 31 75 28 76, Fax: +27 31 75 51 50, E-mail: noël.wright@pixig.co.za.

14. Free Church in Southern Africa (1212)

This is a Xhosa-speaking church, founded originally by the Free Church of Scotland (in 1843). It has been active since that time in Xhosa-speaking areas in the eastern and western Cape regions. When the majority of the Free Church of Scotland reunited with the Church of Scotland in 1900, most missionaries in South Africa joined the union. A minority maintained communion with the continuing Free Church of Scotland. The church became independent in 1982 but continues to be dependent on overseas help in personnel and finances.

TM: **4,000** BM: **4,000** CM: **2,500** Congr: **63** PStations: **6** OrdM: **13** Eld: **115** Deac: **60** EvgHome: **1** Mission: **ne** Women Ord: **no** ChurchOrg: **2 presby, GenAssy** Off/otherLang: **Xhosa, English** DoctrB: **WestConf, WestCat** Infant or believer's baptism: **both** Frequency of the Lord's Supper: **quarterly** Close relations with: **Gereformeerde Kerk van Suid Afrika** NatRel: **nc** RegRel: **nc** IntlRel: **ICRC (1995)** TheolSchool: **Dumisani Bible School** Periodicals: **Umthombo Wamandla (gen/quarterly/ 2,000)**

Address: Free Church in Southern Africa, P.O. Box 681, 15 Leopold Street, King William's Town 5600, South Africa, Tel: +27 433 25537 and 24737, Fax: +27 433 25537

15. People's Church of Africa (1209)

During the early '20s a feeling of discomfort arose within the western Cape with the way the white missionaries ran the affairs of the churches under their jurisdiction. Two like-minded groups, which were originally unaware of each other's existence, met to discuss the role of missionaries in the church. One group was in Stellenbosch and was led by a barber named Paul M. Rhode; the other was in Cape Town and under the leadership of Rev. J. J. H. Forbes. On August 14, 1921, the first group decided to set up the United National Church of Africa, the People's Church (Vereenigd Nasionale Kerk van Afrika, Onze Volkskerk). In 1922 Rev. Forbes, disillusioned with the churches he was serving, joined the Volkskerk. The reasons for establishing the church were not dogmatic but rather socio-political. The Volkskerk was to be a church for the Coloured people, "built on the faith of Jesus Christ, the Son of God and his holy Apostles, church controlled by the people and for the people." Today the church is implanted in the eastern and western Cape.

TM: **21,216** BM: **15,102** CM: **6,114** Congr: **220** PStations: **45** OrdM: **10** Eld: **nc** Deac: **229** EvgHome: **nc** Mission: **nc** Women Ord: **yes** As Ministers: **1990/9** as Deac: **1990/31** as Elders: **nc** ChurchOrg: **nc** Off/otherLang: **English, Afrikaans** DoctrB: **ApC** Ref Infant or believer's baptism: **both** Frequency of the Lord's Supper: **monthly** Close relations with: **American Episcopal Church, UCCSA, URC, Meth** NatRel: **SACC (1987)** RegRel: **SAARC (1992)** IntlRel: **WARC (1994)** TheolSchool: **nc** Service infrastructure: **na** Periodicals: **Year Book (gen/yearly/1,000), Ons Bron (gen/quarterly/1,000)**

Address: Volkskerk van Afrika, P.O. Box 4026, Stellenbosch 7609, 21 Barker Street, Ida's Valley, Stellenbosch 7600, South Africa, Tel: 27 21 883 3710, Fax: +27 21 887 2364

16. Free Reformed Churches in South Africa (1215)

The existence of the Free Reformed Churches owes to Dutch immigration to South Africa after World War II. The churches were founded by immigrants who belonged to Reformed Churches (Liberated) (cf. Netherlands). They want to remain faithful to the Three Formulas of Unity "in a time when most Ref denominations pay only lip-service to their confessions." They are also committed to evangelistic work in South Africa. In recent times the church has attracted members of the Dutch Reformed Church who were dissatisfied with what they considered to be a trend toward liberalism. The Free Reformed Churches maintain close relations with other Reformed Churches (Liberated).

TM. **1,354** BM: **574** CM: **780** Congr: **5** PStations: **5** OrdM: **5** Eld: **34** Deac: **17** EvgHome: **1** Mission: **4** Women Ord: **no** As Ministers: **ne** as Deac: **ne** as Elders: **ne** ChurchOrg: **church order of the Syn of Dordtrecht** Off/otherLang: **Afrikaans** DoctrB: **ApC, AthC, NicC, HeidC, CDort, BelgC** Infant or believer's baptism: **infant** Frequency of the Lord's Supper: **6 times per year** Close relations with: **Free Ch of Southern Africa, Ref Chs in the NL, Free Ref Chs in Australia, Canadian Ref Chs,**

Presb Ch of Korea, Free Ch of Scotland NatRel: **none** RegRel: **none** IntlRel: **ICRC (1985)** TheolSchool: **Theological University of Kampen/NL, Univ. Potchefstroom** Service infrastructure: **2 Ref primary schools** Periodicals: **Kompas (gen/monthly/500)**

Address: Vrye Gereformeerde Kerke in Suid-Afrika, P.O. Box 21232, Helderkruin Johannesburg 1733, South Africa, Tel: +27 11 768-3518, Fax: +27 11 475 3852, E-mail: christo @enet.co.za.

SPAIN

Area in km²	504,750
Population	(July 1996 est.) 39,181,114
Religions in %	RCath 99%, other 1%
Official/other languages	Castilian Spanish/Catalan 17%, Galician 7%, Basque 2%

CECI (Comité Español de Cooperación entre las Iglesias — *Spanish Council of Co-operation between the Churches*)
FEREDE (Federación entitades religiosas evangelicas de España — *Federation of Religious Evangelical Entities*)

Before the short-lived First Republic in 1868, any religious expression deviating from the RCath Church was not tolerated. Prot preaching had begun in various places since the 1850s. With the active help of British, especially Scottish evangelists, Luis de Usoz y Rio began to distribute Bibles and evangelical tracts. Other evangelists were Francisco de Paula Ruet and Manuel Matamoros. Several of them found refuge in Gibraltar, where a small Prot community had been established. Manuel Matamoros and others were arrested in 1860; their trial raised protests throughout Europe. In response to these appeals, the government decided to expel the Prot leaders from the country. The political developments after the Napoleonic wars began to create a new situation. In 1868 freedom of worship was constitutionally guaranteed. In 1868 the **Iglesia Reformada Española** was formed. A year later an assembly was called for the purpose of bringing together the various communities. In 1871 another attempt was made, and, with the addition of new communities, the church became the **Iglesia Cristiana Española**. It adopted its own confession of faith. In 1880 a split took place; one of the pastors left the church and founded, together with a few communities, the **Iglesia Española Reformada Episcopal,** which adopted the liturgy of the Angl churches. In 1890, with the addition of communities in Northern Spain, the name of the church changed again to **Iglesia Evangélica Española (IEE)**. The confession of faith remained unchanged until 1955 when the Meth Church of Catalonia and the Baleares was incorporated into the IEE.

The church went through many difficulties and often suffered persecution. There were periods of relative freedom during the six years of revolutionary government (1868-1874) and the time of the Second Republic (1931-1936). The situation began to change with rapprochement with other European countries and following the Second Vatican Council. In 1967 a law on religious liberty was issued which many Prot considered to be far from satisfactory. With the end of the dictatorial regime and the democratization of Spain in the late seventies, negotiations for a new agreement were initiated. In 1980 a new Law of Religious Freedom was adopted. The majority of Prot groups established the **Federation of Religious Evangelical Entities (FEREDE)** and gave it the mandate to work out the agreement. The agreement was completed and adopted in 1992.

Spanish Evangelical Church (6410)

TM: **10,000** BM: **2,500** CM: **2,700** Congr: **40** PStations: **52** OrdM: **25** Eld: **nc** Deac: **200** EvgHome: **3** Mission: **nc** Women Ord: **yes** As Ministers: **1983/2** as Deac: **nc** as Elders: **nc** ChurchOrg: **local congr, regional synods, national synod** Off/otherLang: **Spanish, Catalan, Castellano** DoctrB: **ApC, NicC, AthC, HeidC, HelvC, Confession of the IEE (1868/1955)** Infant or believer's baptism: **both** Frequency of the Lord's Supper: **monthly** Periodicals: **Cristianismo Protestante (pop/3 per year/2,000), Nuestro Presbiterio Madrid (gen/monthly), Protestantes Aragon (gen/3 per year), Protestantes Andalues (gen/3 per year)** Close relations with: **Spanish Ref Episcopal Church** NatRel: **FEREDE, CECI** RegRel: **CEC** IntlRel: **WMC, WCC (1948), WARC** TheolSchool: **United Ev. Seminary (Madrid)**

Address: Iglesia Evangélica Española (I.E.E.), C.P. 28015, Noviciado 5, Madrid, Spain, Tel: + 34 1 531-3947, Fax: +34 1 523-4137, E-mail: 100774,524@COMPUSERVE.COM

SRI LANKA

Area in km^2	65,610
Population	(July 1996 est.) 8,553,074 Sinhalese 74%, Tamil 18%, Moor 7%, Burgher, Malay, and Vedda 1%
Religions in %	Buddhist 69%, Hindu 15%, Muslim 8%, Christian 8% (of which, RCath 85%, Angl, Meth, Bapt, Presb 15%)
Official/other languages	Sinhala 74%/Tamil (national language) 18%

NCC (National Christian Council of Sri Lanka)

Christian churches have existed in Sri Lanka (until 1948 known as Ceylon) sporadically since the 6th century (Nestorians) and continuously since the arrival of the Portuguese on the island in 1505. The first Prot Church was the **Dutch Re-**

formed Church (no. 1), which was formally founded in 1642 and supplanted the RCath Church in the role of the "established religion" in the maritime provinces of the country until the end of Dutch colonial rule in 1796. Under British domination (1796/1815-1948) several Prot groups started missionary work in Ceylon, among them the American Congreg in the Jaffna peninsula (1816). In 1947 the congr founded by them joined the **Church of South India** as the Jaffna diocese (no. 4). In 1842 the Church of Scotland established **St. Andrew's Church** in Colombo (no. 2) as an overseas congr to serve the Scots community in Ceylon; in 1845 a second church was opened in Kandy. These two Scottish communities came together in the Presbytery of Ceylon. The Dutch Reformed Church subsequently joined the Presbytery of Ceylon. In 1952 doctrinal controversies occurred in the Dutch Reformed Church, which led to a split. The dissenting group founded the Presbyterian Church Colombo, and the Presbytery of Ceylon was eventually broken up. In 1954 the Presbyterian Church Colombo came together with the Scots' Kirk Kandy to form the **Presbytery of Lanka** (no. 3).

Sri Lanka became independent in 1948, and the Christian community had to redefine its role as a minority within a Buddhist majority system. Attempts by the Prot churches (Angl, Meth, Bapt, Presb, and the Church of South India) to form a united church failed in 1975. Since the late '70s attempts have been made by the Ref and Presb churches to bring about common understanding and to work together (Ref and Presb in Dialogue, RAPID). In 1983 ethnic tension in Sri Lanka developed into open civil war. Today national reconciliation is one of the major issues challenging the Christian community.

1. Dutch Reformed Church in Sri Lanka (Ceylon) (4380)

TM: **5,000** Congr: **25** OrdM: **4** Eld: **15** Deac: **20** EvgHome: **8** Mission: **nc** Women Ord: **yes** As Ministers: **no** as Deac: **4** as Elders: **no** ChurchOrg: **gen. consistory; gen. consistory executive committee, local consistory** Off/otherLang: **Sinhalese, Tamil, English** DoctrB: **ApC, NicC, HeidC, CDort, BelgC, WestConf** Infant or believer's baptism: **both** Frequency of the Lord's Supper: **monthly to bi-monthly** Periodicals: **The Herald (English/gen/quarterly/500), The Duthaya (Sinhala/gen/quarterly/l300), The Toothan (Tamil/gen/300)** Close relations with: **Christian Ref Ch in North America, NHK South Africa, Ref Ch of Australia** NatRel: **National Christian Council (1950s), Evangelical Alliance of Sri Lanka (1995)** RegRel: **nc** IntlRel: **REC (1950s), WARC (1950s)** TheolSchool: **Dutch Reformed Church Seminary and Bible Institute**

Address: Dutch Reformed Church in Sri Lanka (Ceylon), 363, Galle Road, Wellawatte, Colombo 6, Sri Lanka, Tel: +94 1 585-861, Fax: +94 1 582-469

2. St. Andrew's Church, Colombo — International and Interdenominational (4383)

Today this church sees its mission as an interdenominational fellowship, serving the international community in Colombo. In the 1970s it participated in the union negotiations, and it continues to seek closer relations with other churches, especially the Presbytery of Lanka.

TM: **nc** BM: **90** CM: **70** Congr: **1** PStations: **1** OrdM: **1** Eld: **10** Deac: **ne** EvgHome: **ne** Mission: **ne** Women Ord: **yes** As Ministers: **1968/nc** as Deac: **ne** as Elders: **1968/5** ChurchOrg: **constituent congregation** Off/otherLang: **English** DoctrB: **ApC, NicC, WestConf** Infant or believer's baptism: **both** Frequency of the Lord's Supper: **monthly and major festivals** Periodicals: **none** Close relations with: **major Prot denominations and Church of Ceylon (Angl)** NatRel: **NCC** RegRel: **CCA** IntlRel: **WCC (both through Church of Scotland)** TheolSchool: **none**

Address: St. Andrew's Church, Colombo — International and Interdenominational, 73 Galle Road, Colombo 3, Sri Lanka, Tel: +94 1 323-765, Fax: +94 1 449-280, E-mail: jyoo@eureka.ik

3. Presbytery of Lanka (4381)

TM: **500** BM: **200** CM: **500** Congr: **3** PStations: **7** OrdM: **5** Eld: **20** Deac: **nc** EvgHome: **4** Mission: **nc** Women Ord: **yes** As Ministers: **none** as Deac: **nc** as Elders: **1970/8** ChurchOrg: **Presby (national level) consisting of 2 elders from each congregation together with all ordained ministers** Off/otherLang: **Sinhalese, Tamil, English** DoctrB: **ApC, NicC, WestConf** Infant or believer's baptism: **both** Frequency of the Lord's Supper: **monthly** Close relations with: **Church of Scotland** NatRel: **National Christian Council of Sri Lanka (1954)** IntlRel: **WARC (1955)** TheolSchool: **Theological College of Lanka, Nandana Uyana, Pilimatalawa**

Address: Presbytery of Lanka, 186 Vauxhall Street, Colombo 02, Sri Lanka, Tel: +94 1 583-458, Fax: +94 1 448-216, E-mail: jfcmb@sri.lanka.net

4. Church of South India (Jaffna) (4385)

After some initial work by the London Missionary Society (1804-1810), American Congreg started missionary work on the Jaffna peninsula in 1816. They engaged in educational and medical work and since 1841 published the journal *The Morning Star*. Until the Second World War the church was confined to the area of the Jaffna peninsula in the extreme north of the country; later it began to expand to other areas, especially the eastern part of the country. In 1947 the church became part of the Church of South India. The church has spread primarily among the Tamil people. In the seventies the church participated in union negotiations. The ethnic strife in Sri Lanka has led to increasing estrangement among the churches. During the years of conflict the church went through many difficulties. Since 1983 many members have migrated to foreign countries.

TM: **18,050** BM: **18,050** CM: **15,165** Congr: **68** PStations: **68** OrdM: **24** Eld: **ne** Deac: **13** EvgHome: **ne** Mission: **ne** Women Ord: **yes** As Ministers: **ne** as Deac: **1992/1** as Elders: **ne** ChurchOrg: **local church committees, diocesan council, Synod** Off/otherLang: **Tamil, English** DoctrB: **ApC, NicC** Infant or believer's **baptism: both** Frequency of the Lord's Supper: **monthly** Periodicals: **The Morning Star (gen/weekly/1,000), Annual Church Bulletin (official newsletter of diocese)** Close relations with: **all member churches of National Christian Councils of Sri Lanka and India** NatRel: **National Christian Council of Sri Lanka (1910), Jaffna Christian Union (1906)** RegRel: **CCA (1979)** IntlRel: **WCC (1948), CWM (from its beginning)** TheolSchool: **Christian Theological Seminary (Jaffna)**

Address: Thenninthiya Thiruchapai Yarlpana Athiyatcha Aatheenam (Bishop's House, Vaddukoddat) for the present: C.S.I. Office, 17 Frances Road, Colombo 6, Sri Lanka, Tel: +94 1 58 4836, Fax: +94 1 58 4836

5. Union Church Nuwara Eliya (4384)

This union church is the result of the missionary efforts of Rev. Arthur Stephen Paynter, who came to Sri Lanka early in this century. It was founded in 1906. The church functions as an interdenominational church. At present the ministers are supplied by the Meth Church in Sri Lanka. Most members are Meth, but there are also Angl, Presb, etc. The church caters to visitors who are holidaying in N'Eliya and to the Paynter Home inmates. Though the Meth Church provides the ministers, the church has its own council to decide concerning church affairs.

TM: **64** BM: **64** CM: **24** Congr: **1** OrdM: **1** Eld: **ne** Deac: **ne** EvgHome: **ne** Mission: **ne** Women Ord: **yes** As Ministers: **nc** as Deac: **nc** as Elders: **nc** ChurchOrg: **nc** Off/otherLang: **English, Sinhalese, Tamil** DoctrB: **nc** Infant or believer's baptism: **both** Periodicals: **none** NatRel: **none** RegRel: **none** IntlRel: **none** TheolSchool: **nc**

Address: Eksath Sabawe Ikiya Thirucwabai, Mission House, 18 Jayetileke Nawatha, Nuwara Eliya none, Sri Lanka, Tel: +94 52-2170, Fax: none, E-mail: none

SUDAN

Area in km^2	2,505,810
Population	(July 1996 est.) 31,547,543 Black 52%, Arab 39%, Beja 6%, foreigners 2%, other 1%
Religions in %	Sunni Muslim 70% (in north), indigenous beliefs 25%, Christian 5% (mostly in south and Khartoum)
Official/other languages	Arabic/Nubian, Ta Bedawie, diverse dialects of Nilotic, Nilo-Hamitic, Sudanic languages, English

SCC (Sudan Council of Churches)
NSCC (New Sudan Council of Churches)
SECA (Sudanese Evangelical Christian Association)

Sudan's population reflects its position as a bridge between the Arab north and the African south of the continent. Today migration caused by civil war has blurred to some degree the historic separation of the two populations. Christianity first spread through the Nubia area in the 6th century. The 19th-century missionary movement did not impact the Sudan until 1890, when the Christian Missionary

Society (Angl) first began to work. The Ref presence began in 1901 with the coming of missionaries from the United Presbyterian Church of North America to Omdurman. The colonial government at the time prohibited Christian evangelization in the North. The South, however, was divided among the three societies seeking to work there. The Presb effort was directed to one of the three southern provinces called Upper Nile.

In the North, work continued in the field of education and health alongside a small church composed mostly of Egyptian expatriates, first connected with the Coptic Evangelical Church of Egypt (cf. Egypt) as the Presbytery of Sudan. It is now independent and known as the **Sudan Presbyterian Evangelical Church (SPEC).**

The work in the South was difficult. Conditions were inhospitable. Travel was largely by boat. It brought missionaries in touch with the Shilluk, Nuer, Dinka, Anuak, and Murle people. The first Sudanese pastor was ordained at Doleib Hill in 1942. An attempt in the '50s to achieve union between the CMS and the Presb mission failed. This good-intentioned plan blocked what could have been a more practical goal: the merger of the Presbyterian Church in the North and the Presbyterian Church in the South now known as the **Presbyterian Church of Sudan (PCOS).** By the time of national independence (1956) the Sudan was in a state of civil war. The new constitution failed to give the South the protection from the Arabs and Muslims which was anticipated. Southern garrisons revolted, and civil war raged until 1972, when the Addis Ababa Peace Agreement, largely negotiated by the WCC and the AACC, was signed. Peace lasted until 1983, when southern garrisons once again revolted because the government had declared that Sharia would become the law of the country and began to transfer southerners in the army to the North. This war continues to this day.

Christian witness everywhere in Sudan is carried out under difficulties. In the North, though freedom of worship is in principle guaranteed, no new buildings are permitted by the government. Christian women are harassed for not wearing Muslim dress, and Christians face discrimination in employment. Nevertheless, churches are crowded. In the South the Presbyterian Church has temporarily been divided into two presbyteries — one for the government areas and one for the rebel-controlled areas. In the latter, there has been a significant movement of the Spirit of God. Though people face enormous suffering, congr are multiplying.

Another branch of the Ref family is the **Sudanese Church of Christ in the Nuba Mountains (SCOC).** The church grew out of the Sudan United Mission from Australia, which started in 1913, and the Sudan United Mission from New Zealand. It became independent in 1962. The roots of the church are among the people of the Nuba Mountains, a remote area which suffered repression from the Sudan government. It developed quickly from 1960 under the leadership of Pastor Samwiil Gangul Angallo. In 1963 some members of the church emigrated to the cities. Accordingly, the name of the church was changed from the Sudanese Church of Christ in the Nuba Mountains (SCNM) to the Sudanese Church of Christ. Today, in the Nuba Mountains, people adhere in about equal numbers to Christianity, Islam, and indigenous religions; they are united in defending their culture, which the government seems determined to Arabize. During the war churches have been burned; many Christians, Muslims, and indigenous people have been killed. Little publicity has been given to these events.

The **Sudan Interior Church** grew out of the Sudan Interior Mission (SIM) from the USA. It was started in 1937 by SIM missionaries who had been expelled from Ethiopia by the Italians. Hoping to keep in touch with the small community they had built in Ethiopia, they began to work in the Sudan along the border in the Blue Nile province, and eventually in the northern part of the Upper Nile province. The Blue Nile province is part of northern Sudan and nominally Muslim. The government is therefore very sensitive to Christian witness. Emphasis was on health care, Bible translation, and literacy work. Efforts to start schools ran into government objection.

The **Trinity Presbyterian Church (TPC)** is the result of a separation from the Presbyterian Church of Sudan (PCOS). Some Dinka leaders felt that the leadership of PCOS was unfair to Dinkas. The leader who rallied people to start TPC was Andrew Wieu Riak, who was raised in the PCOS and became one of the best-known political leaders of Presb background. TPC has grown and started a number of new congr, especially in the North. Some hold out the hope that an eventual union of PCOS, SPEC, and SCOS will pave the way for bringing TPC back into the fold.

1. Presbyterian Church of the Sudan (PCOS) (1360)

The congr of this church are found in Upper Nile province, Juba, and North Sudan. The church became independent in 1956. The statistics cover both presbyteries.

TM: **450,000** BM: **130,000** CM: **320** Congr: **250** PStations: **350** OrdM: **84** Eld: **480** Deac: **530** EvgHome: **540** Mission: **7** Women Ord: **yes** As Ministers: **nc** as Deac: **1972/530** as Elders: **0** ChurchOrg: **Presbyterian (moderator elected every 4 years by GenAssy — 1 presbytery in government-controlled area, 1 in the rebel-controlled area)** Off/otherLang: **Nuer, Shilluk, Dinka, Anuak, Murle, English, Arabic** DoctrB: **ApC, NicC, HeidC, WestConf** Infant or believer's baptism: **both** Frequency of the Lord's Supper: **monthly if war situation permits** Close relations with: **PCUSA, Ref Ch of America, Basel Mission, Ch of Brethren, Presb Ch of Ireland, Ref Ch of NL** NatRel: **SCC (1972)** RegRel: **AACC (1967), MECC (1974)** IntlRel: **WCC (1984), WARC (1969)** TheolSchool: **Nile Theological College (Khartoum)**

Address: Presbyterian Church of the Sudan, P.O. Box 3421, Khartoum, Sudan, Tel: +249 11 445-5148

2. Sudan Presbyterian Evangelical Church (SPEC) (1361)

Work began in 1902, and the church became independent in 1956. Congr exist in northern Sudan.

TM: **8,000** BM: **2,000** CM: **6,000** Congr: **24** PStations: **66** OrdM: **22** Eld: **46** Deac: **40** EvgHome: **35** Mission: **nc** Women Ord: **no** ChurchOrg: **Presbyterian**Off/otherLang: **Arabic, Nuer, Dinka** DoctrB:

ApC, NicC, WestConf Infant or believer's baptism: **both** NatRel: **SCC** RegRel: **none** IntlRel: **none**
TheolSchool: **Nile Theological College (Khartoum) and institutions in Egypt**

Address: Sudan Presbyterian Evangelical Church (SPEC), P.O. Box 57, Khartoum, Sudan, Tel: +249
11 776-807

3. Sudanese Church of Christ (SCOC) (1364)

Work began in 1913, and the church became autonomous in 1962. Congr are located in the Nuba Mountains and the three cities, including the capital.

TM: **11,898** BM: **10,520** CM: **10,520** Congr: **60** PStations: **500** OrdM: **66** Eld: **36** Deac: **60** EvgHome:
62 Mission: **ne** Women Ord: **no** As Ministers: **ne** as Deac: **ne** as Elders: **ne** ChurchOrg: **Presbyterian
(local church committee, district church committee, general church committee)** Off/otherLang:
Arabic and Nuba dialects DoctrB: **ApC, NicC** Infant or believer's baptism: **believer** Frequency of the
Lord's Supper: **monthly** Close relations with: **Sudan Interior Church (SIC)** NatRel: **SCC (1986)**
RegRel: **ne** IntlRel: **ne** TheolSchool: **Gideon Bible School (Khartoum) jointly with SIC**

Address: Sudanese Church of Christ (SCoC), P.O. Box 1235, Omdurman, Sudan

4. Sudan Interior Church (SIC) (1362)

Work began in 1937, and the church became autonomous in 1963. Congr are
found in Khartoum, Upper Nile, and Blue Nile provinces.

TM: **30,000** BM: **20,000** CM: **20,000** Congr: **100** PStations: **30** OrdM: **28** Eld: **na** Deac: **200**
EvgHome: **45** Mission: **0** Women Ord: **yes** As Ministers: **no** as Deac: **200** as Elders: **ne** ChurchOrg:
Reformed (general church conf. executive committee — departments, local sessions) Off/
otherLang: **Arabic, English, Mahaan, Dinka, Uduk, Shilluk** DoctrB: **Trinitarian** Frequency of the
Lord's Supper: **monthly** Periodicals: **none** Close relations with: **SCOC, African Independent
Church** NatRel: **SCC (1979), SECA (1992)** RegRel: **SIM (1936), AEA (1994)** IntlRel: **ne**
TheolSchool: **Gideon Bible School (Modurman)**

Address: Sudan Interior Church (SIC), P.O. Box 220 35, Khartoum, Sudan, Tel: +249 11 47 27 90

5. Trinity Presbyterian Church of Sudan (1363)

This church separated from PCOS in 1986. Congr are in North Sudan and Upper
Nile province.

TM: **16,474** BM: **9,653** CM: **7,266** Congr: **233** PStations: **73** OrdM: **5** Eld: **14** Deac: **6** EvgHome: **24**
Mission: **0** Women Ord: **yes** As Ministers: **0** as Deac: **6** as Elders: **0** ChurchOrg: **Presbyterian (with
congr and elders in session)** Off/otherLang: **English, Arabic, Dinka** DoctrB: **ApC, WestConf** Infant
or believer's baptism: **both** Frequency of the Lord's Supper: **monthly if pastor available** Periodicals:
none Close relations with: **none** NatRel: **SCC (under consideration)** RegRel: **ne** IntlRel: **PCUSA
(pending union between PCoS, SPEC, and TPCS)** TheolSchool: **none**

Address: Trinity Presbyterian Church of Sudan, P.O. Box 935 61, Khartoum Two, Khartoum, Sudan

SURINAM

Area in km²	163,265
Population	(July 1996 est.) 436,418 Hindustani (also known locally as "East" Indians; their ancestors emigrated from northern India in the latter part of the 19th century) 37%, Creole (mixed European and African ancestry) 31%, Javanese 15.3%, "Bush Black" (also known as "Bush Creole," whose ancestors were brought to the country in the 17th and 18th centuries as slaves) 10.3%, Amerindian 2.6%, Chinese 1.7%, Europeans 1%, other 1.1%
Religions in %	Hindu 27.4%, Muslim 19.6%, RCath 22.8%, Prot 25.2% (predominantly Moravian), indigenous beliefs 5%
Official/other languages	Dutch/English (widely spoken), Sranang Tongo (Surinamese, sometimes called Taki-Taki, is the native language of Creoles and large parts of the younger population; it is lingua franca of the country), Hindustani (a dialect of Hindi), Javanese

The Reformed Church of Surinam (2131)

The Reformed Church of Surinam was founded in 1668 after the arrival of Rev. Basseliers. It was from the beginning a church for the Dutch colonists. Most church activities took place in Paramaribo, the capital city of Surinam, and around the various plantations in the countryside. In the second half of the 18th century, as owners of plantations started to move to Paramaribo, the "country churches" which had served them began to disappear. Until the 1850s the church was a state church (the state was paying for pastors and church upkeep) and existed almost exclusively for the elite of the country. The language was Dutch, and the pastors all belonged to the mainline Reformed Church of the Netherlands. Over the following decades this proved to be an asset as numerous streams and splits hit the various Ref denominations in the Netherlands. None of them had any significant influence on Surinam.

After the 1850s the church opened itself to the lower classes and to African slaves alike. "Negro-English" — a pidgin language used by the latter — was introduced in worship services. This was particularly evident in the border town of Nickeri.

In 1876, when a liberal stream created turmoil within the Reformed Church of Surinam, a number of members joined other churches but did not create a new independent church. Through various steps (new rules in 1884 and 1957) the church became fully independent from the Netherlands Reformed Church.

The central church building also functions as the auditorium of the University of Surinam. Here the first president of the state took oath when Surinam became independent in 1975.

TM: **15,000** BM: **15,000** CM: **6,500** Congr: **3** PStations: **5** OrdM: **2** Eld: **12** Deac: **12** EvgHome: **none** Mission: **none** Women Ord: **yes** As Ministers: **1968/1** as Deac: **1958/10** as Elders: **1958/8** ChurchOrg: **congr, synod (also called "board of elders")** Off/otherLang: **Dutch** DoctrB: **ApC, HeidC, CDort** Infant or believer's baptism: **both** Frequency of the Lord's Supper: **3 times a year** Periodicals: **Hervormd Suriname (gen/monthly/300)** Close relations with: **Ev. Luth Church, RCath, Moravian Ch** NatRel: **Committee of Christian Churches (CCK)** RegRel: **CCC** IntlRel: **nc** TheolSchool: **nc**

Address: Hervormde Kerk van Suriname, P.O. Box 2542, Wanicastraat 82 boven, Paramaribo, Surinam, Tel: +597 47 23 44

SWAZILAND

Area in km²	17,363
Population	(July 1996 est.) 998,730 African 97%, European 3%
Religions in %	Prot 23%, RCath 10%, indigenous beliefs 40%, African sects 27%
Official/other languages	English (the language of government business), Siswati, local dialects

CSC (Council of Swaziland Churches)

Swaziland, a British Protectorate until 1968, is a monarchy that has been ruled by King Mswati III since 1986. In October 1993, elections were held for the first time. Prince Mbilini was named Prime Minister. In 1997 Dr. Sibusiso Barabas became Prime Minister of the country. Swaziland relies on agriculture and the mining of natural resources (coal, diamond, and asbestos). Economically it still depends on South Africa, but large parts of the land are now back in the hands of Swazis.

The first church to undertake missionary work was the Meth (1845). Luth followed in 1887, and the RCath church in 1913. Though the country has become Christian, African religions continue to play a significant role.

In 1911 the first mission conference for all Prot churches was held. It was not repeated until 1929, when it was again constituted as the "Swaziland Missionary Council." It met every two years and later changed its name to the "Swaziland Conference of Churches." In 1967 the Council of Swaziland Churches was formed, including the mainline churches. Independent churches set up the League of African Churches in Swaziland in 1937.

Swaziland Reformed Church (1370)

In 1946 the Dutch Reformed Church (cf. South Africa no.1) began missionary work in Swaziland. The first missionary was Rev. Malan. It took fifteen years to set up the first congregation. It became part of the Dutch Reformed Church in Africa, Presbytery of Piet Retief (cf. South Africa no. 4a). In 1983 the three congregations in Swaziland decided to form a presbytery and, later (1989), the synod of Swaziland, which continued to be part of the DRCA. In 1991 the Synod of the DRCA decided to sever itself from the Synod of Swaziland, and the Swaziland Reformed Church was formed.

TM: **570** BM: **190** CM: **380** Congr: **4** PStations: **17** OrdM: **3** Eld: **16** Deac: **22** EvgHome: **7** Mission: **nc** Women Ord: **no** As Ministers: **no** as Deac: **1989/8** as Elders: **nc** ChurchOrg: **wards, congr, synod** Off/otherLang: **English, Swazi (Siswati)** DoctrB: **ApC, NicC, AthC, HeidC, CDort, BelgC, Ref (Dutch)** Infant or believer's baptism: **both** Frequency of the Lord's Supper: **4 times a year** Close relations with: **other churches of CSC** NatRel: **CSC (Council of Swaziland Churches)** RegRel: **nc** IntlRel: **nc** TheolSchool: **nc** Service infrastructure: **5 kindergartens, 4 schools**

Address: Swaziland Reformed Church, P.O. Box 214, Siteki, Swaziland, Tel: +268 34121

SWEDEN

Area in km²	449,964
Population	(July 1996 est.) 8,900,954 white, Lapp (Sami), foreign-born or first-generation immigrants 12% (Finns, Yugoslavs, Danes, Norwegians, Greeks, Turks)
Religions in %	Evangelical Luth 94%, RCath 1.5%, Pent 1%, other 3.5% (1987)
Official/other languages	Swedish

Unsuccessful attempts to evangelize the country were made in 829 and 853 by Saint Ansgar, bishop of Hamburg. In 1020 the Christian King of England and Denmark sent Sigfrid of York to christianize Sweden. Around 1130 Cistercian monks founded several monasteries in the country. On June 6, 1556, the National Church (Luth) was established; Sweden is a constitutional monarchy in which the king must be Luth. There are also Dutch and Korean Ref congregations.

1. The Mission Covenant Church of Sweden (MCCS) (6420)

The church sprang from the spiritual revival in the 19th century. The first local church was founded in 1855, and the denomination in 1878, as a protest against the Luth state church system.

Emphasizing the free association of committed believers in local fellowship, the MCCS adopted a congregational character. It sent representatives to the first meeting of the International Congregational Council in 1891. It regards the Holy Scripture as the sole source of faith and has no creeds. Infant and adult baptism are practiced. Holy Communion is generally led by a pastor, and the elements are distributed by a pastor or a layman. Since 1908 pastors have been trained at the church's own seminary at Lidingö, which, in 1994, in response to a petition from the church, was transformed by the government into a theological faculty, the Stockholm School of Theology, run by the MCCS in cooperation with the Bapt Union of Sweden. The church also runs five "Folkhögskolor" (folk high schools) at Härnösand, Kalix, Karlskoga, Lidingö, and Jönköping. The General Assembly (GA) is the highest decision-making body. The executive board is elected by the GA. The local churches cooperate with the board through seven districts and their superintendents. The MCCS is very involved in political, social, and international issues. A bi-weekly paper, "Sändaren," is published in cooperation with the Bapt Union of Sweden.

The Mission Covenant Youth (SMU/Svenska Missionsförbundets Ungdom) is an independent youth organization, one of the signal youth movements in Sweden, with 58,000 members from toddlers to young adults. It has done extensive international work, in cooperation with youth organizations in sister churches. Mission work overseas began in 1879. Today the MCCS cooperates in mission and development work with churches in the Republic of Congo, Ecuador, India, Japan, Nicaragua, Pakistan, and the Democratic Republic of Zaire. Emphasis is laid on mission work in Sweden itself, which is one of the main issues confronting the MCCS today in the wake of declining membership.

TM: **70,072** Congr: **894** OrdM: **659** Eld: **ne** Deac: **128** EvgHome: **7** Mission: **68** Women Ord: **yes** As Ministers: **1950** as Deac: **1972** as Elders: **nc** ChurchOrg: **geographical districts** Off/otherLang: **Swedish** DoctrB: **ApC, NicC, no emphasis on creeds** Infant or believer's baptism: **both** Frequency of the Lord's Supper: **monthly in gen** Close relations with: **sister churches in Ecuador, India, Japan, Pakistan, both Congos** NatRel: **Sverges Kristna Raad, Sveriges Frikyrkosamraad, Svenska Bibelsällskapet, Frikyrkliga Studieförbundet, Svenska Lausanne kommittén, Svenska Missionsraadet** RegRel: **NER, CEC (1959)** IntlRel: **WARC (1971), WCC (1948), IFFEC (1948)** TheolSchool: **Stockholm School of Theology, Theol. Fac. of Uppsala and of Lund** Service infrastructure: **5 folk high schools, 2 student homes, 1 summer vacation house, 1 printing house, 1 bookshop** Periodicals: **Sändaren (gen/bi-weekly/19,300), Tro och liv (theol. and homiletics/6 per year/1,700), Information (info. to congr and employees /6 per year/2,600)**

Address: Svenska Missionsförbundet, P.O. Box 6302, Tegnérgatan 8, S — 11381 Stockholm, Sweden, Tel: +46 8 151-830, Fax: +46 8 158-757, E-mail: info@smf.se.

2. French Reformed Church (6421)

When Sweden adopted Lutheranism as the state religion, no freedom was granted either to RCath or to "those who share the mistakes of Zwingli and Calvin" (Synod of Upsal 1593). When, in the 1640s, King Gustav Adolph badly needed skilled craftsmen to set up a powerful army, he hired them from the Walloon Province of the Netherlands. These Ref workers came under the condition that they be allowed to bring along their own ministers. Their ministers were paid by Louis de Geer, the rich steel magnate from Liège. The Walloon Period (1640-1696) was followed by the Anglo-British era (1696-1741) when French Huguenots sought refuge in Sweden from King Louis XIV's persecutions of the Prot. They worshiped, together with the Presb, at the residence of the British Ambassador. A third period, the so-called French Period, saw King Frederic I of Hessen-Cassel, a Ref churchman himself, granting the right of public worship to the Ref community. In 1751 the first Ref church was inaugurated. Since 1796 the Ref pastors have had the same "status" as their Luth colleagues.

Over the decades the French Reformed Church lost a sizeable part of its membership through naturalization of the old Ref families. Today the church is heavily involved in social work and asylum issues. It also houses a small French-speaking school.

TM: **310** BM: **na** CM: **na** Congr: **1** OrdM: **1** Eld: **ne** Deac: **1** EvgHome: **ne** Mission: **ne** Women Ord: **ne** As Ministers: **ne** as Deac: **ne** as Elders: **ne** ChurchOrg: **Synod of Scandinavia (Copenhague, Fredericia, Stockholm)** Off/otherLang: **French** DoctrB: **ApC, NicC** Infant or believer's baptism: **both** Frequency of the Lord's Supper: **monthly** Close relations with: **Swedish Luth Church, Bapt Church, CEEEFE** NatRel: **Christian Council of Sweden (1993)** RegRel: **nc** IntlRel: **WARC (membership through Mission Covenant Church)** TheolSchool: **training in Stockholm and Strasbourg (France)** Periodicals: **none**

Address: Eglise réformée française, 13 Humlegärosgatan, S — Stockholm, Sweden, Tel: +46 8 662 8871, Fax: +46 8 662 9817, E-mail: frks@egl.frrer.se.

SWITZERLAND

Area in km²	41,290
Population	(July 1996 est.) 7,207,060 total population: German 65%, French 18%, Italian 10%, Romansh 1%, other 6% Swiss nationals: German 74%, French 20%, Italian 4%, Romansh 1%, other 1%
Religions in %	RCath 47.6%, Prot 44.3%, other 8.1% (1980)
Official/other languages	German, French, Italian, Romanch

AGCK (Conference of the Christian Churches in Switzerland, *Arbeitsgemeinschaft Christlicher Kirchen der Schweiz*)
CER (*Conférence des églises romandes* — Conference of French-speaking Churches in Switzerland)
SEK/FEPS (Federation of Swiss Protestant Churches)
KiKo (Conference of German-speaking churches)

474

The Ref churches in Switzerland came into existence during the 16th-century Reformation. Politically, present-day Switzerland consisted at that time of a number of loosely connected regions or cantons. The Reformation spread primarily in the cities and took a different course in each part of the country. The breakthrough began in the 1520s: in Zurich 1522/23 (under Zwingli 1484-1531), in Bern 1528 (under Berchtold Haller), in Basel 1529 (under John Oekolampad), in St. Gallen 1529 (under Joachim Vadian), in Neuchâtel 1530 (under Guillaume Farel), and in Geneva 1535/36 (under Farel and Calvin). Zurich became the spiritual center of the Zwinglian reform. Under the leadership of John Calvin (1509-1564) Geneva became the spiritual center of the Calvinist reform. Both centers developed a network of manifold relationships; on the one hand among the Swiss cantons which had accepted the Reformation; on the other hand with reform movements in foreign countries. Geneva especially (with its theological academy) had broad international contacts and was sometimes even referred to as the Rome of Protestantism. The strands of the Reformation in Zurich and Geneva actually grew together into a single Ref church family as a result of an understanding reached by Calvin and Heinrich Bullinger, Zwingli's successor, which found expression in the *Consensus Tigurinus,* the Zurich Agreement (1549).

The Swiss Reformation was both a spiritual and a political movement. Since church and society were seen as an integral whole, the reform of the church was a matter to be decided upon by municipal councils. The leaders of the Reformation depended on the agreement and support of the political authorities. The reforms were carried out by magisterial order and enforced with harsh measures against dissidents. The close connection of church and state has remained typical of the Swiss Ref churches, though it was conceived of differently in the various cantons. Throughout his life Calvin sought to limit the power of the magistrate in church affairs.

The Reformation movement also gave birth to the Anabaptist movement (1525). A breach developed among Zwingli's closest companions over the question of baptism and of the right of the government to make decisions regarding the life of the church. Using violent measures, Zwingli and the magistrate of Zurich sought to suppress the movement. For centuries Anabaptist groups continued to suffer persecution from all sides. The Zurich Reformation is thus the cradle both of the Ref and of the Anabaptist-free church tradition.

Just as the political system retained the form of a loose federation of states, the Ref churches never formed a united church. Although they maintained regular and manifold contacts, they remained autonomous regional churches.

A rather unique situation developed in the course of centuries with regard to the authority of confessional statements. In the cities which accepted the Reformation, several confessions were formulated, e.g., the 67 articles in Zurich 1523, Theses of Berne 1528, Berne Synodus 1532, and the Confession of Geneva 1537. The Second Helvetic Confession (*Confessio Helvetica Posterior*), written by Bullinger in 1566, and the Geneva Catechisms by Calvin in 1542 gained importance well beyond the borders of the Ref areas of the Swiss Confederation. The *Formula Consensus* of 1675 was issued as a response to doctrinal controversies at the time of Ref orthodoxy (17th century). It maintains a strict understanding of the doctrines of verbal inspiration and double predestination. With the emergence of Pietism and the Enlightenment (17th/18th centuries) confessions lost much of their credibility. The opposition to the *Formula Consensus* in particular and to every form of enforced confession grew. In the late 18th and in the 19th century the formal obligation to the traditional confessions of faith was gradually abolished. Today the Ref church constitutions name the Bible as the only authoritative document for measuring the Ref faith. The interpretation of the Bible is largely free.

In the course of its history, especially in the 19th century, the Swiss Ref churches often had to fight against secessions. The protest against liberal theology and governmental interference in church life (e.g., the abolition by decree of the traditional confessions of faith) as well as the general impulses of the Revival Movement led to secessions of Ref free churches: 1846 in Vaud, 1849 in Geneva, 1873 in Neuchâtel. The Geneva Free Church still exists today, but the free churches in Neuchâtel and Vaud reunited with the official Reformed Church in 1966 and 1943 respectively. In addition to these Ref free churches, a number of pietistic associations were formed in the wake of the Revival in the 19th century. They were organized as groups within the Ref churches; e.g., Evangelical Societies (the first in Berne in 1831) or the Pilgrim's Mission St. Chrischona (beginning in 1869). The latter has more recently transformed itself into an autonomous free church. The relationship between the Ref churches and the free churches remains strained although mutual relationships have improved substantially in the last decades.

The Swiss Ref churches owe much to Pietism and the Revival Movement. Most of the church-related social-service and missionary organizations go back to the initiative of Revival groups. Although structurally independent, these organizations have spiritual ties to the churches. Thanks to Christian Friedrich Spittler (1782-1867), the founder of the Basel Christian Society, Basel became a center of such organizations. The Basel Mission (founded in 1815) acquired international significance.

In the 18th and 19th centuries the autonomy of church life gradually increased. Today their structures are analogous to the political structures. Just as the course of the political communities in Switzerland is determined by the communal assembly as the legislative body and the community council as the executive body, the congregations (parishes) are led by the parochial assembly and the parochial council. At the cantonal level the church synod and the church council correspond to the cantonal council and the administrative council.

Until well into the 19th century the Ref churches generally remained state churches, i.e., ultimately dependent on the political authorities of the canton. Relationships with the state began to be revised in the 20th century. Today relationships are regulated separately in each canton, which results in major variations among the cantons. Whereas in Basel (since 1905), in Geneva (since 1907), and in Neuchâtel (since 1943) church and state are entirely or partially separated from one another, relationships in Berne, Zurich, Vaud, and also Basel-Land are still very close. The Ref churches continue, however, to regard themselves as the

476

church of their canton. (38.5% of the population belong to the various Ref churches.)

Contacts among the Ref churches in Switzerland remained loose for many centuries. In 1858, following the foundation of the Swiss Confederation (1848), the churches founded a Swiss Church Conference, meeting annually. After World War I, partly in response to the American Federal Council of Churches, which sought a partner to coordinate reconstruction help for war-damaged Europe, the Federation of Swiss Protestant Churches was founded (1920). Two years later it was joined by the Meth Church. The Federation is not itself a church but an alliance of autonomous churches.

In addition, the Swiss Ref churches have created a series of organizations for specific tasks. In the French-speaking area of Switzerland the Département missionnaire des Eglises protestantes de la Suisse romande (DM) and in German-speaking Switzerland the Kooperation evangelischer Kirchen und Missionen (KEM) are responsible for church partnerships. The Hilfswerk der evangelischen Kirchen der Schweiz (HEKS/EPER) was founded as an instrument for church relief work, Brot für alle (Bfa/PPP) is the Ref churches' agency for development work.

The present situation of the Swiss Ref churches is probably best described as transitional. The established church's claim to comprise the majority of the population is no longer accepted as a matter of course. The number of people withdrawing from membership is increasing; many are indifferent. In addition, the uncertainty about the identity of Ref churches is growing. The plurality of theological concepts and spiritual practice is immense. The denominational boundaries in respect to the RCath Church on the one hand and the free churches on the other hand are more permeable. Furthermore, non-denominational movements (evangelical, charismatic, feminist) are being superimposed on the traditional denominational identities. These movements are usually more formative for participants than membership in the Ref tradition. Today the Swiss Ref churches have the task of rediscovering their identity and mission between the poles of unity and diversity, of tradition and innovation, commitment and openness. This task has to be accomplished in an increasingly secular, multi-religious situation, where the church's position is perceived as just one among many offers in the "religious supermarket" of postmodern society.

Federation of Swiss Protestant Churches (*Schweizerischer Evangelischer Kirchenbund — SEK, Fédération de églises protestantes de la Suisse — FEPS, Federazione delle Chiese evangelische della Svizzera*)

Founded in 1920, the Federation includes 22 member churches — twenty cantonal churches and two free churches (Free Church of Geneva and the Evangelical-Methodist Church of Switzerland). It represents these churches nationally vis-à-vis the Swiss government and ecumenical partners. Internationally, it represents the Ref churches in international ecumenical organizations: in the World Alliance of Reformed Churches (since 1922), in the World Council of Churches (since 1948), in the Conference of European Churches (since 1959), and in the Leuenberg Church Fellowship (since 1974).

ChurchOrg: **Federation** Off/otherLang: **German, French, Italian, Roman** Periodicals: **occasional publications, specially of the Institute for Social-Ethics** Close relations with: *Korea:* **PC** (cf. Korea no. 14) **and PROK** (cf. Korea no. 13); *Philippines:* **NCCP;** *Taiwan:* **PCT;** *China:* **CCC;** *Japan:* **Kyodan** (cf. Japan no. 1); *Latin America:* **CLAI; other partnerships via mission and other agencies** NatRel: **AGCK (1971)** RegRel: **CEC (1959), CEPPLE via member churches, CEVAA** IntlRel: **WARC, WCC** TheolSchool: **Theological Faculties of Basel, Bern, Geneva, Lausanne, Neuchâtel, Zürich, Bible School Aarau**

Address: Schweizerischer Evangelischer Kirchenbund (SEK/FEPS), Postfach 36, Sulgenauweg 26, CH-3000 Bern 23, Switzerland, Tel: +41 31 370 25 25, Fax: +41 31 370 25 80

1. Protestant Reformed Church of the Canton Aargau (6431)

TM: **205,000** BM: **205,000** CM: **205,000** Congr: **75** PStations: **150** OrdM: **141** Eld: **500-600** Deac: **50** EvgHome: **nc** Mission: **nc** Women Ord: **yes** As Ministers: **1965/28** as Deac: **1991/35** as Elders: **nc** ChurchOrg: **75 presby, one synod** Off/otherLang: **German** DoctrB: **Bible, Ref tradition, no emphasis on creeds** Infant or believer's baptism: **both** Periodicals: **Kirchenbote (Church Messenger) (monthly/90,000)** NatRel: **SEK/FEPS** RegRel: **CEC** IntlRel: **same as SEK/FEPS**TheolSchool: **various Swiss universities**

Address: Evang.-reformierte Landeskirche des Kantons Aargau, Postfach 5001, Augustin Keller-Str. 1, CH-5000 Aarau, Switzerland, Tel: +41 62 838 00 10, Fax: +41 62 838 00 29

2. Evangelical-Reformed Church of Appenzell (6432)

TM: **30,151** Congr: **20** PStations: **26** OrdM: **21** Eld: **nc** Deac: **1** EvgHome: **none** Mission: **none** Women Ord: **yes** As Ministers: **1967/6** as Deac: **2** as Elders: **nc** ChurchOrg: **parish, convent, synod** Off/otherLang: **German** DoctrB: **Bible, Ref tradition, no emphasis on creeds** Infant or believer's baptism: **both** Periodicals: **Magnet (info/monthly/15,500)** NatRel: **Church in Solidarity with Women, ACK** RegRel: **CEC** IntlRel: **same as SEK/FEPS**TheolSchool: **various Swiss universities**

Address: Evang.-reformierte Landeskirche beider Appenzell, P.O. Box 2, CH-9101 Herisau, Switzerland, Tel: +41 71 351 40 44, Fax: +41 71 351 40 44

3. Evangelical-Reformed Church of the Canton Basel-Landschaft (6433)

TM: **113,537** BM: **113,537** CM: **na** Congr: **35** OrdM: **65** Eld: **nc** Deac: **5** EvgHome: **nc** Mission: **nc** Women Ord: **yes** As Ministers: **since 1966/20** as Deac: **nc** as Elders: **nc** ChurchOrg: **congr — church — church council — synod** Off/otherLang: **German, Swiss-German** DoctrB: **Bible, Ref tradition, no emphasis on creeds** Infant or believer's baptism: **both** Frequency of the Lord's Supper: **6 times per year, but church council has right to ask for more eucharist services** Periodicals: **Kirchenbote (gen/monthly/52,000)** Close relations with: **Ev.-Meth Church** NatRel: **SEK/FEPS (1952)** RegRel: **EECCS, CEC** IntlRel: **same as SEK/FEPS** TheolSchool: **nc**

Address: Evang.-reformierte Kirche des Kantons Basel-Landschaft, Postfach 438, Kirchhof, CH-4410 Liestal, Switzerland, Tel: +41 61 921 22 51, Fax: +41 61 921 28 11, E-mail: none

4. Evangelical-Reformed Church of the Canton Basel-Stadt (6434)

TM: **51,000** Congr: **6** OrdM: **49** Eld: **nc** Deac: **16** EvgHome: **nc** Mission: **nc** Women Ord: **yes** As Ministers: **1656 (single)/1976 (married)/11** as Deac: **nc** as Elders: **always** ChurchOrg: **synod — legislative, church council — executive, parishes** Off/otherLang: **German, French** DoctrB: **Bible, Ref tradition, no emphasis on creeds** Infant or believer's baptism: **both** Frequency of the Lord's Supper: **at major church feasts** Periodicals: **Kirchenbote (gen/weekly/44,000)** Close relations with: **RCath, OldCath, Jewish community** NatRel: **FEPS** RegRel: **CEC** IntlRel: **same as SEK/FEPS** TheolSchool: **Theological Faculty of Basel University, Kirchlich-theologische Schule**

Address: Evang.-reformierte Kirche des Kantons Basel-Stadt, Rittergasse 3, CH-4051 Basel, Switzerland, Tel: +41 61 272 88 11, Fax: +41 61 272 27 94

5. Evangelical-Reformed Churches of the Canton Bern-Jura (6435)

TM: **744,250** BM: **744,250** Congr: **230** PStations: **1,000** OrdM: **500** Eld: **2,200** Deac: **nc** EvgHome: **100** Mission: **ne** Women Ord: **yes** As Ministers: **1929 ord./1963 for preaching/63** as Deac: **120** as Elders: **730** ChurchOrg: **parishes/districts** Off/otherLang: **German, French/some small parishes speaking Korean, Italian, Hungarian, Czech, Slovac** DoctrB: **Bible, Ref tradition, no emphasis on creeds** Infant or believer's baptism: **both** Frequency of the Lord's Supper: **varies according to congregation's tradition** Periodicals: **Circular letter (internal/monthly/3,700)** Close relations with: **RCath, Christian-Catholic, Jewish parishes** NatRel: **SEK/FEPS, AKB (Assembly of Christian Churches in the Canton Bern), IKK (interconfessional conference), CER, KiKo** RegRel: **CEC** IntlRel: **same as SEK/FEPS** TheolSchool: **Theological Faculty of Bern University**

Address: Evang.-reformierte Kirchen Bern-Jura, Postfach 75, Bürenstr. 12, CH-3000 Bern 23, Switzerland, Tel: +41 31 370 28 28, Fax: +41 31 370 28 90, E-mail: kirchenbern@access.ch

6. Evangelical-Reformed Church of the Canton of Freiburg (6436)

TM: **33,111** BM: **33,111** Congr: **11** OrdM: **30** Eld: **nc** Deac: **5** EvgHome: **nc** Mission: **none** Women Ord: **yes** As Ministers: **1969/9** as Deac: **1969/2** as Elders: **nc** ChurchOrg: **synod** Off/otherLang: **German, French** DoctrB: **Bible, Ref tradition, no emphasis on creeds** Frequency of the Lord's Supper: **monthly and special feasts** Close relations with: **RCath Ch, Forum (Plateforme) with Ev. Churches, all Prot Chs** NatRel: **SEK/FEPS (1920), KiKo, CER, "Kirchlicher Hilfsverein Schweiz"** RegRel: **CEC** IntlRel: **same as SEK/FEPS** TheolSchool: **various Swiss theological schools.**

Address: Evang.-reformierte Kirche des Kantons Freiburg, Deutsche Kirchgasse 9, CH-3280 Murten, Switzerland, Tel: +41 26 670 45 40, Fax: +41 26 670 45 40

7. National Protestant Church of Geneva (6437)

TM: **101,608** BM: **101,608** Congr: **43** OrdM: **72** Eld: **nc** Deac: **14** EvgHome: **nc** Mission: **1** Women Ord: **yes** As Ministers: **1930/21** as Deac: **1963/7** as Elders: **nc** ChurchOrg: **consistory (legislative) and council of churches (executive)** Off/otherLang: **French** DoctrB: **Bible, Ref tradition, no emphasis on creeds** Infant or believer's baptism: **both** Frequency of the Lord's Supper: **monthly** Periodicals: **La Vie Protestante (monthly/33,000)** NatRel: **RECG (Assembly of Churches and Christian Commu-**

nities in Geneva), SEK/FEPS (1920) RegRel: **CEC (1959)** IntlRel: **same as SEK/FEPS** TheolSchool: **Autonomous Faculty of Theology (University of Geneva)**

Address: Eglise Nationale Protestante de Genève, C.P. 3078, Rue du Cloître 2, CH-1211 Genève 3, Switzerland, Tel: +41 22 311 85 33, Fax: +41 22 311 13 05

8. Free Evangelical Church of Geneva (6451)

TM: **900** BM: **900** Congr: **7** PStations: **7** OrdM: **7** Eld: **40** Deac: EvgHome: **1** Mission: **1** Women Ord: **no** As Ministers: **no** as Deac: **1** as Elders: **no** ChurchOrg: **synods** Off/otherLang: **French** DoctrB: **nc** Infant or believer's baptism: **believer** Frequency of the Lord's Supper: **weekly** Periodicals: **Courant (pop/mission/homiletics/every 2nd month/100)** NatRel: **SEK/FEPS** RegRel: **CEC** IntlRel: **nc** TheolSchool: **nc**

Address: Eglise évangélique libre de Genève, rue Tabazan 7, A, CH-1204 Genève, Switzerland, Tel: +41 22 310 17 92, Fax: +41 22 310 17 92

9. Evangelical Synod of the Canton of Glarus (6438)

TM: **20,000** BM: **20,000** Congr: **16** OrdM: **15** Eld: **none** Deac: **nc** EvgHome: **none** Mission: **none** Women Ord: **yes** As Ministers: **1990/3** as Deac: **nc** as Elders: **nc** ChurchOrg: **synod** Off/otherLang: **German** DoctrB: **Bible, Ref tradition, no emphasis on creeds** Frequency of the Lord's Supper: **monthly** Periodicals: **Kirchenbote (9,000)** Close relations with: **Ref Ch of Appenzell** NatRel: **SEK/FEPS** RegRel: **nc** IntlRel: **as SEK/FEPS** TheolSchool: **various Swiss theological schools**

Address: Evangelischer Kirchenrat des Kantons Glarus, Wiesli 7, CH-8750 Glarus, Switzerland, Tel: +41 64 026 09, Fax: +41 640 67 02

10. Evangelical-Reformed Church of the Canton of Graubünden (6439)

TM: **70,000** BM: **70,000** Congr: **140** OrdM: **100** Eld: **nc** Deac: **12** EvgHome: **nc** Mission: **nc** Women Ord: **yes** As Ministers: **12** as Deac: **2-3** as Elders: **nc** ChurchOrg: **evangelical council (legislative), synod (assy of all pastors) Colloquium (assy of all parish delegates), parish (assy of all parish-members)** Off/otherLang: **German, Romanch, Italian** DoctrB: **Bible, Ref tradition, no emphasis on creeds** Infant or believer's baptism: **both** Frequency of the Lord's Supper: **minimum 4 times per year** Periodicals: **Bündner Kirchenbote (16,000)** Close relations with: **RCath church** NatRel: **SEK/FEPS** RegRel: **CEC** IntlRel: **same as SEK/FEPS** TheolSchool: **various Swiss theological schools**

Address: Evangelisch-reformierte Landeskirche des Kantons Graubünden, Löestrasse 60, CH-7000 Chur, Switzerland, Tel: +41 81 257 11 00, Fax: +41 81 257 11 01

11. Evangelical-Reformed Church of the Canton of Lucerne (6440)

TM: **43,000** BM: **43,000** CM: **2,500** Congr: **8** PStations: **30** OrdM: **35** Eld: **181** Deac: **6** EvgHome: **none** Mission: **none** Women Ord: **yes** As Ministers: **1970** as Deac: **nc** as Elders: **nc** ChurchOrg: **synod (legislative), council of the synod (executive), parishes with church assemblies and church council**

Off/otherLang: **German** DoctrB: **Bible, Ref tradition, no emphasis on creeds** Infant or believer's baptism: **infant** Frequency of the Lord's Supper: **monthly** Periodicals: **Kirchenbote (gen/monthly/ 20,000)** Close relations with: **RCath Church of the Canton Lucerne, Old Catholic Church/Lucerne, member churches of the SEK/FEPS** NatRel: **SEK/FEPS (1988)** RegRel: **CEC** IntlRel: **same as SEK/FEPS** TheolSchool: **various Swiss theological schools**

Address: Evang.-reformierte Kirche des Kantons Luzern, Steinhofweg 12, CH-6005 Luzern, Switzerland, Tel: +41 41 310 87 24

12. Reformed-Evangelical Church of the Canton of Neuchâtel (EREN) (6441)

TM: **81,684** Congr: **52** PStations: **66** OrdM: **65** Eld: **571** Deac: **14** EvgHome: **none** Mission: **8** Women Ord: **yes** As Ministers: **1970/14** as Deac: **1970/7** as Elders: **1971/264** ChurchOrg: **synod, regional council or consistory, parish** Off/otherLang: **French (except 2 German-speaking congrs)** DoctrB: **Bible, Ref tradition, no emphasis on creeds** Infant or believer's baptism: **both** Frequency of the Lord's Supper: **varies according to congregation's tradition** Periodicals: **La Vie Protestante Neuchâteloise (pop/month/38,000)** Close relations with: **CER/Eglise réformée de France-Est, Luth in Montbéliard, Christian Council in China** NatRel: **CER (1946), SEK/FEPS (1943), AGCK** RegRel: **CEPPLE, CEC** IntlRel: **same as SEK/FEPS** TheolSchool: **Theological Faculty of Neuchâtel University**

Address: Eglise réformée évangélique du canton de Neuchâtel (EREN), C.P. 531, Fbg. de l'Hôpital 24, CH-2001 Neuchâtel, Switzerland, Tel: +41 32 725-7817, Fax: +4132 724-0950

13. Evangelical-Reformed Synod of the Canton of St. Gallen (6442)

TM: **133,000** BM: **133,000** Congr: **55** PStations: **80** OrdM: **120** Eld: **450** Deac: **55** EvgHome: **28** Mission: **nc** Women Ord: **yes** As Ministers: **1949/16** as Deac: **nc** as Elders: **nc** ChurchOrg: **synod (180 members), church council (7 members), 3 church regions with 1 dean and 1 vice-dean** Off/ otherLang: **German, sometimes Swiss-German** DoctrB: **Bible, Ref tradition, no emphasis on creeds** Infant or believer's baptism: **both** Frequency of the Lord's Supper: **10 times per year** Periodicals: **Kirchenbote (gen/monthly/70,000), Synodalamtsblatt (2 times per year/500), Circular Letter (2 times per year/500)** Close relations with: **RCath Church, Evangelical Church of Liechtenstein** NatRel: **SEK/FEPS, AGCK (1972)** RegRel: **nc** IntlRel: **same as SEK/FEPS** TheolSchool: **various Swiss theological schools**

Address: Evang.-reformierte Kirche des Kantons St. Gallen, Oberer Graben 43, CH-9000 St. Gallen, Switzerland, Tel: +41 71 222 38 38, Fax: +41 71 223 22 51

14. Evangelical-Reformed Synod of the Canton of Schaffhausen (6443)

TM: **37,851** BM: **37,851** CM: **37,851** Congr: **30** PStations: **30** OrdM: **28** Eld: **30** Deac: **8** EvgHome: **50** Mission: **nc** Women Ord: **yes** As Ministers: **1966/7** as Deac: **ne** as Elders: **1** ChurchOrg: **synod, parish assembly (each parish is almost autonomous)** Off/otherLang: **German** DoctrB: **Bible, Ref tradition, no emphasis on creeds** Infant or believer's baptism: **both** Frequency of the Lord's Supper: **minimum quarterly** Periodicals: **circular letters (internal info/4-5 times per year/400), Kirchenbote (gen. info./monthly/19,500)** Close relations with: **Ev.-Meth Church, Conference of Churches of the**

481

Rhine NatRel: **SEK/FEPS** RegRel: **CEC Conference of the Churches along the Rhine** IntlRel: **same as SEK/FEPS** TheolSchool: **various Swiss theological schools**

Address: Evang.-reformierte Kirche des Kantons Schaffhausen, Postfach 3150, Pfrundhausgasse 3, CH-8201 Schaffhausen, Switzerland, Tel: +41 52 624 4862, Fax: +41 52 624 4842

15. Reformed Church in the Canton of Solothurn (6452)

TM: **34,781** BM: **34,781** Congr: **14** PStations: **20** OrdM: **17** Eld: **155** Deac: **12** EvgHome: **ne** Mission: **ne** Women Ord: **yes** As Ministers: **1949/1** as Deac: **nc** as Elders: **nc** ChurchOrg: **congr, synod** Off/ otherLang: **German** DoctrB: **Bible, Ref tradition, no emphasis on creeds** Infant or believer's baptism: **both** Periodicals: **Kirchenbote (gen/monthly/18,000)** NatRel: **SEK/FEPS** RegRel: **CEC** IntlRel: **same as SEK/FEPS** TheolSchool: **University of Basel, Zurich, and Bern**

Address: Evangelisch-reformierte Kirche im Kanton Solothurn, Mittelgäu Str. 15, CH Wangen, Switzerland, Tel: +41 62 212 6708, Fax: +41 62 212 6708

16. Protestant Church of Thurgovia (6444)

TM: **103,400** BM: **103,000** CM: **5,250** Congr: **72** PStations: **80** OrdM: **70** Eld: **500** Deac: **10** EvgHome: **none** Mission: **none** Women Ord: **yes** As Ministers: **1966/5** ChurchOrg: **parish (parish assembly, parish council), Canton (synod, executive council)** Off/otherLang: **German and dialect** DoctrB: **ApC, Confession of Thurgovia (1873)** Infant or believer's baptism: **both** Frequency of the Lord's Supper: **at least 10 times per year** Periodicals: **Kirchenbote (gen. and info./monthly/40,000)** Close relations with: **RCath Church** NatRel: **SEK/FEPS (1920)** RegRel: **CEC** IntlRel: **same as SEK/FEPS** TheolSchool: **various Swiss theological schools**

Address: Evangelischer Kirchenrat des Kantons Thurgau, Bankplatz 5, Haus zur "Geduld," CH-8500 Frauenfeld, Switzerland, Tel: +41 52 721 78 56, Fax: +41 52 721 27 51

17. Evangelical-Reformed Church of the Canton of Ticino (6445)

TM: **20,257** Congr: **3** PStations: **10** OrdM: **9** Eld: **31** Deac: **2** EvgHome: **none** Mission: **none** Women Ord: **yes** As Ministers: **1966/1** as Deac: **without ordination** as Elders: **without ordination** ChurchOrg: **parish assemblies, consistories, synod** Off/otherLang: **Italian (also French and German)** DoctrB: **ApC, NicC** Infant or believer's baptism: **both** Frequency of the Lord's Supper: **varies according to congregation's tradition** Periodicals: **Vita Evangélica (church life/monthly/5,200)** Close relations with: **Federazione delle Chiese evangeliche in Italia** NatRel: **SEK/FEPS (1966), KIKO (1966), CER (1966), Conferenza delle Chiese evangeliche di lingua italiana nella Svizzera (1995)** RegRel: **CEC** IntlRel: **same as SEK/FEPS** TheolSchool: **various Swiss theological schools**

Address: Chiesa Evangélica Riformata del Ticino (CERT), Via S. Gottardo, CH-6900 Lugano, Switzerland, Tel: +41 91 922 79 51, Fax: +41 91 923 92 58

18. Reformed Evangelical Church of Valais (6447)

TM: **13,741** Congr: **12** OrdM: **10** Eld: **nc** Deac: **3** EvgHome: **none** Mission: **1** Women Ord: **yes** As Ministers: **1948** as Deac: **1974** as Elders: **1948** ChurchOrg: **synod** Off/otherLang: **French, German**

DoctrB: **ApC, NicC, HelvC, confession of the local church** Infant or believer's baptism: **infant** Frequency of the Lord's Supper: **twice a month** Periodicals: **Présence Protestante/Ev. Stimme (pop/ 7,500)** Close relations with: **RCath Church** NatRel: **AGCK, SEK/FEPS, CER** RegRel: **CEC** IntlRel: **same as SEK/FEPS** TheolSchool: **various Swiss theological schools.**

Address: Eglise réformée évangélique du Valais, rue du Vieux-Moulin 3, CH-1950 Sion, Switzerland, Tel: +41 21 322 69 59, Fax: +41 27 322 69 59

19. Evangelical Reformed Church of the Canton of Vaud (6446)

TM: **481,551** Congr: **158** PStations: **158** OrdM: **276** Eld: **nc** Deac: **56** EvgHome: **nc** Mission: **nc** Women Ord: **yes** ChurchOrg: **synod (legislative), synodal council (executive)** Off/otherLang: **French (except 8 German-speaking congrs)** DoctrB: **ApC, NicC** Infant or believer's baptism: **both** Frequency of the Lord's Supper: **weekly to monthly** Periodicals: **Croire (pop/monthly)** Close relations with: **RCath Church** NatRel: **SEK/FEPS, CER** RegRel: **CEC** IntlRel: **same as SEK/FEPS** TheolSchool: **Theological Faculty of Lausanne University**

Address: Eglise évangélique réformée du Canton de Vaud, C.P. 871, Rue de l'Ale 31, CH-1000 Lausanne 9, Switzerland, Tel: +41 21 323 71 35, Fax: +41 21 323 16 83

20. Evangelical-Reformed Church of the Canton of Zurich (6448)

TM: **532,963** Congr: **179** PStations: **900** OrdM: **520** Eld: **none** Deac: **140** EvgHome: **none** Mission: **0** Women Ord: **yes** As Ministers: **1963/124** as Deac: **1989** as Elders: **nc** ChurchOrg: **parish council, synod (with 180 members)** Off/otherLang: **German, French** DoctrB: **Bible, Ref tradition, no emphasis on creeds** Infant or believer's baptism: **both** Frequency of the Lord's Supper: **usually 4 to 12 times per year** Periodicals: **Kirchenbote (Zürich) (twice a month/270,000), Notabene (6 times a year/6,500)** Close relations with: **through SFPC, churches in Korea and Japan, CEC, HEKS (Eastern Europe)** NatRel: **SEK/FEPS (1920), AGKD — Zürich (1965), KIKO** RegRel: **CEC, EECCS** IntlRel: **same as SEK/FEPS** TheolSchool: **Theological Faculty of Zürich University**

Address: Evangelisch-reformierte Landeskirche des Kantons Zürich, Blaufahnenstrasse 10, CH-80 001 Zürich, Switzerland, Tel: +41 1 258 91 11, Fax: +41 1 258 91 22

21. Evangelical — Reformed Church — Association of Central Switzerland (6449)

TM: **41,000** Congr: **19** PStations: **25** OrdM: **30** Eld: **ne** Deac: **12** EvgHome: **nc** Mission: **nc** Women Ord: **yes** As Ministers: **1967/6** as Deac: **yes** as Elders: **yes** ChurchOrg: **association of individual congr** Off/otherLang: **German** DoctrB: **Bible, Ref tradition, no emphasis on creeds** Infant or believer's baptism: **both** Frequency of the Lord's Supper: **varies according to congregation's tradition** Periodicals: **Kirchenbote (gen/monthly/22,000)** NatRel: **SEK (1920)** RegRel: **CEC** IntlRel: **same as SEK/ FEPS** TheolSchool: **various Swiss theological schools**

Address: Evang.-reformierter Kirchenverband der Zentralschweiz, Terrassenstr. 5, CH-6060 Sarnen, Switzerland, Tel: +41 41 660 33 70, Fax: +41 41 660 39 40

SYRIA

See also LEBANON

Area in km²	185,000
Population	(July 1996 est.) 15,608,648 Arab 90.3%, Kurds, Armenians, and other 9.7%
Religions in %	Sunni Muslim 74%, Alawite, Druze, and Muslim sects 16%, Christian (including various sects) 10%, Jewish (tiny communities lived in Damascus, Al Qamishli, and Aleppo until 1994 when the last 300 left the country)
Official/other language	Arabic (official), Kurdish, Armenian, Aramaic, Circassian, French widely understood

The state of Syria was not established in its present form until 1946, but it is a land which has been inhabited since ancient times by people of various cultures and religions. Archaeologists have unearthed evidence of habitation dating back to about 5000 B.C., and Damascus is probably the world's oldest continuously inhabited city. Greater Syria, a land area incorporating Lebanon, Israel, Jordan, and present-day Syria, was the site of much conflict and conquest throughout its whole history.

Ancient Syria has been successively ruled by the Egyptians, Babylonians, Hittites, Chaldeans, and Persians. It became part of Alexander the Great's empire in 333 B.C., when one of Alexander's generals founded the city of Antioch as its capital. Struggles between the Seleucids and the Ptolemies of Egypt followed until 64 B.C., when Syria became a province of the Roman Empire. Following the decline and collapse of the Romans and the division of the empire in the 4th century A.D., Syria became a Byzantine province and remained so for almost two and a half centuries.

In 636 A.D. Syria was again conquered, this time by the Arabs, and became part of the fast-growing Islamic empire. By the end of the 11th century, the first wave of European Crusaders had arrived in the region and incorporated part of Syria into their Christian Kingdom of Jerusalem. The last Crusaders were defeated by Salah al-Din (Saladin), who took over Syria and Jerusalem at the end of the 12th century.

Syria was then ruled by the Mamelukes and, after 1516, became part of the Ottoman Empire, which continued until the beginning of the First World War. At that time, an alliance between Britain, France, and the Arab people resulted in the expulsion of the Turks from Syria. A French mandate over Syria was declared by the League of Nations in 1922. British troops arrived in the 1940s. When the French and the British left Syria in 1946, the country became both a republic and a charter member of the United Nations. Political instability followed, with one military coup after another. In 1963 the Ba'ath party came to power and the country began to stabilize. Another coup in 1970 brought to power the then Defense Minister Hafez al-Assad, who several times has been re-elected (99%, 98%) President of the Democratic Popular Socialist Republic of Syria.

Christian Churches

Saul from Tarsus is said to have been converted on his way to Damascus. The apostle Thomas, according to tradition, evangelized the region on his way to India. The ancient church was present from its beginning in this part of the Orient. There are still eleven major Christian denominations in Syria, most of them finding their origin in the splits within Oriental Christendom, particularly in the 5th and 6th centuries. Islam in Greater Syria has usually granted privileges and religious freedom to the Christian churches. They have, in return, contributed significantly to the shaping of the national conscience and of the cultural, economic, and commercial development of the country, and continue to do so today.

Among the present-day Christian population of Syria, Greek-Orth (172,000) are the largest group, followed by Melkites (57,000), Jakobites (53,000), Syrian Cath (32,000), Armenian Cath (24,000), Chaldeans (18,000), Maronites (17,000), and Nestorians (12,000). All Prot combined are estimated at about 15,000. Prot mission work started in the early 19th century and was conducted by Ref American and British missionaries. Today the Presb denominations have their headquarters in Lebanon and "sit across the border" while they have congr mainly in Damascus, Aleppo, and Lattaquié.

TAIWAN

Area in km²	35,980
Population	(July 1996 est.) 21,465,881 Hokklo and Hakka Taiwanese 84%, Mainlanders 14%, aboriginal Taiwanese 2%
Religions in %	mixture of Buddhist, Confucian, and Taoist 93%, Christian 4.5%, folk religions and other 2.5%
Official/other languages	Mandarin Chinese/Taiwanese (Min), Hakka dialects, aboriginal languages

Most of the people of Taiwan (called by the Portuguese explorers, Formosa) live in the cities and villages of the lowlands and foothills, largely on the west side of the island. The aborigines, the islands' earliest inhabitants, now a small minority of 340,000, are divided into ten tribes and are culturally and linguistically related to

485

the Malayo-Polynesian people. The largest segment of the population, called Taiwanese, are the descendants of settlers from South East China who began arriving about four centuries ago, escaping hardship in Fujian and Guangzhou. They are either Amoy- or Hakka-speaking. The most recent wave of immigration was the Chinese, who came to Taiwan after World War II.

From 1895 to 1945 Taiwan was occupied by the Japanese. In 1949, after the victory of the revolutionary army under Mao Tse-Tung, the Kuomintang of General Chiang Kai-Shek fled to the island, but still claimed to represent the whole of China. Even after the international recognition of the People's Republic of China, the Kuomintang maintained this claim. Mainland China, on the other hand, regards Taiwan as an integral part of its own territory. For many years now the Taiwanese people have been striving for the recognition of the island as an independent nation.

1. Presbyterian Church in Taiwan (PCT) (4400)

Though Taiwan was occupied by the Dutch in the middle of the 17th century, Prot mission began only in the 19th century. English Presb started work in the south of the island in 1865, and Canadian missionaries followed in 1872 in the north. Both missions were involved in evangelistic and medical work, laying the ground for a church which emphasizes both evangelism and social concern. Under Japanese rule they continued to use the Taiwanese language. Because of the increasing militarism of Japan in the late '30s, it seemed in the best interest of the church that all missionaries be withdrawn, and this gave the church an early experience of autonomy.

The Presb Church in Taiwan has a strong commitment to evangelism. Evangelistic work among the aborigines started in the '30s (about 30% of the aborigines today belong to the Presb Church). The most rapid church growth was experienced in the period from 1955 to 1965 during the "Double the Church Movement." From 1978 the church was engaged in an extensive evangelism effort known as the "Ten One Movement," aimed at a 10% increase in communicant membership each year. In 1990 the church joined other denominations in promoting the "Year 2000 Gospel Movement," whose collective goal is to nurture 2 million Christians in 10,000 churches and send out 200 missionaries to other countries.

The church has maintained a strong sense of political and social concern for the people of Taiwan and the future of the island. It has taken a clear stand in favor of the self-determination of the Taiwanese people. Despite government pressure — in the early '80s, the General Secretary, C. M. Kao, was imprisoned for several years — the church issued several statements on the future of Taiwan: On our National Fate (1971), Our Appeal (1975), On Human Rights (1977), Recommendations Concerning the Present Situation (1990), On the Sovereignty of Taiwan (1991). The church is particularly concerned with the recognition of the rights of aborigines; it also defends, e.g., the interests of exploited fishermen and does rehabilitation work among girls trapped in prostitution. It runs six hospitals and a number of other institutions.

TM: **222,263** BM: **129,354** CM: **99,965** Congr: **1,183** OrdM: **904** Eld: **4,946** Deac: **6,538** EvgHome: **26** Mission: **nc** Women Ord: **yes** As Ministers: **1950/70** as Deac: **2,593** as Elders: **1,420** ChurchOrg: **Presbyterian (20 presby, four districts, GenAssy)** Off/otherLang: **Taiwanese, Hakka, Mandarin Chinese, Japanese, and tribal** DoctrB: **ApC, NicC, HeidC, WestConf** Infant or believer's baptism: **both** Frequency of the Lord's Supper: **4 times per year** NatRel: **Nat. Council of Churches in Taiwan** RegRel: **CCA** IntlRel: **WCC (1951), CWM (1977), WARC (1951)** TheolSchool: **Theological schools in Taipei, Tainan, and Hualien; Bible College in Hsinchu** Service infrastructure: **6 hospitals, 5 schools, 6 social service organizations, lay training center, camps** Periodicals: **Church News (Chinese/gen/weekly/nc), Women's magazine (Chinese/gen/monthly/nc, New Messenger (Chinese/ Church and Society/bi-monthly)**

Address: Tai-OtanKi-Tok Tiu-Lo Kau-Hoe, 3, Lane 269, Roosevelt Rd., Sec. 3, Taipei 106, Taiwan, Tel: +886 2 362-5282, Fax: +886 2 362-8096, E-mail: pctres@tptsl.seed.net.tw/Home:http:/ /www.seed.net.tw/-pctres/.

Other Presbyterian Churches

In addition to the Presb Church in Taiwan, there are several smaller groups. They are due to missionary efforts from various countries. Several groups were founded by Korean missionaries. The majority of these communities belong to the Han people who came over from mainland China.

1. China Presbyterian Church (4411)

Address: China Presbyterian Church, #1, Lane 218, Kuan-Cho, Wan-Hwa, Taipei, Taiwan

2. China Presbyterian Church (4418)

TM: **150** Congr: **nc**

Address: China Presbyterian Church, #1 Lane 218, Kwan-Chou Street, Pan-Chiao, Taipei, Taiwan

3. China Presbyterian Church of Christ (4401)

TM: **900** CM: **450** Congr: **nc** OrdM: **3** Eld: **11** Deac: **22** EvgHome: **nc** Mission: **3** Women Ord: **yes** As Ministers: **1** as Deac: **8** as Elders: **0** ChurchOrg: **nc** Off/otherLang: **Mandarin, Chinese** DoctrB: **nc** Infant or believer's baptism: **believer** Frequency of the Lord's Supper: **monthly** Close relations with: **none** NatRel: **nc** RegRel: **nc** IntlRel: **nc** TheolSchool: **nc** Service infrastructure: **none** Periodicals: **monthly magazine/200**

Address: Hsin-Yi Friendship Presbyterian Church, 5, Lane 269, Roosevelt Road, Sec. 3, Taipei 106, Taiwan, Tel: +886 2 363-1035, Fax: +886 2 363-3343

4. Taiwan Reformed Presbyterian Church (4409)

The church is the result of various conservative Presb missions which started around 1950.

TM: **900** BM: **800** Congr: **29** OrdM: **12** Eld: **45** Deac: **45** EvgHome: **5** Mission: **0** Women Ord: **yes** As Ministers: **no** as Deac: **1950/120** as Elders: **no** ChurchOrg: **2 presby (in process of uniting)** Off/otherLang: **Chinese (Mandarin)** DoctrB: **ApC, HeidC, WestConf** Infant or believer's baptism: **both** Frequency of the Lord's Supper: **4-6 times per year** NatRel: **nc** RegRel: **nc** IntlRel: **ICRC** TheolSchool: **China Reformed Theological Seminary**

Address: Reformed Presbyterian Church in Taiwan, Lane 76-7F, Kuanghwa S. Street, Hsinchu City, Taiwan, Tel: +886 3 542-0674, Fax: +886 3 533-2630, E-mail: tsaies@ms7.hinet.net.

a) Christian Reformed Church (4413)

The work started by Lillian Bode in 1950 led to the foundation of four congregations.

TM: **290** Congr: **4** OrdM: **3** Eld: **7** Deac: **22** EvgHome: **1** Mission: **ne** Women Ord: **no** ChurchOrg: **nc** Off/otherLang: **Chinese** DoctrB: **ApC, WestConf, WestCat, HeidC** Infant or believer's baptism: **both** NatRel: **nc** RegRel: **nc** IntlRel: **nc** TheolSchool: **nc**

Address: Christian Reformed Church, 30 Lane 75, Nanking East Rd., Section 4, Taipeh, Taiwan

b) Orthodox Presbyterian Church (4414)

In 1950 Egbert Andrew and Richard Gaffin of the Orthodox Presbyterian Church in the United States (cf. United States) initiated mission work in Taiwan. It resulted in the foundation of five congregations. The mission agency has been closed.

TM: **250** Congr: **5** OrdM: **2** Eld: **15** Deac: **17** EvgHome: **nc** Mission: **nc** Women Ord: **no** ChurchOrg: **nc** Off/otherLang: **Chinese, Taiwanese** DoctrB: **ApC, WestConf, WestCat, HeidC** NatRel: **nc** RegRel: **nc** IntlRel: **nc** TheolSchool: **nc**

c) Presbyterian Church of Korea — Taiwan Mission (4417)

This community is the result of the missionary efforts of the Presbyterian Church in Korea/KoShin (cf. Korea no. 1). Several missionaries served in Taiwan, e.g., Kim Yong-Jin and Yoo Whan-Joon.

TM: **510** Congr: **11** OrdM: **5** Eld: **10** Deac: **36** EvgHome: **nc** Mission: **nc** Women Ord: **nc** ChurchOrg: **nc** Off/otherLang: **Chinese, Hakas, Taiaru, Amis** DoctrB: **ApC, WestConf, WestCat, HeidC**

Address: Presbyterian Church of Korea — Taiwan Mission, P.O. Box 51-70, Taipei, Taiwan

d) New Zealand Presbyterian Church

Missionary efforts by Presbyterians from New Zealand led to the foundation of one congregation in Taiwan.

TM: **50** Congr: **1** OrdM: **none** Eld: **3** Deac: **6** EvgHome: **nc** Mission: **nc** Women Ord: **no** As Ministers: **no** as Deac: **no** as Elders: **no** ChurchOrg: **nc** Off/otherLang: **Chinese** DoctrB: **ApC, WestC and Cat, HeidC** Infant or believer's baptism: **Infant** NatRel: **nc** RegRel: **nc** IntlRel: **nc** TheolSchool: **nc**

e) Christian Reformed Yung-Men Presbyterian Church (4416)

This church came into existence through missionary efforts of the Presbyterian Church in Korea/HapDong (cf. Korea no.15).

TM: **165** Congr: **5** OrdM: **4** Eld: **4** Deac: **22** EvgHome: **nc** Mission: **nc** Women Ord: **nc** ChurchOrg: **nc** Off/otherLang: **Chinese, Taiaru, Korean** DoctrB: **ApC, WestConf, WestCat, HeidC** Close relations with: **Presb Church in Korea (HapDong)**

Address: Christian Reformed Yung-Men Presbyterian Church, Kuang Fu Street, Lane 2, Alley 11, # 15, Yung-He City, Taipei County, Taiwan, Tel: +886 2 923-1512, Fax: +886 2 929-0124

5. Taiwan Toa-Seng Presbyterian Church (4412)

TM: **381** Congr: **7**

Address: Taiwan Toa-Seng Presbyterian Church, 2F, #288, Rd. Tz-Hsin, Kuan-Du, Beitou, Taipei, Taiwan

6. The General Assembly Evangelical Presbyterian Church (4415)

No historical and statistical data have been made available.

Address: The General Assembly Evangelical Presbyterian Church, #498, Rd. Chin-Hwa, North, Tai-Chong City, Taiwan

THAILAND

Area in km²	514,000
Population	(July 1996 est.) 58,851,357 Thai 75%, Chinese 14%, other 11%
Religions in %	Buddhism 95%, Muslim 3.8%, Christianity 0.5%, Hinduism 0.1%, other 0.6% (1991)
Official/other languages	Thai, English as secondary language of the elite, ethnic and regional dialects

Christianity entered Thailand (or Siam, as it was called until 1949) in 1555 through RCath missionaries. Prot missions began in 1828: the London Missionary Society, the American Bapt Missionary Union, the ABCFM, the American Missionary Association, and the Board of Foreign Mission of the Presbyterian Church in the USA all established mission stations in Bangkok, but, for various reasons (with the exception of the Presb stations), they did not last. By 1850 the American Presb had emerged as the primary mission force in Siam. Their work expanded from Bangkok into the central, northern, and southern regions. In all stations they opened schools, hospitals, and churches; the number of converts increased steadily, especially in the North. Among the Presb missionaries Daniel McGilvray deserves special mention; he translated the Bible into Thai and sought ways to secure theological training.

In the 20th century other missions began working in Siam. In 1903 the British churches of Christ (Disciples) opened a station west of Bangkok. Others arrived later, e.g., missionaries now linked together as the Thailand Bapt Missionary Fellowship, the Marburger Mission from Germany, others from Australia, from the United Kingdom, and more recently from Korea. In the early 1930s, the Presb Mission invited other Prot groups to join together and to form a truly national church. At first only the Bapt congr in Bangkok took up the offer. Later, other communities from Bapt missions, from the Marburger Mission, and from the Disciples followed. In 1934 the Church of Christ in Thailand (CCT) was constituted. After World War II, seeking to fulfill the wish of indigenous leaders who wanted to have an autonomous church which was ruled, administered, and evangelized by Thai people, the Presb (in 1957) and Disciples (in 1962) took their commitment toward a fully autonomous church one step further; they placed their mission work under the jurisdiction of the CCT. During recent decades the CCT has experienced considerable growth both through mission and through new groups joining its fold. The two most recently formed presbyteries are made up of the Lahu and Karen ethnic minorities in the northern part of the country. At the present time eight Korean missionary couples are working with the CCT.

1. Church of Christ in Thailand (CCT) (4430)

TM: **69,000** BM: **60,000** CM: **6,000** Congr: **481** PStations: **139** OrdM: **190** Eld: **nc** Deac: **nc** EvgHome: **nc** Mission: **1** Women Ord: **yes** As Ministers: **1960/16** as Deac: **nc** as Elders: **nc** ChurchOrg: **19 Pahks (presbys), based on geographical and/or ethnic considerations, National GenAssy every 2 years** Off/otherLang: **Thai, Chinese Karen, Lahu, English (2 congr), German, and Korean (1 congr each)** DoctrB: **ApC** Infant or believer's baptism: **both** Frequency of the Lord's Supper: **weekly to monthly** NatRel: **Joint Committee for Prot in Thailand** RegRel: **CCA** IntlRel: **WCC, WARC** TheolSchool: **McGilvary Faculty of Theology, Payap University, Chiang-Mai and Bangkok Institute of Theology** Service infrastructure: **seven hospitals, a leprosy rehabilitation institution, some thirty schools, departments for work with Christian women, youth and evangelism, Christian education and literature.** Periodicals: **Church News (Thai) (gen/monthly), Echoes (English) (newsletter for expatriate workers/monthly)**

Address: Church of Christ in Thailand (CCT), 14 Pramuan Road, Bangkok 10500, Thailand, Tel: +66 2 236-0211, Fax: +66 2 238-3520

2. Evangelical Fellowship of Thailand (EFT) (4432)

There are numerous Prot groups outside the CCT. In 1969 the Evangelical Fellowship of Thailand (EFT) was formed comprising 25 foreign missions and organizations, most of whom are evangelical or Pent. At the present time they represent around 300 churches and 650 worship groups with a total membership of about 25,000. Among them the Gospel Church Foundation of Thailand, a church with close links to the Christian and Missionary Alliance, deserves special mention.The Thailand Bapt Churches Association (related to the Southern Bapt in the USA) and the Advent do not belong to either the CCT or the EFT. Some joint activities between the two organizations have taken place since the 1970s on an ad hoc basis. In 1993 a Joint Committee for Prot in Thailand was set up which consists of the CCT, the EFT, and the Southern Bapt. The EFT runs the Bangkok Bible Seminary and College.

Address: Evangelical Fellowship of Thailand, 485/20 Silom Rd., 662 Bangkok, Thailand, Tel: +66 2
235-2667, Fax: +66 2 237-8264

TOGO

Area in km²	56,790
Population	(July 1996 est.) 4,570,530 native African (37 tribes; largest and most important are Ewe, Mina, and Kabye) 99%, European and Syrian-Lebanese less than 1%
Religions in %	indigenous beliefs 50%, Christian 33% (RCath 70%, Prot 25%, Meth 5%), Muslim 17%
Official/other languages	French, Ewe, and Mina (the two major African languages in the South), Kabye (spoken in the North)

Evangelical Presbyterian Church of Togo (1380)

From 1884 to 1914 the country was under German colonial rule. At the beginning of World War I the Ewe-speaking region was occupied and divided by Britain and France. The western region became part of Ghana; after the War the League of Nations consigned today's Togo to France.

The history of the church goes back to the efforts of German missionaries among the Ewe in the middle of the 19th century (Norddeutsche Mission, Bremen). The first congr (Mission-Tove) on the territory of today's Togo was established in 1893. After the departure of German missionaries, the church sought to

491

maintain its unity. In 1922 the Evangelical Ewe church was constituted which included the whole region (President: Andreas Aku, Secretary Robert Baeta). But more and more the two parts developed their own profile while seeking to maintain a constitutional link by a common synod which met every third year. Increasingly, the "Mission de Paris" accepted responsibility for the church in Togo. In 1929 the church in Togo started its own theological school and began evangelistic work among the Kabye in the North. In 1955 the United Church of Christ in the USA started work in Togo, and from 1960 the "Norddeutsche Mission in Bremen" resumed activities. In 1959 the church gained independence. One year later the country became independent. The following years were a period of renewal and expansion. In 1965, faced with the beginnings of dictatorship in the country, the church issued a statement stressing the duty of the churches to raise their voice in public affairs. Evangelistic work was conducted under the motto "The whole Gospel for the whole human person." In 1984 the church began activities among the Kokomba in the northwest. Ever since 1967 the country has lived under the dictatorship of Gnassingbé Eyadema. Attempts, in 1990, to gain more freedoms for the people did not lead to lasting results.

TM: **300,000** BM: **300,000** CM: **117,525** Congr: **516** PStations: **516** OrdM: **71** Eld: **2,580** Deac: **249** EvgHome: **nc** Mission: **10** Women Ord: **yes** As Ministers: **1989/10** as Deac: **1966/83** as Elders: **1894/ 1,330** ChurchOrg: **Presbyterian (presby, district, region, synod)** Off/otherLang: **Ewe, Kabye, French, English** DoctrB: **ApC, Conf of Ev. Presb Church of Togo** Infant or believer's baptism: **believer** Frequency of the Lord's Supper: **monthly** Periodicals: **none** Close relations with: **Mission of Bremen** NatRel: **Christian Council of Togo (1980)** RegRel: **AACC** IntlRel: **WCC (1976)** TheolSchool: **Ecole Biblique (Atakpamé, Togo)**

Address: Eglise évangélique presbytérienne du Togo, B.P. 2, rue Tokmake 1, Lomé, Togo, Tel: +228 2146 69, Fax: +228 22 23 63

TRINIDAD

Area in km²	5,128
Population	1.2 million Indian 40%, African 41%, Mulattos 17%, White 2%, Syrian/Lebanese, aboriginal population 500
Religions in %	Hindu 30%, Muslim 6%, RCath 30%, Angl 15%, Presb 6%, other groups (Bapt, Meth, Assemblies of God, etc.).
Official/other languages	English

Presbyterianism came to Trinidad in the early 19th century. In 1834, due to the majority of British settlers being Presb Scots, a Trinidad Presb Association was formed to petition the Governor for a Presb ministry to them. The Missionary Society of Greyfriars Original Secession Church decided to choose Trinidad as a mission field. The first church was established in 1836 in Port-of-Spain. In 1846 the church integrated a group of Portuguese Prot of Free Church background who had left Madeira and settled in Port-of-Spain.

Missionary work among the Indian population was started in 1868 by Canadian missionaries, the first being John Morton, a Canadian of Scottish descent. Indians had been brought to Trinidad as cheap labor. They worked on sugar cane plantations. In the beginning they were confined to the plantations they were assigned to. After a certain period they were allowed to move out and were given their own plot of land (usually of second-class quality). Missionaries worked within that system. They preached in the plantations and later helped to build Indian villages providing churches and schools. The first primary school was opened in 1871. In 1892 the Presbyterian Theological College was founded; in the following decades high schools for boys and girls were started. Today the church administers 72 primary schools and five secondary schools.

For Indians, joining the Presb Church meant overcoming dependence, getting a job, acquiring education, and becoming part of the middle or even upper class. The first ordained Indian was Lal Bihari, a highly educated Hindu who had converted to Christianity. Many church buildings are called by Hindi names, and Hindi Bhajans are often used in services.

The communities founded by either Scottish or Canadian missionaries were incorporated into one presbytery in 1891. The presbytery was recognized in Canada but not by the churches in Scotland. Thus two Mission Councils — one Scottish and the other Canadian — continued to exist.

1. Church of Scotland (3341)

This church primarily serves the white and Mulatto populations. In 1969 the Scottish Mission Council was reconstituted as the incorporated Trustees of the Church of Scotland in Trinidad. For many years the ministers were provided by the Church of Scotland. A few years ago the church called a Pent to serve as pastor. There are two congregations in the area of Port-of-Spain and two in other places served by, altogether, three pastors.

TM: **520** BM: **500** CM: **422** Congr: **1** PStations: **3** OrdM: **3** Eld: **27** Deac: **nc** EvgHome: **none** Mission: **none** Women Ord: **yes** As Ministers: **1971/1** as Deac: **nc** as Elders: **21** ChurchOrg: **one overseas charge with four places of worship** Off/otherLang: **English** DoctrB: **WestConf** Infant or believer's baptism: **both** Frequency of the Lord's Supper: **nc** Periodicals: **newsletter (gen/monthly/250) Morning Light (Sunday morning radio broadcast)** NatRel: **Christian Council Council of Evangelical Churches** RegRel: **CCC (observer), CANAC, Caribbean Council of Evangelical Churches** IntlRel: **(same as Church of Scotland)** TheolSchool: **West Indies School of Theology; St. Andrew's Theological College (Trinidad)**

Address: Church of Scotland, 50 Frederick Street, Port of Spain, Trinidad, Tel: +809 623-6684, Fax: +809 624-1727

2. Presbyterian Church in Trinidad and Tobago (3340)

In 1968 the United Church of Canada decided to phase out its work in Trinidad. In 1977 the church became entirely independent and self-supporting. Conversions of Indians have practically ceased. In the meantime Hindus and Muslims have their own schools. Today the church is faced with a strong influence of Pentecostalism.

TM: **40,000** Congr: **105** PStations: **100** OrdM: **20** Eld: **nc** Deac: **9** EvgHome: **nc** Mission: **nc** Women Ord: **yes** As Ministers: **yes/4** as Deac: **yes/0** as Elders: **yes/0** ChurchOrg: **2 presby, Synod** Off/ otherLang: **English** DoctrB: **ApC, NicC, WestConf** Infant or believer's baptism: **both** Frequency of the Lord's Supper: **monthly** Periodicals: **Trinidad Presbyterian (gen/monthly/2,800), Lenten booklets** NatRel: **Christian Council of Churches** RegRel: **CCC** IntlRel: **WARC, WCC** TheolSchool: **St. Andrew's Theological College**

Address: Presbyterian Church in Trinidad and Tobago, P.O. Box 92, Paradise Hill, San Fernando, Trinidad West Indies, Trinidad, Tel: +1 809 652 4829, Fax: +1 809 652 4829

TUNISIA

Area in km²	163,610
Population	(July 1996 est.) 9,019,687 Arab-Berber 98%, European 1%, Jewish less than 1%
Religions in %	Muslim 98%, Christian 1%, Jewish 1%
Official/other languages	Arabic/French (commerce)

The city of Tunis was built near the ruins of Carthage, which was an important center of the early Christian church. Christianity was extinguished in this area by the Arabs by the 12th century.

After 1574 the country became a part of the Ottoman Empire and was governed by a bey. From 1881 to 1956 Tunisia was a French protectorate. Subsequently a republic was set up in 1957 with Bourguiba as president. Islam became the official religion. The government of Tunisia is not favorable toward foreign missions. Open evangelism is now forbidden.

The London Society for Promoting Christianity among the Jews came to North Africa in 1829. The North African Mission, which began working in Tunisia in 1882 and focused mainly on the sale of Bibles, reported some 25 members by 1962. Ref Christians of the French Prot Church have worshiped in Tunisia since 1881 as the result of the work of a French army chaplain. American Meth became active in 1908. Pent arrived in 1912 and in 1957 formed a church with less than thirty members; they no longer have an active presence in Tunisia. St. George's Angl Church has a membership of around 80.

Before the 19th century the RCath Church had made several attempts to establish itself in Tunisia. Between 1820 and 1830 the RCath community counted

2,000 members; it grew to 20,000 by 1860 and 1870. After 1881, when Tunisia had become a French protectorate, the RCath began to expand under the guidance of Archbishop Lavigerie. This growth was largely due to a major influx of European Catholics. Once Tunisia became a republic in 1957, the Catholic Church agreed to close and turn over to the state all but five of its seventy church buildings, together with its cathedral, which became a museum. Thereafter a type of dialogue ensued with Islam.

Reformed Church in Tunisia (1014)

TM: **100** CM: **80** Congr: **1** PStations: **1** OrdM: **1** Eld: **2** Deac: **nc** EvgHome: **nc** Mission: **nc** Women Ord: **no** ChurchOrg: **CEEEFE (Commission des Eglises Evangéliques d'expression Française à l'Extérieur)** Off/otherLang: **French** DoctrB: **ApC, HeidC** Infant or believer's baptism: **both (sprinkling/immersion)** Frequency of the Lord's Supper: **monthly** Periodicals: **none** NatRel: **CEEEFE** RegRel: **nc** IntlRel: **nc** TheolSchool: **Reformed Theological Seminary (Jackson, MS, USA)**.

Address: Eglise Réformée de Tunisie, 36, rue du Général Charles de Gaulle, Tunis, Tunisia, Tel: +216 1 327-886, Fax: none, E-mail: dehoog@compuserve.com

TUVALU

Area in km²	26
Population	(July 1996 est.) 10,146 Polynesian 96%
Religions in %	Church of Tuvalu (Congreg) 97%, Advent 1.4%, Baha'i 1%, other 0.6%
Official/other languages	Tuvaluan, English

Tuvalu, formerly the Ellice Islands, is an independent atoll country with a Polynesian language and culture. Tuvalu consists of a scattered group of nine coral atolls with poor soil located halfway between Hawaii and Australia. The country has no known mineral resources and few exports. Subsistence farming and fishing are the primary economic activities. The islands are too small and too remote for development of a tourist industry. Government revenues come largely from the sale of stamps and coins and worker remittances. National independence was achieved in 1978.

Church of Tuvalu (5170)

Christianity was first introduced in 1861 by Elekana, a deacon of the church in Manihiki in the northern Cook Islands. He was a member of a party of nine people who arrived fortuitously after drifting for eight weeks in a storm. He was given permission by an island chief to teach the Gospel. After four months he went to Malua, Western Samoa, where he trained as an Islander missionary and returned to Tuvalu, which thereafter came under the supervision of the London Missionary Society (LMS). For more than a century LMS missionaries were stationed there. Later Tuvaluan Islander missionaries, trained in Samoa, served on the eight inhabited islands, where 97% of the people now belong to the church. Only a few British missionaries of the LMS have resided for any length of time in Tuvalu. The last among them assisted in the Bible translation into Tuvaluan from the (cognate) Samoan previously used as church language.

Between 1959 and 1968 British missionaries helped to frame a constitution and paved the way to independence for the church in 1969. Many families from Tuvalu have worked abroad, as Islander missionaries within the Pacific, on ships, or in phosphate mines in Kiribati. One of the Tuvalu islands has a dialect close to the language of neighboring Kiribati; the two independent island states and their Prot churches stay in close contact and share similar systems of church government.

TM: **10,000** BM: **10,000** CM: **9,000** Congr: **14** PStations: **17** OrdM: **23** Eld: **none** Deac: **500** EvgHome: **none** Mission: **none** Women Ord: **yes** As Ministers: **no** as Deac: **1980/20** as Elders: **no** ChurchOrg: **congr, executive committee, GenAssy** Off/otherLang: **Tuvaluan, English** DoctrB: **ApC, NicC, Tuvalu Church Creed** Infant or believer's baptism: **both** Frequency of the Lord's Supper: **monthly** Periodicals: **Te Lawa (gen/quarterly/600)** Close relations with: **URCUK** NatRel: **nc** RegRel: **PCC** IntlRel: **WCC, WARC (1997), CWM** TheolSchool: **none**

Address: Te Ekalesia Kelisiano Tuvalu, P.O. Box 2, Pisila Samualu, Funafuti, Tuvalu, Tel: +688 20755/20461, Fax: +688 20651

UGANDA

Area in km²	236,040
Population	(July 1996 est.) 20,158,176 Baganda 17%, Karamojong 12%, Basogo 8%, Iteso 8%, Langi 6%, Rwanda 6%, Bagisu 5%, Acholi 4%, Lugbara 4%, Bunyoro 3%, Batobo 3%, European, Asian, Arab 1%, other 23%
Religions in %	RCath 33%, Prot 33%, Muslim 16%, indigenous beliefs 18%
Official/other languages	English/Luganda, Swahili, Bantu languages, Nilotic languages

Since the late 1970s several Ref groups have been active in Uganda. In 1979 the Presbyterian Church of Uganda was founded. In 1986 a pastor of this church started the Evangelical Free Church. An unfortunate controversy within the Presbyterian Church of Uganda over church discipline led in 1989 to a split which resulted in the formation of the Reformed Presbyterian Church. In the '80s Korean missionaries from the Presbyterian Church (HapDong, cf. Korea) arrived in Uganda and began to work with both churches. Two Bible schools have been opened (All Nations Bible College and Ref Presb Bible College).

In 1992, close to the Kenyan border, the Christian Reformed Church came into existence. Other churches were founded by missionary initiatives from outside. Since 1991 two "All Presb Conferences" have been held. So far they have not led to the formation of a national church.

1. Presbyterian Church in Uganda (1272)

This church came into existence in 1979 through the initiative of the Rev. Dr. Kefa Ssempangi, a Ugandan pastor who had studied in the United States. The first church was built in 1980. The church is active mainly in the area of Kampala.

TM: **4,101** BM: **4,101** CM: **3,379** Congr: **12** PStations: **15** OrdM: **17** Eld: **27** Deac: **15** EvgHome: **nc** Mission: **nc** Women Ord: **no** As Ministers: **nc** as Deac: **nc** as Elders: **nc** ChurchOrg: **sessions/presby** Off/otherLang: **English, Luganda** DoctrB: **ApC, WestConf** Infant or believer's baptism: **both** Frequency of the Lord's Supper: **monthly** Close relations with: **Life Church, Calvary Church** NatRel: **All Presbyterian Conference** RegRel: **none** IntlRel: **nc** TheolSchool: **All Nations Bible College, Westminster Theological College (started in 1996)** Service infrastructure: **3 kindergartens** Periodicals: **none**

Address: Presbyterian Church in Uganda, P.O. Box 31270, Mengo, Butikiro Road, Kampala, Uganda, Tel: +256 41 273 128, Fax: +256 41 259 647, E-mail: actuga@imul.com.

2. Evangelical Free Church in Uganda (1277)

The church was founded in 1986 in Mulago Valley by a pastor of the Presbyterian Church of Uganda, Vicky Atwooki-Wamala, who had gone for studies to the USA. The church has quickly grown and has roots in Kampala and in other parts of the country. The headquarters were originally in Mulago Valley, but they were moved to Muyenga, Kampala, in 1993.

TM: **20,000** BM: **8,000** CM: **12,000** Congr: **10** PStations: **5** OrdM: **12** Eld: **14** Deac: **20** EvgHome: **20** Mission: **none** Women Ord: **no** ChurchOrg: **Presbyterian** Off/otherLang: **English, Luganda, Ruynoro-Rutoro, Rugishu, Iteso** DoctrB: **WestConf, WestCat** Infant or believer's baptism: **both** NatRel: **Evangelical Fellowship of Uganda** RegRel: **none** IntlRel: **none** TheolSchool: **Theological School — Free Church Christian College** Periodicals: **Free Church Faith Link (newsletter)**

Address: Evangelical Free Church in Uganda, P.O. Box 30464, Plot 365/6, Free Church Rd. via Rest Corner Hotel Tank Hill, Muyenga, Kampala, Uganda, Tel: +256 41 266-532, Fax: +256 41 266-974

3. Reformed Presbyterian Church in Uganda (1271)

The church was constituted in 1990. In 1989 a controversy arose over a case of church discipline (divorce of an elder) in the Presbyterian Church (no. 1). After attempts at reconciliation, the separation was formalized a year later. The center of the church's activities is in Kampala.

TM: **5,000** CM: **3,000** Congr: **12** PStations: **11** OrdM: **12** Eld: **20** Deac: **25** EvgHome: **9** Mission: **0** Women Ord: **no** ChurchOrg: **presbys (national level), sessions (regional)** Off/otherLang: **English, local languages** DoctrB: **ApC, HeidC, WestCat, CDort, WestConf** Infant or believer's baptism: **both** Frequency of the Lord's Supper: **every two months** Close relations with: **World Vision International, Back to God Evangelistic Association** NatRel: **none** RegRel: **nc** IntlRel: **REC, WARC** TheolSchool: **Reformed Theological College** Service infrastructure: **2 social service organizations, 1 kindergarten** Periodicals: **none**

Address: Reformed Presbyterian Church in Uganda, P.O. Box 2866, Hoima Road, Kampala, Uganda,
Tel: +256 41 530-384, Fax: +256 41 345-580

4. New Life Presbyterian Church (1273)

This church was founded by American missionaries (World Harvest Mission) working with Ugandan Christians in 1986 in the area of Fort Portal and in 1992 in Bundibugyo. Today the church reports growing church planting in western Uganda and across the Congolese border. It claims to be one of the churches spear-heading efforts to form a united national Ugandan Presb denomination.

TM: **1,000** BM: **500** CM: **150** Congr: **2** PStations: **25** OrdM: **10** Eld: **10** Deac: **10** EvgHome: **5** Mission: **0** Women Ord: **no** ChurchOrg: **presby** Off/otherLang: **Rutooro, Lubhwisi, Rukonjo** DoctrB: **ApC, WestConf** Infant or believer's baptism: **both** Frequency of the Lord's Supper: **4 times per year** Close relations with: **World Harvest Mission** NatRel: **ne** RegRel: **ne** IntlRel: **ne** TheolSchool: **Westminster Bible College (Kampala), All Nations Bible College (Nabwelenga, Uganda)** Service infrastructure: **1 kindergarten** Periodicals: **ne**

Address: Ekanisa Y'obwomeezi Buhyaka, P.O. Box 383, Fort Portal, Uganda

5. Christian Reformed Church in Eastern Africa (1278)

The Christian Reformed Church of East Africa began in Kenya in 1992, when several pastors left the Reformed Church of East Africa, in part to focus on mission fields beyond the Kenyan borders. The church is now registered in Uganda, seeks registration in Kenya, and has mission outposts in Tanzania as well. The church is educating pastors on a full and part-time basis. So far, pastors have all been serving on a voluntary basis; to raise the necessary funds the church makes bricks and does agricultural projects.

TM: **4,000** BM: **330** CM: **3,000** Congr: **80** PStations: **20** OrdM: **12** Eld: **240** Deac: **120** EvgHome: **80** Mission: Women Ord: **yes** As Ministers: **1998/4** as Deac: **1995/10** as Elders: **1998/6** ChurchOrg: **congr, presby, synod, GenAssy** Off/otherLang: **English, Kiswahili, Luhya, Luganda, Kikisu**

DoctrB: **ApC, HeidC, CDort, NicC** Infant or believer's baptism: **both** Frequency of the Lord's Supper: **twice monthly** Close relations with: **CRCNA (1996)** NatRel: **none** RegRel: **none** IntlRel: **REC (1996)** TheolSchool: **Christian Reformed Bible College (Mbale)** Service infrastructure: **5 hospitals, 1 social service, farming projects**

Address: Christian Reformed Church in East Africa, P.O. Box 203, Mbale, Uganda

6. Evangelical Presbyterian Church in Uganda (1276)

This church came into existence in December 1986 and was registered with the Uganda government in 1987. The church was closely connected with the Brainard Presbyterian Church in Tennessee. In its first years the church grew quickly, but after a few years it suffered a split which reduced the membership to 32 adults. The church soon regained strength. Today there are four congregations in the area of Kampala, in the Kasanda in Mubende District, in Kakubo in Mpigi District, and in Buwaya on the island of Lake Victoria.

TM: **169** BM: **78** Congr: **4** PStations: **3** OrdM: **2** Eld: **4** Deac: **4** EvgHome: **2** Mission: **na** Women Ord: **yes** As Ministers: **1989/nc** as Deac: **1992/2** as Elders: **nc** ChurchOrg: **congr, presby** Off/otherLang: **English, Luganda** DoctrB: **ApC, NicC, WestConf** Infant or believer's baptism: **believer** Frequency of the Lord's Supper: **six times per year** Close relations with: **other Ref churches** NatRel: **nc** RegRel: **nc** IntlRel: **nc** TheolSchool: **nc**

Address: Evangelical Presbyterian Church in Uganda, P.O. Box 244, Kampala, Uganda, Tel: +256 41 221-099

7. Calvary Reformed Church (1274)

This church was founded in 1994 by Pastor Nelson Owundo. It was previously called the Presbyterian Evangelical Fellowship. There are three congr in Kampala.

Congr: **3** OrdM: **nc** Eld: **7** Deac: **7** EvgHome: **nc** Mission: **nc** Women Ord: **no** DoctrB: **ApC, WestConf, WestCat**

No other data have been made available.

Address: Calvary Reformed Church, P.O. Box 16362, Kampala, Uganda.

UKRAINE

Area in km²	Ukraine 603,700; Carpatho-Ukraine: 12,900
Population	51 million; Carpatho-Ukraine: 1.3 million (Ukrainian 78%, Hungarian 12.5% = 200,000, Russian 4%, Gipsy 1%, small communities of Germans, Jews, and White Russians)
Religions in %	Orth majority, sizeable RCath minority, Hungarian minority, Ref 70% and RCath 30%
Official/other languages	Ukrainian, languages used by minorities

1. Reformed Church in the Carpatho-Ukraine (6462)

Until the end of World War I the Carpatho-Ukrainian region belonged to Hungary. In 1919 both Carpatho-Ukraine and Slovakia became part of the first republic of Czechoslovakia. In 1938 the region was returned to Hungary. After World War II it became part of the USSR and was incorporated into the Ukrainian Soviet Republic. In 1990 the Ukraine became an independent state.

As long as the Carpatho-Ukraine was part of Hungary, the Reformed Church belonged to the Reformed Church of Hungary (cf. Hungary). In 1923 the Hungarian-speaking Ref congregations in the Carpatho-Ukraine and in Slovakia constituted themselves as the "General Reformed Church of Slovakia and the Carpatho-Ukraine." Though the relation to the Czechoslovakian state could never satisfactorily be settled, the church was able to bear a significant evangelistic and diaconal witness. Orphanages were founded in Munkács and Nagyszöllös. In 1938 the church was reintegrated into the Reformed Church of Hungary.

An even more difficult period began after World War II. For some time it remained unclear in what form the Reformed Church would constitute itself. Attempts by the Soviet authorities to incorporate it into the Association of Bapt congregations met with resistance from the pastors. As a consequence the church was ostracized. Contacts with the Reformed Church of Hungary were prohibited. Many pastors — about 40 out of 106 — fled to Hungary. At the end of the '40s many of those who had decided to stay were arrested and deported. When they returned in 1956, there were 26 pastors serving 81 congregations. There was no opportunity for theological education. Not until the '70s was permission granted to give some theological training to a few candidates for the ministry.

The collapse of the Communist regime led to a radically new situation. The doors to the outside world opened again. Today about 50 young people prepare for the ministry at various theological schools abroad. The church has to live up to the challenges of the post-Marxist society — to make constructive use of the new freedoms in an economically desolate situation (up to 80% unemployment!); to take responsibility for the institutions which have been returned to the church; to ensure a presence in realms of society which had been closed to the church in the past.

TM: **130,000** BM: **110,500** CM: **19,500** Congr: **95** PStations: **95** OrdM: **38** Eld: **1,140** Deac: **15** EvgHome: **80** Mission: **0** Women Ord: **yes** As Ministers: **1994/3** as Deac: **1993/10** as Elders: **1991/190** ChurchOrg: **congreg, presby, counties, Synod** Off/otherLang: **Hungarian/Ukrainian, Russian, English, German,** DoctrB: **ApC, HeidC, HelvC, Calvinism** Frequency of the Lord's Supper: **6 times per year** Close relations with: **Dutch Ref Churches, Ev. Church in Germany, Hungarian Reformed Church, SEK/FEPS** NatRel: **Hungarian Consultative Synod** IntlRel: **WCC (1991), ICRC (1991)** TheolSchool: **none** Periodicals: **Küldetés (gen/monthly/3,000)**

Address: Kárpátaljai Református Egyház, Hmelnickij u. 9, UA-295, 510 Beregszàsz, Ukraine, Tel: +380 3141 234 60, Fax: +380 3141 234 60

2. Ukrainian Evangelical Reformed Church (6465)

Toward the end of the 19th century and early in the 20th century many Ukrainians emigrated to North America. An Independent Ukrainian Orthodox Church was founded in close cooperation with the Presbyterian Church of Canada. It only lasted for a few years (1903-1912). Most of its members joined the Presbyterian Church of Canada. On August 20, 1911, the first Ukrainian Presbyterian Congregation was opened in Edmonton. In 1922 the Ukrainian Evangelical Alliance in North America was established in Rochester, NY. Efforts were made to send a group of preachers to western Ukraine, which was then occupied by Poland. They succeeded in establishing an Ukrainian Evangelical Reformed Church. Ukrainian students were trained in Bloomfield Seminary, which had an Ukrainian department from 1913 to 1931. The church in western Ukraine grew. In 1936 there were 2,780 members in 35 congregations, served by 5 pastors and 8 preachers. World War II and the Soviet occupation of western Ukraine destroyed much of the work. After the change in 1989 the church was able to reconstitute itself.

TM: **52** BM: **52** CM: **52** Congr: **2** OrdM: **1** Eld: **2** Deac: **3** EvgHome: **ne** Mission: **ne** Women Ord: **no** As Ministers: **no** as Deac: **1** as Elders: **3** ChurchOrg: **Reformed (two congr in Rivne and Stepan)** Off/otherLang: **Ukrainian** DoctrB: **ApC, NicC, HeidC, WestConf, CDort** Infant or believer's baptism: **both** Frequency of the Lord's Supper: **at church festivals** Close relations with: **Ref Church of Hatham (NL), Evangelical-Reformed Church of Poland, Evangelical-Reformed Church** (cf. Russia no. 2) NatRel: **none** RegRel: **none** IntlRel: **WARC** TheolSchool: **training place (Tolsto n 13/3, Kiev, 252033)** Periodicals: **The Church (6 times a year/1,000)**

Address: Ukrainian Evangelical Reformed Church, Petra Mohily, UA 266001 Rivne, Ukraine, Tel: +383 62 28 65 70, Fax: +383 62 28 65 70

UNITED KINGDOM

Area in km²	244,820
Population	(July 1996 est.) 58,489,975 English 81.5%, Scottish 9.6%, Irish 2.4%, Welsh 1.9%, Ulster 1.8%, West Indian, Indian, Pakistani, and other 2.8%
Religions in % (est. 1991)	Angl 46%, RCath 15.4%, Muslim 1.7%, Presb 1.4%, Meth 1.3%, Sikh 0.7%, Hindu 0.6%, Jewish 0.5% (note: the UK does not include a question on religion in its census)
Official/other languages	English/Welsh (about 26% of the population of Wales), Scottish form of Gaelic (about 60,000 in Scotland)

ACTS (Action of the Churches Together in Scotland)
BEC (British Evangelical Council)
CCBI (Council of Church for Britain and Ireland)
CTE (Churches Together in England)

Great Britain is not one country, but two or three; and the histories of the Ref churches in these countries are different. In England (and Wales) the church was reformed by order of the crown, but in Scotland it was reformed in spite of Mary Queen of Scots; later attempts to make the church in Scotland Episcopalian were no more successful than the Scottish attempt to make the church in England Presb.

From Reformation to Revolution

In 1534, Henry VIII (1509-1547) began the Reformation in England by breaking the connection with Rome: the Act of Supremacy declared the king to be the supreme head of the Church of England. The pace quickened under Edward VI (1547-1553), with the systematic reformation of doctrine, worship, and discipline. Mary (1553-1558) briefly restored RCath. In the first year of Elizabeth I's reign (1558-1603), the monarch's position as "supreme governor" of the church was restated, and the Act of Uniformity required that worship should follow the Book of Common Prayer; in 1563 standard doctrine was defined in the (Calvinist) 39 Articles.

Wales was formally united with England in 1536. English became the official language and, with the Reformation, the language also of public worship. John Penri died a martyr's death in 1593 for transgressing the Elizabethan Act of Uniformity and for pleading for the preaching of the Gospel in the native language. Scholars and churchmen set about translating the Bible and the Book of

Common Prayer into Welsh, the language most people spoke. The first complete translation of the Bible was published in 1588, and it shaped the further development of the Welsh language — one of the oldest in Europe — just as Luther's Bible shaped German.

In Scotland, meanwhile, John Knox and his associates were busily reforming the national church along Genevan lines. In 1560 the Scottish Parliament rejected papal authority, adopted the Scots Confession, and banned the mass. The Scottish church was now Ref but not yet classically Presb. In response, however, to the resurgence of a form of Episcopacy in the 1570s, Andrew Melville and his colleagues insisted on Presbyterianism, and in 1592 Parliament approved the Presb system. That might have seemed to settle the issue but did not; the battle between Presbyterianism and Episcopacy in Scotland, effectively a battle between church and state, would rage for another century.

In England, the Elizabethan Settlement settled nothing either. Elizabeth's reform was intended to be comprehensive, but it did not comprehend the more radical Reformers, who were labelled Puritans. Controversy broke out almost immediately over worship and ministerial dress. In 1570 Thomas Cartwright lectured in favor of Presbyterianism at Cambridge University and was forced to flee to Geneva. Two years later, John Field and Thomas Wilcox took his ideas further. These Reformers wanted to "tarry for the magistrate," to reform the church by convincing those in power. Separatists like Robert Browne, Henry Barrow, and John Greenwood were convinced that the Elizabethan church would never be truly reformed and broke away to form their own congregations "without tarrying for any." Here are the earliest origins of Presbyterianism and Congregationalism, or Independency, in England.

James VI (1567-1625) had hardly consented to Presbyterianism in Scotland before he began to undermine it, a process completed after he acceded to the English throne as James I (1603-1625). In 1606 he sent Andrew Melville into exile; in 1610 he summoned three of his new Scottish bishops to London for consecration; in 1618, with the Five Articles of Perth, he tried to turn Scottish worship in a more Angl direction. English Puritans presented their grievances to their new king in the Millenary Petition (1603), but were rebuffed by James: "no bishop, no king." During his reign, many Separatists fled to Holland for safety. In 1620 some went from there on the *Mayflower*, with others from England, to found the Plymouth Colony in the New World.

Under Charles I (1625-1649) anti-Puritanism became linked with anti-Calvinism. In 1633, the Arminian William Laud became Archbishop of Canterbury. Four years later he tried to foist on Scotland a version of the Book of Common Prayer. When "Laud's Liturgy" was introduced in the High Kirk of St. Giles in July 1637, the citizens of Edinburgh rioted. A national uprising ensued, culminating in 1638 in the signing of the National Covenant and the restoration of Presbyterianism.

Charles's efforts to put down the Scots led to his own downfall. He was forced to summon an English Parliament, dominated by Puritans and Calvinists, with whom he quickly fell out. In 1642 he entered the House of Commons and attempted unsuccessfully to seize five of its leading members; civil war became inevitable. In September 1643, in need of Scottish help, the English Parliament accepted the Solemn League and Covenant, already approved by the Scots, which pledged its subscribers to bring the churches in the British Isles "to the nearest conjunction and conformity in religion, confession of faith, form of church government, directory for worship and catechizing . . . according to the Word of God and the example of the best Ref churches."

In July 1643, the Westminster Assembly of Divines met to advise the English Parliament on the good government of the church; in August the Church of Scotland appointed Scottish representatives to join their English brethren. The Assembly drew up a Directory for the Public Worship of God, a Confession of Faith, and the Shorter and Larger Catechisms.

In 1645 Parliament accepted the Assembly's Form of Church Government, but nowhere outside London was it seriously implemented. Hopes that the good government of the English church would be Presb were frustrated, in part by Erastians in Parliament, but more by the growing strength of Independency, above all in the New Model Army. In 1616 Henry Jacob had gathered a Separatist congregation at Southwark in London; by 1631 there were eleven such churches in London; in 1639 a church "according to the New England pattern" was formed at Llanfaches in Wales under the leadership of William Wroth. East Anglia, home of Oliver Cromwell, and with easy sea links to Holland, was a stronghold of Independency.

After the execution of Charles I in 1649, the Independent minister John Owen guided a pluralistic religious settlement under Cromwell, in which parishes were occupied by Presb, Independent, Bapt, and moderate Episcopalian ministers. In 1658 a conference of Independent ministers issued the Savoy Declaration of Faith and Order, with an adapted Westminster Confession as their common confession of faith (but "no way to be made use of as an *imposition* upon any"), underlining the central Congreg principle: "Besides these particular churches there is not instituted by Christ any church more extensive or catholic entrusted with power for the administration of his ordinances, or the execution of any authority in his name."

With the restoration of the monarchy (1660) came a harsh drive for Episcopalian uniformity. In Scotland Charles II (1660-1685) declared that "he was resolved to restore the church to its right government by bishops, as it was by law before the late troubles began"; four Scottish ministers were ordained bishop in Westminster Abbey (two having first been reordained as ministers). At the same time, almost 2,000 ministers were driven from their positions in England; most were Presb, but some were Congreg.

Uniformity was impossible on either side of the border. In the South and West of Scotland the great majority of ministers were deprived of their livings; illegal open-air conventicles were held and ruthlessly repressed. Revolts in 1666 and 1679 were quickly crushed. Repression intensified: accepting the ministrations of an ousted minister incurred severe penalties; to preach at a field conventicle was made punishable by death. In 1680 at the market cross in Sanquhar, Dumfriesshire, Richard Cameron, a young field preacher trained in Holland, declared war against the king; and the government sent in its troops, who acted without mercy. Anti-Erastian, and demanding loyalty to the Covenants and Presb church government by divine right, the Cameronians spoke for a minority only of Scottish Presb, but the "Killing Time," which lasted until 1688, made the victory of Presbyterianism in Scotland inevitable.

England and Wales

The "Glorious Revolution" that placed William and Mary (1689-1702) on the throne determined that England and Scotland would go their different religious ways. In England, the Established Church continued to be Episcopal; an Act of Toleration (1689) offered limited freedoms to Nonconformists, but enough disincentives remained to make Dissent unattractive, and the early decades of the 18th century saw English Nonconformity in decline. In the case of the English Presb, decline continued throughout the century, with many Presb congregations becoming Unitarian or turning to Independency. With the Evangelical Awakening later in the century, Dissent began to grow again.

In Wales the Evangelical revival gave renewed impetus to Independency, and many new congregations were formed. In the 19th century Welsh Independents played an important role in nurturing Welsh minds and morals, particularly through their adult Sunday schools. The Union of Welsh Independents was founded in 1872.

The Welsh revival also led to the only Presb church in Britain to take its origins from revival rather than reform. The founders of the Presb (Calvinistic/Meth) Church of Wales, Howell Harris, Daniel Rowland, William Williams, and others (both lay and clerical), were members of the Church of England; but soon after 1735 they established religious societies similar in pattern to the Meth Societies founded in England by John Wesley and George Whitefield. During the years 1735-1752 the societies in all parts of Wales were put under the charge of lay exhorters, and lay and clerical superintendents supervised them.

In the year 1811, under the leadership of Thomas Charles of Bala, an Angl clergyman, a number of exhorters were set aside and ordained to administer the sacraments within the societies; thus the movement became separated from the Church of England. In 1832 the Calvinistic Meth Connexion (as it was then called) formulated its Confession of Faith, Rules of Discipline, and Constitution and Church Government. In general the new Connexion was Presb in polity. The congregations were under the charge of ministers and elders. Under the influence of Lewis Edwards, the Connexion became more and more Presb in outlook and practice, and in 1864 the first General Assembly of the church was held.

The London Missionary Society (1795) was an outstanding result of the Evangelical Revival in English Congregationalism. The Congregational Union of England and Wales was formed in 1832, the Colonial (later Commonwealth) Missionary Society in 1836.

In 1809 Alexander Campbell, son of a minister of the Scottish Secession Church, emigrated from Glasgow to the USA, where he founded the Disciples of

Christ (1827). His ideas were brought back to Britain in 1833 by Peyton Wyeth, who founded a Scotch Bapt congregation in London and introduced them to Campbell's writings. From this almost accidental encounter sprang the movement known in Britain as the Churches of Christ, which grew until 1930, when it had 200 congregations and 16,000 members.

In 1783 Presb congregations in the North of England formed the Presbytery of Northumberland. Depleted English Presb ranks were replenished by Scottish immigration, and in 1836 the Presbyterian Church in England was established. An English Synod of the United Presbyterian Church was formed in 1863; in 1876 it united with the Presbyterian Church in England to form the Presbyterian Church *of* England.

In 1966, following the successful promotion of the idea of a national covenant, the Congregational Union of England and Wales became the Congregational Church of England and Wales; an Evangelical Fellowship of Congregational Churches was formed by those declining to enter the covenant. In the same year the London Missionary Society and the Commonwealth Missionary Society combined to form the Congregational Council for World Mission; after a far-reaching review in 1975, this was relaunched in 1977 as the Council for World Mission, with the old distinction between sending and receiving churches replaced by a new emphasis on partnership.

In 1972 the Congregational Church of England and Wales and the Presbyterian Church of England joined together as the United Reformed Church of England and Wales (URC); those Congreg churches that stayed out of the union formed the Congregational Federation. Proposals for a union between the Association of Churches of Christ and the URC were published in 1976 and approved by the URC the following year. They failed, however, to obtain the assent of the necessary two-thirds majority of the churches in the Association, which dissolved itself in 1979, allowing the Re-formed Association in 1980 to enter what became the United Reformed Church in the United Kingdom.

Scotland

In Scotland Presbyterianism was reestablished by the "Glorious Revolution"; both Episcopalians (Scottish Episcopal Church) and Cameronians (Reformed Presb Church) rejected the Presb settlement. In 1707, when England and Scotland were united as Great Britain, a guarantee of continuing Presb church government in Scotland was written into the Treaty of Union. In 1712 a hostile Westminster Parliament ignored the guarantee in reintroducing patronage (the right to name a candidate to a ministerial charge). This Act, it may be claimed, was at the root of all the Church of Scotland's subsequent troubles. In 1733 Ebenezer Erskine led a first secession from the Kirk in opposition to patronage; in 1761 a second and less bitter secession under Thomas Gillespie led to the founding of the Relief Church.

Erskine's church split in 1747 over whether it was lawful to take the oath, required of burgesses in Edinburgh, Glasgow, and Perth, acknowledging "the true religion presently professed within this realm," which the Antiburgher minority interpreted to refer to the Established Church. At the end of the century both branches became nervous about the Westminster Confession's treatment of the duties of the civil magistrate in church affairs and set about revising their Testimonies to disavow all "compulsory and persecuting principles." The "New Licht" (new light) prevailed in the Burgher Synod in 1799, and in the Antiburgher Synod in 1806, but in both cases it led to further splits. The "Auld Licht" remnants hived off, the "Auld Licht" Burghers rejoining the Church of Scotland in 1839, the "Auld Licht" Antiburghers, or Constitutionalists, continuing as the Original Secession Church until, in 1956, it too rejoined the Church of Scotland. In 1820 the New Lichts united to form the United Secession Church, and further united with the Relief Church in 1847 as the United Presbyterian Church.

At the Disruption in 1843 the Church of Scotland suffered its deepest and most damaging split, once more over patronage. Recognizing that there was no hope of redress by the government in London, those in the Kirk who had spent ten years fighting the intrusion of ministers into charges against the congregation's will walked out of the General Assembly to establish the Church of Scotland Free.

The coming together of daughter churches in England and Australia was one factor encouraging Scottish Presb to think that they might attempt the same. In 1900 the Free Church and the United Presbyterian Church formed the United Free Church, and in 1929 this church united with the Church of Scotland. The key issue lay in defining, and establishing, a church that was at once national and free; not all Scottish Presb were persuaded that the 1929 Articles Declaratory in fact achieved this, but most were.

Congregationalism in Scotland may also be seen, with some justice, as an offshoot of Presbyterianism. Greville Ewing, it is true, was never a Presb; but the Glasites, old Scots Independents, and Bereans, forerunners of Scottish Congregationalism, were all splinters from the Church of Scotland; the Haldane brothers were lay members of the Kirk, and the Evangelical Union was produced by the revolt against Calvinism within the United Secession Church.

At the end of the 18th century two Church of Scotland laymen, Robert and James Haldane, sought to arouse the national church to the need for missionary effort at home and abroad. Their failure led to the formation of independent churches for this purpose. The true architect of Scottish Congregationalism was their associate, Rev. Greville Ewing, who started classes for the training of ministers in 1799 and promoted the formation of the Congregational Union in 1812. In the following eighty years the small denomination learned to become more than an association of autonomous units and pioneered work in local mission, Sunday Schools, women's service, and other areas of outreach. It produced outstanding men like W. L. Alexander, David Livingstone, Robert Moffat, James Chalmers, and P. T. Forsyth.

In 1841 James Morrison was expelled by the Synod of the United Secession Church for a formidable range of disagreements with its Calvinist doctrines. He founded the Evangelical Union, characterized by its Arminian theology and warm evangelical piety. By 1897 the two unions were ready to enter into a new Congregational Union of Scotland, now with explicitly congregational and Presb elements.

At the local community level the churches of the Union were recognized for their social initiative and evangelical effort combined with a liberal theology. At the national level the Union made a significant contribution to ecumenical advance in Scotland. It shared in the agreement between Scottish Ref churches recognizing each other's ministry and membership.

In 1988 proposals for a further union with the United Reformed Church were accepted by the General Assembly of that church almost unanimously, but they failed to obtain the necessary 75% majority in the Congregational Union.

A period of intense self-examination followed, and it was now proposed that the three independent elements of the Congreg family in Scotland (the Scottish Congreg College, the Women's Union, and the Congregational Union) should form a "Voluntary Church" — the Scottish Congregational Church — while retaining their separate identities for legal purposes. The new church was inaugurated in 1993. A minority within the Union, who opposed these changes, broke away and subsequently joined the Congregational Federation.

Denominations are listed in alphabetical order.

1. The Associated Presbyterian Churches of Scotland (APC) (6320)

This church was formed in 1989 as the result of a secession from the Free Presbyterian Church of Scotland. This was over liberty of conscience, which many in the former body were not willing to allow in practice even though it is part of their subordinate standard, the Westminster Confession of Faith. The church was formed by ministers and elders signing a Deed of Separation from the Free Presbyterian Church and then forming a Presbytery. It supports Mediterranean, Hong Kong, and Romanian missions.

TM: **2,200** BM: **2,000** CM: **300** Congr: **21** PStations: **12** OrdM: **14** Eld: **45** Deac: **14** EvgHome: **2** Mission: **2** Women Ord: **no** ChurchOrg: **kirk sessions, presby, assemblies, latter incorporates presbytery in Canada** Off/otherLang: **English, Gaelic** DoctrB: **WestConf, Ref-Ev.** Infant or believer's baptism: **both** Frequency of the Lord's Supper: **2-4 times a year** Close relations with: **Free Ch of Scotland, Church of Scotland** NatRel: **none** RegRel: **none** IntlRel: **none** TheolSchool: **universities, Free Ch College, Highland Theological Institute** Service infrastructure: **none** Periodicals: **APC (news/gen/yearly/3,000), Congregational Newsletter**

Address: The Associated Presbyterian Churches of Scotland, P.O. Box 51, 16 Drummond Road, GB-Innerness-shire AB1 8DN, United Kingdom, Tel: +44 1463 223-983, Fax: +44 1463 223-983, E-mail: mmacinnes@btintemet.com.

2. Church of Scotland (6301)

The Church of Scotland is the largest Christian denomination in Scotland, with its historic roots in the missionary labors of St. Ninian and St. Columba and in the early Celtic Church. It was Ref in the 16th century after the Genevan and Calvinist pattern, but finally established in its Presb polity only with the Revolution Settlement of 1690. Various secessions occurred in the 18th and 19th centuries.

Since 1929 the Church of Scotland has been largely reunited, and is committed to the modern ecumenical movement and to fostering church union. In the Declaratory Articles, which the parliament of the United Kingdom approved as a correct statement of the historic position of the Church of Scotland in matters spiritual, it is described as a "national Church representative of the Christian Faith of the Scottish people." The final authority of the Church of Scotland is the General Assembly.

The church's overseas work includes mission partners in Africa, Asia, and the Caribbean area, and ministers serving in Scots kirks abroad, mostly now in continental Europe, with some in Israel/Palestine.

TM: **1,220,000** CM: **715,571** Congr: **1,619** PStations: **1,619** OrdM: **1,273** Eld: **46,091** Deac: **76** EvgHome: **3** Mission: **78** Women Ord: **yes** As Ministers: **1968/116** as Deac: **nc** as Elders: **1964** ChurchOrg: **presbyteries** Off/otherLang: **English, Gaelic** DoctrB: **ApC, NicC, WestConf** Infant or believer's baptism: **both** Frequency of the Lord's Supper: **once a month encouraged, some still only twice a year** Close relations with: **ACTS, CCBI, WARC** NatRel: **ACTS (1990/1925), CCBI (1990/ 1942), CTE (1993)** RegRel: **nc** IntlRel: **WARC (1970/1975), CEC (1959), WCC (1948), CWM (1978), EECCS (1973)** TheolSchool: **nc** Service infrastructure: **44 rest/nursing homes, Social Responsibility Board** Periodicals: **Life and Work (gen/monthly/nc)**

Address: Church of Scotland, 121 George Street, GB-Edinburgh EH2 4YN, United Kingdom, Tel: +44 131 225 5722, Fax: +44 131 220 3899, E-mail: kirkeculink@gn.apc.org.

3. Congregational Federation (6307)

The Federation was founded in 1972 to link together approximately 200 "continuing Congregational churches" who stayed out of the new United Reformed Church on classic Congreg grounds: "the scriptural right of every separate church to maintain perfect independence in the government and administration of its own particular affairs." It was affirmed that the Federation should not in any case assume legislative authority, or become a court of appeal.

Since 1972 approximately 15 of these churches closed, but the total number of churches increased, particularly through the accession of 25 churches from the Congregational Union of Scotland who declined to join the Scottish Congregational Church.

Integral to the Federation's headquarters in Nottingham are a Christian bookshop, a café, and residential accommodation for 40 people, which is used for training courses and the like. The Federation is active within the Council for World Mission; it has sent missionaries abroad, and has received short-term missionaries from abroad. In 1973 it developed a young people's section, which has steadily grown. In 1993 it appointed a Youth Coordinator to develop the work further. At the end of the 1980s it developed an integrated training program, catering to church members, preachers, pastors, and ministers, which has helped particularly in the training of leaders for its many small churches.

TM: **11,943** Congr: **313** PStations: **313** OrdM: **113** Eld: **ne** Deac: **ne** EvgHome: **nc** Mission: **na** Women Ord: **yes** As Ministers: **1902/13%** as Deac: **0** as Elders: **0** ChurchOrg: **nc** Off/otherLang: **English, Welsh, Irish** DoctrB: **nc** NatRel: **nc** RegRel: **CEC** IntlRel: **CWM, Congreg Fellowship**

TheolSchool: **Theological College or 5-year course with distance learning** Periodicals: **Congregational (quarterly)**

Address: Congregational Federation, 4 Castle Gate, GB-Nottingham NG1 7AS, United Kingdom, Tel: +44 155 941-3801, Fax: +44 155 948-0902

4. Evangelical Fellowship of Congregational Churches (6309)

In 1947 two ministers of the Congregational Union of England and Wales, Harland Brine and Gilbert Kirby, concerned about spiritual decline in their denomination, began the Congregational Evangelical Revival Fellowship (CERF). Open to individual members of Congreg churches, CERF sought to witness to evangelical truth and the need for Holy Spirit revival.

In 1958 the Congregational Union adopted a new constitution. One of the purposes of the Union in the old constitution was "to promote New Testament principles of church fellowship and organization"; this was changed to what CERF saw as a much vaguer aim, "to promote principles of church fellowship and organization that are consonant with the Gospel." CERF was also concerned about the way in which the Union was consolidating and centralizing its power.

In 1961, when the Congregational Union published proposals for covenant and oversight in setting up the Congregational Church in England and Wales, 27 ministers sent out an appeal, on a CERF initiative, calling upon Congregational churches to stand firm on Congregational principles.

In 1967, following the setting up of the Congregational Church, an Evangelical Fellowship of Congregational Churches was established to link those congregations that wished to stay out of the new body.

TM: **6,000** Congr: **130** OrdM: **107** Eld: **na** Deac: **na** EvgHome: **na** Mission: **na** Women Ord: **yes** As Ministers: **na** as Deac: **na** as Elders: **na** ChurchOrg: **Congregational** Off/otherLang: **nc** DoctrB: **historic Reformed Congreg Confessions, Basis of Faith (1971), Savoy Declaration** Infant or believer's baptism: **both** Frequency of the Lord's Supper: **monthly** NatRel: **BEC (1971)** IntlRel: **WECF (1986)** Periodicals: **Congregational Concern (gen/quarterly/2,200)**

Address: Evangelical Fellowship of Congregational Churches, P.O. Box 34, The Manse, GB-Beverley HU17 8YU, United Kingdom, Tel: +44 1 482 860-324, Fax: +44 1 482-860-324, E-mail: efcc@digby.cix.co.uk.

5. Free Church of Scotland (6310)

At the Disruption (1843), under the leadership of Dr. Thomas Chalmers, the Evangelical party in the Church of Scotland as By Law Established withdrew to form the Church of Scotland, Free.

In 1900, when the great majority in the Free Church combined with the United Presbyterian Church to form the United Free Church of Scotland, a small minority elected to continue as the Free Church of Scotland. The adherents of this "constitutionalist" party were to be found mainly, although not exclusively, in the Highlands and islands of Scotland. Union was possible only on the basis of compromise: the minority took the view that doctrines which were being treated as open questions were so vital to the faith that the duty of Christian unity had to yield to the higher duty of fidelity to the truth.

Today the Free Church of Scotland, although much reduced in size, maintains in continuity with the church of 1843 the system of doctrine and the form of worship adopted by the Church of Scotland at the Reformation. The singing of the Scottish metrical psalms, unaccompanied by instrumental music, is, perhaps, the most distinctive feature of its liturgy; but the chief emphasis of its worship is still to be found in the centrality of the pulpit and the proclamation of a free and sovereign salvation.

TM: **20,000** BM: **5,900** CM: **5,900** Congr: **115** PStations: **25** OrdM: **95** Eld: **ne** Deac: **ne** EvgHome: **nc** Mission: **13** Women Ord: **no** ChurchOrg: **9 presby, 3 synods, 1 overseas synod with 2 presby (Canada)** Off/otherLang: **English, Gaelic** DoctrB: **WestConf** Frequency of the Lord's Supper: **2-4 times a year** Close relations with: **federal relations with Presb Ch of Eastern Australia** NatRel: **nc** RegRel: **nc** IntlRel: **ICRC** Service infrastructure: **Maxwell House Eventide Home (rest/nursing)** Periodicals: **Monthly Record of the Free Ch of Scotland (gen/11 times per year)**

Address: Free Church of Scotland, 15 North Bank Street, GB-Edinburgh EH1 2LS, United Kingdom, Tel: +44 131 226 5286 and 4978, Fax: +44 131 220 0597, E-mail: freechurch @compuserve.com.

6. Free Presbyterian Church of Scotland (6313)

The Free Presbyterian Church of Scotland came into separate existence as a result of the passing of the Declaratory Act by the General Assembly of the Free Church of Scotland in 1892. This Act affirmed the full authority of the church to determine what doctrines enter into the substance of the Ref faith. When the 1893 Assembly failed to repeal it, two ministers, Rev. Donald Macfarlane and Rev. Donald Macdonald, left the Free Church, together with many officebearers, members and adherents, to form the Free Presbyterian Church of Scotland. The first presbytery meeting was held in August 1893, when a Deed of Separation was drawn and subscribed. The church now has five presbyteries in the United Kingdom: one in Africa; one in the antipodes, embracing congregations in Australia and New Zealand; and extensive missionary activities in Zimbabwe and Kenya.

The Free Presbyterian Church of Scotland's supreme standard is the inspired, infallible, and inerrant Word of God; its subordinate standard is the Westminster Confession of Faith. In its public worship, the only version of the Bible used is the Authorized Version; it insists on having worshippers stand when addressing God in prayer; it does not admit the use of instrumental music, and its manual of praise is the psalms of David. It supports the Establishment principle acknowledging Christ as "King of Nations" and regards the state as under a divine obligation to support and maintain the Christian religion. It seeks to uphold and teach biblical morality. It is strongly opposed to abortion except in the rare cases where the life of the mother may be at risk, and it advocates the return of capital punishment for the crime of murder. The church is postmillennial in outlook and firmly believes that the whole earth shall yet be "full of the knowledge of the Lord, as the waters cover the sea."

TM: **10,000** CM: **1,000** Congr: **60** PStations: **10** OrdM: **25** Eld: **120** Deac: **0** EvgHome: **1** Mission: **4** Women Ord: **no** ChurchOrg: **presb** Off/otherLang: **English** DoctrB: **WestConf** TheolSchool: Periodicals: **The Free Presbyterian Magazine, The Young People's Magazine**

Address: Free Presbyterian Church of Scotland, 16 Matheson Road, GB-Stornoway Isle-of-Lewis HS1 2LA, United Kingdom, Tel: +44 1851 702-755, Fax: +44 1851 702-755

7. Korean Church London (International Presbyterian Church) (6311)

No data have been made available.

Address: Korean Church London (International Presbyterian Church), 37 Grove Crescent, GB-Kingston upon Thames KT1 2DG, United Kingdom, Tel: +44 1 81 546 9945, Fax: +44 1 81 337 2067

8. Evangelical Presbyterian Church in England and Wales (EPCEW) (6319)

The EPCEW is the child of the Presbyterian Association in England (PAE). The PAE was formed in 1987 as a temporary organization with the expressed intention of forming a new Presb denomination in England. "It was the desire of those who formed the PAE to see a church in England that was biblically based, faithful to the Westminster Confession and connectional," states this church. Membership in the association was open to individuals and groups (churches). The five churches that joined the association worked as an "interim presbytery" until they completed a book of church order. Then they formed a full functioning presbytery in April 1996. The church intends to be not only evangelical in its theological stance but also evangelistic in its practice. It has therefore adopted an aggressive attitude to the planting of new churches. Aware of its small size as a denomination, it has entered into partnership with older and stronger Presb bodies in other countries to help with these church planting projects.

TM: **132** BM: **132** CM: **73** Congr: **5** OrdM: **2** Eld: **6** Deac: **6** EvgHome: **0** Mission: **1** Women Ord: **no** ChurchOrg: **local session, presby, GenAssy (eventually)** Off/otherLang: **English** DoctrB: **WestConf** Infant or believer's baptism: **both** Frequency of the Lord's Supper: **monthly** Close relations with: **Evangelical Presb Church (Northern Ireland), Reformed Church (Liberated, NL), Free Church of Scotland, Presb Church in America** NatRel: **British Evangelical Council** RegRel: **none** IntlRel: **ICRC (1997)** TheolSchool: **Free Church College (Edinburgh), Reformed Presb Seminary (Belfast), Covenant Seminary (St. Louis, USA), Westminster Seminary (Philadelphia, USA)** Service infrastructure: **none** Periodicals: **Presbyterian Network (mag/2 times per year/700)**

Address: Evangelical Presbyterian Church in England and Wales, 14 Longshaw Lane, GB-Blackburn BB2 3LU, United Kingdom, Tel: +44 1 245 450-089, Fax: na, E-mail: 100713.612@compuserve.com.

9. Presbyterian Church of Wales (6305)

This church originated in the Evangelical revival of the 18th century. Originally known as the Calvinistic Methodist Connexion, it held its first General Assembly in 1864.

During the present century it changed its name to the Calvinistic/Methodist Church of Wales, or the Presbyterian Church of Wales, and formulated new Articles Declaratory of the Constitution of the Church in Matters Spiritual. In 1933 its amended Constitution was adopted and received the assent of Parliament.

TM: **53,870** CM: **53,870** Congr: **1,050** OrdM: **141** Eld: **4,104** Deac: **2** EvgHome: **2** Mission: **2** Women Ord: **yes** As Ministers: **1976/17** as Deac: **ne** as Elders: **over 50%/since many years** ChurchOrg: **circuits — 30 presby — 3 provinces — GenAssy** Off/otherLang: **Welsh (26%), English** DoctrB: **Calvinistic Meth Confession of Faith** Frequency of the Lord's Supper: **monthly** Close relations with: **Church Unity, Uniting Congregations which have become weak** NatRel: **Churches Main Committee, Free Churches Council for Wales** RegRel: **nc** IntlRel: **WCC, WARC, CWM** Service infrastructure: **Gwasy Pantycelyn (printing press), Caernarfon Coleg Trefeca (lay training), Coleg y Bala (Youth training), Tresaith Centre (Self-Catering Center)** Periodicals: **Y Goleuad-Welsh (news/weekly/3,000), The Treasury-English (Connexional News/monthly/1,900)**

Address: Eglwys Bresbyteraidd Cymru, 53 Richmond Road, GB-Cardiff/Cymru, Wales CF2 3UP, United Kingdom, Tel: +44 1 222-494913, Fax: +44 1 222 464-293

10. Reformed Presbyterian Church of Scotland (6312)

The Reformed Presbyterian Church of Scotland was a continuation of the Church of Scotland by those in that church (the Covenanters) who saw the Revolution Settlement of 1690 as an Erastian imposition which did not recognize the divine right of Presb church government. The first presbytery meeting was held in 1743, when Rev. John McMillan was joined by another minister. The church grew rapidly during the 18th century but declined after 1863, when the vast majority united with the Free Church of Scotland. During the 20th century the number of congregations has dwindled to the present four, three of which are pastored by Irish ministers.

TM: **90** Congr: **4** OrdM: **5** Eld: **7** Deac: **nc** EvgHome: **nc** Mission: **nc** Women Ord: **no** ChurchOrg: **presby, synod** Off/otherLang: **nc** DoctrB: **WestConf** Frequency of the Lord's Supper: **bi-annual** NatRel: **nc** RegRel: **nc** IntlRel: **nc**

Address: Reformed Presbyterian Church of Scotland, 4 Burnbrae Avenue, GB-Glasgow G61 3ES, United Kingdom

11. Scottish Congregational Church (6302)

The Scottish Congregational Church was inaugurated in 1993, linking the three independent elements of the Congreg family in Scotland (the Scottish Congregational College, the Women's Union, and the Congregational Union) in a "Voluntary Church," i.e., a covenant body in which the three partners would submerge their independent interests and work as one body, while retaining their separate constitutional identities for legal purposes. The reform scheme also involved re-placing all the traditional committees with a simplified threefold structure of mis-sion-driven relationships, comprising mission, pastoral, and educational groups, in every congregation, in area councils (regional groupings of churches), and at the national level. The reform has already proved an outstanding success in renewing concern for mission at the local level.

TM: **7,000** BM: **7,000** CM: **7,000** Congr: **60** OrdM: **74** Eld: **nc** Deac: **nc** EvgHome: **nc** Mission: **2** Women Ord: **yes** As Ministers: **always/7** as Deac: **nc** as Elders: **nc** ChurchOrg: **area councils** Off/ otherLang: **English** DoctrB: **noncreedal** Infant or believer's baptism: **both** Frequency of the Lord's Supper: **monthly to quarterly** Close relations with: **United Reformed Church of Great Britain** NatRel: **CCBI, ACTS** RegRel: **nc** IntlRel: **WCC, WARC, CWM** TheolSchool: **Universities, Scottish Congregational College** Service infrastructure: **none** Periodicals: **Focus (gen/quarterly/5,000)**

Address: Scottish Congregational Church, P.O. Box 189 nc, GB-Glasgow G1 2BX, United Kingdom, Tel: +44 141 332 7667, Fax: +44 141 332 8463, E-mail: 100520,2150@compuserve.com.

12. Union of Welsh Independents (6306)

The Welsh Independent or Congregational Churches stand in the Puritan and Non-conformist tradition. It was the conviction of the churches' founders that the Prot Reformation, which had taken a political turn in England, fell short of the reforma-tion called for in the Scriptures.

The Union of Welsh Independents, founded in 1872, is a voluntary associa-tion of Welsh Congreg churches and individual members. The preservation of the distinctive language and culture of Wales, which have been much influenced by Christianity, continues to be a major concern of the Union.

The Union is presently sharing in discussions on behalf of its churches with other Nonconformist denominations in Wales.

TM: **45,462** BM: **45,462** Congr: **600** OrdM: **368** Eld: **0** Deac: **ne** Mission: **nc** Women Ord: **yes** As Min-isters: **1925/10** as Deac: **1940/unknown** as Elders: **0** ChurchOrg: **18 associations of churches, assem-bly, and council** Off/otherLang: **Welsh, in Anglicized areas bilingual worship, Welsh-English** DoctrB: **no use of confessions in worship** Infant or believer's baptism: **both** Frequency of the Lord's Supper: **once or twice monthly** Close relations with: **Free Church of Walwa, CYTUN** NatRel: **Council of Churches, Britain and Ireland (1990), CYTUN (1900), Free Church Federal Council of Wales, Sunday School Council, Free Church Council of Wales** RegRel: **nc** IntlRel: **WCC (late '50s), WARC (mid '80s), CWM** Periodicals: **Y Tyst (denominational/weekly/1,600), Cristion (gen/ bi-month/2,750)**

Address: Undeb yr Annibynwyr Cymraeg, Ty John Penri, 11 St. Helen Road, GB-Abertawe — Swansea Wales SA1 4AL, United Kingdom, Tel: +44 1 792 652 542, Fax: +44 1 792 650-647

13. United Free Church of Scotland (6303)

In 1900 much of the Free Church of Scotland united with the United Presbyterian Church to form the United Free Church of Scotland, which at that time, like the

Church of Scotland, was a large denomination. In 1929 much of the United Free Church of Scotland united with the Church of Scotland. A small minority continued as the United Free Church of Scotland.

Voluntary support by its members, freedom from state control, and religious equality have always been distinguishing principles of this denomination. Women serve the church as ministers and elders. Mission and evangelism have always been priorities for the church. It takes an active interest in the cultural, social, and political concerns of Scotland and the UK. It is involved in world mission, especially through cooperation with the United Congregational Church of Southern Africa in Botswana and elsewhere. Recently, it has been involved with three other Scottish denominations in a Christian Aid project to assist the people of Cambodia by the clearance of landmines and the rehabilitation of those injured by them.

TM: **6,294** BM: **6,294** CM: **6,294** Congr: **70** OrdM: **37** Eld: **716** Deac: **515** EvgHome: **nc** Mission: **20** Women Ord: **yes** As Ministers: **1929/6** as Deac: **1929/401** as Elders: **1929/227** ChurchOrg: **3 presby** Off/otherLang: **English** DoctrB: **WestConf** Infant or believer's baptism: **both** Frequency of the Lord's Supper: **quarterly** Close relations with: **Church of Scotland, United Ref Church, Bapt, Meth, Episcopal** NatRel: **CCBI, ACTS (1990)** RegRel: **nc** IntlRel: **WCC, WARC (1948)** TheolSchool: **universities** Periodicals: **Stedfast (gen/monthly/3,000)**

Address: United Free Church of Scotland, 11 Newton Place, GB-Glasgow G3 7PR, United Kingdom, Tel: +44 141 332-3435, Fax: +44 141 333-1973

14. United Reformed Church (6304)

The United Reformed Church came into being in October 1972 through the union of the Presbyterian Church of England (PCE) and the Congregational Church in England and Wales (CCEW).

The PCE was formed in 1876 as the end product of a series of unions between various groups, all deriving their origin from the Church of Scotland; by 1972 it was by no means wholly Scottish. Virtually the whole of the PCE entered into the newly formed URC, but a substantial minority of Congreg remained outside the union (cf. Congregational Federation no. 3). In total, however, the URC represents the overwhelming majority of former Congreg and Presb churches in England; it also includes those of the same traditions in Wales but excluding those wholly of Welsh origin, many of which are Welsh rather than English in language.

In 1980 the union was reinforced by the accession of the Reformed Association of Churches of Christ. The proposal to join the URC had not initially secured a sufficiently large measure of support, and the constituent body was dissolved and reformed into two groups so that those wishing to accede might be able to do, and those who opted out could continue as Churches of Christ.

The accession of the Churches of Christ created a new situation in two respects. Firstly, a handful of the new congregations were formed in Scotland; hence the United Reformed Church in England and Wales was renamed the United Reformed Church in the United Kingdom. Secondly, the Churches of Christ, though Presb in background, had from the start adopted a believer's baptist stance. The

URC has in consequence given official recognition to two forms of baptism as equally valid — that of adult believers and that of infants. While this can lead to difficulties in particular cases, it is prized as a contribution, not unique, but still rare, to reconciling different convictions on baptism within one church.

The URC was founded out of conscious ecumenical convictions; it was intended as a temporary creation which would shortly disappear into a wider union. In several ecumenical discussions since, it has played a full part. It has been disappointing to the URC that little fruit has come from such efforts. There has, however, been considerable formation of local ecumenical congregations, with varying relationships between the participating denominations: from simple sharing of premises to the formation of totally united congregations recognized fully by all the churches involved. Such ecumenical congregations form a significant part of the URC constituency.

TM: **nc** CM: **102,582** Congr: **1,768** OrdM: **1,864** Eld: **14,235** Deac: **16** Mission: **14** Women Ord: **yes** As Ministers: **na** as Deac: **no** as Elders: **no** ChurchOrg: **75 districts grouped in 12 provincial synods** Off/otherLang: **English, some Welsh in Wales** DoctrB: **ApC, NicC, Statement concerning Nature, Faith and Order, Statement of Faith at Union in 1972** Infant or believer's baptism: **both** Frequency of the Lord's Supper: **weekly to quarterly** Close relations with: **other 30 members of CWM, Presb Ch in the Rep. of Korea** (no. 13)**, Presb Ch of Ghana, Ev. Presb Ch in Ghana, Ref Ch of Romania, Ref Ch in Hungary, Waldensian Ch of the Rio de la Plata, Ch of Czech Brethren** NatRel: **CCB (1990), CTE (1990), ACTS (1990)** RegRel: **Leuenberg Concord (1973), CEC (1972)** IntlRel: **WARC (1972), WCC (1972), CWM (1972), Disciples Ecumenical Consultative Council (1981)** TheolSchool: **universities** Periodicals: **Reform (gen/monthly/13,000)**

Address: United Reformed Church, 86 Tavistock Place, GB-London WC1H 9RT, United Kingdom, Tel: +44 171 916 2020, Fax: +44 171 916 2021

UNITED STATES OF AMERICA

Area in km²	9,372,610
Population	(July 1996 est.) 266,476,278 white 83.4%, black 12.4%, Asian 3.3%, Native American 0.8% (1992)
Religions in %	Prot 56%, RCath 28%, Jewish 2%, other 4%, none 10% (1989)
Official/other languages	English/Spanish (spoken by a sizeable minority), many languages of other immigrant communities

COCU (Consultation of Church Union)
NAE (National Association of Evangelicals)
NAPARC (National Association of Presbyterian and Reformed Churches)
NCCCUSA (National Council of Christian Churches in the USA)

516

Since the time of its beginnings within European colonialism, the United States has been a place for religious refugees. It nurtured a basic principle of religious freedom, which in the beginning meant local autonomy for several varieties of Christianity. The vast majority of its 260 million people are believers in God, and nearly every variety of Christian expression is found in the USA. The wide diversity of churches reflects the many ethnic communities who have migrated to the USA and retained the church expression of the former homeland. In recent years, Christian cultural dominance has begun to fade, and secularism has pushed Christian life farther into the realm of private conviction only.

A Ref presence came with some of the first European settlers, the Puritans. Dissatisfied with the Church of England, the Puritans fled England under persecution, resided briefly in the Netherlands, and then made their way to America to establish a separate community in Massachusetts. Broadly Calvinist in orientation, some of the Puritans moved toward forming Presb churches, while most formed Congreg churches.

A second substantial immigration came from Scotland, where the church under the leadership of John Knox was more exclusively Calvinistic. Significant numbers came after 1714 and settled in the mid-Atlantic coastal area of New Jersey, Pennsylvania, Delaware, and Maryland. The first presbytery was established in Philadelphia in 1706. The first General Assembly of Presb met in 1789, just as the new nation was formally established.

There were a few presbyteries that did not join the General Assembly. They were known as the Associate Synod and the Associate Reformed Synod. In 1858 these two joined to become the United Presbyterian Church of North America. In 1958 this church merged with the Presbyterian Church USA (the northern Presb), and became part of the United Presbyterian Church in the USA in its formation in 1983.

In the mid-19th century the main course of Presbyterianism was influenced by revivalism. At Yale University Nathaniel Taylor defended the "New School," which was a combination of Enlightenment ideas with revivalist methods. The "Old School" became those characterized by stricter adherence to the Westminster Confession. Some persons in the New School, such as Charles Finney, finally left Presbyterianism for a generic American evangelicalism. Others picked up the strand of Enlightenment thought in the New School and became part of the modernist movement. As for the Old School, some of those embraced ideas of fundamentalism arising in the early 20th century and formed a hybrid fundamentalist Presbyterianism.

While the lines are not continuous, one can still characterize some Presb as Old School. Those holding a fairly strict adherence to the Westminster Confession include the Associate Reformed Presb, the Orthodox Presb, the Ref Presb, the Bible Presb, the Evangelical Presb, the Presbyterian Church of America, and several of the smaller groups that have split from these. Within the larger Presbyterian Church (USA), which dwarfs all the others, there has been a history of strong post-Enlightenment leadership, but recently several minority organizations representing more evangelical and conservative traditions have been exerting enormous influence.

There was an early Ref presence in the Dutch colony of New Amsterdam (1624), which later became New York. These settlers formed the Reformed Church in America (RCA), which slowly spread westward. Additional waves of immigrants beginning in the mid-19th century brought new forms of Reformed Christianity as well as the legacy of the European schisms. An early example is the Christian Reformed Church, whose members had suffered persecution and ostracism when they had tried to reform the Dutch mother church. Following the split in the Netherlands in 1834, immigrants from among the seceders who had settled in the American Midwest could not accept what they saw in the eastern churches of the RCA, and created a separate church in 1857.

In later years new denominations of Ref churches were founded by later immigrants. As the Dutch churches continued to divide, in 1892 and 1944, the immigrants from these new splits kept apart in America (and Canada) as well. Churches such as the American Reformed, the Free Reformed, and Netherlands Reformed Congregations were founded by these immigrant groups from different Dutch traditions.

Other divisions native to North America have come mainly from groups breaking away from the Christian Reformed Church. The first, in 1924, was with the Protestant Reformed Church. Then in the 1960s and 1970s, individual congregations left, some of them forming the Orthodox Christian Reformed after 1979. The largest splits from the Christian Reformed Church have come in the late 1980s and early 1990s, with the breakaway of Koreans in 1991 to form the Christian Presbyterians, and the formation of the Alliance of Reformed Churches and the United Reformed Church from other CRC dissidents.

The movement of European settlers westward led to the formation of some new churches. The settlers required cooperation and flexibility in their church lives, while those staying in the East wanted purity of doctrine and the training offered in the eastern seminaries. Some new Presb groups as well as the Christian Church (Disciples of Christ) were products of this westward movement. The Ameican Civil War of 1861-1865 was another major divider, and southern and northern branches of Presbyterianism persisted for more than a century after the war.

Several other groups of immigrants have formed churches related to their national churches. Immigrant German Ref founded the Reformed Church in the US, and there is a congregation of recent Lithuanian immigrants. Koreans and Hungarians have also formed several ethnic Ref and Presb churches among immigrants and refugees in the twentieth century. Some Koreans maintained links with their mother church, remaining part of the national synods in Korea.

Denominations are listed in alphabetical order.

1. Alliance of Reformed Churches (3244)

The Alliance of Reformed Churches began as a movement within the Christian Reformed Church in 1990. In 1991, when some of its members seceded from the

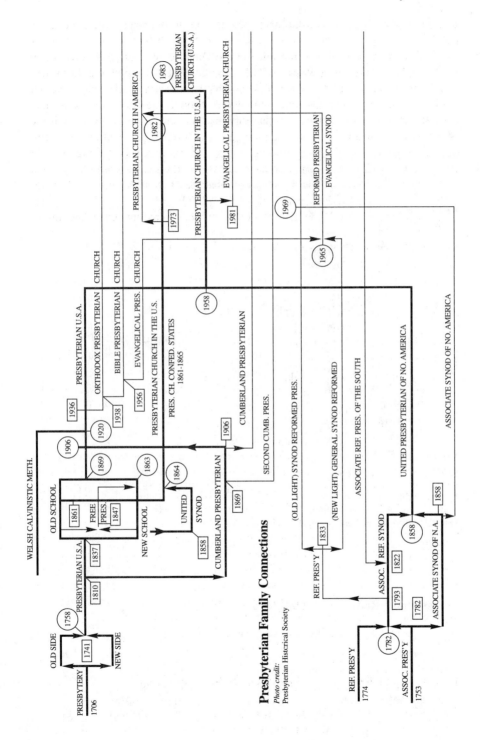

Presbyterian Family Connections

Photo credit:
Presbyterian Historical Society

Christian Reformed Church, and other independent churches expressed interest, the alliance changed its purpose and goals and took on its present name. About 20 of 32 churches are located in Canada. The alliance includes both Ref and Presb creeds as part of its basis. Some members moved toward a tighter federation and eventually formed the United Reformed Churches in 1996 (cf. no. 44). The alliance meets about once a year and continues to struggle with the challenge of its evolving organization. Its members are independent churches, concentrated in the Midwest.

TM: **7,524** BM: **3,271** CM: **4,253** Congr: **32** PStations: **ne** OrdM: **37** Eld: **156** Deac: **142** EvgHome: **6** Mission: **1** Women Ord: **no** ChurchOrg: **regional fellowships, General Alliance** Off/otherLang: **English/Vietnamese** DoctrB: **ApC, HeidC, WestConf, CDort, BelgC, Calvinistic Ref** Infant or believer's baptism: **both** Frequency of the Lord's Supper: **4 times a year** Close relations with: **United Ref Churches** NatRel: **none** RegRel: **none** IntlRel: **none** TheolSchool: **nc** Service infrastructure: **none** Periodicals: **none**

Address: Alliance of Reformed Churches, 10532 Paw Paw Dr., Holland, MI 60438, United States, Tel: +1 616 772-2918

2. American Presbyterian Church (3231)

This church was organized in 1977 by persons leaving the Bible Presbyterian Church, when the Bible Presb, under the influence of Carl McIntire, dissolved the BPC Philadelphia Presbytery. Three congregations reestablished themselves as the American Presbyterian Church. These churches sing psalms only and organize membership by families. They demand that their members abstain from alcohol. The church has a quarterly newsletter, *Katartizo,* aimed at making contact with other small Presb groups. They are seeking others with whom to relate.

TM: **60** BM: **60** CM: **50** Congr: **3** OrdM: **5** Eld: **2** Deac: **nc** EvgHome: **nc** Mission: **nc** Women Ord: **no** ChurchOrg: **Presbyterian** Off/otherLang: **English** DoctrB: **ApC, NicC, AthC, HeidC, WestConf** Infant or believer's baptism: **both** Frequency of the Lord's Supper: **4 times a year** Close relations with: **Presb Ref Church, Ref Presb Church of North America, Ref Presb Church (Hanover Presbytery)** NatRel: **none** RegRel: **nc** IntlRel: **nc** TheolSchool: **nc** Service infrastructure: **none** Periodicals: **Katartizo (Ref ecumenical/quarterly/500)**

Address: American Presbyterian Church, 1674 Dyre St., Philadelphia, PA 19124-1370, United States, Tel: +1 215 744-7488

3. Associate Reformed Presbyterian Church (ARPC) (3222)

The Associate Reformed Presbyterian Church stems from the 1782 merger in America of the Associate Presb and the Ref Presb. The Associate Synod had been formed by Scottish "Seceders" from the Church of Scotland in 1733, and the Ref Presbytery, the "Covenanters," organized in Scotland in 1743.

A southern synod broke away in 1822, first calling itself the ARPC "of the South." This was later dropped when the northern church merged to become the

United Presbyterian Church of North America in 1858. The ARPC has had strong missions in Pakistan and Mexico, whose churches relate closely to this American-based denomination.

Originally, like the Covenanters, the ARPC sang no hymns, but hymns became optional in 1946. The church still has most of its members in the Southeast, but it has congregations scattered across the country and a few in Canada.

TM: **39,000** BM: **33,500** CM: **33,500** Congr: **225** PStations: **15** OrdM: **220** Eld: **ne** Deac: **ne** EvgHome: **ne** Mission: **57** Women Ord: **yes** As Ministers: **no** as Deac: **yes** as Elders: **no** ChurchOrg: **Presbyterian (elders, presby, General Synod (North America)** Off/otherLang: **English** DoctrB: **WestConf** Infant or believer's baptism: **both** Frequency of the Lord's Supper: **quarterly** NatRel: **none** RegRel: **NAPARC** IntlRel: **ICRC** TheolSchool: **Erskine Theological Seminary** Periodicals: **Associate Reformed Presbyterian Magazine, Faith and Practice Magazine**

Address: Associate Reformed Presbyterian Church (ARPC), 3132 Grace Hill Rd., Columbia, SC 29204-3317, United States, Tel: +1 864 232-8297, Fax: +1 864 271-3729, E-mail: leland@piedmont.net.

4. Association of Covenant Charismatic Churches (3216)

The Association is a body that joins Presb congregations that have added a charismatic element. This group of five congregations celebrates communion weekly and publishes *Chalcedon* for its churches. It also operates three Christian schools.

TM: **600** BM: **600** CM: **600** Congr: **5** PStations: **na** OrdM: **8** Eld: **na** Deac: **20** EvgHome: **1** Mission: **3** Women Ord: **no** ChurchOrg: **na** Off/otherLang: **English** DoctrB: **ApC, NicC, AthC, WestConf, WestCat** Infant or believer's baptism: **both** Frequency of the Lord's Supper: **weekly** NatRel: **none** RegRel: **nc** IntlRel: **none** TheolSchool: **nc** Service infrastructure: **3 Christian schools** Periodicals: **Chalcedon**

Address: Association of Covenant Charismatic Churches, 13320 Lake Magdalene Blvd., Tampa, FL 33618, United States, Tel: +1 813 968-2979, Fax: +1 813 969-3701, E-mail: tampacov@aol.com.

5. Association of Free Reformed Churches (3252)

In 1994 several Ref ministers in Cleveland, Ohio, formed an association for the revival and growth of historic Calvinism. The association provides fellowship for confessionally Ref persons, and seeks to apply the law of God in all spheres of life and to promote the biblical unity of the Body of Christ. Not a denomination, the association has both churches and individuals as members.

No data have been made available.

Address: Association of Free Reformed Churches, P.O. Box 42, c/o *The Christian Statesman*, Geigertown, PA 16526, United States, E-mail: weinwechte@aol.com.

6. Bible Presbyterian Church (3210)

The Bible Presb were first part of the movement that formed the Orthodox Presbyterian Church in 1936. However, leaning in a more fundamentalist direction, the Bible Presb formed a new body in 1938. Carl McIntire led a faction out of this church in 1956 to form the Collingswood Synod. After the other Bible Presb joined the Reformed Presbyterian Evangelical Synod in 1965, this group dropped the name Collingswood Synod. Then, in 1984 McIntire again led a group out of the Bible Presbyterian Church. Those remaining claimed the title "General Synod," while the McIntire group took up the designation "Collingswood Synod" once more.

The Bible Presb were influential in the formation of the American Council of Christian Churches in 1941, in opposition to the National Council of Churches. Under the leadership of Carl McIntire, they also started the International Council of Christian Churches. The agencies of the church operate independently. It trains its leaders at Western Reformed Seminary in Tacoma, Washington.

TM: **3,320** BM: **1,840** CM: **1,840** Congr: 29 PStations: 4 OrdM: **80** Eld: **93** Deac: **50** EvgHome: **0** Mission: **7** Women Ord: **no** ChurchOrg: **Presbyterian (local congr — presby — synod)** Off/otherLang: **English** DoctrB: **ApC, WestConf** Infant or believer's baptism: **both** Frequency of the Lord's Supper: **each congregation decides** Close relations with: **Independent Presb Ch of Mexico, Independent Presb Ch of Kenya, American Council of Christian Churches/World Council of Biblical Churches, Ref Presb Ch, Hanover Presbytery** NatRel: **American Council of Christian Churches (1941) (with an interruption between 1970 and 1984)** RegRel: **nc** IntlRel: **ICCC (1948-84), WCBC (1992)** TheolSchool: **Western Reformed Seminary (Tacoma, Washington)** Service infrastructure: **agencies are mostly independent of denominational control** Periodicals: **Mission Banner (mission/monthly)**

Address: Bible Presbyterian Church, P.O. Box 26164, 5804 Hedgecrest Place, Charlotte, NC 282221-6164, United States, Tel: +1 704 596-9000, E-mail: gsellfpp@Perigee.net.

7. Bible Presbyterian Church (Collingswood Synod) (3241)

Under the leadership of Carl McIntire some churches left the other Bible Presbyterians in 1984.

No data have been made available.

Address: Bible Presbyterian Church (Collingswood Synod), P.O. Box 190, Haddon Ave. and Cuthbert Boulevard, Collingswood, NJ 08108, United States, Tel: +1 609 858-0442

8. Calvin Synod — Conference of United Church of Christ (3243)

Hungarian Ref Christians within the United Church of Christ have a special place, with their own bilingual synod. The first Hungarian-speaking congregation was formed in 1890. New congregations were formed both within the Reformed Church in the US and the Presbyterian Church (US). Attempts to create one Hungarian church, through negotiations with independents and the mother church in Hungary, all failed. By 1924 there were four distinct factions.

One of those agreements was the "Tiffin Agreement" between the RCUS and the Hungarian Reformed Church. In this agreement the Hungarian congregations were given relative autonomy. When the RCUS merged with another church in 1934, the new church recognized the Tiffin Agreement. In 1939 the Hungarian congregations formed a separate synod called the Magyar Synod. Several attempts were made to join with the other Hungarian groups, but none succeeded. In the United Church of Christ, formed in 1956, the synod was renamed the Calvin Synod, after unsuccessful efforts by the UCC to have the Hungarian group integrated. Today the Calvin Synod is the largest group of congregations for ethnic Hungarians. As a synod they maintain separate relations with other Hungarian Reformed churches and preserve a distinctly Calvinistic doctrine.

There is a strong feeling among the Hungarians in the United States that they should be united, and there is cooperation and contact among Hungarian Ref. Together pastors and elders from the several traditions have associations where they meet. A common archive is maintained in Ligonier, Pennsylvania.

TM: **3,800** BM: **4,300** CM: **3,800** Congr: 33 OrdM: **54** Eld: **nc** Deac: **nc** EvgHome: **nc** Mission: **nc** Women Ord: **yes** As Ministers: **6** as Deac: **nc** as Elders: **yes** ChurchOrg: **synod with 4 classes** Off/ otherLang: **English, Hungarian** DoctrB: **ApC, HeidC, HelvC, Calvinistic** Infant or believer's baptism: **both** Frequency of the Lord's Supper: **seven times annually** NatRel: **nc** RegRel: **nc** IntlRel: **Hungarian Reformed World Synod, Hungarian Reformed World Federation** TheolSchool: **nc** Periodicals: **Calvin Synod Herald (gen/bi-monthly/3,000/bilingual)**

Address: Calvin Synod — Conference of United Church of Christ, 493 Amboy Ave., Perth Amboy, NJ 08861, United States, Tel: +1 732 826-3513, Fax: +1 732 826-3513, E-mail: none.

9. Canadian and American Reformed Churches, or American Reformed Church (3028a)

There are three congregations of this denomination in the United States, but it is organizationally part of the Canadian Ref Churches. The name American Reformed Church is used for convenience in the American congregations. (Cf. Canada.)

Address: Canadian and American Reformed Churches, 3179 68th St., Dutton, MI 49316. Tel +1 616 698-6360

10. Christian Presbyterian Church (Korean) (3232)

In 1991 a group of Korean churches left the Christian Reformed Church when it decided to ordain women. Together with several independent churches, the Christian Presbyterian Church was formed.

No data have been made available.

Address: Christian Presbyterian Church (Korean), 4741 N. Glen Arden Ave., Covina, CA 91724, United States, Tel: +1 213 665-0224 or 818 332-9686

11. Christian Reformed Church in North America (CRCNA) (3228)

In 1847 a group of Dutch immigrants who had separated from the national Ref church in The Netherlands settled in Michigan and Iowa. In 1857 they founded the Christian Reformed Church, after delegates returned disappointed from a synod of the Reformed Church in America on the east coast. The church grew with several other waves of immigrants, but it was slow to become americanized. Only after World War I did English become commonly spoken in the churches.

After World War I the church began to expand its views. Foreign missions were started, and a widespread system of Christian day schools were begun, organized by the church community but under parental control. These extended to the tertiary level, with Calvin College being the liberal arts college of the church. In the latter half of this century, four other colleges and one graduate school loosely affiliated with the church's members were set up, three of them in Canada.

Since the 1960s the church has gradually changed its Dutch ethnic character. There are now services in up to 14 languages in congregations across the country. About 5% of the members belong to an ethnic and cultural minority. The church is organized in 46 classes, or regional bodies, although the congregations are more numerous in Michigan, Illinois, and Iowa.

In recent years, there have been challenges to its unity, especially over a 20-year debate on the ordination of women. After several approvals and reversals of women's ordination, a local option was accepted in 1995, but many are still dissatisfied.

The church has an active home mission program, a foreign mission program, an international broadcast ministry, "The Back to God Hour," a relief and development agency, and a publications wing that gives it a strong presence on the American church scene.

TM: **279,000** BM: **104,827** CM: **186,403** Congr: **992** OrdM: **1,524** Eld: **6,300** Deac: **5,500** EvgHome: **62** Mission: **300** Women Ord: **yes** As Ministers: **1995/nc** as Deac: **1984/nc** as Elders: **1995/nc** ChurchOrg: **46 classes and synod** Off/otherLang: **English, Cambodian, Chinese, Korean, Zuni, French, Hmong, Indonesian, Khmer, Navajo, Ojibway, Tagalog, Spanish, Vietnamese** DoctrB: **ApC, NicC, AthC, BelgC, CDort, HeidC** Frequency of the Lord's Supper: **quarterly at least** NatRel: **NAPARC (1975), NAE (1988)** RegRel: **nc** IntlRel: **REC (1946)** TheolSchool: **Calvin Theological Seminary** Periodicals: **The Banner (gen/weekly)**

Address: Christian Reformed Church in North America (CRCNA), 2850 Kalamazoo Avenue S.E., Grand Rapids, MI 49560, United States, Tel: +1 616 246-0744, Fax: +1 616 247-5895, E-mail: Engelhard@crcna.org

12. Conservative Congregational Christian Conference (CCCC) (3229)

The Conservative Congregational Christian Conference (CCCC) was established in 1948 to provide fellowship for ministers of evangelical, congregational churches. Some of its churches are community or Bible churches, while others have an evangelical and Ref tradition with congregational government. Its churches trace their roots to the historic Congregationalism of 16th-century England, or to the Christian Church tradition. Their main partners are evangelicals, being part of the National Association of Evangelicals, and through them the World Evangelical Fellowship. They are also part of the World Evangelical Congregational Fellowship.

The CCCC has no official seminary and encourages the use of evangelical seminaries, but it does have a special relationship with Gordon-Conwell Seminary of South Hamilton, Massachusetts, where CCCC denominational standards are taught.

TM: **39,069** Congr: **224** PStations: **ne** OrdM: **508** Eld: **na** Deac: **ne** EvgHome: **na** Mission: **48** Women Ord: **yes** As Ministers: **1960/3** as Deac: **ne** as Elders: **ne** ChurchOrg: **16 regional fellowships** Off/ otherLang: **English** DoctrB: **ApC, NicC, HeidC, WestConf, CCCC Statement of Faith** Infant or believer's baptism: **both** Frequency of the Lord's Supper: **depends on local congregation** NatRel: **NAE (1951)** RegRel: **ne** IntlRel: **WECF (1984), WEF (1951)** TheolSchool: **none; links with Gordon-Conwell Seminary (Massachusetts)** Service infrastructure: **none** Periodicals: **Foresee (gen/ bi-monthly), Yearbook (statistical info/yearly)**

Address: Conservative Congregational Christian Conference (CCCC), 7582 Currell Boulevard, Ste. #108, Maplewood, MN 55125, United States, Tel: +1 612 739-1474, Fax: +1 612 739-0750, E-mail: cccc4@juno.com.

13. Covenanted Reformed Presbyterian Church (Stellite) (3233)

The Stellite group left the Reformed Presbyterians in 1840. Since then they have gone up and down in numbers, and currently they have too few members to form any more than "society meetings." Like other Ref Presb, they sing only psalms and unaccompanied. They refuse cooperation with any government that does not adopt the true Ref religion, nor will they join any voluntary association outside the church for moral or political reform.

TM: **40** Congr: **ne** OrdM: **ne** Eld: **ne** Deac: **ne** EvgHome: **ne** Mission: **ne** Women Ord: nc ChurchOrg: **Presbyterian ("presently disorganized but conducting society meetings")** Off/otherLang: **English** DoctrB: **ne** Infant or believer's baptism: **both** Frequency of the Lord's Supper: **determined by local congr** NatRel: **ne** RegRel: **ne** IntlRel: **ne** TheolSchool: **WestConf; Auchensaugh Renovation of the Covenant (1712), Act, Testimony and Declaration of 1761** Periodicals: **Original Covenanter and Contending Witness (1993-1996)**

Address: Reformed Presbyterian Church, Covenanted (Stellite), P.O. Box 131, Pottstown, PA 19464, United States, Tel: +1 610 327-9662, E-mail: covie@prolog.net.

14. Cumberland Presbyterian Church (3201)

New experiences on the American frontier led to the formation of this church in 1810. It grew from a revival movement in Kentucky and Tennessee around 1800. Three Tennessee ministers led the organization out of the Presbyterian Church because they rejected the doctrine of election and reprobation found in the Westminster Confession. Also included in their statement of faith is a belief that all infants are saved by Christ. The church grew to almost 200,000 members around the turn of the century. A union with the Presbyterian Church USA in 1906 was only partially successful, and a substantial number continued as the Cumberland Presbyterian Church. Most of the congregations are still found in the American South and in the former border states between South and North. In recent years closer links with the Presbyterian Church (USA) have been established.

TM: **88,066** BM: **88,066** CM: **88,066** Congr: **774** OrdM: **826** Eld: **nc** Deac: **nc** EvgHome: **nc** Mission: **11** Women Ord: **yes** As Ministers: **1889** as Deac: **nc** as Elders: **nc** ChurchOrg: **nc** Off/otherLang: **English** DoctrB: **nc** Infant or believer's baptism: **both** NatRel: **nc** RegRel: **CANAAC** IntlRel: **WARC** TheolSchool: **Bethel College, Memphis Theological College** Periodicals: **The Cumberland Presbyterian, The Missionary Messenger, The Digest**

Address: Cumberland Presbyterian Church, 1978 Union Ave, Memphis, TN 38104, United States, Tel: +1 901 276-4572, Fax: +1 901 276-4578

15. Cumberland Presbyterian Church in America (3207)

Also known as the Second Cumberland Presbyterian Church, this church came into being when a black minister successfully appealed to organize a separate African church, so that blacks could learn self-reliance. The 1869 Assembly granted his request, and in 1874 the first General Assembly of the Colored Cumberland Presbyterian Church was held. The church is still mainly located in the South. A few of its 153 congregations are found in Ohio, Illinois, Iowa, and Texas. The Cumberland PCA publishes a monthly mission magazine, *The Cumberland Flag*. In 1993 the church joined the National Council of Churches.

The church sees as a main challenge the move from addressing the survival of the African-American community to sharing in its reconstruction. It is seriously concerned with human rights issues and with women's partnership with men in the church.

TM: **6,500** BM: **6,500** CM: **6,500** Congr: **143** PStations: **10** OrdM: **205** Eld: **615** Deac: **592** EvgHome: **15** Mission: **0** Women Ord: **yes** As Ministers: **1945/65** as Deac: **1945/100** as Elders: **1945/200** ChurchOrg: **congr, presby, synods, GenAssy** Off/otherLang: **English** DoctrB: **ApC, NicC, WestConf** Infant or believer's baptism: **both** Frequency of the Lord's Supper: **monthly** Close relations with: **Cumberland Presbyterian Church** NatRel: **NCCUSA (1993)** RegRel: **nc** IntlRel: **WARC** TheolSchool: **Memphis Theological Seminary (Memphis, TN)** Service infrastructure: **none** Periodicals: **The Cumberland Flag (mission/monthly/500)**

Address: Cumberland Presbyterian Church in America, 226 Church Street, N.W., Huntsville, AL 35 801, United States, Tel: +1 205 536-7481, Fax: +1 205 536-7482

15a. The Evangelical Covenant Church (3215)

The Evangelical Covenant Church of America finds its roots in the Luth traditions of Sweden. After the German pietist movements, the Swedish Mission Covenant

Church was founded with a Ref emphasis. The Evangelical Covenant Church is made up of immigrants from the Mission Covenant Church and is its sister church in North America. Its main challenge has been the process of emerging from its immigrant roots into an American body. The church emphasizes the personal freedom of its members, and thus acknowledges both the practice of infant baptism and the practice of believer's baptism. It is active in mission (Congo-Kinshasa).

TM: **93,139** Congr: **637** PStations: **ne** OrdM: **1,091** Eld: **ne** Deac: **ne** EvgHome: **ne** Women Ord: **yes** As Ministers: **1996/60** as Deac: **ne** as Elders: **ne** ChurchOrg: **congr, regional conferences, annual Assy** Off/otherLang: **English** DoctrB: **none** Infant or believer's baptism: **both** Frequency of the Lord's Supper: **monthly** NatRel: **nc** RegRel: **Confraternity of Evangelical Covenant Churches (CIPE)** IntlRel: **IFFEC** TheolSchool: **North Park University, North Park Theological Seminary (Chicago, Il); Centro Hispano Estudio Teologico (Bell Garden, CA); Covenant Bible College (Strathmore, AB, Canada)** Service infrastructure: **Swedish Covenant Hospital (Chicago), Emmanuel Medical Center (Turlock, CA); see also under theological schools** Periodicals: **Covenant Companion (monthly), Covenant Quarterly**

Address: The Evangelical Covenant Church, 5101 North Francisco Avenue, Chicago, IL 60625, United States, Tel: +1 773 784-3000, Fax: +1 773 784-4366

16. Evangelical Presbyterian Church (EPC) (3202)

The Evangelical Presbyterian Church was formed by 12 congregations leaving the United Presbyterian Church in the USA (the northern Presb) in 1981. This was just prior to the merger of 1983 that formed the large Presbyterian Church USA. Through aggressive evangelism and church planting, the EPC has grown rapidly to become the fourth-largest Presb body in the country. It also maintains one presbytery in Argentina.

The EPC differs from other conservative Presb by its ordination of women, which it has done since its founding. Its evangelical and irenic spirit is described in its motto: "In essentials, unity; in non-essentials, liberty; in all things, charity."

TM: **57,502** BM: **4,402** *(sic)* CM: **53,100** Congr: **183** OrdM: **420** Eld: **1,127** Deac: **798** EvgHome: **nc** Mission: **56** Women Ord: **yes** As Ministers: **1981/2** as Deac: **1981/683** as Elders: **1981/112** ChurchOrg: **Presbyterian (congreg, presby, GenAssy)** Off/otherLang: **English, Spanish** DoctrB: **ApC, NicC, WestConf, WestCat** Infant or believer's baptism: **both** Frequency of the Lord's Supper: **monthly at least** Close relations with: **Christian Ref Ch, Associate Ref Presb Ch, Association of the Charismatic Presb Churches in Puerto Rico** NatRel: **NAE (1981)** RegRel: **nc** IntlRel: **WEF (1986), WARC (1985)** TheolSchool: **nc** Service infrastructure: **none** Periodicals: **EPC Reflections (2-3 per year/30,000)**

Address: Evangelical Presbyterian Church (EPC), 29140 Buckingham Ave., Ste. #5, Livonia, MI 48154, United States, Tel: +1 313 261-2001, Fax: +1 313 261-3282, E-mail: EPCHURCH @aol.com.

17. Federation of Reformed Churches (3247)

No data have been made available.

Address: Federation of Reformed Churches, P.O. Box 107, Harrisonburg, VA 22801, United States, Tel: +1 540 432-2931

18. Free Church of Scotland (3033a)

This Canadian affiliate of the FCS also has one congregation in Detroit (cf. Canada).

Address: Free Church of Scotland, P.O. Box 977, Montague, PEI COA 1RO, Canada

19. Free Presbyterian Church of North America (Irish) (3234)

Ten congregations affiliated with the Free Presbyterian Church of Ulster form this church. There are also seven mission stations which, with the churches, are found in ten states and three provinces of Canada. The church requires total abstinence from alcohol of members and uses the Authorized King James version.

No statistical data have been made available.

Address: Free Presbyterian Church of North America, 209 N. Newtown Street Road, Newtown Square, PA 19073, United States, Tel: +1 215 353-2309

20. Free Reformed Churches of North America (3220)

Immigrants from the Christian Reformed Churches in The Netherlands formed their own church on this continent. The Dutch mother church dates back to a separation of 1834. The current group is the church that continued under the old name after a merger with Abraham Kuyper's church in 1892. Immigrants from the Dutch church after World War II began to gather in separate congregations. They were first named the Old Christian Reformed Church, but in 1974 they took their present name. Most of the congregations are in Canada, with three in the United States. The church has four publications: *The Messenger* and *The Link* for general readers, and two others for youth and students.

TM: **3,662** CM: **1,870** Congr: **15** OrdM: **13** Eld: **77** Deac: **38** EvgHome: **0** Mission: **1** Women Ord: **no** ChurchOrg: **consistory, synod** Off/otherLang: **English, Dutch** DoctrB: **ApC, NicC, AthC, HeidC, CDort, BelgC** Infant or believer's baptism: **both** Frequency of the Lord's Supper: **4 times a year** Close relations with: **Christelijke Gereformeerde Kerken in the Netherlands** NatRel: **Alliance of Reformed Churches (1989)** RegRel: **nc** IntlRel: **ICRC (1989)** TheolSchool: **nc** Service infrastructure: **none** Periodicals: **The Messenger (gen/monthly/2,000), The Link (3 times a year), The Youth Messenger (youth/bi-monthly), Free Reformed Student Journal (gen/quarterly)**

Address: Free Reformed Churches of North America, 950 Ball Ave. NE, Grand Rapids, MI 49503, United States, Tel: +1 616 456-5910, Fax: +1 616 456-5910

21. Heritage Netherlands Reformed Denominations (3221)

The Netherlands Reformed Congregations divided into two groups in 1992. The Heritage congregations operate a seminary from their largest congregation in Grand Rapids, Michigan. This denomination states that "the Ref and Puritan tradition (which stresses preaching and practical living that is biblical, doctrinal, and experimental) is seriously adhered to." The congregations embrace the Three Forms of Unity (BelgC, HeidC, CDort).

TM: **1,750** BM: **850** CM: **900** Congr: **7** PStations: **3** OrdM: **2** Eld: **25** Deac: **25** EvgHome: **none** Mission: **2** Women Ord: **no** ChurchOrg: **consistories, classes, synod** Off/otherLang: **English** DoctrB: **ApC, NicC, AthC, BelgC, HeidC, CDort** Infant or believer's baptism: **both** Frequency of the Lord's Supper: **4 times a year** Close relations with: ne NatRel: ne RegRel: ne IntlRel: ne TheolSchool: **Puritan Reformed Theological Seminary (same address as below)** Service infrastructure: **Plymouth Christian elementary and high schools (12 and 16 staff, 650 children)** Periodicals: **Banner of Sovereign Grace and Truth (gen/10 times a year/1,7000), Gospel Trumpet Sermons (gen/6 times per year/3,000), Inheritance Publishers Sermons (gen/4 times per year/19,000), Reformation Heritage Books (gen/4 times per year/3,000)**

Address: Heritage Netherlands Reformed Congregations, 2912 Leonard NE, Grand Rapids MI 49525, United States, Tel: +1 616 977-0599, Fax: +1 616 977-0889, E-mail: jrbeeke @aol.com.

22. Hungarian Reformed Church in America (3203)

Mission work by the Reformed Church in Hungary started among Hungarian expatriates in the United States in 1904 and was organized into two classes or districts by 1912. However, after the breakup of the Austro-Hungarian Empire, these were transferred to the Presbyterian Church in the United States in 1921. Three of the original congregations refused the transfer, and they formed the Free Magyar Reformed Church in 1924. The present name was adopted in 1958 (cf. also no. 8).

The church follows the Hungarian model and elects a bishop for its three classes. They hold synods yearly and a "constitutional" meeting every three years.

TM: **10,500** Congr: **29** PStations: **4** OrdM: **39** Eld: nc Deac: nc EvgHome: nc Mission: nc Women Ord: nc ChurchOrg: nc Off/otherLang: **English** DoctrB: nc NatRel: **NCCCUSA** RegRel: nc IntlRel: **WCC** TheolSchool: nc

Address: Hungarian Reformed Church in America, 9 Grove St., Poughkeekpsie, NY 12601, United States, Tel: +1 914 454 5735

23. Korean American Presbyterian Church (KAPC) (3224)

The Korean American Presbyterian Church was formed in 1978 from five independent presbyteries of Korean-immigrant churches. Founded on the campus of Westminster Seminary in Philadelphia, the KAPC considers itself a conservative, doctrinally sound Presb church. In 1996 the church had 19 presbyteries, including some in Canada, Russia, and Europe. The church supports 20 missionaries in other countries.

In 1983 the church joined the National Association of Presb and Ref Churches (NAPARC). It has also established its own seminary in California and accepts ministers from other conservative Ref seminaries after examination.

TM: **33,000** BM: **30,000** CM: **20,000** Congr: **332** PStations: **na** OrdM: **520** Eld: **920** Deac: **1,300** EvgHome: **na** Mission: **20** Women Ord: **no** ChurchOrg: **19 presby, North and South America, Canada, Russia, Europe** Off/otherLang: **Korean** DoctrB: **ApC, WestConf, larger and shorter WestCat** Infant or believer's baptism: **both** Frequency of the Lord's Supper: **4 times a year** Close relations with: **Orthodox Presbyterian Church (OPC)** NatRel: **nc** RegRel: **NAPARC (1983)** IntlRel: **none** TheolSchool: **Reformed Presbyterian Seminary** Periodicals: **none**

Address: Korean American Presbyterian Church, 1901 W. 166th St., USA, Gardena, CA 90247, United States, Tel: +1 310 515-7696, Fax: +1 310 515-2741

24. Korean Presbyterian Church in America (3217)

This body was founded in 1976 with the union of three presbyteries of Korean immigrant churches. These congregations were affiliated with the Presbyterian Church of Korea (TongHap) before deciding to become an independent national body. The church cooperates closely in mission with the Korean Christian Church in Japan and the Presbyterian Church (USA).

TM: **29,000** Congr: **263** OrdM: **nc** Eld: **nc** Deac: **nc** EvgHome: **nc** Mission: **several** Women Ord: **nc** ChurchOrg: **nc** Off/otherLang: **English, Korean** DoctrB: **ApC, WestConf** NatRel: **NCCCUSA** RegRel: **nc** IntlRel: **WARC** TheolSchool: **nc**

Address: Korean Presbyterian Church in America, P.O. Box 457, 280 Fairfield Place, USA, Morganville, NJ 07751, United States, Tel: +1 908 591-2771, Fax: +1 908 591-2260

25. Lithuanian Evangelical Reformed Church (3204)

One congregation of this church is located in North America. It maintains ties with the synod of the Reformed Church in Lithuania. It also has local connections with the Presbytery of Chicago (PCUSA) and with ethnic Lithuanian churches in the Luth Church (Missouri Synod). It publishes a Lithuanian-language periodical, *Musu Sparnai.*

TM: **50** BM: **50** CM: **35** Congr: **1** PStations: **1** OrdM: **1** Eld: **31** Deac: **1** EvgHome: **1** Mission: **1** Women Ord: **yes** As Ministers: **nc** as Deac: **1990/1** as Elders: **1921/30** ChurchOrg: **one congregation in USA, annual synod** Off/otherLang: **Lithuanian** DoctrB: **ApC, HeidC, Calvinism, biblical truth** Infant or believer's baptism: **both** Frequency of the Lord's Supper: **4 times a year** Close relations with: **Lithuanian Ev. Church, Lutheran Churches (Zion — Missouri Synod), Evangelical Lutheran Church in America** NatRel: **nc** RegRel: **CANAAC (1970)** IntlRel: **WCC (1948), WARC (1970)** TheolSchool: **nc** Service infrastructure: **none** Periodicals: **Musu Sparnai (Our Wings)(history and current events in Ref Ch in USA and Lith (2 times a year/500)**

Address: Lietuviu Evangeliku Reformatu Baznycia-JAV, 3542 W. 66th Place, Chicago, IL 60629, United States, Tel: +1 714 951 6820

26. National Association of Congregational Christian Churches (3230)

The NACCC was founded in 1955 by some Congreg Christian Churches that elected not to participate in the merger that created the United Church of Christ. Its member churches are autonomous; the NACCC meets annually, but its regional bodies have no authority over member churches. The NACCC provides four periodicals for its membership, *The Congregationalist* being the general bi-monthly. It has no official doctrinal stance and no national or international ecumenical affiliations. The NACCC reports that its own restructuring is the major challenge facing the association.

TM: **nc** Congr: **426** PStations: **na** OrdM: **629** Eld: **na** Deac: **na** EvgHome: **na** Mission: **14** Women Ord: **yes** As Ministers: **since beginning/nc** as Deac: **since beginning/nc** as Elders: **nc** ChurchOrg: **independent congr, annual meeting** Off/otherLang: **English, Spanish** DoctrB: **none** Infant or believer's baptism: **both** Frequency of the Lord's Supper: **varies among churches** Close relations with: **na** NatRel: **none** RegRel: **none** IntlRel: **none** TheolSchool: **none** Periodicals: **The Congregationalist (gen/bi-monthly), News & Needs Newsletter (mission/monthly), Prayer Journal (spiritual resource/monthly), Congregational Contact (ministerial/monthly)**

Address: National Association of Congregational Christian Churches, P.O. Box 1620, 8473 South Howell Ave., Oak Creek WI 53154, United States, Tel: +1 414 764-1620, Fax: 001 414 764-0319, E-mail: naccc@naccc.org.

27. Netherlands Reformed Congregations (3227)

"Reformed Congregations" were a group that left the Netherlands Reformed Church in 1907. Immigrants from that group joined with some dissident congregations of the Christian Reformed Church who were dissatisfied with the influence of the Dutch church leader and politician, Abraham Kuyper. In a dispute in 1992, six congregations left to form the Heritage Netherlands Reformed Congregations (cf. no. 21).

TM: **4,372** Congr: **8** OrdM: **2** Eld: **nc** Deac: **nc**

Address: Netherlands Reformed Congregations, 1255 Covell Rd. NW, Grand Rapids, MI 49504, United States

28. Orthodox Christian Reformed Churches in North America (3016a)

This group of 14 congregations in Canada and the USA broke away from the Christian Reformed Church in North America beginning in 1979. Of these eight are in Canada and six in the USA. They have about 1,400 members.

TM: **1,399** BM: **603** CM: **796** Congr: **6** OrdM: **13** Eld: **nc** Deac: **nc** EvgHome: **nc** Mission: **nc** Women Ord: **no** ChurchOrg: **classes, synod** Off/otherLang: **English** DoctrB: **ApC, NicC, AthC, HeidC, CDort, BelgC, Calvinist, Ref** Infant or believer's baptism: **both** Frequency of the Lord's Supper: **ev-**

ery second month average NatRel: nc RegRel: **Federation of Orthodox Christian Reformed Churches in USA and Canada (1994)** IntlRel: nc TheolSchool: nc Periodicals: **The Trumpet (gen/ monthly/450)**

Address: Orthodox Christian Reformed Churches, 11243 8th Ave. NW, Grand Rapids, MI 49544, United States, Tel: +1 416 741-6035, Fax: +1 416 743-8861, E-mail: trumpetocr@aol.com.

29. Orthodox Presbyterian Church (OPC) (3209)

The Orthodox Presbyterian Church was formed in 1936 by a group leaving the Presbyterian Church USA. Led by J. Gresham Machen, a professor at Princeton Theological Seminary, a group formed a separate foreign mission society. When they refused to disband, the PCUSA suspended them. They first called themselves the Presbyterian Church in America, but had to change their name in 1938. Westminster Seminary, while always an independent school, had close ties with the OPC in the early days and has had a broad impact on conservative Presb churches, including many foreign churches.

The church is active in foreign and domestic missions, with headquarters near Philadelphia.

Members are found in 13 presbyteries across the USA, but the church is strongest in Pennsylvania, New Jersey, and California.

TM: **22,186** BM: **6,181** CM: **15,074** Congr: **192** PStations: **42** OrdM: **366** Eld: **622** Deac: **547** EvgHome: **36** Mission: **15** Women Ord: **no** ChurchOrg: **13 presby, GenAssy** Off/otherLang: **English, some Spanish** DoctrB: **WestConf, WestCat** Infant or believer's baptism: **both** Frequency of the Lord's Supper: **weekly to quarterly** Close relations with: **ARPC (no. 3), PCA (no. 31), RCUS (no. 37), RPCNA (no. 23), KAPC (no. 42)** NatRel: **none** RegRel: **NAPARC** IntlRel: **ICRC (1993)** TheolSchool: nc Service infrastructure: **medical work in East Africa, Eritrea, Ghinda; Great Commission Publications** Periodicals: **New Horizons in the Orth Presb Ch (gen/10 times a year/ 12,200), Directory of the OPC (yearly/7,500)**

Address: Orthodox Presbyterian Church (OPC), P.O. Box P, 607 N. Easton Road, Bldg. E, Willow Grove, PA 19090-092099, United States, Tel: +1 215 830-0900, Fax: +1 215 830-0350, E-mail: info@opc.org.

30. Presbyterian Church (USA) (3205)

The Presbyterian Church (USA) was created in 1983 through a merger of "Northern" and "Southern" Presb, a division dating back to the Civil War. It is by far the largest Presb body and can therefore lay claim to being the mainstream Presb body.

The Presbyterian Church has been subject to both internal and external divisions throughout its history. The 18th-century revival caused a division between the Old Side and the New Side, with the New Side demanding more understanding of the spiritual needs of the people from its ministers. As Americans moved west and required cooperation with their neighbors, there was also cooperation among frontier churches. Suspicion of the orthodoxy of those new churches led to the division of Old School and New School in 1837. Princeton Seminary, founded in 1812, represented Old School thinking, while Union Theological Seminary in New York was founded by persons of the New School in 1836.

While several groups split off from the mainstream in the 19th and 20th century, there were reunions as well. Each reunion left a remnant that continues today. In 1858 two Presb groups, the Associate Synod and the Associate Reformed Synod, each with independent origins, joined to become the United Presbyterian Church in North America (UPCNA). In 1906 the Presbyterian Church USA reunited with the Cumberland Presb, a frontier breakaway. The PCUSA and the UPCNA joined in 1958 to become the United Presbyterian Church in the USA (USA). The Southern group, officially known as the Presbyterian Church in the United States (PCUS), then merged with the UPCUSA in 1983. That merger created the Presbyterian Church (USA), a national Presbyterian church.

From the 1960s on, the PCUSA has found its numbers in decline. Controversies over the 1983 merger led to a loss of about 800,000 members. The church, however, remains the largest body of the Ref and Presb tradition in the USA. Its people are found across the country, although they are more concentrated in the South and East. About 40% of the members live in the Southern states, the area of the former PCUS. There are strong minority caucuses in the PCUSA. The African-American group is the largest, followed by the Korean Presbyterian Council, which has about 50,000 ethnic Koreans in its congregations.

The PCUSA is strongly ecumenical in outlook. Its predecessors were founding members of both the World Council of Churches and of the World Alliance of Reformed Churches. In 1997 agreement was reached with the Evangelical Lutheran Church in America to have full communion and an exchange of ministers. At present the church seeks to establish closer links with the Cumberland Presbyterian Church (cf. no. 14). Among the main challenges facing this church are mission amid pluralism, theology and sexuality, witness in a materialistic culture, and secularization. There are 14 seminaries affiliated with the PCUSA, including two which have covenant agreements with the General Assembly, one being in Puerto Rico.

TM: **3,644,187** CM: **2,698,262** Congr: **12,685** OrdM: **20,624** Eld: **113,654** Deac: **72,685** EvgHome: **nc** Mission: **nc** Women Ord: **yes** As Ministers: **1956/3,026** as Deac: **1915/48,399** as Elders: **1930/52,941** ChurchOrg: **171 presby in 16 synods, annual GenAssy** Off/otherLang: **English, Korean, Spanish, some other locally** DoctrB: **ApC, NicC, HeidC, HelvC, WestConf, Scots Barmen, Confession of 1967, all in the Book of Confessions** Infant or believer's baptism: **both** Frequency of the Lord's Supper: **monthly to quarterly** Close relations with: **hundreds** NatRel: **NCC, COCU** RegRel: **CANAAC** IntlRel: **WARC, WCC** TheolSchool: **14 theological seminaries** Periodicals: **News Brief (reportage/weekly/25,000), Presb Today (gen/monthly/110,000), Monday Morning (minister/21 times per year/21,000), Horizons (women/10 times per year/20,000), Church & Society (social and justice issues/12 times per year/1,500)**

Address: Presbyterian Church (USA), 100 Witherspoon Street, Louisville, KY 40202, United States, Tel: +1 502 569-5346, Fax: +1 502 569-8039, E-mail: clifton_kirkpatrick@pcusa.org.

31. Presbyterian Church in America (PCA) (3213)

In 1973 conservative members of the Presbyterian Church in the United States, the southern Presb, left to form the Presbyterian Church in America (named the National Presbyterian Church for the first year). They left because they perceived theological liberalism growing in the PCUS. They were wary of merger talks, of ecumenical affiliations, and of pressure to make the ordination of women compulsory for all sectors of the church.

In 1982 the Reformed Presbyterian Church, Evangelical Synod joined the PCA, bringing with it two educational institutions, Covenant College and Covenant Theological Seminary. Additional congregations from the Presbyterian Church (USA) came to the PCA after 1983, when the PCUSA was formed by a merger.

The PCA has its headquarters and agencies located in Atlanta, Georgia. Mission to the world, mission to North America, and Christian education are its main agency work. Pastors are also trained at several independent seminaries, such as Westminster Theological Seminary or Reformed Theological Seminary in Jackson, Mississippi. Membership is strongest in the southern USA, but churches are found across the country and in Canada.

TM: **277,899** BM: **277,899** CM: **218,276** Congr: **1,338** PStations: **na** OrdM: **2,573** Eld: **6,041** Deac: **7,276** EvgHome: **186** Mission: **1,201** Women Ord: **no** ChurchOrg: **Presbyterian (church session, presby, GenAssy)** Off/otherLang: **English, Spanish, Portuguese, Korean, Japanese, Chinese** DoctrB: **ApC, NicC, WestConf** Infant or believer's baptism: **both** Frequency of the Lord's Supper: **according to parish decision** Close relations with: **Associate Ref Presb Church (ARPC), Christian Ref Church (CRC), Orthodox Presb Church, Evangelical Presb Church, Ref Presb Church of North America, Ref Church in the US (RCUS)** NatRel: **NAE** RegRel: **NAPARC** IntlRel: **WFRC** TheolSchool: **Covenant Theological Seminary (St. Louis, MO), Covenant College (Lookout Mountain)** Periodicals: **Equip (educational/bi-monthly), Network (mission/quarterly), Multiply (home missions/3 times per year)**

Address: Presbyterian Church in America, 1852 Century Place, Atlanta, GA 30345, United States, Tel: +1 404 320-3366, Fax: +1 404 320-7964, E-mail: Affirmpca@aol.com or Info @AC.PCA-ATL.Org.

32. Presbyterian Reformed Church (3235)

A presbytery was organized in 1965 under the auspices of Professor John Murray of Westminster Theological Seminary (Philadelphia). The two original congregations had been formed 80 years before by Scottish and Irish immigrants to Canada. The presbytery's constitution, composed by Prof. Murray, preserves the simplicity and purity of the worship set forth in the *Westminster Directory of Public Worship,* and practiced in the founding congregations. This includes canonical psalmody without musical instruments. The presbytery has congregations in Ontario, Rhode Island, Maryland, Iowa, and Oregon.

TM: **178** BM: **69** CM: **114** Congr: **5** Eld: **9** Deac: **2** EvgHome: **nc** Mission: **nc** Women Ord: **no** ChurchOrg: **Presbyterian** Off/otherLang: **English** DoctrB: **WestConf** Infant or believer's baptism:

both NatRel: **nc** RegRel: **nc** IntlRel: **nc** TheolSchool: **nc** Periodicals: **Presbyterian Reformed Magazine (quarterly/500)**

Address: Presbyterian Reformed Church, 2107, 320 St., Madrid, IA 50156, United States, Tel: +1
515 795-3676, Fax: +1 515 795-2130, E-mail: Http://members.aol.com/RSISBELL/
church.html

33. Protestant Reformed Churches in America (PRC) (3219)

In 1924 27 congregations separated from the Christian Reformed Church in North
America in a dispute over the doctrine of common grace. In the early 1950s several of the congregations returned to the Christian Reformed Church. The church
continues today primarily in the Midwest. It has its own seminary and supports
churches in Singapore and New Zealand with a missionary pastor.

TM: **6,291** BM: **2,863** CM: **3,528** Congr: 27 PStations: 2 OrdM: 33 Eld: 130 Deac: 96 EvgHome: **1**
Mission: **2** Women Ord: **no** ChurchOrg: **2 classes (East and West, meeting 2-3 times yearly), 1 synod
(meeting yearly)** Off/otherLang: **English** DoctrB: **ApC, NicC, AthC, BelgC, CDort, HeidC** Infant or
believer's baptism: **both** Frequency of the Lord's Supper: **4 times a year** Close relations with: **Evangelical Ref Churches of Singapore** NatRel: **none** RegRel: **none** IntlRel: **none** TheolSchool: **Prot Reformed Seminary (Grandville, MI)** Periodicals: **The Standard Bearer (religious/semi-monthly/
2,500), Prot Ref (theological journal/semi-annual/850)**

Address: Protestant Reformed Churches in America, 4949 Ivanrest Ave., Grand Rapids MI, 49418,
United States, Tel: +1 616 513-1490, Fax: +1 616 531 3033, E-mail: prc@iserv.net.

34. Puritan Evangelical Church of America (3214)

This single congregation left the Orthodox Presbyterian Church in 1973. It has an
evangelism program. Its music is exclusively psalms, sung without instruments.

TM: **100** CM: **38** Congr: **100** PStations: **1** OrdM: **1** Eld: **nc** Deac: **2** EvgHome: **nc** Mission: **nc** Women
Ord: **no** As Ministers: **nc** as Deac: **nc** as Elders: **nc** ChurchOrg: **Presbyterian government** Off/
otherLang: **English** DoctrB: **Bible: Authorized Version, WestConf** Infant or believer's baptism: **both**
Frequency of the Lord's Supper: **quarterly** Close relations with: **none** NatRel: **none** RegRel: **nc**
IntlRel: **none** TheolSchool: **nc** Periodicals: **Trumpet of Truth (gen/bi-monthy/1,200)**

Address: Puritan Evangelical Church of America, 6374 Potomac Street, San Diego, CA 92139,
United States, Tel: +1 619 479-5053

35. Reformation Presbyterian Church (3237)

This church is made up of a few congregations that left the Presbyterian Church in
America in 1994 and formed their own presbytery.

TM: **64** BM: **64** CM: **34** Congr: **1** PStations: **1** OrdM: **1** Eld: **2** Deac: **2** EvgHome: **ne** Mission: **ne**
Women Ord: **no** ChurchOrg: **presbytery** Off/otherLang: **English** DoctrB: **WestConf** Infant or believer's baptism: **infant** Frequency of the Lord's Supper: **weekly** Periodicals: **Blue Banner (monthly)**

Address: Reformation Presbyterian Church, 8210 Schrade, Rowlett, TX 75088, United States, Tel: +1 972 756 7813 or 972 475 9164, Fax: +1 972 475 5317, E-mail: davese@microsoft.com or pastor@fpcr.org

36. Reformed Church in America (RCA) (3206)

Dutch settlers in New Amsterdam, later New York, created the Reformed Church in America in 1628. One of the oldest churches in the United States, it was known as the Reformed Protestant Dutch Church until 1867. The church remained under the authority of the Amsterdam church until 1776. It was an East Coast church, concentrated in New York and New Jersey, until immigration and migration in the 19th century spread the church across the country. It also has a small group of churches in Canada.

Even today, the RCA reflects that history. The East Coast churches tend to have a more liberal ethos, while the Midwest leans toward the conservative side. The church has two seminaries, in New Jersey and Michigan. While its main offices are in New York, there are also regional offices in the Midwest. It is affiliated with three liberal arts colleges, Hope College in Michigan and Central and Northwestern Colleges in Iowa.

The RCA has never been in a merger, but it is involved in major discussions with other mainline Prot in the United States. It has been active ecumenically, and manages a substantial mission organization.

TM: **312,802** BM: **82,096** CM: **189,338** Congr: **956** OrdM: **1,691** Eld: **na** Deac: **na** EvgHome: **nc** Mission: **100** Women Ord: **yes** As Ministers: **1979/144** as Deac: **197/na** as Elders: **1972/na** ChurchOrg: **congrs, 956 consistories (elders and deacons), 46 classes, 8 regional synods, General Synod (bi-national USA and Canada)** Off/otherLang: **primarily English, also Korean, Taiwanese, Hispanic** DoctrB: **ApC, NicC, AthC, HeidC, CDort, BelgC** Frequency of the Lord's Supper: **monthly to quarterly** NatRel: **NCCUSA** RegRel: **CANAAC** IntlRel: **WCC, WARC, CWM** TheolSchool: **two theological seminaries** Periodicals: **The Church Herald (gen/monthly/140,000)**

Address: Reformed Church in America, 475 Riverside Drive, New York, NY 10115, United States, Tel: +1 212 870-2841, Fax: +1 212 870-2499

37. Reformed Church in the United States (3212)

Early German immigrants organized a congregation of Reformed believers in 1725. They were supported by both the Dutch and eventually the Germans, forming a synod of the German Reformed Church in 1793. In 1934 most of the churches merged with the Evangelical Synod to become the Evangelical and Reformed Church. This body eventually became part of the United Church of Christ. The Eureka classis, in North and South Dakota, refused to join the 1934 merger, and continues today as the Reformed Church in the United States. It has now grown to a synod with four classes in the Dakota area. It sees its main challenge as maintaining a biblically Ref worldview in a secular age.

536

TM: **4,250** BM: **1,065** CM: **3,185** Congr: 38 PStations: 3 OrdM: **40** Eld: **97** Deac: **93** EvgHome: **0** Mission: **0** Women Ord: **no** ChurchOrg: **4 regional classes, 1 synod** Off/otherLang: **English, Spanish** DoctrB: **ApC, NicC, AthC, HeidC, CDort, Three Forms of Unity** Frequency of the Lord's Supper: **4 times a year** Close relations with: **Orth Presb Ch, Ref Presb Ch of North America, Ref Confessing Church in Zaire, Ref Church in the Netherlands, Independent Presb Ch of Mexico** NatRel: **nc** RegRel: **NAPARC (1995)** IntlRel: **ICRC (1991)** TheolSchool: **nc** Service infrastructure: **no institutions** Periodicals: **The Reformed Herald (gen/monthly/2,400)**

Address: Reformed Church in the United States, 5601 Spring Blossom St., Bakersfield, CA 95608, United States, Tel: +1 805 827-9885, E-mail: rcuswalk@lightspeed.net.

38. Reformed Congregational Fellowship (3251)

Formerly known as the General Association of Reformed Congreg, the Reformed Congregational Fellowship is an association of congregations that have taken the Savoy Declaration as the base for their theology. They regard themselves as the only confessionally Ref witness in North America among the Congreg. A fairly new organization, the Fellowship held its third convention in 1997 and was still in the process of creating its organizational structure.

TM: **nc** Congr: **nc** OrdM: **nc** Eld: **nc** Deac: **nc** EvgHome: **nc** Mission: **nc** Women Ord: **no** ChurchOrg: **nongeographical association of confessionally Reformed churches** Off/otherLang: **English** DoctrB: **ApC, NicC, AthC, HeidC, Savoy Declaration, Cambridge Platform** Infant or believer's baptism: **both** NatRel: **nc** RegRel: **nc** IntlRel: **nc** TheolSchool: **nc** Periodicals: **The Reformed Congreg (gen/quarterly/nc)**

Address: Reformed Congregational Fellowship, 208 Auburn Ave. E., Bellefontaine, OH 43311, United States, Tel: +1 937 592-6387

39. Reformed Presbyterian Church in America (3242)

A few congregations in Texas and Georgia are linked in this body with a church in England. Congregations use both psalms and hymns for worship.

Address: Reformed Presbyterian Church in America, P.O. Box 888-022, Dunwoody, GA 30356, United States, Tel: +1 404 396-0965

40. Reformed Presbyterian Church General Assembly (RPCGA) (3225)

This group of 12 congregations in four presbyteries in the USA and Canada rejects all state incorporation and excludes any churches chartered by civil authorities. When the Reformed Presbyterian Church, Evangelical Synod, joined the Presbyterian Church in America in 1983, a group that decided not to go along with the union called themselves the Covenant Presbytery. By 1985 this presbytery had grown to four presbyteries and become the Reformed Presbyterian Church in the United States. In 1990 it changed its name to the RPC in the Americas. Within a year, the four presbyteries of this church were in conflict. One presbytery dissolved, another stood alone as the Hanover Presbytery. In 1991 the remainder reorganized as the RPC (General Assembly).

TM: **360** Congr: **12** OrdM: **25** Eld: **14** Deac: **nc** EvgHome: **nc** Mission: **2** Women Ord: **nc** ChurchOrg: **local session, presby, GenAssy** Off/otherLang: **English** DoctrB: **ApC, NicC, WestConf** Infant or believer's baptism: **both** Frequency of the Lord's Supper: **weekly to monthly** NatRel: **nc** RegRel: **nc** IntlRel: **nc** TheolSchool: **nc** Service infrastructure: **none** Periodicals: **none**

Address: Reformed Presbyterian Church (General Assembly), P.O. Box 2757, Belleview, FL 34421, United States, Tel: +1 352 245-1711, E-mail: reut@pig.net.

41. Reformed Presbyterian Church (Hanover Presbytery) (3239)

Hanover Presbytery consists of three congregations and one mission in Northern Virginia. They trace their roots to the Presbyterian Church (US) and to the Reformed Presbyterian Church (General Assembly). They maintain friendly relations with the Bible Presbyterian Church, the RPC of North America, and the Presbyterian Church in America. The church holds to the original standards of the Westminster Confession and the historic covenants of Scotland. It offers support to the diaspora mission of the Reformed Church in Romania.

TM: **400** Congr: **4** PStations: **1** OrdM: **6** Eld: **5** Deac: **4** EvgHome: **nc** Mission: **1** Women Ord: **no** ChurchOrg: **congr, presby meets annually** Off/otherLang: **English** DoctrB: **WestConf** Infant or believer's baptism: **both** Frequency of the Lord's Supper: **decided upon by each local congr** Close relations with: **Bible Presbyterian Church (USA)** NatRel: **nc** RegRel: **nc** IntlRel: **nc** TheolSchool: **nc** Service infrastructure: **ownership above the congregational level is prohibited** Periodicals: **Christian Observer**

Address: Reformed Presbyterian Church (Hanover Presbytery), P.O. Box 10015, 5928 H Coverdale Way, Alexandria, Virginia 22310-5432, United States, Tel: +1 703 971-9437, E-mail: Elliott@jnpcs.com.

42. Reformed Presbyterian Church of North America (3211)

The Reformed Presb originated in Scotland during the Reformation as the Covenanters, who signed "covenants" in resistance to the king. The first Ref presbytery dates to 1752. They merged with the Associate Presbytery in 1782 (cf. no. 3), but a small group reemerged in 1798. After the 1833 split between Old Light and New Light schools, the New Light branch eventually merged first with Bible Presb in 1965 and then with the Presbyterian Church of America in 1982. The Ref Presb today are the continuation of the Old Light School, incorporating a merger with the Associate Presb Church of North America in 1969.

The Old Light church was marked by its refusal to permit members to vote or participate in public affairs. The restriction was removed in 1964. Today the Ref Presb place special emphasis on the inerrancy of Scripture and the Lordship of Christ in every area of life. They sing no hymns and use no instruments in their worship services. They are Presb in government, but they hold no general assemblies. Geneva College in Beaver Falls, PA, is affiliated with the church. Its membership is concentrated in western Pennsylvania and eastern Kansas.

No statistical data have been made available.

Address: Reformed Presbyterian Church of North America, 7408 Penn Ave., Pittsburgh, PA 15208, United States

43. United Church of Christ (3208)

The United Church of Christ was formed by a merger in 1957 of two churches that were themselves products of church unions. The Congreg Christian Churches came from a 1931 union of Congreg churches, dating from the early days of European settlements, and the Christian Churches, a restorationist movement of the 18th century. The Evangelical and Reformed Church was a 1934 union of two Germanic churches, the German Reformed Church descended from Heidelberg, and a Prussian merger of Luth and Reformed Churches. Thus, with the merger of these two churches, the UCC blended four traditions in one body.

That blending affords the UCC's major challenge. It has to work to maintain an ecumenical and theological identity in its diverse membership. Becoming multiracial and multicultural, while the United States itself becomes more pluralistic, is also a challenge for the UCC. The UCC maintains relations with major Presb and Ref churches. It has full communion with the Christian Church (Disciples of Christ) and with the Evangelical Church of the Union, Germany. In 1997 agreement was reached with the Evangelical Luth Church in America to have full communion and exchange of ministers.

The UCC has an immense network of affiliated institutions. It is related to 306 health and welfare organizations, although these have independent operations. There are also 46 affiliated academies, colleges, and theological seminaries, which also operate independently.

TM: **1,880,940** BM: **1,880,940** CM: **1,501,310** Congr: **nc** OrdM: **10,213** Eld: **nc** Deac: **nc** EvgHome: **nc** Mission: **23** Women Ord: **yes** As Ministers: **1850s/1994** as Deac: **nc** as Elders: **nc** ChurchOrg: **associations, organized geographically, ordain, grant ministerial standing; 39 conferences, organized geographically, provide pastoral care to churches; pastors carry out mission regionally** Off/otherLang: **English, Hispanic** DoctrB: **ApC, NicC, HeidC, Statement of Faith of the UCC (1981)** Infant or believer's baptism: **both** Frequency of the Lord's Supper: **weekly to major church festivals** Close relations with: **communion with the Disciples and the Evangelical Ch of the Union in Germany** NatRel: **NCCUSA (1952), COCU (1962)** RegRel: **CANAAC** IntlRel: **WCC (1948), WARC (1970)** Service infrastructure: **historically related to 306 health and welfare institutions that operate independently; related to 46 academies, colleges, theological seminaries, but not run by the church** Periodicals: **United Church News (gen/monthly), New Conversations (mission/quarterly), PRISM (theol/quarterly), Mercersburg Review (theol/twice a year)**

Address: United Church of Christ, 700 Prospect Avenue, East, Cleveland, OH 44115, United States, Tel: +1 216 736-2121, Fax: +1 216 736-2120, E-mail: ThomasJ@ucc.org or http://www.apk.net/ucc.

44. United Reformed Churches in North America (3250)

The United Reformed Churches in North America was formed in October 1996. It is made up of congregations in Canada and the United States that left the Christian Reformed Church in the early 1990s. The main issue in the split was the decision of the Christian Reformed Church to allow ordination of women. There were also disagreements with Christian Ref decisions on creation and evolution. The United Reformed Churches will seek affiliation with the International Conference of Reformed Churches.

TM: **11,500** Congr: **33** OrdM: **61** Eld: **na** Deac: **na** EvgHome: **1** Mission: **1** Women Ord: **no** ChurchOrg: **consistory, classes, synod** Off/otherLang: **English** DoctrB: **ApC, NicC, AthC, HeidC, DortC, BelgC** Infant or believer's baptism: **both** Frequency of the Lord's Supper: **4 times a year at least** NatRel: **none** RegRel: **none** IntlRel: **ICRC** TheolSchool: **nc** Periodicals: **none**

Address: United Reformed Churches in North America, 3646 193rd Place, USA, Lansing, IL 60438, United States, Tel: +1 718 418-5321, Fax: +1 718 418-5591

45. Upper Cumberland Presbyterian Church (3238)

No data have been made available.

Address: Upper Cumberland Presbyterian Church, 172 Country Road 1564, Cullman, AL 35055, United States

URUGUAY

Area in km²	176,220
Population	(July 1996 est.) 3,238,952 white 88%, mestizo 8%, black 4%
Religions in %	RCath 66%, Prot 2%, Jewish 2%, non-professing or other 30%
Official/other languages	Spanish/Brazilero (Portuguese-Spanish mix on the Brazilian border)

FAIE (Federación Argentina de Iglesias Evangélicas)
FIEU (Federación de Iglesias Evangélicas de Uruguay)

The Ref presence in this country owes principally to immigration from Europe. In 1856 several families belonging to the Waldensian Church in Italy (cf. Italy) arrived in Uruguay and founded, after a brief stay in the region of Florida, the settlement Villa de la Paz, on the eastern coast of the Rio Rosario (Colonia) in 1858.

Due to severe economic conditions in the Waldensian valleys in Italy, more families followed their example. In the beginning, the church was forced to rely on lay leadership. A first pastor (Miguel Morel) arrived in 1860, followed in 1877 by Armand Ugon, who succeeded in formally establishing the church; he also founded, together with a Meth pastor, the United Theological Seminary in Buenos Aires (now ISEDET). New immigrants also established colonies in Argentina (provinces of Santa Fe and Entre Rios) and in the beginning of the 20th century the church in Uruguay began to expand to Argentina (provinces of Buenos Aires and La Pampas). In 1895 the congr in the Rio de Plata region began to hold annual conferences; in 1934 they constituted themselves as the Federation of Waldensian Evangelical Churches in Rio de Plata). Until 1965 the church was an integral part of the Waldensian Church in Italy. Finally, in that year, the church held its own synod for the first time; it considers itself as the "South American branch of the Waldensian Church." In the course of time the church was strengthened by Ref immigrants from other countries. The first Hungarians arrived in 1919, and they became a sizeable group after the Hungarian uprising in 1956.

1. Valdensian Evangelical Church of the River Plate (2110)

TM: **13,685** BM: **13,685** CM: **3,165** Congr: **25** PStations: **96** OrdM: **33** Eld: **44** Deac: **70** EvgHome: **nc** Mission: **nc** Women Ord: **yes** As Ministers: **1971/8** as Deac: **1965/109** as Elders: **1965/40** ChurchOrg: **Reformed (seven regions or presby, 3 in Argentina and 4 in Uruguay, Gen Synod)** Off/otherLang: **Spanish** DoctrB: **ApC, NicC, Valdensian Confession of 1655** Infant or believer's baptism: **both** Frequency of the Lord's Supper: **monthly** Periodicals: **Dialogo (gen/2-monthly/1,000), Singular-Memoria Valdense (history/monthly/500), Pagina Valdense (info/monthly/500)** Close relations with: **Ev. Meth Chs in Uruguay and Argentina, Ref Chs in Argentina, Presb Chs in USA** NatRel: **FIEU (1950), FAIE (1958), United Council for Christian Education (1960), Junta Unida de Missiones (1978), Ecumenical Center of Social Action (1985)** RegRel: **CLAI (1978), AIPRAL (1957), CELADEC (1978), CEVAA (1981)** IntlRel: **WARC (1951), WCC (1948), CEVAA (1981)** TheolSchool: **ISEDET (1884)**

Address: Iglesia Evangélica Valdense de Río de la Plata, Armand Ugón 1488, Colonia Valdense 70202, Uruguay, Tel: +598 55 88794, Fax: +598 55 88110, E-mail: mesaval@adinet .com.uy

2. The Reformed Evangelical Uruguayan-Hungarian Church (2111)

Though diminished in numbers, the Hungarian Ref community continues to exist until today with some 30 members.

Address: Iglesia Evangélica Reformada Uruguayo-Hungara, Calle Gutierrez Ruiz 1289, Piso 9, Montevideo, Uruguay

VANUATU

Area in km²	14,760
Population	(July 1996 est.) 177,504 indigenous Melanesian 94%, French 4%, other (Vietnamese, Chinese, Pacific Islanders) 2%
Religions in %	Presb 36.7%, Angl 15%, RCath 15%, indigenous beliefs 7.6%, Advent 6.2%,
Official/other languages	English and French/pidgin (known as Bislama or Bichelama)

Vanuatu consists of a group of over 80 islands in the South Pacific Ocean. It was called the New Hebrides until 1978, when it gained independence as Vanuatu, an Anglo-French condominium. Its economy is based primarily on subsistence farming, which provides a living for the bulk of the population. Fishing and tourism are the other mainstays of the economy, with 43,000 visitors in 1992. A majority of the population does not have access to a potable and reliable supply of water.

Presbyterian Church of Vanuatu (5050)

The Presbyterian Church of Vanuatu was initially formed as a result of missionary activity by British and Samoan Islander missionaries of the London Missionary Society (LMS) between 1839 and 1848. They prepared the way for Presb from Nova Scotia (Canada), Scotland, Australia, and New Zealand. Among them the two most prominent figures were John Geddie from Nova Scotia, who arrived in 1948, and J. G. Paton, from Scotland. Paton's relatives and descendants later figured as an almost legendary "missionary succession." Expansion of the church from origins in the southern island of Aneityum proceeded in a broadly northern direction and featured the training and local employment of indigenous teachers and pastors who worked under exclusively white mission control until the local church became autonomous in 1948 as the Presbyterian Church in the New Hebrides. The presence of a minority of French Prot in the old condominium and the work of the Paris Evangelical Missionary Society in neighboring New Caledonia to the south led to tentative cooperation with a minority of French-speaking people of Ref background, especially during World War II, mainly in the north of the country, where French RCath Marist missionaries were active.

Missionary personnel and material aid have come largely by way of Australia and New Zealand, though the church's Scots origins have not been forgotten. In the postwar period the church contributed national political leadership and helped to promote the adoption of Bislama, a flexible neo-Melanesian pidgin, as the na-

542

tional language by using it in worship, Bible translation, and internal church business. Vanuatu's Presb leaders have also contributed to ecumenical developments in the Pacific Island.

TM: **57,000** BM: **40,000** CM: **40,000** Congr: **400** PStations: **450** OrdM: **121** Eld: **450** Deac: **40** EvgHome: **100** Mission: **4** Women Ord: **yes** As Ministers: **1991/1** as Deac: **1950/20** as Elders: **1950/30** ChurchOrg: **Presbyterian (sessions, presby, GenAssy)** Off/otherLang: **English, Bislama (in urban areas), local languages and dialects in rural areas** DoctrB: **ApC, WestConf, Statement of faith of the Presb Ch of Vanuatu** Infant or believer's baptism: **both** Frequency of the Lord's Supper: **quarterly** Periodicals: **Vanua Press (gen/monthly/600)** Close relations with: **UCC** NatRel: **Vanuatu Christian Council (1960)** RegRel: **PCC (1966)** IntlRel: **WARC, WCC** TheolSchool: **Pacific Theological College (1966)**

Address: Presbiterian Jyos Blong Vanuatu, P.O. Box 150, Port Vila, Vanuatu, Tel: +678 22722, Fax: +678 26480

VENEZUELA

Area in km²	912,050
Population	(July 1996 est.) 21,983,188 mestizo 67%, white 21%, black 10%, Amerindian 2%
Religions in %	nominally RCath 96%, Prot 2%
Official/other languages	Spanish/native dialects spoken by about 200,000 Amerindians in the remote interior

At the end of the 19th century North American missionaries began work in Venezuela. Theodore S. and Julia H. Pond, who had served for 25 years in Syria, were transferred to Colombia and started work in Caracas in 1897. In 1901 they succeeded in founding the first Presb church in Caracas and in inaugurating, in 1912, the first church building (El Redentor). Strong emphasis was placed on educational work. Several schools were opened. The mission station worked in close collaboration with the American School, which had been started in 1896 by Heraclio Osuna. Meth work had started even earlier (1891). After the departure of the Ponds, the young church went through difficult times. The first presbytery was not inaugurated until 1946. In the years following 1956, work began to expand and new churches were founded (Barquisimeto, Maracaibo, Punto Fijo, Valencia, Maracay, Mérida).

In 1958 several Evangelical churches in Venezuela decided to form the Venezuelan Evangelical Council as a means of exchange and collaboration. The organization grew. Its 25th Assembly was held in Carabobo in November 1997.

1. Presbyterian Church of Venezuela (2120)

Between 1970 and 1985 the Presbyterian Church experienced difficult times. The issues of Pentecostalism and liberation theology created a series of conflicts during which the church lost half of its membership and a whole generation of young ministers. In 1983 a split occurred in the oldest and largest congr (El Redentor). More recently another conflict led to a considerable loss of members.

The church then went through a slow recovery process. In 1991 the National Synod was organized with two presbyteries (Western and Central). Mission became a priority and new churches were founded. In 1997 ecumenical work was started with the Luth and Angl churches.

TM: **897** BM: **200** CM: **697** Congr: **20** PStations: **8** OrdM: **12** Eld: **85** Deac: **50** EvgHome: **nc** Mission: **nc** Women Ord: **yes** As Ministers: **1973/2** as Deac: **1910** as Elders: **1910** ChurchOrg: **Presbyterian, having two presby (one central and one western) and a national synod** Off/otherLang: **Spanish** DoctrB: **ApC, NicC, HeidC, WestConf, HeidC, HelvC, Barmen** Infant or believer's baptism: **both** Frequency of the Lord's Supper: **monthly** NatRel: **CLAI-Venezuela** RegRel: **CELADEC (1975), CLAI (1979), AIPRAL (1974)** IntlRel: **WARC (1952)** TheolSchool: **Great Colombia Seminary (Bogotá), Theological Institute (Caracas)** Periodicals: **El Presbiteriano (gen/3 times per year/500)**

Address: Iglesia Presbiteriana de Venezuela, Apartado 75396, Synod Office: Colegio Americano, Caracas 1070-A, Venezuela, Tel: +58 2 930-808, Fax: +58 2 943-3529

2. Presbyterian Church El Redentor (2122)

In 1983 the major part of the largest congr, El Redentor in Caracas, decided to withdraw from the presbytery. Without changing the name Presb, it became, in fact, Pentecostal. Some 60 members of the church did not follow the move and formed a new congr, Principe de Paz. The Presb Church El Redentor went through troubled times but continued to grow and today has two congr and a school functioning in the church building.

No other information has been made available.

Address: Presbyterian Church El Redentor, Carcel a Monzón — Plaza La Concordia, Caracas 1010, Venezuela, Tel: +58 2 484-9283 and 484-9284, Fax: +58 2 484-9282

3. Reformed Faith Christian Church (2121)

The existence of this church is due to the initiative of Pastor César Rodriguez, who discovered the Ref faith in 1984 and decided, together with two friends, to found a Ref church in Barquisimeto on a strictly confessional basis.

TM: **145** BM: **63** CM: **98** Congr: **3** PStations: **2** OrdM: **7** Eld: **7** Deac: **9** EvgHome: **1** Mission: **nc** Women Ord: **yes** As Ministers: **no** as Deac: **1988/6** as Elders: **no** ChurchOrg: **local council, national council** Off/otherLang: **Spanish** DoctrB: **ApC, HeidC, WestConf, CDort** Frequency of the Lord's Supper: **monthly** Close relations with: **Gereformeerde Kerken (Liberated) in the Netherlands** NatRel: **nc** RegRel: **nc** IntlRel: **nc** TheolSchool: **nc**

Address: Iglesia Cristiana de Fe Reformada, Apartado 609, Carrera 19 c/calle 16, Barquisimeto, Edo.
Lara 3001, Venezuela, Tel: +58 51 514-414, Fax: +58 51 514-414

VIETNAM

Area in km²	329,560
Population	(est. July 1996) 73,976,973 Vietnamese 85%-90%, Chinese 3%, Muong, Thai, Meo, Khmer, Man, Cham
Religions in %	Buddhist (est. 80%), Taoist, indigenous beliefs, Islam, RCath (est. 6-10%), Prot (0.8%)
Official/other languages	Vietnamese, French, Chinese, English, Khmer, tribal languages (Mon-Khmer and Malayo-Polynesian)

From 1528 to 1788 Vietnam was divided into two parts: the North was ruled by the Trinh and the South by the Nguyen. After a period of Chinese occupation in the North, the Nguyen dynasty ruled from 1802 to 1945. In 1867, however, French colonial rule began reducing the Nguyen emperors to vassals of France. In protest against the French, Ho Chi Minh (1890-1969) proclaimed the Democratic Republic of Vietnam in 1945. It led to the first Indochina War, which ended in 1954 with the defeat and the withdrawal of the French and led to the division of the country into North and South. The North was ruled by Ho Chi Minh's Vietminh, the South by the anti-Communist regime of Diem, who had the support of the USA. A national liberation front (Vietcong) sought the reunification of the country. The tensions resulting from the conflict led to the second Indochina War (1965-1973) between the Vietcong and the USA. It took a high toll of lives and ended with the withdrawal of the US troops. In 1975 the army of the North conquered Saigon, now Hô Chi Minh City, and in 1976 the country was unified under the Communist regime of the North.

Through the Chinese influence of the Han (2nd century B.C. to 2nd century A.D.) Confucianism was introduced as the state philosophy. Though traditional beliefs survived, it left deep marks on the culture of the country. From the first century A.D. Mahayana Buddhism was increasingly adopted by the people; its influence reached its height in the 10th century. Confucianism was restored in 1802 and remains a major cultural factor until today.

Christianity was brought into the country through the work of Franciscan missionaries from the Philippines in 1580, followed by Jesuits in 1680. Leading Jesuit missionaries advocated a policy of adaptation to traditional culture. Among them, Alexandre de Rhodes, with the help of Vietnamese catechists, conceived the present alphabet. Under French colonial rule, the church, despite severe persecutions, grew at a rate of 2% annually. Hardships continued in the period of the Communist regime. But the church continued to grow both in the North and especially in the South. Growth was mainly in rural areas. Before the fall of Saigon, there had been villages that were entirely RCath. The church remained largely traditionalist, relying on old manuals, and was hardly influenced by Vatican II. In 1975, ties with the Holy See were severed.

Although two Christian and Missionary Alliance (CMA) missionaries visited the North from China in 1895, it was not until 1911 that permission was granted by the French authorities to begin a mission in Da Nang. Success was almost immediate and included influential members of the community. In 1927 the CMA granted the church autonomy, and two years later governmental restrictions on the expansion of the church were withdrawn. Work among tribal peoples (especially the Raday and Koho) of the south-central highlands was initiated in 1934. Theological training has been provided by the Bible and Theological Institute in Nhatrang, which offered a degree program after 1969; Bible institutes have also been active at Dalat and Ban Me Thuot.

Evangelical Churches of Vietnam (Hoi Thánh Tin Lành) (4550)

The Evangelical Church, which has grown out of the missionary efforts of the CMA, has roots throughout the country. Its structure is congregationalist. The individual congregations enjoy considerable autonomy, and there is, at the national level, no synodal authority. Two leaders, one in the North and one in the South, are regarded as spokespersons for the church: Pasteur Hoang Kim Phuc for the North and Pasteur Nguyen Van Quan for the South.

The church is far more numerous in the South than in the North. In the North the church is served by some 25 pastors. Most churches hold evangelistic meetings on Thursdays in addition to the two Sunday worship services. Training classes for new Christians are held for periods of 6 to 8 weeks. Pastors receive their support entirely from their congregations. The seminary was briefly closed because of destruction caused by American bombing, but it was reopened in 1973 (Bible and Theological Institute in Nhatrang). In 1972 contact was made with the National Council of Churches of Christ in the USA, at which time the Vietnamese Prot leaders expressed criticism of America's role in the war. Similar contacts were made with the World Council of Churches in 1973, which resulted in the initiation of aid grants through the WCC to the church.

In 1954 many Christians moved to the South, and new foreign missions, as well as a number of other church-related organizations, entered the country. In 1973 there were 23 foreign missions and agencies with some 275 foreign mission personnel in South Vietnam. Eighteen other foreign missions and agencies provided support but no personnel. As a result of the fall of the Thieu regime in 1975, organized Prot churches and agencies were largely dispersed, and many Prot, including many pastors of the Evangelical Church, left Vietnam as refugees. Some particularly enterprising Vietnamese Christian converts, who became economically affluent, went back and started new churches in Vietnam — both in the North and the South. Today there are in the South about 1,000 local communities served by some 400 pastors; in addition, there are about 1,000 deacons who often fulfill pastoral functions. There are in the region of Hô Chi Minh City alone about 40 communities with 40 pastors and 55 deacons.

In addition to the Evangelical Church of Vietnam, a total of 10 small indigenous groupings, according to some sources, have been established by Vietnamese Christians independent of Western foreign missions. These include small independent denominations formed during the 1960s. Among these are the Church of God and Vietnam Christ's Church (224 Phan Dang Luu, Ho Chi Minh); the latter is the result of a schism in the Evangelical Church in 1964.

Address for the North:
> Hoi Thán Tin Lành, sõ 2, rue Ngo Tram, Hanoi, Vietnam, Tel: +84 8 256-742

Address for the South:
> Hoi Thán Tin Lành, 386 Diên Biên Phu, Quân 3, TP Ho Chi Minh, Viet Nam

---

WESTERN SAMOA

Area in km²	2,860
Population	(July 1996 est.) 214,384 Samoan 92.6%, Euronesians 7% (persons of European and Polynesian blood), Europeans 0.4%
Religions in %	Christian 99.7% (about one-half of population associated with the London Missionary Society; including Congreg), RCath, Meth, Mormons, Advent
Official/other languages	Samoan (Polynesian), English

Western Samoa is made up of a group of islands located in the South Pacific Ocean. Its agriculture employs more than one-half of the labor force, contributes 50% to the GDP, and furnishes 90% of exports. The bulk of export earnings comes from the sale of coconut oil and copra. The economy depends on emigrant remittances and foreign aid to supplement the GDP. It has been independent from a New Zealand-administered UN trusteeship since January 1, 1962.

1. Congregational Christian Church in Samoa (CCCS) (5040)

The majority Congregational Christian Church in Western Samoa began with the arrival in 1830 of John Williams of the London Missionary Society (LMS), which stationed Islander missionaries from Tahiti and the Cook Islands in both eastern and western Samoa. Substantial institutions and village churches were established. At

Malua, on the island of Upoliu, Islander missionaries were trained and sent from there to work on other Pacific islands such as Tuvalu, Niué, Kiribati, and Vanuatu.

The church grew under successive periods of colonial influence: British up to about 1900, German until World War I, New Zealand administration under League of Nations, and UN mandates until independence in 1962. The CCCS developed its own constitution in stages beginning in 1928. The church was called the LMS church until 1962, when it took its present name. The CCCS remained intact until 1980, when delegates to the General Assembly from the two large eastern islands separated to form the Church of Tutuila and Manua, now called the Congregational Christian Church of American Samoa (CCCAS) (cf. American Samoa). Discussions are still proceeding to seek a formula for eventual reunion.

TM: **70,000** BM: **70,000** CM: **32,000** Congr: **285** PStations: **285** OrdM: **335** Eld: **75** Deac: **10,000** EvgHome: **200** Mission: **20** Women Ord: **no** ChurchOrg: **districts, sub-districts, parishes/congregations, all administered by the GenAssy as supreme Council of the church** Off/otherLang: **Samoan, English (second language)** DoctrB: **ApC, NicC, AthC, WestConf** Infant or believer's baptism: **infant** Frequency of the Lord's Supper: **monthly** Periodicals: **O le sulu Samoa (gen/monthly/1,000)** Close relations with: **nc** NatRel: **National Council of Churches of Western Samoa (1964)** RegRel: **PCC (1961)** IntlRel: **WCC (1962), CWM (1977)** TheolSchool: **Malua Theological College**

Address: Ekalesia Fa'apotopotoga Kerisinao I Samoa (EFKS), P.O. Box 468, Vaea Street, Apia, Western Samoa, Tel: +685 22279, Fax: +685 20429

2. Apia Protestant Church (5042)

Since 1849 there has been a church in Apia providing services in the English language. The congregation was first created largely to meet the needs of the many seamen who visited Apia in the middle of the 19th century. The local LMS missionary conducted worship over decades in the tin chapel, "Apia Seamen's Church," erected in 1849. Over the years the whaling fleets moved northward, and fewer seamen came to Apia.

Since 1860 the group which evolved first as the "English Church," then as the Apia Protestant (1895) Church, has met the needs of expatriates in western Samoa. The present church, built in 1895, functions as a trans-denominational center of worship and affiliation, largely for expatriates whose mother tongue is other than Samoan. During the German period (1900-1917) German residents availed themselves of its ministries. The ministers used to come from the LMS. The link continued after 1962, although, more recently, the CCCS has provided a minister. Worship, preaching services, and pastoral care are along lines familiar in the CCCS. Transients, tourists, and residents of other Prot church background usually choose the Apia church.

TM: **102** BM: **nc** CM: **102** Congr: **1** PStations: **1** OrdM: **1** Eld: **na** Deac: **13** EvgHome: **na** Mission: **ne** Women Ord: **yes** As Ministers: **no** as Deac: **1985/4** as Elders: **no** ChurchOrg: **nc** Off/otherLang: **English** DoctrB: **ApC** Infant or believer's baptism: **both** Frequency of the Lord's Supper: **monthly** Periodicals: **none** Close relations with: **nc** NatRel: **Samoa Council of Churches (1994)** RegRel: **nc** IntlRel: **none** TheolSchool: **nc.**

Address: Apia Protestant Church, P.O. Box 1852, Apia, Western Samoa, Tel: +685 21401, Fax: +685 21401

YUGOSLAVIA

Area in km²	Due to the events of the last few years the size of the pop and of the surface of the country is difficult to establish.
Religions in %	The majority religion is the Orthodox faith, though the areas where the Reformed Church has its roots (Baranja and Vojvodina) are confessionally mixed

Reformed Christian Church in Yugoslavia (6470)

Up to the end of World War I the Reformed Church of Yugoslavia was part of the Reformed Church of Hungary.

In the 16th century Michael Sztáray, one of the earliest Hungarian Reformers, was active in the Baranja. When in 1920, after World War I, areas in the South of the Austrian-Hungarian Empire were given to the kingdom of Yugoslavia, the Reformed Christian Church in Yugoslavia was formed (1933). At that time it also included several German-speaking congr among farmers who had immigrated in the 18th century from the south of Germany, and also a congr in Belgrade. After World War II the German-speaking population had to leave Yugoslavia. The church suffered much hardship during the Communist regime. Its membership diminished because of emigration to Hungary and to other countries. The wars which followed the collapse of Communism at the end of the 1980s also created a new situation for the church. The congr in the territory of Croatia established themselves as a separate Reformed Christian Church in Croatia (cf. Croatia). With the massive immigration of Serbian refugees into the Vojvodina, the situation of the Hungarian-speaking minority became precarious and many decided to leave the country.

TM: **17,000** BM: **16,500** CM: **12,000** Congr: **15** PStations: **24** OrdM: **13** Eld: **350** Deac: **0** EvgHome: **none** Mission: **none** Women Ord: **yes** As Ministers: **1982/4** as Deac: **none** as Elders: **1970/65** ChurchOrg: **Synodal (congr, distr, synod)** Off/otherLang: **Hungarian, Czech** DoctrB: **ApC, AthC, HeidC, HelvC** Infant or believer's baptism: **both** Frequency of the Lord's Supper: **5-6 times per year** Periodicals: **Református Elet (gen/weekly/2,200), Reformatus Evkönyv (almanac/annual/3,500)** Close relations with: **Luth, Meth, Serbian, Orthodox church** NatRel: **Yugoslav Ecumenical Council** RegRel: **nc** IntlRel: **WARC (1875), WCC (1948)** TheolSchool: **none**

Address: Reformatska hrisccanska crkva u SRJ, Ul. Bratstva 26, YU-24, 323 Feketic, Yugoslavia, Tel: +381 24 738-070, Fax: +381 24 738-070

ZAÏRE — See CONGO-KINSHASA

ZAMBIA

Area in km²	752,610
Population	(July 1996 est.) 9,159,072 African 98.7%, European 1.1%, other 0.2%
Religions in %	Christian 72% (RCath 42%, Jehovah's Witnesses 21%, Prot 15%, African Independent 14%, Angl 2%, Neo-Apostolic 2%, others 4%), African rel 27%, Hindu and Muslim 1%.
Official/other languages	English (official), major vernaculars — Bemba, Kaonda, Lozi, Lunda, Luvale, Nyanja, Tonga, and about 70 other indigenous languages

CCZ (Christian Council of Zambia)
EFZ (Evangelical Fellowship of Zambia)

For a long period (1870-1924), Zambia, formerly Northern Rhodesia, was governed on behalf of the British Crown by the British South Africa Company of Cecil Rhodes (1853-1902). In 1924 the country became a British Protectorate; under the leadership of the United National Independence Party (UNIP) of Kenneth D. Kaunda, it gained independence in 1964. During the next 27 years it was ruled by UNIP, the state party. The official doctrine was Zambian humanism with three roots — traditional African beliefs, Christianity, and Socialism. In 1991 the Movement for Multiparty Democracy of Frederick Chiluba won the election. Despite its rich resources (copper, agriculture) Zambia is one of the poorest countries of the world. A relatively high percentage of the population lives in the cities, especially Lusaka.

Christianity reached Zambia toward the end of the 19th century. The first Christian missions were the Paris Mission (1877) and the LMS (1883). They were followed by the Presb (1894), the Primitive Methodists (1894), the White Fathers (1895), and the Dutch Reformed mission from South Africa (1899). A number of other churches started work in the 20th century — in particular, the Wesleyan Methodists, the Advent, the Salvation Army, the Brethren, the Church of Christ, and the Angl. The Watchtower Movement, which started in 1911, found a particularly favorable response in the population; while it had, in the beginning, a specifically African character, it is today firmly part of the international organization of Jehovah's Witnesses.

1. United Church of Zambia (UCZ) (1251)

This church is the result of a union of four churches effected in 1965, less than three months after Independence: the Church of Central Africa in Rhodesia (itself a union of the Church of Scotland and the LMS Churches with the Union Church of the Copperbelt), the congregations of the Copperbelt Free Church Council, the Church of Barotseland, and the Meth Church. It is the largest Protestant Church in Zambia.

The components of the United Church of Zambia are the following. In the plains of the Zambesi, in the west of the country, the Paris Mission, with the active participation of people from Lesotho, had started work in 1885. The beginnings were rough. The first group of missionaries, under the leadership of François Coillard, was arrested and mistreated. This mission worked among the Lozi. In 1964, under the name Evangelical Church of Barotseland, the church became independent. In the North the LMS and later the Presbyterians started missionary work. The first LMS station was established in Niamkolo among the Lungu. In 1894 a Scottish missionary, Alexander Dewar, and a Tonga Christian, John Banda, came over from Malawi and began work at Mwenzo near the Tanzanian border. In the early years of the 20th century teams of students from Malawi were making evangelistic journeys into Zambia, among them David Julizya Kaunda, the father of Kenneth Kaunda; he founded the Lubwa mission station. Since 1894 the Methodists have been active in the center of the country among the Ila. In 1920, when copper began to be mined, a mission church was formed among the workers in the Copperbelt. In the '30s the United Missions in the Copperbelt (UMCB) was formed in which both the Presb and the LMS were involved. For a long time Presb and LMS had been in close contact. In 1945 they formed, together with the union churches on the Copperbelt, the Church of Central Africa in Rhodesia (CCAR). In 1958 the Central Free Church Council, which coordinated seven European congregations in the Copperbelt, merged with the CCAR; its name was changed to United Church of Central Africa in Rhodesia. In the following years negotiations began with the Methodists and the Church of Barotseland. In 1965 the United Church of Zambia was inaugurated. The church comprises several tribes — from the Bemba in the northeast to the Lozi in the west.

TM: **1,000,000** CM: **250,000** Congr: **1,200** OrdM: **148** Eld: **nc** Deac: **nc** EvgHome: **nc** Mission: **3** Women Ord: **yes** As Ministers: **1968/15** as Deac: **nc** as Elders: **nc** ChurchOrg: **sections, congr, consistories, 9 presby, 1 synod** Off/otherLang: **English, Zambian languages like Bemba, Nyanja, Tonga, Lozi** DoctrB: **ApC, NicC** Infant or believer's baptism: **both** Frequency of the Lord's Supper: **monthly** Close relations with: **Church of Scotland, Meth Church (UK), URC (UK), Presb Church (USA), United Church of Canada** NatRel: **CCZ** RegRel: **nc** IntlRel: **WCC, CWM, WARC, CEEVA** TheolSchool: **nc** Service infrastructure: **1 hospital, 2 health centers, 3 secondary schools, some kindergartens, Lilelelo youth project, farm college**

Address: United Church of Zambia (UCZ), P.O. Box 50122, Nationalist Road at Burma Road — Ridgeway, Lusaka, Zambia, Tel: +260 1 250-641, Fax: +260 1 252-198, E-mail: uczsynod @zamnet.zm.

2. Church of Central Africa Presbyterian (CCAP) — Synod of Zambia (1252)

This church is closely related to the Church of Central Africa Presbyterian in Malawi (cf. Malawi). It is one of the five synods of this church. The work of the Livingstonia Synod in Malawi extended across the border into today's Zambia. Once the national borders were firmly delineated and Zambia and Malawi became countries, those mission stations and the Christian communities surrounding them, which had been founded inside Zambia — Mwenzo, Lubwa, and Chitambo — under missionary leadership at the time, all became part of the United Church of Central Africa in Rhodesia and later the United Church of Zambia. However, the group of congregations around Lundazi which looked toward the mission station in Malawi, formerly called Louden and now named Embangweni, were cut off from the United Church of Zambia, which had no work in the Eastern Province; they continued their own church life linked with the Synod of Livingstonia. This group has now spread, connecting with other Malawian exiles in the Copper Belt and in Lusaka, and has constituted itself as a synod of the CCAP.

TM: **20,000** Congr: **29** OrdM: **18** Eld: **nc** Deac: **nc** EvgHome: **nc** Mission: **nc** Women Ord: **nc** ChurchOrg: **Synod meets every second year** Off/otherLang: **nc** DoctrB: **Gallican Confession, Scots Confession, BelgC, 39 Articles, CDort, WestConf** NatRel: **CCZ, Evangelical Fellowship of Zambia** RegRel: **SAARC** IntlRel: **REC (1997)** TheolSchool: **Zomba Theological College (Malawi), Justo Mwale Theological College (Zambia)**

Address: Church of Central Africa Presbyterian (CCAP) — Synod of Zambia, P.O. Box 530019, Lundazi, Zambia

3. Reformed Church in Zambia (1250)

The history of this church started in 1898 when a native evangelist started to preach the Gospel among the Ngoni of Chief Mpezeni around Chipata in today's Zambia. Stimulated by this witness, Chief Mpezeni invited missionaries to come to his country. In 1899 a group of Dutch Ref missionaries from South Africa settled in Magwero. Gradually the mission extended westward. In 1929 the first African minister, Justo Mwale, was ordained. In 1943 the church was constituted as the African Reformed Church, but leadership remained in the hands of white missionaries. The first African moderator was elected in 1961. Complete autonomy (Umwini) was granted in 1966, and two years later the church changed its name to Reformed Church in Zambia (RCZ). As a church depending on South Africa, the RCZ was in a delicate situation. In 1971 the moderator declared: "The RCZ is an indigenous church although it originated in South Africa; apartheid is not our inheritance." In 1989 the church threatened to sever ties with the Dutch Reformed Church if it did not change its attitude to apartheid, and in 1991 relations were suspended.

TM: **500,000** BM: **400,000** CM: **290,000** Congr: **145** PStations: **1,450** OrdM: **110** Eld: **1,450** Deac: **1,400** EvgHome: **10** Mission: **0** Women Ord: **yes** As Ministers: **no** as Deac: **1989/30** as Elders: **no**

ChurchOrg: **Presbyterian (congr, 14 presby, national synod every second year)** Off/otherLang:
ChiNyanja (Chew, Nsenga, Ngoni), Chchewa, English DoctrB: **ApC, NicC, HeidC, CDort** Infant
or believer's baptism: **both** Frequency of the Lord's Supper: **4 times a year** Close relations with:
Dutch Reformed Church — Orange County (NGK), Ref Churches of the Netherlands (RCN)
NatRel: **CCZ (1976), EFZ (1977), Bible Society of Zambia** RegRel: **SAARC (1989), AACC (1980s)**
IntlRel: **REC (1971), WARC (1970s), WCC (1991)** TheolSchool: **Justo Mwale Theological College
and two lay training centers** Service infrastructure: **2 hospitals, 1 secondary school, lay training
center** Periodicals: **Dziwani Magazine (monthly)**

Address: Reformed Church in Zambia, P.O. Box 32301, Synod Office, Lusaka, Zambia, Tel: +260 1
231-206, Fax: +260 1 252-651

ZIMBABWE

Area in km²	390,580
Population	(July 1996 est.) 11,271,314 African 98% (Shona 71%, Ndebele 16%, other 11%), white 1%, mixed and Asian 1%
Religions in %	syncretistic (partly Christian, partly indigenous beliefs) 37%, Christian 60% (RCath 12%, Prot and Ev. 40%, Angl, Meth, and Luth 8%), Muslim and other 3%
Official/other languages	English/Shona, Sindebele (also called Ndebele), numer- ous but minor tribal dialects

EFZ (Evangelical Fellowship of Zimbabwe)
ZCC (Zimbabwe Council of Churches)

In Zimbabwe, between the 11th and 15th centuries there was a powerful trading
society. The ruins of Great Zimbabwe, which means "stone building," remain near
Masvingo. The main tribe were the Shona. In the 18th century the Ndebele invaded the country. In 1889 the country was claimed by the British South Africa
Company, and in 1923 it became a colony of the British Crown. From 1953 to
1963 Southern Rhodesia, as it was then called, was, together with Northern Rhodesia (today Zambia) and Nyasaland (today Malawi), part of the Federation of
Rhodesia and Nyasaland. After protracted conflicts it gained independence in
1980. Zimbabwe is rich in resources (coal and iron) and is rather strongly industrialized; it has the largest production of tobacco in Africa. Since independence, the
presidency has been held by Robert G. Mugabe.

The first missionary efforts were undertaken in the 16th century by Portuguese Jesuits. After initial successes Christianity declined again. Until the end of
the 19th century the Christian message found no lasting response. The Ndebele
War of 1893 and the revolts of the Ndebele and Shona in 1896/97 against the colonial regime accelerated missionary efforts because of the increased support the

mission received from the state after these events. The oldest and, today, largest church in Zimbabwe is the RCath Church (1879). The Angl Church was established in 1891 and functioned until independence as the official church. The Meth Church and the Salvation Army started in the same year, and the Luth Church followed in 1903, mainly through the initiative of the Berlin Missionary Society and Church of Sweden. The earliest Ref missionary effort came in 1859 from the LMS. Other Ref groups followed: the Dutch Reformed Church (Cape Synod) in 1891; the ABCFM at Mount Silinda on the eastern border of the country in 1893; the South African General Mission in Rusitu also on the eastern border in 1897; the Presbyterian Church of Southern Africa in Bulawayo in 1898; and the Churches of Christ in Bulawayo and later Dadaya in the Lundi Reserve in 1898.

The Zimbabwe Council of Churches (ZCC) includes in its membership 20 Christian churches.

1. United Congregational Church of Southern Africa (1265)

This church grew out of LMS work initiated in 1859 in Matabeleland under the leadership of the pioneer missionary Robert Moffat. Mission stations were established in Inyati (1859) and Hope Fountain (1870). For many years the efforts seemed to be in vain. Until 1880 no converts were won. The first baptisms took place in the 1880s. During the war of 1893 the two stations were destroyed twice (1893 and 1896/97). After the second war the young church began to grow and educational work developed greatly. By 1927 the church had 2,276 members.

TM: **16,000** BM: **11,000** CM: **11,000** Congr: **10** PStations: **157** OrdM: **10** Eld: **450** Deac: **300** EvgHome: **27** Mission: **0** Women Ord: **yes** As Ministers: **1989/2** as Deac: **1967/200** as Elders: **1967/300** ChurchOrg: **local churches, synod** Off/otherLang: **Ndebele, English in two parishes** DoctrB: **ApC, NicC** Infant or believer's baptism: **both** Frequency of the Lord's Supper: **monthly if possible** Close relations with: **Presbyterian Ch and Ref Ch in Zimbabwe** NatRel: **ZCC, Christian Care** RegRel: **AACC** IntlRel: **WARC, WCC, CWM (through United Congr Church in Southern Africa)** TheolSchool: **United Theological College (Harare)** Service infrastructure: **1 clinic** Periodicals: **Uhambolokukholwa**

Address: United Congregational Church of Southern Africa (Ndebele), P.O. Box 2451, 40 Jason Moyo Street, Bulawayo, Zimbabwe, Tel: +263 9 64935, Fax: +263 9 64935

2. Reformed Church in Zimbabwe (1260)

In 1891, a missionary sent by the Cape Synod of the Dutch Reformed Church in South Africa, Andrew A. Louw, began work among the Shona and established, with the help of African workers, several mission posts in the country (Morgenster, Gutu, Alheit, Makumba, etc.). Later the work expanded among the Nyanja. The church has a strong commitment to evangelism. In 1995 a new center was opened in Dete, and in 1996 another one in Binga among the Tonga people.

TM: **80,000** Congr: **41** PStations: **150** OrdM: **48** Eld: **600** Deac: **130** EvgHome: **12** Mission: **ne** Women

Ord: **yes** As Ministers: **ne** as Deac: **1984/120** as Elders: **1984/160** ChurchOrg: **congr, presby, synod** Off/otherLang: **Shona and English** DoctrB: **ApC, NicC, AthC, HeidC, CDort, Bible creeds** Infant or believer's baptism: **both** Frequency of the Lord's Supper: **six times a year** Close relations with: **CCAP, DRC** NatRel: **ZCC (1982), EFZ** RegRel: **SAARC (1982)** IntlRel: **WARC (1980), REC (1970), WCC (1982)** TheolSchool: **Murray Theological College (PO Morgenster Mission, Masvingo)** Service infrastructure: **2 hospitals 2 rest/nursing homes, 2 social service organizations, 7 kindergartens, 14 schools, 3 training centers** Periodicals: **Munyaiwashe (mission/monthly/500)**

Address: Reformed Church in Zimbabwe, P.O. Box 670, 62 Hughe Street, Masvingo, Zimbabwe, Tel: +263 39 63333, Fax: 263 39 63768

3. Dutch Reformed Church — Synod of Central Africa (1268)

This church is a result of evangelistic efforts of the Dutch Reformed Church in South Africa (cf. South Africa no. 1). In 1895 the first three congregations north of the Limpopo River in what was then Rhodesia were established (Bulawayo, Enkeldoorn, and Melsetter). The congregations whose number was soon increasing were at varying times part of NGK Synods of the Cape, of the Free State, and of Transvaal. In 1957 all congregations north of the Limpopo River became the Synod of Central Africa. In 1962 the various synods of the NGK in Southern and Central Africa united a general Synod, which meets every four years and decides on matters of policy, confession, Bible translation, training of ministers, church order, international ecumenical ties, and other matters of common concern. Subject to its participation in and loyalty to the General Synod, the Synod of Central Africa is autonomous and self-supporting.

TM: **2,585** BM: **570** CM: **2,015** Congr: **16** PStations: **15** OrdM: **12** Eld: **117** Deac: **117** EvgHome: **0** Mission: **0** Women Ord: **yes** As Ministers: **1990/0**, as Deac: **1982/66**, as Elders: **1990/5**, ChurchOrg: **congr, presby, synod, GenSynod** Off/otherLang: **Afrikaans, English** DoctrB: **ApC, NicC, AthC, HeidC, BelgC, CDort** Infant or believer's baptism: **both** NatRel: **Heads of denominations (1966), ZCC (1993)** RegRel: **nc** IntlRel: **REC, WARC** TheolSchool: **University of Stellenbosch (Free State of Pretoria)** Service infrastructure: **senior citizen home** Periodicals: **Die Kerkbode (weekly), Die Voorligter (monthly)**

Address: Nederduitse Gereformeerde Kerk — Sinode van Midde-Afrika, P.O. Box 967, 35 Samora, Machel Ave., Harare, Zimbabwe, Tel: +263 4 722-436 and 744-816, Fax: +263 4 774-739, E-mail: mas@zol.co.zw.

4. The United Church of Christ in Zimbabwe (1264)

The church goes back to efforts of ABCFM missionaries from South Africa. Work started in 1893 in the eastern part of the country, the first stations being established at Mount Silinda and Chikore in 1895. The church became independent in 1973, and experienced considerable growth in the following years. Its successive leaders were Dr. W. M. Mkwakwami, Dr. F. J. Gomendo, and Rev. M. C. Kuchera. The church's strength largely rests on its lay movements — Volunteers (men's association), Ruwadzano (women's association), and the Christian Youth Fellowship.

TM: **30,000** BM: **30,000** Congr: **30** PStations: **130** OrdM: **28** Eld: **1,300** Deac: **130** EvgHome: **5** Mission: **none** Women Ord: **yes** As Ministers: **1973/1** as Deac: **1973/130** as Elders: **1973/1,170** ChurchOrg: **preaching points, congr, circuits, councils, conferences, synod** Off/otherLang: **Shona, English** DoctrB: **ApC, NicC** Infant or believer's baptism: **believer** Frequency of the Lord's Supper: **monthly** Close relations with: **United Congregational Church of Southern Africa** NatRel: **ZCC (founding member 1964)** RegRel: **AACC (1974)** IntlRel: **none** TheolSchool: **United Theological College (UTC), Rusitu Bible Institute** Service infrastructure: **1 hospital and 1 clinic, primary health care centers, 8 primary and 4 secondary schools, agricultural center (Chipinge)** Periodicals: **Mashoko Newsletter (occasional/1,000)**

Address: United Church of Christ in Zimbabwe, Roslin House 316, Nelson Mandela Ave. 48, Harare, Zimbabwe, Tel: +263 4 772-128, Fax: +263 4 772-129, E-mail: uccz@mang.zw

5. Presbyterian Church of Southern Africa (1261)

The initiative for founding the church came from South Africa. The first Presb congregation was formed at Bulawayo in 1896, and in 1903 another at Harare. Others soon followed. Several educational institutions such as David Livingstone Secondary School, Gloag Ranch, and Mondoro Secondary School were started. In due course the two presbyteries of Matabeleland and Mashonaland were constituted. Today the Presb in Zimbabwe are part of the Presbyterian Church of Southern Africa (cf. South Africa no. 8) and form one of its 12 presbyteries (Presbytery of Zimbabwe). The General Assembly Office is located in Johannesburg.

TM: **9,000** CM: **6,700** Congr: **18** PStations: **25** OrdM: **17** Eld: **275** Deac: **ne** EvgHome: **na** Mission: **4** Women Ord: **yes** As Ministers: **1975/nc** as Deac: **ne** as Elders: **1966/nc** ChurchOrg: **congr, presby, GenAssy** Off/otherLang: **English, Shona, Ndebele** DoctrB: **ApC, NicC, AthC, WestConf, 24 Articles of Faith adopted from Presb Ch of England in 1890** Infant or believer's baptism: **both** NatRel: **ZCC** RegRel: **SAARC** IntlRel: **WARC, WCC, CWM** TheolSchool: **Rhodes University (Grahamstown, RSA), UNISA (RSA), Theological Extension College (RSA), United Theological College (Harare, Zimbabwe)** Periodicals: **none**

Address: Presbyterian Church of Southern Africa, P.O. Box 3576, Harare, Zimbabwe, Tel: +263 4 774-730

6. Church of Central Africa Presbyterian (CCAP) — Synod of Harare (1263)

The CCAP Harare Synod was founded in 1965. The church consists mainly of migrant workers from Malawi in search of employment in towns, mining areas, and farms in Zimbabwe. Since they could not speak the local language, worship had to be conducted in Chewa. The first community was formed in 1912. Ministers came from Malawi or were missionaries from South Africa. Today the church conducts services in English, Shona, Chewa, and, to a lesser extent, Ndebele. In recent times candidates for the ministry have been sent from Zimbabwe to Malawi for theological training. The church is part of the CCAP; it is one of the five synods of the Church of Central Africa Presbyterian in Malawi and Zambia (cf. Malawi no. 1).

TM: **11,937** BM: **7,718** CM: **6,173** Congr: **16** PStations: **265** OrdM: **10** Eld: **560** Deac: **416** EvgHome: **28** Mission: **0** Women Ord: **no** As Ministers: **no** as Deac: **276** as Elders: **no** ChurchOrg: **congr, 2 presby, one synod** Off/otherLang: **Chewa, Shona, Ndebele, English** DoctrB: **ApC, NicC, AthC, HeidC, CDort** Infant or believer's baptism: **both** Frequency of the Lord's Supper: **3-4 times a year** Close relations with: **Dutch Ref Church in South Africa, PCUSA, Ref Churches in the Netherlands** NatRel: **ZCC (1995), Heads of Denominations (1991), EFZ (1983)** RegRel: **SAARC** IntlRel: **REC (1976), WARC (1973), WCC (1995)** TheolSchool: **Nkhoma Theological College, Zomba Theological College, Rusitu Bible College** Service infrastructure: **primary school** Periodicals: **none**

Address: Church of Central Africa Presbyterian (CCAP), Gweru, P.O. Box 454, Sibindwane, Gweru, Zimbabwe, Tel: +263 54 51176

7. Churches of Christ in Zimbabwe (1266)

In 1898 Mr. John Sheriff, together with an assistant, F. Hadfield, was sent from New Zealand to undertake the organization of the Churches of Christ in Zimbabwe. The mission had to cope with great financial difficulties. As the situation improved, the work extended to other parts of the country. Headquarters were eventually transferred from Bulawayo to Dadaya in the Lundi Reserve. In 1919 medical work was started at the Dadaya mission station.

TM: **40,000** CM: **14,100** Congr: **120**

Address: Churches of Christ in Zimbabwe, P.O. Box 160, Mapazuli School, Zvishavane, Zimbabwe, Tel: +263 151 207-517

Appendix:
Churches of Christ
(Disciples of Christ)

Though they are, strictly speaking, a separate confessional tradition, the Disciples of Christ churches have much in common with the Reformed family. The church has roots in Presbyterianism; and, today, Disciples' churches in several countries have joined United Churches in which Reformed churches also participate. For a presentation of the origin, history, and present relationship with the Reformed tradition cf. 5.A.2.b, pp. 711f. below.

The Disciples of Christ worldwide number some 3 million. In some countries, particularly in the southern hemisphere, Disciples are known as Churches of Christ. Links among the Disciples are maintained internationally through the Disciples Ecumenical Consultative Council (DECC).

Address: Disciples Ecumenical Consultative Council, General Secretary, 130 E. Washington Street, P.O. Box 1986, Indianapolis, IN 46206, USA, Tel: +1 317 635 3100, Fax: +1 317 635 3700

Disciples churches are today part of the following united churches:

- China Christian Council (cf. China)
- Church of Christ in Thailand (cf. Thailand)
- Church of North India (cf. India no. 2)
- Kyodan (cf. Japan no. 1)
- United Church of Jamaica and Cayman Islands (cf. Jamaica no. 1)
- United Church of Christ in the Philippines (cf. Philippines no. 1)
- United Congregational Church of Southern Africa (cf. South Africa no. 12)
- United Reformed Church in the United Kingdom (cf. United Kingdom no. 14)

In one way or another all these churches are related to the DECC. The following churches have their own existence:

☐ *Argentina:* <u>Evangelical Church "Disciples of Christ"</u>

Founded in 1906. TM: **800** Congr: **10** Institutions: **related to ecumenical institutions in the regions, e.g., the interdenominational seminary ISEDET and various social service agencies and human rights program (United Board of Missions). The church cooperates with five other churches in the Aurora Publishing House** Ecumenical Relations: **DECC, local and national councils of churches. Union discussions have been held with Methodists and Waldensians in Argentina, Uruguay, and Paraguay**

Address: Iglesia Evangélica "Discipulos de Cristo," Arenales 3147-5 "A" 1425, Buenos Aires, Argentina

☐ *Australia:* <u>Churches of Christ (Disciples) in Australia</u>

Founded in 1848. TM: **80,000** Congr: **600 institutions: one seminary and two Bible colleges, cooperative work in state and national seminaries and theological institutions, some cooperative publishing** Ecumenical Relations: **DECC, state and national councils, World Council of Churches. Union discussions have been held in the past with the Uniting Church in Australia; no union plans at present**

Address: Churches of Christ in Australia, 181 Station Street, Aspendale, Victoria 3195, Australia

☐ *Canada:* <u>Christian Church (Disciples of Christ) in Canada</u>

Founded in 1811. TM: **5,000** Congr: **20** Institutions: **involved in local and national ecumenical seminaries and active in interchurch coalitions on social issues** Ecumenical relations: **DECC, local and national councils, World Council of Churches** Union discussions: **long-term conversations with the United Church of Canada, also with Anglicans**

Address: Christian Church (Disciples of Christ) in Canada, Box 64, Guelph, Ontario N1H 6J6, Canada

☐ *Congo:* <u>Democratic Republic of (formerly Zaire): Church of Christ in the Congo (Community of the Disciples of Christ)</u>

Founded in 1899. (Eglise du Christ au Zaire 1956) TM: **900,000** Congr **1,100** Institutions: **participation in ecumenical theological education, social aid institutions** Ecumenical relations: **DECC, regional ecumenical body, World Council of Churches**

Address: Eglise du Christ au Congo, Communauté des Disciples du Christ, B.P. 178, Mbandaka, République démocratique du Congo

☐ *Cook Islands:* **Cook Islands Christian Church (Disciples)**

TM: **13,000** Congr: **50** Institutions: **participation in regional ecumenical theological seminary; locally, in social service agencies.** Ecumenical relations: **DECC, national and regional ecumenical bodies**

☐ *Mexico:* **Association of Christians Churches (Disciples of Christ) in Mexico**

Founded in 1895. TM: **2,000** Congr: **25** Institutions: **Involved in national ecumenical seminary, cooperative publishing house** Ecumenical relations: **DECC, national and regional ecumenical bodies, national organizations of congregational churches, national Bible society**

Address: Iglesias Cristianas Evangélicas (Discipulos de Cristo) Mexico, Ave. Presidente = 604, Col. Ojocaliente 4, 20194 Aguascalientes, Mexico

☐ *New Zealand/Aotearoa:* **Associated Churches of Christ (Disciples) in New Zealand**

Founded in 1844. TM: **3,500** Congr: **50** Institutions: **cooperates for theological training especially with Know College (Presbyterian)** Ecumenical relations: **DECC, national and regional councils, World Council of Churches, national interchurch women's organizations** Union discussions: **Negotiating Churches Unity Council (since 1955) and follow-up, congregations involved in cooperative ventures (joint parishes)**

Address: Associated Churches of Christ in New Zealand, 90A Mount Street, Nelson, New Zealand

☐ *Paraguay:* **Church of the Disciples of Christ in Paraguay**

Founded in 1918 (officially in 1940). TM: **500** Congr: **8** Ecumenical relations: **DECC, national interchurch and pastors' organizations, regional ecumenical body, national Bible Society, national ecumenical educational and youth programs** Union discussions: **with Methodists and Waldensians in Argentina, Uruguay, and Paraguay**

Address: Iglesia Discipulos de Cristo en el Paraguay, Comisión Directiva de la Iglesias, Casilla de Correo 1634, Asunción, Paraguay

☐ *Puerto Rico:* **Christian Churches (Disciples of Christ) in Puerto Rico**

Founded in 1899 (officially in 1901). TM: **15,000** Congr: **80** Institutions: **participation in national Protestant seminary** Ecumenical relations: **DECC, national Protestant and regional ecumenical bodies, national and regional Bible Societies**

Address: Iglesias Cristianas (Discipulos de Cristo) en Puerto Rico, Apartado Postal 4255, Bayamon Gardens, Bayamon, PR 00958-425

☐ *United States:* <u>Christian Church (Disciples of Christ) in the United States</u>

Founded in 1804. TM: **1,500,000** Congr: **4,400** Institutions: **seminaries, colleges, social care institutions, publishing house, wide participation in ecumenical education.** Ecumenical relations: **DECC, local and national councils, World Council of Churches, extensive contacts through academic organizations, women's groups, etc.** Union discussions: **Consultation on Church Union (COCU), Ecumenical Partnership with United Church of Christ**

Address: Christian Church (Disciples of Christ) in the United States, P.O. Box 1986, Indianapolis, Indiana 46206

☐ *Vanuatu:* <u>Churches of Christ in Vanuatu</u>

Founded in 1903. TM: **3,000** Congr: **65** Ecumenical relations: **DECC, national and regional ecumenical bodies**

The following churches consider themselves to be part of the Disciples family. While Disciples have many partner churches through mission relationships, project funding, etc., there are special historical links with the following four:

• Pentecostal Union of Venezuela
• Christian Pentecostal Church of Cuba
• Christian Mission Church of Nicaragua
• Christian Apostolic Holy Spirit Church in Zion of Swaziland

3. THEOLOGICAL SCHOOLS WITH REFORMED TEACHING

The data presented here were collected in 1996 and 1997 and compiled in early 1998. The names of the countries, cities, and schools are listed alphabetically.

AMERICAN SAMOA

• **Pago Pago** — Kanana Fou Theological Seminary (s5048)
Offers training for pastors: **nc** Languages in use: **English**

Address: Kanana Fou Theological Seminary, P.O. Box 456, Pago Pago 96799, American Samoa

---

ANGOLA

• **Gabela** — Biblical Institute "Ebenezer" (s1003)
Type of school: **Undergraduate (Bible school) + Pastor's Inst.** Degrees offered: **Bachelor** Offers training for pastors: **yes** for teachers: **yes** for lay persons: **yes** Type of available practical training: **preaching, pastoral care, religious education** Languages in use: **Portuguese, French, English** Worship life offered: **3 times per week**

Address: Instituto Biblico "Ebenezer," C.P. 464, Gabela, Angola

• **Huambo** — United Emmanuel Seminary (s1004)
Type of school: **Undergraduate/Bible school** Offers training for pastors: **yes** Languages in use: **Portuguese** Full/part-time staff: **9** National/foreign students: **37** /

nc Library size: **3,000** In relations with: **Igreja Evang. Congregational em Angola, Igreja Evang. Reformada em Angola, Igreja Metodista**

Address: Seminário Emanuel Unida, P.O. Box 846, Huambo, Angola, Tel: +244-2575

* **Luanda** — Biblical Institute of Kinkuni — Sanza-Pombo (s1002)
Type of school: **Undergraduate/Bible school** Degrees offered: **basic studies: DiplTh for pastors, biblical cert. for evangelists or to continue studies** Offers training for pastors: **yes** for teachers: **yes** for lay persons: **yes** Type of available practical training: **preaching, pastoral care, religious education** Admission requirements: **6 secondary classes minimum** Languages in use: **Portuguese** Full/part-time staff: **5 basic sem and 4 inst biblico** National/foreign students: **20 / 0** Library size: **less than 100, destroyed during war** Doctrinal basis: **Reformed** Worship life offered: **sometimes** In relations with: **Igreja Evangélica Reformada de Angola-IERA**

Address: Instituto Biblico de Kinkuni — Sanza-Pombo, C.P. 2594-C, Luanda, Angola, Tel: +244 2
394-632 or 394-638, Fax: +244 2 394-586 or 396-872

* **Malange** — Bible School of Quessua (s1005)
Offers training for pastors: **nc** Languages in use: **Portuguese** In relations with: **Ecumenical**

Address: Escola Bíblica de Quessua, C.P. 9, Malange, Angola

AOTEAROA-NEW ZEALAND

* **Auckland** — Congregational College of New Zealand (s5033)
Type of school: **Undergraduate/Bible school** Degrees offered: **degree, e.g., as BMin** Offers training for pastors: **yes** for lay persons: **yes** Type of available practical training: **preaching** Admission requirements: **recommendation from local church and district, council approval of applicant** Languages in use: **English** National/foreign students: **5 / nc** Library size: **300** Doctrinal basis: **no requirement** Worship life offered: **daily** In relations with: **Congregational Union of NZ, Congregational Christian Churches of American Samoa**

Address: Congregational College of New Zealand, c–16 Stanton Terrace — Lynfield, Auckland,
Aotearoa-New Zealand

* **Auckland** — Grace Theological College (s5032)
Type of school: **Undergraduate/Bible school** Degrees offered: **none, courses are credited** Offers training for pastors: **yes** for teachers: **yes** for lay persons: **yes** Type of available practical training: **homiletics, pastoral care, religious education and counseling, effective Bible teaching** Admission requirements: **completed secondary schooling, university degree desirable** Languages in use: **English** Full/part-time staff: **1 / 25** National/foreign students: **10 / 0** Library size: **5,000**

Doctrinal basis: **WestConf** Worship life offered: **weekly** In relations with: **Reformed churches of New Zealand**

Address: Grace Theological College, P.O. Box 534, Manurewa, 1732 Auckland, Aotearoa-New Zealand, Tel: +64 9 268-1469, Fax: +64 9 268-4391

• **Dunedin** — Theological Hall Knox College (s5030)
Type of school: **College** Founded in **1876** Degrees offered: **BTh, BTh(Hons), BD, MTh, PhD** Offers training for pastors: **yes** for lay persons: **yes** Type of available practical training: **pastoral theology, field education, education ministry, communication, hospital, preaching, counseling courses in extensive pastoral theol program** Admission requirements: **ordinands: after church assessment, general students: by University matriculation** Languages in use: **English** Full/part-time staff: **8 / 2** National/foreign students: **44 / 5** Library size: **42,000** Worship life offered: **daily with weekly Holy Communion** In relations with: **Presb Ch of Aotearoa-NZ**

Address: Theological Hall, Knox College, Arden Street, Dunedin, 9001, Aotearoa-New Zealand, Tel: +64 3 473-0109, Fax: +64 3 473-8466

• **Tauranga** — Faith Bible College (s5034)
Type of school: **College** Founded in **1969** Degrees offered: **Dipl (Ministry Development), Dipl (Christian Ministry)** Offers training for pastors: **yes** for teachers: **yes** for lay persons: **yes** Type of available practical training: **each weekend** Admission requirements: **high school education** Languages in use: **English** Full/part-time staff: **8 / 15** National/foreign students: **100 / 15** Library size: **8,000** Worship life offered: **daily**

Address: Faith Bible College, Private Bag, Welcome Bay Rd., Tauranga, Aotearoa-New Zealand, Tel: +64 7 544-2463, Fax: +64 7 544-1923, E-mail: fbc@enternet.co.nz

ARGENTINA

• **Buenos Aires** — Biblical Institute of Buenos Aires (s2003)
Type of school: **Undergraduate/Bible school** Degrees offered: **BTh, MTh** Offers training for pastors: **yes** for teachers: **yes** for lay persons: **yes** Type of available practical training: **preaching, pastoral care, religious education** Admission requirements: **completed secondary school** Languages in use: **Spanish** Full/part-time staff: **7 / 13** National/foreign students: **222 / 31** Library size: **17,300** Doctrinal basis: **Statement of Faith of CMA** In relations with: **Christian and Missionary Alliance (CMA)**

Address: Instituto Biblico Buenos Aires, La Pampa 2975, Buenos Aires, BA 1428, Argentina, Tel: +54 1 784-7501, Fax: +54 1 706-4404, E-mail: ibba@sion.com

- **Buenos Aires** — Higher Evangelical Institute of Theological Studies (ISEDET) (s2001)

Type of school: **Seminary** Founded in **1971** Degrees offered: **BTh, MTh, ThD** Offers training for pastors: **yes** for teachers: **yes** for lay persons: **yes** Admission requirements: **secondary school** Languages in use: **Spanish** Full/part-time staff: **3 / 14** National/foreign students: **120 / 20** Library size: **100,000** Doctrinal basis: **none** Worship life offered: **weekly** In relations with: **Angl Ch, Presb Ch of Argentina, Ref Ch of Argentina, Waldensian Ch of the River Plate, Meth Ch of Argentina, Disciples of Christ, United Lutheran Ch, Evangelical Ch of the River Plate**

Address: Instituto Superior Evangélico de Estudios Teológicos (ISEDET), Camacuá 282, 1406 Buenos Aires, Argentina, Tel: +54 1 632-5039 and 631-0224, Fax: +54 1 633-2825, E-mail: Rectoriael@SEDETI.SATLINK.NET

- **Urdinarrain** — Theological Institute of the Congregational Evangelical Church in Argentina (s2002)

Type of school: **Undergraduate/Bible school** Degrees offered: **BTh** Offers training for pastors: **yes** for teachers: **yes** for lay persons: **yes** Type of available practical training: **preaching, pastoral care, religious education** Admission requirements: **high school senior** Languages in use: **Spanish** Library size: **4,000** Doctrinal basis: **Reformed** In relations with: **Evangelical Congregational Church**

Address: Instituto de Teología de la Iglesia Evangélica Congregacional Argentina, Av. Colón 222, RA 2826 Urdinarrain, Prov. Entre Ríos, Argentina, Tel: +54 446 80218

AUSTRALIA

- **Adelaide** — Parkin-Wesley Theological College (s5007)

Type of school: **Graduate/Uni** Founded in **1969** Degrees offered: **BTh, MTh, PhD, BMin, CertMin, Dipl in Pastoral Studies, all in cooperation with Angl and RCath colleges** Offers training for pastors: **yes** for teachers: **yes** for lay persons: **yes** Type of available practical training: **preaching, pastoral care, chaplaincy, intern year in supervised field education** Admission requirements: **degree-University entrance, certificate — demonstration of ability** Languages in use: **English** Full/part-time staff: **7 plus staff from other colleges plus 10** National/foreign students: **200 / 0** Library size: **23,000** Doctrinal basis: **Basis of Union of Uniting Church in Australia** Worship life offered: **3 to 5 times per week, depending on timetable** In relations with: **Synod of the Uniting Church in Australia**

Address: Parkin-Wesley Theological College, 20 King William Rd., Wayville, Adelaide, SA 5034, Australia, Tel: +61 8 271-8334, Fax: +61 8 373-4874

• **Box Hill North** — Presbyterian Theological College (s5013)
Type of school: **Graduate + Undergraduate Seminary** Founded in **1866** Degrees offered: **Dipl, BTh, BMin MTh** Offers training for pastors: **yes** for teachers: **no** for lay persons: **yes** Type of available practical training: **preaching, pastoral care, religious education** Admission requirements: **university matriculation** Languages in use: **English** Full/part-time staff: **4 / 9** National/foreign students: **65 / nc** Library size: **13,600** Doctrinal basis: **WestConf** Worship life offered: **daily** In relations with: **Presbyterian Church of Victoria**

Address: Presbyterian Theological College, 684 Elgar Rd., Box Hill North, Victoria 3129, Australia, Tel: +61 3 9898-9384, Fax: +61 3 9898-9872, E-mail: prescoll@ozemail.com.au

• **Brisbane** — Trinity Theological College (s5011)
Type of school: **Graduate/Univ+Undergraduate/Bible school** Founded in **1977** Degrees offered: **BA, BTh, MTh, MMin, MPhil, PhD** Offers training for pastors: **yes** for teachers: **yes** for lay persons: **yes** Type of available practical training: **preaching, pastoral care, religious education** Admission requirements: **matriculation** Languages in use: **English** Full/part-time staff: **6 / 9** National/foreign students: **160 / 5** Library size: **25,000** Doctrinal basis: **Basis of Union** Worship life offered: **2 times per week** In relations with: **Uniting Church in Australia**

Address: Trinity Theological College, P.O. Box 674, 47 Candall St., Auchenflower, Brisbane, QLD 4001, Australia, Tel: +61 7 377 9950, Fax: +61 7 377 9824

• **Burwood** — Presbyterian Theological Centre (s5004)
Type of school: **Undergraduate/Bible school** Founded in **1873** Degrees offered: **BTh, DiplTh** Offers training for pastors: **yes** for lay persons: **yes** Admission requirements: **matriculation or equivalent** Languages in use: **English** Full/part-time staff: **4 / 10** National/foreign students: **70 / 12** Library size: **17,000** Doctrinal basis: **WestConf** Worship life offered: **weekly** In relations with: **Presb Ch of Australia**

Address: Presbyterian Theological Centre, 77 Shaftesbury Rd., Burwood, NSW 2134, Australia, Tel: +61 2 744-1977, Fax: +61 2 744-5970

• **Casuarina** — Nungalinya College Darwin (s5010)
Type of school: **Undergraduate/Bible school** Founded in **1973** Degrees offered: **CertTh, Associate DiplTh, Cert in Community Organization** Offers training for pastors: **yes** for teachers: **yes** for lay persons: **yes** Type of available practical training: **preaching, pastoral care, religious education** Admission requirements: **church sponsorship** Languages in use: **English, Kriol, Tiwi, etc.** Full/part-time staff: **14 / 2** National/foreign students: **217 / 0** Library size: **11,000** Doctrinal basis: **none** Worship life offered: **daily** In relations with: **Angl, Uniting Church**

Address: Nungalinya College Darwin, P.O. Box 40371, Drugstore Rd., Casuarina, NT 0811, Australia, Tel: +61 89 271-044, Fax: +61 89 272-332

• **Geelong** — Reformed Theological College (s5009)
Type of school: **Graduate + Undergraduate; Pastor/Evangelist/Missionary** Founded in **1955** Degrees offered: **BD, BTh, Associate Diploma of Theol either**

in mission, evangelism, ministry, or youth work Offers training for pastors: **yes** for teachers: **yes** for lay persons: **yes** Type of available practical training: **preaching, pastoral care, religious education** Admission requirements: **University admission or mature age entrance** Languages in use: **English** Full/part-time staff: **5 / 2** National/foreign students: **40 / 2** Library size: **16,000** Doctrinal basis: **Reformed doctrine** Worship life offered: **weekly** In relations with: **Reformed Churches of Australia, Reformed Churches of New Zealand, Reformed Presbyterian Church**

Address: Reformed Theological College, 55 Maud Street, 3220 Geelong, Victoria, Australia, Tel: +61 52 222-155, Fax: +61 52 221-263, E-mail: rtcoll@deakin.edu.au

- **Griffith** — Griffith University School of Theology (s5003)
Type of school: **Graduate/Univ** Degrees offered: **BTh, Research Master of Philosophy, PhD, Coursework Master of Arts** Offers training for pastors: **nc** Type of available practical training: **no** Languages in use: **English** Full/part-time staff: **30** National/foreign students: **na / na** Library size: **na** Doctrinal basis: **none** Worship life offered: **none** In relations with: **Uniting Church in Australia (Queensland synod)**

Address: Griffith University School of Theology, Faculty of Humanities, Griffith, Sect. 4111, Australia, Tel: +61 7 3875-7573, E-mail: theology@gu.edu.an

- **Mulgrave North** — Churches of Christ Theological College (s5014)
Type of school: **College** Founded in **1907** Degrees offered: **BTh, DiplMin** Offers training for pastors: **nc** Languages in use: **English** Full/part-time staff: **5 / 4** National/foreign students: **120 / nc** Library size: **23,000** In relations with: **Churches of Christ in Australia**

Address: Churches of Christ Theological College, P.O. Box 629, Mulgrave North, Victoria 3170, Australia, Tel: +61 3 790-1000

- **North Parramatta** — United Theological College (s5008)
Type of school: **Graduate/Univ+Undergraduate/Bible school** Founded in **1974** Degrees offered: **BTh, BA or Conversion course, CertTh, MTh, DMin** Offers training for pastors: **yes** for teachers: **yes** for lay persons: **yes** Type of available practical training: **preaching, pastoral care, religious education** Admission requirements: **special application, matriculation at an Australian university or college for advanced education; admission through the Board of Studies** Languages in use: **English** Full/part-time staff: **10** National/foreign students: **180 / 10** Library size: **42,000 + 350 periodicals** Doctrinal basis: **Basis of Union of Uniting Church** Worship life offered: **Mon-Thurs: 15 min. daily chapel/prayer, Friday Eucharist service** In relations with: **Synod NSW of the Uniting Church in Australia**

Address: United Theological College, 16 Masons Drive, North Parramatta, NSW 2151, Australia, Tel: +61 2 683-3655, Fax: +61 2 683-6617

- **Melbourne** — Uniting Church Theological Hall, Ormond College (s5001)
Type of school: **Graduate/Univ+Undergraduate/Bible school** Founded in **1977**

Degrees offered: **BTh, BD, Postgraduate through MC.D. — MTh, MMin, ThD (all through Melbourne College of Divinity as degree-conferring body)** Offers training for pastors: **yes** for teachers: **yes** for lay persons: **yes** Type of available practical training: **preaching, pastoral care; field education, CPE** Admission requirements: **University admission** Languages in use: **English** Full/part-time staff: **9 at Theol Hall / 14 at Univ** National/foreign students: **52 / 4** Library size: **140,000** Doctrinal basis: **none** Worship life offered: **weekly Eucharist** In relations with: **Uniting Church of Australia, member of the United Faculty of Theology**

Address: Uniting Church Theological Hall, P.O. Box 3952, Ormond College, Parkville, Melbourne, Victoria 3052, Australia, Tel: +61 3 9347-7199, Fax: +61 3 348-1982

• **Perth** — Perth Theological Hall (s5002)
Type of school: **Graduate/Univ+Undergraduate/Bible school** Founded in **1915** Degrees offered: **BA, BTh, BD, MPhil, PhD** Offers training for pastors: **yes** for lay persons: **yes** Type of available practical training: **pastoral theology, supervised field education, formation for ministry** Admission requirements: **University admission** Languages in use: **English** Full/part-time staff: **4 from Uniting Church + 6 Angl and RCath** National/foreign students: **150 / 10** Library size: **30,000** Doctrinal basis: **Uniting Basis of Union** Worship life offered: **weekly** In relations with: **Uniting Church of Australia, Western Australian Synod**

Address: Perth Theological Hall, P.O. Box 6150, Murdoch University, Perth, WA 6009, Australia, Tel: +61 8 9360-2651, Fax: +61 9 360-6480, E-mail: creagh@central.murdoch.edu.au

• **Perth** — Westminster Theological College (s5012)
Type of school: **Graduate/Univ+Undergraduate/Bible school** Degrees offered: **BTh** Offers training for pastors: **yes** for teachers: **yes** for lay persons: **yes** Type of available practical training: **communication, homiletics, pastoral care, religious education** Languages in use: **English** Full/part-time staff: **3 / 8** National/foreign students: **20 / nc** Library size: **8,000** Doctrinal basis: **WestConf** Worship life offered: **none** In relations with: **Westminster Presbyterian Churches, Presb Church in Australia**

Address: Westminster Theological College, 32 Bullcreek Dr., Bullcreek, WA, 61490 Perth, Australia, Tel: +61 9 332-6911, Fax: +61 9 332-1991, E-mail: wtc@ami.com.au

• **Sydney** — John Knox Theological College (s5005)
Type of school: **Evangelist/Pastoral Training Institute** Degrees offered: **exit certificate only** Offers training for pastors: **yes** for lay persons: **yes** Type of available practical training: **preaching, pastoral care, religious education** Admission requirements: **none, though students for ministry would have to demonstrate an aptitude to learn** Languages in use: **English** Full/part-time staff: **6** National/foreign students: **40 / 1** Library size: **na** Doctrinal basis: **WestConf** Worship life offered: **none**

Address: John Knox Theological College, 7 Park St., Peakhorst, Sydney, 2210, Australia, Tel: +61 4 294-2579nc

- **Waramanga** — Canberra College of Theology (s5015)
Type of school: **Graduate/Univ+Undergraduate School** Founded in **1970** Degrees offered: **Cert (Biblical Studies), DiplTh, BTh** Offers training for pastors: **yes** for teachers: **no** for lay persons: **yes** Type of available practical training: **preaching, pastoral care, religious education** Admission requirements: **BTh (matriculation)** Languages in use: **English** Full/part-time staff: **3 / 6** National/foreign students: **30 / nc** Library size: **9,500** Doctrinal basis: **CMA** Worship life offered: **twice a week** In relations with: **Christian Missionary Alliance of Australia**

Address: Canberra College of Theology, P.O. Box 42, Waramanga, ACT 2611, Australia, Tel: +61 26 284-366, Fax: +61 26 287-0111, E-mail: rwarnken@pcug.org

AUSTRIA

- **Purkersdorf** — Pastoral School of the Protestant Church in Austria (s6001)
Founded in **1966** Offers training for pastors: **yes** Languages in use: **German** Full/part-time staff: **1** Library size: **5,000**

Address: Predigerseminar der Evangelischen Kirche Augsburgerisches Bekenntnis, Prager Gasse 21, A-3002 Purkersdorf, Austria, Tel: +43 2 2313-708

- **Wien** — Evangelical-Theological Faculty of the University of Vienna (s6002)
Type of school: **Graduate/Univ** Founded in **1821** Degrees offered: **Master, ThD** Offers training for pastors: **yes** Admission requirements: **Matura** Languages in use: **German** Full/part-time staff: **35** National/foreign students: **249 / 58** Library size: **160,000** Doctrinal basis: **German** Worship life offered: **none** In relations with: **for election of new teachers the Ref Church has the right to give advice**

Address: Evangelisch-Theologische Fakultät — Universität Wien, Rooseveltplatz 10, A-1090 Wien, Austria, Tel: +43 1 406-5981, Fax: +43 1 406 59 81 44

- **Wien** — Pedagogical Institute of Religion of the Evangelical Church in Austria (s6003)
Offers training for teachers: **yes** Languages in use: **German** National/foreign students: **nc / 0** In relations with: **Evangelical Church in Austria**

Address: Religionspädagogisches Institut der Evang Kirche A. und H.B. in Oesterreich, Severin Schreiber-Gasse 3, A-1180 Wien, Austria, Tel: +43 2 2247-2523

BANGLADESH

- **Dhaka** — St. Andrews Theological College (s4001)
Type of school: **Undergraduate/Bible school** Degrees offered: **BTh —**

Serampore, India Offers training for pastors: **yes** for lay persons: **yes** Admission requirements: **high school certificate** Languages in use: **Bengali, English** Full/part-time staff: **1/ 8** National/foreign students: **24 / 0** Library size: **2,000** Doctrinal basis: **liberal evangelical** Worship life offered: **daily morning and evening prayer at seminars** In relations with: **Ch of Bangladesh**

Address: St. Andrews Theological College, 54 Johnson Road, Dhaka, 1100, Bangladesh, Tel: +880 2 236-546; 238218, Fax: +880 2 832-915

- **Shaistaganj** — Bible and Leadership Training Programme (BLTP) (s4002) Type of school: **Bible School** Degrees offered: **CertTh** Offers training for pastors: **no** for teachers: **no** for lay persons: **yes** Type of available practical training: **no** Admission requirements: **passed class five** Languages in use: **Bengali, Khasi, Santali** Full/part-time staff: **15** National/foreign students: **150 / nc** Library size: **15,000** Doctrinal basis: **none** Worship life offered: **twice a year** In relations with: **Sylhet Presbyterian Synod (SPS)**

Address: Bible and Leadership Training Programme, Christian Mission Shaistaganj, 3301 Shaistaganj, Habiganj Dt., Bangladesh

---

BELGIUM

- **Bruxelles** — University Faculty of Protestant Theology (s6021) Founded in **1942** Degrees offered: **LicTh, Dipl in higher studies, ThD** Offers training for pastors: **nc** Languages in use: **French, Dutch** Full/part-time staff: **9 / 7** National/foreign students: **163 / nc** Library size: **40,000** In relations with: **Eglise Protestante Unie de Belgique**

Address: Faculté Universitaire de Théologie Protestante, 40, rue des Bollandistes, B-1040 Bruxelles, Belgium, Tel: +32 2 735-6746, Fax: +32 2 735-5037

- **Leuven** — Evangelical Theological Faculty (s6022) Founded in **1595** Degrees offered: **LicDiv, ThD, Lic (MTh)** Offers training for pastors: **yes** for teachers: **yes** for lay persons: **no** Type of available practical training: **preaching, pastoral care, religious education** Admission requirements: **normal admission to university** Languages in use: **Flemish, English** Full/part-time staff: **8 / 18** National/foreign students: **68 / nc** Library size: **20,000** Worship life offered: **weekly**

Address: Bijbelinstituut Belgie, Sint-Jansbergsesteenwe 97, B-3001 Leuven, Belgium, Tel: +32 16 200-895, Fax: +32 16 200943, E-mail: stf@glo.be

BÉNIN

- **Parakou** — Bible Schools (s1086)
Type of school: **Bible School** Degrees offered: **pastoral Dipl only** Offers training for pastors: **yes** for teachers: **yes** for lay persons: **yes** Type of available practical training: **enormous emphasis on practical training, especially church planting** Admission requirements: **Venezuelan literary, extremely high character screening** Languages in use: **French and local languages** Full/part-time staff: **20** National/foreign students: **100 / 5** Doctrinal basis: **Conservative Evangelical, "but not fundamentalist"** Worship life offered: **Sundays** In relations with: **Union des Eglises évangéliques du Bénin**

Address: Bible Schools, P.O. Box 215, c/o Christian Education Department, Parakou, Bénin

- **Porto-Novo** — Protestant Theological School (s1085)
Type of school: **Undergraduate/Bible school** Degrees offered: **BTh, ThD** Offers training for pastors: **yes** for lay persons: **yes** Type of available practical training: **preaching, pastoral care, religious education** Admission requirements: **Bachelor, sent by a church** Languages in use: **French** Full/part-time staff: **10** National/foreign students: **24 / 13** Library size: **4,000** Doctrinal basis: **Principles of Reformation** Worship life offered: **weekly, daily prayer** In relations with: **established by Prot Meth Ch of Bénin, Meth Ch in Togo, Evang. Presb Church of Togo, Prot Meth Ch of Côte-d'Ivoire**

Address: Ecole de théologie protestante, B.P. 176, Adjarra-Dokonkji, Porto-Novo, Bénin, Tel: +229 21 29 30, Fax: +229 21 29 62

BOLIVIA

- **La Paz** — Evangelical Theological Seminary (s2202)
Type of school: **Undergraduate/Bible school** Degrees offered: **BTh** Offers training for pastors: **yes** for lay persons: **yes** Type of available practical training: **preaching, pastoral care, religious education** Admission requirements: **high school graduation** Languages in use: **Spanish** Full/part-time staff: **12** National/foreign students: **80 / 5** Library size: **5,000** Doctrinal basis: **ApC** Worship life offered: **twice a year** In relations with: **Iglesia Presbiteriana en Bolivia, Igl Hermanos Libres, Union Cristiana Evangélica, Alianza Cristiana y Misionera (CMA)**

Address: Seminário Teologico Evangélico, Casilla 4436, Almirante Grau 115, La Paz, Bolivia, Tel: +591 2 340-053nc

- **La Paz** — Union Evangelical University in Bolivia (s2200)
Type of school: **Undergraduate/Bible school** Degrees offered: **undergraduate** Offers training for pastors: **yes** Type of available practical training: **preaching,**

pastoral care, religious education Admission requirements: **senior high school** Languages in use: **Spanish** Full/part-time staff: **60** National/foreign students: **300 / 0** Library size: **4,000** Doctrinal basis: **Reformed** Worship life offered: **weekly** In relations with: **Evangelical Presbyterian Ch in Bolivia**

Address: Universidad Unión Evangélica Boliviana, Casilla 12599, Calle 30, no. 2, La Paz, Bolivia, Tel: +591 2 710-249, Fax: +591 2 710-251

BOTSWANA

- **Gaborone** — Department of Theology and Religious Studies — University of Botswana (s1020)

Degrees offered: **BA, Dipl Th Education** Offers training for pastors: **nc** Languages in use: **Spanish** National/foreign students: **94 / nc**

Address: Department of Theology and Religious Studies — University of Botswana, Private Bag 0022, Gaborone, Botswana

- **Gaborone** — Kgolagano College of Theological Education (s1021)

Type of school: **Undergraduate/Bible school** Founded in **1974** Degrees offered: **DiplTh, CertTh,** Offers training for pastors: **yes** for teachers: **yes** for lay persons: **yes** Type of available practical training: **most students are already church leaders** Admission requirements: **Cambridge School Cert** Languages in use: **English, Setswana** National/foreign students: **117 / 1** Library size: **4,832** Doctrinal basis: **Jesus is Lord** Worship life offered: **daily** In relations with: **Dutch Reformed Church, United Congr Church of Southern Africa**

Address: Kgolagano College of Theological Education, P.O. Box 318, 784 Independence Ave., Gaborone, Botswana, Tel: +267 352-196, Fax: +267 356-122

BRAZIL

- **Anapolis** — Christian Evangelical Theological Seminary of Brazil (s2317)

Type of school: **Seminary** Degrees offered: **Dipl in Biblical Studies, BTh** Offers training for pastors: **nc** Languages in use: **Portuguese** Full/part-time staff: **5 / 12** National/foreign students: **80 / nc** Library size: **4,000** In relations with: **Evangelical Christian Church of Brazil**

Address: Seminario Teologico Cristão Evangelico Brasil, C.P. 465, GO 75001-970 Anapolis, Brazil, Tel: +55 1 62 321-1698, Fax: +55 1 62 321-1698

- **Belo Horizonte** — Theological Presbyterian Seminary "Rev. Denoel Nicodemos Eller" (s2310)

Type of school: **Undergraduate/Bible school** Degrees offered: **BTh** Offers training for pastors: **yes** for lay persons: **yes** Type of available practical training:

preaching, pastoral care, religious education Admission requirements: **high school graduation** Languages in use: **Portuguese** Full/part-time staff: **20** National/foreign students: **115 / nc** Library size: **5,000** Doctrinal basis: **Ref, Calvinist** Worship life offered: **2 times per week** In relations with: **Presb Ch of Brazil**

Address: Seminário Teológico Presbiteriano "Rev. Denoel Nicodemos Eller," Rua Ceará 1434, MG-30150311 Belo Horizonte, Brazil, Tel: +55 31 273-7044, Fax: +55 31 273-7096

- **Brasilia** — Faculty of Christian Theology in Brazil (s2318)
Type of school: **Faculty of Theology** Degrees offered: **Cert of Christian Education, BTh** Offers training for pastors: **nc** Languages in use: **Portuguese** Full/part-time staff: **2 / 10** National/foreign students: **80 / nc** Library size: **10,000** In relations with: **Churches of Christ**

Address: Faculdade Theologica Crista do Brasil, C.P. 14-2296, DF 70349-970 Brasilia, Brazil

- **Campinas** — Southern Theological Presbyterian Seminary (s2303)
Type of school: **Graduate/Univ+Undergraduate/Bible school** Degrees offered: **BTh, M Christian Education and Mission** Offers training for pastors: **yes** for teachers: **yes** Type of available practical training: **preaching, pastoral care, religious education** Admission requirements: **high school graduation** Languages in use: **Portuguese (brasileiro)** Full/part-time staff: **23** National/foreign students: **170 / 2** Library size: **25,000** Doctrinal basis: **WestConf** Worship life offered: **weekly** In relations with: **Igreja Presbiteriana do Brasil**

Address: Seminário Presbiteriano do Sul, C.P. 133, Av. Brasil, no. 1200, S.P. 13075000 Campinas, Brazil, Tel: +55 19 241-9399, Fax: +55 19 241-9399

- **Dourados-Ms** — Presbyterian Biblical Institute "Rev. Felipe Landes"
Type of school: **Mission School** Degrees offered: **Cert** Offers training for indigenous missionaries: **yes** Language in use: **Portuguese** Full/part-time staff: **9** Students **16** Library size: **750** Worship life offered: **daily** Doctrinal basis: **Ref** In relation with: **Presbyterian Church of Brazil, Independent Presbyterian Church of Brazil, Presbyterian Church (USA).**

Address Instituto Biblico Presbiteriano "Rev. Felipe Landes," C.P. 4, 79084-970 Dourados-Ms, Brazil, Tel. +55 67 421 4197

- **Fortaleza** — Theological Seminary of Fortaleza (s2312)
Type of school: **Seminary** Founded in **1986** Degrees offered: **BTh** Offers training for pastors: **yes** for lay persons: **yes** Type of available practical training: **preaching, pastoral care, religious education** Admission requirements: **high school graduation** Languages in use: **Portuguese** Full/part-time staff: **7 / 6** National/foreign students: **80 / nc** Library size: **6,000** Doctrinal basis: **Ref, Calvinist** Worship life offered: **weekly** In relations with: **Independent Presb Ch of Brazil**

Address: Seminário Teológico de Fortaleza, Av. João Pessoa, 5570, CE-60435682 Fortaleza, Brazil, Tel: +55 85 225-9894, Fax: +55 85 225-9894

- **Goiania** — Theological Presbyterian Seminary in Central-Brasil (s2308)
Type of school: **Undergraduate/Bible school** Degrees offered: **BTh** Offers train-

ing for pastors: **yes** for lay persons: **yes** Admission requirements: **high school graduation** Languages in use: **Portuguese** Full/part-time staff: **18** National/foreign students: **120 / nc** Library size: **5,000** Doctrinal basis: **Ref, Calvinist** Worship life offered: **2 times per week** In relations with: **Presb Ch of Brazil**

Address: Seminário Teológico Presbiteriano Brasil-Central, Av. 24 de outobro, 1146, GO-74505011 Goiania, Brazil, Tel: +55 62 291-4677, Fax: +55 62 291-5841

• **Ijuí** — Biblical Institute and Evangelical Congregational Seminary (s2304) Type of school: **Undergraduate/Bible school** Founded in **1962** Degrees offered: **Catechism Cert, DiplTh, BTh** Offers training for pastors: **yes** for teachers: **yes** for lay persons: **yes** Type of available practical training: **preaching, pastoral care, religious education** Admission requirements: **high school graduation** Languages in use: **Portuguese** Full/part-time staff: **6** National/foreign students: **15 / 0** Library size: **3,000** Doctrinal basis: **Ref, Calvinist** Worship life offered: **daily** In relations with: **Igreja Evangélica Congregacional do Brasil**

Address: Instituto Biblico e Seminário Evangélico Congregacional, C.P. 334, Linha 4 Leste, RS-98700000 Ijuí, Brazil, Tel: +55 55 332-4556

• **JI-Parana** — Biblical Institute of Rondania (s2319) Type of school: **Undergraduate/Bible school** Founded in **1989** Degrees offered: **Cert in Bible Studies** Offers training for pastors: **nc** Languages in use: **Portuguese** Full/part-time staff: **5 / 15** National/foreign students: **15 / nc** Library size: **1,000** In relations with: **Presbyterian Church of Brasil**

Address: Instituto Biblico de Rondania, C.P. 293, RO 78958-000 JI-Parana, Brazil, Tel: +55 1 69 421-5547, Fax: +55 1 69 421-5547

• **Londrina** — Theological Seminary of Londrina (s2302) Type of school: **Graduate/Univ** Degrees offered: **BTh, non-degree graduate program** Offers training for pastors: **yes** Type of available practical training: **preaching, pastoral care, religious education** Admission requirements: **high school graduation** Languages in use: **Portuguese** Full/part-time staff: **12** National/foreign students: **101 / nc** Library size: **8,376** Doctrinal basis: **Ref, Calvinist** Worship life offered: **weekly** In relations with: **Independent Presbyterian Church of Brazil**

Address: Seminario Teologico de Londrina, C.P. 588, Av. Madre Leônia Milito 2159, CEP PR-86050180 Londrina, Brazil, Tel: +55 43 339-0276, Fax: +55 43 339-0276

• **Recife** — Theological Congregational Seminary of Recife (s2315) Type of school: **Undergraduate/Bible school** Founded in **1927** Degrees offered: **BTh** Offers training for pastors: **yes** for teachers: **yes** for lay persons: **yes** Type of available practical training: **preaching, pastoral care, religious education** Admission requirements: **high school graduation** Languages in use: **Portuguese** Full/part-time staff: **4 / 5** National/foreign students: **60 / 0** Library size: **4,000** Doctrinal basis: **Reformed** Worship life offered: **daily** In relations with: **Evang Congregational Ch of Brazil**

Address: Seminário Teológico Congregacional do Recife, Rua Arealva, 19 Tejipio, PE-50930190
   Recife, Brazil, Tel: +55 81 251-1486

- **Recife** — Theological Presbyterian Seminary of Norte (s2309)
Type of school: **Undergraduate/Bible school** Degrees offered: **BTh** Offers training for pastors: **yes** for teachers: **yes** Type of available practical training: **preaching, pastoral care, religious education** Admission requirements: **high school graduation** Languages in use: **Portuguese** Full/part-time staff: **25** National/foreign students: **190 / nc** Library size: **12,000** Doctrinal basis: **Ref, Calvinist** Worship life offered: **daily** In relations with: **Presb Ch of Brazil**

Address: Seminário Teólogico Presbiteriano do Norte, Rua Demólclito Souza Filho, 208,
   PE-50610120 Recife, Brazil, Tel: +55 81 227-0986, Fax: +55 81 227-0145

- **Rio de Janeiro** — Theological Congregational Seminary of Rio de Janeiro (s2316)
Type of school: **Undergraduate/Bible school** Degrees offered: **BTh Theol Education, Christian Education** Offers training for pastors: **yes** for teachers: **yes** for lay persons: **yes** Type of available practical training: **preaching, pastoral care, religious education** Admission requirements: **high school graduation** Languages in use: **Portuguese** Full/part-time staff: **12** National/foreign students: **50 / 1** Library size: **5,000** Doctrinal basis: **Reformed** Worship life offered: **weekly** In relations with: **Evang Congregational Ch of Brazil**

Address: Seminário Teológico Congregacional do Rio de Janeiro, Rua Melchior da Fonseca, 151
   Pedra de Guaratiba, RJ-23027260 Rio de Janeiro, Brazil, Tel: +55 21 417-1843

- **Rio de Janeiro** — Theological Presbyterian Seminary of Rio de Janeiro (s2311)
Type of school: **Undergraduate/Bible school** Founded in **1986** Degrees offered: **BTh** Offers training for pastors: **yes** Type of available practical training: **preaching, pastoral care, religious education** Admission requirements: **high school graduation** Languages in use: **Portuguese** Full/part-time staff: **26** National/foreign students: **95 / nc** Library size: **1,500** Doctrinal basis: **Ref, Calvinist** Worship life offered: **weekly** In relations with: **Presb Ch of Brazil**

Address: Seminário Teológico Presbiteriano do Rio de Janeiro, Rua Joaquina Rosa, 199,
   RJ-20710080 Rio de Janeiro, Brazil, Tel: +55 21 201-6734, Fax: +55 21 281-9775

- **Salvador** — Institute for Theological Education of Bahia-Iteba (s2305)
Type of school: **Undergraduate/Bible school** Offers training for pastors: **nc** Languages in use: **Portuguese** Degrees offered: **ThBA** Admission requirements: **high school graduation** Full/part-time staff: **15** National/foreign students: **70 / nc** Library size: **2,000** Worship life offered: **weekly** In relations with: **United Presb Ch of Brazil, Meth Ch of Brazil, Episcopal Ch of Brazil, Evang Luth Confession Ch of Brazil, God's Assembly of Brazil, Brazil for Christ Evang Ch, RCath**

Address: Instituto de Educação Teológica da Bahia, C.P. 350, Av. Lealvigildo Filgueiras, 85, B-
   4000000 Salvador, Brazil, Tel: +55 71 235-0261nc

- **São Bernardo do Campo** — Conservative Presbyterian Seminary (s2314)
Type of school: **Undergraduate/Bible school** Founded in **1954** Degrees offered:
BTh Offers training for pastors: **yes** Type of available practical training: **preaching, pastoral care, religious education** Admission requirements: **high school graduation** Languages in use: **Portuguese** Full/part-time staff: **3 / 6** National/foreign students: **9 / 0** Library size: **3,000** Doctrinal basis: **Ref Calvinist** Worship life offered: **daily** In relations with: **Conservative Presb Ch of Brazil**

Address: Seminário Presbiteriano Conservador, C.P. 7042, Av. Santa Maria, 23 Bo Riacho Grande, SP-9830320 São Bernardo do Campo, Brazil, Tel: +55 11 451-9952, Fax: +55 11 451-9952

- **São Bernardo do Campo** — Postgraduate Ecumenical Institute on Science of Religion (s2301)
Type of school: **Graduate/Univ** Degrees offered: **MDiv** Offers training for pastors: **nc** for teachers: **yes** Type of available practical training: **no** Admission requirements: **College, Master, curriculum vitae** Languages in use: **Portuguese, English** Full/part-time staff: **16** National/foreign students: **119 / 23** Library size: **12,000** Doctrinal basis: **interconfessional** Worship life offered: **none** In relations with: **Iglesia Metodista, Igl Presb Independente, Igl Evangélica de Confissão Luterana, Igl Cristã Reformada, Igl Episcopal Angla, Igl Evangélicás Reformadas, Igl Presbiteriana Unida**

Address: Instituto Ecuménico de pós-Graduação em Ciências da Religião, rua do Sacramento, 230, SP-9735460 São Bernardo do Campo, Brazil, Tel: +55 11 457-3733, Fax: +55 11 457-3349

- **São Luis** — Christian Evangelical Seminary of the North (s2320)
Type of school: **Undergraduate/Bible school** Founded in **1936** Degrees offered:
GTh, BA (Theol), Graduate (Mission), BA (Mission) Offers training for pastors: **yes** for teachers: **yes** for lay persons: **yes** Admission requirements: **BTh** Languages in use: **Portuguese** Full/part-time staff: **9 / 6** National/foreign students: **79 / 0** Library size: **6,000** Doctrinal basis: **Conservative Evangelical** Worship life offered: **5 times per week** In relations with: **Alliance of Evangelical Christian Churches of Brazil, Igreja Evangélica do Brasil**

Address: Seminario Cristão Evangelico do Norte, C.P. 3016, San Jose de Ribamar 220, MA 65045-971 São Luis, 65045-971, Brazil, Tel: +55 1 98 245-2229, Fax: +55 1 98 245-6181

- **São Paulo** — Biblical Institute of the Alliance (s2321)
Type of school: **Undergraduate/Bible school** Founded in **1991** Degrees offered:
LicTh Offers training for pastors: **yes** Type of available practical training: **preaching, pastoral care, religious education** Languages in use: **Portuguese** Full/part-time staff: **2** National/foreign students: **12 / 1** Library size: **4,220** Doctrinal basis: **statement of faith** In relations with: **Christian and Missionary Alliance of Brazil**

Address: Instituto Bíblico Aliança, Rua Princesa Isabel 208, C.P. 21.192, SP-04602-970 São Paulo, Brazil, Tel: +55 11 543-7509, Fax: +55 11 240-4446

577

- **São Paulo** — Biblical Seminary in São Paulo (s2306)
Type of school: **Undergraduate/Bible school** Degrees offered: **BTh** Offers training for pastors: **yes** for lay persons: **yes** Type of available practical training: **preaching, pastoral care, religious education** Admission requirements: **high school graduation** Languages in use: **Portuguese** Full/part-time staff: **18** National/foreign students: **90 / 5** Library size: **3,000** Doctrinal basis: **Reformed** Worship life offered: **weekly** In relations with: **Evangelical Congregational Churches Union of Brazil**

Address: Seminário Bíblico de São Paulo, Rua Pires da Mota, 110, 1529000 São Paulo, SP, Brazil, Tel: +55 11 277-7618, Fax: +55 11 277-7618

- **São Paulo** — Presbyterian Theological Seminary "José Manuel da Conceição" (s2307)
Type of school: **Graduate/Univ+undergraduate/Bible school** Degrees offered: **BTh, MHistory, MTh** Offers training for pastors: **yes** Type of available practical training: **preaching, pastoral care, religious education** Admission requirements: **high school graduation/college** Languages in use: **Portuguese, English** Full/part-time staff: **25** National/foreign students: **140 / 3** Library size: **60,000** Doctrinal basis: **Reformed, Calvinist doctrines** Worship life offered: **weekly** In relations with: **Presb Ch of Brazil**

Address: Seminário Teológico Presbiteriano "José Manoel da Conceição," Rua Pascal, 1165, 4616004 São Paulo, SP, Brazil, Tel: +55 11 542-5676 and 543-3534, Fax: +55 11 542-5676

- **São Paulo** — Theological Seminary of São Paulo (s2313)
Type of school: **Undergraduate/Bible school** Degrees offered: **BTh** Offers training for pastors: **yes** Type of available practical training: **preaching, pastoral care, religious education** Admission requirements: **high school gradutation** Languages in use: **Portuguese** Full/part-time staff: **28** National/foreign students: **130 / 1** Library size: **15,000** Doctrinal basis: **Reformed** Worship life offered: **weekly** In relations with: **Independent Presb Ch of Brazil**

Address: Seminário Teológico de São Paulo, Rua Nesto Pestana, 136, 1303010 São Paulo, SP, Brazil, Tel: +55 11 257-3327, Fax: +55 11 257-3327

CAMEROON

- **Kumba** — Presbyterian Theological Seminary (s1031)
Degrees offered: **DiplTh, BTh** Offers training for pastors: **yes** for teachers: **yes** Type of available practical training: **homiletics, pastoral counseling** Admission requirements: **General Certificate of Education** Languages in use: **English** Full/part-time staff: **11** National/foreign students: **64 / 0** Doctrinal basis: **Reformed**

Address: Presbyterian Theological Seminary, P.O. Box 590, Kumba, South West Province, Cameroon, Tel: +237 35 43 65

• **Lolodorf** — School of Theology Dager (s1038)
Type of school: **Undergraduate/Bible school** Degrees offered: **BTh, LicTh** Offers training for pastors: **yes** for teachers: **no** for lay persons: **yes** Type of available practical training: **preaching, pastoral care, religious education** Admission requirements: **baccalaureate** Languages in use: **French** Full/part-time staff: **5** National/foreign students: **100 / 3** Library size: **5,000** Doctrinal basis: **Calvinism** Worship life offered: **daily** In relations with: **Eglise Presbyterienne camerounaise, Iglesia Presbiteriana de Guinea Ecuatorial, Eglise Evangélique du Gabon**

Address: Ecole de Théologie Dager, 10, Lolodorf, Cameroon

• **Mengong** — Seminary L. Paul Moore (s1036)
Offers training for pastors: **nc** Languages in use: **French** In relations with: **Eglise Presb Camerounaise Orth**

Address: Séminaire L. Paul Moore, B.P. 39, Mengong, Ebolowa, Cameroon

• **Nkongsamba** — Theological School of Ndoungué (s1032)
Type of school: **Graduate/Univ+Undergraduate/Bible school** Degrees offered: **BTh, Dipl in preaching and Bible teaching to lay persons, LicTh** Offers training for pastors: **yes** for lay persons: **yes** Type of available practical training: **preaching, pastoral care, religious education** Admission requirements: **admission test and examination of file** Languages in use: **French** Full/part-time staff: **8** National/foreign students: **50 / 8** Library size: **3,500** Doctrinal basis: **Bible, Protestant faith** Worship life offered: **2 services + 5 meditations per morning** In relations with: **Reformed Church of France, Reformed Church in the NL, Reformed Churches in Switzerland, Evangelical Church of Gabun,**

Address: Ecole de Théologie de Ndoungué, P.O. Box 311, Nkongsamba, Cameroon, Tel: +237 49 35 64nc

• **Yaoundé** — Cameroon Biblical Seminary (s1037)
Type of school: **Graduate/Univ+Undergraduate Seminary** Degrees offered: **BTh, MDiv, MTh** Offers training for pastors: **yes** for teachers: **yes** Type of available practical training: **preaching, pastoral care, evangelism, counseling** Admission requirements: **baccalaureate** Languages in use: **French, English** Full/part-time staff: **3 / 3** National/foreign students: **51 / nc** Library size: **1,500** Worship life offered: **daily**

Address: Séminaire biblique du Cameroun, B.P. 4009, Yaoundé, Cameroon, Tel: +237 30-77-63, Fax: +237 20-52 25

• **Yaoundé** — Faculty of Protestant Theology (s1034)
Type of school: **Graduate/Univ+Mission Institute** Degrees offered: **LicTh, MTh, DiplTh (D.E.T.A.), ThD** Offers training for pastors: **yes** for lay persons: **yes** Type of available practical training: **preaching, pastoral care, religious education** Admission requirements: **with recommendation from the church, baccalaureate for lic, lic for Master, Master for Doctorate** Languages in use: **French** Full/part-time staff: **8** National/foreign students: **125 / 55** Library size: **16,500**

Doctrinal basis: **Resurrection of God in Jesus Christ** Worship life offered: **daily morning worship 8-8:30 h, every Wed evening 18-20 h Eucharist, every last Sun/month 9-11 h**

Address: Faculté de théologie protestante de Yaoundé, B.P. 4011, 237 Yaoundé, Nlong-kak, Cameroon, Tel: +237 21 26 90, Fax: +237 21 26 90

- **Yaoundé** — Theological School of the African Protestant Church E.P.A. (s1033)

Type of school: **Undergraduate/Bible school** Degrees offered: **Dipl of Pastoral Studies** Offers training for pastors: **yes** for lay persons: **yes** Type of available practical training: **formation by alternative periods of internship in parishes and at seminary** Admission requirements: **BEPC, recommendation of the parish** Languages in use: **French (Kwassio)** Full/part-time staff: **2-4** National/foreign students: **6 / nc** Library size: **~950** Doctrinal basis: **Presbyterian** Worship life offered: **in local parish** In relations with: **Eglise Protestante Africaine (E.P.A.)**

Address: Ecole théologique de l'Eglise Protestante Africaine Ê.P.A., B.P. 6754, Yaoundé, Cameroon

CANADA

- **Charny** — Institute Farel (s3024)

Type of school: **Graduate/Univ** Degrees offered: **CertTh, BTh** Offers training for pastors: **yes** for lay persons: **yes** Type of available practical training: **preaching, pastoral care, religious education** Admission requirements: **minimum two years in college** Languages in use: **French** Full/part-time staff: **7** National/foreign students: **10 / nc** Library size: **5,000** In relations with: **Eglise réformée du Québec**

Address: Institut Farel, 5377 Maréchal Joffre, Charny, Québec G6X3C9, Canada, Tel: +1 418 832-9143, Fax: +1 418 832-9143, E-mail: institut.farel@usa.net

- **Edmonton** — St. Stephen's College — University of Alberta (s3022)

Degrees offered: **MTh, MA in Spirituality and Liturgy, DMin** Offers training for pastors: **nc** Languages in use: **English** Full/part-time staff: **4 / 15** National/foreign students: **140 / nc** Library size: **11,000** In relations with: **United Church of Canada**

Address: St. Stephen's College, University of Alberta, 8810-112th St., Bldg. 59, Edmonton, AL T6G 2J6, Canada, Tel: +1 403 439-7311, Fax: +1 403 433-8875

- **Halifax** — Atlantic School of Theology (s3016)

Type of school: **Seminary** Founded in **1971** Degrees offered: **MDiv, MTS, MTh, BTh** Offers training for pastors: **nc** Languages in use: **English** Full/part-time staff: **11 / 13** National/foreign students: **109 / nc** Library size: **70,000** In relations with: **United Ch of Canada, Angl Ch of Canada, RCath Ch**

580

Address: Atlantic School of Theology, 640 Franklin Street, Halifax, NS B3H 3B5, Canada, Tel: +1
902 423-5592, Fax: +1 902 492-4048

• **Hamilton** — Theological College of the Canadian Reformed Churches
(s3012)
Type of school: **Graduate/Univ** Degrees offered: **BDiv, MDiv** Offers training for
pastors: **yes** for teachers: **yes** Type of available practical training: **preaching,
catechetical or religious instruction, evangelism, mission, pastoral care, counseling** Admission requirements: **a Bachelor of Arts degree from a recognized
university** Languages in use: **English, Hebrew, Greek, Dutch, Latin** Full/
part-time staff: **4** National/foreign students: **18 / 3** Library size: **24,000** Doctrinal
basis: **same as Canadian Ref Churches** Worship life offered: **only devotion exercises** In relations with: **Canadian Reformed Churches**

Address: Theological College of the Canadian Reformed Churches, 110 West 27th, Hamilton, Ontario L9C 5A1, Canada, Tel: +1 905 575-3688, Fax: +1 905 575-0799

• **Kingston** — Queen's Theological College (s3014)
Founded in **1842** Degrees offered: **MDiv, MTS, MTh, BTh** Offers training for
pastors: **nc** Languages in use: **English** Full/part-time staff: **17** National/foreign
students: **91 / nc** Library size: **62,800** In relations with: **United Ch of Canada**

Address: Queen's Theological College, Kingston, ON K7L 3N6, Canada, Tel: +1 613 545-2110,
Fax: +1 613 545-6879

• **Montreal** — Faculty of Religious Studies — McGill University (s3010)
Type of school: **Graduate/Univ** Degrees offered: **BTh, BA, MTh, MA, PhD** Offers training for pastors: **yes** Type of available practical training: **no** Languages in
use: **English, French** Full/part-time staff: **11** National/foreign students: **250 / 20**
Doctrinal basis: **Interdenominational** Worship life offered: **weekly**

Address: Faculty of Religious Studies — McGill University, 3520 University St., Montreal, P.Q.
H3A 2A8, Canada, Tel: +1 514 398-4121, Fax: +1 514 398-6665, E-mail: frs@wil-
son.lan.mcgill.ca

• **Montreal** — Presbyterian College (s3025)
Founded in **1865** Degrees offered: **BTh** Offers training for pastors: **nc** Languages
in use: **English** Full/part-time staff: **5 / 2** Library size: **40,000** In relations with:
Presbyterian Church of Canada

Address: Presbyterian College, 3495 University St., Montreal, QU H3A 2A8, Canada, Tel: +1 514
288-5256, Fax: +1 514 398-6665

• **Montreal** — The United Theological College — Le Séminaire Univ (s3017)
Type of school: **Graduate/Univ+Undergraduate/Bible school** Founded in **1925**
Degrees offered: **MDiv, through faculty of McGill: STM, PhD, BTh, MDiv,
MA** Offers training for pastors: **yes** for lay persons: **yes** Type of available practical
training: **field-based In-Ministry year, courses in homiletics, worship, Christian education, counseling, pastoral care, religious education** Admission requirements: **CEGEP or equivalent (e.g., junior college or BA)** Languages in
use: **English, some French** Full/part-time staff: **3 / 6** National/foreign students: **35**

/ 4 Library size: **McGill Univ: 60,000** Doctrinal basis: **Reformed approach** Worship life offered: **2 times per week, also in other denominations (Presb + Angls as well)** In relations with: **United Church of Canada**

Address: The United Theological College — Le Séminaire Univ, 3521 University St., Montréal, QU H3A 2A9, Canada, Tel: +1 514 849-2042, Fax: +1 514 398-6665

- **Ottawa** — Ottawa Theological Hall (s3026)

Type of school: **Seminary** Founded in **1982** Degrees offered: **CertDiv, CertTh, DiplDiv** Offers training for pastors: **nc** Type of available practical training: **pastoral theology, evangelism, church growth, biblical counseling** Admission requirements: **graduate school level and church recommendation** Languages in use: **English** Full/part-time staff: **5 / several** National/foreign students: **12 / nc** Library size: **8,000** Doctrinal basis: **Reformed Presbyterian** Worship life offered: **weekly** In relations with: **Reformed Presbyterian Church of North America**

Address: Ottawa Theological Hall, P.O. Box 23139, 466 Woodland Avenue, Ottawa, K2A 4E2, Canada, Tel: +1 613 596-5566, Fax: +1 613 257-4900, E-mail: adjemian@perth.igs.net

- **Otterburne** — Providence Theological Seminary (s3027)

Type of school: **Seminary** Founded in **1925** Degrees offered: **Cert in Th Studies, MA, MDiv** Offers training for pastors: **nc** Languages in use: **English** Full/part-time staff: **9 / 18** Library size: **50,000**

Address: Providence Theological Seminary, Otterburne, MN R0A 1G0, Canada, Tel: +1 204 433-7488, Fax: +1 204 433-7158

- **Pambrun** — Millar College of the Bible (s3028)

Founded in **1932** Degrees offered: **Dipl in Christian Leadership, BA** Offers training for pastors: **nc** Languages in use: **English** Full/part-time staff: **5 / 3** National/foreign students: **25 / nc** Library size: **10,000** In relations with: **Christian and Missionary Alliance (CMA), Evang and Free Churches**

Address: Millar College of the Bible, P.O. Box 25, Pambrun, SA S0N 1W0, Canada, Tel: +1 306 582-2033, Fax: +1 306 582-2027

- **Paris** — Francis Sandy Theological Centre (s3023)

Type of school: **Undergraduate/Bible school** Founded in **1987** Degrees offered: **Lay Pastoral Ministry Certificate, Dipl** Offers training for pastors: **yes** for teachers: **yes** for lay persons: **yes** Type of available practical training: **na** Admission requirements: **literacy in English + demonstrated leadership in church and community** Languages in use: **English** Full/part-time staff: **3** National/foreign students: **na / na** Library size: **200** Doctrinal basis: **na** Worship life offered: **na** In relations with: **United Church of Canada**

Address: Francis Sandy Theological Centre, P.O. Box 446, Paris, ON N3T 3T5, Canada, Tel: +1 519 442-7725, Fax: +1 519 442-3444

- **Saskatoon** — St. Andrew's Theological College (s3019)

Type of school: **Seminary** Founded in **1912** Degrees offered: **MTS, BTh, MDiv, STM, MPC** Offers training for pastors: **yes** for teachers: **no** for lay persons: **yes**

Type of available practical training: **preaching, pastoral care, religious educa-tion** Admission requirements: **Bachelor's degree** Languages in use: **English** Full/part-time staff: **5 / 2** National/foreign students: **44 / nc** Library size: **36,000** Worship life offered: **4 times per week** In relations with: **United Church of Canada**

Address: St. Andrew's Theological College, 1121 College Dr., Saskatoon, SK S7N 0W3, Canada, Tel: +1 306 966-8970, Fax: +1 306 966-8981, E-mail: bourgeoism@sask.usak.ca

- **Strathmore** — Covenant Bible College (s3029)
Founded in **1941** Degrees offered: **Cert of Christian Studies** Offers training for pastors: **nc** Languages in use: **English** Full/part-time staff: **4 / 1** Library size: **6,000** In relations with: **Evangelical Covenant Church of Canada**

Address: Covenant Bible College, 630 Westchester Road, Strathmore, AL T1P 1H8, Canada, Tel: +1 403 934-6200

- **Swan River** — Living Word Bible College and Theological Seminary (s3030)
Type of school: **Seminary** Founded in **1952** Degrees offered: **Cert in Biblical Studies, BA in Biblical Studies, MTh** Offers training for pastors: **nc** Languages in use: **English** Full/part-time staff: **6** Library size: **4,000** In relations with: **Christians of Ev Faith of Canada**

Address: Living Word Bible College and Theological Seminary, P.O. Box 969, Swan River, MN R0L 1Z0, Canada, Tel: +1 204 734-3836, Fax: +1 204 734-3701

- **Three Hills** — Prairie Bible College (s3031)
Type of school: **Undergraduate/Bible school** Founded in **1922** Degrees offered: **Cert in Bible, Dipl in Bible Studies, BA, BMin, BTh, Assoc. of Arts in Mission Aviation** Offers training for pastors: **yes** for teachers: **yes** for lay persons: **yes** Type of available practical training: **pastoral care, religious education** Admission re-quirements: **be a Christian studying God's Word and completion of 12th grade** Languages in use: **English** Full/part-time staff: **23 / 9** National/foreign students: **438 / na** Library size: **59,834** Doctrinal basis: **none** Worship life offered: **3 times per week**

Address: Prairie Bible College, 319 5th Ave. N, Three Hills, AL T0M 2A0, Canada, Tel: +1 403 443-5511, Fax: +1 403 443-5540, E-mail: Paul.Ferris@PBI.AB.CA

- **Toronto** — Centre for Christian Studies (s3018)
Type of school: **Graduate+Undergraduate Seminary** Founded in **1969** Degrees offered: **Studies for Professional Ministry, Dipl in educational, pastoral, and social ministry** Offers training for pastors: **yes** for teachers: **yes** for lay persons: **yes** Type of available practical training: **preaching, pastoral care, religious edu-cation** Admission requirements: **application and interview** Languages in use: **English** Full/part-time staff: **4 / 1** National/foreign students: **51 / 1** Library size: **4,000** Worship life offered: **weekly** In relations with: **Angl Ch of Canada, United Ch of Canada**

Address: Centre for Christian Studies, 77, Charles Street West, Suite 400, Toronto, Ontario M5S 1K5, Canada, Tel: +1 416 923-1168, Fax: +1 416 923-5496, E-mail: ccs@ecunet.org

• **Toronto** — Emmanuel College of Victoria University (s3015)
Type of school: **Graduate/Univ** Founded in **1928** Degrees offered: **basic degree: MDiv, MRE, advanced degree: MTh, ThD, DMin** Offers training for pastors: **yes** for teachers: **yes** for lay persons: **yes** Type of available practical training: **all basic degree levels have a highly practical component, e.g., homiletics, worship, music, etc., credit "practicums" in worship, education, pastoral theology, homiletics** Admission requirements: **baccalaureate degree from a recognized university, at least 65% average+4 subjects Humanities** Languages in use: **English** Full/part-time staff: **13 / 6** National/foreign students: **225 / 6** Library size: **65,854** Doctrinal basis: **faith in the Triune God** Worship life offered: **6 times per week a 15 min morning prayer, major service every Wednesday afternoon** In relations with: **United Church of Canada**

Address: Emmanuel College — Victoria University, 75 Queen's Park Crescent, Toronto, Ontario
M5S 1K7, Canada, Tel: +1 416 585-4539, Fax: +1 416 585-4516

• **Toronto** — Knox College (s3013)
Type of school: **Graduate/Univ** Degrees offered: **MDiv, MTh, DMin, ThD, PhD** Offers training for pastors: **yes** for teachers: **yes** Type of available practical training: **preaching, pastoral care, religious education** Admission requirements: **Bachelor's degree from a recognized university (for MDiv degree), Bachelor's degree + MDiv for other degrees** Languages in use: **English** Full/part-time staff: **9** National/foreign students: **143 / 28** Library size: **72,000** Doctrinal basis: **Reformed** Worship life offered: **weekly** In relations with: **Presbyterian Church in Canada**

Address: Knox College, 59 St. George St., Toronto, Ontario M5S 2E6, Canada, Tel: +1 416
971-4500, Fax: +1 416 971-2133

• **Toronto** — Toronto School of Theology (s3032)
Type of school: **Graduate Seminary/Univ** Degrees offered: **MDiv, MTS, MTh, ThD, PhD, DMin** Offers training for pastors: **yes** for teachers: **yes** for lay persons: **no** Type of available practical training: **continuing education for ministers** Admission requirements: **BA or equivalent** Languages in use: **English** Full/part-time staff: **90 / 100** National/foreign students: **1,075 / 95** Library size: **400,000** Worship life offered: **weekly** In relations with: **state university**

Address: Toronto School of Theology, 47 Queen's Park Crescent East, Toronto, OT M5S 2C3,
Canada, Tel: +1 416 978-4039, Fax: +1 416 978-7821, E-mail: registrar.tst@utoronto.ca

• **Vancouver** — Vancouver School of Theology (s3011)
Type of school: **Seminary** Founded in **1971** Degrees offered: **MDiv, MPS (Pastoral Studies), MTS, MTh, Dipl in Christian studies (one year)** Offers training for pastors: **yes** for teachers: **yes** for lay persons: **yes** Type of available practical training: **preaching, pastoral care, field education every term** Admission requirements: **Bachelors degree** Languages in use: **English** Full/part-time staff: **12 / 4** National/foreign students: **110 / 20** Library size: **85,000** Worship life offered: **weekly for whole school, Angls 10 times/week, United+Presb. once per week**

584

In relations with: **United Church of Canada, Presbyterian Ch in Canada, United Meth Ch USA**

Address: Vancouver School of Theology, 6000 Iona Drive, Vancouver, B.C. V6T 1L4, Canada, Tel: +1 604 228-9031, Fax: +1 604 228-0189, E-mail: Jim.McCullum@Ecunet.org

• **Winnipeg** — Faculty of Theology — University of Winnipeg (s3021)
Type of school: **Graduate/Univ** Degrees offered: **MDiv, MTS** Offers training for pastors: **yes** for teachers: **yes** for lay persons: **yes** Type of available practical training: **training in preaching and pastoral care, religious education** Admission requirements: **undergraduate degree** Languages in use: **English** National/foreign students: **260 / 4** Library size: **548,572** Doctrinal basis: **Ecumenical** Worship life offered: **special occasions and holidays** In relations with: **all denominations**

Address: Faculty of Theology — University of Winnipeg, 515 Portage Avenue, Winnipeg, MB R3B 2E9, Canada, Tel: 1 204 786-9390, Fax: +1 204 772-2584

CENTRAL AFRICAN REPUBLIC

• **Bangui** — Faculty of Evangelical Theology of Bangui (s1300)
Type of school: **Graduate/Univ** Founded in **1977** Degrees offered: **Licence in Religious Sciences, Licence in Theol, MRelSciences, MTh** Offers training for pastors: **yes** for teachers: **yes** Type of available practical training: **preaching, pastoral care, religious education** Admission requirements: **Bachelor** Languages in use: **French** Full/part-time staff: **18** National/foreign students: **47 / 29** Library size: **12,800** Worship life offered: **occasionally / Free — Evangelical liturgy** In relations with: **Meth, Angl, Mennonite, Reformed, and Lutheran Church**

Address: Faculté de Théologie Evangélique de Bangui, P.O. Box 988, Bangui, Central African Republic, Tel: +263 61 14 93, Fax: +263 61 33 30

CHILE

• **Santiago** — Evangelical Institute of Chile (s2031)
Type of school: **Undergraduate/Bible school** Degrees offered: **BMin, BTh** Offers training for pastors: **yes** for teachers: **yes** for lay persons: **yes** Languages in use: **Spanish** Full/part-time staff: **15** national/foreign students: **39 / 2** Library size: **8,500** Doctrinal basis: **Reformed Calvinist** Worship life offered: **weekly** In relations with: **WARC, Liga Reformada Misionera de Holanda**

Address: Instituto Evangélico de Chile, Casilla 14060, Casa Matriz; Avenida Brasil No. 15, 02 Santiago, Chile, Tel: +56 32 698-4838 & 698-2793

585

- **Santiago** — Evangelical Theological Community of Chile (s2030)
Degrees offered: **DiplTh** Offers training for pastors: **yes** Languages in use: **Spanish**

Address: Comunidad Teológica Evangélica de Chile, Castilla 13596, Santiago, Chile

- **Santiago** — Presbyterian Theological Faculty (s2032)
Type of school: **Evangelist/Pastoral Training Institute** Offers training for pastors: **nc** Admission requirements: **secondary education** Languages in use: **Spanish** Full/part-time staff: **4** Library size: **1,200** Doctrinal basis: **WestConf**

Address: Facultad Presbiteriana de Teologia, C.P. 22-58 (Nueva-Santiago), Exegeuil Fernándes 1144 — Nuñoa-Sontiago, 2 58 Santiago, Chile, Tel: +56 2 238-1188, Fax: +56 2 238-1188

CHINA

- **Beijing** — Yanjing Union Theological College (s4032)
Offers training for pastors: **yes** Languages in use: **Mandarin**

Address: Yanjing Union Theological College, Bing-He Rd., Quing-He Twon, Hai-Ding District, Beijing 100085, China, Tel: +86 10 6292-4272

- **Chengdu** — Sichuan Theological College (s4035)
Founded in **1984** Offers training for pastors: **yes** Languages in use: **Chinese** Full/part-time staff: **10 / 6** Library size: **4,000**

Address: Sichuan Theological College, 19 Sishengci North St., Chengdu, Sichuan Province 610017, China, Tel: +86 28 674-7930

- **Xian** — Shaanxi Bible College (s4045)
Offers training for pastors: **yes** Languages in use: **Mandarin**

Address: Shaanxi Bible College, Zhang-Ba Town, Yan-Ta District, Shaanxi Province 713800, China, Tel: +86 29 4260936

- **Fuzhou** — Fujian Theological College (s4039)
Offers training for pastors: **yes** Languages in use: **Mandarin**

Address: Fujian Theological College, 16 Lequn Road, Chanshan District, Fuzhou, Fujian Province 350007, China, Tel: +86 591 3445-102

- **Guangzhou** — Guangdong Union Theological College (s4044)
Offers training for pastors: **yes** Languages in use: **Mandarin**

Address: Guangdong Union Theological College, 69 Shamian Dajie, Guangzhou, Guangdong Province 510130, China, Tel: +86 20 8186-7950 and 8190-7571

- **Hanzhou** — Zhejiang Theological College (s4038)
Offers training for pastors: **yes** Languages in use: **Mandarin**

Address: Zhejiang Theological College, 104 Jiefang Road, Hanzhou, Zhejiang Province 310009, China, Tel: +86 571 7011303

- **Hefei** — Anhui Theological College (s4037)
Offers training for pastors: **yes** Languages in use: **Mandarin**

Address: Anhui Theological College, 8 Sui-Xi Rd., Hefei, Anhui Province 230041, China, Tel: +86 5538-135

- **Jinan** — Shandong Theological College (s4036)
Offers training for pastors: **yes** Languages in use: **Mandarin**

Address: Shandong Theological College, 67 Jing 2 Road, Jinan, Shandong Province 250001, China, Tel: +86 531 692-6227

- **Kunming** — Yunnan Theological College (s4042)
Offers training for pastors: **yes** Languages in use: **Mandarin**

Address: Yunnan Theological College, 59 Kunsha Road, Kunming, Yunnan Province 650101, China, Tel: +86 871 8182558; 8182775

- **Nanjing** — Nanjing Union Theological Seminary (s4043)
Offers training for pastors: **yes** Languages in use: **English**

Address: Nanjing Union Theological Seminary, 17 Da Jian Yin Xiang, Nanjing, Jiangsu Province 210029, China, Tel: +86 25 664-1439

- **Shanghai** — East China Theological College (s4033)
Offers training for pastors: **yes** Languages in use: **Mandarin**

Address: East China Theological College, 71 Wu Yuan Road, Shanghai, 200031, China, Tel: +86 21 6433-3304

- **Shenyang** — North East Theological College (s4031)
Offers training for pastors: **yes** Languages in use: **Mandarin, Korean**

Address: North East Theological College, 48 North Jing Street, Shen He District, Shenyang, Liaoning Province 110014, China, Tel: +86 24 282-9367; 433-3251

- **Wuhan** — Zhong Nan Theological Seminary (s4034)
Type of school: **Undergraduate/Bible school** Offers training for pastors: **yes** Type of available practical training: **preaching, pastoral care, religious education** Admission requirements: **recommendation by church and entrance exam** Languages in use: **Chinese** Full/part-time staff: **10** National/foreign students: **180 / nc** Library size: **5,000** Worship life offered: **3 times per week, prayers daily** In relations with: **Christian Councils of Hubei, Hunan, Guangdon, Hainan, and Guangxi**

Address: Zhong Nan Theological Seminary, 277 Min Zhu Road, 86 Wuhan, Hubei Province 430061, China, Tel: +86 27 887-6281, Fax: 186 27 891-1368

Hong Kong (Special administrative region of the People's Republic of China)

- **Kowloon** — China Bible Seminary (s4046)
Type of school: **Graduate/Univ** Founded in **1930** Degrees offered: **Cert in Bible**

Studies, BTh, MA in Christian Ministry Offers training for pastors: **yes** for teachers: **yes** for lay persons: **yes** Admission requirements: **Bible College graduate** Languages in use: **Chinese and some English** Full/part-time staff: **5 / 12** National/foreign students: **402 / 1** Library size: **10,000** Worship life offered: **daily**

Address: China Bible Seminary, 3/F Ashley Mansion 10-14 Ashley Rd. TST, Kowloon, Hong Kong, China, Tel: +852 2721-2406, Fax: +852 2724-0685

- **Kowloon Tong** — China Graduate School of Theology (s4047)
Type of school: **Seminary** Founded in **1975** Degrees offered: **Dipl in Christian Studies, MTh, MDiv, MCS (Christian Studies), MCE (Counselor Education)** Offers training for pastors: **yes** for teachers: **yes** for lay persons: **yes** Type of available practical training: **preaching, Christian education, pastoral counseling** Languages in use: **Cantonese, Mandarin, English** Full/part-time staff: **12 / 3** National/foreign students: **222 / nc** Library size: **40,000** Doctrinal basis: **interdenominational** Worship life offered: **daily** In relations with: **interdenominational**

Address: China Graduate School of Theology, 5 Devon Rd., Kowloon Tong, China, Tel: +852 2337-4106, Fax: +852 2794-2337, E-mail: cgst@infolink.net or info@cgst.edu

- **Shatin** — Theology Division, Chung Chi College — The Chinese University of Hong Kong (s4040)
Type of school: **Graduate/Univ+Undergraduate/Bible school** Founded in **1963** Degrees offered: **PhD, ThD, MTh, MDiv, MPhil, BDiv, BDiv(Hons), BA** Offers training for pastors: **yes** for teachers: **yes** for lay persons: **yes** Type of available practical training: **preaching, pastoral care, religious education** Admission requirements: **secondary school graduate, bachelor degree holders** Languages in use: **Chinese, English** Full/part-time staff: **12** National/foreign students: **55 / 2** Library size: **1,279,000** Doctrinal basis: **none** Worship life offered: **2 times per week** In relations with: **Tsung Tsin Mission (Basel Mission), Church of Christ in China, Angl Church, Meth Ch**

Address: Theology Division, Chung Chi College, Shatin, New Territories, 0852 Shatin, China, Tel: +852 2609-6705, Fax: +852 2603-5224, E-mail: lklo@cuhk.edu.hk

---

COLOMBIA

- **Barranquilla** — Presbyterian and Reformed Theological Seminary of Gran Colombia (s2040)
Type of school: **Graduate+Undergraduate+Pastor/Evangelist/Missionary** Founded in **1982** Degrees offered: **BTh, LicTh** Offers training for pastors: **yes** for teachers: **yes** for lay persons: **yes** Admission requirements: **University level and interview** Languages in use: **Spanish** Full/part-time staff: **15 / 8** National/foreign students: **60 / 10** Library size: **7,000** Doctrinal basis: **WestConf** Worship life offered: **weekly + on special occasions** In relations with: **Presbyterian Church of Colombia, Mennonite, Angl, Lutheran churches**

Address: Seminario Teologico Presbiteriano y Reformado de la Gran Colombia, Apartado A 50688, Carrera 46, Nos. 48-50, Barranquilla, 95, Colombia, Tel: +57 5 340-1240 and 341-7708, Fax: +57 5 340-1240; 341-7708, E-mail: precosta@b-quilla.cetcol.net.co

• **Bogotá** — Presbyterian Faculty of the Central Presbytery (s2044)
Offers training for pastors: **nc** Languages in use: **Spanish**

Address: Facultad Presbiterio Corporación Presbiterío Central, Diagonal 49 A, No. 28-06 Sur, Bogotá, Colombia,

• **Ibagué** — Theological Faculty — South Presbytery (s2043)
Offers training for pastors: **nc** Languages in use: **Spanish**

Address: Facultad Teológica Presbiterio del Sur, Carrera 4, Nos. 4-33, Ibagué, Colombia

• **Montería** — Biblical Institute (s2042)
Offers training for pastors: **nc** Languages in use: **Spanish** In relations with: **Presbiterio Noroeste**

Address: Instituto Bíblico, Apartado 01, Montería, Colombia

• **Quindio** — Biblical Seminary of the Alliance in Colombia (s2045)
Type of school: **Seminary** Founded in **1933** Degrees offered: **Dipl in Bible and Theol, BA in Bible and Theol, Lic in Bible and Theol** Offers training for pastors: **nc** Languages in use: **Spanish** Full/part-time staff: **4** National/foreign students: **200 / nc** Library size: **8,000** In relations with: **Christian Alliance of Colombia**

Address: Seminario Biblico Alianza de Colombia, Apartado Aero 516, Armenia, Quindio, Colombia

CONGO (BRAZZAVILLE)

• **Bacongo** — **Brazzaville** — Theological Seminary of Mansimou (s1046)
Offers training for pastors: **nc** Languages in use: **French**

Address: Séminaire Théologique de Mansimou, B.P. 3217, Bacongo — Brazzaville, Congo

• **Loutété** — Biblical Formation Center of Ngouédi (s1045)
Type of school: **Bible school** Degrees offered: **Cert Th** Offers training for pastors: **yes** for lay people: **yes** Type of available practical training: **preaching, pastoral care** Language in use: **French** Full/part-time staff: **6** Students: **20** Library size: **200** Worship life offered: **daily** Doctrinal basis: **Trinitarian**

Address: Centre de Formation Biblique de Ngouédi, B.P. 98, Loutété, Congo-Brazzaville

CONGO

• **Boma** — Boma Evangelical Theological Faculty (s1246)
Type of school: **Graduate/Univ+Undergraduate/Bible school** Founded in **1976**
Degrees offered: **GTh, LicTh** Offers training for pastors: **yes** Languages in use:
French Full/part-time staff: **7 / 8** Library size: **4,000** In relations with: **Christian and Missionary Alliance (CMA)**

Address: Faculté de Théologie évangélique de Boma, B.P. 174, Boma, Bas **Congo**, Congo

• **Bunia** — Bunia Theological Seminary (ISTB) (s1241)
Type of school: **Undergraduate and Graduate Theological Seminary** Founded in **1961** Degrees offered: **Cert, MTh** Offers training for pastors: **yes** for teachers: **yes** Full/part-time staff: **10** National/foreign students: **40 / nc** Library size: **1,000** Doctrinal basis: **Evangelical, interdenominational** Admission requirements: **secondary school** Languages in use: **French Lingala, Swahili**

Address: Institut Supérieur Théologique de Bunia, B.P. 304, Bunia, Congo (or P.O. Box 21285, Nairobi, Kenya)

• **Kananga** — Preachers School (s1240)
Offers training for pastors: **yes** Languages in use: **French** In relations with: **ECC, Communauté presbytérienne**

Address: Ecole des Prédicateurs, Luebo, B.P. 117, Kananga, Congo

• **Kananga** — Reformed Theological Faculty in Kasai (s1237)
Type of school: **Graduate/Univ+Undergraduate/Bible school** Degrees offered: **LicTh, Dipl Rel Studies** Offers training for pastors: **yes** for teachers: **yes** Type of available practical training: **preaching, pastoral care, religious education** Admission requirements: **state dipl and church recommendation** Languages in use: **French** Full/part-time staff: **27** National/foreign students: **97 / nc** Library size: **9,640** Doctrinal basis: **Reformed**

Address: Faculté de Théologie Reformée au Kasai, B.P. 159, Ndesha Mission, Kananga, Congo

• **Kinshasa** — Protestant University of Congo (s1236)
Founded in **1959** Degrees offered: **Lic, MA, ThD, Habil** Offers training for pastors: **nc** Admission requirements: **12 years schooling** Languages in use: **French** Full/part-time staff: **10 / 4** National/foreign students: **130 / nc** In relations with: **ECC**

Address: Université Protestante du Congo, B.P. 4745, Kinshasa 2, Congo

• **Limete** — Presbyterian Pastoral Institute Booth (s1235)
Type of school: **Undergraduate/Bible school** Degrees offered: **Diploma on a level of A2** Offers training for pastors: **yes** Type of available practical training: **homiletics, Sunday school, pastoral care, religious education** Admission requirements: **4-5 years post primary** Languages in use: **French** Full/part-time staff: **8** National/foreign students: **28 / nc** Library size: **152** Worship life offered:

daily 6:00 + 20:00 In relations with: **Faculté de la Théologie reformée au Kasai; Ecoles internationales d'Evangelisation & d'Education Chrétienne**

Address: Institut Pastoral Presbytérien Booth, B.P. 91, Sokwele No. 1 Q Lemba-Salongo, Limete, Congo

• **Luozi** — Theological and Evangelical Seminary of Luozi (s1249)
Type of school: **Evangelist/Pastoral Training Institute** Offers training for pastors: **nc** for lay persons: **yes** Languages in use: **French** In relations with: **Eglise évangélique du Congo, Svenska Missionsförbundet**

Address: Séminaire théologique et évangélique de Luozi (Stel), C.P. 36, Cooreman Siege (CEZ), Luozi, Congo

• **Mbandaka** — Institute of Theology in Bolenge (s1238)
Type of school: **Graduate School** Degrees offered: **GTh** Offers training for pastors: **yes** for teachers: **yes** Type of available practical training: **preaching, pastoral care, religious education 3 times per week in a given parish** Admission requirements: **being a pastor with diploma of the state, being sent by the church** Languages in use: **French** Full/part-time staff: **1 pastor, 5 assistants** National/foreign students: **25 / 0** Library size: **1,272** Doctrinal basis: **Calvinist** Worship life offered: **weekly**

Address: Institut Supérieur de Théologie de Bolenge, B.P. 178, Bolenge Mission, Mbandaka, 378, Congo

• **Mbujimayi** — Bible Training Seminary "Emmaus" (s1245)
Offers training for pastors: **yes** Languages in use: **French**

Address: Séminaire de Formation Biblique — Centre Biblique Emaus, B.P. 875, Mbujimayi, Congo

---

COOK ISLANDS

• **Rarotonga** — Takamoa Theological College (s5100)
Type of school: **Undergraduate/Bible school** Degrees offered: **DiplTh, Cert of Biblical Studies** Offers training for pastors: **yes** Type of available practical training: **preaching, pastoral care, religious education** Admission requirements: **College Entrance Examination** Languages in use: **English, Cook Islands Moari** Full/part-time staff: **6** National/foreign students: **12 / 0** Library size: **500** Doctrinal basis: **ApC, NicC** Worship life offered: **daily** In relations with: **Cook Islands Christian Church**

Address: Takamoa Theological College, P.O. Box 93, Rarotonga, Cook Islands

COSTA RICA

• **San José** — Farel Institute (s2051)
Type of school: **Undergraduate/Bible school** Degrees offered: **DiplTh** Offers training for pastors: **yes** for lay persons: **yes** Admission requirements: **absolved secondary school** Languages in use: **Spanish** Full/part-time staff: **3** National/foreign students: **14 / 0** Library size: **2,800** Doctrinal basis: **HeidC, BelgC** Worship life offered: **none** In relations with: **Christian Reformed Church of Costa Rica**

Address: Instituto Farel, Apartado 10250-1000, San José, Costa Rica, Tel: +506 257-4754, Fax: +506 255-4779

• **San José** — Latin-American Bible Seminary (s2050)
Type of school: **Graduate/Univ** Founded in **1923** Degrees offered: **BTh, LicTh, MTh** Offers training for pastors: **yes** for teachers: **yes** for lay persons: **yes** Admission requirements: **secondary school (Bachillerato) and recommendation of the church** Languages in use: **Spanish** Full/part-time staff: **14 / 3** National/foreign students: **900 / na** Library size: **29,000** In relations with: **Ecumenical**

Address: Seminario Bíblico Latinoamericano, Apartado 901, 3, Av. lt, 1000 San José, Costa Rica, Tel: +506 222-7555, Fax: +506 233-7531, E-mail: bsebila@sol.racsa.co.cr

CUBA

• **Matanzas** — Evangelical Seminary of Theology (s3300)
Type of school: **Graduate/Univ** Degrees offered: **MTh, LicTh, DiplTh** Offers training for pastors: **yes** for teachers: **yes** Admission requirements: **baccalaureate, recommendation of the church** Languages in use: **English in translation, Spanish** Full/part-time staff: **19** National/foreign students: **38 / 5** Worship life offered: **daily** In relations with: **Iglesia Presbiteriana Reformada de Cuba, Iglesia Christiana Reformada de Cuba**

Address: Seminario Evangélico de Teologia, Apartado 149, 53 Matanzas, Cuba, Tel: +53 7 522-866, Fax: +53 7 338-110

CZECH REPUBLIC

• **Hradec Králové** — Bible and Mission School in Hradec Králové (s6030)
Type of school: **Undergraduate/Bible school** Offers training for pastors: **nc** for teachers: **yes** for lay persons: **yes** Type of available practical training: **preaching, Sunday school teaching** Admission requirements: **leaving examination and admission examination** Languages in use: **Czech, English, German, Greek** Full/part-time staff: **10** National/foreign students: **32 / 0** Library size: **2,100** Doctrinal

basis: **4 Confessions of Ceskobratská Ctrken Evang** Worship life offered: **message every day, once per year worship** In relations with: **Ceskobratrská Ctrken Evanglicka, Jungmanova 9, Praha 1**

Address: Biblická a Misijní Skola, Kavci placek 121, CS-50057 50002 Hradec Králové, Czech Republic, Tel: +420 49 27270, Fax: +420 49 27270

• **Praha** — Evangelical Theological Seminary (s6032)
Type of school: **Evangelist/Pastoral Training Institute** Degrees offered: **State Dipl** Offers training for pastors: **yes** for teachers: **yes** Admission requirements: **reference and recommendation by the church** Languages in use: **Czech** Full/part-time staff: **12** National/foreign students: **110 / 5** Library size: **3,000** Doctrinal basis: **Confession of the Evang Alliance** Worship life offered: **weekly** In relations with: **Czech Brethren**

Address: Evangelisch-theologisches Seminar, Soukenická 15, CR-11000 Praha 1, Czech Republic, Tel: +420 2 231-8131, Fax: +420 2 231-8131

• **Praha** — Protestant Theological Faculty of Charles University (s6033)
Type of school: **Graduate / Univ** Degrees offered: **MTh, DTh** Offers training for pastors: **yes** for teachers: **yes** for lay persons: **yes** Admission requirements: **baccalaureate** Languages in use: **Czech, English, German, Hungarian** Full/part-time staff: **30** National/foreign students: **343 / 32** Library size: **150,000** Doctrinal basis: **Reformed perspective** Type of available practical training: **courses in homiletics, catechetics, pastoral care** Worship life offered: **weekly** In relations with: **Evang Church of Czech Brethren, Church of the Brethren, others**

Address: Evangelická teologická fakulta University Karlovy, Cerná 9, P.O. Box 529, 11555 Praha 1, Czech Republic, Tel: +420 2 219 88216 Fax: +420 2 219 88215

DOMINICAN REPUBLIC

• **Santo Domingo** — Theological Seminary (s3313)
Type of school: **Evangelist/Pastoral Training Institute** Degrees offered: **BD, CertTh** Offers training for pastors: **yes** for teachers: **yes** for lay persons: **yes** Admission requirements: **baccalaureate** Languages in use: **Spanish** Full/part-time staff: **12** National/foreign students: **22 / 0** Library size: **2,000** Doctrinal basis: **Reformed** Worship life offered: **2 times daily** In relations with: **Igl Evang. Dominicana**

Address: Seminario Teológico, C.P. 727, Calle Ave. México # 31, Santo Domingo, Dominican Republic, Tel: +1 809 682-4945, Fax: +1 809 689-4088

EGYPT

• **Abbasiah, Cairo** — Evangelical Theological Seminary in Cairo (s1040)
Type of school: **Graduate Seminary** Founded in **1863** Degrees offered: **DiplTh, BTh** Offers training for pastors: **yes** for teachers: **yes** for lay persons: **yes** Type of available practical training: **practical preaching, pastoral care, counseling** Admission requirements: **high school certificate, church recommendation and membership** Languages in use: **Arabic, English, Hebrew** Full/part-time staff: **23** National/foreign students: **96 / 19** Library size: **34,000** Doctrinal basis: **Evangelical Presbyterian** Worship life offered: **2 times per week** In relations with: **Evangelical Presbyterian and Reformed churches**

Address: Evangelical Theological Seminary, 8, El Sekeh el Bedah St., 20 Abbasiah, Cairo, Egypt, Tel: +20 2 282-2162, Fax: +20 2 285-7412, E-mail: etsc@intouch.com

EL SALVADOR

• **San Salvador** — Lutheran University of Salvador (s2060)
Type of school: **Graduate/Univ** Degrees offered: **LicTh** Offers training for pastors: **yes** for teachers: **yes** for lay persons: **yes** Languages in use: **Spanish** Full/part-time staff: **12** National/foreign students: **130 / 5** Library size: **1,200** Worship life offered: **twice each term** In relations with: **Iglesia Reformada de El Salvador**

Address: Universidad Luterana Slavadoreña, C.P. 3039 y 3057, Km. 3 carretera a los planes de Renderos, San Salvador, El Salvador, Tel: +270 7002, Fax: +270 7222, E-mail: Email U.L.S.@euromaya.com.

ETHIOPIA

• **Dembi Dollo** — Gidada Bible School (s1043)
Type of school: **Evangelist/Pastoral Training Institute** Degrees offered: **Certificate** Offers training for pastors: **yes** for teachers: **yes** for lay persons: **yes** Type of available practical training: **preaching, pastoral care, religious education** Admission requirements: **12th grade completion and church recommendation** Languages in use: **Oromo, English** Full/part-time staff: **5** National/foreign students: **31 / nc** Library size: **800** In relations with: **Mekhane Yesus Church (Bethel Synod Coordination), PCUSA, Evangelical Lutheran Churches in Europe**

Address: Gidada Bible School, P.O. Box 16, Dembi Dollo, Wollega, Ethiopia

594

- **Mizan Teferi** — Mizan Teferi Bible School (s1042)
Type of school: **Evangelist/Pastoral Training Institute** Degrees offered: **Certificate** Offers training for pastors: **yes** for teachers: **yes** for lay persons: **yes** Type of available practical training: **preaching, pastoral care, religious education** In relations with: **Mekhane Yesus Church (Bethel Synod Coordination)**

Address: South West Bethel Synod Bible School, P.O. Box 48, Mizan Teferi, Ethiopia

- **Metlu** — Terfa Jarso Bible School (s1044)
Type of school: **Evangelist/Pastoral Training Institute** Degrees offered: **Certificate** Offers training for pastors: **yes** for teachers: **yes** for lay persons: **yes** Type of available practical training: **preaching, pastoral care, religious education** In relations with: **Mekhane Yesus Church (Bethel Synod Coordination)**

Address: Terfa Jarso Bible School, P.O. Box 11, Metlu, Illubabour, Ethiopia

FIJI

- **Suva** — Pacific Theological College (s5200)
Type of school: **Graduate school** Degrees offered: **DiplTh, BTh, MTh** Offers training for pastors: **yes** for teachers: **yes as well as specific women's program** Type of available practical training: **courses in practical theology and field work** Admission requirements: **BA** Languages in use: **English, some French** Full/part-time staff: **9 / nc** students from the Pacific region: **60** Library size: **25,000** Doctrinal basis: **Ecumenical, Basis of Pacific Conference of Churches (PCC)** Worship life offered: **daily** In relations with: **Pacific Conference of Churches**

Address: Pacific Theological College, Private Mail Bag, Suva, Fiji, Tel: +679 311-100, Fax: +679 301-728

FRANCE

- **Aix-en-Provence** — Free Faculty of Reformed Theology (s6055)
Type of school: **Graduate/Univ** Founded in **1974** Degrees offered: **LicTh, MTh, ThD** Offers training for pastors: **yes** for lay persons: **yes** Type of available practical training: **special interest for practical theology, thinking of the diversity of ministries in the church, special efforts on pastoral care, religious education** Admission requirements: **baccalaureate or equivalent** Languages in use: **French, occasionally English** Full/part-time staff: **7 / 4** National/foreign students: **91 / 38** Library size: **20,000** Doctrinal basis: **RochC (art. 1-38), Decl of faith** Worship life offered: **weekly** In relations with: **faculty members come from the ERF and EREI; the faculty is independent in the churches.**

Address: Faculté libre de Théologie Réformée, 33, avenue Jules Ferry, F-13100 Aix-en-Provence, France, Tel: +33 3 42 26 13 55, Fax: +33 3 42 93 22 63

- **Montpellier** — Faculty of Protestant Theology (s6054)
Type of school: **Graduate/Univ** Founded in **1808** Degrees offered: **Dipl of general university studies (DEUG), Lic, Master, Dipl of higher studies (DEA), Dipl of specialized higher studies (DESS), Doctorat, Habilitation** Offers training for pastors: **yes** for lay persons: **yes** Type of available practical training: **preaching, pastoral care, religious education** Admission requirements: **baccalaureate** Languages in use: **French** Full/part-time staff: **8 / 3** National/foreign students: **250 / 80** Library size: **100,000** Doctrinal basis: **pluralistic approach** Worship life offered: **weekly** In relations with: **Eglise réformée de France**

Address: Faculté de Théologie Protestante, Louis Perrier 13, F-34000 Montpellier, France, Tel: +33 4 67 92 61 28, Fax: +33 4 67 58 09 47

- **Nogent sur Marne** — Biblical Institute of Nogent (s6056)
Type of school: **Undergraduate Bible school** Founded in **1921** Degrees offered: **Dipl, Cert** Offers training for pastors: **yes** for teachers: **no** for lay persons: **yes** Type of available practical training: **preaching, pastoral care, religious education** Admission requirements: **high school graduation** Languages in use: **French** Full/part-time staff: **4 / 17** National/foreign students: **74 / 25** Library size: **6,000** Doctrinal basis: **Classic Evangelical** Worship life offered: **4 times per week**

Address: Institut biblique de Nogent, 39 grand-rue Charles de Gaulle, F-94 130 Nogent sur Marne, France, Tel: +33 1 45 14 23 70

- **Paris** — Free Faculty of Protestant Theology (s6050)
Type of school: **Graduate/Univ** Degrees offered: **Lic, Magister, ThD** Offers training for pastors: **yes** for lay persons: **yes** Type of available practical training: **preaching, pastoral care, religious education** Admission requirements: **baccalaureate** Languages in use: **French** Full/part-time staff: **8** National/foreign students: **200 / 45** Library size: **60,000** In relations with: **support by the Ref Ch of France, Evang Lutheran Ch of France**

Address: Faculté libre de Théologie Protestante, 83, bvd. Arago, F-75014 Paris, France, Tel: +33 1 43 31 61 64, Fax: +33 1 47 07 67 87

- **Strasbourg** — Protestant Faculty of Theology — University of Strasbourg (s6051)
Type of school: **Graduate/Univ** Founded in **1538** Degrees offered: **Dipl of general university studies (DEUG), LicTh Prot, MagTh Prot, Dipl of Superior Specialized Studies/DESS, Dipl of Higher Studies /DEA, ThD Prot** Offers training for pastors: **yes** for teachers: **yes** for lay persons: **yes** Type of available practical training: **practical theology and adult education** Admission requirements: **diploma of finished secondary studies (baccalaureate or equivalent)** Languages in use: **French** Full/part-time staff: **24** National/foreign students: **450 / 69** Library size: **100,000** Doctrinal basis: **Protestant** Worship life offered: **none** In

596

relations with: **ERAL and ERF, faculty is not strictly confessional, relations to all churches and communities and also to non-Christians**

Address: Faculté de Théologie Protestante, Palais Universitaire, 9, pl. de l'Université, F-67084 Strasbourg, France, Tel: +33 3 88 25 97 35, Fax: +33 3 88 14 01 37

• **Vaux-sur-Seine** — Free Evangelical Faculty of Theology (s6057)
Type of school: **Seminary** Founded in **1965** Degrees offered: **Dipl, MTh, ThD** Offers training for pastors: **yes** Languages in use: **French** Full/part-time staff: **4 / 7** National/foreign students: **70 / nc** Library size: **15,000**

Address: Faculté libre de Théologie évangélique, 85, avenue de Cherbourg, F-78 740 Vaux-sur-Seine, France, Tel: +33 1 34 74 09 86

FRENCH POLYNESIA

• **Papeete** — Hermon Theological School (s5060)
Type of school: **Bible school** Founded in **1927** Degrees offered: **DiplTh** Offers training for pastors: **yes** Type of available practical training: **no** Admission requirements: **under 31** Languages in use: **French, Máohi** Full/part-time staff: **5 / 8** National/foreign students: **26 / 0** Library size: **2,000** Worship life offered: **daily** In relations with: **Evangelical Church of French Polynesia**

Address: Ecole pastorale d'Hermon, B.P. 667, Papeete, French Polynesia, Tel: +689 41 22 24 and 42 00 93

GERMANY

• **Bad Kreuznach** — Preacher's Seminary of the Church in Rhineland (s6214)
Type of school: **Evangelist/Pastoral Training Institute** Founded in **1959** Degrees offered: **2nd theol exam at the church after the course** Offers training for pastors: **yes** Type of available practical training: **homiletics, liturgy, pastoral care, ecumenics, pedagogical education for working in a parish** Admission requirements: **1st theol exam and admission by the church (EKiR)** Languages in use: **German** Full/part-time staff: **5** National/foreign students: **70 / 0** Library size: **20,000** Worship life offered: **daily** In relations with: **United Institute of the Evang Church in the Rhineland/Düsseldorf**

Address: Predigerseminar der Evang Kirche im Rheinland, Heinrich-Held-Str. 12, D-55543 Bad Kreuznach, Germany, Tel: +49 671 25-507, Fax: +49 671 31-335

• **Berlin** — Pastoral Seminary of Berlin-Brandenburg (s6204)
Offers training for pastors: **yes** Languages in use: **German**

Address: Predigerseminar der Evangelischen Kirche in Berlin-Brandenburg, Schopenhauerstr. 53-55, D-14129 Berlin, Germany, Tel: +49 30 803-45 55nc

597

- **Berlin** — Theological Faculty — Humboldt-University of Berlin (s6223)
Type of school: **Graduate/Univ** Founded in **1810** Degrees offered: **Faculty exam, Mag, Doctorate, MagArt, church exam, exam of religious studies for teachers** Offers training for pastors: **yes** for teachers: **yes** Type of available practical training: **homiletics, pedagogic in religion internships in parish and school** Admission requirements: **Abitur (exam of high school) or finished training with 4 years of work experience** Languages in use: **German** Full/part-time staff: **48** National/foreign students: **750 / 30** Library size: **290,000** Doctrinal basis: **in general Ref confessions** Worship life offered: **weekly devotion, monthly university worship** In relations with: **Evang Ch in Berlin-Brandenburg**

Address: Theologische Fakultät — Humboldt-Universität/Berlin, Burgstr. 25, D-Berlin, 10178, Germany, Tel: +49 30 2093-5693, Fax: +49 30 2093-5778, E-mail: jutta szereiks@theo@hub-ma

- **Bielefeld** — Church Faculty Bethel (s6218)
Type of school: **Graduate/Univ** Degrees offered: **MagTheol, ThD** Offers training for pastors: **yes** for teachers: **yes** Type of available practical training: **no** Admission requirements: **Abitur (Matura), according to German law** Languages in use: **German** Full/part-time staff: **20 / 12** National/foreign students: **380 / 24** Library size: **120,000** Doctrinal basis: **none** Worship life offered: **daily devotion, worship at every new semester (beginning and end)** In relations with: **Evang-Ref Church in Bavaria and NW-Germany, Church of Lippe, United churches, especially of Westphalia and Luth churches**

Address: Kirchliche Hochschule Bethel, Remterweg 45, D-33617 Bielefeld, Germany, Tel: +49 521 144-3948 and 3949, Fax: +49 521 144-4700

- **Bochum** — Evangelical-Theological Faculty — Ruhr-University (s6210)
Type of school: **Graduate/Univ** Degrees offered: **Faculty-exam, Master, 1st state exam for teachers at high school** Offers training for pastors: **yes** for teachers: **yes** Type of available practical training: **no** Admission requirements: **Abitur (Matura)** Languages in use: **German** Full/part-time staff: **29 / 6** National/foreign students: **600 / nc** Library size: **145,000** Worship life offered: **once per term** In relations with: **Church of Lippe, Reformed Alliance**

Address: Evanglisch-Theologische Fakultät — Ruhr-Universität, Universitätsstr. 150, Gebäude, GA/St. 7/8, D-44801 Bochum, Germany, Tel: +49 234 700-2500 and 2501

- **Bonn** — Protestant Theological Faculty — Friedrich Wilhelm University (s6222)
Type of school: **Graduate/Univ** Degrees offered: **Church exam, state exam for teachers, MagTheol** Offers training for pastors: **yes** for teachers: **yes** Type of available practical training: **practical theology** Admission requirements: **Abitur, high school graduation** Languages in use: **German** Full/part-time staff: **16 / 12** National/foreign students: **678 / 22** Library size: **100,000** Doctrinal basis: **Evangelical** Worship life offered: **none** In relations with: **Evang Ch in the Rhineland**

Address: Evangelische-Theologische Fakultät — Rheinische Friedrich-Wilhelm-Univ, Am Hof 1, D-53113 Bonn, Germany, Tel: +49 228 737-345 & 66, Fax: +49 228 73 73 66

598

• **Erlangen** — Protestant Theological Faculty — University of
Erlangen-Nürnberg (s6231)
Type of school: **Graduate/Univ** Founded in **1743** Degrees offered: **First church
exam, exam of the faculty, Mag, Dr, state exam for teacher's education** Offers
training for pastors: **yes** for teachers: **yes** for lay persons: **yes** Type of available
practical training: **partly preaching, Sunday school teaching and pastoral care,
religious education** Admission requirements: **admission for university** Languages in use: **German, sometimes English** Full/part-time staff: **1 Ref chair** Na-
tional/foreign students: **400 / na** Library size: **130,000** Doctrinal basis: **by state
contract** Worship life offered: **seldom** In relations with: **Evang-Ref Church in
Bavaria and NW-Germany**

Address: Evangelisch-Theologische Fakultät — Univ. Erlangen-Nürnberg, Kochstr. 6, D-91045
Erlangen, Germany, Tel: +49 9131 85 22, Fax: +49 9131 85 93 74

• **Frankfurt am Main** — Department of Protestant Theology — Joh. W. Goe-
the-University (s6226)
Type of school: **Graduate/Univ** Degrees offered: **Dipl, 1st state exam for teachers, Mag in Religious, Mag in Philosophy of Religion, diaconal science** Offers
training for pastors: **yes** for teachers: **yes** for lay persons: **yes** Type of available
practical training: **homiletics** Admission requirements: **baccalaureate** Languages
in use: **German** Full/part-time staff: **8** National/foreign students: **643 / 30** Library
size: **85,000** Doctrinal basis: **none** Worship life offered: **none** In relations with:
French-Ref parish/Frankfurt, German-Ref parish/Frankfurt

Address: Fachbereich Evangelische Theologie — Joh. W. Goethe-Universität, Hausener Weg 120,
D-60489 Frankfurt am Main, Germany, Tel: +49 69 7982-2585, Fax: +49 69 7982-8518

• **Friedberg** — Theological Seminary of the Evangelical Church of Hessen
and Nassau (s6236)
Type of school: **Seminary** Offers training for pastors: **yes** Type of available practical training: **homiletics, liturgics, religious education, pastoral care** Languages
in use: **German** Full/part-time staff: **3** National/foreign students: **47 / 0** Library
size: **63,800** Doctrinal basis: **Articles of the Church of Hessen and Nassau** Worship life offered: **only in relation with the Church of Hessen and Nassau**

Address: Theologisches Seminar der Evangelischen Kirche in Hessen und Nassau, Kaiserstr. 2,
D-61159 Friedberg, Tel: +49 6031 9465 Fax: +49 6031 64412

• **Giessen** — Free Theological Academy (s6232)
Type of school: **Seminary** Founded in **1974** Degrees offered: **MDiv, MTh** Offers
training for pastors: **nc** Languages in use: **German** Full/part-time staff: **14 / 2** na-
tional/foreign students: **135 / nc** Library size: **16,000**

Address: Freie Theologische Akademie, Schiffenberger Weg 11, D-35 334 Giessen, Germany, Tel:
+49 641-76001

• **Göttingen** — Protestant Theological Faculty — University of Göttingen
(s6227)
Type of school: **Graduate/Univ** Founded in **1737** Degrees offered: **1) ch exam for**

ministry 2) **Dipl Mag Doktorat Habil** Offers training for pastors: **yes** for teachers: **yes** Type of available practical training: **among the subjects practical theology, but not Ref teacher** Admission requirements: **Abitur (baccalaureate) of high school, immatriculation on the list of the church for those who want to work in the Ref Ch** Languages in use: **German, degrees also possible in English** Full/part-time staff: **40 + 1 chair for Ref theology** National/foreign students: **680 / 40** Library size: **150,000** Doctrinal basis: **none, Ref students are ordained to Barm and HeidC** Worship life offered: **Sunday university worships during semester, 3 times per week devotions at lunchtime** In relations with: **free state university, contract with the confederation of Niedersachsen (Lutherans+minority or Reformed) for education for church employees, 1 chair for Ref theology**

Address: Evangelisch-theologische Fakultät der Univ. Göttingen, Platz der Göttinger Sieben 2,
D-37073 Göttingen, Germany, Tel: +49 551 397-147, Fax: +49 551 397-488

• **Greifswald** — Theological Faculty — E. Moritz-Arndt-University (s6201)
Type of school: **Faculty of Theology** Founded in **1456** Degrees offered: **Dipl, ThD** Offers training for pastors: **yes** for teachers: **yes** Type of available practical training: **homiletics** Languages in use: **German** Full/part-time staff: **15** National/foreign students: **100 / 3** Library size: **50,000** Doctrinal basis: **none** Worship life offered: **monthly**

Address: Theologische Fakultät der E. Moritz-Arndt-Universität, Domstr. 11, D-17487 Greifswald,
Germany, Tel: +49 3834 86-2500, Fax: +49 3834 86-2502

• **Hamburg** — Evangelical Theological Department — University of Hamburg (s6233)
Type of school: **Faculty of Theology** Degrees offered: **ThD, MTh** Offers training for pastors: **nc** Languages in use: **German** Full/part-time staff: **18** National/foreign students: **720 / nc** Library size: **100,000**

Address: Evangelische Theologie — Universität Hamburg, P.O. Box 20, 146, Sedanstr. 19,
D-Hamburg, 13, Germany

• **Hannover** — Evangelical Theology Department — University of Hannover (s6234)
Founded in **1946** Degrees offered: **PhD** Offers training for pastors: **nc** Languages in use: **German** Full/part-time staff: **5 / 6** National/foreign students: **10 / nc**

Address: Evangelische Theologie — Universität Hannover, P.O. Box 30, 173, Bismarckstr. 2,
D-Hannover, 1, Germany, Tel: +49 511 807-8541

• **Heidelberg** — Petersstift, Seminary of the Evangelical Church in Baden (s6211)
Type of school: **Evangelist/Pastoral Training Institute** Degrees offered: **2nd theological exam for ministry** Offers training for pastors: **yes** Type of available practical training: **homiletics, religious education, liturgy, pastoral care, church law** Admission requirements: **1st Theol Exam** Languages in use: **German** Full/part-time staff: **6** National/foreign students: **60 / 0** Library size: **6,000**

600

Doctrinal basis: **Confession of the United Ev Ch in Baden, CA, HeidC** Worship life offered: **prayers at noon and in the evening each day** In relations with: **institution of the United Evangelical Church of Baden**

Address: Petersstift, Predigerseminar der Evang Landeskirche Baden, Neuenheimer Landstr. 2, D-69120 Heidelberg, Germany, Tel: +49 6221 46001, Fax: +49 6221 411-699

• **Heidelberg** — Theological Faculty — University of Heidelberg (s6221) Founded in **1386** Offers training for pastors: **yes** Languages in use: **German** Full/part-time staff: **49 / 11** Library size: **235,000**

Address: Theologische Fakultät — Universität Heidelberg, Hauptstr. 231, D-69117 Heidelberg, Germany, Tel: +49 6221 543-334nc

• **Herborn** — Theological Seminary of the Church of Hessen und Nassau (s6216) Type of school: **Seminary** Founded in **1917** Degrees offered: **Homiletics and Pastoral Theol** Offers training for pastors: **yes** Languages in use: **German** Full/part-time staff: **6 / 1** National/foreign students: **nc / 0** Library size: **70,000** In relations with: **Evang Church of Hessen and Nassau**

Address: Theologisches Seminar der Evang Kirchen Hessen und Nassau, Kirchberg 11, D-35745 Herborn, Germany, Tel: +49 2772 40-021, Fax: +49 2772 40-698

• **Hofgeismar** — Seminary of the Evangelical Church of Kurhessen-Waldeck (s6229) Type of school: **Graduate/Univ+Undergraduate/Bible school** Founded in **1891** Degrees offered: **2nd theological exam for ministry** Offers training for pastors: **nc** Type of available practical training: **homiletics (Sunday school, preparation for confirmation, pastoral care, leading groups, questions of diakonia, church law, counseling) — students spent within 2 years 32 weeks in parishes** Admission requirements: **1st theological exam and being sent by the church** Languages in use: **German** Full/part-time staff: **4 / 19** National/foreign students: **79 / 0** Library size: **48,000** Worship life offered: **2 times per week** In relations with: **Evang Church of Kurhessen-Waldeck**

Address: Predigerseminar der Evang Kirche Kurhessen-Waldeck, Postfach 1120, Gesundbrunnen 10, D-34369 Hofgeismar, Germany, Tel: +49 5671 881-271, Fax: +49 5671 881-250

• **Jena** — Theological Faculty — Friedrich-Schiller-University (s6202) Type of school: **University** Founded in **1548** Degrees offered: **DiplTh, MA, first state exam for teachers** Offers training for pastors: **yes** for teachers: **yes** Type of available practical training: **preaching, pastoral care, religious education, or DipTh during practical theology and pedagogic of religion** Admission requirements: **bachelorship** Languages in use: **German** Full/part-time staff: **22** National/foreign students: **200 / 5** Library size: **about 50,000** Doctrinal basis: **Protestant** Worship life offered: **monthly** In relations with: **Protestant Church in Germany**

Address: Theologische Fakultät — Friedrich-Schiller-Universität, Ibrahimstr. 24, D-7745 Jena, Germany, Tel: +49 3641 638-064, Fax: +49 3641 615-2 92

- **Korntal-Munchingen** — Free School for Mission (s6235)
Type of school: **Seminary** Degrees offered: **MA (Mission, Bible)** Offers training for pastors: **yes** for teachers: **yes** for lay persons: **yes** Admission requirements: **college level** Languages in use: **German** Full/part-time staff: **3 / 7** National/foreign students: **80 / nc** Library size: **20,000** Worship life offered: **daily singing and devotions**

Address: Freie Hochschule für Mission, Hindenburgstr. 36, D-7015 Korntal-Munchingen, 1, Germany, Tel: +49 711 83965-0, Fax: +49 711 8380545, E-mail: cbsinfo@aem.de

- **Landau** — Preacher's Seminary (s6215)
Type of school: **Evangelist/Pastoral Training Institute** Founded in **1926** Degrees offered: **2nd theological exam for ministry** Offers training for pastors: **yes** Type of available practical training: **preaching, pastoral care, religious education** Admission requirements: **1st theological exam** Languages in use: **German** Full/part-time staff: **4** national/foreign students: **66 / nc** Library size: **10,000** Doctrinal basis: **Confessions of the Evang Ch of the Palatinate** Worship life offered: **weekly** In relations with: **Evangelical (United) Church of the Palatinate**

Address: Protestantisches Predigerseminar Landau, Luitpoldstr. 8, D-76829 Landau, Germany, Tel: +49 6341 80-840, Fax: +49 6341 88-989

- **Leipzig** — Theological Faculty — University of Leipzig (s6225)
Type of school: **Graduate/Univ** Founded in **1409** Degrees offered: **Dipl, first church exam, state exam for teachers, MagArt** Offers training for pastors: **yes** for teachers: **yes** Type of available practical training: **in "practical theology": homiletics, pastoral care, liturgy, pedagogic for parish and school** Admission requirements: **baccalaureate** Languages in use: **German** Full/part-time staff: **40 / 2** national/foreign students: **405 / 3** Library size: **85,000** Doctrinal basis: **teachers need to be members of the Ev Ch** Worship life offered: **daily**

Address: Theologische Fakultät der Universität Leipzig, Ernst-Fuchs-St. 1, D-4105 Leipzig, Germany, Tel: +49 341 973-5400, Fax: +49 341 973-5499

- **Mainz** — Evangelical Theological Faculty — Johannes Gutenberg University (s6207)
Type of school: **Graduate/Univ** Founded in **1476** Degrees offered: **DiplTh, 1st theol exam of the Landeskirche/church, state exam for teachers at high school, ThD** Offers training for pastors: **yes** for teachers: **yes** Type of available practical training: **no** Admission requirements: **Abitur (maturity)** Languages in use: **German** Full/part-time staff: **13 profs, 15 assistants** national/foreign students: **400 / na** Library size: **50,000**

Address: Evang Theol. Fakultät — Joh.-Gutenberg Universität, Saarstr. 21, D-55099 Mainz, Germany, Tel: +49 6131 392-217, Fax: +49 6131 392-603

- **Marburg/Lahn** — Department of Protestant Theology —
Philipps-University of Marburg (s6220)
Type of school: **Graduate/Univ** Degrees offered: **DiplTh, ThD, Mag Art., state exam for teacher at high school, church exam for candidates for pastoral**

work Offers training for pastors: **yes** for teachers: **yes** Admission requirements: **Abitur (baccalaureate)** Languages in use: **German** Full/part-time staff: **40** national/foreign students: **800 / 50** Library size: **117,000** In relations with: **scientific university**

Address: Fachbereich Evangelische Theologie — Philipps-Universität Marburg, Lahntor 3,
D-35037 Marburg/Lahn, Germany, Tel: +49 6421 282-441 and 2443-2423, Fax: +49 6421 28 89 68

• **Münster** — Protestant Theological Faculty — Wilhelms-University of Westfalia (s6219)
Type of school: **Graduate/Univ** Founded in **1914** Degrees offered: **Dipl, Mag, ThD, ThD habil, exam of the faculty, state exam for teachers** Offers training for pastors: **yes** for teachers: **yes** for lay persons: **yes** Type of available practical training: **"Practical Theology"** Admission requirements: **General permission for university** Languages in use: **German** Full/part-time staff: **33 / 5** National/foreign students: **1,393 / 40** Library size: **114,475** Doctrinal basis: **none** Worship life offered: **weekly university worship** In relations with: **Church of Lippe, cooperation through the chairs for Ref Theology and Old Testament**

Address: Evangelisch-Theologische Fakultät der Westfälischen Wilhelms-Univ, Universitätsstr. 13
— 17, D-48143 Münster, Germany, Tel: +49 251 832-512, Fax: +49 251 838-460

• **Rostock** — Theological Faculty — University of Rostock (s6203)
Type of school: **Graduate/Univ** Degrees offered: **DiplTh, state exam for teachers of religion** Offers training for pastors: **yes** for teachers: **yes** Type of available practical training: **preaching, pastoral care, religious education** Admission requirements: **Abitur (maturity)** Languages in use: **German** Full/part-time staff: **14** National/foreign students: **150 / 0** Library size: **23,000** Doctrinal basis: **none** Worship life offered: **every 2 weeks university worship**

Address: Theologische Fakultät — Universität Rostock, Schröder Platz 3/4, D-18051 Rostock, Germany, Tel: +49 381 498-3873

• **Tübingen** — Evangelical-Theological Faculty — Eberhard-Karls University (s6206)
Type of school: **Graduate/Univ** Founded in **1477** Degrees offered: **MagTheol, ThD, ThDhabil, Fakultätsexamen, state exam for teachers, theol exam of the Church of Württemberg** Offers training for pastors: **yes** for teachers: **yes** Admission requirements: **Abitur (high school degree)** Languages in use: **German** Full/part-time staff: **65** National/foreign students: **1,011 / nc** Library size: **150,000** Worship life offered: **weekly during the semester** In relations with: **EKD-Germany**

Address: Evang Theol. Fakultät Eberhard-Karls Universität, Liebermeisterstr. 12, D-72076 Tübingen, Germany, Tel: +49 7071 297-2538, Fax: +49 7071 293-318

• **Wittenberg** — Evangelical Preacher's Seminary of the Church of the Union (s6200)
Type of school: **Evangelist/Pastoral Training Institute** Degrees offered: **2nd**

theological exam for ministry Offers training for pastors: **yes** Type of available practical training: **all work to be done in ministry** Admission requirements: **1st theological exam and practical training** Languages in use: **German** Full/part-time staff: **3** National/foreign students: **20 / 1** Library size: **100,000** Doctrinal basis: **Evangelische Kirche der Union** Worship life offered: **daily devotions, Sunday worship** In relations with: **Evangelische Kirche der Union (EKU)**

Address: Evang Predigerseminar der Evang Kirche der Union, Collegienstr. 54, D-06886
  Wittenberg, Germany, Tel: +49 3491 402-196 and 97, Fax: +49 3491 404-103

• **Wuppertal** — Preacher's Seminary of Wuppertal-Elberfeld (s6212)
Type of school: **Evangelist/Pastoral Training Institute** Founded in **1904** Degrees offered: **participation in 4 classes (homiletics, teaching, pastoral care, parish organization) during 16 weeks is obligatory for admission to the 2nd theol exam** Offers training for pastors: **yes** Type of available practical training: **only practical training: homiletics (service, Sunday school), church organization, teaching, pastoral care, religious education** Admission requirements: **1st theol exam + admission from the churches or the Ref Alliance** Languages in use: **German, in special cases English** Full/part-time staff: **3 / 6** National/foreign students: **54 / 3** Library size: **8,250** Doctrinal basis: **Ref confession** Worship life offered: **daily morning meditation, Eucharist service at the end of each course** In relations with: **Evang-Ref Church (Synod of Bavaria + NW-Germany), Landeskirche of Lippe, Evang Ch of the Rhineland, Evang Ch of Westfalia**

Address: Prediger-Seminar in Wuppertal-Elberfeld, Mainzer-St. 16 (Elberfeld), D-42119
  Wuppertal, Germany, Tel: +49 202 421-051, Fax: +49 20 421-061

• **Wuppertal-Barmen** — Church Faculty of Wuppertal (s6230)
Type of school: **Graduate/Univ** Founded in **1935** Degrees offered: **Mag, ThD, HabilTheol** Offers training for pastors: **yes** for teachers: **yes** Type of available practical training: **actually not, but "practical theology" with lessons in homiletics, pastoral care, education, etc.** Admission requirements: **Abitur (maturity)** Languages in use: **German** Full/part-time staff: **15** National/foreign students: **322 / 7** Library size: **95,000** Doctrinal basis: **Evangelical** Worship life offered: **daily devotion, worship with weekly Eucharist** In relations with: **several churches some of which are of the Reformed tradition and with the Reformed Ch (Synod of Bavaria and NW-Germany), which is represented on the Board**

Address: Kirchliche Hochschule Wuppertal, Missionstr. 9B, D-42285 Wuppertal-Barmen, Germany,
  Tel: +49 202 282-00, Fax: +49 202 282-0101

GHANA

• **Accra** — Dept. of Religious Studies — University of Ghana (s1060)
Type of school: **Graduate/Univ** Degrees offered: **from Dipl to PhD** Offers train-

ing for pastors: **nc** for teachers: **yes** Admission requirements: **basic university requirements** Languages in use: **English** Full/part-time staff: **9** National/foreign students: **600 / nc** Library size: **2,000 to 3,000** Doctrinal basis: **none**

Address: Dept. of Religious Studies — University of Ghana, P.O. Box 66, Legon, Accra, Ghana

* **Legon** — Trinity Theological College (s1063)
Type of school: **Undergraduate Seminary** Founded in **1942** Degrees offered: **College Cert, DiplTh, BTh** Offers training for pastors: **yes** for teachers: **yes** for lay persons: **no** Type of available practical training: **preaching, pastoral care, religious education** Languages in use: **English** Full/part-time staff: **8 / 6** National/foreign students: **150 / 10** Library size: **15,000** Worship life offered: **daily** Doctrinal basis: **Ecumenical** In relations with: **Presbyterian Church in Ghana, Meth Church, Evang Presb Church, Ghana**

Address: Trinity Theological College, P.O. Box 48, Legon, Ghana, Tel: +233 21 500-541, Fax: +233 21 502-123

* **Peki V/R** — Evangelical Presbyterian Church Seminary (s1061)
Type of school: **Mission Institute** Degrees offered: **CertTh, Cert church musician** Offers training for pastors: **yes** for lay persons: **yes** Type of available practical training: **course in evangelism, homiletics, pastoral theology, congregational fieldwork, practical attachment to experienced pastors** Admission requirements: **secondary school, B.E.C.E.** Languages in use: **English** Full/part-time staff: **8** National/foreign students: **31 / 0** Library size: **3,053** Doctrinal basis: **Reformed** Worship life offered: **2 times daily** In relations with: **Evangelical Presbyterian Church, Ghana**

Address: Evangelical Presbyterian Church Seminary, P.O. Box 29, Peki V/R, Ghana Fax: +233 11 91 8275

* **Tamale** — Tamale Ecumenical Training Center (s1064)
Offers training for pastors: **nc** Languages in use: **English** Full/part-time staff: **2**

Address: Tamale Ecumenical Training Center, P.O. Box 270, Tamale, Ghana

---

GUATEMALA

* **Guatemala CA** — Central American Theological Seminary (s2070)
Type of school: **Seminary** Founded in **1984** Degrees offered: **DiplTh, LicTh, MTh** Offers training for pastors: **yes** for teachers: **yes** for lay persons: **yes** Languages in use: **Spanish** Full/part-time staff: **25 / 25** National/foreign students: **940 / 75** Library size: **15,000** Doctrinal basis: **own doctrinal statement** Worship life offered: **4 times per week** In relations with: **Evangelical Churches of Central America with Ref government, emphasis on God's sovereignty and salvation**

Address: Seminario Teológico Centro Americano, Apartado 213, Av. Bolivar 30-42, zona 3, 01901

Guatemala CA, Guatemala, Tel: +502 471-0573, Fax: +502 473-5957, E-mail: seteca@gold.guate.net

GUINEA

• **Kissidougou** — Telekoro Biblical Institute (s1050)
Type of school: **Evangelist/Pastoral Training Institute** Degrees offered: **Dipl in Pastoral Studies** Offers training for pastors: **yes** for lay persons: **yes** Type of available practical training: **preaching, pastoral care, religious education** Admission requirements: **high school and recommendation** Languages in use: **French** Full/part-time staff: **5 / 2** National/foreign students: **33 / 2** Library size: **2,000** Worship life offered: **daily** In relations with: **Christian and Missionary Alliance (CMA), Eglise protestante évangélique de Guinée (CMA)**

Address: Institut biblique Telekoro, B.P. 24, Kissidougou, Guinea

HAITI

• **Port-au-Prince** — John Calvin Biblical Institute (s3311)
Type of school: **Evangelist/Pastoral Training Institute** Degrees offered: **Cert of Completion** Offers training for pastors: **yes** Type of available practical training: **preaching, pastoral care, religious education** Admission requirements: **pastoral recommendation, ability to read/write, serving as a leader in church** Languages in use: **Haitian, Creole, French** Full/part-time staff: **5** National/foreign students: **260 / 0** Doctrinal basis: **Reformed Calvinist** Worship life offered: **once a year** In relations with: **Institute independent but professors members/pastors of Christian Ref Church of Haiti**

Address: Institut Biblique Jean Calvin, P.O. Box 1693, N 3, rue Pélican (Delmas 56), Port-au-Prince, Haiti, Tel: +509 461-341, Fax: +509 461-341

HONDURAS

• **Comayaguela** — Presbyterian Institute of Honduras (s3309)
Type of school: **Undergraduate/Bible school** Offers training for pastors: **yes** for teachers: **no** for lay persons: **yes** Admission requirements: **completed secondary school** Languages in use: **Spanish** Full/part-time staff: **6** National/foreign students: **70 / nc** Doctrinal basis: **Reformed** Worship life offered: **2 times per week** In relations with: **Iglesia Presbiteriana de Honduras**

Address: Instituto Presbiteriano de Honduras, Apartado 906, Comayaguela, Honduras, Tel: +504 36
56 78, Fax: +504 27 22 64

- **San Pedro Sula** — Theological Seminary (s3308)
Type of school: **Undergraduate/Bible school** Degrees offered: **BTh** Offers training for pastors: **yes** for teachers: **yes** for lay persons: **yes** Admission requirements: **completed secondary school** Languages in use: **Spanish** Full/part-time staff: **12** National/foreign students: **80 / 0** Library size: **3,000** Doctrinal basis: **Reformed Calvinist** Worship life offered: **occasionally** In relations with: **Iglesia Evangélica Reformada de Honduras**

Address: Seminario Teológico Evangélico Reformado, Apartado 17, San Pedro Sula, Honduras,
Tel: +504 52 67 67, Fax: +504 52 97 15

HUNGARY

- **Budapest** — Faculty of Theology — Károli Gáspár Reformed University (s6335)
Type of school: **Graduate/Univ** Founded in **1855** Degrees offered: **MDiv, MEd, PhD** Offers training for pastors: **yes** for teachers: **yes** for lay persons: **yes** Type of available practical training: **preaching, pastoral care, Christian education** Admission requirements: **high school certificate** Languages in use: **Hungarian** Full/part-time staff: **15 / 14** National/foreign students: **157 / 3** Library size: **150,000** Doctrinal basis: **HeidC, HelvC** Worship life offered: **daily** In relations with: **Ref Ch in Hungary, Ref Ch in Slovakia, Romania, Yugoslavia, Ukraine, and Croatia**

Address: Budapesti Református Theologia Académia, Ráday u. 28, H-1092 Budapest, Hungary,
Tel: +36 1 218-02 66 + 217-2403, Fax: +36 1 217-2403

- **Debrecen** — Debrecen Reformed Theological Faculty (s6338)
Type of school: **Graduate/Univ** Founded in **1549** Degrees offered: **Minister's dipl, qualification for religious instruction in elementary and secondary schools** Offers training for pastors: **yes** for teachers: **yes** Type of available practical training: **preaching, pastoral care, religious education** Admission requirements: **maturity examina, confirmation, recommendation by a Ref minister** Languages in use: **Hungarian** Full/part-time staff: **11** National/foreign students: **173 / 11** Library size: **62,000** Doctrinal basis: **HeidC, HelvC** Worship life offered: **daily twice** In relations with: **Ref Ch in Hungary**

Address: Debreceni Református Theologia Akadémia, Kálvin tèr 16, H-Debrecen, 4044, Hungary,
Tel: +36 52 414-744 and ext 120, Fax: +36 52 414-744 and ext. 122, E-mail:
gbolcskei@tigris.klte

- **Sárospatak** — Reformed Theological Academy (s6336)
Type of school: **Graduate/Univ** Degrees offered: **MTh** Offers training for pastors: **yes** for teachers: **yes** Type of available practical training: **preaching and pas-**

toral care, religious education Admission requirements: **high school grad, one foreign language** Languages in use: **Hungarian** Full/part-time staff: **15** National/foreign students: **141 / 37** Library size: **250,000** Doctrinal basis: **HeidC, HelvC** Worship life offered: **twice daily** In relations with: **Ref Ch of Hungary**

Address: Református Theológia Akadémia, Rákóczy u.1., H-Sárospatak, 3950, Hungary, Tel: +36 47 312-947, Fax: +36 47 312-947

INDIA

• **Aizawl** — Aizawl Theological College (s4055)
Type of school: **Graduate+Undergraduate+Pastor/Evangelist/Missionary** Founded in **1907** Degrees offered: **BD, BTh, BCS (Bachelor of Christian Studies, for private Students), DiplTh, GTh** Offers training for pastors: **yes** for teachers: **yes** for lay persons: **yes** Type of available practical training: **teacher + students regularly visit churches on Sundays, sometimes practical works** Admission requirements: **degree holder for BD, PUC for BTh** Languages in use: **English, Mizo, Khasi** Full/part-time staff: **25** National/foreign students: **260 / 15** Library size: **80,000** Doctrinal basis: **none, but they are Presbyterian colleges** Worship life offered: **daily morning and evening** In relations with: **Mizo synod, PCI**

Address: Aizawl Theological College, P.O. Box No. 167, Durtlang, Aizawl, Mizoram 796001, India

• **Bangalore** — The United Theological College (s4054)
Type of school: **Undergraduate College** Founded in **1910** Degrees offered: **BD — 4 years, MTh — 2 years, Dipl of counseling course — 1 year, ThD — 5 years** Offers training for pastors: **yes** for teachers: **yes** for lay persons: **yes** Type of available practical training: **preaching, pastoral care, religious education** Admission requirements: **a degree** Languages in use: **English** Full/part-time staff: **24 / 7** National/foreign students: **150 / 0** Library size: **73,000, 482 Period, 505 Microfilms** Doctrinal basis: **Ecumenical** Worship life offered: **daily morning and Sunday evenings** In relations with: **CSI, CNI, Lutheran Chs, Mar Thoma Ch, Malankara Syrian Church, Orthodox Syrian Ch, Presb Ch of Mizoram**

Address: The United Theological College, P.O. Box 4613, 63, Miller's Road, Bangalore, 560046, India, Tel: +91 80 333-2844 and 333-3438 and 333-0502, Fax: +91 80 333-0015

• **Calcutta** — Bishop's College (s4053)
Type of school: **Graduate/Univ** Founded in **1820** Degrees offered: **BTh in Bengali (3 1/2 years course), BD in English (3 1/2), MTh in English (2 years)** Offers training for pastors: **yes** for teachers: **yes** for lay persons: **yes** Type of available practical training: **preaching, pastoral care, religious education** Admission requirements: **Secular graduate or BD** Languages in use: **English, Bengali** Full/part-time staff: **9 / 6** National/foreign students: **70 / 0** Library size: **28,000** Doc-

trinal basis: **Ecumenical Biblical** Worship life offered: **daily at 7 a.m.** In relations with: **Church of North India (till 1970 Angl)**

Address: Bishop's College, 224, Acharya Jagadish Chandra Bose Rd., Calcutta, 700 017, India,
Tel: +91 33 247-2779

- **Calcutta** — Calcutta Bible Seminary (s4062)
Type of school: **Undergraduate/Bible school** Founded in **1968** Degrees offered: **GTh, CertTh** Offers training for pastors: **yes** Type of available practical training: **preaching, pastoral care, religious education** Admission requirements: **10th grade** Languages in use: **English** Full/part-time staff: **4 / 6** National/foreign students: **40 / 5** Library size: **1,200** Doctrinal basis: **Evangelical** In relations with: **Evangelical Church of India**

Address: Calcutta Bible Seminary, 16/4/2 Harimohan Dutta Rd., Calcutta, 700 028, India, Tel:
+91-33 551-2262, Fax: +91 33 551-3760

- **Churachandpur** — Dinwiddie Bible College (s4063)
Type of school: **Undergraduate/Bible school** Degrees offered: **DiplTh, BTh** Offers training for pastors: **yes** for teachers: **yes** Type of available practical training: **preaching, pastoral care, religious education** Admission requirements: **10+2** Languages in use: **English** Full/part-time staff: **9 / 1** National/foreign students: **80 / 0** Library size: **4,000** Doctrinal basis: **Evangelical** Worship life offered: **5 times per week** In relations with: **Evangelical Congregational Church of India**

Address: Dinwiddie Bible College, P.O. Box 34, Nehru Marg, Churachandpur, 795 128, India, Tel:
+91 3874 22-468

- **Churachandpur** — Grace Bible College (s4064)
Type of school: **Undergraduate/Bible school** Founded in **1981** Degrees offered: **CertTh, DiplTh, BTh** Offers training for pastors: **nc** Type of available practical training: **preaching, Sunday school teaching** Admission requirements: **pre-university** Languages in use: **English, vernacular** Full/part-time staff: **7 / 3** National/foreign students: **55 / 9** Library size: **4,500** Worship life offered: **5 times per week** In relations with: **Evangelical Convention Church**

Address: Grace Bible College, P.O. Box 44, New Lamka, Churachandpur, Manipur 795 128, India,
Tel: +91 3874 22549

- **Dehra Dun** — Presbyterian Theological Seminary (s4056)
Type of school: **Undergraduate/Bible school** Founded in **1969** Degrees offered: **BTh, GTh** Offers training for pastors: **yes** Type of available practical training: **preaching, pastoral care, religious education** Admission requirements: **high school (12) pass** Languages in use: **English** Full/part-time staff: **7 / 5** National/foreign students: **75 / 10** Library size: **15,000** Doctrinal basis: **WestConf** Worship life offered: **daily** In relations with: **Ref Presb Ch of India + other Ref Churches**

Address: Presbyterian Theological Seminary, 51-C Rajpur Road, 91 Dehra Dun, UP 248001, India,
Tel: +91 135 658-417, Fax: +91 135 655-078

- **Hyderabad** — Andhra Christian Theological College (s4051)
Founded in **1964** Degrees offered: **BTh, BD, MMin** Offers training for pastors: **nc** Languages in use: **Telugu, English** Full/part-time staff: **12** National/foreign students: **124 / nc** In relations with: **CSI and various others**

Address: Andhra Christian Theological College, Gandhinagar P.O., Lower Tank Bund Rd.,
Hyderabad, 500380, India

- **Kolhapur** — Maharashtra Synod Theological College (s4065)
Type of school: **Undergraduate/Bible school** Offers training for pastors: **yes** Type of available practical training: **preaching, pastoral care, religious education** Admission requirements: **12th grade** Languages in use: **Marathi, English** Full/part-time staff: **10** National/foreign students: **15 / nc** Library size: **500** Doctrinal basis: **Presbyterian** In relations with: **Presbyterian Church — Kolhapur Church Council**

Address: Maharashtra Synod Theological College, near Old Church, Kolhapur, Maharashtra, India,
Tel: +91 231 654-738, Fax: +91 231 654-738

- **Madras** — Hindustan Bible Institute and College (s4060)
Type of school: **Graduate/Univ+Undergraduate/Bible school** Founded in **1952** Degrees offered: **Cert in administrative leadership training, Dipl in emerging leadership training, MDiv** Offers training for pastors: **yes** for teachers: **yes** for lay persons: **yes** Type of available practical training: **preaching assignment in college and churches, Sunday school training for orphanage children, mid-week pastoral ministry to houses, hospitals, etc.** Admission requirements: **experience of being spiritually born Christian and commitment to serve the Lord** Languages in use: **English, Telugu** Full/part-time staff: **15** National/foreign students: **85 / 10** Library size: **30,000** Doctrinal basis: **special statement** Worship life offered: **twice daily** In relations with: **interdenominational**

Address: Hindustan Bible Institute and College, 86/89 Medavakka Tamk Road, Kilpauk, 600010
Madras, Tamilnadu, India, Tel: +91 44 642-3664, Fax: +91 44 642-3664, E-mail:
hbi@md2.vsnl.net.in

- **Madurai** — Tamilnadu Theological Seminary (s4058)
Type of school: **Graduate Seminary** Founded in **1969** Degrees offered: **BTh, BD, MTh, MA in Phil and Religion** Offers training for pastors: **yes** for lay persons: **yes** Type of available practical training: **preaching, pastoral care, religious education** Admission requirements: **college degree** Languages in use: **Tamil, English** Full/part-time staff: **23 / 3** National/foreign students: **205 / 12** Library size: **48,580** Doctrinal basis: **Ecumenical** Worship life offered: **daily** In relations with: **Ch of South India, Tamil Evang Lutheran Ch, Arcot Lutheran Ch**

Address: Tamilnadu Iraiyiyal Kalloori, Arasaradi, Madurai, 625 010, India, Tel: +91 452 602-352,
Fax: +91 452 601-424, E-mail: tts@md2.vsnl.net.in

- **Mangalore** — Karnataka Theological College (s4052)
Type of school: **College** Founded in **1847** Degrees offered: **BD, BTh, CertTh, Dipl in Christian Studies** Offers training for pastors: **yes** for lay persons: **yes**

Type of available practical training: **preaching, pastoral care, religious education** Admission requirements: **pre-university** Languages in use: **Kannada, English** Full/part-time staff: **12 / 2** National/foreign students: **103 / 0** Library size: **20,400** Worship life offered: **twice daily** In relations with: **Ch of South India**

Address: Karnataka Theological College, Balmatta, Mangalore, 575 001, India, Tel: +91 824 422-829, Fax: +91 824 429-557

• **Pune** — United Theological Seminary of Maharashtra (s4048)
Type of school: **Seminary** Founded in **1878** Degrees offered: **BTh** Offers training for pastors: **nc** Languages in use: **Marathi** Full/part-time staff: **3 / 3** National/foreign students: **11 / nc** Library size: **6,525** In relations with: **Church of North India, Hindustani Covenant Church**

Address: United Theological Seminary of Maharashtra, 1-A Prince of Wales Drive, 411001 Pune, India, Tel: +91 212 664-864

• **Saiha** — Peniel Bible Institute (s4059)
Type of school: **Evangelist/Pastoral Training Mission Institute** Degrees offered: **CertTh** Offers training for pastors: **nc** for lay persons: **yes** Type of available practical training: **preaching, pastoral care, religious education** Admission requirements: **matriculation** Languages in use: **Mara, Mizo** Full/part-time staff: **7** National/foreign students: **25 / 0** Library size: **200** Doctrinal basis: **yes** Worship life offered: **daily morning and evening** In relations with: **Mara Evang Ch/ Myanmar, Presb Ch Mizoram**

Address: Peniel Bible Institute, College Vaih, Chhimtuipui District, Mizoram, 796901 Saiha, India,

• **Shillong** — John Roberts Theological Seminary (s4057)
Type of school: **Graduate/Univ** Founded in **1887** Degrees offered: **BDiv, BTh of Senate of Serampore College** Offers training for pastors: **yes** for teachers: **no** for lay persons: **yes** Type of available practical training: **preaching, pastoral care, religious education** Admission requirements: **graduate first degree** Languages in use: **English** Full/part-time staff: **5** National/foreign students: **56 / 0** Library size: **10,325** Doctrinal basis: **Ecumenical Evangelical** Worship life offered: **daily** In relations with: **Presbyterian Church of India, Khasi Jaintia Presbyterian Synod**

Address: John Roberts Theological Seminary, Mawklot, P.O. Nonglyer, Shillong, 793 009 Meghalaya, India, Tel: +91 363 722267

• **Trivandrum** — Kerala United Theological Seminary (s4050)
Founded in **1943** Degrees offered: **MTh, MMin, BD, BTh, Dipl in Religious Studies** Offers training for pastors: **nc** Languages in use: **Malayalam, English** Full/part-time staff: **8 / 6** National/foreign students: **146 / nc** Library size: **11,300** In relations with: **Ch of South India**

Address: Kerala United Theological Seminary, Kannammoola Medical College, P.O. Trivandrum, 695 011, Kerala, India, Tel: +91 471 443-410

INDONESIA

- **Abepura** — Theological Seminary GKI I.S. Kijne (s4217)
Type of school: **Undergraduate/College** Degrees offered: **Dipl Christian Education, DegTh, Deg in Christian Education** Offers training for pastors: **yes** for teachers: **yes** Type of available practical training: **Christian religious education in schools** Admission requirements: **completed high school** Languages in use: **Indonesian** Full/part-time staff: **25** National/foreign students: **700 / 0** Library size: **11,558** Doctrinal basis: **Reformed** Worship life offered: **weekly** In relations with: **Evangelical Christian Church in Irian Jaya (GKI-Irja)**

Address: Sekolah Tinggi Theologia (STT) GKI I.S. Kijne, Kotak Pos 115, Jln. Sentani 37,
    Abepura, 99351 Irian Jaya, Indonesia, Tel: +62 81 320-0967

- **Ambon** — Theological Faculty — Christian Moluccan University (s4215)
Founded in **1985** Degrees offered: **BD** Offers training for pastors: **nc** Languages in use: **Indonesian** Full/part-time staff: **34 / 28** National/foreign students: **601 / nc** Library size: **12,103** In relations with: **The Protestant Church in the Moluccas**

Address: Universitas Kristen Indonesia Maluku (UKIM) Fak. Theol., P.O. Box 1014, Jln. Ot
    Pattimaipauw, Ambon, 97115, Indonesia

- **Banjarmasin** — Theological Seminary GKE (s4213)
Type of school: **Graduate/Univ** Founded in **1963** Offers training for pastors: **yes** for teachers: **yes** Type of available practical training: **preaching, pastoral care, religious education** Admission requirements: **senior high school cert, admission text** Languages in use: **Indonesian** Full/part-time staff: **18** National/foreign students: **225 / nc** Library size: **21,500** Worship life offered: **5 times per week** In relations with: **GWE**

Address: Sekolah Tinggi Theologia GKE, P.O. Box 86, Jl. Jend. Sudirman No. 11, Banjarmasin,
    Kalsel, Indonesia, Tel: +62 511 54856, Fax: +62 511 65297

- **DKI Jakarta** — Jakarta Theological Seminary (STTJ) (s4209)
Type of school: **Graduate/Univ** Founded in **1934** Degrees offered: **MDiv, MTh, ThD, Dipl in church music** Offers training for pastors: **yes** for teachers: **no** for lay persons: **yes** Languages in use: **Indonesian, English** Full/part-time staff: **16 / 26** National/foreign students: **292 / 5** Library size: **47,500** Worship life offered: **6 times per week** In relations with: **Javanese Christian Churches: GKI, GKJ, GPIB, GMIM, GPM, GMIT, G TORAJA, GKS, GKP, GKE, GBKP, GMIST, GMIH, GMIBM, GKST, GTM, GKSS, Gepsultra, GKI IRJA**

Address: Sekolah Tinggi Teologi Jakarta (STTJ), P.O. Box 10320, Jalan Proklamasi 27, 62-21
    10320 DKI Jakarta, 10320 62, Indonesia, Tel: +62 21 390-4237, Fax: +62 21 315-3781

- **Kupang** — Theological Faculty of Ukap Kupang (s4201)
Type of school: **Univ** Offers training for pastors: **yes** for teachers: **yes** for lay persons: **yes** Admission requirements: **church recommendation** Languages in use: **Indonesian** Full/part-time staff: **16** National/foreign students: **309 / 0** Library

size: **5,000** Doctrinal basis: **Calvinist** Worship life offered: **2 times per week** In relations with: **Christian Church of Sumba (GKS) GMIT**

Address: Fakultas Theologia Ukap Kupang, P.O. Box 1013, Adi Sucipto Oesapa, 85001 Kupang, NTT, Indonesia, Tel: +62 391 33407, Fax: +62 391 33407

• **Malang** — Institute Pendidikan Theologia "BaleWiyata" (s4210)
Type of school: **Evangelist/Pastoral Training Institute** Founded in **1925** Degrees offered: **Cert** Offers training for pastors: **yes** for teachers: **yes** for lay persons: **yes** Type of available practical training: **preaching, pastoral care, religious education** Languages in use: **Indonesian, Javanese** Full/part-time staff: **6** National/foreign students: **nc / 0** Library size: **1,000** Doctrinal basis: **Calvinism, Presbyterian** In relations with: **Greja Kristen Jawi Wetan (East Java Christian Church)**

Address: Institut Pendidikan Theologia "Balewiyata," P.O. Box 49, Jalan S. Supriadi 18, 65147 Malang, Indonesia, Tel: +62 341 64990, 25846, Fax: +62 341 62604

• **Medan** — Abdi Sabda Theological Institute (ITAS) (s4214)
Type of school: **Seminary and Evangelist/Pastoral Training Mission Institute** Founded in **1967** Degrees offered: **Dipl in Christian Education, BDiv** Offers training for pastors: **yes** for teachers: **yes** Languages in use: **Indonesian** Full/part-time staff: **14 / 30** national/foreign students: **350 / 0** Library size: **10,000**

Address: Institut Teologia Abdi Sabda (ITAS), Medan — Binjai km. 10.8, Medan, Sumatra Utara, Indonesia, Tel: +62 61 851-701, Fax: +62 61 851-930

• **Melolo** — School of Reformed Theology (s4219)
Type of school: **Undergraduate/Bible school** Degrees offered: **no degrees** Offers training for pastors: **yes** for teachers: **yes** Type of available practical training: **preaching, pastoral care, religious education** Languages in use: **Indonesian** Full/part-time staff: **3** National/foreign students: **8 / 0** Library size: **2,000** Doctrinal basis: **same as church** Worship life offered: **none** In relations with: **Gereformeerde Kerk (Liberated), five Reformed churches of Australia**

Address: Sekolah Theologia Reformasi, Melolo, 87181, Indonesia

• **Rantepao** — Rantepao Theological Seminary (s4208)
Type of school: **Graduate Seminary** Offers training for pastors: **yes** for teachers: **yes** for lay persons: **yes** Type of available practical training: **yes** Languages in use: **Indonesian** Full/part-time staff: **12 / 9** National/foreign students: **428 / 0** Library size: **5,253** Doctrinal basis: **none** Worship life offered: **twice a week** In relations with: **Gereja Toraja, Gereja Toraja Mamasa, Gepsultra**

Address: Sekolah Tinggi Teologi Rantepao, Jl Dr. Ratulangi no. 80, Rantepao, 91831 Sulawesi Selatan, Indonesia, Tel: +62 423 21138, Fax: +62 423 25143

• **Salatiga** — Christian University Satya Wacana, Faculty of Theology (s4205)
Founded in **1969** Degrees offered: **BD** Offers training for pastors: **yes** Languages in use: **Indonesian** Full/part-time staff: **12 / 7** National/foreign students: **200 / 0** Library size: **10,000** In relations with: **Javanese Christian Churches, 18 Indonesian Churches**

Address: Universitas Kristen Satya Wacana, Faculty of Theology, Jl Diponegoro 52-60, Salatiga, 50711, Indonesia, Tel: +62 298 81362none

- **Tentena Poso** — Theological Academy GKST (s4202)
Type of school: **Graduate/Univ** Founded in **1986** Offers training for pastors: **yes** for teachers: **yes** for lay persons: **yes** Languages in use: **Indonesian** Full/part-time staff: **23** National/foreign students: **434 / nc** Library size: **3,633** Doctrinal basis: **Reformed Calvinist** Worship life offered: **2 times per week** In relations with: **Christian Church in Central Sulawesi (GKST)**

Address: Sekolah Tinggi Theologia GKST, Jalan Torulemba, 21, 94663 Tentena Poso, Sulawesi Tengah, Indonesia, Tel: +62 458 21019

- **Tobelo** — Theological Seminary — GMIH Tobelo (s4216)
Type of school: **Graduate/Univ** Degrees offered: **CertTh** Offers training for pastors: **yes** for teachers: **yes** Type of available practical training: **preaching, religious education, pastoral care** Languages in use: **Indonesian** Full/part-time staff: **9** National/foreign students: **265 / 0** Library size: **5,143** Doctrinal basis: **Calvinism** In relations with: **GMIH**

Address: Sekolah Tinggi Teologi — GMIH Tobelo, P.O. Box 13, Alamat Kompleks GMIH WARI-Tobelo, 97762 Tobelo (Maluku Utara), Indonesia, Tel: +62 924 21556

- **Tomohon** — Indonesian Christian University Tomohon Kakaskasen III, Faculty of Theology (s4218)
Offers training for pastors: **nc** Languages in use: **Indonesian**

Address: Universitas Kristen Indonesia Tomohon Kakaskasen III, Kotak Pos 4, Tomohon, 95362, Indonesia

- **Ujungpandang** — Jaffray Theological School (s4220)
Type of school: **Graduate/Univ** Founded in **1932** Degrees offered: **STh, MDiv** Offers training for pastors: **yes** for teachers: **yes** Languages in use: **Indonesian** Full/part-time staff: **15 / 8** National/foreign students: **420 / 1** Library size: **15,400** Doctrinal basis: **Christian and Missionary Alliance** Worship life offered: **5 times per week** In relations with: **Christian and Missionary Alliance (CMA)**

Address: Sekolah Tinggi Theologia Jaffray, P.O. Box 1054, Jl Gunung Merapi n 103, Ujungpandang, 90010 Sulawesi Selatan, Indonesia, Tel: +62 411 324-129, Fax: +62 411 311-766

- **Ujungpandang** — Theological School of Eastern Indonesia at Ujungpandang (s4204)
Type of school: **Graduate/Univ** Degrees offered: **BTh, MTh** Offers training for pastors: **yes** for teachers: **yes** Type of available practical training: **preaching, pastoral care, religious education** Admission requirements: **12 years schooling and church recommendation** Languages in use: **Indonesian** Full/part-time staff: **19 / 8** National/foreign students: **549 / 0** Library size: **21,952** Doctrinal basis: **yes** Worship life offered: **twice weekly** In relations with: **PGI and 20 Reformed Churches of Eastern Indonesia**

Address: Sekolah Tinggi Teologi bagi Indonesia bagian Timur, Kotak Pos 1140, Jalan Baji Dakka

No. 7, 90134 Ujungpandang, Sulsel, Indonesia, Tel: +62 411 854-735, Fax: +62 411 856-989, E-mail: zngelow@upandang.wasantara.net.id

- **Yogyakarta** — Theological Faculty — Christian University Duta Wacana (s4203)

Type of school: **Graduate/Univ** Founded in **1962** Degrees offered: **MagTh, BDiv** Offers training for pastors: **yes** for teachers: **yes** Type of available practical training: **preaching, pastoral care, religious education** Admission requirements: **senior high school cert, admission test** Languages in use: **Indonesian** Full/part-time staff: **16 / 20** National/foreign students: **275 / nc** Library size: **26,000** Doctrinal basis: **no** Worship life offered: **daily** In relations with: **10 Reformed churches and 2 Mennonite churches**

Address: Fakultas Teologi Universitas Kristen Duta Wacana, Jalan Dr. Wahidin 15, Yogyakarta, 55224, Indonesia, Tel: +62 274 563-929 and 513-606, Fax: +62 274 513-235, E-mail: infukdw@yogya.wasantara.net.id

---

IRELAND

- **Dublin** — Irish School of Ecumenics (s6540)

Type of school: **Graduate/Univ** Degrees offered: **MPhil in Ec Studies, Dipl in Ec Studies, MPhil in Peace Studies, Cert in Ecumenics** Offers training for pastors: **nc** for teachers: **yes** for lay persons: **yes** Type of available practical training: **fieldwork at parish level** Admission requirements: **undergraduate degree in social sciences or theology** Languages in use: **English** Full/part-time staff: **6** National/foreign students: **50 / 25** Library size: **22,000** In relations with: **URC, Presb Church in Ireland, Church of Scotland, Reformed Church in Germany**

Address: Irish School of Ecumenics, Milltown Park, Dublin 6, Ireland, Tel: +353 1 260-1144, Fax: +353 1 260-1158, E-mail: ise.ecum@tcd.ie

---

ITALY

- **Roma** — Facoltà Valdese di Teologia (s6340)

Type of school: **Faculty of Theology** Founded in **1855** Degrees offered: **Laurea in Teologia, DiplTh** Offers training for pastors: **yes** for lay persons: **yes** Languages in use: **Italian** Full/part-time staff: **5 / 3-6** National/foreign students: **35 / 6** Library size: **78,000** Worship life offered: **daily**

Address: Facoltà Valdese di Teologia, Via P. Cossa, 42, I — 00193 Roma, Italy, Tel: +39 06 321-07 89, Fax: +39 06 320 1040

- **Roma** — Italian Evangelical Bible Institute (s6341)

Type of school: **Undergraduate/Bible school** Degrees offered: **Cert, Dipl** Offers training for pastors: **yes** Languages in use: **Italian** Full/part-time staff: **2 / 9** National/foreign students: **210 / nc** Library size: **3,500**

Address: Istituto Biblico Evangelico Italiano, via de Casale Corvio 50, Finocchio, I — 00132
Roma, Italy, Tel: +39 6 207-62293, Fax: +39 6 207-0151

IVORY COAST

- **Yamassoukro** — Biblical Institute and Faculty of Evangelical Theology (s1340)

Type of school: **Undergraduate/Bible school** Degrees offered: **BTh** Offers training for pastors: **yes** Type of available practical training: **preaching, pastoral care, religious education** Admission requirements: **baccalaureate or elementary certificate (BEPC)** Languages in use: **French** Full/part-time staff: **4 / 5** National/foreign students: **64 / nc** Library size: **7,000**

Address: Institut Biblique & Faculté de théologie évangélique, B.P. 67, Yamassoukro, Ivory Coast, Tel: +225 64 01 37

JAMAICA

- **Kingston 7** — United Theological College of the West Indies (s3330)

Founded in **1966** Degrees offered: **BA, LicTh, MA, DMin, Dipl Cert in Ministerial Studies** Offers training for pastors: **yes** Languages in use: **English** Full/part-time staff: **12 / 8** National/foreign students: **77 / nc** Library size: **22,200** In relations with: **United Ch of Jamaica and Grand Cayman**

Address: United Theological College of the West Indies, P.O. Box 136, Golding Ave., Kingston 7, Jamaica

JAPAN

- **Chiba-Ken** — Tokyo Christian University (s4320)

Type of school: **Univ and Undergraduate Seminary and College** Founded in **1990** Degrees offered: **BTh** Offers training for pastors: **yes** for teachers: **yes** for lay persons: **yes** Type of available practical training: **preaching, pastoral care, religious education** Admission requirements: **Christian, high school graduate** Languages in use: **Japanese, English** Full/part-time staff: **20 / 25** National/foreign students: **160 / 12** Library size: **53,700** Doctrinal basis: **Evangelical** Worship life offered: **daily**

Address: Tokyo Christian University, 301-5 Uchino 3-chome, Inzai-machi, Imba gun, Chiba-Ken, 270-13, Japan, Tel: +81 476 461-131, Fax: +81 476 461-405, E-mail: tci@nrm.root.or.jp

- **Kawagoe** — Nippon Kristo Kyokai Theological Seminary (s4316)
Type of school: **Graduate/Univ** Degrees offered: **BD** Offers training for pastors: **yes** Type of available practical training: **preaching, pastoral care, religious education** Admission requirements: **University graduate** Languages in use: **Japanese** Full/part-time staff: **20** National/foreign students: **20 / nc** Library size: **12,000** Doctrinal basis: **Reformed tradition** Worship life offered: **daily**

Address: Nippon Kristo Kyokai Theological Seminary, 2-2 Yoshida, 350 Kawagoe, Japan

- **Kobe** — Kobe Reformed Theological Seminary (s4318)
Type of school: **Undergraduate/Bible school** Degrees offered: **Diploma equivalent to MDiv** Offers training for pastors: **yes** for lay persons: **yes** Type of available practical training: **preaching, pastoral care, religious education** Admission requirements: **AB degree or equivalent diploma** Languages in use: **Japanese** Full/part-time staff: **2 / 3 and 11 lecturers** National/foreign students: **21 / 7** Library size: **25,500** Doctrinal basis: **Westminster Standards** Worship life offered: **daily** In relations with: **Reformed Church in Japan**

Address: Kobe Reformed Theological Seminary, 3 chome 1-1-3, Sholuga-oka, Kita-ku, Kobe 651-11 Japan, Tel: +81 78 851-4922, Fax: +81 78 851-8274

- **Osaka** — Kansai Bible School K.C.C.J. (s4317)
Founded in **1984** Offers training for pastors: **nc** Languages in use: **Korean, Japanese** Full/part-time staff: **11** National/foreign students: **6 / nc** Library size: **1,500** In relations with: **Korean Christian Ch in Japan**

Address: Kansai Bible School K.C.C.J., 2-11-6, Honjo Higashi, Kita-Ku, Osaka, 531, Japan

- **Tokyo** — Japan Biblical Seminary (s4321)
Type of school: **Seminary** Founded in **1946** Degrees offered: **Cert in Biblical Studies** Offers training for pastors: **yes** Type of available practical training: **pastoral counseling and preaching** Languages in use: **Japanese** Full/part-time staff: **3 / 21** National/foreign students: **39 / 0** Library size: **21,000** Doctrinal basis: **none** Worship life offered: **2 times per week** In relations with: **United Church of Christ in Japan**

Address: Japan Biblical Seminary, 14-16, 3-chome Shimo OchiaiShinjuku-ku, Tokyo, 161, Japan, Tel: +81 3 3951-1101, Fax: +81 3 3951-3044

- **Tokyo** — Tokyo Graduate School of Theology (s4319)
Type of school: **Graduate/Univ** Degrees offered: **MDiv** Offers training for pastors: **yes** for teachers: **yes** for lay persons: **yes** Type of available practical training: **preaching, pastoral care, religious education** Admission requirements: **BA (graduating 4 years university or college)** Languages in use: **Japanese** Full/part-time staff: **12** National/foreign students: **30 / 0** Library size: **10,000** Doctrinal basis: **Westminster Standards** Worship life offered: **daily** In relations with: **the Biblical Church (cf. Japan, no. 9)**

617

Address: Tokyo Graduate School of Theology, 1-12-3 Toyotama-kita, Nerima-ku, Tokyo, 176, Japan, Tel: +81 3 5984-3571, Fax: +81 3 5984-3572

KENYA

- **Bomet** — Bomet Bible Institute (s1087)
Type of school: **Undergraduate/Bible school** Degrees offered: **Dipl of Bible, Cert of Bible** Offers training for pastors: **yes** for lay persons: **yes** Type of available practical training: **preaching, pastoral care, religious education** Admission requirements: **na** Languages in use: **English, Swahili, Kalenjin** Full/part-time staff: **4** National/foreign students: **15 / 0** Library size: **500** Doctrinal basis: **Reformed** Worship life offered: **daily on school days** In relations with: **Africa Gospel Unity Church**

Address: Bomet Bible Institute, P.O. Box 33, Bomet, Kenya, Tel: +254 360 22049

- **Eldoret** — Reformed College of East Africa (s1072)
Type of school: **Undergraduate/Bible school** Founded in **1970** Degrees offered: **DiplTh St. Paul's University (ecumenical)** Offers training for pastors: **yes** for lay persons: **yes** Type of available practical training: **preaching, pastoral care, religious education** Admission requirements: **University Diploma B + Grade** Languages in use: **English** Full/part-time staff: **3 / 2** National/foreign students: **30 / 3** Library size: **5,000** Doctrinal basis: **Barth's Systematic Theology** Worship life offered: **monthly** In relations with: **Reformed Church of East Africa (RCEA) Ref Mission League/NL; Dutch Ref Ch of South Africa; Presb Ch of the Rep of South Africa**

Address: Reformed Theological Colles (E.A.), P.O. Box 746, 3210 Eldoret, Kenya, Fax: +254 321 1 28 70

- **Kapenguria** — B.C.F.C. Bible College (s1078)
Type of school: **Evangelist/Pastoral Training Institute** Offers training for pastors: **yes** for lay persons: **yes** Type of available practical training: **preaching, pastoral care, religious education** Admission requirements: **faith in Christ, secondary school, church recommendations, evidence of financial support** Languages in use: **English, Kiswahili** Full/part-time staff: **3** National/foreign students: **3 / 0** Library size: **100** Doctrinal basis: **WestConf** Worship life offered: **daily morning devotion / 5 days each week**

Address: B.C.F.C. Bible College, P.O. Box 179, Kapenguria, Nairobi, Kenya, Tel: +254 32 42473, Fax: +254 32 43233

- **Kikuyu** — Pastoral Institute (s1079)
Founded in **1978** Degrees offered: **CertTh, DiplTh** Offers training for pastors: **nc** Admission requirements: **primary education** Languages in use: **Swahili, English** Full/part-time staff: **4 / 7** National/foreign students: **33 / nc** Library size: **10,000** In relations with: **Presb Ch of East Africa**

Address: Pastoral Institute, P.O. Box 387, Kikuyu, Kenya

- **Limuru** — St. Paul's United Theological College (s1073)
Type of school: **Undergraduate/Bible school** Degrees offered: **BDiv** Offers training for pastors: **yes** Type of available practical training: **preaching, pastoral care, religious education** Admission requirements: **degree entry as for public universities** Languages in use: **English** Full/part-time staff: **10** National/foreign students: **110 / 22** Library size: **12,000** Doctrinal basis: **own, stating basic Evang doctrine + historic creeds** Worship life offered: **daily except Saturdays** In relations with: **Reformed Church of East Africa, Presb Church of East Africa, Meth Church in Kenya, Church of the Province of Kenya**

Address: St. Paul's United Theological College, Private Bag, Limuru, Kenya, Tel: +254 154 40965 and 40970, Fax: +254 154 40557

- **Mwingi** — Mwingi Bible School IPC (s1075)
Type of school: **Bible school + Pastoral Training Institute** Degrees offered: **DiplTh, CertTh, Cert Attendance** Offers training for pastors: **yes** for teachers: **yes** Type of available practical training: **preaching, pastoral care, religious education** Admission requirements: **std eight to form IV** Languages in use: **English, Kiswahili** Full/part-time staff: **6** National/foreign students: **60 / na** Library size: **na** Worship life offered: **3 times per week** In relations with: **Independent Presbyterian Church**

Address: Mwingi Bible School IPC, P.O. Box 37, Hospital Road, Mwingi, Kenya, Tel: +254 142 22035

- **Mwingi** — Trinity Bible Institute (s1088)
Type of school: **Undergraduate/Bible school** Degrees offered: **Diploma in Christian Ministries** Offers training for pastors: **yes** for teachers: **no** for lay persons: **no** Type of available practical training: **preaching, pastoral care, religious education** Admission requirements: **std eight to form IV, call to serve** Languages in use: **English** Full/part-time staff: **6** National/foreign students: **na / na** Library size: **few, personal volumes** Doctrinal basis: **WestConf** Worship life offered: **none** In relations with: **Orthodox Presbyterian Church, Presbyterian Church of America**

Address: Trinity Bible Institute, P.O. Box 49, Mwingi, Kenya

- **Nairobi** — Bible College of East Africa (s1071)
Type of school: **Bible College** Degrees offered: **DiplTh, Cert of Christian Studies** Offers training for pastors: **yes** for teachers: **yes** for lay persons: **yes** Type of available practical training: **preaching, pastoral care, religious education** Admission requirements: **graduate (12th grade)** Languages in use: **English** Full/part-time staff: **5 / 2** National/foreign students: **90 / 22** Library size: **3,000** Doctrinal basis: **WestConf** Worship life offered: **daily** In relations with: **East Africa Christian Alliance and Independent Board for Presbyterian Foreign Missions**

Address: Bible College of East Africa, P.O. Box 41140, Nairobi, Kenya, Tel: +254 2 802-941, Fax: +254 2 802-044, E-mail: lovegod@form-net.com

- **Nairobi** — Daystar University (s1081)
Type of school: **Graduate/Univ** Degrees offered: **BA, BCom, B in Education** Offers training for pastors: **yes** for teachers: **yes** for lay persons: **yes** Type of available practical training: **6 weeks practical training in Bible and Christian ministries** Admission requirements: **4 years secondary school (same as national universities)** Languages in use: **English** Full/part-time staff: **70** National/foreign students: **1,200 / 300** Library size: **35,000** Doctrinal basis: **Lordship of Jesus Christ** Worship life offered: **2 times per week** In relations with: **interdenominational**

Address: Daystar University, P.O. Box 44400, Nairobi, Kenya, Tel: +254 2 723-003 and 4, Fax: +254 2 728-338, E-mail: daystar@Maf.Org

- **Nairobi** — Faith College of the Bible (s1074)
Type of school: **Undergraduate/Bible school** Degrees offered: **DiplTh** Offers training for pastors: **yes** Type of available practical training: **preaching, pastoral care, religious education** Admission requirements: **12 years of secular education** Languages in use: **English, Kiswahili** Full/part-time staff: **4** National/foreign students: **22 / 8** Library size: **500 (recently started)** Doctrinal basis: **Reformed** Worship life offered: **Sundays** In relations with: **Independent Presbyterian Church**

Address: Faith College of the Bible, P.O. Box 33203, Nairobi, Kenya, Tel: +254 2 799-295

- **Nakuru** — Grace Bible College (s1076)
Type of school: **Undergraduate/Bible school** Degrees offered: **DiplTh** Offers training for pastors: **yes** for teachers: **yes** Type of available practical training: **preaching, pastoral care, religious education** Admission requirements: **academic form IV, born again, recommended by local church** Languages in use: **English** Full/part-time staff: **6** National/foreign students: **11 / 0** Library size: **1,500** Doctrinal basis: **Calvinism** Worship life offered: **daily** In relations with: **Africa Evangelical Presbyterian Church (AEPC)**

Address: Grace Bible College, P.O. Box 2647, 254 Nakuru, Kenya, Tel: +254 37 210-188

KIRIBATI

- **Tarawa** — Tangintebu Theological College (s5180)
Type of school: **Undergraduate/College** Founded in **1900** Degrees offered: **Certificate of Study in Theology, DiplTh** Offers training for pastors: **yes** for teachers: **yes** for lay persons: **yes** Type of available practical training: **weekly in different village churches** Admission requirements: **entrance test, general understanding of the Bible, church culture, English language, etc.** Languages in use: **English, Kiribati** Full/part-time staff: **7** National/foreign students: **40 / 2** Library size: **6,000** Doctrinal basis: **ApC, NicC** Worship life offered: **twice daily** In relations with: **Kiribati Protestant Church, Uniting Church in Australia, United Reformed Church in UK, Presbyterian Church in Aotearoa NZ**

Address: Tangintebu Theological College, P.O. Box 264, TThC Bikenibeu, Tarawa, Kiribati, Tel:
+686 21342nc

KOREA

A. Member Sschools of the Korea Association of Accredited Theological Schools (KAATS)

• **An Yang** — An Yang University and Graduate School (s4602)
Type of school: **Graduate School/Univ** Founded in **1948** Degrees offered: **BA, MDiv** Offers training for pastors: **yes** for teachers: **yes** for lay persons: **yes** Type of available practical training: **Christian Education and Counseling** Full/part-time staff: **88** National/foreign students: **3,000/2** Library size: **100,000** Doctrinal basis: **Calvinism, Conservative Reformed teaching** Worship life offered: **weekly** In relation with: **Presb Ch in Korea (DaeShin, cf. no. 16)**

Address: An Yang University and Graduate School, 708-113 An Yang 5 dong, Man An ku,
430-714 An Yang, Korea, Tel: +82 343 670-700 and 670-856, Fax: +82 343 483-870

• **Chun buk** — Hanil University and Theological Seminary (s4603)
Type of school: **Graduate Seminary/Univ** Founded in **1923** Degrees offered: **BA, BS, BTh, MTh, Dipl in Christ. Studies** Offers training for pastors: **yes** for teachers: **yes** for lay persons: **yes** Type of available practical training: **preaching, pastoral care, religious education, lay training** Admission requirements: **high school** Languages in use: **Korean** Full/part-time staff: **44** National/foreign students: **860** Library size: **38,194** Doctrinal basis: **Presb** In relation with: **Presb Ch in Korea (TongHap, cf. no. 14)**

Address: Hanil University amd Theological Seminary, 694-1 Shin ri, Sangkwan myun, Wanju kun,
Chun buk, Korea, Tel: +82 652 837-011, Fax: +82 652 837-831

• **Kwangju** — Honam Theological University and Seminary (s4606)
Type of school: **Graduate Seminary/Univ** Degrees offered: **BTh, BM, MDiv, MMin, DMin** Offers training for pastors: **yes** for teachers: **yes** for lay persons: **yes** Type of available practical training: **preaching, religious education** Admission requirements: **high school** Languages in use: **Korean** Full/part-time staff: **23** National/foreign students: **838** Library size: **33,659** Doctrinal basis: **Presb** In relation with: **Presb Ch in Korea (TongHap, cf. no. 14)**

Address: Honam Theological University and Seminary, 108 Yangrim dong, Nam ku, Kwangju,
503-756 Korea, Tel: +82 62 651 1552, Fax: +82 62 675 1552 E-mail:
ncsmkims@rsb.chonnam.ac.kr

• **Kyungbuk** — Young Nam Theological College and Seminary (s4600)
Type of school: **Seminary** Degrees offered: **BA, BTh** Offers training for pastors: **yes** for teachers: **yes** for lay persons: **yes** Type of available practical training: **preaching, religious education** Admission requirements: **high school** Languages

in use: **Korean** Full/part-time staff: **18** National/foreign students: **703** Library size: **32,518** Doctrinal basis: **Presb** In relation with: **Presb Ch in Korea (TongHap, cf. no. 14)**

Address: Young Nam Theological Seminary, 117 Bonghoeri, Chinryang-myun, Kyungsan,
Kyungbuk, Korea, Tel: +82 53 850-0500, Fax: +82 53 852-9815

• **Kyungki do** — HanShin University, Faculty of Theology (s4612)
Type of school: **Graduate Seminary/Univ** Degrees offered: **MTh, MDiv, MA, DTh** Offers training for pastors: **yes** for teachers: **yes** for lay persons: **yes** Type of available practical training: **preaching, religious education** Admission requirements: **high school** Languages in use: **Korean** Full/part-time staff: **25** National/foreign students: **750** Library size: **122,649** Doctrinal basis: **Presb** In relation with: **Presb Ch in the Republic of Korea (KiJang, cf. no. 13)**

Address: HanShin University, Faculty of Theology, 411 Yangsan dong, Osan si, Kyungki do,
447-791 Korea, Tel: +82 339 370-6500, Fax: +82 339 723-343

• **Kyungki do** — Kang Nam University, College of Theology
Type of school: **Graduate School/Univ** Degrees offered: **BTh, MTh** Offers training for pastors: **yes** for teachers: **yes** Admission requirements: **high school** Languages in use: **Korean** Full/part-time staff: **9** National/foreign students: **224** Library size: **169,290** In relation with: **Ecumenical**

Address: Kang Nam University, College of Theology, San 6-2, Kugal li, Kyhung eup, Yongin
koon, Kyungki do, Korea, Tel: +82 331 2802-650, Fax: +82 331 2803-650

• **Kyungki do** — Asia United Theological University
Type of school: **Graduate Seminary/Univ** Degrees offered: **BA, BTh, DTh, MTh, MA, MDiv** Offers training for pastors: **yes** for teachers: **yes** for lay persons: **yes** Admission requirements: **high school** Languages in use: **Korean** Full/part-time staff: **23** National/foreign students: **689** Library size: **50,033** In relation with: **ecumenical**

Address: Asia United Theological University, San 151-1, Asinri, Okchun-myun, Yangpyung-kun,
Kyungki do, Korea, Tel: +82 388 725-339, Fax: +82 388 393-3789

• **Pusan** — Pusan Union Theological Seminary
Type of school: **Seminary** Degrees offered: **BTh** Offers training for pastors: **yes** for teachers: **yes** Type of available practical training: **preaching, religious education** Admission requirements: **high school** Languages in use: **Korean** Full/part-time staff: **10** National/foreign students: **357** Library size: **12,000** In relation with: **ecumenical (with roots in the Reformed tradition)**

Address: Pusan Union Theological Seminary, 316-3 Taeyon dong, Nam ku, Pusan, 608-025 Korea,
Tel: +82 51 628 0115

• **Seoul** — Ewha Women's University, Department of Christian Studies (s4608)
Type of school: **Univ** Degrees offered: **BA, MA, PhD** Offers training for teachers: **yes** for lay persons: **yes** Admission requirements: **high school** Languages in use:

Korean Full/part-time staff: **9** National/foreign students: **204** Library size: **674,414** In relation with: **ecumenical**

Address: Ewha University, Department of Christian Studies, 11-1 DaeHyun dong, Sudaemun ku, Seoul, 120-750 Korea, Tel: +82 2 360-2195, Fax: +82 2 393-5903

• **Seoul** — Seoul Women's University, Department of Christian Studies
Type of school: **Univ** Degrees offered: **BA** Offers training for teachers: **yes** for lay persons: **yes** Admission requirements: **high school** Languages in use: **Korean** Full/part-time staff: **4** National/foreign students: **60** Library size: **10,000** In relation with: **Presb Ch in Korea (TongHap, cf. no. 14)**

Address: Seoul Women's University, Department of Christian Studies, 126 Kongnung 2 dong, Nowon ku, Seoul, 139-774 Korea, Tel: +82 2 970-5471, Fax: +82 2 971-0915

• **Seoul** — Presbyterian College and Theological Seminary (s4609)
Type of school: **Graduate Seminary/Univ** Degrees offered: **BA, BTh, MTh, MDiv, MCM, MA, DTh, DD, MDiv, MTh in missions, MA in Christian Education** Offers training for pastors: **yes** for teachers: **yes** for lay persons: **yes** Type of available practical training: **preaching, religious education, liturgics, pastoral care** Admission requirements: **high school** Languages in use: **Korean** Full/part-time staff: **37** National/foreign students: **1,308** Library size: **74,059** Doctrinal basis: **Presb** Worship life offered: **several times a week** In relation with: **Presb Ch in Korea (TongHap, cf. no. 14)**

Address: Presbyterian College and Theological Seminary, 353 Kwangjang dong, Sungdong ku, Seoul, 143-756 Korea, +82 2 450-0700, Fax: +82 2 452-3460

• **Seoul** — Seoul Presbyterian Theological Seminary
Type of school: **Seminary** Degrees offered: **BA** Offers training for pastors: **yes** for teachers: **yes** for lay persons: **yes** Admission requirements: **high school** Languages in use: **Korean** Full/part-time staff: **16** National/foreign students: **1,345** Library size: **35,488** In relation with: **Presb Ch in Korea (TongHap)**

Address: Seoul Presbyterian Theological Seminary, 1370 Soongin dong, Jongro ku, Seoul, 110-150 Korea, Tel: +82 2 238-6305, Fax: +82 2 236-7617

• **Seoul** — Yonsei University, Union Graduate School of Theology (s4617)
Type of school: **Graduate seminary/Univ** Degrees offered: **MTh** Offers training for pastors: **yes** for teachers: **yes** Admission requirements: **college level degrees** Languages in use: **Korean** Full/part-time staff: **20** National/foreign students: **115/5** Library size: **77,000** Worship life offered: **three times every week** In relation with: **ecumenical**

Address: Yonsei University, Union Graduate School, 134 ShinChon dong, Sudaemun ku, Seoul, 120-749 Korea, Tel: +82 2 361-3243 and 361-3244, Fax: +82 2 392-6202

• **Seoul** — Yonsei University, College of Theology
Type of school: **Univ** Degrees offered: **BTh, MTh, PhD** Offers training for pastors: **yes** for teachers: **yes** Admission requirements: **high school** Languages in use:

Korean Full/part-time staff: **15** National/foreign students: **320** Library size: **15,216** In relation with: **ecumenical**

Address: Yonsei University, College of Theology, 134 ShinChon dong, Sudaemun ku, Seoul, 120-749 Korea, Tel: +82 2 361-2895, Fax: +82 2 365-3477

• **Taegu** — Keimyung University, Department of Theology (s4614)
Type of school: **Graduate School/Univ** Degrees offered: **BTh, MTh, DTh** Offers training for pastors: **yes** for teachers: **yes** Type of available practical training: **preaching, religious education** Admission requirements: **high school** Languages in use: **Korean** Full/part-time staff: **7** National/foreign students: **336** Library size: **376,200** In relation with: **ecumenical**

Address: Keimyung University, Department of Theology, 2139 Daemyung 7-dong, Nam ku, Taegu, Korea, Tel: +82 53 580-5785, Fax: +88 53 580-5454

• **Taejon** — Han Nam University (s4601)
Type of school: **Graduate School/Univ** Degrees offered: **BA, MA** Offers training for pastors: **yes** for teachers: **yes** for lay persons: **yes** Admission requirements: **high school, baptism** Languages in use: **Korean** Full/part-time staff: **6** National/ foreign students: **160** Library size: **320,000** Doctrinal basis: **Presb** In relation with: **Presb Ch in Korea (TongHap, cf. no. 14)**

Address: Han Nam University, 133 Ojung dong, Tae Duk ku, Taejon, 300-791 Korea, Tel: +82 42 629-7378, Fax: +82 42 625-5974, E-mail: dalle@eve.hannam.ac.kr

• **Taejon** — Taejon Presbyterian Theological Seminary
Type of school: **Seminary** Degrees offered: **BA** Offers training for pastors: **yes** for teachers: **yes** for lay persons: **yes** Admission requirements: **high school** Languages in use: **Korean** Full/part-time staff: **8** National/foreign students: **378** Library size: **17,935** Doctrinal basis: **Presb** In relation with: **Presb Ch in Korea (TongHap, cf. no. 14)**

Address: Taejon Presbyterian Theological Seminary, 226-22 Ojung dong, TaeDuk ku, Taejon, 306-010 Korea, Tel: +82 42 623-3620, Fax: +82 42 621-0821

B. Reformed Theological Schools Not Members of the Korea Association of Accredited Theological Schools

(ChongHoe means General Assembly)

• **Buchon** — ChongHoe Theological Seminary ((HapDongSungHoe)
Type of school: **Church Seminary** Degrees offered: **Cert** Offers training for pastors: **yes** Type of available practical training: **preaching, religious education, evangelism** Language in use: **Korean** Doctrinal basis: **Presb**

Address: ChongHoe Theological Seminary, 314-8 Samjung dong, Ojung ku, Buchon, 421-150 Korea, Tel: +82 32 672-4621, Fax: +82 32 683-0578

• **Chunju** — YunHap Theological Seminary
Type of school: **Church Seminary** Degrees offered: **Cert** Offers training for pas-

tors: **yes** Type of available practical training: **preaching, religious education, evangelism** Language in use: **Korean** Doctrinal basis: **Presb**

Address: YunHap Theological Seminary, 267-8, Jun dong 1 ga, Wansan ku, Chunju, 560-041 Korea, Tel: +82 652 864 114

• **Inchon** — ChongHoe Theological Seminary (HapDongChong Shin)
Type of school: **Church Seminary** Degrees offered: **Cert** Offers training for pastors: **yes** Type of available practical training: **preaching, religious education, evangelism** Language in use: **Korean** Doctrinal basis: **Presb**

Address: ChongHoe Theological Seminary, 72-1 Kajwa 3 dong, Su ku, Inchon, 404-253 Korea, Tel: +82 32 572-1023, Fax: +82 32 572-1023

• **Inchon** — KoRyu Theological Seminary
Type of school: **Church Seminary** Degrees offered: **Cert** Offers training for pastors: **yes** Type of available practical training: **preaching, religious education, evangelism** Language in use: **Korean** Doctrinal basis: **Presb** In relation with: **Presb Ch in Korea (KoRyuPa, cf. no. 3)**

Address: KoRyu Theological Seminary, 43-46 ManSuck dong, Dong ku, Inchon, 401-060 Korea, Tel: +82 32 764-1839, Fax: +82 32 764-1839

• **Kwangju** — Kwangju GaeHyuck Theological Seminary
Type of school: **Church Seminary** Degrees offered: **Cert** Offers training for pastors: **yes** Type of available practical training: **preaching, religious education, evangelism** Language in use: **Korean** Doctrinal basis: **Presb** In relation with **Presb Ch in Korea (GaeHyuk, cf. no. 23)**

Address: GaeHyuk Theological Seminary, San 70-68, Bonchon dong, Buk ku, Kwangju, 500-210 Korea, Tel: +82 62 571-7251, Fax: +82 62 571-7255

• **Kyungki do** — ChongHoe Theological Seminary (HwanWon)
Type of school: **Church Seminary** Degrees offered: **Cert** Offers training for pastors: **yes** Type of available practical training: **preaching, religious education, evangelism** Language in use: **Korean** Doctrinal basis: **Presb**

Address: ChongHoe Theological Seminary, 406-4 Dukpoong dong, Hanam, Kyungki do, 465-010 Korea, Tel: +82 347 794-0190

• **Kyungki do** — Pierson Theological Seminary
Type of school: **Church Seminary** Degrees offered: **Cert** Offers training for pastors: **yes** Type of available practical training: **preaching, religious education, evangelism** Language in use: **Korean** Doctrinal basis: **Presb**

Address: Pierson Theological Seminary, San 84, YongYe dong, Pyung Taek city, Kyungki do, Korea, Tel: +82 333 541-861

• **Pusan** — Korea Theological Seminary (s4605)
Type of school: **Graduate School and College** Degrees offered: **MDiv** Offers training for pastors: **yes** Type of available practical training: **preaching, religious education, pastoral care, evangelism** Admission requirements: **bachelor's degree** Languages in use: **Korean** Full/part-time staff: **12/7** National/foreign stu-

dents: **500/4** Library size: **35,000** Doctrinal basis: **WestConf** Worship life offered: **four times a week** In relation with: **Presb Ch in Korea (KoShin, cf. no. 1)**

Address: Korea Theological Seminary, 34 AmNam dong, Su ku, Pusan, 602-702 Korea, Tel: +82 51 253-5131, Fax: +82 51 253-5133

• **Pusan** — Pusan Presbyterian Theological Seminary (s4615)
Type of school: **Seminary** Degrees offered: **MDiv** Offers training for pastors: **yes** Type of available practical training: **preaching, religious education, pastoral care, evangelism** Admission requirements: **graduation from high school** Languages in use: **Korean** Full/part-time staff: **25/6** National/foreign students: **232/27** Library size: **11,000** Doctrinal basis: **Presb** Worship life offered: **twice a week** In relation with: **Presb Ch in Korea (TongHap, cf. no. 14)**

Address: Pusan Presbyterian Theological Seminary, 768 Jwachon 1 dong, Dong ku, Pusan, 601-051 Korea, Tel: +82 2 632-1408 and 642-2331 and 634-0130, Fax: +82 2 634-0130

• **Seoul** — ChongShin University (s4618)
Type of school: **Graduate School/Univ** Degrees offered: **BA, BMusic, MA, MTh, PhD, MDiv, DMin** Offers training for pastors: **yes** for teachers: **yes** for lay persons: **yes** Type of available practical training: **preaching, religious education, pastoral care** Admission requirements: **high school, bachelor** Languages in use: **Korean** Full/part-time staff: **63** National/foreign students: **4,000/50** Library size: **150,000** Doctrinal basis: **WestConf, WestCat** Worship life offered: **daily** In relation with: **Presb Ch in Korea (HapDong, cf. no. 15)**

Address: ChongShin University, 31-3 Sadang dong, Dong Jak ku, Seoul, 156-763 Korea, Tel: 82 2 537-5101, Fax: +82 2 536-2602

• **Seoul** — KoRyu GaeHyuck Theological Seminary
Type of school: **Church Seminary** Degrees offered: **Cert** Offers training for pastors: **yes** Type of available practical training: **preaching, religious education, evangelism** Language in use: **Korean** Doctrinal basis: **Presb**

Address: KoRyu GaeHyuck Theological Seminary, 304-43 Sa Jik dong, Chongro ku, Seoul, 110-054 Korea, Tel: +82 2 738-9911, Fax: +82 2 738-0568

• **Seoul** — KoRyu ChongHoe United Theological Seminary
Type of school: **Church Seminary** Degrees offered: **Cert** Offers training for pastors: **yes** Type of available practical training: **preaching, religious education, evangelism** Language in use: **Korean** Doctrinal basis: **Presb**

Address: KoRyu Chong Hoe United Theological Seminary, DaeBang dong, Dong Jak ku, Seoul, 150-092 Korea, Tel: +82 2 826-0301, Fax: +82 2 814-5323

• **Seoul** — ChongHoe Theological Seminary
Type of school: **Church Seminary** Degrees offered: **Cert** Offers training for pastors: **yes** Type of available practical training: **preaching, religious education, evangelism** Language in use: **Korean** Doctrinal basis: **Presb**

Address: ChongHoe Theological Seminary, 877-1 Dok San dong, Kuro ku, Seoul, 142-013 Korea, Tel: +82 2 853-0543, Fax: +82 2 853-3763

- **Seoul** — Presbyterian Theological Seminary (HapDongBoSu)
Type of school: **Church Seminary** Degrees offered: **Cert** Offers training for pastors: **yes** Type of available practical training: **preaching, religious education, evangelism** Language in use: **Korean** Doctrinal basis: **Presb**

Address: Presbyterian Theological Seminary, 311-7 ShinJung 1 dong, Yangchon ku, Seoul, 158-071 Korea, Tel: +82 2 652-9358

- **Seoul** — ChongHoe GaeHyuck Theological Seminary
Type of school: **Church Seminary** Degrees offered: **Cert** Offers training for pastors: **yes** Type of available practical training: **preaching, religious education, evangelism** Language in use: **Korean** Doctrinal basis: **Presb**

Address: ChongHoe GaeHyuck Theological Seminary, 120-3 ChungDam dong, KangNam ku, Seoul, 135-100 Korea, Tel: +82 2 544-6695, Fax: +82 2 514-5801

- **Seoul** — ChongHoe Theological Seminary (GaeHyuck HapDong)
Type of school: **Church Seminary** Degrees offered: **Cert** Offers training for pastors: **yes** Type of available practical training: **preaching, religious education, evangelism** Language in use: **Korean** Doctrinal basis: **Presb**

Address: ChongHoe Theological Seminary, 478-11 Bong Chun 5 dong, KwanAk ku, Seoul, 151-069 Korea, Tel: +82 2 875-5051, Fax: +82 2 875-5055

- **Seoul** — ChongHoe Theological Seminary (KeunBon, fundamentalist)
Type of school: **Church Seminary** Degrees offered: **Cert** Offers training for pastors: **yes** Type of available practical training: **preaching, religious education, evangelism** Language in use: **Korean** Doctrinal basis: **Presb**

Address: ChongHoe Theological Seminary, 414-85 Jangan dong, Dongdaemun ku, Seoul, Korea, Tel: +82 2 215-3004, Fax: +82 2 217-0781

- **Seoul** — ChongHoe Theological Seminary (BoSu HoHun)
Type of school: **Church Seminary** Degrees offered: **Cert** Offers training for pastors: **yes** Type of available practical training: **preaching, religious education, evangelism** Language in use: **Korean** Doctrinal basis: **Presb**

Address: ChongHoe Theological Seminary, 332-32 ChonHo 2 dong, Kangdong ku, Seoul, 134-022 Korea, Tel: +82 2 475-7394, Fax: +82 2 428-8519

- **Seoul** — ChongHoe Theological Seminary (BoSu Chuk)
Type of school: **Church Seminary** Degrees offered: **Cert** Offers training for pastors: **yes** Type of available practical training: **preaching, religious education, evangelism** Language in use: **Korean** Doctrinal basis: **Presb**

Address: ChongHoe Theological Seminary, San 14, SaDang dong, DongJak ku, Seoul, 154-090 Korea, Tel: +82 2 584-0955

- **Seoul** — ChongHoe Theological Seminary (BoSu HapDong)
Type of school: **Church Seminary** Degrees offered: **Cert** Offers training for pastors: **yes** Type of available practical training: **preaching, religious education, evangelism** Language in use: **Korean** Doctrinal basis: **Presb**

Address: ChongHoe Theological Seminary, 877-186 Kil Um dong, SungBuk ku, Seoul, 132-090 Korea, Tel: +82 2 941-0262

• **Seoul** — ChongHoe Theological Seminary (BoSu HapDong)
Type of school: **Church Seminary** Degrees offered: **Cert** Offers training for pastors: **yes** Type of available practical training: **preaching, religious education, evangelism** Language in use: **Korean** Doctrinal basis: **Presb**

Address: ChongHoe Theological Seminary, 251-8 DoRim 2 dong, YoungDeung Po ku, Seoul, 150-082 Korea, Tel: +82 2 835-0567, Fax: +82 2 835-0569

• **Seoul** — ChongHoe Theological Seminary (BoSu HapDong)
Type of school: **Church Seminary** Degrees offered: **Cert** Offers training for pastors: **yes** Type of available practical training: **preaching, religious education, evangelism** Language in use: **Korean** Doctrinal basis: **Presb**

Address: ChongHoe Theological Seminary, 397-16 HongEun 3 dong, Sudaemun ku Seoul, 120-103 Korea, Tel: +82 2 302-3906, Fax: +82 2 302-3906

• **Seoul** — ChongHoe Theological Seminary (SunJang)
Type of school: **Church Seminary** Degrees offered: **Cert** Offers training for pastors: **yes** Type of available practical training: **preaching, religious education, evangelism** Language in use: **Korean** Doctrinal basis: **Presb**

Address: ChongHoe Theological Seminary, 4903-20 ShinKil 4 dong, YoungDeungPo ku, Seoul, 150-054 Korea, Tel: +82 2 845-7711, Fax: +82 2 849-9545

• **Seoul** — ChongHoe Theological Seminary (YunHap YuhMok)
Type of school: **Church Seminary** Degrees offered: **Cert** Offers training for pastors: **yes** Type of available practical training: **preaching, religious education, evangelism** Language in use: **Korean** Doctrinal basis: **Presb**

Address: ChongHoe Theological Seminary, 977-22 ShinJung 4 dong, YangChon ku, Seoul, Korea, Tel: +82 2 698-0583

• **Seoul** — ChongHoe Theological Institute
Type of school: **Church Seminary** Degrees offered: **Cert** Offers training for pastors: **yes** Type of available practical training: **preaching, religious education, evangelism** Language in use: **Korean** Doctrinal basis: **Presb**

Address: ChongHoe Theological Institute, 139-6 SongPa dong, Songpa ku Seoul, 138-170 Korea, Tel: +82 2 413-7460, Fax: +82 2 425-4417

• **Seoul** — ChongHoe Theological Seminary (Asia Theological Seminary)
Type of school: **Church Seminary** Degrees offered: **Cert** Offers training for pastors: **yes** Type of available practical training: **preaching, religious education, evangelism** Language in use: **Korean** Doctrinal basis: **Presb**

Address: ChongHoe Theological Seminary, 717 DaeRim 3 dong, YoungDeunngpo ku, Seoul, 150-070 Korea, Tel: +82 2 847-5091

• **Seoul** — ChongHoe Theological Seminary (YeJang HapBo)
Type of school: **Church Seminary** Degrees offered: **Cert** Offers training for pas-

tors: **yes** Type of available practical training: **preaching, religious education, evangelism** Language in use: **Korean** Doctrinal basis: **Presb**

Address: ChongHoe Theological Seminary, 193-180 EungBong dong, Sungdong ku, Seoul,
133-080 Korea, Tel: +82 2 281-0691

- **Seoul** — JungRib Theological Seminary
Type of school: **Church Seminary** Degrees offered: **Cert** Offers training for pastors: **yes** Type of available practical training: **preaching, religious education, evangelism** Language in use: **Korean** Doctrinal basis: **Presb**

Address: JungRib Theological Seminary, 618-195 YoungDeungPo dong, YoungDeungPo ku, Seoul,
150-020 Korea, Tel: +82 2 846-0069

- **Seoul** — ChongHoe Theological Seminary (YeJung)
Type of school: **Church Seminary** Degrees offered: **Cert** Offers training for pastors: **yes** Type of available practical training: **preaching, religious education, evangelism** Language in use: **Korean** Doctrinal basis: **Presb**

Address: ChongHoe Theological Seminary, 236-488 Shindang 1 dong, Chung ku, Seoul, 100-451
Korea, Tel: +82 2 234-9201, Fax: +82 236-2845

- **Seoul** — ChongHoe Theological Seminary (JeongTong)
Type of school: **Church Seminary** Degrees offered: **Cert** Offers training for pastors: **yes** Type of available practical training: **preaching, religious education, evangelism** Language in use: **Korean** Doctrinal basis: **Presb**

Address: ChongHoe Theological Seminary, 110-78 ShinRim 2 dong, Kwan Ak ku, Seoul, 151-012
Korea, Tel: +82 2 886-2753

- **Seoul** — ChongHoe Theological Seminary
Type of school: **Church Seminary** Degrees offered: **Cert** Offers training for pastors: **yes** Type of available practical training: **preaching, religious education, evangelism** Language in use: **Korean** Doctrinal basis: **Presb**

Address: ChongHoe Theological Seminary, 1-1 Yunji dong, Chongro ku, Seoul, 110-470 Korea,
Tel: +82 2 764-3560

- **Seoul** — ChongHoe Theological Seminary (BokEum)
Type of school: **Church Seminary** Degrees offered: **Cert** Offers training for pastors: **yes** Type of available practical training: **preaching, religious education, evangelism** Language in use: **Korean** Doctrinal basis: **Presb**

Address: ChongHoe Theological Seminary, 1-87 Hyunjuh dong, Sudaemun ku, Seoul, 120-080 Korea, Tel. +82 2 392-8825, Fax: +82 2 932-8828

- **Seoul** — ChongHoe Theological Seminary (JeongTong GaeHyuck)
Type of school: **Church Seminary** Degrees offered: **Cert** Offers training for pastors: **yes** Type of available practical training: **preaching, religious education, evangelism** Language in use: **Korean** Doctrinal basis: **Presb**

Address: ChongHoe Theological Seminary, 114-15 Samsung dong, KangNam ku, Seoul, 135-090
Korea, Tel: +82 2 563-2705, Fax: +82 2 564-6756

- **Seoul** — ChongHoe Theological Seminary (HapDong Gae Hyuck)
Type of school: **Church Seminary** Degrees offered: **Cert** Offers training for pastors: **yes** Type of available practical training: **preaching, religious education, evangelism** Language in use: **Korean** Doctrinal basis: **Presb**

Address: ChongHoe Theological Seminary, 902-23 Bongchun bon dong, Kwanak ku, Seoul, 158-075 Korea, Tel: +82 2 694-9312

- **Seoul** — ChongHoe Theological Seminary (HapDong KyoSung)
Type of school: **Church Seminary** Degrees offered: **Cert** Offers training for pastors: **yes** Type of available practical training: **preaching, religious education, evangelism** Language in use: **Korean** Doctrinal basis: **Presb**

Address: ChongHoe Theological Seminary, 201 Oksu dong, Sungdoch ku, Seoul, 133-100 Korea, Tel: +82 2 299-5948

- **Seoul** — ChongHoe Theological Seminary (HapDong BoSu)
Type of school: **Church Seminary** Degrees offered: **Cert** Offers training for pastors: **yes** Type of available practical training: **preaching, religious education, evangelism** Language in use: **Korean** Doctrinal basis: **Presb**

Address: ChongHoe Theological Seminary, 469 Jayang dong, Sungdong ku, Seoul, 133-193 Korea, Tel: +82 2 455-6936

- **Seoul** — ChongHoe Theological Seminary (HapDong Sun Kyo)
Type of school: **Church Seminary** Degrees offered: **Cert** Offers training for pastors: **yes** Type of available practical training: **preaching, religious education, evangelism** Language in use: **Korean** Doctrinal basis: **Presb**

Address: ChongHoe Theological Seminary, 363-5 Eemun 1 dong, DongDaeMun ku, Seoul, Korea, Tel. +82 2 969-5776, Fax: +82 2 651-0132

- **Seoul** — ChongHoe Theological Seminary (Jae Kun)
Type of school: **Church Seminary** Degrees offered: **Cert** Offers training for pastors: **yes** Type of available practical training: **preaching, religious education, evangelism** Language in use: **Korean** Doctrinal basis: **Presb**

Address: ChongHoe Theological Seminary, 91-7 Sangsung dong, KangNam ku, Seoul, 135-090 Korea, Tel: +82 2 514-8336

- **Seoul** — ChongHoe Theological Seminary (HapDong JeongTong)
Type of school: **Church Seminary** Degrees offered: **Cert** Offers training for pastors: **yes** Type of available practical training: **preaching, religious education, evangelism** Language in use: **Korean** Doctrinal basis: **Presb** In relation with: **Presb Ch in Korea (JeongTong, cf. no. 37)**

Address: ChongHoe Theological Seminary, 981-9 BangBae 3 dong, Sucho ku, Seoul, 137-063 Korea, Tel: +82 2 584-4803

- **Seoul** — ChongHoe Theological Seminary (HapDong JungAng)
Type of school: **Church Seminary** Degrees offered: **Cert** Offers training for pastors: **yes** Type of available practical training: **preaching, religious education,**

evangelism Language in use: **Korean** Doctrinal basis: **Presb** In relation with: **Presb Ch in Korea (JungAng, cf. no. 41)**

Address: ChongHoe Theological Seminary, 448-1 Hongeun 1 dong, Sudaemun ku, Seoul, 120-101 Korea, Tel: +82 2 353-3777, Fax: +82 2 353-0639

• **Seoul** — ChongHoe Theological Seminary (HapDong JungRib)
Type of school: **Church Seminary** Degrees offered: **Cert** Offers training for pastors: **yes** Type of available practical training: **preaching, religious education, evangelism** Language in use: **Korean** Doctrinal basis: **Presb**

Address: ChongHoe Theological Seminary, 1-59 DoRim 1 dong, YoungDeungPo ku, Seoul, 150-081 Korea, Tel: +82 2 841-6061, Fax: +82 2 834-1515

• **Seoul** — ChongHoe Theological Seminary (HapDong BoSu)
Type of school: **Church Seminary** Degrees offered: **Cert** Offers training for pastors: **yes** Type of available practical training: **preaching, religious education, evangelism** Language in use: **Korean** Doctrinal basis: **Presb**

Address: ChongHoe Theological Seminary, 265-339 Hongeun 3 dong, Sudaemun ku, Seoul, Korea, Tel: +82 2 396-4521, Fax: +82 2 396-4528

• **Seoul** — ChongHoe Theological Seminary (HapDong BoSu)
Type of school: **Church Seminary** Degrees offered: **Cert** Offers training for pastors: **yes** Type of available practical training: **preaching, religious education, evangelism** Language in use: **Korean** Doctrinal basis: **Presb**

Address: ChongHoe Theological Seminary, 171-1 Naengchun dong, Sudaemun ku, Seoul, Korea, Tel: +82 2 364-0221, Fax: +82 2 363-4528

• **Seoul** — ChongHoe Theological Seminary (HoHun)
Type of school: **Church Seminary** Degrees offered: **Cert** Offers training for pastors: **yes** Type of available practical training: **preaching, religious education, evangelism** Language in use: **Korean** Doctrinal basis: **Presb**

Address: ChongHoe Theological Seminary, 419-42 HapJung dong, MaPo ku, Seoul, 121-220 Korea, Tel: +82 2 325-7071

• **Seoul** — ChongHoe Theological Seminary (HoHun)
Type of school: **Church Seminary** Degrees offered: **Cert** Offers training for pastors: **yes** Type of available practical training: **preaching, religious education, evangelism** Language in use: **Korean** Doctrinal basis: **Presb**

Address: ChongHoe Theological Seminary, 661-11 Kongnung 1 dong, Nowon ku, Seoul, 139-241 Korea, Tel: +82 2 948-9111

• **Seoul** — ChongHoe Theological Seminary (HapDong BoSu)
Type of school: **Church Seminary** Degrees offered: **Cert** Offers training for pastors: **yes** Type of available practical training: **preaching, religious education, evangelism** Language in use: **Korean** Doctrinal basis: **Presb**

Address: ChongHoe Theological Seminary, 930-42 BongChun dong, Kwanak ku, Seoul, 1511-050 Korea, Tel: +82 2 888-2251, Fax: +82 2 888-2253

• **Seoul** — ChongHoe Theological Seminary (HapDong BoSu)
Type of school: **Church Seminary** Degrees offered: **Cert** Offers training for pastors: **yes** Type of available practical training: **preaching, religious education, evangelism** Language in use: **Korean** Doctrinal basis: **Presb**

Address: ChongHoe Theological Seminary, 284-18 Chunghwa 1 dong, Chungryang ku, Seoul,
131-120 Korea, Tel: +82 2 432-8886

• **Suwon** — HapDong Presbyterian Theological Seminary
Type of school: **Graduate Seminary/Univ** Degrees offered: **BTh, MDiv** Offers training for pastors: **yes** for teachers: **yes** for lay persons: **yes** Admission requirements: **high school, bachelor** Languages in use: **Korean** Full/part-time staff: **19** National/foreign students: **80** Doctrinal basis: **WestConf** In relation with: **Presb Ch in Korea (HapDong GaeHyuck, cf. no. 33)**

Address: HapDong Presbyterian Theological Seminary, 42-3 WonChung dong, Paldal ku, Suwon,
442-791 Korea, Tel: +82 331 212-3694, Fax: +82 331 212-6204

LEBANON

• **Beirut** — Near East School of Theology (NEST) (s4390)
Type of school: **Graduate/Univ+Undergraduate/Bible school** Founded in **1932** Degrees offered: **BA in Christian Educ, BTh + BTh in Christian Educ, MDiv, STM, STM in Ministry** Offers training for pastors: **yes** for teachers: **yes** for lay persons: **yes** Type of available practical training: **seminars in churches in different countries of the Middle East** Admission requirements: **college degree (BA) and church support** Languages in use: **English** Full/part-time staff: **5 / 4** National/foreign students: **45 / 7** Library size: **45,000** Doctrinal basis: **Reformed tradition** Worship life offered: **daily** In relations with: **interdenominational, Union of the Armenian Evangelical Ch in the Near East, Nat Presb Synod of Syria and Lebanon, Evang Luth Ch of Jordan, Angl Ch**

Address: Near East School of Theology (NEST), P.O. Box 13-5780, Sou rati, Chouran, Beirut,
Lebanon, Tel: +961 1 346-708, 349-901, 354-194, Fax: +961 1 347-129

LESOTHO

• **Morija** — Morija Theological Seminary (s1080)
Type of school: **Undergraduate Seminary** Founded in **1882** Degrees offered: **DiplTh** Offers training for pastors: **yes** for teachers: **yes** for lay persons: **yes** Admission requirements: **Cambridge Overseas School Certificate** Languages in use: **English, Sesotho** Full/part-time staff: **6 / 6** National/foreign students: **60 / 0** Library size: **6,500** Worship life offered: **2 times daily** In relations with: **Lesotho Evang Ch, CEVAA, Disciples (USA), PCUSA**

Address: Morija Theological Seminary, P.O. Box 32, 190 Morija, 190, Lesotho, Tel: +266 360-214,
Fax: +266 360-001

LIBERIA

• **Monrovia** — Gbarnga School of Theology (s1400)
Type of school: **Undergraduate Seminary** Founded in **1953** Degrees offered:
DiplTh, BTh, BRE Offers training for pastors: **yes** for teachers: **yes** Languages in
use: **English** Full/part-time staff: **7 / 20** National/foreign students: **240 / 5** Library
size: **since war being slowly replenished** Worship life offered: **bi-weekly** In relations with: **Luth Church, United Meth, Presb, Angl, Pent, Bapt**

Address: Gbarnga School of Theology, P.O. Box 1010, Gbarnga, Bong County, Monrovia, Liberia,
Tel: +231 223-321

MADAGASCAR

• **Antananarivo** — Faculty of Theology (FJKM) (s1102)
Type of school: **Graduate/Univ** Founded in **1979** Degrees offered: **LicTh (3
years), MTh (5 years)** Offers training for pastors: **yes** for lay persons: **yes** Type of
available practical training: **practical theology, dogmatics, ethics** Admission requirements: **baccalaureate of secondary school between 23 and 35 years old**
Languages in use: **Malagasy, French** Full/part-time staff: **6 / 15** National/foreign
students: **138 / 0** Library size: **9,000** Doctrinal basis: **Bible, Christian doctrines**
Worship life offered: **15 minutes every morning before class** In relations with:
Eglise de Jésus Christ à Madagascar, CEVAA

Address: Faculté de Théologie Protestante FJKM — Ambatonakanga, C.P. 642, Place
Rabetafika-Ambatonakanga, Antananarivo, 101, Madagascar, Tel: +261 2 21214

• **Antananarivo** — United Theological College IVATO (s1101)
Type of school: **Undergraduate/Bible school** Founded in **1966** Degrees offered:
BTh Offers training for pastors: **yes** Admission requirements: **concluded high
school** Languages in use: **Malagasy, French** Full/part-time staff: **6 / 7** National/
foreign students: **27 / 0** Library size: **11,200** Worship life offered: **daily morning
+ evening** In relations with: **CWM, CEVAA, FJKM**

Address: Collège théologique uni (Ivato), C.P. 61, Ivato Airport, 105 Antananarivo, Madagascar,
Tel: +261 2 44706, Fax: +261 2 27033

• **Fianarantsoa** — Theological College of Fianarantsoa FJKM (s1100)
Type of school: **Undergraduate/Bible school** Founded in **1875** Degrees offered:
BTh Offers training for pastors: **yes** Type of available practical training: **homiletics, Sunday school, pastoral care, religious education** Admission requirements:

admission test Languages in use: **Malagasy** Full/part-time staff: **3 / 9** National/ foreign students: **43 / 0** Library size: **3,000** Doctrinal basis: **Calvinism** Worship life offered: **daily morning**

Address: Collège théologique de Fianarantsoa FJKM, P.O. Box 1184, 301 Fianarantsoa, Madagascar, Tel: +261 51182

- **Mandritsara** — Theological College of Mandritsara (FJKM) (s1103)
Type of school: **Evangelist/Pastoral Training Institute** Founded in **1923** Degrees offered: **BTh** Offers training for pastors: **yes** Type of available practical training: **preaching, pastoral care, religious education** Admission requirements: **national admission test** Languages in use: **Malagasy, French** Full/part-time staff: **4 / 8** National/foreign students: **38 / 0** Library size: **600** Doctrinal basis: **Calvinist Reformed** Worship life offered: **daily morning before the lessons start** In relations with: **WARC, CWM, CEVAA, Ch of Jesus Christ in Madagascar**

Address: Collège théologique, C.P. 56, 415 Mandritsara, Madagascar

---

MALAWI

- **Nkhoma** — Nkhoma Institute for Continued Theological Training (NIFCOTT) (s1113)
Type of school: **Evangelist/Pastoral Training Institute** Degrees offered: **Cert in applied theology** Offers training for pastors: **yes** for lay persons: **yes** Type of available practical training: **preaching, pastoral care, religious education** Languages in use: **English, Chichewa** Full/part-time staff: **2** National/foreign students: **4 / 0** Library size: **3,100** Doctrinal basis: **Reformed** Worship life offered: **3 times per week** In relations with: **Church of Central Africa Presbyterian — Nkhoma Synod, Dutch Reformed Church in South Africa**

Address: Nkhoma Institute for Continued Theological Training (NIFCOTT), P.O. Box 61, A. C. Murray Rd., Nkhoma, Malawi, Tel: +265 723-688, 723-396, 723-321, Fax: +265 722-901, 720-153

- **Zomba** — Department of Religious Studies — University of Malawi (s1112)
Degrees offered: **BA, B in Education** Offers training for pastors: **nc** Languages in use: **English**

Address: University of Malawi — Dept. of Religious Studies, P.O. Box 280, Chancellor College, Zomba, Malawi

- **Zomba** — Zomba Theological College (s1110)
Type of school: **Undergraduate/Bible school** Degrees offered: **LicTh, DiplTh (to be started in 1997/98), BDiv** Offers training for pastors: **yes** Type of available practical training: **at the campus and local congregations on week-ends, Aug/ Sep students to be located in congr under supervision of the minister** Admission requirements: **high school certificate** Languages in use: **English** Full/

part-time staff: **7** National/foreign students: **37 / 0** Library size: **9,000** Doctrinal basis: **Calvinistic, WestConf** Worship life offered: **daily 7:30-8:00, led by staff and students** In relations with: **jointly established by Churches of Central Africa, Presb in Malawi, Zimbawe, Zambia, Angl Council in Malawi, Ch of Christ and Baptist**

Address: Zomba Theological College, P.O. Box 130, Zomba, Malawi, Tel: +265 522-419, Fax: +265 522-158

MALAYSIA

• **Kota Kinabalu** — Sabah Theological Seminary (s4341)
Type of school: **Graduate+Undergraduate seminary** Founded in **1988** Degrees offered: **BD, BTh, DiplTh, Cert in Th Studies, Cert in Bible Knowledge** Offers training for pastors: **yes** for teachers: **yes** for lay persons: **yes** Type of available practical training: **preaching, pastoral care, religious education** Admission requirements: **senior high and above** Languages in use: **Bahasa Malaysia, Chinese, English** Full/part-time staff: **15 / 4** National/foreign students: **68 / nc** Library size: **25,670** Doctrinal basis: **Ecumenical** Worship life offered: **twice a day** In relations with: **Association of Protestant Chs and Missions in Germany, Angl Ch, Basel Mission, Christian Ch of Malaysia, Borneo Evang Mission, Evang Luth Ch in America, Luth Ch of Australia, United Meth Ch, London Meth Ch, Prot Ch in Sabah**

Address: Sabah Theological Seminary, P.O. Box 11925, 88821 Kota Kinabalu, Malaysia, Tel: +60 88 231-579, Fax: +60 88 232-618, E-mail: semtsab@po.jaring.my

• **Selangor** — Malaysia Bible Seminary (s4342)
Type of school: **Seminary** Founded in **1978** Offers training for pastors: **yes** Languages in use: **English, Chinese** Full/part-time staff: **10 / 9** Library size: **16,500**

Address: Malaysia Bible Seminary, 1-11 Jalan 1, Kaw 16 41300 Klang, Selangor, Malaysia, Tel: +60 3 427-482, Fax: +60 3 412-094

MARSHALL ISLANDS

• **Majuro** — Marshalls Theological College (s5191)
Type of school: **Undergraduate/Bible school** Founded in **1976** Degrees offered: **CertTh, DiplTh** Offers training for pastors: **yes** for teachers: **yes** Type of available practical training: **teaching, Sunday school, preaching** Admission requirements: **be a Christian having tuition** Languages in use: **English, Marshallese** Full/part-time staff: **5** National/foreign students: **22 / no** Library size: **700** Worship life offered: **6 times per week** In relations with: **United Church of Christ, PCC**

635

Address: Marshalls Theological College, P.O. Box 765, Majuro, MH 96960, Marshall Islands, Tel:
(via operator) 625-3931, Fax: 625-5246

MEXICO

- **Akil** — Presbyterian Theological Biblical Institute (s2084)
Type of school: **Undergraduate/Bible school** Degrees offered: **BTh, DiplMusic**
Offers training for pastors: **yes** for teachers: **no** for lay persons: **yes** Admission requirements: **basic education, church member, 16 years old** Languages in use: **Spanish, Maya** Full/part-time staff: **10** National/foreign students: **20 / 0** Library size: **300** Doctrinal basis: **Calvinistic, WestConf** Worship life offered: **daily** In relations with: **Iglesia Nacional Presbiteriana de Mexico — Asamblea General**

Address: Insituto Biblico teológico Presbiteriano, 20 # 62, 97990 Akil, Yucatan, Mexico, Tel: +52
99 48037, Fax: +52 99 48043

- **Comalcalco** — Bible School "Dorcas" (s2087)
Type of school: **Mission Institute** Degrees offered: **Cert in Music and Theol** Offers training for pastors: **nc** for lay persons: **yes** Type of available practical training: **preaching, pastoral care, religious education** Admission requirements: **profession of faith and support of a women's organization** Languages in use: **Spanish** Full/part-time staff: **5** National/foreign students: **15 / nc** Library size: **1,000** Doctrinal basis: **WestConf** Worship life offered: **daily** In relations with: **Nacional Presbiteriana de Mexico**

Address: Escuela Biblica "Dorcas," Sanchez Magallanes No. 503, 86300 Comalcalco, Tabasco,
Mexico, Tel: +52 93 40239

- **Mérida** — St. Paul's Theological Seminary (s2091)
Type of school: **Graduate and Undergraduate/Bible school** Degrees offered: **LicTh, BTh, Director of Music** Offers training for pastors: **yes** for teachers: **yes** for lay persons: **yes** Type of available practical training: **preaching, pastoral care, religious education** Admission requirements: **9 to 12 years of school education** Languages in use: **Spanish** Full/part-time staff: **19** national/foreign students: **76 / 2** Library size: **3,000** Doctrinal basis: **Reformed, WestConf** Worship life offered: **daily** In relations with: **Iglesia Nacional Presbiteriana de Mexico (Sinodo de Yucatán)**

Address: Seminario teológico San Pablo, 136, Cordemex, Kilometro 2 Carretera Dzitya, 97110
Mérida, Yucatán, México, Tel: +52 99 410-070, Fax: +52 99 410-071, E-mail:
dlegters@pibil.finred.com.mx

- **Mérida** — Yucatan Bible Institute (S2099)
Type of school: **Undergraduate/Bible school** Degrees offered: **DiplTh** Offers training for pastors: **yes** for lay persons: **yes** Type of available practical training: **preaching, pastoral care, religious education** Admission requirements: **support by a congregation** Languages in use: **Spanish, Maya** Full/part-time staff: **6** Na-

tional/foreign students: **15 / nc** Library size: **800** Doctrinal basis: **none** Worship life offered: **2 times per week** In relations with: **Iglesia Presbiteriana Independiente de Mexico**

Address: Instituto Bíblico del Sureste, Xocenpich, Mérida, Yucatán, Mexico

• **Mérida** — Presbyterian Bible School "Priscilla" for Women (s2086)
Type of school: **Undergraduate/Bible school** Founded in **1956** Degrees offered: **Dipl** Offers training for pastors: **yes** for lay persons: **yes** Type of available practical training: **preaching, pastoral care, religious education** Languages in use: **Spanish** Full/part-time staff: **9** National/foreign students: **16 / nc** Library size: **1,500** Doctrinal basis: **none** Worship life offered: **daily** In relations with: **Iglesia Nacional Presbiteriana de Mexico (Presby del Mayas)**

Address: Escuela Biblica Presbiteriana "Priscilla," 74 A No. 453 entre 45 y 47, 97000 Mérida, Yucatán, Mexico, Tel: +52 99 242-324

• **Mexico D.F.** — "John Calvin" I Seminary (s2093)
Type of school: **Graduate and Undergraduate/Bible school** Degrees offered: **CertTh, BTh, LicTh, MTh, ThD** Offers training for pastors: **yes** for teachers: **yes** for lay persons: **yes** Admission requirements: **recommendation, interview** Languages in use: **Spanish** Full/part-time staff: **7** National/foreign students: **20 / 0** Library size: **1,500** Doctrinal basis: **WestConf, WestCat** Worship life offered: **3 times per week** In relations with: **Iglesia Presbiteriana Reformada**

Address: Seminario Juan Calvino I, Cuauhtémacy, Allende 117, Coyocan, 04 100 Mexico D.F., Mexico, Tel: +52 5 554-3467

• **Mexico D.F.** — "John Calvin" II Seminary (s2089)
Type of school: **Seminary** Degrees offered: **LicTh, BTh** Offers training for pastors: **yes** for teachers: **yes** for lay persons: **yes** Admission requirements: **completed secondary school** Languages in use: **Spanish** Full/part-time staff: **6** National/foreign students: **12 / nc** Library size: **1,800** Doctrinal basis: **none** Worship life offered: **daily** In relations with: **Iglesia Presbiteriana Independiente de Mexico**

Address: Seminario Juan Calvino II, Viena 99, Col. El Carmen, Mexico D.F., C.P. 04100, Mexico, Tel: +52 5 554-4901, Fax: +52 5 554-4662

• **Mexico D.F.** — Mexico Central Bible Institute for Women Missionaries (s2094)
Type of school: **Mission Institute** Degrees offered: **BTh, DiplEvangelism** Offers training for pastors: **no** for teachers: **yes as well as for missionaries** for lay persons: **yes** Type of available practical training: **preaching, pastoral care, religious education** Admission requirements: **completed secondary school** Languages in use: **Spanish** Full/part-time staff: **7** National/foreign students: **15 / 1** Library size: **1,000** Doctrinal basis: **WestConf** Worship life offered: **twice daily, once a month with communion** In relations with: **Iglesia Nacional Presbiteriana, National Presbyterian Union of Women Associations**

Address: Escuela Biblica Central para Misioneras, Guerrero 13, Col. del Carmen, Coyat, 04100
Mexico D.F., Mexico, Tel: +52 5 547-070, Fax: +52 5 547-070

- **Mexico D.F.** — National Presbyterian Theological Seminary of Mexico (s2088)

Type of school: **Undergraduate/Bible school** Degrees offered: **DiplTh, Cert Theol** Offers training for pastors: **yes** for lay persons: **yes** Type of available practical training: **preaching, pastoral care, religious education** Admission requirements: **completed secondary school** Languages in use: **Spanish** Full/part-time staff: **7** National/foreign students: **15 / nc** Library size: **900** Doctrinal basis: **WestConf** Worship life offered: **daily** In relations with: **Iglesia Presbiteriana Nacional Conservadora**

Address: Seminario teológico nacional presbiteriano de Mexico, Virginia 188, Co. Nativitas, Mexico D.F., Mexico, Tel: +52 5 532-3569, Fax: +52 5 674-8422

- **Mexico D.F.** — Presbyterian Theological Seminary of Mexico (s2097)

Type of school: **Seminary** Founded in **1882** Degrees offered: **Dipl in Sacred Music, BTh, MDiv** Offers training for pastors: **yes** for teachers: **yes** for lay persons: **yes** Admission requirements: **pre-university studies, moral and financial support from a presbytery** Languages in use: **Spanish** Full/part-time staff: **8 / 8** National/foreign students: **65 / 0** Library size: **10,000** Doctrinal basis: **WestConf** Worship life offered: **daily** In relations with: **National Presbyterian Church of Mexico**

Address: Seminario teológico Presbiteriano de Mexico, Arenal 36, Colonia Agricola Chimalistac Deleg. A.O., Mexico D.F., 01050, Mexico, Tel: +52 6 610-397, Fax: +52 6 617-896

- **Monterrey** — Evangelical Presbyterian Theological Seminary "Dr. Leandro Garza-Mora" (s2092)

Type of school: **Graduate and Undergraduate/Bible school** Degrees offered: **LicTh, BTh** Offers training for pastors: **yes** for lay persons: **yes** Type of available practical training: **preaching, pastoral care, religious education** Admission requirements: **completed secondary school** Languages in use: **Spanish** Full/part-time staff: **8** National/foreign students: **15 / 0** Library size: **2,000** Doctrinal basis: **none** Worship life offered: **2 times per week** In relations with: **National Presb Church**

Address: Seminario Teológico Evangélico Presbiteriano "Dr. Leandro Garza-Mora," Hamburgo 307, NL 64000 Monterrey, Nuevo Leon, Mexico, Tel: +52 8 359-1620, Fax: +52 8 359-5071

- **Puebla** — Puebla Bible Seminary (s2100)

Type of school: **Graduate+Undergraduate+Pastor/Evangelist/Missionary** Founded in **1959** Degrees offered: **BD, BTh** Offers training for pastors: **yes** for teachers: **yes** for lay persons: **yes** Admission requirements: **completed secondary school, converted since one year minimum** Languages in use: **Spanish** Full/part-time staff: **5 / 17** National/foreign students: **35 / 0** Library size: **10,000** Doctrinal basis: **own declaration of faith** Worship life offered: **occasionally** In relations with: **Christian and Missionary Alliance (CMA)**

638

Address: Seminario Bíblico de Puebla, 17 Poniente 4113, 72000 Puebla, Pue, Mexico, Tel: +55 22 481-155, Fax: +52 22 480-169, E-mail: 75442.555@compuserve.com

• **Tamazunchale** — Biblical Institute of the Synod of Huastecas (s2085)
Type of school: **Undergraduate/Bible school** Degrees offered: **Dipl** Offers training for pastors: **yes** for lay persons: **yes** Admission requirements: **sixth of primary school, active member in church, 18 years** Languages in use: **Spanish + náhuatl (bilingual)** Full/part-time staff: **6** National/foreign students: **812 / nc** Library size: **700** Doctrinal basis: **none** Worship life offered: **daily** In relations with: **Sínodo Nacional del Centro de la Iglesia Nacional Presbiteriana de México**

Address: Instituto Bíblico Sinódico en las Huastecas, Aquiles Serdán 111, 79960 Tamazunchale, S.L.P., Mexico

• **Tampico** — Eben-Ezer Theological Seminary (s2095)
Type of school: **Seminary** Degrees offered: **LicTheol, Lic in Christian education, MTh** Offers training for pastors: **yes** for teachers: **yes** for lay persons: **yes** Type of available practical training: **preaching, pastoral care, religious education** Admission requirements: **baccalaureate** Languages in use: **Spanish** Full/part-time staff: **7** National/foreign students: **20 / 0** Library size: **2,300** Doctrinal basis: **WestConf, WestCats** Worship life offered: **3 times per week** In relations with: **Associate Reformed Presbyterian Church**

Address: Seminario teológico Eben-Ezer, M. Avila Camacho 501 Col. Vergel, Tampico, Tamaulipas 89150, Mexico, Tel: +52 12 135-999

• **Tampico** — Theological Seminary "Prof. Manuel D. Valencia" (s2101)
Type of school: **Seminary** Degrees offered: **BTh, LicTh** Offers training for pastors: **yes** for lay persons: **yes** Type of available practical training: Admission requirements: **pre-university level** Languages in use: **Spanish** Full/part-time staff: **16** National/foreign students: **10 / 0** Library size: **1,300** Doctrinal basis: **WestConf** Worship life offered: **twice per week** In relations with: **Iglesia Nacional Presbiteriana de Mexico**

Address: Seminario teológico "Pbro. Manuel D. Valencia," Juarez y Emilio Carranza, Tampico, Tamaulipas, Mexico, Tel: +52 121 3 5999

• **Tapachula** — Theological Seminary Dr. Juan R. Kempers (s2098)
Type of school: **Evangelist/Pastoral Training Institute** Founded in **1990** Degrees offered: **DiplTh, LicTh** Offers training for pastors: **yes** for teachers: **no** for lay persons: **yes** Type of available practical training: **preaching, pastoral care, religious education** Admission requirements: **completed secondary school** Languages in use: **Spanish** Full/part-time staff: **8** National/foreign students: **28 / nc** Library size: **1,500** Doctrinal basis: **WestConf** Worship life offered: **3 times per week** In relations with: **Iglesia Nacional Presbiteriana (Sinodo de Chiapas)**

Address: Seminario teológico presbiteriano "Dr. Juan R. Kempers," C.P. 208, Campamento "Getsemani" Canton Providencial Fracc.P, 29130 Tapachula, Chiapas, Mexico, Tel: +52 96 260-679

- **Tlacolula de Matamoros de Oaxaca** — Cultural Training Centre of Tlaclolula (s2096)
Type of school: **Undergraduate/Bible school** Degrees offered: **Cert and Dipl in Biblical Studies** Offers training for pastors: **yes** for lay persons: **yes** Type of available practical training: **preaching, pastoral care, religious education** Admission requirements: **completed secondary school** Languages in use: **Spanish** Full/part-time staff: **4** National/foreign students: **12 / nc** Library size: **400** Doctrinal basis: **none** Worship life offered: **daily** In relations with: **Iglesia Presbiteriana Nacional**

Address: Centro de Capacitación de Tlacolula, Carretera internacional KM. 30, Tlacolula de Matamoros de Oaxaca, Oaxaca, Mexico

- **Villahermosa** — Presbyterian Theological Seminary of the South-East (s2090)
Type of school: **Seminary** Degrees offered: **LicTh, BTh, Dipl in Biblical Sciences** Offers training for pastors: **yes** for lay persons: **yes** Type of available practical training: **preaching, pastoral care, religious education** Admission requirements: **support by presbytery, completed secondary school** Languages in use: **Spanish** Full/part-time staff: **10** National/foreign students: **40 / nc** Library size: **2,000** Doctrinal basis: **WestConf** Worship life offered: **3 times per week** In relations with: **Christian Reformed Church, Reformed Church in America**

Address: Seminario teológico presbiteriano del Sureste, Paseo Usumacinta no. 505, 86000 Villahermosa, Tabasco, Mexico, Tel: +52 93 158-959, Fax: +52 93 158-959, E-mail: biasem@nexus.net.mx

MOZAMBIQUE

- **Maputo** — Theological School of Khovo (s1141)
Offers training for pastors: **nc** Languages in use: **Portuguese**

Address: Escola Nocturna de Teologia de Khovo, C.P. 21, Maputo, Mozambique

- **Maputo** — United Seminary of Ricatla (s1140)
Type of school: **Undergraduate/Bible school** Degrees offered: **Certificate, Diploma, Bachelor** Offers training for pastors: **yes** for teachers: **yes** for lay persons: **yes** Admission requirements: **9-12 classes** Languages in use: **Portuguese, English, French** Full/part-time staff: **17** National/foreign students: **55 / 6** Library size: **8,000** Worship life offered: **daily** In relations with: **Igreja Presbiteriana de Moçambique, Igl Metodista Unida em Moçambique, Igreja de Cristo em M., Ramo Manica e Sofala, Igreja Congregacional Unida de M.**

Address: Seminario Unido de Ricatla, P.O. Box 1057, Maputo, Mozambique

- **Vila Ulónguè Angónia** — Hefsiba, Centro de Treinamento (s1142)
Type of school: **Undergraduate/Bible school and Pastoral Training** Offers

training for pastors: **yes** for teachers: **no** for lay persons: **yes** Type of available practical training: **preaching, pastoral care, religious education** Languages in use: **Portuguese** Full/part-time staff: **4** National/foreign students: **32 / 7** Library size: **430** Doctrinal basis: **HeidC, CDort, Conf of Netherlands** Worship life offered: **5 times per year** In relations with: **Igreja Reformada em Moçambique**

Address: Hefsiba, Centro de Treinamento, CP 3, Samora Machel, Vila Ulónguè Angónia, Tete, Mozambique, Fax: (Malawi) +265 74 33 35 and +265 72 30 90

MYANMAR

- **Tahan-Kalemyo** — Tahan Theological College (s4011)
Founded in **1978** Degrees offered: **BTh, LicTh** Offers training for pastors: **yes** Languages in use: **English** Full/part-time staff: **7 / 2** National/foreign students: **53 / nc** Library size: **4,000** In relations with: **Presb Ch of Myanmar**

Address: Tahan Theological College, Tahan-Kalemyo, Myanmar

- **Yangon** — Bethany Theological Seminary (s4017)
Offers training for pastors: **yes** Languages in use: **English**

Address: Bethany Theological Seminary, 112/B Upper Myinkyi Road, Bogone, Insein, Yangon, Myanmar

- **Yangon** — Far Eastern Fundamental School of Theology (FEFST) (s4016)
Type of school: **Undergraduate College** Founded in **1987** Degrees offered: **BTh, GTh, CertTh** Offers training for pastors: **yes** for teachers: **yes** Type of available practical training: **preaching, pastoral care, religious education** Admission requirements: **minimum matriculation passed** Languages in use: **English** Full/part-time staff: **15 teachers/3 office workers** National/foreign students: **80 / 0** Library size: **500** Doctrinal basis: **Prot Ref theology** Worship life offered: **daily morning worship, Sunday worship** In relations with: **16 denominations from 7 provinces and states in Myanmar (there are 49 Ev churches in Myanmar)**

Address: Far Eastern Fundamental School of Theology (FEFST), P.O. Box 531, 6-D Nanthani Street, Sawbwagyi-gone, Insein, Yangon, Myanmar, Tel: +95 1 41123

- **Yangon** — Reformed Theological Seminary of Discipleship Training Center (s4010)
Type of school: **Undergraduate+Pastor/Evangelist/Missionary** Degrees offered: **BTh in 4 years of study** Offers training for pastors: **yes** for teachers: **yes** for lay persons: **yes** Type of available practical training: **preaching, pastoral care, religious education** Admission requirements: **high school passed** Languages in use: **English** Full/part-time staff: **8** National/foreign students: **7 / nc** Library size: **1,500** Doctrinal basis: **Reformed** Worship life offered: **2 times per week** In relations with: **Reformed Presbyterian Church in Myanmar**

Address: Reformed Theological Seminary of Discipleship Training Center, P.O. Box 1256, 9/30 Shwe Tirih (2), Lane Dagon Myothit (N), Yangon, Myanmar

NAMIBIA

• **Windhoek** — Namibia Evangelical Theological Seminary (NETS) (s1116) Type of school: **Undergraduate/Bible school+Mission Inst** Founded in **1991** Degrees offered: **DiplTh, DiplBible, CertTh I+II** Offers training for pastors: **yes** for teachers: **yes** for lay persons: **yes** Type of available practical training: **practice-possibilities at school devotions, 9 field education units with churches/institutions in and around Windhoek** Admission requirements: **special application forms, recommendation from the applicant's pastor, testimony with Christian witness** Languages in use: **English — Dipl level, Afrikaans — Cert-level, Vernacular** Full/part-time staff: **6 / 4** National/foreign students: **40 / 1** Library size: **4,024** Doctrinal basis: **Statement of Faith (NETS)** Worship life offered: **weekly every Tuesday 9:30-10:40, evening devotions of students with a lecturer 3 times per week** In relations with: **Evangelical Reformed Church in Namibia, Dutch Reformed Church, Evangelical Reformed Church in Afrika**

Address: Namibia Evangelical Theological Seminary (NETS), Witbooi Dr., P.O. Box 158, 9000 Windhoek, Namibia, Tel: +264 61 222-885, Fax: +264 61 222-933

NEPAL

• **Kathmandu** — Nepal Ebenezer Bible College (s4530) Type of school: **Undergraduate/Bible school** Founded in **1992** Degrees offered: **DiplTh, BTh** Offers training for pastors: **yes** for teachers: **yes** for lay persons: **yes** Type of available practical training: **preaching, pastoral care, religious education** Languages in use: **English, Nepali** Full/part-time staff: **3 / 7** National/foreign students: **40 / 1** Library size: **2,000** Doctrinal basis: **World Evangelical Fellowship** Worship life offered: **daily** In relations with: **National Churches Fellowship of Nepal**

Address: Nepal Ebenezer Bible College, P.O. Box 3535, Kathmandu, Nepal, Tel: +977 1 523-423

NETHERLANDS

• **Amsterdam** — Theological Faculty — University of Amsterdam (UvA) (s6357) Type of school: **Graduate/Univ** Degrees offered: **MTh, ThD** Offers training for pastors: **yes** for lay persons: **yes** Type of available practical training: **preaching, pastoral care, religious education** Admission requirements: **high school** Languages in use: **Dutch** Full/part-time staff: **14** National/foreign students: **75 / 2** Library size: **20,000** Doctrinal basis: **none** Worship life offered: **none** In relations with: **Nederlandse Hervormde Kerk, Evangelisch-Lutherse Kerk, Doopsgezinde Broederschap (Mennonite)**

Address: Kerkelijke Opleiding aan de Universiteit van Amsterdam, Oude Turfmerk 147, NL-GC Amsterdam, 1012, Netherlands, Tel: +31 20 525-2010, Fax: +31 20 525-2007

- **Amsterdam** — Free University (s6355)
Type of school: **Graduate/Univ** Degrees offered: **MTh, PhD** Offers training for pastors: **yes** for teachers: **yes** for lay persons: **yes** Type of available practical training: **preaching, pastoral care, religious education are all included in curriculum** Admission requirements: **high school** Languages in use: **Dutch** Full/part-time staff: **60** National/foreign students: **250 / 20** Library size: **60,000** Doctrinal basis: **none** Worship life offered: **twice a year** In relations with: **Reformed Churches in the Netherlands**

Address: Vrije Universiteit, De Boelelaan 1105, 1081 HV Amsterdam, Netherlands, Tel: +31 20 444-6620, Fax: +31 20 444-6635, E-mail: theologie@esau.t-h.un.nl

- **Apeldoorn** — Theological University CGK (s6352)
Type of school: **Graduate/Univ** Degrees offered: **MTh, ThD** Offers training for pastors: **yes** for teachers: **yes** Type of available practical training: **preaching, pastoral care, inherent to the curriculum** Admission requirements: **knowledge of Latin + Greek** Languages in use: **Dutch** Full/part-time staff: **11** National/foreign students: **84 / 7** Library size: **35,000** Doctrinal basis: **Reformed confessions** Worship life offered: **weekly** In relations with: **Christelijke Gereformeerde Kerken in Nederland**

Address: Theological University CGK, Wilhelminapark 4, NL-BT Apeldoorn, 7316, Netherlands, Tel: +31 55 521-3156, Fax: +31 55 522-6339

- **Capelle aan den Yssel** — Theological School of the Reformed Congregations in the Netherlands (s6353)
Offers training for pastors: **yes** Languages in use: **Dutch** In relations with: **Gereformeerde Kerken in Nederland**

Address: Theologische School van de Gereformeede Gemeenten in Nederland, 's-Gravenweg 240, NL-LW Capelle aaw den Yssel, 2903, Netherlands, Tel: +31 10 450-0721

- **Doorn** — Hydepark Theological Seminary (s6356)
Founded in **1951** Offers training for pastors: **yes** Languages in use: **Dutch** Full/part-time staff: **4 / 1** Type of available practical training: **offers training to all students of the Nederlandse Hervormde Kerk** In relations with: **Nederlandse Hervormde Kerk**

Address: Theologisch Seminarium Hydepark, P.O. Box 220, Driebergstraatweg 50, NL-AE Doorn, 3G 4D, Netherlands, Tel: +31 343 814-041

- **Groningen** — Theological Faculty — Rijksuniversiteit (s6354)
Type of school: **Graduate/Univ** Founded in **1614** Degrees offered: **MTh, ThD** Offers training for pastors: **yes** for lay persons: **yes** Type of available practical training: **preaching, pastoral care, religious education** Admission requirements: **secondary school (pre-university education)** Languages in use: **Dutch** Full/ part-time staff: **27** National/foreign students: **119 / nc** Doctrinal basis: **none:** Worship life offered: **weekly** In relations with: **Nederlandse Hervormde Kerk**

Address: Faculteit der Godgeleerdheid — Rijksuniversiteit Groningen, P.O. Box 559, Nieune Kijk in't Jatstraat 104, NL-9212 SL Groningen, 9700, Netherlands, Tel: +31 50 363 5568, Fax: +31 50 363 6200

- **Hellenvoetsluis** — Netherlands Reformed Seminary (s6365)
Offers training for pastors: **yes** Languages in use: **Dutch**

Address: Nederlands Gereformeerd Seminarie, Zeegat 34, NL-SJ Hellenvoetsluis, 3224, Netherlands

- **Kampen** — Theological University Kampen (s6350)
Type of school: **Graduate/Univ** Founded in **1854** Degrees offered: **MTh, ThD** Offers training for pastors: **yes** for teachers: **yes** for lay persons: **no** Type of available practical training: **practical training in preaching, pastoral care, religious education and catechesis** Admission requirements: **secondary school (pre-university education)** Languages in use: **Dutch** Full/part-time staff: **40** National/ foreign students: **230 / 15** Library size: **151,555** Doctrinal basis: **Confessions of the GKN** Worship life offered: **weekly** In relations with: **Gereformeerde Kerken in Nederland (NGK)**

Address: Theologische Universiteit Kampen, P.O. Box 5021, Koornmarkt 1 and Oudestraad 6, NL-GA Kampen, 8260, Netherlands, Tel: +31 38 337-1600, Fax: +31 38 337-1613, E-mail: c.dullemond@thu-k.nl

- **Kampen** — Theological University of the Reformed Churches (Liberated) in the Netherlands (s6358)
Type of school: **Graduate/Univ** Founded in **1854** Degrees offered: **MTh, ThD** Offers training for pastors: **yes** Type of available practical training: **preaching, pastoral care, religious education** Admission requirements: **college with Greek and Latin; for foreign students: graduate of Sem or Univ or BA with at least 2 years of Greek and Latin** Languages in use: **Dutch** Full/part-time staff: **20 / 11** National/foreign students: **110 / 5** Library size: **100,000** Doctrinal basis: **3 Forms of Unity (HeidC, BelgC, CDort)** Worship life offered: **weekly** In relations with: **Reformed Churches (Liberated) in the Netherlands**

Address: Theologische Universiteit van de Gereformeerde Kerken/Vrijgemaakt, P.O. Box 5026, Broederweg 15, NL-GA Kampen, 8260, Netherlands, Tel: +31 38 331-2878, Fax: +31 38 333-0270

- **Leiden** — Faculteit der Godgeleerdheid — Rijksuniversiteit (s6360)
Type of school: **Faculty of Theology** Founded in **1575** Degrees offered: **MTh, ThD** Offers training for pastors: **yes** for lay persons: **yes** Languages in use: **Dutch**

Full/part-time staff: **14 / 7** National/foreign students: **106 / nc** Doctrinal basis: **none** In relations with: **cooperates with the Nederlands Ref Church (cf. Leidschendam and Doorn) and the Remonstrant Brotherhood**

Address: Faculteit der Godgeleerdheid — Rijksuniversiteit Leiden, P.O. Box 9515, NL-RA Leiden, 2300, Netherlands, Tel: +31 71 527-2570, Fax: +31 71 527-2571

• **Leiden** — Seminary of the Remonstrant Brotherhood — Rijksuniversiteit Leiden (s6361)
Type of school: **Graduate Seminary** Degrees offered: **Proponent of the Remonstrant Brotherhood** Offers training for pastors: **yes** for teachers: **no** for lay persons: **no** Type of available practical training: **preaching, pastoral care, religious education** Admission requirements: **completed secondary school** Languages in use: **Dutch** Full/part-time staff: **1** National/foreign students: **10 / 0** Library size: **6,000** Worship life offered: **3 times per week** In relations with: **Remonstrant Brotherhood**

Address: Seminary of the Remonstrant Brotherhood — Rijksuniversiteit Leiden, Postbus 9515, Matthias de Vrieshof 1, NL-RA Leiden, 2300, Netherlands, Tel: +31 71 527-2591, Fax: +31 17 527-2571, E-mail: nil

• **Leidschendam** — Reformed Theological Institute (s6362)
Type of school: **Evangelist/Pastoral Training Institute** Degrees offered: **in cooperation with the faculties of the universities of Leiden, Groningen, Utrecht, and Amsterdam (UvA)** Offers training for pastors: **yes** Type of available practical training: **training is partly theoretical, partly practical; full practical training is given at seminary of Doorn** Admission requirements: **high school** Languages in use: **Dutch** Full/part-time staff: **20** National/foreign students: **800 studying at the various faculties mentioned above / nc** Doctrinal basis: **Reformed confessions** In relations with: **Hervormde Kerk NL**

Address: Hervormd Theologisch Wetenschappelyh Institut, P.O. Box 405, NL-AK Leidschendam, 2260, Netherlands, Tel: +31 70 3131-228, Fax: +31 70 3131-202

• **Rotterdam** — Theological School of the Reformed Congregations (s6366)
Type of school: **Evangelist/Pastoral Training Institute** Founded in **1927** Degrees offered: **ministry** Offers training for pastors: **yes** Type of available practical training: **preaching and pastoral care, religious education** Admission requirements: **personal grace and call** Languages in use: **Dutch** Full/part-time staff: **3** National/foreign students: **7 / nc** Library size: **20,000** Doctrinal basis: **CDort** Worship life offered: **weekly** In relations with: **Reformed Congregations of the Netherlands, United States, and Canada**

Address: Theologische School der Gereformeerde Gemeenten, Boezemsingel 26-27, NL-EC Rotterdam, 3034, Netherlands, Tel: +31 10 412-9329

• **Utrecht** — Theological Faculty, University of Utrecht (s6349)
Type of school: **Graduate/Univ** Founded in **1634** Degrees offered: **MTh, ThD** Offers training for pastors: **yes** for laypersons: **yes** Admission requirements: **high school** Languages in use: **Dutch, English** Full/part-time staff: **33** National/foreign

students: **515 / nc** Doctrinal basis: **none** In relations with: **Nederlandse Hervormde Kerk, Free Evangelical Church (Covenant)**

Address: Faculteit der Godgeleerdheid — Universiteit Utrecht, P.O. Box 80105, NL-3508 TC Utrecht, Tel: +31 30 253 1853, Fax: +31 30 253 3241

• **Utrecht** — Inter-university Institute for Missiology and Ecumenical Research (s6351)
Type of school: **Graduate/Univ** Degrees offered: **none** Offers training for pastors: **yes** for teachers: **yes** Type of available practical training: **as research institute only partially involved in postacademic training of pastors** Admission requirements: **same as for Dutch universities** Languages in use: **Dutch, English** Full/part-time staff: **3** National/foreign students: **na / nc** Library size: **15,000** Doctrinal basis: ecumenical, **same as National Council of Churches in NL** Worship life offered: **no regular teaching schedules and no opening or finishing celebrations** In relations with: **all Prot and RCath theological universities and faculties**

Address: Interuniversitair Instituut voor Missiologie en Oecumenica, Heidelberglaan 2, Transitorium II, room 825 — B, NL-CS Utrecht, 3584, Netherlands, Tel: +31 30 253-2079, Fax: +31 30 253-9434, E-mail: iimo@ggl.ruu.nl

• **Utrecht** — Seminary of the Covenant of Free Evangelical Churches (s6368)
Type of school: **Seminary** Degrees offered: **up to Doctor's degree (in cooperation with the University of Utrecht)** Offers training for pastors: **yes** for teachers: **yes** for lay persons: **yes** Type of available practical training: **preaching** Admission requirements: **advanced secondary education** Languages in use: **Dutch** Full/part-time staff: **5** National/foreign students: **15 / nc** Library size: **na** Doctrinal basis: **none** Worship life offered: **none** In relations with: **Covenant of Free Evangelical Churches**

Address: Seminarie Bond van Vrije Evangelische Gemeenten in Nederland, Heidelberglaan 2, #1221, NL-CS Utrecht, 3584, Netherlands, Tel: +31 30 253-1984, Fax: +31 30 253-3241

• **Zeist** — Wittenberg Christian College (s6367)
Type of school: **Mission Institute** Founded in **1972** Degrees offered: **missionary/evangelistic worker Dipl, BA, BTh** Offers training for pastors: **no** for teachers: **yes** for lay persons: **yes** Type of available practical training: **pastoral care, religious education** Languages in use: **Dutch** Full/part-time staff: **30** national/foreign students: **50 / 1** Library size: **8,000** Worship life offered: **daily**

Address: De Wittenberg Christian College, Krakelingweg 10, NL-HV Zeist, 3707, Netherlands, Tel: +31 30 692-4166, Fax: +31 30 691-3897, E-mail: bterouw@xsyall.nl

NEW CALEDONIA

• **Chépénéhé Lifou** — Theological College of Bethania (s5070)
Type of school: **Undergraduate/Bible school** Degrees offered: **CertTh** Offers training for pastors: **yes** Type of available practical training: **preaching, pastoral**

care, religious education Admission requirements: **CEP** Languages in use: **French** Full/part-time staff: **4** National/foreign students: **17 / 1** Library size: **1,000** Worship life offered: **3 times per week every Monday morning, Wed and Fri evening** In relations with: **Evangelical Church in New Caledonia and Loyalty Islands**

Address: Collège théologique de Béthanie, B.P. 11, 98820 Chépénéhé Lifou, New Caledonia, Tel: +687 45 16 34

• **Ponerihouen** — Institute of the Evangelical Free Church (s5071)
Type of school: **Undergraduate/Bible school** Offers training for pastors: **yes** Type of available practical training: **homiletics** Admission requirements: **to be a convinced practicing Christian** Languages in use: **French** Full/part-time staff: **6** National/foreign students: **8 / 1** Library size: **85** Doctrinal basis: **Trinitarian** Worship life offered: **weekly** In relations with: **Evangelical Free Church**

Address: Institut de l'Eglise libre, Ponerihouen, 98823, New Caledonia, Tel: +687 42 52 44, Fax: +687 42 53 12

NIGER

• **Aguie** — Biblical School of Aguie (s1321)
Type of school: **Undergraduate/Bible school** Degrees offered: **Cert in Basic Bible Studies** Offers training for evangelists: **yes** Type of available practical training: **various practical teachings** Admission requirements: **Cert of basic studies** Languages in use: **Hausa** Full/part-time staff: **9** national/foreign students: **60 / 0** Doctrinal basis: **Evangelical** Worship life offered: **Sundays** In relations with: **Ecole biblique pour la formation locale de nos évangelistes**

Address: Ecole biblique d'Aguie, B.P. 42, Aguie, Niger

NIGERIA

• **Aba** — Aba Bible College (s1181)
Degrees offered: **Dipl** Offers training for pastors: **yes** Admission requirements: **9-10 years of schooling** Languages in use: **English** In relations with: **Evangelical Church in West Africa (ECWA)**

Address: Aba Bible College, P.O. Box 602, Umvokae, Aba, Imo State, Nigeria

• **Abakaliki** — Nigeria Reformed Theological College (NRTC) (s1189)
Offers training for pastors: **yes** Languages in use: **English** In relations with: **Nigeria Reformed Church**

Address: Nigeria Reformed Theological College (NRTC), P.O. Box 538, Abakaliki, Ebonyi State, Nigeria

• **Bukuru** — Theological College of Northern Nigeria (s1177)
Type of school: **Graduate/Univ+Undergraduate** Founded in **1958** Degrees offered: **DiplTh, DCM (Dipl in Christian Ministries), BDiv, MTh** Offers training for pastors: **yes** for teachers: **yes** for lay persons: **yes** Type of available practical training: **teaching, sermon preparation, etc.** Languages in use: **English** Full/part-time staff: **18** National/foreign students: **300 / 10** Library size: **24,000** Doctrinal basis: **Bible, Trinity, ApC, NicC** Worship life offered: **10 times a week** In relations with: **Fellowship of Churches of Christ in Nigeria, CRCN, ERCC, PCN, NKST, EYN, Lutheran, United Meth, United Ch of Christ, etc.**

Address: Theological College of Northern Nigeria, P.O. Box 64, Bukuru, Plateau State, Nigeria
Tel: +234 73 80 958

• **Calabar** — Department of Religion and Philosophy (s1183)
Offers training for pastors: **nc** Languages in use: **English**

Address: Department of Religion and Philosophy, University of Calabar, Cross River State, Calabar, Nigeria

• **Donga** — Veenstra Seminary (s1186)
Type of school: **Undergraduate/Bible school** Degrees offered: **Dipl in Christian Ministry, ThD, Cert of Religious Education** Offers training for pastors: **yes** for teachers: **yes** Type of available practical training: **preaching, pastoral care, religious education** Admission requirements: **secondary school graduates, Bible Colleges** Languages in use: **English, Hausa** Full/part-time staff: **6** National/foreign students: **55 / 0** Library size: **3,450** Doctrinal basis: **Reformed** Worship life offered: **6 times per week** In relations with: **Christian Reformed Church of Nigeria (CRCN), Chr Ref Ch of North America (CRCNA)**

Address: Veenstra Seminary, P.O. Box 75, Donga, Taraba State, Nigeria

• **Harga** — Benue Bible Institute Harga (s1162)
Type of school: **Evangelist/Pastoral Training Institute** Degrees offered: **Dipl Rel Education, Cert Rel Education** Offers training for pastors: **no** for teachers: **yes** for lay persons: **no** Type of available practical training: **preaching, pastoral care, religious education** Admission requirements: **General Certificate of Education (GCE)** Languages in use: **English** Full/part-time staff: **8** National/foreign students: **80 / 1** Library size: **3,200** Doctrinal basis: **ApC, HeidC** Worship life offered: **daily** In relations with: **The Church of Christ in the Sudan among the Tiv (Nongo Kristu u sudan hen TIV NKST), Sudan United Mission, Christian Reformed Church in North America (SUM-CIRC)**

Address: Benue Bible Institute Harga, Harga, Benue State, Nigeria

• **Ibadan** — Department of Religious Studies — University of Ibadan (s1166)
Founded in **1948** Offers training for pastors: **nc** Languages in use: **English**

Address: Department of Religious Studies — University of Ibadan, Oyo State Ibadan, Nigeria

- **Igbaja** — ECWA Theological Seminary (s1180)
Type of school: **Graduate and Undergraduate/Bible school** Founded in **1894**
Degrees offered: **DiplTh, Dipl Rel Education, BTh, B in Rel Education** Offers
training for pastors: **yes** for teachers: **yes** for lay persons: **yes** Type of available
practical training: **focus on professional training for the ministry** Admission requirements: **4 years of post-primary schooling, faith in Christ** Languages in
use: **English** Full/part-time staff: **15** National/foreign students: **315 / 7** Library
size: **23,000** Worship life offered: **twice daily** In relations with: **Evangelical
Church of West Africa**

Address: ECWA Theological Seminary, P.O. Box 20, Seminary Road, Igbaja, Kwara State, Nigeria

- **Ikot Ekang/Ikot Akpabio** — Samuel Bill Theological College (s1185)
Founded in **1941** Offers training for pastors: **yes** Languages in use: **English** Full/
part-time staff: **8** National/foreign students: **53 / nc** In relations with: **Qua Iboe
Church**

Address: Samuel Bill Theological College, P.O. Box 34, Ikot Ekang/Ikot Akpabio, Abak, Cross
River State, Nigeria

- **Ilorin** — UMCA Theological College (s1187)
Type of school: **Undergraduate/Bible school** Degrees offered: **BTh, BA** Offers
training for pastors: **yes** for teachers: **yes** for lay persons: **yes** Type of available
practical training: **preaching, pastoral care, religious education** Admission requirements: **O-level incl English language + knowledge of Christian religion**
Languages in use: **English** Full/part-time staff: **22** National/foreign students: **300 /
4** Library size: **18,000** Doctrinal basis: **Evangelical convictions** Worship life offered: **daily** In relations with: **United Missionary Church of Africa, World
Partners (Box 9127, Fort Wayne, Indiana 46899)**

Address: UMCA Theological College, P.O. Box 171, Muritala Mohammed Way, Ilorin, Nigeria,
Tel: +234 31 221-703

- **Itu** — The Presbyterian Theological College (s1184)
Type of school: **Evangelist/Pastoral Training Institute** Degrees offered: **DiplTh**
Offers training for pastors: **yes** for lay persons: **yes** Type of available practical
training: **preaching, pastoral care, religious education** Admission requirements:
General Certificate of Education, 4 credits Languages in use: **English** Full/
part-time staff: **6** national/foreign students: **51 / 0** Library size: **2,500** Doctrinal basis: **Reformed** Worship life offered: **2 times daily but once on Sundays with
staff and students outside the college** In relations with: **Presbyterian Church of
Nigeria**

Address: The Presbyterian Theological College, P.O. Box 2, Itu, Akwa Ibom State, Nigeria

- **Jos** — Bible School Kulallo-Quan-Pan L.G.C (s1188)
Type of school: **Evangelist/Pastoral Training Institute** Founded in **1968** Degrees
offered: **Cert in Christian Education and in Pastoral Studies** Offers training for
pastors: **yes** for teachers: **yes** for lay persons: **no** Languages in use: **Hausa, English** Full/part-time staff: **6 / 3** National/foreign students: **44 / nil** Library size: **5**

Doctrinal basis: **Evangelical** Worship life offered: **2 times per week** In relations with: **Church of Christ in Nigeria (COCIN)**

Address: Bible School Kulallo-Quan-Pan L.G.C., P.O. Box 003, Quan Pan LGC, Jos, Plateau State, Nigeria

• **Jos** — COCIN Agricultural and Bible Training Institute (s1170)
Type of school: **Undergraduate/Bible school** Founded in **1970** Degrees offered: **Cert in Bible Studies and Agriculture** Offers training for pastors: **nc** Languages in use: **English** Full/part-time staff: **10** In relations with: **Church of Christ in Nigeria**

Address: COCIN Agricultural and Bible Training Institute, P.O. Box 2127, Rockhaven, Jos, Plateau State, Nigeria

• **Jos** — ECWA Theological Seminary (s1171)
Type of school: **Graduate+Undergraduate+Pastor/Evangelist/Missionary** Founded in **1980** Degrees offered: **BTh, MA, MTh, MDiv** Offers training for pastors: **yes** for teachers: **yes** for lay persons: **yes** Type of available practical training: **preaching, pastoral care, religious education** Admission requirements: **equivalent to university requirements** Languages in use: **English** Full/part-time staff: **30** National/foreign students: **350 / 70** Doctrinal basis: **yes** Worship life offered: **daily** In relations with: **ECWA, COCIN, Baptist, Presbyterian, others**

Address: ECWA Theological Seminary, P.O. Box 5398, Zaria-Road Farin-Gada, Jos, Plateau State, Nigeria, Tel: +234 73 53574

• **Jos** — Institute of Church and Society (s1175)
Type of school: **Mission Institute** Degrees offered: **na** Offers training for pastors: **no** for teachers: **no** for lay persons: **yes** Type of available practical training: **no** Admission requirements: **church-nominated persons** Languages in use: **English** Full/part-time staff: **na** National/foreign students: **na / na** Library size: **10** Doctrinal basis: **none** Worship life offered: **none** In relations with: **Christian Council of Nigeria**

Address: Institute of Church and Society, P.O. Box 6485, No. 12, old Bukuru Road, Jos, Plateau State, Nigeria, Tel: +234 73 465-004, Fax: +234 73 465-004

• **Kaduna** — HEKAN Bible Training School Gubuchi (s1163)
Type of school: **Undergraduate/Bible school+Mission Inst.** Degrees offered: **none** Offers training for pastors: **yes** for teachers: **yes** Type of available practical training: **preaching, pastoral care, religious education** Admission requirements: **school leaving certificate and secondary** Languages in use: **Hausa, English** Full/part-time staff: **6** National/foreign students: **24 / 0** Library size: **yet to establish** Worship life offered: **daily devotion and Sunday worship and other occasional services**

Address: HEKAN Bible Training School Gubuchi, P.O. Box 307, Kaduna, Nigeria, Tel: +234 62 210950

- **Kagoro** — Kagoro Bible College (s1178)
Offers training for pastors: **yes** Languages in use: **English** In relations with: **Evangelical Church of West Africa**

Address: Kagoro Bible College, via Kafanchan, Kagoro, Kaduna State, Nigeria

- **Michika** — John Guli Bible School Michika (s1168)
Type of school: **Undergraduate/Bible school** Offers training for pastors: **yes** for teachers: **yes** Type of available practical training: **preaching, pastoral care, religious education** Languages in use: **Hibi, Hausa, English** national/foreign students: **66 / 0** Doctrinal basis: **Church of the Brethren** Worship life offered: **daily** In relations with: **Church of the Brethren in Nigeria (EYN)**

Address: John Guli Bible School Michika, P.O. Box 40, Michika, Adamawa State, Nigeria

- **Mkar** — Reformed Theological College of Nigeria (s1173)
Offers training for pastors: **yes** Languages in use: **English** In relations with: **Church of Christ among the Tiv**

Address: Reformed Theological College of Nigeria, P.O. Box Gboko, Mkar, Benue State, Nigeria

- **Mubi** — Kulp Bible School (s1169)
Type of school: **Evangelist/Pastoral Training Institute** Founded in **1962** Degrees offered: **Dipl in Christian Ministry** Offers training for pastors: **yes** for teachers: **yes** Type of available practical training: **preaching, pastoral care, religious education** Languages in use: **Hausa, English** Full/part-time staff: **17** National/foreign students: **205 / 1** Library size: **3,988** Worship life offered: **daily** In relations with: **Christian Reformed Church in Nigeria (CRCN), Evang Reformed Church of Christ (ERCC)**

Address: Kulp Bible School-Kwharhi, P.O. Box Mubi 1, Mubi, Adamawa State, Nigeria, Tel/Fax: 073 452056

- **Takum** — Smith Memorial Bible College, Baissa (s1154)
Offers training for pastors: **nc** Languages in use: **English** national/foreign students: **nc / 0**

Address: Smith Memorial Bible College, Baissa, P.O. Box 31, c/o CRCN Secretariat, Takum, Taraba Sate, Nigeria

- **Takum** — Veenstra Bible College and Seminary (s1159)
Type of school: **Evangelist/Pastoral Training Institute** Degrees offered: **CertTh, DiplTh** Offers training for pastors: **yes** for teachers: **yes** Type of available practical training: **preaching, pastoral care, religious education** Admission requirements: **secondary school, 3 credits** Languages in use: **English** Full/part-time staff: **5** National/foreign students: **40 / 0** Library size: **1,000** Doctrinal basis: **Reformed persuasion** Worship life offered: **weekly** In relations with: **NKST, CRCN**

Address: Veenstra Bible College and Seminary, P.O. Box 42, Lupwe, Takum, Tabara State, Nigeria

- **Umuahia** — Trinity Theological College (s1174)
Type of school: **Undergraduate/Bible school** Founded in **1948** Degrees offered: **BA in Religious Studies, DiplTh, Dipl in Religious Studies, CertTh** Offers training for pastors: **yes** Type of available practical training: **preaching, pastoral care, religious education** Admission requirements: **4 credits + Dipl in English Language/5 credits + Engl lang undergraduate** Languages in use: **English** Full/part-time staff: **19** National/foreign students: **210 / 0** Library size: **nc** Doctrinal basis: **Angl, Presbyterian, Meth** Worship life offered: **2 times daily** In relations with: **Presbyterian Church of Nigeria**

Address: Trinity Theological College, P.O. Box 97, Umuahia, Abia State, Nigeria

- **Yakubu** — United Missionary Theological College (s1179)
Offers training for pastors: **nc** Languages in use: **English**

Address: United Missionary Theological College, P.O. Box 171, Gowon Way, Yakubu, Kwara State, Nigeria

PAKISTAN

- **Gujranwala** — Gujranwala Theological Seminary (s4350)
Type of school: **Graduate** Founded in **1877** Degrees offered: **BTh, MDiv** Offers training for pastors: **yes** for lay persons: **yes** Type of available practical training: **preaching, pastoral care, religious education** Admission requirements: **Matriculation or BA** Languages in use: **Urdu, English** Full/part-time staff: **12** National/foreign students: **66 / 0** Library size: **20,000** Doctrinal basis: **WestConf, HeidC, ApC, NicC, Ref doctrines** Worship life offered: **daily** In relations with: **Presb Ch of Pakistan, Ch of Pakistan, Associate Ref Presb Ch**

Address: Gujranwala Theological Seminary, P.O. Box 13, 0431 Gujranwala, Pakistan, Tel: +92 431 82617 and 81704, Fax: +92 431 258314

- **Lahore** — Open Theological Seminary (s4351)
Type of school: **Distance Learning College** Founded in **1971** Degrees offered: **CertTh, DiplTh, BTh** Offers training for pastors: **yes** for teachers: **yes** for lay persons: **yes** Type of available practical training: **preaching, pastoral care, religious education** Languages in use: **Urdu** Full/part-time staff: **4 / 240** National/foreign students: **2,445 / 42** Library size: **6,000** Doctrinal basis: **Evangelical (Lausanne)** Worship life offered: **in every tutorial** In relations with: **Pakistan Committee for Theological Education by Extension**

Address: Open Theological Seminary, 8 FC College, Lahore, 54600, Pakistan, Tel: +92 42 757-3608, Fax: +92 42 586-6510, E-mail: post@ots.lhr.erum.com.pk

PALESTINE

• **Bethlehem** — Bethlehem Bible College (s4391)
Type of school: **Undergraduate/Bible school** Founded in **1979** Degrees offered: **2 years: associate degree in Bible studies+Christian education; 3 years: dipl, 4 years: BA in cooperation with Bethlehem University** Offers training for pastors: **yes** for teachers: **yes** for lay persons: **yes** Type of available practical training: **students go to churches to do practical ministries + to church organizations, social organizations, and rehabilitation centers** Admission requirements: **1) high school education, 2) church recommendation** Languages in use: **Arabic** Full/part-time staff: **6 / 5** National/foreign students: **40 / 0** Library size: **1,000** Worship life offered: **2 times per week** In relation with: **interdenominational**

Address: Bethlehem Bible College, P.O. Box 127, Hebron Rd., Bethlehem, Palestine, Tel: +972 2 741-190, Fax: +972 2 743-278, E-mail: 100320.3455@compuserve

PAPUA NEW GUINEA

• **Rabaul** — Rarongo Theological College (s5055)
Type of school: **Graduate** Degrees offered: **Cert of Christian Understanding, DipTh, BD** Offers training for pastors: **yes** for teachers: **yes** Type of available practical training: **preaching, pastoral care, religious education** Admission requirements: **higher educational background, strong Christian faith, church experience, mature and stable character** Languages in use: **English, Pidgin English** Full/part-time staff: **10** National/foreign students: **50-70 / 0** Library size: **30-50,000** Doctrinal basis: **ApC** Worship life offered: **Sundays** In relations with: **United Reformed Church in England, Uniting Church in Australia, United Meth Church in England, United Meth Ch in USA, Presbyterian Church, Meth Church of New Zealand**

Address: Rarongo Theological College, P.O. Box 1510, Rabaul, East New Britain Province, Papua New Guinea, Tel: +675 921-714, Fax: +675 321-4930

PARAGUAY

• **Lambaré** — Presbyterian Reformed Seminary in Paraguay (s2151)
Type of school: **Undergraduate+Pastor/Evangelist/Missionary** Degrees offered: **BTh** Offers training for pastors: **yes** for teachers: **yes** Type of available practical training: **preaching, pastoral care, religious education** Admission requirements: **high school** Languages in use: **Spanish** Full/part-time staff: **6** National/foreign students: **16 / 0** Library size: **2,500** Doctrinal basis: **WestConf** Worship

653

life offered: **weekly** In relations with: **Presbyterian Reformed Ch of Paraguay, KPCA (USA)**

Address: Seminário Presbiteriano Reformado del Paraguay, Casilla D 24024, Lambaré, Paraguay, Tel: +595 21 311-292

• **Nemby** — United Theological Seminary in Paraguay (s2150)
Type of school: **Undergraduate+Pastor/Evangelist/Missionary** Degrees offered: **BTh** Offers training for pastors: **yes** for teachers: **yes** Type of available practical training: **preaching, pastoral care, religious education** Admission requirements: **high school** Languages in use: **Spanish, Guarani** Full/part-time staff: **6** National/foreign students: **11 / 0** Library size: **200** Doctrinal basis: **Reformed** Worship life offered: **weekly** In relations with: **Korean United Ref Ch**

Address: Seminário Unido Teológico del Paraguay, Santa Rosa, 342, Nemby, Paraguay, Tel: +595 21 277-317, Fax: +595 21 332-943

PERU

• **Huánuco** — Higher Biblical Institute of Huánuco (s2083)
Type of school: **Undergraduate/Bible school+Mission Inst** Degrees offered: **BTh, BMissiology** Offers training for pastors: **yes** Type of available practical training: **preaching, pastoral care, religious education** Admission requirements: **high school** Languages in use: **Spanish** Full/part-time staff: **8** National/foreign students: **70 / nc** Library size: **5,000** Doctrinal basis: **Lutheran, Calvinist** Worship life offered: **daily** In relations with: **Evangelical Ch of Peru**

Address: Instituto Bíblico Superior de Huánuco, Apartado 348, Dr. Leonicio Prado, 139, Huánuco, Peru, Tel: +51 64 514-298

• **Lima** — Biblical Institute of Lima (s2081)
Type of school: **Undergraduate/Bible school** Degrees offered: **BTh** Offers training for pastors: **yes** Type of available practical training: **preaching, pastoral care, religious education** Admission requirements: **high school** Languages in use: **Spanish** Full/part-time staff: **7** National/foreign students: **35 / 0** Library size: **1,000** Doctrinal basis: **Lutheran, Calvinist** Worship life offered: **daily** In relations with: **Evangelical Ch of Peru**

Address: Instituto Bíblico de Lima, Casilla 2866, Jr. Nasca 148, Jesus Maria, 100 Lima, Peru, Tel: +51 1 4246955

• **Lima** — Evangelical Seminary of Lima (s2080)
Type of school: **Seminary** Founded in **1933** Degrees offered: **DiplTh, BTh, LicTh** Offers training for pastors: **yes** for teachers: **yes** for lay persons: **yes** Type of available practical training: **preaching, Sunday school teaching** Admission requirements: **high school education and recommendation** Languages in use: **Spanish** Full/part-time staff: **8 / 7** National/foreign students: **110 / nc** Library size:

9,500 Worship life offered: **6 times per week** In relations with: **CMA, Presb, Evangelical Churches**

Address: Seminario evangélico de Lima, Apartado 207, Lima, 12, Peru, Tel: +51 1 348-1202, Fax: +51 1 348-0761, E-mail: jehrich@datast.lima.net.pe

• **Sicuani-Cusco** — Biblical Institute of Sicuani (s2082)
Type of school: **Undergraduate/Bible school+Mission Inst** Degrees offered: **BTh, BMissiology** Offers training for pastors: **yes** Type of available practical training: **preaching, pastoral care, religious education** Admission requirements: **high school** Languages in use: **Spanish** Full/part-time staff: **8** National/foreign students: **70 / nc** Library size: **5,000** Doctrinal basis: **Lutheran, Calvinist** Worship life offered: **daily** In relations with: **Evangelical Ch of Peru**

Address: Instituto Bíblico de Sicuani, Apartado 102, Sicuani-Cusco, Peru

---

PHILIPPINES

• **Cavite** — Presbyterian Theological Seminary (s4365)
Type of school: **Seminary** Founded in **1983** Degrees offered: **BTh, MDiv, MM,** Offers training for pastors: **yes** for teachers: **yes** for lay persons: **yes** Type of available practical training: **field ministry, preaching,** Admission requirements: **recommendations, curriculum vitae, completed high school** Languages in use: **Filipino and English** Full/part-time staff: **10 / 17** National/foreign students: **75 / 4** Library size: **18,900** Doctrinal basis: **Calvinism** Worship life offered: **daily prayers, worships several times a week** In relations with: **Presbyterian Church of the Philippines**

Address: Presbyterian Theological Seminary, P.O. Box 1, Dasmarinas, Cavite, 4114, Philippines, Tel: +63 912 306-7941, Fax: +63 912 631-1437

• **Cotabato** — Southern Christian College, College of Theology (s4363)
Type of school: **Undergraduate/Bible school** Founded in **1949/1979** Degrees offered: **BMin, BSSE (B of Sc in Secondary Education), BAT (B of Agricultural Technology), BBA (B of Business Administration)** Offers training for pastors: **yes** Type of available practical training: **through Field Education Program** Admission requirements: **National College Entrance exams + graduation from the secondary level** Languages in use: **English, Filipino** Full/part-time staff: **7/Col of Theol, 130 /SCC** National/foreign students: **28 / 0** Library size: **35,000** Doctrinal basis: **UCCP Statement of Faith** Worship life offered: **weekly** In relations with: **United Church of Christ in the Philippines (UCCP), linked with Presbyterian, United Brethren, Congregational, Meth, Ch of Christ Disciples, etc.**

Address: Southern Christian College, 9410 Midsayap, Cotabato, Philippines, Tel: +63 6422 98323, Fax: +63 6422 98753

- **Davao** — Davao Apo Alliance Bible College (S4357)
Type of school: **Undergraduate/Bible school** Degrees offered: **BTh, BRS** Offers training for pastors: **yes** for teachers: **yes** Languages in use: **English, Filipino** Full/part-time staff: **17** National/foreign students: **45 / na** Library size: **4,000** Doctrinal basis: **ApC, CMA Statement of Faith** Worship life offered: **2 times per week** In relations with: **Christian and Missionary Alliance (CMA)**

Address: Davao Apo Alliance Bible College, JP Laurel Ave. — Garcia Heights, Bajada, 8000 Davao, Philippines, Tel: +63 82 227-54 55

- **Dumaguete City** — Silliman University Divinity School (s4362)
Type of school: **Graduate/Univ** Founded in **1921** Degrees offered: **BTh, MDiv, MTh** Offers training for pastors: **yes** Type of available practical training: **preaching, pastoral care, religious education** Languages in use: **English, Cehuano** Full/part-time staff: **9** National/foreign students: **120 / nc** Library size: **15,000** Doctrinal basis: **ecumenical creeds, statement of faith of United Church of Christ in the Philippines** Worship life offered: **weekly (Friday) plus Sunday** In relations with: **United Church of Christ in the Philippines (UCCP)**

Address: Silliman University Divinity School, University, Dumaguete City, 6200, Philippines, Tel: +63 35 225-7541, Fax: +63 35 225-4768

- **General Santos City** — Mickelson Alliance Bible Institute (S4352)
Offers training for pastors: **nc** Languages in use: **English, Filipino**

Address: Mickelson Alliance Bible Institute, P.O. Box 44, 9500 General Santos City, Philippines

- **General Santos City** — Shekina Alliance Bible College (S4355)
Offers training for pastors: **nc** Languages in use: **English, Filipino**

Address: Shekina Alliance Bible College, Atis Anonas Street, 9500 General Santos City, Philippines

- **Jaro, Iloilo City** — College of Theology — Central Philippine University, Jaro (s4367)
Type of school: **College** Founded in **1905** Degrees offered: **BTh, BA in Religion, MDiv, MTh** Offers training for pastors: **yes** for teachers: **yes** for lay persons: **yes** Type of available practical training: **preaching, pastoral care, religious education** Admission requirements: **high school diploma** Languages in use: **English** Full/part-time staff: **7 / 8** National/foreign students: **100 / 0** Library size: **16,950** Doctrinal basis: **Evangelical, Reformed** Worship life offered: **2 times per week** In relations with: **Baptist Convention and other denominations through NCC of the Philippines**

Address: College of Theology, Lopez Jaena, Jaro, Iloilo City, 5000, Philippines, Tel: +63 33 329-1971 and 1979

- **Kidapawan** — Mount Apo Alliance Bible College (S4356)
Type of school: **Undergraduate/Bible school** Degrees offered: **BTh, BRE, DiplTh, Dipl Christian Education** Offers training for pastors: **yes** for teachers: **yes** for lay persons: **no** Type of available practical training: **preaching, pastoral**

656

care, religious education Admission requirements: **records of last school, written personal testimony, baptism certificate, and recommendation from applicant's pastor and district superior** Languages in use: **English** Full/part-time staff: **15 / 1** National/foreign students: **121 / nc** Library size: **6,738** Doctrinal basis: **fourfold Gospel of CMA** Worship life offered: **6 times per week** In relations with: **Christian and Missionary Alliance (CMA)**

Address: Mount Apo Alliance Bible College, P.O. Box 37, 9400 Kidapawan, Cotabato, Philippines

• **Laoag City** — Northern Christian College — College of Theology (s4360) Type of school: **Undergraduate/Bible school+Evangelist/Pastor's Inst.** Founded in **1946** Degrees offered: **BTh, Sacred Music** Offers training for pastors: **yes** for teachers: **yes** for lay persons: **yes** Type of available practical training: **preaching, pastoral care, religious education** Admission requirements: **high school graduate** Languages in use: **English, vernacular** Full/part-time staff: **6 / 5** National/foreign students: **42 / nc** Library size: **2,500** Worship life offered: **weekly** In relations with: **United Church of Christ in the Philippines (UCCP), National Council of Churches in the Philippines (NCCP)**

Address: Northern Christian College — College of Theology, P.O. Box 105, Mabini Street, Laoag City, 2900, Philippines, Tel: +63 772 0052, Fax: +63 772 0687

• **Mandaue City** — Visayas Alliance School of Theology (S4358) Offers training for pastors: **nc** Languages in use: **English, Filipino**

Address: Visayas Alliance School of Theology, M.L. Quezon Ave, 6014 Mandaue City, Philippines

• **Manila** — Union Theological Seminary (s4364) Type of school: **Graduate/Univ** Founded in **1907** Degrees offered: **MDiv, BRE, BTh, MTh, BMin, DMin** Offers training for pastors: **nc** Type of available practical training: **preaching, pastoral care, religious education** Languages in use: **English** Full/part-time staff: **14 / 13** National/foreign students: **477 / nc** Library size: **38,000** In relations with: **United Meth Ch, United Ch of Christ in the Philippines**

Address: Union Theological Seminary, P.O. Box 841, Dasmarinas, Cavite 4114, Manila, 1099, Philippines, Tel: +63 2 573-2727, Fax: +63 2 573-2727

• **Metro Manila** — Union Theological Seminary (UTS) (s4361) Type of school: **Graduate Seminary** Degrees offered: **DMin, ThD, MTh, MDiv, BRE** Offers training for pastors: **yes** for teachers: **yes** Type of available practical training: **preaching, pastoral care, religious education** Admission requirements: **records of completed collegiate work, church recommendation** Languages in use: **English, Filipino** Full/part-time staff: **14 / 15** National/foreign students: **353 / 19** Library size: **38,874** Doctrinal basis: **Wesleyan, Reformed** Worship life offered: **3 times per week** In relations with: **United Meth Church, United Church of Christ in the Philippines**

Address: Union Theological Seminary (UTS), Ph. Christian University Taft Avenue, Metro Manila, Dasmarinas, Cavite, Philippines, Tel: +63 2 4160-451, Fax: +63 2 4160-451

- **Quezon City** — Alliance Biblical Seminary (s4368)
Type of school: **Seminary** Founded in **1977** Degrees offered: **Dipl, MA, MDiv**
Offers training for pastors: **yes** for teachers: **yes** for lay persons: **yes** Type of available practical training: **preaching, teaching, pastoral care, religious education**
Admission requirements: **bachelor's degree, testimony of conversion, recommendation from pastor** Languages in use: **English** Full/part-time staff: **11 / 5** National/foreign students: **152 / 26** Library size: **16,000** Doctrinal basis: **CMA doctrinal statement** Worship life offered: **once a week** In relations with: **Christian and Missionary Alliance (CMA)**

Address: Alliance Biblical Seminary, 101 Dangay St., Veterans Village, Quezon City, 1105, Philippines, Tel: +63 2 371-3984, Fax: +63 2 373-6439

- **Zamboanga City** — Ebenezer Bible College and Seminary (s4354)
Type of school: **Bible College** Degrees offered: **BTh, Dipl Church Music** Offers training for pastors: **yes** for teachers: **yes** for lay persons: **yes** Type of available practical training: **preaching, teaching, music** Admission requirements: **high school graduate** Languages in use: **English** Full/part-time staff: **15 / 5** National/foreign students: **144 / 0** Library size: **18,000** Doctrinal basis: **CMA Statement of Faith** Worship life offered: **daily devotions** In relations with: **Christian and Missionary Alliance (CMA)**

Address: Ebenezer Bible College and Seminary, P.O. Box 166, 7000 Zamboanga City, Philippines, Tel: +63 62 991-3039, Fax: +63 62 991-3039, E-mail: ebcs@jetlink.com.ph

- **Zamboanga del Sur** — Lommasson Alliance Bible Institute (s4353)
Type of school: **Undergraduate/Bible school** Degrees offered: **Dipl Pastoral Studies, Dipl Rel Education, Cert Pastoral Studies, Cert Rel Education** Offers training for pastors: **yes** for teachers: **yes** Type of available practical training: **different types** Admission requirements: **recommendation, scholastic records** Languages in use: **English, Philipino** Full/part-time staff: **8** National/foreign students: **60 / nc** Library size: **3,150** Doctrinal basis: **CAMACOP Statement of Faith** Worship life offered: **twice weekly** In relations with: **CMA and Evangelical Churches**

Address: Lommasson Alliance Bible Institute, Lapuyan Poblacion, 7037 Zamboanga del Sur, Philippines

POLAND

- **Warszawa** — Theological Academy (s6395)
Offers training for pastors: **yes** Languages in use: **Polish**

Address: Chrzescijanska Akademia Teologiczna, ul. Miodowa 21, PL-00246 Warszawa, Poland, Tel: +48 22 31 95 97

PORTUGAL

• **Lisboa** — Evangelical Seminary of Theology (s6380)
Type of school: **Undergraduate/Bible school** Founded in **1946** Degrees offered:
BTh Offers training for pastors: **yes** for lay persons: **yes** Type of available practical training: **preaching, pastoral care, religious education** Admission requirements: **secondary school** Languages in use: **Portuguese** Full/part-time staff: **6**
National/foreign students: **25 / nc** Library size: **14,000** In relations with: **Igreja
Evangélica Presbiteriana de Portugal in collaboration with the Meth church**

Address: Seminário Evangélico de Teologia, Rua Tomás da Anunciaçao, 56-1 E, P-1350 Lisboa,
Portugal, Tel: +351 1 397 49 59, Fax: +351 1 395 63 26

PUERTO RICO

• **San Juan** — Evangelical Seminary of Puerto Rico (s3239)
Type of school: **Graduate** Degrees offered: **MDiv, DMin** Offers training for pastors: **yes** for teachers: **yes** for lay persons: **yes** Type of available practical training:
continuing education Admission requirements: **Bachelor's degree** Languages in use: **Spanish** Full/part-time staff: **9** National/foreign students: **200 / 3** Library size:
56,000 Doctrinal basis: **none** Worship life offered: **weekly** In relations with:
Sinodo Boriquen of the Presb Ch (USA) on Puerto Rico

Address: Seminário Evangélico de Puerto Rico, 776 Ponce Pagán de Leon Avenue, San Juan, PR
00925, Puerto Rico, Tel: +1 787 763-6700, Fax: +1 787 751-0847

ROMANIA

• **Cluj-Napoca** — Protestant-Theological Institute (s6390)
Type of school: **Graduate/Univ** Founded in **1895** Degrees offered: **LicTh, ThD**
Offers training for pastors: **yes** Type of available practical training: **theoretical +
practical preparation for parish and pastoral work, also education for teaching** Admission requirements: **confirmation, baccalaureate** Languages in use:
Hungarian, German Full/part-time staff: **25** national/foreign students: **266 / 12**
Library size: **100,000** Doctrinal basis: **HeidC, HelvC, CA** Worship life offered:
daily morning, Saturday afternoon, Sunday: academy worship In relations with: **Reformed Church Cluj, Ref Ch Oradea**

Address: Institutul Teologic Protestant de Grad Universitar, P.O. Box 230, Piata Avram Iancu 13,
RO-3400 Cluj-Napoca, Romania, Tel: +40 64 191-368, Fax: +40 64 191-368

• **Oradea** — The Sulyok István Reformed College (s6391)
Type of school: **Graduate/Univ+Undergraduate/Bible school** Degrees offered:

Diploma Offers training for pastors: **yes** Type of available practical training: **Sunday school, teaching religion in primary schools, pastoral care, religious education (hospital, telephones, etc.), social institutions, etc.** Admission requirements: **exams** Languages in use: **Hungarian** Full/part-time staff: **38** National/foreign students: **270 / nc** Library size: **13,132** Doctrinal basis: **Reformed, respecting confession of other students** Worship life offered: **1 Sunday worship, 4 Bible studies** In relations with: **Reformed Church — Királyhágómelléki Church district Oradea**

Address: The Sulyok István Reformed College, I. Antonescu nr. 27, 3700 Oradea, Bihor, Romania, Tel: +40 59 43 28 37, Fax: +40 59 43 28 37

RUSSIA

• **Moscow** — Moscow Presbyterian Theological Seminary (s6561)
Type of school: **Church Seminary** Degrees offered: **Cert** Offers training for pastors: **yes** For teachers and church workers: **yes** Type of available practical training: **preaching, religious education, evangelism** Full/part-time staff: **5** Languages in use: **Russian, Korean** Doctrinal basis: **Presb** In relations with: **Presb Ch in Korea** (TongHap, cf. Korea no. 14)

Address: Moscow Presbyterian Theological Seminary, 105173 Moscow, Savhoz 1, Maya Dom 11, Russia, Tel/Fax: +7095 407 8504

RWANDA

• **Butare** — United Theological School (s1350)
Degrees offered: **DiplTh** Offers training for pastors: **yes** Admission requirements: **11 years of schooling** Languages in use: **French**

Address: Ecole de Théologie, C.P. 619, Butare, Rwanda, Tel: +250 30 298

• **Gitarame** — Department of Theology of the Presbyterian Church of Rwanda (s1351)
Type of school: **Evangelist/Pastoral Training Institute** Founded in **1980** Offers training for pastors: **yes** Languages in use: **French**

Address: Département de Théologie de l' Eglise Presbytérienne au Rwanda, B.P. 67, Gitarame, Rwanda

SINGAPORE

• **Singapore** — Far Eastern Bible College (s4371)
Type of school: **Undergraduate/Bible school** Degrees offered: **BTh, BRE, MDiv, MRE** Offers training for pastors: **yes** for teachers: **yes** for lay persons: **yes** Type of available practical training: **"Live" homiletics every Wednesday when student preaches to whole school including faculty, most students are involved in Sunday school teaching** Admission requirements: **high school A-level** Languages in use: **English** Full/part-time staff: **10** National/foreign students: **90 / 45** Library size: **10,000** Doctrinal basis: **WestConf** Worship life offered: **daily 8:00 to 8:30 a.m.** In relations with: **Life Bible-Presbyterian Church + other B-P churches in Singapore, Malaysia, Indonesia, Australia, etc.**

Address: Far Eastern Bible College, 9A Gilstead Road, Singapore, 309063, Singapore, Tel: +65 256-9256, Fax: +65 250-6955

• **Singapore** — Trinity Theological College (s4370)
Type of school: **Graduate Seminary** Founded in **1948** Degrees offered: **BTh, BDiv, MDiv, MTh, MMin, DPS, PhD** Offers training for pastors: **yes** for teachers: **yes** for lay persons: **yes** Type of available practical training: **preaching, pastoral care, religious education** Admission requirements: **HSC (English) depending on course applied for, minimum O-level** Languages in use: **English, Chinese** Full/part-time staff: **20** National/foreign students: **170 / 79** Library size: **42,000** Doctrinal basis: **nondenominational** Worship life offered: **daily morning chapel and evening vespers, monthly Holy Communion service** In relations with: **Presb Ch of Singapore, Presb Ch of Malaysia, Basel Christian Church of Malaysia, Angl Ch, Luth Ch, Meth Ch**

Address: Trinity Theological College, 7, Mount Sophia, Singapore, 228458, Singapore, Tel: +65 337-1013, Fax: +65 336-7455

SOUTH AFRICA

• **Alice** — Faculty of Theology — University of Fort Hare (s1232)
Type of school: **Graduate/Univ** Founded in **1920** Degrees offered: **DiplTh, BTh, MTh, ThD** Offers training for pastors: **yes** for teachers: **yes** for lay persons: **yes** Type of available practical training: **preaching, pastoral care, religious education** Admission requirements: **12 years of schooling** Languages in use: **English** Full/part-time staff: **9** National/foreign students: **50 / nc** Library size: **7,000** Worship life offered: **weekly** In relations with: **Reformed Presbyterian, Uniting Reformed, United Congregational**

Address: Faculty of Theology — University of Fort Hare, Private Bag X 1314, Alice, 5700 Eastern Cape, South Africa, Tel: +27 40 422-224, Fax: +27 40 422-224, E-mail: bohnen@ufhcc.ufh.ac.za

661

- **Bellville** — Faculty of Religion and Theology — University of the Western Cape (s1216)

Type of school: **Graduate/Univ** Founded in **1929** Degrees offered: **BA, BTh, BAHons, BD, MA, MTh, ThD, PhD** Offers training for pastors: **yes** for teachers: **yes** for lay persons: **yes** Type of available practical training: **preaching, pastoral care, religious education (as tutors in congregation)** Admission requirements: **matriculation/standard 10** Languages in use: **English, Afrikaans** Full/part-time staff: **20/ 4** National/foreign students: **246 / 10** Library size: **40,000** Doctrinal basis: **none** Worship life offered: **26 times per year** In relations with: **Uniting Ref Ch in South Africa, Apostolic Faith Mission of S Africa, United Congregational Churches of S Africa**

Address: Faculty of Religion and Theology — University of the Western Cape, Private Bag X17, Modderdam Rd., ZA Bellville, 7535, South Africa, Tel: +27 21 959-2206 and 959-2888, Fax: +27 21 959-3355

- **Bellville** — Typerberg Bible School (s1207)

Offers training for pastors: **nc** Languages in use: **English**

Address: Typerberg Bible School, c/o 12 Maroela Street, Loevenstein, 7530, Bellville, South Africa

- **Benoni** — Christian Reformed Theological Seminary (s1200)

Type of school: **Graduate/Seminary+Bible school** Founded in **1961** Degrees offered: **Dipl in Pastoral Theol, Dipl in Missiology, BTh** Offers training for pastors: **nc** Type of available practical training: **preaching, pastoral care, religious education** Admission requirements: **matriculation, senior certificate or equivalent** Languages in use: **Afrikaans, English** Full/part-time staff: **3 / 4** National/foreign students: **95 / nc** Library size: **6,000** Doctrinal basis: **Reformed**

Address: Christian Reformed Theological Seminary, P.O. Box 10, SA Benoni, 1500, South Africa, Tel: +27 11 422-2320, Fax: +27 11 421-1635, E-mail: richarderts@compuserve.com

- **Bloemfontein** — Faculty of Theology — University of the Orange Free State (s1227)

Type of school: **Graduate/Univ** Founded in **1980** Degrees offered: **BTh, study courses A and B, Course A: BTh, MTh, ThD, Course B: BAHons, MA, PhD** Offers training for pastors: **yes** for teachers: **yes** Type of available practical training: **practical theology** Admission requirements: **matriculation exemption, minimum of 26 points in final matriculation examination according to table provided by Univ of OFS, BTh–1st uni-degree** Languages in use: **Afrikaans, English** Full/part-time staff: **16/10** National/foreign students: **444 / 4** Library size: **25,000** Doctrinal basis: **HeidC, BelgC, CDort** Worship life offered: **weekly (teachers+students), once a month — teachers only** In relations with: **Dutch Reformed Church, DRCA, CPSA**

Address: Faculty of Theology — University of the Orange Free State, P.O. Box 339, Bloemfontein, 9300, South Africa, Tel: +27 51 401-2667, Fax: +27 51 489-203, E-mail: TLGPP@RS.UOVS.AC.ZA

• **Durban** — Christian Training Academy (s1213)
Type of school: **Evangelist/Pastoral Training Institute** Degrees offered: **none for the moment** Offers training for pastors: **yes** for lay persons: **yes** Type of available practical training: **preaching, pastoral care, religious education** Admission requirements: **standard 10** Languages in use: **English, Zulu-soto, Xhosa** Full/part-time staff: **6** National/foreign students: **26 / 0** Worship life offered: **daily**

Address: Christian Training Academy, 21, St. Andreas Street, 4001 Durban, South Africa, Tel: +27 31 305-5489, 906-8883

• **Durban** — Department of Divinity — University Durban-Westville (s1217)
Type of school: **Faculty of Theology** Founded in **1969** Degrees offered: **BTh, Postgraduate, MTh, BTh (Hons), ThD, CertTh** Offers training for pastors: **yes** for teachers: **yes** for lay persons: **yes** Type of available practical training: **preaching, pastoral care, religious education** Admission requirements: **South African matriculation certificate** Languages in use: **English** Full/part-time staff: **12** National/foreign students: **150 / 3** Library size: **175,000** Doctrinal basis: **Ecumenical** Worship life offered: **Sundays** In relations with: **Ref Ch in Africa, United Congregational Ch, Baptist**

Address: Department of Divinity — University Durban-Westville, Private Bag X54001, 27 Durban, 4000, South Africa, Tel: +27 31 820-2234, Fax: +27 31 820-2286

• **Durban** — Reformed Church in Africa Bible School (s1205)
Type of school: **Undergraduate/Bible school** Founded in **1991** Degrees offered: **DiplTh (3 years), Cert (1 year without exam)** Offers training for evangelists: **yes** for lay persons: **yes** Admission requirements: **furnish an application signed by his/her pastor; trainee-evangelists must comply with the regulations as laid down by synod** Languages in use: **English** Full/part-time staff: **3** National/foreign students: **30 / nc** Library size: **no library (lack of resources)** Doctrinal basis: **Reformed** Worship life offered: **none** In relations with: **Reformed Church in Africa**

Address: Reformed Church in Africa Bible School, 23, Cactus Lane, Sydenham, 4091 Durban, 4000, South Africa, Tel: +27 31 288-048

• **Grahamstown** — Department of Divinity — Rhodes University (s1214)
Type of school: **Graduate/Univ** Founded in **1948** Degrees offered: **Undergraduate: BTh, Postgraduate: BD, BTh(Hons), BA(Hons), MTh, MA, PhD, DD** Offers training for pastors: **yes** Admission requirements: **South African matriculation certificate or equivalent degree courses, for DiplTh entry at discretion of the dean** Languages in use: **English** Full/part-time staff: **6** National/foreign students: **80 / 3** Library size: **400,000** Doctrinal basis: **ecumenical, therefore no particular confession** Worship life offered: **weekly** In relations with: **Presb Ch of SA, United Congr Ch of SA, Meth Ch of SA, Ch of the Province of Africa (Angl)**

Address: Department of Divinity — Rhodes University, P.O. Box 94, Somerset Street, Grahamstown, 6140, South Africa, Tel: +27 461 318-375 and 6, Fax: +27 461 24010, E-mail: disec@kudu.ru.ac.za

- **King William's Town** — Dumisani Theological Institute and Bible School (s1226)

Type of school: **Undergraduate/Bible school** Degrees offered: **no degree yet, but negotiation with University of Potchefstroom toward affiliation toward one or other of their degree programs** Offers training for pastors: **yes** for lay persons: **yes** Type of available practical training: **full-time theol training and distance learning course for Diploma of Theology or Christian studies. Bible school with excellent correspondence, course program and lay training program, preaching, Sunday school, pastoral care, religious education** Admission requirements: **Std 10 (Matriculation) or above or equivalent** Languages in use: **English** Full/part-time staff: **3 / 2** National/foreign students: **12 / 0** Library size: **1,000** Doctrinal basis: **WestConf, HeidC** Worship life offered: **daily** In relations with: **Gereformeerde Kerk, Free Ch of Scotland**

Address: Dumisani Theological Institute and Bible School, P.O. Box 681, Leopold St., King William's Town, 5600, South Africa, Tel: +27 433 25537 and 24737, Fax: +27 433 25537

- **Kwadlenbezwa** — Faculty of Theology — University of Zululand (s1209)

Type of school: **Graduate/Univ** Founded in **1960** Degrees offered: **BTh (Arts), MTh, DTh** Offers training for pastors: **yes** for teachers: **yes** for lay persons: **yes** Admission requirements: **post grade 12 — university level** Languages in use: **English** Full/part-time staff: **11** National/foreign students: **81 / 0** Library size: **11,500** Worship life offered: **weekly**

Address: Faculty of Theology — University of Zululand, Private Bag X 1001, Kwadlenbezwa, 3886, South Africa, Tel: +27 351 93911, Fax: +27 351 93159, E-mail: asung@pan.uzulu.ac.za

- **Melmoth** — Dingaanstat Theological School (S1206)

Type of school: **Evangelist/Pastor Training + Mission institute.** Degrees offered: **lay training: 5 levels, pastors, and BTh: 6 and 7 levels, Sunday school teacher, elders + deacons, missionaries** Offers training for pastors: **yes** for teachers: **no** for lay persons: **yes** Type of available practical training: **preaching, pastoral care, religious education** Admission requirements: **ability to read/write, member of Uniting Ref Ch/Dutch Reformed Church, assurance of faith** Languages in use: **Zulu, Afrikaans, English** Full/part-time staff: **4** National/foreign students: **16 / 0** Library size: **5,000** Doctrinal basis: **the 3 Reformed doctrines of faith** Worship life offered: **daily morning** In relations with: **Uniting Reformed Church in Southern Africa, Nederduitse Gereformeerde Kerke, Dutch Reformed Church, United Reformed Church of Southern Africa**

Address: Dingaanstat Theological School, Private bag 829, 3855 Melmoth, South Africa, Tel: +27 34 122-676

- **Pietermaritzburg** — School of Theology — University of Natal (s1233)

Type of school: **Graduate/Univ+Undergraduate Seminary** Founded in **1986** Degrees offered: **BTh, BA, BTh (Hons), BA (Hons), MTh, MA, PhD** Offers training for pastors: **yes** for teachers: **yes** for lay persons: **yes** Type of available practical training: **preaching, pastoral care, religious education** Admission requirements: **BTh(Hons), Master's** Languages in use: **English** Full/part-time staff: **13 / 6** National/foreign students: **165 / 35** Library size: **210,000+64,000** Doctrinal basis: **none** Worship life offered: **monthly** In relations with: **secular university**

Address: School of Theology, University of Natal, P/Bag X01, Pietermaritzburg, 3201, South Africa, Tel: +27 331 260-5540, Fax: +27 331 260-5858, E-mail: theo-sec@theology.unp.ac.za

- **Pietersburg** — Turfloop Theological Seminary (s1203)

Type of school: **Graduate** Degrees offered: **BTh** Offers training for pastors: **yes** for teachers: **no** for lay persons: **no** Type of available practical training: **preaching, pastoral care, religious education** Admission requirements: **matriculation exemption** Languages in use: **English** Full/part-time staff: **3** National/foreign students: **33 / 1** Library size: **3,000** Doctrinal basis: **Reformed** Worship life offered: **daily** In relations with: **Uniting Reformed Church**

Address: Turfloop Theological Seminary, P/Bag X1102, 0727 Pietersburg, Sovenga, South Africa, Tel: +27 52 267-0260, Fax: +27 52 267-0226

- **Potchefstroom** — Potchefstroom University for Christian Higher Education (s1223)

Type of school: **Faculty of Theology** Founded in **1869** Degrees offered: **B(Hons), M + D in Arts, Natural Sciences, Theology, Education, Economics, Management, Sciences, Law, Engineering, Pharmacy** Offers training for pastors: **nc** Type of available practical training: **none, aim is to disseminate the Reformation worldview and indicate its relevance to socio-economic-political etc. issues** Admission requirements: **university exemption in the maticulation examination** Languages in use: **Afrikaans, English** Full/part-time staff: **472** National/foreign students: **10,156 / 123** Library size: **500,000** Doctrinal basis: **Bible** Worship life offered: **daily classes and meetings are opened with Scripture reading and prayer** In relations with: **cooperation with Afrikaans and English-speaking Reformed Churches in South Arica**

Address: Potchefstroomsè Universiteit vir Christelike Hoër Onderwys, 11 Hoffman Street, Private Bag X6001, Potchefstroom, 2520, South Africa, Tel: +27 148 299-2222, Fax: +27 148 299-2799, E-mail: irsnk@puknet.puk.ac.za

- **Potchefstroom** — Institute of Reformational Studies (IRS) — Potchefstroom University of Christian Higher Education (s1199)

Type of school: **Mission Institute** Languages in use: **English, Afrikaans** Full/part-time staff: **6 / 0** National/foreign students: **na / na** In relations with: **Afrikaans-speaking Reformed Churches**

Address: Institute of Reformational Studies (IRS), 2520, Potchefstroom, South Africa, Tel: +27 148 2991620, Fax: 127 148 2992799, E-mail: irsnk@puknet.puk.ac.za

- **Pretoria** — Department of Theology — University of South Africa (s1234)

Type of school: **Graduate/Univ** Founded in **1873** Degrees offered: **BTh, BD, MTh, ThD, MA in diaconology** Offers training for pastors: **yes** for teachers: **yes** for lay persons: **yes** Type of available practical training: **Dipl in Christian Services** Languages in use: **English, Afrikaans** Full/part-time staff: **67** National/foreign students: **10,220 / 205** Library size: **90,000** Doctrinal basis: **none** Worship life offered: **none** In relations with: **Ecumenical**

Address: Department of Theology — University of South Africa, P.O. Box 392, Muckleneuk
Ridge, Pretoria, 0003, South Africa, Tel: +27 12 429-4567, Fax: +27 12 429-3332,
E-mail: wolfaja@alpha.unisa.ac.za

- **Pretoria** — Faculty of Theology (B) — University of Pretoria (s1219)
Type of school: **Graduate/Univ** Founded in **1938** Degrees offered: **BTh, BD, MDiv, DD, BA(Hons)(Theol), MTh, PhD** Offers training for pastors: **yes** for teachers: **yes** for lay persons: **no** Type of available practical training: **preaching, pastoral care, religious education** Admission requirements: **matriculation exemption for BA** Languages in use: **Afrikaans, English** Full/part-time staff: **15 / 20** National/foreign students: **440 / 20** Library size: **university library** Doctrinal basis: **Reformed** Worship life offered: **weekly** In relations with: **Dutch Reformed Church (NGK)**

Address: Faculty of Theology (B) — University of Pretoria, Pretoria, 0002, South Africa, Tel: +27
12 420-2322, Fax: +27 12 43-2185, E-mail: teolb@up.ac.za

- **Rondebosch** — Department of Religious Studies — University of Cape
Town (s1212)
Type of school: **Faculty of Theology** Founded in **1969** Degrees offered: **BTh, BA(Hons), MA** Offers training for pastors: **nc** Languages in use: **English** Full/part-time staff: **11/ 1** Library size: **(University) 900,000**

Address: Department of Religious Studies, Private Bag, University of Cape Town, Rondebosch,
7700, South Africa, Tel: +27 21 6650-3452, Fax: +27 21 6650-3761, E-mail: melody@socsciI.uct.ac.za

- **Sibasa** — Iyani Bible School (s1228)
Type of school: **Undergraduate/Bible school** Offers training for lay persons: **yes** Type of available practical training: **preaching, pastoral care, religious education** Admission requirements: **"any person who can read and write"** Languages in use: **Venda, English** Full/part-time staff: **9** National/foreign students: **140 / 0** Library size: **2,500** Doctrinal basis: **HeidC, BelgC, CDort** Worship life offered: **daily** In relations with: **Reformed Church in South Africa (Synod Soutpansberg)**

Address: Iyani Bible School, P.O. Box 74, Sibasa, Venda 0970, South Africa, Tel: +27 159 31402,
Fax: +27 159 31402

- **Sovenga** — Stofberg Theol School at Turfloop (s1221)
Offers training for pastors: **nc** Languages in use: **English** National/foreign students: **nc / 0** In relations with: **Dutch Reformed Church in Africa**

Address: Stofberg Theol School at Turfloop, P.O. Box 1102, Sovenga, 0727, South Africa, Tel:
+27 15 224-201

- **Stellenbosch** — Faculty of Theology — University of Stellenbosch (s1211)
Type of school: **Graduate/Univ** Founded in **1859** Degrees offered: **BTh (4 years), BD (2 years), MTh (2 years), ThD (2 years)** Offers training for pastors: **yes** for lay persons: **yes** Type of available practical training: **preaching, pastoral care, religious education** Admission requirements: **matriculation exception** Languages in use: **Afrikaans, English** Full/part-time staff: **11 / 6** National/foreign students: **321 / 44** Library size: **50,647** Doctrinal basis: **Reformed** Worship life offered: **weekly** In relations with: **training center for ministers of Dutch Ref Ch, Uniting Ref Ch in Southern Africa**

   Address: Fakulteit Teologie — Universiteit of Stellenbosch, Dorpstraat 171, P.O. Box XI, Matieland, Stellenbosch, 7600, South Africa, Tel: +27 21 808-3255, Fax: +27 21 808-3251, E-mail: jc3@maties.sun.ac.za

---

SPAIN

- **Madrid** — United Evangelical Theological Seminary (s6410)
Type of school: **Graduate/Univ** Founded in **1878** Degrees offered: **DiplTh, CertTh, BTh** Offers training for pastors: **yes** for teachers: **yes** for lay persons: **yes** Languages in use: **Castellano** Full/part-time staff: **4 / 5** national/foreign students: **50 / 2** Library size: **6,000** Worship life offered: **weekly** In relations with: **Iglesia Evangélica Española, Iglesia Evangélica Reformada Episcopal**

   Address: Seminario Evangélico Unido de Teologia, Beneficencia 18 bis, E-28004 Madrid, Spain, Tel: +34 1 596-9794, Fax: +34 1 447-9469, E-mail: rpreto@lander.es

---

SRI LANKA

- **Chunnakam** — Christian Theological Seminary of Sri Lanka and Institute for Lay People (s4384)
Type of school: **Undergraduate** Degrees offered: **DiplTh, BTh, BD** Offers training for pastors: **yes** for teachers: **yes** for lay persons: **yes** Type of available practical training: **preaching, pastoral care, religious education** Admission requirements: **Graduate in Christian Education (advanced level) of Dept. of Education, Bachelor's degrees of recognized university** Languages in use: **Tamil, English** Full/part-time staff: **7** National/foreign students: **16 / na** Library size: **10,000** Doctrinal basis: **Faith of the Church of South India** Worship life offered: **daily** In relations with: **CWM, Church of South India (CNI)**

   Address: Christian Theological Seminary of Sri Lanka and Institute for Lay People, c/o Bishop's House, Vaddukoddai, Chunnakam, Sri Lanka, Tel: +94 1 582-015, Fax: +94 1 582-015

- **Dehiwela** — The Association for Theological Education by Extension (TAFTEE) (s4382)

Type of school: **Mission Institute (by extension)** Founded in **1982** Degrees offered: **Bachelor of Theol Studies** Offers training for pastors: **yes** for teachers: **yes** for lay persons: **yes** Type of available practical training: **particularly in preaching, pastoral care, religious education, and biblical study** Languages in use: **English, Sinhalese, Tamil** Full/part-time staff: **3 (volunteers)** National/foreign students: **200 / 0** Library size: **9,000 (joint with Colombo Tehol Seminary)** Doctrinal basis: **evangelical emphasis** Worship life offered: **classes are conducted at various centers, churches, and institutions** In relations with: **Presb Ch Sri Lanka and all denominations**

Address: The Association for Theological Education by Extension (TATREE), 36 Moor Rd., Dehiwela, Sri Lanka, Tel: +94 7 27440

- **Kohuwela** — The Dutch Reformed Church Seminary and Bible Institute (s4380)

Offers training for pastors: **nc** Languages in use: **English** In relations with: **Dutch Reformed Church in Sri Lanka**

Address: The Dutch Reformed Church Seminary and Bible Institute, No. 2 Mudaliyar Ave., Kohuwela, Nogegoda, Sri Lanka, Tel: +94 5 52835

- **Peradeniya** — Lanka Bible College (s4385)

Type of school: **Graduate and Undergraduate School** Founded in **1970** Degrees offered: **DiplTh, BTh, MDiv** Offers training for pastors: **yes** for teachers: **yes** for lay persons: **yes** Admission requirements: **recommendation from church** Languages in use: **English, Sinhala, Tamil** Full/part-time staff: **13 / 7** National/foreign students: **165 / 1** Library size: **15,000** Doctrinal basis: **evangelical** Worship life offered: **daily** In relations with: **Dutch Ref Ch, Presb Ch**

Address: Lanka Bible College, P.O. Box 2, Christopher Rd., KY 20400 Peradeniya, Sri Lanka, Tel: +94 8 388-398, Fax: +94 8 388-682

- **Pilimatalawa** — Theological College of Lanka (s4381)

Type of school: **Undergraduate/Bible school** Founded in **1963** Degrees offered: **BTh, DiplTh, CertTh** Offers training for pastors: **yes** for teachers: **yes** for lay persons: **yes** Type of available practical training: **preaching Sunday, school teaching, pastoral care, religious education** Admission requirements: **General certificate in Education (advanced level)** Languages in use: **English, Sinhala, Tamil** Full/part-time staff: **7 / 5** National/foreign students: **37 / 0** Library size: **16,000** Doctrinal basis: **ecumenical** Worship life offered: **3 times a day** In relations with: **Federation of Angl, Meth, Baptist, Presb Ch in Sri Lanka**

Address: Theological College of Lanka, Nandana Uyana, Pilimatalawa, Sri Lanka, Tel: +94 8 71278, Fax: +94 8 32343

SUDAN

• **Khartoum** — Nile Theological College (s1360)
Type of school: **Graduate school** Founded in **1991** Degrees offered: **BA, CE, BTh** Offers training for pastors: **yes** for teachers: **yes** for lay persons: **yes** Type of available practical training: **preaching, pastoral care, religious education** Admission requirements: **Sudan school certificate with 50% above or its equivalent** Languages in use: **English, Arabic** Full/part-time staff: **5 / 5** national/foreign students: **85 / 3** Library size: **5,000** Worship life offered: **daily morning devotions, Wednesdays: fellowship** In relations with: **Presb Ch of the Sudan, Sudan Evang Presb Ch, other churches sending their students**

Address: Nile Theological College, P.O. Box 632, Khartoum, Sudan, Tel: +249 11 336-530, Fax: +249 11 335 150

• **Malaka** — Giffen Bible School (s1361)
Type of school: **Undergraduate/Bible school** Founded in **1963** Degrees offered: **Junior certificate** Offers training for pastors: **yes** for teachers: **yes** for lay persons: **yes** Type of available practical training: **preaching, pastoral care, religious education** Admission requirements: **Christian Sudanese Nationalist and qualified** Languages in use: **English, Arabic** Full/part-time staff: **8** National/foreign students: **21 / no** Library size: **300-400** Doctrinal basis: **God incarnate and basis of the church** Worship life offered: **daily, weekly, monthly** In relations with: **Ref Ch, Presb Ch of America, Basel Mission, Congregationalist, Baptist Church**

Address: Giffen Bible School, P.O. Box 40, Doleib Hill, Malaka, Sudan, Tel: +249 22260

SWAZILAND

• **Kwaluseni** — Department of Theology and Religious Studies — University of Swaziland (s1371)
Type of school: **Graduate/Univ** Founded in **1964** Degrees offered: **BA, BA +Postgraduate in Christian Education** Offers training for pastors: **nc** for teachers: **yes** Type of available practical training: **no** Admission requirements: **Cambridge Overseas School Certificate, six O-level passes** Languages in use: **English** Full/part-time staff: **4 / 1** National/foreign students: **270 / 5** Library size: **98,000 (plus use of University library)** Doctrinal basis: **none** Worship life offered: **daily by students, main worship on Sunday, denominational services twice a week** In relations with: **na**

Address: Department of Theology and Religious Studies — University of Swaziland, Private Bag 4, Kwaluseni Campus, M 201 Kwaluseni, Swaziland, Tel: +268 85264 and 84747, Fax: +268 85276

SWEDEN

• **Härnösand** — People's Highschool of Härnösand (s6424)
Offers training for pastors: **no** for lay persons: **yes** Type of available practical training: **preaching, pastoral care, religious education** Admission requirements: **18 yrs** Languages in use: **Swedish** Full/part-time staff: **35** national/foreign students: **230 / 0** Doctrinal basis: **none** Worship life offered: **4 times per week** In relations with: **Mission Covenant Church of Sweden**

Address: Härnösands Folkhögskola, Murbergvägen 32, S — 87150 Härnösand, Sweden, Tel: +46
611 220 80, Fax: +46 611 194 32

• **Jönköping** — Mission and Bible School (s6427)
Type of school: **College** Founded in **1919** Degrees offered: **Degree** Offers training for pastors: **yes** Languages in use: **Swedish** Full/part-time staff: **5** national/foreign students: **20 / nc** Library size: **30,000** In relations with: **Swedish Mission Alliance**

Address: Kortoskolan Sam Missionskola och Bibelinstitut, S — 55594 Jönköping, Sweden, Tel:
+46 36 379-205

• **Jönköping** — People's Highschool of Södra Vätterbygens (s6426)
Type of school: **Undergraduate/Bible school** Degrees offered: **PO degree** Offers training for pastors: **no** for lay persons: **yes** Type of available practical training: **after one year of studies the students can practice for one year in a church** Admission requirements: **corresponding college studies** Languages in use: **Swedish** Full/part-time staff: **5** National/foreign students: **40 / 0** Library size: **20,000** Doctrinal basis: **ApC** Worship life offered: **4 times per week** In relations with: **Mission Covenant Church of Sweden**

Address: Södra Vätterbygens Folkhögskola, Fjällgatan 16, S — 55439 Jönköping, Sweden, Tel:
+46 36 306-900, Fax: +46 36 165-575

• **Kalix** — Kalix Folkhögskola (s6425)
Offers training for pastors: **no** Admission requirements: **10th grade** Languages in use: **English** In relations with: **Mission Covenant Church of Sweden**

Address: Kalix Folkhögskola, P.O. Box 10009, S — 95227 Kalix, Sweden, Tel: +46 923 13315,
Fax: +46 923 119 08

• **Karlskoga** — Karlskoga Folk Highschool (s6421)
Type of school: **Undergraduate Bible school** Founded in **1882** Degrees offered: **GCEA, Dipl of leadership, Bible school** Offers training for pastors: **no** for teachers: **yes** for lay persons: **no** Languages in use: **Swedish** Full/part-time staff: **16 / 16** national/foreign students: **265 / 4** Library size: **12,000** Worship life offered: **weekly** In relations with: **Mission Covenant Church of Sweden**

Address: Karlskoga Folkhögskola, P.O. Box 192, S — 69124 Karlskoga, Sweden, Tel: +46 586
64600, Fax: +46 586 64622

- **Lidingö** — Theological Seminary of the Mission Covenant Church (s6422)
Type of school: **Graduate** Founded in **1871/1993** Degrees offered: **DiplTh, Dipl of deacon education, Dipl of leadership, missionary training** Offers training for pastors: **yes** for teachers: **yes** Type of available practical training: **preaching, pastoral care, religious education** Admission requirements: **graduation from high school/upper secondary school** Languages in use: **Swedish (some in English)** Full/part-time staff: **12 / 8** National/foreign students: **150 / 1** Library size: **100,000** Doctrinal basis: **none** Worship life offered: **weekly** In relations with: **Mission Covenant Church, Baptist Union**

Address: Teologiska Högskolan, Stockhom (THS), Kottlavägen 116, S — 18141 Lidingö, Sweden, Tel: +46 8 765-2605, Fax: +46 8 767-0714, E-mail: ths@ths.se

- **Uppsala** — Department of Theology — Uppsala University (s6429)
Type of school: **Faculty of Theology** Founded in **1477** Degrees offered: **BTh, LicTh, ThD** Offers training for pastors: **yes** for teachers: **yes** for lay persons: **yes** Type of available practical training: **no** Admission requirements: **high school exam** Languages in use: **Swedish** Full/part-time staff: **35 / 15** National/foreign students: **700 / nc** Library size: **75,000** Doctrinal basis: **none** Worship life offered: **never** In relations with: **state university**

Address: Uppsala Universitet Teologiska Institutionen, P.B. 1604, Slottgränd 3, S — 751 46 Uppsala, Sweden, Tel: +46 18 471 00 00, Fax: +46 18 710-170, E-mail: teol@teol.uu.se

SWITZERLAND

- **Aarau** — Diaconal Theological Seminary (s6438)
Type of school: **Seminar for diaconal workers in parishes** Founded in **1960** Degrees offered: **Diploma as diaconal worker in a parish (Kirchlich annerkannte/r Gemeindehelfer/in)** Offers training for pastors: **no** for teachers: **yes** for lay persons: **yes** Type of available practical training: **lessons in homiletics, liturgy; pastoral care, religious education (profound), Sunday school — integrated in religious education (deepened)** Admission requirements: **good degree in school education, experience in profession and parish** Languages in use: **German** Full/part-time staff: **4 / 10** National/foreign students: **71 / 0** Library size: **8,000** Doctrinal basis: **Faith basis of the Evangelical Alliance** Worship life offered: **weekly worship, 3 times per week devotions** In relations with: **Ref church of the Canton Aargau**

Address: Theologisch-Diakonisches Seminar, Frey-Herosé-Str. 9, CH-5000 Aarau, Switzerland, Tel: +41 62 824-5051, Fax: +41 62 824-6939

- **Basel** — Theological Church School of Basel (s6439)
Type of school: **Graduate/Univ** Degrees offered: **Theological maturity of the city of Basel, "Propädeuticum" of theological studies** Offers training for pastors: **no** Type of available practical training: **no** Admission requirements: **finished**

formation in one profession, not older than 32, admission exam Languages in use: **German** Full/part-time staff: **9** National/foreign students: **17 / 0** Library size: **50,000** Doctrinal basis: **none** Worship life offered: **none** In relations with: **Ref Chs /Switzerland**

Address: Kirchlich-Theologische Schule Basel, Leimenstr. 48, CH-4051 Basel, Switzerland, Tel: +41 61271-1718

- **Basel** — Theological Faculty — University of Basel (s6441)
Type of school: **Undergraduate** Founded in **1460** Degrees offered: **State exam in Th, LicTh, ThD, Peritia theologiae, Lic Phil I, exams for teachers** Offers training for pastors: **yes** for teachers: **yes** for lay persons: **yes** Type of available practical training: **homiletics, pastoral care, religious education** Admission requirements: **maturity, B.A.** Languages in use: **German** Full/part-time staff: **9 / 3** National/foreign students: **153 / 50** Library size: **40,000** Worship life offered: **none** In relations with: **Reformed churches of Switzerland**

Address: Theologische Fakultät — Universität Basel, Nadelberg 10, CH-4051 Basel, Switzerland, Tel: +41 61 267-2900, 267-3111, Fax: +41 61 267-2902

- **Bern** — Protestant Theological Faculty — University of Bern (s6433)
Type of school: **Graduate/Univ** Founded in **1834** Degrees offered: **state exam in Th, LicTh, ThD, Habil Th** Offers training for pastors: **yes** for teachers: **yes** Type of available practical training: **preaching, pastoral care, religious education** Admission requirements: **maturity or equivalent** Languages in use: **German** Full/part-time staff: **11 / 13** National/foreign students: **223 / 36** Library size: **55,000** Doctrinal basis: **none** Worship life offered: **once per semester** In relations with: **Evang-Ref Church of the Canton of Bern; students can also serve other Evang-Ref Churches**

Address: Evangelisch-theologische Fakultät — Universität Bern, Länggassstrasse 51, Unitobler, 3000 Bern #9, Switzerland, Tel: +41 31 631-8061, Fax: +41 31 631-8224

- **Bettingen** — Theological Seminary St. Chrischona (s6437)
Type of school: **Undergraduate/Bible school** Founded in **1840** Degrees offered: **Dipl, no academic degrees** Offers training for pastors: **yes** for teachers: **yes** for lay persons: **yes** Type of available practical training: **preaching, pastoral care, religious education** Admission requirements: **Abitur (Matura or secondary school with professional degree)** Languages in use: **German** Full/part-time staff: **9+ 8 host-teachers** National/foreign students: **140 / 72** Library size: **26,000** Doctrinal basis: **Declaration of Lausanne** Worship life offered: **daily** In relations with: **Ref Church of Switzerland**

Address: Theologisches Seminar St. Chrischona, Chrischonarain 200, CH-4126 Bettingen, Switzerland, Tel: +41 61 646-4426, Fax: +41 61 646-4575

- **Genève** — Autonomous Faculty of Protestant Theology (s6432)
Type of school: **Graduate/Univ** Founded in **1559** Degrees offered: **LicTh, DiplTh, ThD** Offers training for pastors: **yes** for lay persons: **yes** Type of available practical training: **homiletics, pastoral care, religious education** Admission re-

quirements: **cert art. 4 of the instructions for the licentiate** Languages in use: **French** Full/part-time staff: **11** National/foreign students: **80 / 20** Library size: **30,000** Doctrinal basis: **none** Worship life offered: **weekly** In relations with: **Eglise nationale protestante de Genève**

Address: Faculté autonome de Théologie Protestante, 3, Place de l'Université, CH-1211 Genève 4, Switzerland, Tel: +41 22 705-7111, Fax: +41 22 705-7430

• **Lausanne** — Theological Faculty — University of Lausanne (s6431)
Type of school: **Graduate/Univ** Founded in **1537** Degrees offered: **LicTh, CertTh, Dipl of specialization, ThD, Lic Rel, DRel** Offers training for pastors: **yes** for teachers: **yes** for lay persons: **yes** Type of available practical training: **practical theology** Admission requirements: **baccalaureate or examination** Languages in use: **French** Full/part-time staff: **9 / 5** National/foreign students: **120 / 25** Library size: **180,000-210,000** Doctrinal basis: **Reformed theology** Worship life offered: **weekly, faculty conference begins with a meditation** In relations with: **Evangelical-Reformed Church of the Canton Vaud**

Address: Faculté de Théologie Protestante, Centre Universitaire BFSH 2, CH-1015 Lausanne, Switzerland, Tel: +41 21 692-2700, Fax: +41 21 692-2705, E-mail: Marianne.Rouiller@dtheol.unil.ch

• **Neuchâtel** — Protestant Theological Faculty — University of Neuchâtel (s6442)
Type of school: **Graduate/Univ** Founded in **1530/1873/1980** Degrees offered: **LicTh, CertTh, DiplTh, ThD** Offers training for pastors: **yes** for teachers: **yes** for lay persons: **yes** Type of available practical training: **homiletics (practical theology)** Admission requirements: **baccalaureate, maturity, special exams (varies between different school exams in Switzerland + foreign countries)** Languages in use: **French** Full/part-time staff: **5 / 5** National/foreign students: **82 / 13** Library size: **19,000** In relations with: **state university, Ch of Neuchâtel**

Address: Faculté de Théologie Protestante — Université de Neuchâtel, Faubourg de l' Hôpital 41, CH-2000 Neuchâtel, Switzerland, Tel: +41 38 243-040, Fax: +41 38 240-920, E-mail: Gottfried.Hammann@theol.unie.ch

• **Saint-Légier** — Bible and Missionary Institute Emmaüs (s6434)
Type of school: **Undergraduate/Bible school** Founded in **1926** Offers training for pastors: **yes** for lay persons: **yes** Type of available practical training: **homiletics, children, youth, pastoral care, management, accounting** Admission requirements: **personal faith confession, minimum 18 years old, if possible already with profession** Languages in use: **French** Full/part-time staff: **5 residents, 15 visitors** National/foreign students: **60 / 28** Library size: **32,000** Worship life offered: **weekly**

Address: Institut biblique et missionnaire Emmaüs, Rte. de Fenil 40, CH-1806 Saint-Légier, Switzerland, Tel: +41 21 943-1891, Fax: +41 21 943-4365

• **Zürich** — Theological Faculty — University of Zurich (s6436)
Type of school: **Graduate/Univ** Founded in **1833** Degrees offered: **ThD, LicTh**

Offers training for pastors: **yes** for teachers: **yes** Type of available practical training: **homiletics, religious education, pastoral care** Admission requirements: **maturity** Languages in use: **German** Full/part-time staff: **30** National/foreign students: **200 / 30** Library size: **49,000** Doctrinal basis: **none** Worship life offered: **only on special occasions and, e.g., in homiletics courses** In relations with: **geographically and spiritually to the German-speaking Swiss Ref churches**

Address: Theologische Fakultät — Universität Zürich, Kirchgasse 9, CH-8001 Zürich, Switzerland, Tel: +41 1 257-6721, Fax: +41 1 262-1412

TAIWAN

• **Hsinchu** — Presbyterian Bible College (s4400)
Type of school: **Undergraduate/Bible school** Founded in **1952** Degrees offered: **BTh for church ministry, BA for early childhood education, English, Music majors** Offers training for pastors: **nc** for lay persons: **yes** Type of available practical training: **preaching, pastoral care, religious education are all included in curriculum** Admission requirements: **high school graduation or equivalent** Languages in use: **Taiwanese, Chinese, some English** Full/part-time staff: **7 / 5** National/foreign students: **100 / nc** Library size: **10,000** Worship life offered: **daily mornings Tuesday-Friday, evenings Tuesday + Thursday** In relations with: **Presb Church in Taiwan**

Address: Presbyterian Bible College, P.O. Box 7, 56 Kao-Feng Rd., Hsinchu, 30035, Taiwan R.O.C., Tel: +886 35 217125, Fax: +886 35 217194

• **Shou-Feng** — Yu-Shan Theological College (s4401)
Type of school: **Graduate/Univ** Founded in **1946** Degrees offered: **MDiv, BATh, BA in Christian Education, BA in Church Music** Offers training for pastors: **yes** for teachers: **yes** for lay persons: **yes** Type of available practical training: **after 1st year fieldwork = training in preaching, teaching, etc., prior to going out also practical training in class situation** Admission requirements: **high school graduate, recommended by presbytery, baptized and confessing member of the church, good health** Languages in use: **Mandarin, Chinese** Full/part-time staff: **20** national/foreign students: **168 / 0** Library size: **24,754** Doctrinal basis: **follows the Presb Ch** Worship life offered: **weekly, Sunday worship, daily chapel service, weekly worship in tribal languages** In relations with: **Presb Ch of Taiwan, which has a working relationship with other churches around the world**

Address: Yu-Shan Theological College, 28, Chih Nan Lu Sec. 1, Shou-Feng, Hualien, Taiwan R.O.C., Tel: +886 38 641-1012

• **Tainan** — Tainan Theological College and Seminary (s4402)
Type of school: **Graduate+Undergraduate+Pastor/Evangelist/Mission** Founded in **1876** Degrees offered: **DMin, MDiv, BAR, MTh, or ThD (in assoc. with**

South-East Asian Graduate School of Theology) Offers training for pastors: **yes** for teachers: **yes** for lay persons: **yes** Type of available practical training: **min required for 2 years (6-10 depending on departmental requirements)** Admission requirements: **high school (12th grade), graduate, graduate level** Languages in use: **Taiwanese, Mandarin, English** Full/part-time staff: **19** national/foreign students: **229 / 3** Library size: **52,000** Doctrinal basis: **Confession of the Presb Ch of Taiwan, ApC, NicC, WestConf** Worship life offered: **twice daily** In relations with: **Presb Ch of Taiwan**

Address: Tainan Theological College and Seminary, 117, East Gate, Section 1, Tainan, 701, Taiwan R.O.C., Tel: +886 6 234-1291, Fax: +886 6 234-6060

- **Taipei** — China Reformed Seminary Taipei (s4406)
Offers training for pastors: **nc** Languages in use: **English**

Address: China Reformed Seminary Taipei, P.O. Box 51-70, Taipei, Taiwan, R.O.C.

- **Taipei** — China Reformed Theological Seminary (s4404)
Type of school: **Undergraduate/Bible school+Evang/ Pastor Training** Degrees offered: **BTh, MA, MDiv** Offers training for pastors: **yes** for lay persons: **yes** Type of available practical training: **preaching, pastoral care, religious education in churches for the weekend, practice in all church activities** Admission requirements: **High school + college graduated** Languages in use: **Chinese, English** Full/part-time staff: **10** National/foreign students: **35 / 0** Library size: **3,000** Doctrinal basis: **WestConf, HeidC** Worship life offered: **daily devotions and twice per school session** In relations with: **Reformed Presb Church (Christian Ref Ch, Orthodox Presb Church, Ref Ch of New Zealand, Presb Ch of Korea)**

Address: China Reformed Theological Seminary, P.O. Box 1802, # 30, Lane 75, Nanking E. Rd., Sec. 4, 100 Taipei, Taiwan, Tel: +886 2 712-4385, Fax: +886 2 713-1124

- **Taipei** — China Reformed Theological Seminary (s4405)
Type of school: **Undergraduate/Bible school** Degrees offered: **BA, MDiv** Offers training for pastors: **yes** Type of available practical training: **preaching, pastoral care, religious education** Admission requirements: **graduate from high school + college** Languages in use: **Chinese** Full/part-time staff: **17** National/foreign students: **10 / nc** Library size: **200** Doctrinal basis: **Calvinism** Worship life offered: **4 times per week**

Address: China Reformed Theological Seminary, P.O. Box 51-70, Taipei, Taiwan R.O.C., Tel: +886 2 797-3697, Fax: +886 2 797-4269

- **Taipei** — Taiwan Theological College and Seminary (s4403)
Type of school: **Graduate and Undergraduate/Bible school** Founded in **1872** Degrees offered: **BAR (college), MDiv, DMin (seminary), MTh, ThD (affiliated with SEAGST)** Offers training for pastors: **yes** for teachers: **yes** for lay persons: **yes** Type of available practical training: **preaching, pastoral care, religious education** Admission requirements: **middle school for college level, BA or BS for seminary level** Languages in use: **Taiwanese (major), Chinese** Full/part-time staff: **18** National/foreign students: **235 / 4** Library size: **45,000** Doctrinal basis:

Reformed tradition Worship life offered: **4 times per week** In relations with: **Presb Ch of Taiwan**

Address: Taiwan Theological College and Seminary, 20 Lane 2 — Section 2 Yang Teh Highway, Shilin, Taipei, 11106, Taiwan R.O.C., Tel: +886 2 882-2370, Fax: +886 2 881-6940

THAILAND

• **Bangkok** — Bangkok Bible College and Seminary (s4432)
Type of school: **College** Founded in **1971** Degrees offered: **BTh, MDiv, MBS** Offers training for pastors: **nc** Languages in use: **Thai** Full/part-time staff: **15 / 6** National/foreign students: **94 / nc** Library size: **14,850** In relations with: **CAM, Presb, Indep**

Address: Bangkok Bible College and Seminary, 70 Soi Suksa Wittayu, North Sathorn Rd., Bangkok, 10500, Thailand, Tel: +66 2 235-3852, Fax: +66 2 237-1577

• **Bangkok** — Bangkok Institute of Theology (s4430)
Type of school: **Graduate/Univ** Founded in **1941** Degrees offered: **DiplTh, BTh, MDiv** Offers training for pastors: **yes** for teachers: **yes** for lay persons: **yes** Type of available practical training: **preaching, field education** Admission requirements: **high school graduation, references, exam, interview** Languages in use: **Thai** Full/part-time staff: **10 / 8** National/foreign students: **104 / 0** Library size: **10,462** Doctrinal basis: **NicC** Worship life offered: **5 times per week** In relations with: **Presbyterian Church, 7th District of Church of Christ of Thailand**

Address: Bangkok Institute of Theology, 39-Soi Wachirathamsatit 3, Sukhumvit Rd. 101/1, Bangkok, 10260, Thailand, Tel: +66 2 393-6223, 396-1564, Fax: +66 2 398-7787

• **Chiang Mai** — McGilvary Theological Seminary, Payap University (s4431)
Type of school: **Graduate/Univ** Founded in **1889** Degrees offered: **BTh, MDiv, ThD** Offers training for pastors: **yes** for teachers: **yes** for lay persons: **yes** Type of available practical training: **fieldwork** Admission requirements: **entrance exam, church recommendation, personal interview, BA or equivalent for the MDiv degree** Languages in use: **Thai, English on special occasions** Full/part-time staff: **22 / 3** National/foreign students: **100 / 8** Library size: **16,500** Worship life offered: **daily every weekday, separated service for students and faculty, Thursdays together** In relations with: **Church of Christ in Thailand**

Address: McGilvary Theological Seminary, Payap University, Ampger Mvang LPO Chiang Mai 101, 66 5000 Chiang Mai, Thailand, Tel: +66 53 242-484, Fax: +66 53 241-983

TOGO

• **Atakpamé** — Evangelical Bible School of Atakpamé (s1380)
Type of school: **Undergraduate/Bible school** Degrees offered: **Dipl. for cate-chists and evangelists** Offers training for pastors: **nc** Type of available practical training: **practical theology, permanent formation for lay people and church workers** Admission requirements: **BEPC, exam of entry, recommendation of the church** Languages in use: **French** Full/part-time staff: **6** National/foreign students: **20 / 10** Library size: **2,500** Doctrinal basis: **Protestant** Worship life offered: **daily** In relations with: **Eglise Evang Presb du Togo (Eglise Prot Methe du Bénin)**

Address: Ecole biblique évangélique d' Atakpamé, B.P. 28, Quartier Gnagna, Atakpamé, Togo, Tel: +228 400-177

TRINIDAD AND TOBAGO

• **San Fernando** — St. Andrew's Theological College (s3340)
Type of school: **Undergraduate/Bible school** Offers training for pastors: **yes** for teachers: **yes** for lay persons: **yes** Type of available practical training: **preaching, pastoral care, religious education** Admission requirements: **secondary school completed** Languages in use: **English** Full/part-time staff: **6** National/foreign students: **28 / 0** Doctrinal basis: **Reformed** Worship life offered: **daily** In relations with: **Presbyterian Church in Trinidad**

Address: St. Andrew's Theological College, P.O. Box 92, Paradise Hill, San Fernando, Trinidad and Tobago, Tel: +1 809 657-7554

UGANDA

• **Kampala** — Reformed Theological College (s1356)
Type of school: **College** Degrees offered: **BD, Cert in Christian Ministry** Offers training for pastors: **yes** for teachers: **yes** Admission requirements: **A-level** Languages in use: **English** Full/part-time staff: **14** National/foreign students: **61 / 10** Library size: **6,000** Doctrinal basis: **Evangelical, Reformed** Worship life offered: **daily**

Address: Reformed Theological College, P.O. Box 11701, Kampala, Uganda, Tel: +256 41 271-443, Fax: +256 41 271-443

• **Mbale** — Christian Reformed Bible College (s1357)
Type of school: **Undergraduate/Bible school** Degrees offered: **Cert, Dipl BD (in prep)** Offers training for pastors: **yes** for lay persons: **yes** Type of available practi-

cal training: **practical preaching training, pastoral care, environmental studies, project management** Admission requirements: **O-level and examination** Languages in use: **English** Full/part-time staff: **5** National/foreign students: **50 / 0** Library size: **1,000** Doctrinal basis: **Reformed** Worship life offered: **weekly** In relations with: **Christian Reformed Church in Eastern Africa**

Address: Christian Reformed Bible College, P.O. Box 203, Kumi Rd., Mbale, Uganda

UNITED KINGDOM

- **Aberdeen** — Christ's College Aberdeen (s6318)
Type of school: **Graduate/Univ** Founded in **1843** Degrees offered: **BTh, LicTh, BD, PhD** Offers training for pastors: **yes** for teachers: **yes** Admission requirements: **University admission** Languages in use: **English** Full/part-time staff: **16** National/foreign students: **128 / 62** Worship life offered: **weekly** In relations with: **Church of Scotland**

Address: Christ's College Aberdeen, 25 High Street, GB-Aberdeen, AB24 3EE, United Kingdom, Tel: +44 1224 272-385, Fax: +44 1224 272-136

- **Aberystwyth Ceredigion** — The United Theological College (s6305)
Type of school: **Graduate+Pastor Training Institute** Founded in **1906** Degrees offered: **BD, BTh, PhD, MTh, MPhil (University of Wales)** Offers training for pastors: **yes** for teachers: **yes** for lay persons: **yes** Type of available practical training: **preaching, pastoral care, religious education** Admission requirements: **2 A-level subjects (GCSE)** Languages in use: **Welsh, English** Full/part-time staff: **7** National/foreign students: **85 / 7** Library size: **75,000** Doctrinal basis: **none** Worship life offered: **twice daily** In relations with: **Presb Ch of Wales**

Address: The United Theological College, King St., GB-Aberystwyth Ceredigion, Wales SY23 2LT, United Kingdom, Tel: +44 1970 624-574, Fax: +44 1970 626-350

- **Belfast** — Union Theological College (s6319)
Type of school: **Seminary** Founded in **1978** Degrees offered: **DiplTh, BTh, BD** Offers training for pastors: **yes** for lay persons: **yes** Type of available practical training: **preaching, pastoral care, religious education for ministerial students** Admission requirements: **primary degree (less for special students)** Languages in use: **English** Full/part-time staff: **5 / 5** National/foreign students: **75 / 2** Library size: **50,000** Doctrinal basis: **all staff sign WestConf** Worship life offered: **daily every working day in team time** In relations with: **Presbyterian Church in Ireland**

Address: Union Theological College, 108 Botanic Ave, GB-Belfast, BT7 1JT, United Kingdom, Tel: +44 1232 325-374, Fax: +44 1232 325-397, E-mail: admin@union.org.uk

- **Belfast** — Reformed Theological College (s6541)
Type of school: **Evangelist/Pastoral Training Institute** Founded in **1854** Degrees

offered: **DiplTh, Diploma in Biblical Studies** Offers training for pastors: **yes** Type of available practical training: **one term working with a local pastor** Admission requirements: **University degree or equivalent standard** Languages in use: **English** Full/part-time staff: **5** National/foreign students: **10 / nc** Library size: **5,000** Doctrinal basis: **WestConf** Worship life offered: **daily** In relations with: **Reformed Presbyterian Church of Northern Ireland**

Address: Reformed Theological College, 98, Lisburn Road, Belfast, BT9 6AG, Ireland, Tel: +44 1232 660-689nc

• **Birmingham** — Springdale College (s6320)
Type of school: **Undergraduate/Bible school** Founded in **1980** Degrees offered: **Cert (Christian Min), Cert (Theol Studies), Dipl Mission Theol** Offers training for pastors: **yes** for teachers: **no** for lay persons: **yes** Type of available practical training: **preaching, pastoral care, religious education** Languages in use: **English** Full/part-time staff: **3 / 6** National/foreign students: **15 / nc** Library size: **1,500** Worship life offered: **weekly** In relations with: **Churches of Christ**

Address: Springdale College, 54 Weoley Park Rd., Selly Oak, Birmingham, B29 6RB, United Kingdom, Tel: +44 121 472-0726, Fax: +44 121 472-0726, E-mail: springdale_college@compuserve.com

• **Birmingham** — St. Andrew's Hall Missionary College (s6309)
Type of school: **Mission Institute** Degrees offered: **ThD, PhD in Theol, MTh/ MA in Theol, CertTh, D Missiology, others** Offers training for pastors: **no** for teachers and missionaries: **yes** for lay persons: **yes** Type of available practical training: **Selly Oaks Colleges: development studies, Islam, mission studies; Westhill College: teacher training, religious education, church management, women studies; University of Birmingham: postgrad courses** Admission requirements: **recommendation form of sending church; for undergrad: entrance requirements; for postgrad: min postgrad requirements + evidence of funding** Languages in use: **English** Full/part-time staff: **3** National/foreign students: **50 / 25** Library size: **15,000 and access to Selly Oak Colleges + Westhill** Worship life offered: **daily** In relations with: **United Reformed Church**

Address: St. Andrew's Hall Missionary College, Weoley Park Road, GB-Birmingham, B29 6QX, United Kingdom, Tel: +44 121 472-6144, Fax: +44 121 414-1083

• **Birmingham** — The Queen's College (s6312)
Type of school: **Graduate and Undergraduate School** Founded in **1828/1970** Degrees offered: **MTh, MTh, BDiv, CertTh, BTh (through Birmingham University)** Offers training for pastors: **yes** for lay persons: **yes** Type of available practical training: **full pastoral + practical training for ordination and accredited ministry in the Angl, Meth, United Ref Churches** Admission requirements: **appropriate academic requirements, support from the sponsoring church, admission interview** Languages in use: **English** Full/part-time staff: **8 / 2** National/foreign students: **102 / nc** Library size: **44,000** Doctrinal basis: **none** Worship life offered: **daily** In relations with: **United Ref Ch United Kingdom**

Address: The Queen's College, Somerset Road, Edgbaston, GB-Birmingham, B15 2QH, West Midlands, United Kingdom, Tel: +44 121 454-1527, Fax: +44 121 454-8171

- **Bridgend** — Evangelical Theological College of Wales (s6321)
Type of school: **Graduate/Univ** Founded in **1985** Degrees offered: **Cert (Higher Education), BA, MPh** Offers training for pastors: **yes** for lay persons: **yes** Type of available practical training: **Sunday preaching, evangelism, teaching** Admission requirements: **flexible** Languages in use: **English** Full/part-time staff: **7 / 16** National/foreign students: **108 / 40** Library size: **15,000** Doctrinal basis: **Reformed** Worship life offered: **daily** In relations with: **Grace Baptist Churches, Fellowship of Independent Evangelical Churches, Evangelical Presb Churches, Association of Evangelical Churches in Wales**

Address: Evangelical Theological College of Wales, Bryntirion House, GB-Bridgend, CF31 4DX, United Kingdom, Tel: +44 1656 645-411, Fax: +44 1656 668-709, E-mail: 100667.1273@compuserve.com

- **Cambridge** — Westminster College (s6316)
Type of school: **Graduate and Undergraduate Seminary** Founded in **1899** Degrees offered: **MTh, MA in Theol, certificates in Theol, BA in Theol** Offers training for pastors: **yes** for lay persons: **yes** Type of available practical training: **preaching, pastoral care, religious education** Admission requirements: **min 5 passes in the General, certificate of education combined with being a Christian + educational maturity: many students higher qualified than GCE** Languages in use: **English** Full/part-time staff: **5** National/foreign students: **332 / 35** Library size: **35,000** Doctrinal basis: **the United Ref Ch basis of union** Worship life offered: **daily** In relations with: **United Ref Church in the UK**

Address: Westminster College, Madingley Road, GB-Cambridge, CB3 OA, United Kingdom, Tel: +44 1223 353-997, Fax: +44 1223 300-765

- **Craigavon** — Whitefield College of the Bible (s6542)
Type of school: **Undergraduate/Bible school** Degrees offered: **none** Offers training for pastors: **yes** for lay persons: **yes** Type of available practical training: **preaching, pastoral care, religious education** Admission requirements: **3 matriculation subjects: English language, English literature, history** Languages in use: **English** Full/part-time staff: **12** National/foreign students: **18 / 4** Library size: **7,500** Doctrinal basis: **see Articles of Faith** Worship life offered: **daily** In relations with: **Free Presbyterian Church of Ulster**

Address: Whitefield College of the Bible, 117, Banbridge Road, Gilford, GB-Craigavon, Co Armagh BT63 6 DL, Ireland, Tel: +44 18 2066-2232, Fax: +44 18 2066-2232

- **Edinburgh** — Free Church of Scotland College (s6311)
Type of school: **Undergraduate/Bible school** Founded in **1843** Degrees offered: **DiplTh, Dipl in postgraduate studies** Offers training for pastors: **yes** for teachers: **yes** Type of available practical training: **preaching, pastoral care, religious education** Admission requirements: **degree or equivalent** Languages in use: **English** Full/part-time staff: **5** National/foreign students: **24 / 7** Library size:

40,000 Doctrinal basis: **WestConf** Worship life offered: **daily** In relations with: **Free Church of Scotland**

Address: Free Church of Scotland College, 15 North Bank Str., The Mound, GB-Edinburgh, EH1
2LS, United Kingdom, Tel: +44 131 226-5286, Fax: +44 131 220-0597

• **Edinburgh** — New College — University of Edinburgh (s6313)
Type of school: **Graduate/Univ** Founded in **1583** Degrees offered: **BD, MTh, MPhil, PhD, DD, DiplMin, Cert in Christian Education, Pastoral Studies, BA and MA in Rel Studies** Offers training for pastors: **yes** for teachers: **yes** for lay persons: **yes** Languages in use: **English** Full/part-time staff: **28 / 4** National/foreign students: **500 / 75** Library size: **80,000** Doctrinal basis: **none** Worship life offered: **daily** In relations with: **Church of Scotland, United Free Church**

Address: New College, University of Edinburgh, The Mound, GB-Edinburgh, EH1 2LX, United
Kingdom, Tel: +44 131 650-8959, Fax: +44 131 650-6579

• **Edinburgh** — Scottish Congregational College (s6302)
Type of school: **Undergraduate/Bible school** Founded in **1811** Degrees offered: **none** Offers training for pastors: **yes** for lay persons: **yes** Type of available practical training: **preaching, pastoral care, religious education** Admission requirements: **various** Languages in use: **English** Full/part-time staff: **1** National/foreign students: **6 / 0** Library size: **20,000** Doctrinal basis: **none** Worship life offered: **twice a year** In relations with: **Scottish Congregational Church**

Address: Scottish Congregational College, 20 Inverleith Terrace, GB-Edinburgh, EH3 5NS, United
Kingdom, Tel: +44 131 315-3595, Fax: +44 131 332-2161

• **Edinburgh** — St. Colm's Education Centre and College (s6306)
Type of school: **Undergraduate/Bible school** Founded in **1986** Degrees offered: **Dipl., higher education, BA, MTh** Offers training for pastors: **no** for lay persons: **yes** Type of available practical training: **Sunday school, youth work, worship and preaching, pastoral care, adult education** Admission requirements: **no formal enquirement** Languages in use: **English** Full/part-time staff: **15** National/foreign students: **300 / 4-8** Library size: **20,000** Worship life offered: **daily** In relations with: **Church of Scotland**

Address: St. Colm's Education Centre and College, 18 Inverleith Terrace, GB-Edinburgh, EH3
5NS, United Kingdom, Tel: +44 131 332-0343, Fax: +44 131 315-2161

• **Glasgow** — Trinity College — University of Glasgow (s6314)
Type of school: **Graduate/Univ** Founded in **1451/1856** Degrees offered: **BDiv (academic + church vocation), BTh with teaching qualification, MA (Religious Studies), MTh, PhD (by thesis)** Offers training for pastors: **yes** Type of available practical training: **a lay certificate course in the evenings** Admission requirements: **3 Bs and a C Scottish highers, 2 Cs and a D A-levels** Languages in use: **English** Full/part-time staff: **15** National/foreign students: **249 / 40** Library size: **80,000** Doctrinal basis: **none** Worship life offered: **weekly during term, on voluntary basis for those interested** In relations with: **Ch of Scotland**

Address: Trinity College — University of Glasgow, GB-Glasgow, G12 8QQ, United Kingdom, Tel:
+44 141 330-6526, Fax: +44 141 330-4943

• **Manchester** — Northern College — Luther King House (s6315)
Type of school: **Graduate/Univ and Undergraduate school** Founded in **1756/ 1968** Degrees offered: **MTh, Dipl Th, BTh** Offers training for pastors: **yes** for lay persons: **yes** Type of available practical training: **preaching, pastoral care, also developing now an MA in Missiology** Admission requirements: **ordained and over 25 years** Languages in use: **English** Full/part-time staff: **3 / 2** National/foreign students: **40 / nc** Library size: **25,000** Doctrinal basis: **refer to United Ref Ch** Worship life offered: **daily** In relations with: **United Reformed Church, Congregational Church**

Address: Northern College — Luther King House, Luther King House, Brighton Grove Rusholme,
GB-Manchester, M14 5JP, United Kingdom, Tel: +44 161 224-4381, Fax: +44 161
248-9201

• **Nottingham** — East Midlands Ministry Training Course (s6308)
Type of school: **Graduate+Pastor/Evangelist** Offers training for pastors: **yes** for lay persons: **yes** Type of available practical training: **practical theology** Languages in use: **English** Full/part-time staff: **26** National/foreign students: **76 / nc** Doctrinal basis: **ecumenical** In relations with: **ecumenical course, Ch of England, Meth Ch, United Reformed Ch**

Address: East Midlands Ministry Training Course, The Orchards Annex, University Park, GB-
Nottingham, NG7 2RD, United Kingdom, Tel: +44 115 951-4854, E-mail:
emmtc@Nottingham.ac.uk

• **Old Aberdeen** — Department of Divinity — University Annex of Aberdeen (s6322)
Type of school: **Graduate/Univ** Founded in **1495** Degrees offered: **BD, BTh, MA, LicTh, MTh, MPhil, BD, PhD, DiplM** Offers training for pastors: **yes** for teachers: **yes** for lay persons: **yes** Type of available practical training: **preaching, pastoral care, religious education** Admission requirements: **2 classes at A-level** Languages in use: **English** Full/part-time staff: **14 / 3** National/foreign students: **200 / 50** Library size: **20,000** Doctrinal basis: **none** Worship life offered: **weekly** In relations with: **Church of Scotland**

Address: Department of Divinity — University of Aberdeen, King's College, GB-Old Aberdeen,
AB9 2VB, United Kingdom, Tel: +44 1224 27-2380, Fax: +44 1224 27-3750, E-mail: di-
vinity@abdn.ac.uk

• **Oxford** — Mansfield College Oxford (s6307)
Type of school: **Graduate/Univ** Founded in **1886** Degrees offered: **ThD, PhD in Theol, MA in Theol, BDiv, CertTh, MDiv, BTh** Offers training for pastors: **yes** Type of available practical training: **all normal ministerial training requirements** Admission requirements: **normally 1st degree** Languages in use: **English** Full/part-time staff: **5 / 5** National/foreign students: **47 / 5** Library size: **12,000** Doctrinal basis: **none** Worship life offered: **daily** In relations with: **United Ref Ch, Congregational Federation**

Address: Mansfield College Oxford, Oxford University, Mansfield Rd., GB-Oxford, OX1 3TF, United Kingdom, Tel: +44 1865 270-999, Fax: +44 1865 270-970, E-mail: @Oxford.ac.uk

- **Oxford** — Oxford Centre for Mission Studies (s6323)
Type of school: **Mission Institute** Founded in **1983** Degrees offered: **MPh, MA, PhD** Offers training for pastors: **yes** for teachers: **yes** for lay persons: **yes** Languages in use: **English** Full/part-time staff: **2 / 3** National/foreign students: **83 / nc** Library size: **8,000** Worship life offered: **daily**

Address: Oxford Centre for Mission Studies, P.O. Box 70, Woodstock Rd., Oxford, OX2 6HB, United Kingdom, Tel: +44 1865 556071, Fax: +44 1865 510823, E-mail: 100270.2155@compuserve.com

- **St. Andrews** — Faculty of Divinity — University of St. Andrews (s6301)
Type of school: **Graduate/Univ** Founded in **1439** Degrees offered: **BDiv(Hons), MTh (Hons), MA (Hons), M in Letters, MPhil, PhD** Offers training for pastors: **yes** for teachers: **yes** for lay persons: **yes** Type of available practical training: **preaching, homiletics, pastoral care, counseling, workshops on worship and ministry provided for church candidates** Admission requirements: **previous degree or British A-Level or Scottish Highers (3Bs or 2 Bs and 2Cs) depending upon the degree program** Languages in use: **English** Full/part-time staff: **14** National/foreign students: **210 / 37** Library size: **30,000** Doctrinal basis: **none** Worship life offered: **weekly university chapel service Sun+Thurs**

Address: Faculty of Divinity — University of St. Andrews, St. Mary's College, GB-St. Andrews, KY 16 9JU, United Kingdom, Tel: +44 1334 46-2851, Fax: +44 1334 46-2852, E-mail: rap@st-andrews.ac.uk

UNITED STATES

- **Atlanta** — Johnson C. Smith Theological Seminary (s3228)
Type of school: **Graduate/Univ** Founded in **1867** Degrees offered: **MDiv, MA in Ch Music, MA in Christian Education, MA in Public Health and MDiv, DMin, ThD in pastoral care+counseling** Offers training for pastors: **yes** for teachers: **yes** for lay persons: **yes** Type of available practical training: **preaching, pastoral care, religious education** Admission requirements: **BA degree of bachelor equivalent** Languages in use: **English** Full/part-time staff: **24 / 15** National/foreign students: **450 / 8** Library size: **600,000** Doctrinal basis: **Ref tradition** Worship life offered: **2 times per week during school year** In relations with: **Presb Ch USA**

Address: Johnson C. Smith Theological Seminary, 700 MLKing JR Dr. SW, Atlanta, GA 30314, United States, Tel: +1 404 527-7781, Fax: +1 404 614-6349

- **Austin** — Austin Presbyterian Theological Seminary (s3204)
Type of school: **Seminary** Founded in **1902** Degrees offered: **MA, MDiv, DMin**

Offers training for pastors: **nc** Languages in use: **English** Full/part-time staff: **14 / 14** National/foreign students: **279 / nc** Library size: **150,000** In relations with: **Presb Ch USA**

Address: Austin Presbyterian Theological Seminary, 100, E. 27th Street, Austin, TX 78705-5711, United States, Tel: +1 512 472-6736, Fax: +1 512 479-0438

• **Bangor** — Bangor Theological Seminary (s3213)
Type of school: **Graduate/Univ** Founded in **1814** Degrees offered: **MDiv, BA in Rel, MTS, DMin, MDiv required** Offers training for pastors: **yes** for teachers: **yes** for lay persons: **yes** Type of available practical training: **executive program of supervised practice, course on preaching, counseling, pastoral care, religious education + education** Admission requirements: **depends on degree program** Languages in use: **English** Full/part-time staff: **10** National/foreign students: **200 / 1** Library size: **120,000** Doctrinal basis: **none** Worship life offered: **daily** In relations with: **United Church of Christ**

Address: Bangor Theological Seminary, 300 Union Street, Bangor, Maine 04401, United States, Tel: +1 207 942-6781, Fax: +1 207 990-1267, E-mail: SU-SAN_DAVIES@BTSGATE.CAPS.MAINE.EDU

• **Berkeley** — Pacific School of Religion (s3225)
Type of school: **Graduate/Univ** Degrees offered: **MDiv, MA in Religion, DMin, Joint MDiv/MBA/MAR/MBA** Offers training for pastors: **yes** for teachers: **yes** for lay persons: **yes** Type of available practical training: **preaching pastoral care, religious education (under supervised practice of Ministry program)** Admission requirements: **BA degree** Languages in use: **English** Full/part-time staff: **14 / 30** National/foreign students: **200 / 17** Library size: **295,000** Worship life offered: **5 times per week Mon-Fri** In relations with: **United Church of Christ, multidenominational**

Address: Pacific School of Religion, 1798 Scenic Ave., Berkeley, CA 94709, United States, Tel: +1 510 848-0528, Fax: +1 510 845-8948

• **Boise** — Boise Bible College (s3243)
Founded in **1945** Degrees offered: **Cert Bible, BA, BS** Offers training for pastors: **nc** Languages in use: **English** Full/part-time staff: **7 / 10** National/foreign students: **150 / nc** Library size: **30,000** In relations with: **Church of Christ, Christian Churches**

Address: Boise Bible College, 8695 Marigold Street, Boise, ID 83714, United States, Tel: +1 208 376-7731

• **Cambridge** — Harvard Divinity School (s3216)
Type of school: **Graduate/Univ** Founded in **1816** Degrees offered: **MTh, MDiv, ThD, MTh** Offers training for pastors: **yes** for teachers: **yes** for lay persons: **yes** Type of available practical training: **preaching, pastoral care, religious education** Admission requirements: **depends on program (see catalogue)** Languages in use: **English** Full/part-time staff: **60** National/foreign students: **550 / 55** Li-

brary size: **450,000** Doctrinal basis: **none** Worship life offered: **several times weekly**

Address: Harvard Divinity School, 45 Francis Avenue, Cambridge, MA 02138, United States, Tel: +1 617 495-5761, Fax: +1 617 495-9489, E-mail: ralbert@div.harvard.edu

- **Charlotte** — Reformed Theological Seminary (s3245)
Type of school: **Seminary** Founded in **1992** Degrees offered: **MA, MDiv, DMin** Offers training for pastors: **yes** for teachers: **yes** for lay persons: **yes** Type of available practical training: **400 field hours required for MDiv** Admission requirements: **bachelor** Languages in use: **English** Full/part-time staff: **5 / 3** National/foreign students: **381 / 8** Library size: **35,000** Doctrinal basis: **Evang, Trinitarian, Biblical, WestConf, WestCat** Worship life offered: **twice weekly** In relations with: **PCA, EPC, ARP, Orth Presb Ch**

Address: Reformed Theological Seminary, 2101 Camel Rd., Charlotte, NC 28226-6399, United States, Tel: +1 704 366-5066, Fax: +1 704 366-9295, E-mail: 102336.1507@compuserve.com

- **Chicago** — Chicago Theological Seminary (s3203)
Type of school: **Seminary** Degrees offered: **MDiv, MA, STM, DMin, PhD** Offers training for pastors: **yes** for teachers: **yes** Type of available practical training: **preaching, pastoral care, religious education** Languages in use: **English** Full/part-time staff: **12 / 18** National/foreign students: **233 / 42** Doctrinal basis: **transformative, liberal, left** Worship life offered: **weekly, by subjects more frequently** In relations with: **United Church of Christ (UCC), closely tied/affiliated, yet free-standing**

Address: Chicago Theological Seminary, 5757 S. University Ave., Chicago, IL 60637, United States, Tel: +1 312 752-5757, Fax: +1 312 752-5925

- **Chicago** — McCormick Theological Seminary (s3237)
Type of school: **Graduate Seminary** Founded in **1829** Degrees offered: **MDiv, MATS, DMin** Offers training for pastors: **yes** Type of available practical training: **preaching, pastoral care, religious education** Languages in use: **English, Korean, Spanish** Full/part-time staff: **27** National/foreign students: **175 / nc** Library size: **460,000** Worship life offered: **weekly** In relations with: **Presb Ch USA**

Address: McCormick Theological Seminary, 5555 South Woodlawn Avenue, Chicago, IL 60637, United States, Tel: +1 773 947-6255, Fax: +1 773 947-6273, E-mail: mccormick.seminary@pcusa.org

- **Chicago** — North Park Theological Seminary (s3200)
Type of school: **Graduate/Univ** Degrees offered: **MDiv, MA Chr Education, MATh, DMin** Offers training for pastors: **yes** for teachers: **yes** for lay persons: **yes** Type of available practical training: **preaching, pastoral care, religious education** Admission requirements: **MDiv, MA in Christian Education, MA in Theol Studies, DMin** Languages in use: **English** Full/part-time staff: **15 / 23** National/foreign students: **160 / 0** Library size: **75,000** Worship life offered: **3 times per week** In relations with: **The Evangelical Covenant Church**

Address: North Park Theological Seminary, 3225 W. Foster Ave., Chicago, IL 60625, United
States, Tel: +1 312 244-6210, Fax: +1 312 244-6244

- **Cincinnati** — Cincinnati Bible College and Seminary (s3246)
Type of school: **Graduate College** Founded in **1924** Degrees offered: **Assoc. of
Arts, BA, BS, MA, MMin, MDiv, BMus, MRE** Offers training for pastors: **yes**
for teachers: **yes** for lay persons: **yes** Type of available practical training: **preaching, pastoral care, religious education** Languages in use: **English** Full/part-time
staff: **27 / 39** National/foreign students: **908 / nc** Library size: **101,000** Worship
life offered: **twice a week** In relations with: **Christian Churches, Church of
Christ**

Address: Cincinnati Bible College and Seminary, P.O. Box 04320, 2700 Glenway Avenue,
Cincinnati, OH 45204-3200, United States

- **Decatur** — Columbia Theological Seminary (s3230)
Type of school: **Graduate/Univ** Founded in **1828** Degrees offered: **MDiv, MA,
MTh, DMin, ThD (in pastoral care)** Offers training for pastors: **yes** for teachers:
yes for lay persons: **yes** Type of available practical training: **lay education, continuing education programs** Admission requirements: **Bachelor for MDiv +
MA, Master for ThM, DMin, ThD** Languages in use: **English** Full/part-time
staff: **24 / 23** National/foreign students: **600 / 25** Library size: **125,000** Doctrinal
basis: **nothing formally** Worship life offered: **daily every class day** In relations
with: **Presbyterian Church, USA**

Address: Columbia Theological Seminary, P.O. Box 520, 701 Columbia Drive, Decatur, GA 30031,
United States, Tel: +1 404 378-8821, Fax: +1 404 377-9696

- **Deerfield** — Trinity Evangelical Divinity School (s3247)
Type of school: **Seminary** Founded in **1897** Degrees offered: **MA, MDiv, PhD**
Offers training for pastors: **yes** for teachers: **yes** for lay persons: **yes** Type of available practical training: **preaching, pastoral care, religious education** Admission
requirements: **depends on program** Languages in use: **English** Full/part-time
staff: **44 / 7** National/foreign students: **1,850 / 160** Library size: **240,000** Doctrinal
basis: **Evangelical Free Church of America** Worship life offered: **twice weekly**
In relations with: **Evangelical Free Church of America**

Address: Trinity Evangelical Divinity School, 2065 Half Day Rd., Deerfield, IL 60015, United
States, Tel: +1 847 945-8800, Fax: +1 847 317-8097, E-mail: tedsadm@tiu.edu

- **Dubuque** — Theological Seminary — University of Dubuque (s3224)
Type of school: **Graduate/Univ** Founded in **1852** Degrees offered: **MDiv, MAR,
DMin, Joint MDiv/MBA MAR/MBA** Offers training for pastors: **yes** for teachers: **yes** for lay persons: **yes** Type of available practical training: **under the supervised practice of Ministry program** Admission requirements: **depends on degree sought** Languages in use: **English** Full/part-time staff: **9 / 13** National/
foreign students: **137 / 7** Library size: **160,000** Doctrinal basis: **affiliation with
PCUSA** Worship life offered: **5 times per week (Monday-Friday)** In relations
with: **Presb Ch USA**

Address: Theological Seminary — University of Dubuque, 2000 University Ave., Dubuque, IA
52001-5050, United States, Tel: +1 319 589-3122, Fax: +1 319 589-3110

• **Due West** — Erskine Theological Seminary (s3248)
Type of school: **Seminary** Founded in **1837** Offers training for pastors: **nc** Languages in use: **English** Full/part-time staff: **17 / 7** National/foreign students: **310 / nc** Library size: **145,000**

Address: Erskine Theological Seminary, P.O. Box 172, Due West, SC 29639, United States

• **Dyer** — Mid-America Reformed Seminary (s3233)
Type of school: **Graduate/Univ** Degrees offered: **MDiv, BTh, BTS** Offers training for pastors: **yes** Type of available practical training: **preaching, pastoral care, religious education** Admission requirements: **bachelor's degree** Languages in use: **English** Full/part-time staff: **4** National/foreign students: **25 / 9** Library size: **31,000** Worship life offered: **3 times per week** In relations with: **Trinity Ref Church, Canada**

Address: Mid-America Reformed Seminary, 229 Seminary Drive, Dyer, Indiana 46311, United
States, Tel: +1 219 864-2400, Fax: +1 219 864-2410

• **Edinburgh** — Rio Grande Bible Institute (s3249)
Type of school: **Undergraduate/Bible school** Founded in **1946** Degrees offered: **1 year Dipl, 4 year Dipl in Biblical Studies** Offers training for pastors: **yes** for teachers: **yes** for lay persons: **yes** Type of available practical training: **preaching, pastoral care, religious education** Admission requirements: **born again, 18 years old, high school graduate** Languages in use: **Spanish** Full/part-time staff: **17 / 8** national/foreign students: **132 / 122** Library size: **13,000** Worship life offered: **twice weekly**

Address: Rio Grande Bible Institute, 4300 South Business 281, Edinburgh, TX 78539, United
States, Tel: +1 956 380-8100, Fax: +1 956 380-8256, E-mail: rgbimail@juno.com

• **Edmonds** — Puget Sound Christian College (s3250)
Type of school: **Undergraduate/Bible school** Founded in **1950** Degrees offered: **Bible Cert, Assoc. of Arts, BA in Bible** Offers training for pastors: **yes** for teachers: **yes** for laypersons: **yes** Type of available practical training: **preaching, pastoral care, religious education** Admission requirements: **high school transcript** Languages in use: **English** Full/part-time staff: **19 / 6** National/foreign students: **215 / nc** Library size: **20,000** Doctrinal basis: **Evangelical** Worship life offered: **2 times per week** In relations with: **founded by Christian Churches / Churches of Christ**

Address: Puget Sound Christian College, 410 Fourth Ave. N, Edmonds, WA 98020-3171, United
States, Tel: +1 425 775-8686, Fax: +1 425 775-8688

• **Enid** — Phillips Theological Seminary (s3251)
Type of school: **Seminary** Founded in **1906** Degrees offered: **MA in Pastoral Care, Religious Education and Counseling, MTh, MDiv, DMin** Offers training for pastors: **yes** for teachers: **yes** for lay persons: **yes** Type of available practical training: **preaching, pastoral care, religious education** Admission requirements:

baccalaureate degree Languages in use: **English** Full/part-time staff: **20** National/foreign students: **230 / 3** Library size: **110,000** Doctrinal basis: **none** Worship life offered: **3 times per week** In relations with: **Christian Church (Disciples)**

Address: Phillips Theological Seminary, P.O. Box 2335, 102 University Dr., Enid, OK 73702, United States, Tel: +1 405 548-2238, Fax: +1 405 237-7686, E-mail: president@ptsem.org

- **Eugene** — Northwest Christian College (s3252)
Type of school: **College** Founded in **1895** Degrees offered: **BA, Pastoral Min, BS, Youth Min, MA in Marriage and Family Therapy** Offers training for pastors: **yes** Languages in use: **English** Full/part-time staff: **16 / 31** National/foreign students: **85 / nc** Library size: **46,000** In relations with: **Christian Church (Disciples of Christ)**

Address: Northwest Christian College, 828 E 11th Avenue, Eugene, OR 97401-9983, United States, Tel: +1 503 343-1641

- **Gardena** — Reformed Presbyterian Seminary (s3207)
Type of school: **Graduate** Degrees offered: **MDiv, ThM, DMin, MAR** Offers training for pastors: **yes** for teachers: **yes** Type of available practical training: **training young men for gospel ministry, women are trained for Sunday school, school, and Christian education ministries** Admission requirements: **Bachelor of Arts degree** Languages in use: **Korean, English** Full/part-time staff: **20** National/foreign students: **40 / 0** Library size: **20,000** Doctrinal basis: **WestConf, WestCats** Worship life offered: **daily** In relations with: **North American Presbyterian and Reformed Council (NAPARC), Korean American Presbyterian Church (KAPC)**

Address: Reformed Presbyterian Seminary, 1901 W. 166th St., Gardena, CA 90247, United States, Tel: +1 310 515-7696, Fax: +1 310 515-2747

- **Grand Rapids** — Calvin Theological Seminary (s3222)
Type of school: **Graduate Seminary** Founded in **1876** Degrees offered: **MDiv, MA Church Education, MA Missions, MTS, MTh, PhD** Offers training for pastors: **yes** for teachers: **yes** Type of available practical training: **preaching, pastoral care, religious education** Admission requirements: **stated in catalog, BA degree or equivalent** Languages in use: **English** Full/part-time staff: **21 / 3** National/foreign students: **260 / 50** Library size: **600,000** Doctrinal basis: **BelgC, HeidC, CDort** Worship life offered: **3 times per week** In relations with: **Christian Reformed Church in North America**

Address: Calvin Theological Seminary, 3233 Burton Street SE, 1 Grand Rapids, MI 49546-4387, United States, Tel: +1 616 957-6036, Fax: +1 616 957-8621, E-mail: kprg@calvin.edu

- **Grand Rapids** — Puritan Reformed Theological Seminary (s3212)
Type of school: **Graduate School** Degrees offered: **MDiv equivalent** Offers training for pastors: **yes** Type of available practical training: **preaching, pastoral care, religious education** Admission requirements: **knowing the Bible, special inter-**

view Languages in use: **English** Full/part-time staff: **3** National/foreign students: **4 / 0** Library size: **18,000** Doctrinal basis: **3 Forms of Unity** Worship life offered: **weekly** In relations with: **Heritage Netherlands Reformed Congregations/USA**

Address: Puritan Reformed Theological Seminary, 2115 Romenece NE, Grand Rapids, MI 49503, United States, Tel: +1 616 459-6565, Fax: +1 616 459-7709, E-mail: jrbeeke@aol.com

• **Grand Rapids** — Reformed Bible College (s3211)
Type of school: **Undergraduate/Bible school** Founded in **1939** Degrees offered: **Bible Knowledge, Cert of Religious Education, Associate in Religious Education** Offers training for pastors: **yes** for teachers: **yes** for lay persons: **yes** Type of available practical training: **preaching, pastoral care, religious education** Admission requirements: **high school or equivalent** Languages in use: **English** Full/part-time staff: **11** National/foreign students: **245 / 19** Library size: **47,000** Doctrinal basis: **Reformed Standards of Unity** Worship life offered: **3 times per week** In relations with: **Christian Reformed, Ref Church in America**

Address: Reformed Bible College, 3333 East Beltline, NE, Grand Rapids, MI 49525-9749, United States, Tel: +1 616 222-3045, +1 616 222-3000, Fax: +1 616 363-9771

• **Grandville** — Theological School of the Protestant Reformed Churches (s3209)
Type of school: **Graduate School** Degrees offered: **not degree-granting, 4 year program is the equivalent of a MDiv** Offers training for pastors: **yes** Type of available practical training: **practice preaching, half-year internship in catechism teaching and pastoral care, religious education** Admission requirements: **Bachelor-level degree (including certain required courses)** Languages in use: **English** Full/part-time staff: **3** National/foreign students: **10 / 1** Library size: **6,000** Doctrinal basis: **HeidC, CDort, BelgC** Worship life offered: **daily** In relations with: **Protestant Reformed Churches in America**

Address: Theological School of the Protestant Reformed Churches, 4949 Ivanrest Ave., Grandville, MI 49418, United States, Tel: +1 616 531-1490, Fax: +1 616 513-3033, E-mail: 74170.3215@compuserve.com

• **Hartford** — Hartford Seminary (s3253)
Type of school: **Graduate/Univ** Founded in **1833** Degrees offered: **MA (Min, Leadership), MA (Islamic Studies), DMin** Offers training for pastors: **yes** for teachers: **yes** for lay persons: **yes** Admission requirements: **transcripts, personal statement, recommendations** Languages in use: **English and Spanish** Full/part-time staff: **12** National/foreign students: **181 / 6** Library size: **74,100** Doctrinal basis: **none** Worship life offered: **weekly on Monday mornings** In relations with: **historical relationship with Congregationalism through the United Church of Christ**

Address: Hartford Seminary, 77 Sherman Street, Hartford, CT 06105-2260, United States, Tel: +1 860 509-9500, Fax: +1 860 509-9509

• **Holland** — Western Theological Seminary (s3231)
Type of school: **Graduate/Univ** Founded in **1866** Degrees offered: **MDiv, MRE,**

MTh (for international students degrees in Ministry, DMin) Offers training for pastors: **yes** for teachers: **yes** for lay persons: **yes** Type of available practical training: **preaching, pastoral care, religious education** Admission requirements: **College/University degree from accredited College/University** Languages in use: **English** Full/part-time staff: **12 / 10** National/foreign students: **140 / 6** Library size: **250,000** Doctrinal basis: **see Ref Ch in America** Worship life offered: **5 times per week** In relations with: **Ref Church in America**

Address: Western Theological Seminary Beardslee Library, 101 East 13th Street, Holland, MI 49423, United States, Tel: +1 616 392-8555, Fax: +1 616 392-7717

• **Indianapolis** — Christian Theological Seminary (s3254)
Type of school: **Seminary** Founded in **1958** Degrees offered: **MA in Sacred Theol, MDiv** Offers training for pastors: **nc** Languages in use: **English** Full/part-time staff: **18 / 1** National/foreign students: **160 / nc** Library size: **30,000** In relations with: **Christian Church (Disciples of Christ)**

Address: Christian Theological Seminary, 1000 W. 42nd St., Indianapolis, IN 46208-0267, United States

• **Jackson** — Reformed Theological Seminary (s3241)
Type of school: **Graduate Seminary** Founded in **1964** Degrees offered: **DMissiology, DMin, MDiv, MA, MTh** Offers training for pastors: **yes** for teachers: **yes** for lay persons: **yes** Type of available practical training: **preaching, pastoral care, religious education** Admission requirements: **Bachelor's** Languages in use: **English** Full/part-time staff: **42 / 5** National/foreign students: **1,200 / 60** Library size: **195,000** Doctrinal basis: **WestConf, WestCats** Worship life offered: **2 times per week** In relations with: **na**

Address: Reformed Theological Seminary, 5422 Clinton Blvd., Jackson, Mississippi 39209, United States, Tel: +1 601 922-4988, Fax: +1 601 922-1153, E-mail: afreundt@aol.com

• **Johnson City** — Emmanuel School of Religion (s3255)
Type of school: **Graduate Seminary** Founded in **1961** Degrees offered: **MA in Religion, MDiv, DMin** Offers training for pastors: **yes** for teachers: **yes** for lay persons: **yes** Type of available practical training: **preaching, pastoral care, religious education** Admission requirements: **baccalaureate degree** Languages in use: **English** Full/part-time staff: **10 / 4** National/foreign students: **165 / 14** Library size: **96,000** Worship life offered: **4 times per week** In relations with: **Christian Churches, Church of Christ**

Address: Emmanuel School of Religion, 1 Walker Dr., Johnson City, TN 37601-9989, United States, Tel: +1 423 926-1186, Fax: +1 423 926-6198, E-mail: http://www.esr.edu

• **Kissimee** — Florida Christian College (s3256)
Type of school: **College** Founded in **1976** Degrees offered: **Assoc. of Science, BA, BS, BTh** Offers training for pastors: **nc** Languages in use: **English** Full/part-time staff: **8 / 10** National/foreign students: **165 / nc** Library size: **31,000** In relations with: **Christian Churches, Church of Christ**

Address: Florida Christian College, 1011 Bil Beck Blvd., Kissimee, FL 34744, United States, Tel:
+1 407 847-8966, Fax: +1 407 847-8966

- **Kosciusko** — Magnolia Bible College (s3258)
Type of school: **Undergraduate Bible College** Founded in **1976** Degrees offered:
BA in Bible, BTh Offers training for pastors: **yes** for teachers: **yes** Admission re-
quirements: **high school diploma** Languages in use: **English** Full/part-time staff:
4 / 7 National/foreign students: **60 / nc** Library size: **35,000** Doctrinal basis: **Bible**
Worship life offered: **daily** In relations with: **Churches of Christ**

Address: Magnolia Bible College, P.O. Box 1109, Kosciusko, MS 39090, United States

- **La Mirada** — Talbot School of Theology (s3259)
Type of school: **Graduate/Univ+Undergraduate/Bible school** Founded in **1952**
Degrees offered: **Cert in Bible Studies, MA, MDiv, MTh, DM, MTh, EdD** Of-
fers training for pastors: **yes** for teachers: **yes** for lay persons: **yes** Type of available
practical training: **preaching, pastoral care, religious education** Admission requirements: **Bachelor's degree; statement of conversion; 3 reference forms**
Languages in use: **English** Full/part-time staff: **36 / 16** National/foreign students:
576 / 81 Library size: **196,000** Worship life offered: **3 times per week** In relations
with: **Covenant, Friends, Christian and Missionary Alliance (CMA)**

Address: Talbot School of Theology, 13800 Biola Ave., La Mirada, CA 90369, United States, Tel:
+1 562 903-6000, Fax: +1 562 903-4759, E-mail: dennis-gaines@peter.biola.edu

- **Lakeland** — Whitefield Theological Seminary (s3240)
Type of school: **Graduate Seminary** Degrees offered: **MDiv, BD, MA, MA in
Religion, MTh, PhD, ThD, DMin** Offers training for pastors: **yes** for teachers:
yes Type of available practical training: **ministerial practicums** Admission re-
quirements: **BA or equivalent** Languages in use: **English** Full/part-time staff: **20**
National/foreign students: **65 / 10** Library size: **8,000** Doctrinal basis: **WestConf**
Worship life offered: **weekly** In relations with: **Reformed Presbyterian Church
General Assembly**

Address: Whitefield Theological Seminary, P.O. Box 6321, 1347 Ariana St., Lakeland, FL 33807,
United States, Tel: +1 941 683-7899, Fax: +1 941 607-6211

- **Lancaster** — Lancaster Theological Seminary (s3236)
Type of school: **Graduate/Univ** Degrees offered: **MDiv, MA in Religion, DMin**
Offers training for pastors: **yes** for teachers: **yes** for lay persons: **yes** Type of available practical training: **preaching, pastoral care, religious education** Admission
requirements: **Bachelor's degree** Languages in use: **English** Full/part-time staff:
12 / 2 National/foreign students: **200 / 1** Library size: **132,600** Worship life offered: **daily** In relations with: **United Church of Christ**

Address: Lancaster Theological Seminary, 555 W. James St., Lancaster, PA 17603-2897, United
States, Tel: +1 717 393-0654 Fax: +1 717 393-4254

- **Lexington** — Lexington Theological Seminary (s3260)
Type of school: **Seminary** Founded in **1865** Degrees offered: **MDiv, MA, MA in
Pastoral Studies, DMin** Offers training for pastors: **yes** for teachers: **yes** for lay

persons: **yes** Type of available practical training: **preaching, pastoral care, religious education** Admission requirements: **baccalaureate** Languages in use: **English** Full/part-time staff: **13** National/foreign students: **220 / 6** Library size: **125,000** Doctrinal basis: **none** Worship life offered: **6 times per week** In relations with: **Christian Church (Disciples of Christ)**

Address: Lexington Theological Seminary, 631 S. Limestone St., Lexington, KY 40508, United States, Tel: +1 606 252-0361, Fax: +1 606 281-6042

• **Louisville** — Louisville Presbyterian Theological Seminary (s3227)
Type of school: **Graduate Seminary** Founded in **1853** Degrees offered: **MDiv, MA, DMin, MTh** Offers training for pastors: **yes** for lay persons: **no** Type of available practical training: **preaching, pastoral care, religious education** Admission requirements: **BA** Languages in use: **English** Full/part-time staff: **18 / 25** National/foreign students: **250 / 13** Library size: **127,741** Doctrinal basis: **Reformed** Worship life offered: **4 times per week** In relations with: **PCUSA**

Address: Louisville Presbyterian Theological Seminary, 1044 Alta Vista Road, Louisville, KY 40205, United States, Tel: +1 502 895-3411, Fax: +1 502 895-1096

• **Memphis** — Memphis Theological Seminary (s3214)
Type of school: **Graduate Seminary** Founded in **1852** Degrees offered: **MA in Religion, MDiv, DMin** Offers training for pastors: **yes** for teachers: **yes** for lay persons: **yes** Type of available practical training: **preaching practicum, supervised clinical practicum, supervised parish practicum (required in MDiv courses)** Admission requirements: **Bachelor's degree from accredited college 2.5 G.P.A.** Languages in use: **English** Full/part-time staff: **12 / 5** National/foreign students: **268 / nc** Library size: **80,000** Doctrinal basis: **none** Worship life offered: **daily** In relations with: **Cumberland Presb Church**

Address: Memphis Theological Seminary, 168 East Parkway South, Memphis, Tennessee 38104, United States, Tel: +1 901 458-8232, Fax: +1 901 452-4051, E-mail: http://www.magibox.net/~Jerizholmts-page.htm/

• **New Brighton** — United Theological Seminary of Twin Cities (s3218)
Type of school: **Seminary** Founded in **1962** Degrees offered: **MDiv, MA Theol, MA Religious Leadership, MA Religious Studies/Worship and Arts/Women's Studies, DMin** Offers training for pastors: **yes** for teachers: **yes** for lay persons: **yes** Type of available practical training: **preaching, pastoral care, contextual studies requirements, involving placement in churches of other ministry settings** Admission requirements: **ordinarily, BA or equivalent** Languages in use: **English** Full/part-time staff: **14** National/foreign students: **215 / 2** Library size: **78,000** Worship life offered: **3 times per week** In relations with: **United Church of Christ**

Address: United Theological Seminary of Twin Cities, 3000 Fifth Street NW, New Brighton, MN 55112, United States, Tel: +1 612 633-4311, Fax: +1 612 633-4615

• **New Brunswick** — New Brunswick Theological Seminary (s3223)
Type of school: **Seminary** Founded in **1784** Degrees offered: **MDiv, MA, MTh**

692

and **Pastoral Care** Offers training for pastors: **yes** for teachers: **yes** for lay persons: **yes** Type of available practical training: **preaching, pastoral care, religious education** Admission requirements: **college degree from accredited college/university** Languages in use: **English, Korean** Full/part-time staff: **14 / 33** National/foreign students: **210 / 30** Library size: **150,000** Doctrinal basis: **see Ref Ch in America** Worship life offered: **5 times per week** In relations with: **Ref Ch in America**

Address: New Brunswick Theological Seminary, 17 Seminary Place, New Brunswick, New Jersey 8901, United States, Tel: +1 908 247-5241, Fax: +1 908 249-5412, E-mail: house@pilot.njin.net

• **New Haven** — Yale University (s3205)
Type of school: **Graduate/Univ** Degrees offered: **STM, MAR, MDiv** Offers training for pastors: **yes** Languages in use: **English** Full/part-time staff: **30 / 16** National/foreign students: **395 / 0** Library size: **375,000**

Address: Yale University Divinity School, New Haven, Connecticut 06511, United States, Tel: +1 203 432-5307, Fax: +1 203 432-5356

• **Newton Centre** — Andover Newton Theological School (s3235)
Type of school: **Seminary** Founded in **1807** Degrees offered: **MDiv, MA, DMin, STM** Offers training for pastors: **yes** for teachers: **yes** for lay persons: **yes** Languages in use: **English** Full/part-time staff: **16 / 8** National/foreign students: **470 / 16** Library size: **225,000** Worship life offered: **once a week** In relations with: **United Church of Christ, American Baptist Churches**

Address: Andover Newton Theological School, 210 Herrick Rd., Newton Centre, MA 02159, United States, Tel: +1 617 964-1100, Fax: +1 617 965-9756

• **Oakland** — Patten College (s3262)
Type of school: **Graduate School** Founded in **1944** Degrees offered: **BA in Biblical Studies** Offers training for pastors: **yes** Languages in use: **English** Full/part-time staff: **16 / 18** Library size: **30,000** In relations with: **Christian Evangelical Churches of America**

Address: Patten College, 2433 Coolidge Ave., Oakland, CA 94601, United States, Tel: +1 510 533-8306, Fax: +1 510 534-8564

• **Philadelphia** — Westminster Theological Seminary (s3263)
Type of school: **Seminary** Founded in **1929** Degrees offered: **MA in Religion, MDiv, DMin, PhD** Offers training for pastors: **yes** for teachers: **yes** for lay persons: **yes** Type of available practical training: **preaching, pastoral care, religious education** Admission requirements: **BA** Languages in use: **English** Full/part-time staff: **14 / 28** national/foreign students: **631 / 90** Library size: **102,600** Doctrinal basis: **WestConf** Worship life offered: **daily** In relations with: **Orthodox Presb Church, Presb Ch in America, CRCNA**

Address: Westminster Theological Seminary, P.O. Box 27009, Chestnut Hill, Philadelphia, PA 19118, United States, Tel: +1 215 887-5511, Fax: +1 215 887-5404

• **Pittsburgh** — Pittsburgh Theological Seminary (s3229)
Type of school: **Graduate Seminary** Founded in **1794** Degrees offered: **MDiv, MA, STM, DMin** Offers training for pastors: **nc** for teachers: **yes** for lay persons: **yes** Type of available practical training: **preaching, pastoral care, religious education** Admission requirements: **bachelor's degree** Languages in use: **English** Full/part-time staff: **22 / 19** National/foreign students: **302 / 6** Library size: **325,000** Doctrinal basis: **Reformed** Worship life offered: **3 times per week** In relations with: **PCUSA**

Address: Pittsburgh Theological Seminary, 616 N. Highland Ave., Pittsburgh, PA 15206-2596, United States, Tel: +1 412 362-5610, Fax: +1 412 363-3260

• **Pittsburgh** — Reformed Presbyterian Theological Seminary (s3264)
Type of school: **Graduate Seminary** Founded in **1810** Degrees offered: **MDiv, MTS** Offers training for pastors: **yes** for missionaries: **yes** for lay persons: **yes** Type of available practical training: **preaching, pastoral care, religious education** Admission requirements: **undergraduate degree** Languages in use: **English** Full/part-time staff: **5 / 6** National/foreign students: **85 / 4** Library size: **43,500** Doctrinal basis: **Westminster Standards and Testimony of Reformed Presb Ch of North America** Worship life offered: **3 times per week** In relations with: **Reformed Presbyterian Church of North America**

Address: Reformed Presbyterian Theological Seminary, 7418 Penn Ave., Pittsburgh, PA 15208, United States, Tel: +1 412 731-8690, Fax: +1 412 731-4834, E-mail: rpseminary@aol.com

• **Princeton** — Princeton Theological Seminary (s3219)
Founded in **1812** Degrees offered: **MDiv, MA, MTh, DMin, PhD** Offers training for pastors: **yes** Languages in use: **English** Full/part-time staff: **48 / 22** National/ foreign students: **824 / many** Library size: **390,000** In relations with: **PCUSA**

Address: Princeton Theological Seminary, P.O. Box 111, CN 821, Princeton, NJ 08542, United States, Tel: +1 609 921-8300, Fax: +1 609 924-2973

• **Richmond** — Union Theological Seminary and Presbyterian School of Christian Education (s3221)
Type of school: **Graduate/Univ** Founded in **1871** Degrees offered: **MDiv, DMin, MTh, PhD** Offers training for pastors: **yes** for teachers: **yes** Type of available practical training: **preaching, pastoral care, religious education** Admission requirements: **college degree from an accredited institution** Languages in use: **English** Full/part-time staff: **36** National/foreign students: **244 / 28** Library size: **291,560** Doctrinal basis: **PCUSA Book of Confession** Worship life offered: **5 times per week and a dozen or more other services** In relations with: **PCUSA**

Address: Union Theological Seminary in Virginia, 3401 Brook Road, Richmond, VA 23227, United States, Tel: +1 804 255-3919, Fax: +1 804 355-3919

• **San Anselmo** — San Francisco Theological Seminary (s3206)
Type of school: **Graduate/Univ** Founded in **1871** Degrees offered: **MDiv, MA (Theol Studies)** Offers training for pastors: **yes** for teachers: **yes** Admission re-

694

quirements: **bachelor's degree** Languages in use: **English, Korean** Full/part-time staff: **23 / 120** National/foreign students: **700 / 300** Worship life offered: **5 times per week** In relations with: **PCUSA**

Address: San Francisco Theological Seminary, 2 Kensington Rd., San Anselmo, CA 94960, United
        States, Tel: +1 415 258-6500, Fax: +1 415 258-1608, E-mail: sftsinfo@sfts.edu

• **San José** — San José Christian College (s3265)
Type of school: **College** Founded in **1939** Degrees offered: **Cert in Bible, Assoc. of Arts, BA** Offers training for pastors: **yes** Languages in use: **English, Korean, Cambodian** Full/part-time staff: **11 / 35** National/foreign students: **295 / nc** In relations with: **Christian Churches**

Address: San José Christian College, P.O. Box 1090, San José, CA 95108, United States, Tel: +1
        408 293-9058

• **St. Bonifacius** — Crown College (s3266)
Type of school: **Graduate/Univ** Founded in **1916** Degrees offered: **BA, BS, MA** Offers training for pastors: **yes** for teachers: **yes** for lay persons: **yes** Type of available practical training: **preaching, pastoral care, religious education** Admission requirements: **evangelical Christian commitment** Languages in use: **English** Full/part-time staff: **25 / 22** National/foreign students: **625 / 5** Library size: **98,000** Doctrinal basis: **Evangelical (NAE)** Worship life offered: **4 times per week** In relations with: **Christian and Missionary Alliance (CMA)**

Address: Crown College, 6425 County Rd. 30, St. Bonifacius, MN 55375, United States, Tel: +1
        612 446-4100, Fax: +1 612 446-4149, E-mail: crown@crown.edu

• **Tacoma** — Western Reformed Seminary (s3202)
Type of school: **Graduate/Univ** Degrees offered: **MDiv (3 years), Master of Arts in Biblical Studies (OT or NT emphasis = 2 years), MTh, MRS (2 years)** Offers training for pastors: **yes** for teachers: **yes** for lay persons: **yes** Type of available practical training: **preaching, pastoral care, counseling** Admission requirements: **proficiency in English; students without a BA equivalent enter on probation** Languages in use: **English** Full/part-time staff: **5** National/foreign students: **31 / 2** Library size: **25,000** Doctrinal basis: **Westminster Standards, covenantal and premillennial** Worship life offered: **weekly** In relations with: **Bible Presbyterian Church/USA**

Address: Western Reformed Seminary, Five South G St., Tacoma, WA 98405, United States, Tel:
        +1 206 272-0417, E-mail: clensch@AOC.Com

• **Webster Groves** — Eden Theological Seminary (s3232)
Type of school: **Seminary** Founded in **1850** Degrees offered: **MDiv, MTh, DMin** Offers training for pastors: **yes** for teachers: **yes** for lay persons: **yes** Type of available practical training: **field education is an essential part of MDiv program, 7 units required** Admission requirements: **bachelor's degree, church recommendations, references, autobiographical essay** Languages in use: **English** Full/part-time staff: **13** National/foreign students: **200 / 2** Library size: **204,421** Doctrinal basis: **not for admission, teaching in evang/ecumen tradition** Worship life

offered: **3 times per week** In relations with: **United Church of Christ (Congregational Christian, Evangelical, Reformed)**

Address: Eden Theological Seminary, 475 East Lockwood Ave., Webster Groves, MO 63119, United States, Tel: +1 314 961-3627, Fax: +1 314 961-5738

URUGUAY

• **Montevideo** — Latin American Faculty of Theological Studies (s2130)
Type of school: **Seminary** Degrees offered: **CertTh, Cert in Pastoral Training, Dipl in Biblical Studies** Offers training for pastors: **yes** Languages in use: **Spanish** National/foreign students: **550 / nc**

Address: Facultad Latinoamericana de Estudios teológicos, Av Agraciada 3452, Montevideo, 11700, Uruguay, Tel: +598 2 386-905, Fax: +598 2 386-905

VANUATU

• **Luganville** — Talua Ministry Training Centre (s5050)
Type of school: **Evangelist/Pastoral Training Institute** Founded in **1971/1977/ 1986** Degrees offered: **CertTh (accredited by South Pacific Association of Theology school); DiplTh (accredited; see above); Women's Program Certificate** Offers training for pastors: **yes** for teachers: **yes** for lay persons: **yes** Type of available practical training: **preaching, pastoral care, Christian education, discipleship, evangelism and mission, field education — 8 weeks for certificate students, 1 year for diploma students** Admission requirements: **Certificate Program: 6 years primary school, Diploma Program: 10 years high school or certificate program** Languages in use: **English (some Bislama, Pidgin English)** Full/part-time staff: **6 / 2** National/foreign students: **65 / 0** Library size: **6,500** Doctrinal basis: **statement of Presbyterian Church of Vanuatu** Worship life offered: **daily ½ hour worship, every Sunday whole community gathers for worship morning and evening** In relations with: **owned by the Presbyterian Church of Vanuatu, partnership with PC Australia, PC NewZealand, PCUSA**

Address: Talua Ministry Training Centre, P.O. Box 242, Luganville, Vanuatu, Fax: +678 22-910

VENEZUELA

• **Maracay** — Evangelical Seminary of Venezuela (s2140)
Founded in **1969** Degrees offered: **Lic in Prot Worship** Offers training for pas-

tors: **yes** Languages in use: **Spanish** Full/part-time staff: **12 / 2** National/foreign students: **210 / nc** Library size: **8,000**

Address: Seminario evangélico de Venezuela, Apartado 2050, Maracay, 2101.A Estado Aragua, Venezuela, Tel: +598 43 839-273, Fax: +58 9 43 832-687, E-mail: 76671.3326@compuserve.com

VIETNAM

• **Nha Trang** — Biblical and Theological Institute (s4550)
Type of school: **Undergraduate/Bible school/Theological Education by Extension Program** Founded in **1973** Degrees offered: **Cert of Biblical Theol, DiplTh** Offers training for pastors: **yes** Type of available practical training: **homiletics** Admission requirements: **high school graduate** Languages in use: **Vietnamese, English** Full/part-time staff: **3 / 5** National/foreign students: **120 / nc** Library size: **2,000** Doctrinal basis: **evangelical** In relations with: **Evangelical Protestant Church of Vietnam, CMA**

Address: Institut théologique et biblique, P.O. Box 73, Nha Trang, Vietnam

WESTERN SAMOA

• **Apia** — Malua Theological College (s5040)
Type of school: **Seminary** Degrees offered: **DiplTh, BTh, BDiv** Offers training for pastors: **yes** for teachers: **yes** Type of available practical training: **preaching, pastoral care, religious education** Admission requirements: **entrance examination** Languages in use: **English, Samoan** Full/part-time staff: **12** National/foreign students: **91 / 3** Library size: **10,000** Doctrinal basis: **Reformed** Worship life offered: **daily** In relations with: **Congregational Christian Church in Samoa**

Address: Malua Theological College, P.O. Box 468, Private Bag, Apia, Western Samoa, Tel: +685 42303, Fax: +685 42301, E-mail: maluatc@talofa.net

ZAMBIA

• **Kitwe** — Mindolo Ecumenical Foundation (s1250)
Type of school: **Mission Institute** Degrees offered: **DiplTh** Offers training for lay persons: **yes** Admission requirements: **school certificate** Languages in use: **English** Full/part-time staff: **24** National/foreign students: **118 / 50** Library size: **45,000** Worship life offered: **beginning of every workday**

Address: Mindolo Ecumenical Institute, P.O. Box 21493, Kitwe, Zambia, Tel: +260 2 211 488, 214 572, 211 269, Fax: +260 2 211001

- **Kitwe** — United Church of Zambia Theological College (s1251)

Type of school: **Undergraduate College** Founded in **1961** Degrees offered: **DiplTh, CertMin** Offers training for pastors: **yes** Type of available practical training: **pastoral care, religious education through visitation and counseling, worship, preaching, regular, funerals, baptism, special church functions, activities of youth, men + women, community functions** Admission requirements: **O-level certificate with 5 passes, including English** Languages in use: **English** Full/part-time staff: **6** National/foreign students: **25 / 4** Library size: **9,000** Doctrinal basis: **Presbyterian / Congregational** Worship life offered: **daily morning chapel worship, Holy Communion service twice during the term** In relations with: **United Church of Zambia**

Address: United Church of Zambia Theological College, P.O. Box 20429, Kitwe, Zambia, Tel: +260 2 210-218, Fax: +260 2 210-218

- **Lusaka** — Justo Mwale Theological College (s1252)

Type of school: **Undergraduate/Bible school** Founded in **1961** Degrees offered: **DiplTh, BTh, Orientation in Theol, Women's Ministry Cert, Women's Ministry Cert. Advanced** Offers training for pastors: **yes** Type of available practical training: **very intensive: preaching, pastoral care, religious education** Admission requirements: **DiplTh for O-level GCE including English, BTh, Five GCE O-level credits including English** Languages in use: **English** Full/part-time staff: **10** National/foreign students: **57 / 4** Library size: **12,500** Doctrinal basis: **BelgC, HeidC, CDort** Worship life offered: **daily morning before class starts, every Friday whole students body + staff** In relations with: **Reformed Ch in Zambia, Reformed Ch in Zimbabwe, Presb Ch in Zambia, Church of Central Africa Presbyterian (Zambia Synod), Ch of Central Africa Presb (Livingstonia Synod), Dutch Reformed Ch in Botswana**

Address: Justo Mwale Theological College, P.O. Box 310199, Lusaka, 10101 Zambia, Tel: +260 1 294-252, Fax: +260 1 294-252, E-mail: jvanwyk@zamnet.zm

- **MuFumbwe** — Chizela Bible Institute (s1254)

Type of school: **Undergraduate/Bible school** Founded in **1948** Degrees offered: **Cert in Biblical Instruction** Offers training for pastors: **yes** for teachers: **no** for lay persons: **yes** Type of available practical training: **preaching, pastoral care, religious education** Admission requirements: **grade 7 (for Kaonde-speaking), grade 9 (for English-speaking), leadership potentials** Languages in use: **Kikaonde, English** Full/part-time staff: **4 / 7** National/foreign students: **29 / 3** Doctrinal basis: **Evangelical Church of Zambia** Worship life offered: **occasional** In relations with: **Evangelical Church in Zambia**

Address: Chizela Bible Institute, P.O. Box 130015, MuFumbwe, Zambia, Tel: ncechzmuk@zamnet.zm

698

ZIMBABWE

- **Harare** — Department of Religious Studies and Philosophy — University of Zimbabwe (s1262)
Type of school: **Graduate/Univ+Undergraduate/Bible school** Founded in **1967** Degrees offered: **BA Hons Rel Studies, MA Rel Studies, PhD Rel Studies** Offers training for pastors: **yes** for teachers: **yes** for lay persons: **yes** Type of available practical training: **preaching, pastoral care, religious education by affiliated colleges** Admission requirements: **Cambridge University A-levels or Diploma in Religious Studies** Languages in use: **English** Full/part-time staff: **24** National/ foreign students: **814 / 25** Doctrinal basis: **none** Worship life offered: **often**

Address: Dept. of Religious Studies and Philosophy — University of Zimbabwe, P.O. Box MP, 167 Mount Pleasant, Harare, Zimbabwe, Tel: +263 4 303-211 ext. 1248, Fax: +263 4 333-407, E-mail: rscp@esanet.zw

- **Harare** — United Theological College (s1260)
Type of school: **Graduate/Univ** Founded in **1956** Degrees offered: **DiplTh** Offers training for pastors: **yes** Admission requirements: **4 O-level subjects** Languages in use: **English** Full/part-time staff: **7 / 3** National/foreign students: **90 / nc** Library size: **4,875** Doctrinal basis: **yes** In relations with: **Presbyterian Ch, United Congreg Ch of Zimbabwe (UCCZ), UCC of Southern Africa**

Address: United Theological College, P.O. Box H.97, Hatfield, Harare, Zimbabwe, Tel: +263 4 57-3629

- **Masvingo** — Murray Theological College — Morgenster Mission (s1261)
Type of school: **Pastor/Evangelist/Missionary** Founded in **1925** Degrees offered: **DiplTh** Offers training for pastors: **yes** for teachers: **no** for lay persons: **yes** Type of available practical training: **preaching, pastoral care, religious education** Admission requirements: **O-level and above** Languages in use: **English** Full/ part-time staff: **5 / 2** National/foreign students: **16 / 2** Library size: **+4,000** Doctrinal basis: **Reformed** Worship life offered: **daily** In relations with: **Reformed Church in Zimbabwe, REC, SAARC, WARC**

Address: Murray Theological College Morgenster Mission, P.O. Morgenster, Masvingo, Zimbabwe, Tel: +263 4 7225

4. INTERNATIONAL REFORMED ORGANIZATIONS

1. WORLD ALLIANCE OF REFORMED CHURCHES (WARC)

The World Alliance of Reformed Churches is the oldest international association of Reformed churches. It was founded by Presbyterian and Reformed leaders from North America and Britain who met in July 1875 in London. Their intention was to establish a forum of exchange and coordination. The Alliance was to manifest the fundamental unity of the Reformed churches and to facilitate common action, in particular in missionary outreach. Constitutionally the Alliance is not a church but a federation of churches. The fellowship is not based on a single common confession. Attempts in the history of the Alliance to formulate a common confession based on the many Reformed confessions did not lead to any tangible results. Article 2 of the constitution states: "Any church which accepts Jesus Christ as Lord and Saviour, holds the Word of God given in the Scriptures of the Old and New Testaments to be the supreme authority in matters of faith and life, acknowledges the need for the continuing reformation of the Church catholic, whose position in faith and evangelism is in general agreement with that of the historic Reformed confessions, recognizing that the Reformed tradition is a biblical, evangelical and doctrinal ethos, rather than any narrow and exclusive definition of faith and order, shall be eligible for membership."

In the early stages of its life the Alliance included primarily Presbyterian and Reformed churches from North America and Britain. Gradually, membership expanded to the European continent and later, especially after World War II, to Asia, Africa, and Latin America. At the first General Council 49 churches were represented; the number increased to 211 in 1997.

An important stage in the history of the Alliance was the union of the "Alliance of Reformed Churches thoughout the World holding the Presbyterian Order" and the "International Congregational Council" founded in 1892. After several years of negotiations they decided to combine efforts at the General Council in Nairobi in 1970 (see 5.A.2.a, p. 711 below).

In the beginning, the Alliance was loosely structured. Headquarters were in Edinburgh. General Councils were organized every five to eight years. The first General Council was held in 1877. One hundred and twenty years later the 23rd General Council took place in Debrecen, Hungary (August 1997).

To facilitate activities the Alliance originally operated through two practically independent sections. The first was the Western section; it grouped the Reformed churches in North America. The second, or Eastern section, comprised the churches in Britain and Ireland. In the years after World War I the churches on the European continent began to acquire more weight. In 1946 important decisions were taken. In order to give maximum support to the World Council of Churches, then in process of formation, headquarters were moved to Geneva. The Alliance adopted the policy not to duplicate any activity which could be accomplished within the framework of the World Council of Churches. The regional organizations continued in a renewed form. Today five regional organizations enrich the activities of the Alliance: The Caribbean and North American Region (CANAAC), the European Region, the Alianza de Iglesias Presbiterianas y Reformadas de America Latina (AIPRAL), the Southern Africa Alliance of Reformed Churches (SAARC), and the Region of the Far East.

Today the activities of the Alliance take place in four departments (Theology, Cooperation and Witness, Partnership, and Finances). In 1997 the secretariat in Geneva employed 12 staff members.

Throughout its history the Alliance sought to maintain communication with its member churches through the publication of a journal, first called *The Catholic Presbyterian* (1879), then *The Quarterly Register* (1886), *The Presbyterian Register* (1937), *The Presbyterian World* (1949), *The Reformed and Presbyterian World* (1956), and after the union with the Congregational churches *The Reformed World* (1970).

At different stages of its history the Alliance has taken a clear stand on public issues, e.g., on slavery or on the Armenian massacres. In the 1970s the Alliance developed a strong emphasis on the protection of human rights. Despite its loose organization it declared in 1982 the status confessionis on racism and the apartheid system and suspended two white member churches from the exercise of membership rights. While one of these churches (Nederduitsch Hervormde Kerk) left the Alliance, the larger Nederduitse Gereformeerde Kerk (NGK) maintained its membership. The suspension was lifted in 1997 on condition that the General Synod of the NGK recognize unequivocally that apartheid was in its essence wrong and sinful.

Address: World Alliance of Reformed Churches, 150 route de Ferney, P.O. Box 2100, 1211 Geneva 2, Switzerland, Tel: +41 22 791 6238, Fax: +41 22 791 6505, E-mail: Info-warc @wcc-coe.org

2. REFORMED ECUMENICAL COUNCIL (REC)

The Reformed Ecumenical Council (REC) is a council of 29 Reformed and Presbyterian churches from 21 countries around the world. Founded in 1946, it was first named Reformed Ecumenical Synod, but began calling itself a council in 1988. Its member churches include more than five million Christians.

The churches of the REC joined for closer fellowship on the basis of a shared confession of faith. The REC was formed, as its constitution says, to promote "the confessional integrity and well-being of its member churches in a continuing reformation in teaching and life, and to present to the world and to other churches a united and uniting witness" of our historic Christian faith. Membership is open to all churches who build their church life on the foundation of one of several Reformed confessions.

The REC wishes to build a growing, unified family of Reformed churches for mutual support and for an instrument to share the resources and heritage of the Reformed faith with the whole church. They support one another in the areas of ecumenical calling, biblical and confessional integrity, bearing of burdens, and healing of wounds.

The REC holds an Assembly every four years. Between assemblies, the affairs of the Council are decided by an interim committee. A permanent secretariat handles the daily business of the Council. Three major commissions assist the member churches to cooperate in the areas of mission and diakonia, theological education, and youth and Christian education.

The Commission for Mission and Diakonia (1) publishes a quarterly *Mission Bulletin* available from the secretariat. In addition, there are two important subcommittees, one on communications and media and the other on sharing resources. Through these committees the REC works to assist and build up the communities of which our churches are members.

The Commission for Theological Education and Interchange (2) works to increase cooperation in developing leadership for the churches. The Commission has a program to build up library resources for the emerging training centers of our younger churches, called the Library and Textbook Program. It also publishes a quarterly journal of exchange, called the *Theological Forum,* which is aimed at helping both pastors and theologians in learning about Reformed theology in its various forms and cultural expressions around the world.

The Commission for Youth and Christian Education (3) promotes mutual support among youth leaders in member churches. The REC also encourages a growing movement for Christian education, sometimes within the churches, but more and more frequently expressed in full-time day schools for Christian youth. The Youth Commission is assisted by a secretary for Youth and Christian Education.

The REC's secretariat is based in Grand Rapids, Michigan. The secretariat produces a monthly *News Exchange* to enhance communication among the member churches, and for individuals interested in news of Reformed churches and other ecumenical activities.

The REC sees confessional integrity as essential to its calling and purpose, and assists its member churches to maintain unity even amidst the diversity of different cultures. The REC believes its member churches embody a holistic Reformed spirituality that takes seriously public and private means of grace, and prepares God's people for works of service in every area of life to promote a unifying witness in the world.

Addresss: The Reformed Ecumenical Council, 2050 Breton Road SE, Ste. 102, Grand Rapids, MI 49546-5547, USA, Tel and Fax: +1 (616) 949-2910, alternate Fax: +1 (616) 493-9058, E-mail: rvhrec@aol.com, http://www.recweb.org

3. INTERNATIONAL FEDERATION OF FREE EVANGELICAL CHURCHES (IFFEC)

The International Federation of Free Evangelical Churches provides a loose international forum for Free Churches and Covenant Churches. It was formally organized in 1948 in Berne, Switzerland.

In 1834 the oldest Free Evangelical Church in Berne, formed in 1829, had already federated with 45 churches in Switzerland, France, and Northern Italy. In 1854 the first German Free Evangelical Church joined the association. The constitution, adopted in 1860, was built on the conviction that the Holy Scriptures, both Old and New Testaments, are inspired by God and serve as the only valid basis for faith and life.

In the middle of the 19th century a spiritual awakening led to the formation of Free Evangelical Churches (Mission Covenant Churches) in Norway, Sweden, and Denmark. Church leaders began meeting annually after the First World War (1921). They were later joined by the Evangelical Covenant Churches in the United States. Primarily at the initiative of Augustinus Keijer from the Swedish Covenant Church (1901-1969), international conferences were held in the '30s (Göteborg 1934, Prague 1936). From 1926, youth meetings were regularly held. Immediately after the War a first meeting was organized in Malmö (1945), and in 1948 the International Federation was founded. Additional churches were received into membership — from Greece, Spain, the Evangelical Free Church of the USA, — and friendly relationships were developed with churches in Belgium, Great Britain, Poland, and Romania, as well as India, Peru, and Brazil. The Federation especially cultivates contacts with churches which are the result of missionary work of member churches, primarily in Africa.

A long series of international conferences has been organized: Oslo 1950, Witten 1952, Helsinki 1953, Hilversum 1954, Hamburg 1956, Jöngköping 1958, Aeschi 1960, Aarhus 1962, Barcelona 1966, Lidingö 1967, Ewersbach 1970, Chicago 1971, Ewersbach 1974, Cap Sounion 1978, Oslo 1980.

The International Federation comprises 15 national federations: Czechia, Denmark, Finland (2), France, Germany (2), Greece, Netherlands, Norway, Spain,

Sweden, Switzerland, United States (2). Altogether the 15 federations include more than 3,200 congregations.

Address: General Office of the International Federation, Tégnergatan 8, S-11381 Stockholm, Tel: +46 8 15 18 30

4. INTERNATIONAL CONGREGATIONAL FELLOWSHIP (ICF)

This is a fellowship of individuals concerned to bear witness to the Congregational Way, rather than an association of denominations or unions of churches. Accordingly, the emphasis of its conferences, which have been held every four years since 1977, is upon witness and fellowship rather than upon ecclesial joint action. Some personal members belong to denominations which are members of the World Alliance of Reformed Churches (e.g., to the Union of Welsh Independents), while others belong to denominations which are not so affiliated (e.g., the National Association of Congregational Christian Churches of the United States, NACC). A corporation registered in Illinois raises funds to support the activities of the Fellowship.

The origins of the Fellowship lie in the failure of the NACC to secure membership of the International Congregational Council in 1962, and in the formation of the Congregational Federation in England and Wales ten years later. The latter body comprises some of the Congregational churches which declined to enter the United Reformed Church on its inception in 1972 (others who declined are the members of the Evangelical Fellowship of Congregational Churches and a number of unaffiliated churches).

Prompted by the efforts of David Watson of England and John Alexander of the United States, a group of 25 people from six countries assembled at Chiselhurst, Kent, in May 1975. They resolved to constitute the Fellowship and planned their first conference (regarded as the spiritual legatee of the International Congregational Council), which was held at General Booth College, London, in 1977. They also drew up and on May 13 signed "The Chiselhurst Thanksgiving," in which they reaffirmed their allegiance to God and to the Congregational Way.

Addresss: International Congregational Fellowship, Rev. Graham Adams, The Congregational Centre, 4, Castle Gate, Nottingham NG1 7AS, Great Britain, Tel: +44 115 941 41 33

5. INTERNATIONAL COUNCIL OF CHRISTIAN CHURCHES (ICCC)

The ICCC seeks to promote fellowship among fundamentalist churches and to provide a militant common front against theological liberalism and the ecumenical movement. It was founded by Carl McIntire in 1948 in Amsterdam a few days before the foundation of the World Council of Churches with the explicit aim "to give constructive testimony to the Lord Jesus Christ and to stand against the World Council of Churches." Carl McIntire and his movement have sought to spread the fundamentalist message to conservative Christians. In many places their activities have led to divisions. The movement is characterized by radical anti-Communism.

Before founding the ICCC Carl McIntire, born in 1906, was for several years (1933) pastor of a congr in Collingswood, NJ, USA. He then started the Bible Presbyterian Church and in 1940 founded the American Council of Christian Churches, a counterforce to the Federal Council of Churches, which, in his eyes, was too liberal and ecumenical. His criticisms also extended to the evangelical camp.

The first Assembly in Amsterdam was attended by delegates of 58 churches in 29 countries; by the 12th congress in 1988 ICCC reported 490 churches from 100 countries. In recent years several churches have withdrawn from membership. ICCC publishes the *Reformation Review*.

Its doctrinal statement reads as follows: "Among other equally Biblical truths we believe and maintain the following: a) The plenary divine inspiration of the Scripture in the original languages, their consequent inerrancy and infallibility, and, as the Word of God, the supreme and final authority in faith and life; b) The triune God, Father, Son and Holy Spirit; c) The essential absolute, eternal Deity, and the real and proper, but sinless, humanity of our Lord Jesus Christ; d) His birth of the Virgin Mary; e) His substitutionary, expiatory death, in that he gave his life 'a ransom for man'; f) His resurrection from among the dead in the same body in which he was crucified and the second coming of this same Jesus in power and great glory; g) The total depravity of man through the fall; h) Salvation, the effect of regeneration by the Spirit, not by works but by grace through faith; i) The everlasting bliss of the saved, and the everlasting suffering of the lost; j) The real spiritual unity in Christ of all redeemed by his precious blood; k) The necessity of maintaining, according to the Word of God, the purity of the Church in doctrine and life; still, believing the Apostles' Creed to be a statement of scriptural truth, we therefore incorporate it in these articles of faith."

Address: ICCC, 756 Hadden Avenue, Box 190, Collingswood, New Jersey 08108, USA

6. INTERNATIONAL CONFERENCE OF REFORMED CHURCHES (ICRC)

The organization brings together Reformed churches of conservative persuasion. Today, it includes about 21 churches. The constituent meeting was held in Groningen, the Netherlands, in 1982. Invited by the Reformed Churches in the Netherlands (Liberated), delegates from nine conservative Reformed and Presbyterian churches came together to discuss ways to promote the unity of the faith in

Christ Jesus as revealed in the Scriptures and confessed by the Reformed creeds. The churches were concerned about what they considered a growing undermining of the authority of God's Word in Reformed circles and increasing attacks on the validity of the creeds of the Reformation. The meeting resulted in the provisional adoption of a constitution. Three years later, in Edinburgh, the First Assembly was held with eleven member churches. Subsequent meetings took place in Langley, B.C., Canada (1989) and Zwolle, Netherlands (1993). The Fourth Assembly took place in 1997 in Seoul, Korea.

As its basis the ICRC has adopted the Holy Scriptures of the Old and New Testament as confessed in the Three Forms of Unity (Belgic Confession, Heidelberg Catechism, Canons of Dort) and the Westminster Standards (Westminster Confession of Faith, Larger and Shorter Catechisms). The Constitution stipulates that membership is open to churches that "are faithful to the confessional standards stated in the Basis" and "are not members of the World Council of Churches or any other organization whose aims and practices are deemed to be in conflict with the Basis."

The purpose of the ICRC is fivefold: 1. To express and to promote the unity of faith that the member churches have in Christ; 2. To encourage the fullest ecclesiastical fellowship among the member churches; 3. To encourage cooperation among the member churches in the fulfillment of the missionary and other mandates; 4. To study common problems and issues that confront the member churches and to aim for recommendations with respect to these matters; 5. To present a Reformed testimony to the world.

A semi-annual newsletter of the ICRC Mission Committee is published, and regional mission conferences are promoted in several areas of the world.

Addresss: International Conference of Reformed Churches, Rev. M. van Beveren, 13904 - 26th Street, Edmonton, Alberta T5E 3C1, Canada, Tel: +1 403 478 5852, E-mail: vanbever @compusmart.ab.ca

7. WORLD FELLOWSHIP OF REFORMED CHURCHES (WFRC)

This Association of Reformed churches was founded in 1994 by the National Presbyterian Church of Mexico, the Presbyterian Church of Brazil, and the Presbyterian Church in America. The WFRC is not a council but a fellowship of churches. It seeks to promote an atmosphere in which the churches make mutually beneficial, cooperative agreements. It also encourages the training of pastors and laymen and fosters mutual cooperation in missions. The Fellowship exists under the umbrella of the World Evangelical Fellowship (WEF) although it operates independently. Assemblies are held in conjunction with WEF Assemblies, e.g., in May 1997 in Abbotsford, British Columbia. Any Presbyterian and Reformed church may join which endorses one of the classic Reformed creeds or confessions and (1) is a member of its national WEF-related association of evangelicals or (2)

707

has leaders who participate in their nation's WEF-related association or (3) does not have a WEF connection but the WFRC Executive Committee votes to admit the church. The WFRC also encourages the formation of regional fellowships. In 1995 14 Reformed churches from 11 Latin American countries formed Confraternidad Latinoamericana de Iglesias Reformadas (CLIR). Through CLIR the WFRC plans several missionary consultations in Latin America.

Addresss: World Fellowship of Reformed Churches, K. Eric Perrin, President, 5637 Bush River Road, Columbia, SC 29212, Tel: +1 803 772 1000, Fax: +1 803 772 1003, E-mail: corner1 @aol.com

8. INTERNATIONAL REFORMED FELLOWSHIP (IRF)

The IRF was recently founded as an international association of conservative Reformed Churches with a strong Korean participation. The founding act took place in Pasadena, California, USA.

The inaugural resolution says in part: "Whereas, we, members and representatives of those who hold to the revelation of God infallibly recorded in the Holy Scriptures, accept the expression of these teachings in the historic documents of the Reformation, particularly the Westminster Confession, the Heidelberg Catechism, and Belgic Confession and whereas we recognize that there are organizations whose faith and practice are in apparent contradiction to the faith embodied in the historic confessions stated above, such as the World Council of Churches and similar international and national associations and whereas we realize that the church is anaemic and faltering away from the truth of God in His Word. . . ."

Address: International Reformed Fellowship, Rev. Aranda Perera, 332 South Vigil Ave., Los Angeles, CA 90020, USA

5. UNIONS, UNION NEGOTIATIONS, AND DIALOGUES WITH CHURCHES OF DIFFERENT CONFESSIONAL BACKGROUNDS

From the beginning, the Reformers had to face the issue of the unity of the church. In their understanding, the movement of reform was to restore the true face of the church; it was not to divide but to renew the church by gathering it around God's Word. For a long time they continued to hope for a reform without division. But gradually it became clear that the conflict could not be resolved. In the eyes of the Reformers, the Church of Rome, by persisting in its errors, was primarily responsible for the loss of unity.

Even more disquieting for the Reformers was the fact that the movement of reform itself led to the formation of different churches. Among the Reformers, John Calvin was particularly active in promoting mutual understanding and proposing ways of union. It was in response to a proposal for a conference of representatives of various Reformation churches that he wrote the famous statement: "If I can do anything for the unity of the churches I am prepared to cross a thousand seas."

Throughout the centuries attempts have been made to heal the fragmentation associated with the Reformation. In the 20th century significant changes have occurred in relationships with other churches. Where do Reformed churches stand today in this respect?

There is among Reformed churches a wide range of attitudes toward ecumenical efforts. While some regard the Reformed tradition as the only adequate interpretation of the Gospel and, therefore, are reluctant to engage in ecumenical dialogue and cooperation, others are prepared to consider not only conversations but even union with other churches. There is, in particular, a wide divergence in the assessment of the status of the Roman Catholic Church. While some Reformed

709

churches continue to consider the Roman Catholic Church as heretic and even as the Antichrist, the large majority of Reformed churches recognizes that the Roman Catholic Church has changed and has become a partner in ecumenical endeavors.

Reformed ecumenical initiatives have mostly taken place within the World Alliance of Reformed Churches — undertaken either by member churches of the Alliance or by the Alliance itself. The agreements so far reached are therefore not necessarily representative of all Reformed churches. Even within the membership of the Alliance they are not appropriated by all churches to the same degree. The following survey does not follow chronological order but groups negotiations and conversations according to the degree of commonality or mutual understanding achieved.

A. ACHIEVING UNITY AMONG CHURCHES OF THE REFORMATION

1. United Churches at the National Level

In the course of the last decades Reformed and Presbyterian Churches have partic-ipated in union negotiations and unions. Partners in unions are primarily Congre-gationalist and Methodist churches. In a number of countries Reformed churches share membership in a united church with the Churches of Christ (Disciples). In the Churches of South India and of North India, Anglican Churches are involved. Reformed churches are part of the following (transconfessional) united churches: United Churches in Germany (19th and 20th centuries), Evangelical Church of the Augsburg and Helvetic Confessions, Austria (1891), Evangelical Church of the Czech Brethren (1918), United Church of Canada (1925), Church of Christ in China/China Christian Council (1927), Church of Christ in Thailand (1934), United Church of Christ in Japan (1941), Church of South India (1947), United Church of Christ in the Philippines (1948), United Church of Christ, USA (1957), Church of Jesus Christ in Madagascar (1968), Church of North India (1970), Church of Pakistan (1970), Church of Bangladesh (1971), Church of Christ in Zaire (1971), Uniting Church of Australia (1977), United Protestant Church in Belgium (1979), Waldensian Evangelical Church (1979), United Reformed Church in the United Kingdom (1981), United Church in Jamaica and the Cayman Islands (1992). In some cases Reformed and Presbyterian churches were unable to make a unanimous decision on a proposed union and split in the course of joining the united church. From the point of view of the World Alliance of Reformed Churches, churches joining a united church do not cease to be Reformed; they are invited to continue their membership in the Alliance. Today 15 united churches are members of the Alliance.

Publications:

Michael Kinnamon, "United and Uniting Churches," in *Dictionary of the Ecumenical Movement*, Geneva and Grand Rapids 1991, pp. 1032-1036

Thomas E. Best (ed.), "Sixth International Consultation of United and Uniting Churches," Faith and
   Order Paper 174, Geneva 1996

2. Unions and Mutual Recognition at the International Level

a) Union of WARC and the International Congregational Council (1970)

Theologically the two families had always been very close to one another. At the
suggestion of WARC, the two bodies started conversations in 1958. Soon it became clear that there was sufficient common ground between them to envisage
further steps. A Joint Committee was appointed in 1960, and in the following
years the two bodies quickly advanced in mutual understanding. Union took place
in 1970 at the Uniting General Council in Nairobi. To recall the different roots of
the member churches the new body was given the name World Alliance of Reformed Churches (Presbyterian and Congregational). The union was accepted by
all member churches of the WARC and the great majority of the Congregational
Churches. A minority of congregational churches continue as members of the International Congregational Fellowship (see 4, p. 705 above).

Publications:
Marcel Pradervand, *A Century of Service,* Edinburgh 1975

b) Dialogue and Agreement of Mutual Recognition with the Disciples Ecumenical Consultative Council (DECC)

A special relationship has developed between the World Alliance of Reformed
Churches and the Disciples Ecumenical Consultative Council, the body representing
the Disciples churches in intentional dialogues. The Disciples, though a separate
confessional tradition, have many affinities with the Reformed churches. The church
emerged on the United States frontier, then western Pennsylvania and Kentucky, in
the years 1800-1840. Fundamentally a movement for the unity and renewal of the
church, the Disciples were formed by believers from various churches (including
Presb, Bapt, Meth) who rejected sectarian divisions within their own traditions — divisions imported from Europe which, they felt, were irrelevant to Christian life and
witness within the context of the "new world." They combined an evangelistic zeal
with an appeal to reason and an emphasis upon Christian moral formation. Seeking
to express their common identity as *Christians,* they took their characteristic beliefs
and practices from the New Testament picture of the early Christian communities;
the baptism of professing believers by immersion, the celebration of the Lord's Sup
per during worship on each Lord's day, and an emphasis upon the fellowship and
witness of the locally governed congregation, complemented by a lively sense of the
unity of the Body of Christ throughout the world. Lay leadership, exercised particularly through the offices of elder and deacon, is significant in the life and worship of

711

Disciples churches. Historically, Christian mission, social witness, and higher education have been important concerns. A series of internal discussions and, occasionally, divisions — particularly in the mid-19th and early 20th centuries — have clarified the churches' identity, with the mainstream of Disciples rejecting biblical literalism, affirming their links with Christian tradition, and increasingly acknowledging the need for structures of oversight at local, regional, and national levels. While Disciples are keenly aware of the Reformed dimension of their heritage, these diverse characteristics link them not only to Presbyterians and Congregationalists but also to Anglicans, Baptists, Methodists, and even Roman Catholics. Since the end of the 19th century Disciples have been actively involved in mission work. The movement has spread to many countries. The strongest Disciples church outside the USA has developed in Congo-Kinshasa.

Conversations with the Churches of Christ (Disciples) were initiated in 1984. In several countries, in the course of the last decades, Reformed churches and Disciples have established close relations, or have even united. Naturally, therefore, the question arose whether a rapprochement could also take place at the international level. Encouraged by the findings of a first encounter in 1984, the WARC and the DECC called a larger consultation in Birmingham in 1986. The participants came to the conclusion that "there are no theological or ecclesiological issues which need to divide us as churches" and requested the WARC and the DECC to call upon their member churches to say whether or not they could accept the following declaration: "The Disciples of Christ and the Reformed Churches recognize and accept each other as visible expressions of the one Church of Christ." The response to this question was positive on both sides. At its General Council in Seoul (1989), the WARC explicitly affirmed the special relationship between the two families. It was agreed that representatives of the Disciples should participate in both decision-making and study of the World Alliance of Reformed Churches. At the national level the movement toward unity has since advanced further. In recent times the DECC has also sponsored official dialogues with the Roman Catholic Church and the Orthodox Church of Russia.

Publications:
Alan P. F. Sell (ed.), *Reformed and Disciples of Christ in Dialogue,* Studies from the WARC 6, 1985
Towards Closer Fellowship, Report of the Dialogue between Reformed and Disciples of Christ, Studies
     from the WARC 11, 1988; *Reformed World* 39/8 (December 1987)
"Papers from the Birmingham Consultation," *Mid-Stream* 27/2 (April 1988)

c) Dialogue and Agreement of Mutual Recognition with Lutheran Churches and the Lutheran World Federation

A breakthrough in the relations between Reformed and Lutheran churches was accomplished with the completion of the Leuenberg Agreement in 1973. After extended theological conversations, representatives of Reformed and Lutheran churches were able to propose to the Reformed and Lutheran churches in Europe a declaration of church fellowship. "The participating churches are convinced that they have part together in the one Church of Jesus Christ and that the Lord liberates them for, and lays upon them the obligation of, common service." Church fellowship was to include pulpit and table fellowship and the mutual recognition of the ordained ministry. Most Reformed churches in Europe officially accepted the agreement and engaged in continuing doctrinal conversations. In 1994 the Methodist churches in Europe also affirmed the agreement. Reformed-Lutheran conversations in North America came to similar conclusions. In 1984 a Joint Commission proposed mutual recognition as churches, mutual recognition of the celebration of the Lord's Supper and mutual recognition of the ordained ministries; it also suggested that a process of reception be initiated. Further talks were started in more recent years. They led to the adoption in 1997 of the Formula of Agreement, which established full communion between the two church traditions. In addition, it must be remembered that, in some countries, Reformed and Lutheran churches have joined in united churches (Germany, Czechia, Ethiopia, Indonesia). After a series of preliminary talks the WARC and the Lutheran World Federation decided in 1984 to set up a dialogue at the international level with the aim of reflecting on the implications of all these developments for their mutual relation. The principal recommendation they came to was to "urge Lutheran and Reformed churches throughout the world who are members of the WARC and LWF to declare full communion with one another."

Publications:

Agreement between Reformation Churches in Europe (Leuenberg Agreement), Trilingual Edition Frankfurt 1993

James E. Andrews and Joseph A. Burgess (ed.), *An Invitation to Action,* The Lutheran-Reformed Dialogue, Series II, 1981-1983, Philadelphia 1984

Lutheran-Reformed Joint Commission, *Towards Church Fellowship,* Geneva 1989

d) Dialogue and Doctrinal Agreement with the World Methodist Conference

Encouraged by the fact that in many parts of the world Reformed and Methodist churches had come together in church unions, the WARC and the World Methodist Council decided to start an official dialogue. Two joint meetings were held in 1985 and 1987. The report speaks of "a new-found confidence that our traditions witness to a common gospel and embody authentic forms of obedience and faithful discipleship." The report also encourages member churches on both sides to take steps toward unity and to collaborate in mission.

Publication:

Reformed and Methodists in Dialogue, Studies from the WARC 12, Geneva, 1988

e) Dialogue with the Anglican Communion

Conversations with the Anglican Communion were proposed by the WARC in 1976 in order to reflect on the experience of both sides in union negotiations. The

Joint Commission, which after a preliminary exchange was appointed in 1978, concentrated its attention on the theme of the church. An attempt was made to understand the nature of the church and its mission in the perspective of the kingdom of God. The report recommends to the churches on both sides to consider seriously steps toward union.

Publications:
God's Reign and Our Unity, The Report of the Anglican-Reformed International Commission, London and St. Andrews, 1984

f) Dialogue with Mennonites

On March 5, 1983, a joint communion service was celebrated in the Grossmünster in Zürich between representatives of the WARC, the World Baptist Alliance, and the World Mennonite Conference. On this occasion a spokesperson of the Swiss Reformed Churches expressed deep regret for the mistreatment of Anabaptists and Mennonites in the past and asked officially for forgiveness. This event was followed in 1984 by theological conversations between the WARC and World Mennonite Conference in Strasbourg which dealt with the condemnations of Anabaptists in Reformed confessions.

Publications:
Mennonites and Reformed in Dialogue, Studies from the WARC 7, Geneva 1986

g) Dialogue with Baptists

Theological conversations between the WARC and the World Baptist Alliance took place from 1973 to 1977. There was fundamental agreement on recognizing the central function of the Holy Scriptures in the life of the church. An attempt was made to approach divergences in the understanding of both the church and baptism in the perspective of pneumatology and the mission of the church. The report was shared with member churches on both sides, and in 1982 the responses were evaluated at a joint meeting. The agreement was that the dialogue needed to be continued at the level of the individual churches in each country.

Publications:
Baptists and Reformed in Dialogue, Studies from the WARC 4, Geneva 1983

h) Conversations with Pentecostals

Conversations with Pentecostals were initiated by the World Alliance of Reformed Churches in 1996 with the aim "to increase mutual understanding and respect, identify areas of theological agreement, convergence or disagreement, and explore possibilities of common witness. The first meeting took place in May 1996 in Torre Pellice (Italy), and centered around the theme "Spirituality and the Challenges of Today." A second meeting in 1997 in Chicago was devoted to "The Role and Place of the Holy Spirit in the Church." The consultation was able to affirm the following statement: "The Good News of Jesus Christ is received through the community of the faithful. The community furthers the message and mission of God rooted in the Word of God and guided by the Holy Spirit. The members of the community offer their eyes, ears, mouths and hands to God and are sustained and nurtured by the Spirit and the Word. Furthermore, it is the Spirit whose sovereignty bestows charismata upon the faith community as it seeks to address the diverse needs which arise in the church, society and the world." Further meetings are envisaged.

i) Dialogue of the Reformed Ecumenical Council with Seventh Day Adventists

Two meeting were held in 1985 and 1987. At the second, more substantive meeting, the partners exchanged views on the authority of Scripture, on the Gift of Prophecy, and on the status of Ellen G. White's writings within the Seventh Day Adventist Church. The two groups have exchanged observers at international assemblies and have proposed further conversations, but none have been scheduled as of 1997.

B. Theological Conversations with the Roman Catholic Church

a) Conversations at the International Level

After the conclusion of the Second Vatican Council, the question arose how to redefine the relationship to the Roman Catholic Church. After initial hesitation, the WARC decided to engage in an official dialogue. Theological conversations were conducted in two phases from 1970-1977 and from 1984-1990. Together with the Lutheran World Federation, a tripartite commission also discussed the issue of mixed marriages. The Joint Theological Report, completed in 1990, emphasizes the common ground Reformed and Catholics share. Without minimizing the remaining differences, especially in the understanding of the church and its ministry, it urges the two traditions to live in a new openness to one another. Main recommendations concern the mutual recognition of baptism, the "reconciliation of memories," and common witness in the world of today.

Publications:
Towards a Common Understanding of the Church, Studies from WARC 21, Geneva 1991

b) Conversations at the National Level

Conversations at the national level were conducted mainly in countries with a long history of relationships with the Roman Catholic Church: Australia, Austria, Belgium, France, the Netherlands, North America, Scotland, and Switzerland. In

715

some countries agreements on the mutual recognition of baptism were adopted, and in others certain passages in Reformed confessions concerning the Roman Catholic Church were revised (Heidelberg Catechism, Westminster Confession).

Publications:
Reformed and Roman Catholic in Dialogue, A Survey on Dialogues at National Level, Studies from the WARC 10, Geneva 1988

C. Theological Conversations with Orthodox Churches

a) Official Dialogue with the Eastern Orthodox Church

In order to reach a deeper level of mutual understanding, in 1977 the WARC proposed to the Ecumenical Patriarchate of Constantinople to start an official dialogue. After an exploratory phase of several years, the Patriarchate recommended that all Orthodox churches participate in an official dialogue. Primary attention was to be given to the Trinitarian teaching of the church. So far, five meetings of the Joint Commission have taken place (1988, 1990, 1992, 1994, and 1996). Two agreed statements on the Trinity and on the Incarnation have been formulated.

Publications:
T. F. Torrance, *Theological Dialogue between Orthodox and Reformed Churches,* 2 vols., Edinburgh, 1985, 1993
Agreed Statements from the Reformed/Orthodox Dialogue, Studies from the WARC 38, Geneva 1998

b) Dialogue with Oriental Orthodox Churches

On August 27, 1992, a group of representatives of the Oriental Orthodox Churches and the WARC met in Geneva for an exploratory conversation and decided to initiate a theological dialogue. Three meetings have taken place so far. The first was hosted by Pope Shenouda III in May 1993 at Anba Bishoy Monastery, Wadi-El-Natroun, Egypt; the second took place in September 1994 in Driebergen, the Netherlands; and the third in January 1997 in Kottayam, Kerala, India. After getting mutually acquainted at the first meeting, it was decided to devote primary attention to the themes of Christology and the relationship of Holy Scripture and Tradition. From the common investigations into these themes the dialogue will proceed to address the theme "The Nature and Mission of the Church." The delegation from the Oriental Orthodox side includes representatives from most Oriental Orthodox Churches, i.e., the Coptic Orthodox Church, the Ethiopian Orthodox Church, the Syrian Orthodox Church of Antioch, the Malankara Orthodox Syrian Church, and the Armenian Orthodox Church.

Publications:
Oriental Orthodox / Reformed Dialogue, The First Four Sessions, Studies from the WARC 40, Geneva 1998.

6. LIST OF CONTRIBUTORS

Names of main contributors are listed in italics. Members of the editorial board are identified by *

Name	First name	Country of origin/of residence
Ada	Samuel	Togo
Balasundaran	Franklyn	India
Baynard	Chuck	USA
Beveren	M. van	Canada
Birri	Debela	Ethiopia
Bonneville	Henri	Reunion Island
Brinks	Ray	USA
Brown	John	Australia
Brown	G. Thompson	USA
Butselaar	Jan	Netherlands
Camps	Carlos	Cuba
Cardoso	Manuel Pedro	Portugal
Chamango	Simão	Mozambique
Chiphangwi	Saindi	Botswana
Choe	Il Sik	South Korea
Chon	Jeng-Hong	Taiwan
Chung	Byung-Joon	South Korea
Vasquez Clemente	Abel	Mexico
Cox	Elizabeth	UK/Nepal

LIST OF CONTRIBUTORS

Name	First name	Country of origin/of residence
Crespo	Maritza	Venezuela/Costa Rica
Dah	Jonas N.	Cameroon
Dengthuama		Myanmar
Dezsö	Buzogany	Romania
Dilger	Otto	Germany
Dinkelaker	Bernhard	Germany
Doezema	Don R.	Jamaica/USA
* Doom	John	French Polynesia/Switzerland
Dupertuis	Sylvain	Switzerland
Elliott, Jr.	Edwin P.	USA
Falconer	Alan	Scotland/Switzerland
Farrell	Hunter	USA
Flores Amaya	Santiago	El Salvador
Garrett	*John*	*American Samoa*
Gimenez Perez	Buenaventura	Paraguay
Glüer	Winfried	Germany
Gonnet-Griot	Hugo	Uruguay
Gonzalez Roca	Hernán	Dominican Republic
Gounelle	Yves	France
Gsell	Brad K.	USA
Guhrt	Joachim	Germany
* *Guimarães*	*Hircio de Oliveira*	*Brazil*
Han	Buyung-Huh	Gambia
Hegemann	Neal	Canada
Heideman	Eugene	USA
Holtrop	Pieter	Netherlands
Hopkins	Paul	USA
Huyser	Joel	Nicaragua/USA
Inhauser	Marcos Roberto	Brazil
Iverson	Lee	USA/Chile
Jagessar	Michael and Leonora	Curaçao
* *Jongeneel*	*Jan A.*	*Netherlands*
Jonsson	Anita	Sweden
Jordan	Roberto H.	Argentina

Name	First name	Country of origin/of residence
Kabongo Mbaya	Philippe	Congo (Kinshasa)/France
Karamaga	André	Rwanda
Kimhachandran	Sint	Thailand
Klamer	J.	Netherlands
Koll	Karla Ann	USA
König	Robert	French Polynesia
Koschorke	Klaus	Switzerland
Koulouris	Antonio	Greece
Kyasooka	Hosea Nelson	Uganda
Lautenbach	Hugo	Switzerland
Lima	Eber F. S.	Brazil/USA
Lutz	Hans	Switzerland/China Hong Kong (SAR)
Lyons	Keith	Australia
Mahecha	Guidoberto	Colombia/Brazil
Makari	Victor	USA
Marais	Clem	Namibia
Maritz	Frans	Zimbabwe
Matze	Pauline J.	Surinam
Merino Boyd	Pedro	Peru
Miquel	Bruno	New Caledonia
Mocong Onguene	Carmelo	Equatorial Guinea
Monsarrat	Jean-Pierre	France
Morvant	Nivo	Switzerland
Murray	John	Aotearoa New Zealand
Nishimura	Katsuyoshi	Japan
Opocensky	Milan	Czech Republic/Switzerland
* *Park*	*Seong-Won*	*South Korea/Switzerland*
Pattiasina	Joseph M.	Indonesia
Pereira Guimarães	Tirza	Brazil
Perrin	Eric K.	USA
Peyer	Fritz	Switzerland
Pilatuña	Luis Alfredo	Ecuador
Poerwowidagdo	Judo	Indonesia
Ravalitera	Jean	Madagascar

Name	First name	Country of origin/of residence
* *Réamonn*	*Paraic*	*United Kingdom*
Regard	Pierre	Switzerland
Rooy	Sidney	USA/Costa Rica
Rubio	Pablo Garcia	Spain
Rüegger	Heinz	Switzerland
Ruun	Haruun L.	Sudan
Ryan	Edward A.	Bahrain/USA
Saayman	Willem A.	South Africa
Schäfer	Heinrich	Costa Rica
Schneider	Vreni	Switzerland
Schoon	Simon	Netherlands
Schubert	Benedikt	Switzerland
Scudder	Lewis R.	USA/Cyprus
Senner	Edward L.	Taiwan
Shepherd	Henry A.	Bermuda
Siyachitema	Rosemary	Zimbabwe
Slomp	Jan	Netherlands
Smith	Dennis	Guatemala
Spindler	Marc	France
Staal	Harvey	USA
Stenström	Gösta	Sweden
Tamás	Bertalan	Hungary
Thompson	Eileen	Bangladesh
Uidam	Cornelis	Australia
Van Beveren	M.	USA
van den End	*Thomas*	*Netherlands/Indonesia*
* *Van Houten*	*Richard*	*United States*
Van Tol	William	USA
van Wyngaard	Arnau	South Africa
Wagenveld	Louis	El Salvador/USA
Weber	Jacques	Switzerland
Wills	Omar	Honduras
Wind	John	Honduras/USA
Woodruf	Archibald Mulford	Brazil

7. MAPS

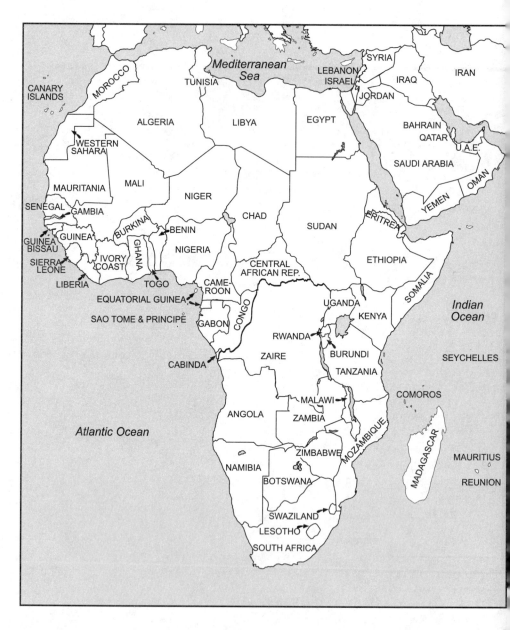

Africa general

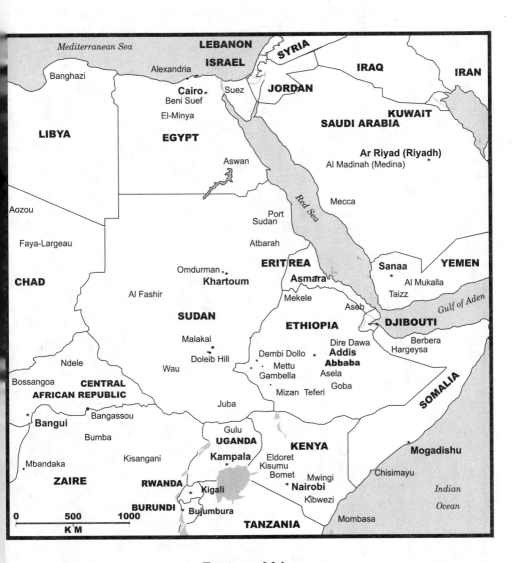

Eastern Africa

723

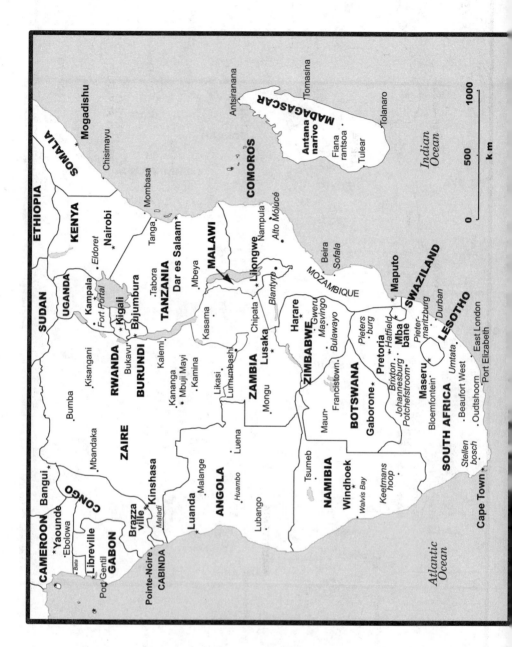

Southern Africa

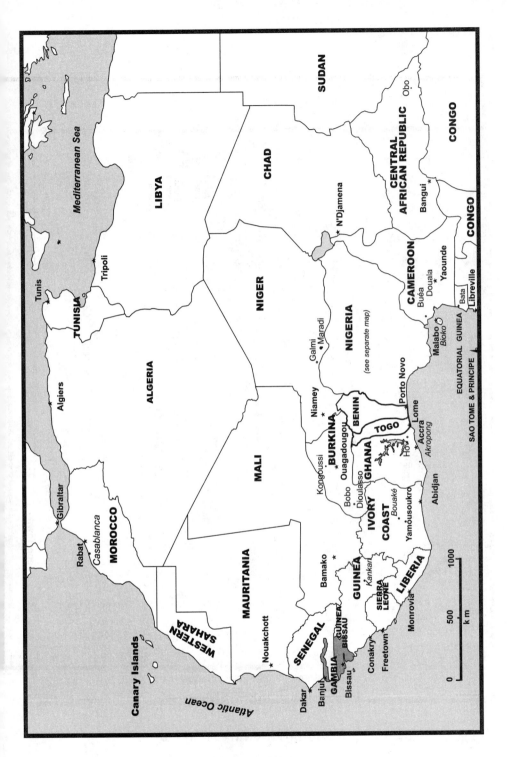

Western Africa

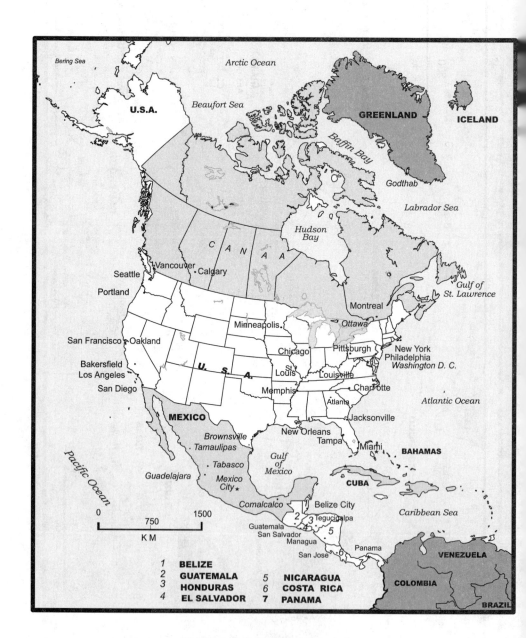

North and Central America

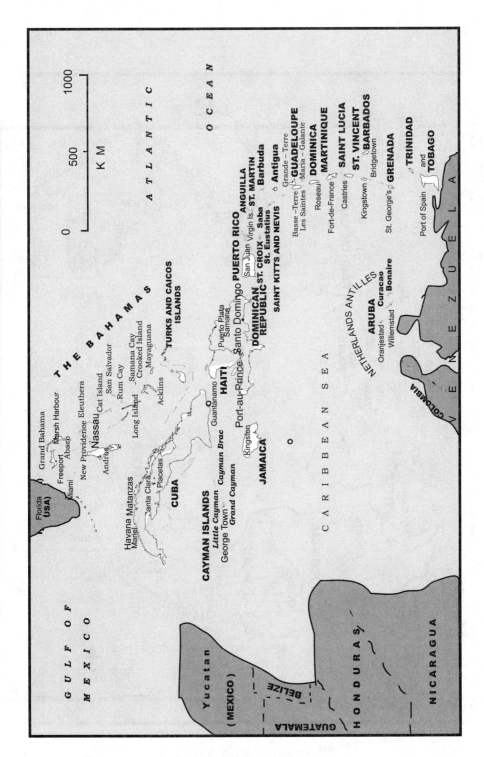

Caribbean Sea

727

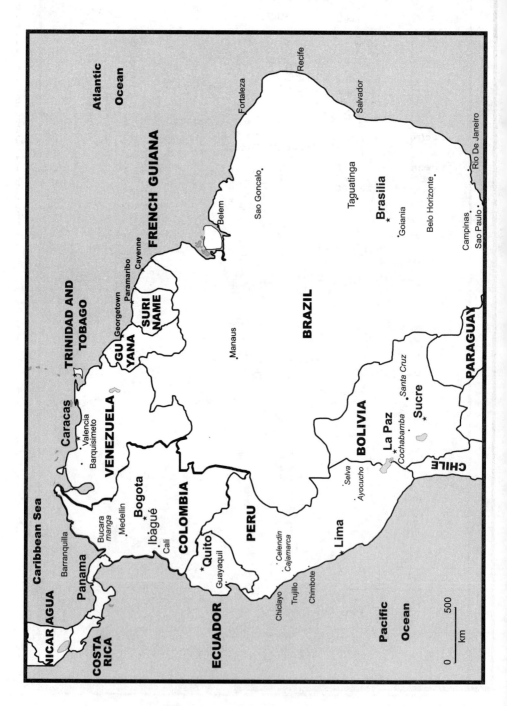

Northern South America

Southern South America

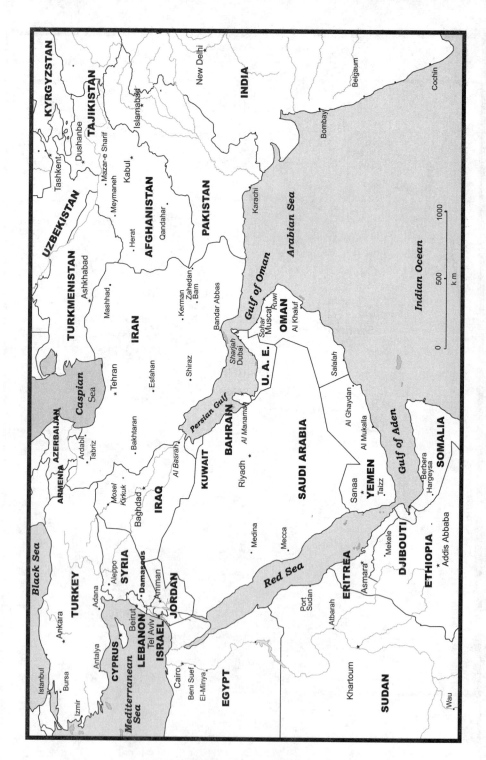

Middle East and Western Asia

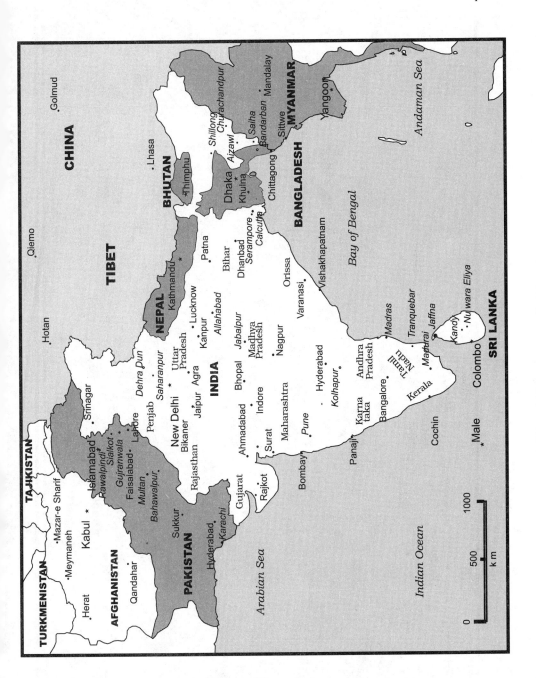

South West Asia

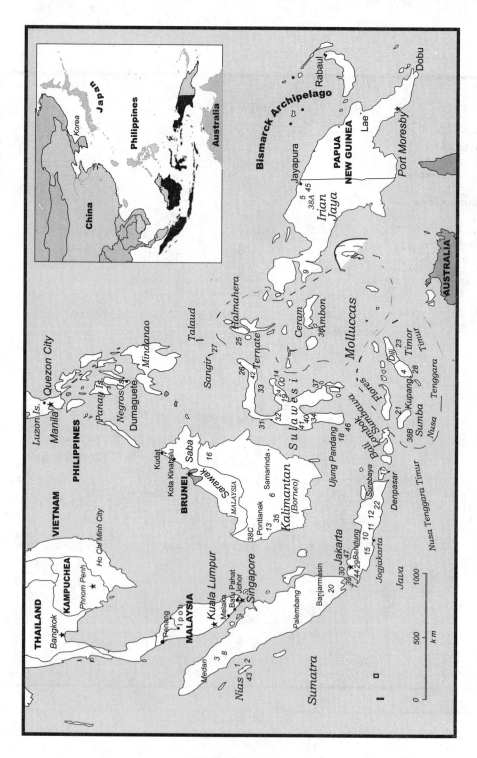

Southern Asia

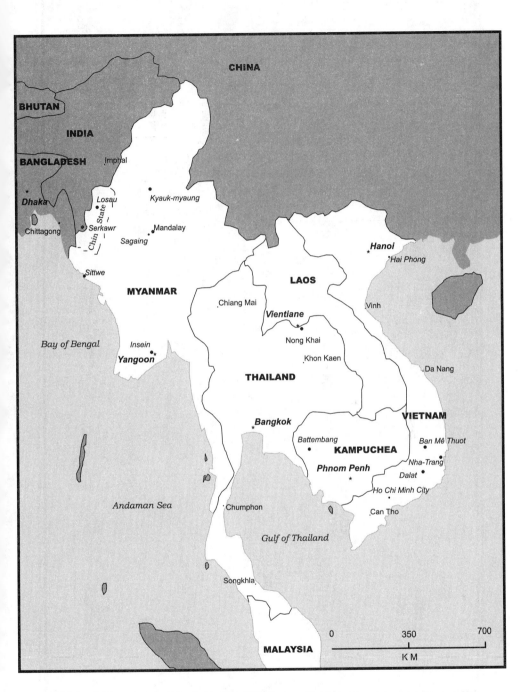

Indochina Peninsula

733

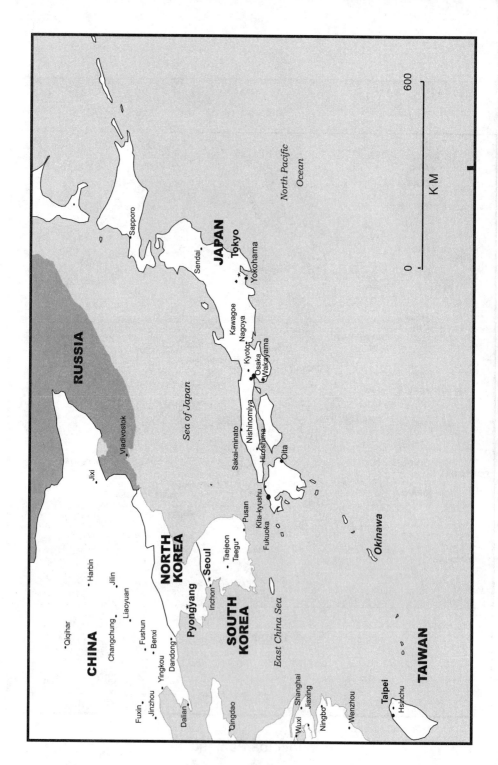

East Asia

Europe general

Europe West

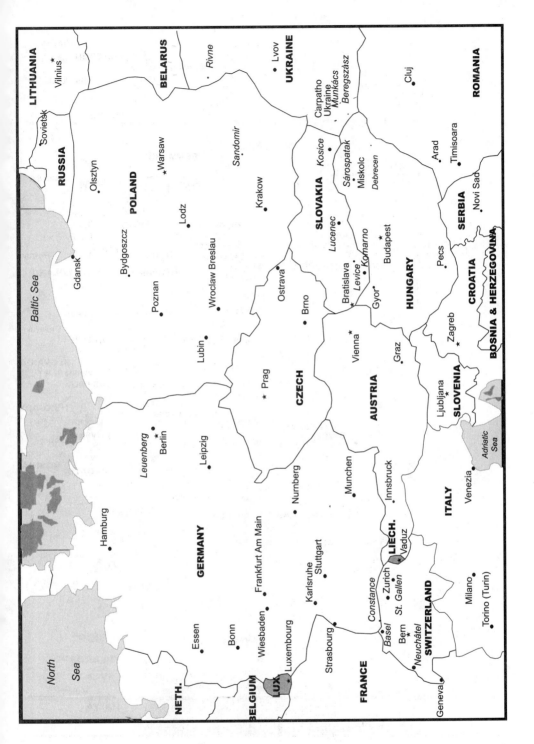

Europe Central West and Central

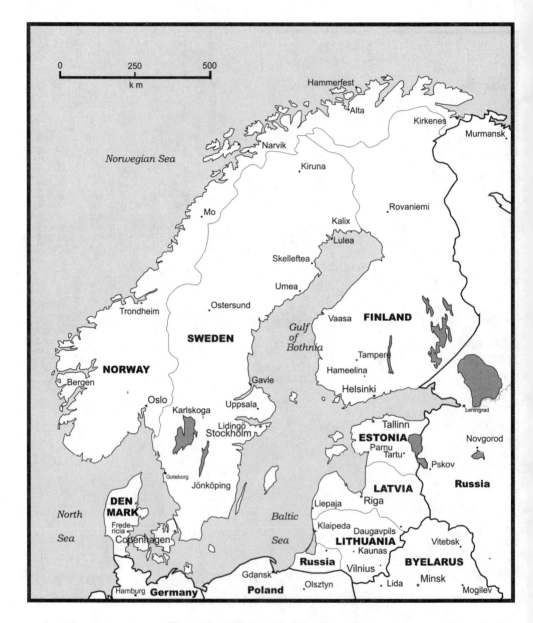

Scandinavian and Baltic States

Europe and the Balkans

739

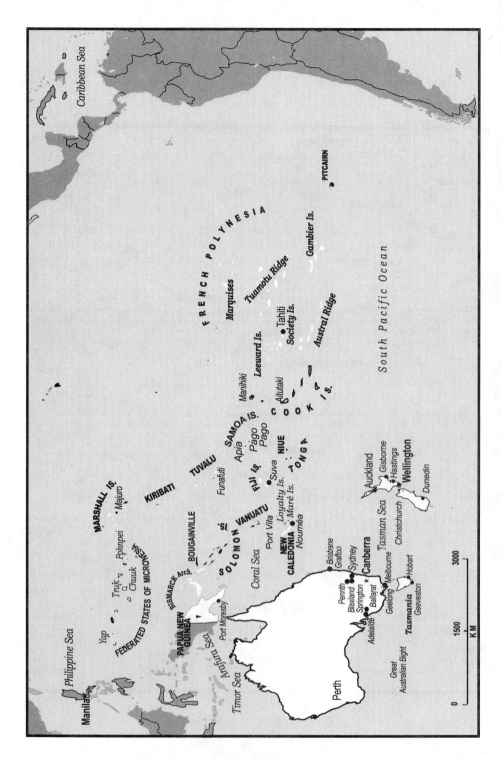

Australia and South Pacific

740